The Hollywood.com Guide to Film Directors

The Hollywood.com Guide to Film Directors

Baseline Hollywood Film Director Directory

Edited by the
Staff of Hollywood.com

CARROLL & GRAF PUBLISHERS
NEW YORK

THE HOLLYWOOD.COM GUIDE TO FILM DIRECTORS
Baseline Hollywood Film Director Directory

Carroll & Graf Publishers
An Imprint of Avalon Publishing Group Inc.
245 West 17th Street, 11th Floor
New York, NY 10011

First Carroll & Graf edition 2004

Library of Congress Cataloging-in-Publication Data is available.

ISBN: 0-7867-1131-0

Printed in the United States of America
Interior design by Paul Paddock
Distributed by Publishers Group West

Preface

Ever since the new-wavers over at Cahier du Cinema pointed out that Hollywood directors aren't simply foremen at a punch-the-clock movie factory, but rather visionaries with the creative brio to turn celluloid images into high art (auteurs they liked to call them), directors have become as celebrated as the celebrities themselves. No longer simply relegated to the annals of film studies like so many of their forefathers, today's purveyors of cinematic hiptitude like Quentin Tarantino, Wes Anderson, and the Coen Brothers have become bona fide Page Six stars in their own right. When we go to the movies, it's no longer just because of a popular actor or actress; we go to the theaters to see "a Ridley Scott Film" or "the new Darren Aranofsky movie." Director's names are now as synonymous with the films they make as Julia Roberts and Jim Carrey are with the movies in which they star. And yet regardless of iconic renown, no one is capable of influencing a film more than the director, and by having access to information about these men and women, we are subsequently able to inform our viewing experience. With that in mind, we give you *The Hollywood.com Guide to Film Directors.*

A historic addition to the ever-growing library of film reference material, what makes this guide so special is right there in the title—Hollywood.com. Baseline.Hollywood.com is the definitive source of film information for not only the industry at large, but for the movie-going public as well. And for the first time, that remarkable multitude of information on the men and women behind the camera is available in convenient book form. At over nine hundred pages, the guide offers not only a comprehensive look at the heavyweights of movie making, but also indie heroes like John Sayles, foreign directors like Werner Herzog, B-movie grinders like Herschell Gordon Lewis, and exciting newcomers like Sophia Coppolla. While it is nearly impossible to include the names of anyone and everyone who ever directed a film, *The Hollywood.com Guide to Film Directors* boasts over three hundred meticulously detailed and informative entries, and provides a sweeping examination of filmmaking's great artists. They're all here: Hitchcock, Copolla, Truffaut, Cukor, etc.

This book is more than just a standard reference tool. In addition to the vital biographical data that one would expect like date and place of birth, religious and organizational affiliations, and awards, there are also concise and informative biographies that provide everything a film buff or even a producer du jour needs to know about a given director. The entries are entertaining too. Let's face it, directors can be an outlandish, narcissistic bunch of deranged geniuses, and Hollywood.com takes all of the essential moments and concentrate them into enjoyable, easily accessible entries that offer fresh perspectives on not only the men and women that make the movies, but the movies themselves.

Thanks for listening . . . and action!

—Nate Knaebel
2003

Chantal Akerman

BORN: Chantal Anne Akerman in Brussels, Belgium, 06/06/1950

SOMETIMES CREDITED AS:
Chantal Anne Akerman

NATIONALITY: Belgian

EDUCATION: Institut Superieur des Arts du Spectacle et Techniques de Diffusion (INSAS), Brussels, Belgium, 1967–68; did not complete four-year course

International University, Paris, France, theater, 1968–69

BIOGRAPHY

Considered one of the most significant independent filmmakers of the 1970s, 80s and 90s, Chantal Akerman possesses a pronounced visual and narrative style, influenced by structuralism and minimalism, which offers astute insights into women's role in modern culture.

Akerman's interest in film was sparked at the age of 15 by a viewing of Jean-Luc Godard's "Pierrot le Fou", prompting her to enroll in the Belgian film school, INSAS. After about two years' study she quit school, eager to begin making films rather than sitting in a classroom. Akerman saved money from clerical and waitressing jobs to make several short films which received minimal recognition.

It was not until she moved to New York in 1972 that Akerman began to develop her distinctive visual style and to deal with those themes which have dominated her work thus far. In America she became acquainted with the films of the avant-garde, specifically those of Michael Snow, which influenced her perception of the relationship between film, space and time. Her first two features, "Hotel Monterey" (1972) and "Je Tu Il Elle" (1974), with their studiously static camerawork and minimal dialogue, were early indications of the visual style which came to full flowering in "Jeanne Dielman, 23 quai du Commerce, 1080 Bruxelles" (1975). This 200-minute, minimally plotted film scrutinized three days in the life of a woman (Delphine Seyrig) who adheres to a regimented schedule of cleaning, cooking and caring for her teenage son. Every day she also takes in one male caller to make ends meet. On the third day her schedule is interrupted, and she later experiences an orgasm with her male caller. Her response to these unfathomable alterations in her routine is to thrust a pair of scissors into the man's throat.

Reception for "Jeanne Dielman" was mixed. It was criticized by many as a boring and meaningless minimalist exercise; Akerman's defenders, however, were awed by her visual aesthetic and use of real time to emphasize the routine of her protagonist's world. Thanks to the film's exposure, Akerman was able to secure financial backing from the Gaumont company and from German TV for the striking "Les Rendezvous d'Anna" (1978). Her first semi-commercial effort, it featured popular French actors Aurore Clement and Jean-Pierre Cassel in a story of a female director trekking across Europe to promote her latest film. Again, static camerawork and minimal dialogue created a sense of alienation which mirrored the emptiness and insincerity of the protagonist's encounters.

After failing to raise $25 million for an adaptation of Isaac Bashevis Singer's 1969 novel "The Manor", Akerman returned to independent production with "All Night Long" (1982), an insightful drama contrasting romantic illusions with harsh realities. Akerman's most accessible film to date is "Golden Eighties" (1986), a satire of musicals set completely within the confines of a Brussels shopping mall. Here too her concern is with idealized notions of romance; unlike her earlier works, however, the central story is complemented by several subplots and the film's pacing is a little more sprightly. Akerman's signature camera does remain static, providing a unique perspective on the structured world of the shopping mall.

In 1988 Akerman returned to New York to film "American Stories/Food, Family and Philosophy", an exploration of her Jewish heritage through a series of stories told by immigrants. To support herself, Akerman has held a number of teaching posts; she has stated a desire to make more commercially viable films because of the financial constraints now on independent production.

MILESTONES:

At age 15, after seeing Jean-Luc Godard's "Pierrot le fou" (1965), decided to become a filmmaker

1968: Made first film, "Saute ma ville/Blow Up My City" (35mm, 13mins); shown at Oberhausen Film Festival in 1971

1971–1973: Made four non-feature-length films, most notably "Hotel Monterey" (16mm, 65mins)

1972: Lived in New York for a short time before returning to France

1972: Feature film directing, writing, acting and producing debut, "Je tu il elle"

1975: Wrote and directed "Jeanne Dielman, 23 Quai du Commerce, 1080 Bruxelles", what she has referred to as a "love letter" to her mother

1980: Helmed the TV-movie "Dis-moi/Tell Me"

1982: Wrote and directed "Toute une nuit/All Night Long"

1987: Co-directed "Seven Women, Seven Sins"

1991: Directed and co-wrote "Nuit et jour/Night and Day"

1996: Helmed "Un Divan a New York/A Couch in New York", starring Juliette Binoche and William Hurt

1996: Helmed, wrote and starred in "Chantal Akerman by Chantal Akerman"

1999: Directed "Sud", an examination of the US South

2000: Wrote and directed "The Captive"

Robert Aldrich

BORN: Robert Burgess Aldrich in Cranston, Rhode Island, 08/09/1918

DEATH: in Los Angeles, California, 12/05/1983

NATIONALITY: American

EDUCATION: Moses Brown School, Providence, Rhode Island
University of Virginia, Charlottesville, Virginia, economics; played football; dropped out in 1941 to pursue film career

AWARDS: Venice Film Festival Silver Prize "The Big Knife" 1955; one of four films cited
Venice Film Festival Italian Critics Award "Attack!" 1956
Berlin Film Festival Best Director Award "Autumn Leaves" 1956

BIOGRAPHY

Famed for his macho mise-en-scene and resonant reworkings of classic action genres, Robert Aldrich became a model for many younger directors in the 1960s and 70s. Along with such figures as Roger Corman and Sam Arkoff, he was also a symbol of the free-spirit of independent filmmaking (although Aldrich had more interest in quality, and became renowned for substantive content and the interior meanings of his works). He is best recalled for such horror classics as "Whatever Happened to Baby Jane?" (1962), and "Hush, Hush, Sweet Charlotte" (1964), both starring Bette Davis. But, the director also tried his hand at more literary works, such as "The Killing of Sister George" (1968), and even commercial comedies like "The Longest Yard" (1974), starring Burt Reynolds.

Dropping out of college and the career in banking or politics expected by his prominent Republican family (John D Rockefeller Jr was an uncle by marriage), Aldrich entered film as a clerk at RKO in 1941. He rose through the ranks as a second assistant director, first assistant (working with Chaplin and Renoir, among others), production manager, studio manager and screenwriter under contract to Enterprise Studios (1946–48).

In the early 1950s, Aldrich directed episodes of several TV series, including the syndicated "China Smith" and NBC's "The Doctor", before finally making his feature film debut in 1953 with "The Big Leaguer." This low-budget film starred Edward G Robinson in one of his first roles after being cleared of the "red" taint by the House Committee on un-American Activities. The actor was sorely miscast as the manager of a training camp for baseball players, not to mention, Aldrich would later recall, low on self-confidence after being away from the screen for nearly two years. The result was not stellar in Robinson's canon, but it did establish that Aldrich could direct a film under budget and ahead of schedule. The director soon formed his own

company, Associates and Aldrich, to assume more control of his career; he then produced most of the films he directed and also contributed to their screenplays. Aldrich's work aggressively confronted controversial social and political issues. Taking uncompromising positions in familiar genres and revising genre conventions, he challenged both the studio system and audience expectations.

Aldrich's dominant theme was man's efforts to prevail against both impossible odds and institutional oppression. In "Apache" (1954), the only tribal leader left unconquered after the defeat of Geronimo refuses to be subjugated by the white man but is also, ultimately, alienated from his own people. Aldrich returned to the same subject 18 years later in "Ulzana's Raid" (1972), in which an Apache leader breaks the reservation's institutional constraints, vowing to recapture lost land. In depicting the brutal savagery of the white soldiers, who are oblivious to the hostility they cause, Aldrich refuses to allow his characters the traditional redemption offered by the Western genre.

In "The Big Knife" (1955), the Hollywood studio system was shown as nurturing dictatorial leaders who push individuals to compromise and suicide. (The film, which won the Silver Award at the Venice Film Festival, contains blatant allusions to real-life moguls Harry Cohn and Jack Warner.) "Whatever Happened to Baby Jane?" (1962) and "The Legend of Lylah Clare" (1968) continued to present a Hollywood breeding jealousy and empty myths rooted in egomania.

In "Attack!" (1956), the combination of cowardice and political compromise displayed by military officers destroys the common soldiers under their command. "Attack!" was criticized for Aldrich's violent, often frantic mise-en-scene: for example, a soldier's arm is slowly crushed under a tank in a shot that can be taken as a metaphor for the results of institutional military incompetence. "The Dirty

Dozen" (1967) reiterated Aldrich's contemptuous view for a military machine which dehumanized its subjects in order to make them capable of killing. The violent "heroics" of Robert Jefferson (Jim Brown)—dropping grenades that engulf trapped German officers in flames—illustrated how vicious men become under adversity.

Cynicism and pessimism permeated Aldrich's work. In the fatalistic "Kiss Me Deadly" (1955), private detective Mike Hammer attempts to track down the "great whatsit," a suitcase-sized atomic device which has been stolen by a spy; but the spy's greedy mistress opens the case, unleashing the device's deadly power in an apocalyptic finale. The film is arguably the director's most aesthetically striking and original, a hyper-kinetic reworking of the film noir genre that has become something of a cult favorite.

The abuse of institutional power motivates a terrorist in the political thriller "Twilight's Last Gleaming" (1977). A rogue general captures a nuclear missile silo and demands that the President read on national TV a Joint Chiefs of Staff memo admitting that over 50,000 Americans and 100,000 Southeast Asians died in a war the government knew America could never win. He insists that the President restore public confidence by calling the Vietnam war a "theatrical holocaust perpetrated by the criminally negligent." In Aldrich's cynical world-view, the Joint Chiefs sacrifice the President in order to maintain the credibility of the military complex.

On a smaller scale, "Hustle" (1975) reflects Aldrich's bleak vision of institutional betrayal. Gus, a police detective, can't win justice for the parents of a girl who accidentally drowned after an orgy with a protected leader of organized crime. Gus breaks the law to effect vengeance for the girl's father, then is himself killed by a petty criminal holding up a convenience store.

"All The Marbles" (1981), Aldrich's last film, was largely neglected by critics and audiences. It depicted two women wrestlers who confront the greed, sexism and humiliation of the wrestling world. Aldrich explicitly equated the physical abuse suffered by the women in the ring with the social abuse they suffered struggling for success and respect in a male-dominated field.

FAMILY:

grandfather: Nelson W Aldrich. Former US Senator

father: Edward B Aldrich. Newspaper publisher

mother: Lora Lawson.

aunt: Mrs. John D Rockefeller.

daughter: Adell Aldrich. Filmmaker, born in 1943; mother, Harriet Foster

son: William Aldrich. Producer, born in 1944; produced 1991 TV remake of "What Ever Happened to Baby Jane?"; mother, Harriet Foster

daughter: Alida Aldrich. Appeared as a child in "Hush Hush . . . Sweet Charlotte"; mother, Harriet Foster

son: Kelly Aldrich. Film transportation driver; appeared as a child in "Hush Hush . . . Sweet Charlotte", later worked as a driver on his father's films; mother, Harriet Foster

MILESTONES:

Through an uncle, got a job as a production clerk at RKO

1944–1952: Worked as assistant director on films by directors such as Lewis Milestone, Abraham Polonsky, Joseph Losey and Charles Chaplin; first film as assistant director, Jean Renoir's "The Southerner"

1951: First film as producer (associate), "Ten Tall Men"; also had bit part in Joseph Losey's "The Big Night"

Wrote and directed episodes of such TV series as "The Doctor" and "China Smith"

1953: Feature directing debut, "The Big Leaguer"

1954: Formed production company

1955: Co-wrote (uncredited) "The Gamma People"

1957: Directed most of "The Garment Jungle"; (film completed by, and credited to, Vincent Sherman)

1962: Produced and directed "Whatever Happened to Baby Jane?"

1967: Scored immense financial success with "The Dirty Dozen"; subsequently bought studio facility

1973: Reverse in fortunes lead to sale of studio facility

1981: Directed final film, "The Angry Hills"

QUOTES:

He served as president of the Directors Guild of America from 1975 to 1979. A special award presented by the Guild was created posthumously.

While being interviewed for "Little Caesar: A Biography of Edward G. Robinson" (New English Library, 1983), Aldrich said that he thought the only reason he had not been blacklisted along with many Hollywood notables was because he was only a low-level assistant director at the time of the red hunt.

Woody Allen

BORN: Allen Stewart Konigsberg in Brooklyn, New York, 12/01/1935

SOMETIMES CREDITED AS:
Heywood Allen

NATIONALITY: American

EDUCATION: Midwood High School Brooklyn, New York

New York University, New York, New York 1953; attended for one semester

AWARDS: National Board of Review Special Citation Best Screenplay "Sleeper" 1973

Berlin Film Festival Special Silver Bear 1975; presented for body of work

New York Film Critics Circle Award Best Director "Annie Hall" 1977

Directors Guild of America Award Outstanding Directorial Achievement in Feature Film "Annie Hall" 1977

BAFTA Award Best Director "Annie Hall" 1977

Oscar Best Director "Annie Hall" 1977

Los Angeles Film Critics Association Award Best Screenplay "Annie Hall" 1977; shared award with Marshall Brickman

New York Film Critics Circle Award Best Screenplay "Annie Hall" 1977; shared award with Marshall Brickman

National Society of Film Critics Award Best Screenplay "Annie Hall" 1977; shared award with Marshall Brickman

BAFTA Award Best Screenplay "Annie Hall" 1977; award shared with Marshall Brickman

Oscar Best Original Screenplay "Annie Hall" 1977; award shared with Marshall Brickman

O. Henry Award Best Short Story "The Kugelmass Episode" 1978; originally published in *The New Yorker*

New York Film Critics Circle Award Best Director "Manhattan" 1979

National Society of Film Critics Award Best Director "Manhattan" 1979; tied with Robert Benton who was cited for "Kramer vs. Kramer"

BAFTA Award Best Screenplay "Manhattan" 1979; award shared with Marshall Brickman

Cesar Best Foreign Film "Manhattan" 1980

Venice Film Festival Italian Critics Pasinetti Prize "Zelig" 1983

BAFTA Award Best Original Screenplay "Broadway Danny Rose" 1984

Cannes Film Festival FIPRESCI Prize for Non-Competing Film "The Purple Rose of Cairo" 1985

New York Film Critics Circle Award Best Screenplay "The Purple Rose of Cairo" 1985

Golden Globe Award Best Screenplay "The Purple Rose of Cairo" 1985

BAFTA Award Best Original Screenplay "The Purple Rose of Cairo" 1985

Cesar Best Foreign Film "The Purple Rose of Cairo" 1986

National Board of Review Award Best Director "Hannah and Her Sisters" 1986

New York Film Critics Circle Award Best Director "Hannah and Her Sisters" 1986

Los Angeles Film Critics Association Award Best Screenplay "Hannah and Her Sisters" 1986

BAFTA Award Best Original Screenplay "Hannah and Her Sisters" 1986

Oscar Best Original Screenplay "Hannah and Her Sisters" 1986

BAFTA Award Best Original Screenplay "Husbands and Wives" 1992

Venice Film Festival Golden Lion 1995; for lifetime achievement

Directors Guild of America D W Griffith Award 1996; for lifetime achievement

BAFTA Fellowship 1996

Catalan International Film Festival of Sitges Award to the Gran Angular Best Film "The Curse of the Jade Scorpion" 2001

Prince of Asturias Prize 2002

BIOGRAPHY

Woody Allen is one of a handful of American filmmakers who can rightly be labeled as an auteur. His films, be they dramas or comedies, are remarkably personal and are permeated with Allen's preoccupation with art, religion and love. While the comedies are generally upbeat and the dramas rich in detail, most of his films are fiercely personal, betraying a yearning for physical beauty, a traditional sense of machismo, intellectual and professional acceptance and knowledge. Allen's obsessions with Judaism, the WASP world that eludes the Jew, and the balm of psychiatry—which may or may not chase these devils—are also never far beneath the surface of his work.

The Brooklyn-born Allen purportedly failed a film course at NYU during his first semester. Dropping out of college, he joined the NBC Writer's Program and began contributing material to such programs as "The Colgate Comedy Hour" and "Your Show of Shows". Allen also started a lucrative secondary career as a gag writer for such comics and nightclub performers as Carol Channing, Art Carney, Herb Shriner and Buddy Hackett. By 1960, he had begun his own successful career as a stand-up comedian, honing what would become his screen persona, the intellectual "schnook". Inspired by Hope, Nichols and May and Mort Sahl, Allen created humor that was based in the urban Jewish mentality, guilt-ridden and anxious. In his halting stammer, he would deliver monologues that would poke fun at everything from sex and marriage to religion and politics. His routines proved popular not only in Greenwich Village cabarets but also on college campuses and recordings. So successful was Allen that his audience came to believe he was that person on stage. (Despite protestations, he continued to nourish this belief in his onscreen characterizations.)

In 1965, Allen made his feature film acting and writing debut with the farcical, but uneven, "What's New, Pussycat?", directed by Clive Donner. This film introduced recurring themes found in his work: romantic complications and the reliance on psychotherapy. Shortly thereafter, he debuted as a filmmaker of sorts by re-tooling a minor Japanese spy thriller with his own storyline and with English dialogue dubbed by American actors. The amusing result was "What's Up Tiger Lily?" (1966) that, along with the James Bond spoof "Casino Royale" (1967), he co-wrote and acted in, launching Allen on one of the most successful and unusual filmmaking careers.

For a period in the mid- to late-1960s, Allen concentrated on the Broadway stage. "Don't Drink the Water" (1966), about a family from New Jersey caught up in spying in an unnamed Iron Curtain country, was a modest success. "Play

It Again, Sam" (1969) was more successful. The central character, a film critic, invokes the spirit of Humphrey Bogart as his guide through life and love. Successfully treading the fine line between fantasy and reality, the play was filmed in 1972 and began Allen's long association with actress Diane Keaton.

In 1969, Allen created two short films for a television special, "Cupid's Shaft", an homage of Charlie Chaplin's 1931 classic "City Lights" that co-starred Candice Bergen, and a loose adaptation of "Pygmalion" in which Allen as a fake rabbi hired to teach a beautiful, but stupid woman (Bergen). That same year, he wrote, directed and starred in the feature "Take the Money and Run" which parodied both gangster films and cinema verite documentaries. The loose structure, lack of technical polish, and indebtedness to his nightclub routines are also evident in his next two features as well. "Bananas" (1971) was a south-of-the-border satire that lambastes both politics and mass media while "Everything You Always Wanted to Know About Sex* (*but were afraid to ask)" (1972) consisted of a series of skits loosely related to a title borrowed from a then-popular self-help book.

While Allen's films were not blockbusters, they did turn enough of a profit for the writer-director-star to begin creative control of his work. As the 70s progressed, Allen found his voice as a filmmaker. "Sleeper" (1973), about a 20th-century health food store owner who is cryogenically frozen and thawed out after two hundred years is filled with sight-gags yet has a curiously apolitical tone. "Love and Death" (1975) marked a leap forward for Allen as he interwove serious themes with the comedy. Set during the Napoleonic wars, the film not only spoofed Russian literature and culture as well as numerous classic films (e.g., "Alexander Nevsky") but also raised serious philosophical questions. "Love and Death" signaled Allen's higher aspirations and desire to be considered a "serious" moviemaker.

The bittersweet "Annie Hall" (1977) was a further step toward this goal. While still anchored in comedy, Allen utilized sophisticated narrative devices (such as direct address to the camera), relied less on slapstick and sight gags and clearly tackled themes and problems that were reflective of his concerns and his life. In Alvy Singer, the writer-director-actor solidified his screen persona as the urban, Jewish intellectual outsider. For many, the film defined the quintessential Allen movie: personal and thoughtful yet satiric and entertaining. Critically acclaimed, "Annie Hall" received numerous accolades, including four Academy Awards: Best Picture, Best Actress (Diane Keaton), Best Director (Allen) and Best Original Screenplay (Allen and Marshall Brickman).

As a surprising follow-up, Allen shifted to more dramatic material and focused on the starchy, repressed WASP milieu in "Interiors" (1978). Owing more than a debt to Ingmar Bergman, Shakespeare and Eugene O'Neill, "Interiors" probed the angst and petty betrayals of an upper-class family with three daughters. Many critics and audience members were confounded by the deadly earnest tone Allen adopted; it was a film that one either loved or hated. Beautifully shot by cinematographer Gordon Willis and strongly acted by a cast that included Geraldine Page, E.G. Marshall, Diane Keaton and Maureen Stapleton, "Interiors" earned a surprising five Oscar nominations, including nods to Allen for direction and writing.

Again teaming with Marshall Brickman, Allen wrote what is his most profitable, and arguably his best, film, "Manhattan" (1979). With its lush Gershwin score, gorgeous black-and-white photography (again by Willis) and brilliant ensemble cast, the film marked a return to comedy peppered with autobiographical and romantic elements. It was also notable as Allen's last film with Diane Keaton for many years (their off-screen relationship was ending around the same time). The film engendered mild controversy over his celluloid love interest, a teenager played by Mariel Hemingway.

Allen moved on to the somewhat self-indulgent Felliniesque "Stardust Memories" (1980), made in part to counter-act those critics who felt he was becoming too serious a filmmaker. (Throughout the film, Allen's character, a film director, is exhorted to "make funny movies", something the character is adamant about no longer doing.) Beginning with the slight "A Midsummer Night's Sex Comedy" (1982), Allen found a new leading lady (both on and off screen) in Mia Farrow. (She went on to headline a dozen more films during the next ten years, proving to be both a strong dramatic performer as well as a gifted comedienne.) "Zelig" (1983) melded Allen's fascination with celebrity with his growing grasp of cinematic methods. A marvel of technical wizardry, this mock documentary inter-cut and merged new footage with old to recreate vintage newsreels and sound recordings. (In many ways, a precursor of the techniques utilized by Robert Zemeckis in 1994's "Forrest Gump".) The Runyonesque "Broadway Danny Rose" (1984) was primarily dismissed by critics as a minor outing, yet it contains a marvelous performance from Farrow who was virtually unrecognizable as the Brooklyn-accented former mistress of a gangster. "The Purple Rose of Cairo" (1985), in which Allen did not appear, was another technical tour de force. Set in the Depression, Farrow was cast as the timid wife of an abusive husband who finds refuge at the movie theater. Her life is complicated when the matinee idol lead (Jeff Daniels) of a film one day steps off the screen and into her life. Tying together several of Allen's major themes (fame, romance, fantasy and art), the film earned respectable notices and a modest box office.

Except for the nostalgia-laden "Radio Days" (1987), for much of the remainder of the decade, Allen concentrated on dramatic material, peaking with the Chekhovian "Hannah and Her Sisters" (1986), which focused on New York family relationships. Allen received his third Oscar for its brilliant original script. The bloodless "September" (1987) and the Bergmanesque "Another Woman" (1988, with a virtuoso leading turn from Gena Rowlands) were further examinations of the emotionally bereft worlds of WASPy New Yorkers. With "Crimes and Misdemeanors" (1989), Allen closed the decade with a pessimistic examination of the morality of murder.

The early 90s found Allen in a lighter mode. The New Age–themed "Alice" (1990), a riff on Lewis Carroll's "Alice and Wonderland", that cast Farrow as a distaff WASPy version of Allen's familiar flustered, neurotic self-conscious screen persona. The critically reviled "Shadows and Fog" (1992) was an allegory about anti-Semitism that combined homages to 1930s German expressionism and 1950s European art films and was plagued by one-note characterizations. "Husbands and Wives" (also 1992), though not without humor, was one of the director's most emotionally violent films. Highlighted by jittery, hand-held cinema verite camerawork and a pessimistic view of enduring love, the film was released early by its distributor in part to capitalize on its uncanny parallels with the real-life turmoil between Allen and Farrow. Their very public break-up, spurred by Allen's romantic involvement with Farrow's adopted daughter, was followed by Farrow's public accusations that Allen had molested their adopted daughter. In the midst of all the Sturm und Drang, Allen made the frothy "Manhattan Murder Mystery" (1993), which reunited him with Marshall Brickman and Diane Keaton. A comic thriller that attempted to recreate the banter and urbanity of such seminal films as "The Thin Man", "Manhattan Murder Mystery" proved to be a financial disappointment, overshadowed by Allen's personal troubles.

By the time "Bullets Over Broadway" was released in 1994, audiences were ready to embrace his work anew. Working with writer Douglas McGrath, Allen fashioned a period comedy about a playwright (John Cusack as Allen's screen alter ego) who achieve success through connections with gangsters. A meditation on what defines an artist, "Bullets Over Broadway" benefited from fine performances, notably Dianne Wiest's Oscar-winning turn as a past-her-prime stage diva. "Mighty Aphrodite" (1995) was an uneven attempt that baldly proclaimed its indebtedness to Greek theater with the use of a chorus. Allen played a middle-aged sportswriter searching for the birth mother of his adopted child, who turns out not to be the cultured woman he imagined but rather a vulgar prostitute. With "Everyone Says I Love You" (1996), he combined frothy 30s musical sensibilities with his familiar themes to a mixed result that divided audiences and critics. "Deconstructing Harry" (1997) was a critically praised, scatological and complex look at a writer's life that employed black comedy and dramatizations of the author's works to comment on the function of the artist in society.

Alone among contemporary independent filmmakers, Allen has had a constant stream of highly personal films produced and distributed with "mainstream" money, while still exerting creative control over the product. He has also enjoyed long and fruitful collaborations with talents both in front of and behind the camera. In the former category would be such performers as Diane Keaton, Mia Farrow, Tony Roberts, Dianne Wiest and Alan Alda; in the latter, cinematographers Gordon Willis and Carlo Di Palma, producers Jack Rollins, Robert Greenhut and Jean Doumanian, designers Mel Bourne and Santo Loquasto, editors Ralph Rosenblum and Susan E Morse. A remarkable businessman, Allen has protected himself with low budgets that allow him to reach his like-minded, intelligent and mostly urban audience on a regular basis.

In addition to his impressive body of work as writer-director, Allen has occasionally acted in films directed by others. He proved quite effective as the titular "The Front" (1977), a shill willing to put his name on the scripts written by blacklisted writers. Allen fared less well as Bette Midler's husband in Paul Mazursky's seriocomic look at contemporary marriage "Scenes From a Mall" (1991). Allen returned to TV to adapt, direct and co-star in a small screen remake of "Don't Drink the Water" (ABC, 1994). He and Peter Falk filmed a TV version of Neil Simon's "The Sunshine Boys" for CBS in 1995, that finally aired in December 1997 to generally unfavorable notices. Allen is also an accomplished author, penning essays and short stories for *The New Yorker* and other magazines, and a musician. For many years, he has spent his Monday evenings playing clarinet with a jazz band. Noted documentarian Barbara Kopple filmed "Wild Man Blues" (1998), which followed Allen and the band on a European tour.

Allen continued to put out one movie per year for the next five years. He dappled in different genres, with his comic heist pic "Small Time Crooks" (2000) and the mystery "Curse of the Jade Scorpion" (2001). A running theme for his most recent films, however, seems to eerily mimic his real life romance with step-daughter and wife, Soon Yi Previn. In "Jade Scorpion" Allen becomes romantically involved with starlet Charlize Theron, entangled with the youthful Tea Leoni in "Hollywood Ending," and 2002's "Anything Else" couples Allen with Christina Ricci, who is 45 years his junior.

COMPANIONS:

Mia Farrow. Actor; began relationship in 1980; mother of Allen's son Satchel/Seamus; separated in 1992 after Allen admitted to a romantic involvement with her adopted daughter Soon-Yi Previn in the winter of 1991

wife: Soon-Yi Previn. Just before Allen's suit to gain custody of his three children with Mia Farrow came to court, it was revealed that Allen had fallen in love with Previn at the end of 1991; she is one of the children Farrow adopted while married to conductor Andre Previn during the 1970s; born October 8, 1970; married on December 23, 1997 in Venice, Italy

MILESTONES:

At age 15, began sending jokes to columnists Walter Winchell and Earl Wilson

Worked at a public relations firm supplying comedy material to Bob Hope and Arthur Murray, among others

1953: After flunking out of NYU, joined the NBC Writer's Program; contributed to "The Colgate Comedy Hour"

1955: Hired as a writer for "Your Show Of Shows" at age 19; began writing gags for such comedians as Herb Shriner, Buddy Hackett and Art Carney (date approximate)

1960: Stage writing debut for revue, "From A to Z"

1960: Debut as stand-up comedian at The Blue Angel in NYC (October)

Became staff writer on "The Tonight Show" (NBC)

1964: First guest-host to replace Johnny Carson on "The Tonight Show" (NBC)

1965: Feature film acting and writing debut, "What's New Pussycat?", directed by Clive Donner

1966: First play produced on Broadway, "Don't Drink the Water"

1966: Made feature film, "What's Up, Tiger Lily?" using existing footage of a Japanese film, creating new story by dubbing in voices

1969: TV writing and acting debut with the short film, "Cupid's Shaft"

1969: Headlined "Woody's First Special" (CBS) and "The Woody Allen Special" (NBC)

1969: Feature film directing debut (also screenwriter; actor), "Take the Money and Run"

1969: Broadway acting debut in "Play It Again, Sam"; also playwright

1970–1971: Debut as TV series regular on the NBC children's show "Hot Dog"

1971: Published first collection of comic material "Getting Even"

1972: First of six films opposite Diane Keaton, "Play It Again, Sam"

1976: Rare acting appearance in a film which he did not direct, "The Front"

1977: Breakthrough film, "Annie Hall"; film won four Academy Awards, including Best Picture and Best Director

1978: Directed first film drama, "Interiors"

1979: Last film opposite Diane Keaton for 14 years (except for her cameo in "Radio Days" 1987), "Manhattan"; also most successful film

1981: Wrote the full-length stage comedy "The Floating Light Bulb"

1982: First film with Mia Farrow, "A Midsummer Night's Sex Comedy"

1986: Won third Oscar for Best Original Screenplay for "Hannah and Her Sisters"

1987: Had cameo in Jean-Luc Godard's "King Lear"

1991: Co-starred with Bette Midler in Paul Mazursky's "Scenes from a Mall"

1991: Signed an agreement with Italy's National Association of Consumer Cooperatives (COOP) to write and direct of series of five TV commericials (his first); fee for the package rumored to be 3 million lire ($2.5 million)

1991: Signed deal with TriStar Pictures (September); began first film for them, "Husbands and Wives"

1992: Separated from Mia Farrow after admitting to having fallen in love with Farrow's adopted daughter Soon-Yi Previn during the winter of 1991; accused by Farrow of having molested her children; filed for custody of his three children Moses, Satchel and Dylan (August)

1993: Lost custody suit for his three children against Farrow

1993: Completed a second film for TriStar, "Manhattan Murder Mystery" (reteaming him with Diane Keaton); ended multi-picture deal with the company; signed with Sweetland Films in July

1993: Charges of molestation dropped

1994: Had modest success with the period comedy "Bullets Over Broadway"; first of three films distributed by Miramax period comedy

1994: Made rare TV acting appearance in small screen remake of "Don't Drink the Water"; also directed and wrote

1995: Co-starred with Peter Falk in TV remake of Neil Simon's "The Sunshine Boys"; production aired in December 1997

1997: First film distributed by Fine Line, "Deconstructing Harry"; nominated for a Best Original Screenplay Oscar; Allen's 20th Academy Award nomination and 13th for screenwriting, making him the most nominated screenwriter in Academy history

1998: Made unbilled cameo appearance in Stanley Tucci's film "The Imposters"

1998: Voiced the characters of the worker ant Z in the DreamWorks–produced animated film "Antz"; character romanced the princess ant Bala voiced by Sharon Stone

1998: Released his 30th film as director, "Celebrity"

1999: Wrote and directed "Sweet and Low-down", focusing on a 1930s jazz guitarist

2000: Starred opposite Sharon Stone in the black comedy "Picking Up the Pieces"

2000: Wrote and directed the comedy "Small Time Crooks"

2000: In March, signed distribution deal with DreamWorks

2001: Wrote and directed "The Curse of the Jade Scorpion"

2002: Wrote, directed and starred in "Hollywood Ending"

QUOTES:

As of 2000, Allen has been nominated for 20 Academy Awards: once for Best Actor; six times for Best Director and 13 times for Best Screenplay

"I just keep my nose to the grindstone. I don't listen to people who criticize me, don't listen to them tell me my films are bad, or listen to people who tell me I'm a comic genius. I don't worry about getting rich or about what people say. I focus on the work with the same fanaticism that a Muslim fundamentalist might focus on religion. If I was giving advice to younger people, I would tell them to not listen to anything—not read what's written about you, don't listen to anybody, just focus on the work." Allen quoted in a rare interview in New York *Daily News*, October 22, 1995.

Allen has played New Orleans jazz clarinet with his group, the New Orleans Funeral and Ragtime Orchestra, almost every Monday at Michael's Pub in New York since 1971 (and skipped the 1978 Oscar ceremonies so as not to miss a Monday night set).

"I didn't want to play Bogart. I didn't want to play John Wayne. I wanted to be the schnook. The guy with the glasses who doesn't get the girl, who can't get the girl but who's amusing."—Woody Allen to John Lahr in *The New Yorker*, December 9, 1996.

Denis Hamill: What are your feelings toward Mia Farrow now?

Woody Allen: I haven't had any contact with her for years. Although we've had our many conflicts, I have no further or lingering feelings about it. I wish her well. No, I haven't read her book, don't intend to. Not interested in the whole thing. To me, now it's history. I know what happened and what she thinks. As it turned out, in that period of my life, more people that I care about became closer to me than became estranged. People I thought of as acquaintances became friends. Some rose to the occasion in heroic fashion for me. Which was great. My relationship with Soon-Yi is the best one of my life. So it wasn't all bad."— "Deconstructing Woody", *Daily News*, October 5, 1997.

"After the treadmill and breakfast, I lie down on the bed with a pad and pencil or pad and pen and write for two hours and then have a shower. Write for another two hours and break for lunch, Then write all afternoon. I could write all the time. I love to write. All I need are little breaks to practice the clarinet and to get a breath of fresh air. Then I can't wait to get back to it because I'm refreshed. I'd be happy to write all day and all night. If I didn't make movies, I could easily write four screenplays a year."—Allen to Denis Hamill in *Daily News*, October 7, 1997.

"I've been blessed. It's like fool's luck. From the day I made my first film, nobody at United Artists and then Orion expected anything. I've had nothing but support, freedom, final cut, nobody tells me who to cast. It's nothing that I did to earn it. It was given to me by magnanimous people."—Woody Allen in conversation with Martin Scorsese, *The New York Times Magazine*, November 16, 1997.

"Working with Woody is like holding a puppy. It's warm and nice, but you know if you hold on too long he's going to piss all over you."—an unnamed source quoted in Marion Meade's biography, "The Unruly Life of Woody Allen" (Scribner's, 2000).

About his break up with Mia Farrow, Allen told London's *The Daily Telegraph* (March 18, 2002): "It was big and messy and it could have been handled better and had better consequences. But I didn't have any choice. I was put in that position and I had to respond. Normally I like to handle everything quietly and discreetly and I'm a, you know, a friendly and forgiving private type. But I will always . . . There are certain situations where you are forced to act.

"It was a terrible, terrible, terrible situation. My not having access to the children is completely cruel and unfair. Not in their best interests. But these dreadful things happen in life. To balance that I had parents with good longevity [his father lived to 100, his mother was 95]. I've been healthy. I've been blessed with a talent."

In June, 2002, Allen sued longtime friend and producer Jean Doumanian and her business partner and boyfriend, Jacqui Safra, saying they cheated him out of his share of profits on eight movies made since 1993. Allen said the pair owed him more than 12 million dollars. The parties reached an undisclosed settlement after 9 days in court.

DISCOGRAPHY:

"Woody Allen" Colpix, 1964
"Woody Allen, Volume 2" Colpix, 1965
"Woody Allen: Stand-Up Comic—1964–68" United Artists; 1978

BIBLIOGRAPHY:

"Getting Even" Woody Allen, 1971, Random House
"Without Feathers" Woody Allen, 1975, Random House
"Woody Allen: Clown Prince of American Humor" Bill Adler and Jeff Feinman, 1975, Pinnacle Books
"On Being Funny: Woody Allen and Comedy" Eric Lax, 1975, Charterhouse
"Non-Being and Somethingness" Woody Allen, 1978, Random House
"Woody Allen: A Biography" Lee Guthrie, 1978, Drake
"Side Effects" Woody Allen, 1980, Random House
"Woody Allen: His Films and Career" 1985, Citadel Press
"Woody Allen on Location" Thierry De Navacelle, 1987, William Morrow
"Woody Allen" Eric Lax, 1991, Alfred A. Knopf; authorized biography
"Woody Allen at Work: The Photographs of Brian Hamill" Brian Hamill, 1995, Harry N. Abrams Inc. with an introduction by Charles Champlin
"Woody: Movies From Manhattan" Julian Fox 1996, Overlook Press
"Reconstructing Woody: Art, Love and Life in the Films of Woody Allen" Mary Nichols, Rowman & Littlefield

"Woody Allen: A Biography" John Baxter, 1998, HarperCollins

"The Unruly Life of Woody Allen" Marion Meade, 2000, Scribner

Pedro Almodovar

BORN: Pedro Almodovar Caballero in Calzada de Calatrava, La Mancha, Spain, 09/25/1949

SOMETIMES CREDITED AS:
Patti Diphusa

NATIONALITY: Spanish

EDUCATION: educated in Caceres, Spain

AWARDS: Rio Film Festival Glauber Rocha Award Best Director "Law of Desire" 1987

Los Angeles Film Critics Association New Generation Award "Law of Desire" 1987

Rio Film Festival Glauber Rocha Award Best Director "Law of Desire" 1987

Venice International Film Festival Prize Best Screenplay "Women on the Verge of a Nervous Breakdown" 1988

Cesar Best Foreign Language Film "High Heels" 1993

Honorary Cesar 1998

Cannes Film Festival Best Director Award "Todo Sobre Mi Madre/All About My Mother" 1999

FIPRESCI Grand Prize "Todo Sobre Mi Madre/All About My Mother" 1999; presented at the San Sebastian Film Festival

British Independent Film Award Best Foreign Independent Film "All About My Mother" 1999

European Film Award European Film "All About My Mother" 1999

European Film Award People's Choice for Best Director "All About My Mother" 1999

British Independent Film Award Best Foreign Independent Film—Foreign Language "All About My Mother" 1999

National Board of Review Best Foreign Film "All About My Mother" 1999

Los Angeles Film Critics Association Award Best Foreign Film "All About My Mother" 1999

Boston Society of Film Critics Award Best Foreign Film "All About My Mother" 1999

New York Film Critics Circle Award Best Foreign Language Film "All About My Mother" 1999

Broadcast Film Critics Association Award Best Foreign Film "All About My Mother" 1999

Golden Satellite Best Foreign Language Film "All About My Mother" 1999; tied with Tony Bui's "Three Seasons"

Golden Globe Award Best Foreign-Language Film "All About My Mother" 1999

Goya Best Director "All About My Mother" 1999; also cited as Best Film

Lumiere Best Foreign Film "All About My Mother" 1999

Cesar Best Foreign Film "All About My Mother" 2000

London Film Critics Circle Award Best Foreign Language Film "All About My Mother" 2000

BAFTA Award Best Film Not in the English Language "All About My Mother" 2000

BAFTA David Lean Award for Best Achievement in Direction "All About My Mother" 2000

David di Donatello Prize Best Foreign Film "All About My Mother" 2000

Los Angeles Film Critics Association Awards Best Director "Talk To Her" 2002

BAFTA Best Screenplay (Original) "Talk To Her" 2002

BAFTA Film not in the English Language "Talk To Her" 2002

Oscar Best Screenplay (Original) "Talk To Her" 2002

BIOGRAPHY

The most internationally popular and important Spanish director since Luis Bunuel, Pedro Almodovar fled the stifling Roman Catholicism of his provincial La Mancha at the age of 17 to do battle with the windmills of Madrid. Lacking the money to enter college, he peddled books and made jewelry before settling into a decade-long run as a clerk at the National Telephone Company during which he contributed comic strips and stories to underground magazines like *Star*, *Vibora* and *Vibraciones*. As the most visible exponent of "la movida" (the cultural ferment in Madrid post-Franco), he would eventually act with the avant-garde theater group Los Goliardos, meeting actors like Carmen Maura and Antonio Banderas who would become key players in his movie repertory company. Additionally, he would publish parodic memoirs under the pen name 'Patti Diphusa' (a fictitious international porn star) in LA LUNA and record and perform (in drag) with his own band (Almodovar and McNamara), although not before shooting his first Super-8 shorts, beginning with "Dos Putas, o Historia de Ampor que Termina en Boda" (1974).

While other directors of his generation were making somber films about the Franco years, Almodovar made the conscious intellectual decision to never allude to the specter of the generalisimo, recording instead the vibrant explosion of wild behavior and hedonism expressed in the giddy rush of freedom following the old fascist's death in 1975. In fact, his first mainstream feature "Pepi, Luci, Bom and Other Girls Like Mom" (1980), shot in 16mm and blown up to 35mm, was an instant success, due in large part to the marked absence of Franco's shadow. Almodovar continued to develop his eye-popping colorful style, making affectionately off-the-wall movies chronicling the dark, bawdy and ultimately lonely misadventures of people living on the fringes of society—heroin-shooting nuns in "Dark Habits" (1983); a speed-addicted

cleaning woman in "What Have I Done to Deserve This?" (1984); a murderous bullfighter in "Matador" (1986); and lovelorn homosexuals and transsexuals in "Law and Desire" (1987), a film which drew fire for its depiction of unprotected gay sex.

Though openly gay, Almodovar took umbrage at what he considered the pejorative label of "gay filmmaker", arguing that the homosexual sensibility in his films did not make them "gay films", but rather films depicting universal passion to which both homosexuals and heterosexuals could relate. The director successfully transcended these early attempts to classify him, and when people refer to him today as the undisputed leader of the New Spanish Cinema, there is no tag regarding his sexual orientation. Funny, outrageous, sexy, even kinky, his early movies driven by headstrong (and high-strung) heroines earned him a reputation as a fine director of women (a contemporary George Cukor) and culminated in the wackily exuberant farce "Women on the Verge of a Nervous Breakdown" (1988). Almodovar painted the manic Madrid of the 80s as a playground for wit—above all, women's wit—and audiences responded enthusiastically, making it the most successful film in Spanish box-office history, one that won international acclaim and an Academy Award nomination for Best Foreign Film.

Of all his films to date, "Women" faired the best with Americans, grossing a phenomenal $7 million in the States. Almodovar's attempt at high comedy à la "How to Marry a Millionaire" (1953) resulted in what he called an "absolutely white" movie covering 48 hours in the lives of several women who are so hysterical, they don't have time for sex and drugs. Though seemingly at odds with the uninhibited signature of his earlier work, the lack of oral sex acts and dope that made it in the words of leading lady Maura "a film that our nephews will be allowed to see" also made it more accessible to conservative US audiences. His next film

"Atame!/Tie Me Up! Tie Me Down!" (1990), however, earned an X rating for its one prolonged sex scene, which showed the two lovers only from the waist up and focused primarily on the woman's sexual fulfillment. Perhaps the success of "Women" had made him a target of the MPAA, but the advocacy of William Kunstler on the picture's behalf did not dissuade the ratings board. The X stood, causing the incensed director to compare MPAA's tactics to fascist techniques under Franco.

"Tie Me Up! Tie Me Down!", Almodovar's fifth and last movie with Banderas, grossed $4 million in the States but since then his US box office has been in a downward spiral. Americans loved the campy "Women" but responded less enthusiastically to the kidnapping central to "Tie Me Up!". "High Heels" (1991) started out in the helmer's typically irreverent, wacky style but ran out of steam about halfway through, and the lengthy rape scene of "Kika" (1993), which earned the film its NC-17, did not strike US audiences as funny, once again causing the director to decry Americans as puritanical and lacking a sense of humor for their inability to see rape as a laughing matter. "The Flower of My Secret" (1995), while true to Almodovar's typically sympathetic focus on the plight of the contemporary Spanish woman, also revealed a more mature artist at work. Audiences expecting the enfant terrible's familiar, off-beat black humor saw a return to the masterful high comedy of urban life, accompanied by the sad notes of resignation and compromise that signaled a new austerity.

With "Live Flesh" (1998), Almodovar moved beyond his stance of never referring to the Franco years while showing he could fuse visual and sexual anarchy with the most elegant of plots. He also for the first time filmed material which he had not originated, loosely adapting Ruth Rendell's novel into a completely Spanish sensibility. The movie opens with the birth of Victor on a bus in 70s Madrid, its streets bare because of the restrictions of the Franco regime, and comes full circle with the birth of Victor's son 26 years later in the middle of a Madrid street choked with traffic, symbolic of the better life Victor's son will enjoy in a democratic Spain. In an ominous note for Spanish audiences, the voice heard announcing the state of emergency at the picture's beginning belongs to Manuel Fraga Iribane, formerly Franco's minister of information and grand old man of the conservative party ruling Spain today. Almodovar's concerns about that new right-wing government prompted his use of this device to remind viewers that "we are not so far from it (the awful past)."

Though American audiences have not embraced the more political and sober Almodovar, the change of mood has proved popular in Spain, where critics who previously attacked the unevenness of his plotting and superficiality of his characters proclaimed "Live Flesh" a masterpiece, qualifying it with adjectives like consistent and cohesive. No longer the overgrown kid who sprang from the thick of Madrid's anything-goes night life, armed with a hand-held camera, to record the intoxication of Spain's post-Franco freedoms, he has reinvented himself triumphantly as a consummate stylist with a serious touch. The departure from his wildly comedic storylines represents the evolution of a director who needed to tackle fresh and dangerous territory to escape becoming mannered. What interests Almodovar as he enters this period of maturity is a narrative that truthfully reveals his characters' emotions, and the fully-developed masculinity of "Live Flesh" that replaces the crude and flat males of his recent work is just one indication of an auteur beginning to demonstrate complete command of the art form.—Written by Greg Senf

MILESTONES:

1962: Won a prize at the age of 10 for essay about the Immaculate Conception (date approximate)

1968: Moved to Madrid (date approximate)

Wrote comic strips and articles for underground Spanish publications, *Star, Vibora* and *Vibraciones*

1970–1981: Worked for the National Telephone Company

Joined theater group Los Goliardos, where he met Carmen Maura and Antonio Banderas

Made numerous short super-8 films; first short, "Dos Putas, o Historia de Amor que Termina en Boda/Two Whores, or a Love Story Which Ends in Marriage" (1974)

Regular contributor to newspapers *El Pais, Diario 16* and *La Luna*; for the latter created popular cartoon character, "Patti Diphusa" whose fictionalized confesssions he published under the eponymous female pseudonym

1978: Made first feature-length film (in super-8), "Folle, Folle, Folleme, Tim/Fuck, Fuck, Fuck Me, Tim"

1978: Made first 16mm film, "Salome"

1980: Directed first commercial feature (16mm, blown up to 35mm), "Pepi, Luci, Bom and Other Girls on the Heap"; first feature with Maura

1981: Composed and performed score for film, "Labyrinth of Passions"; also directed; retired from Telephone Company

Performed with rock group, Almodovar and McNamara (with friend Fabio, known as Fanny McNamara)

1982: First feature film with Banderas, "Labyrinth of Passion"

1983: Attracted attention outside of Spain (for the first time) with third feature, "Dark Habits"

1984: First international hit, "What Have I Done to Deserve This?"

1985: Formed production company, El Deseo, with brother Agustin

1987: "Law of Desire" (starring Banderas) drew criticism for depicting unprotected gay sex; first producing credit (associate producer) and only credit as production designer

1988: Biggest US success, "Women on the Verge of a Nervous Breakdown" netted more than $7 million in ticket sales; fourth film with Banderas; final feature (to date) with Maura; nominated for Oscar as Best Foreign Film; won New York Film Critics Circle Award as Best Foreign Film

1990: Fifth and last collaboration to date with Banderas, "Tie Me Up! Tie Me Down!"; US box office fell to $4 million

1991: Appeared in the documentary charting Madonna's world tour "Truth of Dare"

1995: Began departing from his typically comedic story lines for "The Flowers of My Secret"; grossed $1 million in the USA

1998: Revealed continued attraction for austere and sober narratives with noirish crime drama, "Live Flesh", very loosely adapted from the Ruth Rendell novel; first film based on material by another

1999: Helmed "Todo Sobre Mi Madre/All About My Mother" which premiered at the Cannes Film Festival to postive notices and garnered the director's prize; won the Best Foreign Language Film Academy Award

2002: Wrote and directed the romantic comedy "Hable Con Ella/Talk To Her"

QUOTES:

Some sources list 1951 as the year of Mr. Almodovar's birth.

"Women on the Verge of a Nervous Breakdown" received the 1989 Orson Welles Award as best non-English film, the Goya as Best Film and that same year the Spanish magazine *Cambio 16* named Almodovar as Man of the Year.

"All About My Mother" was named the Best Foreign-Language Film by the Academy of Motion Picture Arts and Sciences.

"It's something magical. To me it has become an obsession that sort of parallels a great love story. When you start a love story, you're moved by something very concrete. Perhaps a physical attraction. And then with time you discover the reasons why you are with that person. And a great love story begins to happen as the years pass. As if you have a disease that finally ends up consuming you entirely. Film has become something like that for me. At first it was a love story with a very immediate pleasure. And it has become something much more painful as time passes, but also something much more complete. Something I couldn't live without. I wonder where that need to make films and to narrate stories comes from. I don't know. Perhaps it is a fight against death, a fight against all the limitations we face."—Pedro Almodovar quoted in *Los Angeles Times,* May 6, 1990.

"I want [the characters] to live in a universe that belongs only to them, as if they were alone in the world, and where pain becomes the only protagonist in their life.

"It's not that I have any sympathy for murderers. But in my films, when one of my characters kills, as a writer I try to understand and explain it. And from that moment forward you're taking guilt away. And my characters—as I do—feel a natural antipathy towards authority and the police. So my characters end up winning."—Almodovar to *New York Post,* December 17, 1991.

"Women on the Verge . . . " exemplified the classic Almodovarean technique of blending kitsch, melodrama, fantasy and salacious humor into a nimble and assured exploration of human feeling: Gabriel Garcia Marquez crossed with John Waters crossed with Virginia Woolf. Almodovar knows how to create female characters that are finely nuanced and surprisingly complex. Like Hitchcock, he is also a master at depicting the life of objects: typewriters, blenders, answering machines. And then there are touches that show no influence, that belong only to Almodovar."—From "Almodovar on the Verge" by David Leavitt in *The New York Times Magazine,* April 22, 1990.

"He is a very courageous, brave man. He doesn't have any kind of fear when he is behind the camera. There is no self-censorship.

"Almodovar has always been afraid of Hollywood's control . . . But I think finally he has found some people and studios that will take a risk with him. I don't see Pedro Almodovar directing somebody else's scripts or somebody else's ideas. It must be something that comes from his heart."—Antonio Banderas quoted in *Chicago Tribune,* February 19, 1998.

"I would like to work with him [Banderas], but I don't know if that's possible—he's become too expensive for me."—Pedro Almodovar to *New York,* January 19, 1998.

"My first films coincided with a moment of absolute, vital explosion in the city. Madrid in the beginning of the 1980s was probably the most joyful, the most fun, the most permissive city in the world. It was really the rebirth of the city after such a horrible period as the Franco regime. If there was something characteristic about Madrid, about the culture of Madrid that I belonged to, it was the night life. That was my university, and the university for many others . . .

"Young people now are very preoccupied with the market, which is natural. But I remember in the early 80s, everything we did we did for pleasure, because we liked to, for the joy of doing it. Now people are not doing that, and it is a pity. Because when you are starting out, that is when you need to do exactly what you want, with no responsibility."—Almodovar quoted in *The New York Times,* January 18, 1998.

BIBLIOGRAPHY:

"El Sueno de la Razon/The Sleep of Reason" Pedro Almodovar; anthology of stories

"Fuego en las Entranas/Fire in the Guts" Pedro Almodovar, 1972; novella

"Todo Tuya/All Yours" Pedro Almodovar; pornographic photo-novel

BORN: in Kansas City, Missouri, 02/20/1925

NATIONALITY: American

EDUCATION: St Peter's Catholic School Kansas City, Missouri

Rockhurst High School, Kansas City, Missouri; Jesuit-run preparatory high school

Wentworth Military Academy, Lexington, Missouri

AWARDS: Cannes Film Festival Palme d'Or "M*A*S*H" 1970

New York Film Critics Circle Award Best Picture "Nashville" 1975

New York Film Critics Circle Award Best Director "Nashville" 1975

National Society of Film Critics Award Best Picture "Nashville" 1975

National Society of Film Critics Award Best Director "Nashville" 1975

National Board of Review Award Best Picture "Nashville" 1975; shared award with Stanley Kubrick for "Barry Lyndon"

National Board of Review Award Best Director "Nashville" 1975; shared award with Stanley Kubrick for "Barry Lyndon"

Berlin Film Festival Golden Bear "Buffalo Bill and the Indians, or Sitting Bull's History Lesson" 1976

Emmy Outstanding Directing in a Drama Series "Tanner '88" 1988/89 episode entitled "The Boiler Room"

John Cassavetes Award 1992 given to filmmakers whose work extends the possibilities of the medium; presented by Independent Feature Project

Cannes Film Festival Best Director Award "The Player" 1992

New York Film Critics Circle Award Best Director "The Player" 1992

Boston Society of Film Critics Award Best Director "The Player" 1992

Chicago Film Critics Association Award Best Director "The Player" 1992

Directors Guild of America D. W. Griffith Award 1994 for lifetime achievement

Independent Spirit Award Best Director "Short Cuts" 1993

Independent Spirit Award Best Screenplay "Short Cuts" 1993; shared award

American Cinema Editors Golden Eddie Award 1995 for "an individual who has significantly advanced the art of film"

Venice Fim Festival Golden Lion Award for Lifetime Achievement 1996

American Society of Cinematographers Board of Governors Award 1998

British Film Institute Fellowship 2001

New York Film Critics Circle Award Best Director "Gosford Park" 2001

National Society of Film Critics Award Best Director "Gosford Park" 2001

American Film Institute Award Director of the Year "Gosford Park" 2001 initial presentation of the award

Golden Globe Award Best Director "Gosford Park" 2001

Evening Standard Award Best Film "Gosford Park" 2001; shared award

Berlin Film Festival Golden Bear for Lifetime Achievement 2002; actress Claudia Cardinale also cited; first time in festival's 52-year history that more than one career achievement award was presented

BAFTA Award Best British Film "Gosford Park" 2002; Altman was one of the film's producers

BIOGRAPHY

Long recognized in Europe as a true auteur, Robert Altman brings an ironic, spare, irreverent gaze to bear on many long-standing

American values through his ongoing project of reconsidering film genres. His style—very much part of what one might call "American art cinema"—is full of quirks and surprises, all the more striking in light of his early training in TV and industrials.

Altman's apprenticeship began in 1947 in his native Kansas City with the Calvin Company, a leading producer of industrial films. "The Delinquents" (1957); his first feature, was followed by "The James Dean Story" (1957), a docudrama that mapped out his intentions of using film to explore the harsh reality behind pop culture icons.

From 1957 to 1965, Altman worked in Hollywood on a wide variety of television programs including "Combat", "Alfred Hitchcock Presents", and "Bonanza"; his resistance to conformity, however, delayed his progression into feature filmmaking for another decade. "Countdown" (1968) and "That Cold Day in the Park" (1969) garnered some critical attention, but Altman's career took a dramatic turn with "M*A*S*H" (1970), a box-office and critical smash which won the Palme d'Or at Cannes. Altman's defining characteristics were already emerging: the episodic structure, the penchant for black comedy, the ability to use a minute and detailed setting (here a medical unit during the Korean War) as a vehicle for broader social concerns. Success led him to expand his own Lion's Gate production company—complete with state-of-the-art editing and sound recording facilities—where the creative process was once described as "controlled chaos."

Altman's ensuing films, "Brewster McCloud" (1970), "McCabe & Mrs. Miller" (1971), "The Long Goodbye" (1973) and "Thieves Like Us" (1974), added to his reputation as an artist, but were all disappointments at the box-office. They also demonstrated his interest—doubtless nurtured during his restless TV days—in revising genre conventions to better reflect "reality", hence the downbeat turns of the grim yet humorous western, "McCabe", and the oddly relaxed quality of his excursion into film noir with "The Long Goodbye".

"Nashville" (1975), though, won back the audience, was nominated for several Oscars, and invariably appears on critics' "Best of the 1970s" lists for its layered narrative, breezy character treatment and witty use of music. Technically, the film was perhaps most remarkable for its dense, multi-track sound, which enabled Altman to subtly merge a diverse and often savagely satirical group of stories set in the world of country music and contemporary politics. The accolades stopped, however, with the still underrated "Buffalo Bill and the Indians, or Sitting Bull's History Lesson" (1976), Altman's Bicentennial film which explored the marketing of American history. His feud with producer Dino de Laurentiis over its editing led to his dismissal from "Ragtime" (1981), eventually directed by Milos Forman.

Altman debuted as a producer with "Welcome to L.A." (1976), by his protege Alan Rudolph, and "The Late Show" (1977), by screenwriter Robert Benton, both films echoing his fondness for quirky characters and situations. Altman's own directorial style continued to evolve and diversify with "Three Women" (1977), a film very much influenced by European art cinema, which won Shelley Duvall the Best Actress prize at Cannes; the freewheeling and also underrated satire "A Wedding" (1978); and "Quintet" (1979), an obscurely poetic film set in a snowbound post-apocalyptic world. Two comedies of this period, the offbeat romance "A Perfect Couple" (1979) and "Health" (1980), a send-up of America's health food craze, ran into distribution problems and were not widely seen. His final Lion's Gate effort, "Popeye" (1980), was a curious but off-the-mark cartoon re-creation that, like all Altman films, has its champions. The critical consensus, however, was hostile and the box office was disappointing. It would mark Altman's last mainstream Hollywood studio feature for more than a decade.

In 1981, Altman sold Lion's Gate and turned his attention to the theater. He staged and then filmed the drama "Come Back to the 5 & Dime, Jimmy Dean, Jimmy Dean" (1982). "Secret Honor" (1984) portrayed Richard Nixon (Philip Baker Hall) delivering an "apologia pro vita sua" monologue, while "Streamers" (1983), a film of David Rabe's play about stateside barracks life in the early days of the Vietnam War, garnered some critical support and a Venice Film Festival award for its ensemble cast. These films were a dramatic departure from the freewheeling, relatively improvisational, large canvas films of the preceding decade. These rigorous experiments tended to explore character in miniature with surprising fidelity to the theatrical sources. Paradoxically, Altman then returned to carving a niche in the small screen, having worked on several made-for-TV productions including "The Caine Mutiny Court-Martial" (CBS, 1988) and "Tanner '88" (HBO, 1988), for which he won an Emmy.

Treading water as a film director for much of the 80s, Altman helmed such little-seen misfires as "Beyond Therapy" and "O.C. and Stiggs" (both 1987) before regaining critical attention with his handsomely filmed, quietly intense portrait of the van Gogh brothers, "Vincent and Theo" (1990). He followed up with his most acclaimed film in years and one of his most commercially successful ever, "The Player" (1992), a bravura, scathing look at Hollywood opportunism which reunited Altman's restless camera stylistics with his ironic take on popular culture. The maverick filmmaker found himself restored to the A-list.

Apparently reinvigorated by success, Altman followed up with "Short Cuts" (1993), a return to the collage of portraits from the "Nashville" era. Twenty-two actors in nine different stories enacted Altman's take on writer Raymond Carver's stories of families and marital problems in a darkly rendered vision of Southern California life. Altman faltered a bit

as he proceeded in a lighter but similar panoramic vein with "Ready to Wear (Pret-a-Porter)" (1994), in which another highly varied collection of contemporary and past stars and character players enacted roles in a satirical look at the world of haute couture during the Paris shows. Unlike his two previous films, however, "Ready to Wear" failed to provide any insight into the subject matter and characters. Reviewers and audiences rejected the glitzy but shallow proceedings.

Having survived far worse career reversals, Altman continued to tackle new projects beginning with "Kansas City" (1996), a period urban gangster film set in the era of his earlier rural "Thieves Like Us." Miranda Richardson, Jennifer Jason Leigh and Harry Belafonte starred in this tale of a telegraph operator who kidnaps the wife of a leading politician to secure her husband's release from death row.

In 1997, Altman made a short-lived return to the small screen as creator, executive producer and occasional director of "Gun" (ABC), an anthology series that followed individuals who came into contact with the titular weapon. Some critics were impressed, but audiences stayed away and only six episodes were aired. The following year, the director tackled "The Gingerbread Man" (1998), a legal thriller that marked the first original screenplay by author John Grisham. Grisham, however, objected to the changes made by Altman and removed his name (the final screenplay was credited to the pseudonymous Al Hayes), and the releasing studio (PolyGram) was reportedly unhappy with the director's ending and did not really support the movie on its release. Despite receiving respectful reviews, the film was a box-office failure. Altman's next two films, the Southern Gothic "Cookie's Fortune" (1999) and the satirical "Dr. T and the Women" (2000), were praised by critics but failed to spark a response with the movie-going public.

Altman had virtually tackled—and inverted the conventions of—nearly every genre in his long and distinguished career. Longtime friend Bob Balaban proposed an idea for a murder mystery along the lines of an Agatha Christie novel and together Altman and Balaban hammered out a sketchy outline. They hired actor Julian Fellowes—whose previous screenwriting credits had been for the small screen—to flesh out their outline of a shooting party at an English country house in 1932. The result, "Gosford Park" (2001), was Altman's most accessible and successful picture in years. The standard touches were all employed: an all-star ensemble (in this case the cream of British talent including Sir Michael Gambon, Dame Maggie Smith and Helen Mirren as well as rising talents like Clive Owen and Kelly Macdonald); a terrifically designed production (sets by Stephen Altman, the director's son, and costumes by Oscar-winner Jenny Beavan); sweeping camera movements (captured by director of photography Andrew Dunn); and a literate screenplay delivered with overlapping dialogue. The film earned seven Academy Award nominations including Best Picture and Best Director. Capitalizing on his renewed success, Altman announced plans to shoot his next project "Voltage" (lensed 2002), an adaptation of the novel "A Shortage of Engineers".

MILESTONES:

1943–1947: Joined the US Army at age 18; became a B24 pilot (dates approximate)

1948: First feature screen credit ("from story", co-written by George W George), "The Bodyguard", a crime film directed by Richard Fleisher

Moved to NYC and attempted to make a living as a writer of stories and screenplays

Tried living as a writer on the West Coast

Returned to Kansas City; made industrial films for the Calvin Company, serving as designer, cinematographer, producer, director, writer and editor

1955: Raised $63,000 to direct his first independently produced fiction feature, "The

Delinquents" (acquired by United Artists for $150,000 and released in 1957)

Completed over 65 industrial films and documentaries

1957: Co-produced and co-directed (with George W. George) first commercial documentary, "The James Dean Story"

1957: On the strength of "The James Dean Story", hired by Alfred Hitchcock to direct episodes of "Alfred Hitchcock Presents"; made TV directing debut with episode entitled "The Young One"; also completed episode entitled "Together" before being fired in 1958

Directed (and occasionally produced and wrote) episodes for some 20 TV series including "Combat," "Kraft Mystery Theater" and "The Roaring Twenties"

1963: Formed (with Ray Wagner) Lion's Gate Films (approximate date)

1964: Two-episode TV movie "Nightmare in Chicago"—made for "Kraft Mystery Theater"—edited together for feature release

1968: First studio-backed fiction feature, "Countdown" (Warner Bros.)

1970: Critical and popular breakthrough feature, "M*A*S*H"; earned first Best Director Academy Award nomination

1971: Helmed the revisionist western "McCabe & Mrs. Miller"

1973: Took on the detective genre with "The Long Goodbye"

1974: Buddy gambling picture "California Split" marked first credit for "Lion's Gate 8-Track Sound"; allowed Altman to record sound live from microphones planted on set or on location thereby eliminating the need for postdubbing while allowing the sound to be mixed or unmixed at will

1975: Earned second Best Director Oscar nomination for "Nashville", arguably his masterpiece

1976: Stumbled a bit with "Buffalo Bill and the Indians"

1977: Produced first film, "Welcome to L.A.",

directed by Alan Rudolph; also produced "The Late Show", directed by Robert Benton

1978: Helmed the ensemble comedy-drama "A Wedding"

1980: Directed the fantasy musical "Popeye", starring Robin Williams

1981: Sold Lion's Gate

1981: Debut as stage director, "Precious Blood" and "Rattlesnake in a Cooler" in "Two By South", Actors Theatre, Los Angeles

1982: Directed Broadway production of "Come Back to the Five & Dime, Jimmy Dean, Jimmy Dean"; filmed production and released movie in 1982

Formed Sandcastle 5 Productions

1983: Won acclaim for film adaptation of David Rabe's "Streamers"

1984: Helmed the one-man drama "Secret Honor", with Philip Baker Hall starring as Richard Nixon

1985: Directed the film adaptation of Sam Shepard's play "Fool for Love"

1985: Returned to TV work after 17 years as director of "The Laundromat" (HBO)

1987: Made another feature based on a play, "Beyond Therapy", adapted from Christopher Durang

1987: Produced and directed the ABC TV specials "The Dumb Waiter" and "The Room"

1988: Helmed the HBO series "Tanner '88", about a presidential candidate; won Emmy Award

1988: Directed the CBS remake of "The Caine Mutiny Court-Martial"

1990: Earned praise for "Vincent & Theo", a biography of the Van Gogh brothers

1992: Earned critical praise for "The Player"; nominated for Best Picture and Best Director Academy Awards

1992: Staged William Bolcom's "McTeague" (libretto by Arnold Weinstein and Robert Altman), based on Frank Norris' 1899 novel of the same name, for the Lyric Opera of Chicago; the novel was the basis of Eric von Stroheim's "Greed"

1993: Garnered fourth Oscar nomination as Best Director for "Short Cuts"; also co-wrote the screenplay adapted from short stories by Raymond Carver

1994: Honored with a Gala Tribute by the Film Society of Lincoln Center

1994: Had critical and box-office failure with "Ready to Wear (Pret-a-Porter)"

1996: Helmed the jazz-era set comedy-drama "Kansas City"

1997: Produced the Alan Rudolph-directed "Afterglow"

1997: Executive produced, created series and helmed episodes of the ABC series "Gun"

1998: Directed and co-scripted "The Gingerbread Man", a legal drama based on a screenplay by John Grisham; Grisham had his name removed from the final script which was rewritten by Altman; the onscreen credit was to the pseudonymous Al Hayes

1999: Returned to form with the comedy "Cookie's Fortune"

2000: Directed "Dr. T and the Women", with Richard Gere as a gynecologist

2002: Helmed "Gosford Park", a period mystery; earned Best Picture and Best Director Academy Award nominations

AFFILIATION: Raised Roman Catholic
Democrat

QUOTES:
Named a Knight of the Legion of Honor in 1996.

After "Popeye", which Altman still refuses to acknowledge was the failure critics labeled it, he changed his style. The master of the ensemble movie, he was often reduced to a cast of five, or two, or even—in the case of his extraordinary Richard Nixon monologue film, "Secret Honor"—just one. The blithe deconstructionist of screenplays, he stuck almost religiously to texts by David Rabe and Harold Pinter. The mixed celebrator/debunker of male camaraderie, he began to focus more on women and gay themes. He went from widescreen to regular aspect ratio, foggy colors to sharp contours. The Altman of the 80s was often a very different director from the Altman of the 70s: arguably less inventive, but far more exacting, less of a virtuoso, more of a polished craftsman."—Michael Wilmington in *Los Angeles Times*, November 11, 1990.

"When you can direct great individual scenes, you can end up with some beautiful pearls. Then you can say, 'O.K., put them on a strand'. And you put them on a strand, and something is missing. It's just not a beautiful necklace. Altman is one of the few directors I've worked with who makes beautiful necklaces, not just the pearls."—Jack Lemmon on Altman's style of directing, from *Interview*, October 1993.

On Hollywood studio executives, Altman was quoted in *The Hollywood Reporter* (January 9, 2002): "I don't think I know any of their names. They make shoes, I make gloves."

"If there is any aspect of Robert Altman's work that fascinated me more than any other, it is his grasp of visual narrative. He has the eye of a choreographer grafted onto the brain of a dramatist, the heart of a dancer and the soul of a poet. So, he can steer the audience through incredibly complicated scenes, in which many different actors all have their own agenda and yet, somehow, and I don't know how, make it all perfectly clear on the screen. Part of this comes from a genuine love of, and respect for, actors. This is, believe me, rare among directors and as a result the cast all strive to do their best in the certain knowledge that their contribution is being appreciated (it really is) but, even so, how he can throw the camera at five or six different things going on at once without losing the thread of any of them must remain something of a sacred mystery."—"Gosford Park" screenwriter Julian Fellowes at OscarCentral.com.

"I try to give them [actors] confidence and try to earn their trust . . . and I won't let them make fools out of themselves. In other words, I will protect them so they are not afraid to go over the top."—Altman in *Entertainment Weekly* 2002.

BIBLIOGRAPHY:

"Persistance of Vision: Films of Robert Altman" Neil Feineman, 1978, Ayer

"Robert Altman" Jean-Loup Bourget, c. 1980; Edilig biography; published in France

"The Films of Robert Altman" Alan Karp, 1981, Scarecrow Press

"American Skeptic: Robert Altman's Genre-Commentary Films" Norman Kagan, 1982, Pierian Press

"Robert Altman" Gerard Plecki, 1985, Twayne

"Robert Altman: Jumping Off the Cliff: A Biography of the Great American Director" Patrick McGilligan, 1989; biography

"The Nashville Chronicles: The Making of Robert Altman's Masterpiece" Jan Stuart, 2001, Simon & Schuster

Alejandro Amenabar

BORN: in Santaiago, Chile, 1972

NATIONALITY: Chilean

CITIZENSHIP:
 Chile, Spain

EDUCATION: enrolled in a film studies program; dropped out

AWARDS: Goya Best New Director "Tesis" 1997
 Goya Best Original Screenplay "Tesis" 1997
 Online Film Critics Society Award Best Original Screenplay "The Others" 2001; tied with David Lynch ("Mulholland Dr.")
 Goya Best Director "The Others" 2001; the film had been nominated for 15 awards and won eight, including Best Film
 Goya Best Original Screenplay "The Others" 2001

BIOGRAPHY

With only a pair of thrillers under his belt, Chilean-born filmmaker Alejandro Amenabar was already considered a wunderkind in Spain when he successfully crossed over to English-language films with the spooky box-office success "The Others" (2001). With just a handful of films that rely on thought-provoking suspenseful narratives with surprise twists, the movie maker has emerged as the 21st century heir to Alfred Hitchcock.

Amenabar demonstrated his creative bent early in life. As a child, he composed guitar music that was to be played as accompaniment for short stories he had penned. By age 10, he had begun studying piano and then considered a career as either a musician or an illustrator. As a lark, he enrolled in film studies at the University of Madrid and began making short films (but ironically failing courses). While still an undergraduate, he collaborated on a screenplay with Mateo Gil about a cinema student who discovers what appears to be a snuff film. That script caught the attention of veteran director Jose Luis Cuerda, who encouraged Amenabar to make the feature "Tesis/Thesis" (1996, co-written with Mateo Gil). The resulting movie garnered widespread acclaim in Spain, earned several Goyas (the Spanish equivalent of the Oscar) and announced the arrival of a potent new voice in Spanish cinema.

With his follow-up feature, "Abre los Ojos/Open Your Eyes" (1997, also co-written with Gil), Amenabar solidified his standing. Because the film—which was tinged with science fiction and fantasy—did not delve into Spanish history or examine the faults and failings of contemporary people, some rejected it. More open-minded audiences and critics, however, were rewarded with a strong narrative, solid production values and terrific lead performances from Penelope Cruz and Eduardo Noriega, who was a frequent collaborator with the director. "Abre los Ojos" centered on a playboy (Noriega) who survives a horrific car crash and finds himself caught in a world that may or may not be real. When it was screened at the 1998 Sundance Film Festival, "Abre los Ojos" garnered good notices and caught the eye of actor-producer Tom Cruise who secured the American remake rights and went on to team with writer-director Cameron Crowe on "Vanilla Sky" (2001). Cruise also served as executive producer of Amenabar's English-language debut, "The Others", which featured Nicole Kidman in a bravura lead performance as a high-strung woman who inhabits a large mansion on the remote Isle of Jersey during WWII. Despite his success in the USA, the filmmaker has stated he has no plans to relocate to Los Angeles or pursue a Hollywood career.

Before segueing to his American debut, Amenabar provided the lilting underscores for two 1999 films made by close collaborators. He penned the music for "Butterfly/La Lengua de las mariposas", directed by Jose Luis Cuerda, and for "Nadie conoce a nadie/Nobody Knows Anything", helmed by Mateo Gil.

MILESTONES:

1973: Family fled military dictatorship of Pinochet in Chile; settled in Madrid, Spain

As a child, began composing music on guitar to accompany short stories he had written

At age 10, began studying piano

1991: Made first short film, the thriller "Himenoptero"

1995: Wrote and directed the short thriller "Luna"; first collaboration with actor Eduardo Noreiga

1996: Co-wrote (with Mateo Gil), directed and composed the score for debut feature "Tesis/Thesis", starring Ana Torrent and Eduardo Noriega; film produced by Jose Luis Cuerda

1997: Directed, co-wrote (with Gil) and composed the score for the fantasy thriller "Abre los Ojos/Open Your Eyes"; screened at the World Cinema section of the 1998 Sundance

Film Festival; Noriega starred as a man left disfigured after an accident; Penelope Cruz co-starred

1998: Penned the music for Mateo Gil's short thriller "Allanamiento de morada"; Noriega co-starred

1999: Composed the the scores for the acclaimed film "Butterfly/La Lengua de las mariposas", directed by Jose Luis Cuerda, and for "Nadie conoce a nadie/Nobody Knows Anything", directed by Mateo Gil and starring Eduardo Noriega

2001: English-language directorial debut, "The Others", starring Nicole Kidman and executive produced by Tom Cruise; also wrote the screenplay and composed the score

AFFILIATION: Roman Catholic

QUOTES:

"I'm not really terrified by the possibility of seeing a ghost. It is human beings—and the things they're capable of—that really scare me."—Alejandro Amenabar quoted in *Los Angeles Times*, August 8, 2001.

"Alejandro has got a lot of depth, he's very smart and he has integrity in the way Stanley (Kubrick) had integrity. It's unusual, too, for a director to have such strong belief in his actors. It would have been so easy to fill ['The Others'] with special effects."—actress Nicole Kidman quoted by Anthony Breznican of the Associated Press, August 8, 2001.

"Eventually I'd love to free myself from surprise endings. Hitchcock didn't like them. He avoided them as much as he could. But I can't seem to shake them off. A big discovery at the end of the picture helps me guide my protagonist to the culmination of the journey, to the lesson that's waiting to be learned."—Amenabar to *Los Angeles Times*, August 8, 2001.

"For me, the hardest part of the process is writing and composing. Directing is just suffering too much work every day, but it doesn't really demand a creative point of view. When I write, I'm thinking of the music. Sometimes, I even compose previous to the shooting of the film. That really helps me have a whole vision of the story, a whole technical concept."—Amenabar quoted in *The Hollywood Reporter*, August 7–13, 2001.

Allison Anders

BORN: in Ashland, Kentucky, 11/16/1954

NATIONALITY: American

EDUCATION: attended junior college, despite having not finished high school

University of California at Los Angeles' School of Theater, Film and Television, Los Angeles, California; graduated summa cum laude

AWARD: New York Film Critics Circle Award Best New Director "Gas Food Lodging" 1992

BIOGRAPHY

Described by one writer as a cross between a

60s earth mother and a Hell's Angels biker chick, indie filmmaker Allison Anders weathered a rough childhood and young adult life that not only encouraged an escapist penchant for making up characters but also an insider's sympathy for the strong but put-upon women who have peopled her films. Abandoned by her father at age five, sexually abused by a number of different men while growing up and gang-raped at the age of 12, she eventually retreated into a fantasy relationship with "dead Paul" (McCartney), a flight of fancy which helped get her admitted to a mental hospital at 15. Anders, who had written prior to being institutionalized, rediscovered her voice with the help of a poet she met "inside" and learned "to make people who aren't there really stand up and talk." At 17, she dropped out of high school in Los Angeles and ventured back to the rural Kentucky of her birth, moving soon afterwards to London to live with the man who would father her first child.

Upon her return to the USA, Anders finally began to pick up the pieces of her life. Despite not having a high school diploma, she attended junior college and later the UCLA film school, managing to stick to her dreams when a second daughter came along. Enchanted with Wim Wenders' films, the welfare mother so deluged the filmmaker with correspondence that he gave her a job as a production assistant on "Paris, Texas" (1984). Afterwards, with fellow UCLA colleagues Dean Lent (who also worked as a production assistant on "Paris, Texas") and then-lover Kurt Voss, Anders made her feature co-writing and co-directing debut with the cult hit "Border Radio" (1988), a black-and-white 16mm study of the L.A. punk scene, revealing the "artistic" sensibilities of the trio who expressed their difficulties getting the film made in its final credit—"Many Curses on: Those Who Tried To Thwart Us." Anders reteamed with Lent (this time as cinematographer) for her first solo effort, "Gas Food Lodging" (1992), drawing from her own personal life to tell the compelling, multilevel story of a single mother (Brooke Adams) and her two teenage daughters (Fairuza Balk and Ione Skye).

Set in the milieu of a southwestern hardscrabble life, "Gas Food and Lodging" was tour de force filmmaking, its tone of poignant hope amidst disappointment starkly convincing. Like Anders' 1994 follow-up, "Mi Vida Loca/My Crazy Life", which depicted girl gangs in the Echo Park neighborhood of L.A. where she lived, it showcased her ability to capture on camera a genuineness that made audiences feel they were watching real people, not actors. In "Mi Vida Loca", they actually were watching real Latina gang members sprinkled in with the actors (some of whom were Spanish soap opera stars). Anders had won their trust over time ("At first . . . they thought I was a cop") by approaching them without judgment, and in addition to appearing in the film, they worked closely with the director, advising her on script changes and characterizations and serving as consultants on costumes, language, music and location. The strength of both films lies in the emotionally rich portrayals of women battling the odds (i.e., dead-end jobs, vanishing men) to bond with one another, but "Mi Vida Loca", in its attempt to develop too many characters, provided a too frequently shifting point-of-view that worked to undermine the picture's power.

Despite the unwieldy episodic structure, Anders had successfully captured the frustrations, social rituals and violence affecting her "Girlz 'N the Hood". She also got to work out some of her own frustrations by killing-off former love-who-broke-her-heart John Taylor (guitarist of Duran Duran) in the guise of the fictional character El Duran (Taylor, who had actually remained friends with the director, survived to provide the music for "Mi Vida Loca" and headline 1999's "Sugar Town"). When one of her extras/consultants died of a drug overdose shortly after filming wrapped, Anders began caring for the woman's young son (eventually adopting him) and dedicated the film to the deceased, establishing a scholarship fund in her name through a community service group in Echo Park, to which she donated the proceeds from the movie's Los Angeles premiere. Anders next directed the "Strange Brew" episode of the omnibus "Four Rooms" (1995), which starred Madonna as a lesbian witch and Alicia Witt as her love-slave. The embarrassing compilation wasted the talents of all involved (including the directors of the other segments—Quentin Tarantino, Alexandre Rockwell and Robert Rodriguez), with the sole point of interest being "Which one is the worst?"

"Grace of My Heart" (1996), a project teaming her with Martin Scorsese (executive producer) and his then-girlfriend Illeana Douglas (as a Carole King–like songwriter-singer), was Anders' first attempt at a period piece. Set against the backdrop of the pop music world centered around NYC's Brill Building during the 50s and 60s, it featured some pleasant sound-alike songs from the period, plus one showstopper, "God Give Me Strength", which inaugurated the collaboration between Elvis Costello and pop veteran Burt Bacharach. Anders may have compromised this fabulous idea by again trying to cover too much, but the predictable structure of scene-song-scene-song also exacerbated the film's superficiality. Fortunately, the score and a wonderful performance by John Turturro as a Jewish record company owner helped save what must be considered Anders-lite compared to her previous work. "Sugar Time" then reunited her with ex-beaux Voss (as co-director and co-writer) and Taylor making his feature debut in the art-imitating-life role of a rock musician suffering through a mid-life crisis. An amusing, polished look at L.A.'s rock'n'roll subculture, it did not, however, mark a return to the hard-hitting substance of either "Gas Food Lodging" or "Mi Vida Loca."

FAMILY:

son: Reuben Goodbear Anders. Adopted; born c. 1990; mother Nica Rogers was a Latina gang member who had played a small role and served as one of Anders' advisors on "Mi Vida Loca" (1994) when she died of a drug overdose at age 19 before movie's completion; Anders brought home the motherless child and eventually began adoption procedures

COMPANIONS:

John Taylor. Rock musician; member of the band Duran Duran; had relationship with Anders in the 1980s and stayed friends after they broke up; supplied the music for Anders' film "Mi Vida Loca" (1994) and starred in "Sugar Town" (1999)

Quentin Tarantino. Screenwriter, director; no longer together

Kurt Voss. Screenwriter, director; involved with Anders in the 1980s; classmate of Anders at the UCLA film school; co-wrote and co-directed (with Anders and Dean Lent), "Border Radio" (1987) and "Sugar Town" (1999)

MILESTONES:

Raised in Kentucky until father left family when Anders was five; mother moved her around a great deal thereafter

1967: Was gang-raped at age 12 (date approximate)

1970: Family settled in Los Angeles when Anders was 15; stepfather at one point pulled a gun on her (date approximate)

1970: Was placed in a mental hospital in Los Angeles at age 15 because of suicidal feelings and a retreat into a fantasy world; depression exacerbated by, among other things, the widely circulated rumors of the death of her favorite Beatle, Paul McCartney

1972: Dropped out of high school at age 17; headed back to Kentucky by bus to live with other relatives (date approximate)

1973: Moved to London at age 18 to live with an English-born philosophy student she had met on the Greyhound she took to move back to Kentucky (date approximate)

1973–1974: Worked as a barmaid in London until she got pregnant; when lover did not want her to have baby, moved back to Los Angeles alone and supported herself and child with welfare and with work as a waitress

Attended junior college (dates approximate)

Returned to junior college for another two years after the birth of her second daughter (dates approximate)

Was accepted by, and attended, UCLA's film school, beginning in the early 1980s

Became fascinated with the films of Wim

Wenders; sent the filmmaker dozens of letters, some of which were as long as 60 pages, as well as audiocassettes of music she liked; Wenders only wrote back a few times, but the two began to communicate by telephone

1984: First feature film credit, as a production assistant on Wim Wenders' film, "Paris, Texas"

1986: Moved to the Echo Park section of Los Angeles shortly after graduating from UCLA; supported herself and her daughters for a time with money from a screenwriting grant she had received

1987: Feature film directorial and screenwriting debut, "Border Radio" (b&w, 16mm), co-directed and co-written with fellow UCLA film students Kurt Voss and Dean Lent

1992: First solo directorial effort, "Gas Food Lodging", for which she also wrote the screenplay, based on a novel by Richard Peck; Lent served as director of photography

1994: Actor Hugh Grant backed out of Anders' "Paul Is Dead" project a scant month before shooting was to start, and funding disappeared with him

1994: Won praise for "Mi Vida Loca/My Crazy Life", her authentic picture about Latina gang members; shot film only a month after the Los Angeles riots of 1992

1995: Awarded a MacArthur "genius" grant ($255,000)

1995: Signed two-year deal with Miramax Films to write, produce and direct features

1995: Helmed and scripted the "Strange Brew" segment of "Four Rooms"

1996: Wrote and directed "Grace of My Heart", about a female singer struggling to make it in the music business in the 1950s and 1960s; executive produced by Martin Scorsese

1997: Executive produced "Lover Girl", on which Lent was director of photography

1999: Reteamed with Voss to co-write and co-direct the comedy-drama "Sugar Town", about a group of aging musicians; premiered at the Sundance Film Festival

2001: With Voss, co-wrote "Things Behind the Sun", a drama about a young female rock musician coping with a rape; also directed; premiered at Sundance Film Festival; sold to Showtime; inspired by events from Anders' own life

QUOTES: Received a Nicholl Fellowship in screenwriting from the Academy of Motion Picture Arts and Science in 1986.

According to *Elle* (July 1996), Anders once "did phone sex to finance a project and could do it again."

"When I was a teen-ager, everybody told me being an unwed mother was going to ruin my life. And in fact it was my opportunity." —Allison Anders to *The New York Times*, July 26, 1992.

"There's a certain kind of feminist who doesn't like my stuff. And there's enough of 'em to to, you know, bum me out. But I always felt like feminism was about empowering yourself by knowing yourself. And that means not just exploring work, but also relationships and desire. But for some reason, there's this attitude—which is changing a little bit—that if you're looking for intimacy with a man, that's like selling out your feminism, which I think is so bizarre. In Hollywood, you can do two types of women characters: the objectified female, who's always saying something smart, or the butch female. I feel like we encountered that a couple times making this film ('Grace of My Heart')—people wanted Denise to behave more like a guy. You know, being bitter and aggressive, as though somehow that's strength that's very male."—Allison Anders in *Time Out New York*, September 11–18, 1996.

"The first record I bought was 'Johnny Get Angry' by Joanie Sommers, a good start for a feminist: 'I want a brave man/I want a cave man' . . . I learned to write female characters from Paul McCartney's songwriting. I'm amazed at how he gets into women's minds: a young woman going her own way in 'She's

Leaving Home', or a lonely old woman in 'Eleanor Rigby'—and 'For No One', the most incredible example, where the guy being dumped chooses to get inside her feelings, writing the song from her point of view. My other favorites were The Shangri-Las: those amazing narrative songs about rebellious teenagers. I love the voiceover on 'I Can Never Go Home Any More', it's so melodramatic, pure Douglas Sirk. I'd study the sleeves of my favorite records for hours and wonder who these people (Barry-Greenwich, Goffin-King) were. When Carole King's 'Tapestry' came out, you could suddenly connect her to the writer of 'Will You Love Me Tomorrow'."—Anders to *Sight and Sound*, April 1997.

Wes Anderson

BORN: in Harris County, Texas, 1969

NATIONALITY: American

EDUCATION: St John's High School. Houston, Texas, prep school; Anderson used school as inspiration for the one depicted in "Rushmore"

University of Texas at Austin, Austin, Texas, philosophy, BA, 1991; met Owen Wilson; pair roomed together

AWARDS: MTV Movie Award Best New Filmmaker "Bottle Rocket" 1996

Los Angeles Film Critics Association New Generation Award "Rushmore" 1998

Independent Spirit Award Best Director "Rushmore" 1999

BIOGRAPHY

Texas filmmaker Wes Anderson cut his directing teeth making Super-8mm movies with his brothers and went on to cable access television before meeting frequent collaborator Owen Wilson at the University of Texas in the late 1980s. The two made their film debut with the 1992 short "Bottle Rocket", a sparse, black-and-white film about two young burglars starring Wilson and his younger brother Luke. Championed by screenwriter-actor-director L. M. 'Kit' Carson and screened to acclaim on the festival circuit, the project gained the attention of producers Polly Platt and James L. Brooks and Columbia Pictures eventually offered Anderson a $6 million budget to fashion a full-length version of the story. Following two Texans who try their hand at a life of crime in search of some focus or sense of belonging, the 1996 film (co-scripted with Owen Wilson and co-starring both Owen and Luke Wilson) bombed at test screenings and opened to mostly positive critical notices but disappointing box office numbers. Weird, warm and at times riotously funny, the quirky, atmospheric piece didn't connect with most moviegoers but it found a devout cult audience, even earning a place on esteemed filmmaker Martin Scorsese's list of the best films of the 1990s. Anderson had already found his voice with "Bottle Rocket", his evocative use of color and music making the film something of a transcendence for those who caught on, while the feature also effectively launched the careers of stars Luke and Owen Wilson.

Anderson's second feature effort "Rushmore" (1998) was afforded about twice the budget of "Bottle Rocket" despite its predecessor's relative failure. With this film, Anderson and Owen Wilson revisited the misguided but tenacious enthusiasm espoused by "Bottle Rocket"'s Dignan. In "Rushmore" the well-meaning maniac in question was fifteen-year old Max Fischer (Jason Schwartzman), a prep-school student with an overwhelming slate of extracurricular activities but lackluster grades who loves first grade teacher Miss Cross (Olivia Williams) almost as much as he loves the titular school itself. Max's journey of friendship (relationships with Bill Murray's bemused businessman and Mason Gamble's earnest and wise fourth grader blur the line between mentor and mentored), loss and self-awareness is handled with both an unwavering eye and palpable affection, the audience learning to love him as they note his missteps. Full of the kind of singularly evocative and empathetic moments (most tied inextricably to the seminal soundtrack) that have set Anderson apart from his contemporaries from the beginning, "Rushmore" reached a much wider audience than "Bottle Rocket", bringing in over $17 million in box-office grosses and becoming a favorite of many critics and movie fans alike.

Anderson's next project "The Royal Tenenbaums" was set in NYC, the filmmaker's adopted home since 1999. A story about a family of child prodigies who never reach their potential, the film boasted Anderson's most impressive cast, with Gene Hackman as the eponymous patriarch, Anjelica Huston as the graceful mother, Danny Glover as her gentlemanly suitor, Ben Stiller, Gwyneth Paltrow and regular Luke Wilson as the three siblings in a state of arrested genius and Owen Wilson, Bill Murray and Anderson's unlikely staple Kumar Pallana (an Austin yoga instructor who befriended Anderson and the Wilsons and has appeared in every feature) with fully realized supporting turns. Continuing to use music and setting as characters in and of themselves, Anderson outdid himself. Breathtaking moments between strangely attracted siblings Margot (Paltrow) and Richie (Luke Wilson) were created through precise employment of music (including Nico's "These Days" and The Rolling Stones' "She Smiled Sweetly") and a perfectly restrained touch while Anderson's Manhattan is hyperbolic, almost cartoonish, a New York City where New Yorkers are from

pages of *The New Yorker,* all cabs are dispatched by the Gypsy Cab Co. and people swim and stay at the 375th St Y. Mixing the colorful characters with hyperrealistic surroundings, Anderson succeeded in setting the scene and bringing his script to life though mixed critical reception seemed to indicate that the film didn't resonate with people quite the way "Rushmore" had.
—Written by Jane O'Donnell

MILESTONES:

Raised in Houston, Texas

Began making Super-8mm films with his brothers

1990: Began writing script for "Bottle Rocket" with college roommate Owen Wilson

1992: Directed 13-minute short "Bottle Rocket"; also co-wrote; film played at the Sundance FIlm Festival

1994: Moved to Los Angeles

1996: Feature film debut, "Bottle Rocket"; also co-wrote

1998: Directed and co-wrote (with Wilson) second feature "Rushmore"

1999: Relocated to New York City

2001: Co-wrote (with Owen Wilson) and directed third feature "The Royal Tenenbaums"

AFFILIATION: Episcopalian

QUOTES:

Wes Anderson on his debut feature "Bottle Rocket": "It didn't quite get the studio push, but I guess that's what everybody says when their movie doesn't make any money."
—quoted in *Daily Variety,* January 15, 1997.

James L. Brooks on Wes Anderson to *Time Out New York* (December 10–17, 1998): "All thse words that are tossed around—filmmaker, auteur—you gag on them, but Wes is for real. I mean, he's not going to do 'one for them'. Other directors are always thinking, 'Gee, if I do three for them, I'll get to do one for me.' Every one Wes does is going to be for him, out of his sensibility."

"I like characters that are trying to realize their projects. They have a strong idea of something they want to execute and they just won't let anybody shut 'em down. It might seem ridiculous or it might seem too big—I mean, building an aquarium, that's crazy; putting on a Vietnam play with explosions from the stage is crazy—but ["Rushmore' "s Max Fischer] does that. Of course, it's a movie, so I can have whatever I want to have happen. But I do like that kind of thing of people with unrealistic ambitions and their ambitions are not just to be rich. They have ideas and projects that they want to do. So that has a strong appeal to it." —quoted in *Salon*, January 21, 1999.

"He's a shy guy, the kind of guy who never dances, but when it came to the movie, he was tenacious. It reminded me a lot of working with John Cassavetes. They're both directors that get actors to trust them. That's why Wes got such good performances from Jason [Schwartzman], who'd never acted before, and [Bill] Murray, who usually wants to be the only funny guy on the set, but was really restrained for this part."—"Rushmore" co-star Seymour Cassel on Anderson, to *Los Angeles Times*, January 29, 1999.

Olivia Williams, co-star of "Rushmore" on Anderson: "He doesn't play games with his actors. He'd come up and say, 'The thing you do with your face when you smile—don't do it.' "—quoted in *The New York Times*, January 31, 1999.

Owen Wilson on working with Anderson: "He's not doing anything to let you know that he knows how to move the camera—you don't have to worry that he's gonna do anything affected or tricky, or show that he's seen all of Scorsese's movies. It's exciting to watch, but not pretentious."—to *Premiere*, February 1999.

"The darkest hour was the evening of our first test screening, in Santa Monica, at which we had 85 walkouts. The head of the studio said, 'Congratulations. Seriously.' [My agent]

Jim Berkus said that our goal for the next screening should be for someone to say 'congratulations' without having to say 'seriously' afterward. And then later that night, my girlfriend broke up with me."—Anderson in *Premiere*, March 1999.

Martin Scorsese quoted in the *Esquire* feature "The Next Scorsese" (March 2000): "Wes Anderson, at age thirty, has a very special kind of talent: He knows how to convey the simple joys and interactions between people so well and with such richness. This kind of sensibility is rare in movies . . . I remember seeing [Jean] Renoir's films as a child and feeling connected to the characters through his love for them. It's the same with Anderson. I've found myself going back and watching 'Bottle Rocket' several times. I'm also very fond of his second film, 'Rushmore'—it has the same tenderness, the same kind of grace. Both of them are very funny, but also very moving."

Wes Anderson, explaining to *Film Comment* (November-December 2001) his decision to dress many of the characters in "The Royal Tenenbaums" in the same clothes throughout the film, even as it spans time: "That's something I've done in all the movies. In 'Rushmore', Max wears his school uniform, and then goes through his depressed barber phase. Bill Murray wears the same thing but his shirt colors change. In this one, there are many more characters and it's much more noticeable because their outfits are more extreme. I like them to have a uniform. I feel like if there's a uniform for the actors, then every time they put it on, they can make their shift from what they were like before they arrived on the set. And it sort of unifies them throughout the movie."

On the real-life inspiration for "The Royal Tenenbaums": "Owen had always been pushing me to do something about my parents' divorce, xwith this. The movie ends up being something totally different from what I would have envisioned, because the father in the movie is nothing like my father. The family dynamic is quite different than mine. That opening scene in the movie is Royal [telling] the kids that they're going to get a divorce, and the questions they're asking are the questions we asked."—quoted in New York's *Daily News*, December 9, 2001.

Paul Thomas Anderson

BORN: Paul Thomas Anderson in Studio City, California, 06/26/1970

SOMETIMES CREDITED AS:
Paul Anderson
P. T. Anderson

NATIONALITY: American

EDUCATION: Montclair College Prep, North Hollywood, California

Emerson College Boston, Massachusetts; dropped out

New York University, New York, New York, attended for one and a half days before dropping out

AWARDS: Los Angeles Film Critics Association New Generation Award 1997

Boston Society of Film Critics Award Best New Filmmaker "Hard Eight" and "Boogie Nights" 1997

PEN Center USA West Literary Award Best Screenplay "Boogie Nights" 1998

British Independent Film Award Best Foreign Independent Film in English "Boogie Nights" 1998

Toronto Film Critics Association Award Best Picture "Magnolia" 1999

Toronto Film Critics Association Award Best Director "Magnolia" 1999

Toronto Film Critics Association Award Best Screenplay "Magnolia" 1999; tied with Charlie Kaufman for "Being John Malkovich"

Berlin Film Festival Golden Bear "Magnolia" 2000

Golden Bug Best Foreign Film "Magnolia" 2000

Cannes Film Festival Award Best Director "Punch-Drunk Love" 2002; tied with Kwon-Taek for "Chihwaeseon"

BIOGRAPHY

From the debut of his short film "Coffee and Cigarettes" at the 1993 Sundance Film Festival, Paul Thomas Anderson was on a trajectory to success. An ambitious featurette that focused on five characters interacting in a Las Vegas diner, "Coffee and Cigarettes" set the mold for his later films: multiple storylines, dazzling camerawork and a detailed emphasis on character. A brash, gutsy moviemaker, Anderson has tackled big themes but paradoxically allowed them to unfold via intimate moments onscreen. As Chris Vognar of *The Dallas Morning News* pointed out in his January 9, 2000, profile of the wunderkind writer-director, "Remorse, regret and redemption, played out in a family or surrogate-family setting, have been key elements in all three of Mr. Anderson's films [to that date]. The stakes get higher, and the canvas grows wider, with each one."

The son of TV host and voice actor Ernie Anderson (perhaps best remembered as the announcer on the long-running ABC series "The Love Boat"), Anderson spent his formative years in Studio City, California. The admittedly poor student had begun making amateur movies after his father purchased a Betamax camera in 1982. He has said in interviews that when he was about nine he discovered a stash of pornographic tapes belonging to his father and the lasting effect could be seen in one of his amateur films "The Dirk Diggler Story" (1988) and its feature incarnation "Boogie Nights" (1997). Despite a self-admitted contempt for film schools, Anderson briefly attended Boston's Emerson College and New York University before leaving academia in favor of obtaining practical experience. Upon his return to Southern California, he found employment in various production capacities on independent films as well as TV programming (including a stint on the short-lived syndicated "Quiz Kid Challenge" in 1990). While working as a production assistant on a PBS special on political correctness, he met character actor Philip Baker Hall and promised to write something for him. The result was the character of Sydney, one of the coffee shop denizens in 1992's "Cigarettes and Coffee". After the short screened at Sundance, Anderson fielded offers, including one to expand it into feature length. Concentrating on Hall's character, he fashioned "Sydney", a drama of love, revenge and ultimately redemption set against a seedy Las Vegas backdrop. Because he insisted on Hall for the lead, raising the financing was a bit problematic until Gwyneth Paltrow accepted the role of a cocktail waitress who becomes a part of Sydney's world. The film premiered at Cannes in 1996 to mixed to positive reviews (particularly for Hall's central performance). The distributor, however, re-cut the film and released it under the title "Hard Eight" (1997). Despite it not being exactly his vision, it earned respectful reviews although it wasn't a big box-office hit.

The fight over the control of "Hard Eight/Sydney" left the writer-director with a somewhat dim view of the Hollywood suits. ("It was the most painful experience I've ever gone through," Anderson has been quoted as saying.) While waiting for the financing for his first film, Anderson wrote a sprawling 300-page script that served as the basis for his second feature, "Boogie Nights" (1997), which

expanded on ideas he first addressed in his short, "The Dirk Diggler Story" (which in turn owed its inspiration to real-life porn star Johnny Holmes), Anderson was invited to participate at the Sundance Institute's Filmmakers Workshop and was mentored by Michael Caton-Jones. The script eventually found its way to New Line Productions, where it was greenlit by executive Michael De Luca. Although ostensibly set in the world of pornography, "Boogie Nights" was more of a coming-of-age drama centered on an unhappy Southern California youth named Eddie Adams (rapper-turned-thespian Mark Wahlberg) who happened to blessed with a large physical endowment. Working under surrogate father Jack Horner (played by Burt Reynolds) and co-starring with the maternal Amber Waves (Julianne Moore), Adams rechristens himself Dirk Diggler and enjoys fame within the industry yet descends into a personal maelstrom fueled by drugs. Extremely well-acted (both Reynolds and Moore snagged supporting Oscar nominations) and well-written (Anderson too garnered an Academy nod), the film did suffer some diffusion. In following numerous characters, it paid some (like Don Cheadle's Buck) short shrift and there were several subplots that either went nowhere or bogged the proceedings down. Stylistically, Anderson paid his due to Robert Altman, particularly in the long opening shot that recalled Altman's first scene in "The Player" (1992), but he also demonstrated a command of the camera that was an improvement over "Hard Eight". "Boogie Nights" for all its faults, clearly announced the arrival of an intriguing new voice in film.

Anticipation rode high as to how Anderson would follow his first flush of success. In an almost unprecedented move, New Line practically offered him carte blanche. Inspired by the songs of Aimee Mann (he even used one of her lines, "Now that I've met you, would you object to never seeing me again?" as a jumping-off place for the story), Anderson penned "Magnolia" (1999). Again like Altman, the filmmaker hired many of the same actors (Philip Baker Hall, John C. Reilly, William H. Macy, Julianne Moore, Philip Seymour Hoffman, Melora Walters) and undertook the ambitious idea of telling nine stories, some of which interconnect, (not unlike several of Altman's films) that transpire over the course of one very unique day. In addition to his stock players, the script attracted the likes of Oscar-winner Jason Robards and Oscar nominee Melinda Dillon. But the biggest coup was landing Tom Cruise for a pivotal role as a foul-mouthed, cable TV sex guru. "Magnolia" was Anderson's most ambitious work to date and although it dealt with similar themes of parent-child relations and redemption, they were tempered with more humanity. In an essay in *The Washington Post* (January 23, 2000), Stephen Hunter deconstructed the religious imagery and undertones to the film, calling it "a God-mad chunk of pure American magic realism" and "a meditation on the intricacy of whimsical patterns". Like Julio Medem's "Lovers of the Arctic Circle" (1998), "Magnolia" owed much of the thrust of its plot to odd coincidences. (Anderson sets this up in a brilliant prologue in which he reconstructs three strange but true examples of the capriciousness of fate.) Because he employed a biblical deus ex machina and refused to tie up the loose ends neatly, "Magnolia" polarized critics and audiences; one either wholeheartedly gave in to it or one resisted and despised it. For his part, Anderson used bold camerawork that kept the three-hour opus moving and incorporated one of Mann's songs in a moving and audacious coup de cinema. If nothing else, this brash moviemaker established a level of personal best that would challenge his future work, begging the question of how he would top himself.

Anderson's next move was certainly a bold one, refashioning the well-established sad sack image of hugely successful comedian Adam Sandler, whose familiar shtick was beginning to bore

audiences. Anderson wrote the lead role in his 2002 film "Punch-Drunk Love" specifically for Sandler, casting him in a romantic comedy with dark overtones about a soft-spoken man beset by seven domineering sisters whose involvement in a phone sex scheme leads him to find love in the form of Emily Watson. Anderson scored critical kudos, including a Best Directing award at the Cannes Film Festival, for the atypically restrained and whimsical film, and Sandler earned high marks for segueing near-seamlessly into a more mature role.

FAMILY:

father: Ernie Anderson. TV host, voice actor; born on November 12, 1923; died on February 6, 1997, at age 73; former partner of Tim Conway

COMPANION:

Fiona Apple. Singer; dating as of 1998

MILESTONES:

Raised in the San Fernando Valley in Studio City, California

1979: Reportedly found his father's collection of pornographic tapes at age nine (date approximate)

1982: Began making movies with a Betamax video camera purchased by his father

1988: Made first amateur short film "The Dirk Diggler Story", about a male porno star

Briefly attended Emerson College; dropped out to pursue film career

Began career working as a production assistant on music videos and on independent films

1990: Was a messenger and production assistant on the syndicated game show "Quiz Kid Challenge"

Met Philip Baker Hall while working as a production assistant on the 1993 PBS special "Campus Culture Wars: Five Stories About PC"

1992: Directed short film "Coffee and Cigarettes", starring Philip Baker Hall; premiered at the 1993 Sundance Film Festival

1996: Expanded his short "Cigarettes and Coffee" into the full-length "Sydney", again starring Philip Baker Hall; premiered at the Cannes Film Festival

1997: "Sydney" was retitled "Hard Eight" and released theatrically in the USA

1997: Directed second feature, "Boogie Nights", an expanded version of his early short "Dirk Diggler"; earned an Oscar nomination for Best Original Screenplay

1997: Helmed the music video for Michael Penn's song "Try"

1998–1999: Directed two music videos featuring his off-screen companion Fiona Apple, "Across the Universe" and "Fast as You Can"

1999: Wrote and directed third feature, "Magnolia"; film received wildly divergent reviews, with critics either lavishing praise or decrying its excess; film was inspired by songs of Aimee Mann; also helmed the music video for Mann's original song "Save Me" featured in the movie

2002: Directed and scripted "Punch-Drunk Love" starring Adam Sandler and Emily Watson; won Best Direction award at the Cannes Film Festival

QUOTES:

Not to be confused with either the British director Paul Anderson ("Shopping", "Mortal Kombat") or the porno director Paul Thomas who works for Vivid Video.

There's a web site devoted to him at www.ptanderson.com

"As a kid, I became obsessed by pornos. I searched them out, obsessing over the humor and camp—how bad the acting was, how odd it all was. By the time I was sixteen, I had seen so much that it was no longer funny—it actually became quite sad. [Laughs] That's what 'Boogie Nights' should be doing: It's funny for the first part, but then it transforms."—Paul Thomas Anderson quoted in *Details*, September 1997.

"He's so in love with everything you do. . . .

Paul is obsessed with you while you're working with him. And it makes you free, totally confident."—Gwyneth Paltrow to *The New York Times*, October 12, 1997.

"One thing that impressed me about him [Anderson] was how specific he was. I've worked with much older directors who were floundering."—Don Cheadle in *Premiere*, September 1997.

"I count Paul among the great directors that I've worked with—Spielberg, Todd Haynes, the Coen Brothers, Louis Malle. He has a very strong sense of what he wants to accomplish as a person and there's a gravity that you don't often find in people his age."—Julianne Moore quoted in *Us*, February 1999.

"When Paul Thomas Anderson was 7, growing up in the San Fernando Valley, he wrote in a notebook: 'My name is Paul Anderson. I want to be a writer, producer, director, special effects man. I know how to do everything and I know everything. Please hire me.' Philip Seymour Hoffman, who, like the other members of the Anderson repertory company, is a close friend, says: 'You get the sense that Paul was always a director. He was born to the job.' "—From "His Way" by Lynn Hirschberg, *The New York Times Magazine*, December 19, 1999.

"When I watch 'Magnolia' or 'Boogie Nights', I see Paul in all the characters—the selfish Paul, the caretaking Paul, the little-kid Paul, the mature Paul—he is all those things at a given time, and I see him telling a story about all aspects of himself."—actor Philip Seymour Hoffman quoted in *Rolling Stone*, February 3, 2000.

"I do feel an obligation to not be a jackass in my life only because that will infringe on the view of the movie. I remember when 'Husbands and Wives' came out and Woody Allen was going through that whole thing and it was so terrible because that was one of his best movies. But everybody would look at it and see all the mistakes he was making—it polluted the movie. I guess my goal is to do everything I can to not pollute my movie. It is a hard thing because you want to promote them. You want to have attention. You want to be interviewed and be liked. But at the same time you want to balance out, step back, and have the movie . . . I just want the film to survive."—Anderson quoted in *IFP/West Calendar*, December 1999.

"Most people don't share my moral sense, which is, I'll masturbate, but I have to clean it up very quickly afterwards."—Paul Thomas Anderson to *The New York Times Magazine*, December 12, 1999.

"You get criticized for being self-indulgent, but if I weren't self-indulgent, they'd be p——off because I'd be making something very slight. Aren't I supposed to try and indulge who I am, to try to put that on the screen? They're mad if you don't put enough heart in your movie, and they're REALLY mad if you put too much heart in it."—Paul Thomas Anderson to *USA Today*, January 7, 2000.

"In lots of ways, Anderson's life is like one of those foreign-language books that have the original text on one page and the English translation on the facing page. There is his actual life, which remains largely opaque, and there is the cinematic translation that he puts up there on the screen. In some cases, the correspondence is discernible. 'Oh, fucking hell, that's the problem with a third movie,' says Anderson. 'You start to become a big, clear, naked thing.' As Dylan Tichenor ["Magnolia' 's editor] pointed out when we were cutting the scene where Donnie [William H. Macy] is professing his love for Brad the bartender, 'Here we are with a second time in a movie of yours where the gay character has to get drunk to profess his love.' And I said, 'Well, great, here comes the chapter on my closet homosexuality.' I thought that was a good one. I was sort of excited about that."—From *Rolling Stone*, February 3, 2000.

" 'Magnolia' is a singularity in American movies: a big, self-important, overreaching, but fundamentally sweet picture that fancies itself a major achievement, by a young director who's probably read one too many Don DeLillo novels . . . "—From "Kent Jones Tours P.T. Anderson's *Magnolia*" in *Film Comment*, January–February 2000.

"Directing a movie doesn't mean anything. It's only 50 percent of the job. The other 50 percent is this gene of protectiveness and parenting and evil that safeguards your movie. It's not a gene I love having, but I have to use it."—Paul Thomas Anderson quoted in *The New York Times Magazine*, December 19, 1999.

"What I've come to realize is that if the script is good, the actors will just show up. I think I'm an OK director, but I think I'm a good writer. My job as a director is just to write really well, because that makes it all so much easier. They get it when they read it, so you don't have to talk about it too much."—Anderson to *The Dallas Morning News*, January 9, 2000.

"I think when the movie gets bigger and costs more and more, it becomes harder to be a control freak. But I'm doing a pretty good job of maintaining all the proper paranoia and control that I should. That's why movie directors either go crazy or start making crap, because you could lose your mind if you realize that you can make it rain and you can change that sign from red to green. It's a scary thing when you finish shooting a movie and you're still driving a little too fast because you used to be able to drive that fast because you had to get on the set and 'Goddamnit, cars, get out of my way.' You kind of go to a maniacal, egotistical place in your own little mind. . . . "—Anderson quoted in *Rolling Stone*, February 3, 2000.

BORN: Kenneth Wilbur Anglemyer in Santa Monica, California, 02/03/1927

NATIONALITY: American

EDUCATION: Maurice Kossloff Dancing School, Hollywood, California 1935; studied tap dancing

Santa Monica High School, Santa Monica, California

University of Southern California, Los Angeles, California, cinema studies

AWARD: American Film Institute Maya Deren Award 1996

BIOGRAPHY

One of the major figures of the avant-garde "New American Cinema" of the 1950s and 60s, Kenneth Anger (born Kenneth Anglemyer) grew up in Hollywood, was a child actor (most notably in "A Midsummer Night's Dream" 1935) and was allegedly making films by the age of ten (e.g., the short "Ferdinand the Bull" 1937; "Who Has Been Rocking My Dream Boat?" 1941). After meeting famed underground filmmaker Harry Smith in 1947, he adopted the name 'Kenneth Anger' and, over two weekends, completed his first important work, "Fireworks" (1947). This personal psychodrama received a public screening and won critical acclaim in 1949 at Jean Cocteau's "Festival of the Damned" in Biarritz. Its protagonist, played by Anger, is a guilt-ridden homosexual who dreams of being viciously beaten by a group of sailors and his punishment leads to images of sexual liberation and fertility. The film's final images are of Anger asleep with another man, the dream only temporarily abating his internal anguish over his homosexuality. Shocking in its time for its sexual content, "Fireworks" was praised as a imaginative and daring personal expression.

After moving to France in 1950, Anger shot his next major work, "Eaux d'Artifice" (1953), in the gardens of the Villa d'Este in Tivoli, Italy. "Eaux d'Artifice" is a beautifully photographed, single-character exercise in symbolism. Wandering through the garden, a woman in baroque evening dress becomes frightened by hypnotic fountains and ominous gargoyles and tries to flee the labyrinth. The film begins with her emergence from a spurting fountain and ends as water engulfs her. While in Italy, he also shot "Thelema Abbey", a no longer extant documentary of an expedition headed by Dr. Alfred C. Kinsey to the Sicilian home of occultist Aleister Crowley. Before leaving France, Anger completed 20 minutes of "Histoire d'O/The Story of O" (1958–61), footage he has claimed is still locked in the Cinematheque Francaise because the character "O" was played by the 20-year-old daughter of the then-Minister of Finance.

"Inauguration of the Pleasure Dome" (1954, 1966) depicts an imaginative world of gods invoked and controlled by the untamed desires of Lord Shiva and his female self, the Scarlet Woman. It has been shown in several versions, including one with three-screen projection inspired by Abel Gance's "Napoleon" (1927). Lord Shiva's mythical world is paced with ritualistic pomp, from the slow entrance of the gods and the deceitful intoxication of Pan to the orgiastic finale set among the flames of hell.

Thirteen popular songs from the period provide the framework for Anger's most influential film, "Scorpio Rising" (1962–64). Each song is juxtaposed ironically with startling visual images. The song "Blue Velvet" accompanies men ritualistically dressing up in blue jeans and black leather. As the audience hears the lyrics to

"I Will Follow Him", the screen flashes a montage of images that includes Adolf Hitler at military rallies, disciples following Jesus Christ in clips from a low-budget educational feature "The Road to Jerusalem", Marlon Brando leading a motorcycle gang in "The Wild One" and Anger's Scorpio figure directing his followers in a motorcycle race. While these juxtapositions may seem jejune to contemporary audiences, the "poetic" symbolism of "Scorpio Rising" was striking to the audiences of the new art-houses in America in the early 60s.

"Invocation of My Demon Brother" (1969) presents a pastiche of images as seen through the mind's eye of a male albino: marijuana smoked through a skull pipe, soldiers in Vietnam, a burning cat, naked males wrestling in bed, and Mick Jagger performing on stage. Inserted throughout are shots of Anger as Magus, performing occult rites on stage in celebration of the Autumnal Equinox.

Anger made "Invocation" with scraps of footage originally photographed for "Lucifer Rising" (1980). His childhood fascination with fairy tales led to a lifelong dedication to the occult, specifically Aleister Crowley's religion, Thelema. In "Lucifer Rising", the forces of nature (e.g., volcanic eruptions, lightning, turbulent water, an eclipse of the moon) awaken Lucifer. Anger includes numerous symbols drawn from alchemy and imagistic references to the cosmology of Crowley. Stunningly photographed in Egypt, Germany and England at the sites of sun worship by ancient cultures, "Lucifer Rising" culminates with the spiritual rebel of the title conjuring up a luminous flying object over the pyramids and pharaohs of Egypt.

Anger has equated filmmaking with "casting a spell," or invocation. "Lucifer Rising" marked his attempt to move from the solipsistic visions and images of his earlier films to the invocation of a higher spiritual and intellectual order. Anger appeared the sketches of Jonas Mekas' 1985 film "He Stands in the Desert Counting the Seconds of His Life" and was among the notables who honored Mekas in a documentary, "Jonas in the Desert" (1993).

Those who do not know of Anger as filmmaker may be aware of his book "Hollywood Babylon", in which he related numerous scandals in the film industry. Throughout his life, he has shown a penchant for embellishment and fantasy. He recreated himself, casting off his childhood and adopting a new persona complete with new name. Anger often claimed that the source of the stories for "Hollywood Babylon" was his grandmother, a studio costume mistress. (In reality, she was an interior decorator.) Anger had a love-hate relationship with Hollywood and harbored some bitterness toward the film industry for not recognizing his talent. The disappointments he felt over his failed acting career somewhat fueled his writings. He wrote and published the book while living in penury in France. Inspired by the lurid tabloid *Confidential*, Anger embellished on gossip he had heard as a child; while the less lurid stories tend to be more truthful, many of the stories in his book generally detailed sexual exploits or described brutal and horrifying deaths. Subsequent research, however, has disproved many of his accounts, yet the success of the book and its sequel and a short-lived 1992 syndicated TV version hosted by Tony Curtis has allowed many of the tales to enter popular consciousness as fact.

MILESTONES:

Appeared in Baby Burlesk musical shorts; reportedly appeared in one with Shirley Temple; Anger later claimed to have attended dancing school with Temple

1935: Played the role of a changeling in Max Reinhardt's film, "A Midsummer Night's Dream"

1937: Made first film at age ten, the short "Ferdinand the Bull"

1941: Directed, photographed, edited and conceived short subject, "Who Has Been Rocking My Dream Boat?" at age fourteen

1944: Made silent film "Demigods"

1946: First exhibited film, sound version of "Demigods" now titled "Escape Episode"

With USC classmate Curtis Harrington, formed Creative Film Associates

1946: First arrested for homosexual behavior

1947: Changed name to Kenneth Anger

1947: Met renowned underground filmmaker Harry Smith

1947: Completed first extant film, "Fireworks"

1948: Completed "Puce Moment" (fragment of unfinished feature "Puce Women," about Hollywood in the 1920s)

1950: Went to France

1953: Shot "Eaux d'artifice" in Italy

1954: Returned to California

1955: Made "Thelema Abbey" (no longer extant) in Sicily for the BBC

1958: Appeared in Stan Brakhage's "The Dead"

1959: Published book "Hollywood Babylon" in France

1959–1961: Worked on, but never completed, feature "Histoire d'O"

1964: Received Ford grant to make a feature but completed only fragment (until death of actor playing protagonist), "KKK/Kustom Kar Kommandos"

1966: Began feature, "Lucifer Rising", but abandoned project after rough cut was stolen

1967: Placed ad in *Village Voice*: "In Memoriam Kenneth Anger 1947–67", announcing end of filmmaking career

1974: Completed second version of "Lucifer Rising" ("Invocation", released 1980)

1985: Acted in experimental film "He Stands in a Desert Counting the Seconds of His Life"

1992: Was advisor on TV series derived from "Hollywood Babylon"

QUOTES:

He received a Ford Foundation Fellow Grant in 1964.

BIBLIOGRAPHY:

"Hollywood Babylon" Kenneth Anger, 1959; anecdotal portrait of the underbelly of Hollywood, first published in France

"Hollywood Babylon II" Kenneth Anger, 1984; sequel

"Anger: The Unauthorized Biography of Kenneth Anger" Bill Landis, 1995, HarperCollins

Jean-Jacques Annaud

BORN: in Juvisy-sur-Orge, France, 10/01/1943

SOMETIMES CREDITED AS:
Jean Jacques Annaud

NATIONALITY: French

EDUCATION: Ecole de Vaugirard, Paris, France; valedictorian; school specialized in teaching the technical aspects of cinema

Ecole Nationale de Photo et Cinema, Paris, France, 1964, graduated

Institut des Hautes Etudes Cinematographiques, Paris, France, 1966

Sorbonne, University of Paris, Paris, France, literature 1967

AWARDS: Cesar Best Director "Quest for Fire" 1982

Cesar Best Motion Picture "Quest for Fire" 1982

Cesar Best Foreign Film "The Name of the Rose" 1987

Cesar Best Director "L'Ours/The Bear" 1989

BIOGRAPHY

Pioneering French director Jean-Jacques Annaud has often seemed as much anthropologist as filmmaker, taking great pains to faithfully create the disparate cultures that have driven his films. Time after time he has depicted the conflict that occurs when one culture bumps up against another and the resultant emotional transformations that arise from these clashes. His globetrotting has taken him from Vietnam (where he became the first non-Asian in 50 years to shoot anything but live ammunition) to the Andes (substituting for the Himalayas), the Canadian Rockies (standing in for the Andes) to colonial Africa, pursuing a recurrent theme—the quest for humanity in a world that has lost all sense of what being human is.

Annaud began collecting cameras and projectors at an early age, studied at the Vaugirard film technical school and later IDHEC and first made educational films for the French Army while fulfilling his mandatory military requirement in Africa. He subsequently became an acclaimed and extremely prolific director of TV commercials, making over 500 during the late 1960s and early 70s and acquiring the clout to venture into features. His debut, "Black and White in Color" (1976)—sparked by his compassion for the people of Africa during his Army days and wittily satirizing a group of French colonialists around the Ivory Coast circa 1914—though unsuccessful in his own country was a surprise hit in the USA, winning the Oscar as Best Foreign Film. His follow-up film, "Coup de tete/Hot Head" (1979), amusingly debunked the world of professional soccer and gave him a popular success in his native land.

For "Quest for Fire" (1981), a grueling portrait of primitive man that earned him two Cesar awards, Annaud invented four primitive tribes and then, with the help of the late Anthony Burgess and renowned anthropologist Desmond Morris, invented a culture—from body language to dress to implements—for each tribe. One tribe's discovery and use of fire to vanquish its enemies perfectly presaged

modern man's exploiting his advantage whenever possible. His first English-language film, "The Name of the Rose" (1986), adapted from the Umberto Eco novel, introduced him to the world of the box-office star (Sean Connery) and the big budget ($18 million). Its tale of intrigue and murder in a medieval monastery continued his collaboration with screenwriter Gerard Brach which was begun on "Quest for Fire." Brach would also script "The Bear" (1988) and share screenwriting credit for "The Lover" (1992) with Annaud.

"The Bear", a cub's coming of age story told from the cub's point of view, pitted sympathetic beast against villainous man, imparting a real sense of nature's magnificence in the bargain. Annaud spent nearly six years finding the right animals (including a 2000-pound Kodiak bear named Bart) and training them for their "roles" in the film. For his film version of Marguerite Duras' novel "The Lover", Annaud revisited European colonialism and its prejudices, brilliantly recreating a 1929 Saigon backdrop for the steamy romance between a young French girl and a wealthy Chinese man. The passion he acquired for Vietnam during "The Lover" ensured that he would return to an Asian setting for a subsequent movie.

With "Wings of Courage" (1995), Annaud became the first director to shoot a feature in the 3D IMAX format, telling in spectacular fashion the true story of a downed aviator who trekked back to civilization across six Andes mountain peaks in 1930. Then it was East meets West once again in "Seven Years in Tibet" (1997). Annaud's film starred Brad Pitt as Austrian mountaineer Heinrich Harrer, who escaped from a British prisoner of war camp during World War II by climbing over the Himalayas into Tibet, where he served as advisor to the young Dalai Lama while discovering Buddhism. Thwarted in his attempts to film in northern India, Annaud spared no expense rebuilding Tibet in Argentina, putting every bit of the movie's $70 million budget on the screen.

MILESTONES:

Fulfilled mandatory period of military service in Cameroon, Africa

Began career as film director making educational films while serving in French Army

Directed over 500 commercials (for which he won numerous Clio and Silver Lion Awards)

1976: First film as director and screenwriter, "Victoire en chantant/Black and White in Color"; won Oscar as Best Foreign-Language Film

1978: Co-wrote (with Alain Godard and director Pierre Richard) the screenplay for a film he did not direct, "Je suis timide, mais je me soigne/I'm Shy But I'm Treating It"

1979: Last screenplay credit for 13 years, "Coup de Tete/Hot Head", which he also directed

1981: First collaboration with screenwriter Gerard Brach, "Quest for Fire"

Founded Paris-based production company, Reparge Productions

1986: First English-language film, "The Name of the Rose"

1988: Helmed "The Bear", a wildlife coming-of-age movie told from the bear's point of view

1992: First screenplay credit in 13 years, "The Lover", adapted from Marguerite Duras's novel in collaboration with Gerard Brach

1993: Signed a three-year deal with Sony Pictures to direct English-Language movies

1995: Wrote and directed the first IMAX 3-D fiction film, the 40-minute "Wings of Courage"

1997: Directed Brad Pitt in the $70 million biopic "Seven Years in Tibet"

2001: Helmed "Enemy at the Gates"; screened at the Berlin Film Festival

QUOTES:

Awarded the Cinema Prize from French Academy in 1989 for career's work and the Grand Prix National du Cinema (1990).

Named Best Director by the Japanese Critic Association for "The Lover" (1993).

Made Officier des Arts et Lettres, Merite National

When asked if he was among the Hollywood Buddhists: "No. No. In a way, I resent those people who are parading in front of His Holiness [the Dalai Lama], bent in obedience. I respect the man immensely, but I'm not a Buddhist, I'm a filmmaker. I don't want to convert people. I want to entertain them and give them a glimpse at another civilization. I have seen a lot of Hollywood Buddhists who produce violent movies and give three percent of the gross to nonviolent organizations. That doesn't work for me. I think, if you want to promote nonviolence, don't make violent movies."—Jean-Jacques Annaud in *Movieline*, October 1997.

Michelangelo Antonioni

BORN: in Ferrara, Italy; 09/29/1912

NATIONALITY: Italian

EDUCATION: University of Bologna, Bologna, Italy; economics and commerce, 1935; helped found a student theater company; attempted to make first film

Centro Sperimentale di Cinematografia, Rome, Italy; direction, 1940; attended for a brief three months but made a short documentary

AWARDS: Italian Guild of Film Journalists Silver Ribbon "Nettezza Urbana" 1948

Italian Guild of Film Journalists Silver Ribbon "L'amoroso Menzogna" 1949

Venice Film Festival Silver Lion "Le Amiche/The Girlfriends" 1955; one of four films cited

Locarno Film Festival Critic's Grand Prize Best Film "Il Grido/The Outcry" 1957

Cannes Film Festival Special Jury Prize "L'Avventura" 1960

Berlin Film Festival Golden Bear "La Notte" 1961

Cannes Film Festival Special Jury Prize "L'Eclisse" 1962

Venice Film Festival Lion of St Mark for Best Film "Red Desert" 1964

Venice Film Festival International Film Critics Award "Red Desert" 1964

National Society of Film Critics Award Best Director "Blow-Up" 1966

Cannes Film Festival Palme d'Or "Blow-Up" 1967

Cannes Film Festival Special Prize of the 35th Anniversary "Identificazione di una Donna" and entire body of work 1983

Honorary Oscar 1995 presented for lifetime achievement

Venice Film Festival International Critics Prize "Beyond the Clouds" 1995; tied with "Cyclo"; shared award with Wim Wenders

BIOGRAPHY

Michelangelo Antonioni began writing about film as a student at Bologna University, mercilessly criticizing the fatuous Italian comedies of the 1930s. In 1940, he studied direction at the Centro Sperimentale di Cinematografia in Rome and two years later co-wrote the scenario for "Un piloto ritorna" with director Roberto Rossellini before working as an assistant director on films directed by Enrico Fulchignoni and Marcel Carne. His first directorial effort was a documentary, "Gente del Po", begun in 1943 and completed in 1947. For two other documentaries in the late 40s he solicited music from Giovanni Fusco, initiating and cementing a collaboration with the man whose scores would enhance his own pessimism in eight films.

Antonioni's minimalist yet poignant style, which critics described as "structured absence," and his disdain for vulgar commercialism, made him an important influence on post-neorealist Italian cinema. His first feature, "Story of a Love Affair" (1950), used complex camerawork to tell the simple tale of a wealthy woman whose husband dies, an approach that would typify his subsequent work. "The Vanquished" (1952) focused on the youth of postwar Europe in three separate stories set and shot in Rome, Paris and London. The Italian section displeased the Italians by depicting their youngsters as neo-Fascists, and censors in France and England banned their respective portions of the film. Antonioni's episode of the anthology film "Love in the City" (1953) dealt with suicide, a preoccupation that also provided the uneasy resolution to "The Girl Friends" (1955), a study of several women and their disappointing relationships with men.

After the release of "The Outcry" (1957), a study of the inept men of the Po Valley, Antonioni's developing assurance with the medium led him to look beyond the proletarian subjects favored by neorealism. "L'Avventura" (1959) began a phase of non-narrative, psychological cinema, examining the barren eroticism of a bourgeoisie (Antonioni was himself from the middle class) which had abandoned its traditional social and cultural values. The film attracted a political critique that equated Antonioni's work with the writings of Andre Gide. Critics, citing the united thematic concerns of "L'Avventura", "La Notte" (1961) and "L'Eclisse" (1962), have grouped them as a trilogy in which mankind reaches unsuccessfully for love as the last refuge in the modern world. Antonioni made one more film directly charting the same universe, although "The Red Desert" (1964), in which Antonioni working for the first time in color, had an entire landscape painted red to underline his theme of despair, focused so intensely on the character of Giuliana as to lose the trilogy's sense of alternative possibilities. Heroine Monica Vitti's palpable frustration signaled the end of her four-film collaboration with Antonioni, which had made her an international star.

"Blow-Up" (1966) marked Antonioni's departure from Italy to "swinging London," where he dramatized the paradoxes of its nervous hip consciousness. The film's finale—a ball-less tennis match—became a reference point of 60s cinema. The success of "Blow-Up" (Antonioni won the National Society of Film Critics' Best Director award and was nominated for Oscars for Best Director and Best Screenplay) brought the director to California for "Zabriskie Point" (1970), an elegiac view of the intersection of materialism and hippiedom. "The Passenger" (1975) featured Jack Nicholson as an American reporter who adopts the identity of a deceased fellow guest in a North African hotel. The director's virtuoso use of Gaudi's architecture echoed the unresolved angles of the protagonist's world. Neither "Mystery of Oberwald" (1980) nor "Identification of a Woman" (1982) found distribution in the USA.

In 1985, Antonioni suffered a heart attack that left him partially paralyzed and over the next decade managed to produce only the eleven-minute documentary short, "Volcanoes and Carnival" (1992). However, with the encouragement of his wife Enrica and the financial backing provided by French producer Stephane Tchalgadjieff, Antonioni returned triumphantly with "Beyond the Clouds" (1995). German director Wim Wenders, who had become involved because Antonioni's precarious health made him uninsurable, shot the prologue, epilogue and linking shots between the four episodes comprising the movie and otherwise stayed out of the way, totally fascinated by Antonioni at work.

Based on stories in Antonioni's book "That Bowling Alley on the Tiber: Tales of a Director" (1985), "Beyond the Clouds" proved a brilliantly unified movie on par with the director's best work, evoking such familiar themes as alienation in the modern world while also exploring a religiosity not previously found in his films. Employing his signature fluency of camera movement and shots sustained much longer than the norm in the creation of an impeccable visual composition, "Beyond the Clouds" demonstrated that the old master had lost none of his technical expertise and was in fact still growing artistically at the age of 83. His wife chronicled the experience and edited her nearly 85 hours of film into a 52-minute documentary titled "For Me, to Make a Film Is to Live" (1995). The director was presented with an honorary Academy Award for lifetime achievement at the 1995 ceremony.

MILESTONES:

While at university began first documentary (shot in an insane asylum); later abandoned

1935: Wrote for newspaper, *Il Corriere Padano* in Ferrara

1935–1939: Worked in bank

1939: Moved to Rome

1940: Began writing for magazine *Cinema*, fired for political reasons after only a few months; magazine's director was Mussolini's son Vittorio

1942: First film as co-screenwriter, "Un piloto ritorna"; director and co-screenwriter was Roberto Rossellini

1942: Worked as assistant director on Enrico Fulchignoni's "I due Foscari" and in France on Marcel Carne's "Les visiteurs du soir"

Served in Italian army; sneaked out of camp to work with Fulchignoni and contrived trip to Paris to work with Marcel returning to Italy when military leave expired

1943: Worked as a translator of French literature

Directed and wrote 11 short films; debut, "Gente del Po" (shot in 1943, completed 1947)

1950: Feature film directing debut (also co-screenwriter; from story), "Cronaca di un Amore/Story of a Love Affair"

1955: Sole producing credit, Nicolo Ferrari's "Uomini in piu"

1955: "Le amici/The Girlfriends," widely agreed to be director's first truly outstanding achievement

1957: Directed Monica Vitti on stage in "I Am a Camera"

1958: Worked as uncredited co-director on "La tempesta" (Alberto Lattuada) and "Nel segno di Roma" (Guido Brignone)

1960: Achieved new level of international recognition and success with his "L'Avventura"

1964: Used color film for first time in "Il deserto russo/The Red Desert"

1966: First English-language film, "Blow-Up", made in Great Britain; received Oscar nominations for Best Director and Best Screenplay

1970: Directed only US film, "Zabriskie Point"

1975: "The Passenger", starring Jack Nicholson, brought renewed critical recognition and some degree of commercial success

1982: Last film for a decade, "Identificazione di una donna/Identification of a Woman"

1985: Suffered heart attack that left him partially paralyzed

1992: Completed the documentary short, "Noto—Mandorli—Vulcano—Stromboli—Carnevale/Volcanoes and Carnival"

1995: Returned triumphantly to form directing "Beyond the Clouds"; Wim Wenders directed linking sequences (including a prologue and epilogue)

1995: His wife directed a documentary "For Me, to Make a Film Is to Live" chronicling the making of "Beyond the Clouds"

1995: Presented with honorary Oscar for lifetime achievement

QUOTES:

"I shot so much film that when I began editing, I didn't know where to start. The real value of my film was the possibility I had for my camera to be in the closest proximity possible to Michelangelo, who wouldn't have allowed anyone else's camera to be so intimate while he was working."—Enrica Antonioni on making "For Me, to Make a Film Is to Live", her documentary of filmmaker husband Michelangelo Antonioni.

When asked what he wants to do next [after "Beyond the Clouds"], Antonioni replied, "It's all said by the director character in my film: 'When I have finished a film, I start thinking about the next one, and for me, being silent is not just the only thing, it is the best thing—to be silent in the darkness and then the lights come up.'"

BIBLIOGRAPHY:

"That Bowling Alley on the Tiber: Tales of a Director" Michelangelo Antonioni and William Arrowsmith" 1985 Oxford University Press

"Antonioni: The Poet of Images" William Arrowsmith 1995 Oxford University Press

"My Time with Antonioni" Wim Wenders 2000 Faber and Faber

Michael Apted

BORN: Michael David Apted in Aylesbury, Buckinghamshire, England, 02/10/1941

NATIONALITY: English

EDUCATION: City of London School London, England

Downing College, University of Cambridge, Cambridge, England, law and history; BA 1963

AWARDS: International Emmy "The Collection" 1976

BAFTA Robert Flaherty Documentary Award "28 Up" 1984

Grammy Best Music Video, Long Form "Bring on the Night" 1987; shared award with Sting

International Documentary Association Career Achievement Award 1999

BIOGRAPHY

Versatile director Michael Apted's fondness for both documentaries and dramas has provided him with a balance and perspective matched by few of his contemporaries. Beginning his career with England's Granada Television first as a researcher, then director, notably of the long-running soap "Coronation Street", he branched into features at the helm of "Triple Echo" (1973), an off-beat wartime romance in which Oliver Reed falls for an AWOL soldier disguised as a woman. Apted displayed his enthusiasm for the music scene with his follow-up, "Stardust" (1974), chronicling the rise and fall of a Beatles-like pop group, and continued to show his eclectic tastes, as well as a talent for action sequences, with the gritty British crime thriller "The Squeeze" (1977), starring Stacy Keach as a burnt-out, alcoholic ex-cop offered a chance at redemption when called upon to rescue his former spouse from kidnappers. His last effort before crossing the pond to work in Hollywood, "Agatha" (1979), was an intriguing speculation on the 11-day disappearance of Agatha Christie in 1926 and starred Vanessa Redgrave as the famous mystery writer and Dustin Hoffman as the smooth Yankee reporter who tracks her down.

Apted gained instant credibility with his American film debut, "Coal Miner's Daughter" (1980), one of the finest musical bios ever made. The rags-to-riches story of country star Loretta Lynn earned star Sissy Spacek a well-deserved Best Actress Oscar (for a performance that saw her do her own singing) and featured equally outstanding work from Tommy Lee Jones, Beverly D'Angelo and Levon Helm in supporting parts. He stumbled with his next outing, "Continental Divide" (1981), despite the presence of potent collaborators like Lawrence Kasdan (screenwriter) and Steven Spielberg (executive producer), and returned to England for the so-so adolescent comedy "Kipperbang" (1982, made for British TV but released theatrically in the USA) before finally scoring at the box office with the absorbing murder mystery "Gorky Park" (1983). A very bad Richard Pryor vehicle, "Critical Condition" (1986), proved a momentary bump in the road, but he recovered his bearings with "Gorillas in the Mist" (1988), an intriguing blend of documentary and career-woman melodrama starring Sigourney Weaver as Dian Fossey, a ferocious and antisocial recluse whose fanatical protecting of "her" gorillas led to her murder.

His success in features not withstanding, Apted may be best remembered as a documentarian, particularly for the interview series started when he was a researcher for Granada's "World in Action" program. Although just an assistant on "7 Up" (1963), Paul Almond's attempt to document the effects of social and economic disparities among English schoolchildren of radically different backgrounds, Apted took over the project and made it his own, directing follow-up portraits of the same group of subjects at seven-year intervals in the sequels "14 Up" (1970) "21 Up" (1977), "28 Up" (1984), "35 Up" (1991) and "42 Up" (1998). The popularity of the series led to an American spin-off, "Age Seven in America" (CBS, 1992) and its later installment "14 Up in America" (Showtime, 1998), both directed by Phil Joanou with Apted behind the scenes as first producer, then executive producer. He subsequently set loose a Russian crew, which has completed its own versions of "7 Up" and "14 Up", and the franchise has since spread to South Africa, Japan and Germany.

Although there was a time when the "Up" films were his only break from fiction, Apted has increasingly expanded his scope as a non-fiction filmmaker. "Bring on the Night" (1985), his look into the formation of Sting's rock-jazz band culminating in their first concert performance, earned a Grammy for Best Music Video, Long Form, and he similarly profiled Russian rock star Boris Grebenshikov in "The Long Way Home" (Granada TV, CBS Music Video, 1989). After getting crackling performances from Gene Hackman and Mary Elizabeth Mastrantonio as father and daughter lawyers on opposite sides of a "Class Action" (1991) court case, he journeyed to Sioux country and exercised both his loves with the incisive documentary "Incident at Oglala" and the related "Thunderheart" (both 1992), a drama based loosely on those events of the 70s which occurred at the Pine Ridge Reservation in South Dakota and led to the framing of Indian activist Leonard Peltier. The engrossing thriller starred Val Kilmer as an FBI man who discovers his own Indian roots while investigating murder on the reservation. He then traveled to China for "Moving the Mountain" (1994), a documentary look inside the inner circles of that country's pro-democracy circles.

Apted's penchant for dramas revolving around the fairer sex continued with his two 1994 features. In "Blink" the protagonist was a blind woman who regains her sight after twenty years, only to witnesses a murder, which she then doubts she has seen. For "Nell" Apted adopted a documentary tone to tell its story of a young woman (Jodie Foster) raised in isolation who becomes the center of controversy when a kindly doctor (Liam Neeson) and an ambitious psychologist (Natasha Richardson) take opposing views on whether she should be integrated into society. Following "Extreme Measures" (1996), a conspiracy thriller set in the medical world that tipped its hand too soon, the director embarked on back-to-back documentaries, "Inspirations" (1997) and "Me and Isaac Newton" (1999), the former detailing the creative process of celebrated artists while the latter looked at individuals who find solace in the answers provided by science. His reputation for helming character-driven projects prompted producers Michael G Wilson and Barbara Broccoli to invite him to take on James Bond in "The World Is Not Enough" (also 1999). Apted concentrated on providing a strong story to go with all the action and reinvigorated the franchise, elevating the Bond girls above their usual sexual ornamentation.

Apted directed the thriller "Enigma" in 2001 and the Jennifer Lopez vehicle "Enough" in 2002. Also in 2002, he embarked on a documentary series on marriage called "Married in America." Using the same format as his seminal "Seven Plus Seven" series, the nine couple's lives will be documented over ten years.

MILESTONES:

Joined Granada TV as a trainee, then worked as researcher for current-affairs program "World in Action"; later directed episodes of "All Our Yesterdays" and "Coronation Street" in the mid-1960s

1963: Served as assistant to director Paul Almond on "7 Up" (Granada TV); broadcast on PBS in 1987

1965: Became producer-director for local programs and current affairs; then staff director of TV series, plays (directed over 50) and serials

1970: Helmed "Seven Plus Seven", a documentary update for Granada TV of Almond's "7 Up"

1973: Feature directorial debut, "Triple Echo"

1975: Directed "Stardust", a provocative and believable look at a fictional, Beatles-like rock group

1977: American TV directorial debut, the PBS special "Childhood"

1977: Helmed "21 Up" (Granada TV), a continuing update of "7 Up"

1978: Debut as stage director, "Strawberry Fields" at the National Theatre, London

1979: Directed "Agatha", a fictional speculation on Agatha Christie's famous 11-day disappearance in 1926

1980: American feature directorial debut, "Coal Miner's Daughter", star Sissy Spacek earned a Best Actress Oscar; first collaborations with Tom Rickman, who scripted and Tommy Lee Jones, who co-starred

1981: Teamed with screenwriter Lawrence Kasdan and executive producer Steven Spielberg on "Continental Divide"; only interesting in its unusual casting of John Belushi as a romantic lead opposite Blair Brown

1983: Turned Helsinki into Moscow for

"Gorky Park", an absorbing murder mystery set in Russia starring John Hurt

1984: Helmed "28 Up" (Granada TV)

1985: Executive produced Tom Rickman's feature directing debut, "The River Rat", starring Tommy Lee Jones

1985: Consolidating the four TV documentaries begun by Almond 21 years before in "7 Up", produced feature version of "28 Up" (based on the TV documentary), incorporating footage from interviews of the same children at ages 7, 14, 21 and 28

1985: Directed "Bring On the Night", a first-rate documentary about the formation of Sting's rock-jazz band; shared Grammy with Sting for Best Music Video, Long Form

1985: Appeared as Ace Tomato Agent in John Landis' "Spies Like Us"

1987: Missed with "Critical Condition", starring Richard Pryor as a con artist who takes charge of a prison hospital

1988: Redeemed himself at the helm of "Gorillas in the Mist", a compelling drama based on the life of Dian Fossey (Sigourney Weaver in an Oscar-nominated turn)

1989: Filmed "The Long Way Home" (Granada TV, CBS Music Video), a documentary about Russian rock star Boris Grebenshikov

1991: Helmed "Class Action", featuring top-notch performances from Gene Hackman and Mary Elizabeth Mastrantonio as father-daughter lawyers on opposite sides of a class-action lawsuit against a negligent auto company

1991: American TV debut, directing the premiere episode of "My Life and Times" (ABC)

1991: Produced and directed "35 Up" for Granada TV and feature release, receiving first screenplay credit

1992: Brought the franchise to America, producing "Age Seven in America/7 Up in America" (CBS), directed by Phil Joanou

1992: Executive produced the CBS miniseries "Intruders", directed by Dan Curtis

1992: Directed the pilot episode and served as executive producer of the ABC series "Crossroads"

1992: Journeyed into Sioux Indian country, directing "Thunderheart" (co-produced by Robert De Niro) and "Incident at Oglala" (co-executive produced and narrated by Robert Redford)

1992: Co-executive produced "Bram Stoker's Dracula", directed by Francis Ford Coppola

1993: Served as co-executive producer of Forest Whitaker's directing debut, "Strapped" (HBO)

1994: Scripted and helmed "Moving the Mountain", a documentary look inside the inner circle of China's pro-Democracy leaders

1994: Helmed "Nell", starring Jodie Foster (who also produced); Foster received a Best Actress Oscar nomination

1996: Stepped inside the emergency room to helm "Extreme Measures"

1997: Produced and directed "Inspirations", a documentary detailing the creative process of seven celebrated artists

1998: Directed the modern urban fable "Always Outnumbered" (HBO)

1998: Executive produced Joanou's "14 Up in America"; American series projects a theatrical release in 2012 when its subjects are 28

1998: Produced and helmed "42 Up" (Granada TV)

1999: Helmed "Me and Isaac Newton", a documentary profiling six individuals who find solace in the answers provided by science

1999: Directed "The World Is Not Enough", featuring Pierce Brosnan as James Bond

2001: Helmed the thriller "Enigma"; premiered at the Sundance Film Festival

2002: Directed Jennifer Lopez as an abused woman who strikes back in "Enough"

2002: Created the documentary series "Married in America" following nine newlywed couples over ten years

2003: Replaced Martha Coolidge as President of the DGA

QUOTES:

"I've always had this double interest. I was able, largely because of the 'Up' films, to keep the two strands going, and I do it as much as I can. There was a period when I would do only the 'Up' films other than fictional films, but then they became so successful around the world that they opened the doors for me to keep the [other] documentaries going. Now I find I do more and more, maybe because it's harder to find fiction films to resond to. I respond to the documentaries more because they're my statement, they're very personal to me. They're my films, whereas getting caught up in the studio system, sometimes it's hard not to think of yourself as a hired gun."—Michael Apted quoted in *Moviemaker*, April 1998.

"And another interesting thing is, 'How important is the scene?' Because I'm also of the belief, that not all scenes are as important as others. In terms of—how much time am I going to spend on this scene? I'm very careful about that, when I do my schedule, I think that's part of the job to be able to make those value judgments about where you want to spend your time.

"When I've produced stuff, and I've produced first-time directors, it's something I try to instill in them but it's very hard to get because they want everything to be good. But I say to them, 'Don't waste a lot of time on this scene. It's going to be in the movie but it's not that important. Don't cover that scene from here to Christmas. Just move on.' And that's a hard thing to grasp. The more experience you get, the more comfortable you are with that."—Apted, in *DGA Magazine*, December 1997–January 1998.

On joining the James Bond franchise for "The World Is Not Enough": "At first I was surprised they wanted to make any change to the formula. But their appetite for something new coincided with my views and when I saw what was in the back of their minds, all doubts were removed about my involvement. They knew the action would be in good hands with regulars like second unit director Vic Armstrong and stunt co-ordinator Simon Crane. They've got it down pat, so the action would take care of itself. It was a daunting prospect, I won't deny it. There's a lot of expectation that comes with a Bond film which can be intimidating. But going in, my one major worry was could I handle such a scale of movie on a tough 110-day schedule.

"Looking back . . . the biggest surprise is I'm not tired or worn out from it all. I've still got all my marbles. I've learned such bad habits, though. How can I go back to an ordinary 50-day shoot?"—quoted in *Cinemafantastique*, December 1999.

"Americans want to be in show business . . . Whereas it's a nightmare for me to persuade these good [English] souls to do it every seven years. Doing it in America, it's fighting them off. America is much more celebrity-conscious than England. We will see whether the subjects of the American one can have a kind of serious life, or get swallowed up. I doubt it. In England they're celebrities for about six weeks after it's broadcast, but it doesn't really affect their lives in the celebrity sense."—Apted quoted in *Daily News*, November 16, 1999.

BORN: Gregg Y Araki in Los Angeles, California, 12/17/1959

NATIONALITY: American

EDUCATION: University of California at Santa Barbara, Santa Barbara, California; film studies, BA 1982

University of Southern California Los Angeles, California; film production, MFA 1984

AWARD: Los Angeles Film Critics Association Award Best Independent/Experimental Film "The Long Weekend (o' Despair)" 1989

BIOGRAPHY

A self-styled "guerrilla filmmaker" (because he often films without permits and pays his actors very little), Gregg Araki's features are tinged with ironic nihilism and reflect the boredom, despair and inadequacy of segments of American youth who consider themselves outside the mainstream. The openly gay Asian-American was born and raised in Southern California and made his first feature, "Three Bewildered People in the Night" (1987), on a budget of $5000. Shot in grainy black and white with a stationary camera, the film was a character study of a love triangle between an aspiring video artist, her gay male friend and her boyfriend. His second feature, "The Long Weekend (o' Despair)" (1989), shot in similar style on the same budget, depicted a reunion of college friends who come to realize that they cannot recapture the feelings of the recent past. Both films depicted disintegrating relationships in a starkly stylized, claustrophobic manner.

Araki achieved a breakthrough with his third feature, "The Living End" (1992), which also earned him the label as a pioneer of the 'Queer New Wave Cinema'. Shot in bright colors on a budget of over $20,000, "The Living End" follows two HIV-positive men who, in the midst of a casual affair, embark on a road trip after one murders a policeman. The film exploits and explodes the cliches of the road picture to create a controversial exploration of life in a society where AIDS and homophobia are inescapable realities.

Araki's fourth film, "Totally F***ed Up" (1993), was actually shot before "The Living End" but delayed because of funding difficulties. "Totally F***ed Up" portrays, in a fragmented structure, the lives of six gay and lesbian teenagers contending with AIDS, suicide, homophobia, despair, depression and drugs. "The Doom Generation" (1995), subtitled "A Heterosexual Movie", was a return to the road picture. Essentially a riff on "The Living End", it focuses on two alienated teenagers, aimlessly driving around California, whose lives are transformed when they become involved with a mysterious drifter. The supporting cast was filled with odd cameos by such diverse personalities as former madam Heidi Fleiss and 1970s TV icons Lauren Tewes ("The Love Boat") and Christopher Knight ("The Brady Bunch"). The visually striking "Nowhere" (filmed in 1995; released in 1997) is Araki's take on the interrelationships among post–high school youth in Los Angeles and is meant to be an antithetical version of TV's "Beverly Hills, 90210."

MILESTONES:

Raised in Santa Barbara, California

1987: Directed first feature (reportedly for $5,000), "Three Bewildered People in the Night"

1992: Breakthrough feature "The Living End" released

1993: Began his "teenage" trilogy with "Totally F***ed Up"

1995: First feature with budget of $1 million, "The Doom Generation"

1997: Completed unofficial trilogy with the nihilistic "Nowhere"

1999: Shifted gears and directed the romantic comedy "Splendor"

2000—2001: Produced and directed the MTV series "This Is How the World Ends"

QUOTES:

Araki freely admits that his films frequently refer to Godard: "Totally F***ed Up" borrows the intertitle device and the lesbian leads Michele and Patricia are named after the characters played by Jean-Paul Belmando and Jean Seberg in "Breathless"; the male leads in "The Living End" are named John and Luc, etc.—Noted by Chris Chang in "Absorbing Alternative" in *Film Comment*, September-October 1994.

"I taught a class in independent film at my old school in Santa Barbara and we talked about this idea of 'the mainstream' versus ideas of 'the outside' and 'the edge'. We came up with this metaphor of an amoeba or giant blob absorbing everything. Punk culture, which starts way out there with The Sex Pistols and safety pins through your nose, all becomes accountants driving around listening to Nirvana. Everything out there eventually comes around. Being on the outside, being a part of alternative culture, being gay and away from the middle of the road has always struck me as a very scary and hypocritical thing. I've always distrusted popular culture, Top 40, hit TV shows, and I don't like being in a huge faceless crowd, or a mob. I just feel more comfortable outside than inside but, at the same time, as the margins get pushed further and further, they're slowly drifting towards you."—Araki in *Film Comment*, September–October 1994.

"None of my films are autobiographical, [but] I make films about a very specific subculture or milieu which is directly related to my experience."—Araki in "Absorbing Alternative" in *Film Comment*, September–October 1994.

"I'm very interested in sex and violence. Not in a slasher, T&A way, but violence as bizarre action."—Araki quoted in *Elle*, December 1993.

"One thing I hate about contemporary movies is that most of them clearly lack any visual conception or style. They're flat, lifeless and predictable. A lot of things influence me visually besides other films—magazines, photography, MTV, advertising."—Araki quoted in *UGC News*, February 1995.

Alfonso Arau

BORN: in Mexico City, Mexico, 1933

NATIONALITY: Mexican

EDUCATION: studied medicine before quitting to study dance and drama
    studied pantomime in France

AWARDS: Ariel Best Film "Like Water for Chocolate" 1992
    Ariel Best Director "Like Water for Chocolate" 1992

BIOGRAPHY

Multi-talented Mexican artist who began as a dancer before turning to acting and eventually writing, directing and producing motion pictures. Arau made his feature directing debut with the Mexican-lensed "The Barefoot Eagle" (1967), before playing what would be the first in a series of somewhat stereotypical characters for Hollywood in Sam Peckinpah's landmark Western "The Wild Bunch" (1969). Subsequently, the thin, handsome and often mustached Arau alternated between acting assignments in the US and producing, directing, writing and starring in his own projects in Mexico. Arau's better known American credits include Kirk Douglas' "Posse" (1975), as a bandit, "Romancing the Stone" (1984), as a friendly drug-dealing bandit, and "Three Amigos!" (1986), as El Guapo the "jefe" of a group of bandits.

Arau's greatest success came as the producer-director of the sensuous art-house hit, "Like Water for Chocolate" (1992). Adapted by his former wife, Laura Esquivel, from her acclaimed novel, "Chocolate" went on to become the most successful film in Mexican history and received ten of 12 possible Ariel Awards (Mexico's Oscar equivalent). This success caught the attention of Hollywood and projects began coming his way.

COMPANION:

wife: Laura Esquivel. Author, screenwriter; wrote the novel and screenplay of "Like Water for Chocolate"; second wife; divorced

MILESTONES:

Born and raised in Mexico City, Mexico

Studied medicine before switching to dance and drama

Worked as a professional classical dancer

Toured for four years in a one-man pantomime show

1967: Feature directing debut, "The Bearfoot Eagle"

1969: Feature acting debut, Sam Peckinpah's "The Wild Bunch"

1974: Wrote, directed, produced and acted in "Calzonzin Inspector"

1992: Directed and produced the art-house hit "Like Water for Chocolate", adopted by his wife Lara Esquival from her novel

1995: Helmed the period romance "A Walk in the Clouds"

2000: Directed the black comedy "Picking Up the Pieces", starring Woody Allen and Sharon Stone; film premiered on Cinemax in lieu of theatrical release

2002: Helmed the three-hour A&E TV remake of "The Magnificent Ambersons", utilizing Orson Welles' screenplay adaptation; production edited as international theatrical release

Denys Arcand

BORN: in Deschambault, Quebec, Canada, 06/25/1941

NATIONALITY: Canadian

EDUCATION: attended Jesuit school for nine years

University of Montreal Montreal, Quebec, Canada; history 1963

AWARDS: Canadian Film Award Best Children's Film "Quebec 1603" 1965

Canadian Film Award Best Original Screenplay "Rejeanne Padovani" 1973; co-winner with Jacques Benoit

Cannes Film Festival FIPRESCI Prize "The Decline of the American Empire" 1986

Genie Best Director "Le Declin de l'empire americain/The Decline of the American Empire" 1986; film won 9 awards

Genie Best Original Screenplay "Le Declin de l'empire americain/The Decline of the American Empire" 1986

Cannes Film Festival Jury Prize "Jesus of Montreal" 1989

Genie Best Director "Jesus of Montreal" 1990; film won 12 Genies

Genie Best Original Screenplay "Jesus of Montreal" 1990

BIOGRAPHY

Montreal-based Denys Arcand is one of Canada's most successful screenwriter-directors. Arcand was raised in a strict Catholic home (his mother had wanted to be a Carmelite nun) and spent nine years in Jesuit school. He produced his first film, the short "Seul ou avec d'autres" (1962), while at university.

After graduation, Arcand went to work for the National Film Board of Canada where, between 1964 and 1965, he made a trilogy of short historical documentaries about the early explorers and settlers of North America. In 1970, he directed "On est au coton", a feature-length documentary about abuses in the textile industry that was officially banned, allegedly because of its "biased" point of view. Another politically-oriented documentary followed, "Quebec: Duplessisz et apres . . . " (1972).

In 1972, Arcand directed his first fiction feature, "Une maudite galette", an ironic thriller involving theft and murder. "Rejeanne padovani" (1973), set against the construction of Montreal's Ville-Marie superhighway, also dealt with murder and greed. For "Gina" (1975), the director drew upon his experiences filming "On est au coton" to fashion a tale of violence and revenge about a stripper and a film crew working on a documentary about the textile industry.

Following some work for TV and the production of a controversial documentary for the National Film Board about Quebec's 1980 referendum for secession from Canada, Arcand returned to features with "Le crime d'ovide plouffe" (1984) and his breakthrough film, "The Decline of the American Empire" (1986).

Marked by Arcand's typically cynical humor, "Decline" focuses on a group of Quebecois artists and intellectuals—four men and four women—coming to grips with the problems of sexuality, success, fidelity, intimacy and aging in contemporary society. Mirroring the baby-boomer angst of John Sayles' "Return of the Secaucus Seven" and Lawrence Kasdan's

"The Big Chill", "Decline" became Canada's biggest worldwide screen success. A hit on the festival circuit and with critics and filmgoers in the States, the film won nine Genies (the Canadian Oscar), the FIPRESCI prize at Cannes and an Oscar nomination for Best Foreign Language Film. (Paramount even announced the development of a US remake.)

"Jesus of Montreal" (1988) is a tragicomic account of a group of struggling Montreal actors who support themselves by giving revisionist nighttime performances of a passion play. The film was allegedly inspired by an actor who auditioned for "Decline"; he told Arcand that he was portraying Jesus in an old French play being performed for tourists visiting the city's famed Mont Royal peak. The director became fascinated with the lives of these Montreal artists who made a living as biblical figures by night and in beer commercials and porno films by day.

A dazzling mix of passion play drama, Catholic ideology and contemporary satire, "Jesus of Montreal" takes an unblinking look at the plight of the struggling actor. It is a highly personal work, influenced by Arcand's rigorous Catholic education and disillusionment with the church, and reflecting his view that "the Catholic hierarchy is completely opposed to Christ's purest teachings." It earned a 1989 Oscar nomination as Best Foreign Language Film.

After contributing a segment to the omnibus film "Montreal Vu Par . . . " (1991) which celebrated the 350th anniversary of the founding of the city, Arcand helmed the screen version of Brad Fraser's controversial play "Love and Human Remains" (1993). Following a disparate group of twentysomethings searching for meaning and fulfillment in their lives, this comedy was Arcand's first English language film and successfully adapted the dark, quirky, highly theatrical original material (which employed the metaphor of a serial killer randomly striking victims with AIDS).

FAMILY:
brother: Gabriel Arcand. Actor has appeared in brother's films

MILESTONES:

1962: Made first short film, "Seul ou avec d'autres", while still in school

1963–1968: With National Film Board of Canada, made short documentaries including the trilogy "Champlain" (1964), "Les Montrealistes" (1965) and "La route de l'ouest" (1965); became founding member of Les Cineastes Associes (Associated Filmmakers)

1970: Made banned feature-length documentary "On est au coton" (released 1976)

1971: First feature film as director, "La maudite galette"

1972: Was director, screenwriter and editor of the feature "Rejeanne Padovani"

1974: Directed "Gina", a controversial look at filmmaking and action-packed revenge movies

1977: TV directing debut, "Duplessis"

1981: Helmed the documentary "Le Confort et l'indifference", a look at the 1980 Quebec Referendum top secession

1984: Directed brother Gabriel in "Le Crime d'Ovide Plouffe"; also penned screenplay

1986: Was director and screenwriter of the roundly acclaimed, witty and dialogue-heavy feature "The Decline of the American Empire"

1987: Had a cameo in Jean-Claude Lauzon's gritty Genie-winning melodrama "Un Zoo la nuit"

1989: Wrote and directed the award-winning drama "Jesus of Montreal"; also acted in a small role

1991: Contributed his film "Vue d'Ailleurs/Seen From Elsewhere" to the anthology "Montreal Vu Par . . . ", celebrating the city's 350th anniversary

1992: Had a cameo in Jean-Claude Lauzon's "Leolo"

1993: Directed the darkly atmospheric and somewhat comedic feature "Love and Human Remains"

1996: Helmed the docudrama "Joyeux Calvaire", a portrait of Montreal's homeless

2000: Was director of "Stardom", an aptly titled look at celebrity, screened at the famed film festivals in Cannes and Toronto

AFFILIATION: Member of the National Film Board of Canada.

Darren Aronofsky

BORN: in Brooklyn, New York, 02/12/1969

NATIONALITY: American

EDUCATION: Edward R Murrow High School, Brooklyn, New York, 1987; graduated early in order to move to Israel for kibbutz

Harvard University Cambridge, Massachusetts; met Sean Gullette as an undergraduate

Center for Advanced Film Studies, American Film Institute Los Angeles, California

AWARDS: Sundance Film Festival Filmmakers Trophy (Drama) "Pi" 1998

IFP Gotham Open Palm Award "Pi" 1998

Florida Film Critics Circle Award Newcomer of the Year "Pi" 1998; cited with Chris Eyre and Sherman Alexie ("Smoke Signals")

Independent Spirit Award Best First Screenplay "Pi" 1999

New York Film Critics Online Award Breakthrough Director "Requiem for a Dream" 2000

Online Film Critics Society Award Best Director "Requiem for a Dream" 2000

American Film Institute Franklin J Schaffner Alumni Medal 2001

BIOGRAPHY

Brooklyn-born Darren Aronofsky received the director's award at the 1998 Sundance Film Festival for "Pi", his thought-provoking debut feature about a mathematics genius studying the numerical patterns in the stock market who runs afoul of a group of Jewish mystics and shady Wall Street types. Part-thriller, part-character study, this visually and aurally stunning black-and-white feature amazingly was crafted on a minuscule budget ($60,000).

The child of schoolteacher parents, Aronofsky was raised in Coney Island and graduated from high school early so he could travel to Israel and live on a kibbutz. Once there, however, he found things were not what he expected. Instead of farming avocados, the work was in a plastics factory. After two days, Aronofsky left, traveled to Jerusalem and encountered Hassidim who offered food and shelter in return for his taking classes on the Torah. After returning to the USA, Aronofsky graduated from Harvard (where he met future collaborator Sean Gullette) and then attended the American Film Institute for two years. After a year of employment in the film industry, he returned to NYC and began to work on his script for "Pi", fashioning the leading role for Gullette. A workshop period followed before producer Scott Franklin hit on the novel idea of selling $100 units to family and friends. Executive producer Randy Simon provided a much-needed cash infusion and the film was shot in just under a month in the fall of 1996. At Sundance, the distribution rights were purchased by Artisan Entertainment (formerly known as LIVE Entertainment) for a figure reportedly in excess of $1 million. Even before the July 1998 release of "Pi", Aronofsky made further trade headlines when he signed a pay-or-play contract with Dimension Films for "Proteus", a historical sci-fi thriller he co-wrote with Lucas Sussman.

The deal also included first-look at a follow-up film should "Proteus" go into production.

Despite his deal for "Proteus", Aronofsky opted to follow-up his first feature with the harrowing "Requiem for a Dream" (2000), an adaptation of Hubert Selby Jr.'s fiction. Centering on a mother and son who both are struggling with addiction, she to diet pills, he to heroin, the film is a powerful character study. Aronofsky employed a highly distinctive visual style that is becoming his trademark. Although he had several projects in the development pipeline, the writer-director agreed to another high profile feature, the latest in the Batman franchise to be called "Batman: Year One" detailing Bruce Wayne's initial forays into crime fighting.

MILESTONES:

Raised in Coney Island, Brooklyn, New York

After high school, moved to Israel to live on a kibbutz

In Israel, worked in a plastics factory; ran away after two days

Attended Harvard

1991: Senior thesis film "Supermarket Sweep" was a national finalist in the Student Academy Awards

Moved to L.A. to study at the American Film Institute

1998: Feature directing and screenwriting debut, "Pi"

1998: Signed pay-or-play deal for feature "Proteus"

1998: Inked deal to script and direct a feature based on the comic book "Ronin" (not to be confused with 1998 feature of the same name)

1999: Selected to participate in Sundance Screenwriters Lab, working on script "Requiem for a Dream"

2000: Wrote and directed "Requiem for a Dream", adapted from the novel by Hubert Selby Jr.; screened at Cannes

2000: Signed to direct and write and develop the screenplay for "Batman: Year One"

AFFILIATION: Jewish

QUOTES:

"The great thing about Sundance is that I came here two years ago. Very lost. I had been trying to set up a film in New York for a long time. It's just too big for me . . . I came to Sundance and I really saw the films they were praising were really great films made by directors who were really doing their films. Here are these bad-assed people who went out, made out their own projects and Sundance is praising them, and you know what, if you go out, you do what you want to do, if you're not a copycat and you

just do it, you'll get recognized. That's the only way to do it well."—Darren Aronofsky to www.Indiewire.com, January 21, 1998.

"Ultimately I would classify myself as existential humanist. I think we're here for some reason, but that reason we'll never, ever know. But while we're here there is hope and promise of the great things that we can do. [In "Pi"], Max's tragic flaw is searching for the unknown and for God and for what we're all going to share when we're dead before our time. Life isn't about order; it's about chaos. And that's what makes life worth living."—Aronofsky quoted in *Filmmaker*, Winter 1998.

Miguel Arteta

BORN: in Puerto Rico, 1964

NATIONALITY: Puerto Rican

CITIZENSHIP: United States

EDUCATION: Harvard University, Cambridge, Massachusetts; studied in the documentary program; attended for two years before transferring to Wesleyan

Wesleyan University, Middletown, Connecticut; film, BA, 1989

American Film Institute, Los Angeles, California, directing, 1993

AWARD: Independent Spirit Award Best Feature—Under $500,000 "Chuck & Buck" 2001

BIOGRAPHY

"Star Maps" (1997) mirrored Miguel Arteta's own observations about desperation in Hollywood absorbed while a student at the American Film Institute, He spent four years raising money and shooting this film about a young Latino with dreams of becoming a movie star, who is forced into prostitution by his own

father. Premiering out of competition at the Sundance Film Festival, "Star Maps" was purchased by Fox Searchlight and opened later in the year amid much publicity, if not gushing critical acclaim. In the long run, though the film proved to be a bit of a financial disappointment for the studio.

The son of a Peruvian father and Spanish mother, Arteta was born in Puerto Rico and spent his teenage years in Costa Rica. He moved to the USA to attend college, where he began making films, including the short "Every Day Is a Beautiful Day", a satire of Hollywood musicals. Arteta then entered the world of filmmaking as a location assistant on Sidney Lumet's "Q & A" (1990) and as a second camera assistant to Jonathan Demme on the documentary "Cousin Bobby" (1991), before heading to Los Angeles to study at the American Film Institute (AFI). Feeling alienated as a Latino and disenchanted with the atmosphere at AFI, which Arteta perceived as full of insiders and/or people willing to sell their mother's souls to make a film, Arteta chose instead to make a film with Latino characters who weren't stereotypical, "Star Maps." After making the film Arteta told the *Village Voice* he was taking time off to become "aware of my Latin heritage and the pain that that entails".

MILESTONES:

Raised in Puerto Rico and Costa Rica

1990: Short film, "Every Day is a Beautiful Day" premiered at Berlin Film Festival; also nominated for a student Academy Award

1990: Was location coordinator assistant on Sidney Lumet's "Q & A"

1991: Worked as a second camera assistant to Jonathan Demme on "Cousin Bobby"

1993: Directed AFI thesis film "Lucky Peach"

1996: Invited to participate in the Sundance Institute Writer's Lab; worked on a script "Ball and Chain" with Ron Nyswaner

1997: Feature directorial and screenwriting debut, "Star Maps"

2000: Second feature, the digitally shot "Chuck & Buck", scripted by and starring Mike White; premiered at the Sundance Film Festival

Reteamed with White on "The Good Girl" (lensed 2001)

QUOTES:

"My goal was to make a personal film about the insane world of Hollywood. I wanted to show how extreme this culture really is from the point of view of people's dreams, expectations and their sexual perversions. These are dysfunctional people living in a melodramatic world."—Miguel Arteta.

"As a Latino artist it is hard to live in Los Angeles without satirizing Hollywood and the racism inherent within."—Miguel Arteta.

"I was very lucky. My car mechanic introduced me to Jonathan Demme, and I showed him one of my student films."—Arteta in *Time Out New York*, July 24–31, 1997.

"I've been a foreigner all my life, looking at cultures from the outside. I lived in San Juan 'til I was 13. Then we moved to Costa Rica when my father sold his auto-parts shop. Previously, he worked for Chrysler during the revolution in Cuba, and Che Guevara put him in jail for working for a U.S. company".—Arteta in in *Time Out New York*, July 24–31, 1997.

"I feel like there hasn't been a Latino independent voice out there. Robert Rodriguez is really a Hollywood director."—Miguel Arteta in in *Time Out New York*, July 24–31, 1997.

Dorothy Arzner

BORN: in San Francisco, California, 01/03/1897

DEATH: in La Quinta, California, 10/01/1979

NATIONALITY: American

EDUCATION: Westlake School for Girls, Beverly Hills, California 1915

University of Southern California, Los Angeles, California; pre-med, dropped out

BIOGRAPHY

As a young woman growing up in Hollywood, Dorothy Arzner often spent time in the Hoffmann Cafe, a restaurant owned by her father that was frequented by the top pioneering filmmakers (e.g., Mack Sennett, Charlie Chaplin, D. W. Griffith). Although drawn to the world of show business, she enrolled at USC as a medical student and even signed on to be an ambulance driver during WWI (although she never left the USA). In 1919, having decided to pursue a career as a film director, Arzner was hired by William de Mille to work as a typist in the script department of Famous Players—Lasky (soon to become Paramount). While still in its infancy, the film industry allowed women more opportunities then for work behind the camera, although Arzner did get pigeonholed for a time as an editor, in part because of her exemplary work cutting the bullfighting sequence of "Blood and Sand" (1992) which convinced James Cruze to hire her to edit "The Covered Wagon" (1923). Arzner went on work on several films for the director including "Ruggles of Red Gap" (1923), "Merton of the Movies" (1924) and "Old Ironsides" (1926), also functioning as his co-scenarist on the latter film.

Using an offer from Harry Cohn at Columbia as leverage, Arzner finally convinced Paramount head B. P. Shulberg to give her a shot at directing. Her first assignment was 1927's "Fashions For Women", a lightweight comedy that she completed on time and which earned respectable reviews. She went on to handle similar chores on "Ten Modern Commandments" and "Get Your Man" (both 1927) broke into talking pictures with 1929's "The Wild Party," one of the quintessential "flapper" pictures starring Clara Bow.

Arzner had begun to develop a reputation for films built around spunky women and her ability to elicit strong performances from the actresses in those roles. Beginning a multiple film collaboration with screenwriter Zoe Akins, she continued in this vein with such efforts as "Sarah and Son" (1930), which brought star Ruth Chatterton an Academy Award nomination as Best Actress, and "Anybody's Woman" (also 1930). After Arzner left Paramount, she and Akins reteamed once more for one of her more interesting efforts, "Christopher Strong" (1933), starring Katharine Hepburn as an aviatrix modeled on Amelia Earhart. When her character falls in love and becomes pregnant with the married title character (Colin Clive), Hepburn's flier purposely crashes her plane to earth during a test flight, killing both herself and her unborn child. The film's bleak subtext—the independent woman must die

because she has flouted moral convention—is complemented by stunning visuals echoing both Lubitsch's "Trouble in Paradise" and Lang's "Dr. Mabuse der Spieler."

Hired by Samuel Goldwyn to direct the screen adaptation of "Nana" (1934), Arzner had to overcome one major obstacle—her leading lady Anna Sten, a protege of Goldwyn's. "The only thing I could do was not let her talk so much," the director is reported to have said. Still, the film has its moments. The helmer found a more satisfactory leading lady in Rosalind Russell in "Craig's Wife" (1936). That movie offered Russell a meaty role as a shrew who drives away husband and friends with her incessant need to control the people and things around her; in contrast to the Broadway play on which the film is based, "Craig's Wife" treats the heroine sympathetically, raising her to almost tragic status. For "The Bride Wore Red" (1937), the primary female part fell to Joan Crawford. Arzner did what she could with the underdeveloped script and overproduced decor forced on her, claiming that the end result was unsatisfactory. (The only good thing to come out of the experience was her friendship with Crawford.)

"Dance, Girl, Dance" (1940) features Lucille Ball in one of her best straight performances, as a vain stripper who accepts the grimy environment in which she works with no illusions. Although visually unremarkable, its critique of the inherent sexism of the world of burlesque was far ahead of its time, especially when, in a remarkable sequence, Maureen O'Hara confronts a burlesque theater audience about their pleasure in leering at and mocking the women performers.

After a stint making training films for the US Army during WWII, Arzner made one last studio film for Columbia, the little known "First Comes Courage" (1943), starring Merle Oberon. Oberon as a Norwegian double agent who pretends to be in love with a Nazi commandant (Carl Esmond) in order to pry secrets from him, the film contains a number of remarkable set pieces, including a memorable wedding sequence set in a converted chapel with a regiment of SS officers in attendance; "Mein Kampf" is substituted for the Bible, and the vows are exchanged in the name of Hitler rather than God. Significantly, the sequences featuring Oberon and her character's true love (Brian Aherne) are the weakest elements of the narrative yet Oberon's spy is a typical Arzner heroine, a courageous woman who lives by her wits and neither welcomes nor depends on the aid of a man.

After completing "First Comes Courage", Arzner fell ill with pneumonia and was bedridden for more than a year. With societal changes and the after-effects of women working during WWII, changes in Hollywood were taking place. Women were no longer finding the opportunities they had in the halcyon early days as the studios began adopting a more bottom line approach to the business. Certainly a woman in her mid-40s was also problematic. Undoubtedly, Arzner could have returned to the editing room or might have been allowed a chance to write scripts but the idea of a female film director was becoming more rare. Faced with these harsh realities, Arzner opted to "retire" and instead turned to teaching, first at the Pasadena Playhouse and later at USC (where Francis Ford Coppola was among her students). Old friend Joan Crawford, then married to the chairman of PepsiCo, got her hired to direct over 50 television commercials for the soft drink.

At her death in 1979, Arzner had been "rediscovered" by a new generation of film historians and her uneven body of work became fodder for discussion for its targeting of feminist issues that prefigured the concerns of contemporary directors like Lizzie Borden, Joyce Chopra and Agnes Varda. While there were female directors before Arzner, she holds the unique distinction of being the only woman to compile a significant body of work within the studio system of the 1930s and 40s.

MILESTONES:

During WWI, worked as an ambulance driver

1919: Began career as a stenographer at Famous Players-Lasky Corporation (later Paramount)

Trained as an assistant film cutter

1921: Appointed as chief editor at Realart Studios; cut and edited at least one film per week

1922: Attracted attention at Paramount for her editing of the Rudolph Valentino vehicle, "Blood and Sand", particularly the bullfight sequence that used stock footage as well as reels of Valentino

1924: Early screenplay credits included "The Breed of the Border" and "The No-Gun Man"

When Harry Cohn offered a contract as director at Columbia, B. P. Schulberg agreed to let her helm a film for Paramount

1927: Film directorial debut at Paramount with "Fashions for Women"

1928: Used music and sound effects but no dialogue in "Manhattan Cocktail"

1929: First talking picture, "The Wild Party", starring Clara Bow

1930: First collaborations with screenwriter Zoe Akins, "Sarah and Son" and "Anybody's Woman", both starring Ruth Chatterton

1930: Reportedly offered uncredited directorial assistance to Robert Milton on "Behind the Makeup" and "Charming Sinners"

1932: Ended full-time affiliation with Paramount Studios; freelanced for the rest of her career

1933: Helmed "Christopher Strong", starring Katharine Hepburn; also written by Akins

1934: Hired by Samuel Goldwyn to direct "Nana"

1936: Directed remake of "Craig's Wife", starring Rosalind Russell

1937: Was director of "The Bride Wore Red", starring Joan Crawford

1940: Steered Maureen O'Hara and Lucille Ball in "Dance, Girl, Dance"; film received belated attention in the 1980s and 1990s for its feminist overtones

Directed instructional films during WWII

1943: Made last feature, "First Comes Courage"

1943: Contracted pneumonia and was an invalid for more than a year

Initiated first film classes at the Pasadena Playhouse

Hired at the suggestion of Joan Crawford (then married to the company's president) to direct more than 50 television commericals for Pepsi Cola in the 1950s

Taught at UCLA for four years in the 1960s; among students was Francis Ford Coppola

1975: Feted in a tribute given by the Directors Guild of America

QUOTES:
Sources are divided over the year of Arzner's birth. While most claim that she was born in 1900, her death certificate lists 1897.

"My philosophy is that to be a director you cannot be subject to anyone, even the head of the studio. I threatened to quit each time I didn't get my way, but no one ever let me walk out."—Dorothy Arzner.

BIBLIOGRAPHY:
"The Work of Dorothy Arzner: Towards a Feminist Cinema" Claire Johnston and Pam Cook, 1975

"Directed By Dorothy Arzner" Judith Mayne, 1994

Richard Attenborough

BORN: in Cambridge, England, 08/29/1923

SOMETIMES CREDITED AS:
Lord Attenborough

NATIONALITY: English

EDUCATION: Wyggeston Grammar School for Boys Leicester, England

Royal Academy of Dramatic Art, London, England 1941; won Leverhulme Scholarship and won the Bancroft Silver Medal in 1942

AWARDS: British Film Academy Award Best British Actor "Seance on a Wet Afternoon" and "Guns at Batasi" 1964; cited for both films

San Sebastian Film Festival Best Actor Award "Seance on a Wet Afternoon" 1964

Golden Globe Award Best Supporting Actor "The Sand Pebbles" 1966

Golden Globe Award Best Supporting Actor "Doctor Dolittle" 1967

Golden Globe Award Best English Language Foreign Film "Oh! What A Lovely War" 1969; award shared with co-producer Brian Duffy

British Film Academy United Nations Award "Oh! What A Lovely War" 1969; award shared with co-producer Brian Duffy

New York Film Critics Circle Award Best Picture "Gandhi" 1982

Golden Globe Award Best Director "Gandhi" 1982

Directors Guild of America Award Outstanding Directorial Achievement in Feature Film "Gandhi" 1982

Oscar Best Picture "Gandhi" 1982; Attenborough was a producer of the film

Oscar Best Director "Gandhi" 1982

BAFTA Award Best Film "Gandhi" 1982 as producer

BAFTA Award Best Director "Gandhi" 1982

BAFTA Fellowship 1983

BAFTA Award Best British Film "Shadowlands" 1993; award shared with Brian Eastman

BIOGRAPHY
A short, and later chunky, star character

performer since the 1940s, Richard Attenborough made a transition to the director's chair in the late 60s. He won Oscars for directing and producing "Gandhi" (1982), but as an actor may be better known to American audiences for playing the brains behind "The Great Escape" (1963) and the millionaire builder of "Jurassic Park" (1993).

With his vulnerable baby face, Attenborough entered film while still a RADA student as the faint-hearted seaman in "In Which We Serve" (1942). Although often typecast as weak or blustery youths, he displayed his brash intensity and great versatility as the menacing psychotic hood in the superb "Brighton Rock/Young Scarface" (1948), as the laborer sent to Coventry in the social drama, "The Angry Silence" (1959) and most notably as the accommodating, pathetic kidnapper in "Seance on a Wet Afternoon" (1964).

Frustrated by the British film industry, Attenborough teamed with actor-writer Bryan Forbes to form Beaver Films in 1959, which produced a slew of small, ambitious and often socially-conscious films often directed by Forbes. Their sympathy for "the little people" came through best in the delicately offbeat "Whistle Down the Wind" (1961), produced by Attenborough and directed by Forbes, in which three children mistake a fugitive murderer for Jesus Christ. The duo enjoyed another triumph with the story of an unwed, expectant mother and the motley crew she meets in a shabby London boardinghouse, "The L-Shaped Room" (1962).

Since his boisterous, if uneven, directing debut, "Oh! What a Lovely War" (1969), a satirical anti-war musical revue, Attenborough has frequently made films involving social and political issues, often as large-scale epics with star-studded casts. Typical in this respect was his lavish but overlong, war epic "A Bridge Too Far" (1977). Attenborough also has a fondness for screen biography, first evidenced in his helming of the early days of Churchill, "Young Winston" (1972). Following in this vein, Attenborough in 1982 realized his long-held dream to film "Gandhi", winning numerous awards for his stately handling of the life of the pacifist Indian ruler.

Attenborough's subsequent direction of overblown "prestige" projects has, however, been less well received. His most notable talent would seem to be his sympathetic, detailed direction of actors. "Gandhi" benefited enormously from Ben Kingsley's fascinating performance in the title role, "Magic" (1978) gave Anthony Hopkins a good scenery chew, and Attenborough's later biopic, "Chaplin" (1992), only garnered acclaim for Robert Downey Jr.'s splendid star turn in the title role. "Cry Freedom" (1987), meanwhile, benefited from Denzel Washington's presence and its obvious sincerity in reconstructing the anti-apartheid struggles of activist Stephen Biko, but was bogged down by talk and choppy exposition. Among his smaller films, "A Chorus Line" (1985) suggested that Attenborough, though often possessing a bit of the "showman", was not the right director to bring the long-running Broadway musical to the big screen. (Attenborough later suggested that the failure of "A Chorus Line" was due to an American anger at a Brit being chosen to make the film, and not because of the abysmal casting and camerawork.) "Shadowlands" (1993), though, a biopic of writers C. S. Lewis and Joy Gresham, featured poignant work from Hopkins and Debra Winger and proved Attenborough a director capable of some subtleties. He backslid, though, with his study of the war experiences of Ernest Hemingway, "In Love and War" (1996). The miscasting of Chris O'Donnell and Sandra Bullock and their lack of screen chemistry torpedoed what might have been a sweeping romance in the vein of "The English Patient" (1996).

In 1993, bearded and almost unrecognizable compared to his early screen incarnations, Attenborough seemed to have fun when he returned to screen acting as the cuddly billionaire ringmaster of a unique theme park in Steven Spielberg's "Jurassic Park". He proved even cuddlier when he played Kris Kringle in a 1994 remake of the popular comedy-drama, "Miracle on 34th Street". Attenborough was briefly seen in a cameo as the English Ambassador in Kenneth Branagh's all-star "Hamlet" (1996) and was on screen only slightly longer reprising his billionaire role in Spielberg's monster sequel "The Lost World: Jurassic Park" (1997). He next portrayed one of the monarch's advisors, Sir William Cecil, in the lavish biopic of the Tudor Queen, "Elizabeth" (1998).

Attenborough has not appeared extensively on the small screen, although he was effective as Mr. Tungay in "David Copperfield", which played in the USA on NBC in 1970 and was released in Britain as a feature film. Knighted in 1976 and eventually raised to the peerage, the feisty Attenborough has been affectionately dubbed "the Chairman of London" for his involvement as president or board member of up to several dozen arts, media or charitable organizations at any one time. He has been long married to actress-turned-magistrate Sheila Sim, with whom he appeared onstage and in several films in the 40s and 50s.

MILESTONES:

At age 12, hired public hall in Leicester and mounted an evening of harmonica solos, comic songs, and sketches

Semi-professional debut in small roles with Leicester's Little Theatre (of which his mother was president)

1941: Professional stage debut in "Ah, Wilderness!" at Palmers Green

1942: West End debut, "Awake and Sing"

1942: Film debut, "In Which We Serve" (while still RADA student)

1943: First major stage success as Pinkie in "Brighton Rock"

1943: Joined Royal Air Force (RAF)

1944: Sent to RAF Film Unit to play a leading role opposite Edward G. Robinson in John Boulting's propaganda drama, "Journey Together"

1947: Achieved star status when he reprised his role as Pinkie in the film version of "Brighton Rock"

1956: Acted with Bryan Forbes in the film, "The Baby and the Battleship"

1959: Formed Beaver Films with Forbes

1959: Co-produced (with Forbes) first film, "The Angry Silence"

1963: Made first Hollywood film, "The Great Escape"

1964: Beaver Films dissolved after the making of "Seance on a Wet Afternoon"

1969: Film directing debut with "Oh! What a Lovely War"

1970: Played Mr. Tungay in NBC rendition of "David Copperfield"

1976: Knighted by Queen Elizabeth II

1979: Last screen appearance for nearly 15 years, in Otto Preminger's "The Human Factor"

1982: Directed and produced "Gandhi"; film won 8 Oscars including Best Picture and Best Director

1985: Served as a consultant for, and provided the narration to, the feature-length documentary, "Mother Teresa"

1988: Appeared on television in the all-star "Freedomfest: Nelson Mandela's 70th Birthday Celebration"

1993: Returned to screen acting in Steven Spielberg's "Jurassic Park"

1994: Played Kris Kringle in remake of "Miracle on 34th Street"

1996: Was Cameron Mackintosh Visiting Professor of Contemporary Theatre at Oxford

1997: Briefly reprised role in Speilberg's "The Lost World: Jurassic Park"

1998: Acted role of Sir William Cecil, one of the advisors to the monarch, in "Elizabeth"

AFFILIATIONS: Served as president of the British Film Year (1985)

Served as chairman of Royal Academy of Dramatic Art

Served as chairman of the Actor's Charitable Trust

Served as vice president of BAFTA

QUOTES:

He was named Commander of the British Empire in 1967

Awarded the Martin Luther King Jr. Peace Prize (1983)

Received India's Padma Bhusan (1983)

Worked as pro-chancelllor of Sussex University

He was honored with a BBC/BAFTA Lifetime Achievement Tribute on December 19, 1999

Hector Babenco

BORN: Hector Eduardo Babenco in Buenos Aires, Argentina, 02/07/1946

NATIONALITY: Argentine

CITIZENSHIP: Brazil

AWARD: Los Angeles Film Critics Association Award Best Foreign Film "Pixote" 1981

BIOGRAPHY

Hector Babenco became Brazil's leading post-"cinema novo" director in the 1970s and an acclaimed Hollywood director in the 80s. All his films deal with social issues, and are best seen as personal and subjective accounts of "marginalized" people—the homeless, prostitutes, political prisoners, homosexuals.

Born to poor Russian and Polish Jewish immigrant parents, Babenco was 18 when he left Argentina on a "divine mission," inspired by Beat and existential writers, to "know the world." For seven years he traveled throughout Africa, Europe and the Americas, working at odd jobs. In Spain and Italy he pursued his interest in film, working as an extra in spaghetti westerns.

In 1971, Babenco emigrated to Brazil to make films. Having grown up watching Hollywood and European films with subtitles, he was impressed by the new, indigenous

Brazilian cinema. The year he arrived, however, Brazil's rightist military regime instituted strict censorship, forcing most "cinema novo" directors into exile. Babenco, who had never formally studied cinema, spent the next four years filming documentaries, shorts and commercials while he worked on his first feature, "King of the Night" (1975).

His next film, "Lucio Flavio" (1978), made at the height of political repression in Brazil, depicted the life and death of a real-life thief/folk hero who had threatened to expose the police death squads. Although Babenco used dream sequences and attached a disclaimer to the film in order to appease the censors, he was the target of death threats and his house in Sao Paulo was machine-gunned. In addition, the prisoner who had killed the real Lucio Flavio for the police was himself murdered on the eve of the film's opening. Despite these intimidations, "Lucio Flavio" became Brazil's fourth-highest grossing feature, reviving the fortunes of the Brazilian film industry and picking up both the New York and the Los Angeles Film Critics Association Award for Best Foreign Film. Babenco became disillusioned, however, when he realized that the film had brought no concrete political changes.

Babenco's first international success was "Pixote" (1981), about the plight of Brazil's three million abandoned children. The director originally intended to film a documentary, and had completed 200 hours of interviews with children in reformatories. When he was refused further access, however, he turned to the streets and hired slum children to portray themselves. The result, although scripted, displays a documentary-like attention to detail and perspective. Rather than having the children read lines, Babenco built scenes around improvisation workshops that allowed them to contribute their own experiences to the picture.

Babenco's next two projects were English-language films. With "Kiss of the Spider Woman" (1985), he had difficulty finding American investors and was forced to defer salaries for himself and the lead actors. Its success (star William Hurt won an Oscar for his performance) ensured major Hollywood studio support for "Ironweed" (1987). Ironically, Babenco's experience in the USA convinced him that Brazilian political censorship offered greater artistic freedom than Hollywood's economic censorship and studio bureaucracy.

MILESTONES:

Raised in Argentina

1963: Moved to Sao Paulo, Brazil at age 17 (date approximate)

1975: Feature film directing debut, "King of the Night"

1981: Gained international recognition with third feature, "Pixote"

1985: First English language film, "Kiss of the Spider Woman"; received Oscar nomination as Best Director

1987: Helmed "Ironweed", starring Jack Nicholson and Meryl Streep

1991: Directed "At Play in the Fields of the Lord"

Underwent treatment for a virulent strain of lymphoma; had bone marrow transplant in 1995

1998: First film in seven years, "Corazon Illuminato"

AFFILIATION: Jewish

Michael Bay

BORN: Michael Benjamin Bay in Los Angeles, California, 02/17/1965

NATIONALITY: American

EDUCATION: Crossroads High School, Santa Monica, California

Wesleyan University, Middletown, Connecticut; film, BFA 1986; made thesis short "Benjamin's Birthday" which won the Frank Capra Award

Art College Center of Design, Pasadena, California; film MFA; made commercial for Coca-Cola while student

AWARDS: Directors Guild of America Award

Commercial Direction "Aaron Burr" for California Milk; "Deion Sanders" for Nike; "Vending Machine" for California Milk; "Big Lawyer Round-Up" for Miller Lite; "Baby and Cat" for California Milk 1994

BIOGRAPHY

Like many aspiring filmmakers, Southern California native Michael Bay began making films with his family's Super-8mm camera while still a teenager. At age 15, he scored a clerical job at Lucasfilm and attempted to absorb whatever he could. Following college (where he made the thesis short "Benjamin's Birthday" in 1986) and post-grad work at the Art College Center of Design in Pasadena, Bay made his first music video at age 24. The result, "Soldier of Love", reinvigorated the moribund career of singer Donny Osmond and put the tyro director on the map, landing him a spot with Propaganda Films. He subsequently handled similar chores for acts as diverse as Tina Turner, The DiVynals and Wilson Phillips and branched out to TV commercials for clients like Nike, Coca-Cola and Miller Light. In 1994, Bay received the Directors Guild of America Award for commercial work further raising his profile.

Hollywood inevitably came calling in the form of producers Don Simpson and Jerry Bruckheimer. Bay had already impressed the duo with his work on the music video for their race car movie "Days of Thunder" (1990). So, at the age of 30, Bay crossed over to features at the helm of "Bad Boys" (1995), about two cops that featured Martin Lawrence and Will Smith. Bay demonstrated an ability to stage impressive action sequences (albeit at the expense of the story) but audiences were impressed enough to the tune of $70 million-plus in grosses in the USA alone and over $160 million worldwide.

Like many filmmakers who came from commercials and music videos, Bay relied on razzmatazz editing and a frenetic pace to the story. He tapped into the same sort of vein for his follow-up "The Rock" (1996). Although the cast was a bit more high brow (featuring two Oscar-winners, Nicolas Cage and Sean Connery), the dazzling effects still held center stage. "The Rock" became a summer blockbuster and typecast Bay as one of Hollywood's premiere action helmers. "Armageddon" (1998), about a meteor on a collision course with the earth, did nothing to dispel that image. The testosterone-driven script revolved around a select group chosen to fly to outer space to save the world, and while Liv Tyler appeared as the nominal love interest, she was underutilized.

For his next project, Bay undertook one that he hoped would confound expectations. "Pearl Harbor" (2001) was a big-budget war epic built around a love triangle. With Bruckheimer once again producing, the director set about recreating that fateful day in December 1941. Clashes with Disney over the film's budget, however, led Bay to walk away from the project four different times during pre-production. It took Bruckheimer's persuasion to convince the helmer to see the project through. Working with a relatively tight budget (estimated at $140 million) and forfeiting his usual fee of $6 million, Bay undertook the biggest risk of his career. Advance word praised the spectacular effects and the battle scenes, but criticized the love story as maudlin and trite. Although the studio heavily hyped the film, there were negative comments by some involved. Writer Randall Wallace was vocal about the changes to his original screenplay and how he and the director did not see eye to eye on things. (Wallace eventually walked away from the project and was replaced by two uncredited scribes.) The actresses, including star Kate Beckinsale along with Sara Rue and Catherine Kellner, were quoted as saying the director was hardly sympathetic to their ideas. Whatever the case, the film dominated the early summer box office but "Pearl Harbor" didn't necessarily do for Bay's career what "Titanic" had done for James Cameron's. Rather than follow "Pearl Harbor" up with another strenuous, sweeping mega-action film—like the long awaited new "Superman" movie he was rumored to be considering—Bay instead opted for a more commerically safe road, reteaming with Jerry Bruckheimer and stars Martin Lawrence and Will Smith to helm the loud, explosive-packed sequel "Bad Boys II" (2003).

MILESTONES:

Raised in Westwood, California

Used parents Super-8mm movie camera to make films as a teenager

At age 15, worked in a filing job at Lucasfilm

Was one of the principals in Propaganda Films;

directed TV commercials for The Red Cross, Milk, Coca Cola, Nike, many others

1988: Began directing music videos, relaunching Donny Osmond's career and also directing for Meatloaf, Tina Turner, and others

First collaboration with Don Simpson and Jerry Bruckheimer, the music video for "Days of Thunder"

1995: Made feature film directorial debut with "Bad Boys"; produced by Simpson and Bruckheimer

1996: Leaped onto "A" list of directors with "The Rock"

Formed Bay Films

1998: Helmed the big-budget actioner "Armageddon", produced by Bruckheimer

1998: Announced plans to develop a TV series "Quantico" for Fox; still in development as of 2001

1998: Signed two-year multimillion dollar producing and directing deal with Disney

2001: Directed the big-budget WWII-era set "Pearl Harbor"; again produced by Bruckheimer

Formed Platinum Dunes, a production company designed to produce lower-budgeted films; announced first project in January 2002, a "reconceptualization" of the 1974 horror film "The Texas Chainsaw Massacre"

QUOTES:

In a July 1998 profile in *Entertainment Weekly*, Bay claimed to have tracked down his birth parents and indicated that his father was a famous Hollywood director. Speculation ran rampant until some revealed it was thought to be John Frankenheimer. In a May 2001 article that appeared in the *New York Post*, Frankenheimer addressed the topic, confirming that he had had a one-night stand with Bay's birth mother who then tried to extort money from him by claiming to have been pregnant with his child. Frankenheimer paid the hush money and the woman went on to believe that he was the father of her child, but Frankenheimer insists he is not Bay's natural father, even telling the *Post* that "tests" had determined that wasn't the case.

"I think a lot of times I'm a little bit misunderstood. I mean, from what I read in the press, they just make it sound so harsh. I don't know why that image comes across. I think one of the things is, basically, I've got a very soft heart and I'm a very shy person.

"There are times I can go out on the set and direct 600 extras and I can have 14 planes flying in and know exactly what I'm doing in terms of take charge with a loud voice out there, and there are times I can lecture to 600 students, but there are times when I can just be meeting someone and just be shy."—Michael Bay quoted in *Los Angeles Times*, May 20, 2001.

"I love doing big movies. It's awesome! You have all these toys. . . . The thing I like about this movie is, like they always say, directors have the biggest train sets.! Don't tell anyone but I'd do this for free."—Michael Bay to *USA Today*, July 2, 1998.

"Working with Michael is very much about presenting stuff that looks cool to the audience."—"Pearl Harbor" digital effects supervisor Eric Brevig quoted in *Premiere*, May 2001.

"I don't take shit from actors. Getting 12 women into lipstick was the hardest thing about making this movie ["Pearl Harbor"]. I would have a shit fit. I'm the type of guy who will personally go knock on actors' trailers."—Bay quoted in *Premiere*, May 2001.

"The script [for "Pearl Harbor"] just felt so romantic, like a war epic. Then you get there, and you realize you are in a Michael Bay-Jerry Bruckheimer movie, and you find out what a blockbuster means."—actress Kate Beckinsale in *Premiere*, May 2001.

"There are stories that I'm tough. You know what? I know what I'm doing."—Michael Bay to *Movieline*, May 2001.

Asked what his strengths as a director are, Bay replied to *Movieline* (May 2001): "I am very good at handling a huge movie, with a million things going on. I'm very decisive, clear in what I want. I'm very cost-conscious, in terms of how to get the big bang on screen. I'm very good at making things happen fast."

Asked then what his weaknesses are, Bay replied: "Patience. Politics. I just want to shoot."

"I was talking to one of the writers about our target audience, and he was insulted that I used that term. But if you're given $60 million to make a film, you'd better know who your target audience is. That's who's going to pay back the bills you run up."—Bay quoted in *The New York Times*, June 16, 1996.

"Commercials were a great training ground. I became a very fast shooter."—Bay in *Los Angeles Times*, June 11, 1996.

"One day I'm going to grow up as a filmmaker and do something as powerful as "Schindler's List". But right now my strength is in entertaining audiences, in making them escape for two hours."—Bay in *Los Angeles Times*, June 11, 1996.

"I go out there to win, People don't care if you DIE in this business. The only way I get back is with success."—Bay in *Premiere*, July 1996.

Roberto Benigni

BORN: in Arezzo, Tuscany, Italy, 10/27/1952

NATIONALITY: Italian

EDUCATION: attended a seminary in Florence, Italy with plans to become a priest; dropped out when a flood damaged the school

graduated from an accounting school in Prato, Italy

AWARDS: Cannes Film Festival Grand Prix "La Vita e Bella/Life Is Beautiful" 1998

David di Donatello Prize Best Actor "La Vita e Bella/Life Is Beautiful" 1998

David di Donatello Prize Best Director "La Vita e Bella/Life Is Beautiful" 1998

David di Donatello Prize Best Screenplay "La Vita e Bella/Life Is Beautiful" 1998; shared with Vincenzo Cerami

European Film Academy Award Best Picture "Life Is Beautiful/La Vita e Bella" 1998

European Film Academy Award Best Actor "Life Is Beautiful/La Vita e Bella" 1998

National Board of Review Award Special Achievement in Filmmaking "Life Is Beautiful/

La Vita e Bella" 1998; cited for writing, directing and acting in film

San Diego Film Critics Award Best Foreign Language Film "Life Is Beautiful" 1998

Online Film Critics Award Best Foreign Film "Life Is Beautiful" 1998

Lumiere de Paris Best Foreign Film "Life Is Beautiful" 1998

Dallas-Fort Worth Film Critics Association Award Best Foreign Language Film "Life Is Beautiful" 1998

Prix Moussinac Best Foreign Film Released in France "La Vita e Bella/Life Is Beautiful" 1998

Chicago Film Critics Award Best Foreign-Language Film "Life Is Beautiful" 1998

Florida Film Critics Circle Award Best Foreign Film "Life Is Beautiful" 1998

American Comedy Award Funniest Actor in a Motion Picture "Life Is Beautiful" 1999

Cesar Best Foreign Film "La Vita e Bella/Life Is Beautiful" 1998

The Actor Outstanding Performance by a Male Actor in a Leading Role "Life Is Beautiful" 1998

Oscar Best Actor "Life Is Beautiful" 1998; only second performer and first male to be honored for a performance in a foreign language

BAFTA Award Best Actor "Life Is Beautiful" 1999

German Film Award Best Foreign Film "Life Is Beautiful" 1999

Australian Film Institute Award Best Foreign Film "Life Is Beautiful" 1999

Goya Best European Film "Life Is Beautiful" 1999

European Film Academy Award European Achievement in World Cinema 2000

Razzie Award Worst Actor "Pinocchio" 2002

BIOGRAPHY

Widely hailed as one of the world's funniest men, this loquacious, rubber-faced comic has been one of Italy's most popular actors for much of the last decade. At age 19, Benigni moved from working as a small-town street performer in his native Tuscany to performing stand-up comedy and acting in "experimental" theater in cosmopolitan Rome. Collaborating with Giuseppe Bertolucci, Benigni co-wrote the comic monologue "Cioni Mario Di Gaspare Fu Giulia/Mario Was Julia." This provided the foundation for his feature debut, "Berlinguer, Ti Voglio Bene/Berlinguer, I Love You" (1976), helmed by Bertolucci and a TV special "Onda Libera/Free Wave" about a critic who either misunderstands or misses seeing the films he's assigned to review. Benigni started his own successful career as an actor-writer-director with a collection of four comic sketches entitled "Tu Mi Turbi/You Disturb Me" (1983). This film also marked the first of his many screen collaborations with actress Nicoletta Braschi. (The pair married in December 1991.)

Benigni continued to work with notable European filmmakers including Constantin Costa-Gavras ("Clair de Femme", 1979), Bertolucci ("Luna" 1979) and Federico Fellini ("Voice of the Moon", 1990) before finding his greatest success writing, directing and starring in his own productions. In the US, Jim

Jarmusch has been his primary helmer, featuring him as a cheerful, jailed Italian tourist in New Orleans in "Down by Law" (1986), a talkative Roman cabbie in "Night on Earth" (1991) and half the cast (opposite comedian Steven Wright) of "Coffee and Cigarettes" (1986), a six-minute comedy short which Benigni co-wrote with Jarmusch and Wright. He may have been more widely seen in "Blake Edwards' Son of the Pink Panther" (1993), a failed effort to revive the lucrative "Pink Panther" series. Playing the illegitimate son of Peter Sellers' Inspector Clouseau, Benigni was as enthusiastic as ever but the story was weak and much of the humor heartless.

Writing about Jarmusch's "Down by Law", Roger Ebert raved, "The discovery in the picture is the redoubtable Roberto Benigni, who has an irrepressible, infectious manner and is absolutely delighted to be himself . . . He's like a show-off kid who gets you laughing and then starts laughing at himself, he's so funny, and then tries to top himself no matter what." In addition to such usual comedy suspects as Charlie Chaplin and Buster Keaton, Benigni has drawn inspiration from French film comics Jacques Tati and Louis de Funes.

Benigni's successful career in his native Italy skyrocketed in the 1990s with two wildly successful comedies about mistaken identity: "Johnny Stecchino" (1991) and "The Monster" (1994; US release 1996). The first, presenting the funny man in dual roles as an innocent bus driver and a notorious mobster, displaced Bernardo Bertolucci's 1972 "Last Tango in Paris" as Italy all-time domestic box-office champ. "Johnny Stecchino", in turn, was supplanted by "The Monster" in which Benigni played a harmless small-time con man wrongly suspected of being a serial killer. The red-hot comic co-wrote and directed both films and made his producing debut on the latter. Both were being developed as Hollywood remakes as of the spring of 1996. At the 1998 Cannes Film Festival, Benigni received the Grand Prix for his somewhat sentimental "La Vita e Bella/Life Is Beautiful", about a man trying to shield his child from the horrors of the Holocaust. The film proved a critical and art-house hit, becoming the highest-grossing foreign film and earning a record seven Academy Award nominations (including Best Picture, Best Foreign-Language Film, and three for Benigni for his acting, direction and as co-scenarist, the most for a non-English-language movie. The irrepressible Benigni went on to triumph as Best Actor and also took home the statue for Best Foreign Film.—Written by Kent Greene

FAMILY:

father: Luigi Benigni. Farmer, carpenter, brick-layer; born c. 1918; was prisoner in Bergen-Belsen concentration camp for two years (c. 1943–45); Benigni used his memories as basis for "La Vita e Bella/Life Is Beautiful"

COMPANION:

wife: Nicoletta Braschi. Actor; co-starred in "Down By Law" (1986), "Johnny Stecchino" (1991), "The Monster" (1994) and "Life Is Beautiful" (1998); married in December 1991

MILESTONES:

Raised in Tuscany

1963: Introduced to performing at age 10 or 11 by farming relatives who involved him in an improvised song and poetry act

Worked as a clown and magician's assistant in his early teens

1969: Discovered at age 16 by the director of an experimental theater group while delivering an improvised satirical political speech in a Tuscan town square (date approximate)

1971: Moved to Rome at age 19 (date approximate)

Joined an experimental theater group and worked as a stand-up comic

1972: Debuted at the Satiri in Rome in the comedy "I Burosaui" by Silvano Amobrogi

Co-wrote (with Giuseppe Bertolucci) the monologue "Cioni Mario Di Gaspare Fu Giulia/Mario Was Julia" from which pieces were taken for the feature "Berlinguar, Ti Voglio Bene/Berlinguer, I Love You" and the TV series "Onda Libera/Free Wave"

1976: Feature acting debut, "Berlinguer, Ti Voglio Bene/Berlinguer, I Love You", directed by Giuseppe Bertolucci

Starred in a TV show as a critic who misunderstands or fails to see the films he's assigned to review

1982: Began cultivating a reputation for anti-clericalism with with an irreverant quip about Pope John Paul II on Roman TV

1983: Feature writing and directing debut (also actor), "Tu Mi Turbi/You Disturb Me", a collection of four comic sketches; first film collaboration with future wife Nicoletta Braschi

1985: Starred and played guitar in "TuttoBenigni", a concert film of his one-man show helmed by Giuseppe Bertolucci

1986: English-language acting debut, Jim Jarmusch's "Down By Law"; first collaboration with writer-director Jarmusch

1986: US screenwriting debut, co-wrote (with Jarmusch and Steven Wright) and co-starred (with Wright) in "Coffee and Cigarettes", a six-minute short helmed by Jarmusch

1991: "Johnny Stecchino", became the most profitable film in Italy up to that date

1993: American debut as a lead, Blake Edwards' "Son of the Pink Panther"

1994: Feature producing debut, "The Monster" (also co-wrote, directed and starred); grossed 55 billion lire (approximately $35 million) thereby becoming the highest-grossing film in Italian film history up to that date

1998: Earned international acclaim for his comedy-drama "La Vita e Bella/Life Is Beautiful"; co-wrote, directed and starred; film received seven Oscar nominations, including Best Picture, Best Foreign Language Film, Best Actor, Best Director and Best Screenplay, a record for a non-English-language picture; film won three Academy Awards, Best

Foreign Language Film, Best Actor and Best Original Dramatic Score; became only the second person in Oscar history to direct himself to a Best Actor win

2002: Returned to feature films as star and director of a live-action "Pinocchio" (lensed 2001); with a budget of $45 million movie is reportedly the most expensive ever produced in Italy

AFFILIATION: Roman Catholic

QUOTES:

" 'My family is wonderful,' he said. 'It is composed of a lot of women. Three sisters, older than me, and a mother, older than me too. And my father was always looking for some job, so I was alone sleeping in the same bed with four women.' Pause. Punchline: 'And I never repeated this in my life.' Laughter."—From "Roberto Benigni Readies More Laughs for Export" by Alan Cowell, *The New York Times* July 19, 1992.

"Mr. Benigni relies, he said, on body movement and the pitch of his voice to make people laugh, regarding himself as a comedian from an older school, not a humorist. 'Buster Keaton never told a joke,' he said. 'A humorist, like Oscar Wilde—he wrote some good jokes. But I am not able to tell a joke.' Ask Mr. Benigni which comics he reveres most and, almost predictably, the answers include Charlie Chaplin, Groucho Marx, Stan Laurel and Oliver Hardy."—From "Roberto Benigni Readies More Laughs for Export" by Alan Cowell in *The New York Times,* July 19, 1992.

Ingmar Bergman

BORN: Ernst Ingmar Bergman in Uppsala, Sweden, 07/14/1918

SOMETIMES CREDITED AS:
Buntel Eriksson

NATIONALITY: Swedish

EDUCATION: Palmgren's School, Stockholm, Sweden

University of Stockholm, Stockholm, Sweden; literature and art history, 1937–40; did not complete degree; began directing for student and amateur theater groups

AWARDS: Cannes Film Festival Special Mention "A Ship to India/Frustration" 1947

Cannes Film Festival Prix de l'Humour Poetique "Sommarnattens Leende/Smiles of a Summer Night" 1956

Cannes Film Festival Special Jury Prize "Det Sjunde Inseglet/The Seventh Seal" 1957; shared with Andrzej Wajda's "Kanal"

Cannes Film Festival Direction Award "Brink of Life" 1958

Berlin Film Festival Golden Bear "Wild Strawberries" 1958

National Board of Review Award Best Foreign Film "Wild Strawberries" 1959

Golden Globe Award Best Foreign Film "Wild Strawberries" 1959; one of 5 films cited by Hollywood Foreign Press Association

Venice Film Festival Special Jury Prize "The Magician" 1959

Cannes Film Festival Special Homage Award "The Virgin Spring" 1960

Golden Globe Award Best Foreign-Language Foreign Film "The Virgin Spring" 1960; shared award with "La Verite" (France)

Erasmus Award 1965

National Society of Film Critics Award Best Picture "Persona" 1967

National Society of Film Critics Award Best Director "Persona" 1967

National Society of Film Critics Award Best Picture "Shame" 1968

National Society of Film Critics Award Best Director "Shame" and "Hour of the Wolf" 1968

National Board of Review Award Best Foreign-Language Film "Shame" 1969

National Society of Film Critics Award Best Director "The Passion of Anna" 1970

Irving G. Thalberg Memorial Award 1970; presented by the Academy of Motion Picture Arts and Sciences; accepted by Liv Ullmann

New York Film Critics Circle Award Best Picture "Cries and Whispers" 1972

New York Film Critics Circle Award Best Director "Cries and Whispers" 1972

New York Film Critics Circle Award Best Screenwriting "Cries and Whispers" 1972

National Society of Film Critics Award Best Screenwriting "Cries and Whispers" 1972

National Board of Review Award Best Foreign-Language Film "Cries and Whispers" 1973

National Board of Review Award Best Director "Cries and Whispers" 1973

Cannes Film Festival Technical Prize "Cries and Whispers" 1973 "for the use of color to serve thought"

New York Film Critics Circle Award Best Screenplay "Scenes From a Marriage" 1974

National Society of Film Critics Award Best Picture "Scenes From a Marriage" 1974

National Society of Film Critics Award Best Screenplay "Scenes From a Marriage" 1974

Golden Globe Award Best Foreign Film "Scenes From a Marriage" 1974

National Society of Film Critics Special Award "The Magic Flute" 1975; cited "for demonstrating how pleasurable opera can be on film"

National Board of Review Special Citation "The Magic Flute" 1975; for outstanding translation of opera to film

Goethe Award 1976

Los Angeles Film Critics Association Award Best Foreign Film "Face to Face" 1976

Golden Globe Award Best Foreign-Language Film "Face to Face" 1976

National Board of Review Award Best Foreign-Language Film "Autumn Sonata" 1978

National Board of Review Award Best Director "Autumn Sonata" 1978

Golden Globe Award Best Foreign Film "Autumn Sonata" 1978; award shared with Lew Grade and Martin Starger, co-producers

National Board of Review Best Foreign Film "Fanny and Alexander" 1983

New York Film Critics Circle Award Best Foreign Film "Fanny and Alexander" 1983

New York Film Critics Circle Award Best Director "Fanny and Alexander" 1983

Los Angeles Film Critics Association Award Best Foreign Film "Fanny and Alexander" 1983 director

Golden Globe Award Best Foreign-Language Film "Fanny and Alexander" 1983

Venice Film Festival International Critics Prize "Fanny and Alexander" 1983 shared with Alexander Kluge's "Der Macht der Gefuhle/The Power of Emotion"

Cesar Best Foreign Film "Fanny and Alexander" 1984

BAFTA Fellowship 1988

OBIE Award Direction "Hamlet" 1988/89

Directors Guild of America D. W. Griffith Award 1990, awarded for lifetime achievement

Dorothy and Lillian Gish Prize 1995; for creativity and outstanding contributions to the arts

OBIE Award Sustained Excellence in Direction 1995/96

Cannes Film Festival Palme des Palmes Award 1997; initial presentation of the award instituted to commemorate the 50th Anniversary of the festival; award to honor great directors whose work had previously been overlooked by the festival juries

Cannes Film Festival Ecumenical Jury Award (Special Mention) "In the Presence of a Clown" 1998

BIOGRAPHY

The extraordinary and unparalleled career of Swedish filmmaker Ingmar Bergman can be divided into four periods: his apprenticeship (1946–55), his first flowering (1955–64), his maturity, during which he produced several masterpieces (1965–83) and post-retirement (1983–). Throughout the years, the prolific director and writer also managed to stage numerous theatrical and television productions. Acknowledged as one of the masters of cinema, Bergman concentrated on themes of spiritual and psychological conflicts complemented by a distinctly intense and intimate visual style. As he matured as an artist, he shifted from an allegorical to a more personal cinema, often revisiting and elaborating on recurring images, subjects and techniques.

The middle child born to a Lutheran minister and his wife, Bergman became enamored of the theater at a young age. After seeing his first stage production, he built a puppet playhouse complete with revolving stage and elaborate lighting system where he and his sister would produce entertainments. Trips to the cinema with his older brother instilled a love for film. By the time he broke with his parents over their restrictions, Bergman had decided to pursue a career in theater and film.

As an undergraduate, Bergman began directing stage plays and in 1944 began his professional career at the Helsingborg City Theatre. Over the course of his long and distinguished theatrical career, he held similar posts at the Goteberg City Theatre and Malmo City Theatre, culminating in a three year (1963–66) stint as chief director at the Royal Dramatic Theatre in Stockholm. For the next thirty odd years, Bergman continued to stage acclaimed and innovative productions, several of which were presented at the Brooklyn Academy of Music.

In 1943, Bergman began his film career when he was hired in the script department of Svensk Filmindustri. The following year, his first effort, "Torment" was filmed by director Alf Sjoberg. He was given his first chance to direct with "Kris/Crisis" (1946), adapted from a play by Dane Leck Fischer. In this film, the nascent stylings can be evidenced: There is a trace of latent sadism that runs through much of his work. Although it was not a box-office success, the film did launch his directing career. In the 16 films he directed in this apprenticeship period, one see Bergman struggling to master the medium, honing his craft, developing his trademark stylings and introducing themes that he would explore in detail in later masterpieces (e.g., "Summer Interlude" 1951 and "Monika" 1953, both studies of adolescent love and its disappointments). "Sawdust and Tinsel/The Naked Night" (1953) introduced the recurring theme of humiliation and the utter loneliness of the human condition.

With "Smiles of a Summer Night" (1955), Bergman entered into a period of international recognition which saw him experimenting and solidifying his technical prowess. "Smiles of a Summer Night" is an ironic comedy that examines sexual frustration, lost loves and debasement. Two year later, he won further acclaim with "The Seventh Seal", a medieval allegory in which a knight plays chess with Death. The silhouetted long shot of Death leading a group of peasants across the horizon has become one of the most famous images in modern cinema. That same year, Bergman wrote and directed the journey narrative "Wild Strawberries", considered one of his masterworks. Following the events of a day in the life of an aging professor (played by veteran director Victor Sjostrom), the film is a model of fluidity, with flashbacks and dream sequences creating a penetrating investigation of life and death, emphasizing the relationships between desire, loss and guilt contrasted with compassion, restitution and celebration. It is not accidental that these two films were made back-to-back; Bergman has stated he was exploring how an individual may find "peace and clarity of soul" and concluding a) that God is silent and b) the individual must examine the truth of his/her existence by careful consideration of both the past and the present. Bergman further explored religion symbolically in "The Magician" (1958) and overtly in "The Virgin Spring" (1960), which earned a Best Foreign Film Oscar. The former starred Max Von Sydow as a Christ-like occultist who appears to die and is resurrected while the latter, set in the Middle Ages, depicts the rape and murder of a virginal maiden and the avenging of the crime by her father father. God "speaks" to the farmer through a miraculous spring of water that spouts when the dead girl's body is moved.

Bergman gradually moved to a more intimate chamber style of filmmaking as the 60s progressed, beginning with his trilogy that intensely examined psychological and spiritual themes: "Through a Glass Darkly" (1961), in which love proves to be a virtue and is an example of God's presence. "Winter Light" (1962), in which love is depicted as cold and sterile but where there is possibility, and "The Silence" (1963), which depicted a world without love and therefore without God.

Over the next decade, Bergman moved to a deeper probing of the human psyche and a closer examination of male-female relationships. "Persona" (1966) was the first of his great films that examined how individuals play roles in their lives. By using actors or artists at the core of the story, he demonstrated his beliefs that there is a harrowing separateness between people, even in the most private relationships. "Persona" is about an actress who undergoes a psychological breakdown and refuses to speak. Gradually, she assumes the persona of the loquacious nurse caring for her, much in the same way she assumed the identities of the characters she portrayed onstage. "Hour of the Wolf" (1968) shows a painter gradually descending into madness despite or because of those around him. "Shame" (also 1968) depicts the breakdown of a marriage between a musician and his wife as war rages around them. He further explored the same themes on a grander scale in "The Ritual/The Rite" (1969).

The 70s saw Bergman at the height of his powers culminating in "Cries and Whispers" (1973), a Gothic period piece revolving around three sisters, one of whom, Agnes, is dying, and their maid. Each of the sisters is symbolic of a particular theological concept and the film uses overt religious symbolism. Agnes reclines in a cruciform position and seems to be resurrected. There is an exquisite shot of her held by the maid that invokes the Pieta that is a highlight of this masterwork. Bergman returned to exploring the relations between the sexes in the superb six-part TV drama "Scenes From a Marriage" (1973) which was edited for theatrical release. The well-acted film depicts in a straightforward manner the disintegration of a seemingly perfect marriage. An anomaly for the period was his excellent rendering of Mozart's opera "The Magic Flute" (1975). "Face to Face" (1976) was another TV drama reshaped for theatrical release that followed the psychological disintegration of a therapist who is driven to attempt suicide. After helming his first English-language film, the flawed melodrama "The Serpent's Egg" (1977), Bergman returned to surer ground with "The Autumn Sonata" (1978). A chamber piece about a woman (Liv Ullmann) and her neglectful pianist mother (Ingrid Bergman), it was a gem-like character study of an artist who could not love. In 1982, Bergman announced his intention to retire and his last feature (actually made for Swedish TV) was the autobiographical "Fanny and Alexander." Perhaps the director's most personal film, it was infused with memories of childhood.

While he has not directed a feature film, Bergman has remained busy directing for the stage (although in 1995 he announced plans to curtail that activity). Several of his TV projects ("After the Rehearsal", 1983; "In the Presence of a Clown", 1998) have received theatrical release. He has also scripted semi-autobiographical projects helmed by others, including the Bille August–directed "The Best Intentions" and "Sunday's Children" (both 1992), directed by his son Daniel. In 1998, he announced that Liv Ullmann would be directing his script "Faithless" (set to lens in 1999 for release in 2000), to star Lena Endre and Erland Josephson as Bergman.

MILESTONES:

1930: Attended the theater for the first time; inspired to create own plays at home with his sister Margareta

Wrote first play as a teenager

1938: Amateur stage directing debut, "Outward Bound," in May

1939: Hired as production assistant at Stockholm Opera

1940: Broke with parents over family constrictions

1943: Joined Svensk Filmindustri

1944: Hired as director of Helsingborg Town Theatre in April

1944: Screenwriting debut with "Hets/Frenzy/Torment" (dir. Alf Sjoborg)

1946: Film directing debut (also writer), "Kris/Crisis"

1946: Made radio debut as director and playwright, adapting "Requiem"

1955: Had first international success with "Smiles of a Summer Night"

1957: Won prize at Cannes for "The Seventh Seal"

1959: Received first Academy Award nomination for the screenplay to "Smultronstallet/Wild Strawberries"

1960: First Bergman film to win a Best Foreign Film Oscar "The Virgin Spring"

1962: Earned second Oscar nomination for the script to "Through a Glass Darkly"

1963: Hired as Chief Director of Royal Dramatic Theatre, Stockholm; resigned 1966

1968: Directed and wrote "Skammen/Shame"; first film for own production company, Cinematograph AB

His teleplay "The Lie" aired on American television

1973: Received Oscar nominations as producer, director and screenwriter of "Cries and Whispers"

1973: Wrote and directed the the six-part Swedish TV series "Scenes From a Marriage"; edited version released theatrically

1974: Directed "The Maigc Flute" for Swedish television; released theatrically

1976: Left Sweden after encountering tax problems; booked but never tried; traveled to USA before settling in Munich

1976: Earned second Best Director Oscar nomination for "Face to Face"

1977: Made English language directing debut with "The Serpent's Egg," a US-German co-production

1978: Returned to Sweden

1978: Teamed Ingrid Bergman and Liv Ullmann in "The Autumn Sonata"; earned Best Screenplay Academy Award nomination

1982: Announced retirement from filmmaking; released last film as director "Fanny and Alexander", an edited version of the Swedish TV production; film won four 1983 Academy Awards including Best Foreign Film; received Oscar nominations as Best Director and Best Screenplay

1983: Made short film "Karin's Face" as a tribute to his mother

1987: Published memoirs

1991: Staged the Royal Dramatic Theater of Sweden's Swedish-language production (starring Lena Olin) of "Miss Julie" at Brooklyn Academy of Music

1991: Scripted "The Best Intensions", directed by Bille August

1992: Wrote the screenplay for the autobiographical "Sunday's Children", directed by son Daniel

1994: Penned the teleplay for "The Last Scream"

1995: Announced retirement from the theater

1997: Scripted "Larmar och gor sig till/In the Presence of a Clown" for Swedish TV; shown at the 1998 Cannes Film Festival

1998: Announced plans to produce "Trolosa/Faithless", a semi-autobiographical project he scripted to lens in 1999 for a 2000 release; to be directed by Liv Ullmann and to star Lena Endre and Erland Josephson as Ingmar Bergman

2000: Participated in a rare television interview in Sweden in which he suggested he would rather commit suicide than "become a vegetable and a burden on other people. A soul slowly dying out, trapped in a body in which the insides gradually sabotage me, that I think would be terrifying."

QUOTES:

"I really should be done with this, but I'm like an old actor who gives at least 50 farewell appearances. It's nice to be able to stand to the side of the camera, and I have stopped directing. But writing is fun, and I will continue to do it as long as I live."—Ingmar Bergman announcing plans for "Faithless", quoted in the *New York Post*, May 10, 1998.

In a 1999 interview, Bergman revealed that he was briefly a Nazi sympathizer in his youth.

Awarded an honorary PhD from University of Stockholm in 1975

Received the Japan Art Association's Praemium Imperiale prize (1991); award was set up in 1989 to honor artists whose works fall outside the Nobel Prize.

BIBLIOGRAPHY:

"The Magic Lantern" Ingmar Bergman, 1988 autobiography

"Private Confessions" Ingmar Bergman, translated by Joan Tate, 1997, Arcade

Busby Berkeley

BORN: William Berkeley Enos in Los Angeles, California, 11/29/1895

DEATH: in Palm Springs, California, 03/14/1976

NATIONALITY: American

EDUCATION: Mohegan Lake Military Academy, New York, 1914

BIOGRAPHY

Busby Berkeley is known primarily as an innovative choreographer who freed dance in the cinema from the constraints of theatrical space. In Berkeley's musical numbers, the confining proscenium of the stage gives way to the fluid frame of the motion picture image, and dances are choreographed for the ideal, changing point of view of a film spectator, rather than for the static position of a traditional theatergoer.

After enlisting in the army during WWI, Berkeley found himself conducting trick parade drills for as many as 1200 men and training as an aerial observer—two experiences that clearly shaped his approach to dance on film. After the war Berkeley worked in the theater, acting in and choreographing some numbers for touring musicals. His reputation grew steadily, and in 1928 he choreographed five Broadway shows, a considerable accomplishment for a man who had seriously studied neither choreography nor dance.

Berkeley's substantial success on Broadway led in 1930 to the opportunity to work in Hollywood on the newest movie genre, the film musical, then in its first flush of popularity after the recent arrival of sound. Sam Goldwyn hired him to direct the musical sequences of "Whoopee!" (1930), starring Eddie Cantor. In one sequence, Berkeley filmed the Goldwyn Girls, deployed in symmetrical fashion, from overhead—a technique that would become perhaps his most famous trademark.

Berkeley worked on several other musicals for MGM before settling in at Warner Bros. for seven years in 1933. His most famous Warner films included "42nd Street" (1933), "Gold Diggers of 1933" (1933) and "Dames" (1934). When he returned to MGM in 1939, Berkeley demonstrated that good musicals could be made with smaller budgets, but the development of the integrated dramatic musical left little room for his bravura approach. Berkeley doubled as director and choreographer on some of his films, and even directed the occasional dramatic feature, as with "They Made Me a Criminal" (1939), starring John Garfield.

The plots of Berkeley's musicals usually serve as little more than narrative pretexts for the the dance numbers, in which the camera soars through space, achieving a variety of startling surrealist effects. He choreographed dancing skyscrapers in "42nd Street" and 56 white pianos in "Gold Diggers of 1935." In "Small Town Girl" (1953) only the arms and instruments of an orchestra are visible through the floors and walls.

Berkeley's choreography is also notable for its humorous and voyeuristic eroticism. "Golddiggers of 1933" opens with chorines, including a young Ginger Rogers, singing "We're in the Money" clad in nothing but large coins—a striking image of women as objects of exchange within a patriarchal society, and thus a metaphorical reinforcement of the film's central theme. The "Pettin' in the Park" number from the same movie features Dick Powell using a can opener to gain access to Ruby Keeler's metal-clad body. The famous sequence from "The Gang's All Here" (1943), featuring Carmen Miranda ("The Lady in the Tutti-Frutti Hat") and a line of chorus girls waving giant bananas, may be the essential Berkeley sequence; it combines his surreal visual style with an overblown Freudian symbolism that prefigures the sensibility of Camp.

There is an almost cubist element to Berkeley's penchant for breaking up the physical world into aesthetically pleasing, abstract visual patterns—as in the giant jigsaw puzzle of Ruby Keeler's face carried by the chorines in the

"I Only Have Eyes for You" number in "Dames." Berkeley's greatest achievement was that, in an era dominated by the illusionist style of the classical Hollywood film, he attempted to free the camera from the mere recording of surface reality.

MILESTONES:

Moved with family to New York aged three; first stage appearance aged five in "Under Two Flags"

Worked as management trainee with a Massachusetts shoe factory

1917: Enlisted in US Army the day before USA entered WWI; served as second lieutenant in the artillery where he worked out trick precision drills for 1200 men in parade formation; served with Third Army of Occupation in Germany as entertainment officer

1920: Acting debut in stock company production of "The Man Who Came Back" (date approximate)

1923–1926: Performed and directed on Broadway and in stock before going to Hollywood

1927: First success on Broadway as dance director, Rodgers and Hart's "A Connecticut Yankee in King Arthur's Court"

Choreographed four films for United Artists; first film, "Whoopee!" (directed by Thornton Freeland)

1932: Loaned to Warner Bros. to choreograph "42nd Street" (1933)

1933: For First National, made co-directing debut (with George Amy), "She Had to Say Yes"

1933: Signed with Warner Bros.

1934: Provided dances for "Dames"

1935: Solo directing debut (also choreographer), "Gold Diggers of 1935"; received Oscar nomination in the dance direction category

1936: Received second dance direction Academy Award nomination for "Gold Diggers of 1937"

1937: Earned third Oscar nomination for

dance direction of "Varsity Show"; category discontinued after this year

Was involved in a fatal three-car automobile accident; charged with second-degree murder in the deaths of three people as well as with driving under the influence; lawyers made plea to jury playing up his care of his then 80-year-old mother; cleared of all charges after three trials

Left Warner Bros. and put under contract at MGM

Briefly worked on "The Wizard of Oz" (1939)

1943: Choreographed the MGM remake "Girl Crazy"

Left MGM and moved to Fox

1943: Served as dance director for "The Gang's All Here"; choreographed the "Lady With the Tutti Frutti Hat" number for Carmen Miranda

1946: Attempted suicide and was temporarily placed in a Los Angeles psychiatric hospital (date approximate)

1949: Last film as director, "Take Me Out to the Ball Game"

1962: Worked as second unit director on "Jumbo/Billy Rose's Jumbo" (directed by Charles Walters)

1970: Appeared in feature film "The Phynx"

1971: Returned to Broadway as supervisor of revival of "No, No, Nanette"

QUOTES:

Nicknamed after turn-of-the-century New York stage star Amy Busby

Alain Berliner

BORN: in Belgium, 1963

NATIONALITY: Belgian

EDUCATION: Insitut de Radioelectricite et de Cinematographie (INRACI), Brussels, Belgium, 1987; graduated with honors

AWARDS: European Film Award Best Screenwriter "Ma Vie en Rose" 1997; award shared with Chris Vander Stappen

Golden Globe Award Best Foreign Language Film "Ma Vie en Rose (My Life in Pink)" 1997

BIOGRAPHY

Belgian-born filmmaker Alain Berliner grew up to be a proponent of "magical realism", a mixture of fantasy and the everyday pioneered by fellow countryman Andre Delvaux in the late 1960s and early 70s. ("Every time there's a plot point, it can be solved in a magical way. It's much more interesting than solving a situation in a Hollywood way.") After his first directing experience as a student convinced him he did not handle actors well, Berliner initially contented himself with writing, first for commercials and later for Belgian features and French TV. After co-scripting the very successful "Koko Flanel" (1990), he wrote and helmed the shorts "Le Jour du chat" (1991) and "Rose" (1993), and his sure handling of the latter's off-beat tale of a music teacher who falls in love with a flower pricked the interest of a French executive who thought he might possess the sensibility to helm what would become "Ma Vie en Rose/My Life in Pink" (1997), a sensitive story of gender confusion.

Berliner had already begun a screenplay he hoped would mark his feature directing debut, but Chris vander Stappen's initial draft completely entranced him and altered his course. The two writers worked their way through 13 more drafts before arriving at a final screenplay, and Berliner shot the film over nine weeks in the summer of 1996. His authentic "Levittown" location at Mennecy, 30 miles south of

Paris, provided the candy-colored suburban neighborhood (with each garage door painted a different pastel) that was his first tip of the hat to director Tim Burton (remember "Edward Scissorhands"), and the exploration of the main character's fantasy world via dreamlike computer-animated sequences recalled the Burton-produced "The Nightmare Before Christmas" (1993). In this "Ozzie and Harriet" world where conformity is de rigueur, a seven-year old boy upsets the balance by wearing dresses, playing with dolls and insisting: "I'm a boy now, but one day I'll be a girl." The heartfelt, uplifting story of this boy and his identity problem elicited sympathy for both the child and parents as they cope with the fallout the situation provokes. Though the film's homosexual undertones may have prevented it from receiving an Academy Award nomination (after winning the Golden Globe as Best Foreign Language Film), the overriding theme of family closeness gave "Ma Vie en Rose" its universal appeal, and its generalized study of difference sounded a clarion call for tolerance.

The need for tolerance was also at the root of Berliner's next film, "The Wall" (1998), a featurette which aired on the French-German cultural station Arte as part of the omnibus "2000 as Seen by . . . " In "The Wall", the hostilities between Flemish and French-speaking Belgians become embodied (through a fanciful touch of surrealism) by the brick structure which suddenly appears down the middle of a small Brussels' chip wagon straddling the linguistic border. Berliner also contributed to the screenplay of the disappointing French-Canadian children's fantasy "Babel" (1999). He fared better with his English-language directing debut "Passion of Mind" (also 1999), starring Demi Moore as a New York publisher who falls asleep and wakes up in the French countryside of Provence as a widow with two small children. Her subsequent quest to discover which of her two lives is real and which is imaginary

was right up the alley for this accomplished disciple of Delvaux.

MILESTONES:

When young, escaped to screenings at Brussels' cinematheque (favorite directors were Billy Wilder, Federico Fellini and Tim Burton)

1987: Made a short movie while in film school and decided he was a bad communicator not suited for directing (date approximate)

Worked briefly on TV commercials before settling into screenwriting for Belgian features and French TV

1990: Was co-screenwriter of feature "Koko Flanel", starring Belgian funny-man Urbanus ("sort of our regional Chevy Chase"); film sold one million tickets in Belgium and another million in Holland

Earned living as a "reparateur de scenario" (script doctor)

1991: Wrote and directed eight-minute short, "Le Jour du chat"

1993: Directed and wrote "Rose", an original short about a music teacher who secretly falls in love with the titular inhabitant of his garden

1997: Had international success with feature directorial debut, "Ma Vie en Rose/My Life in Pink"; received co-screenwriting credit and shared the European Film Award for Best Screenplay with Chris vander Stappen, whose provided original story; also co-produced

1998: Second movie (a featurette), "The Wall", aired on the French-German cultural television channel Arte as part of the omnibus "2000 as Seen by . . . ", showcasing 10 directors from around the world (Hal Hartley represented the USA)

1999: Received a screenwriting credit (along with others) on the disappointing French-Canadian children's fantasy "Babel"

2000: Helmed English-language debut, "Passion of Mind", starring Demi Moore; screenplay by Ronald Bass

QUOTES:

"Ma Vie en Rose/My Life in Pink" won the best picture award at Seattle's 1997 Gay and Lesbian Film Festival.

"I like when magic comes on the screen. In Belgium we like 'le realisme magique.' Surrealism. It's day and night at the same time."—Alain Berliner quoted in *Variety*, January 14, 1998.

"I wanted to make a film that was open, not one directed at a specific public of, say, homosexuals or transvestites. Afterall, Ludovic may just be going through a phase. And, remember, he is too young to be sexually aware. That's why we don't suggest what hapopens when he grows up. That's for the public to decide. But I must say, homosexuals have come up to me after some screenings and said, 'It's my story.' "—Berliner to Alan Riding, quoted in *The New York Times*, December 22, 1997.

On the ending of "Ma Vie en Rose": "I don't know if it's such a happy ending. The family accepts, but you don't find out what happens later—whether he really chooses to be a girl. We left it open because medically it's impossible to determine at the age of nine, and because we wanted to focus on the principal question, which was whether or not the parents are going to accept their child like he is."—Berliner quoted in *Time Out New York*, December 24, 1997–January 8, 1998.

"He [Berliner's father] didn't want to talk about it [the Holocaust]. He was hiding from the Germans during the war. He was one of those people who lost all faith. He raised me with the idea that being a Jew is not important, we're just normal people. I didn't have a bar mitzvah. I rarely met Jewish women. So I don't know why the woman I married was a Jew! Her family tree goes back to the 12th century, in Lebanon. But my family [he makes a chopping gesture] there is a great cut."—Berliner to Betsy Sherman, *The Boston Globe*, February 1, 1998.

Bernardo Bertolucci

BORN: in Parma, Italy, 03/16/1940

NATIONALITY: Italian

EDUCATION: Rome University, Rome, Italy; modern literature dropped out in 1962 to begin film career

AWARDS: Viareggio Prize "In cerca del mistero" 1962 collection of poems

National Society of Film Critics Award Best Director "The Conformist" 1971

Directors Guild of America Award Outstanding Directorial Achievement in Feature Film "The Last Emperor" 1987

Oscar Best Director "The Last Emperor" 1987

Oscar Best Screenplay (Based on Material from Another Medium) "The Last Emperor" 1987; award shared with Mark Peploe

Cesar Best Foreign Film "The Last Emperor" 1988

National Board of Review Freedom of Expression Award 1998

India Film Festival Lifetime Achievement Award 1999; initial presentation of the award

BIOGRAPHY

The childhood of Italian director-scenarist Bernardo Bertolucci couldn't have been more idyllic. Existing simultaneously in two worlds, he experienced the earthiness of the peasant's life courtesy of his grandfather, padrone of a small farm near Parma, while receiving an equal dose of the refined artistic life from his parents. Yet despite the big, comfortable house, the servants and an atmosphere that encouraged creativity, he would grow up disaffected, chafing against his life of privilege and the tradition of his father's poetry, which he eventually viewed as being based on repression. Initially, the son competed in the father's arena (after all, poetry was part of the daily diet), publishing his first poems by the age of 12 and later winning the prestigious Viareggio Prize for his first book of verse, "In Cerca del Mistero/In Search of Mystery" (1962), a work full of nostalgia for the lost Eden of his country boyhood. By then he was busy seeking his liberation as a neophyte filmmaker, lyrically revealing the dark side of human nature via the poetry of movies.

Bertolucci's first foray into cinema came as the assistant director on family friend Pier Paolo Pasolini's inaugural film, "Accattone" (1961). The following year, he made his own distinguished debut at the helm of "La Commare Secca/The Grim Reaper", a script Pasolini had originally written to direct but which Bertolucci rewrote extensively with Sergio Citti. The central narrative event was the murder of a prostitute, around which he wove flashbacks to the lives of witnesses and potential suspects, all leading up to the time of the killing. Though influenced by the French New Wave, the film showed an even greater allegiance to Italian neorealism in its concentration on behavioral detail, location shooting and use of nonprofessional actors. With his second film, "Before the Revolution" (1964), the precocious director became a name internationally and established his distinctive visual style of bold camera movements, moody lighting and expressive mise-en-scene, typically backed with an evocative score.

For the first time, Bertolucci's preoccupation with politics, sex and Freud was on display, and "Before the Revolution" also introduced what would become a favorite thematic element of the director, the conflict between freedom and conformity, placing him on the cutting-edge of 1960s sensibilities. In this reworking of Stendhal's "The Charterhouse of Parma", the leading character is a well-to-do boy who fancies himself a Marxist but ultimately learns he is nothing of the sort. Forced to decide between radical political commitment and an irreproachably bourgeois marriage, he opts for the latter, conducting an incestuous affair with an apolitical aunt along the way and renouncing his communist mentor (and totemic father figure). The film evoked comparisons to Orson Welles but stalled at the box office, and Bertolucci turned to television, making a prize-winning series of three documentaries about the Italian petroleum industry. "The Partner" (1968), which continued the political argument begun in "Before the Revolution", started to explore the director's fascination with the psychological double but suffered for its polemical excess, finding few admirers.

Angry and disillusioned, Bertolucci joined the Italian Communist Party and went about resurrecting his career with two 1970 films beginning his long collaboration with director of photography Vittorio Storaro. "The Spider's Stratagem", commissioned by the enlightened Italian television company RAI, returned to the doubling theme, tracing a son's search for his father through a surrealistic, complex narrative that incorporated Verdi's "Rigoletto" and the work of Borges and Magritte. (A later film, 1981's "Tragedy of a Ridiculous Man", reverses that narrative premise, following a father's search for his son.) In the end, the son discovers that his father had not heroically opposed the Italian Fascists but was in fact a traitor (as in Freudian terms fathers always are). In "The Conformist" (1970), considered by many critics to be Bertolucci's masterpiece, the leading character Marcello (Jean-Louis Trintignant) becomes a Fascist in order to suppress his growing recognition of his homosexuality. Here, the Oedipal imagery is even more powerful as Marcello plans to kill his anti-Fascist teacher and have sex with the teacher's wife (Dominique Sanda), but after botching the assassination attempt, he is powerless to prevent her murder by his Fascist comrades.

Firmly in control of the lighting, decor, costume and music, Bertolucci reveled in the elaborate tracking shots, the opulent color photography and the odd, surrealistic, visual incongruities that give his work its distinctive surface. The classic sequence in which the two central women characters perform a tango became a Bertolucci signature, and the dance as metaphor served as a bridge to his controversial "Last Tango in Paris" (1972). Considered obscene by some viewers, "Last Tango" was for others a breakthrough in its depiction of sexual politics as a presentation of the passionate, conflicted relationship between an older man (Marlon Brando) and a younger woman (Maria Schneider) in the enclosed psychological space of chamber cinema. Railing against the hypocrisy of cultural institutions such as family, church and state as his protagonist assails the girl's body, Bertolucci purposefully cast someone old enough to be her father, making Schneider's murder of Brando at the end of the film yet another Oedipal killing. It was a sterling showcase for the helmer's moving camera (earning him an Oscar nod as Best Director), and the performance by Brando ranks among the best of the actor's career.

The world acclaim (and notoriety) garnered by "Last Tango" enabled Bertolucci to get financing for his long-planned Marxian epic, "Novocentro/1900" (1976), which featured an international cast and a length of nearly six hours (cut dramatically for American and British release). Returning to his northern Italian roots, the director charted 45 years of social history and class struggle through the friendship and political enmity of two men (Robert De Niro and Gerard Depardieu) born on different sides of the social fence at the turn of the century. Envisioning the culture of the peasant farmers as an idealized form of communism, he showed their exploitation at the hands of first the aristocracy and later the Fascists, ending with an agrarian revolt that seems to promise a socialist utopia, though the revolution they

are celebrating is already doomed. Despite mixed reviews and a woeful box office, Bertolucci was still able to acquire backing for "La Luna/Luna" (1979), swinging back to Freudian concerns for its graphic portrayal of mother-son incest, but following its critical and commercial failure, the money finally dried up. He was unable to find anyone to release "The Tragedy of a Ridiculous Man."

Having hit rock bottom, Bertolucci went into seclusion and did not work on a movie for four years. Unhappy with the state of filmmaking in Italy (and unable to get arrested in Hollywood), he looked to the East and was somehow, miraculously able to mount his expensive, ambitious epic masterpiece "The Last Emperor" (1987). Winner of nine Academy Awards including Best Director and Best Picture, the film follows the shifting fortunes of Pu Yi, who begins his life as the last emperor of China and ends it as a gardener in post-revolutionary Beijing. Like the deposed Pu Yi, Bertolucci was an exile from his own culture, and his passion for the project overcame such logistical nightmares as having the privilege of filming in China. (He became the first Westerner granted access to shoot in Beijing's Forbidden City since the Communists came to power in 1949.) Again, the relationship between individual psychology and the political and historical forces that mold it formed the center of the film, linking it to "Before the Revolution", "The Conformist" and "1900."

Bertolucci's much-anticipated adaptation of Paul Bowles' cult favorite "The Sheltering Sky" (1990), starring John Malkovich and Debra Winger, proved a critical and financial disappointment, though he and Storaro may have done more for desert landscapes than anyone since David Lean. His fascination with epic form undimmed, he reteamed with Jeremy Thomas, the producer of "The Last Emperor" and "The Sheltering Sky", to complete what he calls his Eastern trilogy with "Little Buddha" (1994). The visually stunning production (owing much to Storaro and the designs of multiple Oscar-winner James Acheson) focused on a dual story: the modern-day search for the reincarnation of Buddha and the ancient tale drawn from the life of Prince Siddhartha (portrayed strikingly by Keanu Reeves). Operatic in execution, the film failed in its attempt to synthesize a script which functioned meaningfully for both children and adults, as intended by the director. Despite the lush look of the canvases, there was a hollowness to these pictures as the director seemed to be losing his way amidst the spectacle.

"Stealing Beauty" (1996) signaled a change in direction for Bertolucci, from large-scale epics to smaller, more personal films. Centering on a teenage American girl sent to Tuscany to stay with family friends after her mother's death, it featured a dead-on, star-making turn by Liv Tyler and a touching performance by Jeremy Irons as the dying man who finds renewed life through his young visitor. For only the second time since 1970, Bertolucci chose not to employ Storaro as director of photography, using instead Darius Khondji, who avoided the cliched sun-drenched photography in favor of a softer, more painterly tone. Scaling-down further, he shot "Besieged" (1998), essentially a two-person piece with minimal dialogue, in 28 days for less than $3 million, but the pic originally intended as a one-hour TV project suffered in its expansion to feature length with most critics decrying the dearth of believable character development. Though his films have lost none of their surface polish, an older and mellower Bertolucci seems unable to recapture that sense of danger that so captivated audiences in the 60s and 70s.

COMPANION:

wife: Clare Peploe. Director, screenwriter; married in 1978

MILESTONES:

Had poems published in magazines by age 12

Made amateur 16mm films as a teenager, the first one showing a pig being slaughtered

1961: Worked as assistant director to family friend Pier Paolo Pasolini on the latter's feature directing debut, "Accattone"

1962: Published first collection of poems, "In cerca del mistero/In Search of Mystery" (winner of the Viareggio Prize)

1962: Film directing and co-writing (with Pasolini and Sergio Citti) debut, "La commare secca/The Grim Reaper"; shot on location with a cast of nonprofessionals

1964: Came into his own directing "Before the Revolution"; critical acclaim, however, did not translate to box office success

1965–1966: For Italian TV directed three-part documentary "La Via del Petrolio," about an Italian oil company in Iran

1968: Continued the political argument begun in "Before the Revolution" with "The Partner" (based on Fyodor Dosteyevsky's novel "The Double"); also marked first collaboration with actress Stefania Sandrelli

1968: Joined the Italian Communist Party; resigned ten years later

1969: Co-wrote story (with director and Dario Argento) for Sergio Leone's "Once Upon a Time in the West"

Initial collaborations with director of photography Vittorio Storaro, "The Spider's Stratagem" (originally made for Italian television) and "The Conformist"

1970: Soared to international prominence with "The Conformist"; picture brought him acclaim in the USA; earned first Oscar nomination for Best Adapted Screenplay; first film with actress Dominique Sanda

1972: Helmed "Last Tango in Paris", arguably the most controversial film of its era; garnered Oscar nod as Best Director; film was originally banned in Italy; after finally being released, it was again banned for 11 years; tried for blasphemy, Bertolucci received a suspended prison sentence and lost the right to vote for five years

1975: Made first film appearance in documentary, "Bertolucci Secundo il Cinema/The Cinema According to Bertolucci/The Making of '1900'", co-directed by his brother and Gianni Amelio

1976: Assembled an international cast, including Robert De Niro, Gerard Depardieu and Sanda, for the epic "1900"

1979: First collaboration with screenwriter (and wife) Clare Peploe, "Luna"

1982: Initiated by a lama into the Tibetan practice of meditation

1982: Producing debut, "Sconcerto Rock"

1987: English language directing debut, "The Last Emperor"; first teaming with screenwriter (and brother-in-law) Mark Peploe; film won nine Academy Awards including Best Picture and two for Bertolucci, as Best Director and for the Best Screenplay

1990: Co-wrote (with Mark Peploe) and directed "The Sheltering Sky", adapted from the Paul Bowles novel; executive produced by William Aldrich whose director father Robert Aldrich had first optioned the 1949 novel but failed to obtain studio financing after years of trying

1993: Third film with Mark Peploe, "Little Buddha"; eighth and final collaboration (to date) with Storaro

1996: Began moving away from the epic format with "Stealing Beauty" (picture's budget—under $15 million—was less than half that of "Little Buddha" at $35 million), starring Liv Tyler; first film made in his native Italy since 1981's "The Tragedy of a Ridiculous Man"; also reunited with Sandrelli for the first time since "1900"

1998: Reteamed with wife on screenplay for "Besieged" (filmed for less than $3 million), adapted from a short story by James Lasdun

QUOTES:

About the role of his father, Attilio (one of Italy's most respected poets), in his films: "My father is the sweetest man, but also very strong. One way to make him less menacing was to make weak fathers in my movies . . . All my characters are searching for liberation from my father, but this is the first time (in 'Little Buddha') that someone has been able to free himself.

"When I grew up I found poetry was belonging to him. He already had my mother so I wanted something all mine. Maybe the real reason this Oedipal syndrome wasn't resolved earlier was because my parents are so close. They're kind of impenetrable, always together, no way to sneak in, no way to win. Maybe one way was to do movies, because it was different."—Bernardo Bertolucci quoted in *Premiere*, May 1994.

On his experience directing Brando in "Last Tango in Paris": "When you work with Marlon Brando you discover what is beyond the great actor is something else—a man who is so omnivorous in his curiosity it's contagious. His questions force you to be as curious as he is. It was an incredible lesson—and I was attempting to take off his Actors Studio mask.

"About a year ago we were talking up at his house—I had not seen him in a long time.

"We were so greedy to talk to each other we sat there—3 p.m., 7 p.m., 8 p.m.—it got dark, but we didn't stop to turn on the lights. At a certain point I said, 'Do you agree that I got something of you in the film?' He said, 'Do you think that man up there on the screen is me? Ha! Ha!' There will always be another 'beyond' with Brando. Doing 'Last Tango' was an initiation into adulthood. I was dealing with an American icon—the American icon."— Bertolucci to Kevin Thomas in *Los Angeles Times*, October 18, 1996.

"After I made '1900', my great monument to communism, I started to lose faith in it. Communism was a terrible failure. I'm disappointed, but I recognize that to allow me to have my great dreams and utopia, millions of people would have to suffer.

"I'm no longer interested in making political films. There's something old-fashioned about them. Young people now don't care for politics. It isn't present in life as it used to be. And increasingly I like films which reflect present-day reality."—Bertolucci quoted in *Los Angeles Times,* May 16, 1999.

Luc Besson

BORN: in Paris, France, 03/18/1959

NATIONALITY: French

EDUCATION: dropped out of secondary school at age 17 to begin work in films

AWARDS: Lumiere Best Director "Le Cinquieme element/The Fith Element" 1997

Cesar Best Director "Le Cinquieme element/The Fifth Element" 1998; had been nominated four times before as Best Director

BAFTA Alexander Korda Award for Outstanding British Film "Nil by Mouth" 1998; awarded to the outstanding British film of the year; shared with Douglas Urbanski and Gary Oldman

Lumiere Best Director "The Messenger: The Story of Joan of Arc" 1999; movie also cited as Best Film

BIOGRAPHY

Called "the French Steven Spielberg" by some, Luc Besson made an impressive debut at age 24 with "Le Dernier Combat" (1983), an apocalyptic drama noted for its striking black-and-white photography and bold lack of dialogue (a clever low-budget strategy). His subsequent films were box-office hits at home, more popular for their exhilarating visuals than for their thin storylines. After going underground to helm "Subway" (1985), starring Christopher Lambert and Isabelle Adjani, this son of scuba divers mined his first love (the sea) to make the underwater epic "The Big Blue" (1988), a huge commercial success in France and his international breakthrough, excluding the US market. Besson's next project, the aggressively violent and wildly improbable "La Femme Nikita" (1990), provided a great part for his then wife Anne Parillaud and finally registered with American audiences. An entertaining story of a hedonistic young woman who becomes an undercover assassin for the French government, the film did so well in the USA that it spurred the dreadful remake "Point of No Return"(1993).

Besson returned underwater to film the stunning "Atlantis" (1991), a documentary tone-poem focusing on the beauty of marine life (with no intrusions from humanity this time around), for which Eric Serra's music passed as the text. His first Hollywood film, "The Professional" (1994), followed the blossoming relationship between a hitman (frequent collaborator Jean Reno) and an orphan (Natalie Portman in her screen debut), and the filmmaker again garnered praise for skillful direction and stylish action sequences that overshadowed the less than satisfactory story development. Besson followed with the blockbuster sci-fi extravaganza "The Fifth Element" (1997), a visually stunning triumph of sophisticated production (Dan Weil) and costume (Jean-Paul Gaultier) design starring Bruce Willis, future wife Milla Jovovich and Gary Oldman. Based on Besson's visions of the future that had been distilling for two decades, "The Fifth Element" was a delight to watch (if only eyeball-deep), a comic book with Willis' jocular finesse at its center. He also produced Oldman's impressive writing-helming debut

"Nil By Mouth" that year and the following year produced and scripted Gerard Pires' "Taxi".

Besson established on "Le Dernier Combat" the hands-on approach of operating the camera himself, a practice he has continued on all his successive films. "Why lose time explaining everything to someone else? He's going to be slightly off, and then I'm going to freak out and say, 'No this is not what we discussed. I want the camera here!' So it's better for everyone involved if I just do it myself" (*American Cinematographer*, May 1997). His first foray into historical drama, "The Messenger: The Story of Joan of Arc" (1999), was no exception as he plunged with his camera into the midst of battle scenes, presenting the furious, close-quarters fighting which was the best reason to see the film. With names like John Malkovich, Faye Dunaway and Dustin Hoffman, the picture boasted his most Hollywood star-studded cast to date (apologies to Willis and Oldman). Unfortunately, his use of Jovovich as his leading lady did nothing to elevate his otherwise eye-catching version of the frequently filmed story. (The couple separated soon after filming was completed.) He then produced Fred Garson's "The Dancer" (2000), as well as providing the idea for the film.

COMPANIONS:

wife: Anne Parillaud. Actor; met c. 1986; starred in title role of Besson's "La Femme Nikita"; divorced

wife: Milla Jovovich. Actor, model, recording artist; Ukranian; appeared in Besson's "The Fifth Element" and "The Messenger: The Story of Joan of Arc"; married in Las Vegas in December 1997; separated in April 1999

MILESTONES:

1976: Dream of following in his parents' footsteps shattered by a serious diving accident at age 17 (date approximate); told he would never dive again, he has since resumed diving

1976: Turned down by France's national film school at age 17 (date approximate)

Moved to Hollywood, where he worked doing various jobs

1982: Founded production company, Les Film du Loup

1983: Worked as second unit director on "Le Grand Carnaval"

1983: At age 24, directed, produced and co-wrote (with Pierre-Alain Jolivet) first film, "Le Dernier Combat"

1985: Introduced Christopher Lambert with "Subway", which also starred Isabelle Adjani

1986: Produced first film which he did not also direct, "Kamikaze"; also wrote screenplay

1988: Returned to his first love (the sea) with "The Big Blue" about famed diver Jacques Mayol; his first English-language film, it was a huge commercial success in France (the biggest to that date), but failed to reach its intended US audience, thanks to the butchered cut which debuted there

1990: Directed and wrote the stylish and compelling "La Femme Nikita", heads above its American remake "Point of No Return" (1993)

1991: Made little-seen documentary, "Atlantis", ("The Big Blue" without humans), sharing cinematography duties as well as directing

1993: Executive produced Patrick Grand-perret's "L'Enfant Lion"

1994: Produced, directed and wrote first American film, "The Professional"; initial collaboration with Gary Oldman; fifth film with actor Jean Reno

1997: Scored big hit with the sci-fi comic book "The Fifth Element"; directed and scripted but did not produce; film starred future wife Milla Jovovich

1997: Produced Oldman's writing-directing debut "Nil By Mouth"

1998: Scripted and produced Gerard Pires' "Taxi"

1999: Helmed "The Messenger: The Story of Joan of Arc", starring Jovovich in the title role; Eric Serra provided the music, his ninth collaboration with the director

2000: Produced and provided the idea for Fred Garson's (second assistant director on "The Fifth Element") feature directing debut, "The Dancer"

2000: Served as jury president at the Cannes Film Festival

2000: Director's cut of "The Big Blue" released in USA

2001: Produced and co-wrote "Kiss of the Dragon", starring Jet Li and Bridget Fonda

2001: Scripted "Wasabi", about a French detective on a case in Tokyo

QUOTES:

Besson served as president of the jury at the 2000 Cannes Film Festival

"Luc Besson has been praised and disparaged as one of the new breed of high-tech, high-gloss, Americanoid anti-auteur filmmakers who do not wish to provide an alternative to Hollywood's blockbuster confections, but merely to embellish them with some Gallic sauce. Mr. Besson has even been described as the French Steven Spielberg."—Andrew Sarris, quoted in the *New York Observer*, April 1, 1991.

About dreaming up the world that would become "The Fifth Element" as a bored adolescent: "I was living in the country, 60 miles from Paris, and I was pretty lonely—no VCR, no TV, no cinema where I was. I didn't have so many friends. I tried to invent how this world works, what the police are like, how the buildings work. This world, where I can fly in my flying cab, was more fun for me. It was my companion. It was a way to escape instead of taking drugs and stealing motorbikes.'—Luc Besson to Andy Seller in *USA Today*, May 8, 1997.

Kathryn Bigelow

BORN: Kathryn Ann Bigelow in San Carlos, California, 11/27/1951

SOMETIMES CREDITED AS:
Kathy Bigelow

NATIONALITY: American

EDUCATION: San Francisco Art Institute, San Francisco, California; painting, 1970–72 (dates approximate); attended for two years before winning a scholarship to the Whitney Museum Independent Study Program

Independent Study Program, Whitney Museum, New York, New York, 1972; studied and produced conceptual art in an independent study program

School of the Arts, Columbia University, New York, New York, film studies, MFA, 1979; attended on scholarship

BIOGRAPHY

Perhaps too easily pigeonholed as the female filmmaker with a flair for traditionally masculine genres, Bigelow entered the cinema by way of the art world. Hailed as one of the preeminent stylists of contemporary Hollywood filmmaking, she has proven her mettle and placed her distinctive stamp on several male-dominated arenas. Bigelow has crafted a languorous biker flick ("The Loveless" 1981), a Country & Western–flavored vampire movie ("Near Dark" 1987), a distaff crime drama ("Blue Steel" 1990), a surfing-oriented heist picture ("Point Break" 1991) and a would-be millennial sci-fi thriller ("Strange Days" 1995). She augmented her genre credentials with her marriage to action auteur—and sometime collaborator—James ("The Terminator") Cameron in 1989. They divorced in 1991 but continued to work together.

The tall (5'11"), statuesque and strikingly beautiful Bigelow once modeled for a Gap ad and acted in Lizzie Borden's ironically militant feminist fantasy "Born in Flames" (1983). What's more, by peppering her interviews with allusions to post-structuralist theoreticians and other high-brow sorts, she has cultivated a reputation as an intellectual while charming journalists with her learned takes on her own work. All these factors have conspired to give Bigelow more status in the industry that one might expect for an artist with a relatively modest body of work.

The only child of a paint store manager and a librarian, Bigelow began her creative life as a painter in her teens. She took up formal studies at the San Francisco Art Institute for two years before winning a prestigious scholarship to the Whitney Museum Independent Study Program in 1971. Moving to NYC, the 19-year-old was set up with a studio in a former off-track betting office. Her paintings and conceptual art pieces were critiqued by the likes of Richard Serra, Robert Rauschenberg and Susan Sontag. The Whitney displayed one of her works in which viewers listened to a recording of pipes clanging together while all they saw was a still arrangement of chrome pipes on the floor. The piece was intended to illustrate "potentiality."

Bigelow ventured further into the realm of the avant-garde as the assistant of conceptual artist Vito Acconci. Among her duties was filming slogans to run behind the artist's performance pieces. Bigelow entered the graduate film program at Columbia University but focused on theory and criticism rather than production. Nonetheless she gained some attention with her first short, "Set-Up" (1978), a 20-minute piece in which two men fight while, on the soundtrack, someone reads an essay on violence. Bigelow segued into feature filmmaking as the co-writer-director (with Monty Montgomery) of "The Loveless", an outrageously mannered meditation on 1950s juvenile delinquent movies. (The film also marked the feature acting debut of Willem Dafoe.) This eccentric art movie generally bored or baffled the few who saw it but deeply impressed producer-writer-director Walter Hill who gave Bigelow a development deal when she moved to Los Angeles.

Bigelow became a cult figure with the 1987 release of "Near Dark", a stylish, atmospheric tale of modern-day vampires on the Great Plains which even prompted New York's Museum of Modern Art to mount a "retrospective" of her brief career. "Blue Steel" provided a strong vehicle for Jamie Lee Curtis and the wild and woolly "Point Break" first introduced Keanu Reeves as an action star. "Strange Days" won some rapturous reviews and a screening at the 1995 New York Film Festival. The film, however, quickly fizzled at the box office.

While she was absent from the big screen for five years. Bigelow was hardly idle. Since 1992, she had been developing a feature about the life of Joan of Arc and at one time Luc Besson was involved. When Besson went on to make his version of the story (1999's "The Messenger: The Story of Joan of Arc"), she cried foul and filed a lawsuit alleging fraud, breach of contract and breach of fiduciary duty. Rather than face a protracted legal battle, Besson settled out of court. Additionally during her absence from the big screen, Bigelow saw her script for the thriller "Undertow" produced and aired on Showtime in 1996 and she also helmed three episodes of the critically acclaimed NBC drama "Homicide: Life on the Street", the two-part season finale in 1998 and one of the series' final episodes in 1999. The following year, she was back at the multiplexes with "The Weight of Water", a psychological thriller that *Variety* (September 12, 2000) called "her richest, most ambitious and personal work to date". A drama that interwove two separate stories—the breakup of a contemporary marriage and a 19th-century murder—"The Weight of Water" was a visual stunning, well-acted film anchored by the superlative performances of its female leads.

Bigelow's next project was directing Harrison

Ford and Liam Neeson in 2002's "K-19: The Widowmaker." Her direction of the movie was well recieved, though the film itself was not a huge box office or critical success.—Written by Kent Greene

COMPANION:

husband: James Cameron. Director; married in August 1989; divorced in 1991

MILESTONES:

1971–1983: Lived in NYC variously as a student, artist and filmmaker

1971: Had one of her first "exhibitions" at the Whitney Museum in NYC

First professional art job, worked as the assistant to conceptual artist Vito Acconci

1978: Short film writing, producing and directing debut, "Set-Up" (a 20-minute-long Columbia student project)

Posed for a Gap advertisement

1980: Served as script supervisor, "Union City"

1981: First feature as co-writer-director (with Monty Montgomery), "The Loveless"; feature debut for star Willem Dafoe

1983: Feature acting debut (as Kathy Bigelow), Lizzie Borden's "Born in Flames"

1983: Moved to Los Angeles

Landed a development deal with producer-writer-director Walter Hill (who had been impressed by "The Loveless")

1987: Solo directorial debut (also co-writer with Eric Red), "Near Dark"

1991: First collaboration with producer-writer-director James Cameron (to whom she was then married), "Point Break" (Cameron executive produced)

1992: Began developing "Company of Angels", a film about Joan of Arc; at one time Luc Besson was involved with project; after he completed "The Messenger: The Story of Joan of Arc", Bigelow filed a lawsuit charging fraud, breach of contract and breach of fiduciary duty; settled out of court for an undisclosed amount of money

1993: TV directing debut, helmed the second hour of the sci-fi thriller miniseries "Wild Palms"

1995: Directed "Strange Days", a stylish but overambitious sci-fi epic that was screened at the New York Film Festival

1996: Penned the script for the thriller "Undertow"; aired on Showtime

1998: Helmed a two-part episode of "Homicide: Life on the Street" (NBC); directed a third episode in 1999

2000: Directed "The Weight of Water", a contemporary psychological thriller; premiered at Toronto Film Festival

2002: Helmed "K-19: The Widowmaker", a drama about a Russian submarine trapped at the bottom of the ocean

QUOTES:

"Film requires nothing but time. Two hours. . . . I thought it could be this great social tool. The challenge became how to create something accessible with a conscience. I'm still working on that. That's where I am. You know, rules are meant to be broken, boundaries are meant to be invaded, envelopes are meant to be pushed, preconceptions challenged. One of the things the film is about is watching, the consequences of watching, the political consequences of experiencing someone else's life vicariously, of having your art consist of pieces of other people's experience. It's sort of like a Rorschach, sort of like the monolith in '2001.' You will project onto it. But hopefully you'll also take away thought. Human nature prevents us from standing still. If you're pushing the envelope and challenging the system, that's the tenet of art."—Kathryn Bigelow quoted in *The Boston Globe*, October 8, 1995.

"The nice thing with a genre like horror is that it's a definite grid on which to hang a piece and give the audience a familiarity before you kind of subvert it. In the case of 'Near Dark,' I was interested in this sort of marginal ad hoc family unit doing no more than trying to survive as any family unit will do. They're not like serial killers or someone killing for pleasure; they're killing for survival. And so I kept thinking of them as this marginal family structure—I wanted to see how they could function in an alternative universe."—Bigelow to *The Washington Post*, October 17, 1995.

"The filmmakers I admire most like Oliver [Stone] and Scorsese and Kurosawa—they always have an edge, a complexity. Their movies aren't comforting; they're not pacifying. They bring out the audience's strength."—Kathryn Bigelow quoted in *Vogue*, October 1995.

On the images she creates in her films, Bigelow told Graham Fuller in *Interview* (November 1995); "I simply try to visceralize the psychology of the characters. . . . I create the visuals in a way that seems absolutely inevitable to me. There's nothing aesthetized about them."

"She's great. She's kind of an insane combination of things. She's like both this excited little girl who's beside herself with excitement of being on a film set and then this kind of tiger who is so tough and so fierce and knows exactly what she wants."—Sarah Polley, star of "The Weight of Water" on Kathryn Bigelow.

Peter Bogdanovich

BORN: in Kingston, New York, 07/30/1939

SOMETIMES CREDITED AS:
Derek Thomas

NATIONALITY: American

EDUCATION: Collegiate School, New York, New York; missed graduating for failing to make up an algebra exam

Stella Adler Conservatory, New York, New York, 1954–58

AWARDS: New York Film Critics Circle Award Best Screenwriting "The Last Picture Show" 1971; award shared with Larry McMurtry; tied with Penelope Gilliatt for "Sunday, Bloody Sunday"

British Film Academy Award Best Screenplay "The Last Picture Show" 1972; award shared with Larry McMurtry; tied with Paddy Chayefsky's "The Hospital"

Silver Shell Award (Mar del Plata) "Paper Moon" 1973; award of Spain

Brussels Film Festival Best Director Award "Daisy Miller" 1974

Venice Film Festival Pasinetti Award "Saint Jack" 1979

Venice Film Festival Critics Circle Prize "Saint Jack" 1979

BIOGRAPHY
The Peter Bogdanovich story is a Hollywood tale through and through, replete with memorable associations and fantastic success mitigated by mediocrity, tragedy and bankruptcy. Though his talent was never as great as the hubris that allowed him to believe his own press clippings and compare himself to Orson Welles after critics called his breakout movie, "The Last Picture Show" (1971), "the most impressive work by a young American director since 'Citizen Kane'," he did enjoy a brief run as a 70s wunderkind before slipping into a Welles-like decline that made his earlier words ("I hope I'm not repeating what happened to Orson") almost a self-fulfilling prophecy. In fact, Bogdanovich's eye for younger ladies separated him from perhaps his greatest asset (first wife Polly Platt whose production designs and story input played no small part in his greatest triumphs) and ultimately proved to be his

Achilles' heel to tragedy, while living fabulously above his means and avoiding fiscal responsibilities led to the second of his two bankruptcies.

Bogdanovich was a teenage actor in NYC and directed and produced an Off-Broadway production of Clifford Odets' "The Big Knife" at age 20. He worked as a film critic for such magazines as *Film Culture, Movie* and *Esquire* and began interviewing directors in the early 60s, writing monographs for the Metropolitan Museum of Art on Howard Hawks, Orson Welles and Alfred Hitchcock and publishing elsewhere the results of his talks with other luminaries like John Ford, Fritz Lang and Allan Dwan. Despite his reported megalomania, it is a mark of his humanity that Bogdanovich continued to care about and seek out "old directors" during his glory days of the 70s, compiling a storehouse of anecdotal information about the pioneering days of Hollywood which found its way into "Who the Devil Made It?", a huge and valuable collection of his interviews with 16 great Hollywood directors (including such first-person tidbits as Raoul Walsh's account of stealing John Barrymore's body from a morgue and leaving it for a drunken Errol Flynn to discover on his couch) that was published in 1997.

Fed up with waiting for Broadway to discover his genius, Bogdanovich and wife Platt relocated to Hollywood where he entered film production under the aegis of Roger Corman who hired him (on the strength of his film criticism) as a second unit director on "The Wild Bunch." His next assignment for Corman was to cut some "T & A" footage of Mamie Van Doren into a somber Russian sci-fi movie, resulting in "Voyage to the Planet of Prehistoric Women" (both 1966) and his first film credit. Bogdanovich's feature directing debut came at the helm of another Corman project, "Targets" (1968), in which he and Platt improved on the more pedestrian idea of creating a movie around 20 minutes from the 1963 Corman

stinker "The Terror", coming up instead with an original and brilliant melodrama which relied on less than three minutes of "Terror" footage and gave its star Boris Karloff his best part in years. Karloff, essentially playing himself (in his last American film), is an old veteran of horror flicks, who heroically disarms a sniper near a drive-in theater where one of his movies is playing.

Though a commercial failure, the belated critical success of "Targets" convinced the backers of "Easy Rider" and "Five Easy Pieces" to give him artistic carte blanche on "The Last Picture Show", Larry McMurtry's coming-of-age novel about a group of high school seniors in a dying Texas town during the Korean War. Platt, who had come up with the idea to film the novel, provided the production design, and Bogdanovich, seeing it as a Texas version of Welles' "The Magnificent Ambersons", proceeded to produce a brooding, laconic black and white "masterpiece" that resonated the period. If "Picture Show" was his hymn to Welles, then "What's Up, Doc?" (1972) was his tribute to the screwball comedies of Howard Hawks. Although Barbra Streisand was no Carole Lombard or Katharine Hepburn (both of whom Hawks directed at their madcap apex) and Ryan O'Neal was doing an obvious Cary Grant imitation, "What's Up, Doc?" was a huge success, just the prescription for a country weary of the Vietnam War. Bogdanovich followed with the Depression-era comedy-drama "Paper Moon" (1973), which marked the peak of his filmmaking fame and his last picture with Platt as production designer, By then, his liaison established with Cybill Shepherd during "Picture Show" had kicked her to the curb.

Bogdanovich's fortunes began to flag with the ill-conceived costume drama "Daisy Miller" (1974), which Shepherd nearly single-handedly sunk with her lackluster performance. He rebounded for "Nickelodeon" (1976), recreating the early days of motion pictures, but the slide had already begun;

although he regrouped somewhat for the low budget "Saint Jack" (1979) before the murder of the "love of his life" Dorothy Stratten by her jealous husband sent his life spinning out of control. His failed attempt to distribute "They All Laughed" (1981), his "record of Dorothy," led to his first bankruptcy, and though "Mask" (1985) opened to good reviews, whatever cachet it might have restored dissipated amid reports of his bratty behavior on the set, coupled with revelations of his financial difficulties. Of his subsequent features, "Texasville" (1990), a sequel to "The Last Picture Show" released to mixed reviews, and "Noises Off" (1992), adapted from the hit stage play, did not flop whereas the stench raised by "Illegally Yours" (1988) and "The Thing Called Love" (1993) has pretty much relegated him to the status of TV-movie director.

In a twist stranger than fiction, Bogdanovich married Stratten's half-sister, Louise Hoogstraten, a contemporary of his daughters, on December 30, 1988, and has managed to remain on good terms with both Platt and Shepherd. The director, who has seen his love life thinly, or not so thinly disguised in at least four movies, claims to have "more pictures that I want to make now than I ever did and I'm afraid I won't get to them." Of course, his work at the helm of TV-movies could earn him another shot at directing a feature film, but if he never makes another great movie, he will always have those few exceptional pictures from the glory days of the early 70s to anchor his reputation. "The Last Picture Show", "What's Up, Doc?" and "Paper Moon" stand as monuments to his (and Platt's) genius, but his lasting legacy may be as a link to the "old directors," providing in "Who the Devil Made It?" an indispensable text for anyone interested in Hollywood filmmaking.—Written by Greg Senf

MILESTONES:

1956: Performed with American Shakespeare Festival in Stratford, Connecticut

1958: Acted with New York Shakespeare Festival, NYC

1958: Began writing film criticism for publications including *The New York Times, Esquire* and *Film Culture*

Worked as a film programmer for the New Yorker Theater in Manhattan

1959: Directed and co-produced the Off-Broadway staging of "The Big Knife"

1961–1963: Wrote monographs for the Museum of Modern Art Film Library on Orson Welles, Alfred Hitchcock and Howard Hawks

1964: Moved to California

Hollywood correspondent to Britain's *Movie* magazine

1966: Hired as second unit director by Roger Corman for "Wild Angels"; claims to have done rewrites (uncredited), location scouting and editing; also a bit actor in the rumble (hired after Corman read some of his film criticsm)

1966: First feature film credit (as additional sequence director; credited as Derek Thomas), "Voyage to the Planet of Prehistoric Women"; also narrated; paid by Corman to cut some "T & A" footage of Mamie Van Doren into a somber 1962 Russian pic

1968: Feature directing and producing debut, "Targets" (also writer and actor), starring Boris Karloff and featuring clips from Corman's "The Terror" (1963), starring Karloff; Corman executive produced

1971: Release of first documentary, "Directed by John Ford" (commissioned by the American Film Institute)

1971: Won acclaim for "The Last Picture Show"; received Oscar nominations for Best Director and Best Screenplay (shared with Larry McMurtry); film won Academy Awards for supporting actors Ben Johnson and Cloris Leachman

1972: Produced and directed "What's Up, Doc?", starring Ryan O'Neal and Barbra Streisand

Formed Directors Company with Francis Ford Coppola and William Friedkin

1973: Reteamed with O'Neal for "Paper Moon" (producer, director); 10-year-old Tatum O'Neal picked up Best Supporting Actress Oscar; Directors Company's first offering

1974: Provided companion Cybill Shepherd with starring vehicle, "Daisy Miller", though her hollow performance as an American courting European society in the late 1800s nearly sank this adaptation of a Henry James' story

1976: Wrote and directed the heartfelt valentine to early days of moviemaking, "Nickelodeon", based on reminiscences of such veterns as Raoul Walsh and Alan Dwan; third film with Ryan O'Neal; second with Tatum O'Neal

1979: Made a movie version of Paul Theroux's novel "Saint Jack" for $1.5 million; an absorbing character study that made excellent use of Singapore location

1981: "They All Laughed" released after Dorothy Stratten's murder; wrote screenplay and contributed music, in addition to directing; distributed movie himself

1985: Directed "Mask", starring Cher and Eric Stoltz

1985: Filed for bankruptcy in November

1986: Founded Crescent Moon Productions, Inc., Los Angeles

Weekly film commentator for CBS News program, "CBS This Morning"

1990: Returned to "Last Picture Show" territory with the sequel "Texasville"; produced, directed and wrote screenplay

1992: Came as close as anybody has come to translating a door-slamming British sex farce from the stage to the screen as director of "Noises Off"

1993: Directed "The Thing Called Love", an ordinary drama about a country singer-songwriter who wants to make it big in Nashville; of interest as one of River Phoenix's last films

1995: Helmed "Song of Songs" segment of "Picture Windows" and "A Dime a Dance" segment of "Fallen Angels", both Showtime anthology series; each segment 30 minutes in length

1996: Directed "To Sir With Love II" (CBS), a sequel to 1967 feature film "To Sir With Love", with Sidney Poitier reprising his role

1997: Helmed another CBS movie, "The Price of Heaven"

1997: Directed "Rescuers: Stories of Courage: Two Women" for Showtime; executive produced by Barbra Streisand

1997: Acted in CBS miniseries "Bella Mafia"

1997: Filed Chapter 7 bankruptcy

1998: Appeared as the leader of therapy group in "Mr. Jealousy", co-starring and produced by Eric Stoltz

1998: Made cameo appearance in the feature "54"

2000: Played recurring role of a psychiatrist in the HBO series "The Sopranos"

2001: Returned to filmmaking with "The Cat's Meow", a drama that examined the shooting of silent filmmaker Thomas Ince aboard a yacht owned by William Randolph Hearst; released theatrically in 2002

QUOTES:

"I always looked at them [Bogdanovich and Polly Platt] like a replay of the old saying about Fred Astaire and Ginger Rogers: 'He gave her class, she gave him sex.' With Peter and Polly, it was: 'He gave her the nerve, she gave him all her best ideas.' "—an unidentified former friend of the couple, quoted in *Movieline*, c. 1995.

"I think [Fritz] Lang said he was advised don't have an affair with an actress. And Lang said, 'I didn't listen.' And I thought when I was doing the interview, I didn't know what was in store. That was five years before "The Last Picture Show" (and the affair with Cybill Shepherd). Well, it's an occupational hazard—you're creating somebody in a way."—Peter Bogdanovich to the *Los Angeles Times*, May 15, 1997.

" . . . The generation that we're dealing with in my book, which covers 16 directors who were born between 1885 and 1924, grew up either with no films or silent films. Silent film was a medium in which the goal was to convey everything visually without dialogue and without titles.

"When sound came in, the whole question of 'how do you convey this fleeting thought, this plot point, this nuance of character visually' became, 'What kind of dialogue can we write?' There's the difference right there. It's only because the great veterans of the silent era—most of them—continued well into the talking era that the talkies from '29 to '61 or '62 had as much visual power and impact as they did. Despite the fact that sound or dialogue came to dominate, the most effective moments in all their films are still silent moments, and they knew that."—Bogdanovich in *Moviemaker,* January 1998.

BIBLIOGRAPHY:

"The Cinema of Orson Welles" Peter Bogdanovich, 1961, Film Library of the Museum of Modern Art, distributed by Doubleday

"The Cinema of Howard Hawks" Peter Bogdanovich, 1962, Film Library of the Museum of Modern Art, distributed by Doubleday

"The Cinema of Alfred Hitchcock" Peter Bogdanovich, 1963, Film Library of the Museum of Modern Art, distributed by Doubleday

"John Ford" Peter Bogdanovich, 1968, University of California Press

"Fritz Lang in America" Peter Bogdanovich, 1969, Praeger

"Allan Dwan—The Last Pioneer" Peter Bogdanovich, 1971, Praeger

"Pieces of Time" Peter Bogdanovich, 1973, Arbor House; published in 1975 in England by Allen and Unwin under title "Picture Shows: Peter Bogdanovich on the Movies"; re-issued in 1985

"Bogdanovich's Picture Shows" J. Harris Thomas, 1990, Scarecrow Press

"The Killing of the Unicorn: Dorothy Stratten (1960–1980)" Peter Bogdanovich, 1984, William Morrow

wrote 1991 desk diary based on the book "The White Goddess" and other writings by Robert Graves (published by Overlook Press and distributed by Viking-Penguin)

"This Is Orson Welles" Orson Welles and Peter Bogdanovich; Jonathan Rosenbaum (editor), 1992, HarperCollins; reissued in 1998 with a new introduction by Bogdanovich and published by Da Capo Press

"Picture Shows: The Life and Films of Peter Bogdanovich" Andrew Yule, 1992, Limelight Editions

"A Moment with Miss Gish" Peter Bogdanovich, 1995, Saint Teresa Press

"Who the Devil Made It?: Conversations with Robert Aldrich, George Cukor, Allan Dwan, Howard Hawks, Alfred Hitchcock, Chuck Jones, Fritz Lang, Joseph H. Lewis, Sidney Lumet, Leo McCarey, Otto Preminger, Don Siegel, Josef von Sternberg, Frank Tashlin, Edgar G. Ulmer, Raoul Walsh" Peter Bogdanovich (editor and complier), 1997, Alfred A. Knopf; compilation of interviews with film directors

"Peter Bogdanovich's Movie of the Week: 52 Classic Forms for One Full Year" Peter Bogdanovich, 1999, Ballantine

BORN: in Shepperton, Middlesex, England, 01/18/1933

NATIONALITY: English

EDUCATION: Jesuit Salesian School Chertsey, England

AWARDS: Cannes Film Festival Best Director Award "Leo the Last" 1970

Cannes Film Festival Artistic Contribution to the Poetics of Cinema Award "Excalibur" 1981

Los Angeles Film Critics Association Award Best Film "Hope and Glory" 1987; award shared with co-producer Michael Dryhurst

Los Angeles Film Critics Association Award Best Director "Hope and Glory" 1987

Los Angeles Film Critics Association Award Best Screenplay "Hope and Glory" 1987

National Society of Film Critics Award Best Director "Hope and Glory" 1987

Cannes Film Festival Best Director Award "The General" 1998

Boston Society of Film Critics Award Best Director "The General" 1998

BIOGRAPHY

Renowned for pushing actors (and crews) to their very limit in order to achieve transcendent results, director John Boorman is a committed filmmaker who has refused to settle into fixed genres and remains as commercially unpredictable as he is artistically fascinating. Though he dismisses realism, the location shooting on his movies that pit man against the environment creates conditions that promote it, and his pronounced mystical bent drives him to explore the power of myth in his work. Profoundly influenced by Carl Jung's writings about archetypal imagery, Boorman

has often said that all his films use the Arthurian legend as a template. His filmmaking is a substitute for the experience of adventure, a quest, and he has constantly put himself in situations of physical and mental hardship to satisfy a longing for a challenge. Abstract, dreamlike and surrealistic, his movies have consistently displayed a cinematic virtuosity that sometimes triumphs over substance.

Boorman demonstrated an early entrepreneurial spirit by leaving school at the age of 16 and setting up a successful dry cleaning business with a friend. He also worked as a film critic on the side, and though his involvement with dry-cleaning ended when he entered military service, Boorman continued to pursue journalism. He joined the newly-formed Independent Television News (ITN) in 1955 as an assistant film editor and later produced documentaries for Southern Television. Boorman's early dissatisfaction with realistic documentaries led him while head of the BBC's Bristol Film Unit to begin making poetic or impressionistic documentaries, films about atmosphere and the search for cinematic moments that rejected the strictly journalistic approach. He was responsible for two highly-acclaimed documentary series while there, "Citizen 63" (1963) and the even more ambitious "The Newcomers", a six-part study of a newly married Bristol couple and their friends with "an Antonioni-esque flourish in which twelve cameras filmed what went on in Bristol in the last half-hour as the birth of twins took place."

Boorman's first feature, "Having a Wild Weekend" (1965), was a competent, exuberant 1960s musical featuring the Dave Clark Five, which unsuccessfully attempted to duplicate the success of the Beatles/Richard Lester groundbreaker "A Hard Day's Night" (1964). After "The Great Director" (1966), a documentary on D.W.

Griffith for the BBC, Boorman moved to the USA and directed the genre-bending "Point Blank" (1967), a taut, violent thriller marked by a complex flashback narrative structure. Starring a palpably sexy Angie Dickinson and a somnambulistically intense Lee Marvin, the film exhibited a sustained brilliance of camerawork and editing no one expected from the sophomore director. Ignored at the box office, it has since acquired the status of masterpiece, one many critics feel the director has not surpassed. Marvin played to perfection the archetypal Boorman protagonist, a disruptive loner with a lip-curling distaste for all forms of authority, and the picture managed to bridge the two halves of his future oeuvre, functioning as a stylized, artificial universe of the mind as well as depicting the struggle with nature.

"Hell in the Pacific" (1968), also starred Marvin and mined the director's WWII experiences, which included guilt about surviving an ambush on Saipan that wiped out his entire platoon except for one other person. Playing a stranded flyer on a tiny Pacific island, Marvin encounters a Japanese naval officer (Toshiro Mifune), and the two first stalk each other, then come to a temporary truce before the clash of cultures drives them apart again. The film approached the completely silent movie Boorman had hoped to make after his Griffith documentary. Most critics believed he had beat his anti-war message to death, but some praised his ability to sustain a two-character story-line over feature length. For "Leo the Last" (1970), the director upped the allegorical content to a level considered excessive by most with his story of an expatriate prince (Marcello Mastroianni) who eventually becomes emotionally involved with his poor black neighbors and joins them in their struggle against heartless property speculators. The picture brought Boorman the director's award at Cannes and was a hit in France but flopped in Britain and America.

Boorman made a strong recovery with "Deliverance" (1972), in which four Atlanta businessmen take off on a weekend canoe trip down a wild (but soon to be tamed) Appalachian river, deliberately pitting themselves against the imperiled wilderness. The adventure becomes a nightmare when a couple of hate-filled, near-mutant hillbillies sodomize one of the travelers (Ned Beatty), turning the game into a real struggle for survival and revenge. Creative (and personal) differences with screenwriter James Dickey (who had adapted his novel and also played the sheriff in the film) led Boorman to ban the writer from the set, protecting his vision for a far more ambiguous ending than exists in the book. On the level of allegory, the director may have erred by again hammering his message relentlessly home, and as for complex character studies, he was content (as always) to examine archetypes, not individuals. However, the visual account of the journey and the irrational hostility of the hill people was stunning, thanks to outstanding cinematography (featuring extremely long takes) by Vilmos Zsigmond, guaranteeing its box-office success.

Boorman's next two films missed the mark. The sci-fi pic "Zardoz" (1974) earned kudos for its special effects but plunged into myth without creating a satisfactory context for it, leaving audiences confused. On the other hand, "Exorcist II: The Heretic" (1977) was a fiasco of monumental proportions, containing some decent f/x but offering nothing in the way of its predecessor's strong suits (like a somewhat believable story). Of course "The Exorcist" (1972) was a tough act to follow, but Boorman's ambitious, exclusively visual film put people off, though some critics began seeing it in a more forgiving context once the stench of its scornful reception died down. The director turned to the Arthurian legend for his next picture, writing (with Rospo Pallenberg) "Excalibur" (1981), based mostly on Thomas Malory's "Le Morte d'Arthur." Although the cast included Nicol Williamson (Merlin) and

Helen Mirren (Morgana), Boorman for the most part went with lesser known actors, beginning a practice he would follow thereafter to ensure that no star would ever be bigger than the picture.

Although "Excalibur" struck some critics as humorless, thematically heavy-handed and overlong, it was still a spellbinding, sexually aware rendition of the King Arthur legend by a stylish filmmaker working at the peak of his powers. Effectively evoking the dreams, the magic, the imagery and the romance, Boorman fashioned arguably the best movie about Camelot, and his next film, "The Emerald Forest" (1985), followed in logical progression exploring the same thematic territory. The story (written by Pallenberg) of a white child raised for ten years by a primitive Amazon tribe provided his biggest challenge since "Deliverance" and a superb showcase for his virtuosity with the camera. Shot at great hardship on location along the Xingu River in Brazil, it starred the director's son Charley and Powers Boothe as his engineer father who finds him after a ten-year search. Initiated in the tribe's shamanistic rituals, Boothe recognizes the barrenness and cruelty of his own culture, and after father and son destroy a dam together that threatens the rain forest, they part, the boy remaining with his adoptive people. Giving the impression it was every bit as suspenseful to make as watch, it was his biggest box-office success in more than a decade.

In a real change of pace, Boorman followed with the most conventional film of his career, the delightful, autobiographical "Hope and Glory" (1987), which captured a child's innocent delight at the disruption of the Blitz mirroring the director's own experience of living through the London air raids of World War II. Although there were a few examples of the visual flourishes expected from Boorman, he remained content to tell a simple, loving story, and audiences responded to the material. That success, however, would be his last for more than a decade. "Where the Heart Is" (1990), a disappointing farce about 80s values with faint echoes of Shakespeare's "King Lear" co-written with his daughter Telsche, was just a little too outlandish to take seriously, and he missed again with "Beyond Rangoon" (1995), an examination of the political intrigues in 1980s Burma (Myanmar). The picture fell short in its analysis of the little-known political situation, but Boorman and production designer Anthony Pratt (in the pair's fifth collaboration) were right at home capturing the tropical milieu and delivering exciting large-scale action sequences. The film's biggest negative was leading lady Patricia Arquette's inability to carry the ball, though all characters were uniformly one-dimensional.

While Lady Luck refused to smile on his large screen projects, Boorman delivered two very fine efforts for TV. First, he made the remarkable one-hour film "I Dreamt I Woke Up" (1991), a personal essay-meditation on cinema, landscape and myth for a BBC Scotland series, "The Director's Place", and on the other side of the pond, he directed the "Two Nudes Bathing" segment of Showtime's "Picture Windows" (1995). Pouring out all his love for his adopted homeland Ireland, the director startlingly rejuvenated his career with "The General" (1998), a biopic of Irish crime lord Martin Cahill (a perfect Boorman protagonist). Working in black-and-white for the first time since his feature debut, he reestablished himself as a major creative force in critics' eyes, winning the Best Director Award at Cannes, though commercially the picture was primarily a specialty item for urban audiences and movie buffs. Director of photography Seamus Deasy contributed mightily with his widescreen lensing, as did Ron Davis, his editor since "The Emerald Forest", but the real star was Boorman, rediscovering the vitality and freshness of his earlier work and reasserting himself as a unique, visionary filmmaker.—Written by Greg Senf

MILESTONES:

Left school at age 16, going into partnership with a friend to open what became a thriving dry-cleaning business

1951–1953: Served in British Army

1955: Began working for Independent Television News as assitant editor; while there launched ITN magazine program "Day by Day"

1958: Moved to Southern Television; began producing documentaries

1960: Moved to BBC-TV, where he became head of the Documentary Film Unit in Bristol

1965: Feature film directing debut, "Having a Wild Weekend/Catch Us If You Can"

1966: Made documentary on D.W. Griffith, "The Great Director," for BBC

1967: US directing debut, "Point Blank", a gangster film starring Lee Marvin; subsequently hailed as a genre landmark

1968: Reteamed with Marvin for "Hell in the Pacific", also starring Toshiro Mifune

1969: First screenwriting credit, "Leo the Last", starring Marcello Mastroianni; also directed; a hit in France, it was a box-office disaster in Britain and America

1972: Made a strong recovery directing "Deliverance"; first credit as producer but would produce all pictures from here on; received two Oscar nominations for Best Picture and Best Director

1974: Wrote and directed "Zardoz", an unconventional piece of science fiction starring Sean Connery

Served as Chairman of the National Film Studios of Ireland

1977: Bombed horribly with sequel, "Exorcist II: The Heretic"

1981: Achieved dream project, a film based on Arthurian legend, "Excaliber"

1985: Had box office success with "The Emerald Forest"; completely convincing performance by director's son Charley as the kidnapped son raised by rain forest Indians

1985: Became governor of British Film Institute

1987: Scored a hit with "Hope and Glory", an autobiographical tale of growing up in Britain during "the Blitz"; served as narrator, in addition to directing, writing and producing; received three Oscar nominations

1990: Became a co-editor and contributor to *Projections*, an annual British film journal (date approximate)

1991: Made a remarkable one-hour film, "I Dreamt I Woke Up", a personal essay-meditation on cinema, landscape and myth made for a BBC Scotland series, "The Director's Place"

1994: Named Commander of the British Empire

1995: Returned to tropical environs and political realities for "Beyond Rangoon"

1995: US TV directing debut, "Two Nudes Bathing" segment of Showtime's "Picture Windows"

1998: Named Best Director at Cannes Filme Festival for "The General" (also wrote screenplay); black-and-white film (first since his debut feature) reteamed him with actor Jon Voight

1998: Helmed "Lee Marvin: A Personal Portrait by John Boorman" (aired on AMC in November)

2001: Helmed "The Tailor of Panama" based on the John Le Carre novel

Produced and directed "Knight's Castle" (lensed 2002)

QUOTES:

"All my films use the Arthurian legend as a template; it happens to a large extent unconsciously."—John Boorman in *Film Comment*, July–August 1995.

"People often ask me, 'Why do you take these difficult projects—the jungle, battling rivers?' and I give various answers. But the real answer is that the only way I'm able to achieve momentarily this kind of transcendence we're talking about is when I'm making a picture in extraordinarily difficult circumstances, when

I'm extended to the very limits. Then, from time to time, I'm able to reach that condition where I'm not looking at myself; I'm unself-conscious and fearless. That to me is the ultimate joy of filmmaking, when I occasionally reach that level.

"I had spent my childhood on rivers and with boats, so I handle these things fairly well, but when we started shooting the canoe sequence in 'Deliverance', when it came to it to get these actors into these boats and do this stuff, I reached a level where I could canoe those rapids myself with absolute confidence. I just knew I could do it and I did. I would always canoe the stretch of rapids first so that the actors could see that even I could do it. That's one example."—John Boorman, interviewed by Gavin Smith, Film Society of Lincoln Center (1995).

Asked whether he was flattered or agitated by the Mel Gibson vehicle "Payback" (1999), which is a remake of his "Point Blank": "When I was trying to get 'Point Blank' made with Lee Marvin, I had the producer send him the script and when I met with him (afterward), I said, 'What do you think?' He said, 'It's terrible, but the character's fascinating.' We had a number of meetings and one night, about two in the morning, he said to me, 'Well, here's what I'll do. I'll do the picture with you on one condition . . .' He took the script and threw it out the window, and it fell to the ground where, apparently Mel Gibson picked it up.

"I take the view that I made the remake and Mel Gibson is doing the original."—John Boorman to *Los Angeles Times*, May 20, 1998.

On James Dickey during the "Deliverance" shoot: "He was drunk all the time, and he was losing his distinction between fact and fantasy. He said to me, 'Everything in that book happened to me.' Well, when I saw him get into a canoe, I realized it wasn't true."—Boorman in GQ, October 1998.

"I prepared that picture ['A Simple Plan']. I cast it. I did rewrites with the author . . . and then Paramount canceled it two weeks before we were to start shooting. . . . the studio decided to make 'A Simple Plan' after all, and then decided to start production much earlier than I could possibly do it, and they brought in someone else to direct it [Sam Raimi]. He only had four weeks to prepare. He used my cast, my script, my locations . . . People say a director has done 70 percent of the work on a film before shooting starts—so I feel it's as much my film as his."—John Boorman quoted by Marilyn Beck and Stacy Jenel Smith in their syndicated column "Hollywood", October 14, 1998.

BIBLIOGRAPHY:
"Zardoz" John Boorman (with Bill Stair), 1974; novel based on the movie

"Money into Light" John Boorman; account of the filming of "The Emerald Forest"; published in US under title "The Emerald Forest Diary"

BORN: in Radcliffe, England, 10/20/1956

SOMETIMES CREDITED AS:
Daniel Boyle

NATIONALITY: English

EDUCATION: attended a Salesian school in England

AWARD: BAFTA Alexander Korda Award for Outstanding British Film "Shallow Grave" 1995

BIOGRAPHY

A product of a working-class background in Manchester, England, Danny Boyle came out of both politically-charged and mainstream theater to make his feature directing debut with "Shallow Grave" (1994), an intense study of how greed can affect people who are otherwise chums. Boyle claims not to have been in a theater until he was 18, yet by the time he was in his 20s he was already directing at the Joint Stock Theatre Company, known in Britain for being both controversial and for producing new and cutting edge plays. In 1982, he moved to London's Royal Court Theatre Upstairs as artistic director, in charge of putting on smaller productions. During this period, he directed "The Genius" by Howard Brenton and "Saved" by Edward Bond, which won a coveted *Time Out* Award. Boyle became deputy director of the Royal Court Theatre (main stage) in 1985, serving in that capacity until 1987 when he made the leap into TV. Other productions he directed included "The Pretenders" and "The Last Days of Don Juan" for the Royal Shakespeare Company.

Boyle's work in TV was mostly in drama, including the 1991 "Masonic Mysteries" installment of the "Inspector Morse" series, in which Morse is arrested on suspicion of murder. Boyle also directed the TV-movies "The DeLorean Tapes" and "For the Greater Good" and produced the controversial "Elephant" by Alan Clarke for the BBC. His series credits include "Mr. Wroe's Virgins."

Collecting about $1.5 million from Channel 4 and a Glasgow Film Grant, Boyle went on to make "Shallow Grave" from a script by John Hodge. From its kinetic opening shots through its denouement, the film announced the arrival of a major talent. Boyle assuredly handled the black comedy of the script with a stylized theatricality that has become a hallmark of his features. The performances of the lead trio of actors (Kerry Fox, Ewan McGregor and Christopher Eccleston) blossom and grow; at the start of the movie, they act almost as one, but as the story progresses each becomes a defined personality. Boyle managed to create a number of brilliantly shot comic set pieces (including a series of interview sessions with prospective roommates and the disposal of a dead body). The feature's violent undercurrents are also successfully navigated up to its tour-de-force surprise ending. Aiding in the film's success is its production design (especially the apartment that is its primary setting), editing and atmospheric score. Boyle won a Silver Shell at the San Sebastian Film Festival and the Golden Hitchcock at Dinard for Best Direction.

Reteaming with screenwriter Hodge and producer Andrew Macdonald, Boyle directed "Trainspotting" (1996), a look at the drug-infested underworld of Glasgow. Again employing a hyper-active camera and working with many of the same behind-the-scenes personnel, the director established an unique visual style that matched the storylines. Each set piece successfully commented on and enhanced the characters and their situations; not only did the film depict the addicts it captured the complexity of addiction itself. There are a number of memorable scenes, most involving Ewan McGregor's Renton; notably a sequence in which he seemingly dives head first into a public toilet and his harrowing attempt to quit heroin cold turkey. In the latter sequence, the room takes on a fantastic life and character of its own. As with "Shallow Grave", Boyle, abetted by a cast that included Jonny Lee Miller, Robert Carlyle and Ewen Bremner, created a world populated with venal, yet oddly, charismatic characters. A box-office hit in the UK and a cult hit in the USA, it firmly established the creative team in films.

In fact, Boyle has reportedly spurned offers from Hollywood (including a chance to helm the fourth installment in the "Alien" series) to concentrate on his own vision. His third feature, the oddball comedy "A Life Less Ordinary" (1997), once again teamed him with Hodge and Macdonald and also featured McGregor. This time the actor was cast as a man who takes revenge on his employer by kidnapping the employer's daughter (Cameron Diaz).

MILESTONES:

Raised in Radcliffe, Lancashire, England

Began career as theater director with the radical Joint Stock Company

1982–1985: Served as artistic director of the Royal Court Theatre Upstairs

Was deputy director of the Royal Court Theatre

1991: Directed "Inspector Morse: Masonic Mysteries" for TV

1993: Directed the BBC series "Mr. Wroe's Virgins"

1994: Feature directorial debut, "Shallow Grave", written by John Hodge and produced by Andrew Macdonald

1996: Made second feature, "Trainspotting", adapted by Hodge and produced by Macdonald

1997: Directed "A Life Less Ordinary", scripted by Hodge and produced by Macdonald

2000: Helmed "The Beach", starring Leonardo DiCaprio and Virginie Ledoyen; scripted by Hodge and produced by Macdonald

2003: Directed the feature "28 Days Later," which co-starred Brendan Gleeson and Cillian Murphy

AFFILIATION: Raised Roman Catholic

QUOTES:

"I get scripts written by Americans that are technically brilliant, but there is something unconfident about the writing. Despite their technical expertise, they know that [the script they are writing] for a Hollywood producer or star will be rewritten by others."—Danny Boyle in *Screen International*, January 27–February 2, 1995.

"When I was a kid I used to go to cinemas, and I was never in a theatre until I was 18. Ironically, theatre seemed a much easier and more accessible way of getting into the arts, so that's how I started . . . As a director, your ultimate goal is to make something for the big screen, because it tests your craft more than any other way."—Danny Boyle.

"It's about being a transgressor. It's about doing something that everybody says will kill you—YOU WILL KILL YOURSELF. And the thing that nobody understands is, it's not just that you don't hear that message, it's just that it's irrelevent. The film ["Trainspotting"] isn't about heroin. It's about an attitude, and that's why we wanted the film to pulse, to pulse like you DO in your twenties, before you get ground down by whatever grinds you down—be it heroin or all the other things that wipe you out."—Boyle quoted in *New York*, July 15, 1996.

BORN: in Bressuire, France, 07/13/1948

NATIONALITY: French

EDUCATION: passed bacclaureate degree in 1964

AWARD: Berlin Film Festival Manfred-Salzberger Film Prize "A Ma soeur!" 2001

BIOGRAPHY

Dubbed "the bad girl intellectual of French cinema" by Amy Taubin of the *Village Voice*, writer-director Catherine Breillat seemingly has courted controversy since her career began. While still in her teens, she published her first novel, the erotic "L'Homme facile", which was not sold to anyone in France under 18 years of age. Breillat's film acting debut was alongside her sister Marie-Helene in 1973's frank and groundbreaking "Last Tango in Paris", helmed by Bernardo Bertolucci. Her own feature directorial debut based on one of her novels, "Une Vraie jeune fille", was originally shot in 1975 but through a combination of the bankruptcy of her producers and its shocking content that caused it to be banned, the film did not receive a release for 25 years. As with several of her works, "Une Vraie jeune fille" centered on the sexual coming of age of a woman—here a 14-year-old boarding school student. Over the next decade, Breillat continued to make her mark as both a fiction writer and in films. She penned the story for and contributed to the script of "Police" (1985), a cop drama-cum-romance starring Gerard Depardieu and Sophie Marceau.

Breillat gained a measure of international attention with "36 Fillette" (1988), yet another finely observed tale of a teenage girl's awakening to her sensuality. She has stated that her inspiration for this film came from repeated viewings of the 1956 movie "Baby Doll." For Breillat, one of the central issues in the male-female dynamic stems from the manner in which a woman must learn harsh truths about sexuality. "In love, the respect of a man is the worst humiliation a girl could experience," she has written. Indeed, one of the recurring motifs in her work is the heroine's sense of shame regarding her sexuality. Breillat revisited it in "Parfait amour!" (1996) and more baldly in "Romance" (1999). The latter proved quite controversial as it straddled the fine line between art and pornography. The filmmaker's more untraditional approach to her material (which hearkens back to Godard and Cassavetes) set her apart from most of her contemporaries. In her personal and idiosyncratic features, Breillat continued to push the envelope. "A ma soeur/Fat Girl" (2001) revisited was yet another graphic exploration of an underage girl's attempt to lose her virginity. When it screened at Berlin, audiences and critics were divided in reaction to it, with some hailing the film while others feeling the director had begun to repeat herself and ran the risk of falling into self-parody.

MILESTONES:

1973: Played Mouchette in "Last Tango in Paris"; sister Marie-Helene Breillat played Monique

1975: First film as screenwriter, "Catherine et Cie/Catherine & Co."

1975: Feature directorial debut, "Une Vraie jeune fille"; also wrote script based on her novel "La Soupirail"

1983: Wrote English-language adaptation of Fellini's "And the Ship Sails On"

1985: Co-scripted and provided the original

story for "Police", a well-received romance-cum-cop drama directed by Maurice Pialat

1988: Engendered controversy and divided critics with "36 Fillette", which detailed the sexual coming of age of a chunky teenage girl

1991: Wrote and directed "Sale comme un ange/Dirty Like an Angel", about policemen partners, one of whom may be dying

1996: Directed and wrote "Parfait amour!/Perfect Love!", a disturbing examination of a May–December relationship that ends in murder

1999: Courted controversy with the sexually explicit "Romance", a drama centered on one woman's exploration of her sensual nature

2000: Contributed to the screenplay of "Selon Matthieu/According to Matthew"

2001: Garnered attention and praise for "A mon soeur!/Fat Girl", which centered on a teenager losing her virginity; screened at Berlin

QUOTES:

"A script is only the 'bare bones' of a film, because what matters in the most important moments is silence. Words are there to fill in the most violent exchanges between the characters."—Catherine Breillat quoted in *Positif*, June 1988.

"Women are not simple human beings. They are a lot more complicated than men. In violence, they have no physical strength, but they have incredible mental strength. When a woman becomes free, a liberated woman, what she actually does is free herself of all her alienation. A great tenderness and weakness often coexist in women who are emotional, confused, and fragile. At the same time, they are capable of tremendous violence and aggression in their relationships, in their love life as well, and that includes physical and romantic relationships. Men cannot portray women like that, so it's fairly new to see that in film."—Breillat in an interview in *Cineaste*, Volume XXV, No. 1.

" . . . movies are both an industry and an art. Sometimes, the industry moves closer to the art, sometimes the art moves closer to the industry. You can't work in film without butting up against this reality. The only thing I'm against is the idea that a film is simply a replica of what's on the page. The actual shooting of the film seems like a formality, as if creation doesn't take place on the set. Instead, it happens everywhere else—on paper, in the writer's den, in the producer's office, over lunch, whatever, but not on the set. In this view, the filmmaker is something of a pitiful employee who's simply there to obey orders. It's a horrible way of thinking about film-making. I try not to believe in the dominance of the screenplay. It makes for very boring cinema."—Breillat quoted at IndieWire.com, September 23, 1999.

BIBLIOGRAPHY:

"L'Homme facile" Catherine Breillat, 1967; novel; English title was "A Man for the Asking"

"Le Silence, apres . . . " Catherine Breillat, 1970; second novel

"La Soupirail" Catherine Breillat, 1974; third novel; made into a film by Breillat in 1975 as "Une Vraie jeune fille"

"Police: roman" Catherine Breillat novel

BORN: in Bromont-Lamothe, Puy-de-Dome, France, 09/25/1901

DEATH: in Paris, France, 12/18/1999

NATIONALITY: French

EDUCATION: Lycee Lakanal Sceaux, France, classics and philosophy attended from ages 13–17
at University studied classics and philosophy

AWARDS: Grand Prix du Cinema Francais "Les Anges du peche" 1943
Venice Film Festival Grand Prize "Le Journal d'un cure de campagne/Diary of a Country Priest" 1951; one of three films cited
Prix Louis Delluc "Diary of a Country Priest" 1951
Cannes Film Festival Best Director Award "Un condamne a mort s'est echappe/A Man Escaped" 1956
Cannes Film Festival Special Jury Prize "The Trial of Joan of Arc" 1962
Venice Film Festival Special Jury Prize "Au Hasard Balthazar" 1966; one of three films cited
Cannes Film Festival Special Homage Award 1967
British Film Institute Award for Most Original Film "Quatre nuits d'un reveur/Four Nights of a Dreamer" 1971
Cannes Film Festival FIPRESCI Prize "Lancelot of the Lake" 1974
National Society of Film Critics Award Best Director "L'Argent" 1983
Cannes Film Festival Grand Prix du Cinema de Creation "L'Argent" 1983
Felix Lifetime Achievement 1994

BIOGRAPHY

Bresson originally pursued a career as a painter but turned to film in the early 1930s, gaining his first experience as a script consultant on "C'etait un musicien" (1933), directed by Frederic Zelnick and Maurice Gleize. In between other, unexceptional assignments as a screenwriter, he made a medium-length film, the long-lost "Les Affaires publiques", in 1934. During WWII, Bresson was a prisoner of war from June 1940 to April 1941—an experience which profoundly marked his subsequent work in the cinema.

Bresson made a stunning feature debut with "Les Anges du peche" (1943), scripted by him and with dialogue by Jean Giraudoux. A melodramatic tale of a convent novice who sacrifices her life to save the soul of a murderer, it nevertheless defined the thematic territory of grace and redemption which Bresson would continue to explore. Like "Les Anges", "Les Dames du Bois de Boulogne" (1945) featured dramatic cinematography, atmospheric music and professional actors—all elements which Bresson would later shun in his quest to forge a purer cinematic art.

Bresson's next three films marked the development of his own personal, mature style. "Diary of a Country Priest" (1950) is an account, adapted from the 1936 novel by Georges Bernanos, of an awkward young priest who saves the souls of others while he himself is dying of stomach cancer. "A Man Escaped" (1956) is based on the real-life experiences of Andre Devigny, a French resistance fighter imprisoned by the Nazis. "Pickpocket" (1959) tells of a lonely young thief who finds redemption in love.

All three films are narrated in the first person and bear what are now known as the hallmarks of Bresson's work: a spare, abstract visual style which concentrates on objective details to create a sense of timelessness; natural sounds in place of mood-creating music; elliptical narrative structures which preclude suspense and invoke spiritual isolation; an absence of character psychology; and nonprofessional actors giving flat, expressionless "performances." ("What I am seeking is not so much expression by means of gesture, speech, mimicry, but expression by means of the rhythm and combination of images, by position, relation and number," Bresson explained.)

Perhaps the ultimate expression of Bresson's unique cinematic voice is "The Trial of Joan of Arc" (1962) which, with his films of the late 1950s, was much admired by the filmmakers of the New Wave. In the austere documenting of Joan's imprisonment and trial, physical objects—chains, stones, walls, windows—become metaphors for her spiritual isolation and sounds—the scratching of a pen during her hearing—contribute to the minimalist musicality of the experience.

In "Balthazar" and "Mouchette" (both 1966), a mule and a young girl, respectively, endure the indignities, cruelty and callousness of existence. Balthazar is exploited and mistreated by a series of owners before finding peace in a memorable death sequence, on a hillside surrounded by sheep. Mouchette drowns herself to escape the abuse and humiliation she suffers at the hands of her parents. (The film was Bresson's second to be adapted from the work of Bernanos.)

"Une Femme douce" (1969) tracks the failure of a marriage between an inquisitive, self-educated wife interested in the arts and archeology and a husband who values money and security. The wife takes her own life, marking the director's increasing concern with suicide; he went on to articulate the theme in such color films as "Four Nights of a Dreamer" (1971).

In "Lancelot du Lac" (1974), Bresson found his most fitting subject matter since "Joan of Arc". Lancelot and the Knights of King Arthur undertake a fruitless search for the Holy Grail in an age of chivalry defined by clumsy, episodic bloodshed, cumbersome armor and jealous infighting. At the film's conclusion Lancelot's horse, an arrow impaled in its neck, surveys the human carnage, as if recognizing a futility and horror to which the humans are blind.

Bresson's last masterpiece was "L'Argent" (1983). Chance events lead to the arrest of Yvon, an oil delivery man, for using counterfeit bills palmed off on him by a store clerk (perjury and a bribe protect the guilty). Now unemployable, Yvon commits a crime. While in jail his daughter dies, his wife abandons him and he unsuccessfuly attempts suicide. Upon release Yvon kills the family of an old lady who shelters him in a horrific ax-murder, for which Bresson refuses to provide a motivation.

No filmmaker has had a darker vision of man's inhumanity to man, nor has portrayed it with such consistent and remarkable style. In 1975, Bresson published "Notes on Cinematography", an apologia for his singular cinematic vision which argues that film is a blend of music and painting rather than—as traditionally understood—theater and photography.

MILESTONES:

1933: First film credit as script consultant, "C'etait un musicien"

1934: First short film as director, writer, co-photographer and editor, "Les Affaires Publiques"

1939: Joined French army

1940–1941: Spent year in German POW camp

1943: Feature film directing debut (also co-writer), "Les Anges du peche"

AFFILIATION: Roman Catholic

BIBLIOGRAPHY:

"Notes on Cinematography" Robert Bresson, 1975; theory of film

BORN: Albert Einstein in Los Angeles, California, 07/22/1947

SOMETIMES CREDITED AS:
A. Brooks

NATIONALITY: American

EDUCATION: Carnegie Institute of Technology Pittsburgh, Pennsylvania, 1966–68; school later renamed Carnegie-Mellon University; dropped out after attending for two years on an acting scolarship

AWARDS: New York Film Critics Circle Award Best Screenplay "Mother" 1996; award shared with co-writer Monica Johnson

National Society of Film Critics Award Best Screenplay "Mother" 1996; award shared with co-writer Monica Johnson

NATO/ShoWest Screenwriters of the Year 1997; award shared with Monica Johnson; presented by the National Association of Theater Owners

BIOGRAPHY
Called the West Coast Woody Allen for his cerebral brand of comedy, actor-writer-director Albert Brooks turned down the Billy Crystal role in "When Harry Met Sally . . . " (1989) precisely because "it read to me like a Woody Allen movie, verbatim. And I thought that was not something I should be in." Though both are tortured insecure geniuses of Hebraic descent who changed their names and abandoned brilliant stand-up careers to make movies, Brooks is by far the slower worker, helming on average only one movie every 3.5 years (six in 21 years), compared to Allen who cranks out at least one picture per annum. Yet, Brooks wouldn't have it any other way. As an actor, he's rejected countless projects from "Dragnet" (1987) and "Midnight Run" (1988) to "Sgt. Bilko" (1996). After pitching a sitcom ("Our Man in Rattan") to Michael Eisner at ABC in 1976, calling for him to play a lowly TV correspondent in the armpit of Africa, he was just about to sign on the dotted line when Eisner's "Albert, where do you see the character in seven years?" elicited "Suicide. I don't think I'm ready to do this." He also turned down Lorne Michaels' offer to be the sole host of the original "Saturday Night Live" (NBC) in 1975.

Brooks' life has been a comedy act since coming into the world christened Albert Einstein. His father (who couldn't resist the gag of saddling him with the famous scientist's moniker) was Eddie Cantor's zany sidekick Harry Einstein, and growing up around the dinner table, Albert had to compete for laughs with his dad and two older brothers, one of whom (Bob) went on to become daredevil comedian Super Dave Osborne. The funniest kid in his class at Beverly Hills High, where he acted in plays with fellow classmate Richard Dreyfuss, Brooks also had a knack for cracking up adults at the tender age of 16 as director Rob Reiner recalled: "He'd come to our house, and my father [Carl Reiner] would be convulsing from his routines." Soon after leaving college to take his shtick on the road, he made his TV debut in 1968, performing his act on "The Steve Allen Show", and his manic, sardonic wit and satirical stylings quickly made him a regular on NBC's "The Tonight Show." Two acclaimed comedy albums followed, but Brooks found the life of a comic wanting, the constant repetition of material anathema, and eventually walked out on a thriving career in the 70s.

Having already picked up his first TV writing credit for the ABC variety series "Turn On" in 1969, Brooks tried his hand at directing with a segment for PBS' "The Great American Dream Machine" (1971), adapting an essay he wrote for *Esquire* magazine entitled "Albert Brooks's Famous School for Comedians." Despite turning down the offer to host "SNL", he did write, direct and produce six short films for its first season. After making his feature acting debut as a presidential campaign co-worker of Cybill Shepherd in Martin Scorsese's riveting "Taxi Driver" (1976), Brooks took his first stab at full-length helming with "Real Life" (1978), a satirical take on the PBS series "An American Family", in which he starred as a documentarian who, in his search for the typical American family, alters real events to make them more cinematic. Though his first feature did not sustain its comic premise as well as his hilarious short subjects, it struck a balance between humor and social criticism that remains the hallmark of his work. He followed with "Modern Romance" (1981), an extremely funny look at one neurotic man's (Brooks) attempt to find love in Hollywood, complete with wonderful in-jokes about moviemaking.

Finding strong and funny identification with the urban impulse to chuck the rat race and hit the open road, Brooks' "Lost in America" (1985) brought him many new fans who had missed his first two features. Its meticulous observation of two disillusioned yuppies (Brooks and Julie Hagerty) who liquidate their assets and buy a Winnebago ("We'll be like 'Easy Rider'—with a nest egg") struck a chord with people who secretly longed to act on youthful, irresponsible fantasies to drop out of society. Across the country they go, experiencing one misadventure after another in their ill-fated attempt to "find themselves," and by the time Brooks takes a job as an Arizona school crossing guard and Hagerty is slinging hamburgers, the inevitable and sobering "sellout" is just around the corner. Co-writer Monica Johnson, director of photography Eric Saarinen and editor David Finfer had all worked on the previous features, and the

well-oiled unit delivered Brooks' best film to that time. His fourth feature, "Defending Your Life" (1991), picked up where "Lost in America" left off, with Brooks as a self-obsessed, recently deceased executive who, having never accomplished his life goals, must face his past in order to continue in the after-life. Boasting enjoyably broad performances by Brooks and Rip Torn, the one-joke script did wear thin but was still hard to dislike.

Although Brooks the auteur stars in his own pictures, he does act for other directors. For his writer-director friend James L. Brooks (no relation), he played the talented but luckless TV journalist who sweats a lot in "Broadcast News" (1987), earning a Best Supporting Actor Oscar nomination and raising his public profile a notch higher. He also provided a voice for Brooks' Oscar-winning Best Picture "Terms of Endearment" (1983) and portrayed a strident Hollywood producer of slick action films (à la Joel Silver) in "I'll Do Anything" (1994), most notable for having been filmed as a musical before test audience reactions convinced the director to pull the music. That year also saw Brooks star as "The Scout", an old Andrew Bergman baseball script which he and Johnson "doctored" for director Michael Ritchie. Unfortunately, the major league baseball strike conspired to sink the slim commercial chances of a comedy that never quite recovered from its detour to drama. Brooks also acted in Sidney Lumet's "Critical Care" (1997, as a 65-year-old alcoholic surgeon) and Steven Soderbergh's "Out of Sight" (1998, as a Wall Street guy put in prison), not to mention voicing the suicidal tiger of the live-action "Dr. Dolittle" (also 1997).

It was five years between directing efforts but well worth the wait when Brooks finally delivered "Mother" (1996), co-writing (with Johnson) and starring in the comedy about a twice-divorced man who decides to move back in with Mom (Debbie Reynolds in a well-modulated, non-jokey performance), attempting to understand the root of his problems with women. Brooks considered Nancy Reagan, Doris Day and Esther Williams for the eponymous part before finally choosing Reynolds, who put her Vegas career on hold to play her first significant film role in 25 years. Three years later, he helmed, co-wrote (again with Johnson) and starred as a Hollywood screenwriter struggling for inspiration who meets "The Muse" (Sharon Stone), a romantic comedy that also featured Jeff Bridges and Andie MacDowell plus a slew of celebrity cameos, including Martin Scorsese, Rob Reiner and James Cameron. Brooks once said, "Being a screenwriter in Hollywood is like being a eunuch at an orgy. Worse, actually, at least the eunuch is allowed to watch." By directing his own scripts, he has avoided such powerlessness and guaranteed that his fractured vision reaches the audience in tact.

Stepping outside of his own genre again, Brooks received an abaundance of critical praise for his turn in director Christine Lahti's unassuming indie debut "My First Mister" (2001), playing a finicky clothing store owner who embarks on a relationship with a 17-year-old employee (Leelee Sobieski), and then took on a comedy classic by teaming with Michael Douglas for a remake of the eccentric "The In-Laws" (2003), playing a neurotic and nebbishy dentist opposite Douglas' die-hard CIA agent. The actor—or at least his distinctive voice—was introduced an entirely new generation of fans when he lent his vocal talents to Marlin the Clownfish, the dyspeptic dad searching for his son in Disney/Pixar's CGI-animated underwater comedy-adventure "Finding Nemo" (2003).

FAMILY:
father: Harry Einstein. Comedian, actor; born in 1904; died in 1958; best known for his Greek dialect character Parkyarkarkus; appeared in "Strike Me Pink" (1936), "New Faces of 1937" (1937), "Night Spot" (1938), "Sweethearts of the U.S.A." (1944), "Out of

This World" (1945), and "Earl Carroll's Vanities" (1945); had Paget's disease, a rare spinal cord problem, but died of a heart attack at a Friars Club banquet roast of Lucille Ball and Desi Arnaz

COMPANIONS:
Carrie Fisher. Actor, writer; Carrie's mother Debbie Reynolds used to try to convince the pair to wed, prompting her daughter's retort: "Mother, there can't be two neurotic parents!"
Linda Ronstadt. Singer; lived with her for two years during the 1970s
Kathryn Harrold. Actor; co-starred with her in "Modern Romance" (1981)
Julie Hagerty. Actor; acted opposite her in "Lost in America" (1985)

MILESTONES:
1962–1963: Worked as a sportswriter for KMPC in Los Angeles
Worked as a stand-up comic
1968: TV debut, performing his stand-up act on "The Steve Allen Show" (syndicated)
1969: Performed as a regular on the summer variety series, "Dean Martin Presents the Golddiggers" (NBC)
Provided the voices of Mickey Barnes and Kip for the ABC animated series, "Hot Wheels"
1969: First TV writing credit for the ABC variety series "Turn On"
1971: First directorial effort, adapting his *Esquire* article, "Albert Brooks' Famous School for Comedians", for the PBS series "The Great American Dream Machine"
1973: Released first comedy album, "Comedy Minus One"
Wrote, produced and directed six short films during the first season of NBC's "Saturady Night Live"
1975: Released second comedy album, "A Star Is Bought"; received Grammy nomination
1976: Film acting debut in "Taxi Driver"; played campaign worker for a presidential candidate

1979: Feature directing and co-writing (with Monica Johnson and Harry Shearer) debut, "Real Life"; also starred

1980: Acted in "Private Benjamin", starring Goldie Hawn

1981: Reteamed with Johnson to co-write "Modern Romance"; also directed and starred; in a bit of life-imitating-art, writer-director James L. Brooks (no relation) played a director

1983: Credited as A. Brooks for supplying Rudyard's voice in James L. Brooks' "Terms of Endearment"

1985: Co-wrote (with Johnson), and directed "Lost in America"; also co-starred opposite Julie Hagerty

1987: Initial appearance in a co-starring role in a film he did not direct, "Broadcast News", written and helmed by James L. Brooks; garnered a Best Supporting Actor Oscar nomination

1991: Teamed with Meryl Streep for the comedy "Defending Your Life", again directing and co-writing with Johnson

1994: Reteamed with James L. Brooks for "I'll Do Anything", notorious for being shot initially as a musical before test screenings convinced the director to drop the musical numbers

1994: Starred as "The Scout", rewriting (with Johnson) an Andrew Bergman script that director Michael Ritchie had been trying to get made for several years; that year's baseball strike destroyed its commercial prospects

1996: Co-wrote (with Johnson), directed and co-starred with Debbie Reynolds in "Mother"; first major film role for Reynolds since 1971

1997: Played a 65-year-old alcoholic surgeon in Sidney Lumet's "Critical Care"

1998: Provided the voice of a suicidal tiger in the live-action "Dr. Dolittle", starring Eddie Murphy

1998: Appeared as a Wall Street guy put in prison in "Out of Sight", starring George Clooney

1999: Co-wrote (with Johnson), directed and co-starred with Sharon Stone in the romantic comedy "The Muse"

2001: Starred in the independent dark comedy "My First Mister"

2003: Co-starred in the Andrew Fleming comedy "The In-Laws"

QUOTES:

About why he came aboard as star and script doctor for "The Scout": "I like to write, but I wanted to take a job. In Hollywood, people thought I would work only for myself or Jim Brooks. I wanted to say, 'That's not true.'

"I came across this script which had been around a long time and was inspired by Roger Angell's *The New Yorker* article on Fernando Valenzuela.

"Most Hollywood comedies are miserable. There are 80 laughs in this—and not one from fart jokes. In this day and age, that's something."—Albert Brooks, to Stephen Schaefer from *New York Post*, September 26, 1994.

On turning down Lorne Michaels' offer to be the sole host of the original "Saturday Night Live": "Fame isn't the goal. It's better to be known by six people for something you're proud of than by 60 million for something you're not."—Brooks quoted in *People*, January 27, 1997.

About his feature acting debut in Martin Scorsese's "Taxi Driver": "My role was only indicated in the script, so I had to write it. Paul Schrader [the film's screenwriter] once said the funniest thing to me. He said, 'Thank you, I didn't understand that character.' And I thought, That's the character you don't understand? You understand Harvey Keitel and Travis Bickle perfectly, but the guy who works at the campaign office you're not sure of?"—Brooks to *Premiere*, January 1997.

"I've always felt like I work in a small little area that doesn't represent ANYTHING like the rest of society."—Brooks quoted in *Entertainment Weekly*, April 30, 1999.

DISCOGRAPHY: "Comedy Minus One" Albert Brooks, ABC, 1973, comedy

"A Star Is Bought" Albert Brooks, Electra-Asylum, 1975, comedy; earned Grammy nomination

Mel Brooks

BORN: Melvin Kaminsky in Brooklyn, New York, 06/28/1926

NATIONALITY: American

EDUCATION: Eastern District High School, Brooklyn, New York, 1944

AWARDS: Oscar Best Animated Short Subject "The Critic" 1963

Emmy Outstanding Writing Achievement in Variety "The Sid Caesar, Imogene Coca, Carl Reiner, Howard Morris Special" 1966/67; co-winner

Writers Guild of America Award Best-Written Original Screenplay "The Producers" 1968

Oscar Best Screenplay "The Producers" 1968

Writers Guild of America Award Best-Written Comedy Written Directly for the Screen "Blazing Saddles" 1974; shared award

NATO Director of the Year Award 1977 awarded by the National Association of Theater Owners

American Comedy Award Funniest Male Guest Appearance in a Television Series "Mad About You" 1997

Emmy Outstanding Guest Actor in a Comedy Series "Mad About You" 1996/97

Emmy Outstanding Guest Actor in a Comedy Series "Mad About You" 1997/98

Grammy Spoken Comedy Album "The 2000 Year Old Man in the Year 2000" 1999; shared with Carl Reiner

Emmy Outstanding Guest Actor in a Comedy Series "Mad About You" 1998/99

American Comedy Award Funniest Male Guest Appearance in a Television Series "Mad About You" 2000

New York Drama Critics Circle Award Best Musical "The Producers" 2000/01

Drama Desk Award Outstanding Musical "The Producers" 2001; Brooks was a producer

Drama Desk Award Outstanding Book "The Producers" 2001; shared with Thomas Meehan

Drama Desk Award Outstanding Lyrics "The Producers" 2001

Tony Best Musical "The Producers" 2001; award shared; Brooks was a producer

Tony Book of a Musical "The Producers" 2001 award shared with Thomas Meehan

Tony Score of a Musical "The Producers" 2001

Grammy Best Musical Show Album "The Producers" 2002; award shared with producer Hugh Fordin

BIOGRAPHY

Mel Brooks is a former stand-up comic who, together with Woody Allen and Bill Cosby, set the stage in the 1960s for the entire post-burlesque, TV generation of comedians. Allen was personal and self-deprecating, Cosby eschewed shtick in favor of witty commentary, and Brooks—often working with Carl Reiner—embraced the craziness at the root of all ethnic burlesque and reshaped it for decades to come.

Brooks graduated from 1950s TV writer (Sid Caesar's "Your Show of Shows") to successful 1960s series creator ("Get Smart!") before breaking into features with "The Producers" (1968), which set the zany, comedic tone of all his subsequent films and brought him an Oscar for the screenplay. His two greatest commercial successes, "Blazing Saddles" and "Young Frankenstein" (both 1974), were broad send-ups of the Western and horror genres, respectively. As with other comedy performers who also made their own films—Chaplin, Keaton, Lloyd, Tati, Allen—the persona was more important than the filmmaking regardless of its degree of sophistication and expressiveness.

In 1979, Brooks formed his production company, BrooksFilms, Ltd., which has been responsible for such diverse works as David Lynch's "The Elephant Man" (1980), Graeme Clifford's "Frances" (1982), Freddie Francis's "The Doctor and the Devils" (1985), David Jones' "84 Charing Cross Road" and David Cronenberg's "The Fly" (both 1986).

"High Anxiety" (1977), an engaging if imprecise homage to Hitchcockian thrillers, was his last largely acceptable film. Since the early 80s, Brooks' track record as a writer-director has been less distinguished than his work as an executive producer. There has been a marked and depressing decline in quality, freshness, and relevance in his films. "History of the World Part I" (1981), a scattershot parody of overblown historical epics, had some undeniably funny gags and sequences but these were overwhelmed by the sheer volume of comic misfires and relentless scatalogical material. Six years elapsed before the release of the regrettable "Spaceballs" (1987), a small-minded and uninspired spoof of the "Star Wars" films. Obviously not a labor of love, "Spaceballs" felt like a desperate attempt to connect with the youthful audience he no longer understood. Brooks aimed higher with his next feature, "Life Stinks" (1991), an admirable if wildly uneven attempt to tackle homelessness in a satirical format. The film, however, died at the box office.

While recent features have fizzled, Brooks continued to delight audiences with his riotous appearances on TV as a talk show guest, such as his memorable turn on one of the last install-ments of the Johnny Carson "Tonight Show" in 1992. While promoting "Life Stinks", he appeared on three consecutive nights of "Later", the late night talk show hosted by Bob Costas, where he rattled off many hilarious showbiz anecdotes. In a more serious vein, as a guest on the revealing cable documentary series, "Naked Hollywood", Brooks spoke can-didly about the machinations necessary to remain a player in contemporary Hollywood.

Brooks returned to the familiar ground of movie parody with "Robin Hood: Men in Tights" (1993) staring Cary Elwes and Richard Lewis. In the film's press kit, Brooks stated "I think you must have affection for whatever you tease. I love Westerns. I love monster movies. And I love the story of Robin Hood." While certainly not in the league of "Blazing Saddles" and "Young Frankenstein", this spoof was buoyed somewhat by this good-natured approach. Reviewers, however, thought otherwise, as apparently did the public.

Brooks, however, disproved the adage that there are no second acts in American lives. In 2000, he collaborated with Thomas Meehan (the award-winning librettist of "Annie" who had previously worked with Brooks on the remake of "To Be or Not to Be" and "Space-balls") in adapting the comedy classic "The Pro-ducers" for the stage. In addition to his work on the show's book, Brooks composed a battery of new songs (19 in all). Under the skillful direc-tion of Susan Stroman and with Nathan Lane and Matthew Broderick in the lead roles, "The Producers" began a pre-Broadway tryout in Chicago where it became an immediate hit. Arriving in New York, the musical became the most acclaimed show in years and went on to amass numerous accolades, including a record 15 Tony Award nominations.

COMPANION:

wife: Anne Bancroft. Actor; married on August 5, 1964; second wife; acted with Brooks in "To Be or Not to Be" (1983)

MILESTONES:

Worked variously as jazz drummer, stand-up

comedian, handyman and social director for a Catskills resort after World War II

1949–1958: Worked as sketch writer for Sid Caesar, collaborating on television shows Like "Your Show of Shows" (NBC, 1950–1954)

1954: Film writing debut with "New Faces" (sketches)

1957: Co-wrote the book for the Broadway musical "Shinbone Alley"

1960: Earned a Grammy nomination with Carl Reiner for Best Spoken Word Comedy for "2,000 Years"

1961: Nominated for Best Comedy Performance Grammy for "2,000 and One Years"

1962: Wrote the book for the Broadway musical "All-American"

1963: Created and narrated first film, the cartoon, "The Critic"; won Academy Award for Best Short Subject

1963: Nominated for Grammy Award for Best Comedy Performance for "At the Cannes Film Festival"

1964: Earned Emmy nomination with Buck Henry for Best Writing Achievement in Comedy for penning an episode of "Get Smart!"

1967: Won Emmy Award for Outstanding Writing Achievement in a Variety Comedy for "The Sid Caesar, Imogene Coca, Carl Reiner, Howard Morris Special" (CBS)

1968: First film as director and screenwriter, "The Producers"; also composed song "Springtime for Hitler"; won Academy Award for Best Originaly Screenplay

1970: Wrote, directed and starred in the comedy "The Twelve Chairs"

1974: Played Governor Lepetomane and Indian Chief in the Western movie parody "Blazing Saddles"; also co-wrote and directed

1974: Wrote and directed the horror movie spoof "Young Frankenstein"; earned Academy Award nomination for Best Adapted Screenplay

1977: First film as producer, "High Anxiety"; also acted in and directed

1979: Formed production company Brooksfilms Ltd

1979: Had cameo in "The Muppet Movie"

1980: Served as uncredited executive producer of "The Elephant Man", a heartwrenching drama about a man with physical deformities; film was nominated for Best Picture Academy Award

1981: Played various roles, including Moses and King Louis XVI, in "History of the World, Part I"; also directed, wrote and produced

1982: Served as uncredited executive producer on the Frances Farmer biopic "Frances"

1982: Executive produced the film "My Favorite Year", loosely inspired by the behind-the-scenes action at "Your Show of Shows"

1986: Served as executive producer on a successful remake of the 1958 sci-fi flick "The Fly" and the less-than-stellar fantasy "Solarbabies"

1987: Played President Skroob and Yogurt in the "Star Wars" spoof "Spaceballs"; also co-wrote, directed and produced

1989: Served as uncredited executive producer on "The Fly II"

1991: Starred in, directed and wrote the unpopular comedy "Life Stinks"

1992: Executive produced the misfire "The Vagrant"

1993: Made rare TV sitcom appearance on NBC's "Frasier"

1993: Featured as Rabbi Tuckman in "Robin Hood: Men in Tights"; also directed, produced and co-wrote

1994: Played Mr Welling in the big-screen version of "The Little Rascals"

1995: Featured as vampire hunter Abraham Van Helsing in "Dracula: Dead and Loving It"; also directed, wrote and produced

1995: Played himself on an episode of the Fox animated series "The Simpsons"

Had recurring role as Paul's Uncle Phil on the hit NBC sitcom "Mad About You"; won three Emmy Awards for appearances

1997: With Carl Reiner wrote the book "The 2000 Year Old Man in the Year 2000"

1999: With Reiner won Grammy for Spoken Comedy Album for the recording of "The 2000 Year Old Man in 2000"

2000: Wrote the score (including 17 new songs) and adapted his Oscar-winning screenplay for the stage musical version of "The Producers"; opened in Chicago to rave reviews and moved to Broadway in April 2001, where it also earned critical kudos and a record 15 Tony Award nominations, including Book and Score; won a record 12 Tony Awards including Best Musical, Book and Score

QUOTES:

With his 2001 Tony wins for the book and score for "The Producers", Brooks joined the elite club of Helen Hayes, John Gielgud, Rita Moreno, Audrey Hepburn, Richard Rodgers and Marvin Hamlisch as one of the few individuals to earn all four of the major entertainment prizes (Oscar, Tony, Emmy, Grammy) in competition. Later that year, Mike Nichols joined the group when he earned an Emmy for "Wit."

Tod Browning

BORN: Charles Albert Browning, Jr in Louisville, Kentucky, 07/12/1880

DEATH: in Santa Monica, California, 10/06/1962

NATIONALITY: American

EDUCATION: Boys High School, Louisville, Kentucky; dropped out at age 16 to join the circus

AWARD: Directors Guild of America Honorary Life Membership 1948

BIOGRAPHY

Tod Browning helped to create the genre now known as "horror films" as evidenced by his ten-film collaboration with actor Lon Chaney, the first sound version of "Dracula" (1931, starring Bela Lugosi) and most particularly with what is arguably his master work "Freaks" (1932). The latter, which included real carnival sideshow performers, was considered so frightful by contemporary standards that some 20 minutes were edited from the US version and it was banned in Great Britain for some three decades. Ironically, it was only after the director's death in 1962 that the film was "rehabilitated"; a screening at that

year's Venice Film Festival led to its reappraisal by film historians.

Born and raised in Louisville, Kentucky, Charles Albert Browning Jr. spent part of his youth producing and performing in theatricals in his back yard. An accomplished singer, the youngster literally ran away from home at age 16, adopted the new first name of Tod and joined the circus, working in various capacities from carnival barker to contortionist to head-liner (as "The Living Corpse", an act that had him buried alive for up to two days at a time). Browning later turned to vaudeville as a singer, dancer and comedian, earning attention for playing the popular comic strip character Mutt (of "Mutt and Jeff") in the burlesque show "The Whirl of Myth" (1913). A former vaude-ville partner, Charles "Charlie" Murray, who had found a niche working in films at Bio-graph, introduced Browning to D. W. Griffith in 1913. The director cast him in a bit role as an undertaker in "Scenting a Terrible Crime" and incorporated the budding thespian into the "family." Browning's versatility and physical prowess made him ideal for the demanding comic roles and when Griffith headed west so too did Browning.

Once in Hollywood, Browning began to

work behind the cameras helming a series of one- and two-reel comedies. His career was nearly ended, though, by a June 1915 automobile accident in which he was driving while intoxicated. One passenger, comic actor Elmer Booth, was killed and another, George A. Seigmann, was seriously injured. Browning had suffered massive injuries and spent a long convalescence, during which he penned screenplays. When he had recovered sufficiently, Griffith put him to work as one of the many assistant directors on "Intolerance" (1916). The following year, in tandem with star Wilfred Lucas, he co-directed the Civil War drama "Jim Bludso." Over the next seven years, Browning directed a string of films for Metro and Universal, many of which are no longer extant and have been described as routine melodramas, doing little to advance his career. It was a fortuitous collaboration with actor Lon Chaney (beginning with 1919's "The Wicked Darling") that pulled him from the rank and file into a position as one of Hollywood's bankable directors.

Much of Browning's reputation as one of the top directors of horror films rests largely on the Chaney silents. Most, however, remain largely inaccessible ("The Unholy Three" 1925, "The Road to Mandalay" 1926, "The Unknown" 1927, etc.) or completely lost ("London After Midnight" 1927). "The Unholy Three", made under the seal of approval of MGM production boss Irving Thalberg, was built around a trio of criminals—Chaney as a transvestite ventriloquist (in a silent film!), a dwarf (Harry Earles) and a strongman (Victor McLaglen)—and perhaps was the best and most successful of this partnership. Still, film historians are divided over whether it was the brilliance of Chaney that made the films with Browning so stunning. For his part, the director sensed a kindred spirit in the actor and the duo crafted fascinating character studies of damaged men filled with emotional anguish. "The Black Bird" (1926) gave Chaney an opportunity to transform himself into a cripple merely by contorting his body. "London After Midnight" (1927) was Browning's first flirtation with the myth of the vampire while "The Unknown" (also 1927), was a truly disturbing tale of a circus knife-thrower who pretends to have no arms who undergoes an amputation to avoid detection as a murderer. As critic Stuart Rosenthal pointed out, the physical mutilation of a Browning protagonist often mirrors a mental or spiritual one that leads to the characters eventual destruction without losing the audience's sympathy.

Without Chaney, Browning directed "The Show" (1927), an upsetting tale of carnival performers (played by Renee Adoree and John Gilbert) who nightly re-enact the story of Salome and John the Baptist while a jealous rival (Lionel Barrymore) plots to win the woman. Browning's use of camera angles and shifts in perspective heighten the film's tension and prefigure many of the techniques now commonplace in suspense films. Contemporary audiences, however, did not respond to the film and it proved a box-office failure. While MGM allowed Browning to continue to work, the studio had no qualms about loaning him to Universal in 1929 to make "Outside the Law" (1930). Universal then tapped him to helm "Dracula" (1931), which was intended as a starring vehicle for Lon Chaney but the actor's ill health precluded his taking the part. (Chaney died of throat cancer in 1930.) Instead of using an unknown as Browning had wanted, the studio hired Bela Lugosi to recreate his popular stage role.

Browning's vision for the story was apparently at odds with Universal's. The resultant film plays as slightly plodding and seemingly harmless. Lugosi's distant, stylized portrayal of the vampire lends an elegance to the film, but Browning's camera remains static, as if waiting for the actors to bring the piece alive. (He reportedly clashed often with the great cinematographer Kurt Freund who suggested more movement.) Browning clearly was still not fully comfortable shooting sound and the infusion of that element seems to have confounded his technique, lending an awkwardness to the proceedings. In contrast, the Spanish-language version shot on the same sets with a different cast and crew captures a sensuality and danger that is missing from the US release.

In undertaking "Freaks", Browning achieved notoriety and later cult status. The film, which employs and even celebrates real circus "freaks" via voyeuristic appeal, unfortunately suffers from the amateurism of its cast. With the exception of the leading lady (Olga Baclanova) few of the performers were trained actors and it shows. With its limited camera angles and woodenly-delivered dialogue, "Freaks" takes on the aura of a 1950s B-grade horror movie, which was decidedly not its intent. Browning was making a statement: in his collaborations with Chaney, a "normal" man becomes mutilated and turns into a monster, with "Freaks", the process is reversed. The grotesque are not the monsters, but Baclanova and her ilk are. Some critics argued that the film humanized the freaks, while others made claims of exploitation. Still, the film's "one of us" claustrophobically unnerving sequences possesses the requisite terror quotient as does its incendiary climax when Olga Baclanova appears in quite a different form. Although by contemporary standards where computer-generated special effects are the norm, the movie appears dated and almost quaint, in its time, "Freaks" was truly agitating. During a preview, one female patron ran screaming up the aisle and out of the theater. MGM cut some 20 minutes from the film and it was banned in Great Britain for some three decades. As punishment, the studio assigned Browning to the routine "Fast Workers" (1933), starring John Gilbert.

Browning's later work in sound horror films is often obscured by the reputations of "Dracula" and "Freaks". "Mark of the Vampire" (1935), a remake of "London After Midnight",

maintains a consistently eerie atmosphere and contains several understated scenes of chilling beauty featuring Lugosi and the ethereal Carol Borland as a "vampire" couple. Despite the fact that the film's supernatural elements give way by the conclusion to a standard mystery story, Browning here displays more control and visual polish than in his prior work. "The Devil Doll" (1936), in which Devil's Island escapee Lionel Barrymore shrinks the partners who framed him for embezzlement to the size of toys, is in many ways a standard revenge melodrama. But the director makes inventive use of a wide variety of cinematic tools—canted shots, a moving camera, montages—to enhance the suspense and charge of the science fiction trappings. Tastes in the movie business change rapidly, and Browning intuited that his era had passed when he announced his retirement in the early 1940s. Although he received screen credit for the story to 1946's "Inside Job", he spent his remaining years as a recluse. When his wife died in 1944, it was erroneously reported that he had died. Browning developed throat cancer in the 1950s and underwent an operation on his tongue. He died in 1962 at age 82.

MILESTONES:

As a child in Louisville, Kentucky, performed in and produced amateur theatricals

1896: At age 16, joined the Manhattan Fair and Carnival Company; changed first name to Tod

Billed as "The Living Corpse" in one carnival act; would be buried alive for up to two days at a time

Briefly appeared as a clown with the Ringling Brothers Circus

Performed in vaudeville as a contortionist and clown as well as a singer and dancer and a comic, the latter in partnership with several other performers including Charles Murray; traveled throughout the world

1913: Introduced to D W Griffith by former partner Charles Murray; joined Biograph Studios as a performer

1913: Feature acting debut, had bit role as an undertaker in "Scenting a Terrible Crime", directed by Griffith

Moved to Hollywood with Griffith

1915: Began directing career, helming two-reel shorts like "The Living Death" and "The Lucky Transfer"

1915: Involved in an automobile accident while driving drunk that resulted in the death of comic Elmer Booth, a passenger in the car (June 17)

1916: Was an assistant director to D.W. Griffith on "Intolerance"; also acted in the film

1916: Wrote and directed the comedy short, "The Mystery of the Leaping Fish"

1917: Feature film directing debut, the Civil War romance "Jim Bludso"; co-directed with star Wilfred Lucas

1917–1918: Helmed several films for Metro, many with Edith Storey as star

1918: Began directing for Bluebird Photoplays; later joined Universal by year's end

1918: Initiated collaboration with actress Priscilla Dean with "Which Woman" and "The Brazen Beauty"

1918: Received screenplay credit for "Set Free"; also directed

1919: First collaboration with Lon Chaney, "The Wicked Darling", starring Priscilla Dean

1924: Last film under Universal contract, "White Tiger"

Struggled with alcoholism for roughly two years

1925: Career turned around after directing "The Unholy Three" for MGM; film starred Chaney, Victor McLaglen and Harry Earles

1926: Helmed "The Black Bird", starring Chaney

1927: Clashed with studio heads over "The Show", featuring John Gilbert and Chaney; dark subject matter (a circus sideshow) offended many critics

1929: Last collaboration with Chaney, "Where East Is East"; also last silent film

1929: First sound film, "The Thirteenth Chair"; also released as a silent; first film with Bela Lugosi

Loaned out to Universal

1931: Directed, "Dracula" (for Universal); director's first choice for part was Chaney who was too ill to work; title role eventually played by Bela Lugosi who had originated it on Broadway

1932: Status at MGM lessened after the box-office failure of "Freaks"; studio cut 20 minutes after a disastrous preview; contemporary critics and audiences dismissed film; banned from screenings in Great Britain until 1962

1933: Reteamed with John Gilbert on "Fast Workers", a drama about construction workers that proved a flop

1936: Directed the intriguing "The Devil Doll"

1939: Last film, "Miracles for Sale"

1942: Formally retired from filmmaking

1946: Received screen credit for the story for "Inside Job"

Developed throat cancer in the 1950s and underwent an operation on his tongue

QUOTES:

"When I quit a thing, I quit. I wouldn't walk across the street now to see a movie."—quote attributed to Tod Browning at the time of his "retirement" from movie making in the early 1940s.

BIBLIOGRAPHY:

"Dark Carnival: The Secret World of Tod Browning, Hollywood's Master of the Macbre" David J. Skal and Elias Savada, 1995, Anchor Books

BORN: in Calanda, Teruel, Spain, 02/22/1900

DEATH: in Mexico City, Mexico, 07/29/1983

NATIONALITY: Spanish

CITIZENSHIP: Mexico 1949

EDUCATION: Colegio del Salvador, religion, entomology and zoology; attended for seven years

Instituto Nacional de Ensenanza Media 1915–17

University of Madrid, agricultural engineering, natural sciences and history, 1917–25

Academie du Cinema, Paris, France

AWARDS: Cannes Film Festival International Critics Prize Best Director "Los Olvidados" 1951

Cannes Film Festival International Critics Prize "Subida al Cielo/Mexican Bus" 1952

Cannes Film Festival Special Jury Prize "Nazarin" 1959

Cannes Film Festival Special Hommage Award "The Young One" 1960

Cannes Film Festival Grand Prix "Viridiana" 1961; co-winner

Cannes Film Festival International Critics Prize "El Angel Exterminador/The Exterminating Angel" 1962

Venice Film Festival Silver Lion "Simon of the Desert" 1965

Venice Film Festival International Film Critics Award "Simon of the Desert" 1965; cited along with Carl Dreyer's "Gertrud"

Venice Film Festival Lion of St Mark for Best Film "Belle du Jour" 1967

National Society of Film Critics Award Best Director "The Discreet Charm of the Bourgeoisie" 1972

British Film Academy Award Best Screenplay "The Discreet Charm of the Bourgeoisie" 1973; award shared with Jean-Claude Carriere

National Board of Review Award Best Director "That Obscure Object of Desire" 1977

Los Angeles Film Critics Association Award Best Foreign Film "That Obscure Object of Desire" 1977

National Society of Film Critics Award Best Director "That Obscure Object of Desire" 1977

BIOGRAPHY

One of the founders of surrealist cinema, Luis Bunuel enjoyed a career as diverse and contradictory as his films: he was a master of both silent and sound cinema, of documentaries as well as features; his greatest work was produced in the two decades after his 60th year, a time when most directors have either retired or gone into decline; and although frequently characterized as a surrealist, many of his films were dramas and farces in the realist or neo-realist mode. Yet despite all the innovations and permutations of his work, Bunuel remained suprisingly consistent and limited in the targets of his social satire: the Catholic Church, bourgeois culture, and Fascism. As he once commented, "Religious education and Surrealism have marked me for life."

Bunuel described his childhood in Calanda, a village in the Spanish province of Aragon, as having "slipped by in an almost medieval atmosphere." Between the ages of six and fifteen he attended Jesuit school, where a strict educational program, unchanged since the 18th century, instilled in him a lifelong rebellion against religion.

In 1917 Bunuel enrolled in the University of Madrid and soon became involved in the political and literary penas, or clubs, that met in the city's cafes. His friends included several of

Spain's future great artists and writers, including Salvador Dali, Federico Garcia Lorca and Rafael Albertini. Within a few years the avant-garde movement had reached the penas and spawned its Spanish variants, "creacionismo" and "ultraismo". Although influenced by these, Bunuel was often critical of the Spanish avant-garde for its allegiance to traditional forms.

In 1925 Bunuel left Madrid for Paris, with no clear idea of what he would do. When he saw Fritz Lang's "Destiny" (1921), however, he realized where his vocation lay. He approached the renowned French director, Jean Epstein, who hired him as an assistant. Bunuel began to learn the techniques of filmmaking but was fired when he refused to work with Epstein's own mentor, Abel Gance, whose films he did not like. In a prophetic statement, Epstein warned Bunuel about his "surrealistic tendencies."

In 1928, with financial support from his mother, Bunuel collaborated with Dali on "Un Chien Andalou", a "surrealist weapon" designed to shock the bourgeois as well as criticize the avant-garde. As in his earlier book of poems, "Un Perro Andaluz", Bunuel rejected the avant-garde's emphasis on form, or camera "tricks," over content. Instead, his influences were commercial neo-realism, horror films and American comedies.

Bunuel's three early films established him as a master of surrealist cinema, whose goal was to treat all human experience—dreams, madness or "normal" waking states—on the same level. The critical success in some quarters of the strange and provocative "L'Age d'or" (1930) secured Bunuel a contract with MGM, which he turned down after a visit to Hollywood in 1930. His next film, "Las Hurdes: Tierra Sin Pan" (1932) was a documentary financed with money won in a lottery and shot with a camera borrowed from Yves Allegret. Ostensibly an objective study of a remote, impoverished region in western Spain, the film constituted such a militant critique of both church and state

that it was banned in Spain. The stage had been set, however, for Bunuel's later work, in which realism—with its pre-established mass appeal—provided an accessible context for his surreal aesthetic and moral code.

After "Las Hurdes", Bunuel would not direct another film until 1947. Although still critical of commercial cinema, he spent the next 14 years within the industry, learning all aspects of film production. From 1933 to 1935 he dubbed dialogue for Paramount in Paris and then Warner Bros. in Spain; between 1935 and the outbreak of the Spanish Civil War in 1936 he produced popular musical comedies in Spain; during the Civil War he served the Republican government, compiling newsreel material into a documentary about the war, "Espana leal en armas" (1937). In 1938, while he was in Hollywood supervising two other documentaries, the Fascists assumed power at home. Unable to return to Spain, Bunuel went to work for the Museum of Modern Art in New York, re-editing and dubbing documentaries for distribution in Latin America. He was forced to resign in 1942, however, because of his suspected Communist background—a suspicion which he later claimed had been aroused by Dali. In order to survive, Bunuel narrated documentaries for the Army Corps of Engineers until 1944, when Warner Bros. hired him to produce Spanish versions of their films.

In 1946 Bunuel moved to Mexico, where many of Spain's intellectuals and artists had emigrated after the Civil War. He would live there for the rest of his life, becoming a citizen in 1949 and directing 20 films by 1964. This period is often described as an "apprenticeship" in which Bunuel was forced to shoot low-budget commercial films in between a handful of surreal "classics." Indeed, Bunuel's supposed indifference to style—his minimal use of non-diegetic music, close-ups or camera movement—is often judged to be largely the result of the limited resources available to him. Yet his Mexican films can more accurately be seen as a refinement of the often unobstrusive aesthetic style that had been evident since "Un Chien Andalou." As Bunuel himself insisted, "I never made a single scene that compromised my convictions or my personal morality."

Bunuel's third Mexican film, "Los Olvidados" (1950), brought him to international attention once again. Although hailed as a surrealist film, it owes much to postwar neorealism in its unsentimental depiction of Mexico's slum children. As in his other Mexican films before "Nazarin" (1958), dream sequences and surreal images are introduced at strategic moments into an otherwise realist narrative. (Contributing to the relative neglect of these films has been their unavailability outside Mexico, and perhaps their proletarian and "ethnic" focus.)

In 1955 Bunuel began to direct international—and more openly political—co-productions in Europe. In 1961 he was invited to Spain to film "Viridiana." The completed film was a direct assault on Spanish Catholicism and Fascism and was banned by its unwitting patron; a "succes de scandale", it won the Palm d'Or at Cannes and secured long overdue international acclaim for its director. After "Viridiana", Bunuel worked mostly in France. The growth of his new international (and consequently educated and middle-class) audience coincided with his return to a surrealist aesthetic. "The Exterminating Angel" (1962), "The Discreet Charm of the Bourgeoisie" (1972) and "The Phantom of Liberty" (1974) depict a bourgeoisie trapped within their own conventions, if not—in the first film's metaphorical conceit—their own homes. "Belle de jour" (1967), "Tristana" (1970) and "That Obscure Object of Desire" (1977) explore sexual obsessions and preoccupations. "The Milky Way" (1969) launches a frontal assault on the Church, in a summation of Bunuel's lifelong contempt for that institution.

In 1980, Bunuel collaborated with Jean-Claude Carriere, his screenwriter since "Diary of a Chambermaid" (1963), on his autobiography, "My Last Sigh" (France 1982; USA 1983).

MILESTONES:

Grew up in Saragossa

1922: Began contributing to literary journals

1925: Went to Paris; invited by director Jean Epstein to be his assistant

1926: First film as assistant director "Mauprat"

1926: Film acting debut in "Carmen"

1927: Debut as playwright with Spanish "Hamlet"

1927: Stage directing debut (Amsterdam) with "El Retablo de Maese Pedro"

1929: First film as director and co-screenwriter (with Salvador Dali) "Un chien Andalou"

1930: Hired for six months by MGM after he made "L'Age d'Or" with the idea that he would be involved in making foreign-language versions of other MGM films

1931: Returned to France

1932: Hired by Paramount (Europe) as dubber

1935: Becomes executive producer for Filmofono Films in Madrid, supervising musicals and comedies

1936–1939: Hired as cultural attache by Republican government (Paris); returned to Hollywood to supervise (ultimately unrealized) documentaries on Spanish Civil War

Worked at Museum of Modern Art, New York, re-editing, dubbing, directing documentaries for Latin American distribution

1942: Dismissed because of suspicion of Communist background

1944: Returned to Hollywood to produce Spanish versions of Warner Brothers films

1946: Moved to Mexico; made films there for next fifteen years

1950: "Los Olvidados" set record by winning 11 Ariel awards

1961: Invited by Spanish government to return; made "Viridiana"; film suppressed in Spain

BIBLIOGRAPHY:

"My Last Sigh" Luis Bunuel and Jean-Claude

Carriere, 1982; autobiography; first published in France

"An Unspeakable Betrayal: Selected Writings of

Luis Bunuel" 2000, University of California Press; translated by Garrett White with an foreword by Jean-Claude Carriere

Tim Burton

BORN: Timothy W. Burton in Burbank, California, 08/25/1958

NATIONALITY: American

EDUCATION: California Institute of the Arts, Valencia, California, animation, 1979–80; in the Disney animation program; received scholarship for second year

AWARD: Daytime Emmy Outstanding Animated Program "Beetlejuice" 1989/90; shared award; Burton was one of the executive producers

BIOGRAPHY

A pale and lonely dark-eyed boy, out of place in the suntanned Burbank world of his youth, filmmaker Tim Burton refused to yield to the cookie-cutter homogeneity demanded by suburbia (and later by Disney), translating his alienation into a dark and highly personal vision that would resonate resoundingly with movie audiences. He drew great inspiration from Roger Corman's movies starring Vincent Price and as a natural progression immerse himself in the German expressionism of the 1920s and the Gothic horror of the 1930s. Ill-equipped to do things the Disney way while briefly toiling at the studio as an apprentice animator, he impressed future collaborators Henry Selick and Rick Heinrichs with his brilliant doodles. Despite being perceived as a weirdo, he also managed to make his own six-minute animated short, "Vincent" (1982), a wryly amusing little film portraying the dual life of a tortured, but seemingly normal suburban

child who lives in a fantasy world of Gothic horror and imagines he is Vincent Price (who incidentally served as narrator). The autobiographical character was a prototype for the misunderstood, sympathetic outsider at the center of all the director's subsequent films.

Burton's follow-up, the 29-minute, partially live-action "Frankenweenie" (1984), was an inventive twist on the "Frankenstein" story. A young boy (Victor Frankenstein) brings his dead dog Sparky back to life (à la his namesake) thanks to the wonders of electricity, even jump-starting the canine later with a little jolt from a car battery, and Sparky eventually finds love with a poodle that recalls Elsa Lanchester's famous hairdo from 1935 classic "The Bride of Frankenstein." Considered too outre for a Disney product, it did not receive a proper release until 1992 when it finally became available on video and on The Disney Channel. A private showing for Paul Reubens, however, landed Burton his first feature directing assignment on the superlatively silly "Pee-Wee's Big Adventure" (1985). Though his first two films had been in black and white, the director adjusted readily, using primary colors to create Pee Wee's surreal, cartoon-like world without completely abandoning the dark side revealed in Pee Wee's nightmares. Though most critics savaged it, "Pee-Wee's Big Adventure" found a sizable audience, and a surprised industry duly took notice.

Building on the live-action cartoon style of his debut, Burton's "Beetlejuice" (1998) employed a fantastic array of outstanding special effects to tell its campy ghost story. When it, too, became a sleeper hit, Burton became an intriguing choice to direct "Batman" (1989), a project which allowed him, together with Oscar-winning set designer Anton Furst, to return to his beloved long shadows, jagged angles and distorted perspective for the imagery of the appropriately named Gotham City. If it had not been apparent before, "Batman" and Burton's even darker "Batman Returns" (1992) made it evident that a coherent narrative was an afterthought when compared with the director's remarkable visual style. For the former feature, that capability overcame the clunky story and somewhat leaden action sequences to bring in more than $400 million worldwide and a cool billion in merchandising. Unfortunately, the latter's performance at the box office (a mere $150 million), was decidedly lackluster, particularly considering it cost more than the first one. His decision to pass the reins to Joel Schumacher for "Batman Forever" (1995) probably brought a sigh of relief from studio execs, ecstatic to be free from the grim Burton vision.

In between "Batman"s, Burton delivered a strikingly original fable about a man-made boy whose creator dies before attaching hands to his body. Visually, the pastel plasticity of suburbia in "Edward Scissorhands" (1990) contrasted sharply with the Gothic angles of the scientist's mountaintop home, just as that dayglo community's superficial welcome vanished in the face of mob frenzy when Edward's difference became too threatening for the close-knit society. As the title character, former teen idol Johnny Depp was extremely effective in his mute, wide-eyed performance, and Burton's mentor Price provided a real emotional context in his cameo as the inventor. Despite his success, Burton has remained the misunderstood outsider, and "Scissorhands", a moderate hit in commercial terms, represents the movie that is perhaps closest to his heart. Expressing his deep affection for fairy tales, he weaves an underlying threat of love being a fatally attractive lethal weapon as Edward can't hold the girl

he adores most (Winona Ryder), fearing he will cause her harm.

Burton returned to animation for the first time since "Vincent" as producer, creator and guiding sensibility behind "Tim Burton's 'The Nightmare Before Christmas' " (1993), the first full-length stop-motion (three-dimensional figures, not drawings, repositioned from frame to frame) animated film produced by Disney. Burton had come up with the idea while employed by the studio in the early 80s, and when he tried to rescue it from the black hole it had fallen into there, he found Disney loathe to part with it and also leery of his ability to helm it what with his commitment to "Batman Returns." He got the project green-lighted when he turned it over to friend Selick, who had himself left Disney long ago but was a stop-motion veteran, having directed Pillsbury "Doughboy" commercials and an award-winning short called "Slow Bob in the Lower Dimensions" (1981), among other credits. Wildly imaginative in its excursion to the macabre, this twisted cousin to the cuddly Disney classics normally unveiled at Christmas featured trademark Burton designs and thematic concerns and had execs holding their collective breath waiting for the bomb to explode. The success of "Nightmare" again confounded the supposed experts and confirmed Burton as a commercial wunderkind.

The director's decision to shoot the biopic "Ed Wood" (1994) in black and white caused Columbia to pull out, leaving the field clear for Disney. Starring Depp as "the world's worst director", Burton's first period piece also featured Martin Landau in an astonishing, Academy Award–winning supporting turn as an aged and impoverished Bela Lugosi. (Rick Baker also won an Oscar for his makeup.) While smaller in scope than his last three outings, "Ed Wood" was also the first Burton movie grounded in a truthful, if bizarre, historical reality, unlike the internally consistent but fictional worlds of "Scissorhands" and the

"Batman" movies. The cinematic love letter to Hollywood's Poverty Row, like "Scissorhands", was an extremely personal film, and many critics cited parallels between Wood's relationship with Lugosi and Burton's with Price. Despite its vivid recreation of time and place, it unfortunately did not appeal to mass tastes, bringing his string of box office successes to an end. Perhaps Columbia had been right about black and white not being commercial, or maybe the project just missed the touch of Danny Elfman, whose music had provided the perfect complement for Burton's vision on all his previous films.

Burton turned his attention next to "Mars Attacks!" (1996), a high-budget, special effects laden adaptation of a series of bubble gum trading cards spoofing the sci-fi thriller of the 50s and 60s. Boasting an all-star cast (including Annette Bening, Glenn Close, Michael J. Fox and Jack Nicholson in a dual role), the film combined live-action with superb animation (the Martian characters) to tell its overly self-satisfied, ultimately one-note tale of alien invasion. A fabulous production design could not carry the day, proving that Burton's unquestioned visual genius had not yet mastered or found a way of doing without narrative. Its American box office failure, due in part to the success of the similarly themed blockbuster "Independence Day" released some five months earlier, though not branding the wunderkind an overnight pariah, certainly gave studios pause to wonder whether his delightfully demented vision would continue to sell. (European receipts vindicated him somewhat.) Undaunted by his inability to get his troubled "Superman" off the ground, he rebounded with "Sleepy Hollow" (1999, loosely based on Washington Irving's famous story), starring Depp as discredited professor Ichabod Crane, exiled for his outrageous theories to Sleepy Hollow, where he confronts the local myth of the headless horseman.

COMPANIONS:

wife: Lena Gieseke. Painter; German; married in February 1989; separated in spring 1992

Lisa Marie. Model, Actor; appeared as Vampira in Burton's "Ed Wood", an alien in "Mars Attacks!" and in "Sleepy Hollow" and "Planet of the Apes"; together from 1992 until 2001; reportedly were engaged

Helena Bonham Carter. Actor; co-starred in "Planet of the Apes" (2001); began dating in October 2001

MILESTONES:

1970: At age 12, decided he didn't want to live with his parents and moved in with his grandmother (date aproximate)

In ninth grade, designed anti-litter poster that won top prize in local California refuse company contest; Burton's artwork adorned Burbank garbage trucks for one year

After graduating from art school, worked as animator at Walt Disney Studios

1981: Working on Disney's "The Fox and the Hound" prompted him to say, "I was just not Disney material. I could not draw cute foxes for the life of me. I couldn't do it . . . "

1982: Release of first animated (stop-motion) short film, "Vincent" (six minutes), narrated by Vincent Price; won several film festival awards

1984: Made live-action short, "Frankenweenie" (29 minutes), which inspired Paul Reubens to give him his first feature directing assignment

1985: Feature directing debut at age 25, "Pee-Wee's Big Adventure", starring Reubens (aka Pee Wee Herman); film also marked first collaboration with music composer Danny Elfman

1988: First collaboration with Michael Keaton, Wynona Ryder and Jeffrey Jones, "Beetlejuice"

1989: Founded Tim Burton Productions

1989: Helmed the enormously popular "Batman", starring Jack Nicholson as the Joker and Keaton as the caped crusader

1990: First feature producing credit, "Edward Scissorhands", starring Johnny Depp and Ryder; also directed; Price, in his final feature role, portrayed the man-made boy's creator

1992: Directed "Batman Returns", featuring Danny DeVito as the Penguin; Keaton's last time as Batman; Reubens showed up in cameo as the Penguin's father; first pic with Christopher Walken

1992: Feature acting debut in Cameron Crowe's "Singles"

1993: Produced and provided the vision for "Tim Burton's The Nightmare Before Christmas", a 72-minute animated musical directed by stop-motion guru and friend Henry Selick; Elfman sang the lead role of Jack Skellington (in addition to writing the score); required a staff of 120, the stop-action process was so time-consuming that each of the 13 animators produced no more than five to ten seconds of footage a week

1994: Second feature with Depp, "Ed Wood", a cinematic love letter to Hollywood's Poverty Row that was not a hit with audiences; only feature film to date for which Elfman did not write the music; second film with Jones; co-star Martin Landau won Best Supporting Actor Oscar portraying Bela Lugosi

1995: Turned the directing reins over to Joel Schumacher but retained his connection to the franchise as a producer of "Batman Forever"

1996: Produced Selick's stop-motion animated feature "James and the Giant Peach"

1996: Stumbled again at the US box office with "Mars Attacks!", a blend of live action and animation which he produced as well as directed; overseas popularity redeemed him to a degree; second film with Nicholson, who played dual role of US President and a sleazy Las Vegas car dealer

1998: Directed first TV commercial, pitching Hollywood Gum for the European market

1999: Reteamed with Depp (as Ichabod Crane), Jones and Walken on "Sleepy Hollow", freely adapted from Washington Irving's "The Legend of Sleepy Hollow"; as part of the production design of longtime collaborator (in varying capacities) Rick Heinrichs, constructed a picturesque version of a Dutch colonial town

2001: Helmed the remake of "Planet of the Apes", starring Mark Wahlberg

QUOTES:

On the apoplectic response to "Batman Returns" and parental upset about a McDonald's merchandising tie-in: "I mean, I'm sorry, but I didn't ask to put this stuff on the side of a McDonald's carton. Besides, why aren't these people objecting to the junk McDonald's is pushing as food? I felt the whole controversy was simply remnants of the whole family values baloney. These movies are people running around in bad costumes. How relevant are we being here?"—Tim Burton, quoted in *Daily News*, October 12, 1993.

"If you take all these guys in a row—Batman, Beetlejuice, Pee-wee, Scissorhands, Skellington—they define Tim. The characters in his movies have an emptiness, they have soul and they have heart. They're trying to become accepted for their own weirdness. And they end up doing it . . . Just like their creator."—David Hoberman, president of Walt Disney Pictures and Touchstone Pictures quoted in "Writing Music to Horrify in a Disney Nightmare" by Joseph Gelmis in *New York Newsday*, November 12, 1993.

"Kind of sad, really, the way they experience the seasons in California, walking down the aisles at Thrifty's."—Burton on Christmas in California, quoted in *People*, November 22, 1993.

About his experience as an assistant animator on Disney's "The Fox and the Hound": "I felt they were saying, 'Okay, this is Disney—this is supposed to be the most incredible gathering of artists in the world.' At the same time they were saying, 'Just do it this way; shut up and become like a zombie factory worker.' After a while I was thinking, Is my restaurant job still available? I realized I'd rather be dead than work for five years on this movie."—Burton to Mimi Avins in *Premiere*, November 1993.

"Tim is a genius and I don't use that word lightly. The definition of a great artist is someone who doesn't care much what other people think. Tim cares what people think of his movies but he has that core essence, that compulsion, to do his art. I accept that about him. And his instincts are unerring. I've never seen them to be wrong on any small or large decision. Ever. His instincts emanate from a place that's very pure, truly artistic."—Producer Denise Di Novi on Burton's talent quoted in *Movieline*, June 1994.

"There's something beautiful in the catharsis of doing something, which a lot of people don't understand. I grew up around people who were afraid to do anything, and hid behind these masks of normality, just falling into line, not saying anything of their own, but just sort of together, like the angry villagers in 'Frankenstein'. Talent is secondary,

really. If people ask, 'Who's your favorite filmmaker?' I don't have any favorites. I like anybody, I don't care if I've seen their movies or not . . . They should get a certain amount of credit for just fighting through things.

"I grew up in this puritanical American Dream kind of thing where everybody's suppose to be normal, and people attacked anybody who tried to make something . . . I shielded myself from that, and punched through it. Because I couldn't draw either. If I had listened to those people, I'd have ended up like everyone else. 'I can't do this, I can't do that.'"—Tim Burton to *Village Voice*, October 4, 1994.

BIBLIOGRAPHY:

"Burton on Burton" Tim Burton (with contributions from Mark Salisbury), 1995, Faber and Faber

"The Melancholy Death of Oyster Boy and Other Stories" Tim Burton, 1997, William Morrow

"Tim Burton: An Unauthorized Biography of the Filmmaker" Ken Hanke, 1999, Renaissance Books

James Cameron

BORN: in Kapuskasing, Ontario, Canada, 08/16/1954

NATIONALITY: Canadian

EDUCATION: California State University, Fullerton, Fullerton, California, physics; left school before graduation

AWARDS: NATO/ShoWest Director of the Year Award 1986; presented by National Association of Theater Owners

MTV Movie Award Best Movie "Terminator 2: Judgment Day" 1992

MTV Movie Award Best Action Sequence "Terminator 2: Judgment Day" 1992

NATO/ShoWest Producer of the Year Award 1994 presented by National Association of Theater Owners

Broadcast Film Critics Association Award Best Director "Titanic" 1997

Golden Globe Award Best Picture "Titanic" 1997; award shared with Jon Landau

Golden Globe Award Best Director "Titanic" 1997

Golden Satellite Best Motion Picture (Drama) "Titanic" 1997

Golden Satellite Best Director "Titanic" 1997

Golden Satellite Best Film Editing "Titanic" 1997; shared award

Producers Guild of America Darryl Zanuck

Theatrical Producer of the Year Award "Titanic" 1997

Japanese Academy Award Best Foreign Film "Titanic" 1997

Directors Guild of America Award Outstanding Directorial Achievement in Feature Film "Titanic" 1997

American Cinema Editors Eddie Award Theatrical Film Editing "Titanic" 1997; shared award

Oscar Best Picture "Titanic" 1997; award shared with Jon Landau

Oscar Best Director "Titanic" 1997

Oscar Best Film Editing "Titanic" 1997; shared with Conrad Buff and Richard A Harris

MTV Movie Award Best Picture "Titanic" 1998; award shared with Jon Landau

People's Choice Award Favorite Dramatic Motion Picture "Titanic" 1999

People's Choice Award Favorite Motion Picture "Titanic" 1999

American Cinema Editors Golden Eddie Award 1999

BIOGRAPHY

Since the mid-1980s, Canadian-born James Cameron became established as a leading sci-fi auteur and a visionary of cinematic special effects. He shrewdly mixes and matches genre conventions, potent cultural signifiers and top-notch FX to comment on both big issues (i.e., fears of nuclear holocaust) and interpersonal relationships, transforming spectacles into personal films. Each film, however, ups the ante, pushing the limits of what is affordable and what is cutting-edge. A key theme of a Cameron film is the loss of humanity because of modern technology. There is a sense of the inevitable that emerges in his work that reached its apotheosis in the blockbuster "Titanic" (1997), which was both an FX-laded spectacle as well as an old-fashioned romance.

Born in Kapuskasing, Ontario, Canada to an electrical engineer father and an artist mother, Cameron crossed the border with his family to live first in Niagara Falls, NY, and later Brea, CA. As a youngster, he was interested in astronomy and science fiction, even penning his own short stories. Cameron was so astounded by a screening of Stanley Kubrick's "2001: A Space Odyssey" (1968) that he reportedly viewed the film ten times and became inspired to experiment with 16mm film-making and model building. He enrolled in a local college to study physics but instead dropped out, married a waitress, and got work as a truck driver. After viewing George Lucas' "Star Wars" (1977) he decided he should be making his own epics. Cameron raised private financing and directed, shot, edited and built miniatures for his first short film. The talent evident in this effort landed him an interview with Roger Corman's New World Pictures, where he began as a special effects technician and soon evolved into an art director and production designer.

Cameron received his first directing credit on the better-off-forgotten "Piranha II: The Spawning" (1981), an ill-conceived "sequel" to an amusing "Jaws" knockoff. The experience was memorably unpleasant for the neophyte director who arrived on the Jamaican set to find a crew that spoke only Italian and a shockingly underfinanced production. Cameron had no control over the film, a situation he would successfully avoid during his subsequent career. Late in the production, he had a vivid nightmare about a robot assassin from the future, which served as the basis for a screenplay that would evolve into "The Terminator" (1986).

Cameron approached producer Gale Anne Hurd, former head of marketing at New World, and sold her the rights to his screenplay for one dollar, on the condition that he would be allowed to direct the film, The result was a classic thriller crafted on a modest budget of about $6.5 million. Boasting sleek compositions, expertly edited action sequences, and a career-transforming performance by Arnold Schwarzenegger, "The Terminator" was a critical and commercial triumph. Many Cameron hallmarks were already present, including intelligent scripting, strong characters, particularly the female lead, and a seriousness of purpose. The imagery and situations were resonant without resorting to trumpeting their allusions; Cameron's approach to the mythic material was often witty without descending into camp.

Hardly the standard Hollywood liberal, Cameron worked as a screenwriter (sharing credit with star Sylvester Stallone) on the landmark revisionist war fantasy "Rambo: First Blood II" (1985). His follow-up as a writer-director was "Aliens" (1989), a galvanizing sequel to Ridley Scott's memorably horrific 1979 outing, which many found superior to the original. Cameron reimagined the scary material as an action flick that begins as a "can-do" WWII-style story but quickly descends into a Vietnam-inflected vision of chaos. He also turned the already formidable Sigourney Weaver into a no-nonsense warrior for this box-office smash. "Aliens" snared seven Oscar nominations, including a Best Actress nod for Weaver, and won two statues for Best Sound Effects Editing and Best Visual Effects.

Cameron's victorious march faltered a bit with the ambitious, but underperforming, underwater epic "The Abyss" (1991). This waterlogged tale of first contact with alien life was a special effects landmark that also depicted the demise of a marriage (paralleled in real-life as Cameron's marriage to producer Gale Ann Hurd was ending). Cameron had already developed a reputation for the extreme demands he makes on both cast and crew and "The Abyss" proved to be a notoriously difficult shoot as much of the story is set underwater. In order to achieve the director's vision, Cameron and crew had to invent much of the equipment used to shoot the film. Nominated for four technical Oscars, "The Abyss" swallowed one up for Best Visual Effects.

Cameron went on to establish his own production company, Lightstorm Entertainment, in partnership with former Vestron production executive Larry Kasanoff as executive vice president. Initially based in northern Burbank, CA, Lightstorm was conceived by Cameron as "a place for passionate filmmaking" by the writer-director and others. The first expression of this passion was the eagerly awaited 1991 blockbuster sequel "Terminator 2: Judgment Day" which recast Schwarzenegger's mechanical hitman as a hero and showcased a newly-buffed Linda Hamilton as the guerrilla heroine dead set on saving the world. The computer-generated "morphing" effects first seen briefly in "The Abyss" were perfected here for the many transformations of Robert Patrick's sinister T-1000. Described by Cameron as a "violent movie about world peace", the film contains a nightmare-inducing sequence of nuclear destruction. Rumored to be one of Hollywood's most expensive films up to that time ($88–95 million), "T2" gave the world its money's worth and earned over $200 million domestically. The film won four of its six Oscar nominations (Best Visual Effects, Best Sound, Best Makeup and Best Sound Effects Editing). The success of "T2" led to Lightstorm signing an exclusive five-year, twelve-picture financing distribution deal with 20th-Century Fox worth over $500 million. Under this deal, Fox would advance a percentage of the negative costs of films produced, directed or written by Cameron and would also handle North American distribution of all Lightstorm productions.

In April 1993, Cameron founded the special effects company Digital Domain with former Industrial Light and Magic staffer Scott Ross and creature-maker/special makeup FX artist Stan Winston. This firm would handle the full FX spectrum with an emphasis on the computer-generated digital variety. Their first feature assignment was 1994's "True Lies", which marked an elaborate change-of-pace for the modern master of sci-fi action films. Described by Cameron as a "domestic epic", the film is loosely based on "La Totale!", a 1991 French comedy about a bored librarian who learns that her apparently ho-hum hubby is actually a secret agent. Schwarzenegger and Jamie Lee Curtis starred in this mega-budget (reportedly $120 million) mock-Bond film that also told the comic story of a marriage in crisis. Curtis shone as a demure housewife who evolves into a sexy and crafty heroine. Reviewers and audiences were divided over the merits of the extensive comedy sequences but everyone was bowled over by the over-the-top stunts and FX. Cameron had helmed another solid hit that managed to turn a healthy profit despite its Olympian budget.

Production costs on "True Lies" had exceeded Fox's mandated limit of $60 million, so Cameron and Company had to scramble to obtain completion financing. Lightstorm restructured its deal with Fox thereby necessitating Cameron to rein in the scope of his business aspirations. Fox became the sole financier of Lightstorm's productions in return for ownership to their worldwide rights. Cameron would henceforth focus on filmmaking rather than being an international film financier.

Cameron co-produced and co-wrote the futuristic "Strange Days" (1995), which was directed by his third wife Kathryn Bigelow. Instead, he turned his attention to the project which would consume him for nearly two years, "Titanic." Given Cameron's interest in technology as a theme in his work, it seemed only natural he would turn his attentions to one of the first symbols of engineering failures of the Twentieth Century. In 1995, the director participated in a series of underwater dives at the wreckage of the ocean liner. Using special cameras encased in titanium, he shot footage of the wreckage at the bottom of the sea, (Some of these shots ended up in the finished film.) While "Titanic" ran over schedule (by 22 days), the major challenges for Cameron were to build both a model of the grand liner (which was created at 90 percent of scale) and the tank in which to sink it (accomplished in

Rosarita, Mexico); these were built simultaneously and under a tight construction schedule. He also had to fashion a workable romantic story at the film's heart (achieved through the performances of Leonardo DiCaprio and Kate Winslet). During the laborious shoot, Cameron often clashed with representatives of the two studios (Fox and Paramount) who were sharing costs. Originally intended for release in July 1997, the film was delayed because of the painstaking state-of-the-art FX technology, which employed the most FX shots ever, including all scenes of the ship at sea and most spectacularly, its sinking.

Almost from the outset of filming, the press speculated on the movie's commercial appeal and each rumor was duly reported, every little difficulty noted and occasionally exaggerated. (Admittedly, there were some problems: someone spiked the on-set food with PCP early in the shoot; the Screen Actors Guild investigated to ensure the safety of the cast, etc.) Cameron faced innumerable odds in completing "Titanic" and by his own accounts, it was not easy or pleasurable. But it proved to be a labor of passion for him and to guarantee his vision, he relinquished all fees except a salary as screenwriter. When "Titanic" was released in December 1997 at a running time of over three hours, it received generally favorable critical notices. (Those who did pan the film carped at its somewhat cliched romance between a socialite expected to marry for money and a poor artist.) But audiences responded to Cameron's ideal and "Titanic" proved to be a surprising blockbuster, eventually becoming the top grossing film in history earning over $470 million within three months of its release. It received 14 Academy Award nominations, matching the record held by 1950's "All About Eve", and went on to win 11 Oscars, including Best Picture and Best Director, tying the record set by the 1959 remake of "Ben-Hur."

COMPANIONS:

wife: Susan Williams. Waitress, worked at a Bob's Big Boy restaurant; married after Cameron dropped out of California State University, Fullerton; inspiration for Sarah Connor in "The Terminator"; divorced

wife: Gale Anne Hurd. Producer, screenwriter; produced and co-wrote (with Cameron) "The Terminator" (1984), also produced "Aliens" (1986), "The Abyss" (1989), and "Terminator 2: Judgment Day" (1991) for Cameron; divorced

wife: Kathryn Bigelow. Director, screenwriter; Cameron produced her "Point Break" (1991); produced and scripted her "Strange Days" (1995); married in 1989; separated in 1991; divorced

wife: Linda Hamilton. Actor; directed her in starring roles in both "Terminator" films; together from 1991–94 (end date approximate); moved out with their infant daughter during pre-production on "True Lies" but continued the relationship for a period; reunited and in March 1997, Hamilton announced their plans to marry; married on July 24, 1997; separated in May 1998; Hamilton filed for divorce on December 14, 1998

MILESTONES:

Moved with family to Niagara Falls, New York, as a child

1966: At age 12, wrote a sci-fi short story that was reportedly a precursor for "The Abyss" (date approximate)

1968–1969: Saw Stanley Kubrick's "2001: A Space Odyssey" ten times (dates approximate)

Started building models and experimenting with 16mm film

Made first film "Niagara: Or How I Learned to Stop Worrying and Love the Falls"

1971: Moved with family to Brea, California

Enrolled in college to study physics

Dropped out, married a waitress, and worked as a truck driver for the local school district

1977: Inspired to become a filmmaker after seeing "Star Wars"

Raised private financing and directed, shot, edited and built miniatures for first short film

Joined Roger Corman's New World Pictures as a special effects person, and later became art director and production designer

1980: Credited as set dresser assistant on "Happy Birthday, Gemini"

1980: First film as art director, "Battle Beyond the Stars"

1981: Feature debut as production designer and second unit director, "Galaxy of Terror"

1981: Feature directing debut, "Piranha II: The Spawning/Piranha II: Flying Killers"

Wrote first draft of screenplay for what would become "The Terminator"; sold rights to producer Gale Anne Hurd for $1 on the condition that he would direct

1984: Gained recognition with feature screenwriting debut, "The Terminator" (co-written with producer and future wife Gale Anne Hurd); also directed

Hemdale and Orion gave veteran fantasy writer Harlan Ellison an "acknowledgement to the works of" credit on "The Terminator" and a cash settlement lest he sue for plagiarism of two episodes he wrote for "The Outer Limits" in the 1960s and a Hugo award winning sci-fi story

1985: Co-wrote (with Sylvester Stallone) the hugely successful "Rambo: First Blood II"

1986: Became a hot writer-director after the success of "Aliens"

1989: Wrote and directed "The Abyss"

1990: Formed production company Lightstorm Entertainment Inc.

1991: Produced, directed and scripted the sequel "Terminator 2: Judgment Day"

1992: Lightstorm signed an exclusive five-year, 12-picture distribution deal with 20th Century Fox valued at $500 million; Lightstorm Entertainment was given total creative control and a large share of the profits

1993: With Stan Winston and Scott Ross and substantial financing from IBM, started the special effects company Digital Domain to further develop the field of digital FX

1993: Released a "restored" print of "The Abyss" including approximately 27 minutes of scenes omitted from the original

Production costs on "True Lies" exceeded Fox's mandated limit of $60 million

Renegotiated deal with Fox so as to get them to increase their funding of "True Lies" while Cameron retained creative control; new deal involved three films and worked on a film-by-film basis

1994: Wrote, produced, and directed the action-comedy "True Lies", the first release under Lightstorm's deal with 20th Century Fox

1995: Provided the story for and served as a producer on "Strange Days"; also reportedly assited in the editing for which he did not receive onscreen credit

1995: Became the first feature film director to shoot underwater footage of the wreck of the Titanic; used a specially-designed, state-of-the-art camera encased in titanium; footage was incorporated into the feature "Titanic"

1997: Co-edited, co-produced, wrote and directed the lavish spectacle "Titanic", reported to be the most expensive film made to date (budgeted at $200 million); went on to become the top grossing film in history; film received 14 Academy Award nominations (matching the record set by 1950's "All About Eve"), including Best Picture, Best Director and Best Editing; awarded 11 Oscars, including Best Picture and Best Director, tying the record set by 1959's "Ben-Hur"

1998: With Stan Winston, resigned from board of Digital Domain

1998: Signed exclusive deal with 20th Century Fox TV to develop programming; co-wrote five-hour miniseries on the colonization of Mars to air in the spring of 2001

2000—Present: Executive produced and co-wrote the Fox fall drama series "Dark Angel"; helmed the finale of the 2001–2002 season

Co-produced (with Jean-Michel Cousteau) a series of undersea specials for ABC under the umbrella title of "Ocean Challenge"

QUOTES:

In 1998, Cameron became the fifth recipient of the Beatrice Wood Film Award.

"I'm fascinated by the end of the world. The idea of the end of the world and the idea of either the fabric of reality unraveling, or literally the cataclysm. 'Strange Days' plays around with that from the millennial standpoint, and 'Terminator' palys around with it quite literally—this has happened, but it just hasn't happened yet. . . . the folding of time thing."—James Cameron quoted in *Written By*, December 1997–January 1998.

"I think I'm a good director, but I never claimed to have the PERSONALITY for directing. It brings out the worst in me, and it's the aspect of the work I hate the most. It should be noted that I am never megative with the actors, absolutely and religiously. In many ways they have the most difficult job on the set, and I make it my mission to be supportive and collaborative."—Cameron to *Time*, December 8, 1997.

"He's a genius and a maniac. A genius in terms of his vision, a maniac in terms of getting what he wants. But that's to be absolutely admired, because to be the controller of a thing that's so absolutely huge is amazing. Some of the visions he had in his head I found really frustrating, because I couldn't quite understand what he meant. I finally came to realize, though, My God, this man has been visualizing nothing but this for the last two years."—"Titanic" co-star Kate Winslet on Cameron to *Movieline*, March 1998.

"The funny thing is, I'm always OBSESESSED. Whatever film I make it's the same. I was obsessed on 'True Lies' and that was an action comedy. I'm always obsessed with details. I think it's the strength of any good film-maker—and really part of the job description—to be obsessed like that."—James Cameron quoted in "Heading for Shore" by John Anderson in *Newsday*, December 14, 1997.

"Filming underwater [for 'The Abyss']

proved to be incredibly arduous. The water was so highly chlorinated that it burned skin and turned hair white. Even the mundane details were complicated. . . . The actors were stretched to the breaking point. When the camera ran out of film in the middle of her death scene, Mary Elizabeth Mastrantonio stormed off the set, screaming, 'We are not animals!' Ed Harris tells [in "The Abyss' "s fascinating laserdisc special edition] of a day so hard, he burst into tears on the drive home."—From "Iron Jim" by John H. Richardson in *Premiere*, August 1994.

"One aspect of that drive that sets him apart from other action filmmakers is his meticulous attention to the composition of shots, even in stunt scenes. Where many directors are happy just to get the stunt committed to celluloid, Cameron looks both for a spectacular thrill and a carefully sculpted image, which means demanding, nearly impossible camera work."—From "Can He Do Side-Splitting Action?" by David Kronke in *Los Angeles Times Calendar*, July 17, 1994.

"With Cameron anything is possible. Fired from his first film, he broke into the editing room and cut the film back to his original vision. That was before the runaway success of the two "Terminators" and "Aliens" gave him imperial power. Nowadays he directs his crew through a bank of speakers pitched to concert volume: THAT'S EXACTLY WHAT I WANT, he booms. If they mess up, he says, THAT'S OKAY. I'VE WORKED WITH CHILDREN BEFORE. The crews respond by printing up T-shirts with semi-jokey slogans: YOU CAN'T SCARE ME—I WORK FOR JIM CAMERON."—From "Iron Jim" by John H. Richardson in *Premiere*, August 1994.

"Like the others, 'T2' spawned its own crew T-shirt: TERMINATOR 3—NOT WITH ME."—From *Premiere*, August 1994.

"Mr. Cameron is the master of movies that put women at the center of the action. He is responsible for the macho Sigourney Weaver in 'Aliens' and the pumped-up, rifle-toting

Linda Hamilton in 'Terminator 2: Judgment Day'. . . . Traditionally, action films have been directed at male viewers; adding a character with whom women can identify broadens the audience appeal. But pop culture always reflects mainstream attitudes, if only inadvertently, and in their exaggerated ways these films hint at how women's lives have changed.

"The heroines of 'Aliens' and 'Terminator 2', however, developed their biceps between movies, in the time lapse between the original films and the sequels. By showing Helen's transformation in 'True Lies', Mr. Cameron charts the comic course of a female stereotype falling to pieces."—From "Film View: The Woman in 'True Lies', a Mouse That Roared" in *The New York Times*, July 17, 1994.

" 'True Lies' is able to effectively kid itself, to playfully mock the conventions of espionage thrillers. Casting the breezy Tom Arnold as Harry's partner Gib helps, but more important is Cameron's unerring ability to find the humor in Schwarzenegger, something the people at 'Last Action Hero,' for instance, were unable to manage."—Kenneth Turan in *Los Angeles Times Calendar*, July 14, 1994.

BIBLIOGRAPHY:

"James Cameron: An Unauthorized Biogrpahy of the Filmmaker" Marc Shapiro, 2000, St. Martin's Press

Jane Campion

BORN: in Wellington, New Zealand 04/30/1954

NATIONALITY: New Zealander

EDUCATION: Victoria University, Wellington, New Zealand, structural anthropology, BA

studied art in Venice and Italian in Perugia

Sydney College of the Arts, Sydney, Australia, painting and sculpture; began making Super-8 films; directed short film "Tissues" in 1980

Australian Film Television and Radio School, Sydney, Australia, 1981–84, graduated; completed short films "Peel" (1982), "Passionless Moments" (1984), and her thesis film, "A Girl's Own Story" (1984)

AWARDS: Melbourne International Festival XL Elder Award "After Hours" 1984

Australian Film Institute Award Best Experimental Film "Passionless Moments" 1984

Cannes Film Festival Palme d'Or Short Film "Peel" 1986

Australian Film Institute Award Best TV Director "Two Friends" 1987

Australian Film Institute Byron Kennedy Award 1989

Film Critics Circle of Australia Award Best Director "Sweetie" 1989

Los Angeles Film Critics Association New Generation Award "Sweetie" 1990

Chicago Film Critics Association Award Best Foreign Film "An Angel at My Table" 1991

Cannes Film Festival Palme d'Or "The Piano" 1993; shared award with Chen Kaige who won with "Farewell to My Concubine"; first Palme d'Or awarded to either a woman or a Chinese filmmaker

Film Critics Circle of Australia Award Best Director "The Piano" 1993

Film Critics Circle of Australia Award Best Screenplay "The Piano" 1993

Australian Film Institute Award Best Director "The Piano" 1993; film won a record 11 Australian Film Institute awards

Australian Film Institute Award Best Screenplay "The Piano" 1993

Los Angeles Film Critics Association Award Best Director "The Piano" 1993

Los Angeles Film Critics Association Award Best Screenplay "The Piano" 1993

New York Film Critics Circle Award Best Director "The Piano" 1993

New York Film Critics Circle Award Best Screenplay "The Piano" 1993

National Society of Film Critics Award Best Screenplay "The Piano" 1993

London Film Critics Circle Award Best Film "The Piano" 1993

Writers Guild of America Award Best Screenplay Written Directly For the Screen "The Piano" 1993

Oscar Best Screenplay Written Directly for the Screen "The Piano" 1993

Cesar Best Foreign-Language Film "The Piano" 1994

BIOGRAPHY

Along with Australian directors Gillian Armstrong, Jocelyn Moorhouse and Shirley Barrett, Jane Campion has emerged as a major feminist filmmaker. She has been responsible for some of the most acclaimed films to have originated from Down Under since the late 1980s. Her features all have one thing in common: a powerful, courageous woman as a central figure. From Genevieve Lemon's unhinged "Sweetie" (1989) to Kerry Fox's mentally troubled Janet Frame in "An Angel at My Table" (1990) to Holly Hunter's mute Ada in "The Piano" (1993) to Nicole Kidman's manipulated Isabel Archer in "The Portrait of a Lady" (1996), the lead in a Campion film provides a showcase for the actress and advances the director's desire to display private, often erotic, sides of women rarely portrayed in conventional Hollywood fodder. Although some critics have found her work self-conscious, the majority have praised her originality. The roots of her skill can be traced to her upbringing and education. Born in Wellington, New Zealand, to theatrical parents (her father was a director, her mother, an actress), Campion displayed an early interest in art; she was also an accomplished, but idiosyncratic artist, with an eye toward the unusual. (This would later manifest in her use of camera angles and in the set pieces she created in her films.) Although interested in acting, Campion studied anthropology in college and later ventured to Europe where she studied art in Venice. Migrating to London, she found work as an assistant to a director of commercials and documentaries before she moved to Australia. Enrolling in art school, Campion began to experiment with film and shot her first short, "Tissues", about a father who had been arrested for child molestation. Furthering her education at the Australian Film, Television and Radio School, Campion went on to complete several award-winning shorts, including "Peel" (1982), centering on a power struggle over discipline between a child and his father, and her thesis, "A Girl's Own Story" (1984), which introduced her themes of women, sexuality and rites of passage.

After marking time in the Women's Film Unit, a government-sponsored program for which she directed the short "After Hours" (1984), about sexual harassment, and a detour to TV with the longform "Two Friends" (1986), Campion made her feature debut with the darkly stylish "Sweetie", a disturbing study of familial tensions brought about by a mentally unstable young woman. Acclaimed for its visual style, strong performances and comic originality, "Sweetie" earned prizes from the Film Critics Circle of Australia and the Los Angeles Film Critics Association.

Campion's second feature "An Angel at My Table" was originally intended as a TV-movie. Working from a script by Laura Jones, adapted from the autobiography of New Zealand writer Janet Frame, the director fashioned a biopic that detailed an unconventional story. Tracing Frame from her awkward childhood through a nervous breakdown and stay in a mental institutions to her eventual fulfillment as a writer, Campion once again displayed a flair for observant detail and lush visuals. It is an intimate look at an atypical central figure, a shy, plain woman who defines herself through her writing.

In 1984, fresh out of film school, Campion began working on a screenplay about the colonial past of New Zealand. Over nearly a decade, she developed the project into what became her most acclaimed feature to date, "The Piano", an intensely erotic story told from the female perspective. The story is fairly simplistic: a mute woman (Holly Hunter) enters into an arranged marriage and moves halfway around the world with her illegitimate daughter (Anna Paquin) and her piano. Her new husband (Sam Neill) refuses to transport the instrument and sells it to a settler gone native (Harvey Keitel). The purchaser agrees to return the piano if the woman teaches him how to play. Again Campion's hallmarks of gorgeous photography (the landscape almost becomes another character) and strong performances align to produce a remarkably original Gothic drama. "The Piano" earned numerous awards, including the Palme d'Or at Cannes (the first for a woman director). Campion became only the second woman nominated for the Best Director Academy Award. Although she lost in that category, she did win for her screenplay, as did Hunter for Best Actress and Paquin for Best Supporting Actress.

Campion's long awaited follow-up was an adaptation of Henry James' novel "The Portrait of a Lady", written by Laura Jones and starring Nicole Kidman. Critics were divided; some found it static and miscast, while others praised its intelligence and the director's injection of sexual matters hinted at in the original.

MILESTONES:

Raised in Wellington, New Zealand

1970: Moved with family to a farm when she was aged 16 (date approximate)

Received degree in anthropology from Victoria College in Wellington, New Zealand

After graduating college, travelled to Europe; lived in Venice where she studied art; moved to Perugia to study Italian; later moved to London where she worked as an assistant to filmmaker of documentaries and commercials; eventually moved to Sydney, Australia

1980: Directed first short film, "Tissues", while a student at Sydney College of the Arts

Enrolled in Australia Film Television and Radio School

1982: Directed, wrote, and edited "Peel", a short film

1984: Directed and wrote short, "After Hours" (for the Women's Film Unit in Australia)

1985: Directed first TV-movie, "Two Friends"

1989: Feature film directing debut, "Sweetie"; also co-wrote with Gerald Lee

1990: Second feature, "Angel at My Table", won an unprecedented eight prizes at the Venice Film Festival, including the Silver Lion

1990: Acted in the comedy short, "The Audition", directed by her sister Anne Campion and opposite their mother Edith Armstrong

1993: Had international breakthrough hit, "The Piano"; became the first female director to win the Palme d'Or at Cannes and only the second female nominated for the Best Director Oscar

Formed Big Shell Films with her husband Colin Englert

1996: Returned to features with "The Portrait of a Lady"

Entered into production agreement with Miramax for at least one film

1997: Signed three-year, first-look agreement with Propaganda Films to begin after Campion fulfilled terms of agreement with Miramax

1999: With sister Anna co-wrote "Holy Smoke", starring Harvey Keitel and Kate Winslet; also directed

Helmed "In the Cut" (lensed 2002), an erotic thriller based on Susanna Moore's novel

QUOTES:

"I'm really interested in issues of love and superstition—family love, romantic love, reality and illusion, New Age-ism, misconceptions of New Age-ism . . . I'm interested in all those things. But when I write, I don't think like this. I just think, 'What would be fun to have happen next?' I think in a playful way, and then later I try to examine what's happened."—Jane Campion in *Premiere*, March 1990.

"I think she really writes about what is exquisite in human beings but not necessarily about the perfection. She writes about the things that are hard to come to terms with in us and those things may be good and the may have elements of evil, or they may have elements of desire."—Holly Hunter, on the lyrical writings of Jane Campion, quoted in *Filmmaker*, Fall 1993.

"Jane is Isabel Archer—but she's also Madame Merle. She's reasonably manipulative. She is intensely competitive. She has always managed to get what she's wanted. She will do absolutely what she wants to do, in her life and in her movies."—"The Portrait of a Lady" star Nicole Kidman on her friend Jane Campion, quoted in "Heroine Chic" by Howard Feinstein in *Vanity Fair*, December 1996.

"Here is the key to her personality and way of working—the conspiracy of great friendship that has its own secrets."—actor Richard E. Grant quoted in *Vanity Fair*, December 1996.

BIBLIOGRAPHY:

"Holy Smoke" Anna Campion and Jane Campion, 1999, Miramax/Hyperion; novel

Frank Capra

BORN: Francesco Capra in Bisaquino, Sicily, Italy, 05/18/1897

SOMETIMES CREDITED AS:
Frank R. Capra

DEATH: in La Quinta, California, 09/03/1991

NATIONALITY: Italian

CITIZENSHIP: United States

EDUCATION: Manual Arts High School, Los Angeles, California

California Institute of Technology, Pasadena, California, chemical engineering, BS, 1918; school then called the Throop Polytechnic Institute; worked his way through college running the student laundry, waiting tables and wiping engines at the Pasadena power plant

AWARDS: Oscar Best Director "It Happened One Night" 1934

National Board of Review Award Best American Film "Mr. Deeds Goes to Town" 1936

New York Film Critics Circle Award Best Picture "Mr. Deeds Goes to Town" 1936

Oscar Best Director "Mr. Deeds Goes to Town" 1936

Oscar Best Picture "You Can't Take It With You" 1938 Capra produced the film

Oscar Best Director "You Can't Take It With You" 1938

Directors Guild of America Honorary Life Membership 1941

Golden Globe Award Best Director "It's a Wonderful Life" 1946

Directors Guild of America D. W. Griffith Award 1959

Society of Motion Picture and Television Engineers Award 1973

American Film Institute Life Achievement Award 1982

BIOGRAPHY

During the dark decade of the 1930s, Frank Capra became America's preeminent filmmaker, leavening Depression-era despair with the laughter of his irrepressible optimism. Packaging hope for the hopeless, his "fantasies of goodwill" were as important to national morale as FDR's "fireside chats" and well-deserving of the three Best Director Oscars they brought him. Twenty years later when the *Cahiers du Cinema* critics launched an auteurist reassessment of American films, his reputation suffered, despite the unarguable fact that his "name above the title" signified his absolute artistic control of the project, a rarity in the studio-dominated Hollywood culture of his heyday. Subsequent voices followed suit, taking great delight in decrying his work as dangerously simplistic in its populism, its patriotism and its celebration of all-American values, but the content of his films should not be judged too harshly out of the context of their time, the pulse of which Capra accurately measured. Fortunately, most contemporary critics look past the ideology to his undeniable strengths as a filmmaker.

Capra celebrated his sixth birthday alongside fellow immigrants in steerage of a ship bound for the United States. The classic rags-to-riches story, which saw this son of a fruit picker become one of his adopted country's most celebrated directors, was pure Horatio Alger, complete with his putting himself through the future CalTech by running the student laundry and waiting on tables, among other money-making endeavors. After service in the army, the unemployed engineer (and only college graduate among seven siblings) knocked about the

West, hustling a living as a poker player and selling wildcat oil stocks before achieving a measure of respectability peddling Elbert Hubbard's "Little Journeys" in a 14-volume deluxe edition. Seeing an ad for a new movie studio in San Francisco, he managed to talk his way into helming his first short, "Fultah Fisher's Boarding House" (1922), a one-reeler based on the poem by Rudyard Kipling. In order to learn more about his new chosen profession, Capra apprenticed in a film lab, eventually working as a prop man, film editor and gag writer for director Bob Eddy, then joined first Hal Roach and later Mack Sennett, climbing the ladder of film comedy.

Though remembered primarily today for his social comedies of the 30s and 40s, Capra developed his craft at the helm of a diverse body of work, his first 21 features (made between 1926 and 1932) bearing almost none of the trademarks of his signature films. When Harry Langdon left Sennett for First National, Capra tagged along, successfully directing three vehicles for the popular silent comic, whose decline seemingly coincided with his decision to direct himself. Capra's big break came in 1928 when Harry Cohn at struggling Columbia Pictures made him a company director, giving him carte blanche on the strength of his Langdon pictures. Over the next ten years he would direct 25 films (nine features in his first 12 months alone), raising that studio almost single-handedly from Poverty Row to the ranks of MGM, Paramount, RKO and United Artists. At Columbia, Capra became known as a reliable craftsman of efficient and profitable productions, regardless of genre, his early work including military/action dramas ("Submarine" 1928, "Flight" 1929, "Dirigible" 1931); newspaper stories ("The Power of the Press" 1928); Barbara Stanwyck melodramas ("Ladies of Leisure" 1930, "The Miracle Woman" 1931, "Forbidden" 1932); and tearjerkers ("The Younger Generation" 1929).

"Platinum Blonde" (1931) heralded the beginning of Capra's long-standing collaboration with screenwriter Robert Riskin, with whom his social conscience suddenly emerged on "American Madness" (1932), the prototype for much of their work to come. Their first idealistic hero (Walter Huston) is a dedicated community banker who, much like James Stewart in "It's a Wonderful Life" (1946), lends money to people whose only collateral is honesty and averts a bank run by rallying faithful depositors as he battles the impersonal and corrupt machinery of big business. Capra demonstrated his mastery of the medium, using overlapping speeches that emphasized the naturalistic quality of the dialogue as increased crosscutting and jump cuts registered the panic and hysteria of the mob. However, having discovered a winning 30s formula, he abandoned it (and Riskin) for "The Bitter Tea of General Yen" (1933), his most elaborately designed film recalling the style of Josef von Sternberg in its chiaroscuro lighting and its exoticism. Considered by some his masterpiece, it failed to generate enthusiasm, and Capra returned to Depression-era sentimentality with Riskin on "Lady for a Day" (also 1933), earning his first Oscar nomination as Best Director.

Though some critics blame Riskin for all that is saccharine and simplistic in the "Capriskin" oeuvre, he did write the pioneering "screwball comedy", "It Happened One Night" (1934), which swept the five major Academy Awards and established Capra as a major director. Following this unprecedented success, Capra began to produce as well as direct all of his projects, creating the string of celebrated films championing the common man most closely associated with his name. First came "Mr. Deeds Goes to Town" (1936), whose innocent and truly virtuous bumpkin, Longfellow Deeds (Gary Cooper), confronts a corrupt and crazy world which does not cotton to his decision to give away his inherited millions. A key player in the film's success was the character played by Jean Arthur, a cynical reporter who anticipates audience skepticism and leads Deeds down a primrose path to his potential undoing, while managing to fall in love along the way. Of course, the eventual resolution at the sanity hearing is as unbelievable as the prosecution's punk case against Deeds, but the movie's message that goodness can ultimately triumph over evil was a perfect tonic for the times. Oscar smiled again on the director.

Adaptations of "Lost Horizon" (1937, from the James Hilton novel) and "You Can't Take It With You" (1938, from the George S. Kaufman-Moss Hart play) perpetuated the director's utopian vision of the world. The former added "Shangri-La", a strange Tibetan land where health, peace and longevity reign, to the lexicon and the latter (according to some reports Capra's most profitable film) celebrated individualism as embodied by the eccentric Grandpa Vanderhof (Lionel Barrymore) and clan. (It also earned Capra his third Best Director Academy Award.) "Mr. Smith Goes to Washington" (1939), his last film for Columbia, then introduced James Stewart as his representative of small-town idealism, with Arthur reprising her hard-boiled dame routine. When crooked politicians send head "boy scout" Stewart to the Senate, he turns the tables on them, making the world safe again for "truth, justice and the American way." Though such easy cures for the political and press corruption so visibly illustrated were not readily available, the film exhibited the master at work, using all the techniques at his disposal to pack an emotional wallop in every scene. Long shots, quick cuts in close-up and montages that conveyed an accelerated storyline without disrupting it complemented a stellar cast delivering yet another Capra masterpiece.

Gary Cooper was back as the "barefoot fascist" of "Meet John Doe" (1941), the director's first independent film, which warned of influential native elements like the pro-Nazi German-American Bund operating in pre-World War II America. His only commercial film to appear during the war was "Arsenic and Old Lace" (filmed in 1941 but released in 1944), adapted from the Joseph Kesselring play, as he reentered the service and devoted his filmmaking talent to the American propaganda effort, directing the Oscar-winning "Prelude to War" (1942). It and its six sister "Why We Fight" information films shown to every G.I. helped remove any doubts in servicemen's minds that they were fighting for America against inhuman foes devoid not only of morality, but of common decency. Called the most powerful "statement of our cause" by Winston Churchill, these textbooks of found-footage montage and other documentaries earned Colonel Capra the Distinguished Service Medal (the highest American military decoration for noncombat service). The French (or anybody else for that matter) can say what they want about being simplistic or overly patriotic. Capra was the right man at a black-and-white time, pitting his goodness against unspeakable evil.

Back in civilian clothes, the director went to work on the perennial Christmas classic, "It's a Wonderful Life" (1946), a picture that lost money at the box office during its initial release. Capra considered it his greatest achievement, and time has borne him out as the sentimental tale continues to improve with age. For his examination of the human heart, he tapped Stewart (who also ranked it his favorite film) for small-town Everyman George Bailey, Barrymore for Bailey's evil nemesis Potter and Donna Reed as the loyal trusting wife who knew since childhood she would be Mrs. George Bailey, surrounding his principals with stalwart supporting players like Thomas Mitchell, Henry Travers, Beulah Bondi and Ward Bond. Is it too uncritical to call this the perfect movie? Certainly it ranks among the greatest pictures ever made. In someone else's hands, a story of a man stopped from committing suicide by his guardian angel would have been trite, but Capra's contagious optimism and faith in the basic goodness of people turned it into an emotionally and spiritually uplifting experience. Simple? Not at all. Only a master filmmaker like Capra could pull it off so well.

The box-office failure of "It's a Wonderful Life" presaged the fate of his subsequent five features, none of which found much success. The best of these were probably the first (1948's "State of the Union", based on the Broadway hit) and last (1961's "A Pocketful of Miracles", a remake of "Lady for a Day"), though the in-betweeners starring Bing Crosby (twice) and Frank Sinatra yielded two Oscar-winning songs, "In the Cool, Cool, Cool of the Evening" (Bing in "Here Comes the Groom" 1951) and "High Hopes" (Frank in "A Hole in the Head" 1959). Originally slated as the second project of his Liberty Films, "State of the Union" starred Spencer Tracy as a wealthy politician who sickens of the corruption around him and pulls out of the race for president, but for Capra, his selling-out of Liberty (to Paramount) represented a different kind of turning-point. "I fell never to rise to be the same man again either as a person or a talent . . . I lost my nerve . . . for fear of losing a few bucks." "Pocketful of Miracles" proved to be just a little too dated, though it boasted arguably the greatest array of character actors assembled since the 30s and a bravura performance by Bette Davis as Apple Annie.

Capra would try one more time to mount a feature film, but studio interference caused him to pull out of "Marooned", eventually released in 1969 with John Sturges at the helm. His last picture, "Rendezvous in Space" (1964), written, produced and directed for the Martin-Marietta Corporation (builders of the Titan rocket boosters), was in the tradition of his great wartime documentaries and the lesser-known series of educational science documentaries he wrote, produced and directed for the Bell System between 1952 and 1957, exhibiting his remarkable skill for manipulating mundane images into inspirationally charged, optimistic visions of human life. Capra made movies with a message, a simple message which often required a suspension of disbelief in order to respond to them. His genius as a moviemaker was getting the audience past that hurdle and then pulling mercilessly at the heart-strings. Francois Truffaut said of him: "In recognizing the facts of human suffering, uncertainty, anxiety, the everyday struggles of life, Capra with his unquenchable optimism, was a healing force. This good doctor, who was also a great director, became a restorer of men's spirits."—Written by Greg Senf

COMPANIONS:

wife: Helen Howell. Actor; married in 1924; divorced in 1928

Barbara Stanwyck. Actor; acted in five of Capra's films, beginning with "Ladies of Leisure" (1930) and ending with "Meet John Doe" (1941); had relationship in the early 1930s while she was still married to Frank Fay; Capra wanted to marry her but she refused him

wife: Lucille Florence Reyburn. Married engineer Francis Clarke Reyburn in 1928; widowed c. 1929; married Capra in 1932; had four children together; born on April 23, 1903; died on July 1, 1984; claimed to be a descendent of Horatio, Lord Nelson and Sir Thomas More

MILESTONES:

1903: Spent sixth birthday in steerage on the "Germania" en route from Italy to USA; moved with family to California; sold newspapers and played banjo in Los Angeles honky-tonks to pay for education

1918–1919: Enlisted in US Army as a private after college graduation; taught ballistics and mathematics to artillerymen at Fort Scott, San Francisco; demobilized with rank of second lieutenant

Hustled a living as a poker player and sold wildcat mining stocks

1922: Became a book salesman, selling Elbert Hubbard's "Little Journeys" door-to-door

1922: Short film directing debut, "The Ballad of Fultah Fisher's Boarding House/Fultah Fisher's Boarding House"; made in San Francisco for Shakespearean actor Walter Montague's new studio

Apprenticed at Walter Bell's small film lab where he printed, dried and spliced amateur films and dailies for Hollywood comedy director Bob Eddy

1923: Worked as prop man, film editor and gagman for Bob Eddy

Co-wrote—but did not direct—numerous shorts and two features; joined Hal Roach studios as a gagman of "Our Gang" comedies; hired as gag writer by Mack Sennett for Harry Langdon comedies

1926: Co-directed (uncredited) and co-wrote Harry Edwards' "Tramp Tramp Tramp", starring Langdon

1926: Solo feature directing debut, "The Strong Man", starring Langdon

1927: Co-scripted (with Arthur Ripley) Edwards' "His First Flame", starring Langdon

1927: Last film with Langdon, "Long Pants"

1927: Went to NYC where he directed Claudette Colbert in her film debut, "For the Love of Mike"

Briefly Returned to work for Sennett

1928: Joined Harry Cohn's Columbia Pictures as a director; contract called for relatively paltry sum of $1000 a picture but gave Capra complete control of his projects, the first being "That Certain Thing"; helmed eight more features that year with "Submarine" establishing him as a bankable director

1929: First real talkie, "The Younger Generation"; "Submarine" had sound effects and snatches of dialogue

1930: First collaboration with screenwriter Jo Swerling, "Ladies of Leisure"

1931: First collaboration with screenwriter Robert Riskin, "Platinum Blonde"

1932: Fifth and last collaboration for 14 years with Swerling, "Forbidden"

1933: Earned first Academy Award nomination for Best Director for "Lady for a Day", adapted by Riskin from a Damon Runyan story

1934: First blockbuster hit, "It Happened One Night"; became first fim to sweep the top five Oscars: Best Picture, Best Director, Best Screenplay (Riskin), Best Actor (Clark Gable) and Best Actress (Colbert)

1936: Weighed in with the first of his social comedies, "Mr. Deeds Goes to Town", winning second Best Director Academy Award

1938: Earned third Best Director Oscar for film version of George S Kaufman and Moss Hart's stage hit, "You Can't Take It with You"; first of three films with actor James Stewart

1939: Earned Oscar nomination as Best Director for "Mr. Smith Goes to Washington", with Stewart in the title role; last film for Columbia

1939: Formed Frank Capra Productions with Riskin

Commissioned as a major in the US Army Signal Corps; produced all, and directed some, of the films in the "Why We Fight" and "Know Your Ally/Know Your Enemy" documentary series; discharged after WWII with rank of colonel

1945: Formed Liberty Films with production head Samuel Briskin, William Wyler and George Stevens which made only one film, "It's a Wonderful Life" (1946); Liberty Films sold to Paramount in 1948

1946: Received last Academy Award nomination as Best Director for "It's a Wonderful Life", starring Stewart; Swerling contributed additional scenes

1950: Directed "Riding High", a remake of his earlier "Broadway Bill" (1934), starring Bing Crosby

1951: Reteamed with Crosby for "Here Comes the Groom"; 11th and last collaboration with Riskin

1952: Retired to his ranch; worked with Cal-Tech on Defense Department project studying psychological warfare; went to India as US State Department emissary to a film festival that the USA feared would be controlled by Communists; had security clearance delays due to content of "State of the Union" (1948)

Produced, directed and wrote four educational science documentaries for Bell Telephone: "Our Mr. Sun", "Hemo The Magnificent", "Strange Case of Cosmic Rays" and "Unchained Goddess"

1961: Directed last feature "A Pocketful of Miracles", a remake of "Lady for a Day"

1964: Shot last film, "Rendezvous in Space", a short made for the Martin-Marietta Corporation

1964: Moved back onto the Columbia lot to begin pre-production on "Marooned"; blaming then-studio chief Mike Frankovich for forcing him to submit to what he considered unreasonable script approvals and budgets, left this pet film project and officially retired; picture eventually released in 1969 with John Sturges at the helm

1967: Left Hollywood with his wife to settle in La Quinta, California

Suffered a series of minor strokes and was under 24-hour nursing care in the late 1980s

AFFILIATIONS: President of the Academy of Motion Picture Arts and Sciences (1938–40)

Founder and president (1938–40) of Screen Directors Guild

President of the Directors Guild of America (1959)

QUOTES:

Credited as Frank R. Capra on early films

"It Happened One Night" (1934) was the first film to win Oscars for Best Picture, Best Actress, Best Actor, Best Director and Best Screenplay. No other film won all five major awards until "One Flew Over the Cuckoo's Nest" in 1975.

"I always felt the world cannot fall apart as long as free men see the rainbow, feel the rain and hear the laugh of a child."—Frank Capra (From "The Name Above the Title").

Capra often attributed his conversion to "social comedy" to a visit from a "faceless little man" introduced to him during a period of illness by a Christian Scientist friend. The man, whose name he never learned, pointed out that he was able to "talk to hundreds of millions, for two hours—and in the dark. The talents you have, Mr. Capra, are not your own, not self-acquired. God gave you these talents; they are His gifts to you, to use for his purpose." Inspired, the director set about conveying a message to the American people: "My films must let every man, woman, and child know that God loves them, that I love them, and that peace and salvation will become a reality only when they all learn to love each other."—Frank Capra (quoted in "World Film Directors", Volume One).

About "It's a Wonderful Life": "I thought it was the greatest film I ever made. Better yet, I thought it was the greatest film anybody ever made. It wasn't made for the oh-so-bored critics or the oh-so-jaded literati. It was my kind of film for my kind of people."—Frank Capra.

"I respect films, because I know what goes into them. Nobody starts out to make a bad film. I take my hat off to anyone who can complete a picture. They can't all be successes, because we're dealing with an art form, and there are no formulas. Mathematics and art don't speak the same language.

"The best pictures are yet to be made."—Frank Capra, on "The Merv Griffin Show", August 14, 1973 (From "The Complete Films of Frank Capra" by Victor Scherle and William Turner Levy. Citadel Press: 1992).

"Frank Capra made old-fashioned American values and crying in the movies a national pastime. He celebrated the noblest impulses of woman and man, showed all of us our dark side and then pointed a flashlight at the way out."—Steven Spielberg quoted in USA Today, September 4, 1991.

"Capra innovations included accelerated, faster-than-life pacing with overlapping dialogue;

unaffected, conversational speech; removal of men's makeup, and the tape recording of previews to gauge audience reactions that might necessitate revisions.

"Noted for getting actors to perform at the top of their talent, Mr. Capra made stars of Harry Langdon, Jean Harlow and Barbara Stanwyck."—From *The New York Times* obituary by Peter B. Flint, September 4, 1991.

Received Distinguished Service Medal from the US Army Forces in 1945

Awarded France's Legion of Merit Honor and the Order of the British Empire

In 1952, Capra was named US delegate of the International Film Festival in Bombay

BIBLIOGRAPHY:
"Frank Capra: The Name Above the Title" Frank Capra, 1971, Macmillan; autobiography
"Frank Capra" Richard Griffith, 1951; biography
"Frank Capra: One Man—One Film" James Silke, 1971
"The Films of Frank Capra" Donald Willis, 1974
"Frank Capra: The Catastrope of Success" Joseph McBride, 1992, Simon & Schuster

John Carpenter

BORN: John Howard Carpenter in Carthage, New York, 01/16/1948

SOMETIMES CREDITED AS:
Frank Armitage
James T. Chance
John T. Chance
Martin Quatermass
Rip Haight

NATIONALITY: American

EDUCATION: Western Kentucky University, Bowling Green, Kentucky; dropped out in 1968

University of Southern California, Los Angeles, California, film, 1968–72

AWARD: Los Angeles Film Critics Association New Generation Award "Dark Star", "Assault on Precinct 13" and "Halloween" 1979; cited for all three films

BIOGRAPHY
John Carpenter became known in the late 1970s for his expert handling of action and suspense sequences in masculine genre fare.

But unlike some of his contemporaries, he used violence to provide a comic-book texture that advanced the plot rather than grounds for moral dilemmas or stylistic excess. In fact, his signature film, the horror classic "Halloween" (1978), has nary a drop of blood. Drawn to filmmaking by youthful viewings of relatively innocent entertainments like "It Came From Outer Space" (1953) and "Forbidden Planet" (1956), Carpenter has worked primarily in the horror, thriller and science fiction genres. He has been most comfortable and effective when working on modestly budgeted projects.

While a graduate student at USC, Carpenter also produced, helmed and co-wrote with classmate Dan O'Bannon the sci-fi black comedy "Dark Star", a memorable Master's thesis project which he expanded into his first feature—and a minor classic—in 1974. Shot on a budget of only $60,000, the film offered a witty yet quite bleak alternative to Stanley Kubrick's high-minded "2001: A Space Odyssey" in its vision of man in space overwhelmed by technology. British culture magazine *Time Out* proclaimed it "arguably the last great hippy movie with its jokey references to drugs, the Absurd and California surfing. . . . "

Described by its creator as " 'Waiting for Godot' in space", "Dark Star" alerted genre fans of the arrival of a distinctive new sensibility that was smart, playful and technically assured. Sadly, relatively few had a chance to see the film. Though well received at the 1974 Filmex, "Dark Star" was mishandled by several different distributors. Its cult status was attained only after it became popular on the 16mm college circuit in the late 70s.

With no directing offers forthcoming, Carpenter turned to writing screenplays—with some success. He sold "Eyes" to Columbia, "Blood River" to John Wayne's Batjac Productions and "Black Moon Rising" to producer Harry Gittes. "Eyes" metamorphosed into Irvin Kershner's "The Eyes of Laura Mars" (1978), starring Faye Dunaway; "Blood River" galloped onto the small screen as a 1991 CBS Western telefilm starring the unlikely trio of Rick Schroder, Wilford Brimley and Adrienne Barbeau; and "Black Moon Rising" became a forgettable 1986 caper film starring Tommy Lee Jones and Linda Hamilton.

Carpenter enhanced his reputation with the remarkable exploitation flick "Assault on Precinct 13" (1976), which he directed and scripted and for which he composed the catchy minimalist score. "Assault" ingeniously mixed Howard Hawks' "Rio Bravo", George A. Romero's "Night of the Living Dead" and film history references galore to create a deliciously stressful exercise in screen suspense. Though a failure at the box office, the film helped establish Carpenter with European cineastes fond of tough American auteurs. A last-minute addition to the London Film Festival in December 1977, the film garnered a huge audience response. London critics anointed Carpenter the major new "find" of the festival. Unfortunately, this critical success did not translate into directing offers, so Carpenter resumed screenwriting with "Escape" for 20th Century-Fox and "High Rise" and "Prey" for Warner Brothers. Of the three (as of 1996),

only "High Rise" was subsequently produced (as the superior 1978 NBC telefilm "Someone's Watching Me!").

Producer Irwin Yablans—whose Turtle Releasing had distributed "Assault on Precinct 13" in the US—had attended the successful London screening. Then setting up a new production company, Compass International, he offered Carpenter a chance to direct a feature. The project would be a thriller based on a concept by Yablans called "The Babysitter Murders". The struggling writer-director thought the idea might prove commercial.

Carpenter finally gained a firm foothold in the industry with the enormous success of the influential thriller "Halloween" (1978) which introduced Jamie Lee Curtis and helped to establish the grammar and thematic preoccupations of the modern "slasher" film. To the accompaniment of his most celebrated film score, Carpenter skillfully employed a gliding Steadicam that unexpectedly turned elegant tracking sequences into menacing point-of-view shots. Having more in common with a carnival funhouse than the charnel house air of many of its would-be imitators, the film tantalized with the possibility of cheap thrills on the periphery of each carefully composed widescreen frame. Produced by co-writer Debra Hill for $300,000, "Halloween" has reportedly grossed over $75 million worldwide, making it one of the most profitable films ever made.

The success of "Halloween" launched a series of inferior sequels (directed by others), as well as Carpenter's entry into mainstream Hollywood production. The Los Angeles Film Critics Association hailed Carpenter with the 1979 New Generation Award for "Dark Star", "Assault on Precinct 13" and "Halloween."

Carpenter began working in TV during the late 70s, starting with co-scripting the innocuous teen romance "Zuma Beach" (NBC, 1978). He strutted his stuff a few months later as writer-director of NBC's "Someone's Watching Me!", a dazzling suspenser starring

Lauren Hutton as a career woman being preyed upon by an unseen voyeuristic neighbor. With a nod to Hitchcock's "Rear Window", Carpenter achieved his claustrophobic effects with subtle framing and deep focus compositions. He gained more attention and kudos with "Elvis" (ABC, 1979), a three-hour biopic starring Kurt Russell as the legendary rocker. A trimmed version was released theatrically overseas.

Carpenter's overall approach rests firmly in the American tradition of genre filmmaking embodied by directors like John Ford, Raoul Walsh, Alfred Hitchcock and Howard Hawks. His greatest skill is an uncluttered depiction of action in a way that almost transcends narrative constraints, such as the famous lengthy POV shot that opens "Halloween" or the astronaut's chase of a mischievous alien creature through the ship's elevator shaft in "Dark Star." His stylistic trademark is a driving pace, enforced by a powerful sense of montage and insistent music, often electronic compositions by the director. Carpenter favors two-fisted yet intelligent heroes and equally tough heroines.

Once a leading contender to become modern Hollywood's version of the old genre master Hawks, Carpenter, since moving into bigger-budget productions, has found his stylistic strengths and modest thematic interests (e.g., issues of communication and isolation; questioning authority) being sometimes smothered by an excess of production values or poorly served by inadequate scripting. Even a relatively early and low-budget outing like "Escape From New York" (1981) soon dropped its intriguing premise to settle for the conventional heroics required by the plot. Similarly, in "The Thing" (the first film over which Carpenter did not have contractual control), Rob Bottin's impressive special effects stole the spotlight from an ostensibly humanist theme. "Christine" (1983) began as a promising exploration of America's automobile fetish and its relationship to male youth culture only to dissolve into a spectacle of the eponymous

car's several physical metamorphoses and murderous rampages. "Starman" (1984) attempted to retell "E.T. The Extra-Terrestrial" as an adult love story. Neither Jeff Bridges' Oscar-nominated performance as an amorous alien nor his peculiar, but engaging, chemistry with leading lady Karen Allen was sufficient to overcome the sketchy and derivative screenplay (which Carpenter did not script). "Starman" served as a gentle reminder that characterization is not one of Carpenter's strengths as a filmmaker.

"Big Trouble in Little China" (1986) was a lavish but uneven homage to supernatural Hong Kong action flicks. Memorable for Kurt Russell's broad spoof of John Wayne and for a deftly edited kidnapping sequence, the film eventually succumbed to an overdose of special effects. The commercial and critical failure of this project sent Carpenter temporarily back to the world of low-budget filmmaking.

"Prince of Darkness" (1987) was a likably goofy return to low-budget horror and a knowing tribute to the works of British fantasy screenwriter Nigel Kneale (best known for the "Quatermass" films). Absurd but compelling, the film told the story of Satan's return to Earth couched in the terminology of technological sci-fi. "They Live" (1988) presented professional wrestler Roddy Piper in an initially subversive consideration of the dark underpinnings of the "Reagan revolution" before degenerating into all-too-familiar fisticuffs and shoot-outs. Nonetheless, budget restrictions seemed to reawaken some quality that had been fading in Carpenter's filmmaking. Shorn of production bloat, his films had again become fairly dependable if unambitious fun.

The $40 million "Memoirs of an Invisible Man" (1992) boasted state-of-the-art invisibility effects from Industrial Light and Magic but was undermined by poor casting—it was a Chevy Chase vehicle—and an indecisive tone. Carpenter briefly returned to the small screen as executive producer, segment director, composer and host of "John Carpenter Presents Body Bags" (Showtime, 1993), a horror anthology telefilm. Playing a ghoulish, pun-happy morgue attendant, Carpenter introduced three horrific stories, "Gas Station", "Hair" and "Eye." He helmed the first two while Tobe Hooper directed the third. The effort was generally deemed well-crafted but uninspired.

"In the Mouth of Madness" (1995) was an enormously entertaining trifle about a skeptical insurance investigator (Sam Neill) pursuing a hugely successful horror writer whose books literally create a world of their own. The film benefited from a terrific cast that also included David Warner, Charlton Heston, Jurgen Prochnow and John Glover. The film's pleasures were undercut by an annoyingly obscure last third and a silly ending. Carpenter's remake of one of the beloved films of his youth, "Village of the Damned" (also 1995) opened to mixed reviews and tepid box office.

The sequel that no one demanded, "John Carpenter's Escape From L.A." (1996) arrived 15 years after its predecessor on a wave of hype. Carpenter, Kurt Russell and Debra Hill collaborated on the screenplay and Hill produced. Though a stylized cipher, "Escape from New York" 's Snake Plissken may be the most memorable character in all of Carpenter's films. Russell was still convincing in black leather as the reluctant mercenary sent into a nightmarish futuristic Los Angeles where the terminally politically incorrect are consigned. Though budgeted at $50 million, the film was deemed "cheesy" and "crappy" by much of the press but these words were delivered with affection. The cast featured such exploitation icons as Peter Fonda, Bruce Campbell and Pam Grier and the film opened to healthy box office.

By the mid-90s, John Carpenter was a hardy survivor of the vicissitudes of the movie business. One of the few young genre auteurs of the 70s to continue to work in genre fare (unlike David Cronenberg)—and work regularly (unlike George Romero and Tobe Hooper), he has remained busy producing, helming and penning works for film and TV. But, he has had difficulty rediscovering and packaging his strengths in a modern commercial cinema that encourages the presentation of action as overblown visual spectacle. A consummate craftsman, Carpenter delivers solid entertainments that always boast at least a few outstanding sequences. Unfortunately, while his career has continued, there is little evidence of artistic growth. Carpenter's name figures prominently in advertising as a "brand-name" assurance of a certain level of quality, but he has clearly failed to live up to the promise of his early work.—Written by Kent Greene

FAMILY:

father: Howard Ralph Carpenter. College music professor; session musician as a session player in Nashville, played with Roy Orbison, Frank Sinatra and Brenda Lee; one of the originators of the "Nashville sound"

COMPANIONS:

Debra Hill. Producer, screenwriter; met Carpenter while working as script supervisor on "Assault on Precinct 13" (1976); produced and co-scripted Carpenter's "Halloween" (1978) and "The Fog" (1980), produced "Escape From New York" (1981), produced and co-scripted "Escape From L.A."

wife: Adrienne Barbeau. Actor; married January 1, 1979; divorced November 1988; appeared in several of Carpenter's film and TV projects

wife: Sandy King. Producer; has collaborated with Carpenter on many of his films and some TV projects

MILESTONES:

1952: At four years old, saw his first theatrical feature, John Huston's "The African Queen"

1953: Interest in fantastic film ignited by a screening of Jack Arnold's black-and-white 3-D sci-fi feature, "It Came From Outer Space"

1956: At age eight, began making his own action-oriented movies using his father's 8mm Brownie camera

Moved to Bowling Green, Kentucky

Graduated to using a Eumig 650 8mm camera

First substantial film, the 40-minute featurette, "Revenge of the Colossal Beasts"

While a teen, formed own production company, Emerald Productions, for which he purchased two projectors, still cameras, floodlights and a rear projection screen for stop-motion work

By the age of 14, had filmed three additional shorts: "Gorgo vs. Godzilla", featuring clay figures manipulated live; "Terror From Space", a science fiction Western; and "Sorceror From Outer Space", a comedy

Made his "first really promising film", a 40-minute short entitled "Warrior and the Demon"; featured Carpenter's first use of stop-motion animation

Made his last—and reportedly best—short, "Gorgon the Space Monster"

1965: Deferring plans to concentrate on producing a feature, Emerald Productions published the first issue of a film fanzine entitled *Fantastic Films Illustrated*; mag ran for three mimeographed issues; Carpenter drew the covers himself, even hand painting the first in water colors

Published two one-shot fanzines *King Kong Journal* and *Phantasm—Terror Thrills Of The Films*

Met future collaborator Dan O'Bannon while both were graduate film students at USC

1969: Served as co-writer, editor, composer (and sometimes co-director) on the Oscar-winning short, "The Resurrection of Bronco Billy" (date approximate)

1970: With O'Bannon, began work on their Master's thesis project, "Dark Star"

1974: Feature film directing debut (also screenwriter; producer; composer), "Dark Star", an expanded version of their Master's thesis, made for $60,000

Wrote and sold several screenplays: "Eyes", "Blood River" and "Black Moon Rising"

1976: Wrote, directed and scored second feature, the crime thriller, "Assault on Precinct 13"

1977: "Assault" garnered wildly positive audience and press reaction as a surprise addition to the London Film Festival

Resumed writing and selling screenplays with "Escape", "High Rise" and "Prey"

1978: TV-movie writing debut (co-scripter), "Zuma Beach", a teen romance

1978: First mainstream Hollywood feature credit: co-wrote story and screenplay for "Eyes of Laura Mars"

1978: Directed, scripted and composed score for his breakthrough commercial and critical success, "Halloween", a landmark horror film

1978: TV-movie directing debut, "Someone's Watching Me!", starring Lauren Hutton; first screen collaboration with future wife Adrienne Barbeau; first union shoot; gained him his DGA card

1979: Helmed the TV biopic "Elvis", starring Kurt Russell in their first collaboration

Formed own production company Hye Whitebread Productions with wife Barbeau

1980: Screen acting debut, "The Fog" (also directed, wrote story and screenplay and composed score); marked the feature starring debut of his then-wife Adrienne Barbeau

1981: First feature starring Kurt Russell, "Escape From New York"

1982: Directed first feature without writing screenplay, "The Thing" (also starring Russell)

1984: Feature debut as executive producer, "The Philadelphia Experiment"

1985: Turned down a chance to direct the Eddie Murphy vehicle "The Golden Child" in favor of helming "Big Trouble in Little China" (date approximate)

1987: After the expensive failure of "Big Trouble in Little China", returned to low-budget filmmaking with "Prince of Darkness", a sci-fi-tinged supernatural outing

1990: TV-movie producing debut, executive produced and scripted "El Diablo", a Western comedy on HBO

1993: Executive produced, directed two

segments, composed score and acted in "John Carpenter Presents Body Bags", a Showtime cable TV horror anthology
1996: Reteamed with Kurt Russell for sequel, "John Carpenter's Escape From L.A."

AFFILIATION: Member, board of directors, The Horror Hall of Fame

QUOTES:

"Carpenter best sums up the influence of his fannish preoccupations, in a letter he wrote to the fanzine PHOTON shortly after the release of "Dark Star": 'My young life was filled with the pulp and pablum of "Not of This Earth", "It Conquered the World" and "Enemy From Space". I was only eight years old when I saw "Forbidden Planet", but I still haven't gotten over it. The young eyes that watched the invisible id creature make its huge footprints in the sand of Altair IV and finally saw the thing fully illuminated in the glowing laser beams would never be the same.' "—From "Roots of Imagination" by Frederick S. Clarke, *Cinefantastique*, Volume 10, Number 1.

From "Carpenter: Riding High on Horror" by Jordan R Fox, *Cinefantastique*, Volume 10, Number 1:

[Fox:] What's your view on the resurgence of the horror film in recent years?

[Carpenter:] I don't think it's just the horror film. We're going back to escapist entertainment; the "B" film is coming back. By "B" I don't mean less expensive, good, or important, but a film whose primary purpose is to entertain. There was a great deal of pretension in film during the '60s and '70s: filmmaking is ART. The idea was that you were delivering a message of great importance. This goes back to Antonioni and Fellini, the influence of the European film. Now we're going back to the American cinema, filmmakers like Howard Hawks, Hitchcock and John Ford—entertainment movie-makers. I'm happy, because this is the best kind of film there is.

His [Carpenter's] early work was a fond and felicitous tribute to the aura of RKO in the forties: very low-budget pictures full of visceral excitement and rich cinematic texture that belie their cost. He adores and refers to the style of Hitchcock and the atmosphere of Hawks, and he made "Dark Star" as a rebuke to "2001" and an affirmation of the innocent wonder of "The Thing" or "Forbidden Planet." With effect, for "Dark Star" is the best space-travel film since the early fifties.—David Thomson, "A Biographical Dictionary of Film" (NY: Alfred A. Knopf, 1994).

From Fox, *Cinefantastique* Volume 10, Number 1:

[Carpenter:] You want a philosophy? Filmmaking is not people sitting and talking. That's recording—like what we're doing here. Movies MOVE—M-O-V-E—they move. Cutting, camera movement—that's what they're about.

At the same time, technique is not an end in itself. It is the means through which you reach your audience. I don't want to make a film where the story is subordinated to technique. We're all storytellers here.

"I am a writer, and a director, and let me tell you something, a screenplay is not a movie, it's a bunch of words. The director makes the movie. All this other bullshit can just go away. I've had my screenplays directed by other people. "The Eyes of Laura Mars" was directed by Irvin Kershner and he is the author of that movie, not me. As a director, I am the author of my movies. I know that's not a popular view with the writers, but I'm sorry. If the writer thinks he's an auteur, then let him thread up his screenplay in a projector and we'll take a look at it."—John Carpenter interviewed in "Fires . . . Floods . . . Riots . . . Earthquakes . . . John Carpenter!: Hollywood's Prince of Darkness Destroys L.A." by Ted Elrick, *Dga Magazine*, July-August 1996 (Vol. 21, No. 3).

From Fox, *Cinefantastique*, Volume 10, Number 1:

[Fox:] That brings up the question of the

'director's hand.' A good example would be Brian De Palma and "The Fury", where you have some very fancy shots that show off his camera virtuosity.

[Carpenter:] It's called masturbation. Now, to be fair, I must admit that I have been masturbatory in my work also, but I do try not to be too self-conscious. A director get's a few tricks under his belt and says 'Hey, watch this! See what I can do!' But it's hollow isn't it? There's no substance underneath. Take a film like "Vertigo." The underlying emotions are so strong, the technique just amplifies them (without calling attention to itself)."

"If I had three wishes, one of them would be 'Send me back to the 40s and the studio system and let me direct movies.' Because I would have been happiest there. I feel I am a little bit out of time. I have much more of a kinship for older-style films, and very few films that are made now interest me at all. I get up and walk out on them."—Carpenter quoted in "A Biographical Dictionary of Film" by David Thomson.

From Army Archerd's column, "Just for Variety" in *Daily Variety*, October 9, 1995:

" . . . Sandy and John Carpenter's home in the Point Reyes National Forest area was one of 40 destroyed by the forest fire last week. John bought the house when he was making "The Fog". It was their 'retreat from the world', also the site of his "Village of the Damned". 'It's the last anyone will see of that forest with its 200-foot-tall trees', Sandy said. The house was in *Architectual Digest*. They are more saddened about the loss of the forest and its animals than their house."

"In . . . "They Live", aliens have settled on Earth, offering material success to a chosen few while the rest of the population becomes poor and homeless. In one of the most chilling moments of the film, the hero stumbles upon some special sunglasses which, when worn, reveal subliminal messages hidden in billboards and magazines. Everywhere there are messages ordering the subconscious to 'Consume' and 'Marry and Reproduce.' Dollar bills reveal the message, 'This is your God.' The sunglasses also reveal the aliens' true identity.

"As he rides across the Paramount lot in a studio golf cart on his way to a photo shoot, Carpenter, wearing sunglasses given to him from a French fan which have the 'They Live' logo on the frames, suddenly spots a fellow in jeans and work shirt. After a beat Carpenter says, 'He's human.' As his golf cart turns a corner, he spots another fellow, this time wearing a suit and tie. 'I'm not sure about him,' he says."—From Elrick, *DGA Magazine*, July-August 1996.

Carpenter should not be confused with the stage actor of the same name who has also appeared in films including "Network" and "Tootsie."

DISCOGRAPHY: "Dark Star" John Carpenter, Varese Sarabande soundtrack

"Halloween" John Carpenter, Varese Sarabande soundtrack

"Christine" John Carpenter, Varese Sarabande soundtrack

"Body Bags" John Carpenter with Jim Lang, Varese Sarabande soundtrack

"John Carpenter's Greatest Hits" John Carpenter, Varese Sarabande soundtrack compilation; performed by Carpenter

"Halloween—The Best of John Carpenter" John Carpenter, Silva Screen soundtrack compilation; performed by Daniel Cane

BORN: in New York, New York, 12/09/1929

DEATH: in Los Angeles, California, 02/03/1989

NATIONALITY: American

EDUCATION: Mohawk Valley Community College, Utica, New York, English
  Colgate University, Hamilton, New York, English; transferred
  American Academy of Dramatic Arts New York, New York, 1950

AWARDS: Venice Film Festival Critics Award "Shadows" 1960
  Venice Film Festival Award "Faces" 1968; won five awards
  National Society of Film Critics Award Best Screenplay "Faces" 1968
  Venice Film Festival Golden Lion "Gloria" 1980
  Berlin Film Festival Golden Bear "Love Streams" 1984
  Taormina Film Festival Best Actor Award "Love Streams" 1984
  Los Angeles Film Critics Association Career Achievement Award 1986

BIOGRAPHY

For 35 years, John Cassavetes held a unique position in American film, maintaining dual careers as a highly regarded actor in popular movies and as a director of independent films which themselves explored the art of acting. Like Orson Welles, he fused the roles in a truly remarkable way.

From 1953 through 1956 the "Golden Age" of TV afforded Cassavetes a unique opportunity to experiment as an actor; he essayed more than 80 roles during this three-year period. He began almost immediately to take on more filmmaking responsibilities, writing the teleplays for "The Night Holds Terror" (1955) and "Crime in the Streets" (1956). Shortly after performing opposite Sidney Poitier in Martin Ritt's "Edge of the City" (1957), a groundbreaking portrait of interracial bonding, Cassavetes began work on his own first feature, "Shadows"—also an interracial story, but with a profoundly different style.

Shot in 16-mm black-and-white on location in the streets of New York, "Shadows" (1960) began a new era in American film. As an actor turning to directing, Cassavetes displayed many of the same concerns that characterized the approach of the film critics-turned-auteurs who were revolutionizing French cinema. In a way, Cassavetes was the American New Wave, but with a difference. Instead of a critic's perspective, he brought an actor's understanding to the director's chair. Cassavetes' work is often mistaken as improvisational, or even as cinema verite. In fact, his films are thoughtful celebrations of the art of acting and, in most cases, are shot from precise scripts (even if those scripts are based on extensive improvisational exercises).

"Shadows", according to Cassavetes, "emanates from characters" thoroughly analyzed by the actors before improvisation. It is a family drama: jazz musician Hugh, the older brother, is dark-skinned; his younger brother Ben and sister Lelia are light-skinned. Hugh must confront racial tensions while Ben and Lelia can pass as whites, avoiding them. Hugh struggles with Lelia and Ben over their denial of color in a racist society, avoiding any comfortable resolution to a sensitive issue.

Despite its underground quality, "Shadows" was successful enough to gain the attention of Hollywood studio executives. "Too Late Blues" (1961) and "A Child Is Waiting" (1962), both studio productions, frustrated Cassavetes. He returned to acting to finance has next film, the independently produced "Faces" (1968).

"Faces", like most Cassavetes films, focuses intently on family and friends—on both sides of the camera—as the director tracks the breakdown of a marriage. Like "Shadows", it was an underground hit. (Throughout his career, Cassavetes was able to garner a much wider audience for his independent films than one might expect.) The late 60s witnessed some of his most memorable commercial film roles, in "The Dirty Dozen" (1967) and "Rosemary's Baby" (1968).

By 1970, the pattern was established, with fees for acting jobs paying for the occasional independent production. "Husbands" (1970), "Minnie and Moskowitz" (1971), "A Woman Under the Influence" (1974), "Opening Night" (1977), "Gloria" (1980) and "Love Streams" (1984) each celebrate relationships—mostly middle-aged—from different perspectives, and usually with the same group of acting family and friends collaborating.

For Gus (Cassavetes), Archie (Peter Falk) and Harry (Ben Gazzara), "Husbands" is a chance to explore their own lives as well as their chosen professions. These three suburbanites react to a friend's death by flying off to London for a drunken weekend. Along the way, they get to do some tour-de-force ensemble acting.

Having provided a vehicle for himself in "Husbands", Cassavetes offered a couple to his wife, Gena Rowlands, in "Minnie and Moskowitz" and "A Woman Under the Influence". "Minnie and Moskowitz" is a romantic duet between Rowlands, who works in a museum, and Seymour Cassel, a garage attendant. "A Woman Under the Influence" is a tragic duet between Rowlands and Peter Falk, who plays her husband, and remains an insightful essay on sexual politics. As Rowlands delicately crosses the line of sanity it becomes apparent that imposed social roles are the cause.

"The Killing of a Chinese Bookie" (1976) stars old friend and collaborator Ben Gazzara as Cosmo, a loner up against the mob.

"Opening Night" (1977) is more directly about the job and art of acting. Rowlands, as star, superbly limns the complex relationships between actor and character, actor and collaborators. "Gloria", like "Bookie", is one of the more accessible Cassavetes works, featuring a relatively strong storyline. It also encourages audience identification with a tough, independent woman (Rowlands again), who learns to love a child that she is obliged to protect from the mob. "Love Streams" is a free-form, off-beat look at the emotional interdependence of a brother and sister.

Throughout his career, Cassavetes as a filmmaker was absorbed with the work he did as an actor. His style and concerns are so powerful they often come through just as strongly in his acting vehicles as in the films he wrote and directed. Elaine May's "Mikey and Nicky" (1976) stars Cassavetes and Falk in what looks like a sequel to "Husbands" with a bit of "Bookie" thrown in. And Paul Mazursky's "Tempest" (1982) stars Cassavetes as the Prospero figure in this reworking of Shakespeare's highly personal play about the life of the stage. Gradually, Cassavetes, the actor-director, overwhelms colleague Mazursky, the director-actor. No one in contemporary cinema has so eloquently illuminated the relationships of the stage, the bonds between the family of players.

FAMILY:

son: Nicholas Cassavetes. Actor, director, screenwriter; born in 1959

daughter: Zoe Cassavetes. Actor, filmmaker, model; born in June 1970

COMPANION:

wife: Gena Rowlands. Actor; married from March 19, 1958 until his death February 3, 1989

MILESTONES:

1950–1952: Professional acting debut with a Providence, Rhode Island stock company

1951: First film as extra, "14 Hours"

1953: First film as supporting actor, "Taxi"

1953: First Broadway play as stage manager, "The Fifth Season"

1953: Television acting debut in "Paso Doble" on "Omnibus" series

1955: First film as star, "The Night Holds Terror/Crime in the Streets"

Starred in TV series "Johnny Staccato"

Taught method acting at Burt Lane's Drama Workshop, NYC

1960: Film directing debut with "Shadows"

1961: Hired by Paramount to direct; contract terminated after failure of "Too Late Blues"

1961: Debut as film producer, "Too Late Blues"

1962: Directed wife Gena Rowlands in "A Child Is Waiting"; also featured Judy Garland

1967: Received Best Supporting Actor Oscar nomination for "The Dirty Dozen"

1968: Began practice of previewing films on college campuses with "Faces", co-starring Rowlands; earned Best Original Screenplay Oscar nomination

1968: Co-starred as Mia Farrow's husband in the thriller "Rosemary's Baby"

1970: Directed himself in "Husbands"

1974: Received Academy Award nomination as Best Director for "A Woman Under the Influence"; film starred Rowlands and Peter Falk; Rowlands also nominated for a Best Actress Oscar

1980: Debut as playwright, "The East/West Game" produced in Los Angeles

1980: Helmed "Gloria", with Rowlands as a tough gun moll who reluctantly cares for an orphan

1981: Refurbished theater in Hollywood ("Center Theater") and built acting company

1986: Directed final film "Big Trouble"

BIBLIOGRAPHY:

"Cassavetes on Cassavetes" Ray Carney (editor), Faber and Faber

"John Cassavetes: Lifeworks" Tom Charity, 2001, Omnibus Press published in United Kingdom

William Castle

BORN: William Schloss in New York, New York, 04/24/1914

DEATH: in Beverly Hills, California, 05/31/1977

NATIONALITY: American

BIOGRAPHY

Eccentric director of routine low-budget horror films, with a flair for self-promotion. Castle's standout efforts include the B thriller, "When Strangers Marry" (1944), with Robert Mitchum in his first important role and the camp gem, "House on Haunted Hill" (1958). Like latter-day P.T Barnum, upon whom he modeled himself, Castle lured audiences to his chillers by appearing in their trailers and psyching the audience up to be scared. Most of his films included outrageous gimmicks such as an insurance policy against death by fright for "Macabre" (1957), skeletons that whistled over the audience in a process called "Emergo" during critical scenes in "House on Haunted Hill" and his most audacious stunt, "Percepto", which literally shocked the audience by wiring selected seats in the theater with electricity and administering mild jolts during moments in "The Tingler" (1959). Castle is also noted as the producer of the psychological thriller, "Rosemary's Baby" (1968).

MILESTONES:

1929: Broadway acting debut at age 15

1932: Directed Bela Lugosi in a Broadway production of "Dracula"

1932–1939: Worked as director and actor on Broadway and in summer stock

1937: Film acting debut

Wrote and directed radio series, "Lights Out" and "The Romance of Helen Trent"

1939: Brought to Hollywood by Harry Cohn; worked for Columbia (1943–1963)

1943: Film directing debut with the short, "Mr. Smug"

1943: Directed first feature film, "The Chance of a Lifetime"

1948: First film as producer (co-associate with Richard Wilson), Orson Welles' "The Lady from Shanghai"

1955: Formed own production company

1968: Produced "Rosemary's Baby" and "The Riot"

1972: Produced TV series, "Circle of Fear"

1975: Played a producer in the film, "Shampoo" and a director in "The Day of the Locust"

BIBLIOGRAPHY:

"Step Right Up! I'm Gonna Scare the Pants Off America" William Castle, 1976, autobiography

Laude Chabrol

BORN: Claude Henri Jean Chabrol in Paris, France, 06/24/1930

NATIONALITY: French

EDUCATION: Sorbonne, University of Paris, Paris, France, pharmacy, literature

AWARDS: Locarno Film Festival Grand Prix "Le Beau Serge/Handsome Serge" 1958

Berlin Film Festival Golden Bear "Les Cousins/The Cousins" 1959

Los Angeles Film Critics Association Award Best Foreign Film "Story of Women" 1989; tied with director Terence Davies for "Distant Voices, Still Lives"

Los Angeles Film Critics Association Award Best Foreign Film "La Ceremonie" 1996

National Society of Film Critics Award Best Foreign-Language Film "La Ceremonie" 1996

Prix Louis Delluc "Merci pour le chocolat/Nightcap" 2000

BIOGRAPHY

An upstart critic for *Cahiers du Cinema* in the 1950s and a financial force behind early French New Wave films in the early 60s, Claude Chabrol himself became a key director of the movement, Chabrol's filmmaking career spans nearly 35 years and some 45 films. They range from uninspired commercial projects (1964's "Marie-Chantal Contre le Docteur Kha"), to costly financial flops (1962's "Bluebeard"), to some of the darkest and most penetrating studies of obsession and, especially, murder ever to reach the screen.

Chabrol had just co-written, with Eric Rohmer, his celebrated monograph on "Hitchcock" (1957) and was working as a critic for *Cahiers Du Cinema* when money from his wife's inheritance allowed him to leave the magazine and make his first film, "Le Beau Serge/Bitter Reunion" (1958). A tragic, rural drama shot in black-and-white, "Le Beau Serge" helped define the New Wave of filmmaking that would posit the "auteur," or director, as key creator of his or her cinematic work.

Chabrol immediately followed "Le Beau Serge" with the equally dark and cruelly ironic "Les Cousins/The Cousins" (1959), a decadent tale of Parisian student bohemians. Again Chabrol served up the New Wave hallmarks of realism and intimacy, informal, sometimes iconoclastic, style and bold content. Jean-Claude Brialy starred as the cousin who is as evil as he is appealing; the Brialy character was the first of many ambiguous Chabrol creations who would subvert traditional concepts of the "bad guy."

The financial success of "Les Cousins" allowed Chabrol to set up AJYM, his own production company, which financed the first films of Rohmer, Philippe De Broca and Jacques Rivette. Chabrol's own next films as a director, however, did not fare well at the box office.

The highly stylized "A Double Tour/Leda" (1959) and "Les Bonnes Femmes" (1960) dealt with psychopaths and underlined the director's fascination with murder. The commercial disappointment of the expensive "Landru/Bluebeard" (1962), however, based on the story of the real-life murderer, made it difficult for Chabrol to find backing for his own projects. In the Hollywood tradition, he became a director-for-hire, crafting a number of lightweight films which included several spy spoofs.

Chabrol enjoyed his "golden era" in the late 60s, triumphing with a string of highly successful thrillers noted for their subtlety and quiet yet momentum-building dramatic power: "La Femme infidele/Unfaithful Wife" (1968); "Que la Bete Meure/This Man Must Die!" (1969); and "Le Boucher" (1969). Both "Les Biches/The Girl-friends" (1967) and "La Rupture/The Breakup" (1970), though not strictly thrillers, explored the director's signature themes of obsession and compulsion. Ironically, one of Chabrol's biggest commercial successes of the 60s was one of his least favorite films—"La Ligne de Demarcation" (1966), a drama about French Resistance heroes which he deemed "naive."

It was also during this period that Chabrol cemented long-standing professional relationships, including those with cinematographer Jean Rabier, actress Stephane Audran (who had appeared in "Les Cousins" and whom Chabrol married in 1964), leading man Michel Bouquet, character players Attal and Zidi, composer Pierre Jansen and screenwriter Paul Gegauff, who co-scripted "Les Cousins." The celebrated Chabrol/Gegauff collaborations often reflected a cynical view of relationships and of the bourgeois values that fostered hypocrisy and violence. (Ironically and tragically, Gegauff was brutally murdered by his wife in 1983.)

After a number of professional frustrations and disappointments in the 70s, Chabrol turned to TV work. He resumed his theatrical career toward the end of the decade with the stunning features, "Violette" (1977)—another real-life tale of murder—and "The Horse of Pride" (1979), a poetic look at Breton peasant life.

From 1984 to 1987, Chabrol teamed with producer Marin Karmitz to make a trio of Hitchcockian thrillers, "Poulet au vinaigre/Cop Au Vin" (1985), "Inspector Lavardin" (1986) and "Masques" (1987). The two collaborated again in 1988 on the critically acclaimed "Story of Women," a bleak tale of a woman (Isabelle Huppert) who performs illegal abortions in order to support herself during the Nazi occupation of France.

His film adaptation of "Madame Bovary" (1991), lushly realist and unlike the many other films to use Flaubert's text, was obsessively true to the text—and thus received a lukewarm critical reception as ornate and lifeless. Also starring Isabelle Huppert, the cold pageantry of "Bovary" was something of a dull echo of the chilling immediacy of his strangely similar, earlier work, "Story of Women." The hardest working of Frenchman subsequently directed a documentary, "The Eye of Vichy" (1993), and two features, "Betty" (1992) and "L'enfer" (1994), in the early 90s.

With a typically Gallic zest for life and moral inquiry, Chabrol has largely worked in his native land and language. His films have taken him to the far corners of his own country—Brittany, Provence, Alsace, etc.—as much, it has been said, for the fine cuisine as the fine locations. Chabrol has, however, also directed several films in English, including "Ten Days Wonder" (1972), "The Twist" (1976) and the 1984 HBO made-for-cable feature, "The Blood of Others."

MILESTONES:

During WWII, family moved to Sardent; Chabrol operated a film club

Worked as a film critic for *Arts* and *Cahiers du Cinema* during the 1950s

1956: Short film acting, producing, co-writing and co-scoring debut, "Le coup de Berger" (dir. Jacques Rivette)

Worked for 20th Century-Fox as press attache

1958: Formed production company AJYM, which supported not only his own early features, but those of other New Wave directors

1958: Film directing debut (also screenwriter; producer), "Le Beau Serge/Bitter Reunion/ Handsome Serge"

1958: First collaboration with Paul Gegauff,

"Les cousins", for which Gegauff provided dialogue; film also marked his first with actress Stephane Audran

1971: Made first English-language feature, "Ten Days' Wonder"

1975: Last collaboration with Gegauff, "Les magiciens"

1985: American TV directorial debut, "Les sang des autres/The Blood of Others"; a French-Canadian co-production made for HBO

BIBLIOGRAPHY:

"Hitchcock" Claude Chabrol and Eric Rohmer 1957 critical study of the first 44 films of Alfred Hitchcock

Gurinder Chadha

BORN: in Kenya, 1960

NATIONALITY: British

CITIZENSHIP: United Kingdom

EDUCATION: wrote dissertation on the representation of Indian women in British cinema

AWARD: Evening Standard Award Best British Newcomer "Bhaji on the Beach" 1994

BIOGRAPHY

The output of Anglo-Indian director Gurinder Chadha up until her first feature "Bhaji on the Beach" (1993) consisted primarily of TV documentaries as well as film and video shorts on Anglo-Asian themes. Among Chadha's early work, with which she began her fruitful alliance with British Film Institute and Channel 4 as producers, was the 30-minute documentary, "I'm English But . . . " (1989), which followed young English Asians who, unlike their parents, listen to Acid Bhangra, a mix of Punjabi

bhangra and rap. Her first dramatic film short was the 11-minute "Nice Arrangement" (1990), about a British-Asian wedding.

Chadha's feature directorial debut, "Bhaji on the Beach" was an Asian feminist comedy with a cheeky wit and a more serious political thematic underpinning, tracing the adventures of a busload of Anglo-Asian women on holiday in the vacation spot of Blackpool. The film's subjects momentarily leave their lives, which while full of humor, interconnectedness, and polycultural, are also marked by male sexism, English racism, personal traumas and numbing stases.

After turning out the 1994 short "What Do You Call an Indian Woman Who's Funny?" and making a cameo appearance in friend John Landis' "The Stupids" (1996), Chadha returned to features with "What's Cooking?" (2000), selected as the opening night film at the Sundance Film Festival. Following four ethnically diverse families as they prepare for a Thanksgiving celebration, the movie took a comic look at the trials and tribulations of the holidays in an urban setting.

COMPANIONS:

husband: Paul Mayeda Berges. Screenwriter; divorced

husband: Jeffrey Taylor. Producer

MILESTONES:

1967: Left Kenya with family; moved to Southall, London (date approximate)

Worked as a radio news reporter for the BBC

1989: Short film directorial debut, "I'm British But . . . "

Directed several TV documentaries for BBC, Channel 4 and the British Film Institute, including "Acting Our Age" (1991) and "Pain, Passion & Profit" (1992)

1993: Feature directorial debut, "Bhaji at the Beach"

1994: Directed the short "What Do You Call an Indian Woman Who's Funny?"

1995: Helmed the British TV-movie "Rich Deceiver" (BBC)

1996: Had small role as a reporter in John Landis' "The Stupids"

2000: Second feature, "What's Cooking?", premiered at Sundance Film Festival

2002: Helmed the sports-themed "Bend It Like Beckham"

QUOTES:

"I love to tell stories about people who rarely make it to the screen—to take people who are often on the margins of the frame and put them in the center."—Gurinda Chadha quoted in the press notes for "What's Cooking?

Charlie Chaplin

BORN: Charles Spencer Chaplin in London, England, 04/16/1889

SOMETIMES CREDITED AS:

Charles Chaplin

Sir Charles Chaplin

DEATH: in Corsier-sur-Vevey Switzerland, 12/25/1977

NATIONALITY: English

EDUCATION: attended various schools in London, Manchester, Liverpool and Newington

AWARDS: Honorary Oscar "The Circus" 1927/28 "for versatility and genius in writing, acting, directing and producing 'The Circus' "

National Board of Review Award Best Acting "The Great Dictator" 1940; one of twelve performers cited

New York Film Critics Circle Award Best Actor "The Great Dictator" 1940; Chaplin refused the award

National Board of Review Award Best Picture "Monsieur Verdoux" 1947

World Peace Council Prize 1954; Chaplin donated the monetary value to benefit the poor of Lambeth and Paris

Writers Guild of America Medallion Award 1971; initial presentation of award

Honorary Oscar 1971 for his "incalculable effect . . . in making motion pictures the art form of this century"

Oscar Music-Scoring (Best Original Dramatic Score) "Limelight" 1972; shared with Raymond Rasch and Larry Russell; also producer; eligible for award because the 1952 film was not released in the Los Angeles area until 1972

Directors Guild of America Honorary Life Membership 1974

BIOGRAPHY

Recognized as one of the greatest actors in movie history, Charlie Chaplin drew from his impoverished childhood in South London to create the 'Tramp', an undaunted cavalier from the 19th century trying to survive the materialistic, isolating, technologically-driven 20th century. Thanks to the endearing charm and spirit of the Tramp, he became the industry's first superstar, signing a contract with the First National Exhibitors Circuit for $1 million in 1918. A life-size cardboard figure of the icon—outfitted in tattered baggy pants, a cutaway coat and vest, impossibly large, worn-out shoes and a battered derby hat—bearing the inscription I AM HERE TODAY was enough to produce a line around the block during the late 1910s. He controlled every aspect of the filmmaking process (producing, casting, directing, writing, scoring and editing the movies in which he starred) and by 1917 was exposing 50,000 feet of film for a two-reel (2000 feet) Mutual comedy, an astonishing shooting ratio of 25 to 1, which would later swell to 100 to 1.

Born into a home of enough gentility to keep a maid, Chaplin watched his family lose everything at a very early age. Both parents were music hall entertainers and his father, who eventually died from alcoholism in 1901, abandoned the family for another woman when Charlie was three years old. His mother's continued performing led to his own debut at the age of five, but it wasn't long before mental illness forced her from the stage into an asylum, condemning Chaplin and older half-brother Sydney to a childhood spent between public charity homes and fending for themselves on the streets. Avid fan Sigmund Freud remarked: "He always portrays one and the same figure . . . himself as he was in his early, dismal youth." His observations of the little jobs and stratagems that allowed the least fortunate members of society to survive would pay off handsomely in later years, though the cruel deprivation scarred him irrevocably. His son Sydney said of him: "He was the most insecure man I ever knew. I wanted to tell him, 'Dad, you made it!' "

Though not from Lancashire, Chaplin began his career in earnest in the summer of 1898 as one of the Eight Lancashire Lads, a children's musical troupe touring England's provincial music halls. By the age of 16 he was playing the featured role of Billy in William Gillette's West End production of "Sherlock Holmes" (1905). At the prompting of his brother, Chaplin then secured a spot in Fred Karno's music hall revue, quickly becoming its star attraction. He remained with the Karno troupe for seven years until film producer Mack Sennett discovered him during his second tour of America in 1913 and signed him to the Keystone Company. Chaplin's European music hall style was out of place in the mechanized world of Sennett, who ran his studio with production-line efficiency, churning out two films a week and allowing no more than ten camera set-ups per film. For an actor used to refining a set character night after night with the Karno company, the Sennett method seemed careless, sloppy and crude.

Chaplin's first film for Sennett, "Making a Living" (1914), was mediocre, featuring him in standard English music hall garb racing across the frame for the entire reel. "Kid Auto Races at Venice" (1914), however, was a different story. Borrowing a bowler hat, reedy cane and baggy pants (from Fatty Arbuckle) to go with floppy shoes (from Fred Sterling), he assembled his trademark Tramp costume, forever transforming the cinema. Arriving to watch the races, he discovers a movie camera and crew recording the event, and in an unstructured half-reel of improvised clowning made himself the star of the newsreel while resisting all attempts of the crew to throw him out of the frame. After a four-month apprenticeship, Chaplin, now directing and scripting his shorts, began separating himself from the Sennett style. He moved the camera closer than Sennett permitted, focusing on character to bring a comedy of emotions to the frenetic Keystone world. He also slowed the breakneck

Keystone pace, reducing the number of gags per film and increasing the time devoted to each. Though his technique tended to be invisible, he gradually evolved a principle of cinema based on framing: finding the exact way to frame a shot to reveal its motion and meaning completely, thus avoiding disturbing cuts.

By the end of his Keystone year, Chaplin had become so popular that Sennett's offer of $750 per week (five times his 1914 salary) was not enough to keep him in the fold. Within that year, he had revolutionized film comedy by introducing characterization, mime and slapstick pathos, his emphasis on character paving the way for the subsequent achievements of Buster Keaton, Harold Lloyd, Stan Laurel and Oliver Hardy. Joining the Essanay Company for $1250 per week plus a $10,000 signing bonus, he embarked on a transitional year between the knockabout Sennett farces and the more subtle comedies of psychological observation and moral debate that mark the mature Chaplin. Though early films for Essanay recalled Sennett, "The Tramp" (1915) looked to the future, firmly establishing the relationship of his screen persona to the respectable social world. After protecting his idealized woman (Edna Purviance) from harm, Chaplin at first mistakes her kindness for another type of love but ultimately realizes the respectable Ednas of the world are not for tramps like him. Taking to the road, his back to the camera, he walks briskly to his future, with a kick of his feet and a twirl of the cane, providing the ending that would dominate his films for the next two decades.

Ranking among his greatest achievements, Chaplin's twelve Mutual two-reelers of 1916 and 1917 were so inventive, intimate and hilariously clever that they brought him worldwide popularity. In "One A.M." (1916), he once again tailored his Karno drunk for the camera. "Behind the Screen" (1916) glimpsed life inside a movie studio, and "The Rink" (1916) put him on roller skates for the first time. "Easy

Street" (1917) cast him in his only performance as a policeman while converting the most sordid subjects (i.e., wife-beating, drug addiction, police brutality and rape) into surprisingly funny material for comic routines. He brought drunken chaos to an entire health spa for "The Cure" (1917) before ending his Mutual run with two remarkable films, "The Immigrant" (1917), which identified the plight of a whole class with the solitary tramp, and "The Adventurer" (1917). His non-stop race to escape his police pursuers in the latter was his ultimate tribute to the kind of chase that former boss Sennett had made intrinsic to film comedy. The Mutual films revealed a master at work, stitching mime, satire, sentimentality and slapstick into a seamless whole.

As an independent filmmaker distributing through First National, Chaplin broke out of his popular two-reel format. Though his contract called for 12 two-reelers in one year, he actually took five years to deliver eight films, of which only three were of the specified length. His initial film for First National, ("A Dog's Life" 1918), longer (a three-reeler) and richer than any he had attempted, introduced the mongrel Scraps, an outcast like the Tramp, who must fight to survive in a world of tougher, bigger dogs. He followed with another three-reeler, "Shoulder Arms" (1918), which transported the Tramp to the battlefields of Europe, before suffering a major disappointment with "Sunnyside" (1919), his first not to find favor with the public. More than 18 months elapsed before the appearance of "The Kid" (1921), his most ambitious film yet, which to the consternation of First National had grown from its planned three-reel length into a six-reeler. Elaborating on the friend-ally embodied by Scraps, Chaplin worked hard with his child co-star Jackie Coogan, shaping the boy into a mirror of himself. The result was the biggest hit in motion picture history to that time, excluding D.W. Griffith's "Birth of a Nation" (1915).

In 1919, Chaplin along with fellow stars

Douglas Fairbanks and Mary Pickford and director Griffith founded United Artists, for whom his first film was the atypical (Tramp-less) "A Woman of Paris" (1923), a comedy of manners and swan song for long-time co-star Purviance. Though quite sophisticated for its time, it flopped commercially but became a powerful influence on Ernst Lubitsch, the eventual grand master of the genre. His next four features returned to the Tramp and his conflict with "normal" social expectations, forming what might be called the "marriage group." "The Gold Rush" (1925), featuring the famous feasting on shoe leather scene, suggested that his striking it rich might make him an acceptable mate, but he was back on the road in "The Circus" (1928) after failing to fulfill the heroine's vision of romance. Audiences rewarded the director's bold move of resisting sound for "City Lights" (1931), proving they would still see a silent film if Charlie Chaplin was the star. The fourth-biggest grosser of the year tells the story of his love for a blind flower girl, and though he facilitates the operation that gives her sight, the abrupt conclusion seems to suggest she will not share her life with a lowly tramp.

Silence was the medium in which the Tramp lived, but for "City Lights", Chaplin's concession to sound was providing musical scoring and sound effects. From this point on, he would compose the scores for all his sound films, as well as adding musical tracks to silent classics. No longer able to resist synchronized sound, he bid farewell to the Tramp in "Modern Times" (1936), allowing him his only talking sequence on film, a jumble of gibberish in the form of a song. When he took to the road this last time, it was also finally in the company of another, Paulette Goddard (Chaplin's wife at the time). He had made only four films in eleven years, but his output would slow further with his final three American films coming in the next 16 years. "The Great Dictator" (1940), his first full-talkie, combined slapstick, satire and social

commentary, casting Chaplin in the dual role of a Tramp-like Jewish barber and Adenoid Hynkel, the Hitler-like dictator of Tomania. In addition to the send-up of Hitler as a maniacal clown, Jack Oakie weighed in unforgettably as Benzino Napaloni of rival country Bacteria, a hysterical take-off of Mussolini.

The Tramp had been a character of 19th century sensibilities, a leftover from a Dickensian world, but with "Monsieur Verdoux" (1947), Chaplin proved he was firmly in the 20th century with a resonant film of his times. Another political fable, "Verdoux" presents him as a man who marries rich, repellent ladies and murders them to support his beloved wife on an idyllic farm. The startling transformation of their precious tramp into a murderous Bluebeard turned his once adoring public against him, but his creative expression was right on-target for a post-Holocaust world. "Wars, conflict, it's all business. One murder makes a villain; millions a hero. Numbers sanctify." Equating Verdoux's murderous trade with acceptable professions—munitions manufacturing, stock trading, banking—was clearly years ahead of its time, and its wry humor and pacifist sentiments make it quite contemporary when seen today. Under fire for his liberal views in an era defined by Joe McCarthy's anti-Communist tirades, Chaplin released a final affectionate tribute to his art and its traditions, "Limelight" (1952). Having never become an American citizen, he found his re-entry permit to the USA revoked after he had attended its London premiere and settled with his family in Switzerland.

Public reaction against Chaplin was so rabid that his first European film ("A King in New York" 1957), a slight satire on American consumerism and political paranoia, remained unreleased in the United States until 1973. Chaplin's final film, "A Countess From Hong Kong" (1967), in which he merely made a cameo appearance as a waiter, was even more disappointing, suffering as had its predecessor at the hands of a low budget, tight schedule and a production team of strangers. "Limelight" functions as his cinematic swan song. In his most autobiographical and most underrated work, Chaplin played Calvero, an old, drunken has-been, commenting superbly on his own fabulous career, one which saw the triumph and decline of the physical comedy he had brought to silent films from the English music hall. For the last time on celluloid, he exercised classic pantomime bits recalling the Tramp, like taming a flea and imagining himself a great lion tamer. Chaplin's hilarious routine with the great Keaton (the only time the two appeared together) before Calvero collapses and dies is his last significant screen image, a fitting finale to a wondrous career. Everything after it was strictly denouement.

Twenty years later Hollywood welcomed the Tramp back, presenting Chaplin with an Honorary Academy Award amid the loudest and longest ovation in its history. The frail man of 82, who had long since given up radical politics, also picked up an Oscar the following year for writing the score of "Limelight" (including its hit ballad "Eternally"), eligible since the movie had not played the Los Angeles area before 1972. His final great tribute came when Queen Elizabeth II knighted him in 1975. Chaplin had his dark side. His idealization of women masked his penchant for young girls. His first two wives were 16 when he married them, and his last, 18. He was a total autocrat on the set, demonstrating every bit of business for his actors to copy, and his need to control all aspects of production cut him off from meaningful collaboration. We can forgive him all his failings because of the Tramp and the joy that sublime creature brought to the world. James Agee perhaps said it best: "Of all comedians, he worked most deeply and most shrewdly within a realization of what a human being is, and is up against. The Tramp is as centrally representative of humanity, as many-sided and as mysterious, as Hamlet, and it

seems unlikely that any dancer or actor can ever have excelled him in eloquence, variety, or poignancy of motion."—Written by Greg Senf

FAMILY:

father: Charles Chaplin. Music hall entertainer, born in 1863; left family when Chaplin was a young child; died of alcoholism in 1901

mother: Hannah Chaplin. Music hall entertainer, born in 1865; had breakdown after husband left; institutionalized for most of her remaining years; died in 1928; portrayed by her granddaughter Geraldine in the biopic "Chaplin" (1992)

COMPANIONS:

Hetty Kelly. First love; met in 1908; died in 1918 in England

Peggy Pearce. Actor; dated in 1914

wife: Mildred Harris. Married in 1918; divorced in 1920; born on November 29, 1901; died on July 20, 1944

Pola Negri. Actor; had on-again, off-again romance from c. 1923 to 1924

wife: Lillita MacMurray. Actor; born on April 15, 1908; married in 1924; divorced in 1927; died at age 87 on December 29, 1995 in Woodland Hills, California; Chaplin cast her in his "The Kid" when she was 12 and the two were married when she was 16; when they divorced Grey received $825,000, the then-largest divorce settlement in American history

Louise Brooks. Actor, dancer; had relationship in summer 1925

wife: Paulette Goddard. Actor; married c. 1933, divorced in 1942; some controversy has surrounded exactly when the two were married; Goddard acted opposite Chaplin in his films "Modern Times" (1936) and "The Great Dictator" (1940); born on June 3, 1911; died on April 23, 1990

wife: Oona O'Neill. Married, from June 1943 until Chaplin's death in 1977; daughter of American playwright Eugene O'Neill; met Chaplin in 1942 at age 17 when a Hollywood agent recommended her for a part in the unfilmed "Shadow and Substance"; renounced her American citizenship in 1954; died of pancreatic cancer at age 66 on September 27, 1991 in Corsier-sur-Vevey, Switzerland

MILESTONES:

Began music hall career at age 5

1898: Toured as one of the Eight Lancashire Lads

1903: First featured stage role in "Sherlock Holmes"; toured English provinces

1905: Appeared in London West End production of "Sherlock Holmes", starring its American author, William Gillette

1907: Joined Fred Karno's Pantomime Troupe in England; quickly rose to Karno's star attraction, specializing in a dexterous portrayal of a comic drunk

1910: Made first trip to America with Karno's Speechless Comedians

1913: Hired by Mack Sennett's Keystone Company while on tour with Karno; left for Hollywood, arriving on Sennett's lot in December with a contract for $150 per week

1914: Film acting debut in Keystone's "Making a Living"

1914: First appearance of the tramp in "Kid Auto Races at Venice"

1914: Directed, acted in and wrote over 20 shorts

1915: Left Keystone Company; signed with Essanay Company for $1250 per week (Sennett had offered $750) plus a $10,000 signing bonus; met key collaborator, cameraman Rollie Totheroh, who would shoot every Chaplin film (and only Chaplin films) until his death in 1946

1915: First film with Edna Purviance; she would play the idealized woman in every Chaplin film for the next eight years, remaining on the Chaplin payroll until her death in 1958

1916: Moved to Mutual Film Corporation; the popularity of such Mutual two-reelers as

"The Pawnshop", "The Immigrant" and "Easy Street" (only pic in which he ever played a cop) made him an international star

1918: Signed by First National Exhibitors Circuit, producing his films independently; contract allowed him to build his own studio, which he alone used until 1952

1919: Co-founded United Artists Corporation (with Mary Pickford, Douglas Fairbanks and D.W. Griffith)

1921: Strayed from First National contract calling for two-reelers to make "The Kid" (a six-reeler), his longest and most ambitious film to that time

1923: Wrote and directed (appearing only briefly as a railway porter) "A Woman of Paris" (first full-length film), a comedy of manners starring Purviance (her final film with Chaplin); first UA release

1925: Tramp's feature debut for UA, "The Gold Rush"; Chaplin called it "the picture I want to be remembered by"

1928: Awarded an honorary Oscar for "versatility and genius in writing, acting, directing, and producing 'The Circus' "

1931: First feature of the sound era, "City Lights" (a silent film); fourth biggest grosser of the year

1936: Voice first heard in a commercial film, "Modern Times", when he sang a nonsense song; mild left-wing point of view signaled his growing political convivtion; year's second biggest money-earner after "San Francisco"

1940: First full talkie, "The Great Dictator"; received Oscar nominations for best actor, best screenplay and best picture; refused New York Film Critics Award as Best Actor

1942: His appearance at a rally supporting a Russian counterattack of Germany (a second front) led to his becoming a target of investigation by the FBI

1943: Named in paternity suit by actress Joan Barry, who claimed that Chaplin had been her lover for several years and was the father of her child; though Chaplin denied Barry's claims and genetic evidence suggested that he was not the father of her child, the court ruled in Barry's favor

1947: Played "lady killer" in "Monsieur Verdoux"; Oscar-nominated for his screenplay

Refused to testify before House Committee on Un-American Activities

1952: Denied reentry into America after attending the London premiere of "Limelight" (only film in which he appared with Buster Keaton); settled in Switzerland

Sold interest in United Artists

1957: First film outside the US, "A King in New York"

1963: Orchestrated a festival of his films in NYC

1967: Last film, "The Countess of Hong Kong", starring Sophia Loren and Marlon Brando; Chaplin had cameo as waiter

1972: Returned to the USA after nearly 20 years to accept an honorary Academy Award

1975: Knighted by Queen Elizabeth II

1978: Body dug up by two grave robbers on March 2; found 2 1/2 months later and reburied

1992: Subject of a biographical motion picture "Chaplin", directed by Richard Attenborough and starring Robert Downey Jr.

1995: Voted the greatest actor in movie history by a worldwide survey of film critics

QUOTES:

"Halfway through, a shower of money poured on the stage. Immediately I stopped and announced that I would pick up the money first and sing afterwards. This caused much laughter. The stage manager came on with a handkerchief and helped me gather it up. I thought he was going to keep it. This thought was conveyed to the audience and increased their laughter, especially when he walked off with it with me anxiously following him. Not until he handed it to Mother did I return and continue to sing. I was quite at home. I talked to the audience, danced and did several imitations including

one of Mother singing her Irish march song."—Charles Chaplin, remembering his stage debut at the age of five in "My Autobiography"

BIBLIOGRAPHY:

"Charles Chaplin: My Autobiography" 1964

"Chaplin: Last of the Clowns" Parker Tyler, 1972, Garland Publishing

"My Life in Pictures" Charlie Chaplin, 1974

"Chaplin and American Culture" Charles Mayland, scholarly study of Chaplin's films, his star image, and his public notoriety

"Tramp: The Life of Charlie Chaplin" Joyce Milton, 1996, HarperCollins

"Charlie Chaplin: Comic Genius" David Robinson, 1996, Harry N. Abrams Inc.

"Charlie Chaplin and His World" Kenneth S. Lynn, 1998, Aurum Press; published in Great Britain

"Oona: Living in the Shadows" Jane Scovell, 1998, biography of Oona O'Neill Chaplin

"The Intimate Charlie Chaplin" May Reeves and Claire Goll, 2001, McFarland

BORN: Elizabeth Cholodenko in California, 06/05/1964

NATIONALITY: American

EDUCATION: San Francisco State University, San Francisco, California

Film Division, Graduate School of the Arts, Columbia University, New York, New York, film, MFA

AWARDS: Sundance Film Festival Waldo Salt Screenwriting Award "High Art" 1998

Deauville Festival du Cinema Americain Prix du Jury "High Art" 1998

BIOGRAPHY

A native of Southern California, Lisa Cholodenko began her career in film as a post-production assistant on John Singleton's acclaimed "Boyz N the Hood" (1991). After work as an assistant editor on such films as "The Lawnmower Man" and "Used People" (both 1992), she moved to NYC to attend graduate school. While at Columbia University, Cholodenko was mentored by Milos Forman and wrote, produced and directed two widely seen short films, "Souvenir" (1994) and "dinner party" (1996), both of which involved lesbian themes. With her first feature "High Art" (1998), the filmmaker explored a budding same-sex romance set amid the art and publishing worlds, the vagaries of fame and the compromises exacted by success. Cholodenko received the Waldo Salt Screenwriting award at the 1998 Sundance Film Festival and garnered particular praise for her direction of a cast that included Ally Sheedy as a heroin-addicted photographer, Patricia Clarkson as her German lover and Radha Mitchell as an ambitious magazine staffer.

MILESTONES:

Raised in California

1991: Served as post-production assitant on John Singleton's "Boyz N the Hood"

1992: Was assistant editor on "The Lawnmower Man" and "Used People"

1992: Moved to NYC to attend Columbia University

1994: Produced, wrote and directed the short film "Souvenir"; premiered at the London Film Festival

1996: Wrote, edited, produced and directed second short "dinner party"

1998: Feature directorial and screenwriting debut "High Art"

1999: TV directing debut, an episode of NBC's "Homicide: Life on the Street"

2001: Helmed an episode of the HBO series "Six Feet Under"

Made second feature, "Laurel Canyon" (lensed 2001); also wrote screenplay

QUOTES:

"I think there have been a lot of people in the arts who have had that experience of just not wanting to succumb to the pressures or conventions of the marketplace—either they made an ethical choice or it was emotionally impossible for them. For whatever specific reason, but mainly because they weren't able to cope with the pressures of commercial success, they drop out or drift into obscurity—I find that a fascinating character and, I think, an archetypical character in modern culture."—Lisa Cholodenko in the press notes for "High Art"

"It's the rare person who can have a thriving professional life and a rich, intact love life."—Cholodenko quoted in *Detour*, June–July 1998

Larry Clark

BORN: in Tulsa, Oklahoma, 1943

NATIONALITY: American

EDUCATION: Layton School of Art, Milwaukee, Wisconsin, attended after high school

BIOGRAPHY

Outlaw photographer-turned-filmmaker Larry Clark influenced the likes of Martin Scorsese, Francis Ford Coppola and Gus Van Sant long before he directed a picture. Inspired by his seminal photo essay, "Tulsa" (1971), they stole shamelessly in creating respectively "Taxi Driver" (1976), "Rumble Fish" (1983) and "Drugstore Cowboy" (1989), acknowledging their debt to Clark's realistic portrayal of the Tulsa drug and street milieu of the 1960s and early 70s. Clark was injecting amphetamines at the age of 16 and, after a tour of Vietnam, returned to his boyhood home to record its seamier side, snapping photographs off and on from 1962 to 1971. He shocked with pictures of penises protruding from pants and needles hanging from junkies' arms, but his own wild ways were responsible for his distinctive oeuvre and also contributed to his slow growth as an artist. Drug addiction and alcoholism got in the way as did several brushes with the law, including a 19-month prison stay for shooting a man in the arm during a card game.

As a child, Clark had once had his picture taken with Walt Disney, but Miramax, a division of Disney, would have to create an independent company (Excalibur) to distribute his debut film "Kids" (1995) in order to distance it from the parent studio. Called everything from "a masterpiece" to "nihilistic pornography," it bore a far greater resemblance to "A Clockwork Orange" (1971) than to "Pocahontas" (1995) and proved Clark had not lost his power to shock. Armed with a script penned by a then-19-year old Harmony Korine, the director zeroed in on "kidspeak" and teenage culture, following a group 90s youths throughout the course of one NYC day as the specter of AIDS hovered over them. A telling portrait of children growing up without proper parental guidance, "Kids" is utterly matter-of-fact, brutal and nonjudgmental about its sexual frankness and violence. Clark was able to gain his charges' trust, drawing phenomenal performances from nonactors, particularly his stars Leo Fitzpatrick, Justin Pierce and Chloe Sevigny, all of whom have gone on to acting careers.

Clark returned to the streets of Tulsa for "Another Day in Paradise" (1998), based on the book by Eddie Little. More conventional and arguably more satisfying than his debut film, it was a bit raw and unflinching for some tastes but found an audience ready to respond to its gritty aesthetic. Featuring an emotionally engaging Melanie Griffith in an uncharacteristic, deglamorized role and a sometimes over-the-top James Woods, this more traditional narrative seemed to spring directly from the director's Midwestern background and experience of the renegade life, depicting a surrogate family brought together by drugs and crime and its eventual unraveling. Natasha Gregson Wagner registered sympathetically in the most tragic role, but the real revelation was Vincent Kartheiser as Bobbie, previously only in children's films.

Clark's downbeat but surprisingly warm slice of life on the edge proved an anomaly. His third feature was "Bully" (2001), an affecting and disturbingly nihilistic portrait of contemporary teenagers in southern Florida. Inspired by a true story, the film depicted the antisocial behavior of the tyrannical Bobby Kent who was eventually murdered by his best friend. Clark displayed a taut control over the material and elicited strong performances from his cast (including Brad Renfro, Rachel Miner and Nick Stahl) and the film earned considerable critical acclaim.

MILESTONES:

As a child, posed for a photograph with Walt Disney

1959: Began shooting drugs as a 16-year old (date approximate)

Among the first US troops to go to Vietnam

1962–1971: Photographed Oklahoma drug culture for first documentary book "Tulsa" (1971); cited as inlfuence or inspiration for films by directors Martin Scorsese ("Taxi Driver" 1976), Francis Ford Coppola ("Rumble Fish" 1983) and Gus Van Sant ("Drugstore Cowboy" 1989)

Ran afoul of the law and arrested for driving under the influence and later possession of a firearm

1976: Convicted of assault and battery after shooting a man in the arm during a card game; served 19 months in prison; of the shooting, he said, "I was doing speed; it seemed like the right thing to do"

1983: Issued second book of photographs, "Teenage Lust"; also wrote text; had received an NEA grant in the 1970s for the book

1989: Met Harmony Korine in San Francisco, California; the two corresponded and later hooked up in NYC

1995: Feature directing debut, "Kids", scripted by Korine

1998: Made second feature, "Another Day in Paradise"; first credit as producer; story revolved around a pair of drug-abusing scam artists who take a young couple under their wing and form a surrogate family

1998: Checked into a rehab center for treatment for heroin and alcohol addiction

2001: Directed third film "Bully", based on true story of a Florida teenager who murdered his best friend; also had cameo role as the father of one of the teens involved in the murder

QUOTES:

"I've always said that the only reason I make my photographs is because I can't see them anywhere else and I have a psychological need to see these images. Why make them if they're already there? But I'd see these films, and I'd say, 'Why don't they go further? If I'd done that film, I would have done it differently.' "

" . . . My dear mother in Oklahoma sent me this newspaper clipping when 'Drugstore Cowboy' came out, and it said in the production notes Gus Van Sant credits Larry Clark's book 'Tulsa' as an inspiration for the film. I grudgingly liked it, but I didn't like it too much, and I was pissed. I said, 'Man, this guy's on my turf!' "

"And I said, 'I'm gonna make a film and show these motherfuckers how it's done.' That's how it was. It was a macho don't-fuck-with-me kind of thing, and I thank you, Gus, for getting me to make this film. You're more responsible for 'Kids' than you know."—Larry Clark to Gus Van Sant in *Interview*, July 1995.

"Hollywood sucks. . . . Hollywood's the lowest place in the United States. . . . Man, the people suck, they all have agendas and agendas and agendas, and they're all lying cocksuckers and the lowest scum of the earth. But you know, I was in the penitentiary, so I know those people. I was ready for 'em. And when it came down to the shit, I said, 'Man, you need to spend some time in the joint, man, you need to smarten up.' "—Larry Clark quoted in *Time Out New York*, January 21–28, 1999.

BIBLIOGRAPHY:

"Tulsa" Larry Clark, 1971; book of photographs begun in 1963

"Teenage Lust" Larry Clark, 1983; essay and photographs

"The Perfect Childhood" Larry Clark, 1993; published in the United Kingdom

"The River Phoenix Book" Larry Clark, 1994; compilation of teen-magazine pictures of Phoenix interspersed with collages of teen murderers

"Heroin" Larry Clark, 1999, Thea Westreich

BORN: Jean Maurice Eugene Clement Cocteau in Maisons-Lafitte, France, 07/05/1889

DEATH: in Milly-La-Foret, France, 10/11/1963

NATIONALITY: French

EDUCATION: Lycee de Condorcet France

BIOGRAPHY

Jean Cocteau is a preeminent figure in 20th-century French culture. A major contributor to the history of the cinema, he is also noted for his work as a novelist, poet, painter, sculptor and playwright.

Cocteau wrote, directed, narrated, edited and performed in his first film, "The Blood of a Poet", shot in 1930. Privately financed by the Vicomte de Noailles, the film's release was delayed for two years due to the scandal that surrounded another 1930 Noailles production, Dali and Bunuel's "L'Age d'or", which was denounced as "sacrilegious" when first screened.

"Blood of a Poet" was certainly influenced by the work of Dali and Bunuel, as well as other surrealist films by Man Ray and Rene Clair. But in its unprecedented use of sync-sound dialogue, narration and music (by the prolific and accomplished Georges Auric), juxtaposed with free-form episodic imagery, Cocteau's debut marked a watershed in non-narrative, personal filmmaking. Bracketing the beginning and end of the work with a shot of a factory chimney collapsing (to show that the events represented actually take place in an instant of "real time"), Cocteau designed the piece as a series of disparate sections, each centering on the adventures of a young poet/artist condemned to walk the halls of the "Hotel of Dramatic Follies" for his crime of having brought a statue to life. Perhaps the most famous of the film's striking images is the sequence in which the young man, having created a drawing with a moving mouth, wipes the mouth onto his hand in an effort to erase it from the picture; whereupon the mouth takes on a life of its own, begging for air and later drinking from a bowl of water. Another memorable—and much-imitated—conceit is that of the poet passing through a mirror which turns into a pool of water.

Cocteau worked only intermittently in film for the next 15 years, one reason being his recurring addiction to opium. His return to directing in 1945, with "Beauty and the Beast", was partly due to the efforts of his favorite actor and close associate Jean Marais, who played the Beast in the film.

Relentlessly romantic, beautifully mounted (despite the problems attendant on film production in post-war France) and flawlessly acted, "Beauty and the Beast" marked a triumphant return to the screen for Cocteau. With its linear narrative and familiar mythic structure, the film was less experimental than "Blood of a Poet." Yet Marais's unforgettable performance, the beast's (pre-prosthetic) make-up and Cocteau's inspired visual conceits (the beast's fingers smoking after a kill, human hands used as candelabras in his castle), made the film one of the director's most memorable—and most enduringly popular—works.

Cocteau directed two films adapted from his own plays, "The Eagle with Two Heads" and "The Storm Within" (both 1948). "Eagle" is a rather ordinary palace romance which the director later claimed he had created solely to please Marais. "The Storm Within", on the other hand, is perhaps the finest of all Cocteau's narrative films. At the center of the work is the magnetic performance of Yvonne de Bray as Marais's violently possessive, drug-addicted mother, who kills herself when her son decides to marry. Shot almost entirely in one apartment, "The Storm Within" achieves an unparalled sense of claustrophobic melancholy, highlighted by brilliant camera movement within the confines of the small, cramped flat.

In 1950 Cocteau made the film for which he is perhaps best known, "Orpheus", again starring Marais, this time as a young poet beset by artistic and romantic rivals. When his wife dies, Orpheus descends to Hell to rescue her, only to be brought before a tribunal where his final fate is determined. Once again, Cocteau makes considerable use of liquid mirrors through which his protagonists enter and leave rooms. Attacked in some quarters as being too mannered and occasionally pretentious (a charge that followed Cocteau throughout his career), the film is on the whole a successful blend of the real and the fantastic, "a realistic document of unrealistic events," as Cocteau had termed "Blood of a Poet" many years earlier.

Over the next ten years Cocteau worked on several projects, providing dialogue and/or off-screen narration for a number of features by other directors and contributing to several short films. His one-act, one-person play "The Human Voice" was made into an excellent short film ("L'Amore") in 1948 by Roberto Rossellini and also provided the inspiration for Pedro Almadovar's 1988 farce, "Women on the Verge of a Nervous Breakdown". Cocteau also adapted his novel "Les Enfants Terribles" into the screenplay for Jean-Pierre

Melville's 1950 film of the same name. Like Jean Delannoy's "L'Eternel Retour" (1943), the work bears Cocteau's stamp far more than that of its nominal director.

In 1959, with private financing (part of it coming from Francois Truffaut), Cocteau made his last film as a director, "The Testament of Orpheus". A rather elaborate home movie starring its director, the work features cameos from numerous celebrities including Pablo Picasso, Yul Brynner and Jean-Pierre Leaud. A nostalgic return to the legend of Orpheus in the manner and style of "The Blood of a Poet", the film lacks the earlier work's imagination and intensity.

MILESTONES:

1925: Made short 16mm film "Jean Cocteau fait du cinema"; no prints extant and never shown in public

1930: Film directing debut (also writer; editor; sets; voices), "Le sang d'un poete/The Blood of a Poet" (58mins)

1940: First feature as screenwriter, "La comedie du bonheur"

1942: Worked with Marcel Carne on adaptation of "Juliette ou la cle des songs" (later filmed by Carne with other collaborators)

1943: Appeared in Sacha Guitry's "La malibran"

BIBLIOGRAPHY:

"L'Inconcevable Jean Cocteau" Jean Marais; biography

Ethan Coen

BORN: in St. Louis Park, Minnesota, 09/21/1957

SOMETIMES CREDITED AS:
Roderick Jaynes

NATIONALITY: American

EDUCATION: attended high school in Minnesota; left early

Simon's Rock of Bard College, Great Barrington, Massachusetts

Princeton University, Princeton, New Jersey, philosophy

AWARDS: United States (Sundance) Film Festival Grand Jury Prize (Dramatic) "Blood Simple" 1985

Cannes Film Festival Palme d'Or "Barton Fink" 1991 shared award with Joel Coen, brother

IFP Gotham Filmmaker Award 1994; award shared with brother Joel

Australian Film Institute Award Best Foreign Film "Fargo" 1996 producer

New York Film Critics Circle Award Best Picture "Fargo" 1996

Los Angeles Film Critics Association Award Best Screenplay "Fargo" 1996 award shared with brother Joel Coen

Society of Texas Film Critics Award Best Picture "Fargo" 1996

Broadcast Film Critics Association Award Best Picture "Fargo" 1996

Golden Satellite Best Motion Picture (Drama) "Fargo" 1996; initial presentation of the award

Florida Film Critics Circle Award Best Picture "Fargo" 1996

Florida Film Critics Circle Award Best Screenplay "Fargo" 1996; shared with Joel Coen

Chicago Film Critics Association Award Best Picture "Fargo" 1996

Chicago Film Critics Association Award Best Screenplay "Fargo" 1996; shared with Joel Coen

London Film Critics Circle Award Best Screenwriter "Fargo" 1996; shared award with Joel Coen

Writers Guild of America Award Best Screenplay Written Directly for the Screen "Fargo" 1997 award shared with Joel Coen

Independent Spirit Award Best Screenplay "Fargo" 1996; award shared with Joel Coen

Independent Spirit Award Best Feature "Fargo" 1996

Oscar Best Screenplay Written Directly for the Screen "Fargo" 1996; award shared with Joel Coen

BIOGRAPHY

With his director brother Joel, producer Ethan Coen has become one of the most highly regarded talents on the contemporary American film scene. Each of the writing team's first three films paid homage to a classic cinematic genre with a knowing quality born of many hours spent in darkened theaters. The Coen brothers have watched a lot of movies, and it clearly shows.

The Coen brothers began writing screenplays soon after college. Joel also worked as an editor on some low-budget horror movies, including Sam Raimi's popular "Evil Dead" (1983). Raimi later collaborated with the Coens on the screenplays for the manic comedy "Crimewave" (1985) and the screwball-inspired "The Hudsucker Proxy" (1994). Additionally, he made a cameo appearance in their "Miller's Crossing" (1990).

The Coen magic began with "Blood Simple" (1984), a tough and witty modern film noir starring John Getz, Frances McDormand, Dan Hedaya, and, in an indelible portrayal of a seedy Texan private eye, M. Emmet Walsh. From the early shots of a rain-spattered windshield through a harrowing (and artfully composed) finale, "Blood Simple" created an atmosphere of suspense and mutual suspicion to rival any film of its kind. It was followed, in a bravura display of technical and artistic versatility, by "Raising Arizona" (1987), a zany dysfunctional family comedy about a childless couple (Nicolas Cage and Holly Hunter) who decide to kidnap a quintuplet. Superb performances, dazzling camera pyrotechnics and some brilliantly conceived scenes—John Goodman literally bursting up out of the earth during a rainstorm—helped create a world as far removed from that of "Blood Simple" as was possible.

Loosely based on Dashiel Hammett's "The Glass Key", "Miller's Crossing" (1990) starred Albert Finney as a mob boss and Gabriel Byrne as the advisor from whom he becomes estranged during a period of inter-gang conflict. Though it was largely well received, some critics felt the film suffered from an excess of style—that the brothers were too concerned with showing off their familiarity with earlier, landmark gangster films to successfully forge their own contribution to the genre. Others hailed it as a genre classic. In any event, the film solidified the team's reputation as leading stylists in the American cinema.

"Barton Fink" (1991) garnered the Palme d'Or at the 1991 Cannes Film Festival and a directing prize for Joel. This jet black comedy told the story of a leftist New York playwright (allegedly modeled on Clifford Odets) who hits it big on Broadway, moves out to Hollywood, and suffers writer's block while attempting to craft a screenplay for a wrestling vehicle for Wallace Beery. Fink (John Turturro) starts to go a bit mad in his creepy hotel room, where his neighbor is an amiable traveling salesman (John Goodman) who may be a serial killer. With its striking depiction of mental decay, "Barton Fink" echoed the concerns and tone of "The Tenant" (1976), Roman Polanski's darkly comic psychological horror film. Unfortunately, the Coens also ventured into thematic pretension as the film touched upon issues of anti-Semitism, leftist hypocrisy, and the banality of evil. While devilishly clever, "Barton Fink" seemed to lack an organizing intelligence as it raised more questions than it answered. Some critics condemned the film as thoughtlessly anti-intellectual and even anti-Jewish.

Though "Barton Fink" grossed less than $6 million, hot-shot producer (and Coen Brothers fan) Joel Silver raised somewhere between $25 and $40 million (depending on which report one believes) for "The Hudsucker Proxy." This lavish take on Hollywood screwball comedies of the 30s and 40s lovingly recreated a 50s period NYC skyline with sets, costumes and patter to match. The Coens' reputation snared several big names for the high stakes comedy, including Paul Newman, Tim Robbins and Jennifer Jason Leigh. Reviews were mixed and box office was next to nothing as the film brought in a paltry $2.8 million domestically.

The brothers followed this massive disappointment with a little film that allowed them to get back to basics—with quite successful results. "Fargo" (1996) was a black comedic crime film about a down-on-his-luck Minneapolis used car salesman (William H. Macy) who hires two inept thugs (Steve Buscemi and Peter Stomare) to stage a "fake" kidnapping of his wife in hopes of extorting ransom money from his wealthy father-in-law (Harve Presnell). Unfortunately, things go spectacularly wrong. Reviewers noticed both thematic and subject links between this effort and their celebrated debut outing, "Blood Simple." The flashy camerawork was kept to a minimum as longer takes and a more detached observational style was adopted.

Budgeted at a thrifty $6.5 million, "Fargo" emerged as the Coens' breakthrough feature: a major arthouse hit as well as a critical darling. The film garnered numerous awards and seven Oscar nominations including three each for the duo. For Ethan, this consisted of a nod for Best Picture (as producer) in addition to sharing two for Best Film Editing (under the joint pseudonym of Roderick Jaynes) and Best Original Screenplay, winning the latter.

The Coens continued to indulge their fascination with kidnapping in their next project, a comedy thriller entitled "The Big Lebowski" (late 1997) which boasted an unusually impressive cast including John Goodman, Jeff Bridges, Steve Buscemi and John Turturro.—Written by Kent Greene

MILESTONES:

Grew up in St. Louis Park, a suburb of Minneapolis, Minnesota

Left high school early

Transferred to a private school in Massachusetts, Simon's Rock of Bard College

Attended Princeton University as a philosophy major

1980: Left college to join brother Joel in NYC

1980: Did temp work as a statistical typist at Macy's department store in NYC

1984: First film as co-screenwriter (with brother Joel and Sam Raimi), Raimi's "Crimewave (released 1985)

1984: First film as producer and co-screenwriter, "Blood Simple"

1984: Began co-writing (with brother Joel and Sam Raimi) the screenplay for "The Hudsucker Proxy" (released 1994)

1994: Signed a five-commercial deal with brother Joel for Budweiser Ice Draft Beer

1996: Breakthrough feature, "Fargo"

QUOTES:

See Joel Coen's bio for more of an overview of the Coen brothers films.

Together, the Coens edit their own films under the pseudonym Roderick Jaynes.

"The enigmatic brothers have created a tiny body of crazily proficient movies, full of comic-book humor, lizard-like alertness, deadpan wit and cosmic images. . . . Their movies, dark and foreboding as they are, are full of glee. There are 'in' jokes, comments on moviemaking itself, products of the kind of cool, bratty intelligence the Coens are known for."—From Jami Bernard's "Barton Fink" review in the New York Post, August 21, 1991.

BIBLIOGRAPHY:

"Blood Simple: An Original Screenplay" Joel Coen and Ethan Coen, 1988, St. Martin's Press published screenplay

"Raising Arizona: An Original Screenplay" Joel Coen and Ethan Coen, 1988, St. Martin's Press; published screenplay

"Barton Fink; Miller's Crossing" Joel Coen and Ethan Coen, 1991, Faber and Faber; published screenplay

"Gates of Eden" Ethan Coen, 1998, fiction

"Joel & Ethan Coen" Peter Korte and Georg Seesslen Titan

Joel Coen

BORN: in St. Louis Park, Minnesota, 11/29/1953

SOMETIMES CREDITED AS:
Roderick Jaynes

NATIONALITY: American

EDUCATION: attended high school in Minnesota; left early

Simon's Rock of Bard College, Great Barrington, Massachusetts

Institute of Film and TV, New York University, New York, New York

University of Texas at Austin, Austin, Texas; briefly did post-graduate work in film

AWARDS: Independent Spirit Award Best Director "Blood Simple" 1985; tied with Martin Scorsese for "After Hours"

Cannes Film Festival Palme d'Or du Festival International du Film (Long Metrage) "Barton Fink" 1991; shared award with Ethan Coen

Cannes Film Festival Prix de la Mise en Scene au Festival International du Film (Long Metrage) "Barton Fink" 1991; awarded for best direction

IFP Gotham Filmmaker Award 1994; award shared with brother Ethan Coen

Cannes Film Festival Best Director Award "Fargo" 1996

National Board of Review Award Best Director "Fargo" 1996

Los Angeles Film Critics Association Award Best Screenplay "Fargo" 1996; award shared with brother Ethan Coen

Golden Satellite Best Director "Fargo" 1996; initial presentation of award

Film Critics Circle of Australia Award Best Foreign Film in English "Fargo" 1996

Florida Film Critics Circle Award Best Director "Fargo" 1996

Florida Film Critics Circle Award Best Screenplay "Fargo" 1996; shared with Ethan Coen

Chicago Film Critics Association Award Best Director "Fargo" 1996

Chicago Film Critics Association Award Best Screenplay "Fargo" 1996; shared with Ethan Coen

London Film Critics Circle Award Best Screenwriter "Fargo" 1996; award shared with Ethan Coen

Writers Guild of America Award Best Screenplay Written Directly for the Screen "Fargo" 1997; award shared with Ethan Coen

Golden Satellite Best Director "Fargo" 1996; initial presentation of the award

Independent Spirit Award Best Screenplay "Fargo" 1996; award shared with Ethan Coen

Independent Spirit Award Best Director "Fargo" 1996

Oscar Best Screenplay Written Directly for the Screen "Fargo" 1996; award shared with Ethan Coen

BAFTA David Lean Award for Best Achievement in Direction "Fargo" 1996

Cannes Film Festival Best Director Award "The Man Who Wasn't There" 2001; tied with David Lynch ("Mulholland Drive")

BIOGRAPHY

With producer and co-writer Ethan, Joel Coen has been part of the most celebrated brother act in recent entertainment memory. He has helmed a series of stylish, irreverent and cinema-savvy movies that have charmed critics while thrilling an initially small but loyal band of viewers. Though they evince a powerful fascination with Hollywood genres, the Coens' work gets the Serious Film treatment from the Hollywood community. These are self-conscious movie-movies with style to spare: manic, witty yet sinuous camera movements, slick yet richly textured cinematography and powerhouse performers spouting smart and beautifully artificial dialogue. Some have complained, however, that one may leave their films with the sense that the Coens believe in nothing but style.

Like Alfred Hitchcock, the Coens have relied heavily upon detailed preproduction and storyboarding. With the notable exception of "Raising Arizona" (1987), they have favored chilly irony in the grand tradition of Hitchcock and Stanley Kubrick. "Fargo", their belated 1996 commercial/critical breakthrough may be the ultimate example of this tendency as it veers eccentrically from low-key quirky comedy to hard-edged violence and serious consequences. One could quibble, however, that they lack Hitchcock's obsessiveness and moral seriousness and fail to match Kubrick's intellect and profound pessimism. Nonetheless, their undeniable virtuosity and terminal cool have propelled them to the front ranks of the generation of filmmakers who emerged since the halcyon days of the 1970s American auteurs (Altman, Coppola, Spielberg, Scorsese, et al.). Though they are visually oriented and allow little deviation from their scripts, actors love to work with them due to the trust they inspire with their low-key directing style. (Though Joel is officially the director, they collaborate on all aspects of their productions. Reportedly they tend to be perceived as an interchangeable unit on their film sets, as they chuckle together at private jokes and complete each other's sentences.) Most impressively, studios scramble to back their distinctive projects though the first four of them cumulatively grossed less than "Ace Ventura: Pet Detective" (1994).

The Coens have collaborated with writer-director Sam Raimi (best known for "Darkman" and the "Evil Dead" series) on several projects. Though Joel Coen and Raimi have similar sensibilities—hellzapoppin' camerawork and a weakness for genre—the latter has yet to gain comparable critical cachet. This may be due to the Coens' excellent track record with actors and their shrewd avoidance of the more disreputable popular genres, like horror and action. Moreover, while Raimi's movies don't pretend to be about anything much, the brothers' films have an ineffable patina of depth. One hungers for the day when they tackle a project which finally reveals their heretofore concealed passions—their "Vertigo", their "Paths of Glory." Nevertheless, the lack of an official masterpiece on his resume did not prevent Joel from garnering the official recognition of a Best Director nod for his work on "Fargo" (1997). He also shared nominations with his brother for Best Editing (under the joint pseudonym of Roderick Jaynes) and Best Original Screenplay, winning the latter.—Written by Kent Greene

COMPANION:

wife: Frances McDormand. Actor; directed by Coen in "Blood Simple" (1984); together from 1987; married 1994; second wife

MILESTONES:

Grew up in St. Louis Park, a suburb of Minneapolis, MN

Transferred to a private school in Massachusetts, Simon's Rock of Bard College

1980: Feature debut, assistant editor on "Fear No Evil"

1980: Served as assistant editor on "The Evil Dead" (released 1983)

1984: First film as co-screenwriter (with brother Ethan and Sam Raimi), Raimi's "Crimewave (released 1985)

1984: First film as director and screenwriter, "Blood Simple"

1984: Began co-writing (with brother Ethan and Sam Raimi) the screenplay for "The Hudsucker Proxy" (released 1994)

1985: First film appearance, played a security guard in John Landis' "Spies Like Us"

1994: Signed a five-commercial deal with brother Ethan for Budweiser Ice Draft Beer

1996: Breakthrough feature "Fargo"

1997: Helmed "The Big Lebowski"

2000: Shared a Best Adapted Screenplay Oscar nomination with brother Ethan for "O Brother Where Art Thou?"

2001: Helmed "The Man Who Wasn't There"; premiered at Cannes

QUOTES:

See Ethan Coen biography for a film-by-film evaluation

"Maybe the Coens are just the most un-self-conscious self-conscious artists in history. Their evasive and jokey approach to interviews . . . reveals as much as it conceals. For the Coens's disdain of abstract thinking goes far beyond the traditional artist's distrust of ideas. It goes, finally, as deep as style itself—which in many ways is what the Coens are all about. Theirs is a style that's exuberantly attentive to surfaces, to the look of things, to style itself."—John H. Richardson, "The Joel & Ethan Story," in *Premiere*, October 1990.

BIBLIOGRAPHY:

"Blood Simple: An Original Screenplay" Joel Coen and Ethan Coen, 1988, St. Martin's Press; published screenplay

"Raising Arizona: An Original Screenplay" Joel Coen and Ethan Coen, 1988, St. Martin's Press; published screenplay

"Barton Fink; Miller's Crossing" 1991, Faber and Faber; published screenplay

"Joel & Ethan Coen" Peter Korte and Georg Seesslen Titan

BORN: in Cornwall-on-Hudson, New York, 03/12/1949

NATIONALITY: American

EDUCATION: Amherst College Amherst, Massachusetts attended

Harvard University, Cambridge, Massachusetts, visual and environmental studies, BA, 1971, graduated magna cum laude

BIOGRAPHY

This busy producer-director of film and TV became one of Hollywood's "baby moguls" of the 1970s. At age 24, Cohen headed up the motion picture producing arm of Motown Records, overseeing some notable and/or popular black-oriented films: "Mahogany" (1975), "The Bingo Long Traveling All-Stars and Motor Kings" (1976), "Scott Joplin: King of Ragtime" (1977), "Thank God It's Friday" and Sidney Lumet's notorious "The Wiz" (both 1978). At age 28, he formed his own production company and set to work on his directorial debut, "A Small Circle of Friends" (1980), a nostalgic comedy set at Harvard (Cohen's alma mater) in the 60s, starring Brad Davis and Karen Allen and more than inspired by Francois Truffaut's superior "Jules et Jim" (1962). Cohen followed with "Scandalous" (1984), a farce starring Robert Hays and John Gielgud. He also executive produced the high-minded remake of "The Razor's Edge" (1984), starring a miscast Bill Murray, and produced the teen drama "The Legend of Billy Jean" (1985).

By 1985, Cohen had become a significant director of TV commercials and programs, with credits including "Miami Vice", "A Year in the Life" and "thirtysomething. He juggled these tasks with ongoing feature production as the president and, later, vice chairman and partner

of Keith Barish Productions. In this capacity, he produced or executive produced such diverse fare as Paul Schrader's "Light of Day", with Michael J. Fox and Gena Rowlands, the sci-fi thriller "The Running Man", the sober and atmospheric "Ironweed" (all 1987), and Wes Craven's creepy tale of voodoo, "The Serpent and the Rainbow" (1988).

In October 1988, Cohen and longtime friend John Badham merged their two separate deals with MCA to form The Badham/Cohen Group. Their first two ventures were slickly produced star packages, "Bird on a Wire" (1990), with Mel Gibson and Goldie Hawn, and "The Hard Way" (1991), with James Woods and Michael J. Fox. Cohen continued to work in 90s TV, racking up credits on "Eddie Dodd", "The Antagonists" and "The Wonder Years." He returned to feature directing with the fanciful biopic "Dragon: The Bruce Lee Story" (1993), a surprise critical and commercial hit (which Cohen co-wrote). Featuring an inspirational central performance by the half-Hawaiian Jason Scott Lee, the film confounded easy categorization. Nearly equal parts old-fashioned biography, touching romance, sensitive problem pic (dealing with anti-Asian prejudice and the strains of interracial romance) and rousing chopsocky adventure, the film delighted even those with no interest in martial arts.

Cohen returned to the small screen in a producing capacity, serving as executive producer, creator, screenwriter and—fleetingly—performer on a series of "Vanishing Son" TV-movies as part of the syndicated "Action Pack" series in 1994. The original, its three sequels and a 1995 syndicated spin-off series—a routinely inferior modern-day fusion of "Kung Fu", "The Incredible Hulk" and "The Fugitive"—well displayed Cohen's interest in issues confronting Asian immigrants in the

US. "Vanishing Son" began in mainland China where two brothers caught up in the turmoil of the Tiananman Square demonstrations are forced to flee for the safety of the US. The elder, Jian-Wa (Russell Wong), is torn between a career as a concert violinist and further developing his already formidable martial arts skills. The younger, Wago (Chi Muoi Lo), mesmerized by glitz and power, becomes a gangster. Like "Dragon", the "Vanishing Son" movies were sometimes corny yet satisfying offerings of romance, social commentary and impressive fighting sequences.

After the success of his Bruce Lee biopic, Cohen shifted gears considerably to helm "Dragonheart" (1996), a big-budget, special effects-driven period fantasy. Dennis Quaid played an itinerant dragonslayer who teams with Draco (memorably voiced by Sean Connery), the last dragon on Earth, to bring down a tyrannical king (David Thewlis). Reviews were wildly mixed and business was disappointing. Nonetheless, Cohen remained on the A-list, directing Sylvester Stallone in the high-profile disaster thriller "Daylight" (1996). Cohen directed a few television projects including the television series, "The Guardian" (1997) and the HBO drama, "The Rat Pack" (1998). He then returned back to the big screen to direct two summer blockbusters, "The Fast And The Furious" (2001) and "xXx" (2002) both starring rising action star Vin Diesel.—Written by Kent Greene

MILESTONES:

1969: While a college sophomore, assisted director Daniel Petrie on the Universal/NBC TV movie "Silent Night, Lonely Night"

Hired by producer Martin Jurow to try writing screenplays

Worked as a reader for the International Famous Agency (now part of ICM)

Evaluated the script for "The Sting" and recommended it; the project was set up at Universal within a week

Hired as an assistant to Richard Berger, vice president of 20th Century-Fox TV

Served as director of made-for-TV movies at 20th Century-Fox

1973: Named executive vice president of the motion picture divsion of Motown Records at age 24

1975: First film as producer, "Mahogany" (for Motown)

1978: Left Motown to form his own production company

1980: Feature film directing debut, "A Small Circle of Friends"

1984: First film as screenwriter, "Scandalous"

1985: Appointed president of Keith Barish Productions

1985: Began directing regularly for episodic TV

Directed TV commercials

Served as vice chairman of Keith Barish Productions

Formed The Badham/Cohen Group with director John Badham, merging their two separate deals with MCA

1990: First film released by The Badham/Cohen Group, "Bird on a Wire"

1993: Breakthrough directorial outing, "Dragon: The Bruce Lee Story"

1998: Directed the HBO movie "The Rat Pack"

2000: Helmed the lame thriller "The Skulls"

2001: Enjoyed a box-office hit as director of "The Fast and the Furious", starring Vin Diesel

2002: Reunited with Diesel on the spy thriller "xXx/Triple X"

BORN: Christopher Columbus in Spangler, Pennsylvania, 09/10/1958

NATIONALITY: American

EDUCATION: Tisch School of the Arts, New York University, New York, New York, film production, BFA, 1980

AWARDS: Las Vegas Film Critics Society Award Best Family Film "Harry Potter and the Sorcerer's Stone" 2001

Broadcast Film Critics Association Award Best Family Film (Live-Action) "Harry Potter and the Sorcerer's Stone" 2001

BIOGRAPHY

One of the more successful filmmakers to "graduate" from the Spielberg School of Genre Moviemaking, Chris Columbus emerged as a specialist in combining a sensitivity for feelings of young people with a rousing adventure yarn. The only child of a coal miner father, Columbus sold his first script while still in college and went on to pen three highly imaginative and commercially popular films ("Gremlins" 1984; "The Goonies" 1985; "Young Sherlock Holmes" 1985) for producer Steven Spielberg before making a competent directorial debut with the engaging teen comedy "Adventures in Babysitting" (1987).

Columbus directed his own screenplay for "Heartbreak Hotel" (1988), a whimsical romp set in 1972 about an Ohio teen who kidnaps Elvis Presley to cheer up his divorced Mom (Tuesday Weld). That feature bombed but Columbus explored the box-office heavens as the director of "Home Alone" (1990), the most popular comedy in movie history. Produced and scripted by John Hughes, another kidcult auteur, this sentimental yet amazingly violent Christmas adventure made adorable blond tyke Macaulay Culkin a male Shirley Temple for the times. He also handled similar chores on the inevitable sequel, "Home Alone 2: Lost in New York" (1992).

Between blockbusters, Columbus discovered a flair for gentle romantic comedy, scripting and directing "Only the Lonely" (1991), an uncharacteristic film for grown-ups from producer John Hughes. John Candy and Ally Sheedy were the romantic leads and the lovely Maureen O'Hara returned to the screen after an 18-year absence to play Candy's emotionally dependent mother who finds romance with Anthony Quinn. Returning to his roots as an animation maven, Columbus contributed to the script of the Japanese feature "Little Nemo: Adventures in Slumberland" (1990; released in the USA in 1992), inspired by Windsor McCay's celebrated comic strip from the early 1900s.

The director again hit box-office gold when he directed "Mrs. Doubtfire" (1993), a nuanced if extremely mild family comedy starring Robin Williams as a divorced dad who dons drag to see his kids. The actor, who was in top form (underneath Oscar-winning makeup) disguising himself as a dowdy sixtyish British housekeeper, also provided the high points for Columbus' next project, "Nine Months" (1995), this time in a small role as a Russian obstetrician. Unfortunately, its story of a five-year marriage blindsided by an unexpected pregnancy was a bit too pat, and Hugh Grant's boyish charm and Julianne Moore's radiant beauty were not enough to raise it above mediocrity.

Having produced the Brian Levant-directed Christmas comedy "Jingle All the Way" (1996) and tried his hand at a failed ABC pilot (1996's "For the People"), Columbus returned to the director's chair putting Susan Sarandon, Julia Roberts and Ed Harris through their paces in the maudlin "Stepmom" (1998). Once again, though, the helmer proved a master with his younger stars, Jena Malone and Liam Aiken, both of whom gave unaffected performances. A reteaming with Robin Williams, "Bicentennial Man" (1999), an adaptation of an Isaac Asimov short story, proved ill advised, though. After a promising start, the film devolved into the kind of sentimentality that marred "Stepmom."

From his early career penning screenplays for Spielberg through such directorial efforts as the "Home Alone" series and "Mrs. Doubtfire", Columbus has shown an ease with younger actors that few can match, except perhaps his mentors Spielberg and Hughes. His incredible success in the family genre may well be a blessing and a curse: despite trying to explore other areas of filmmaking like sci-fi and horror, Hollywood appeared to have pigeonholed him as the director of "Home Alone" and its ilk. All that was altered, however, when he landed the plum assignment of directing the first two feature adaptations of the popular series of books about a young British boy named Harry Potter who discovers that he is actually a wizard and not just a mere mortal. While many wanted to handle the directing chores (including Spielberg), Columbus emerged as something of a surprise victor. It was his dedication and his passion that won over producer David Heyman and author J.K. Rowling. When "Harry Potter and the Sorcerer's Stone" opened in November 2001, it set box-office records (grossing a record $93.5 million in its opening weekend). Having had the near impossible task of crafting a film that honored its source material, Columbus more than succeeded (although some critics carped because he did not put his imprint on the material, feeling a stronger directorial hand was required). Within days of the first film's opening, Columbus was back on set shooting the second in the series "Harry Potter and the Chamber of Secrets" (2002). When it was released the sequel was largely received as an improvement on the first installment, brisker and bolder while still exceedingly faithful to the source material.

MILESTONES:

Raised in Warren, Ohio

1973: Inspired to become a filmmaker after seeing "The Godfather" (date approximate)

Began making short Super-8 films in high school

Sold first screenplay, "Jocks", for $5,000 while at NYU; never produced

Sold screenplay for "Gremlins" to producer Steven Spielberg; produced in 1984

1984: First produced screenplay, "Reckless"

1985: Last realized collaboration with producer Spielberg, the screenplay for "Young Sherlock Holmes", directed by Barry Levinson

1986–1988: Developed and wrote for TV cartoon series, "Galaxy High School"

Fired as the screenwriter of "Indiana Jones and the Last Crusade" by Spielberg and George Lucas

1987: Formed production company, 1492 Productions

1987: Feature directorial debut, "Adventures in Babysitting"

1988: Wrote and directed the personal film "Heartbreak Hotel", about a boy who brings Elvis Presley home to meet his mother

1990: Breakthrough directing assignment, the megahit "Home Alone", scripted and produced by John Hughes

1991: Wrote and directed the sweet and sentimental "Only the Lonely", which shone with right-on-target performances, including Maureen O'Hara's first since 1973; produced by Hughes

1992: Helmed sequel, "Home Alone 2: Lost in New York", scripted and produced by Hughes

1993: Directed the crowd-pleasing comedy "Mrs. Doubtfire", starring Robin Williams and Sally Field

1995: Stumbled with utterly predictable and silly "Nine Months", which he produced, directed and wrote; Williams, as a nervous, malaprop-spouting Russian obstetrician, provided film's high points

1996: Produced "Jingle All the Way", directed by Brian Levant and starring Arnold Schwarzenegger

1996: Wrote and executive produced the ABC pilot "For the People"

1998: Directed "Stepmom", starring Julia Roberts, Susan Sarandon and Ed Harris

1999: Reteamed with Robin Williams as producer and director of "Bicentennial Man"

2001: Directed screen version of popular children's book "Harry Potter and the Sorcerer's Stone"; movie broke all box-office records on its opening weekend, earning in excess of $90 million; went on to set record as the film that earned over $100 million in the shortest time

2002: Helmed the second installment in the series, "Harry Potter and the Chamber of Secrets"

QUOTES:

When Chris Columbus met with Warner Bros. executives in order to "audition" for the the assignment of directing the Harry Potter movies, he brought along his annotated copy of Steve Kloves' screenplay. As Columbus told the *Daily News* (November 11, 2001): "I essentially put stuff back from the book and restructured [the script] to show them how I would make the movie, and I made the descriptions much more flowery so they would know what I was trying to do. I said, 'I'm actually so passionate about this that I've rewritten it to show you what I would do for free. I don't think anyone else in Hollywood would do that.' "

"There are a couple of things I WON'T do—you won't find me making a '9 1/2 Weeks', he says, smiling at the very idea. "I would start laughing if I was doing it. Movies like 'Basic Instinct'—I can understand the validity of showing people the ugliness of the world, but I also think there is a place for movies to leave people with a sense of hope for life. If your film

isn't going to do that, then I just don't think it's worth making."—Chris Columbus, quoted in "Columbus' New Adventure" by Blaise Simpson, *Los Angeles Times*, November 7, 1993.

As Spielberg's protege, Columbus had an office just down the hall from his mentor. He was welcome to interrupt whenever he pleased to discuss characters and to go over his pages. Their collaboration ended when Columbus was fired as the screenwriter of "Indiana Jones and the Last Crusade" (1989).

"The mistake I made was that Steven asked me to do 'Indiana Jones' and I was scheduled to go into meetings with Steven and George Lucas. Just the three of us in a room. Now if you want to talk about intimidating . . . So I went into this room for about eight days in New York and I just took notes on every aspect of the story." Columbus was so awed at working with the two screen legends that he transcribed the notes almost word for word, adding nothing of himself—which resulted in what he calls a "very flat screenplay."

"They tossed me off the project, but I understood," he continues. "I learned a very valuable lesson, which is that if you're going to do something, you always have to do it from your own inspiration, even if you're rewriting someone else's work." He has remained close to Spielberg and says, "I still make my films hoping to please Steven."—quoted in "Columbus' New Adventure" by Blaise Simpson, *Los Angeles Times*, November 7, 1993.

Actor Richard Harris on Columbus' technique on the set of "Harry Potter and the Sorcerer's Stone": "Chris quite rightly concentrated on the kids. He said, 'You guys are pros, you can do it.' He was like the Pied Piper with them. They absolutely worshipped him. He never once lost his cool."—quoted in *Daily News*, November 11, 2001.

Columbus states that his father gave him Christopher as a first name because, "He thought people would remember it. He had a good sense of humor."

BORN: William Condon in New York, New York, 1956

SOMETIMES CREDITED AS:
William Condon

NATIONALITY: American

EDUCATION: Regis High School, New York, New York

Columbia College, Columbia University New York, New York, philosophy, BA

AWARDS: Golden Satellite Best Motion Picture Screenplay (Adaptation) "Gods and Monsters" 1998

Oscar Best Adapted Screenplay "Gods and Monsters" 1998

BIOGRAPHY

Native New Yorker Bill Condon has been a film buff since childhood. After earning a degree in philosophy, he began contributing to such publications as *American Film* and *Millimeter*. In the early 1980s, he teamed with director Michael Laughlin as co-scenarist on a pair of cult thrillers, "Dead Kids/Strange Behavior" (1981), which focused on the mysterious murders of teenagers in a Midwestern town, and "Strange Invaders" (1983), a spoof of 50s sci-fi films that received generally positive notices. Moving to the director's chair, Condon steered the atmospheric, "Sister, Sister" (1987), a Southern gothic tale about two siblings who have converted their family's Louisiana plantation into a bed-and-breakfast. While many critics carped over the story (deemed too derivative of Hitchcock's work), there was grudging admiration for the lead performances of Judith Ivey and Jennifer Jason Leigh.

As "Sister, Sister" was a critical and box-office disappointment, Condon retreated to cable TV, helming a trio of 1991 films for the USA Network. In interviews, the writer-director has stated "that's where I learned to make movies. You have to do them in 20 day, you have $2 1/2 million, including the money they spend on 'stars', so you don't have much money to make them. Other than that, they leave you alone. I worked in all these different genres and put together a team. I got to learn how to do it all." Indeed, "Murder 101" focused on a mystery author and college professor (Pierce Brosnan) who finds himself framed for a murder. "White Lie" was a provocative story about a contemporary political aide (Gregory Hines) who returns to the South and looks into the 1961 lynching of his father. "Dead in the Water" was a taut thriller featuring a murder plan than goes awry. Moving to network television, Condon helmed the based-on-fact "Deadly Relations" (ABC, 1993), about an abusive and controlling father, as well as the unsold pilot "The Man Who Wouldn't Die" (ABC, 1995) which teamed a crime writer (Roger Moore) with a psychic waitress (Nancy Allen) in the search for a master criminal (Malcolm McDowell).

Having served his apprenticeship, Condon returned to feature films first as one of the screenwriters on "FX2—The Art of the Deadly Flesh" (1991) and later as director of the middling sequel "Candyman: Farewell to the Flesh" (1995). His previous work hardly prepared audiences and reviewers for what proved to be a triumph, "Gods and Monsters" (1998). In adapting "Father of Frankenstein" Christopher Bram's 1995 novel about the last days of British expatriate filmmaker James Whale, Condon fashioned a minor masterpiece, melding a gay theme with historical Hollywood and eliciting a towering central performance from Ian McKellen as the ailing director.

Deliberately invoking Whale's style and making numerous inside references to the moviemaker's work, Condon brought wit and style to the material. This complicated, emotional story of, in the writer-director's words, "somebody in his decline, facing the loss of power . . . and coming face to face with certain regrets and failures in his life" ranked as one of the year's best films and earned Condon a well-deserved Academy Award for his script.

MILESTONES:

Raised in NYC

Wrote for such publications as *American Film* and *Millimeter*

1981: Screenwriting debut, co-wrote the thriller "Dead Kids/Strange Behavior" with director Michael Laughlin; billed as William Condon

1983: With Laughlin, co-wrote the sci-fi spoof "Strange Invaders"

1988: Feature directorial debut, "Sister, Sister"; also co-wrote screenplay

1991: TV debut as director with first of three USA Network movies, "Murder 101"; also scripted

1993: Made network debut as director with the ABC drama "Deadly Relations"

1995: Helmed the feature thriller sequel "Candyman: Farewell to the Flesh"; initial screen collaboration with Clive Barker

1998: Wrote and directed the superior "Gods and Monsters", a fictionalized meditation on the last days of expatriate British director James Whale; executive produced by Barker; received Oscar for Best Adapted Screenplay

2002: Wrote screenplay adaptation of the stage musical "Chicago"; received nominations for both a Golden Globe and an Oscar for Best Screenplay (Adapted)

AFFILIATION: Raised Roman Catholic

QUOTES:

"Although I was inspired by James Whale for the expressionistic elements in the flashbacks, the film is really a '50s film, when they did everything in color and widescreen. It's like James Whale is really an anachronism in that time, and finds himself inside a Douglas Sirk movie . . . "—Bill Condon speaking about "Gods and Monsters", quoted in *Cinefantastique*, November 1998.

Bruce Conner

BORN: in McPherson, Kansas, 1933

NATIONALITY: American

EDUCATION: University of Nebraska

AWARD: American Film Institute Maya Deren Award 1988

BIOGRAPHY

Leading figure in the American avant-garde of the 1960s. His short experimental works rely on rhythmic editing, often of "found" footage, to create both humorous and politically challenging statements, as with "A Movie" (1958), "Cosmic Ray" (1961)—in which Ray Charles' "What'd I Say" accompanies a semi-nude go-go dancer—and "Report" (1965), which repeatedly shows the assassination of John F. Kennedy.

MILESTONES:

1958: Produced, directed, and edited first feature, "A Movie"

BORN: in New Haven, Connecticut, 08/17/1946

NATIONALITY: American

EDUCATION: trained as actor with Lee Stras-berg, Stella Adler and Joanne Baron

Rhode Island School of Design Providence, Rhode Island animation BFA made six student films, including "Mondo Linoleum" in which she acted opposite Martin Mull

School of Visual Arts, New York, New York

Columbia University, New York, New York

Institute of Film and Television, New York University, New York, New York, MFA, 1970–71; reportedly worked on 15 student films, including producing and editing "Passing Quietly Through"

AWARDS: Chicago Film Festival Gold Hugo Award "Passing Quietly Through"

John Grierson Award Best Young Director "David: Off and On" 1972

American Film Festival Blue Ribbon "More Than a School" 1973

American Film Festival Blue Ribbon "Old Fashioned Woman" 1973

American Film Festival Blue Ribbon "Not a Pretty Picture" 1976

Women in Film Crystal Award 1992

Directors Guild of America Robert Aldrich Award 1997; presented for extraordinary service to the DGA and its membership

Directors Guild of America Robert Aldrich Award 1998; presented for extraordinary service to the DGA and its membership

BIOGRAPHY

A proficient director of mainstream Hollywood fare, Martha Coolidge began her career in her native Connecticut as a stage actress appearing with a local theater company. While attending the Rhode Island School of Design, she began to make films and found her true calling, turning out six student films. After further studies at NYC's School of Visual Arts and at Columbia University, she landed her first professional gig as a writer and producer of the Canadian daily children's show "Magic Tom." Returning to the USA, Coolidge enrolled at NYU's Institute of Film and Television and went on to turn out several award-winning documentary portraits, including two of family members, "David: On and Off" (1972), about her brother, and "Old Fashioned Woman" (1974), about her grandmother. These, along with the pseudo-documentary "Not a Pretty Picture" (1976) which reconstructed her high school date rape, helped establish her reputation as a filmmaker.

Coolidge first broke into Hollywood studios as a screenwriter receiving credit as one of several writers who contributed the story to the spy comedy "The Omega Connection" (1979). Her directorial debut, "Valley Girl" (1983), proved to be an above-average teen comedy and quickly established her as one to watch. She had elicited a fine comic turn from Nicolas Cage in that film and her sophomore effort, "The City Girl" (1984) was an underrated gem featuring fine work from Laura Harrington as the titular character, a photographer with a penchant for unwise romantic pairings. With her growing reputation as an actor's director and given a "big budget" ($13 million), Coolidge helmed "Real Genius" (1985), a smart satire that featured a star-making turn by Val Kilmer and gave William Atherton a meaty supporting role. If overall the film was somewhat lacking in consistent character development, it did provide solid laughs and boded well for its director. Further adding to her reputation was "Rambling Rose" (1991), a meticulously performed character piece about an eccentric Southern family and their housemaid. The mother and daughter team of Diane Ladd and Laura Dern each received Oscar nominations under Coolidge's assured handling.

An active member of the Directors Guild of America, Coolidge divided her time between TV and features and working within the union. While her film work in the 1990s hasn't exactly yielded a blockbuster, she has done yeoman work, often giving actresses rare chances to shine: consider Mercedes Ruehl in "Neil Simon's Lost in Yonkers" (1993), Geena Davis in "Angie" (1994) and Mary Elizabeth Mastrantonio in "Three Wishes" (1995). Even in "Out to Sea" (1997), a film built around the comic pairing of Jack Lemmon and Walter Matthau, Elaine Stritch, Rue McClanahan, Dyan Cannon and Gloria DeHaven won critical kudos. Coolidge continued to demonstrate an affinity for pulling strong performances from her leading ladies in her small screen work as well. Her best-known telefilms were "Crazy in Love" (TNT, 1992), which focused on three generations of women (Herta Ware, Gena Rowlands and Holly Hunter) in the Pacific Northwest, and "Introducing Dorothy Dandridge" (HBO, 1999), a biopic of the black sex symbol produced by and starring Halle Berry.

MILESTONES:

Raised in New Haven, Connecticut

Acted with a local theater company in Connecticut

1968: Wrote and produced daily children's TV show, "Magic Tom" in Canada

1972: Wrote, produced, directed and edited the documentary "David: Off and On", about her brother

1973: Edited, produced, wrote and directed "Old Fashioned Woman", a documentary portrait of her octogenarian grandmother

1975: Feature film debut, the semi-autobiographical, pseudo-documentary, "Not a Pretty Picture", about date rape; produced, wrote, directed, edited and starred

Helped start the Association of Independent/ Video and Filmmakers

1976: As American Film Institute/Academy intern, worked with Robert Wise on his film, "Audrey Rose"

1978: Worked on rock and roll love story, "Photoplay" for Coppola's Zoetrope Studio (project abandoned when studio began its collapse c. 1980)

Returned to work on Canadian television

1983: Breakthrough feature, "Valley Girl" starring Nicolas Cage and Deborah Foreman

1985: First big budget ($13 million) Hollywood film, "Real Genius"

1986: Helmed the pilot for the ABC sitcom "Sledge Hammer!"

1989: TV-movie directing debut, "Trenchcoat in Paradise"

1991: Won acclaim for her direction of "Rambling Rose"; real-life mother and daughter co-stars Laura Dern and Diane Ladd received Oscar nominations for their performances

1992: Helmed the well-received made-for-cable movie "Crazy in Love" (TNT)

1993: Steered the uneven film version of "Neil Simon's Lost in Yonkers", an semi-autobiographical look at the author's upbringing based on his Pulitzer-winning play

1994: Appeared as a security guard in "Beverly Hills Cop III"

1995: Directed the family drama "Three Wishes", starring Al Pacino and Mary Elizabeth Mastrantonio

1997: Helmed the feature comedy "Out to Sea", starring Jack Lemmon and Walter Matthau

1999: Directed the HBO biopic "Introducing Dorothy Dandridge", produced by and starring Halle Berry; received Emmy nomination

2000: Helmed one segment of the tripart "If These Walls Could Talk 2" (HBO), examining the lesbian experience in America

2001: Helmed "The Ponder Heart" for PBS

Signed to direct a five-hour miniseries about the colonization of Mars, co-written and executive produced by James Cameron

AFFILIATION: Member, Board of Trustees, American Film Institute

President, Directors Guild of America (2002–03)

Chair, DGA's Creative Rights Committee (1992–); since 1996, served as co-chair with John Frankenheimer

QUOTES:

She is a distant cousin of former president Calvin Coolidge.

In March 2002, Coolidge became the first female president of the Directors Guild of America when she succeeded Jack Shea who resigned.

Awarded the Crystal Award by Women in Film.

Awarded the Breakthrough Award by Women, Men & Media.

"If a man is demanding and doesn't stand for inefficiency, if he wants things done in a certain way, he will frequently get forceful, Many directors get angry and yell. They may be difficult. And on some level they are worshipped for that.

"If I do that, I run the risk of being 'shrill', 'a screamer' or 'a bitch'. This is a big dilemma for women directors. There are more people questioning what we can do every day. There are more people thinking they can push us around than there are thinking they can push men around. A director must be demanding and tough. When a woman gets that way she can run into criticism which I consider to be gender-based."—Martha Coolidge to *DGA Magazine*, November 1998.

Francis Ford Coppola

BORN: Francis Ford Coppola in Detroit, Michigan, 04/07/1939

SOMETIMES CREDITED AS:

Thomas Colchart

Francis Coppola

Albert Posco

NATIONALITY: American

EDUCATION: Great Neck High School, Great Neck, New York

Hofstra College, Hempstead, New York ,drama BA, 1960; now Hofstra University; attended on scholarship; wrote, directed and produced student play, "Inertia"; classmates included Lainie Kazan

School of Film, University of California at Los Angeles, Los Angeles, California, MFA, 1967; noted 1930s Hollywood director Dorothy Arzner, who was his instructor, said he was her "most promising" student, if "rather eccentric"

AWARDS: Writers Guild of America Award Best-Written American Drama Written Directly for the Screen "Patton" 1970; award shared with Edmund H. North

Oscar Writing (Best Story and Screenplay Based on Factual Material or Material Not Previously Published or Produced) "Patton" 1970; shared award with Edmund H. North

Golden Globe Award Best Director "The Godfather" 1972

Golden Globe Award Best Screenplay "The Godfather" 1972; award shared with Mario Puzo

Writers Guild of America Award Best-Written Drama Adapted from Another Medium "The Godfather" 1972; award shared with Mario Puzo

Directors Guild of America Award Outstanding Directorial Achievement in Feature Film "The Godfather" 1972

Oscar Writing (Best Screenplay Based on Material from Another Medium) "The Godfather" 1972; award shared with Mario Puzo

Golden Globe Award Best Motion Picture (Musical or Comedy) "American Graffiti" 1973; Coppola was a producer

Cannes Film Festival Palme d'Or "The Conversation" 1974

National Board of Review Award Best English Language Film "The Conversation" 1974; Coppola was a producer

National Board of Review Award Best Director "The Conversation" 1974

National Society of Film Critics Award Best Director "The Godfather, Part II" and "The Conversation" 1974; cited for two films

Directors Guild of America Award Outstanding Directorial Achievement in Feature Film "The Godfather, Part II" 1974

Writers Guild of America Award Best-Written Drama Adapted from Another Medium "The Godfather, Part II" 1974; award shared with Mario Puzo

Oscar Best Picture "The Godfather, Part II" 1974; producer

Oscar Best Director "The Godfather, Part II" 1974

Oscar Best Screenplay Adapted from Another Medium "The Godfather, Part II" 1974; award shared with Mario Puzo

Cannes Film Festival Palme d'Or "Apocalypse Now" 1979; co-winner with Volker Schlondorff's "The Tin Drum"

Cannes Film Festival FIPRESCI Prize for Competing Film "Apocalypse Now" 1979

Golden Globe Award Best Director "Apocalypse Now" 1979

Golden Globe Award Best Musical Score "Apocalypse Now" 1979; shared with his father Carmine Coppola

BAFTA Award Best Direction "Apocalypse Now" 1979

Venice Film Festival Career Award 1992; cited along with Jeanne Moreau and Paolo Villaggio

American Cinema Editors Golden Eddie Award 1992 "for distinguished contributions to the art and craft of film"; Coppola was also made an honorary member of the American Cinema Editors

Directors Guild of America D. W. Griffith Award 1998; awarded for distinguished achievement in motion picture directing

American Society of Cinematographers Board of Governors Award 1997

Mary Pickford Award 2000 initial presentation of award by International Press Academy

BIOGRAPHY

One of America's most erratic, energetic and controversial filmmakers, Francis Ford Coppola has enjoyed stunning triumphs and endured monumental setbacks, then resurrected himself, rising Phoenix-like to begin the process over again. Known primarily for his successful "Godfather" trilogy ("The Godfather" 1972, "The Godfather, Part II" 1974 and "The Godfather, Part III" 1990), Coppola breathed life into a generation of filmmakers, promoting and subsidizing the likes of George Lucas, John Milius, Willard Huyck and Gloria Katz, while indirectly influencing Martin Scorsese and Brian De Palma. He continued his patriarchy as an executive producer, championing the work of Wim Wenders, Paul Schrader and Akira Kurosawa, to name a few, and played an important part in the restoration of Abel Gance's classic silent film, "Napoleon" (1927). The quality of his directing fell off throughout the 80s and 90s, however, and the big studios, remembering his colossal box-office failures, became leery of backing his more personal projects, preferring instead to employ him as a hired gun.

Winner of five Academy Awards before he was 40, Coppola grew up in a creative, supportive Italian-American family. His father Carmine was a flutist who during the course of his career played in several orchestras including Toscanini's NBC Symphony Orchestra, which he often conducted on tour. His mother, the former Italia Pennino, had been an actress. Although his fascination with film had begun early (he made his first movies at the age of 10 with his father's 8 mm camera and tape recorder), he chose to seek a rounded theatrical education "because Eisenstein had started like that" and attended Hofstra University, where he capped his collegiate career by conceiving, producing and directing the first play ever written and staged entirely by Hofstra students. From there, Coppola entered UCLA film school in 1960, eventually earning a Masters Degree (1967), but his discontent with the classroom led him to direct some soft-core porn films, then hire himself out to low-budget king Roger Corman. His first job for Corman was to dub and re-edit a Russian science fiction film, turning it into a sex-and-violence monster movie entitled "Battle Beyond the Stars" (1962).

Coppola directed his first feature, the unremarkable Corman-produced "Dementia 13", while in Ireland in the summer of 1963, and, on the strength of his Samuel Goldwyn award-winning UCLA screenplay "Pilma Pilma", secured a job as a scriptwriter with Seven Arts. He made significant contributions to "Is Paris Burning?" (1966) and "This Property is Condemned" (1966) and eventually won his first Oscar for co-writing Franklin Schaffner's "Patton" (1970). Frustrated at not seeing his vision on the screen, though, Coppola bought the rights to a David Benedictus novel and fused it with a story idea of his own. His adaptation of "You're a Big Boy Now" (1966) became his UCLA thesis project and received a theatrical release via Warner Brothers. Critics praised the funny and fast-paced film, applauding the appearance of a new director of great talent and promise, but a more polished movie with a related theme, Mike Nichols' "The Graduate" (1967), dwarfed it at the box office.

Coppola agreed to direct a screen version of "Finian's Rainbow" (1968), a musical starring Fred Astaire, and though it bombed on release (the studio blew it up from 35mm to 70mm chopping off Astaire's feet), it did introduce him to George Lucas who would work as a production assistant on his next movie, "The Rain People" (1969). Written, directed and financed by Coppola (until his money ran out and the studio had to help out), it starred Shirley Knight as a distressed housewife who takes to the road and befriends along the way the brain-damaged football player James Caan (who had also attended Hofstra). Coppola next launched American Zoetrope as an idealistic alternative to the way studios operated. The company intended to produce mainstream pictures to finance "off-the-wall" projects and give first-time directors their chance to direct, but when Warner Bros. disliked Zoetrope's initial offering, Lucas' futuristic "THX-1138", and demanded their money back, Coppola was $300,000 in debt and unsure of his future as a filmmaker.

"The Godfather" changed all that, but only after Coppola had fought tooth and nail for the cast of his choice and narrowly avoided dismissal by a skittish Paramount that feared he was in over his head. Thanks to producer Bob Evans' faith in him and a timely Oscar for "Patton", Coppola survived to bring his monumental epic to the screen, earning his second Oscar for the screenplay he co-adapted with Mario Puzo from the latter's bestseller. One of the highest-grossing films in movie history, "The Godfather" captured the country's imagination by skirting the traditional gangster territory and reinventing itself as a family chronicle. When family is so strong, so loving, it does not matter that their trade is slaughter and graft. Coppola's brilliant opening juxtaposed the brightly-lit wedding outside with the dark interior of the Don's court, and the finale intercut murder with baptism, closing a visual feast of nearly three hours containing not an ounce of fat. Marlon Brando presided over the festivities (and rekindled his career), aided ably by an extraordinary supporting cast, including Caan, Al Pacino, Robert Duvall, Coppola's sister Talia Shire and Diane Keaton. "The Godfather" ushered in the era of the blockbuster, making Coppola a rich man, and his career soared on the wings of his revived prospects.

Coppola launched his friend Lucas' career, producing the 60s nostalgia flick "American Graffiti" (1973) and, following work on the screenplay for "The Great Gatsby" (1974), directed the "The Conversation" (1974), his own script about a lonely surveillance expert (Gene Hackman) whose obsessive eavesdropping leads to tragedy. The film, which brought Coppola two Oscar nominations and won the Palme d'Or at Cannes, featured the high-tech gadgetry that would fascinate him throughout his career. The real star turned out to be sound designer Walter Murch who, besides providing the superb soundtrack, also ran post-production when the director had to abandon the project to work on "Godfather II." Coppola again co-wrote with Puzo that hugely successful sequel, winner of six Oscars, including three for Coppola as producer, director and writer. "Godfather II" daringly intercut the story of the rise to power of Vito Corleone (Robert De Niro), a prelude to the first film, with the parallel, contrasting story of his son Michael's ascendance 30 years later. (Both parts of "The Godfather" were later recut in chronological sequence for a TV miniseries.)

By the end of 1975, Coppola had begun work on "Apocalypse Now" (1979)—a version of Joseph Conrad's "Heart of Darkness" updated to the Vietnam War. John Milius had written the original script years earlier under Coppola's sponsorship and George Lucas was to have directed it before Coppola assumed control. The film tracked a CIA operative (Martin Sheen) traveling up a Cambodian river in search of the legendary Colonel Kurtz (Marlon Brando), who had established a bizarre empire deep in the jungle. Everything that could conceivably go wrong during production went wrong. Coppola replaced his leading actor after shooting began, the replacement Sheen had a heart attack delaying the production at length and Typhoon Olga destroyed the sets. The

director's personal journey into self mirrored the story he was filming. The cost overrun was staggering, and Coppola had to mortgage everything he owned to cover some $16 million of the $30 million budget. His wife who had gone to the Philippines to make a documentary about the process wrote of her husband in a March 1977 entry in her diary: "I guess he has had a sort of nervous breakdown." Coppola has remarked of the experience that "little by little we went crazy." After many months of difficult jungle shooting and strenuous editing, the long-awaited production enjoyed an emotional premiere at the Cannes Film Festival, where it won the Palme d'Or. Parts of the movie (like the helicopters attacking to the music of Wagner's "The Ride of the Valkyries") were sheer genius, and despite its overall lack of unity, "Apocalypse Now" was undeniably visually breathtaking and a modest hit at the box office, winning two Oscars and once again saving Coppola from ruin. It also took its toll on the director, perhaps doing irreparable damage to his psyche and permanently undermining his confidence.

"Apocalypse Now" marked the end of Coppola's "golden period", and a succession of box-office disappointments ensued, his films often suffering as a result of his megalomania. The $26 million production of the movie musical "One From the Heart" (1982) was a major financial and critical bomb, due largely to Coppola's preoccupation with costly high-tech gadgets and experimental computer and video techniques at the expense of storytelling. "One from the Heart" brought him to the brink of personal as well as business bankruptcy, and he would spend the rest of the decade working to pay his debts. (Zoetrope Studios finally filed for Chapter 11 bankruptcy in 1990). In 1983, Coppola directed two adaptations of teenage-themed novels by S.E. Hinton, "The Outsiders" and "Rumble Fish", both criticized as overly-stylized and lacking in strong narrative impact. Both also lost money. Nevertheless, they captured the writer's world, as Coppola had intended, and provided screen introductions for an astonishing number of young actors who would, within a few years, dominate the Hollywood scene, including Matt Dillon, Mickey Rourke, Nicolas Cage, C. Thomas Howell, Ralph Macchio, Patrick Swayze, Rob Lowe, Emilio Estevez, Tom Cruise, Christopher Penn and Diane Lane.

Coppola's run of bad luck continued with "The Cotton Club" (1984), an ambitious musical set in the famous Harlem jazz club of the 1920s. Despite putting the script through nearly 40 drafts before the trouble-plagued production began, Coppola was hamstrung by the predetermined character of white cornetist Dixie Dwyer (dictated by Richard Gere's contract), which led to an improbable and incoherent story. Coupled with that was his unmitigated fascination with huge state-of-the-art production methods that ballooned costs to $48 million and had him spending most of his time in his customized high-tech trailer, the "Silverfish", surrounded by cameras, monitors, consoles and computers. It was a pure recipe for disaster. Still, he continued his love affair with technology for his TV directing debut, "Rip Van Winkle" (Showtime, 1985), crafting many of the fantastic scenes with computer imaging systems, and he was really able to indulge himself making "Captain Eo" (1985), a 12-minute space fantasy for Disney theme parks starring Michael Jackson and produced by Lucas.

Coppola next helmed the light time-travel comedy, "Peggy Sue Got Married" (1986), and though it suffered for its inevitable comparisons to "Back to the Future" (1985), it managed a respectable box office. In spite of a weak script, Coppola constructed the tale around a series of poignant encounters, the most powerful (i.e., when Peggy sees her grandparents as they were 25 years earlier) causing the audience to choke-up right along with the time-traveling heroine. A high school student himself in the 50s, Coppola effectively conveyed an authentic look and feel for the period. The film solidified Kathleen

Turner's reputation and made a star of Coppola's nephew, Nicolas Cage, although some thought him grating in his turn as Peggy Sue's husband. An aura of tragedy surrounded "Gardens of Stone" (1987), a well-acted Vietnam War–era drama played out on the home front, which pleased some critics but not audiences. During its filming, Coppola's son Gian-Carlo was killed in a boating accident. The far more impressive "Tucker: The Man and His Dream" (1988) starred Jeff Bridges in the role of the real-life 40s auto-industry visionary. Coppola had been planning to make this film since the early 70s, when he had become fascinated with the story of Tucker, the brash but intelligent entrepreneur who dared to challenge the Detroit establishment. The story is not without parallels to Coppola's own career in Hollywood but, more importantly, "Tucker" focused attention on entrepreneurship and innovation at a time in American history when those qualities were sorely lacking. Like "Peggy Sue", "Tucker" also revealed a striking sense of period. Because Coppola used the cinematic conventions of the 40s to capture the look and feel of the time, "Tucker" was as much about his (and our) memory of the period as it was about the period itself.

Coppola was working in Rome when the opportunity arose to direct "Godfather III." In desperate need of a hit, Coppola acceded to Paramount chairman Frank Mancuso's pleas for a third installment in the series. Bargaining for full artistic control over the project, he began what was to become a $55-million rumor-bound production in November 1989, reuniting screenwriters Coppola and Puzo and stars Pacino, Keaton and Shire. Coppola's decision to cast daughter Sofia in a pivotal role backfired; her failure to capture the part was widely cited as one of the film's worst flaws. (Winona Ryder has originally been cast but withdrew because of illness.) Studio pressure to meet a December release terminated the editing process prematurely, leaving essentially an unfinished product that seemed aimless and uncertain. The revised "Godfather III" available in the videotape version of all three parts of "The Godfather", though not as good as the first two parts, is far superior to the theatrical release, thanks to Walter Murch's additional cutting during assembly. Autumnal, sad, and full of confessions, it is one of Coppola's most candid films and better than originally believed.

Coppola scored a huge success at the helm of "Bram Stoker's Dracula" (1992) with the help of a stunning production design (Thomas Sanders) and superb cinematography (Michael Ballhaus) and music (Wojciech Kilar). A sumptuous visual extravaganza that more than compensated for lapses in the story, the film grossed $200 million worldwide and carried home Oscars for makeup, sound effects editing and costume design. His 9-year-old granddaughter's asking when he was going to make a movie for kids influenced his next directorial choice. "Jack" (1996) starred Robin Williams as a child with a disorder that caused him to grow four times faster than normal and have the appearance of a 40-year-old man when he was only 10. The fable, a kind of "Peggy Sue Got Married" premise dealing with Jack's diminished life expectancy, appealed to Coppola for its parallel to his son Gian-Carlo's tragically short but full life. He also related to Jack, the outsider, having felt cut off from other children as a result of a bout with polio at the age of 9. Regrettably, this movie, which he dedicated to Gian, and for which he had so much personal feeling, did not resonate with audiences, pulling up lame at the box office. He picked a proven winner as his next mount, scripting and helming the film adaptation of "John Grisham's 'The Rainmaker' " (1997).

Throughout Coppola's career, shaky business ventures magnified the problems of his box-office flops. In the 60s, he poured profits from screenwriting into an ill-fated venture called Scopitone, a precursor of music videos, which showed short movies on a jukebox, and the 70s saw him quickly lose $1.5 million on the San Francisco-based *City Magazine* during his stewardship. Though the bankruptcy of American Zoetrope (the studio) signaled his ultimate failure to establish himself independent of the Hollywood power structure, the success of "Dracula" restored Coppola's fortune, and subsequent investments have thrived. He bought Blancaneaux, a 50-acre property on the banks of the Privassion River in Belize, and began operating it as a luxury hotel in 1993. The following year, he opened (along with partners Robert De Niro, Robin Williams and restaurateur Drew Nieporent) Rubicon, a San Francisco restaurant. Coppola paid $10 million in 1995 to purchase the balance of the old Inglenook wine-producing property, completing his dream estate and expanding his wine company Niebaum-Coppola. He has a food line, "Francis Coppola Selects", reflecting his love of cooking, that features olive oils, vinegars and sun-dried tomatoes. Continuing to serve as an executive producer on projects as mixed as his own films, Coppola also launched *Zoetrope*, a literary magazine, in 1997. Doubling as a film development lab, *Zoetrope* hearkens back to the golden age of film, a time of greater respect for the short-story form as an impetus for movies.

Coppola's latest rebirth has been much more monetary than artistic, and the big studios have remained reticent to back the movies he really wants to make. Whatever he does in the future, the "Godfather" series will stand as the monument of his career, the first two installments alone earning more than $800 million at the international box-office. The pervasive "Godfather" theme of the sanctity of the family is what has mattered most to Coppola throughout his life, both as paterfamilias to his filmmaking community of the early 70s and as advocate for his relatives, including father Carmine, sister Talia Shire, nephew Nicolas Cage and daughter Sofia, as key contributors to his films. With prospects for financial ruin growing dimmer and dimmer, one hopes that

Coppola's many interests don't spread him so thin that he can't devote himself to a personal project and shepherd it to a conclusion worthy of his best work. Then will the great bird rise again from the ash heap in all its artistic glory, flapping its golden wings majestically for all to see.—Written by Greg Senf

FAMILY:

grandfather: August Coppola. Pianist; emigrated to USA from Naples as Enrico Caruso's piano accompanist

father: Carmine Coppola. Flutist, composer, musical arranger; born on July 11, 1910; died on April 26, 1991; Italian-American; played in Toscanini's NBC Symphony Orchestra; scored some of son's films, including "The Godfather, Part II" for which he shared an Oscar

mother: Italia Coppola. Actor

uncle: Archimedes Coppola. Engineer, musician; born in 1909; died in 1927

uncle: Michael Coppola. Inventor born in 1914

uncle: Antonio Coppola. Conductor, music teacher; conductor of symphony orchestras and opera with the San Francisco Opera and New York City Opera; also conducted Broadway musicals like "My Fair Lady"; was opera advisor on "The Godfather, Part III" (1990)

father-in-law: Clifford Neil. Artist, inventor; born in 1891; died in 1945

brother: August Floyd Coppola. Writer, professor; born in 1934; dean of the School of Creative Arts at San Francisco State University; involved with "Audio Vision" which provides a taped soundtrack of a narrator describing visual information for blind filmgoers; father of Marc and Christopher Coppola and Nicolas Cage

sister: Talia Rose Coppola. Actor, producer, director; born on April 25, 1945; has acted in films directred by brother; formerly married to composer David Shire who scored "The Conversation" (1974); subsequently wed to the late producer Jack Schwartzman with whom she had two sons, actors Jason and Robert Schwartzman

brother-in-law: William Neil. Special effects technician; born in 1939

nephew: Marc Coppola. Actor; born in 1957; son of August Coppola; acted in "Cotton Club", "Jack" and "Deadfall"

nephew: Christopher Coppola. Director, screenwriter; son of August Coppola; born on January 25, 1962

nephew: Nicolas Cage. Actor; son of August Coppola; has acted in films directed by uncle; born on January 7, 1964; won Oscar for "Leaving Las Vegas"

son: Gian-Carlo Coppola. Born on September 17, 1963; killed in boating accident in May 1986

son: Roman Coppola. Production head, visual effects technician, 2nd unit director, sound mixer, music video director; born in 1965; heads Black Diamond Productions; first feature as executive producer, "The Spirit of '76" (1990)

daughter: Sofia Coppola. Director, screenwriter, fashion designer, former actor; first screen appearance as infant in "The Godfather" (1972); born in May 1971; played Kathleen Turner's younger sister in "Peggy Sue Got Married"; co-author, costume designer and main title designer of Coppola's segment, "Life Without Zoe" in "New York Stories" (1989); replaced Winona Ryder in "The Godfather, Part III" (1990); directed first film "The Virgin Suicides" (1999); married to director Spike Jonze in June 1999

nephew: Jason Schwartzman. Actor, musician; son of Talia Shire and late producer Jack Schwartzman; born on June 26, 1980; star of comedy hit "Rushmore" (1998)

granddaughter: Gian Carla Coppola. Daughter of the late Gian-Carlo Coppola and Jackie De La Fontaine, born six months after Gian-Carlo's death in 1986

MILESTONES:

1947–1948: Stricken with polio as a child (dates approximate)

Worked on various non-mainstream and "nudie" movies (e.g., "The Playgirls and the Bellboy" 1962, "Tonight For Sure" 1962) before being hired by Roger Corman

1962: For Corman, re-wrote, dubbed and re-edited two Soviet films; credited as Alfred Posco for adapting "Sadko (1952) into "The Magic Voyage of Sinbad" and credited as Thomas Colchart on adaptation of "Nebo zovyot/The Heaven's Call" (1960) into "Battle Beyond the Sun"; served as assistant to director Roger Corman on "The Premature Burial" and as dialogue director on "Tower of London"

1962: Won the Samuel Goldwyn Award for his UCLA screenplay "Pilma, Pilma" (never produced)

1962: Joined Seven Arts (later Warner Brothers-Seven Arts) as scriptwriter

1963: Directed and co-wrote first "legitimate" feature, "Dementia 13"

1966: Directed and wrote UCLA thesis feature, "You're a Big Boy Now" (received theatrical release)

1969: Established American Zoetrope (later Zoetrope Studios) for which he executive produced John Korty's 1972 TV thriller, "The People"

1970: Co-wrote the Academy Award–winning screenplay for Franklin Schaffner's "Patton"

1971: First American Zoetrope film, George Lucas' futuristic "THX-1138"

1972: Scored huge success with "The Godfather", winning Oscar for co-writing (with Mario Puzo) the screenplay

1973: Directed revival of Noel Coward's "Private Lives" at the American Conservatory Theater (San Francisco) and Gottfried von Einem's opera, "The Visit of the Old Lady", for the San Francisco Opera Company

1973: Formed The Directors Company (with Peter Bogdanovich and William Friedkin), which produced only two films: Bogdanovich's "Paper Moon" (1973) and Coppola's "The Conversation" (1974) (date approximate)

1974: Co-wrote (with Puzo) and directed sequel "The Godfather, Part II"; won Oscars for Best Screenplay and Best Director

1974: Scripted the film adaptation of F. Scott Fitzgerald's novel "The Great Gatsby"

Published *City Magazine*

1979: "Apocalypse Now" released to mixed reviews but great box office; Coppola had mortgaged everything to personally cover some $16 million of the $30 million cost

1982: American Zoetrope dealt a crippling blow by the failure of the extravagant musical film "One From the Heart"

1983: Directed two film adaptations of S.E. Hinton novels, "The Outsiders" and "Rumble Fish"

1985: TV directing debut with "Rip Van Winkle" (Showtime)

1988: Directed "Tucker: The Man and His Dream"

1989: Co-wrote (with daughter Sofia) and directed the "Life Without Zoe" segment of "New York Stories" and received the weakest reviews of the three participating directors (also Martin Scorcese and Woody Allen)

Founded the Niebaum-Coppola winery

1990: Returned to the Corleone saga for "The Godfather, Part III"; considered the weakest of the trilogy

1992: Produced and directed "Bram Stoker's Dracula"

1993: Appointed to the board of directors at MGM

1993: Opened a hotel in Belize

1996: Served as president of jury at Cannes Film Festival

1996: With Wayne Wang and Tom Luddy, formed production company Chrome Dragon

1996: Dedicated "Jack" (which he produced and directed) to granddaughter Gian (Gian Carla), daughter of his son, the late Gian-Carlo

1997: Launched the literary magazine *Zoetrope*

1997: Announced first feature to be produced through Chrome Dragon, Sherwood Hu's

"Lanai-Loa: The Passage", starring Angus Macfadyen

1997: Directed and scripted screen adaptation of "John Grisham's 'The Rainmaker' ", starring Danny Glover and Danny DeVito

1998: Won lawsuit against Warner Bros. claiming the studio had stolen his idea for a live-action version of "Pinocchio"; awarded $20 million in compensatory damages by a jury; further awarded $60 million in punative damages; on appeal, however, $60 million damages were dismissed; appellate judge let stand the $20 million award

Served as one of the executive producers of the Sci-Fi Channel series "First Wave"

AFFILIATION: Roman Catholic

QUOTES:

He was given his middle name because his father was playing flute on the "Ford Sunday Evening Hour" at the time of his birth.

In 1974, Coppola was the first director to receive two nominations from the Directors Guild of America for their annual award. He was cited for "The Conversation" and "The Godfather, Part II." He won for the latter.

"Really, the way the movie business has evolved, there are six companies that own the basketballs, and if you want to play, you have to either talk one of them into doing [your project] or accept one of their jobs. When you talk a studio into doing one of your films, immediately it's, 'But of course, you're going to do this for half your fee, or no fee.' Or, 'Of course, well, let's see, you've got to work on the script a little bit.' They totally control it, so they can have you take a year in rewriting and reworking and casting, and ultimately, you're sort of trying to hang on to doing it the way you want to do it, but they're running everything."—Francis Ford Coppola in an August 1996 interview with the website Mr. Showbiz (www.mrshowbiz.com).

BIBLIOGRAPHY:

"Francis Ford Coppola" Jean-Paul Chailet and Elizabeth Martin, 1985, St. Martin's Press

"Notes" Eleanor Coppola, 1979, Simon & Schuster

"The Godfather Legacy" Harlan Lebo, 1997, Fireside; evaluation of Coppola's film

"A Sense of Place: An Intimate Portrait of the Niebaum-Coppola Winery and the Napa Valley" Steve Kolpan, 1999, Routledge

Sofia Coppola

BORN: Sofia Carmina Coppola in New York, New York, 05/12/1971

SOMETIMES CREDITED AS:
Domino

NATIONALITY: American

EDUCATION: St Helena High School Napa Valley, California, graduated

BIOGRAPHY

A member of the filmmaking dynasty that includes such heavy hitters as father Francis Ford Coppola and cousin Nicolas Cage, Sofia Coppola parlayed her Hollywood clout and calling into various ventures, working as an actress, costume designer, screenwriter and later most notably, a director. Debuting onscreen not long after her on-location birth, Coppola was featured in the climactic scene of her father's epic "The Godfather" (1972), playing the male infant being baptized. She went on to appear in several other of her father's films (credited as Domino) playing bit parts in the features "Rumble Fish" and "The Outsiders" (both 1983) and "The Cotton Club" (1984). Next, Coppola took a supporting role as the younger sister of Kathleen Turner's title character in the 1986 comedy "Peggy Sue Got Married", co-starring cousin Nicolas. The father-daughter team worked together behind the scenes on the "Life Without Zoe" segment of "New York Stories" (1989), with Sofia earning screenplay, costume designer and main title design credits. The following year, the young Coppola replaced Winona Ryder as Mary Corleone in "The Godfather, Part III", reportedly as a favor to her father who was at a loss to find a replacement after Ryder's abrupt departure. Coppola's Mediterranean good looks were fitting for the role, but her California girl accent was less appropriate and her otherwise stilted turn sparked one of the more vicious rounds of movie criticism in recent memory. Being cast in such a high-profile role could have served as Coppola's breakthrough, but her unimpressive turn transformed it into just the opposite, a hurdle that she would struggle to overcome throughout her career, her name now notorious and almost synonymous with badly placed nepotism. Understandably, in a move that would prove auspicious down the line, she set her sights on goals other than acting, save for a part as Patricia Arquette's lover in the little-seen comedy "Inside Monkey Zetterland" (1992) and a cameo role as a handmaiden to Princess Amidala in "Star Wars: Episode I—The Phantom Menace" (1999).

Although she wasn't appearing onscreen, Coppola stayed in the public eye with various artistic ventures. Her interest in fashion (she interned with Karl Lagerfeld at Chanel while in high school) was employed in film again in 1990 when she added a costume design credit for "Spirit of '76" (produced by brother Roman) to her résumé. Coppola's next endeavor was Milk Fed, her own line of designer clothing. Joining the ranks of other "celebutots" like Zoe Cassavetes and Donovan Leitch and musicians like Sonic Youth and the Beastie Boys, Coppola was a noted mover on the Los Angeles/New York young hipster scene, a hot-list favorite often seen on the pages of magazines. She and Cassavetes even hosted their own tongue-in-cheek magazine show "Hi-Octane" (1994), a limited run series aired on Comedy Central in 1995, covering music, fashion and lifestyles. Coppola cemented her status as a consistent pop culture presence, additionally enjoying exposure as a music video star, starting with a cameo role in Madonna's "Deeper and Deeper" and moving up to memorable featured turns in "Sometimes Salvation" by The Black Crowes and "Elektrobank" by The Chemical Brothers. The latter (directed by future husband and fellow auteur Spike Jonze) starred Coppola as a gymnast while the former showed her in the midst of a breakdown. While her turn in "The Godfather, Part III" may have indicated a less than stellar screen presence, she was striking and inherently watchable in this capacity, and generated even more underground buzz.

Coppola began to broaden her range of behind the scenes work, beginning with the 28-minute short "Bed, Bath and Beyond" (shot on video), which she edited and co-directed along with Ione Skye and Andrew Durham. She subsequently produced, wrote and directed the black-and-white comedy short "Lick the Star" (1998), which screened at festivals and aired on both Bravo and the Independent Film Channel. Now a driven filmmaker, Coppola next endeavored to make her feature debut, and courageously chose "The Virgin Suicides" (2000), Jeffrey Eugenides' atmospheric hit novel about a family of teenage girls dealing with their younger sister's shocking death, told from the point of view of a group of neighborhood boys obsessed with them. Oddly structured, sincerely moving and irreverently comedic, the multifaceted novel was an ambitious choice for adaptation. Coppola deftly handled the intricacies of the source material and captured the spirit of Eugenides' fiction, imparting the undercurrents of both innocent enthusiasm and heartbreaking hopelessness. She set the film in suburban Michigan in the 1970s and managed to steer clear of broad stereotypical era markers, giving this singular and yet transcendent tale an appropriately subtle Everyman air. Starring her "Peggy Sue Got Married" co-star Kathleen Turner as the girls' overprotective mother, James Woods as the defeated father, and hot young players Kirsten Dunst and Josh Hartnett, "The Virgin Suicides" also introduced a cast of newcomers, and following its acclaimed screenings at Cannes and Sundance, would introduce Coppola into the ranks of esteemed new filmmakers.—Written by Jane O'Donnell

FAMILY:

great-grandfather: August Coppola. Pianist; emigrated to USA from Naples as Enrico Caruso's piano accompanist

grandfather: Carmine Copppola. Flutist, composer and musical arranger; born on July 11, 1910; died on April 26, 1991; Italian-American; played in Toscanini's NBC Symphony Orchestra; scored some of Francis Ford Coppola's films, including "The Godfather, Part II", for which he shared an Oscar

grandmother: Italia Coppola. Actor

grandfather: Clifford Neil. Inventor; born in 1891; died in 1945

great-uncle: Archimedes Coppola. Engineer, musician; born in 1909; died in 1927

great-uncle: Michael Coppola. Inventor; born in 1914

great-uncle: Antonio Coppola. Conductor; born in 1917 conductor of symphony orchestras; also with the San Francisco Opera and New York City Opera; also conducted Broadway musicals like "My Fair Lady"; was opera advisor on "The Godfather, Part III"

uncle: August Coppola. Writer, professor; dean of the School of Creative Arts at San Francisco State University; involved with "Audio Vision" which provides a taped soundtrack of a narrator describing visual information for blind filmgoers

father: Francis Ford Coppola. Director; directed daughter in films including "Peggy Sue Got Married" and "The Godfather, Part III"; collaborated on the "Life With Zoe" segment of "New York Stories"

mother: Eleanor Coppola. Set decorator, artist; born c. 1936; married Francis Ford Coppola in February 1963; co-directed documentary "Hearts of Darkness: A Filmmaker's Apocalypse"

uncle: William Neil. Special effects technician; born in 1939

aunt: Talia Rose Coppola. Actor, producer, director; born on April 25, 1945; formerly married to composer David Shire who scored Francis Ford Coppola's "The Conversation"; subsequently wed to producer Jack Schwartzman from August 23, 1980 until his death from cancer in 1994

cousin: Marc Coppola. Actor; born in 1957; son of August Coppola

cousin: Christopher Coppola. Director, screenwriter, producer; born in 1962; son of August Coppola

cousin: Nicolas Cage. Actor; son of August Coppola; born on January 7, 1964; won Oscar for "Leaving Las Vegas"; married to and divorced from actress Patricia Arquette

brother: Gian-Carlo Coppola. Born on September 17, 1963; killed in boating accident in May 1986

brother: Roman Coppola. Producer, director, visual effects technician, sound mixer; born in 1965; headed Black Diamond Productions

cousin: Jason Schwartzman. Actor, musician; son of Talia Shire and late producer Jack Schwartzman; born on June 26, 1980; star of comedy hit "Rushmore"

cousin: Robert Schwartzman. Actor; born on

December 24, 1982; son of Talia Shire and the late Jack Schwartzman

niece: Gian Carla Coppola. Daughter of late Gian-Carlo Coppola and Jackie De La Fontaine; born six months after Gian-Carlo's death in 1986

COMPANION:

husband: Spike Jonze. Director; married on June 26, 1999; collaborated with Coppola on Comedy Central's "Hi-Octane"; directed her in The Chemical Brothers' "Elektrobank" music video

MILESTONES:

1971: Born in New York during the filming of father Francis Ford Coppola's epic "The Godfather"

1972: Made film debut as an infant in the climactic baptism scene in "The Godfather"

Raised primarily in Napa Valley, California, but moved around frequently with father on movie locations

1983: Had small roles in her father's adaptations of the S.E. Hinton novels "Rumblefish" and "The Outsiders"; credited as Domino

1984: Appeared in Coppola's "The Cotton Club", credited as Domino

1984: Acted in Tim Burton's short "Frankenweenie"

1986: Played the younger sister of Kathleen Turner's character in the comedy "Peggy Sue Got Married", directed by her father

Worked as an intern at Chanel under Karl Lagerfield while in high school

1987: Appeared in Yurak Bogayevicz's drama "Anna", starring Sally Kirkland and Paulina Porizkova

1989: Contributed to the "Life Without Zoe" segment of "New York Stories", with credits for screenplay, costume design and main title design

1990: Was costume designer for the flashback comedy "The Spirit of '76", produced by her brother Roman Coppola

1990: Made her lead acting debut quite notoriously as Mary Corleone in "The Godfather, Part III"

1992: Had a featured role as Patricia Arquette's lover in the comedy "Inside Monkey Zetterland"

1992: Appeared in the music video for Madonna's "Deeper and Deeper"

1992: Was featured in the music video "Sometimes Salvation" by The Black Crowes

Began designing her own clothing line Milk Fed

1994: Along with Zoe Cassavettes, hosted the limited run lifestyle magazine series "Hi-Octane"; director Spike Jonze worked on the project

1996: Edited and co-directed (with Ione Skye and Andrew Durham) the 28-minute video production "Bed, Bath and Beyond"

1997: Starred as a gymnast performing a routine to the song "Elektrobank" by The Chemical Brothers in the music video directed by Jonze

1998: Produced, directed and wrote the black and white comedy short "Lick the Star", screened at festivals and aired on Bravo and the Independent Film Channel

1999: Played Sache, one of Queen Amidala's handmaidens in "Star Wars Episode I—The Phantom Menace"

2000: Made feature directorial debut with "The Virgin Suicides", a 1970s suburbia-set adaptation of Jeffrey Eugenides' cult novel; also scripted

QUOTES:

Coppola on the opportunities afforded her by her famous lineage: "I couldn't have worked at Chanel when I was 15 if I'd grown up on a farm."—quoted in *USA Today*, February 3–5, 1995.

Coppola on using the teenage perspective in "The Virgin Suicides": "Your memory of being young is very simple and I wanted it to look like that. I wanted the movie to be from a kid's point of view, a kid's world. You can get away with obsessiveness then, I feel like when you're at that age, everything is really melodramatic, everything is a huge deal."—to director Wes Anderson in *Interview*, October 1999.

On her much maligned turn in "The Godfather III": "After that, I definitely did not want to be an actress."—quoted in *Time*, January 24, 2000.

Mark Ebner: With "Virgin Suicides," have you finally found your metier?

Sofia Coppola: Directing? Yeah, I think so. I spent most of my 20s worrying, "Oh no. I don't know what I want to do" and "I'll try this and try that." It's really huge to find something that you really enjoy, something that you can really contribute something to. And I really love doing it, and I feel like it's something that combines so many other things that I love.

—From *Salon* magazine (www.salon.com), February 1, 2000.

Roger Corman

BORN: Roger William Corman in Detroit, Michigan, 04/05/1926

SOMETIMES CREDITED AS:
Henry Neill

NATIONALITY: American

EDUCATION: Beverly Hills High School, Beverly Hills, California

Stanford University, Stanford, California engineering 1947; wrote film reviews for the school newspaper

Balliol College, Oxford University, Oxford, England, English, attended six months

AWARDS: Los Angeles Film Critics Association Career Achievement Award 1996

American Cinema Editors Golden Eddie Award Filmmaker of the Year 1997

Casting Society of America Lifetime Achievement Award 1997

BIOGRAPHY
Roger Corman is known primarily for his low budget, highly profitable films, but also for providing in-house training to young filmmakers who went on to become masters of the Hollywood cinema. Working outside the studio system, Corman has established a record as one of the most commercially successful filmmakers in Hollywood history, with over 200 films to his credit, 90 percent of which have turned a profit.

After graduating from Stanford in 1947, Corman broke into the film business, first as a messenger boy and later as a story analyst and screenwriter. After his first script ("Highway Dragnet" 1954) was altered by a studio, he decided to make his own movies, beginning with "Monster from the Ocean Floor" in 1954. American Releasing Corporation, which later became known as American International Pictures, distributed Corman's second film, "The Fast and the Furious" (1954), as part of an unusual deal: ARP advanced the filmmaker cash to make additional movies. Corman later employed this arrangement with other distributors such as Allied Artists.

By 1955, when he made his directorial debut, the Corman formula was in place: quirky characters; offbeat plots laced with social commentary; clever use of special effects, sets and cinematography; employment of fresh talent; and above all, miniscule budgets (under $100,000) and breakneck shooting schedules (5–10 days). Corman titles from the 1950s and 60s include such genre films as "Swamp Women" (1956), "Machine Gun Kelly" (1958), "Little Shop of Horrors" (1961), "The Wild

Angels" (1966) and "The Trip" (1967). His films based on the stories and poems of Edgar Allan Poe ("The Pit and the Pendulum" 1961, "Tales of Terror" 1962, "The Raven" 1963, "Masque of the Red Death" 1964) were typically shot in three weeks on only slighly higher budgets, yet have become classics of the horror genre.

Dissatisfied with increasing studio and AIP interference in both the content and budgets of his films, Corman decided to start his own company in order to exert total control over his product. In 1970 he formed New World Pictures, which produced and distributed, not only exploitation movies such as "Death Race 2000" (1975), but also sophisticated European art films by celebrated directors such as Truffaut, Bergman and Fellini. Corman once again demonstrated his Midas touch; New World became the largest independent production and distribution company in the US and in January 1983 he sold it for $16.5 million.

In 1983 Corman founded Concorde/New Horizons, a production company which continues to be both prolific (over 20 films annually) and commercially prodigious (1987 gross earnings: $94 million). Taking full advantage of "ancillary" markets (videocassete, pay TV and foreign sales), Corman continues his lucrative practice of releasing successful, cut-rate exploitation films such as "Not of this Earth" (1988), "Nightfall" (1988) and "The Lawless Land" (1989).

Corman's legendary success is attributed to the fact that he operates outside the usual Hollywood constraints. He does not shrink from hiring unconventional actors such as pornography film stars like Traci Lords; he was one of the first producers to recognize the financial advantages of shooting in Europe; and he has even used sets discarded from other lavish, expensive movies for his own films.

In addition to his successful business innovations, Corman is recognized for his sponsorship of new talent. His ability to locate, and then provide a training ground for young filmmakers has produced an impressive roster of directors and performers. Francis Ford Coppola, Peter Bogdanovich, Martin Scorsese, John Sayles, Robert Towne, Jack Nicholson, Robert De Niro, Dennis Hopper and Charles Bronson are but a few of the names associated with Corman films early in their careers.

MILESTONES:

Joined 20th Century Fox as messenger

1949: Became story analyst for Fox

1954: First film as co-producer (also co-story), "Highway Dragnet"

1954: First film as producer for own production company (Palo Alto), "Monster from the Ocean Floor"

1954: First film distributed by American International Pictures, "The Fast and the Furious"

1955: Feature directing debut (also producer), "Five Guns West"

1974: Acted in Francis Ford Coppola's "The Godfather Part II" as one of the senators on the congressional committee

BIBLIOGRAPHY:

"How I Made a Hundred Movies in Hollywood and Never Lost a Dime" Roger Corman and Jim Jerome, 1990, Random House; autobiography

"Roger Corman: Brilliance on a Budget" Ed Naha, 1982, Arco Press

"Roger Corman: The Best of the Cheap Acts" Mark McGee Thomas, 1988, McFarland

"The Films of Roger Corman: 'Shooting My Way Out of Trouble'" Alan Frank, 1998, Batsford

"Roger Corman: An Unauthorized Bioography of the Godfather of Indie Filmmaking" Beverly Gray, 2000, Renaissance Books

Constantin Costa-Gavras

BORN: Konstantinos Gavras in Klivia, Greece, 02/13/1933

SOMETIMES CREDITED AS:
"Costa-Gavras" Costa-Gavras
Constantin Costa-Gavras
Costi Costa-Gavras

NATIONALITY: Greek

CITIZENSHIP: France 1956

EDUCATION: Sorbonne, University of Paris Paris, France, literature; switched to IDHEC before completing degree
Institut des Hautes Etudes Cinematographiques, Paris, France, producing; and directing

AWARDS: Cannes Film Festival Jury Prize "Z" 1969
New York Film Critics Circle Award Best Film "Z" 1969
New York Film Critics Circle Award Best Director "Z" 1969
Cannes Film Festival Direction Award "Special Section" 1975
Oscar Best Screenplay (based on material from another medium) "Missing" 1982; shared with Donald Stewart
Cannes Film Festival Palme d'Or "Missing" 1982

BIOGRAPHY

Constantin Costa-Gavras made his reputation as the preeminent director developing the political thriller from the late 1960s through the 80s. Several of his films ("State of Siege" 1973, "Missing" 1982) are archetypes of the genre and "Z" (1969) is a crucial fictional account of political repression in the 20th century.

Born to a Russian father and a Greek mother, Costa-Gavras was mesmerized as a boy by the energy and movement of the many American films he saw. Because of his father's activities in the Greek resistance during WWII, Costa-Gavras's educational and occupational opportunities were stifled when the rightist Greek government blacklisted him. When he failed to obtain a visa to the US, Costa-Gavras went to Paris, where he studied at the Sorbonne. Like other young cineastes such as Francois Truffaut and Jean-Luc Godard, he haunted the Cinematheque Francaise and the Left Bank repertory film theaters. In November 1954 he enrolled in IDHEC, the French national film school.

After completing his formal training in 1958 Costa-Gavras started work as a directorial trainee, receiving valuable mentorship from, among others, Rene Clement, Rene Clair and Jacques Demy. His first film, "The Sleeping Car Murder" (1965), a detective thriller starring Yves Montand and Simone Signoret, was followed by the overtly political "Shock Troops", a tale of the French Maquis starring Michel Piccoli. Shown at the Moscow Film Festival in 1967, "Shock Troops" was re-edited and given a happy ending by United Artists prior to its American release in 1969.

While preparing another project, Costa-Gavras discovered Vassilis Vassilikos's novel "Z", based on the events surrounding the assassination of Greek reformer Grigoris Lambrakis in 1963. His film version, starring Yves Montand, Irene Papas and Jean-Louis Trintignant, was released as a French/Algerian co-production in 1969 and touched the consciousness of young cineastes, critics and political activists around the world. "Z" won the jury and best actor prizes at Cannes as well as the Oscar for best foreign film. It also spawned a host of imitations in France and the US. The film deals with the themes which have remained central to Costa-Gavras's work: the mechanics and repercussions of tyranny and the subtle varieties of guilt. Hugely successful in France and abroad (but banned in Greece), it remains a landmark of recent cinema.

"The Confession" (1970) followed, again based on a true incident in which a spurious confession was tortured out of a Czech Communist Party functionary (Yves Montand) and used in a sham trial. With "State of Siege", Costa-Gavras completed an intensely creative period. Another fictionalized treatment of an actual event, the film tells the story of a clandestine American intelligence agent (Montand) assassinated by Uruguayan political terrorists. "State of Siege" also witnessed the maturation of Costa-Gavras' working method: beginning with a novelistic retelling of a single event and working in close collaboration with his screenwriter, the director meticulously researches the details of the incident, which is then brought to the screen via a highly disciplined but visually eclectic shooting style.

"Special Section" (1975) reunited Costa-Gavras with Jorge Semprun, the screenwriter of "Z", on a project devoted to the activities of the French Vichy government. Roundly criticized by French patriots who had hoped for a melodramatic rewriting of wartime events, "Special Section" is a meditative and even-handed study of one of the most painful periods of French history. "Clair de femme", an emphatically apolitical film starring Montand and Romy Schneider, was released in 1979.

Costa-Gavras was able to weave his fascination with American political culture into the fabric of his first United States–produced film "Missing" (1982), starring Jack Lemmon and Sissy Spacek. "Missing" told of the kidnapping and death-squad murder of Charles Horman, a leftist American journalist, in Chile in 1973. The film attracted criticism (as have all Costa-Gavras's films since "Z") from doctrinaire Marxists for its use of dramatic devices to invoke sympathy for an individual victim of political repression. Yet "Missing" was well calibrated for its American audience, which responded enthusiastically to the most significant political thriller made in the US since "The Manchurian Candidate."

Although many of Costa-Gavras's French films have not gotten much play in this country, "Hanna K" (1983) generated controversy here for its pro-Palestinian stance but beyond pushing that button, the unsatisfying melodrama was an artistic disappointment. "Betrayed" (1988) marked Costa-Gavras's first collaboration with screenwriter Joe Ezsterhas, and judging from its considerable implausibility and lack of dramatic tension, one wonders why the director trusted Ezsterhas' vision. Starring Tom Berenger and Debra Winger, "Betrayed" explored the underworld of racist politics in rural America, important and unsettling subject matter which deserved better than the pedantic treatment it received from the Costa-Gavras–Ezsterhas team. Their second film together, "The Music Box" (1989), related the trial of an alleged Hungarian war criminal (Armin Mueller-Stahl) and US citizen for 40 years, who is defended in court by his daughter (Jessica Lange). Though decidedly better than "Betrayed", director and screenwriter allowed a potentially crackling political thriller to degenerate into high-gloss melodrama.

In 1982, Costa-Gavras took over the directorship of the Cinematheque Francaise, then badly in disarray. During his tenure, he proved a tireless champion of both film preservation and artistic freedom, furthering the institution's international renown even as he continued to work on his own films. Costa-Gavras demonstrated his continuing social conscience in 1992 by contributing (as one of 30 French filmmakers) his plea on behalf of people suffering human rights violations in the documentary "Lest We Forget." "The Minor Apocalypse" (1993), a French film about a writer who gets an offer to be published only if he commits suicide on TV, served as a dry run for the American release of "Mad City" (1997), a supposedly scathing look at the electronic media's ability to manipulate (and manufacture) breaking news, which elicited yawns and indifference before quickly departing theaters. Fans of Costa-Gavras can only hope for a return of the storytelling prowess that brought them "Z", "State of Siege" and "Missing."

MILESTONES:

1959: First feature as assistant director, Yves Allegret's "L'ambitieuse"

1965: Feature directing debut, "The Sleeping Car Murders"

1969: Received two Oscar nominations (Best Director and Best Adapted Screenplay) for "Z"

1973–1974: Made commericals for TV-Hachette

1977: Film acting debut in "La vie devant soi/Madame Rosa"

1982: First US-produced film, "Missing"; won Academy Award for Best Adapted Screenplay (shared with Donald Stewart)

1982: Took over directorship of Cinematheque Francais

1985: Acted in John Landis' "Spies Like Us", portraying a Tadzhic Highway Patrolman

1988: First collaboration with screenwriter Joe Eszterhas, "Betrayed"

1989: Reteamed with Eszterhas for "Music Box"

1992: One of 30 French filmmakers who delivered their short pleas on behalf of people who had suffered human rights violations in the documentary "Lest We Forget"

1997: "Mad City" disappeared quickly from theaters

2002: Engendered controversy in Europe with "Amen.", a drama about two men, real-life German soldier Kurt Gerstein and a fictionalized priest, who attempt to warn the world about the Nazis' plan to exterminate Jews during WWII

QUOTES:

In 1995 Costa-Gavras received the Irene Diamond Lifetime Achievement Award for commitment to human rights. "It's a huge honor because I believe the organizations taking care of human rights are the people I completely trust more than any other ethical movement. The way they work, the reasons for which they do it; not for money or career, just for human rights."—Costa-Gavras to *Daily News*, June 16, 1995.

"For a little Greek immigrant who came from nothing, I feel I've been extrememly lucky. I've been a director for 30 years, doing exactly what I want to do. I still can't believe it. I think one day someone will say it's all been a mistake."—Costa-Gavras in *New York Post*, October 29, 1997.

Wes Craven

BORN: Wesley Earl Craven in Cleveland, Ohio, 08/02/1939

NATIONALITY: American

EDUCATION: wrote and edited his high school's newspaper, including a regular comedy column

Wheaton College, Wheaton, Illinois, English and psychology, BA; editor of literary magazine which was eventually banned; evangelist Billy Graham's alma mater

Johns Hopkins University, Baltimore, Maryland, creative writing and philosophy, MA, 1964; attended on full scholarship to the Johns Hopkins Graduate Writing Seminars, studying under the Baltimore poet-scholar Eliot Coleman; earned degree in one year

AWARDS: French Science Fiction and Horror Film Festival Critics' Choice Award "A Nightmare on Elm Street" 1984

    MTV Movie Award Best Movie "Scream" 1997

    ShowEast Lifetime Achievement Award 1997

BIOGRAPHY

A former humanities professor turned brand name fright-master, producer, writer, director Craven is clearly an intellectual artist trapped in a disreputable genre. He entered filmmaking as an editor and assistant producer to exploitation producer Sean Cunningham (who would later create Jason for the "Friday the 13th" movies) on several low-budget comedies and skin flicks before graduating to the position of writer-director with a modestly budgeted ($87,000), feature "Last House on the Left" (1972). Still a potent shocker, this grimly realistic tale of rape, murder, and revenge was loosely based on Ingmar Bergman's 1960 classic, "The Virgin Spring." The intensity of the film shocked many—Leonard Maltin's "Movie Guide" damns it as "repugnant" and "really sick"—including its creator.

Craven spent the next five years working as a film editor and unproduced screenwriter. He tried his hand at numerous genres including biopic, war, romance, and comedy but there were no takers. Finally as his savings ran out, a reluctant Craven accepted an offer to make another horror film. His infamy in polite filmgoing circles grew with the extraordinary thriller "The Hills Have Eyes" (1977). Brought in for an impressive $225,000, this profoundly troubling tale of an All-American family becalmed in the desert and beset by cannibalistic mutants became a genre classic of the 1970s. According to the British magazine *Time Out*, "exploitation themes are used to maximum effect. . . . A heady mix of ironic allegory and seat-edge tension." For better or worse, Craven was firmly typed as a horror filmmaker.

Four years passed before Craven was able to complete another feature, but he did manage to helm a TV-movie "Stranger in Our House" (NBC, 1978) starring B-queen Linda Blair in a tale of teenage witchcraft. He returned to features with "Deadly Blessing" (1981), an uneven but frightening tale of a woman terrorized by a rural religious sect. (This project may have had a personal dimension for the filmmaker. Craven himself was the product of a strict fundamentalist Baptist upbringing that taught that movies were a tool of the Devil. In fact he did not see his first film until college.)

Craven finally gained some measure of success and industry clout with "A Nightmare on Elm Street" (1984), in which the horrific Freddy Krueger haunts the dreamscapes of small-town American teens. The hard-edged and strikingly surreal original was followed by five popular and increasingly campy sequels. The franchise generated over a half a billion dollars but the creator received a paltry $400,000 after signing away his rights so as to secure the director's chair for the first film. Nonetheless, having his name associated with the successful series led to expanded career opportunities.

Craven began working regularly in TV in the mid-80s. His projects included helming first season episodes of the 1985 CBS revival of "The Twilight Zone" and the TV-movie "Chiller" (CBS, 1985), and creating and producing the short-lived anthology series "The Nightmare Cafe" (NBC, 1992), which reunited Craven with "Elm Street" star Robert Englund. His next feature, the oddball teen horror romance "Deadly Friend" (1986), was seriously marred by censorship and studio interference. "The Serpent and the Rainbow" (1988), an ambitious and atmospheric but ultimately half-baked period piece set in a pre-revolutionary Haiti, has its fair share of admirers.

Craven attempted (and failed) to create another Freddy Krueger in serial killer Horace Pinker, the persistent villain of the engagingly silly thriller "Shocker" (1989). He attempted to comment on the exploitation of the poor in "The People Under the Stairs" (1991), with uneven results. Craven finally returned to classic filmmaking form with "Wes Craven's New Nightmare" (1994). He crafted a complex and highly reflexive narrative about the nature and function of horror films that incorporated dreams he had while making the film. Set in the "real" world of filmmaking, he and his main stars played themselves in a project that felt like "The Player" with a bigger body count. Craven wisely eliminated the camp aspects that had overtaken the series, and it garnered some respectful notices. The same cannot be said for his follow-up feature, a relatively high-profile horror comedy vehicle for Eddie Murphy, then in the midst of a serious career slump.

Unlike his last Freddy opus, "Vampire in Brooklyn" (1996) was clearly a work-for-hire assignment for Craven. A horror fan himself, Murphy contacted the genre auteur with a script he had co-written with his brothers. Though marketed as "a comic tale of horror and seduction", the film played like an uneven vampire outing with moments of comic relief. Both press and public were unimpressed and the film found an early grave. Nonetheless, Craven emerged from the project not only unscathed but on something of a roll. The following year found him with half a dozen projects in various stages of development. Craven helmed, but did not script, "Scream" (1996), a mainstream comedy-thriller hit boasting a fashionable young cast that included Courteney Cox, Drew Barrymore and David Arquette. While such a project was clearly good for Craven's ascendant career as an industry player, longtime fans may feel that something vital had been lost. Nevertheless, he was on to a new franchise, helming the concluding installments "Scream 2" (1997) and "Scream 3" (2000). In between, Craven completed an unusual project, "Music of the Heart" (1999) with Meryl Streep, a biopic of music teacher Roberta Guispari-Tzavaras who had been profiled in the 1995 Oscar-nominated documentary "Small Wonders."—Written by Kent Greene

MILESTONES:

Raised in a working-class fundamentalist Baptist family in Cleveland, Ohio

As a teen, read the complete works of Dostoyevsky, Poe, and Dickens

Taught that movies were tools of the Devil; never saw a film until reaching college

After graduate school, taught Humanities at Westminster College in New Wilmington, Pennsylvania

1964: Taught Humanities and modern drama at Clarkson College in Potsdam, New York (date approximate)

Became interested in experimental, art, and documentary cinema

Purchased a 16mm camera from a NYC pawnshop

Began making short films with his students

1966: At age 27, decided not to pursue a doctorate, opting to become a filmmaker instead (date approximate)

Left teaching and took a job as a messenger for a film post-production company on 25th Street in NYC for $60 a week

1971: First feature film as editor, "You've Got to Walk It Like You Talk It or You'll Lose That Beat"

1971: First "adult" documentary feature as assistant producer (co-produced with director Sean Cunningham), "Together/Sensual Paradise"

1972: Feature directing and writing debut, "The Last House on the Left" (produced by Sean Cunningham)

1972–1977: Spent five years as an editor and unproduced screenwriter

Wrote various unsold scripts including "American Beauty", a comedy about beauty pageants; "Mustang", a biopic about Col. Anthony Herbert, an Army inspector general who reported American atrocities in Vietnam; and a love story

1977: Wrote, directed, and edited his second horror feature, "The Hills Have Eyes"

1978: TV-movie directing debut, "Stranger in Our House"

1984: Voluntarily signed a contract with New Line Pictures in which he gave up up rights to all sequels and merchandising "and everything else" to "A Nightmare on Elm Street" in return for completion money and assurance that he would to direct the picture (date approximate)

1984: Wrote and directed the popular and influential feature, "A Nightmare on Elm Street"; inaugurated a $500-million-grossing film franchise

1987: Provided story and co-wrote screenplay for "A Nightmare on Elm Street Part III: Dream Warriors"

1989: TV producing debut, executive producer of short-lived fantasy sitcom, "The People Next Door"; also wrote the story for the pilot

1992: Created and executive produced short-lived fantasy TV series, "Nightmare Cafe"; also wrote pilot and several episodes

1993: Collaborated with producer-director Tim Burton on "Laurel Canyon", an unsold pilot

1996: Had box-office hit with the self-reflexive horror film "Scream"

1997: Helmed the sequel "Scream 2"; the second in a projected trilogy

1998: With Shaun Cassidy, co-created the Fox series "Hollyweird"; Cassidy withdrew from project after conflicts with network; project put on hold pending further development

1998: Signed four-year production deal with Miramax; projects include "Scream 3"

1999: Directed non-horror film "Music of the Heart", a biopic of music teacher Roberta Guaspari-Tzavaras, who had been profiled in the Oscar-nominated documentary "Small Wonders"

2000: Helmed the concluding segment of the trilogy, "Scream 3"

AFFILIATION: Baptist

QUOTES:
According to Robert 'Freddy Krueger' Englund (*New York Post*, October 10, 1994), Craven lives on a cliff in Hollywood Hills in a house once owned by Steve McQueen.

"The horror film consistently bucks censorship, the sort of censorship of the mind that tries to normalize the chaos of life itself. The middle class wants things nice, neat and normal with all the corners squared. Horror films are the brush fires that make room for new trees to grow."—Craven, quoted in *The Hollywood Reporter*, October 30, 1992.

Wes Craven talking about his feature debut as a writer-director, "Last House on the Left" (1972): " 'The way I was raised, which was basically as a law-abiding, Bible-following person, a lot of the rage and wildness is kept out from your conscious mind,' Mr. Craven says. 'Finally when I had gone through a divorce and left teaching, abandoning everything everyone was pleased that I was doing, and somebody said just make something wild and crazy, suddenly all this came out of me very easily. It just gelled in a way that astonished everyone, including me.' "—From "Freddy Krueger's Creator Breaks Out of His Genre" by James Greenberg, *The New York Times*, October 9, 1994.

Wes Craven talking about his feature debut as a writer-director, "Last House on the Left" (1972): " 'I found that I had never written anything like this, and I'd been writing for ten to twelve years already. I'd always written artistic, poetic things. Suddenly, I was working in an area I had never confronted before. It was almost like doing a pornographic film if you'd been a fundamentalist. And I found that I was writing about things that I had very strong feelings about. I was drawing on things from very early in my own childhood, things that I was feeling about the war, and they were pouring into this very simple B-movie plot.' "—From "Neglected Nightmares", a chapter of *Hollywood from Vietnam to Reagan* by Robin Wood (New York: Columbia University Press, 1986)

"Rape, disembowelment and death by

chainsaw are now standard horror fare, but Craven's cold, flat style of filming emphasizes the fact that the violence dehumanises not only the victims but the aggressors. Craven fans will also note an early use of the domestic booby traps and dream sequences which were to be central to the later 'Nightmare on Elm Street.'"—From Nigel Floyd in *The Time Out Film Guide*, edited by Tom Milne (Penguin Books, 1993 edition).

"I dream in colors, I dream in scene cuts, dissolves sometimes. Quite often I'll have a dream that is very specific to what I'm working on."—Wes Craven quoted in "Meeting Mr. Fright" by Manohla Dargis, *Village Voice*, October 25, 1994.

"In 1978, Craven's interest in dreams led him to a series of news reports which served as the inspiration for the original "A Nightmare on Elm Street". The articles detailed the mysterious case of three boys who, after experiencing a horrific nightmare one night, died the next time they slept. 'The last time it happened the kid literally tried to stay awake as long as he could. His family was very concerned. He was getting more and more distraught. The doctor prescribed sleeping pills and he threw them away. They gave him warm milk and he threw it in the sink. Finally, he fell asleep and the whole family breathed a sigh of relief. Then in the middle of the night they heard screams and ran in and found him dead.' "—From "Craven's Nightmare: Dream Director" by Dale Kutzera, *Imagi-Movies*, Fall 1994.

"Craven followed his dreams throughout the course of filming, often incorporating actual incidents of the real shoot into the cinematic depiction of the film's production. 'The tricky part came when we were ready to shoot and I was still writing down scenes and new scenes were coming to me, which made New Line crazy. It was a pretty bold experiment just in the sense of filming what was happening in my dream life even if it hadn't been dreamed yet. We had a loose schedule, and in some way

the dreams came through on time.' "—From "Craven's Nightmare: Dream Director" by Dale Kutzera, *Imagi-Movies*, Fall 1994.

" 'Horror has affected me deeply, and it hasn't always been in a positive way,' he says. 'In certain circles, I've become a pariah for making this kind of film. I've had a lot of suspicion and resentment directed at me because I choose to deal with horror and for having to come back to it more than once. I've found that horror can be a lonely watch, and this film ("Wes Craven's New Nightmare" 1994) addresses some of that loneliness."—"Wes Craven's Psycho Analysis" by Marc Shapiro, *Fangoria*, October 1994.

" 'I would have hoped that the "Elm Street" films would have been treated with absolute respect all along the way,' he says. 'That's not a snipe against New Line (Pictures), but I would have liked to see somebody sit down each time they set out to make one of the sequels and really get into the philosophy and the heart behind it.

'My first film was about some very serious and important subjects. I felt that with "2", they immediately threw all the important issues out the window and made it a series of strange freaky events and the same old raunchy teenagers. I tried to wrestle it back with "3", and then the series tended to wander, depending on the talent of the directors and the commitment of the writers. Sometimes I had the feeling that they just went with somebody who could knock out a script rather than somebody who had a true vision.' "—"Wes Craven's Psycho Analysis" by Marc Shapiro, *Fangoria*, October 1994.

BIBLIOGRAPHY:

"Screams & Nightmares: The Films of Wes Craven" Brian J. Robb, 1999, Overlook Press

BORN: in Toronto, Ontario, Canada, 03/15/1943

NATIONALITY: Canadian

EDUCATION: Drewson Street Public School, Canada

Kent Senior School, Canada

Harbord College, Canada

North Toronto Collegiate, Toronto, Ontario, Canada

University of Toronto, Toronto, Ontario, Canada, English, 1963–67; switched to English from science; Ontario scholar; won Gertrude Lawler Scholarship for graduating at the head of the class; won Epstein award for best short story; made two experimental 16 mm short films

AWARDS: Genie Best Director "Videodrome" 1984; tied with Bob Clark ("A Christmas Story")

Los Angeles Film Critics Association Award Best Director "Dead Ringers" 1988

Golden Horse Award Best Director "Dead Ringers" 1989 Taiwanese film award

Genie Best Picture "Dead Ringers" 1989; shared with Marc Boyman

Genie Best Director "Dead Ringers" 1989

Genie Best Adapted Screenplay "Dead Ringers" 1989; shared with Norman Snider

New York Film Critics Circle Award Best Screenplay "Naked Lunch" 1991

National Society of Film Critics Award Best Director "Naked Lunch" 1991

National Society of Film Critics Award Best Screenplay "Naked Lunch" 1991

Boston Society of Film Critics Award Best Screenplay "Naked Lunch" 1991

Genie Best Director "Naked Lunch" 1992

Genie Best Adapted Screenplay "Naked Lunch" 1992

Cannes Film Festival Special Jury Prize "Crash" 1996 "for daring and originality"

Genie Best Director "Crash" 1996

Genie Best Adapted Screenplay "Crash" 1996

Berlin Film Festival Silver Bear Jury Prize for Outstanding Artistic Achievement "eXistenZ" 1999

BIOGRAPHY

Hailed as one of the most original and sophisticated of the generation of horror filmmakers that came to prominence during the 1970s, David Cronenberg went on to transcend the limitations of his somewhat disreputable genre. By the 90s, after helming the critically lauded features "Dead Ringers" (1988), "Naked Lunch" (1991) and "Crash" (1996), he had attained status as one of the most intelligent and interesting contemporary auteurs working in English language films. Cronenberg began building his reputation with a series of vivid explorations of biological terror and sexual dread. He shed the label of "exploitation director" by de-emphasizing his trademark graphic and revolting special effects to concentrate instead on theme and character. In an industry glutted by anonymous big-budget films, it is no small feat that he has turned out such hauntingly artistic movies, reflecting his preoccupations with reality and creativity as played out through stories of telepathy, drug addiction, transvestitism and virtual reality.

While attending university, Cronenberg made two short experimental science fiction features, "Stereo" (1969) and "Crimes of the Future" (1970), both demonstrating his penchant for stylistic and thematic quirkiness, as well as a flair for utilizing architectural space for expressive purposes. The stomach-churning shocker "The Parasite Murders" (1975, subsequently retitled "Shivers" in English Canada and Great Britain, "They Came From Within" in the USA, and "Frissons" in the French version prepared for Quebec and France), co-produced by fellow Canadian Ivan Reitman, marked his entry to the commercial marketplace. In its depiction of an artificially created parasite that releases uncontrollable sexual desire in the residents of an antiseptic luxury apartment complex, Cronenberg fashioned a wry commentary on the sexual liberation of the time. Playing on the same theme, "Rabid" (1977) cleverly cast Marilyn Chambers, former Ivory Snow Girl and porn star, as the unfortunate victim of an operation that leaves her with a vampiric appetite for blood and a murderous phallic spike protruding from her armpit.

Inspired by the painful breakup of Cronenberg's first marriage, "The Brood" (1979) was a more ambitious exercise in biological horror that revealed the filmmaker reaching for some measure of respectability. With his biggest budget up to that point ($1.4 million), he was finally able to afford established actors with international reputations, in this instance Oliver Reed and Samantha Eggar. Placing his players within a gruesome tale in which biological mutation is a metaphor for emotional rage, he handled them with surprising skill. He demonstrated a similar sense of directorial assuredness with "Scanners" (1981), a sci-fi conspiracy thriller involving an underground community of telepaths. Though the screenplay shows signs of being rewritten on the run, Cronenberg's filmmaking savvy and special effects made up for its deficiencies, the picture containing arguably the key shock image from his early career, that of a telepath's head exploding.

"Videodrome" (1983) was a self-reflexive, McLuhanesque nightmare about the effects of television on its viewers. The film tells the story of an opportunistic TV producer, played by James Woods, who grows obsessed with a sadistic-erotic program emanating from a mysterious pirate station. His fantasies, stimulated by the show, grow increasingly out of control and seem to represent the consciousness of the typical male TV viewer shaped by that medium's emphasis on violence, sex and spectacle. "Videodrome" is a formal tour de force in which fantasy merges with reality to the point where the viewer of the film, like the protagonist himself, cannot separate the two. It drives home the degree to which we are all "programmed" by the media—a theme strikingly visualized by the image of a newly evolved orifice in the producer's stomach for receiving video software. For his next film "The Dead Zone" (1983), Cronenberg truly rose above the level of horror exploitation. Adapted from a Stephen King novel about a man able to predict future events in people's lives simply by touching them, atmosphere and acting—especially a fine central performance by Christopher Walken—took precedence over special effects.

Cronenberg has had to struggle for the critical recognition his work deserves, largely because of the nature of his material. Early response in his native Canada ranged from MPs in Parliament railing about government funding for a "disgusting" movie like "Shivers", to critic Robert Fulford's review entitled "You Should Know How Bad This Film Is. After All, You Paid For It". Robin Wood's influential 1979 essay "An Introduction to the American Horror Film", which set the terms for serious discussion of the genre in the 80s, identified Cronenberg as a prime example of the horror film's "Reactionary Wing." Many have followed Wood in viewing Cronenberg's work as motivated by sexual disgust. Cronenberg's 1986 remake of "The Fly" would seem to endorse such a view. The hero, a scientist whose atomic structure has been confused with that of a housefly, undergoes a gradual physical disintegration that has been read as a metaphor for AIDS. Nonetheless, in marked contrast to the director's customary detached and clinical tone, "The Fly" is a very emotionally affecting work. Beginning as a gently playful romance laced with ominous intimations of the horrors to come, the film eventually escalates to the level of a full scale human tragedy. Cronenberg elicited a profoundly moving performance from Jeff Goldblum that is central to the film's success.

Cronenberg's somber and deliberately paced follow-up, "Dead Ringers" (1988), a resounding critical and commercial success, would seem to refute the persistent sexual disgust interpretation. In this impressively accomplished work, Cronenberg's biological horror is almost entirely submerged within the psychological exploration of character and the director's precise command of color, decor and camera movement. A bravura performance by Jeremy Irons makes this grisly story of twin gynecologists who descend into drugs, madness and, finally, death, a chilling examination of masculine sexual dread and a powerful critique of the patriarchal control of the medical profession. In retrospect, much of Cronenberg's earlier work can be seen as an ironic critique of the fears and repression that inform our apparently liberated society, rather than merely a visualization of the director's personal obsessions.

Cronenberg turned to a legendary literary source for his next feature "Naked Lunch" (1991). Realizing that a faithful adaptation of William S. Burroughs' resolutely unfilmable novel would be impossible, he utilized elements of Burroughs' own remarkable life to craft a hallucinatory meditation on the writing of the novel and the shaping of the writer. Easily Cronenberg's greatest critical success to date, "Naked Lunch" garnered awards from several major critics' associations (mostly for its screenplay), 11 Canadian Genie awards (including Best Picture, Best Adapted Screenplay and Best Editing) and placement on many "best of the year" lists. Cronenberg's surprisingly subdued direction of "M. Butterfly" (1993), David Henry Hwang's adaptation of his hit Broadway show that confronted issues of identity, gender roles, and ethnic stereotyping, met with mixed and disappointed reviews. Still, the filmmaker's move from the grindhouse to the art house was complete.

Cronenberg again chose seemingly unfilmable material for "Crash" (1996, based on J. G. Ballard's 1973 novel), creating his most disturbing, sexually explicit and controversy-provoking film yet. "Crash" presented a psychological futurescape populated by characters who, having lost the ability to connect on an emotional level, engage in fetishistic sex and bizarre car-crash rituals, their preference for coupling from behind exacerbating the distance between individuals and heightening the atmosphere of alienation pervading the film. Howls of protest decried his take on the depersonalizing modern world as pornographic and nihilistic (Ted Turner stalled its release in the USA until March 1997 while "Crash" narrowly avoided censorship for its June 1997 opening in England). But the film was honored as a modern masterpiece with the 1996 Cannes Special Jury Prize ("for daring and originality"). The director viewed the characters' desperate quest for feeling, despite their dangerous flirtation with death, as very human and ultimately life-affirming.

Cronenberg's "eXistenZ" (1999), his first original screenplay since "Videodrome", picked up right where that film left off, the orifice in the stomach to receive video software replaced by a "bioport" at the base of a person's spine to interphase with the virtual reality game of the title. Inspired by the Fatwa against Salman Rushdie (and perhaps a little by the furor over "Crash"), the picture presented a futuristic world where gameplaying rules and its creators are society's superstars. Allegra (Jennifer Jason Leigh), whose "eXistenZ" effectively erases the boundaries between fantasy and reality, finds a $5 million Fatwa on her head and embarks with security man Jude Law on a synaptic road movie into the very heart of her game where nothing is as it seems. Once again addressing the consequences of radical bio-technology, Cronenberg imagined a Game Pod that was an organic creature grown from fertilized amphibian eggs stuffed with synthetic DNA, in its way analogous to actual ongoing experimentation with animal proteins to replace metals as the basis of computer chips.

Cronenberg is nothing like his movies. He's just a normal guy from Toronto who looks like a college professor, a gray-haired Blue Jays fan with a wife and kids. Although his films have always exhibited a sense of humor, the tone of "eXistenZ" was markedly lighter than previous fare, and the mixture of blood-stained schlock and self-referential black humor disappointed some fans of his more ghoulish productions. However, the unmistakable Cronenberg style was evident, his vision as always enhanced by long-term collaborators. Beginning with "Fast Company" (1978), he has worked exclusively with two cinematographers, replacing Mark Irwin with Peter Suschitzsky on all projects beginning with "Dead Ringers", and "eXistenZ" marked his eleventh and ninth collaborations respectively with production designer Carol Spier and composer Howard Shore whose contributions are integral components of the director's signature.

MILESTONES:

Submitted fantasy and science fiction stories to magazines for publication as a youth; none purchased

1966: As a college student, directed, wrote, shot and edited first film, the 16mm, seven-minute short "Transfer"

1967: Wrote, directed, shot and edited the 14-minute 16mm short "From the Drain"

1969: First feature and first film in 35mm, "Stereo" (produced, directed, wrote, shot and edited)

1970: Completed second feature, "Crimes of the Future"

1971: Traveled to Europe on Canadian Council Grant

1971: While living in France, directed, scripted, and shot three fillers for television

1972: Returned to Canada

1972: Made six fillers for TV (directed, scripted, and shot)

1972: Episodic TV directing debut, "Secret Weapons" for the Canadian series "Project X"

1974: First commercial feature, "Shivers/They Came from Within/Frissons"; also wrote script

1976: Cast Marilyn Chambers (the "Ivory Snow" porn queen) as a woman with an unsatiable thirst for blood in "Rabid"

1979: Used Samantha Eggar's bodily-manifested anger in "The Brood" as a reflection of own anger over divorce from first wife

1980: Wrote and directed the sci-fi horror flick "Scanners"; among film's assets were the noteworthy special effects; spawned a host of sequels (none of which Cronenberg directed)

1983: Wrote last original screenplay for 16 years, "Videodrome"; starred James Woods in a dynamic performance as head of a soft-core TV channel mesmerized by bizarre, untraceable "snuff" transmissions that have a hallucinatory power

1983: First feature directed from another's screenplay, "The Dead Zone", based on a Stephen King novel; first Hollywood film

1985: Acting debut in John Landis' "Into the Night"

1986: Scored biggest commercial success to date with "The Fly", a reworking of the 1958 cult sci-fi movie starring Jeff Goldblum; made cameo appearance as a gynecologist

1988: "Dead Ringers" starred Jeremy Irons in fascinating dual role as twin gynecologists who share each other's lives—and lovers; based on the true story of the Marcus brothers

1990: First major acting role in a feature, Clive Barker's "Nightbreed"

1991: Brilliantly adapted William S. Burroughs' supposedly unfilmable novel "Naked Lunch"

1993: Reteamed with Irons for "M. Butterfly", a tame, disappointing adaptation of David Henry Hwang's Tony-winning Broadway play

1996: Turned another unfilmable novel, J. G. Ballard's "Crash", into an intriguing, distubing, enigmatic motion picture

1999: Directed first original script in more than 15 years, "eXistenZ"

1999: Served as jury president at the Cannes Film Festival

2000: Signed agreement with Internet studio ExFlix to provide content; announced plans to create "David Cronenberg's Film Skool" featuring a character called Rant Quealy

QUOTES:

"Roger, I had a very strange dream last night. In this dream, I found myself making love to a strange man. Only I'm having trouble, you see, because he's old and dying, and he smells bad, and I find him repulsive. But then he tells me that EVERYTHING is erotic, that everything is sexual. You know what I mean? He tells me that even old flesh is erotic flesh, that disease is the love of two alien creatures for each other—that even dying is an act of eroticism. That talking is sexual. That breathing is sexual. That even to physically exist is sexual. And I believe him. And we make love BEAUTIFULLY."—A monologue from Cronenberg's "Shivers" (1975), his first commercial feature, quoted in *The Shape of Rage*, edited by Piers Handling.

"It's a small field, Venereal Horror, but at least I'm king of it."—David Cronenberg talking about "Rabid" (1976) in *Monthly Film Bulletin*, February 1987.

About Ted Turner's reaction to "Crash": "The film is a meditation on sex, death and technology, but it's beyond articulating. So somebody like Turner slips to the next available notch, which is about teenagers and cars and sex, or something silly like that—especially coming from a guy whose network shows 'The Dukes of Hazzard' all the time."—David Cronenberg quoted in *Daily News*, March 19, 1997.

"Kids have been masturbating and crashing cars for years; I don't think I'm going to contribute to that. It's ridiculous to think we are realigning society in order to trigger psychotics. People fasten their seatbelts after they see this film. I've probably saved lives."—Cronenberg quoted in the London *Times*, May 28, 1997.

"It's always amusing to me, and maybe a little sad, when people say to me, 'Why did you choose that to be your next film?' And I say, 'Because the money came together.' It's not as though I snap my fingers. People have this

wonderful delusion, because your name is known, that you're rich, incredibly powerful, and can do whatever you want. None of these is true.

"When you talk about power, you can also talk about influence, and then it's the body of work, perhaps, that's an influence, and that's not for me to decide. The influence of my first couple of movies still resonates. They're still remaking 'Shivers' with parasites; even the influence it had on 'Alien' is obvious. So, in the sense of that kind of power, that's really more for the critics to decide than for me. It's not something I feel, except that I'm now at an age when people can say I inspired them."—David Cronenberg to *Cinefantastique*, June 1997.

About why MGM (who initially developed project) dropped "eXistenz": "Their own demographics tell them this kind of movie is going to be attractive to young men—because it's sci-fi and about games—and young men don't want the lead to be a girl. They want it to be them. Suddenly you realize you've not written quite so commercially viable script as you thought. Feminist so-called paranoia about Hollywood is absolutely justified."— From *Sight and Sound*, April 1999.

Cautiously hopeful about the reactions to "eXistenZ", he still worried: "It's depressing to think that it might be too much, too confusing, too complex, for people. One feels in danger of losing an audience. There might come a time when there is no audience who can understand what I'm doing. Then I'm no longer a filmmaker—I mean you need an audience."—From *The Guardian*, April 1, 1999.

BIBLIOGRAPHY:

"The Shape of Rage: The Films of David Cronenberg" Handling Piers (editor), 1983, General Publishing/New York Zoetrope, Inc. collection of critical essays; the first book produced by the Academy of Canadian Cinema

"Cronenberg on Cronenberg" Chris Rodlet, (editor), Faber and Faber

BORN: Cameron B. Crowe in Palm Springs, California, 07/13/1957

NATIONALITY: American

EDUCATION: attended a Catholic high school
California State University, San Diego, San Diego, California; dropped out

AWARDS: People's Choice Award Favorite Dramatic Motion Picture "Jerry Maguire" 1998; award shared with James L. Brooks, Laurence Mark and Richard Sakai

Boston Society of Film Critics Award Best Film "Almost Famous" 2000

Boston Society of Film Critics Award Best Director "Almost Famous" 2000

New York Film Critics Online Award Best Original Screenplay "Almost Famous" 2000

Broadcast Film Critics Association Award Best Original Screenplay "Almost Famous" 2000

San Diego Film Critics Award Best Director "Almost Famous" 2000

San Diego Film Critics Award Best Original Screenplay "Almost Famous" 2000

Online Film Critics Society Award Best Picture "Almost Famous" 2000

Online Film Critics Society Award Best Screenplay "Almost Famous" 2000

Southeastern Film Critics Association Award Best Picture "Almost Famous" 2000

Southeastern Film Critics Association Award Best Original Screenplay "Almost Famous" 2000

Phoenix Film Critics Society Award Best Picture "Almost Famous" 2000; initial presentation of the award

Phoenix Film Critics Society Award Best Screenplay—Original "Almost Famous" 2000; initial presentation of the award

Golden Globe Award Best Picture (Musical or Comedy) "Almost Famous" 2000

BAFTA Award Best Original Screenplay "Almost Famous" 2001

Chicago Film Critics Award Best Picture "Almost Famous" 2000

Chicago Film Critics Award Best Screenplay "Almost Famous" 2000

Oscar Best Original Screenplay "Almost Famous" 2000

BIOGRAPHY

The eclectic career of Cameron Crowe has encompassed a wide variety of occupations, including journalism, writing liner notes for albums and filmmaking. As a teenager, the California native began writing freelance pieces for such publications as *Playboy* and *Creem*. By age 16, Crowe was on the staff of *Rolling Stone*, profiling such artists as Bob Dylan, David Bowie, Neil Young and Kris Kristofferson. He made an "undercover" return to high school in 1979 to research a book on teen life. The result, "Fast Times at Ridgemont High", was optioned by Universal Studios before it hit the bookstores and Crowe was hired to write the screenplay adaptation. Amy Heckerling's 1982 film version was an honest and entertaining evocation of suburban high school culture and remains vastly superior to the slew of similar teen films (including Crowe's sophomore scripting effort 1984's "The Wild Life") that followed in its wake. "Fast Times" is also notable for its impressive cast, including Judge Reinhold, Phoebe Cates, Jennifer Jason Leigh, Sean Penn, Forest Whitaker, Anthony Edwards and Eric Stoltz.

Crowe moved to the director's chair with "Say Anything" (1989), a superior, insightful study of teen angst finely acted by John Cusack, Ione Skye and John Mahoney as a seemingly perfect father whose exposure as a crook shatters his daughter's world. The equally engaging "Singles" (1992) saw Crowe shift his focus to a slightly older (twentysomething) age group embarking on the adult life in Seattle. Good performances, fine comic timing and a soundtrack featuring the music of Seattle's popular rock scene, however, failed to translate into box-office success.

Crowe waited for four years before returning to the big screen, writing, directing and producing "Jerry Maguire" (1996), a mature examination of the fall and redemption of a flawed but essentially noble sports attorney. Partly inspired by the films of Billy Wilder, particularly 1960's "The Apartment", "Jerry Maguire" opened to excellent notices and a healthy box office. It also provided star Tom Cruise (as Jerry) with one of his best screen roles, tapping a depth and vulnerability rarely seen in the actor's performances. The feature also provided star-making turns for Cuba Gooding Jr. (as Jerry's one loyal client) and Renee Zellweger (as the love interest).

Crowe followed up with a dream project, "Almost Famous" (2000), which followed the adventures of a teenage rock journalist. Although fictionalized, the writer-director mined his own life to create a true-to-life portrait of the world of early 1970s music. While critically acclaimed, "Almost Famous" proved to be somewhat disappointing in its box office but it brought the filmmaker a Best Original Screenplay Oscar. Crowe followed by reteaming with Cruise on the romance "Vanilla Sky" (2001), an Americanized version of the Spanish film "Open Your Eyes" (1998).

COMPANION:

wife: Nancy Wilson. Singer, guitarist, songwriter; with her sister, was part of the rock group, Heart; co-wrote and performed one song from soundtrack album for "Say Anything"; wrote the score for "Jerry Maguire"

MILESTONES:

Raised in San Diego, California
Began journalism career at age 15, eventually

writing on freelance basis for such publications as *Playboy, Circus, Creem* and *Penthouse*
Joined staff of *Rolling Stone* at age 16; worked as contributing and associate editor; wrote profiles on Bob Dylan, David Bowie, Neil Young, Led Zeppelin and Eric Clapton, among others

1979: Returned to high school (undercover) to do research for book on teenagers; result was top-selling "Fast Times at Ridgemont High"; optioned by Universal Studios in galley form, with Crowe slated to write screenplay

1982: Feature writing debut, "Fast Times at Ridgemont High"

1984: First film as co-producer (also writer), "The Wild Life"

Co-directed and produced MTV special, "Heartbreaker Beach Party", a profile of Tom Petty and the Heartbreakers

1986: Served as creative consultant for TV series, "Fast Times"

1986: Wrote album notes for Bob Dylan's "Biograph"; earned Grammy nomination

1989: First film as director (also writer), "Say Anthing"

1990: Wrote album notes for a boxed set of recordings by Led Zepplin

1996: Breakthrough feature as writer-director, "Jerry Maguire"; earned Oscar nomination for Best Original Screenplay

1997: Signed three-year, first-look deal with DreamWorks SKG

2000: Wrote and directed the autobiographical "Almost Famous", based on his years as a teen reporter for *Rolling Stone* ; earned Best Original Screenplay Academy Award

2001: Reteamed with Tom Cruise on "Vanilla Sky"

QUOTES:

"John Cusack once told me while making 'Say Anything' that my writing is not easy to act. The key is to play it as if it is real life . . . and real life is not easy to act because real life is mostly boring."—Crowe in "The 'Jerry Maguire'

Journal", *Rolling Stone*, December 26, 1996–January 9, 1997.

BIBLIOGRAPHY:
"Fast Times at Ridgemont High" Cameron

Crowe, 1981, Simon & Schuster; made into a 1982 film, with a screenplay by Crowe
"Conversations With Wilder" Cameron Crowe, 1999

Alfonso Cuaron

BORN: in Mexico, 1961

NATIONALITY: Mexican

EDUCATION: Cooperativa Universitaria Editrice Cagliaritana Mexico City, Mexico, film

AWARDS: CableACE Award Best Directing in a Drama Series "Murder Obliquely" episode of "Fallen Angels" 1993

Los Angeles Film Critics Association New Generation Award "A Little Princess" 1995

Venice Film Festival Best Screenplay Award "Y Tu Mama Tambien" 2001; shared with brother Carlos Cuaron

Los Angeles Film Critics Association Awards "Y Tu Mama Tambien" 2002

Independent Spirit Awards Best Foreign Film "Y Tu Mama Tambien" 2003

BIOGRAPHY

A Mexican director who has had a rapid rise in Hollywood, Alfonso Cuaron became established in Mexican TV and made a heralded film about AIDS, "Solo Con Tu Pareja/Love in the Time of Hysteria" (1991). Hollywood, in the form of Sydney Pollack, took notice and brought Cuaron to the US to helm an episode of the Showtime series "Fallen Angels." The director earned a CableACE Award for his work and moved into features with "The Little Princess" (1995), a critically acclaimed box office dud that was the third go-around for the Frances Hodgson Burnett story. First shot in 1917 as a silent starring Mary Pickford and

remade as a Shirley Temple vehicle in 1939, the story centers on a young girl of privilege forced into servitude at an austere boarding school as she searches for her lost father. Critics championed Cuaron's version, a beautifully photographed version that captured the charm and grace of the original story. Warner Brothers attempted to garner audience support by re-releasing the film, but audiences stayed away. Nevertheless, at year's end, Cuaron was cited by the Los Angeles Film Critics for his efforts.

After studying at Mexico's CUEC, Cuaron gained experience working as an assistant director on many English-language films shot in Mexico and Latin America. He was first AD to Luis Mandoki on "Gaby-A Love Story" (1987) and served the same function for "Romero" (1989), in which Raul Julia was a doomed Salvadoran priest. For his follow-up to "A Little Princess", he directed "Great Expectations" (1997), a modern update of the Dickens classic, now set in Florida fishing villages and New York art's scene. Still a tale of a young man making his way in the world, the film stars Ethan Hawke, Robert De Niro and Gwyneth Paltrow.

Cuaron seemed to find his niche with the release of "Y Tu Mama Tambien (And Your Mother Too)"(2001). The frank portrayal of two adolescent boys and their road trip with an older woman was a runaway success. The movie's intoxicating spirit seemed to flow off the screen and swept audiences away. Although the film was met with some controversy over its graphic sex scenes, the overwhelming response was positive. Cuaron had captured the passion of youth and showed it to audiences in an authentically tender, albeit raw, manner. And perhaps it was treading in the wild and isolated land of his native Mexico that allowed Cuaron to find this charmingly honest story of the unspoiled hearts of two boys before they are men.

MILESTONES:

1991: Made first feature, a comedy about AIDS, "Solo Con Tu Pareja/Love in the Time of Hysteria"

1993: Directed episode of Showtime series "Fallen Angels"

1995: Won widespread critical acclaim for "A Little Princess"

1997: Directed version of Dickens' "Great Expectations"

2002: Co-wrote (with brother Carlos) and directed "Y Tu Mama Tambien/And Your Mother Too", first Spanish-language film in

more than a decade; received nominations for a BAFTA for for Best Screenplay (Original) and an Oscar nomination for Original Screenplay

QUOTES:

"I have to admit that if I saw an ad in the paper for something called 'A Little Princess' and only knew it was about little girls at a boarding school at the turn of the century, I'm not sure I'd want to see it."—Alfonso Cuaron in *Daily Variety,* January 15, 1997.

"Being close or far from Mexico doesn't mean much to me. Not as much as working on films that are close to my heart."—Cuaron in *Daily Variety,* January 15, 1997.

"You'd hear folks saying, 'You guys are perverts, because my son is not like that and teenagers are not like that.' What it only proves is when the innocence of children ends, the innocence of the parent begins.—Cuaron on response to "Y Tu Mama Tambien" as quoted in *Premiere,* April 2002.

Michael Cuesta

BORN: Michael Cuesta, Jr. in Bronx, New York, 1963

SOMETIMES CREDITED AS:
Michael Cuesta, Jr.

NATIONALITY: American

EDUCATION: School of Visual Arts, New York, New York, photography and graphic design

AWARD: Boston Society of Film Critics Award Best New Filmmaker "L.I.E." 2001

BIOGRAPHY
Following in his father's stead, Michael Cuesta began his career as a photographer before segueing to directing commercials. Eventually,

though, he moved into writing and directing feature films and he earned nearly unanimous praise for the well-crafted, controversial "L.I.E." (2001). Raised on Long Island in the tony community of Dix Hills, Cuesta spent two high school summer vacations working as a newspaper intern and photojournalist in Puerto Rico. After attending NYC's School of Visual Arts, he marked time as a photographer's assistant before eventually opening his own shop (as his father had). The Michael Cuesta Studio shot advertising campaigns for such clients as Coca-Cola and Dupont. By 1992, though, Cuesta has made the move to film, shooting tabletop work for the now-defunct London-based firm Jennie & Co. Within six months, he had switched employers and became ensconced at A+R

New York and went on to create hundreds of commercials.

In 1995, Cuesta began to write a semi-auto-biographical drama about growing up on Long Island. By his own admission, he had run "with a crowd and we caused a little trouble, but I was always much more into books and movies and I always carried a camera." Still, the seed for what would become his first full-length feature was sown. Over the next five years, Cuesta would refine the screenplay with help from his brother Gerald and college pal Steve Ryder. Eventually what emerged was a contemporary snapshot of disaffected sub-urban teens. The film's protagonist is a young boy on the cusp of manhood struggling with his burgeoning sexual feelings, his attraction to his charismatic best friend and his odd but chaste relationship with an ex-Marine who happens to be a pedophile. Shot almost like a documentary, "L.I.E." (which stands for Long Island Expressway as well as the obvious) gar-nered strong notices at Sundance and was picked up for distribution by Lot 47 Films.

MILESTONES:

Raised in Dix Hills, New York

1979–1980: During summers worked in Puerto Rico as a newspaper intern and pho-tojournalist for *El Nuevo Dia* in San Juan, Puerto Rico

Attended School of Visual Arts in NYC

Worked as a photographer's assistant

Opened own photography shop, Michael Cuesta Studio; shot print commercials for clients like Coca-Cola and Dupont

1992: Made transition to filmmaking shooting tabletop work for the now-defunct London-based Jennie & Co.

After six months, moved to A+R New York

1995: Began writing script for what eventually became his feature debut

Shot numerous commercials

2000: Feature film directorial debut "L.I.E"; chosen for the Dramatic Competition for the 2001 Sundance Film Festival; also co-wrote screenplay with brother Gerald and Stephen M. Ryder and served as one of the producers; released theatrically in 2001

George Cukor

BORN: George Dewey Cukor in New York, New York, 07/07/1899

DEATH: in Los Angeles, California, 01/24/1983

NATIONALITY: American

EDUCATION: DeWitt Clinton High School, New York, New York

AWARDS: Golden Globe Award Best Director "My Fair Lady" 1964

Directors Guild of America Award Out-standing Directorial Achievement in Feature Film "My Fair Lady" 1964

Oscar Best Director "My Fair Lady" 1964

Emmy Outstanding Directing in a Special Program—Drama or Comedy "Love Among the Ruins" 1974/75

Los Angeles Film Critics Association Special Award "Love Among the Ruins" 1975

Directors Guild of America D. W. Griffith Award 1981

BIOGRAPHY

One of Hollywood's brightest talents, George Cukor has often been dismissed as a "woman's director." Accurate or not, he was responsible for some of the greatest treasures of Holly-wood's golden era.

The plump, bespectacled Cukor was born and raised in New York City. Stage-struck from childhood, he haunted Broadway and got his first professional work as assistant stage manager in a Chicago company of "The Better 'Ole" (1919). From 1920–1927, he directed for his own stock company in Rochester, NY, then relocated to manage the Empire Theater on 42nd Street. It was there he worked with such stage divas as Ethel Barrymore, Jeanne Eagels and Laurette Taylor.

The movies came calling in 1929, and Cukor joined Paramount (as dialogue director on the early talkie "River of Romance"). He worked on "All Quiet on the Western Front" (Universal, 1930) before debuting as a director on "Grumpy" (1930, sharing credit with Cyril Gardner). From there on, there was no holding Cukor back.

Cukor made a handful of films (including Tallulah Bankhead's 1931 "Tarnished Lady", his first solo flight), before decamping to RKO over a disagreement with Ernst Lubitsch about "One Hour with You" (1932). His career really took off at RKO (1932–35). "What Price Hollywood?" (1932) was a brilliant precursor to "A Star is Born", a dark yet sparkling indictment of the star-making machinery. He fought to cast Katharine Hepburn in her screen debut, "A Bill of Divorcement" (1932), and went on to make another eight films (and two TV-movies) with her, including "Little Women" (1933), a sweet cameo of a film, and the financial flop (but subsequent cult favorite) "Sylvia Scarlett" (1936). He was loaned to MGM in 1933, where he marshaled such stars as Jean Harlow, Marie Dressler, John and Lionel Barrymore and Wallace Beery in the delightful "Dinner at Eight" (1933)—filmed in an amazing 28 days.

Despite a loan-out to Columbia for a sterling adaptation of Philip Barry's "Holiday" (1938, with Hepburn and Cary Grant), Cukor finally settled down at MGM for the bulk of his career. His 1930s hits there included "David Copperfield" (1935), a lush if flawed version of "Romeo and Juliet" (1936), Garbo's transcendent "Camille" (1937) and the brittle all-star comedy "The Women" (1939). That same year, he was fired from "Gone With the Wind" and replaced by Victor Fleming—a move that caused much speculation and gossip (such as Clark Gable's demanding another director because of Cukor's homosexuality).

In 1942, Cukor enlisted—at the age of 43—in the Army Signal Corps, where he directed training and propaganda films. He was honorably discharged (because of his age) the following year. Cukor made only a dozen theatrical films in the 1940s, but several were among his most fondly remembered and featured tour-de-force roles for top actresses. He directed Hepburn's comeback vehicle, "The Philadelphia Story" (1940), one of Joan Crawford's better performances, "A Woman's Face" (1941), Ingrid Bergman's Oscar-winning turn in "Gaslight" (1944) and the Tracy-Hepburn comedy "Adam's Rib" (which provided a wonderful part for neophyte Judy Holliday, 1949). But even the best of directors has his flops; Cukor's included Garbo's career-killing comedy "Two-Faced Woman" (1941) and Norma Shearer's "Her Cardboard Lover" (1942).

Despite his few ventures into film noir, Cukor was best known for a light-hearted mixture of sophistication and bandbox Hollywood corn at its best. Even his darkest works ("What Price Hollywood?", "Gaslight") have a glamorous sheen. His amazing ability to coax performances from divas (male and female) made him both a valuable team player and the savior of more than one film career. He also brought a theatrical sensibility to films, never interrupting the flow of dialogue with fast cuts or self-conscious film techniques.

Cukor continued working until 1981; his last film was "Rich and Famous", a remake of "Old Acquaintance" (1943), starring Candice Bergen and Jacqueline Bisset. Among his latterday hits were three Judy Holliday vehicles, "Born Yesterday" (for which she won an Oscar in 1950), "The Marrying Kind" (1952) and the delightful "It Should Happen to You" (1954);

the Tracy-Hepburn comedy "Pat and Mike" (1952); Judy Garland's comeback, "A Star is Born" (1954, his first color film and a musical remake of his 1932 "What Price Hollywood?"); and Audrey Hepburn's immensely popular "My Fair Lady", which won Cukor his only Best Director Oscar (1964). He continued mixing hits with misses, including Marilyn Monroe's unsuccessful "Let's Make Love" (1960) and the expensive Russian-American flop "The Blue Bird" (1976). He was also directing Monroe in "Something's Got to Give" (1962) at the time of her death.

Cukor made much-heralded ventures into TV with "Love Among the Ruins" (1975), for which he won an Emmy, and "The Corn is Green" (1979), both starring his old friend Katharine Hepburn. The highly sociable director, discreet but long known as gay to his Hollywood peers, lived in a huge art-deco mansion for most of his career, and was famed in the film community for his sparkling gourmet dinner parties and weekend salons.— Written by Eve Golden

MILESTONES:

1917–1918: Served in sudent Army Training Corps

1919: Hired as stage manager in Chicago for "The Better 'Ole"

1919: Became a Broadway stage manager, first for Edgar Selwyn organization, then for the Shuberts

1922: General manager and actor with the Lyceum Players (Rochester, New York) where he made stage directing debut

1925: Broadway directorial debut, credited as co-stager of "Antonia"

1926: Enjoyed first success as a Broadway director with "The Great Gatsby"

1929: Went to Hollywood under contract to Paramount and earned first screen credit, as dialogue director for "River of Romance"

1930: First film as co-director (with Cyril Gardner), "Grumpy"

1931: Solo film directing debut, "The Tarnished Lady"

1932: Put under contract by RKO

1932: First film with Katharine Hepburn, "A Bill of Divorcement"

1933: Loaned to MGM for "Dinner at Eight"

1933: Directed Hepburn in "Little Women"; received first Best Director Oscar nomination

1935: Signed contract with MGM

1936: Helmed both "Camille" with Greta Garbo and "Romeo and Juliet" with Norma Shearer and Leslie Howard

1938: Guided Hepburn and Cary Grant through "Holiday", an engaging adaptation of Philip Barry's romantic comedy

1939: Directed an all-star cast in "The Women"

1939: Did uncredited tests for "The Wizard of Oz"

1939: Was fired from "Gone With the Wind"

1940: Reteamed with Hepburn and Grant for another Philip Barry adaptation "The Philadelphia Story"; earned second Academy Award nomination as Best Director; James Stewart received the Best Actor Oscar

1941: Directed Garbo in her final screen appearance in "Two-Faced Woman"

1942: Enlisted in Army Signal Corps at age of 43; honorably discharged a year later and returned to MGM

1944: Helmed "Gaslight", a thriller starring Ingrid Bergman (in an Oscar-winning performance), Charles Boyer and Angela Lansbury

1947: Received third Best Director Oscar nod for "A Double Life", a drama about an actor who takes playing Othello a little too close to heart; star Ronald Coleman picked up a Best Actor Oscar

1949: Helmed "Adam's Rib", which teamed Hepburn and Spencer Tracy

1950: Guided Judy Holiday to a Best Actress Oscar in "Born Yesterday"; received fourth Best Director nomination

1952: Again directed Holiday in "The Marrying Kind"

1952: Reunited with Tracy and Hepburn for "Pat and Mike"

1954: Last film with Holiday, "It Should Happen to You"

1954: Made first color film, "A Star Is Born", teaming Judy Garland and James Mason

1957: Helmed the musical "Les Girls", with Gene Kelly and Mitzi Gaynor

1960: Directed Marilyn Monroe in "Let's Make Love"

1962: Signed to direct Marilyn Monroe in "Something's Got to Give"; film never completed

1964: Won Best Director Oscar for helming "My Fair Lady", starring Rex Harrison and Audrey Hepburn; last film for five years

1969: Returned to features as director of "Justine", adapted from one of Lawrence Durrell's novels that comprised "The Alexandria Quartet"

1972: Helmed "Travels with My Aunt"; star Maggie Smith garnered a Best Actress Oscar nomination

1975: First TV-movie, "Love Among the Ruins" (ABC), starring Katharine Hepburn and Laurence Olivier; won Emmy Award

1976: Went to Russia to direct the first Soviet-US co-production, the misguided "The Blue Bird", starring Elizabeth Taylor, Ava Gardner and Jane Fonda

1979: Final TV-movie, a remake of "The Corn Is Green" (CBS) starring Katharine Hepburn

1981: Final feature film, "Rich and Famous"

AFFILIATION: Jewish

QUOTES:

"Women's director! Well, I'm very pleased to be considered a master of anything, but remember, for every Jill there was a Jack. People like to pigeonhole you—it's a shortcut, I guess, but once they do, you're stuck with it."—George Cukor in 1979, quoted in his *The New York Times* obituary, January 26, 1983.

"You have to know when to shut up. A director can talk a lot and theorize and shut off whatever creative thing they [actors] have. You can be quiet, but you can't be inhibited."—George Cukor, quoted in his *The New York Times* obituary, January 26, 1983.

BIBLIOGRAPHY:

"Cukor" Carlos Clarens, 1976, Secker & Warburg

"George Cukor: A Critical Study and Filmography" James Bernardoni, 1985, McFarland

"On Cukor" Gavin Lambert, 1972, G.P. Putnam's Sons; review of his film career based on interviews with the director

"George Cukor: A Double Life" Patrick McGilligan, 1991, St. Martin's Press; biography; alleges that a rumored homosexual encounter between Clark Gable and a friend of Cukor's was indirectly responsible for Cukor's being fired from "Gone With the Wind" (1939)

"George Cukor, Master of Elegance: Hollywood's Legendary Director and His Stars" Emanuel Levy, 1994, William Morrow

Michael Curtiz

BORN: Mihaly Kertesz in Budapest, Hungary, 12/24/1888

SOMETIMES CREDITED AS:
Kertesz Mihaly
Michael Kertesz

Mahala Kurtez
Michael Courtice
Mihaly Kertesz
Kertesz Mihaly

DEATH: in Hollywood, California, 04/11/1962

NATIONALITY: Hungarian

CITIZENSHIP: United States

EDUCATION: Markoszy University Budapest, Hungary
　　Royal Academy of Theater and Art Budapest, Hungary

AWARDS: National Board of Review Award Best Director "Casablanca" and "This Is the Army" 1943; cited for both films; William A. Wellman and Tay Garnett also named as winners
　　Oscar Best Director "Casablanca" 1943

BIOGRAPHY

One of the most prolific directors in the history of the cinema, Hungarian-born Michael Curtiz has often received short shrift from proponents of the auteur theory for his willing participation in the studio system as the top helmsman at Warner Bros. in the 1930s and 40s. He tirelessly hammered out four or five films a year for the studio through the 30s, as ready to take on low-budget programmers as more prestigious assignments, and was amazingly adept at creating lavish results on minimal budgets in a wide variety of genres. He also earned a reputation as one of the most hated directors in Hollywood. Autocratic and overbearing to the extreme, Curtiz clashed constantly with his actors, and his most famous player, Errol Flynn, finally refused to work for him. Yet for all his unsympathetic treatment of performers, Curtiz had a knack for detecting and fostering unknown talents, including Flynn, John Garfield and Doris Day, among others. His highly developed visual approach combined with his technical mastery could elevate the most mundane material, and three of his finest films, "Yankee Doodle Dandy" (1942), "Casablanca" (1943) and "Mildred Pierce" (1945), make a virtue of melodrama and sentimentality.

No complete evaluation of the director can ignore his European work, which numbered well over 50 films before Jack L. Warner imported him to Hollywood at the ripe old age of 38. Curtiz participated in the beginning of the Hungarian film industry, usually receiving credit for directing that country's first feature film ("Today and Tomorrow" 1912). After he apprenticed at Denmark's Nordisk Studios, his Hungarian films exhibited a Scandinavian influence, particularly in the naturalism of their outdoor settings. With the nationalization of Hungary's film industry by Bela Kun's communist regime, he fled the country, eventually working for Vienna's Sascha Films where he came in contact with German expressionism as embodied by the work of Fritz Lang and F.W. Murnau. He established his reputation with two DeMille-style biblical spectaculars, "Sodom and Gomorrah" (1922) and "Moon of Israel" (1924), the latter prompting Jack Warner's job offer. Curtiz's first US film, "The Third Degree" (1926), revealed a mastery of the moving camera in its flashy expressionistic sequences, at one point presenting the action from the perspective of a lethal bullet. It also marked the first of eight collaborations with Dolores Costello, one of the studio's few established female stars.

Warner Bros. thrust Curtiz into its attempts at sound innovation, and two part-talkies "Tenderloin" (1927) and "Noah's Ark" (1928), both starring Costello, achieved considerable popularity and garnered millions in box office revenues. In 1930, he directed no less than six Warner talkies, but the studio's attempt to partially introduce color that year in Curtiz's commercially successful "Mammy" (a backstage murder vehicle for Al Jolson with songs by Irving Berlin) fell short of expectations. Warners was the fastest-growing studio in Hollywood, and the director's fortunes rose with them. "The Cabin in the Cotton" (1932) delivered the first of Bette Davis' malicious Southern belles while "20,000 Years in Sing Sing" (1933) presented her in a more sympathetic light as the girlfriend of noble Spencer

Tracy, who sacrifices his life for the murder she committed. He also helmed two of the studio's rare excursions into horror, "Dr. X" (1932) and "The Mystery of the Wax Museum" (1933), both all-color and both exhibiting the influence of Lang and Murnau in their vividly atmospheric scenes.

Despite his early penchant for Swedish naturalism, Curtiz in the USA followed in the footsteps of the great German studio directors, transporting his audiences to distant lands while all the time remaining on the back lots of Hollywood. He began his 12-film collaboration with Errol Flynn (often paired with Olivia de Havilland) in "Captain Blood" (1935), and together director and actor became synonymous with the "swashbuckler" genre, which they reprised marvelously in "The Adventures of Robin Hood" (1938) and "The Sea Hawk" (1940). Flynn was no great actor, but his sheer vitality as personified by his swordsmanship made him a star, and the pair continued working together despite their animosity. "Dodge City" (1939) marked the first of three big-budget Westerns, and they followed with perhaps their best, "Virginia City" (1940), rounding out the trilogy with that year's "Santa Fe Trail." By then, Flynn had had it with the director, and the mediocre "Dive Bomber" (1941) closed out their association.

One actor who apparently did not mind the director's imperious ways was Claude Rains, appearing in 10 Curtiz films, including three sentimental small-town soapers ("Four Daughters" 1938 and its two 1939 sequels "Daughters Courageous" and "Four Wives") which introduced Garfield to the public. He also elicited some of the finest work from both Edward G. Robinson and James Cagney, the former giving a bravura performance as the tough, sardonic, ultimately soft-hearted boxing manager of "Kid Gallahad" (1937) and providing perhaps an even richer portrayal as the intellectual, rampaging captain of "The Sea Wolf" (1941, the quintessential adaptation of

the Jack London novel). As for Cagney, Rocky Sullivan in "Angels with Dirty Faces" (1938) represented a high point from the actor's gangster oeuvre, and his Academy Award–winning turn as George M. Cohan in "Yankee Doodle Dandy" (1942) stands at the very pinnacle of his career. Though Curtiz's prodigious output slowed some during the 40s, his films reflected the efficiency of the studio system at its best, and "Casablanca" (1943), the cult classic that earned him his only Oscar as Best Director, is a shining example of what could go right in that setting.

Originally scheduled as a low-budget melodrama starring Ann Sheridan and Ronald Reagan, "Casablanca" acquired some cachet when Warners upgraded it to major-budget status and brought in Humphrey Bogart and Ingrid Bergman as the leads. The supporting actors were all first rate, led by Rains as Vichy police chief Louis Renault, Paul Henreid as resistance leader Victor Lazlo (and ultimate winner of the Bergman sweepstakes), Sidney Greenstreet, Peter Lorre, Conrad Veidt and Dooley Wilson, playing that haunting melody again for Rick, the character in which Bogie, more than in any other, established his iconographic screen persona. Longtime Curtiz screenwriting collaborators Julius and Philip Epstein fresh from scripting the director's "Mission to Moscow" (also 1943), worked alongside Howard Koch to provide what was often pure schmaltz ("I remember every detail—the Germans wore gray, you wore blue."). If the result was not great art, beyond all doubt, it was great cinema. Legend has it that shooting was only days ahead of the script. What clearer proof could there be of a director's instinct working within the American studio system at its most stable and powerful.

"Casablanca" was a tough act to follow. "Passage to Marseille" (1944) rounded up some familiar suspects (Bogart, Rains, Greenstreet and Lorre) but fell far short of its precursor. There still remained the wonderful

"Mildred Pierce" (1945), which earned Joan Crawford a Best Actress Oscar, but after that, consensus has it that the master fell victim to the sheer volume of his output. People didn't stop going to his movies. In fact, some of his biggest moneymakers lay ahead. "Night and Day" (1946), a sanitized biopic of Cole Porter (with a miscast Cary Grant), which pales in comparison with "Yankee Doodle Dandy", and "Life with Father" (1947) were optimistic, upbeat fare that enjoyed a healthy box office, and the Bing Crosby–Danny Kaye vehicle "White Christmas" (1954), sad to say, was the biggest commercial success of his career (ironically made for Paramount soon after he ended his 28-year run with Warner Bros.). Curtiz shouldered on, directing more than 20 additional pictures, after his excellent film noir (and last with Garfield) "The Breaking Point" (1950), including "King Creole" (1958), which starred box-office monarch Elvis Presley.

In the saddle nearly to the end, Curtiz died six months after the release of his final film, "The Commancheros" (1961), a well-paced actioner with John Wayne as a Texas Ranger out to bring in the gang supplying liquor and guns to the Comanches. Though he may not have demonstrated the easily identifiable style demanded by the "politique des auteurs" of the *Cahier Du Cinema*, Curtiz left behind an impressive body of work possessing an incredibly consistent narrative energy. He scoffed at attempts to delve beneath the polished surface of his films: "I put all the art into my pictures I think the audience can stand. I don't see black-and-white words in a script when I read it. I see action." The director displayed his "personal vision" in the "look" of his films. Curtiz instinctively understood where to put the camera in relation to the action to achieve maximum emotional identification from his audience. Perhaps only John Ford and William Wyler enjoyed comparable success directing within the studio system.—Written by Greg Senf

MILESTONES:

1897: Made first stage appearance in an opera starring his mother

1906: Ran away to join a traveling circus at age 17, performing with them as strongman, acrobat, juggler and mime

After completing studies, joined the Hungarian National Theatre, eventually working as actor and director

Reputedly was a member of the Hungarian fencing team at the 1912 Stockholm Olympic Games

1912: Film directing debut (although no director credited), "Today and Tomorrow"; also played a leading role; film announced as "The First Hungarian Dramatic Art Film"

Worked at Nordisk Studios in Denmark learning filmmaking techniques; assisted both Victor Sjostrom and Mauritz Stiller

1914: Returned to Hungary

1914–1919: Directed at least 37 films, many of which—following the Scandinavian example—showed a preference for outdoor locations

Drafted into Austo-Hungarian artillery, but through use of connections obtained transfer to the film unit and then was discharged

1917: Worked as managing director of Hungarian Phoenix Studios; helmed several films which starred first wife Lucy Doraine

1919: Fled Hungary when Bela Kun's Communist regime nationalized film industry

Helmed at least 21 films for Sascha Films of Vienna, credited as Michael Kertesz

1923: Directed the acclaimed "Sodom and Gomorrah", featuring Walter Slezak

1926: Brought to Hollywood by Jack Warner who had been impressed by Curtiz's camera work for "Moon of Israel" (1924), produced by Alexander Korda; directed first US film, "The Third Degree"; first of eight collaborations with Warner Bros. star Dolores Costello

1929: Scored substantial box-office success with "Noah's Ark"; Erich Wolfgang Kornholder provided the first of his six scores for the director

1932: Directed Hollywood's first all-color horror film, "Doctor X"

1933: Helmed the well-regarded, all-color horror flick "The Mystery of the Wax Museum"

1934: First film with James Cagney, "Jimmy the Gent"

1935: Initial collaboration with screenwriter Julius Epstein, "Little Big Shot"

1935: Directed first film with Errol Flynn and Olivia de Havilland, "Captain Blood"

1936: Reteamed Flynn and de Havilland in "The Charge of the Light Brigade"; climactic charge was then one of the most dangerous scenes ever filmed with one man dying, several more badly injured, and so many horses killed that the SPCA raised a public protest

1936: First of 10 films with Claude Rains, "Stolen Holiday"

1937: Directed "Kid Galahad", featuring a bravura performance by Edward G. Robinson as a ruthless (but ultimately soft-hearted) boxing manager

1938: Reunited with Cagney for "Angels With Dirty Faces"

1938: Helmed perhaps the finest swashbuckler, "The Adventures of Robin Hood", starring Flynn and de Havilland; Korngold earned his second Oscar for the film's score

1938: First of five films with John Garfield, "Four Daughters"; Garfield's feature debut

1939: Phillip G. Epstein teamed with brother Julius on screenplay for "Daughters Courageous"

1939: Directed the Academy Award-winning two-reel short "Sons of Liberty", a Warner Historical Featurette

1939: Helmed "The Private Lives of Elizabeth and Essex", with Bette Davis and Errol Flynn

1941: 12th and last film with Flynn, "Dive Bomber"; director and star were barely speaking, and Flynn refused to work with Curtiz afterwards

1941: Reteamed with Robinson for "The Sea Wolf", adapted from the Jack London novel

1942: Fourth and last film with Cagney, "Yankee Doodle Dandy", superb biopic of George M. Cohan which earned Cagney the Best Actor Oscar; scripted (with others) by the Epstein brothers

1943: Last film with Costello, "This Is the Army"

1943: Earned Best Director Academy Award for the classic Oscar-winning Best Picture "Casablanca"; the Epstein twins and Howard Koch picked up Best Adapted Screenplay statue as well

1944: "Passage to Marseilles" reunited him with four from the "Casablanca" cast (Humphrey Bogart, Sidney Greenstreet, Peter Lorre and Rains)

1945: Directed "Mildred Pierce", starring Joan Crawford who won a Best Actress Oscar

1947: Formed Michael Curtiz Productions, an in-house company headquartered at Warner Bros.

1947: Last film with Rains, "The Unsuspected"; initial movie made under the Michael Curtiz Productions banner

1948: First of four films with Doris Day, "Romance on the High Seas"; marked Day's film debut

1949: Final film from Michael Curtiz Productions, "Flamingo Road"; sold company to Warners, tired of exercising a nominal independence that gave final say to the studio

1950: Fifth and final film with Garfield, "The Breaking Point", a remake of "To Have and Have Not" that was more faithful to the Hemingway novel

1952: Fourth and last film with Day, "I'll See You in My Dreams", the formulaic musical biopic of Gus Kahn (played by Danny Thomas)

1954: After almost 28 years, ended exclusive affiliation with Warner Bros.; asked to accept a 50-percent cut in pay, refused and quit studio; also embroiled at this time in a paternity suit with a young actress which ultimately went expensively against him

1954: Enjoyed biggest commercial success of career, "White Christmas", for Paramount

1958: Ninth and last film with de Havilland, "Proud Rebel"

1960: Helmed "A Breath of Scandal", adapted from fellow Hungarian Ferenc Molnar's play "Olympia"

1961: Directed last film, "The Comancheros", starring John Wayne

Honored posthumously with a career retrospective at New York's Museum of Modern Art entitled "Michael Curtiz: From Hungary to Hollywood"

AFFILIATION: Jewish

QUOTES:
All his life Curtiz retained a strong Hungarian accent, and his creative mishandlings of the English language deserve to be as famous as those of Sam Goldwyn. He once stormed at a confused prop man: "Next time I send a damn fool, I go myself!" He expressed dissatisfaction with a child actor by remarking scathingly: "By the time I was your age, I was fifteen."—from "World Film Directors", Volume One 1890–1945, edited by John Wakeman (New York: H.W. Wilson Company, 1987).

"Bring on the empty horses!"—Curtiz on the set of "The Charge of the Light Brigade." When co-stars Errol Flynn and David Niven broke out in laughter, Curtiz reportedly responded, "You people, you think I know fuck nothing; I tell you, I know fuck all!" Niven later titled one of memoirs "Bring on the Empty Horses"

"Don't talk to me when I'm interrupting."—a reported "Curtizism."

BIBLIOGRAPHY:
"The Casablanca Man" James C. Robertson, 1993, Routledge
"The Warner Brothers Directors" William R. Meyer, 1978, Arlington House

John Dahl

BORN: in Billings, Montana, 1952

NATIONALITY: American

EDUCATION: University of Montana, Missoula, Montana; music and art attended for two years

Montana State University, Bozeman, Montana, film, BS; directed first feature, "The Death Mutants" (1980), a send-up of horror and science fiction films

American Film Institute Los Angeles, California, 1982; attended as a directing fellow; wife attended as a cinematography student

AWARD: Los Angeles Film Critics Association New Generation Award "Red Rock West" and "The Last Seduction" 1994; cited for both films

BIOGRAPHY
Assured director of modern film noirs who has injected new life into the genre with a series of tough, economical, and atmospheric tales. Dahl tells unsentimental stories of hopelessly stupid men who take the fall for beautiful dames. Whereas most movies of this ilk are set against the backdrop of urban L.A. or NYC, this Montana native finds the darkness in the heart of middle America, in claustrophobic towns surrounded by great open spaces. In an era of imitations, both cheap and lavish, he offers the real deal.

Dahl entered the industry as a storyboard artist on "A" films ("Something Wild" 1986; "Married to the Mob" 1988) and an assistant director on "B" genre fare ("The Dungeonmaster" 1983). He made his first feature as a student at Montana State University—"The

Death Mutants" (1980), a horror/sci-fi send-up. Dahl moved to L.A. where he attended the American Film Institute as a directing fellow. After making some well-received shorts, including "The Ugliest Family in the World", he shifted to music videos filming such artists as Kool and the Gang and Joe Satriani.

Dahl found his voice as a director with the moody "Kill Me Again" (1989), featuring Joanne Whalley-Kilmer as a femme fatale who tours the West double-crossing the mob and luring unsuspecting men into her web. Largely ignored by the public, the film raised eyebrows among industry insiders. His follow-up, "Red Rock West" (1993), told a familiar hard-boiled story: seduction, double-crosses, and murder ensue when a stranger pulls into town and gets confused for a hit man hired to kill the slyly adulterous wife of the local sheriff. The film garnered at least as much attention for the way it reached the big screen as for its considerable merits. Originally acquired for TV distribution by HBO, the film received such raves on the festival circuit that it was picked up for theatrical release on a platform basis.

Staying with the familiar, Dahl's next effort "The Last Seduction" (1994), once again found its way to the silver screen via the back roads of TV. This time out, Linda Fiorentino starred as a cold-hearted woman who steals drug money from her weasel of a husband (Bill Pullman) and lures a bumpkin from the country into a world of treachery and murder. The film received numerous accolades with many critics hailing Dahl as a filmmaker to watch.

FAMILY:

brother: Rick Dahl. Screenwriter, producer; co-wrote "Red Rock West" (1993) with Dahl

MILESTONES:

1980: First feature, a student film entitled "The Death Mutants" and made for $12,000 dollars Moved to Los Angeles, attended AFI's directing program

Directed music videos for Kool and the Gang and Joe Satriani

1983: Worked as an assistant director on the omnibus horror film, "The Dungeonmaster"

1987: First produced screenplay, "Private Investigations"; also served as 2nd unit director

1988: Served as a visual consultant and storyboard artist on Jonathan Demme's "Married to the Mob"

1989: Professional feature directing debut, "Kill Me Again" (also wrote screenplay)

1993: Helmed the feature "Red Rock West"; acquired by HBO for domestic TV distribution then picked up for theatrical release by Roxie Releasing

1993: Made third film, the acclaimed "The Last Seduction"; rights sold to HBO which premiered film before its theatrical release

1998: Directed Matt Damon and Edward Norton in "Rounders"

2001: Helmed the thriller "Joy Ride"

BORN: in Dorset, England, 1960

NATIONALITY: British

EDUCATION: Sheffield University, Sheffield, England; joined program run by the Royal Air Force; served as chair of the university's drama club; met Eddie Izzard

apprenticed to clown Elder Milletti at It Circo di Nando Orfei in Italy c. 1984

AWARDS: Plays and Players Best Director "Damned for Despair" 1991

London Critics' Circle Award Best Director "An Inspector Calls" 1992

Evening Standard Award Best Director "An Inspector Calls" 1992

Olivier Award Best Director of a Play "An Inspector Calls" 1993

Drama Desk Award Outstanding Director of a Play "An Inspector Calls" 1994

Tony Director of a Play "An Inspector Calls" 1994

Olivier Award Best Director of a Play "Machinal" 1994

British Independent Film Award Best British Independent Film "Billy Elliot" 2000

British Independent Film Award Best Director "Billy Elliot" 2000

London Film Critics' Circle Award Best British Director "Billy Elliot" 2000

BAFTA Alexander Korda Award for Outstanding British Film "Billy Elliot" 2001

Lumiere Best Foreign Film "Billy Elliot" 2001

BIOGRAPHY

Along with contemporaries like Sam Mendes, Deborah Warner and Matthew Warchus, British stage director Stephen Daldry moved from the theater to film. After spending some 15 years honing his craft and amassing numerous accolades, he stepped behind the cameras to helm the feature "Billy Elliot" (2000), a drama about a preteen boy struggling with grief over his mother's premature death and finding a measure of solace in dancing.

The son of a singer and a bank manager, Daldry spent part of his formative years as a member of a youth drama group in Taunton, England. While at Sheffield University, he excelled at dramatics and after an apprenticeship with Italian clown Elder Milletti, began his theatrical career in earnest. Daldry served an apprenticeship at the Crucible Theatre in Sheffield from 1985 to 1988. His initial directorial work was in repertory before he joined The Gate Theatre where he garnered attention for his work on "Damned for Despair" in 1991.

Daldry moved to the National and immediately served notice as one to watch with an acclaimed deconstructionist staging of J. B. Priestley's "An Inspector Calls." The collaboration with designer Ian McNeill yielded a highly stylized approach to what was considered a heavy-handed drama about a family's involvement in a young woman's suicide. The curtain opened to an onstage rainstorm, shrill air raid sirens and a dollhouse-like main setting that by play's end resulted in a brilliant coup de theatre. Daldry picked up numerous accolades for his staging including a Tony Award when the production transferred to Broadway in 1994.

Continuing to work at the Royal Court Theatre where he served as artistic director from 1992 to 1995, he guided Fiona Shaw in an acclaimed revival of "Machinal" (1994) and directed "Rat in the Skull" (1995), with Tony Doyle and Rufus Sewell. In 1997, Daldry signed a three-year, first look deal with Working Title Films, anticipating his move to film. He worked on the 1998 BAFTA-nominated short "Eight" before returning to the theater to direct David

Hare's monologue "Via Dolorosa", about Hare's trip to the Middle East. Playwright Lee Hall showed Daldry his screenplay about a youngster from a coal mining family who wants to be a ballet dancer instead of a miner. Hooked by the writing and the story, Daldry selected the project as his debut film "Billy Elliot" (originally called "Dancer"). For his follow-up, the director attracted top-drawer talent like Meryl Streep, Julianne Moore and Ed Harris as co-stars in his powerful, emotional film version of Michael Cunningham's Pulitzer-winning "The Hours" (2002). Telling three loosely inter-related stories about author Virginia Woolf, a Los Angeles housewife and a middle-aged lesbian coping with the terminal illness of her best male friend, the film allowed its leading ladies to shine and transitioned nimbly and cleverly between the three storylines and historical eras without feeling forced or gimmicky. Daldry's skill with both his actresses and his storytelling techinque was recognized with a wealth of critical accolades and awards nods, including an Academy Award nomination as Best Director.

MILESTONES:

Joined youth drama group in Taunton

1985–1988: Worked as associate artist for Crucible Theatre in Sheffield

1988: Acted in a production of "Prometheus in Evin"

1989: Began directing stage productions at The Gate Theater in West London; remained associated with The Gate until 1992

Served as artistic director at the Royal Court Theater

1992: First came to international prominence with the revival of "An Inspector Calls"

1994: Broadway debut, repeating his staging of the acclaimed revival of "An Inspector Calls"; won Tony Award

1995: Staged the acclaimed revival of "Rat in the Skull", starring Tony Doyle and Rufus Sewell

1996: Helmed a BBC documentary on The Royal Court Theatre

1997: Signed a three-year, first-look directing deal with Working Title Films

Formed Stephen Daldry Productions

1998: Co-directed the short film "Eight", which received a BAFTA nomination

1998: Directed David Hare in the one-person show "Via Dolorosa" in London and on Broadway

2000: Feature film debut as director, "Dancer"; premiered at the Cannes Film Festival; title later changed to "Billy Elliot"; nominated for a Best Director Oscar

2000: Directed the British stage production "Far Away" at The Royal Court; moved to the West End in January 2001

2002: Helmed second film, an adaptation of Michael Cunningham's Pulitzer-winning novel "The Hours"; received nominations for a Golden Globe, a BAFTA and an Oscar for his achievement in directing

AFFILIATION: Member of charitable trust which purchased the Old Vic Theatre in London

QUOTES:

"To his admirers, Daldry is a hyeractive bubble of charm, brains and balls. . . . "—From the London *Times*, September 2, 1998.

"At a very basic level, Stephen took a total non-actor and taught me the craft. From the first day, he was saying, 'You cannot do this as an animated lecture; you have to act it, whatever it means.' And I basically recoiled. But Stephen made it clear that unless I put myself on the line and made myself the subject, the play wouldn't work. He was forever encouraging me to be bolder and more emotional."—David Hare on his collaboration with Daldry on "Via Dolorosa", quoted in *The New York Times*, March 14, 1999.

On his approach to his first film, Daldry told the *Los Angeles Times* (January 23, 2000): "My plan on this was quite consciously to go with a vey simple filmic language, just to learn what the language was. I decided not to try to be very clever, not to do self-conscious shots or move the camera around for no particular reason. It's not that I don't like films like that. I do. But for a first-time film director, the danger is in trying to run before you can walk."

About "Billy Elliot", Daldry told *The Guardian* (October 3, 2000): "To be frank about it, it was—is—a small budget British film that faced struggles in its making. But it was also a good working context, in that it became very special to the people working on it. It was a real surprise the way the Cannes audience responded to it; in Croatia they responded in the same way. I've just come back from three weeks touring it in the US, and it amazes me that what is essentially a small British film can have such a cross-cultural, cross-nationality reaction."

BIBLIOGRAPHY:

"A Director Calls: Stephen Daldry and the Theatre" Wendy Lesser, 1997, University of California Press

Frank Darabont

BORN: in France, 01/28/1959

NATIONALITY: Hungarian

CITIZENSHIP: United States

EDUCATION: Hollywood High School, Hollywood, California

AWARDS: Humanitas Prize Best Screenplay "The Shawshank Redemption" 1995; prize given by Human Family Institute included $25,000 cash award which Darabont gave to charity

Broadcast Film Critics Association Award Best Adapted Screenplay "The Green Mile" 1999

People's Choice Award Favorite Motion Picture "The Green Mile" 2001

People's Choice Award Favorite Dramatic Motion Picture "The Green Mile" 2001

BIOGRAPHY

A screenwriter-turned-director, Frank Darabont initially entered the film industry as production assistant and set dresser before he got a break when he sold an original screenplay (eventually produced in 1997 and aired on HBO) to producer Jere Henshaw and Apollo Pictures. The son of Hungarian refugees, he was born in a French relocation camp and raised in Chicago and Southern California. Eschewing college for a crack at a career in films, Darabont was driven by his goals. With several friends, he acquired the rights to a Stephen King short story "Woman in the Room" and fashioned a 30-minute short that eventually aired on cable outlets and was released to video. Darabont received his first screenplay credit when he helped director Chuck Russell rewrite "A Nightmare on Elm Street III: Dream Warriors" (1987). The film's popularity and Darabont's long-standing love of horror films led to his penning screenplays for the remake "The Blob" (1988), the sequel "The Fly II" (1989) and several episodes of TV's "Tales from the Crypt." He cut his teeth as a producer on a TV horror flick, "Buried Alive" (USA Network, 1990) and began to branch out from scary material writing for the ABC adventure series, "The Young Indiana Jones Chronicles" (1992).

Darabont crafted his most ambitious, adult work to date adapting another Stephen King work, the novella "Rita Hayworth and the Shawshank Redemption." (The feature's title was shortened to "The Shawshank Redemption") Offered a healthy $2.4 million for his adaptation, he held out for the chance to direct—the result was a critically praised prison story about an unusual but powerful friendship between a level-headed banker convicted of murdering his wife and a seasoned lifer with a knack for acquisitions. The film earned seven Oscar nominations including Best Picture, and for his efforts, Darabont earned nominations from the Directors Guild, the Writers Guild and the Academy (for Best Adapted Screenplay).

Despite several projects in development, it took four years before his next film reached theaters. Darabont reportedly assisted on the screenplay for the WWII drama "Saving Private Ryan" (1998) for director Steven Spielberg, but final screen credit went to writer Robert Rodat. He returned to the director's chair to undertake the screen adaptation of another Stephen King opus, "The Green Mile" (1999), starring Tom Hanks and relative newcomer Michael Clark Duncan. Set on death row in a Louisiana prison in the 1930s, the film focused one particular prisoner with seemingly miraculous powers (Duncan) and his relationship with the other inmates as well as the senior guard (Hanks). Darabont once again proved to be the perfect adapter for King's work, crafting a script that was entirely faithful to the original. His direction stressed the relationships in the film and allowed each actor (including David Morse, Doug Hutchison, Michael Jeter and Sam Rockwell) to contribute solid performances.—Written by David Lugowski

MILESTONES:

Born in a French relocation camp after parents fled their home following the 1956 Hungarian Uprising

Moved with family to Chicago while still an infant

Raised in Illinois and California

1981: First film credit, working as a production assistant on the horror film, "Hell Night"

1983: With a group of friends, acquired the rights to a Stephen King short story, "Woman in the Room"; eventually wrote, produced and directed a 30-minute adaptation of the story which was later aired on some cable stations and released to video

1984: Received credit as a set dresser on Ken Russell's "Crimes of Passion"

Sold a screenplay entitled "Black Cat Run" to producer Jere Henshaw and Apollo Pictures

1987: First screenplay credit, "A Nightmare on Elm Street III: Dream Warriors"

1990: Received a nomination for a Writers Guild of America Award for "The Ventriloquist's Dummy", an episode of the HBO horror anthology series, "Tales from the Crypt"

1990: First credit as producer, the USA Network TV-movie, "Buried Alive"

1992–1993: Wrote several episodes of the ABC adventure series, "The Young Indiana Jones Chronicles"

1993: Was offered $2.4 million for his screenplay adaptation of Stephen King's short story, "Rita Hayworth and the Shawshank Redemption" by Rob Reiner of Castle Rock Productions, with the chance to also direct another film; Darabont turned it down because he also wanted to direct the film based on his screenplay (date approximate)

1994: Did screenplay rewrites for Kenneth Branagh's feature, "Mary Shelley's Frankenstein"

1994: Release of feature directorial debut, "The Shawshank Redemption"; film earned seven Oscar nominations including Best Picture and Best Adapted Screenplay for Darabont

Reportedly assisted on the scripts for the prequels to "Star Wars"

1997: Had small role in the TV miniseries version of King's "The Shining", directed by Mick Garris

1998: Executive produced and scripted the HBO film "Black Cat Run"

1998: Reportedly worked on the script to "Saving Private Ryan", directed by Steven Spielberg and starring Tom Hanks; Robert Rodat, however, received sole credit

1999: Returned to filmmaking at the helm of "The Green Mile", an adaptation of Stephen King's novel starring Hanks; also produced and scripted; received Oscar nominations for Best Picture and Best Screenplay

Reportedly did rewrites on the script for "Minority Report"; project put on hold and then later shot with a screenplay credited to other writers

2001: Returned to filmmaking at the helm of "The Majestic", starring Jim Carrey; also co-wrote screenplay

QUOTES:

Frank Darabont did not go to college, he explains, because "it was either be a bag person sleeping in a cardboard box, or make it in the film industry."—From *Premiere*, October 1994.

"If you're going to succeed, you've got to be like one of those punch-drunk fighters in the old Warner Bros. boxing pictures: too stupid to fall down, you just keep slugging and stay on your feet."—Frank Darabont in *Premiere*, October 1994.

Darabont earned nominations from the DGA in both 1994 and 1999 for "The Shawshank Redemption" and "The Green Mile" respectively. In both instances, he was overlooked in the Oscar category of Best Director, but received nods for Best Picture and Best Screenplay.

Julie Dash

BORN: in New York, New York, 10/22/1952

SOMETIMES CREDITED AS:
Julie Dash Fielder

NATIONALITY: American

EDUCATION: Studio Museum, New York, New York; studied film making in Harlem in the late 1960s

City College of New York, New York, New York, film production graduated

American Film Institute Los Angeles, California; studied film as an undergraduate

University of California at Los Angeles, Los Angeles, California; studied at film school in the 1970s

AWARD: American Film Institute Maya Deren Award 1993

BIOGRAPHY

Independent African-American filmmaker whose first short, "Diary of an African Nun" (1977), was adapted from a short story by Alice Walker. "Four Women" (1978) is a "choreopoem" based on the Nina Simone song of the

same title and "Illusions" (1982) is about a black woman executive passing for white in 1940s Hollywood.

After almost six years of fundraising, Dash completed her first feature, "Daughters of the Dust" (1992). Set at the turn of the century, the stunningly photographed film is an impressionistic portrait of an African-American family—descendants of West African slaves—just as they are about to give up their insular customs and unique "Gullah" language to travel north to the newly industrialized land of "milk and honey". "Daughters" was the first feature-length film by an American-born black female filmmaker to be released commercially in the United States.

MILESTONES:

Raised in the Queensridge housing projects in Long Island City, New York

1968: First became interested in film making when she visited a friend at a film workshop at the Studio Museum in Harlem

1978: Directed first film, "Four Women"

1991: Directed, wrote and co-produced first feature film, "Daughters of the Dust"

1999: Helmed the TV-movie "Funny Valentines" (BET/Starz!)

QUOTES:

"It is a matter of black people putting up money to finance their own projects . . . and a matter of getting Hollywood to put its marketing dollars—and its faith—into offbeat black films or those not centered on hormone-driven adolescents. 'Waiting to Exhale' made $100 million worldwide. Where's our 'English Patient'? Where's our 'Schindler's List'? Where's our 'Unbearable Lightness of Being'? I know alternative films are appreciated. They are life-enhancing, if you will. I know how I feel when I see a good film."—Julie Dash to *The New York Times*, December 3, 1997.

"I like telling stories and controllng worlds. In my world, black women can do anything. They ride horses and fly from trapezes; they are in the future as well as in the past."—Julie Dash in *The New York Times*, February 13, 1992.

"The image of the black revolutionary was neutralized through caricature during the blaxploitation era. He was made to seem weak and a phony. Now there exists a fear of black people using our culture to make statements in code. It's the modern variation on the fear that led slaveholders to take our drums away."—Julie Dash quoted in *Village Voice*, April 12, 1988.

"Dash's personal demeanor suggests both dreamy-eyed fabulist and focused professional. Her attitude on the set is casual but only because her preproduction work is meticulous . . . Day charts detail the entire two-week shoot [her grant monies only carrying her part way through production]. Once Dash sets up her shots, and sound and camera get rolling, the action plays until the takes sync with her vision. Her mood on the set is chillmaximus."—Greg Tate (*The Village Voice*, April 12, 1988).

Tamra L Davis

BORN: Tamra L Davis in Los Angeles, California, 11/26/1962

NATIONALITY: American

EDUCATION: Los Angeles City College, Los Angeles, California, cinema

BIOGRAPHY

Prolific video director Tamra Davis showed promise with her initial leap to feature filmmaking "Guncrazy" (aired on Showtime in 1992 in lieu of theatrical release), though her subsequent directorial efforts didn't entirely live up to those high expectations. Married to Mike D of the Beastie Boys, Davis earned a reputation as a hipster auteur with credits on several videos by Sonic Youth and The Lemonheads as well as films like "Guncrazy" and "Best Men" (1997), but remained commercially viable thanks to work with Hanson

("Mmmbop"), Cher ("I've Got You Babe") and Adam Sandler ("Billy Madison").

The California native served an apprenticeship under Francis Ford Coppola at his Zoetrope studios early on in her career and racked up experience there and with her own independent projects, including the documentary look at Latino gangs "Vida Loca" and shorts starring Ione Skye and Bette Midler. Though the artist-oriented market of 1980s videos meant she didn't get much fame or even credit as the director of such hit music videos as Tone Loc's "Wild Thing" and The Bangles' "In Your Room", the projects were a good start for the budding director.

In 1992, Davis made her feature film debut with "Guncrazy", an ambitious and offbeat crime thriller starring Drew Barrymore and James Le Gros. Screened at festivals, the film won the director accolades before it found an audience on Showtime. The following year,

Davis helmed "CB4", a comedy chronicling the rise and fall of a fictional gangsta rap group hailing from the suburbs. Starring Chris Rock and featuring some well-observed bits of truly inspired comedy, many critics opined that the film fell short of its mark due to a lack of cohesion. 1994 saw Davis return to music with "No Alternative Girls", a behind-the-scenes look at female rock bands including Luscious Jackson, Bikini Kill and the Courtney Love–fronted Hole.

After being replaced by director Jonathan Kaplan during the making of the fashionable western "Bad Girls", Davis reached the mainstream and had great box-office success with 1995's "Billy Madison", a broad comedy that marked Adam Sandler's starring debut. She followed up with the quirkier "Best Men", a character-driven bank robbery film that reunited Davis with "Guncrazy" and "Bad Girls" star Drew Barrymore. Having consistently moonlighted as a video director, Davis gained a higher profile when outlets like MTV began crediting helmers onscreen, and her sunny 70s take on the oddly accomplished bubble gum pop of Hanson with the 1997 videos "Mmmbop" and "Where's the Love?" introduced the director to a new, younger audience. In 1998, she directed the decidedly more R-rated "Half-Baked", an at times very funny but ultimately less-than-satisfying update of the stoner comedy.

The reviews of Davis' period romance "Skipped Parts" (released direct-to-video in 2001) were mixed, with most critics conceding that the 60s-set coming-of-age tale had its heart in the right place, but missed something in the execution. Davis followed up with "Crossroads" (2002), a road movie about three young women and one young man on a cross-country car ride. The premise sounded innocuous enough, but cast in the lead role was pop superstar Britney Spears, a fact that would bring many running into the theater but would also send many others fleeing in the opposite direction. The negative initial response from critics and the cringe-inducing trailer didn't help to put non-fans in seats, but Davis' determination to taking on a project reviled from its outset showed what might have been described as a fiercely independent spirit despite the film's obvious commercial focus.—Written by Jane O'Donnell

COMPANION:
husband: Mike Diamond. Musician; member of the Beastie Boys

MILESTONES:
Served an apprenticeship under Francis Ford Coppola at his Zoetrope Studios
1988: Directed the videos for the crossover rap hit "Wild Thing" by Tone Loc and "In Your Room" by The Bangles
Directed "Vida Loca", a documentary about Latino gang culture
Helmed several videos for seminal indie rock band Sonic Youth including 1990's "Kool Thing" and 1994's "Bull in the Heather"
1992: Made feature directorial debut with the independent crime drama "Guncrazy", starring Drew Barrymore (debuted on Showtime in lieu of theatrical release)
1993: Directed "CB4", the comedic story of the rise and fall of a fictional middle class "gangsta" rap group
1993: Was set to direct the western "Bad Girls", featuring Drew Barrymore; replaced by Jonathan Kaplan
1994: Helmed the music documentary short "No Alternative Girls"; screened at the 1995 Toronto International Film Festival
1995: Directed the popular Adam Sandler vehicle "Billy Madison"; replaced original director Stephen Kessler who left over "creative differences"
1997: Helmed the quirky crime drama "Best Men"
1997: Directed the videos for the Hanson hits "Mmmbop" and "Where's the Love?"
1998: Directed the marijuana-fueled comedy "Half-Baked"

2000: Was executive producer and director of the period romance "Skipped Parts"; released direct-to-video in 2001

2002: Helmed "Crossroads", a road movie starring Britney Spears

Jan de Bont

BORN: in Amsterdam, The Netherlands, 10/22/1943

NATIONALITY: Dutch

EDUCATION: studied at film academies in Amsterdam and Cologne

AWARDS: Kodak Camera Award given for his cinematography work in Holland

Rembrandt Award 1992; given for his cinematography; the Dutch equivalent of the "People's Choice Award"

MTV Movie Award Best Action Sequence "Speed" 1995

MTV Movie Award Best Action Sequence "Twister" 1997

BIOGRAPHY

An experienced Dutch director of photography who began his career in 1961 before collaborating with Paul Verhoeven on the director's first film, "Wat Zien Ik/Business Is Business" (1971), De Bont subsequently worked with Verhoeven on films including "Turkish Delight" (1973) and "Keetje Tippel" (1975). De Bont also worked with other Dutch filmmakers, notably George Sluizer ("Joao" 1972), and developed a reputation as a talented, indeed often flamboyant, craftsman.

De Bont first worked in the US on the teen comedy-drama "Private Lessons" (1981), already suggesting the voyeuristic nature of many of his later films, as a randy teenager stalks his father's housekeeper with a camera. The drug addiction drama, "I'm Dancing as Fast as I Can" (1981), did not quite seem like suitable material, but after reuniting with Verhoeven for the lurid but striking erotic thriller "The Fourth Man" (1982), De Bont became one of Hollywood's leading cinematographers, specializing in rough-and-tumble action drama and often outlandish sex-themed material. The formulaic sports picture "All the Right Moves" (1983) had suitably gritty cinematography, but De Bont did better with the rollicking adventure "Jewel of the Nile" (1985) and the garishly colored farce "Ruthless People" (1986).

De Bont's deliberately intrusive visual style calls attention to his slick frame compositions and glossy mise en scene, while also indulging a formidable prowess at camera movement. "Die Hard" (1988), a punchy action pic, embodied all these qualities and offered a strong argument that contemporary Hollywood's one true forte is an intoxicating flair for creating all the thrills that technological know-how can provide. "Black Rain" (1989), a collaboration with another visually authoritative artist, Ridley Scott, had little to offer but its look. "The Hunt for Red October" (1990) was a very popular reteaming with "Die Hard" director John McTiernan while "Lethal Weapon 3" (1992) was at least a watchable, workmanlike example of its genre. "Basic Instinct" (1992) again reunited De Bont with Verhoeven for for another flashy psychodrama, with camera angles designed as the last word in empty-headed kinkiness.

Having provided such showy craftsmanship on so many hit films, it was no surprise when the veteran De Bont was finally given a chance to direct a film. Situating himself solidly in the realm in which he has been most assured—the visceral—he came up with

"Speed" (1994), widely categorized as "Die Hard on a Bus." Critical acclaim was unanimous: of course no one expected rich characterizations, complex thematics or a heart on a sleeve. What people hoped for were some exciting variations on film narrative's oldest formula, the chase, and that is what De Bont delivered—in spades. Modestly budgeted for a large-scale Hollywood action pic—$30 million—"Speed" proved the first sleeper hit of that summer and greatly improved the fortunes of stars Keanu Reeves and Sandra Bullock. Offers also poured in for the suddenly hot director. De Bont was attached to a ultra-big-budget remake of "Godzilla" before he got swept up into "Twister" (1996), a special-effects oriented thriller from Amblin Entertainment about scientists who chase and study tornadoes. As with "Speed", De Bont avoided casting the usual "bankable" big names, opting instead for Bill Paxton, Helen Hunt and Cary Elwes. With "Speed 2: Cruise Control" (1997), the director stumbled a bit. Instead of a simple thrilling story as in the original, the sequel upped the ante. Set on a hijacked luxury liner, the film was merely a series of overstaged set pieces that overshadowed its stars Sandra Bullock and Jason Patric. Based on the film's disappointing box-office performance, it was unlikely a third entry in the series would be on De Bont's slate. Instead, he tackled a lackluster remake of the 1963 cult horror classic "The Legend of Hill House" titled "The Haunting" (1999) that despite an all-star ensemble that included Liam Neeson, Catherine Zeta-Jones, Owen Wilson and Lili Taylor played to only ghostly audiences. De Bont also developed a reputation as something of an autocrat on his sets. He eased away from directing briefly, instead lending his producing skills to the sci-fi films "Minority Report" (2002), directed by Steven Spielberg, and writer-director Kurt Wimmer's "Equalibrium" (2002). De Bont returned to the director's chair in 2003 to helm "Lara Croft, Tomb Raider: The Cradle of Life," a superior sequel starring Angelina Jolie as the pneumatic video game heroine.—Written by David Lugowski

MILESTONES:

1967: Began working as a director of photography in his native country, the Netherlands; first film, "Paranoia", directed by Adrian Ditvoorst

1971: Began successful collaboration with Paul Verhoeven as the director of photography on Verhoeven's feature debut, "Wat Zien Ik/Business Is Business"

1977: Moved to Los Angeles

1981: First American film as cinematographer, "Private Lessons"

1982: Earliest American TV work included credit as cinematographer on a presentation of the "CBS Afternoon Playhouse", "Help Wanted"

1983: Shot first US TV miniseries, "Sadat"

1985: Served as cinematographer on his first US TV-movie, "Heart of a Champion: The Ray Mancini Story"

1992: Nominated for a CableACE Award for best direction of photography in a comedy or dramatic series for "Split Personality", an episode of HBO's "Tales from the Crypt" directed by producer Joel Silver

1994: Feature directorial debut, "Speed"

1994: Signed a two-year first look deal with Fox

BORN: Brian Russell de Palma in Newark, New Jersey, 09/11/1940

SOMETIMES CREDITED AS:
Brian DePalma

NATIONALITY: American

EDUCATION: Friends Central School, Philadelphia, Pennsylvania, a Quaker institution

Columbia University, New York, New York, fine arts and physics, BA, 1962; member of drama group, the Columbia Players; after making two movies switched major from physics to fine arts

Sarah Lawrence College, Bronxville, New York, MA; attended on MCA writing fellowship; made first feature film

BIOGRAPHY

Brian De Palma has attained an unusual position in contemporary Hollywood filmmaking over the last several decades. Straddling generic and critical categories, his work has claimed fervent supporters and detractors. Now often hailed (and marketed) as the 'Modern Master of Suspense', De Palma has roots in the rarefied soil of the NYC avant-garde theater. He began as a "committed" New York–based independent filmmaker whose left-leaning countercultural comedies of the late 1960s and early 70s owed much to the early films of Jean-Luc Godard (e.g., the 1966 political comedy "Masculine-Feminine"). Later dismissed in some quarters as a purveyor of bloody, misogynistic generic sleaze, he graduated to helming a number of big-budget A-list films with such top-drawer stars as Al Pacino, John Travolta, Sean Connery and Robert De Niro. Rarely classified as an actors' director, De Palma has elicited an impressive number of acclaimed performances (e.g., Sissy Spacek in "Carrie", Sean Penn in "Carlito's

Way"). Not one to be pinned down, De Palma has continued to confound categories.

De Palma earned "street" credibility among action fans by helming slick yet tough crime dramas ("Scarface" 1983; "The Untouchables" 1987; "Carlito's Way" 1993) but his fluent, inventive and defiantly excessive cinematic style also made him a darling of cineastes. The now-classic prom sequence in "Carrie" (1976), with its use of the split screen, slow-motion and cross-cutting, typified the rich versatility of De Palma's craft. The "alternative" politically-minded press gave serious attention to "Casualties of War" (1989), an ambitious cinematic excursion into Vietnam. Even his most notorious flop, a problematic adaptation of Tom Wolfe's novel "Bonfire of the Vanities" (1990), was deemed a significant cultural event worthy of a book-length chronicle of its production.

De Palma's thrillers have paid extensive homage to Hitchcock—indeed they often flirt with plagiarism. Examples abound: "Sisters" (1973) owed a large debt to both "Psycho" (1960) and "Rear Window" (1954); "Obsession" (1976) reworked "Vertigo" (1958); "Dressed to Kill" (1980) was a slick take on "Psycho"; and "Body Double" (1984) was a gratuitous return to the themes of "Vertigo" and "Rear Window." De Palma's films, however, differ strikingly in subject matter and technique. Furthermore, Hitchcock has hardly been his sole cinematic reference—Eisenstein, Antonioni and Michael Powell have been similarly referenced. De Palma presented his own version of the Odessa Steps sequence from "Potemkin" (1925) in "The Untouchables", "Blow-Up" (1966) informed "Blow Out" (1981) and "Peeping Tom" (1960) was just one of the sources evoked by "Raising Cain" (1992). Although he has been criticized for portraying graphic violence, De Palma has retorted that he has incorporated Eisenstein's theory of montage as conflict, that "film 'is' violence." Stylization acts to aesthetically distance De Palma's violence so that it becomes a visual effect rather than a naturalistic detail.

De Palma began making films as a student, first at Columbia, later at Sarah Lawrence. His 1962 short, "Wotan's Wake", won him several awards and his first feature film. "The Wedding Party" (produced in 1966; released in 1969) is best remembered as the feature debut of Robert De Niro and Jill Clayburgh. "Greetings" (1968) and its sequel, "Hi, Mom" (1970), were inventive, uneven, and exceedingly low-budget ($43,000 and $120,000 respectively) films shot on the streets of NYC during the tumultuous Vietnam era. These works revealed the young De Palma attempting to be an American Godard, making challenging and critical films that commented on contemporary politics, film history and the nature of the medium. The films had a raw documentary immediacy that was enhanced by improvisatory performances, long takes and location shooting.

Beginning with "Carrie", his commercial breakthrough, De Palma's work began to explore recurrent themes and narrative patterns. The framing device of the dream/nightmare brackets films as diverse as "Dressed to Kill" and "Casualties of War." Many of his features have portrayed a failed attempt to rescue an endangered female, as most tragically played out in "Blow Out." De Palma's fascination with the dual role of the gifted young person as a heroic ideal and outsider is illustrated in "Carrie" and "The Fury" (1978) while a subtext of family romance and Oedipal conflict underlies the psychological power of De Palma's vision. Such elements as the search for the father, repressed incestuous desire and sibling rivalry appear in several of his films. The complex narrative structures of "Obsession", "The Fury" and "Raising Cain" examine these themes with particular force. De Palma also explores the dynamics of sadomasochism and voyeurism in "Body Double", "Dressed to Kill" and "Blow Out."

De Palma has utilized genre to explore social and ethical tensions that deconstruct the American mythos. Possible paranoid conspiracy and power politics shape the ethical dilemmas of the several of his young heroes (e.g., "Mission: Impossible" 1996). While De Palma may peripherally examine larger social issues of institutional, professional and political corruption (notably "The Untouchables") the director regards himself as an artist and not a polemicist. Even "Carrie", which explores the social conformity and cruelty of teenage bonding, essentially parodies itself through De Palma's characteristic black humor. Moreover, one can argue that even an overtly political thriller like "Blow Out" is as much about a film artist's disenchantment with technique as it is about a citizen losing faith in the System.

Although De Palma has worked primarily in the psychological thriller genre—a frankly commercial move after the nearly career destroying debacle of "Get to Know Your Rabbit" (1972)—elements of comedy, romance, horror and gangster melodramas are explored as well. Adept at urban location shooting, De Palma has brought to the screen the visual ambiance of such cities as Chicago, New York, Philadelphia, New Orleans and Florence. Even "Casualties of War", an anomaly in genre and location, nevertheless begins and ends on a San Francisco train.

De Palma's most important contributions to contemporary cinema lie in his inventive, visually-dynamic style. He frequently employs such techniques as the stalking, searching camera, split screens, slow motion, "God's eye" point-of-view shots, and an expressively detailed mise-en-scene. A master of rhythmic editing, he has often opened his films with extended, viscerally composed sequences that confirm his status as one of the great stylists of contemporary American cinema (most recently in "Snake Eyes" 1998). Nonetheless, his commercial status has remained inconstant.

The success of "The Untouchables" raised De Palma's stock in Hollywood and gave him the freedom to direct "Casualties of War." This worthy project was probably not expected to rake in box-office receipts but "Bonfire of the Vanities", prior to release, showed every sign of being commercial. After that debacle (which still has its devoted admirers), De Palma returned to his once reliable medium budget thriller mode, helming "Raising Cain" as if in penance for the excesses of "Bonfire." When this underrated jet black comedy failed to win over critics or audiences, he reteamed with "Scarface" star Al Pacino (who had just won the Best Actor Oscar) to make a presumably popular gangster movie ("Carlito's Way") which fizzled at the box office. De Palma then directed superstar-producer Tom Cruise in "Mission: Impossible", and though his first excursion into the high-tech world of special effects-driven action spectaculars necessitated his spending five months of post production at friend George Lucas' Industrial Light and Magic Land, the result was his biggest hit since "The Untouchables", earning him carte blanche in choosing his next picture, "Snake Eyes" (1998). This thriller, however, disappeared quickly after opening with a bang on the strength of De Palma and star Nicolas Cage's names. Even more poorly received was 2000's "Mission to Mars," which contained a handful of powerful kicky images that were in line with De Palma's bag of visual tricks, but they—and the top-flight cast of Tim Robbins, Gary Sinise, Don Cheadel and Connie Neilson—were not enough to pump life into the longwinded, uninspired script. Continuing to reaffirm his reputation for adding visual panache and razzle-dazzle to material clearly beneath his cinematic talents, De Palma attempted to return to erotic thriller territory in 2002 with his self-penned "Femme Fatale," which was ultimately received as an anemic version of his more effective work.—Written by Kent Greene

COMPANIONS:

Margot Kidder. Actor; had relationship in early 1970s

Betty Buckley. Actor, Singer; had relationship before filming of "Carrie"

wife: Nancy Allen. Actor; married in 1979; divorced

Beth Broderick. Actor; appeared in "The Bonfire of the Vanities"; together c. 1989–90

wife: Gale Anne Hurd. Producer; married on July 20, 1991; separated in September 1992; divorced

wife: Darnelle De Palma. Ballerina; met c. 1993; married in October 1995; filed for separation in April 1996; divorced

MILESTONES:

Raised in Philadelphia

1960: Made first film, "Icarus" (16mm, 40 mins), while at Columbia

1962: Earned MCA writing fellowship to Sarah Lawrence on strength of third student film, "Wotan's Wake"

1963: Began co-directing, co-writing, and co-editing (with Wilford Leach and Cynthia Munroe) first feature, "The Wedding Party" (completed in 1966; released in 1969); also initial collaboration with actor Robert De Niro

Shot "The Responsive Eye", a record of the opening of the 'Op' art show at the Museum of Modern Art in NYC, in four hours

Made documentaries for the US Treasury Department

1968: Directed, wrote and edited his first theatrical feature, "Greetings", featuring De Niro

1972: Directed first Hollywood production for Warner Bros., "Get To Know Your Rabbit", a vehicle for Tommy Smothers; fired from the film; reworked by studio before release

1973: Directed "Sisters", his first thriller; also scripted from his story

1976: Commercial breakthrough, "Carrie", based on the Stephen King novel and starring Sissy Spacek as a teenager with psykokinetic powers; first of five movies directing then-wife

Nancy Allen; also marked initial collaborations with composer Pino Donaggio and actors John Travolta and Amy Irving

1978: Continued his study of psychokinetic powers with "The Fury", starring Kirk Douglas and Amy Irving

1979: Debut as a producer, "Home Movies"; also directed and contributed story; second teaming with Douglas, Allen and Donaggio

1980: Wrote and directed high tension melodrama "Dressed to Kill", featuring a chilling score by Donaggio and an appearance by Allen

1981: Emulated Michelangelo Antonioni with "Blow Out", which reteamed him with Travolta; last film directing Allen

1983: First pairing with Al Pacino, "Scarface"

1987: Scored huge commercial success with "The Untouchables"; film featured Robert De Niro as Al Capone

1989: Directed compelling Vietnam War tale, "Casualties of War"; first collaboration with Sean Penn

1990: Bombed with "Bonfire of the Vanities"

1992: Returned to the world of the medium budget thriller for "Raising Cain" with little success; sixth and (to date) last collaboration with Donaggio

1993: Reteamed with Pacino and Penn for "Carlito's Way"

1996: Raised stock considerably helming the blockbuster "Mission: Impossible", produced by and starring Tom Cruise

1998: Fizzled with "Snake Eyes", despite promising opening: a 12-minute continuous steadicam shot

2000: Directed the little-seen sci-fi film "Mission to Mars"

2002: Wrote and directed the erotic thriller "Femme Fatale" starring Rebecca Romijn-Stamos and Antonio Banderas

QUOTES:

A film by De Palma is never accidental in any detail. He can offer a financier a precise prospectus: "Those are the actors, there's every shot of the picture, there's the script. You get exactly what you see there. I'm not a director like Francis Coppola or Marty Scorsese, who shoot so much material and work variations on a theme, trying to discover something as they are shooting. That's fine. but that's a whole different way of working. For Francis and Marty, their movies are almost created in the editing. For me, it's just finishing the design."—From *The Movie Brats* by Michael Pye and Lynda Myles (New York: Holt, Rinehart and Winston, 1979).

"I think I first saw the irony when I was out on a publicity tour for "Greetings," he says. "I am in the midst of a society that is very capitalist, and whose values I completely reject. But I, too, became a capitalist. The problem is that by dealing with the devil, you become devilish to a certain extent. You need the machine. And once you use it, you are a tainted human being. . . . You can make message pictures, you can lead a Simon-pure life, but the very fact that you are in that world at all makes you a compromised individual. People who think they're going to sanitize this business, make it straight and honorable, are absolutely crazy."—From *The Movie Brats* by Michael Pye and Lynda Myles (New York: Holt, Rinehart and Winston, 1979).

His example, still, is Orson Welles, the master he cast as a magician and teacher in "Get to Know Your Rabbit". "Just look at our gods," he says, "Look at Welles. He's the greatest director in the world, and he can't get a job and he's sold out. Totally. Orson Welles on the Johnny Carson show doesn't give us much to hope for. That is the story of this business."—From *The Movie Brats* by Michael Pye and Lynda Myles (New York: Holt, Rinehart and Winston, 1979).

"There is a self-conscious cunning in De Palma's work, ready to control everything except his own cruelty and indifference. He is the epitome of mindless style and excitement swamping taste or character. Of course, he was a brilliant kid. But his usefulness in an historical survey is to point out the dangers of movies falling into the hands of such narrow movie-mania, such cold-blooded prettification. I daresay there are no 'ugly' shots in De Palma's films—if you feel able to measure 'beauty' merely in terms of graceful or hypnotic movement, vivid angles, lyrical color, and hysterical situation. But that is the set of criteria that makes Leni Riefenstahl a 'great' director, rather than the victim of conflicting inspiration and decadence." —David Thomson, *A Biographical Dictionary of Film* (NY: Alfred A. Knopf, 1994).

"De Palma's eye is cut off from conscience or compassion. He has contempt for his characters and his audience alike, and I suspect that he despises his own immaculate skill. Our cultural weakness admires and rewards technique and impact bereft of moral sense. If the thing works, it has validity—the means justify the lack of an end. De Palma is a cynic, and not a feeble one; there are depths of misanthropy there."—David Thomson, *A Biographical Dictionary of Film* (NY: Alfred A. Knopf, 1994).

BIBLIOGRAPHY:

"Brian De Palma" Michael Bliss, 1983, Scarecrow Press

"Devil's Candy: The Bonfire of the Vanities Goes to Hollywood" Julie Salamon, 1991, Houghton Mifflin

Vittorio de Sica

BORN: in Sora, Italy, 07/07/1902

DEATH: in Paris, France, 11/13/1974

NATIONALITY: Italian

CITIZENSHIP: France 1968

AWARDS: National Board of Review Award Best Film "The Bicycle Thief" 1949

National Board of Review Award Best Director "The Bicycle Thief" 1949

New York Film Critics Circle Award Best Foreign Film "The Bicycle Thief" 1949

Golden Globe Award Best Foreign Film "The Bicycle Thief" 1949

British Film Academy Award Best Film "The Bicycle Thief" 1949

New York Film Critics Circle Award Best Foreign Film "Miracle in Milan" 1951

Cannes Film Festival Grand Prize "Miracle in Milan" 1951; shared award with Alf Sjoberg's "Miss Julie"

New York Film Critics Circle Award Best

Foreign Film "Umberto D." 1955, tied with Clouzot's "Diabolique"

Berlin Film Festival Golden Bear "The Garden of the Finzi-Continis" 1971

BIOGRAPHY

Italian director Vittorio De Sica was also a notable actor who appeared in over 100 films, to which he brought the same charm and brightness which infused his work behind the camera.

By 1918, at the age of 16, De Sica had already begun to dabble in stage work and in 1923 he joined Tatiana Pavlova's theater company. His good looks and breezy manner made him an overnight matinee idol in Italy with the release of his first sound picture, "La Vecchia Signora" (1931). De Sica turned to directing during WWII, with his first efforts typical of the light entertainments of the time. It was with "The Children are Watching Us" (1942) that he began to use nonprofessional actors and socially conscious subject matter. The film was also his first of many collaborations with scenarist Cesare Zavattini, a combination which shaped the postwar Italian Neorealist movement.

With the end of the war, De Sica's films began to express the personal as well as collective struggle to deal with the social problems of post-Mussolini Italy. "Shoeshine" (1946), "The Bicycle Thief" (1948) and "Umberto D" (1952) combined classic neorealist traits—working-class settings, anti-authoritarianism, emotional sincerity—with technical and compositional sophistication and touches of poignant humor.

De Sica continued his career as an actor with sufficient success to finance some of his directorial projects, playing a host of twinkling-eyed fathers and Chaplinesque figures in films such as "Pane, amore e gelosia" (1954). His later directorial career was highlighted by his work with Sophia Loren and Marcello Mastroianni in "Yesterday, Today & Tomorrow" (1963), which won the Oscar as best foreign film. After a period of decline in which he came to be perceived as a slick, rather tasteless master of burlesque, De Sica resurfaced with "The Garden of the Finzi-Continis" (1971), a baroque political romance which won him another Oscar for best foreign film.

Active to the end, De Sica appeared as himself in Ettore Scola's "We All Loved Each Other So Much" (1975), which was released after his death.

MILESTONES:

1918: Screen acting debut in "The Clemenceau Affair"

1919–1925: Acted exclusively on the stage

1940: First film as co-director (with Giuseppe Amato), "Rose Scarlatte"

1941: Solo directing debut, "Maddalena zero in condotta"

1942: First collaboration with scenarist Cesare Zavattini, "I bambini ci guardano/The Children Are Watching Us"

1954: Directed "The Gold of Naples", first of eight films with Sophia Loren

QUOTES:

"Do you know how was born the neo-realist style? After the war we have no studio, no negative, nothing. And a newspaperman ask me: 'What picture do you want to make?' And I say: 'I don't know. Maybe the boys.' Because I watch the boys on the street, the shoeshine boys. And they steal some money for a horse. And I look in Rome and find someone to give me money to make this picture.

"And I look at a man, a colleague of mine, Roberto Rossellini. And I sit on the steps and I ask Roberto: 'What you do there?' And he says: 'A lady will maybe give me some money to make a picture about a priest in Rome during the liberation. And you, Vittorio?' And I say: 'I don't know, maybe about shoeshine.' He says: 'Ah, good luck.' "—Vittorio De Sica in a 1972 interview with Jerry Tallmer quoted in *New York Post*. October 3, 1991.

Donna Deitch

BORN: Donna Eleanor Deitch in San Francisco, California, 06/08/1945

NATIONALITY: American

EDUCATION: University of California at Berkeley, Berkeley, California, art, MA

University of California at Los Angeles, Los Angeles, California, film

AWARD: Daytime Emmy Outstanding Directing in a Children's Special "The Devil's Arithmetic" 1999/2000

BIOGRAPHY

Though her feature credits have been scant to date, Donna Deitch has earned a very small but honorable place in American film history. More specifically, she has been a pioneer in the area of gay and lesbian cinematic representation as the producer and director of "Desert Hearts" (1985), generally acknowledged as the first "mainstream" feature to deal sympathetically and realistically with the lesbian experience.

Deitch purchased the film rights to Jane Rule's 1964 novel "Desert of the Hearts" and spent the next five years raising money for the production. She slowly acquired $850,000 through the sale of $1000 units to small investors and friends. Deitch also threw parties for wealthy women and persuaded them to pitch in financially. Their investment paid off as the film went on to critical acclaim and art-house success. Set in 1959, the romantic story starred Helen Shaver as a repressed, older college professor who arrives in Reno for a six-week divorce and falls for a free-spirited younger cartoonist (Patricia Charbonneau). The lush production values and accomplished performances belied the modest budget. The film inspired a generation of lesbian film-makers and audience members.

The success of "Desert Hearts" did not lead to a high-profile Hollywood feature directing career for its openly lesbian producer-director. Dissatisfied with the sexually exploitative feature screenplays she was receiving, Deitch accepted an offer from producer-actor Oprah Winfrey's Harpo Productions to direct the TV miniseries version of Gloria Naylor's lesbian-themed novel "The Women of Brewster Place" (ABC, 1989). She found TV to be a more hospitable medium than features and has continued to work there regularly, often directing episodes of such highly acclaimed drama series as "NYPD Blue", "ER" and "Murder One."

Deitch was able to more directly address her feminist concerns in her TV-movie projects. These include "Esperanza", a segment of "Prison Stories: Women on the Inside" (HBO, 1991), about an imprisoned Latina drug dealer whose son is arrested for the same crime. Another such project was "Sexual Advances" (ABC, 1992) which dealt with a female manager facing sexual harassment on the job. Deitch also helmed a female-centered genre piece, "A Change of Place" (CBS, 1994), for "Harlequin Romance Movies" on the "CBS Sunday Afternoon Showcase". Similarly, her direct-to-video erotic thriller "Criminal Passion" (1994) featured a distaff protagonist.

Hailed as one of the defining events in queer cinema, "Desert Hearts" was honored with a tenth anniversary celebration at the Los Angeles Gay and Lesbian Center. Deitch has considered making a sequel but her busy TV career gives her the luxury to wait until she can get it made her way.—Written by Kent Greene

FAMILY:

mother: Eleanor Green. Born in Hungary; died in the mid-1970s

COMPANION:

Terri Jentz. Writer; together since 1992; keep separate apartments

MILESTONES:

1971: Feature debut, served as still photographer for "Billy Jack"

1974: Filmaking debut, served as producer, director, cinematographer and editor on "Woman to Woman", a documentary "featurette"

1978: Directed the ten-minute black-and-white short, "The Great Wall of Los Angeles", about the world's longest mural

Secured the film rights to Jane Rule's 1964 novel, "Desert of the Hearts"

Spent more than five years raising the budget for the film adaptation by throwing parties for affluent women and persuading them to contribute and selling $1000 units of the film to small investors and friends

1985: Produced, directed and acted in "Desert Hearts", a landmark in the history of lesbian representation in American film

1989: TV directing debut, helmed "The Women of Brewster Place", an ABC dramatic miniseries produced by and starring Oprah Winfrey

1991: Directed "Esperanza", a segment of "Prison Stories: Women on the Inside" on "HBO Showcase"

1994: Directed the direct-to-video erotic thriller "Criminal Passion"

Directed episodes of "NYPD Blue", "ER", and "Murder One"

1996: Helmed the pilot for the ABC drama series "Second Noah"

1997: Released documentary "Angel on My Shoulder," which profiled actress Gwen Welles during her battle with, and subsequent death from, cancer in 1993

2000: Directed the Showtime drama "Common Ground"

QUOTES:

Deitch is openly lesbian.

Deitch shares a 1909 craftsman-style home in Los Angeles with two cats and a chocolate-color Labrador retriever.

" . . . Deitch has learned to draw a sharp line between her personal vision and her work for hire. 'When I'm executing someone else's vision, it's not my movie,' she says. 'It's my job. In this business that's something you have to learn to remember.'"

" 'Some directors will do only their own stuff, and they just go to meeting after meeting trying to get something off the ground—they don't work for months at a time,' Deitch observes. 'I did that for a while. But I don't want to be just pushing my own projects and not working at all if they don't get going. So now I try to find a happy medium.' "—Donna Deitch quoted in "Ten Years Gone" by Barbara Pepe, *The Advocate*, August 20, 1996.

Cecil B DeMille

BORN: Cecil Blount De Mille in Ashfield, Massachusetts, 08/12/1881

DEATH: in Hollywood, California, 01/21/1959

NATIONALITY: American

EDUCATION: Pennsylvania Military College, Pennsylvania, 1896

American Academy of Dramatic Arts, New York, New York, 1898

AWARDS: National Association of Plumbers Award "for giving the industry professional status in the eyes of the world"

Honorary Oscar 1949 to a "distinguished motion picture pioneer, for 37 years of brilliant showmanship"

Cecil B DeMille Award 1952 presented by the Hollywood Foreign Press Association; special lifetime achievement award that was named in DeMille's honor

Golden Globe Award Best Director "The Greatest Show On Earth" 1952

Golden Globe Award Best Motion Picture (Drama) "The Greatest Show on Earth" 1952

Oscar Best Picture "The Greatest Show on Earth" 1952 producer

Irving G. Thalberg Memorial Award 1952 presented by the Academy of Motion Picture Arts and Sciences

Directors Guild of America D W Griffith Award 1953 awarded for lifetime achievement

BIOGRAPHY

As the ace director in the mid-1910s for

Famous Players-Lasky, a company he had a hand in creating, DeMille was a crucial figure in the early development of the classic Hollywood narrative filmmaking style. Although less critically revered than D.W. Griffith, DeMille actually played a more important role in shaping the structure of the Hollywood system.

One of DeMille's most influential films of the 1910s was "The Cheat." Released the same year (1915) as "The Birth of a Nation", "The Cheat" was instrumental in developing the rules of classic Hollywood filmmaking. This melodrama is the story of a society woman, Mrs. Richard Hardy, who attempts to save her husband from financial ruin by borrowing needed funds from a wealthy Japanese acquaintance. When the man demands sexual favors in return, Mrs. Hardy returns the money, but this enrages him and he brands her on the shoulder with a red-hot iron. When Richard Hardy attacks the Japanese man (his nationality was changed to Burmese in later prints to increase foreign export potential), he is put on trial. In a final courtroom sequence, he is about to be judged guilty when his wife reveals the wound on her shoulder. DeMille worked wonders with what could have been a hackneyed melodrama by giving it a unique visual style, featuring complex lighting and patterns of shadow suggestive of jail bars. Characters are surrounded by smoke, silhouetted behind screens and appear from nowhere amidst pitch black. In DeMille's hands, "The Cheat" became an intricate study of individual responsibility, handled with subtlety and sophistication. The film is entirely free of sentimentality and the acting of stars Fanny Ward and Sessue Hayakawa is remarkably modern, direct but without sweeping gestures. With this extremely profitable feature, DeMille proved his mastery of film narrative. Over the next eight years, his output would include comedies and dramas that captured American society in transition.

DeMille's initial works brought famous plays and novels to the screen for Famous Players—

"Joan the Woman" (1917), "Old Wives for New" (1918) and "Male and Female" (1919). These and other films of the period starred such proven players as James O'Neil, from Broadway, and Geraldine Farrar, from the operatic stage. In the postwar period came a series of comedies, unlike "The Cheat" in story form, but very similar in faithfulness to the newly established Hollywood rules: "We Can't Have Everything" (1918), "Why Change Your Wife?" (1920) and "Saturday Night" (1922). Ernst Lubitsch, much more famous for his comedies of manners, has singled out the DeMille films from this era as a major influence.

DeMille the innovator became DeMille the moneymaker with "The Ten Commandments" (1923). Budgeted at more than a million dollars, the film proved immensely profitable for Paramount. By the middle of the decade DeMille, with his Germanic swagger, boots and riding crop, had come to represent the archetypal director to the moviegoing public. Chafing under the strictures of the studio system, he quit Paramount in 1925 to set up his own studio, buying the old Ince Studios to form Cinema Corporation of America. Later the company merged with the Keith vaudeville chain, then into Pathe.

The independent DeMille's greatest film was "King of Kings" (1927), a two-million-dollar rendering of the life of Christ. However, the company's lack of other such successes forced DeMille to sign with MGM in 1928. The contrast could not have been greater; he went from autonomy to the strict control of Louis B. Mayer and Nicholas M. Schenck. In 1932 DeMille returned to Paramount, where he would stay for the remainder of his remarkable career.

During the 1930s and 1940s DeMille was Paramount's most bankable director, turning out such hits as "The Sign of the Cross" (1932), "The Plainsman" (1937), "The Buccaneer" (1938), "Union Pacific" (1939), "Northwest Mounted Police" (1940), "Reap the Wild Wind" (1942), "The Story of Dr. Wassell"

(1944), "Unconquered" (1947) and "Samson and Delilah" (1949). He was at his best with historical costume epics such as "Cleopatra" (1934) and "The Crusades" (1935). Under president Barney Balaban and studio boss Y. Frank Freeman, DeMille helped make Paramount the most profitable of the studios during Hollywood's Golden Age.

DeMille also directed and hosted a successful radio show, "Lux Radio Theatre," on CBS from 1936 until 1945, when he refused to join the radio union and quit the program instead. In the late 40s and early 50s, he would become a leader of the Hollywood right wing and the anti-communist witch hunt. His directorial career ended with his spectacular remake of "The Ten Commandments" (1956). Most of his later directorial efforts were forgettable, save for the charming "The Greatest Show on Earth" (1952), a film with an untypically contemporary—though hardly realistic—setting.

In the final analysis, DeMille's big-budget spectacles, made at Paramount from 1932 through 1956, emerge as less significant than those films he made in the pioneering days of the Hollywood studio system. If his early partner Adolph Zukor taught the world how to use movies to fashion a corporate empire, the Cecil B. DeMille of the 1910s must take credit as a key shaper of the classic Hollywood narrative film—a filmmaking form which remains dominant to this day.

MILESTONES:

1900: Broadway acting debut in "Hearts Are Trumps"

Member of the Standard Opera Company as director-actor

1907: Acted for David Belasco

1910: Made general manager of mother's DeMille Play Company

1913: Formed motion picture firm Lasky Feature Play Company with Jesse L. Lasky, Samuel Goldfish (later Goldwyn) and Arthur Friend

1914: First film as co-producer and co-director (with Oscar C. Apfel) "The Squaw Man" (first US feature film)

1916: Helped devise a mechanical color tinting process for his "Joan the Woman"

1919: Formed California's first commercial airline, Mercury Aviation Company

1921: Formed Cecil B. DeMille Productions

1925: Left Paramount (previously Jesse L. Lasky Feature Play Company)

1925: Formed Cinema Corporation of America

1925: First film as independent producer, "The Road to Yesterday"

Cinema Corporation of America merged with Pathe

1928–1931: With MGM

1931: Helped form the Screen Directors Guild

1937: Hired by Lever Brothers as sponsor of "Lux Radio Theater"

1938: Offered Republican senator nomination (California)

1945: Left "Lux Radio Theater"

Formed DeMille Foundation for Political Freedom in late 1940s

1953: Helmed the Oscar-winning Best Picture "The Greatest Show on Earth"

BIBLIOGRAPHY:

"Autobiography" Cecil B DeMille, 1959, Prentice-Hall

BORN: in Baldwin, New York, 02/22/1944

SOMETIMES CREDITED AS:
Rob Morton

NATIONALITY: American

EDUCATION: University of Florida, Gainesville, Florida; chemistry attended a few semesters; film reviewer for student newspaper *The Florida Alligator* and a weekly shopper, *Coral Gables Times*

AWARDS: New York Film Critics Circle Award Best Director "Melvin and Howard" 1980

National Society of Film Critics Award Best Documentary "Stop Making Sense" 1984

IFP Gotham Filmmaker Award 1991

Berlin Film Festival Best Director Award "The Silence of the Lambs" 1991

National Board of Review Award Best Director "The Silence of the Lambs" 1991

New York Film Critics Circle Award Best Director "The Silence of the Lambs" 1991

Chicago Film Critics Association Award Best Director "The Silence of the Lambs" 1991

Directors Guild of America Award Outstanding Directorial Achievement in Feature Film "The Silence of the Lambs" 1991

Oscar Best Director "The Silence of the Lambs" 1991

BIOGRAPHY

An incredibly energetic, optimistic and versatile director of character-driven films, Jonathan Demme emerged from the crucible of B-moviemaking at Roger Corman's New World Pictures in the early 1970s to become one of Hollywood's most critically admired filmmakers in the 80s and 90s. He cut his teeth on a few cheapie action pics like "Caged Heat"

(1974) and "Crazy Mama" (1975) before Corman pushed him from the nest and subsequently enhanced his reputation as a chronicler of post-modern Americana with acclaimed features like "Handle With Care/Citizens Band" (1977) and "Melvin and Howard" (1980), an endearing, bittersweet fable which earned Oscars for Mary Steenburgen (Best Supporting Actress) and Bo Goldman's screenplay. After experiencing the greatest disappointment of his career with "Swing Shift" (1984), Demme rebounded with the brilliant concert film "Stop Making Sense" (1984) and continued to garner critical praise for such diverse pictures as "Something Wild" (1986), "Swimming to Cambodia" (1987) and "Married to the Mob" (1988), all helping to set the stage for the mainstream commercial success he would finally achieve with "The Silence of the Lambs" (1991) and "Philadelphia" (1993).

Unable to master the most basic concepts of college chemistry, Demme had given up on his dream of being a veterinarian and was writing film reviews for his college newspaper when his father arranged an introduction to producer Joseph E Levine. Charmed by Demme's rave review of "Zulu" (1964), Levine hired him to write press releases. Demme moved to New York, where he would later meet and befriend French director Francois Truffaut, in town promoting "The Bride Wore Black" (1968). Though Truffaut's influence on the aspiring director can be seen in the sly humor and oddball style of his early films, Demme opted foremost to concern himself with exploring humanity rather than crafting an image as an auteur. In addition to his work as a publicist, he had written movie and rock reviews while in NYC, but a move to London opened the door for his first feature film credit. Hired by producers Paul Maslansky and Irwin Allen to create a rock score for "Eyewitness/Sudden Terror" (1970), he engaged the services of two British rock groups, Vandergraf Generator and Kaleidoscope, with whom he developed the score in the capacity of "music coordinator."

It was also in England that Demme came to the attention of Corman while working as a unit publicist on the director's "Von Richtofen and Brown" (1971). At Corman's invitation, he relocated to Los Angeles to write screenplays for the recently-formed New World Pictures, completing his first script with friend Joe Viola. The pair then co-produced (with Viola directing) their biker flick "Angels Hard as They Come" (also 1971) under Corman's auspices. Demme graduated to second unit director on "The Hot Box" (1972) before making his full-fledged directorial debut with the tongue-in-cheek "Caged Heat", a fairly typical women's prison flick, in which the director inserted a socially conscious secondary plot about the medical exploitation of prisoners. He helmed two more pictures for Corman, New World's "Crazy Mama", a rich movie full of his trademark music, back country and wild women on an absurdist crime spree from California to Arkansas, and "Fighting Mad" (1976, for 20th Century-Fox), starring Peter Fonda as a man driven to violence by a ruthless landowner who wants to take over his farm.

"Citizen's Band" was an adventurous comedy which wavered between glorifying, lampooning and seriously questioning the implications of the CB radio craze of the era. Retitled "Handle With Care", its series of mundane, whimsical and disturbing vignettes featuring a gang of loony CB operators dominated by their radio personae prompted President Carter to say, "That's America!" but generated little box office, despite good reviews. After making "Last Embrace" (1979), an expert thriller in the Hitchcockian mold, Demme continued his exploration of the American condition in "Melvin and Howard", a relaxed yet revealing account of an unlikely encounter

between a working-class Everyman (gas station owner Melvin Dummar) and an eccentric billionaire (Howard Hughes, whom Dummar claimed named him sole heir to his fortune). Named Best Picture by the National Society of Film Critics, this satiric, tolerant look at the American class structure also won Demme the New York Film Critics' Best Director award but again failed to ignite the box office.

Demme envisioned "Swing Shift" as a probing look at women factory workers during WWII (his grandmother had worked on the assembly line making fighter planes), but the film's executive producer and female lead Goldie Hawn saw it as a star vehicle Hating the director's print emphasizing female camaraderie and endurance in the face of domineering male employers, the actress presented the director with 28 pages of new material, which he half-heartedly shot. As soon as the picture had been through two previews in its original form, the contractual period of the director's creative control was over, and Hawn decided to re-cut the film, playing up the doomed love affair between a married woman and her supervisor. Demme and his editor Craig McKay quit the project rather than insert the new scenes, and though its critical and commercial failure vindicated him in a way, the pain of the experience lingered for well over a year. Pauline Kael, who gave "Swing Shift" a negative review, would later say, "I saw his cut recently, on videotape, and thought it was wonderful," and her words echoed those of almost everyone who ever saw his version.

During the early stages of editing "Swing Shift", Demme had attended a Talking Heads concert in Los Angeles and been knocked out by their performance. Coming out of the show, he realized "My God, that's a movie waiting to be filmed." He sold the band's leader David Byrne on his vision of honoring the excitement of the live performance by avoiding tricky shots, flashy editing techniques, anything that would constitute a digression from the performance itself (like cutaways to the audience). Compiled from three concerts, "Stop Making Sense" was a joyously energetic, yet cool showcase which helped propel the Talking Heads (and Byrne) to mainstream acceptance. Demme also directed several rock videos for other bands including UB40, New Order ("Perfect Kiss" 1985) and Fine Young Cannibals ("Ever Fallen in Love?"). These artists and quite a few others contributed songs to the lively and memorable soundtrack of "Something Wild", for which Laurie Anderson and John Cale wrote the fine score.

"Something Wild" was Demme's contribution to the disaffected yuppie genre, which had already yielded Albert Brooks' "Lost in America" and John Landis' "Into the Night" (both 1985). The darkly comic road movie examined contemporary America through the metaphoric relationship between a spontaneous gamine and a staid stockbroker, and its rapid editing, sharp camera angles and bouncy pace made for a breathless, dizzying experience. The film's hip urban sensibility seemed a change for Demme, as did the return to violence largely unseen since his early days with Corman, but the film was actually consistent with the director's examination of self-determination begun with the women prisoners of "Caged Heat" and continued with the munitions workers of "Swing Shift". His concern with the "heroic" struggles of the central female characters of "Something Wild" (Melanie Griffith) and "Married to the Mob" (Michelle Pfeiffer) as they attempt to establish themselves against patriarchal attitudes helped contribute to his reputation as a feminist filmmaker.

Demme showed his mettle with another artful and subtle performance film, "Swimming to Cambodia", featuring the celebrated monologist Spalding Gray, before spoofing the Mafia in "Married to the Mob", another dark comedy more garishly colored and cheerful than "Something Wild", which had lost many viewers with the violence and sheer malevolence of Ray Liotta

in its final act. Dean Stockwell's brilliant comic turn as Mafioso Tony "The Tiger" Russo and the right-on performance of Pfeiffer were standouts among a formidable cast, boasting Matthew Modine, Mercedes Ruehl, Alec Baldwin and frequent Demme player Charles Napier. Popular music (Byrne provided the score) again contributed to the movie's success with audiences and critics alike, and for the first time production designer Kristin Zea joined the team, which included Tak Fujimoto, Demme's longtime director of photography, paving the way for subsequent collaborations on the director's upcoming blockbusters.

It finally all came together for Demme, critically and commercially, with "The Silence of the Lambs", superbly adapted from the novel by Thomas Harris. A genuinely terrifying thriller, the film centers on an FBI trainee (Jodie Foster) who enlists the help of one psychopath (Anthony Hopkins) in order to track down another (Ted Levine). Despite the grisly nature of the story—one killer who eats his victims, another who skins them—Demme resisted the possibilities for exploitation and instead fashioned a compelling and impressively sensitive psychological drama with a courageous, independent female protagonist. He also elicited landmark performances from both Foster and Hopkins, who manages to make a hero out of the unruly demon Hannibal Lecter. (At film's end, we are actually rooting for the cannibal as he goes off stalking his "dinner".) Following in the footsteps of "It Happened One Night" (1934) and "One Flew Over the Cuckoo's Nest" (1975), the film went on to win the five top Oscars—Best Picture, Best Actor, Best Actress, Best Director and Best Adapted Screenplay—an immense accomplishment for what is essentially a big-budget splatter film.

Often associated with progressive causes, Demme has lent his talents to projects that reflect his political concerns such as "Haiti Dreams of Democracy" (1988), which he co-wrote, co-produced, and co-directed. He also helmed and appeared in "Cousin Bobby" (1992), a documentary about his relative, the Reverend Robert Castle, a radical, Harlem-based clergyman. Though many viewed the director's decision to film "Philadelphia" as a mea culpa in response to the charges of homophobia leveled at "The Silence of the Lambs" from some members of the gay press who decried the complex sexuality of the film's killer, Demme had actually been working on the project with "Swing Shift" screenwriter Ron Nyswaner as early as 1988. In any event, the moving courtroom drama dealing with discrimination against gays and PWAs (People with AIDS) was a landmark in mainstream Hollywood history. Greeted with mixed reviews, "Philadelphia" provided an attention-getting (and Oscar-winning) role for Tom Hanks as the afflicted homosexual lawyer who loses his job when he becomes symptomatic but lacked the strong character development, mischief and sense of the unexpected that characterizes Demme's best work.

In the 90s, Demme, like his mentor Corman, increasingly concentrated on producing, beginning with George Armitage's "Miami Blues" (1990). He upped his output considerably after 1993, executive producing, producing or "presenting" 10 pictures in five years. He finally returned to the director's chair for the film version of Toni Morrison's Pulitzer Prize–winning "Beloved" (1998), reinforcing the novel's best insights with a startling breadth of vision (and a tip of the hat to Sidney Lumet's "The Pawnbroker") that is the best part of the film. It was no nightmare directing his producer-star this time as he and Oprah Winfrey, whose presence legitimized the project as authentic black self-expression and took away the onus of hiring a white urbanite as director, were on the same page from the start. Demme had been looking for a project that addressed race relations for a long time, and "Beloved" fit the bill with its story about the disfiguring effects of slavery and its aftermath. As a reflection of his lifelong passion for

rock'n'roll in particular and music in general, he also helmed that year's "Storefront Hitchcock", a documentary about legendary rocker Robyn Hitchcock. Demme has said, "There's nothing I'd rather do than direct because directing combines three of my favorite things in life: people, imagery, and sound—not just music, but the sounds of life."

After a lengthy hiatus away from the camera, Demme returned in 2002 to helm "The Truth About Charlie," a remake of one of his favorite films, 1963's "Charade" starring Cary Grant and Audrey Hepburn and directed by the legendary Stanley Donen. Demme set upon an eclectic path, alternately faithful and radically different (casting Mark Wahlberg in the Grant role, for example), to bring the story to new life. Essentially casting the central locale of Paris as a third lead character, Demme reunited with some longtime collaborators such as Tak Fujimoto and paid tribute to the influences of the French New Wave that have long guided his sensibility by including cameos from Anna Karina, Agnes Vardas, Charles Aznavour and Magali Noel.

MILESTONES:

Raised in Rockville Centre, New York

1953: At age nine, became the youngest card-carrying member of the American Ornithologist's Union

1959: Moved to Miami, Florida at age 15 (date approximate)

1964: Introduced by his father to producer Joseph E Levine who, pleased by Demme's review of "Zulu" (1964), hired him to write press releases; moved to New York City

1966: Served briefly in US Air Force

1966: Worked as a publicist for Avco Embassy

1966–1967: Sold films for Pathe Contemporary Films in NYC

Wrote for exhibitor trade paper *Film Daily*

Made 16mm short "Good Morning, Steve"

Worked in New York publicity department of United Artists

1968: Met and befriended Francois Truffaut, who was then publicizing "The Bride Wore Black" (1968) in NYC; chauffered Truffaut to all of his interviews

1969: Moved to London as sales representative and producer for small company; also wrote music reviews for a Boston underground newspaper

1970: First film credit as musical coordinator on the Irwin Allen production "Sudden Terror/Eyewitness"

While working in London, met producer-director Roger Corman

1971: Feature debut as co-screenwriter, co-producer and second unit director, "Angels Hard as They Come", directed by Joe Viola; produced by Corman's New World Pictures

1972: Reteamed with Viola to make "The Hot Box" for New World Pictures

1974: Feature directing debut for New World Pictures "Caged Heat", made for $160,000; also wrote screenplay; first collaboration with director of photography Tak Fujimoto

1977: First association with actor Paul Le Mat, "Citizens Band/Handle With Care"

1978: TV directorial debut, "Murder Under Glass", an NBC TV-movie episode of the Peter Falk "Columbo" series

1978: Acted in the film "The Incredible Melting Man"

1979: Directed fine Hitchcockian suspense thriller "Last Embrace", starring Roy Scheider

1980: Reteamed with Le Mat (as Melvin Dummar) in "Melvin and Howard", a wonderful slice-of-life comedy which earned Oscars for Mary Steenburgen (Best Supporting Actress) and screenwriter Bo Goldman; first association with Jason Robards Jr. (as billionaire recluse Howard Hughes)

1981: Helped photograph Adam Brooks' independent film "Ghost Sisters" (date approximate)

1982: First credit as Rob Morton for his contributions to the screenplay of "Ladies and Gentleman . . . The Fabulous Stains"

1982: Withdrew from the rock documentary, "Urgh! A Music War"

1982: Directed the PBS teleplay, "Who Am I This Time?", based on a short story by Kurt Vonnegut Jr. and starring Susan Sarandon and Christopher Walken

1984: Credited as Rob Morton for his contributions to the screenplay of "Swing Shift"; also directed, but executive producer Goldie Hawn took over final cut of film, hiring another director to reshoot at least a half-hour's worth of footage altering the tone of the film

1984: Shot outstanding concert film, "Stop Making Sense", featuring David Byrne and his band Talking Heads

1984: Directed "A Family Tree", the pilot for PBS' "Trying Times", written by Beth Henley and starring Byrne and Rosanna Arquette

1985: Contributed a cameo to John Landis' "Into the Night"

1986: Produced and directed comedy thriller "Something Wild"; Byrne contributed opening song

1987: Helmed "Swimming to Cambodia"; his artful (and subtle) directing, combined with Spalding Gray's storytelling skills, made a fascinating film out of a 90-minute monologue

1988: Directed amiable, entertaining Mafia farce "Married to the Mob"; Byrne wrote the score; first collaboration with production designer Kristi Zea

1988: Co-produced, co-wrote, and co-directed "Haiti Dreams of Democracy", a documentary on post-Duvalier Haiti, for Great Britain's Channel 4

1990: Produced George Armitage's "Miami Blues"

Formed production company, Clinica Estetico Ltd. (ungrammatical Portuguese for "beauty parlor")

1991: Directed first blockbuster, "The Silence of the Lambs"; film became only the third to win the top five Oscars, including Best Picture and Best Director

1992: First film produced under the Clinica

Estetico banner, "Cousin Bobby", a highly personal documentary of radical Harlem clergyman Robert Castle, the director's cousin

1993: Produced and directed "Philadelphia", a politically correct, mainstream Hollywood look at the AIDS epidemic and American homophobia; Reverend Castle played Oscar-winner Tom Hanks' father; third collbration with Zea, who served as a second unit director as well as production designer; film also reunited him with "Swing Shift" co-screenwriter Ron Nyswaner and actors Steenburgen and Robards

Served in various producing capacities on 10 films, executive producing (i.e., "Amos & Andrew" 1993), producing (e.g., Hanks' directorial debut "That Thing You Do!" 1996) and "presenting" (i.e., "Ulee's Gold" 1997)

1994: Provided the funding so that his wife's best friend, AIDS-stricken artist Juan Botas, could make his documentary "One Foot on a Banana Peel, the Other Foot in the Grave"

1997: Executive produced and helmed "Subway Car From Hell" segment of HBO's anthology movie "Subway Stories: Tales From the Underground"

1997: Winnowed his colllection of Haitian art for an exhibition of more than 100 paintings called "Island on Fire: Passionate Visions of Haiti From the Collection of Jonathan Demme" at NYC's Equitable Gallery

1998: Directed "Storefront Hitchcock", a documentary of legendary rocker Robyn Hitchcock

1998: Helmed adaptation of Toni Morrison's Pulitzer Prize-winning novel "Beloved", starring and co-produced by Oprah Winfrey; also served as a producer; 13th collaboration (as either director or producer) with Fujimoto; fourth collaboration with Zea (again as second unit director and production designer); Robards contributed a cameo

2002: Directed "The Truth About Charlie," a remake of the classic "Charade"; 14th collaboration with Fujimoto

Agreed to develop a thriller to star Jodie Foster with writer Richard Price, producer Scott Rudin and Paramount Pictures (deal 2002)

AFFILIATION: Member of the American Ornithologist's Union since age nine

QUOTES:

Demme used the pseudonym Rob Morton for screenwriting credit on the films "Swing Shift" (which he directed under his real name) and "Ladies and Gentleman . . . The Fabulous Stains."

Awarded an honorary degree by Wesleyn University June 3, 1990

"The most important thing Roger [Corman] did for me was to sit down with me right before I directed 'Caged Heat' and run down just how to do a job of moviemaking. He hit everything: have something interesting happening in the background of the shot; try to find good motivation to move the camera, because it's more stimulating to the eyes; if you're shooting the scene in a small room where you can't move the camera, try to get in different angles, because cuts equal movement; respect the characters and try to like them, and translate that into the audience liking and respecting the characters. To me, those are the fundamentals."—Jonathan Demme on making "Caged Heat" (1974) quoted in "Righteous & Outrageous—Jonathan Demme" by Paul Taylor, *Monthly Film Bulletin*, July 1989.

"Jonathan Demme's domain is America itself—a vibrant, polychromatic, up-to-the-second place. But there isn't a slick or pat frame in any of his movies. When Jason Robards and Paul Le Mat, as Howard Hughes and Melvin Dummar, sing 'Bye Bye Blackbird' as they drive through the desert at night in "Melvin and Howard"; . . . when Jeff Daniels, pretending to be the husband of his kinky kidnapper, Melanie Griffith, goes to meet her small-town mother in "Something Wild"— Demme's films cross the line from entertainment into poetry. They contain a warmth, a largeness of spirit, a deadpan humor, and a visual and narrative unpredictability that are indebted equally to the eye-pleasing kineticism practiced by Demme's mentor, Roger Corman, the master of horror and action pictures, and to the cinematic intelligence of his early friend and influence Francois Truffaut"—from "Jonathan Demme's Offbeat America" by James Kaplan, *The New York Times,* 1988.

"It's amazing. I'm an Oscar-winning director. And I love it. I'm proud of it. But I honestly didn't expect to win. I came out here to have some fun, to see the event up close, to visit friends. I don't feel it's going to be a part of my identity, or change a second of my life. But, man, it sure puts the spotlight on you."—Jonathan Demme, quoted in *New York Newsday,* April 1, 1992.

"I didn't go to film school; I didn't work toward being a filmmaker. I stumbled into writing movie reviews so I could get into the movies for free. Then my father introduced me to Joseph E. Levine, and Levine offers me a job in the movie business. 'A huge stroke of luck' doesn't catch it.

"Then I wind up crossing paths with Roger Corman, and Corman has just started New World Pictures and needs scripts. My best friend is Joe Viola, one of the most gifted storytellers I've ever known. So Joe and I write a script for Corman, and then, because Joe directs commercials, suddenly Roger wants us to make this motorcycle movie. Again, 'an enormous stroke of good fortune' doesn't fully chacterize it. I mean, people bust their butts for decades to get to make a picture, and I fell backward into it."—Demme quoted in *Rolling Stone,* March 24, 1994.

On deciding to make "Beloved": "I loved the script, the characters, the story. It's a great love story, a great ghost story, a great historical epic. It also had the dimension of addressing race relations in America, which is a subject that's very close to my heart. So I just dove in.

"I met with Oprah and asked her if she was at all concerned that because of her prominence as a public figure audiences might have some difficulty accepting her as a 19th-century farm woman haunted by her past.

"She thought that was a fair question, but felt she was capable of giving a performance and undergoing a not just physical but kind of cosmic transformation through the channeling of ancestors that would make what she could do rise above such concerns.

"And I believed her. So, we went to work on it."—Demme to *Newsday,* October 10, 1998.

The aftermath of "Beloved": "I feel haunted—in the best sense of the word—by the experience of making this film. It wasn't a difficult shoot; it was a joyful shoot. I still miss the filming so much. And the dailies every night—it was a celebration. There'd be a certain point where you'd hear Oprah go, 'I ain't ever seen no movie like this before.'"—Demme to *Premiere,* November 1998.

BIBLIOGRAPHY:
"What Goes Around Comes Around: The Films of Jonathan Demme" Michael Bliss and Christina Banks, 1996, Southern Illinois University Press

Jacques Demy

BORN: in Pontchateau, France, 06/05/1931

DEATH: in Paris, France, 10/27/1990

NATIONALITY: French

EDUCATION: attended a technical college in Nantes, studying to be a mechanic

Ecole des Beaux Arts Nantes, France painting and drawing

Ecole de Vaugirard Paris, France filmmaking 1949

AWARDS: Cannes Film Festival Catholic Film Office Award "Les Parapluies de Cherbourg/The Umbrellas of Cherbourg" 1964

Cannes Film Festival Grand Prix "Les Parapluies de Cherbourg/The Umbrellas of Cherbourg" 1964

Grand Prix of Cinema Award "Chambre en Ville/A Room in the City" 1982

BIOGRAPHY

Versatile director whose films such as "Lola" (1961) are generally noted for their stylish, bittersweet yet often optimistic romanticism. Demy made several musicals, including "The Umbrellas of Cherbourg" (1964)—in which all the dialogue was sung—and worked often with actress Catherine Deneuve and composer Michel Legrand. He married fellow New Wave director Agnes Varda in 1962. Varda paid tribute to her ailing husband with the wistful, biographical "Jacquot/Jacquot de Nantes" (1991). Demy grew up in Nantes, and originally was expected to follow in his father's footsteps and trained as a mechanic. Instead, he headed into the arts. After earning a degree from L'Ecole Technique de Photographie et de Cinematographie, Demy worked on publicity films and as an assistant to animator Paul Grimault, then as assistant to director Georges Rouquier on "Lourdes et ses miracles" (1954). In 1955, he also secured the backing of Pathe for his own short film, "Le Sabotier du Val du Loire," which was a slow-paced documentary about the family of clog makers with who Demy had lived when he was a child during World War II. He made his first short fiction film "Le Bel indifferent" in 1957, based on a short play by Jean Cocteau. After several other short films came "Lola" in 1960, set in his own home town and starring Anouk Aimee as a beautiful, fearless nightclub singer. Though not a commercial success, "Lola" won the Prix de L'Academie du Cinema and critic Eric Rohmer called it the "most original film of the New Wave" in France. (Although technically, Demy was not a New Wave director. Having worked his way up as an assistant on other's films and not as a critic, he was considered one of the "Left Bank School" director.) Demy's next feature was "La Baie des anges/Bay of Angels" (1962), written in three days and telling the story of a bank employee who becomes fascinated with gambling and Jeanne Moreau, the woman he meets in the casino. "The Umbrellas of Cherbourg," starring Catherine Denueve, followed in 1964, gaining Demy an international reputation. In the film all the dialogue is sung, amidst imaginative use of color and design. Also with Deneuve—and her sister, Francoise Dorleac—Demy did the all-sung "Les Demoiselles de Rochefort" (1967), but the reception was not as strong. Still, "The Young Girls of Rochefort" (as it was called in English), includes a performance by Gene Kelly whose work on the screen as a director and performer greatly influenced Demy. Demy made "Model Shop" in English, in which Anouk Aimee reappears as Lola, but then flopped with "Peau d'Ane" (1967), "The Pied Piper of Hamelin" (US/1972), and "A Slightly Pregnant Man" (1973). It was not until 1979—a six year absence—that Demy again directed. He chose "Lady Oscar" (1979), financed by Japanese interests and based on a Japanese comic strip. He then turned to TV, directing "La Naissance du jour," an adaptation of a story by Colette. Demy bounced back in feature films in 1982, again with sung dialogue, with "Une Chambre en ville." Like "The Umbrellas of Cherbourg," it was about an ill-fated love affair, this time starring Dominique Sanda. Although honored with the Grand Prix du Cinema, Demy failed to impress the critics in France with the effort. His work after showed a decline in originality. "Parking" (1985), was a retelling of the Orpheus tale, and was a disappointment, even with its score by Michel Legrand. Three years later, Demy made his final film, "Trois place pour le 26." Demy can also be seen briefly in the films of other directors. He played a policeman for Francois Truffaut in "400 Blows" (1959), and also appears in "Paris nous appointment" (1960).

COMPANION:

wife: Agnes Varda. Director; together from 1959; married from 1962 until his death; mother of Mathieu; directed such films as "Cleo from 5 to 7" (1962), "One Sings, the Other Doesn't" (1976) and "Vagabond" (1985)

MILESTONES:

Raised in Nantes, France

1945: At age 14, tried to make first feature "L'Aventure de Solange" using neighborhood children; film returned from the processing lab was overexposed (date approximate)

1952: Worked as assistant to Paul Grimault making advertising cartoons

1952: First film as assistant director, "Lourdes et ses miracles", directed by Georges Rouquier

1955: First short film as director, "Le sabotier du Val de Loire"; also scripted

1959: Acted in Truffaut's "The 400 Blows"; played bit part of a policeman

1961: Feature directing debut, "Lola"

1964: Had greatest success with the all-sung, color feature "Les parapluis de Cherbourg/The Umbrellas of Cherbourg"; wrote, directed and supplied lyrics to Michel Legrand's music; received Oscar nomination as Best Foreign-Language Film, Best Screenplay, Best Score and Best Song

1967: Stumbled at the box-office with "Les demoiselles de Rochefort/The Young Ladies of Rochefort", another all-sung film

1970: Directed Catherine Deneuve in the fairy tale-inspired "Peau d'ane/Donkey Skin/The Magic Donkey"

1972: Co-wrote and directed "The Pied Piper", starring Danny Kaye; film made for UNICEF; first-English language film

1976: Staged first Cesar Awards ceremony

1979: Made English-language film "Lady Oscar"

1981: Turned briefly to TV, directing "La Naissance du jour"

1982: After several years of critical decline, bounced back somewhat with the musical tragedy "Une chambre en ville"

1983: Hired to direct the cable TV-movie "Louisiana" (Cinemax); withdrew for "personal and family reasons" and was replaced by Philippe de Broca

1985: Reinterpreted the Orpheus myth as "Parking"

1988: Last film, "Trois Places Pour le 26"

QUOTES:

"There is in the best of his work an underlying strain of melancholy, a unique fusion of lust and wanderlust, an intensity one has no right to expect from material as fey as this."—Critic Gilbert Adair. Demy's films often began with an iris opening, a signature he chose because "I'd seen it at the cinema, especially in silent films, and . . . I found it very fascinating, this little circle that encompasses a face, isolates it, and makes the picture disappear. The fade-in is really a picture that you remove, that you erase, whereas what I like with the iris shot is that the picture stays behind it, it's not quite finished."

"In New York I met Warhol and the Factory people, and I must say that all those people were much more interesting than the major companies that weren't producing much of interest at the time. In fact, Warhol was reinventing cinema in his way, like Godard, going back to the beginning. I was very tempted (to work with them), but I think the differences between their culture and civilization, and mine were too big, and although I was fascinated by the underground movement, there was no place for me in it. Maybe I was mistaken but that I felt at the time."—Demy in *Film Dope*, Number 10.

"Perhaps I would not have remained in films or pursued acting if it hadn't been for Jacques Demy. He was a single-minded man who never let me think about anything but my career."—actress Catherine Deneuve to columnist Liz Smith in August 1998.

Claire Denis

BORN: in Paris, France, 04/21/1948

NATIONALITY: French

EDUCATION: Institut des Hautes Etudes Cinematographiques, Paris, France, film, 1971

AWARD: Locarno Film Festival Golden Leopard Award "Nenette Et Boni" 1996

BIOGRAPHY

A key member of the new wave of female French directors, Claire Denis toiled for more than 10 years as an assistant director before winning international acclaim with her first feature film, "Chocolat" (1988), a semi-autobiographical tale of a young French girl in Africa. "Chocolat", co-written with Jean-Pol Fargeau, was a meditation on colonialism. The woman returning to Africa is driven by an American black and the intertwining of their stories links the pair to the continent through issues of native identity. It was the official French entry in the Cannes Film Festival.

A graduate of the prestigious IDHEC, Denis began her professional career making short films, including one with the Great Magic Circus at the Arles Festival in Provence. Other shorts were produced by Pathe for the Chronicles of France series. In 1974, she was hired as a production assistant on "Le Vieux fusil/The Hidden Gun", directed by Robert Enrico, and by 1978 was assistant director to Alain Fleischer on "Zoo-Zero." She was AD to Costa-Gavras on "Hannah K" (1983) and to indie filmmaker Jim Jarmusch on "Down By Law" (1986). It was her connection with German Wim Wenders that triggered "Chocolat." Working as Wenders' AD on "Paris, Texas" (1984), Denis thought the terrain of the American Southwest was similar to that of

Cameroon, where she had spent her childhood. While working on "Wings of Desire" (1998), she began to seek financing and eventually Wenders became one of her backers.

Following the success of "Chocolat", Denis directed "Man No Run" (1989), a concert film with the Cameroon band Les Tetes Brulees. Africa was again part of Denis' motif in "S'en fout la mort/No Fear, No Die" (1990), about two Africans involved in cock fighting and again the director explored issues of racism and colonialism. She wrote and directed "J'ai pas sommeil/I Can't Sleep" (1993), a thriller which examined the intersection of seemingly unrelated, yet overlapping lives, and "U.S. Go Home" (1994), a coming of age story about teens who want to lose their virginity. In 1996, Denis scripted and helmed "Nenette et Boni", the story of a sister and a brother forging a new relationship after the death of their mother.

Denis has also worked occasionally for French TV, including "Jacques Rivette, le veilleur" (1989) and "La Robe a cerceaux" (1992). Additionally, she acted in "Mais ou et donc ornicar" (1979) and as the teen lead's mother in "En avoir (ou pas)/To Have (Or Not)" (1995).

MILESTONES:

1948–1962: Lived with civil servant father and family in Africa

1962: Sent back to France to live with her grandfather in Paris

1973: Produced short film with the Great Magic Circus

1974: Worked as production assistant for director Robert Enrico on "Le Vieux fusil/The Hidden Gun"

1978: Was first assistant director for Alain Fleischer on "Zoo-Zero"

1979: Acting debut in "Mais ou et donc ornicar"

245

1984: Was first assistant director for Wim Wenders on "Paris, Texas"

1988: Again worked with Wenders on "Wings of Desire"

1988: Co-wrote and directed first feature film, "Chocolat"

1989: Made "Man No Run", a documentary on the tour of the African band Les Tetes Brulees

1989: Directed first TV project, "Jacques Rivette, le veilleur"

1990: Returned to fiction, scripting and directing "No Fear, No Die"

1996: Directed and wrote "Nenette et Boni"

1999: Received widespread praise for her lyrical "Beau Travail", loosely adapted from "Billy Budd"

2000: Helmed the thriller "Trouble Every Day", starring Vincent Gallo; released theatrically in USA in 2002.

QUOTES:

"For many whites, I think Africa remains the magic continent. But the experience of whites is always the same: we approach, approach, approach, but we never quite reach the heart of Africa. In 'Chocolat', I always tried to maintain only the perspectives of the whites. I just didn't think I should pretend to understand the black point of view."—Claire Denis in *The New York Times*, c. 1988.

Ernest Dickerson

BORN: in Newark, New Jersey 1952

SOMETIMES CREDITED AS:
Ernest R. Dickerson

NATIONALITY: American

EDUCATION: Howard University architecture, photography, BA

Tisch School of the Arts, New York University, New York, New York, film, MFA; met Spike Lee

AWARDS: New York Film Critics Circle Award Best Cinematography "Do the Right Thing" 1989

IFP Gotham Award Cinematographer 1991

BIOGRAPHY

Gifted African American cinematographer who established himself on financially modest but artistically ambitious independent features before shifting to major motion pictures as a d.p. and genre films as a director. Dickerson became known as the ace director of photography for fellow NYU alumnus Spike Lee. His vibrant painterly camerawork enhanced Lee's student film "Joe's Bed-Stuy Barbershop: We Cut Heads" (1980) and his subsequent first six features. His first feature credit was John Sayles' "The Brother From Another Planet" (1984), an engaging social parable about a mute alien stranded in Harlem, which benefited greatly from Dickerson's soulful portraits of the faces and places of Black folks. He has achieved great success in conveying the full spectrum of African American coloring by utilizing various tinted lights and colored backdrops. Dickerson has also shot films by Michael Schultz ("Krush Groove" 1985), Robert Townsend ("Eddie Murphy Raw" 1987) and John McNaughton ("Sex, Drugs, Rock & Roll" 1991).

Dickerson has also worked in TV as a d.p. and director. He lensed the first season of "Tales From the Darkside", a low-budget syndicated horror anthology series from Laurel Entertainment. Dickerson's subsequent cinematography credits on TV include "H.E.L.P." and "Law & Order." He made his directing debut helming a popular musical special,

"Spike & Co.: Do It A Cappella", for "Great Performances" (PBS, 1990). Dickerson made his feature debut as a director and screenwriter with the $3 million independent feature, "Juice" (1992) about four young black friends from Harlem whom become involved in a tragic robbery. Inspired by "The Most Dangerous Game", an oft-filmed 20s short story by Ragnar Benson, "Surviving the Game" (1994) was standard action fare for the director. Still it boasted a strong cast including Ice-T, Rutger Hauer and Charles S. Dutton.

MILESTONES:

Began career filming surgical procedures for Howard University Medical School

1980: Shot Spike Lee's student films, beginning with "Sarah" and including "Joe's Bed-Stuy Barbershop: We Cut Heads"

1984: Shot first major feature, "Brother From Another Planet"

1984–1985: Served as the director of photography for the first season of "Tales From the Darkside", a low-budget syndicated horror series

1985: Worked as a camera operator and 2nd unit director on George A. Romero's "Day of the Dead"

1986: Appeared in Spike Lee's "She's Gotta Have It" (also shot)

Network TV debut as d.p., "H.E.L.P."

Shot Nike commercials and music videos including "Born in the USA" by Bruce Springsteen, "Stir It Up" by Patti LaBelle, and "Tutu" by Miles Davis

1990: TV directing debut, "Spike & Co.: Do It A Capella" ("Great Performances" PBS)

1990: Shot six episodes of cop/legal series "Law & Order"

1991: Directed and co-wrote first feature. "Juice"

1993: Directed the premiere episode of "The Untouchables", the syndicated revival derived from the 1987 feature

1998: Helmed "Blind Faith"; played at various film festivals and aired on Showtime

Directed the TNT movie "Monday Night Mayhem" (lensed 2001), with John Turturro as Howard Cosell

QUOTES:

Received graduate fellowships from Academy of Motion Picture Arts and Sciences and from Louis B. Mayer Foundation.

Saluted for his cinematography at the 34th San Francisco Film Festival.

"A lot of the directors that I worked with also worked in front of the camera as actors: Spike Lee, John Sayles, Peter Wang. And so I had a chance to really find out what directing is like. Directors also entrusted me with designing entire sequences of their movie in terms of shot structure, and I think seeing how these sequences worked in the final films taught me I should trust my instincts."—Ernest Dickerson in *The New York Times*, May 24, 1991.

"The type of individual who would brandish a semi-automatic weapon at a movie theater where Ernest Dickerson's 'Juice' is playing . . . is the best argument for the reasonableness of what Mr. Dickerson has to say. His film addresses the peer pressures at work on a group of Harlem high school students, one of whom eventually develops a taste for murderous mayhem and viciously attacks his friends.

"The irrational bravado and macho posturing displayed by Bishop (Tupac Shakur), the film's bad-boy character, are undoubtedly shared by those gun-toting, knife-wielding moviegoers who have put 'Juice' in the news."—Janet Maslin in *The New York Times*, January 22, 1992.

Stanley Donen

BORN: in Columbia, South Carolina, 04/13/1924

NATIONALITY: American

EDUCATION: graduated from high school at age 16

AWARDS: Los Angeles Film Critics Association Career Achievement Award 1989

National Board of Review Billy Wilder Award 1995; for career achievement in direction; second recipient

Honorary Oscar 1997 "in appreciation of a body of work marked by grace, elegance, wit and visual innovation"

American Society of Cinematographers Board of Governors Award 2002

BIOGRAPHY

Stanley Donen was sixteen when he left his native South Carolina and moved to NYC to pursue a stage career. He landed in the chorus of George Abbott's "Pal Joey" (1940), which made a star of Gene Kelly. Donen and Kelly became friendly and when Kelly was choreographing the Broadway show "Best Foot Forward" (1941), he hired Donen as his assistant. When the feature version was made, Donen was hired as a chorus boy. He and Kelly worked on choreography for "Cover Girl" (1944). The following year, Donen worked on "Anchors Aweigh" (1945) and broke new ground with the now famous sequence wherein Kelly danced with the animated Jerry the mouse (of "Tom and Jerry"). He continued to act as choreographer on a variety of films in the 1940s until making his film directing debut as Kelly's full-fledged collaborator with the energetic "On the Town" (1949). Along with Vincente Minnelli, Donen became the star director of MGM musicals in the 50s. Among his best work are: "Singin' in the Rain" (1952), considered to be one of the greatest musical films ever made; "Seven Brides for Seven Brothers" (1954); his post-MGM romantic fairy tale, "Funny Face" (1956); and his spirited George Abbott collaborations, "The Pajama Game" (1957) and "Damn Yankees" (1958).

In 1958, he began working in England, turning out sophisticated comedies and thrillers, such as the polished "Charade" (1963) and the stylish romantic drama, "Two for the Road" (1966). His subsequent films, however, have met with lukewarm critical response. "The Little Prince" (1974), complete with a Lerner and Loewe score, attempted to film the unfilmable. "Lucky Lady" (1975) was a nostalgic throwback to the films of the 30s that seemed quaint and out of place with the grittier fare embraced by mid-70s audiences ("One Flew Over the Cuckoo's Nest", "Nashville"). Another exercise in nostalgia, "Movie Movie" (1978) was a gentle send-up of 30s-era Hollywood staples: the Warners melodramas and the Technicolor movie musical. His films in the 80s ("Saturn 3" 1980 and "Blame It on Rio" 1984) were box office and critical disappointments.

In 1993, Donen made his stage musical directing debut with the unsuccessful adaptation of the classic dance film "The Red Shoes." He briefly romanced Elizabeth Taylor in 1951 and was formerly married to dancer Jeannie Coyne, who later wed Gene Kelly. His son Joshua, from his second marriage to actress Marion Marshall, is a film producer. Donen was also formerly married to actress Yvette Mimieux.

FAMILY:

son: Joshua Donen. Agent, producer; born in 1955; mother, Marion Marshall; producer of

"The Quick and the Dead" (1995); named senior vice president at William Morris in July 1996

COMPANIONS:

wife: Jeannie Coyne. Dancer, assistant choreographer; married in 1948; divorced in 1949; met through mutual friendship with Gene Kelly (Coyne had been Kelly's student and later his assistant in the 1940s); married to Kelly from 1960 until her death in 1973

Elizabeth Taylor. Actor; together briefly in 1951

MILESTONES:

1940: Broadway debut (as chorus boy) in "Pal Joey", which starred Gene Kelly

1941: Worked as assistant choreographer (to Kelly) on Broadway musical, "Best Foot Forward"

1943: Went to Hollywood as assistant choreographer and member of dancing chorus of film version of "Best Foot Forward"

1944: Worked with Kelly on choreography for "Cover Girl"

1949: Debut as co-director and co-story writer (with Kelly) of "Strictly USA" number in "Take Me Out to the Ball Game"

1949: Film co-directing debut (with Kelly) "On the Town"

1951: Solo film directing debut, "Royal Wedding"

1957: First film as producer, "The Pajama Game"

1963: Produced and directed the stylish comedy-mystery "Charade", starring Cary Grant and Audrey Hepburn

1967: Directed Audrey Hepburn and Albert Finney in "Two for the Road"

1978: Helmed the homage to old Hollywood "Movie Movie"

1984: Produced and directed last feature "Blame It on Rio"

1993: Made Broadway debut as director of ill-fated musical "The Red Shoes"

1998: Awarded honorary Academy Award for career achievement in March

1999: TV directorial debut with adaptation of A.R. Gurney's "Love Letters" (ABC)

AFFILIATION: Jewish

QUOTES:

"If we remade 'Singin' in the Rain' today, when Gene Kelly sings in the rain I think he'd be looking around to make sure he wasn't going to get mugged."—Donnen quoted in *The New York Times*, February 9, 1996.

BIBLIOGRAPHY:

"Stanley Donen" Joseph Andrew Casper, 1983, Scarecrow Press

"Dancing on the Ceiling: Stanley Donen and His Movies" Stephen Silverman, 1996, Alfred A. Knopf

---

Richard Donner

BORN: Richard Donald Schwartzberg in Bronx, New York, 1930

NATIONALITY: American

EDUCATION: Parker Junior College
New York University, New York, New York, business and theater

AWARD: MTV Movie Award Best Action Sequence "Lethal Weapon 3" 1993

BIOGRAPHY

A former Off-Broadway actor who began directing commercials and industrial films in the late 1950s, Richard Donner caught his first big break directing Steve McQueen in the TV series "Wanted: Dead or Alive." Throughout the

60s and into the 70s, he helmed numerous episodes of classic shows ("The Twilight Zone", "The Man From U.N.C.L.E" and "The Fugitive" to name just a few) and also dabbled in feature work (his low-budget directorial debut "X-15" 1961; "Salt and Pepper" 1968). He scored his first commercial if not critical success with "The Omen" (1976) and followed that with the enjoyable box-office smash "Superman" (1978).

After the success of "Superman", Donner attempted a film with more substance, "Inside Moves" (1980), an offbeat picture examining a suicide survivor's recovery. Featuring David Morse, John Savage, Amy Wright and Diana Scarwid among its 70s dark horse cast, this well-meaning but flawed film failed to generate much business. Donner, who started out as director of "Superman II" (1981) before giving way to Richard Lester, had a much more positive experience on the fantasy-adventure film "Ladyhawke"(1985), sharing producing duties with his future wife Lauren Shuler in addition to directing. He also co-produced the exciting teen hit "The Goonies"(1985) with Steven Spielberg.

Donner produced and directed "Lethal Weapon" (1987), introducing one of the cinema's most popular crime fighting duo, Mel Gibson and Danny Glover, and subsequently repeated his duties for the popular and cartoonish sequels, "Lethal Weapon 2" (1989) and "Lethal Weapon 3" (1992). At the same time, Donner returned to television as executive producer/producer and sometime director of the HBO series "Tales From the Crypt" (1989–91).

In 1990, Donner took over the direction of the hotly bid-upon project "Radio Flyer" (1992) for a reportedly record fee of $5 million, replacing fired screenwriter and first-time director David Mickey Evans. This odd film, half sentimental journey, half an exploration of child abuse, flopped commercially and raised critical hackles for its questionable notion that living in fantasy alone is enough for abused kids.

He and his wife's successful production company, Donner/Shuler-Donner Productions, has been responsible for a growing list of films, including the family hit "Free Willy" (1993) and its sequels "Free Willy 2: The Adventure Home" (1995) and "Free Willy 3: The Rescue" (1997); two predictable feature spin-offs from the HBO "Crypt" series, "Tales from the Crypt Presents Demon Knight (1995) and "Tales from the Crypt Presents: Bordello of Blood" (1996); "Maverick" (1994), a cliched but money-making adaptation of the old TV show starring Gibson, Jodie Foster and James Garner (directed by Donner); and "Conspiracy Theory" (1997), an action-adventure fare once again directed by Donner and teaming Gibson with Julia Roberts.

MILESTONES:

Raised in Mount Vernon, New York

Began career as an actor Off-Broadway

1950–1951: Worked with director Martin Ritt on TV production of W Somerset Maugham's "Of Human Bondage" for "The Teller of Tales"

Debut as TV director, episode of "Wanted: Dead or Alive"

1958: Moved to Los Angeles; began directing commercials, industrial films and documentaries

Directed numerous episodes of TV series including "Perry Mason", "The Detectives", "Route 66", "The Fugitive", "The Man From U.N.C.L.E.", "Get Smart", "The Six-Million-Dollar Man", as well as the pilots for "Kojak" and "Bronk"

1961: Feature directing debut, "X-15", starring Charles Bronson

1975: TV-movie producing and directing debut, "A Shadow in the Streets" (NBC)

1976: First major feature, "The Omen" was box office hit

1978: Directed "Superman"; replaced on the sequel "Superman II" by Richard Lester

1981: First film as executive producer, "Omen III: The Final Conflict"

1985: First film as producer (with Lauren Shuler), "Ladyhawke"; also directed

1987: Introduced cop team of Mel Gibson and Danny Glover in "Lethal Weapon"; produced and directed

Served as executive producer and producer on cable series, "Tales From the Crypt" (HBO); also directed various episodes

1990: Paid the then-record fee of $5 million to take over the direction of "Radio Flyer" (1992) from screenwriter and first-time director David Mickey Evans after ten days of shooting; Donner replaced cast and added more upbeat ending

1994: Produced and directed summer smash "Maverick", movie version of old TV series; starring Mel Gibson

1997: Reunited with Gibson for "Conspiracy Theory", co-starring Julia Roberts

1998: Helmed "Lethal Weapon 4"

Directed the feature adaptation of Michael Crichton's novel "Timeline" (lensed 2002); also co-produced

QUOTES:

Among Donner's acting jobs was a role in Martin Ritt's TV production of W Somerset Maugham's "Of Human Bondage." "Marty told me I'd never make it as an actor because I couldn't take direction, but he thought I could give it, so he offered me a job as his assistant.

"He's known for being loud and blustery and funny. But inside is this wonderful, pure child that comes out beautifully in some of his films. Anything to do with mythos or mysticism, he's drawn to. As sophisticated as he is, he retains this sense of innocence that he tries to cover up. He believes. He has this boundless energy. Before there was the Energizer bunny, there was Dick Donner."—screenwriter Tom Mankiewicz quoted in *Daily Variety*, July 31, 1997.

Carl Theodor Dreyer

BORN: in Copenhagen, Denmark, 02/03/1889

SOMETIMES CREDITED AS:
'Tommen/Inch'

DEATH: in Copenhagen, Denmark, 03/20/1968

NATIONALITY: Danish

AWARDS: Venice Film Festival Special Homage "Dies Irae/Day of Wrath" 1947

Venice Film Festival Lion of St. Mark for Best Film "Ordet" 1955

Venice Film Festival International Film Critics Award "Gertrud" 1965 cited along with Luis Bunuel's "Simon of the Desert"

BIOGRAPHY

Carl Theodor Dreyer was born the illegitimate son of a Danish farmer father and a Swedish mother; when he was a young boy his mother died and he was adopted by a Danish family named Dreyer. He embarked upon several careers before becoming a journalist in 1909. In this position, he wrote a series of articles profiling Danish celebrities which put Dreyer in touch with the world of film and theater. In the tradition of other Scandinavian directors, he began his film career by writing scripts; he joined the Danish state studio, Nordisk Films, in 1913 and became a full time screenwriter two years later, scouting for and adapting literary material, writing intertitles and editing film.

With 23 scripts to his credit, Dreyer was given a film to direct in 1919, beginning a career that would virtually span the history of cinema. "The President", like each of Dreyer's subsequent films, was based on a literary work that Dreyer himself had selected. Adaptation was essential to his aesthetic, in which film was envisioned as an extension of literature and theater, and narrative and psychological truth were paramount. "The President" is memorable for its simple sets, carefully created to reflect each character's personality. Perhaps most significantly, Dreyer believed that it was a personal work of art, unlike the assembly-line product of the day.

"Leaves from Satan's Book/Blade at Satan's Bog" (1919) solidified Dreyer's reputation as a director with an uncompromising personal vision. This elaborate project, which Dreyer had been planning for years, faced numerous production difficulties and was altered without the director's permission when it was shown. Even so, "Leaves" was praised for its sophisticated composition and for the subtlety of its character portrayals; it also raised controversy for its treatment of socialism and its depiction of Christ.

Dreyer left Nordisk and made "The Parson's Widow" (1920) for the Swedish company, Svensk Filmindustri, before filming "Love One Another" in Berlin in 1921. The latter film employed Russian emigre actors from Stanislavsky's troupe as well as some of Max Reinhardt's performers. At this time Dreyer began his lifelong habit of collecting and studying prints and photographs to get ideas for sets. Although he returned to Denmark to make "Once Upon a Time" (1922), a beloved operetta filmed with theatrical actors, he would spend the rest of his career as a freelance director, working for any film company that would offer him artistic freedom.

In Berlin, Dreyer made "Mikael" (1924) for UFA, a film known for its ambitious and scrupulously designed sets, which Dreyer helped to dress with items bought throughout the city. Unhappy that the film's ending was changed without his consent, Dreyer returned to Denmark to make "The Master of the House" (1925). For this film, which established Dreyer's reputation in France, a fully functioning two-room apartment was built in the studio to provide the actors with a realistic space in which to perform. "The Bride of Glomdal" (1925) was made in Norway with the mere outline of a script and much improvisation.

During the 1920s and 1930s, when many of Europe's great directors emigrated to Hollywood, Dreyer remained in Europe. Under contract to the French firm Societe Generale des Films, Dreyer was given a seven-million franc budget to make "The Passion of Joan of Arc" (1927). He rejected the original script, based on Joseph Delteil's biography of the heroine, in favor of the actual trial records. Preparations for the eight-month production included the construction of a vast concrete recreation of Rouen castle, complete with sliding walls to facilitate shooting. The realism of the sets extended to every aspect of the production; actors were cast according to facial type; makeup was rejected; and the film was shot in exact sequence. On the unusually silent and intense set, the actors—ruled by Dreyer's belief that the face was the mirror of the soul—were left alone to find the essence of their character, which was then captured in closeup. The film remains one of the most closely examined, and highly acclaimed, in the history of cinema.

With the Danish film industry in financial ruins, Dreyer turned to private financing from Baron Nicholas de Gunzburg to make "Vampyr" (1932), an hypnotically photographed supernatural tale with an elliptical narrative which brilliantly blends fantasy and reality in a uniquely nightmarish manner. After abandoning "Mudundu," an African project that was completed by another director, Dreyer returned to Denmark to work as a journalist.

After the Nazi invasion of Denmark and the subsequent ban on film imports, Danish films were once again in demand. Dreyer worked on a number of documentary shorts for the government before embarking on "Day of Wrath" (1943), a somber, slowly-paced account of a woman who is wrongly burned as a witch.

Over the next decade Dreyer assumed the job

of managing a film theater. He also wrote a script for a film about Mary, Queen of Scots, with his son and started research for a film about Christ which would preoccupy him for the rest of his life.

In 1954, Dreyer made the award-winning "Ordet/The Word", based on the Kaj Munk play. It is noteworthy for its unusually long takes, shot with the continual smooth camera movement that Dreyer believed to be characteristic of modern film technique, as opposed to the short scenes and quick cutting of silent cinema.

After a ten-year silence, the much-anticipated "Gertrud" (1964) appeared, only to face a disastrous reception. Dreyer used silence and softly-spoken dialogue to portray the failure of communication in this story of a middle-aged woman who leaves her home and husband to live alone in Paris. The film still divides critics 25 years later. Dreyer's last years were spent researching "Jesus," as he scouted locations in Israel, learned Hebrew and collected crates of photographs and notes. Although financial backing finally came through in 1967, Dreyer died before he could start the film.

Dreyer's transcendental aesthetic, his search for a spiritual truth beyond the surface of everyday life, marks him as a quintessentially Romantic artist. Yet, as critics have pointed out, his later films are among the most modern ever made, conveying the tension between a conservative vision and an experimental style. The integrity of his vision, combined with his consummate grasp of the film medium, make him one of the greatest directors in the history of cinema.

FAMILY:

mother: Josefin Bernhardin Nilsson. Housekeeper; Swedish; had son illegitimately; died from accidental phosphorus poisoning in 1891

MILESTONES:

1891: Adopted by the Dreyer family
1906: Left home
Worked as a theater critic
1910: First passenger to fly between Denmark and Sweden
1912: Hired as newspaper columnist for *Ekstrabladet*
1912: Screenwriting debut with "Bryggerens Datter/The Brewer's Daughter"
1913: Hired by Nordisk Films Kompagni as screenwriter
1919: Film directing debut with "Praesidenten/The President" (also screenwriter)
1920: Left Nordisk Films Kompagni
Formed independent production company with Baron Nicholas de Gunzburg in early 1930s
1928: Made last and most notable silent film, "The Passion of Joan of Arc"
1932: First sound film as director, "Vampyr"
1952: Made manager of Copenhagan cinema house, Dagmar, by Danish government
1964: Last film, "Gertrud"

Clint Eastwood

BORN: Clinton Eastwood, Jr. in San Francisco, California, 05/31/1930

NATIONALITY: American

EDUCATION: attended eight elementary schools
Oakland Technical High School, Oakland, California, 1948; graduated

Los Angeles City College Los Angeles, California business attended on the GI Bill; never graduated

AWARDS: Golden Globe Award World Film Favorite-Male 1970
People's Choice Award Favorite Motion Picture Actor 1981

People's Choice Award Favorite Motion Picture Actor 1984; tied with Burt Reynolds

People's Choice Award Favorite Motion Picture Actor 1985

People's Choice Award Favorite Motion Picture Actor 1987

People's Choice Award Favorite All-Time Motion Picture Star 1988

Cecil B. DeMille Award 1988; presented by the Hollywood Foreign Press Association

Cannes Film Festival Technique Award "Bird" 1988

Golden Globe Award Best Director "Bird" 1988

Los Angeles Film Critics Association Award Best Film "Unforgiven" 1992; Eastwood was producer

Los Angeles Film Critics Association Award Best Director "Unforgiven" 1992

Los Angeles Film Critics Association Award Best Actor "Unforgiven" 1992

National Society of Film Critics Award Best Picture "Unforgiven" 1992

National Society of Film Critics Award Best Director "Unforgiven" 1992

Golden Globe Award Best Director "Unforgiven" 1992

American Cinema Editors Golden Eddie Award 1993; awarded for distinguished contribution to the art and craft of film

NATO/ShoWest Director of the Year "Unforgiven" 1992; honored by the National Association of Theater Owners

Directors Guild of America Award Outstanding Directorial Achievement in Feature Film "Unforgiven" 1992

Oscar Best Picture "Unforgiven" 1992

Oscar Best Director "Unforgiven" 1992

British Film Institute Fellowship 1993; awarded for his unique contribution as an actor and director to the world of film

Irving G Thalberg Memorial Award 1994; presented by the Academy of Motion Picture Arts and Sciences

American Film Institute Life Achievement Award 1996

Honorary Cesar 1998 for directorial achievement

Producers Guild of America David O. Selznick Theatrical Lifetime Achievement Award 1998

National Board of Review Career Achievement Award 1999

Venice Film Festival Golden Lion for Lifetime Achievement 2000

Kennedy Center Honors Lifetime Achievement Award 2000

The Actor Lifetime Achievement Award 2002

BIOGRAPHY

A tall, soft-spoken and leathery leading man since the 1960s who diversified into directing and producing after achieving iconic status, Clint Eastwood arose from the world of TV Westerns to become the number-one box-office star in the world, subsequently earning critical acclaim as a director. His production company, Malpaso, crafts moderate-budget features that range from the bluntly commercial to the impressively personal and ambitious. Eastwood is not entirely part of the Hollywood establishment; his business is run out of Carmel, California, on the Monterey Peninsula, where he has served as mayor and run a restaurant.

Eastwood grew up in Depression-era California, where his parents were itinerant workers. After high school, he worked as a lumberjack in Oregon, played honky-tonk piano and was a swimming instructor in the US Army. On the GI Bill, he studied at Los Angeles City College. Signed by Universal, one of his first experiences with the indignity actors must suffer was in a "Francis the Talking Mule" movie, "Francis in the Navy" (1955). Many B-movies later, he moved to New York and gained recognition as trail boss Rowdy Yates in the successful TV series "Rawhide" (1959–66).

Tight TV schedules and good training helped him develop the minimalist acting style for which he is famous; it was first appreciated in Europe where he starred in a trilogy of popular spaghetti westerns directed by Sergio Leone in Spain. Sinewy, laconic and lethal, he embodied to Europeans the maverick, unpredictably violent American, whose philosophy in "A Fistful of Dollars" (1964) was "everybody gets rich or dead." "For a Few Dollars More" (1965) and "The Good, the Bad, and the Ugly" (1966) became classic revisionist Westerns and made Eastwood an international star. He returned stateside and starred in "Coogan's Bluff" (1968), a smart urban Western that marked the beginning of his long and successful collaboration with director Don Siegel.

Eastwood's second famed screen incarnation was "Dirty" Harry Callahan, the cop of Don Siegel's "Dirty Harry" (1971) who found it easier to shoot suspects than interrogate them. Hence Harry's immortal line in "Sudden Impact" (1983) when a crook threatens him: "Go ahead—make my day," calmly intoned from the responsible end of a massive handgun. Nonetheless these films were sufficiently ambiguous to defy easy ideological categorization. Eastwood has stated "My characters are usually callused men with a sensitive spot for right and wrong." He has also noted that "My movies add up to a morality, not a politics." His friendship with Ronald Reagan has attracted criticism from some, but Eastwood's concern for the environment, he claims, would make him befriend any President and his Department of the Interior.

Eastwood became a fixture of masculine action fare but he also fared well in several popular comedies ("Every Which Way But Loose" 1978; Any Which Way You Can" 1980). Though he could have coasted on his established persona, Eastwood chose to take chances with his material and subjected his image to thoughtful and not always flattering scrutiny. His portraits of tormented men with intense inner lives and little ability to communicate with others found an apogee in "Bird" (1988), his moody acclaimed portrait of jazz musician Charlie

Parker. Virtual "auteurist" control has enabled him to make unusual Westerns ("High Plains Drifter" 1973; "Pale Rider" 1985) and cop movies exploring feminist concerns ("Sudden Impact 1983"; "Tightrope" 1984).

Eastwood's commercial viability seemed to be in marked decline by the late 80s, The fifth "Dirty Harry" movie, "The Dead Pool" (1988), was far less successful than its predecessors. 1990 saw the box-office failures of both "The Rookie", a formula cop outing, and "White Hunter, Black Heart", an interesting, semi-fictional account of the making of "The African Queen." Eastwood enjoyed a triumphant popular and critical rehabilitation, though, with "Unforgiven" (1992), a Western which earned Eastwood Oscars for Best Picture and Best Director as well as several other major awards. A spellbinding morality tale originally written by David Webb Peoples in 1976, "Unforgiven" took an ironic view of, as well as paid homage to, several of Eastwood's earlier gunfighter incarnations. Dedicated to his directorial mentors, "Sergio" (Leone) and "Don" (Siegel), the film was a solid commercial hit, grossing over $100 million over the course of its long run.

Eastwood's next star vehicle, "In the Line of Fire" (1993), was an immediate blockbuster. This satisfying political thriller—which pitted veteran Secret Service man Clint against a brilliant assassin played to the hilt by John Malkovich—passed the $100 million mark in just a few months. Eastwood directed his subsequent feature, "A Perfect World" (also 1993) wherein he portrayed an experienced law man tracking down a dangerous escaped convict (Kevin Costner) with a seven-year-old hostage/companion.

Surprising even the most jaded critics praised Eastwood's restrained film adaptation of "The Bridges of Madison County" (1995) which took a treacly best-seller and transmuted into a well-acted adult love story. A detailed, mature look at passion, "Bridges" not only exhibited Eastwood's directorial skill but also provided him with a romantic lead that he inhabited with confidence and charm. Playing opposite Meryl Streep, he exudes sex in a charming, low-key manner and reveals a softer yet still very masculine side. Eastwood contributed compositions to the soundtrack and he also launched Malpaso Records, a predominantly jazz label. The first album released was the soundtrack to "Bridges." That same year, Eastwood made an uncredited cameo in the fantasy "Casper."

With "Absolute Power" (1997), Eastwood began to address the issue of age. In that thriller, he portrayed an thief out to commit one last crime before retirement who witnesses a murder involving the US President. Similarly "True Crime" (1999) saw him portray a burntout reporter who finds a last shot at redemption when he becomes convinced a Death Row inmate is innocent. "Space Cowboys" (2000) perhaps was his most blatant attempt to come to terms with the aging process; he played the leader of a quartet of veteran astronauts called out of retirement to fix a satellite first sent into space some forty years earlier. In 2002, Eastwood took on the title of director and star of the crime mystery feature "Bloodwork."

MILESTONES:

Worked as a lumberjack and forest firefighter in Oregon

1948–1951: Worked as a steelworker in Seattle

1955: Film acting debut in "Revenge of the Creature"

1956: Dug swimming pools in Beverly Hills

Made several appearances on the anthology series "The West Point Story" (CBS 1956–1957; ABC 1957–1958)

Starred as Rowdy Yates in the popular TV Western, "Rawhide" (CBS)

1964: Breakthrough screen role as the man with no name in "A Fistful of Dollars", directed by Sergio Leone

1966: Reteamed with Leone for the sequel "For a Few Dollars More"

1968: First film with director Don Siegel, "Coogan's Bluff"

1969: Made singing debut in the film musical "Paint Your Wagon"

1970: Starred opposite Shirley MacLaine in "Two Mules for Sister Sara", directed by Siegel

1970: Directed first film, a documentary short about the filming of "The Beguiled" (1971)

1971: Feature film directorial debut, the thriller "Play Misty For Me"; also starred

1971: First played the role of detective Harry Callahan in "Dirty Harry" after Frank Sinatra turned down the part

1972: Starred in title role of "Joe Kidd"

1973: Helmed the May-December romance "Breezy", starring William Holden and Kay Lenz; first directing assignment in which he did not also act

1973: Reprised Harry Callahan in "Magnum Force"

1975: Moved production company, Malapaso Co. to Warner Bros. on a "handshake deal"

1975: First of six films with off-screen companion Sondra Locke, "The Outlaw Josey Wales"

1976: Third outing as Callahan in "The Enforcer"

1978: Teamed with an orangutan in the comedy "Every Which Way But Loose"

1980: Sang on the soundtrack to "Bronco Billy"; also directed and starred

1982: Producing debut, "Firefox"; also starred in and directed

1983: Last feature with with Sondra Locke, "Sudden Impact"

1984: Earned critical praise for playing a troubled police detective in "Tightrope"; also produced

1985: TV directorial debut, "Vanessa in the Garden", an episode of NBC's "Amazing Stories" starring Harvey Keitel, Sondra Locke and Beau Bridges; story by Steven Spielberg

Won a landslide victory as mayor of Carmel, California; served for two years

1988: First credit as an executive producer, "Thelonius Monk: Straight, No Chaser"

1988: Helmed "Bird", the biopic of jazz legend Charlie Parker

1990: Portrayed a John Huston-like film director in "White Hunter, Black Heart"; also produced and directed

1992: Re-established his superstar status and won widespread acclaim with "Unforgiven"; film won the Best Picture and Best Director Oscar

1993: Had the Clint Eastwood Scholarship Award named after him by Warner Bros.

1993: Documentary "Clint Eastwood—The Man From Malpaso" aired on Cinemax

1993: Played an aging Secret Service agent in "In the Line of Fire"

1993: Teamed with Kevin Costner in the taut "A Perfect World"; also directed and composed a song for the soundtrack

1994: Filed suit against *The National Enquirer* for fabricating an interview between Eastwood and the tabloid; awarded $150,000 in damages by jury in October 1995

1995: Launched new record label, Malpaso Records; first project the soundtrack to "The Bridges of Madison County"; also directed and starred opposite Meryl Streep in the film

1995: Produced "The Stars Fell on Henrietta", featuring Frances Fisher and Robert Duvall

1996: Honored by Film Society of Lincoln Center

1997: Portrayed a thief who becomes embroiled in a murder with political overtones in "Absolute Power"

1997: Documentary "Eastwood on Eastwood" aired on TNT

1997: Directed the uneven film adaptation of the popular non-fiction bestseller "Midnight in the Garden of Good and Evil"

1999: Produced, directed and starred in "True Crime", about a journalist who becomes convinced a man on Death Row is innocent

2000: Teamed with James Garner, Tommy Lee Jones and Donald Sutherland for the sci-fi adventure "Space Cowboys"; also produced and directed

2000: Was subject of documentary "Clint Eastwood: Out of the Shadows", directed by David Ricker; screened at Venice Film Festival

2002: Starred in and directed "Blood Work"

QUOTES:

Eastwood has a number of business interests including the Hog's Breath Inn in Carmel, California, a line of sportswear Tehama Clint and an alcoholic beverage, Pale Rider Ale.

"Maybe being an introvert gives me, by sheer accident, a certin screen presence, a mystique."—Eastwood on his screen persona quoted in *The New York Times,* November 21, 1993.

He was named Harvard's Hasty Pudding Man of the Year in 1991.

Eastwood was sued by former lover Sondra Locke in 1994 for fraud and contractual interference stemming from what she claimed was a bogus production deal made with Warner Bros in return for her declining to pursue a palimony case against Eastwood. In 1996, the matter went to trial, but Eastwood settled out of court for an undisclosed amount of money.

While speaking at the 92nd Street Y in NYC, Eastwood was reported to have said: "When I was doing 'The Bridges of Madison County', I said to myself 'This romantic stuff is really tough. I can't wait to get back to shooting and killing.' "—From *Daily News,* November 15, 1996.

BIBLIOGRAPHY:

"Clint Eastwood" Richard Schickel, 1996, Alfred A. Knopf; biography

BORN: William Blake Crump in Tulsa, Oklahoma 07/26/1922

SOMETIMES CREDITED AS:
Sam O. Brown
William Blake McEdwards

NATIONALITY: American

EDUCATION: Beverly Hills High School Beverly Hills, California

AWARDS: Cesar Best Foreign Film "Victor/Victoria" 1983

Los Angeles Film Critics Association Career Achievement Award 1990; tied with Chuck Jones

Preston Sturges Award for Outstanding Achievements in Both Writing and Directing 1993; presented jointly by the Directors Guild of America and the Writers Guild of America West

American Comedy Award for Lifetime Achievement 1988

Art Directors Guild Contribution to Cinematic Imagery Award 2000

Writers Guild of America Screen Laurel Award 2002

BIOGRAPHY

While best known for his "Pink Panther" comedies starring Peter Sellers as the bumbling Inspector Clouseau, Blake Edwards has also written and directed such hit films as "10" (1979) and "Victor/Victoria" (1982) and created the popular TV series "Peter Gunn" (NBC, 1958–60; ABC, 1960–61). Much of his screen work has been in collaboration with his wife (since 1969) Julie Andrews.

The grandson of silent film director J. Gordon Edwards, Blake Edwards began his career as an actor, first appearing in "Two Gentlemen From West Point" (1942) and playing a supporting role in William Wyler's Oscar-winning "The Best Years of Our Lives" (1946). He turned to screenwriting in 1948 with "Panhandle", providing a role for himself onscreen as well. By the 50s, Edwards was concentrating on writing. Perhaps his most commercially successful screenplay was that for "My Sister Eileen" (1955), the same year Edwards made his directorial debut with "Bring Your Smile Along", a thin musical romance in which Constance Towers is a schoolteacher and would-be songwriter who finds love in the big city. Edwards had written the screenplay for that film, although he did not fill that task on three of his early directorial successes: the Cary Grant classic, "Operation Petticoat" (1959); the exceptional "Breakfast at Tiffany's" (1961); and the more serious "The Days of Wine and Roses" (1963). Though primarily associated with comedies, Edwards has also been responsible for some fine thrillers, including the taut, strikingly photographed "Experiment in Terror" (1962).

In 1964, Edwards co-wrote and directed "The Pink Panther", the first of his many Inspector Clouseau comedies starring Peter Sellers and featuring an infectious theme by Henry Mancini. A sequel, "A Shot in the Dark" (also 1964) followed quickly, but it would be eleven years before Edwards and Sellars reteamed for another go at Clouseau. In the meantime, Edwards' output included the all-star comedy "The Great Race" (1965) and "The Party" (1968), which featured Sellers as an Indian who is accidentally invited to a Hollywood fete—a film which has found a new cult audience in the 90s.

Continual disputes with the Hollywood establishment led Edwards to spend five years in Europe in the 70s, and his critical reputation has since fluctuated. He first directed wife Julie Andrews in "Darling Lili" (1970). Critically dismissed upon its release, this espionage spoof has gained admirers in the last 20 years, partly due to a "director's cut" that Edwards prepared in 1990. The duo collaborated again on an other spy/romance "The Tamarind Seed" (1974) before Edwards turned his attention to the "Pink Panther" sequels. Teaming with Tony Adams (who has risen form production manager to producer), Edwards helmed with varying results "The Return of the Pink Panther" (1975), "The Panther Strikes Again" (1976), "Revenge of the Pink Panther" (1978) and "Trail of the Pink Panther" (1982).

In 1979, Edwards returned triumphantly to the Hollywood fold after the stunning box office and critical success of "10", a film about middle-aged angst which starred Andrews, Dudley Moore and Bo Derek. Edwards followed this with the biting satire of Hollywood, "S.O.B." (1981), most notable for Andrews first topless scene which finally laid to rest her saccharine screen image, and "Victor/Victoria" (1982), based on a 1933 German film about a woman pretending to be a man performing in drag. The film was an artistic triumph for Edwards and Andrews, earning eight Oscar nominations.

Most of Edwards output in the late 80s and 90s seemed to emanate from his own psyche and ran the risk of being labeled self-obsessed. "The Man Who Loved Women" (1983) was a weak remake of the 1977 Francois Truffaut film and "That's Life!" (1986) focused on a man (Jack Lemmon) and his fear of turning 60 while his wife (Andrews) worries whether or not she has cancer. It was perhaps Edwards most personal film, filmed at his and Andrews' Malibu home, with much of the dialogue improvised. "That's Life!" met with a mixed critical reception and indifference from audiences. "Switch" (1991), in which a macho man awakes as a woman (Ellen Barkin) was resoundingly panned by critics. Edwards' attempted to resurrect his most successful franchise with "Son of the Pink Panther" (1993) which had Roberto Benigni stepping in as Clouseau's son. The reviews unfavorably compared this effort with the originals and it sank at the box office.

Edwards had written and directed for radio, including "Richard Diamond, Private Detective" (NBC, 1949) which was revived for TV on ABC from 1950–52. In the late 50s and early 60s, Edwards kept busy on the small screen as well. He produced the syndicated series "City Detective" (1953), created, directed and produced "Peter Gunn" and directed "The Dick Powell Show" (NBC, 1961–63). He also directed and produced the TV-movie "The Monk" (ABC, 1969). Most of his subsequent small screen efforts have been projects designed to showcase his wife, including "Julie!" (ABC, 1972), a documentary on her career, "Julie and Dick in Convent Garden" (ABC, 1974), which reteamed Andrews with her "Mary Poppins" co-star Dick Van Dyke, "Julie-My Favorite Things" (ABC, 1975), and even Andrews' ill-fated sitcom "Julie" (ABC, 1992).

In 1995, Edwards fulfilled a decade-long dream of writing and directing a stage musical adaptation of "Victor/Victoria" for Andrews. After a bumpy start in Chicago, the show arrived on Broadway with a score by Henry Mancini and Leslie Bricusse (supplemented with songs composed by Frank Wildhorn). Critics were reserved in their judgment on the show's overall quality, however, Andrews received personal raves. Many reviews faulted Edwards direction and musical book. The show went on to become a box office success (due in no small part to Andrews' presence). A minor furor arose over the 1996 Tony Award nominations as only Andrews was cited for Best Actress in a Musical. She chose to refuse the nomination which caused a small brouhaha on Broadway.

Edwards' son Geoffrey is a screenwriter and daughter Jennifer is an actress.

COMPANION:

wife: Julie Andrews. Actor; author; married on November 12, 1969; met on the set of "Darling Lili" (1970), married shortly after filming

MILESTONES:

1942: Film acting debut (bit part) in "Ten Gentlemen from West Point"

1948: First film as co-writer (with Lesley Selander) and producer, "Panhandle" (also actor)

1948: Final film as an actor "Panhandle"

1953: TV debut as a producer, "City Detective"

1953–1955: TV debut as a writer, "Hey Mulligan"

1955: Film directing debut, "Bring Your Smile Along" (also writer; songwriter)

TV debut as a director (also creator, producer and writer), "Peter Gunn"

First collaboration with Henry Mancini, "Peter Gunn"

1964: First collaboration with Peter Sellers, "The Pink Panther"

1975: First collaboration with Tony Adams (as producer), "Return of the Pink Panther"

1978: Final film with Peter Sellers, "Revenge of the Pink Panther"

1981: Had box office hit with "S.O.B."

1982: Scored international success with "Victor/Victoria"

1992: Executive producer of short-lived series for Julie Andrews

1993: Returned to the "Pink Panther" series with "Son of the Pink Panther"

1995: Had Broadway box office success with "Victor/Victoria: The Musical"; final collaboration with Henry Mancini

QUOTES:

Edwards used the pseudonym Sam O Brown for his story and screenplay for the film "City Heat" (1984).

Edwards is connected by marriages to the family of screen great Douglas Fairbanks. Donald Crump, Edwards' natural father, was the brother-in-law of Lucile Fairbanks Crump, niece of Douglas Fairbanks and Fairbanks family historian.

"In what business in the world can you have more fun, be creative while you're having fun, be funny and work at being funny, work really nice hours and get paid a lot of money for doing it?"—Blake Edwards in *The Hollywood Reporter* tribute to him.

"He's easygoing as opposed to other directors who dictate and take away the spontaneity."—Dudley Moore.

"Before I became a director, when I would go to another country and go through customs, the airlines handed out little cards for your to fill out. I wrote 'writer'. Now I write 'writer-director'. But the great thing about being a writer is that it's not limited to a soundsage and equipment and a crew of people. I wrote 'S.O.B.' in the middle of the Alps."—Blake Edwards.

"He has great taste. He married Julie."—James Garner.

Atom Egoyan

BORN: in Cairo, Egypt, 07/19/1960

NATIONALITY: Armenian

CITIZENSHIP: Canada

EDUCATION: Trinity College, University of Toronto, Toronto, Ontario, Canada, international relations and classical guitar, 1982

AWARDS: Mannheim International Filmweek Golden Ducat "Next of Kin" 1984

Locarno Film Festival FIPRESCI Prize "Family Viewing" 1988 award also known as the International Critics Award

Moscow International Film Festival Second Prize "The Adjuster" 1991; shared prize with Chinese filmmaker Wang Jin; offered the equivalent of $500,000 to make a film in the Soviet Union within 18 months

National Film Board Award Best Canadian Film "The Adjuster" 1991 awarded at Cinefest '91 in Sudbury Ontario

MCTV Best Ontario Film Award "The Adjuster" 1991

Toronto Festival of Festivals Toronto-City Award for Best Canadian Film of the Year "The Adjuster" 1991; Egoyan handed the prizes of $25,000 cash award to first-time feature director John Pozer of Montreal in recognition of his film "The Grocer's Wife"

Genie Best Picture "Exotica" 1994

Genie Best Director "Exotica" 1994

Genie Best Original Screenplay "Exotica" 1994

Cannes Film Festival Grand Prix du Jury "The Sweet Hereafter" 1997

Genie Best Picture "The Sweet Hereafter" 1997; shared award

Genie Best Director "The Sweet Hereafter" 1997

Toronto Film Critics Association Award Best Picture "The Sweet Hereafter" 1997; initial presentation

Toronto Film Critics Association Award Best Director "The Sweet Hereafter" 1997; initial presentation

Toronto Film Critics Association Award Best Canadian Film "The Sweet Hereafter" 1999; initial presentation

Society of Texas Film Critics Award Best Picture "The Sweet Hereafter" 1997; shared award

Society of Texas Film Critics Award Best Director "The Sweet Hereafter" 1997

Independent Spirit Award Best Foreign Film "The Sweet Hereafter" 1998

Genie Best Adapted Screenplay "Felicia's Journey" 1999

BIOGRAPHY

A stylish and highly assured filmmaker, Egoyan has produced work that combines self-reflexive meditations on the nature of film and video, examinations of psycho-sexual behavior and a black, ironic sense of humor. Director Wim Wenders was so impressed with Egoyan's third feature, "Family Viewing" (1987), an irreverent study of familial breakdown, cultural alienation, sexual frustration and the disposability of the past all linked together by an omnipresence of video technology, that, when awarded the Prix Alcan for "Wings of Desire" at the 1987 Montreal New Cinema Festival, Wenders publicly turned the prize over to the younger filmmaker.

Egoyan has subsequently continued making his own idiosyncratic, often satirical brand of brightly-hued and darkly-themed musings on sexuality, politics and the media. While his films generally divide audiences, he has emerged as a thought-provoking filmmaker unafraid to explore seeming taboo subjects. "Speaking Parts" (1989) examined the sexual intersection of and communications between three disparate individuals: a dour woman (Arsinee Khanjian) obsessed with an aspiring actor (Michael McManus) who, in turn, becomes involved with a novice screenwriter (Gabrielle Rose). In 1991's "The Adjuster", Egoyan furthered explored such issues, adding voyeurism and censorship into the mix and laced them with symbolic images and sequences that were striking but not always comprehensible. "Calendar" (1993) was essentially a two-hander, in which the director starred as a photographer who travels to Armenia with his dissatisfied wife (Khanjian). The film explored themes of national identity and heritage, commitment and separation, and the cold effect of a camera lens. While not inaccessible, it was hardly mainstream either. In 1994, Egoyan wrote and directed the intriguing "Exotica", an intricately-plotted, haunting look at human despair. The stories of five individuals become interwoven as they cross paths at the titular strip club. As with many of his works, the themes of observation and desire mixed with his metaphorical and literal use of mirrors.

With "The Sweet Hereafter" (1997), an adaptation of Russell Banks' novel about the aftermath of a tragic schoolbus accident, Egoyan created his most complex work to date.

Eschewing the inherent sentiment of the material in favor of a more restrained approach, the writer-director retained some of the more unconventional storytelling aspects of his work, but added a layer of emotional weight lacking in his previous screen outings. As in his other films, "The Sweet Hereafter" raised a number of disturbing (and perhaps unanswerable) questions ranging from how to grieve for loved ones to how to cope with societal changes. As it did not offer pat answers or Hollywood-style happy endings, the film proved compelling and disturbing. Surprisingly Egoyan received two Academy Award nominations for the film, as Best Director and for Best Adapted Screenplay.

In 1997 Egoyan directed a one-hour film featuring renowned cellist Yo-Yo Ma as himself in series of chance encounters with people who had no connection to one another except through his music; the film was shown at Venice International Film Festival. In 1999 the writer-director saw the release of his next major motion picture, the potent psychological thriller "Felicia's Journey" (adapted from William Trevor's novel), which focused on a seemingly kind and genteel caterer (Bob Hoskins) who hides a secret life—even to himself—as a serial killer, and his relationship with 17-year-old, pregnant Felicia, who seems poised to either become his next victim or awaken him to his hideous crimes. Another perfect exercise in masterfully atmospheric direction, the film was a critical and art house favorite and won four Genie Awards, including Best Adapted Screenplay for Egoyan and Best Actor for Hoskins. Egoyan's next major work was 2002's "Ararat," which chronicled the estranged members of a contemporary Armenian family as they faced both Turkey's denial of their catastrophic past and with their own complicated future.

MILESTONES:

1963: At age two, moved with his family from Egypt to Canada

1979–1982: While at the University of Toronto, made four short films: "Howard in Particular" (1979; 15 mins), "After Grad with Dad" (1980; 25 mins), "Peep Show" (1981; 8 mins), "Open House" (1982; 25 mins)

Formed Ego Arts Films

1984: Feature film directing debut, "Next of Kin"

1989: His feature "Speaking Parts" was shown at the New York Film Festival

1993: Produced, wrote, directed, edited and acted in "Calendar"

1994: Acted in "Camilla", starring Bridget Fonda and Jessica Tandy

1995: With Patricia Rozema, served as executive producer on "Curtis's Charm"

1996: Stage opera directing debut, "Salome"

1997: Won widespread critical acclaim for his adaptation of Russell Banks' novel "The Sweet Hereafter"; received Academy Award nominations as Best Director and for Best Adapted Screenplay

1999: Helmed "Felicia's Journey", the first of his films not shot in Canada

2000: Directed the film adaptation of Samuel Beckett's play "Krapp's Last Tape", starring John Hurt

2002: Devised the art installation "Steenbeckett"; opened in London in February

2002: Wrote and directed "Ararat", about a director making a movie about the Armenian genocide of the early 20th century

QUOTES:

Named "Atom" by his parents because there was a nuclear power plant built in Egypt the year he was born. "My parents thought it would be cool to name their son after what was going to be a predominant source of energy for the future. As opposed to calling me 'television monitor' "
—Egoyan quoted in *Interview*, March, 1995.

"I have worked in a hotel for five years. I have worked in film for ten. Both of these professions involve the creation of illusion. In one, the territory of illusion is a room. In the other, it is a screen. People move in and out of rooms.

Actors move in and out of screens. "Speaking Parts" explores a terrain which moves between rooms and screens; a terrain of memory and desire. Somewhere in the passage from a room to a screen, a person is transformed into an image. I am fascinated by this crucial moment, and by the contradictions involved in making images of people."—Atom Egoyan (PR/ "Speaking Parts" 1989).

Sergei Eisenstein

BORN: Sergei Mikhailovich Eisenstein in Riga, Latvia, 01/23/1898

DEATH: in Moscow, Russia, 02/10/1948

NATIONALITY: Russian

EDUCATION: Realschule Riga, Latvia
School of Fine Arts Riga, Latvia
Institute of Civil Engineering Petrograd (now St. Petersburg), Russia architecture, 1914–17)
Officers Engineering School Russia
General Staff Academy Moscow, Russia Oriental languages 1920
State School for Stage Direction Moscow, Russia 1921

AWARDS: Order of Lenin Award "Alexander Nevsky" 1939
Stalin Prize Award "Ivan the Terrible, Part I" 1945

BIOGRAPHY

As a youth, Sergei Eisenstein attended the science-oriented Realschule, to prepare himself for engineering school. However, he did find time for vigorous reading in Russian, German, English and French, as well as drawing cartoons and performing in a children's theater troupe which he founded. In 1915, he moved to Petrograd to continue his studies at the Institute of Civil Engineering, his father's alma mater. On his own, he also studied Renaissance art and attended avant-garde theater productions of Meyerhold and Yevreinov.

After the February 1917 Revolution, he sold his first political cartoons, signed Sir Gay, to several magazines in Petrograd. He also served in the volunteer militia and in the engineering corps of the Russian army. Although there is little record that Eisenstein was immediately affected by the events of October 1917, in the spring of 1918 he did volunteer for the Red Army. His father joined the Whites and subsequently emigrated. While in the military, Eisenstein again managed to combine his service as a technician with study of theater, philosophy, psychology and linguistics. He staged and performed in several productions, for which he also designed sets and costumes.

In 1920 Eisenstein left the army for the General Staff Academy in Moscow where he joined the First Workers' Theater of Proletcult as a scenic and costume designer. After he gained fame from his innovative work on a production of "The Mexican," adapted from a Jack London story, Eisenstein enrolled in his idol Meyerhold's experimental theater workshop and collaborated with several avant-garde theater groups, all of whom shared a mistrust of traditional art forms and "high" culture in general. The new theater's contribution to the revolutionary cause was to destroy the old art entirely and create a new, democratic one. The young Soviet artists resorted to "low" culture—circus, music hall, sports, fair performances—to educate the largely illiterate Russian masses in a "true" communist spirit.

Eisenstein's studies of "commedia dell'arte" paid off in his 1923 staging of "The Sage," a huge success not only as propaganda but also as sheer entertainment. For that production he made a short comic film, "Glumov's Diary" (1923), a parody of newsreels whose hero's grotesque metamorphoses anticipated the metaphors of "Strike" (1925), Eisenstein's first feature. But even more important for his career as a filmmaker was the structure of "The Sage." Eisenstein took an old Ostrovsky play and reassembled it as a series of effective, circus-like attractions. The assemblage of such shocking scenes, as he claimed in his 1923 manifesto, "The Montage of Attractions," would lead the public's attention in a direction planned by the "montageur."

Having studied the films of Griffith, Lev Kuleshov's montage experiments and Esfir Shub's re-editing techniques, Eisenstein became convinced that in cinema one could manipulate time and space to create new meanings, especially if the images were not to be merely linked, as Kuleshov suggested, but juxtaposed. Because at that time he believed that his duty as an artist was to contribute to the forging of the new life for his country, Eisenstein eagerly embraced the film medium as the most efficient tool of communist propaganda. However, as much as "Strike" was a condemnation of czarism, it was also an innovative work of art. With this film, an inexperienced director immediately caught up with the work of Soviet, German and French avant-garde filmmakers. "Strike" is filled with expressionistic camera angles, mirror reflections and visual metaphors. In a story of police spies, the camera itself turns into a spy, a voyeur, a trickster. The film was the first full display of Eisenstein's bold new cinematic grammar, a montage of conflicting shots that served as words and sentences endowed with the maximum power of persuasion. Although his command of this new technique was shaky—some sequences did not convey the intended message—"Strike" was a groundbreaking accomplishment.

As Eisenstein's second film, the enormously successful and influential "Battleship Potemkin" (1925), demonstrated, his art could be even more powerful when it achieved a balance between experimental and traditional narrative forms. If "Strike" was an agitated visual poem arousing emotions within a receptive audience, "Potemkin," the fictionalized story of one of the tragic episodes of the 1905 Russian revolution, was a work of prose, highly emotional but clear in its logical, public speech. The close-ups of suffering human faces and the soldiers' boots in the now legendary "Odessa steps" sequence carried such impact that some screenings of the film outside the USSR provoked clashes with police when audiences were convinced they were watching a newsreel.

Later in his career Eisenstein would compare the film director's art with the craft of a shaman. But in the 20s he was trying hard to find a rational basis for it: in Bekhterv's reflexology, in Russian formalist literary theory, in Marxist dialectics. As his films became more complex, they raised the ire of the new breed of ideologues who called for art accessible to the masses and flexible enough to illustrate the latest party line. However, Eisenstein was too deeply involved with his personal research to follow everyday politics. Thus, "October," commissioned for the tenth anniversary of the October revolution of 1917 was not released until 1928; for one thing, all sequences featuring Trotsky, one of the leaders of the revolt, had to be deleted. Then too, the authorities were disappointed with Eisenstein, for while the edited "October" was considered ideologically correct, its confusing structure and abundance of abstract metaphors were thought to diminish its propagandistic message, and it did not carry the same impact as "Potemkin." Attacking him for the "sins of formalism," critics claimed that he "lost his way in the corridors of the Winter Palace" and pointed to the more intelligible anniversary films shot by his colleagues on more modest budgets and in less time. In a way, the critics were correct; in none of his other films was Eisenstein's search for the new cinematic language so nobly radical.

After "October," Eisenstein was able to resume work that had been interrupted on "The General Line" (1929), a film meant to demonstrate the advantages of collective labor in the village. However, during the production of "October," the party policy toward peasantry had drastically changed from persuasion to coercion, and the film's surrealistic imagery and sophisticated montage, which anticipated Godard, were considered inappropriate. Stalin summoned Eisenstein and his co-director Grigori Alexandrov and ordered them to make radical changes. They made a few cuts and immediately embarked on a trip abroad to investigate the new sound technology. With Eisenstein out of the country, the film was released under the neutral title "Old and New" to vicious attacks. His claim that the film was an experiment which could be understood by the millions was ridiculed as wishful thinking; according to one of his critics, the public needed "simple, realistic pictures with clear plot."

Meanwhile, Eisenstein's reception in Europe nurtured his opinion that he could be both avant-garde artist and creator of popular and ideologically "correct" films. In every country he visited he was hailed by radical students and intellectuals. He met with Joyce, Cocteau, Abel Gance, Marinetti, Einstein, Le Corbusier, Gertrude Stein, all of whom seemed excited about his work. In May 1930 Eisenstein arrived in the United States, where he lectured at several Ivy League schools before moving on to Hollywood, where he hoped to make a film for Paramount. Although he was welcomed by leading Hollywood figures, including Fairbanks, von Sternberg, Disney and especially Chaplin, who became his close friend, his proposal for an adaptation of "An American Tragedy" was rejected as too complicated, as were several other highly original projects.

Just before he left America, Eisenstein was encouraged by Robert Flaherty and Diego Rivera to make a film about Mexico, and in December 1930, with funding from writer Upton Sinclair, he began work on "Que Viva Mexico." This project, which promised to become Eisenstein's most daring, took a tragic turn when Sinclair, caving in to pressures from his family, who cited financial reasons, and Stalin, who was afraid that Eisenstein might defect, cancelled the film with shooting almost finished. Although Eisenstein was told the footage would be sent to Moscow for editing, he was never to see it again.

Upset over the loss of his footage and shocked at the differences in the political and cultural climate that he noticed after three years abroad, he suffered a nervous breakdown. One after another, his ideas for projects were bluntly rejected, and he became the target of intense hostility from Boris Shumyatsky, the Soviet film industry chief whose objective was to create a Stalinist Hollywood. With his bitter memories of commercial filmmaking and strong ties to European modernism, Eisenstein could not make the switch to directing cheerful "agitkas" and was thus perceived as a threat. He took an appointment to head the Direction Department at the Moscow film school and became a devoted teacher and scholar. In January 1935, he was vilified at the All-Union Conference of Cinema Workers but eventually was allowed to start working on his first sound film, "Bezhin Meadow."

On this notorious project Eisenstein tried to create a universal tragedy out of the true story of a young communist vigilante who informed on his father and was murdered in retaliation by the victim's relatives. The authorities wanted to demonstrate that family ties should not be an obstacle to carrying out one's duty—a theme common to Soviet and German cinema of the time. Why Eisenstein agreed to deal with such dubious subject matter is not clear, but what has been saved from the allegedly destroyed film suggests that he once again confounded the Soviet authorities' expectations. After

"Bezhin Meadow" was banned, Eisenstein had to repent for his new "sins of formalism." As one Soviet film scholar put it, "Eisenstein was apologizing for being Eisenstein."

As if to save his life, Eisenstein next made "Alexander Nevsky" (1938), a film about a 13th-century Russian prince's successful battle against invading German hordes. This monumental costume epic starring familiar character actors was a striking departure from Eisenstein's principles of montage and "typage" (casting non-professionals in leading roles). "Nevsky" was a deliberate step back, in the direction of old theater or, even worse, opera productions which Eisenstein has been fiercely opposed to in the 20s. Still, the film demonstrated Eisenstein in top form in several sequences, such as the famous battle scene on the ice. Also significant were his attempts to achieve synthesis between the plastic elements of picture and music with the film's memorable score by Prokofiev, possibly reflecting Eisenstein's prolonged admiration for the cartoons of Walt Disney.

The exciting and stirring "Nevsky" was a huge success both in the USSR and abroad, partially due to growing anti-German sentiment, and Eisenstein was able to secure a position in the Soviet cinema at a time when many of his friends were being arrested. On February 1, 1939, he was awarded the Order of Lenin for "Nevsky" and shortly thereafter embarked on a new project, "The Great Fergana Canal," hoping to create an epic on a scale of his aborted Mexican film. Yet after intense pre-production work the project was cancelled, and following the signing of the non-aggression treaty between the USSR and Germany, "Nevsky" was quietly shelved as well. In February 1940, in a Radio Moscow broadcast to Germany, Eisenstein suggested that the pact provided a solid basis for cultural cooperation. At that time he was commissioned to stage Wagner's opera "Die Walkure" at the Bolshoi theater. At the November 21, 1940, premiere, the German diplomats in Moscow, not unlike Stalin's henchman before them, were dismayed by Eisenstein's artistry. They accused him of "deliberate Jewish tricks." Yet when the Nazis attacked Russia less than a year later, it was "Die Walkure' "s turn to be banned while "Nevsky" could once again be screened.

In 1941 Eisenstein was commissioned to do an even larger scale historic epic, a three-part film glorifying the psychopathic and murderous 16th-century Russian czar, Ivan the Terrible. However, Part I of "Ivan the Terrible" (1945) was an enormous success and Eisenstein was awarded the Stalin Prize. But "Ivan the Terrible Part II" (1946) showed a different Ivan: a bloodthirsty tyrant, the unmistakable predecessor of Stalin. Naturally, "Part II" was banned and the footage of "Part III" destroyed. Eisenstein was hospitalized with a heart attack, but he recovered and petitioned Stalin to be allowed to revise "Part II" as the bureaucracy wanted, only to be dismissed. In fact, Eisenstein was too weak to resume shooting, and he died in 1948, surrounded by unfinished theoretical works and plans for new films. "Ivan the Terrible Part II" was first shown in 1958 on the 60th anniversary of Eisenstein's birth. In 1988, at the international symposium at Oxford marking Eisenstein's 90th anniversary, Naum Kleiman, the director of the Eisenstein Museum in Moscow, showed a scene that survived from "Part III." In it, Ivan is interrogating a foreign mercenary in a manner resembling one of Stalin's secret police. With the abundance of literature on Stalin's crimes now available even in the USSR, the significance of "Ivan the Terrible Part II" as a document of its tragic time has diminished, but as a work of art it is still significant. In his last completed film, Eisenstein achieved what he had dreamt of since 1928, when he saw a Japanese Kabuki troupe performance: the synthesis of gesture, sound, costume, sets and color into one powerful, polyphonic experience. Both "Nevsky" and "Walkure" were steps in that direction, but only the celebrated danse macabre of Ivan's henchmen comes close to the synthesis of the arts which has haunted artists for ages.

Eisenstein's death prevented him from summing up his theoretical views in the areas of the psychology of creativity, the anthropology of art and semiotics. Although not many filmmakers have followed Eisenstein the director, his essays on the nature of film art have been translated into several languages and studied by scholars of many nations. Soviet scholars published a six-volume set of his selected works in the 60s. 1988 saw the publication of a new English-language edition of his writings.

COMPANION:

wife: Pera Fogelman. Married in 1934; reportedly a marriage of convenience as Eisenstein was a homosexual

MILESTONES:

1917: Joined Red Army

1920: Debut as stage producer and director

1922: Hired by Peredvizhaniya Trupa as administrative head and artistic director

1922: First film as co-editor "Dr. Mabuse der Spieler"

1923: Debut as screenwriter and actor with five-minute short film "Glumov's Diary" from Pere Tru's stage production "The Wise Man"

1925: First feature film as director and co-screenwriter, "Stachka/Strike"

1928: Hired by State Institute of Cinematography to teach filmmaking

1928: He also wrote a sound film manifesto with Vsevolod Pudovkin and Grigori Aleandrov that was published in 1928.

1930: Hired by Paramount

1930: Fired by Paramount, left for Mexico to film "Que Viva Mexico!"

1932: Made head of directing department, State Institute of Cinematography, in Russia

1940: Joined Mosfilm (Moscow) as artistic director

AFFILIATION: Jewish

BIBLIOGRAPHY:

"Immoral Memories: An Autobiography" Segei Eisenstein (translated by Herbert Marshall), 1983, Houghton Mifflin

"Eisenstein: A Life in Conflict" Ronald Bergan, 1998, Overlook Press

Nora Ephron

BORN: in New York, New York, 05/19/1941

NATIONALITY: American

EDUCATION: Beverly Hills High School, Beverly Hills, California

Wellesley College, Wellesley, Massachusetts, BA, 1962

AWARDS: Women in Film Crystal Award 1994

ShowEast George Eastman Award 1996 presented by the National Association of Theater Owners

Writers Guild of America, East Lifetime Achievement 2002

BIOGRAPHY

This oldest daughter of screenwriters Henry and Phoebe Ephron originally intended to avoid following in her parents wake and chose to head East for college and a career in journalism. Nora Ephron spent five years as a reporter at the *New York Post* before making her mark as an essayist and practitioner of the "New Journalism" prevalent in the early 1970s. Skewering such pop culture figures as Betty

Friedan and Gail Sheehy, she quickly became an in demand writer, eventually joining the staff of both *Esquire* and *New York*. Her first collection of essays, "Wallflower at the Orgy" was published in 1970 and she earned notable praise for her second, "Crazy Salad: Some Thing About Women" published in 1975.

Ephron has stated that she was lured into writing scripts because it seemed to be in vogue and she began by contributing to the short-lived 1973 ABC sitcom "Adam's Rib." She penned the caper TV-movie "Perfect Gentlemen" (CBS, 1978) which teamed Lauren Bacall, Ruth Gordon, Sandy Dennis and Lisa Pelikan as women desperately in need of cash who plan a $1 million heist. Ephron garnered much press over her first novel, "Heartburn" a 1983 roman a clef about the breakup of her second marriage to journalist Carl Bernstein. Segueing to the big screen, she came to be known for creating strong central roles for women. evidenced by the Oscar-nominated script (co-written with Alice Arlen) of "Silkwood" (1983), Mike Nichols' biopic of anti-nuclear activist Karen Silkwood (portrayed by Meryl Streep). Nichols agreed to film "Heartburn" (1986), casting Streep in the role based on the author. Ephron continued to create feisty women's roles including a mobster's daughter in "Cookie" (1989) and the clear-eyed heroine of "When Harry Met Sally . . . " (also 1989). The latter brought Ephron her second Academy Award nomination for Best Original Screenplay.

Moving to the director's chair, Ephron oversaw "This Is My Life" (1992). Co-written with her sister Delia, it was a comedy starring Julie Kavner that traced how a single mother struggled to become an established stand-up comic. Ephron followed with the box office hit "Sleepless in Seattle" (1993), which she helmed and co-wrote (with David S. Ward and Jeff Arch). Less about love than about love in motion pictures, the film drew its inspiration from Leo McCarey's 1957 tearjerker "An Affair to Remember" with Tom Hanks and Meg Ryan in the leading roles. Her 1994 follow-up "Mixed Nuts" was a black comedy about a suicide hot line at Christmas and suffered from its holiday release. Ephron bounced back co-producing, co-writing (with Delia Ephron) and directing the genial "Michael" (1996), about tabloid reporters investigating a possible angelic visitation. She reteamed with "Sleepless" stars Hanks and Ryan for "You've Got Mail" (1998), which put a modern spin on Ernst Lubitsch's charming 1940 classic "The Shop Around the Corner."

COMPANIONS:

husband: Carl Bernstein. Journalist; born in 1944; married on April 14, 1976; divorced in 1979; Ephron is legally enjoined by the terms of the divorce settlement from using anything about their life together or the children as material in her work

husband: Nicholas Pileggi. Author, screenwriter; married on March 28, 1987

MILESTONES:

1944: Moved to Beverly Hills, California, at age three (date approximate)

Parents reportedly used her college letters to home as the inspiration for the 1961 Broadway hit "Take Her, She's Mine" (filmed in 1963)

1963–1968: Worked as reporter for the *New York Post*

Was a freelance writer, contributing to such publications as *The New York Times Magazine* and *Good Housekeeping*

1970: Published collection of essays, "Wallflower at the Orgy"

1972: Named a columnist and contributing editor at *Esquire*

1973: Wrote scripts for the short-lived ABC sitcom "Adam's Rib"

Was contributing editor at *New York* magazine

1974: Promoted to senior editor at *Esquire*

1975: Published second collection of essays, "Crazy Salad: Some Things About Women"

1978: Wrote the teleplay for the TV comedy-drama "Perfect Gentlemen", a comic caper about four women who attempt a $1 million heist

1983: Feature screenwriting debut, "Silkwood", co-written with Alice Arlen; received first Academy Award nomination for Best Original Screenplay

1983: First novel published, "Heartburn"; loosely based on the break-up of her second marriage

1986: Wrote screenplay adaptation of "Heartburn", directed by Mike Nichols

1989: Appeared in a small role as a wedding guest in Woody Allen's "Crimes and Misdemeanors"

1989: Produced first films "Cookie" (executive producer) and "When Harry Met Sally . . . " (associate producer); also scripted; earned second Oscar nomination for the latter

1992: Directorial debut, "This Is My Life"; co-written with sister Delia Ephron

1992: Played a party guest in Woody Allen's "Husbands and Wives"

1993: Had box office success with the romantic comedy "Sleepless in Seattle"; directed and co-wrote with David S. Ward and Jeff Arch; garnered third Best Original Screenplay nomination; film starred Tom Hanks and Meg Ryan

1994: Had minor setback with the critically-derided box office disappointment "Mixed Nuts", co-scripted with sister Delia

1996: Regained career momentum as producer, co-screenwriter (with Delia Ephron) and director of "Michael", a comedy about tabloid reporters investigating an angel sighting

1998: Reteamed with Tom Hanks and Meg Ryan for "You've Got Mail", a modern day remake of "The Shop Around the Corner"; co-written with sister Delia

2000: Produced and co-wrote screenplay (with sister Delia) for "Hanging Up", loosely based on their father's life

2002: Play "Imaginary Friends", about the relationship between writers Lillian Hellman and Mary McCarthy, set to premiere at the Old Globe Theatre in San Diego; includes songs by Marvin Hamlisch and Craig Carnelia

AFFILIATION: Jewish

QUOTES:

"The hugest smile I ever saw was when Nora said 'Action!' for the first time. It was a smile of complete pleasure. She loves to be able to control things. Francis Coppola said that being a director is one of the last dictatorships you can have in an increasingly democratic world. Without being a dictator in the evil sense of the word, Nora is, in a postitive sense. I think Nora was born to direct."—Julie Kavner on Ephron's directorial debut, quoted in *Vanity Fair,* February 1992.

"When I started out writing screenplays, it was during a period of time when anyone who could type was writing them. I already knew how to do journalism with my hands tied behind my back. Suddenly, I was doing something that I didn't know much about and it was very interesting."—Nora Ephron quoted in *Daily Variety,* October 21, 1996.

"All of movie making consists of making a choice about one detail after another. But in the end the details don't matter. That's the really shocking thing."—Ephron quoted in *The New York Times,* April 10, 1994.

"Question: As a child, did you crave to be a screenwriter and director?

"Answer: No, I craved to be a journalist. My parents were terrific screenwriters and that's why I didn't want to be one. I mean, who wants to do what your parents do? My parents did have some influence on my choice of career. My parents were writers. I wanted to be a writer. I just didn't want to have anything to do with the movie business. I didn't want to live 'out there.' I grew up 'out there.' And I thought in order to be in the movie business, you had to live 'out there.' And it turns out you don't. It turns out you can be in the New York and be in the movie business."—Nora Ephron in *The Hollywood Reporter,* June 11, 1996.

"Look, people can be whatever they want to be in Hollywood. They can be complete babies and do brilliantly or they can be fascists and do brilliantly. But I have found it very useful not to let a lot of things bother me, because you eventually learn that most of them get sorted out, and if you react to every little thing, you could go crazy in the movie business."—Ephron in the 1996 special "Women in Film" issue of *Premiere*.

BIBLIOGRAPHY:

"Wallflower at the Orgy" Nora Ephron, 1970, Viking; collection of essays

"Crazy Salad: Some Things About Women" Nora Ephron, 1975, Alfred A. Knopf; collection of essays

"Scribble, Scribble: Notes on the Media" Nora Ephron, 1979, Alfred A. Knopf

"Heartburn" Nora Ephron, 1983, Alfred A. Knopf; novel; reportedly loosely based on the break-up of her marriage to Carl Bernstein

"Crazy Salad Plus Nine" Nora Ephron, 1984; revised collection of essays

"Nora Ephron Collected" 1991, Avon

"The Women Who Write the Movies: From Frances Marion to Nora Ephron" Marsha McCreadie, 1994, Birch Lane Press

Bobby Farrelly

BORN: Robert Leo Farrelly, Jr., 1958

NATIONALITY: American

EDUCATION: Rensselaer Polytechnic Institute, Troy, New York, geological engineering, BS; attended on a hockey scholarship

AWARDS: ShoWest Screenwriters of the Year 1999; shared with brother

Producers Guild of America Golden Laurel Todd-AO Nova Award Most Promising Film Producer "There's Something About Mary" 1998; shared with brother

BIOGRAPHY

Sometimes described erroneously as the smaller, quieter, less affable of the Farrelly filmmaking duo, the cherubically preppy Bobby Farrelly has teamed with his slightly more sinister older brother Peter to reach new heights (or depths) of low-brow comedy. Though he went to college on a hockey scholarship and came away with a degree in geological engineering, he was just another slacker-in-waiting when he arrived in Hollywood to partner with his brother and Bennett Yellin writing screenplays, one of which eventually became the comedy hit "Dumb and Dumber" (1994). Growing up in a Rhode Island town without a movie theater, the Farrellys developed their brand of humor at the family dinner table "and just trying to crack each other up all of our lives." They had a feeling that audiences wanted to laugh long and hard at idiots in absurd situations, and after finally breaking through with two 1992 episodes of NBC's "Seinfeld", "Dumb and Dumber" proved their fingers were solidly on the nation's comic pulse.

With Peter at the helm and Bobby co-producing, "Dumb and Dumber" teamed Jim Carrey and Jeff Daniels as dimwitted buddies going cross-country to return a briefcase, which they don't realize (until much later) contains a lot of money. A flat-out celebration of stupidity, bodily functions and pratfalls, the picture succeeded on the strength of its uniformly strong performances and by not overplaying its vulgarity. The Farrellys concocted some crazily original humor instead of relying on the same, tired, recycled gags, and audiences laughed until it hurt, with the film eventually earning in excess of $300 million. They were back in gross-out form for the crass bowling farce "Kingpin" (1996), which marked Bobby's debut as co-director with Peter, but despite the presence of Woody Harrelson, Randy Quaid and Bill Murray, the picture tanked at the box office, perhaps due to faulty marketing by MGM. The brothers had to wonder whether audiences truly loved their unhinged humor or if the success of "Dumb and Dumber" was merely part of the Jim Carrey phenomenon.

"There's Something About Mary" (1998) passed the acid test, proving their earlier hit was no fluke and that the Farrelly sickness was quite contagious. As Bobby told the *Daily News* (July 14, 1998), "We did something drastically different in this: we added a plot." They also had a female lead (Cameron Diaz) for a change, making their antics more palatable for the ladies, and the most outrageous, gross-out gags of their short career as masters of taste-lessness. There was the brilliant genitalia-in-the-zipper bit and the arguably even more inspired "hair gel" routine. The Farrellys spared no one, wrenching laughter from its audience at the expense of a helpless animal and the handicapped while lampooning gays and serial killers. Though far from a perfect film, "Mary" had five or six extremely hysterical scenes, more than enough saving grace to make it the comedy hit of the summer and one of the year's top-grossers.

As directors, the Farrelly style is pretty style-less, which seems to suit their material. "We never think of any swooping camera moves," Bobby admitted to the *Los Angeles Times* (July 18, 1998). "But the director of photography likes to do that, so we sort of go along with him, let him do it, then cut it out in the end." They're famous for their loose sets and for employing lots of friends and family in minor roles, including the wheel-chair bound Danny Murphy, whose take on how the handicapped should be portrayed colors their movies. The brothers wrote and produced "Outside Provi-

dence" (1999), based on Peter's 1988 novel, but turned the reins over to fellow Rhode Islander Michael Corrente. More a coming-of-age story than that wacky new Farrelly comedy as promoted by Miramax, it stalled at the box office after recouping its small investment. The Farrellys then returned behind the camera for "Me, Myself and Irene" (2000), reteaming with the zany Carrey for more high art of the low brow.

MILESTONES:

Raised in Cumberland, Rhode Island

Joined with team of Peter Farrelly and Bennett Yellin to write screenplays

1992: Co-wrote two episodes of "Seinfeld" with brother Peter

1994: Co-wrote (with brother and Yellin) and co-produced first feature film, "Dumb and Dumber", starring Jim Carrey and Jeff Daniels

1996: Co-directed (with brother) feature film "Kingpin"

1998: Made third film "There's Something About Mary", sharing producing, directing and writing responsibilities with brother

1999: Produced and scripted "Outside Providence" with brother and director Michael Corrente, adapting from Peter's 1988 novel; first film the brothers produced which they did not also direct

2000: Reteamed with Carrey for "Me, Myself and Irene", again sharing directing, producing and scripting honors with his brother

QUOTES:

Asked what got used as prop semen, Farrelly told *Movieline* (August 1998): "Promise not to tell Ben [Stiller], because we told him it was a mixture of hand cremes. But that was all mine."

About Matt Dillon agreeing to play the jerky detective in "There's Something About Mary": "It was an act of courage for Matt to take the part. And it did not come naturally to him. I think he was wondering, even as late as editing, if there was any way we could cut the film so he got the girl."—Bobby Farrelly to Stephen Talty in *Time Out New York,* July 16–23, 1998.

"You won't earn laughs if somebody is going to be hurt by something—meaning what's offensive to us, what we don't do, is any gay-bashing or racism. But who gets hurt by a guy sitting on the dumper letting a huge one rip? Growing up in the Rhode Island/Massachusettes area influ-

enced us, the basic sense of humor there. Almost every gag in our movies comes from real-life incidents. Even our parents' sense of humor is very out there. The other day I told my father a tasteless joke about the similarity between a woman and a washing machine, and he was, like, 'You've gotta tell your mother that one!' "—Farrelly quoted in *Movieline,* August 1998.

Peter Farrelly

BORN: Peter John Farrelly in Phoenixville, Pennsylvania, 12/17/1956

NATIONALITY: American

EDUCATION: Kent School, Kent, Connecticut; boarding school located on the Housatonic River in northwestern Connecticut 55 miles west of Hartford; Farrelly got the idea for "Outside Providence" while attending

Providence College, Providence, Rhode Island, accounting, BA, 1979

Columbia University, New York, New York, MFA, 1987

AWARDS: ShoWest Screenwriters of the Year 1999; shared with brother

Producers Guild of America Golden Laurel Todd-AO Nova Award Most Promising Film Producer "There's Something About Mary" 1998; shared with brother

BIOGRAPHY

Half of arguably the second most-famous brother act in filmmaking (after the Coens), Peter Farrelly developed his comic chops competing for laughs around the family dinner table in Cumberland, Rhode Island. Together with his equally underachieving brother Bobby, he lived the slacker life to the hilt before moving to Los Angeles in 1985, landing a development deal with writing partner Bennett

Yellin soon after. Bobby joined the process, and the brothers remained constantly employed, going from one deal to the next, though none of the movies ended up getting made. Peter did score a credit and some valuable insight to comedy writing with the Zucker brothers (among others) for the 1987 NBC special "Our Planet Tonight" before seeing his first novel, "Outside Providence", published the following year. The brothers' first big break, however, came when they scripted two 1992 episodes of NBC's wildly popular "Seinfeld." Having seen so many projects go down the developmental drain, he opted to direct his first feature, "Dumb and Dumber" (1994, written with Yellin and Bobby, who also served as a co-producer), despite the daunting fact that neither brother had ever picked up a camera.

Farrelly, who credits Mel Brooks' "Blazing Saddles" (1974), John Landis' "Animal House" (1978) and the breakthrough Abraham-Zucker brothers collaboration "Airplane!" (1980) as inspirations, had grown tired of smart aleck comic heroes who are wiser than everyone else. The brothers instead presented two doofus buddies and benefited from the hot streak of Jim Carrey, riding his coattails to improbable grosses, ultimately in excess of $300 million on an investment of $16 million. The low-brow "Dumb and Dumber" showcased Carrey (dumb) and Jeff Daniels (dumber) as they traveled cross-country to return a briefcase which, unbeknownst to them, contains a fortune in ransom money. Along the way, the stunts included the very politically incorrect selling of a dead bird to a crippled, blind kid and inadvertently giving a cop who has stopped them for speeding a beer bottle containing urine to drink. Though critics looked askance, the laidback Farrellys had definitely cultivated a fun atmosphere in which their actors could work, and that real enjoyment translated to the screen, putting their careers on firm footing.

The brothers did less well with "Kingpin" (1996), which they co-directed but did not write, barely managing to recoup its $25 million budget. The fault may well have been with MGM's lackluster marketing (as Peter has claimed) since many critics (i.e., Roger Ebert) who had not exactly warmed to "Dumb and Dumber" came onboard, howling at the Farrellys' audacious vulgarity. Establishing their working method of Peter directing the actors from behind the camera while Bobby positioned himself at the monitor, they elicited first-rate performances from Woody Harrelson as a former bowling champion who bottoms out after losing his hand, Randy Quaid as the Amish prodigy he discovers and manages, and Bill Murray as the smug Ali of pro bowling, sporting an hilarious combover from hell. There were prosthesis jokes, badteeth jokes, ugly-women jokes and sight gags involving vomiting, not to mention throwaway jokes in the background, such as the performance of "The Jeffersons on Ice." In a nod to Don Knotts, another comic inspiration, an unseen person at the bowling tournament yells "Attaboy, Luther!", which also rang out in "The Ghost and Mr. Chicken" (1965) every time Knotts spoke in public. If they erred, the Farrellys erred on the side of tastelessness as they had intended.

Taking gross-out jokes to a whole new level in "There's Something About Mary" (1998), they struck box office gold again, delivering some truly outrageous gags that managed not to cross the line. (The Farrellys test their material on many audiences and cut the bits that fail

the laugh-out-loud test.) First up was the magnificent money shot of Ben Stiller's private parts caught in a zipper, one which they milked relentlessly for every drop of humor available. There was silly slapstick involving the handicapped and lampooning of gay sex and serial murder, not to mention Matt Dillon's ludicrous overbite and two memorable scenes with a dog, one on sedatives, the other on speed. Perhaps best of all was that seminal film moment when Stiller answers the door with an egregious gob of ejaculate hanging from his ear, and Cameron Diaz mistakes it for styling mousse and puts it on her tresses, setting up the tremendous, sticky-hair follow-up. The Farrellys, who had geared their first two movies to sixteen-year-old males, had women splitting their sides with this questionable entry to the romantic comedy genre, proving that a picture can be far from perfect as long as it delivers in its big scenes.

For "Outside Providence" (1999), which they adapted from Peter's 1988 novel, the brothers stayed behind the scenes as producers, turning the reins over to fellow Rhode Islander Michael Corrente. Missing, however, from this coming-of-age story set during the 70s was the Farrellys' trademark zaniness, and Miramax's marketing campaign put the brothers in an awkward position. Miramax president Mark Gill defended his company's position to the *Los Angeles Times* (August 30, 1999): "The first job is to get an audience in . . . Every time we've done a screening for this movie, we've told audiences it's the outrageous new comedy from the Farrelly brothers . . . They see the movie and, far from being disappointed, they really like it. This is what gets them through the door and then once they see it, they're really satisfied. Is it a little bit different than we told them? Sure, but that's common." The studio's disingenuousness backfired, and the picture suffered at the box office, though it did manage to recoup its investment. The Farrellys then returned behind the camera for the more typical "Me, Myself and Irene" (2000), reteaming with ace funnyman Carrey, whose character's split personalities war with each other over the love of a woman (Renee Zellweger).

MILESTONES:

Raised in Cumberland, Rhode Island

1979–1981: Worked as salesman for US Lines, Inc in Boston, Massachusetts

Tended bar in Boston

1985: Moved to Los Angeles and began writing screenplays with Bennett Yellin; younger brother Bobby later joined the process

1987: First writing credit (with Jerry and David Zucker and Yellin, among others), the NBC TV special "Our Planet Tonight"

1988: Published first novel, "Outside Providence"

1992: With brother Bobby, wrote two episodes for the NBC sitcom "Seinfeld"

1994: Made feature directorial debut with "Dumb and Dumber"; co-scripted with Yellin and brother; film starred Jim Carrey and Jeff Daniels

1996: With brother Bobby, co-directed the feature comedy "Kingpin"; also co-wrote

1998: Made third film, the summer hit "There's Something About Mary"; executive produced and co-directed with brother Bobby; reportedly, the brothers rescued the project from development hell and worked on the script with original writers Ed Decter and John J. Strauss

1998: Appeared in Brad Kane's feature directing debut, "Say You'll Be Mine", produced by Michael Corrente and filmed on location in Providence and NYC

1999: Produced (with brother Bobby) "Outside Providence", based on his 1988 novel; adapted screenplay with brother and film's director Corrente; first time the brothers produced without directing

2000: Produced, directed and scripted (sharing all responsibilities with brother) "Me, Myself and Irene", reteaming with Jim Carrey

QUOTES:

"We agree on most things; we have the same vision. The big blowups come when no one wants to back off from his point of view. And when the smoke clears, we realize we're both wrong. But that doesn't happen very much. We know each other too well. I've been sleeping in the same room with him since I was 2 years old."—Peter Farrelly on working with his brother, quoted in *The New York Times,* February 27, 1998.

On MGM dropping the promotional ball on the Farrelly's second movie, "Kingpin": "It was a shock and a disappointment. MGM released it, and they suck—they're the worst. They dropped it in the middle of the Olympics, and they did one television ad. [They told us,] 'That's not your audience.' The whole fucking world is watching, and it's not our audience?"

About the inspiration for the famous "zipper" scene in "There's Something About Mary": "My sister had her 12th birthday party at our house. This guy named Al, the cool kid in the class, went to the bathroom and didn't come out for like an hour. My parents went in there, and his thing was all tangled up in the zipper. It was a one and a two and a whoop."—Farrelly to Stephen Talty in *Time Out New York,* July 16–23, 1998.

Regarding his penchant for displaying his penis: "It's a joke. It's not like I make a habit of just whipping it out and saying, 'Hey! Look! My cock!' We do a joke where, it's like, Bob says, 'Pete's been really crazy, he went out and spent $500 on a belt buckle.' I go, 'Bob, it's an investment, it's not a big deal.' He says you're stupid! $500 on a belt buckle!' I say it's not stupid . . . Finally she [in this case Cameron Diaz] says, 'Let me see it.' And I lift my shirt and have it . . . hanging over . . .

"I don't like it when they laugh at my penis . . . But I do like it when they stare."—Farrelly, quoted in the *The Observer,* September 27, 1998.

BIBLIOGRAPHY:

"Outside Providence" Peter Farrelly, 1988, Atlantic Monthly Press; first novel and basis for the 1999 movie of the same name

"The Comedy Writer" Peter Farrelly, 1998, Doubleday; second novel

Rainer Werner Fassbinder

BORN: in Bad Worishofen, Bavaria, Germany, 05/31/1945

SOMETIMES CREDITED AS:
Franz Fassbinder
Franz Walsch
R. W. Fassbinder

DEATH: in Munich, Germany, 06/10/1982

NATIONALITY: German

EDUCATION: Rudolph Steiner Elementary School, left high school before graduating in 1964

AWARD: Cannes Film Festival FIPRESCI Prize "Ali: Fear Eats the Soul" 1974

BIOGRAPHY

By far the best-known director of the New German Cinema, Fassbinder has also been called the most important filmmaker of the post-WWII generation. Exceptionally versatile and prolific, he directed over 40 films between 1969 and 1982; in addition, he wrote most of his scripts, produced and edited many of his films and wrote plays and songs, as well as acting on stage, in his own films and in the films of others. Although he worked in a variety of genres—the gangster film, comedy, science fiction, literary adaptations—most of his stories employed elements of Hollywood melodrama from the 1950s overlayed with social criticism and avant-garde techniques. Fassbinder's expressed desire was to make films that were both popular and critical successes, but assessment of the results has been decidedly mixed: his critics contend that he became so infatuated with the Hollywood forms he tried to appropriate that the political impact of his films is indistinguishable from conventional melodrama, while his admirers argue that he was a postmodernist filmmaker whose films satisfy audience expectations while simultaneously subverting them.

Fassbinder often described his early years as lonely and lacking in love and affection. His father, a physician, and his mother, a translator, were divorced in 1951, and Fassbinder had little contact with his father after that. From around the age of seven, Fassbinder would be sent by his mother to the cinema so that she could work on her translation projects. He would later claim that during this period of his life he went to the movies almost every day, sometimes two or three times a day. He attended private and public schools at Augsburg and Munich but left before graduating in 1964 to enroll in a private drama school.

In the summer of 1967 Fassbinder joined the Action Theater, modeled on American Julian Beck's Living Theater. Two months later, he had become the company's co-director, and when it reorganized under the name "antitheater," he emerged as its leader. The group lived together and staged a number of controversial and politically radical plays in 1968 and 1969, including some of Fassbinder's original works and adaptations.

Fassbinder's work in the theater, however, was primarily a means toward his goal of making films. He had applied in 1965 to the Berlin Film and Television Academy but failed the entrance exam. In the same year he wrote and directed his first film, a ten-minute short entitled "The City Tramp." During his "antitheater" period he made ten feature films, including "Love is Colder Than Death" (1969), "Katzelmacher" (1969), and "Beware of a Holy Whore" (1971). Influenced by Jean-Luc Godard, Jean-Marie Straub and the theories of

Bertolt Brecht, these films are austere and min-imalist in style, and although praised by many critics, they proved too demanding and inac-cessible for a mass audience. It was during this time, however, that Fassbinder developed his rapid working methods. Using actors and tech-nicians from the "anti-theater" group, he was able to complete films ahead of schedule and often under budget and thus compete success-fully for government subsidies.

In search of a wider, more sympathetic audience, Fassbinder turned for a model to Hollywood melodrama, particulary the films of German-trained Douglas Sirk, who made "All That Heaven Allows," "Magnificent Obses-sion" and "Imitation of Life" for Universal Pic-tures during the 1950s. Fassbinder was attracted to these films not only because of their entertainment value but also for their depiction of various kinds of repression and exploitation. This mixture of melodrama and politics is evident in Fassbinder's first commer-cially successful film, "The Merchant of Four Seasons" (1972). But the film that brought him international acclaim was "Ali: Fear Eats the Soul" (1974), which won the International Critics Prize at Cannes in 1974.

"Ali" relates a love story between a German cleaning woman in her fifties and a young Moroccan immigrant worker. The two are drawn to each other out of mutual loneliness. As their relationship becomes known, they experience various forms of hostility and public rejection. Fassbinder makes it apparent that social and economic factors constrain the couple, through his favorite techniques of double-framing shots and extremely long takes of characters looking with objectifying gazes. At the end, Fassbinder withholds a "happy solution" and directs our attention to the ongoing problems of migrant workers. The overall effect of the film is to foreground the tenuous boundaries between public and pri-vate life and to stimulate the audience to find a solution to the couple's problems.

Enthusiasm for Fassbinder's films grew quickly after "Ali." Vincent Canby paid tribute to Fassbinder as "the most original talent since Godard," and in 1977, Manhattan's New Yorker Theater held a Fassbinder Festival. That same year saw the release of "Despair." Shot in English on a budget that nearly equalled the cost of his first fifteen films, "Despair" was based on a novel by Vladimir Nabokov, adapted by Tom Stoppard, and starred Dirk Bogarde. Favorable comparisons with such revered directors as Ingmar Bergman, Luis Bunuel, and Luchino Visconti soon followed.

But even as enthusiasm for Fassbinder grew outside of Germany, his films seemed to make little impression on German audiences. At home, he was better known for his work in tele-vision ("Eight Hours Are Not a Day," 1972 and the 15 1/2 hour "Berlin Alexanderplatz" 1980) and for a certain notoriety surrounding his lifestyle and open homosexuality. Coupled with the controversial issues that his films took up—terrorism, state violence, racial intolerance, sexual politics—it seemed that everything Fass-binder did provoked or offended someone. Charges leveled against him included anti-Semi-tism, anti-Communism, and anti-feminism.

With "The Marriage of Maria Braun" (1978) Fassbinder finally attained the popular accept-ance he sought, even with German audiences. The film recounts and assesses postwar German history as embodied in the rise and fall of the main character, played by Hanna Schygulla. Its story of manipulation and betrayal exposes Germany's spectacular postwar economic recovery in terms of its cost in human values. In the years following "Maria Braun," Fassbinder made "private" films like "In a Year with Thir-teen Moons" (1978) and "The Third Genera-tion" (1979), two of his greatest works, stories that translated personal experiences and atti-tudes, as well as big budget spectacles like "Lili Marleen" and "Lola" (both 1981). By the time he made his last film, "Querelle" (1982), based on the Jean Genet novel, heavy doses of drugs and alcohol had apparently become necessary to sustain his unrelenting work habits. When Fassbinder was found dead in a Munich apartment on June 10, 1982, the cause of death was reported as heart failure resulting from interaction between sleeping pills and cocaine. The script for his next film, "Rosa Luxemburg," was found next to him. He had wanted Romy Schneider to play the lead.

MILESTONES:

1965: First short film as director, writer and actor, "Der Stradtstreicher/The City Tramp"

1967: Joined Munich Action-Theater

1968: Founded acting company Anti-Theater Debut as playwright, "Katzelmacher"

1969: First feature film as director, co-art director and actor, "Liebe ist kalter als der Tod/Love Is Colder Than Death"

1982: Last film, "Querelle"

BIBLIOGRAPHY:

"Rainer Werner Fassbinder" edited by Laurence Kardish, with Julianne Lorenz, 1997, Museum of Modern Art

Federico Fellini

BORN: in Rimini, Italy, 01/20/1920

DEATH: in Rome, Italy, 10/31/1993

NATIONALITY: Italian

EDUCATION: attended schools in Rimini, Italy

AWARDS: Nastro d'Argento Award "Luci del varieta/Variety Lights" 1950

New York Film Critics Circle Award "L'Amore/The Miracle" 1950

Venice Film Festival Silver Lion Award "I Vitelloni" 1953; one of six films cited

Venice Film Festival Silver Lion Award "La Strada" 1954; award shared with Kazan's "On the Waterfront," Kurosawa's "Seven Samuai" and Mizoguchi's "Sansho the Bailiff"

New York Film Critics Circle Award Best Foreign Film "La Strada" 1956

Cannes Film Festival Golden Palm Award "La Dolce Vita" 1961

New York Film Critics Circle Award Best Foreign Film "La Dolce Vita" 1961

Moscow Film Festival First Prize "Otto e Mezzo/8 1/2" 1963

Golden Globe Award Best Foreign Language Foreign Film "Juliet of the Spirits" 1965

New York Film Critics Circle Award Best Director "Amarcord" 1974

Directors Guild of America Golden Jubilee Special Award 1986 cited with Akira Kurosawa and the late Oscar Micheaux

Cannes Film Festival Prix du 40th Anniversaire "Federico Fellini Intervista" 1987

Honorary Oscar Life Achievement 1992; honored "in recognition of his cinematic accomplishments that have thrilled and entertained worldwide audiences"; award presented by Sophia Loren and Marcello Mastroianni

BIOGRAPHY

Italian humanist director Federico Fellini was among the most intensely autobiographical film directors the cinema has known. "If I were to make a film about the life of a soul", said Fellini, "it would end up being about me." Born in Rimini, a resort city on the Adriatic, Fellini was fascinated by the circuses and vaudeville performers that his town attracted. His education in Catholic schools also profoundly affected his later work, which, while critical of the Church, is infused with a strong spiritual dimension. After jobs as a crime reporter and an artist specializing in caricature, Fellini began his film career as a gag writer for actor Aldo Fabrizi.

In 1943, Fellini met and married actress Giulietta Masina, who has appeared in several of his films and whom Fellini has called the greatest influence on his work. In 1945, he got his first important break in film, when he was invited to collaborate on the script of "Open City," Roberto Rossellini's seminal work of the neorealist movement. In 1948, Rossellini directed "L'Amore", one part of which was based on Fellini's original story "Il Miracolo/The Miracle" about a peasant woman (Anna Magnani) who thinks that the tramp (played by Fellini) who has impregnated her is St. Joseph and that she is about to give birth to Christ.

"Variety Lights" (1950), detailing the intrigues of a group of travelling entertainers, was Fellini's directorial debut, in collaboration with the established Alberto Lattuada. "The White Sheik" (1952) and "I Vitelloni" (1953) followed; the former was a comedy about a woman's affair with a comic strip hero, the latter a comedy-drama about the aimless lives of a group of young men. Though Fellini's earliest films were clearly in the neorealist tradition, from the start his interest in and sympathy for characters' eccentricities and his penchant for absurdist, sometimes clownish humor, makes them distinctive.

Fellini's international breakthrough came with "La Strada" (1954). One of the most memorable and moving films of world cinema, it told the story of an innocent, simple young woman (Masina) who is sold by her family to a brutish strongman in a traveling circus. Because Fellini infused his film with surreal scenes, he was accused of violating the precepts of neorealism. Ultimately, "La Strada", Fellini's first unquestioned masterpiece, is a poetic and expressive parable of two unlikely souls journeying toward salvation. The film's impact is bolstered immeasurably by Nino Rota's unforgettable music,

marking the beginning of a collaboration between the two men which would end only with Rota's death in 1979. A luminous performance by Masina, and the moving Jungian imagery of earth, air, fire and water, are also memorable elements of "La Strada."

After two very strong but less important works—"Il Bidone/The Swindlers" (1955) and "Nights of Cabiria" (1956), the latter providing Masina with a hallmark role as the hapless but ever hopeful prostitute—Fellini directed his two most influential masterworks: "La Dolce Vita" (1959) and "8 1/2" (1963). "La Dolce Vita" was a three-hour, panoramic view of contemporary Italian society as seen from the perspective of a journalist, played by Fellini's alter ego, actor Marcello Mastroianni. A savage, if subtle satire which exposes his perception of the worthless hedonism of Italian society, "La Dolce Vita" provided a wealth of unforgettable images, from its opening—a parody of the Ascension as a helicopter transports a suspended statue of Christ over rooftops with sunbathing women in bikinis—to its signature scene of bosomy Anita Ekberg bathing in the Trevi Fountain. The film was a scandalous success, a worldwide box-office hit that was condemned by both the Catholic Church for its casual depiction of suicide and sexual themes and by the Italian government for its scathing criticism of Italy.

Celebrated as a brilliant social critic, Fellini now found himself under careful scrutiny by the international community, which anxiously awaited his next film. "8 1/2" represented a brilliant gamble: as a filmmaker who did not know what film to make next, Fellini decided to make a film about an internationally acclaimed director who does not know what film to make next, thus confronting his personal confusions head-on; Mastroianni again played the director's alter ego. Having directed six features, co-directed another (counting as one half) and helmed episodes of two anthology films (each one also counting for a half), one of which was "Boccaccio '70" (1962), Fellini realized he had made 7 1/2 films and hence chose the title "8 1/2" for his most reflexive film. For the first time, surreal dream imagery clearly dominated, with no clear demarcation between fantasy and reality in this groundbreaking and exceptionally influential film.

Fellini's next film, "Juliet of the Spirits" (1965), was his first in color. Again starring Masina, whose career was at a low ebb and with whom Fellini had been having personal problems, "Juliet" applied the methods of his previous two films to examine the psyche of a troubled upper-class housewife. For the first time, the voices of those critics who attacked Fellini for self-indulgence were louder than those who praised him for his perceptive vision. A feminist film ahead of its time, which necessarily complicates dismissals of Fellini as a "dirty old man", "Juliet of the Spirits" seems today even stronger than when released. One sequence, Juliet's memory of a religious pageant of school-girls directed by unknowingly sadistic nuns, certainly stands among the most memorable and terrifying sequences in world cinema.

Many critics called Fellini's next film his "ne plus ultra." "Fellini Satyricon" (1969), loosely based on extant parts of Petronius's "Satyricon", was the most phantasmagorical of all Fellini's works, following the bawdy adventures of bisexual characters in the pre-Christian world. Fellini has himself described the film as science fiction of the past; and indeed the whole film moves with the logic of a dream: fragmentary, at times incomprehensible, and ending, literally, in the middle of a sentence. The abandonment of relatively conventional narrative which increased over the course of "Juliet" as its protagonist's psychical world took over came completely to the fore, and much of Fellin's subsequent work does not reverse the pattern. "Fellini Satyricon" is also unusually sensuous, more so than his other works; there is a constant tension between the film's sense-pleasing surface and its often disturbing elements, which include sex and

nudity, dwarves, an earthquake, a hermaphrodite, a decapitation, an erotic feast and orgy, suicides, mythological creatures, violence and hundreds of the most grotesque extras ever assembled. "Satyricon" polarized critics: some attacked the film as proof that Fellini's self-indulgence had run amuck, and others praised it as a great fountainhead of a new kind of non-linear cinema, a head-trip (not unlike Stanley Kubrick's "2001: A Space Odyssey") representing the aesthetic culmination of the 1960s and the ultimate comment, through an examination of the imaginary past, on the present.

Fellini's work since "Satyricon" has been seen by many as less focused, his international acclaim less consistent. Retreating from the splendid excess of "Satyricon," he created several very fine, more modest films, all marked by striking imagery, which diminished the distinctions between fiction film and documentary: "The Clowns" (1970), which deals with Fellini's life-long love of circuses; "Fellini's Roma" (1972), centering on his love/hate relationship with the the Eternal City which recurs in many of his films; and the critical and potent but little-seen "Orchestra Rehearsal" (1978), his most overtly political work, portraying the orchestra as a metaphor for discordant Italian politics. Perhaps Fellini's most acclaimed post-"Satyricon" film was "Amarcord" (1973), an accessible work which can be seen as a summation to that point of his autobiographical impulse (the title means "I remember"). Lovingly describing Fellini's Rimini boyhood, peppered with offbeat but gentle humor, "Amarcord" organized its images through a strong emphasis on the natural cycle and a coherent narrative, though it also contained such memorable flights of fancy as the peacock who appears during the winter snow.

"Amarcord" was the fourth Fellini film to win an Oscar as Best Foreign-Language Film, but as he continued making films in the 80s he found it increasingly difficult to find financial backing and distributors. The downturn in his critical reputation and the inaccessibility of several key films led many to dismiss them as unimportant or as further signs of his "self-indulgence." "Fellini's Casanova" (1976), while perhaps not one of his most important films, was unusually, indeed strikingly, cold, filled stunning imagery which cannot be easily dismissed. "And the Ship Sails On" (1983), meanwhile, proved that his flair for flamboyant characterization had not lost its comic or satiric prowess in its commentary on self-absorbed artists and motley others (including a homesick rhinoceros). "Ginger and Fred" (1985), though heavily criticized by many upon its release (the last to get a full art-house run in the US), has more than its share of touching and amusing moments as his two most important actors, Masina and Mastroianni, play a dance team reunited for what can only be described as "Fellini TV."

Fellini's "Intervista" (1987) carried the reflectiveness of his later years around full circle. A fitting companion piece to "8 1/2" and a revisitation (with Mastroiannai and Anita Ekberg) of that other landmark, "La Dolce Vita", Fellini again directly confronted his own position and status as a filmmaker, this time with a sadder, more wistful nostalgia than he had as a younger man. Now the aging "Il Mago" ("the magician" as he was sometimes called in Italy) and his aging actors watch clips of their earlier triumphs in scenes that are extremely moving. His last completed film, "Voice of the Moon" (1990), considered by some critics as his most surreal film, was, like "Intervista", a small film chock-full of references and last-minute thoughts, alternately strange and sad, an appropriate postscript to a film career filled with laughter and wonder at the bizarre circus of life.

COMPANION:

wife: Giulietta Masina. Actor; married on October 30, 1943 after a four-month courtship; died on March 23, 1994 at age 73; appeared in seven of husband's films from "Luci del Varieta/Variety Lights" (1950) to "Ginger et Fred/Ginger and Fred" (1986)

MILESTONES:

Attended religious boarding schools as a child

1937: Was a contributor to satirical magazine, "Il 420" in Florence; also worked for a time as a proofreader

Went to Rome where he worked as secretary for newspaper, "Il Popolo di Roma"

1938–1939: Enrolled in the University of Rome Law School; did not attend classes but used his student status to avoid conscription; sold stories and cartoons to weekly magazine, "Marc Aurelio" (also became story editor in 1939) (date approximate)

1939: Travelled with a vaudeville troupe, writing gags and doing general support work; later recalled the year as "the most important of his life"

1939: First film as gag writer, "Lo Vedi come soi . . . lo vedi come sea?!"

1940: Debut as radio gag writer for comedian Macario

1941: First film as uncredited screenwriter, "Documento Z 3"

1944: Set up "Funny Face Shop" to make caricatures of GIs; shop also took photographs and let soldiers make voice recordings that they could send home to families

1945: First film as assistant director, "Roma Citta aperta/Open City" (also co-wrote)

Set up "Funny Face Shop" to make caricatures of GIs

1946: First film as co-scenarist "Paisan" (also assistant director)

1948: Screen acting debut in "Il Miracolo/ The Miracle"

1950: Formed Capitolium production company with Alberto Lattuada

1950: First feature film as co-director and co-screenwriter (with Alberto Lattuada), "Luci del Varieta/Variety Lights"

1953: First feature film as solo director, "Lo Sceicco Bianco/The White Sheik"

1961: Formed Federiz production company with Angelo Rizzoli; company went bankrupt in one year without making any films

1969: Directed and narrated, "Fellini: A Director's Notebook" for NBC-TV

1970: First appeared in one of his own films, "The Clowns"

1970: Made an appearance as himself in the American feature, "Alex in Wonderland"

1987: Last appearance in a feature film, "Intervista", which he also directed

1990: Last completed film, "Voices of the Moon"

1993: Suffered a stroke in August; later suffered from heart failure; en route to recovery in October, suffered another stroke when he gagged on a piece of cheese while dining in a restaurant

QUOTES:

Four films directed by Fellini were awarded the Best Foreign-Language Film Academy Award: "La Strada" (1956), "Nights of Cabiria" (1957), "Fellini's 8 1/2" (1963) and "Amarcord" (1974).

For a number of years Fellini told interviewers that he ran away from home to join a circus when he was either seven or eight years old, but in his later years he admitted that the story was a fabrication "to help journalists" who wanted to explain or autobiographically justify Fellini's fascination with circuses and carnivals and their recurring presence in his films.

"I have the feeling that all my films are about women. . . . They represent myth, mystery, diversity, fascination, the thirst for knowledge and the search for one's own identity. . . . I even see the cinema itself as a woman, with its alternation of light and darkness, of appearing and disappearing images. Going to the cinema is like returning to the womb, you sit there still and meditative in the darkness, waiting for life to appear on the screen. One should go to the cinema with the innocence of a fetus."—Fellini in 1981.

The November 1, 1993 *New York Post* quotes director Spike Lee's response to seeing his first Fellini film when he was still a student in high school: "It really just for me emphasized . . . what you could do. There are no boundaries. There are no limits."

Honored by the Film Society of Lincoln Center (1985).

Given a honorary doctor of humane letters degree from Columbia University in 1970.

BIBLIOGRAPHY:

"Federico Fellini: Essays in Criticism" Peter Bondanella

"I, Fellini" Charlotte Chandler, 1995, Random House; biography based on taped interviews with Fellini

"Federico Fellini" Lietta Tornabuoni (editor), 1995, Rizzoli; catalog of Roman exhibition

Abel Ferrara

BORN: in Bronx, New York, 07/19/1951

SOMETIMES CREDITED AS:
Jimmy Laine

NATIONALITY: American

EDUCATION: went to the same high school in Peekskill, New York as future screenwriting partner Nicholas St John, with whom he explored Super-8 during this time

Rockland Community College Suffern, New York political science enrolled to avoid the Vietnam War

State University of New York, Purchase Purchase, New York briefly studied film

AWARD: IFP Gotham Award Filmaker 1995

BIOGRAPHY

A prolific, driven writer-director known for his highly atmospheric, stylized portraits of an ultra-violent, crime-ridden New York City, Abel Ferrara works on a metaphorical and allegorical level exploring the battle between good and evil. Aided by his screenwriting partner Nicholas St. John (and other collaborators who comprise his filmmaking family), he depicts essentially an evil world that contains the hope for salvation. Ferrara starred in his first feature, the exploitation flick "Driller Killer" (1979), on which he also served as editor and songwriter under the pseudonym Jimmy Laine. He followed with the cult hit "Ms. 45/Angel of Vengeance" (1980), about a retribution-seeking rape victim, in which he played one of the rapists (again credited as Jimmy Laine). His next three features did little to advance his reputation. Despite a good cast, "Fear City" (1984) repelled viewers as overly gratuitous and "Cat Chaser" (1989) never made it to the theaters, but "China Girl" (1987) exhibited Ferrara's tremendous trademark energy along with over-the-top violence and perhaps deserved more respect than it received.

Ferrara proved his mainstream mettle in an association with TV producer Michael Mann, beginning with his direction of two episodes during the first season (1984–85) of NBC's "Miami Vice", which led to his helming the critically-acclaimed two-hour pilot of "Crime Story" (NBC, 1986). Although Ferrara's wife Nancy walked out on the premiere of "King of New York" (1990) because of its treatment of women, the film attracted more interest than any of his features to that time, helped by the presence of screen heavyweights Christopher Walken, Wesley Snipes and Laurence Fishburne. 1992 marked the release of Ferrara's ambitious "Bad Lieutenant", starring Harvey Keitel in a tour-de-force performance in this relentless character study of a disillusioned NYC cop descending into a colorful hell of drugs, alcohol, and corruption when the brutal rape of a nun forces him to confront personal issues of faith and redemption. Long-time writing partner St. John, a devout Catholic, refused to work with Ferrara on the picture due to its blasphemous images but was back on board for the next four flicks.

For his next two films, Ferrara found himself out of low-budget waters for the first time. Madonna's $4 million salary alone for 1993's "Dangerous Game" (originally given the more interesting title "Snake Eyes") could have financed two Ferrara films and swelled the budget to $12 million. An unconventional account of the process of filmmaking, also starring Keitel and James Russo, it received decidedly mixed reviews, but at least it got a wide release. His sci-fi thriller, "Bodysnatchers" (1994), the second remake of Don Siegel's 1956 classic "Invasion of the Body Snatchers", suffered inexplicably at the hands of Warner Brothers. Although favorably reviewed at several major film festivals, the studio mysteriously shelved it for a time and marketed it pitifully upon its release. Consequently, the $20 million picture did relatively little business when finally exhibited and helped make Ferrara an even more resolute independent filmmaker and foe of the studios.

Refusing to be compromised by money matters, Ferrara returned to the low-budget viscerality of his early work with "The Addiction" (1995), on the surface a tale of vampirism. Filmed in black and white, it is really a theological tale probing the corrupt human condition while allowing Lili Taylor's character a way out through Jesus Christ. He continued in the same vein with the 1930's gangster piece "The Funeral" (1996). Christopher Walken, the oldest of three brothers, wrestles with a Catholic conscience at odds with his need to revenge his younger brother's death. Chris Penn turned in a riveting portrayal of the insane middle brother and Isabella Rossellini, Annabella Sciorra, Vincent Gallo and Benicio del Toro all contributed notable performances to a movie of hypnotic intensity rooted in the behavioral nuances of the characters. For "The Blackout" (1997), Ferrara temporarily abandoned his usual NYC locale for a warmer Miami but returned to New York where Matthew Modine, comfortably settled in domestic stability with his girlfriend Claudia Schiffer, must confront the trace memories of a murder he committed during an alcoholic blackout 18 months before in Miami.

MILESTONES:

Moved from Fordham section of the Bronx to Peekskill, NY at age 13

Inspired by the success of "The Texas Chainsaw Massacre" (1975), decided to make "Driller Killer"

1979: Feature directing debut, "Driller Killer"; also starred, edited and wrote songs under pseudonym Jimmy Laine

1981: Played first rapist (again credited as Jimmy Laine) in second directorial effort "Ms. 45"

1985: Directed two first season episodes of Michael Mann's "Miami Vice" (NBC)

1986: Directed the two-hour pilot for the Michael Mann-produced cop series, "Crime Story" (NBC)

1990: "King of New York", featured at various international festivals (including New York), caught the attention of mainstream critics; first collaboration with Christopher Walken

1992: "Bad Lieutenant" released; repelled by its blasphemous imagery, devout Catholic St. John refused to work on film with long-time partner; first collaboration with Harvey Keitel

1994: Helmed "Body Snatchers", a slick remake of the 1954 classic horror flick

1995: Returned to low-budget viscerality of early work with "The Addiction", filmed in black and white

Honored with a career retrospective during the 22nd annual Rotterdam Film Festival

1996: Directed period gangster piece "The Funeral"

1997: "The Blackout", starring Mathew Modine, debuted at Cannes Film Festival

1997: Contributed 10-minute segment featuring Rosie Perez ("Love on the A Train") to Jonathan Demme-produced HBO anthology film "Subway Stories"

1997: Directed "The New Rose Hotel"; Ferrara co-scripted with Zoe Lund (who also co-scripted "Bad Lieutenant")

2001: Helmed "R-Xmas"

QUOTES:

"If I was gonna make an NC-17 film, those people would be dead in the screening room"—Abel Ferrara on the ratings board insisting he cut his films to a more "suitable" R, from the *Daily News*, October 27, 1993.

"He's fabricated his reputation, Abel loves to provoke people."—Nancy Ferrara on her husband's reputation with the press from *The New York Times*, January 2, 1994.

"Abel is one of the most interesting visual stylists in contemporary American cinema. He has an extraordinary sense of style in terms of sound and image. Even when his films don't work, he's a bright light on the scene."—Richard Pena, program director of the Film Society of Lincoln Center from *The New York Times*, January 2, 1994.

When asked if he thinks he's getting better making films: "I hope so. We're tryin' to. We're goin' through some hard times lately, but hopefully we're gettin' better and that's balancin' out how much wear and tear is happenin' to us. Gettin' the money's tough. Real tough. That's the hardest part, financin' the film. Financin' the film on your own fuckin' terms. That's what it's about, man. That's what these movies are about, tryin' to come to terms with your own existence. What else? Be righteous. If you make the movies, you be righteous in your work. For me it's the process of makin' 'em. If the process is righteous, then the films are gonna make sense on some level. This is the business we're in. This is what we chose to do, so I'm not gonna stand here and start bellyachin' about it. That's the fuckin' deal."—Abel Ferrara, *GQ*, c. 1996 (post-"The Addiction", prior to "The Funeral" shoot).

BORN: Michael Figgis in Kenya, 1948

NATIONALITY: British

EDUCATION: studied music in London

AWARDS: San Sebastian Film Festival Best Director Award "Leaving Las Vegas" 1995

Los Angeles Film Critics Association Award Best Director "Leaving Las Vegas" 1995

Los Angles Film Critics Circle Best Director Award "Leaving Las Vegas" 1995

National Society of Film Critics Best Director Award "Leaving Las Vegas" 1995

Independent Spirit Award Best Director "Leaving Las Vegas" 1995

FilmFour Special Jury Prize 2000; presented at the British Independent Film Awards

BIOGRAPHY

With his roots in experimental theater and music, it is perhaps surprising that Kenyan-born writer-director Mike Figgis started out as such a conventional filmmaker, but his dissatisfaction with the Hollywood studio system eventually led to his true calling as one of the most innovative auteurs working in contemporary cinema. After studying music in London, he became a member of Gas Board, an English rhythm-and-blues band (which also featured a pre-fame Bryan Ferry), and later went on tour for nearly a decade with an experimental theater group The People Show first as a musician, then also as an actor. Undaunted by his unsuccessful application to London's National Film School, Figgis began writing and directing his own stage productions, visually striking works like "Redheugh", "Slow Fade" and "Animals of the City", which combined music with filmed segments and live performance. He developed "Slow Fade" into a one-hour piece ("The House") for Britain's Channel 4, capturing the attention of producer David Puttnam, for whom he wrote a treatment that would become his feature writing-directing debut, "Stormy Monday" (1988).

Although Puttnam would pass on the project, Figgis did finally get backing for his tale set in the seamy world of Newcastle jazz clubs. The atmospheric homage to Hollywood film noir featured a score by the director, who also persuaded B.B. King to record the title track, a career first for the great bluesman. His impressive American debut, "Internal Affairs" (1990), was a striking portrait of police corruption featuring powerhouse performances by a creepy silver-haired Richard Gere and a seething Andy Garcia. The studio demanded control over the music and chose two composers to help execute Figgis' vision, even though he had already done a temporary track to accompany the film. His follow up, "Liebestraum" (1991), made precious little sense—something about a 40-year-old sex scandal, corruption, and family madness—but had style to spare, and with Brit backing, he was able to write his own score, a more or less "wall-to-wall" affair, often almost inaudible but always a presence. Figgis then tangled with the studio and producers who insisted that "Mr. Jones" (1993), a change-of-pace romance with Gere as a manic depressive charmer who gets involved with his psychiatrist (Lena Olin), be more upbeat. "I thought it was a ludicrous idea," he told *The New York Times* (November 1, 1995). "Manic-depression isn't something to dismiss lightly."

Once again a hired gun on the well-mounted, though stodgy remake of "The Browning Version" (1994), Figgis was at the creative center of his next project, "Leaving Las Vegas" (1995), and acquired foreign financing to protect the integrity of his noirish character study of an alcoholic, suicidal screenwriter (Nicolas Cage in an Oscar-winning turn) and his relationship with an abused prostitute (Elisabeth Shue). The actors and director took virtually no money, and Figgis began his love affair with the cheaper, grittier, "more impressionistic" Super 16 film (later blown up to 35 mm) normally used in documentaries, perfectly capturing the seamy trappings of the powerful love story. He also composed the score, and Sting, who had starred in "Stormy Monday", volunteered to sing on the soundtrack. When the movie opened, he had no expectations for commercial success, but "Leaving Las Vegas" became a critical darling, earning him the best reviews of his career as well as two Oscar nominations for Best Director and Best Adapted Screenplay.

After serving as executive producer of Annette Haywood-Carter's "Foxfire" (1996), Figgis then produced his own "One Night Stand" (1997), which he extensively rewrote from a Joe Eszterhas script (so much so that Eszterhas took no credit). Despite a too-pat ending, it continued to show him as a filmmaker firmly in control, expertly matching his moody score to his complex take on relationships and reassessing life choices. His next film, "The Loss of Sexual Innocence" (1999), may have completed a trilogy of sexual obsession and human frailty begun with "Leaving Las Vegas", but it was also a labor of love 17 years in the making. Rejecting the linear three-act structure ("the filmmaker's Bible"), Figgis presented a fragmented narrative relying more on music and images than dialogue, intercutting a coming-of-age tale with the Adam and Eve story. His ambitious attempt to restore art to the medium was his most personal film yet and, despite its problems, successfully demanded audience participation in a way few pictures can. Like the preceding two films, it featured improvisation, energetic camera work and a fearlessness to delve into the human psyche that had become the director's trademark.

Figgis continued his experimentation with "Miss Julie" (also 1999), an adaptation of August Strindberg's 19th-century play about sexual obsession, filming in 16mm in 16 days on one set with two hand-held cameras. His decision to split the screen and show the love scene from both camera perspectives prefigured the four-camera point-of-view he would employ on "Time Code" (2000), arguably his most innovative picture to date. Working only from an outline, he equipped his actors with digital watches, and as they hit their prescribed marks at the prearranged times, he followed the action with four hand-held digital video cameras, shooting the entire 93-minute movie in one complete take. Though there were multiple takes, Figgis eschewed editing, opting to simultaneously show the images from all four cameras of what he deemed the best take. The director drew inspiration from the Dogma '95 movement and from the success of "The Blair Witch Project" (1999) to come up with this seminal work of the digital revolution, and the actors involved embraced its guerilla aspect. "This is the most incredible experience I've ever had—and the most stressful," Selma Hayek told the *Los Angeles Times* (November 8, 1999). "Nothing is really set. And there is no room for mistake. The danger of it, the experimental quality of it, really turned me on."

COMPANION:

Saffron Burrows. Actor; born c. 1973; directed by Figgis in "One Night Stand" (1997), "The Loss of Sexual Innocence" and "Miss Julie" (both 1999) and "Time Code" (2000)

MILESTONES:

1957: Moved to Newcastle, England at the age of eight

Performed with R&B group, Gas Board, which also included Bryan Ferry

Recorded with a band produced by Charlie Watts of the Rolling Stones

Toured with experimental theater group, The

People Show, in 1970s; joined as a musician but was soon acting

1980: Left The People Show to concentrate on writing and directing for film and the theater

Made 15-minute 16mm short film "Redheugh"; followed with stage productions "Slow Fade" and "Animals of the City" which combined music and film with live action

Toured the major European capitals; won various European theatrical awards

Commissioned by Channel 4 to write and direct

First TV-movie as director, "The House", adapted from the performance piece "Slow Fade"

Taught film part-time at London Polytechnic

1988: Feature writing and directing debut, the jazz-infused noir "Stormy Monday"; also wrote music

1990: Helmed "Internal Affairs", starring Richard Gere; also co-wrote music, received credit as a musician and acted in film in the part of Hollander

1991: Directed and wrote screenplay and composed music for the psychological erotic drama "Liebestraum"

1991: Helmed, scripted and wrote music for "Mara" segment of HBO's "Women & Men II"

1993: Clashed with producer Ray Stark over the final cut of "Mr. Jones", which reteamed him with Gere; this dark look at mental illness became a love story set in a hospital for the mentally ill, though executives at Tri-Star insisted that the movie was always a love story, that he had failed to follow the script and asked the actors to improvise their lines, and that the ending presented by the director was incoherent, necessitating the studio take over the final editing

1994: Helmed remake of "The Browning Version"

1995: Received widespread acclaim and two Oscar nominations for Best Director and Best Adapted Screenplay for "Leaving Las Vegas"; also wrote original score and played Mobster No 1; featured as musician (trumpet and keyboards) on soundtrack

1996: Executive produced Annette Haywood-Carter's "Foxfire"

1997: Produced, directed, wrote screenplay and music for "One Night Stand"; also appeared as Hotel Clerk and credited as trumpet player

1998: Signed an exclusive two-year production deal with Columbia Pictures

1999: Rejected linear narrative form to tell "The Loss of Sexual Innocence"; directed, scripted, wrote music and played trumpet

1999: Produced, directed and wrote music for film adaptation of August Strindberg's "Miss Julie"; shot on 16mm in 16 days with two hand-held cameras on one set; used split-screen technique for the love scene, prefiguring his innovative four camera point-of-view in "Time Code"

1999: Helmed two 50-minute documentaries ("Flamenco Women" and "Just Dancing Around"); screened at NYC's Anthology Film Archives as "Two Dance Videotapes by Mike Figgis"

2000: Produced, scripted and directed "Time Code", in which four digital video cameras were employed to capture different perspectives; shot in sequence in real time entirely with hand-held cameras over the course of one day; has the distinction of being the first feature filmed in one take (there were several "takes", but what the audience sees is one complete take selected by Figgis as the best); also operated one of the four cameras

QUOTES:

"I was in pre-production on the film ["Leaving Las Vegas"] when I got a call that John [O'Brien, author of the source material] had committed suicide. Obviously, I was quite upset and considered not making the film, but eventually I decided that John wrote a great book, and the most I could do for him was to go ahead and make the film."—Mike Figgis to the *Los Angeles Times*, October 29, 1995.

On the nightmare of "Mr. Jones": "I've never

experienced anything so degrading, so humiliating, so completely lacking in respect. Had it been anywhere but a film studio, people would have been on the floor bleeding."—Figgis quoted in *The New York Times*, November 1, 1995.

"I'm not disgusted with working with Hollywood, just realistic . . . The problem isn't Hollywood or the independent market—it's about how much money you're expecting to earn. There's the potential for a successful director to earn between $1 million and $7 million per film . . . So directors coming out of film schools or commercials or going to Hollywood having made a moderately successful British film have in their minds the mathematical possibility of becoming a very rich person very quickly. It's the oldest temptation in the book. How hard is it to say no to that? How easy is it to delude yourself you're doing good work in the studio system?

"The answer is, why bother? If you want to do good work . . . as the 'Dogma' people have also proved, you can make a film for virtually nothing if you're passionately interested in film-making as opposed to passionately interested in becoming a rich film-maker . . . "
—Figgis quoted in *Sight and Sound*, May 1999.

About working in Hollywood: "It was something I was excited to fall into because I was suddenly in a position of such power, and I was suddenly earning such money and meeting world-famous actors on a casual basis. And it feels terribly cool. You start regarding yourself as a very special individual. But then at a certain point you suddenly feel: 'I am so frustrated and bored by this', and you see the British people who have gone there and become so homogenised. And I guess I had a fear of that.

"Hollywood destroys people and ages people and throws them out on a weekly basis."—Figgis quoted in *The Guardian*, January 8, 2000.

"I have a theory that film has replaced religion, because it's projected in temples, basically, and seems the ultimate corruption of a pure religious ideal in that it's about excessive sensuality on a cheap level . . . My hope is that these new [technical] developments will dignify the temple and turn film into an amateur thing. The idea that anyone can make a movie is healthy. You don't have to have a mark from God."—Figgis in *The Guardian*, January 8, 2000.

"I prefer small films and rarely get excited by big expensive films. I feel shut out of big films, as if I am not being asked to participate in the event. It would be true to say that I feel the same about big theatre and big music. There comes a point where you know you are being manipulated by tricks rather than connecting with emotions and ideas and truths. It is much harder to tell the truth to a lot of people than a few. Glenn Gould retreated to the recording studio rather than play the big concert halls. It is a bald fact that bigger means more expensive to produce—as soon as you cross that line, you have to make compromises.

" . . . the biggest problem with studio films is that they are not good enough any more. And the reason they are not good enough is because they cannot trust the individual vision of the film-maker. There is simply too much money at stake. An interesting date is the day 'Fatal Attraction' was tested in front of an invited audience. As a result of the test the ending was re-shot amd the film was a huge hit. This proved . . . whatever the studio wanted it to prove. The theory now is that any film can be fixed by spending money on it. And very few execs will have the courage to back a film that is not right in the middle of the taste-buds of an average audience. It is far simpler to say no to an idea than to say yes to an idea."—Figgis quoted in *The Guardian*, February 25, 2000.

"I never wanted to be an epic filmmaker. I never get jealous when I see hugely extravagant vistas and all that. It's like a different world to me. I like it very, very simple—where all the focus goes into the psychology of the acting."—Figgis to the *Chicago Sun-Times*, March 6, 2000.

David Fincher

BORN: in Colorado, 1962

NATIONALITY: American

EDUCATION: Ashland High School, Ashland, Oregon

AWARDS: MTV Music Video Award Director "Express Yourself" 1989; video starring Madonna

MTV Music Video Award Director "Vogue" 1990; starred Madonna

Grammy Best Music Video, Short Form "The Rolling Stones' 'Love Is Strong' " 1995

BIOGRAPHY

One of contemporary cinema's most dazzling visual stylists whose dark vision of human nature colors his images, David Fincher knew he was going to be a director at the tender age of eight when he began experimenting with an 8mm camera. The sight of neighbor George Lucas picking up his paper in the morning helped demystify the process, too, proving that ordinary people made the magic happen. Filmmaking seemed the perfect outlet for a kid who could spend all day drawing and loved to make sculptures, take pictures and tape-record stuff. Fincher eschewed the film school route, getting a job loading cameras and doing other hands-on work for an animation company. He next finagled a position with Lucas' esteemed special effects production company, Industrial Light and Magic (ILM), when he was only 18, and stayed there for four years, learning the trade from the ground up and earning some screen credits, including one for matte work on "Indiana Jones and the Temple of Doom" (1984).

Fincher, however, was not cut out for technical subservience. As he told *The New York Times* (September 2, 1997), "I have problems with authority, and I'm definitely not a team player. I.L.M. was very team-oriented. But it was a good place to try things out." He left the company to helm TV commercials, shooting his first one for the American Cancer Society, a grim hint of things to come showing a fetus smoking a cigarette. Though he would go on to direct spots for Revlon, Converse, Nike, Pepsi and Levi's, Fincher soon discovered that the slightly expanded format of music videos was an even better place to try things out. As a founder of Propaganda Films in 1986, he quickly took that company to the top of the field, helming memorable rock videos for Don Henley ("The End of the Innocence"), Paula Abdul ("Straight Up", "Cold Hearted"), Billy Idol ("L.A. Woman") and Aerosmith ("Janie's Got a Gun"). He did some of his best work for Madonna, creating a sleek noir world of muscle hunks, black cats and bondage for "Express Yourself" (1989) and staging the equally memorable "Vogue" (1990), with its gorgeous black-and-white photography evoking a variety of movie divas of yore, slickly edited to Madonna's pop appropriation of the "vogue" dancing of Harlem's drag queens.

Having always wanted to direct science-fiction movies, Fincher jumped at the chance to make his feature debut with "Alien3" (1992), naively assuming Fox would let him make the movie he had pitched to get the job. He soon learned that his music video skirmishes had not prepared him for the all-out war of piloting a lucrative franchise previously steered by Ridley Scott and James Cameron. With the shooting script a scant 45 pages on Day 1, he knew he was in trouble but soldiered on when his agent told him he'd never work again if he quit, remaining allies with star Sigourney Weaver throughout while clashing repeatedly with studio executives nervous about their jobs. Individual sequences had much to recommend them, and Fincher sustained his dark visual assurance over a full-length film, but too much interference from higher-ups worried about production costs and trying to imitate past formulas resulted in a less-than-stellar release. Doubting he would ever direct another feature, Fincher returned to music videos, earning a Grammy for the Rolling Stone's "Love Is Strong" (1994).

Fincher kept reading screenplays though, and one finally crossed his desk that excited him from beginning to end. Unlike "Alien3", "Seven" (1995) was a coherent script by Andrew Kevin Walker without any baggage, and the director pulled no punches delivering an extraordinarily gripping, unrelenting story of a serial killer murdering his victims according to the seven deadly sins. Dark, moody and malicious, it was unsettling from its mind-bending opening credits straight through to its downbeat ending which Fincher had fought to keep, informing reluctant producer Arnold Kopelson: "Forty years from now, nobody's gonna remember you and nobody's gonna remember Brad Pitt, but they're gonna be talking about a bad guy delivering the good guy's head in a box. Nobody's going to forget that." (From *Entertainment Weekly*, September 19, 1997.) Often only the flashlights of the two detectives could penetrate the gloom of its inky-black darkness (a trick Fincher first used in Aerosmith's "Janie's Got a Gun"), and many critics dismissed the picture as murky and pretentious. Audiences, however, did not agree. Almost overnight, on the strength of its overwhelming box office, Hollywood's favorite whipping boy became arguably the town's hottest director.

Next came "The Game" (1997), a nightmarish, "Twilight Zone"-style thriller which projected the same sense of suffocating enclosure and mounting despair as had "Seven." The sterile universe of ruthless tycoon Nicholas Van Orton (Michael Douglas) spirals out of control

when he accepts the invitation of his younger brother (Sean Penn) to indulge in an unusual "entertainment", courtesy of the mysterious Consumer Recreation Services. Sucked into a vortex of paranoia and uncertainty, Van Orton eventually wakes up somewhere in Latin America as a penniless nobody and spends the rest of the film trying to get to the bottom of things. Admittedly a stunning technical achievement, audiences still found the movie a little too coolly cerebral, and after a strong first week, word-of-mouth kept the crowds away. With "Fight Club" (1999), Fincher latched on to his most disturbing material yet, delivering an adrenaline-charged satire sending-up both corporate-consumer culture and the men's movement. The complacent, well-ordered world of Edward Norton comes apart when he encounters the destabilizing force of Brad Pitt, who prescribes brutality and mayhem as an antidote to the inauthenticity and mediocrity of modern life. Whether zeitgeist item or cult movie, "Fight Club" is pure Fincher, an inventive and bold visual display that begs the question: "What's next?"

MILESTONES:

Grew up in San Rafael, Marin County, California; began experimenting with an 8mm camera at age eight; saw George Lucas' "American Graffiti" when he was ten, and months later Lucas moved into his neighborhood two doors down, making the magical medium seem more accessible

Entered the film industry by getting a job with an animation company loading cameras

1981–1984: Got a job at age 18 with George Lucas' special effects production company Industrial Light and Magic (ILM); stayed for about four years, working on the special effects of the animated "Twice Upon a Time" and as an assistant cameraman in the miniature and optical effects unit (involved in go-motion photography) of "Return of the Jedi" (both 1983)

1984: Received screen credit as an assistant on the matte photography work of "Indiana Jones and the Temple of Doom" and "The Neverending Story"

Left ILM to begin making commercials

1985: Made first commercial, a spot for the American Cancer Society which showed a fetus smoking (date approximate)

1986: Co-founded Propaganda Films with Steve Golin

Began directing music videos, including Madonna's stylish "Express Yourself" (1989) and "Vogue" (1990)

1992: Feature film directorial debut, "Alien3"

1994: Helmed the music video for the Rolling Stones' "Love Is Strong"; received Grammy Award

1995: Had surprise box office success with the dark drama "Seven", starring Morgan Freeman and Brad Pitt

1997: Helmed third feature, "The Game", starring Michael Douglas and produced by Golin

1999: Directed "The Fight Club", adapted by Jim Uhls from the novel by Chuck Palahniuk; picture boasted potent performances by its three leads Pitt, Edward Norton and Helena Bonham Carter

2001: Executive produced a series of short film advertisements for BMW shown over the Internet at bmwfilms.com

2002: Helmed "Panic Room", a thriller about a trio of men terrorizing a woman and her child in the search for missing money; project began filming with Nicole Kidman in the lead but was jeopardized by her recurring knee injury which forced her withdrawal; Jodie Foster replaced Kidman

QUOTES:

"I don't know how much movies should entertain. I'm always interested in movies that SCAR. The thing I love about 'Jaws' is the fact that I've never gone swimming in the ocean again."—David Fincher quoted in *Empire*, February 1996.

"David Fincher is a Baudelairean aesthete in reverse: a modernist with stunning control over the great modernist medium, abandoning himself to romanticism, finding beauty in rotting corpses and reeking cities. Now in his early thirties, Fincher has made two features—'Alien3' and 'Seven'—and each of them has at least one sequence (Sigourney Weaver's final plunge into the abyss in 'Alien3' and the shadowy Brad Pitt/Morgan Freeman/Kevin Spacey chase in 'Seven') that's as ravishing as anything in the history of American movies."—From "Seven Seal" by Amy Taubin in *Village Voice*, January 9, 1996.

On his music video work: "I just make these things and try to live them down. It's just creating a context for understanding a song. These are not windows into somebody's soul. For me, this is my film school, and, quite honestly, I'm embarrassed by a lot of my work."—Fincher to David Wild in *Rolling Stone*, October 17, 1996.

"I had a meeting once with a famous commercial director who was running off to direct a movie, and he wanted me to join his company. He said, 'I'm going off to do this movie.' I said, 'Well, what is it?' 'Oh, it's this cop thing.' I thought to myself, 'Oh, my God, I don't ever want to be in a situation where I'm going off to do some 'cop thing.'

"You know, the best analogy for moviemaking is you're doing a watercolor from three blocks away through a telescope, with 40 people holding the brush, and you have a walkie-talkie."—Fincher to Fred Schruers in *Rolling Stone*, April 3, 1997.

"I look for patterns in coverage, and for ways to place the camera to see what you need to see, from as far away as possible. I try to remain semi-detatched; I want to present the material without becoming too involved. I'll say to myself, 'Am I getting too involved in the action? Am I presenting this to someone who's uninitiated to these people, and doesn't want to be in the middle of this argument? Maybe we should be doing over-the-shoulders, as if the spectator is experiencing the scene after returning from the water cooler.' My visual approach comes from a more voyeuristic place."—Fincher quoted in *American Cinematographer*, September 1997.

"I thought 'Alien3' was an opportunity to make my mark, but it didn't quite work. I learned a lot: never to shoot a movie without a script, and the more money you have, the more trouble you're likely to run into."—Fincher to David Hochman in *Entertainment Weekly*, September 19, 1997.

" . . . to hear Fincher's friends and associates tell it, [Michael] Douglas' character [in 'The Game'] isn't so different from the director himself, whom they describe as intense, controlling, manipulative, arrogant and—oh, yes—extraordinarily talented. . . . "—From " 'The Game' Spins Into David Fincher's Control" by Patrick Goldstein in *Los Angeles Times*, September 17, 1997.

"I never feel comfortable on set. I don't know why I do it—honestly, I don't know. It's the most unpleasant part of the whole thing— collecting all the stuff and going through it like the military part of an operation when you have to show up early and marshall the forces and shoot stuff and argue with people and cajole and cheat and do whatever you have to do . . .

"I like the initial design and rehearsal, all the possibilities. Then when you go to shooting, it's, 'We can't put a wide enough lens on,' or, 'We can't get the wall further back.' That's always so unpleasant and has not gotten any easier."—Fincher quoted in *Empire*, November 1997.

"I've had days of shooting where I went, Wow, that's what it is, that's what it's like to be making a movie. Everything's clicking, people are asking questions, and the clock's ticking, but you feel like you're making progress. But most of the time it isn't that. Most of the time it's, How do you support the initial intent of what it is you set out to do, and not undercut that by getting pissed off and letting your attention get away on that? It's priority management. It's problem solving. Oftentimes you walk away from a scene going, Wasn't what I thought it was going to be. Often. But it's also knowing that you don't have to get it exactly the way you see it."—From "Inside Out, Gavin Smith Goes One-On-One with David Fincher" in *Film Comment*, September–October 1999.

Robert J. Flaherty

BORN: Robert Joseph Flaherty in Iron Mountain, Michigan, 02/16/1884

SOMETIMES CREDITED AS:
Robert J. Flaherty

DEATH: in Vermont, 07/23/1951

NATIONALITY: American

EDUCATION: Upper Canada College, Toronto, Ontario, Canada

Michigan College of Mines, Michigan; expelled after 7 months

AWARDS: Venice Film Festival Best Foreign Film Award "Man of Aran" 1934

Venice Film Festival Best Director Award "Elephant Boy" 1937 award shared with co-director Zoltan Korda

Venice Film Festival International Prize "Louisiana Story" 1948 cited "for its lyrical beauty"

British Film Academy Award Best Documentary "Louisiana Story" 1948 producer

BIOGRAPHY

A mineralogist and explorer turned pioneering documentarist, Robert Flaherty shot material for his first film, a study of the Belcher Islands, in 1917 but the footage was accidentally destroyed by fire. Undeterred, he planned another film, on Eskimo life, and received backing from the Revillon Freres fur company to make "Nanook of the North" (1922). An engaging chronicle of the day-to-day existence of one family, "Nanook" became an international success despite initial skepticism on the part of distributors. It also represented a landmark in the development of the documentary, thanks to its use of elements associated with narrative film: Flaherty structured the work around a storyline, directed the Eskimos in scenes "staged" for the benefit of the camera, and made sophisticated use of techniques including close-ups, tilts and pans. The success of "Nanook" earned Flaherty studio backing to make the lyrical Polynesian documentary "Moana" (1926), which was praised by critics but justly attacked by anthropologists as a poetic fantasy rather than an accurate representation of island life.

Flaherty went on to co-direct the narrative feature "White Shadows of the South Seas" (1928) with W.S. Van Dyke and to collaborate with F.W. Murnau on "Tabu" (1931), though he withdrew from both projects before completion. In 1931 he immigrated to England, where he exerted a significant influence on John Grierson and the British "social documentary" movement of the 1930s. Flaherty's best-known British film was "Man of Aran" (1934), a lyrical study of an Irish fisherman and his daily struggle for survival.

Flaherty later returned to the US and made two more highly acclaimed documentaries, "The Land" (1942), for the US Information Service, and "Louisiana Story" (1948), for Standard Oil.

MILESTONES:

Served as explorer, surveyor and prospector for Candian Grand Trunk Railway and Canadian mining syndicates in the early 1900s

1910–1916: Carried out series of expeditions searching for iron ore deposits in Nastapoka Islands, east of the Hudson Bay in Northern Canada for industrial entrepreneur, Sir William Mackenzie of the Mackenzie-Mann Company

Took motion picture camera along on expedition for first time

1916: Made first documentary film (negative destroyed by cigarette fire in editing room)

1920: Returned to Eskimo country to make film

1922: Made first feature documentary film, "Nanook of the North"

1926: Hired by Jesse L. Lasky to make a film about Polynesian tribal life for Paramount, "Moana"

1928: Began co-directing (with Willard S. Van Dyke) first dramatic feature film, "White Shadows of the South Seas" (left before production completed) for MGM

1937: Went to Great Britain; first worked for John Grierson at Empire Marketing Board, then for Gaumont-British and finally for Alexander Korda's London Films

1939: Returned to US and made "The Land" for Pare Lorentz's US Film Service

1942: Joined Frank Capra's War Department Film Division

1944: Commissioned by Standard Oil to film "Louisiana Story"

1950: Formed Robert Flaherty Film Associates Inc. (date approximate)

AFFILIATION: Robert Flaherty Foundation established 1953; later renamed International Film Seminars Inc.

QUOTES:

Awarded the Doctor of Fine Arts degree by the University of Michigan (1950).

The Robert Flaherty Foundation established in 1953 and later renamed International Film Seminars, Inc.

BIBLIOGRAPHY:

"The Drawings of Ennoesweetok of the Sikosilingmiut Tribe of the Eskimo" Robert Flaherty, 1915

"The Captain's Chair" Robert Flaherty 1938 novel

"The White Master" Robert Flaherty 1939 novel

"My Eskimo Friends" Robert Flaherty 1942 in collaboration with Frances Hubbard Flaherty

Andrew "Andy" Fleming

BORN: 1964

SOMETIMES CREDITED AS:
Andy

NATIONALITY: American

EDUCATION: New York University, New York, New York, film, BFA, 1984; received the Peter Stark Scholarship for two years; directed the short films "In the Dark", which won the NYU Best Film Award; "Prisoner", combining live action and animation; and "P.P.T." (which featured Bridget Fonda), for which he was awarded a fellowship at Warner Bros.

BIOGRAPHY

Openly gay "Generation X" filmmaker Andrew Fleming acquired a reputation as a wunderkind shortly after leaving New York University's prestigious film school. The last of his three award-winning student films there, "P.P.T.", earned him a fellowship at Warner Bros., and he teamed with no less a producer than Gale Ann Hurd ("Terminator" 1984; "Aliens" 1986) for his feature directing and writing debut "Bad Dreams" (1988), a largely ignored psychological horror film. Although some found it stylish in a sort of David Cronenbergian way, many questioned Hurd's involvement in an "entertainment" so clearly celebrating doom and utterly devoid of hope, aimed shamelessly at the teen market.

Prior to "Bad Dreams", Fleming's interests had primarily lain in the technical side of filmmaking, but after a hiatus to learn how to write, he resurfaced with his follow-up feature, "Threesome" (1994), an amusing coming-of-age college story. Boasting an attractive young cast (Lara Flynn Boyle, Stephen Baldwin and Josh Charles) caught up in a somewhat unconventional love triangle, the movie outstandingly and believably expressed the sex-saturated state-of-mind of 20-year-olds and represented a giant leap forward for the screenwriter. Solid tech contributions gave the independent feature the polished look of a bigger budget studio effort.

The refreshingly unpretentious writer-director "nailed" the high school experience for "The Craft" (1996), a supernatural thriller and black-comedy clone of "Heathers" (1989), featuring four toothsome "witches" (Fairuza Balk, Robin Tunney, Neve Campbell, Rachel True) grounded in a realistic setting. Fleming's ship ran aground when it abdicated its strong narrative in favor of well-executed special effects, culminating in a showdown battle between Balk (in full-blown punk Medusa frenzy) and Tunney, the recent convert with a conscience. He continued in the high school milieu with "Dick" (1999), a period piece bringing two teenagers in contact with such Watergate era characters as President Nixon (Dan Hedaya), James Dean (Jim Breuer) and G. Gordon Liddy (Harry Shearer), among others.

MILESTONES:

Directed the short student film "P.P.T", featuring Bridget Fonda; won fellowship to Warner Bros.

Worked in several production facilities on commercials

Directed several music videos

1988: Feature directorial and co-screenwriting debut, "Bad Dreams"

Studied acting in order to improve as a writer

1994: Helmed and co-scripted "Threesome", a triangular relationship comedy-drama set on a collge campus

1996: Directed and co-wrote boxoffice success "The Craft", featuring Fairuza Balk and Robin Tunney as battling witches

1999: Co-wrote and directed the satirical comedy "Dick", which posited the idea that the Watergate scandal was broken by two high school students

AFFILIATION: Raised as a Baptist; became an agnostic

QUOTES:

"When I was young, my father was a talent agent who represented directors. It did not look like a good life to me—directors are divorced, alcoholic, not a happy bunch. So I never envisioned being a director as some glamorous job; you're a mess, you never have time to bathe, you smell—it's the worst."—Fleming to *Movieline*, March 1995.

"Well, when somebody came up to me to say, " 'Threesome' is my favorite movie ever,' I said, 'You know if that's true, you really need to see a few more movies.' "—Andrew Fleming quoted in *Movieline*, March 1995.

About "The Craft": "It just seemed like a nice, new way to offend people. I didn't really know anything about witchcraft when we started, but we had a witch technical consultant, and I learned. It's really in no way more preverse than Catholicism is, and makes as much or more sense because it's grounded in worshipping the earth. It has a lot more to do with day-to-day life than nailing somebody to the cross, to be perfectly honest."—Fleming quoted in *Out*, March 1996.

"I sometimes amaze myself how bitchy I can be."—Andrew Fleming in *Out*, March 1996.

Victor Fleming

BORN: in Pasadena, California, 02/23/1883

DEATH: in Cottonwood, Arizona, 01/06/1949

NATIONALITY: American

AWARD: Oscar Best Director "Gone With the Wind" 1939

BIOGRAPHY

Former race car driver and chauffeur who began his film career as a cinematographer, working with Allan Dwan, Douglas Fairbanks and D.W. Griffith before graduating to directing in 1919. Fleming's talent for spectacular action and his ability to elicit strong performances from leading stars made him one of the most popular directors of the 1930s. He is most widely known for "The Wizard of Oz" (1939) and for taking over the direction of "Gone With the Wind" (1939) from George Cukor.

MILESTONES:

1910: Began film career as assistant cameraman to Allan Dwan (at American Film Company)

1915: Hired as director of photography at Triangle

Served with the photographic section of US Army Signal Corps during WWI and was Walter Wanger's cameraman at the 1919 Versailles Peace Conference

1919: First film as director (with Ted Reed) "When the Clouds Roll By"

1920: First film as solo director with "The Mollycoddle"

1932: Joined MGM as contract director

BORN: Sean Aloysius O'Fearna in Cape Elizabeth, Maine, 02/01/1895

SOMETIMES CREDITED AS:
"Pappy" Ford
Jack Ford
Sean O'Feeney
Sean Aloysius O'Feeney

DEATH: in Palm Desert, California, 08/31/1973

NATIONALITY: American

EDUCATION: Portland High School, Portland, Maine

AWARDS: New York Film Critics Circle Award Best Director "The Informer" 1935; first year of awards

Oscar Best Director "The Informer" 1935

New York Film Critics Circle Award Best Director "Stagecoach" 1939

New York Film Critics Circle Award Best Director "The Grapes of Wrath" and "The Long Voyage Home" 1940

Oscar Best Director "The Grapes of Wrath" 1940

New York Film Critics Circle Award Best Director "How Green Was My Valley" 1941

Oscar Best Director "How Green Was My Valley" 1941

Oscar Best Documentary Film "The Battle of Midway" 1942

Oscar Best Documentary Film "December 7th" 1943

Venice Film Festival International Prize "The Fugitive" 1948 cited "for its drama"

Locarno Film Festival Critic's Grand Prize Best Film "When Willie Comes Marching Home" 1950

Oscar Best Director "The Quiet Man" 1952

Directors Guild of America Award Outstanding Directorial Achievement in Feature Film "The Quiet Man" 1952

Venice Film Festival International Prize "The Quiet Man" 1952; one of three films cited

Directors Guild of America D W Griffith Award 1954; for career achievement

Golden Globe Pioneer Award 1954

American Film Institute Life Achievement Award 1973; initial recipient of annual award

BIOGRAPHY

John Ford grew up with the American cinema. In the early days of filmmaking, his older brother Francis moved to Hollywood to work for Universal Pictures and John joined him in 1914, forging his apprenticeship as a moviemaker during the formative period of the classical Hollywood cinema. By 1917 he had been promoted to contract director, fashioning westerns which often starred Harry Carey, Sr. Ford moved to the Fox studio in 1921 and established his reputation with such films as the western spectacular "The Iron Horse" (1924). In his silent films, Ford composed images with a formality and a symmetry that valued order; even at this stage, he had acquired the mantle of a Hollywood master.

Although best known for his westerns such as the landmark "Stagecoach" (1939), Ford worked in many other genres through his long career. Early in the 1930s, he led Fox's top comedy star, Will Rogers, through "Doctor Bull" (1933)," Judge Priest" (1934) and "Steamboat 'Round the Bend" (1935). Ford also set a number of his films in his parents' native Ireland. "The Informer" (1935), a drama of the Irish rebellion, won him the first of four Academy Awards for his direction. In retrospect, the film seems stylistically stodgy and thematically preachy, especially next to the vitality of "The Quiet Man" (1952), an unpretentious film about an Irish-American returning to settle in his native land. Ford also dealt with American history in "The Prisoner of Shark Island" (1936), "Young Mr. Lincoln" (1939), "Drums Along the Mohawk" (1939) and "The Grapes of Wrath" (1940).

After WWII Ford fashioned some of the best westerns ever to come out of Hollywood, including "She Wore a Yellow Ribbon" (1949), "Wagonmaster" (1950), "The Searchers" (1956) and "The Man Who Shot Liberty Valance" (1962). In creating the archetype for the genre in "My Darling Clementine" (1946), Ford focused on the classic cinematic shoot-out, the famous final gunfight at OK Corral, where Wyatt Earp (Henry Fonda) and his brothers avenge the murder of their youngest brother. Against the harsh background of the buttes and desert of Monument Valley, Ford had the Earps ally with Easterner Doc Holiday (Victor Mature) to rid Tombstone of the evil Clantons and bring civilization to the town. In reshaping these familiar elements, Ford demonstrated that Hollywood genre films could be transformed into complex artifacts of popular culture and history.

Ford's postwar westerns examined all facets of the settling of the West. He began with a shared optimism in "My Darling Clementine" and "She Wore a Yellow Ribbon" and ended with a close examination of the dark side of manifest destiny in "The Man Who Shot Liberty Valance."

Possibly his most underrated film, "She Wore a Yellow Ribbon", should be singled out for its brilliant use of color: rich and muted hues blended into an often somber aura. In this transitional work, part of a trilogy (including "Fort Apache" 1948 and "Rio Grande" 1950) about life in the United States cavalry, Ford praises the work of the military in settling the West, while undercutting the role of war in settling disputes." The Searchers," now highly regarded by critics, historians, and such contemporary directors as Steven Spielberg,

Martin Scorsese and George Lucas, presents not only a rousing adventure tale, but also a melancholy examination of the contradictions of settling the old West. At the center of the film stands Ethan Edwards (John Wayne), a bitter, ruthless and frustrated veteran of the Civil War who engages in an epic quest to retrieve an orphaned niece abducted by a Comanche raiding party. This neurotic man belongs neither to the civilized world of settlers hanging on at the edge of Monument Valley nor to the proud but doomed Native Americans he doggedly pursues. Torn between his respect for, but racist hatred of, Indians, Edwards speaks their language and is at home with their customs but is not deterred from seeking revenge for his murdered sister-in-law and her daughter. In "The Searchers" the wilderness never seemed so brutal nor civilization so tenuous and threatened. There are no towns, only outposts and isolated homesteads. The towering buttes of Monument Valley, in vivid Technicolor, are stunning but seem terribly threatening at the same time. After years of searching, Ethan gently lifts his niece in his arms to take her home, back to a family which is long dead, a homestead long deserted. The western myth persists above all.

If the latter film is one of the most beautiful color films ever made," The Man Who Shot Liberty Valance", in black and white, is surely one of the most bleak and barren. This dark vision of a West of deceit and lying, abandons the stunning Technicolor vistas of the buttes of Monument Valley for the rickety buildings of a ramshackle town continually cast in shadow. The heroic shooting by Ranson Stoddard (James Stewart) of evil Liberty Valance (Lee Marvin), revealed in flashback, is shown by the end of the film to be a lie and a sham. Still, society hails Stoddard as a hero and elevates him to a position of power as a United States Senator. The true Western hero, Tom Doniphon (John Wayne), dies a pauper, unknown, save to his closest friends.

Although his final film was "Seven Women" (1965), "Cheyenne Autumn", released in 1964 and his final film shot in Monument Valley, seems a more fitting cap to a career begun some fifty years earlier. Ford made many of the best films ever to come out of Hollywood, even as he managed to make a few of the worst. By focusing on the aforementioned works, one overlooks the wretched excess of "Wings of Eagles" (1957). How he could make this film just after his masterpiece, "The Searchers", is a paradox that suggests a great deal about working in Hollywood.

MILESTONES:
1913: Hired by Universal
1917: Contract director at Universal

1917: First feature film as director on "Straight Shooting"
1921: Contract director at Fox
Made Chief of Field Photographic Branch, Office of Strategic Services (rank as lieutenant commander, rear admiral) during WWII

AFFILIATION: Roman Catholic

BIBLIOGRAPHY:
"Directed By John Ford" Peter Bogdanovich, 1971
"Pappy: The Life of John Ford" Dan Ford, 1979, biography written by grandson
"Print the Legend: The Life and Times of John Ford" Scott Eyman, 1999, Simon & Schuster

Milos Forman

BORN: in Caslav, Czechoslovakia, 02/18/1932

SOMETIMES CREDITED AS:
Tomas Jan

NATIONALITY: Czech

CITIZENSHIP: United States 1977

EDUCATION: attended boarding school in Prodebrady where he met Ivan Passer, Vaclav Havel and Jerzy Skolimowski
    completed high school in Dejvice, 1950
    FAMU, Prague, Czechoslovakia, screenwriting, 1950–55; studied under Milan Kundera

AWARDS: Czechoslovak Film Critics Award Best Picture "Cerny Petr/Black Peter" 1963
    Locarno Film Festival Golden Sail Award "Cerny Petr/Black Peter" 1964
    Venice Film Festival Jury Prize "The Loves of a Blonde" 1965
    French Film Academy Award Best Film "The Loves of a Blonde" 1966

Cannes Film Festival Jury Prize "Taking Off" 1971; awarded to the film
    Golden Globe Award Best Director "One Flew Over the Cuckoo's Nest" 1975
    Directors Guild of America Award Outstanding Directorial Achievement in Feature Film "One Flew Over the Cuckoo's Nest" 1975
    Oscar Best Director "One Flew Over the Cuckoo's Nest" 1975
    BAFTA Award Best Director "One Flew Over the Cuckoo's Nest" 1976
    Los Angeles Film Critics Association Award Best Director "Amadeus" 1984
    Golden Globe Award Best Director "Amadeus" 1984
    Directors Guild of America Award Outstanding Directorial Achievement in Feature Film "Amadeus" 1984
    Oscar Best Director "Amadeus" 1984
    Cesar Best Foreign Film "Amadeus" 1985
    Eastman Kodak Second Century Award 1990, fourth annual presentation; awarded annually by Eastman Kodak Company in recognition of support for emerging filmmakers;

previous recipients were Lucille Ball, David Putnam and Steven Spielberg

National Board of Review Freedom of Expression Award "The People vs. Larry Flynt" 1996; shared with Oliver Stone

Golden Globe Award Best Director "The People vs. Larry Flynt" 1996

John Huston Award for Artists Rights 1997; fourth recipient; cited for his efforts to have broadcasters label films which have been altered before airing; presented by the Artists Rights Foundation

Berlin Film Festival Golden Bear "The People vs. Larry Flynt" 1997

European Film Academy Award for Achievement in World Cinema 1997

Berlin Film Festival Silver Bear Best Director "Man on the Moon" 2000

BIOGRAPHY

Milos Forman stands as one of the few established foreign directors to find success within the American film industry. Like Fritz Lang, Forman was an influential filmmaker in his homeland who went on to achieve comparable influence in Hollywood. Forman's Czechoslovakian films, including "Loves of a Blonde" (1965) and "The Fireman's Ball" (1967), marked a distinct thematic and stylistic break with the prior generation of filmmaking in that country and played a major role in shaping the Czech New Wave of the 1960s. These films were characterized by an ironic humor and detailed observation of character for which Forman has become well known.

A persistent theme in Forman's work is generational conflict, particularly as it is played out within a family or family-like context. Some critics have suggested that Forman's preoccupation with parent-child relationships may stem from the loss of his own parents in Nazi concentration camps. In Forman's first two features, "Black Peter" (1963) and "Loves of a Blonde", he deals with the theme in a gentle and humanistic manner, using it for subtle criticism of the socio-political climate in Czechoslovakia of the mid-60s. The political content of Forman's Czech films is rarely overt, but rather suggested through the harshly authentic depiction of a bleak environment and inflexible social order. To achieve this authenticity, Forman has routinely used non-professional actors who were often instructed to improvise their dialogue to achieve a sense of spontaneity. The political implications of Forman's realism have been complemented by his narratives, which, as in "Loves of a Blonde", often tell the story of young people struggling to find happiness and meaning within an established social order that has not provided for their personal and emotional fulfillment. In all his Czechoslovakian films, the political critique is gently ironic and the humanism abundant.

Forman's first two American films bear strong thematic and stylistic resemblance to his Czechoslovakian work. "Taking Off" (1971), a critical if not commercial success, developed the generation gap theme: a set of parents go in search of their runaway daughter in NYC. "One Flew Over the Cuckoo's Nest" (1975), explored the struggle of the individual against the establishment. This film solidified his stature in the US, became a box-office smash and was the second film in history to sweep the top five Academy Awards, earning Best Picture, Director, Actor (Jack Nicholson), Actress (Louise Fletcher) and Screenplay (Bo Goldman and Lawrence Hauben).

Forman continued to develop these themes in his subsequent work. Switching gears, he explored the musical genre in "Hair" (1979), adapting the quintessential anti-establishment stage show. Forman had originally been drawn to the material in the late 60s, but the rights were then unavailable. By the time the film was made, it had become a period piece and its loose, revue-like structure posed problems. Working with screenwriter Michael Weller, Forman reinterpreted the material, fashioning yet another tale of young people seeking something more than the conventions provided by society. The tribal aspects of the hippie lifestyle provided a familial context against which the main action played out. Forman staged several brilliant set pieces, particularly the "be-in" in Central Park and Cheryl Barnes' heartbreaking solo "Easy To Be Hard." Abetted by the exquisite camerawork of Miroslav Ondricek and Twyla Tharp's energetic choreography, "Hair" remains one of the best screen adaptations of a stage musical. Unfortunately, despite strong reviews, the film was not a box-office success. Too much time had passed and other films had significantly dealt with the 60s and the Vietnam experience.

Forman followed with the period drama "Ragtime" (1981) that was noted more for marking the screen return of veteran actor James Cagney. Again collaborating with screenwriter Weller, he undertook the daunting task of translating E. L. Doctorow's sprawling, multi-character novel. Forman chose to concentrate on a few of the book's storylines, notably that of Coalhouse Walker Jr., a proud black musician who faces a choice of humiliation or defiance. The resulting film, while visually stunning and featuring several fine performances (including Cagney's police commissioner and the late Howard E. Rollins Jr.'s Coalhouse), was a financial failure. Forman's original cut ran close to three hours; it was edited at the urging of the studio and producer Dino Di Laurentiis and the narrative structure somehow suffered.

For his next project, the director undertook adapting Peter Shaffer's award-winning play "Amadeus" (1984). The film played upon one of Forman's favorite themes, generational conflict (e.g., an older composer, Salieri, jealous of the youthful upstart Mozart; Mozart and his prickly realtionship with his father). Filming provided the helmer with an emotionally fraught set of circumstances. In his memoir, "Turnaround" (Random House, 1993), Forman details obtaining a visa to visit his homeland and the resulting sentiments of working in Prague. "Amadeus" was another visually stunning,

well-acted piece and the American public responded to it. The film earned eight Oscars, including Best Picture, Actor (F Murray Abraham as the embittered Salieri), Screenplay (Shaffer) and a second Best Director Award for Forman.

Forman moved to academia in the late 1970s, teaching at Columbia University and eventually becoming co-director of its film program. After a five year break (during which time he had acted in two films, Mike Nichols' "Heartburn", 1986 and Henry Jaglom's "New Year's Day", 1989), he returned to features to helm an adaptation of Choderlos de Laclos' epistolary novel "Les Liaisons Dangereuses." Forman had first become interested in the material while an undergraduate studying with Milan Kundera. Despite a competing project, "Dangerous Liaisons" (1988), Stephen Frears' adaptation of Christopher Hampton's play, the director pushed on. Casting more youthful actors (Annette Bening, Colin Firth, Meg Tilly), Forman helmed a less pungent version of the story. Audiences had embraced Frears' acerbic take and high powered cast (Glenn Close, John Malkovich, Michelle Pfeiffer) and all but ignored Forman's. Its disappointing box office was tempered for the director by the democratic revolution in his homeland that saw his old friend, Vaclav Havel become president.

Much of Forman's attention in the early 90s was occupied with his duties at Columbia University and with developing his first original screenplay, the unproduced "Hell Camp", which focused on two Americans attending a school for managers in Japan. Forman was also at one time attached to direct "Disclosure" (1994), but he left the project in 1993 and was eventually replaced by Barry Levinson. He finally returned to the screen with the biopic, "The People vs. Larry Flynt" (1996). Again, Forman's themes of political conflict are baldly played out in this somewhat sanitized depiction of pornographer Flynt's First Amendment lawsuit. Produced by Oliver Stone, the film, which utilizes humor to make social commentary, won critical attention and audiences in big cities, although it failed to attract viewers in the South and Midwest.

FAMILY:

father: Rudolf Forman. Professor of education; Jewish; arrested by Nazis in 1940; died in Buchenwald concentration camp in 1944

mother: Anna Forman. Protestant; arrested by Nazis in 1940 for suspicion of being Jewish or having Jewish blood; died in Auschwitz concentration camp in 1943

COMPANIONS:

Beverly D'Angelo. Actor; met during the filming of "Hair" (1979); no longer together

MILESTONES:

Raised by two uncles and one family of friends of his parents after parents were arrested

1945: Became a film buff after the occupation ended

1950: While a senior at Dejvice high school, organized a drama club and staged an avant-garde musical about Francois Villon which toured small halls near Prague

1950: Enrolled in newly founded Film Institute at the University of Prague (FAMU)

1954–1956: Directed documentaries for Czech TV

Collaborated on script of Martin Fric's feature comedy, "Leave It to Me" (1955) while still a student at FAMU

1956: First onscreen appearance in Alfred Radok's "Old Man Motorcar"

1957: Wrote and was assistant director on Ivo Novak's film, "Puppies"

Joined theater group Laterna Magika (Magic Lantern) as an assistant writer; worked with Alfred Radok on presentations that mixed film with live actors to be performed for the Brussels World Fair

1963: Medium-length 16mm semi-documentary directing debut with "Konkurs/Competition"; Forman's first collaboration with Ivan Passar and cinematographer Miroslav Ondricek

1963: Feature film directing debut with "Cerny Petr/Black Peter"

1967: Made first trip to the US; negotiated to make first US feature; wanted to produce a film adaptation of the stage musical "Hair", but rights were not available

1968: Was in Paris at time of Russian occupation of Czechoslovakia in August and the fall of the Dubcek regime in September and stayed there until moving to New York in 1969

1971: Made first US film, "Taking Off"

1971: Subject of Mira Weingarten's documentary short, "Meeting Milos Forman"

1972: Contributing director for "Visions of Eight" (documentary covering Munich Olympics)

Directed a failed play for the NY stage

1973: Was suffering from acute depression when approached by producers Saul Zaentz and Michael Douglas to direct film adaptation of Ken Kesey's novel, "One Flew Over the Cuckoo's Nest"

1975: Directed breakthrough US feature, "One Flew Over the Cuckoo's Nest"; won first Oscar as Best Director

1975: Named co-director of Columbia University film division

1977: Became a US citizen (November 30)

1978: Made professor, Columbia University film division

1979: Helmed adaptation of stage musical "Hair"

1981: Directed "Ragtime"; convinced James Cagney to come out of retirement to play final screen role

1984: Reteamed with producer Saul Zaentz to direct the film adaptation of Peter Shaffer's "Amadeus"; returned to Czechoslovakia for the first time since 1968 to film on location; earned second Oscar as Best Director

1986: Made US acting debut in small role in Mike Nichols' "Heartburn"

1989: Was subject of a segment of the PBS series "American Masters"

1989: Last film released for seven years, "Valmont"

1989: Acted in Henry Jaglom's "New Year's Day"

Worked on unproduced film, "Hell Camp", about Americans in Japan

Began pre-production on "Disclosure"; withdrew from film in the fall of 1993 (eventually replaced by Barry Levinson)

1996: Returned to feature directing with "The People vs. Larry Flynt"

1999: Helmed "Man on the Moon", the biopic of comedian Andy Kaufman starring Jim Carrey

QUOTES:

Forman has notably cast non-actors in prominent film roles. For example, author Norman Mailer played Stanford White in "Ragtime" and poitical pundit James Carville was cast as a prosecuting attorney in "The People vs. Larry Flynt."

BIBLIOGRAPHY:

"Turnaround" Milos Forman and Jan Novak, 1993, Random House; memoir

"Milos Forman: A Bio-Bibliography" Thomas J. Slater, 1987, Greenwood Press

John Frankenheimer

BORN: in Malba, New York, 02/19/1930

SOMETIMES CREDITED AS:
Alan Smithee

DEATH: in Los Angeles, California, 07/06/2002

NATIONALITY: American

EDUCATION: Foxwood School Flushing, New York

LaSalle Military Academy, Oakdale, New York, 1947; was captain of the tennis team

Williams College, Williamstown, Massachusetts, English, BA, 1951; discovered acting

Cordon Bleu, Paris, France; studied for two years

studied with chef Michel Guerard

AWARDS: Emmy Outstanding Individual Achievement in Directing for a Miniseries or a Special "Against the Wall" 1993/94

Golden Globe Award Best Made-for-Television Movie or Mini-Series "The Burning Season" 1994

Emmy Outstanding Individual Achievement in Directing for a Miniseries or a Special "The Burning Season" 1994/95

American Cinema Editors Golden Eddie Award Filmmaker of the Year 1995

Emmy Outstanding Individual Achievement in Directing for a Miniseries or a Special "Andersonville" 1995/96

CableACE Award Miniseries "George Wallace" 1996; shared award; Frankenheimer was the producer

CableACE Award Directing of a Movie or Miniseries "George Wallace" 1996

Golden Globe Award Best Motion Picture Made for Television or Miniseries "George Wallace" 1997; shared award

Emmy Outstanding Directing for a Miniseries or a Movie "George Wallace" 1997/98

ShowEast Lifetime Achievement Award 1999

BIOGRAPHY

The John Frankenheimer story contains one of the great second acts of American filmmaking. The wunderkind who left his Air Force film unit and talked his way into an assistant director's job at CBS established himself as one of the most brilliant talents to emerge from TV's "Golden Age", helming more than 150 live dramas between 1954 and 1960, prestigious contributions like "The Last Tycoon" (starring Jack Palance), "For Whom the Bell Tolls" (Jason

Robards, Maureen Stapleton and Eli Wallach), the original "Days of Wine and Roses" (Cliff Robertson and Piper Laurie), "The Turn of the Screw" (Ingrid Bergman) and "The Browning Version", featuring Sir John Gielgud's first television appearance. Frankenheimer then made a seamless transition to film, inaugurating a collaboration with Burt Lancaster that would span five pictures, and became on the strength of work like "Seven Days in May" (1964), "The Train" (1965) and "Grand Prix" (1966) one of Hollywood's most sought after action directors. Much of his 60s work (as the 1988 re-release of 1962's "The Manchurian Candidate" revealed) has stood the test of time remarkably well, but he floundered during the 70s and 80s before returning to the small screen and reinventing himself as an Emmy-winning director of cable movies and miniseries.

His debut feature, "The Young Stranger" (1957), was an expanded version of a one-hour TV drama he had directed called "Deal a Blow" (1955). A prototypically Frankenheimer picture with its protagonist (young James MacArthur in his feature debut) persecuted by authority figures, the film was well-received, though he personally had a horrible experience. The cameraman would not cooperate and give him what he wanted, and he didn't get along with the producer either. Chagrined to learn that the film producer had much more power to second guess the director than in TV, he happily returned to the small screen and, growing ever surer, became more selective in the assignments he accepted or proposed, showing a flair for adapting the work of celebrated writers like F. Scott Fitzgerald, Ernest Hemingway and Henry James, to name a few. Sidney Lumet (his mentor on CBS' "You Are There" series), Arthur Penn and he are arguably the three best directors TV's "Golden Age" produced, and Frankenheimer later stated: "I enjoyed television more than I can really tell you and I think everything I am today I owe to it . . . I drew a tremendous amount of experience from five years as a

television director, more I think than many film directors get in their entire career."

In 1961, Frankenheimer directed the taut, visually striking feature "The Young Savages" (1961), adapted from Evan Hunter's novel "A Matter of Conviction." Set in East Harlem and starring Burt Lancaster as an idealistic prosecutor out to save the lives of three innocent gang members, it (like his debut and so many subsequent films) mined the theme of a lone male up against "the system" and was the first of a string of successes that included three movies in 1962 ("All Fall Down", "The Birdman of Alcatraz" and "The Manchurian Candidate"). Frankenheimer recruited actual teen gang members for "Savages" and gave Sydney Pollack his first Hollywood job coaching the young non-professional actors. Producer-star Lancaster then called him to take over "Bird Man" from Charles Crichton, and the director elicited an unusually restrained performance from the actor as real-life Robert Stroud, some of whose problems owed to his appallingly possessive mother (Thelma Ritter). Equally destructive examples of the breed, played in both cases by Angela Lansbury, surfaced in his other two movies that year. Ironically, both Lansbury (as the sinister mother of Laurence Harvey in "Manchurian Candidate") and Ritter were nominated for the Best Supporting Actress Oscar that year, although neither took the prize.

"The Manchurian Candidate" is one of Frankenheimer's finest films, the first he instigated and had complete control over. A tingling Cold War thriller called by Richard Corliss "an eccentric and spectacularly assured tightrope walk between sci-fi and satire, paranoia and prophecy," it gave him the clout to enlarge the scale of his pictures, and he cast around for some time before seizing on "Seven Days in May" (1964) as his next project. Featuring an all-star cast of Lancaster, Kirk Douglas, Fredric March and Ava Gardner and a screenplay by Rod Serling (adapted from the Fletcher Knebel and Charles W. Bailey novel),

"Seven Days" told an absorbing, believable story of a military scheme to overthrow the government, perfectly accompanied by the ominous notes of its Jerry Goldsmith score. No sooner had he completed the film when Lancaster called him to Paris to replace Arthur Penn as director of "The Train" (1965), a flawlessly executed adventure story full of spectacular wrecks filmed entirely without models or process shots. Like it or not, Frankenheimer was suddenly in demand as an action director.

His first taste of failure came on "Seconds" (1966), a film which ironically has grown in critical estimation through the years. Although Frankenheimer doesn't rank it among his top six films, he has remarked, "It's the only picture that's gone from failure to classic without having success." Starring Rock Hudson as a frustrated middle-aged businessman who has transformed his identity (thanks to science) only to find himself at odds with his new role, "Seconds" was just a little too "out there" for its time and received a thrashing at the hands of the European critics when it debuted at Cannes. Paramount then panicked and dumped the film, fearing audiences would not respond to Hudson's unusual performance. In light of the actor's personal tragedy, his stepping out of his usual role may have provided some of his most genuine moments on screen as he displayed the anguish, sorrow and regret of a man trying to lead a secret identity. An amateur racer for many years, Frankenheimer derived his greatest pleasure from "Grand Prix" (1966), a technically brilliant actioner featuring an international cast headed by James Garner, Yves Montand and Toshiro Mifune. His first film in color scored well with critics and audiences alike and temporarily restored his damaged reputation.

Things began to unravel for Frankenheimer in June 1968 when his close relationship with Robert F. Kennedy ended in tragedy. Kennedy was staying with the director at the time of his assassination at Los Angeles' Ambassador Hotel and had wanted his friend next to him

that fateful night, but Frankenheimer had demurred, thinking the presidential hopeful should not highlight his Hollywood connection. In the aftermath of the slaying, the director plunged into a deep depression. He and third wife Evans Evans moved to Europe, and while he continued to make movies (e.g., "The Fixer" 1968; "The Gypsy Moths" 1969; "The Horsemen 1971), they were not the hits he had enjoyed before. He directed the 1973 version of Eugene O'Neill's "The Iceman Cometh" (a personal favorite), which few saw despite good reviews, and showed signs of box-office life with the sequel "French Connection II" (1975), but the commercial failure of "Black Sunday" (1977) pretty much spelled an end to any A-list considerations. Quality scripts did not come his way, and offerings like "Prophecy" (1979), "The Holcroft Covenant" (1985) "52 Pick-Up" (1986), "The Fourth War" (1989) and "Year of the Gun" (1991) hardly seemed the work of the same man who had directed "The Manchurian Candidate."

Frankenheimer had begun an association with HBO on the remake of "The Rainmaker" (1982), starring Tommy Lee Jones and Tuesday Weld, and had subsequently directed an episode of that cable network's "Tales From the Crypt" (1992), but it was the HBO TV-movie "Against the Wall" (1994), about the 1971 prison uprisings at Attica told from a hostage's point of view, which finally provided him the best material he had helmed in years. Although he had received five Emmy nominations for his direction of live TV shows, "Against the Wall" earned him his first statue and his next three TV projects, "The Burning Season" (HBO 1994), the biopic of South American activist Chico Mendes (Raul Julia); "Andersonville" (TNT, 1996), a miniseries about the notorious Civil War prison camp; and "George Wallace" (1997), starring Gary Sinise, all returned him to the winner's circle, giving him four directing Emmy Awards in five years. His TV success refreshed Hollywood's notoriously short memory, and he once again came to the rescue and replaced original director Richard Stanley on "The Island of Dr. Moreau" (1996), sorting out the chaos and enabling its release.

Frankenheimer returned triumphantly to the big screen in 1998, delivering "Ronin", a sly action masterpiece which featured his trademark—holding a large number of people at different depths in his frames (a technique developed during his live TV days)—and another specialty (à la "Grand Prix"), a fondness for sending vehicles screeching through narrow European streets. "Ronin" (the Japanese word for samurai who have lost their master and must hire themselves out as amoral and dispassionate mercenaries) sets its band of international thugs (including Robert De Niro, Jean Reno and Stellan Skarsgard) in expensive, nonstop pursuit of an oddly-shaped aluminum suitcase (its contents never revealed). Uncluttered by boring details, it showed off its extreme stylishness, the juxtaposition of its script's verbal acrobatics and Frankenheimer's bold visual manner. The man who had redefined the suspense film with "The Manchurian Candidate", who had refused to give up his quest for the elusive big-budget picture, had finally weighed in with a movie that displayed his mastery of the medium.—Written by Greg Senf

MILESTONES:

During his last two summer vacations of college, acted in summer stock at the Highland Playhouse in Falmouth, Massachusetts

1951–1953: Served in US Air Force; eventually joined its newly formed film squadron

Short film about a California cattle farm brought him first assignment from the private sector, writing and producing a local TV show, "The Harry Howard Ranch Roundup"; served unofficially as director for drunken title holder

1953: Arrived in NYC with $150 and talked his way into an assistant director's job at CBS

1954: TV directing debut, "The Plot Against King Solomon" episode of the CBS series "You Are There"

After directing additional episodes of "You Are There" and "Danger", moved to CBS' California studios to direct for "Climax!" and "Playhouse 90"

1956: Feature directorial debut, "The Young Stranger"; had also filmed live TV version ("Deal a Blow") for "Climax!"; preferred that version because he had worked with familiar TV crew

1957: Helmed "The Comedian" for "Playhouse 90", considered by some the finest live drama from TV's "Golden Age" because of its depiction of the fledgling medium itself; written by Rod Serling and starring Mickey Rooney

1959: Directed Broadway production, "The Midnight Sun"

1961: Second feature, "The Young Savages", adapted from a novel by Evan Hunter; first of five films with Burt Lancaster; also first of five films with director of photography Lionel Lindon

1962: Helmed William Inge's adaptation of James Leo Herlihy's novel "All Fall Down", starring Warren Beatty; first of two films that year with Angela Lansbury

1962: Replaced Charles Crichton as director of "The Birdman of Alcatraz", starring Lancaster

1962: Directed and co-produced (with screenwriter George Axelrod) "The Manchurian Candidate"; second film with Lansbury

1964: Initial collaboration with producer Edward Lewis, "Seven Days in May", starring Lancaster, Fredric March, Kirk Douglas and Ava Gardner

1965: Replaced Arthur Penn as director of "The Train", starring Lancaster and Paul Scofield

1966: After "Seconds" received harsh treatment at Cannes, Paramount panicked and dumped the film; critical esteem for film has grown over the years

1966: Success of actioner "Grand Prix" restored bankability; international cast included James Garner, French actor Yves Montand and Japanese actor Toshiro Mifune

1968: First collaboration with screenwriter Dalton Trumbo, "The Fixer", adapted from the Bernard Malamud novel

1968: Directed campaign commercials for Robert F. Kennedy during presidential primary season

1969: Last film with Lancaster, "The Gypsy Moths"

1971: Reteamed with Trumbo on "The Horsemen", adapted from the Joesph Kessel novel

1973: Seventh and last film with Lewis, the highly esteemed "The Iceman Cometh"; also Fredric March's last film

1975: Helmed the sequel "French Connection II"

1977: Seized upon the Goodyear Blimp as an instrument of unpredictable menace in action disaster pic "Black Sunday"; feature acting debut as TV Controller

1982: Reteamed with Mifune for "The Challenge", martial arts movie co-scripted by John Sayles; Steven Seagal worked as a stunt coordinator

1982: Directed HBO TV-movie remake of "The Rainmaker", starring Tommy Lee Jones and Tuesday Weld

1985: Second collaboration with screenwriter George Axelrod, "The Holcroft Covenant"

1988: Career received boost with re-release of "The Manchurian Candidate"

1992: Returned to TV at helm of "Maniac at Large" episode of HBO's "Tales of the Crypt"

1994: Began career turnaround with "Against the Wall" (HBO); produced by Axelrod's son Jonathan; received first of four Emmy Awards for Outstanding Achievement in Directing for a Miniseries or Special

1994: Produced and directed the HBO biopic "The Burning Season", starring Raul Julia; received second Emmy

1996: Picked up third Emmy Award for the acclaimed TNT miniseries "Andersonville", set in the notorious Civil War prison camp; also served as an executive producer

1996: First feature in five years, "The Island of Dr. Moreau"; took over production from

fired South African director Richard Stanley, salvaged the film and made it releasable

1997: Received fourth Emmy for helming the TNT biographical miniseries "George Wallace"; also produced

1998: Delivered sly action masterpiece, "Ronin", a triumphant feature return; boasted international cast including Robert De Niro, Jean Reno and Stellan Skarsgard

1999: Appeared as an Army general in the thriller "The General's Daughter"

2000: Helmed the thriller "Reindeer Games", starring Ben Affleck and Charlize Theron

2001: Directed the short "Ambush", one of five featurette advertisments for BMW shown over the Internet at bmwfilms.com

Helmed an as yet untitled prequel to "The Exorcist" (lensed 2002), focusing on Father Merrin's missionary work in Africa

AFFILIATION: Member, Board of Governors of Academy of Motion Picture Arts and Sciences

QUOTES:
Actors John Scott and Don Galloway portrayed Frankenheimer in the TV productions "Robert Kennedy and His Times" (CBS, 1985) and "Rock Hudson" (NBC, 1990) respectively.

Frankenheimer used the pseudonymous Alan Smithee credit on the 1987 TV-movie "Riviera"

"It was very exciting. If they had live television right now, I'd still be doing it. You had total control as a director. It was live, so we had final cut. And you had no such thing as a difficult actor."—John Frankenheimer in *Los Angeles Times,* November 5, 1989.

On the death of his friend Robert Kennedy: "He wanted me up there on the podium with him, but I said I didn't think this was the kind of image he wanted—a movie director beside him on the night of the primary.

"It was a tremendous sense of loss. I had spent my life dealing with make-believe. And here was somebody trying to make a huge difference in people's lives. I was really left very disillusioned, and went through a period of deep depression."—From *The New York Times,* March 24, 1994.

About signing on to direct Marlon Brando in "The Island of Dr Moreau": "We missed each other during our careers. I've worked with a lot of people and I always thought I really wanted to work with Brando before we both hang it up. I said that during an interview with Australian TV. Lo and behold, two weeks later the phone call came asking, 'Would you like to take over this movie?' "—John Frankenheimer quoted in *Entertainment Today,* August 23–29, 1996.

On what TV offers that film doesn't: "First it offers me more time to tell a story. Long form is fabulous for me. Secondly, the material that I've been lucky enough to do on these four cable movies has been controversial, cutting-edge material that I don't think would have been made into a feature film today. Certainly not a mainstream feature film, because mainstream studios aren't making that kind of material."—Frankenheimer to *Buzz,* August 22–28, 1997.

About the alcoholism that threatened his life as well as his career: "I had a drinking problem. It took a toll on me. And the state of mind you're in when you have a problem like that, even when you're not drunk, is the most dangerous time. Because you make decisions that are not totally in your best interest—about your life, about your career choices and everything."

He stopped drinking c. 1981. "I said, 'I can't go on like this'—I figured I'd better do something about it because otherwise I was going to die."—From *The New York Times,* September 14, 1998.

In May 2001, Frankenheimer addressed rumors that he was actually the biological father of film director Michael Bay. Frankenheimer admitted to a brief relationship with Bay's birth mother who later contacted the director's representatives and claimed to be pregnant. Frankenheimer reportedly payed her a sum of money (about $7500) when he learned she was expecting. After the rumors surfaced that Bay's natural father was a filmmaker, there was much speculation and Frankenheimer's name often came up. In the May 2001 interviews, the director firmly stated that he was NOT the father of Michael Bay and that it had been verified by "tests."

BIBLIOGRAPHY:

"The Cinema of John Frankenheimer" John Frankenheimer with Gerald Pratley 1969 A.S. Barnes & Co. Inc.

Carl Franklin

BORN: Carl Michael Franklin in Richmond, California, 04/11/1949

SOMETIMES CREDITED AS:
Carl Mikal Franklin

NATIONALITY: American

EDUCATION: University of California at Berkeley, Berkeley, California, dramatic arts, 1967

American Film Institute, Los Angeles, California, 1986; enrolled in directors program

AWARDS: Los Angeles Film Critics Association New Generation Award "One False Move" 1991

Independent Spirit Award Best Director "One False Move" 1992

MTV Movie Award Best New Filmmaker "One False Move" 1993

American Film Institute Franklin J. Schaffner Alumni Medal 1996

BIOGRAPHY

Those who watched far too much bad TV in the 1970s and 80s may remember Carl Franklin as a rugged African-American character player. Those who value thoughtful and solidly crafted genre films may give more weight to his second career as a filmmaker in the 1990s. Franklin first acted as student at UC-Berkely and honed his skills off-Broadway at the Public Theater before becoming a familiar face on TV. He made one film appearance in the family comedy "Five on the Black Hand Side" (1973) before landing steady work on the small screen with numerous guest shots, roles in TV movies, miniseries and busted pilots and stints as a regular on several unsuccessful series including the cop shows "Caribe" (ABC, 1975), co-starring Stacy Keach and "McClain's Law" (NBC, 1981–82), with James Arness as well as the sci-fi adventure "The Fantastic Journey" (NBC, 1977).

With his handsome yet serious features, Franklin tended to be cast as men of authority such as military officers, scientists and police detectives. He may have been most widely seen as the recurring character Captain Crane on the hit comedy adventure series "The A-Team" (NBC, 1983–87). Nonetheless, such roles soured Franklin on acting. He enrolled in the American Film Institute's directing program in L.A. in 1986. Franklin's master thesis film, "Punk" (1989), was a riveting portrait of a black boy from a broken home coping with both societal norms and his own emerging sexuality. Over the course of 30 minutes, the neophyte writer-director dealt with such issues as single female parenting, codes of masculinity and gay-bashing, all without resorting to cliches or easy answers.

"Punk" caught the eye of legendary exploitation producer Roger Corman who hired Franklin in 1989 for a brief but intense "apprenticeship" (six films in two years) in low-budget filmmaking. The inexperienced filmmaker entered features working variously (and in combination) as a director, screenwriter and/or actor in a series of genre quickies that received brief regional releases before finding their rightful homes on video store shelves. Franklin made his directorial breakthrough with the highly acclaimed crime drama "One False Move" (1992). This tough noir-ish thriller efficiently told the story of the manhunt of three small-time criminals on the lam after a botched drug deal. The film opened with a memorable and disturbing bloodbath that eschewed the glamorization of violence so prevalent in much of Hollywood's genre fare. Moreover, Franklin focused on what critic Sheila Benson described as "subtle shifts and balances in racial and sexual relationships."

Franklin followed his film success with an unexpected return to TV. He again won kudos for his sensitive direction of "Laurel Avenue" (HBO, 1993), a superior made-for-cable miniseries depicting a weekend in the lives of a working-class black family in St. Paul, Minnesota. Franklin's next feature was "Devil in a Blue Dress" (1995), a high-profile period mystery about a Negro detective in 40s L.A. He directed his own adaptation of Walter Mosley's acclaimed novel and landed a major star— Denzel Washington—and a healthy $20 million budget.—Written by Kent Greene

MILESTONES:

Raised the youngest of three children in Richmond, California

Acted off-Broadway at Joseph Papp's Public Theater

1973: Feature acting debut, "Five on the Black Hand Side", credited as Carl Mikal Franklin

1974: TV acting debut, "It Couldn't Happen to a Nicer Guy", a TV-movie comedy about a male rape victim

1975: TV series debut, "Caribe" (ABC), an exotic cop drama with Stacy Keach

1977: Co-starred on "The Fantastic Journey", a short-lived NBC sci-fi series

1977: First TV special, NBC team member in "Battle of the Network Stars II"

1978: TV miniseries debut, "Loose Change/ Those Restless Years" on NBC-TV

1979: Co-starred in the unsold Western

TV-movie/pilot "The Legend of the Golden Gun" on NBC

1981–1982: Cast as a regular on "McClain's Law" on NBC, a cop drama vehicle for James Arness

Played the recurring role of Captain Crane on the popular NBC action comedy series "The A-Team"

1989: Debut as a writer-director, "Punk", a short film made as Franklin's masters thesis at AFI (broadcast in 1993 as a presentation of "Alive TV" on PBS)

1989: Feature directing and screenwriting debut, "Eye of the Eagle II: Inside the Enemy"; also acted in first feature appearance in 16 years; first feature made in association with Roger Corman's Concorde Pictures (here acting as a distributor)

Scripted, directed and/or acted in subsequent genre quickies for Corman: "Nowhere to Run", "Last Stand at Lang Mei" (both 1989); "Full Fathom Five" (1990); "Eye of the Eagle 3"; and "In the Heat of Passion" (both 1992)

1993: Breakthrough feature directing assignment, the critically acclaimed crime drama "One False Move"

1993: TV miniseries directing debut, "Laurel Avenue" on HBO

1995: Wrote and directed an acclaimed but little seen adaptation of Walter Mosley's "Devil in a Blue Dress", starring Denzel Washington

1998: Helmed the moving adaptation of Anna Quindlen's autobiographical novel "One True Thing", starring Renee Zellweger and Meryl Streep

QUOTES:

"With "Punk" and "Laurel Avenue", Carl Franklin has made the best American movies I have seen so far this year. "Punk" is great enough to make Franklin seem to be the Black filmmaker everyone has been waiting for. Charles Burnett and Wendell B. Harris are idiosyncratic artists out of left field (so is Spike Lee, who comes from the infield), but Franklin works in a plain, linear mode, on ostensibly topical matters that he gives the imaginative richness of artistry. His specialty is not the violent hysterics of kid directors like The Hughes Brothers, Mario Van Peebles, Matty Rich, but wisdom and beauty."—From "Carl Franklin Rises to the Top with 'Punk' " by Armond White, *The City Sun*, August 18–August 24, 1995.

Stephen Frears

BORN: Stephen Arthur Frears in Leicester, England, 06/20/1941

NATIONALITY: English

EDUCATION: Greshams School Holt, Norfolk, England, public school; attended for five years; Frears has characterized it as uninspiring as his home town

attended a state-run school with "a very, very good headmaster, who, in the space of about three months, opened my mind. He taught me about the world, about politics, about literature . . . enough to help me pass an exam to get into Cambridge" (The New York Times Magazine, December 18, 1988)

University of Cambridge Cambridge, England law 1960–63 graduated with a law degree but had become involved in student theater

AWARDS: Cesar Best Foreign Film "Les Liaisons Dangereuses/Dangerous Liaisons" 1990

Berlin Film Festival Silver Bear for Best Director "The Hi-Lo Country" 1999

BIOGRAPHY

Armed with a keen visual awareness and compelling ability to tell a story, Stephen Frears became established as a leading director in British cinema and TV in the 1980s. While studying law at Cambridge, Frears' interest in the stage was peaked and soon after obtaining his degree, he joined London's Royal Court Theater. He did not become involved in film until 1966 when Karel Reisz offered an unemployed Frears a job as assistant director on "Morgan" setting the stage for his apprenticeship as assistant director to Reisz, Lindsay Anderson and Albert Finney before he had the opportunity to step into the director's chair for "Gumshoe" (1971), a satire on American detective films with Finney as a romantic dreamer who envisions himself a private eye.

It was not until 1984 that Frears would work on another project intended specifically for theatrical release. During this interval, he worked continuously in TV, refining his craft while developing a reputation for workmanlike efforts and an ability to get along with both writers and actors. Frears returned to feature filmmaking with "The Hit" (1984), a taut, well-crafted thriller which, like "Gumshoe", provided an interesting twist to the crime genre. Terence Stamp played an informer living out his days in Spain, with John Hurt as a hard-boiled hit man hired to take him back to Paris to receive his comeuppance from the crime boss he had snitched on. This downbeat film regarded its characters and their predicaments with a biting sense of humor, a quality which has marked all of Frears' films.

With "My Beautiful Laundrette" (1985), shot in 16mm on a budget of only $900,000 for British television, Frears achieved a breakthrough. Working with writer Hanif Kureishi, the director portrayed the effects of racism and underemployment on working-class London through the eyes of a young Pakistani attempting to carve his own place in the world. The next Kureishi/Frears effort, "Sammy and Rosie Get Laid" (1987), dealt with these same themes in a multi-layered look at the social relations revolving around a liberal, educated, mixed-race

couple (Pakistani and upper-middle-class British) living in a poor section of London. Though the themes were not explored to their fullest, the rich visuals and good performances made for an entertaining film that exposed many of the inequities of British society.

Between these two efforts, Frears directed Alan Bennett's adaptation of John Lahr's biography of playwright Joe Orton, who was brutally murdered at the height of his fame by his longtime lover and roommate Ken Halliwell. Rather than a standard biography, "Prick Up Your Ears" (1987) concentrated mainly on the relationship of these two men as a study of marriage gone tragically sour. In 1988, Frears fulfilled his longtime wish to work in the Hollywood system, a move he hoped would broaden his potential while providing greater financial rewards. "Dangerous Liaisons", an adaptation of Christopher Hampton's play (which itself was based on Choderlos de Laclos' 18th-century novel), displayed the customary Frears trademarks: good performances and witty dialogue. But it was also his most glossy, stylized film, lacking the conviction and force of his earlier efforts.

As if in response to this, Frears' next Hollywood outing, "The Grifters" (1990), retained the stylization (a timeless Southern California floating somewhere between the 1950s and the 80s), but added the grittiness that had informed his British features. Adapted from the novel by Jim Thompson and starring John Cusack, Annette Bening, and Anjelica Huston, the film garnered critically acclaim and confirmed Frears' bankable status in Hollywood, capped by a Best Director Oscar nomination. He followed with "Hero" (1992), a lightweight Capraesque fable about the power of the media and the nature of heroism. Starring Dustin Hoffman, Geena Davis and Andy Garcia, the film received some positive reviews but fizzled at the box office. Moreover, it broke little new ground for the director who reportedly clashed on set with star Hoffman.

Frears had better luck when he returned to England to direct "The Snapper" (1993). Based on a novel by Roddy Doyle and made for British television, this film was a sequel to Alan Parker's "The Commitments" (1991) centering on an Irish working-class family coping with the teenager daughter's pregnancy. It featured a literate script and strong performances, particularly from Colm Meaney as the father confused by circumstances. Frears directed the third installment "The Van" (1996), again starring Meaney, which screened at the Cannes Film Festival. Before its release, however, the helmer had spent almost two years on "Mary Reilly" (1996). Adapted from Valerie Martin's novel that recounted the Dr. Jekyll/Mr. Hyde story from the point of view of a parlor maid, "Mary Reilly" opened to lackluster box office and harsh reviews, with critics carping over the miscast Julia Roberts as Mary and John Malkovich as Jekyll/Hyde.

"The Hi-Lo Country" (1998) reteamed Frears with producers Barbara De Fina and Martin Scorsese from "The Grifters" and revealed the director completely at home with the Western genre. Overwhelmed by the weight of responsibility studio money entailed, he insisted the movie be made as an independent and successfully grafted film noir onto the Western, benefiting from a superb, charismatic turn by Woody Harrelson as the "last real cowboy." Keeping to his penchant for variety, Frears next helmed "High Fidelity" (2000), a quirky comedy exploring the romantic misfortunes of its main character. John Cusack starred in a fearless and ferociously funny performance, as well as co-adapting and remaining faithful to Brit writer Nick Hornby's excellent source material, despite switching the London locale to Chicago. The director continued to push the envelope in his career by making his American TV debut at the helm of a live small screen remake of "Fail Safe". The two-hour, black-and-white CBS project was a personal project for producer-star George Clooney and although Frears did yeoman work, capturing the drama's inherent suspense, it proved too old-fashioned to audiences raised on the razzmatazz of MTV. Frears surprised Hollywood with his next career move, heading back to Europe to direct the French film "Liam" (2000), which chronicled the effects of Liverpool's Depression on the family of sprightly, if stuttering, 8-year-old (Anthony Borrows). He remained in Europe to make the dark, critically-trumpeted morality meditation "Dirty Pretty Things" (2002; US release 2003) featuring Chiwetel Ejiofor and Audrey Tatou as immigrants caught up in the shadowy secrets of a hotel's black market underbelly.

COMPANION:

Annie Rothenstein. Painter; together since c. 1974; mother of one son and one daughter

MILESTONES:

1964: Directed "Waiting for Godot" and "Inadmissible Evidence" at the Royal Court Theatre, London

1966: Worked as assistant director on Karel Reisz's "Morgan"

1967: Directorial debut with "The Burning", a half-hour film made for the British Film Institute's Production Board

1967: Served as assistant director to Albert Finney on Finney's directorial debut "Charlie Bubbles"

1968: Was assistant director to Lindsay Anderson on "If . . . "

1971: Directed first feature film, "Gumshoe" (scripted by Neville Smith), starring Finney; commissioned original score from Andrew Lloyd Webber

1971: Directed first TV film scripted by playwright Alan Bennett, "A Day Out"; first of many small screen collaborations with Bennett, including "Sunset Across the Bay" (1973), "A Visit from Miss Protheroe" (1977) and a series of six plays for London Weekend Television in 1978

1972: Reteamed with Neville Smith on tele-film, "Match of Day"; would also collaborate with Smith on 1979 TV-movie "Long Distance Information"

1975: Collaborated with playwright Tom Stoppard on BBC-TV film, "Three Men in a Boat"

1978: Appeared as the Biscuit Man in Maurice Hatton's "Long Shot"; frequent collaborators Smith and Bennett were also cast members

1983: Two made-for-television presentations which he directed, "Bloody Kids" (1979) and "Saigon: Year of the Cat", scripted by David Hare, received theatrical releases

1984: Helmed sly, unpredictable thriller, "The Hit", which contained memorable theme music composed by Eric Clapton (with an assist from Pink Floyd's Roger Waters)

1985: Breakthrough feature, "My Beautiful Laundrette"; first feature collaboration with screenwriter Hanif Kureishi

1987: Reteamed with Kureishi on "Sammy and Rosie Get Laid"

1987: Lone feature to date scripted by Bennett, "Prick Up Your Ears", a chillingly realistic biopic of British playwright Joe Orton

1988: First American feature, "Dangerous Liaisons", starring John Malkovich; first film with playwright-screenwriter Christopher Hampton, who had first adapted the 18th-century French novel "Les Liaisons Dangereuses" to the stage

1990: First film with actor John Cusack, "The Grifters", adapted from the novel by Jim Thompson; earned Oscar nomination for Best Director

1992: Third US feature, the $42 million "Hero", starring Dustin Hoffman Geena Davis and Andy Garcia (Cusack's sister Joan was also in cast); reportedly feuded on set with star Hoffman

1993: Disgusted with studio excess, returned to the United Kingdom and directed "The Snapper" (budgeted at less than $2 million), adapted by Roddy Doyle from his novel about a working-class Irish family; starred Colm Meaney; second in Doyle's Barrytown Trilogy, following Alan Parker's "The Commitments" (1991), which also featured Meaney

1995: Co-directed (with Mike Dibb) documentary, "Typically British", a survey of a century of British filmmakers, their films and their industry

1996: Reunited with Malkovich and Hampton for misfire, "Mary Reilly", also starring Julia Roberts

1996: Reteamed with Meany, Doyle and Clapton for "The Van", completing Doyle's Barrytown Trilogy

1997: Narrated feature documentary, "Howard Hawks: American Artist"

1998: Helmed "The Hi-Lo Country", a handsome postmodern Western starring Woody Harrelson; project reteamed him with "The Grifters" producing team of Barbara De Fina and Martin Scorsese

2000: Reteamed with Cusack for "High Fidelity"; Cusack co-adapted British writer Nick Hornby's novel, changing the setting from London to Chicago

2000: Directed small screen remake "Fail Safe" (CBS), a live, two-hour, black-and-white adaptation of the bestselling 1962 Cold War novel by Henry Wheeler and Eugene Burdick; George Clooney starred and was one of the executive producers; Walter Bernstein wrote the screenplay as he did for the 1964 movie version directed by Sidney Lumet; received Emmy nomination

2000: Garnered good reviews for the small-scale "Liam", a drama about an 8-year-old Liverpudlian

QUOTES:

Created an Officer of the Order of Arts and Letters by the French government in 1998

About winning the race to be the first director to release a film based on Choderlos de Laclos' 1782 novel "Les Liaisons Dangereuses": "It's amazing what you can do when you've got an Oscar-winning director staring over your shoulder.

"I knew that Milos [Forman, who was simultaneously helming "Valmont"] takes a long time to make his movies. But it does work wonders—I mean, it's a very good thing to have somebody else making the same film a few days later after you. I would thoroughly recommend it as a way of geting things done."—Stephen Frears quoted in *The New York Times Magazine*, December 18, 1988.

"This black hole that people talk about in my career in the 70s, when I didn't make any films—in retrospect what I was doing was learning my job. But I was learning it on very, very good material. We were, as they say, grinding it out, but we were doing it with the very best writers and the very best actors.

"In the BBC, we were trained that it was the writer's voice we were filming; I know that's clearly not the case in America, but it's not my job to alter a writer's story.

"I wouldn't cross the road if a script isn't good."—Frears in *The New York Times Magazine*, December 18, 1988.

"I didn't want to go into filmmaking. I went into theater because a couple of actors came into town, and I just wanted to run away and join them. Then I met a film director and he said come and work on my film. I went and worked on his film. That was the first time I was ever on a film set. It wasn't at all a plan. It wasn't like it is now. There weren't people called film directors in those days. Film directors weren't part of normal life. That is all quite

new. Films were things you saw in the cinema. They weren't made by people I knew. They came by magic."—Frears to Michelle Bryant in *FP West Calendar*, December 1998.

Why he does not go back and look at his previous work: "All you ever do is wonder if someday you'll lose your talent. That's what I lie in bed and worry about. I might look at something and say, 'God, I can't do that anymore.' "—Frears to *The Washington Post*, January 10, 1999.

On his entry to the Western genre, "The Hi-Lo Country", adapted by Walon Green from Max Evans' 1961 novel celebrating both the end of the true cowboy era and the author's friendship with fellow cowboy Big Boy Matson: "It's really about the mythology and the reality. This is not a kid's cowboy movie, it's a grown-up film . . .

"My head was full of all those stories about [Howard] Hawks bringing Montgomery Clift out to act opposite John Wayne in 'Red River' and the contrast between them. That was what I was looking for. Woody [Harrelson] was a country boy, an outsider in the right way and charismatic. Billy [Crudup]'s a New York actor, he's pretty young but he looks as though he's experienced something of life. What you realize is that these people are strong and silent; they don't sit around and discuss their feeling or emotions as we do today, and the landscape becomes the way you tell the emotional story of the character."—quoted in the London *Times*, July 21, 1999.

William Friedkin

BORN: in Chicago, Illinois, 08/29/1935

NATIONALITY: American

EDUCATION: Senn High School Chicago, Illinois on Chicago's North Side

AWARDS: Golden Globe Award Best Director "The French Connection" 1971

Directors Guild of America Award Outstanding Directorial Achievement in Feature Film "The French Connection" 1971

Oscar Best Director "The French Connection" 1971

Golden Globe Award Best Director "The Exorcist" 1973

NATO Director of the Year Award 1974 presented by the National Association of Theater Owners

BIOGRAPHY

Noted for the documentary quality of his dramas, William Friedkin began his career in the mail room of a local Chicago TV station and quickly worked his way up to director, reportedly helming over 2,000 live shows before tackling his first TV film, the documentary "The People vs. Paul Crump" (1962), designed to convince the governor of Illinois to commute the death sentence of an inmate who had his confession beaten out of him by the Chicago police. Although the film never aired on TV, it did accomplish its purpose, as well as winning the Golden Gate Award at the San Francisco Film Festival and paving the way for future documentary work for the filmmaker. After directing segments (including the final episode) of NBC's "Alfred Hitchcock Presents" in 1965, Friedkin graduated to features with "Good Times" (1967), an enjoyable little pic starring Sonny and Cher, which he followed with the more ambitious burlesque nostalgia piece "The Night They Raided Minsky's" and the static screen adaptation of playwright Harold Pinter's "The Birthday Party" (both 1968).

Friedkin fared better with his adaptation of Mart Crowley's Off-Broadway play about gay men "The Boys in the Band" (1970). Sensationally acted by the original stage cast, the film was a rare case where a single, claustrophobic set was an asset, though some critics complained that the little "opening up" of the piece by the director had dissipated its atmosphere. Crowley, who also produced "Boys", had introduced Friedkin to Kitty Hawks, daughter of legendary filmmaker Howard Hawks, who advised the young director: "People don't want stories about somebody's problems or any of that psychological s—.

What they want is action stories. Every time I made a film like that, with a lotta good guys against bad guys, it had a lotta success, if that matters to you." The words stuck with Friedkin, and when Fox production president Richard D Zanuck told him he could make "The French Connection" (1971), as long as he kept the price under $2 million, he jumped at the chance. The budgetary restraints forced him to cast relative no-names Gene Hackman and Roy Scheider, and the rest is movie history.

Friedkin instructed his cameraman to eschew traditional lighting and blocking and to film the events before them as if they were news reporters arriving at the scene of the crime. The resultant "induced documentary" style was perfect for the gritty, urban drama, which catapulted him to the front rank of American directors. Perhaps best remembered for its renowned car chase, considered by many to be the most exciting chase sequence ever filmed, "The French Connection" garnered five Oscars for Best Picture, Best Director, Best Actor (Hackman), Best Screenplay (Ernest Tidyman) and Best Editing (Jerry Greenberg). His next picture, "The Exorcist" (1973), ushered in a new kind of horror film and earned him a reputation as a bully on the set for such antics as slapping a non-actor (a real priest) to get an appropriate line reading and showing open disregard for the safety of his actors, leading to a permanent back injury for star Ellen Burstyn. Still, there was method to his madness, and the powerfully suggestive movie topped $100 million, accompanied by reports that audience members were fainting, having fits and regurgitating their popcorn in response to the ocean of pea soup spewed forth from Linda Blair and the devilish utterings of Mercedes McCambridge. The film received ten Academy Award nominations including one for Friedkin as Best Director.

Fast on the heels of success came the prodigious failures. 1977's "Sorcerer", Friedkin's remake of Henri-Georges Clouzot's "The Wages of Fear" (1952), was a colossal bust, considered by most everybody a pretentious waste of time. "The Brink's Job" (1979) assembled a notable cast (i.e., Peter Falk, Warren Oates, Paul Sorvino) but also lost money, despite its excellent period and location favor. Then came "Cruising" (1980, his first screenplay), which elicited widespread protest from the homosexual community for what was perceived as a negative expose of gay club culture and even louder howls from the MPAA, which refused to rate it until after substantial editing, described by the director in Sight and Sound (November 1998) as "butchery on the scale comparable to 'The Magnificent Ambersons'—we must have lost about 40 minutes of material." Friedkin missed again with his satire of international weapons merchants, "Deal of the Century" (1983), and his attempt to fashion a West Coast equivalent of "The French Connection" as director and co-author of "To Live and Die in L.A." (1985) also fell short. Despite its spectacular car chase and excellent cast, the intense vulgarity of the characters and stylistic overkill doomed the film with mainstream audiences. Perhaps "Rampage" (1987) and its thoughtful exploration of the insanity defense could have restored some luster to his name, but the demise of its production house delayed its release until 1992.

In 1986, Friedkin returned to television to direct Barbra Streisand's HBO special "Putting It Together: The Making of 'The Broadway Album' " and to produce and direct an action adventure series pilot "C.A.T. Squad" (NBC, as well its 1988 sequel). Inspired by personal experiences with people hired to look after his son, Friedkin wrote and directed "The Guardian" (1990), a return to the horror genre depicting a baby in supernatural danger from a new nanny. He delivered scares with a comic twist helming an episode of "Tales From the Crypt" (HBO, 1992) and directed Shannen Doherty and Antonio Sabato Jr. in the made-for-cable outing "Jailbreakers" (1994), one of Showtime's "Rebel Highway" remakes of 1950s and 60s teen drive-in movies. After helming

the Ron Shelton-scripted basketball pic "Blue Chips" (1994), Friedkin directed "Jade" (1995), the third installment of scripter Joe Eszterhas' series of San Francisco-set erotic thrillers that began in 1985 with "Jagged Edge" and continued with 1992's "Basic Instinct." The convoluted story boasted a solid cast and one of the filmmaker's trademark long, dizzying car chases but died at the box office. His acclaimed remake of "12 Angry Men" for Showtime in 1997 earned another shot at a big Hollywood project, but "Rules of Engagement" (2000) proved he had not yet rediscovered the magic that made "The French Connection" and "The Exorcist" such blockbusters in the 70s.

COMPANIONS:

Kitty Hawks. Model; also worked in an advertising agency; daughter of Howard Hawks; introduced to Friedkin by playwright Mart Crowly c. 1969 during the filming of "Boys in the Band"; lived together; announced engagement but separated in June 1971

Jennifer Nairn-Smith. Dancer; met in 1972; together for four years; twice announced engagement; mother of Friedkin's son Cedric

Ellen Burstyn. Actor; worked together on "The Exorcist" (1973); Burstyn claims they had an affair c. 1976; Friedkin disputes it claiming they were "just friends"

wife: Jeanne Moreau. Actor, director; married in 1977; divorced in 1979

wife: Lesley-Anne Down. Actor; married in 1982; divorced in 1985; mother of Friedkin's son Jack; engaged in bitter custody dispute over son

MILESTONES:

Began career in mailroom of WGN-TV, Chicago after finishing high school; eventually graduated to floor manager, then director

1962: Directed first TV film, "The People vs. Paul Crump", a 16mm documentary; received funding for project from rival Chicago station WBKB-TV, and though film never aired on the station, was subsequently hired to head a documentary unit established at WBKB; picture won Golden Gate award at San Francisco Film Festival; producer David Wolper offered him jobn which he declined at the time

1965: Moved to L.A.

1965: Hired to direct episodes of NBC's "Alfred Hitchcok Presents", including the final broadcast

Eventually went to work for Wolper, reportedly working on the TV documentaries "The Thin Blue Line" (about law enforcement), "Mayhem on Sunday Afternoon" (a report on professional football) and "The Bold Men" (which dealt with people who risk their lives for money, adventure or science)

1967: Directed first feature, "Good Times", starring Sonny and Cher

1968: Helmed "The Night They Raided Minsky's", an affectionate look at burlesque; production was slightly hampered by death of co-star Bert Lahr during filming

1968: Filmed a somewhat static feature adaptation of Harold Pinter's stage play "The Birthday Party"

1970: Helmed "The Boys in the Band", adapted from the Mart Crowley play

1971: Won the Best Director Oscar for "The French Connection"

1973: Had box-office hit with screen version of "The Exorcist"

1973: Formed partnership with Peter Bogdanovich and Francis Ford Coppola called the Directors Company; organization disbanded after one year

1977: Suffered career setback with the box-office failure of "Sorcerer", a remake of Henri-Georges Clouzot's "The Wages of Fear"

1978: Helmed comic period piece, "The Brink's Job", about the infamous 1950 Boston heist

1980: Wrote first screenplay, "Cruising"; also directed; film engendered controversy over its depiction of aspects of the gay community in NYC

1983: Attempted satire of international weapons merchants in "Deal of the Century", starring Chevy Chase

1985: Helmed and co-scripted "To Live and Die in L.A."

1986: Returned to TV to direct Barbra Streisand's HBO special, "Putting It Together—The Making of 'The Broadway Album' "

1986: Executive produced, created and directed the NBC pilot "C.A.T. Squad" and its 1988 TV-movie sequel

1987: Completed "Rampage", which dealt with the death penalty and the complexity of the insanity plea; release delayed when De Laurentis Entertainment went bankrupt; released in 1992; also underwent change in ending; the original was more blatantly anti–capital punishment; final version proved more favorable to the victims

1990: Returned to horror with "The Guardian"; also co-scripted

1992: Continued in the horror vein directing "On a Dead Man's Chest" episode of HBO's "Tales From the Crypt"

1994: Helmed "Jailbreakers" segment of Showtime's "Rebel Highway" series

1994: Returned to features as director of the sports-themed "Blue Chips", scripted by Ron Shelton

1995: Helmed third film in Joe Eszterhas' "sleaze" trilogy, "Jade"

1997: Directed the acclaimed small screen remake of "12 Angry Men" (Showtime)

1997: Received star number 2,093 on the Hollywood Walk of Fame (August 14)

1998: Directed Alban Berg's opera "Wozzeck" in Florence, Italy with Zubin Mehta conducting

2000: Helmed "Rules of Engagement"; produced by Richard D Zanuck, the 20th Century-Fox executive who greenlit "The French Connection"

2002: Staged two productions for the Los Angeles Opera

2002: Directed "The Hunted"; film was forced to shut down in June 2001 when star Benicio

Del Toro was injured days before principal photography was due to end; completed several months later

AFFILIATION: Jewish

QUOTES:
"I always aim at the stars and sometimes I hit Dresden. But I set out, as Wernher Von Braun did with every rocket, to take it to the moon."—William Friedkin on aiming his films at the widest possible audience to *Los Angeles Times,* November 19, 1989.

Although it never aired on the small screen, Friedkin's first TV film, "The People vs. Crump", was instrumental in saving the life of its subject, a man who had spent several years on death row.

"I never made the film ["Cruising"] to have anything to do with the gay community other than as a background for a murder mystery. It was not meant to be pro or con, gay rights, or gay anything. It was an exotic background that people, I knew, hadn't seen in a mainstream film. That's what intrigued me about it. I had never seen it, but heard about it and decided to go around to the various clubs and saw what was going on. I decided to write the story based on what I'd seen and on a story that one of the 'French Connection' cops told me that he'd experienced when he was sent as a decoy in the gay world to catch a killer who was targeting gays. That situation really screwed him up. It made him start to question his sexuality. Some of the best stuff was cut out of it. It was compromised severely. It should've gone out as an 'X' picture, but they couldn't."—Friedkin quoted in *Venice,* August 1997.

"I burned a lot of bridges. I treated Diller and Sheinberg and Eisner with contempt. The more powerful they got, the easier it was for them to remember the way I had carried on with them. Those people on the elevator going up were the ones I met going down. There was a lot of resistance to my doing films at some of these studios.

"I never set out to make a bad film. I thought in each case they were going to be as good or better than anything I had done. I went through this long period of wondering why I wasn't being received in the same way. Now I've reached the point where I know why. These films just weren't any fucking good. They have no soul, no heart—they don't even have any technical expertise. It's as though someone reached up inside of an animal and pulled the guts out. The thing that drove me and still keeps me going is 'Citizen Kane'. I hope to one day make a film to rank with that. I haven't yet." —Friedkin to Peter Biskind in *Premiere,* May 1998.

On his ruthless treatment of Mercedes McCambridge (vocal double for Satan) on the set of "The Exorcist": "I had her tied to a chair for a month while we recorded. I squeezed her, I tortured her, I shoved raw eggs and whisky down her throat and made her chain-smoke so we could get the sounds we wanted. She was a lapsed Catholic and a reformed drunk, so it really whipped her out of shape. She had two friends of hers who were priests, and when she'd start to blubber after takes, they'd give her counseling. Did it bother me? Nah, I was just making a movie."—Friedkin to *The Guardian,* October 18, 1998.

About meeting Alfred Hitchcock: "Hitchcock came over and I told him I was really honored to meet him and I extended my hand. And he gave me his hand like a royal hand show. He handed it to me like a dead fish to shake and he said: 'Mr. Friedkin, I see that you're not wearing a tie.' And I thought he was putting me on. I said: 'No sir, I didn't put on a tie today.' And he said: 'Usually our directors wear ties.' And he walked away.

" . . . a few years later . . . I was at the Directors Guild Awards in Los Angeles and the film ["The French Connection"] had won and I came down the platform with this director's award in my arms. It was in a banquet room and there at the first table was Hitchcock. I had a tuxedo with one of those flashy string bow ties, and I went down to Hitchcock, holding my award and I snapped my tie and said: "How do you like the tie, Hitch?' And he sort of stared at me. Of course he didn't remember at all."—Friedkin quoted in *The Guardian*, October 22, 1998.

On the famous car chase from "The French Connection": "We'd been shooting for a number of days on elements for the chase, and it occurred to me that we didn't have anything really dangerous, and not a lot of speed. Bill Hickman, who was the stunt driver on 'Bullit', was our man, and one night I got him drunk and told him, 'You know, Bill, you're a pussy. You've shown me nothing, and I don't think we have much of a chase.' He immediately rose to the challenge and said, 'You wanna see some hairy driving? Have you got the balls to get in my car?' So next day we strapped a camera to the front of the car, I got in the back with a handheld, and my memory is that he just drove through 26 blocks of traffic . . . just kept his foot on the gas. One take. And this one take is cut into . . . the chase over and over, Bill going in the wrong lane and cutting off opposing traffic. It's only by the grace of God we didn't kill ourselves or somebody."—quoted in *Sight and Sound*, January 2000.

BIBLIOGRAPHY:

"William Friedkin: Films of Aberration, Obsession and Reality" Thomas D. Clagget, 1990, McFarland

Samuel Fuller

BORN: Samuel Michael Fuller in Worcester, Massachusetts, 08/12/1911

SOMETIMES CREDITED AS:
Sam Fuller

DEATH: in Hollywood Hills, California, 10/30/1997

NATIONALITY: American

AWARDS: Writers Guild of America Award Best-Written American Low-Budget Film "The Steel Helmet" 1951

Venice Film Festival Bronze Prize "Pickup on South Street" 1953; one of four films cited

Los Angeles Film Critics Association Career Achievement Award 1987; cited with Joel McCrea

Independent Spirit Lifetime Achievement Award 1995

BIOGRAPHY
Sam Fuller has always been Hollywood's bad boy. A director with a wide streak of independence, strangely contradictory politics and a pugnacious visual style, he has often been described as a cinematic primitive. Fuller worked as a newspaperman and a crime reporter for many years before turning in the late 1930s to screenwriting. (Even after he began directing, Fuller continued to write most of his own scripts.) During WWII he enlisted in the army, serving with the First Infantry Division throughout the European theater, earning numerous decorations. Fuller's experiences in the newsroom and on the front lines would mold his film work.

Fuller's first film as a director was "I Shot Jesse James" (1949), a low-budget reworking of the James legend concentrating on Bob Ford, the bandit's murderer, and characterized by a startling use of closeups. However, the fundamentally dull cast and lack of action hinder the overall effect. The film did well enough to establish Fuller and was followed by an intriguing oddity based on the true story of a man who tried to prove that he owned practically an entire state, in effect making himself, "The Baron of Arizona" (1950). His first war film, "The Steel Helmet" (1951), was rushed into production to capitalize on the outbreak of hostilities in Korea, and became his first box-office hit. It was succeeded by "Fixed Bayonets" (also 1951), another gritty Korean War film about a corporal forced to take command of a rear guard action as his superiors are killed off. "Park Row" (1952), a period newspaper story, was a successful blend of history, action, and romance.

"Pickup on South Street" (1953) remains Fuller's best film. Richard Widmark stars as a pickpocket who accidentally steals a roll of microfilm intended for communist agents. He soon finds himself caught between the FBI and the communists before finally shirking off his cynicism to help defeat the foreign agents. The film features numerous Fuller touches: a shrill anti-Communist line, a protagonist who is a borderline psychopath, "film noir" sensibilities, bursts of graphic violence, unapologetic sentimentality, and fluid, almost athletic, camerawork. It also benefits from a more polished look than many of his previous, independently produced films.

Fuller's concern with identity, whether racial or national, is the underlying focus of many of his films. His sympathetic treatment of Indians in "Run of the Arrow", the Eurasian heroine in "China Gate" (both 1957), and the Japanese-American cop in "The Crimson Kimono" (1959) seem at odds with his anti-Communist, gung-ho American attitudes. Yet such treatments are fully in keeping with Fuller's respect for the myth of the great American melting pot. Such thematic concerns, however, are always secondary to Fuller's primary impulse as a storyteller with pulp sensibilities. This trait is best displayed in such primal melodramas as "Forty Guns" (1957), a horse opera in the truest sense of the term, with Barbara Stanwyck as a black-clad woman with a whip, and in the crime expose "Underworld U.S.A." (1961).

Fuller's tabloid style was most evident in "Shock Corridor" (1963) and "The Naked Kiss" (1964). Revealing a darker take on American life, the former followed a self-serving reporter who has himself confined to an asylum to uncover a murder so he can win the Pulitzer Prize. The asylum is revealed as a microcosm of contemporary society, and the reporter is eventually sucked into its maelstrom, losing his mind. In "The Naked Kiss," a reformed prostitute moves to a small town to take a job working with hospitalized children. She becomes engaged to one of the community's leading citizens, only to discover that he is a child molester. In both movies Fuller plays the cinematic bully, confronting us with unpleasant characters and situations—and yet both films are oddly compelling. Critics most often split on Fuller over these films, one camp hailing him as an unpolished genius, the other dubbing him a sensationalist hack.

With the exception of "The Big Red One" (1980), an episodic paean to his WWII squadron, Fuller's output since the mid-1960s has been uneven, sporadic, and in some cases virtually unreleased. The bizarre detective saga, "Dead Pigeon on Beethoven Street" (1972), has its champions, but Fuller's most controversial film, "White Dog", was made in 1982 yet remained unreleased until 1991 due to undeserved charges of racism in its story of a dog trained to attack black people. Fuller had aimed, rather, to make a film critical of racism but, as was typical of much of his work, "White Dog" was misunderstood by many and consequently overrated by those few who got to see it. During these leaner years Fuller has made several films in France and has taken cameo roles in a number of films, notably as an American film director in Paris in Jean-Luc Godard's "Pierrot le fou" (1965), a gangster in Wim Wenders' "The American Friend" (1977), an aged cinematographer in Wenders' "The State of Things" (1982) and as Gabriel Byrne's father in "The End of Violence" (1997).

MILESTONES:

1922: Moved with mother to NYC after father's death (date approximate)

1923: Became a copyboy at *New York Journal*

1928: Began journalistic career as reporter for *The New York Evening Graphic*

Moved to California and worked as crime reporter for *The San Diego Sun*

1935: Published first novel, "Burn Baby Burn"

1936: Screenwriting debut with "Hats Off"

Served in North Africa and Europe during World War II; awarded Bronze Star, Purple Heart and Silver Star

Returned to Hollywood after military service

1949: Film directing debut with "I Shot Jesse James"; also scripted

1951: Producing debut (also directed) "The Steel Helmet"

1953: Directed "Pickup on South Street"

Directed occasional episodes of TV series like "The Dick Powell Show" and "The Virginian"

1965: Played himself in Jean-Luc Godard's "Pierrot le Fou"

1971: Cast as 'Movie Director' in Dennis Hopper's ill-fated "The Last Movie"

1977: First collaboration with Wim Wenders, "The American Friend"

1980: Wrote and directed "The Big Red One", based on his wartime experiences in Northern Africa

1982: Directed and co-wrote (with Curtis Hanson) the controversial "White Dog", about a stray dog that had been trained to attack blacks; film was not released in the USA until 1991 and even at that time, only in limited areas; NBC purchased rights to air the film, but never did; edited version has aired on US cable stations

1988: Directed final feature, "Street of No Return"

1997: Final acting role in Wenders' "The End of Violence" as Gabriel Byrne's father

QUOTES:

Fuller has received the Bronze Star, the Silver Star and a Purple Heart.

BIBLIOGRAPHY:

"Burn Baby Burn" Samuel Fuller, 1935, novel

"Test Tube Baby" Samuel Fuller, 1936, novel

"Make Up and Kiss" Samuel Fuller, 1936, novel

Antoine Fuqua

BORN: in Pittsburgh, Pennsylvania, 05/30/1965

NATIONALITY: American

EDUCATION: West Virginia University, West Virginia

AWARD: MTV Award Best Rap Video

BIOGRAPHY

Armed with good looks and a cool demeanor, Antoine Fuqua was a well-known award-winning commercial and music video director, well before his hype hit the film-arena. But after directing his film short titled, "Exit" and gaining valuable experiences from Propaganda Films, Fuqua's plans of becoming an engineer quickly changed to becoming a director. And if there were any lingering doubts, those were soon diminished after the Fuqua's feature debut, "The Replacement Killers" (1998) was released. Closely compared to director John Woo, Fuqua provided non-stop action and constant visual stimulation, which made it virtually impossible not to be entertained. "The Replacement Killers", which starred Chow Yun-Fat and Mira Sorvino, was simple in form but rich with visuals. Two years later, Fuqua returned with the action feature "Bait", which starred comedian Jamie Foxx as a trash-talking thief who is used as 'bait' to lure a cyber-villian.

In 2001, Fuqua confirmed his place as a young director of unique vision and craft when he released the LAPD corruption drama, "Training Day." Filmed entirely on location in Los Angeles, "Training Day" told the story of an idealistic young cop (Ethan Hawke) who gets a hard lesson about life in the streets from a veteran (Denzel Washington). The shining star power of Denzel Washington (who played the most morally ambiguous role of his thriving career) and Ethan Hawke, made the edgy drama crackle with energy. Fuqua's ability to capture the "raw-ness" of the Washington's character and the innocence of Hawke's was accomplished as the two were awarded a leading man Oscar and supporting role Oscar nomination (respectively). Fuqua returned, in 2003, with the Navy SEAL drama "Tears of the Sun," a heroic tale for which Fuqua dedicates to the men and women in the military.

MILESTONES:

1987: Relocated to New York to direct music videos

Directed his debut short "Exit"

1998: Directing feature debut in the action drama "The Replacement Killers."

2000: Directed the action dram-edy "Bait", which co-starred Jamie Foxx and David Morse.

2001: Directed the crime feature "Training Day"; it was in this feature that Denzel Washington received an Oscar for Best Actor In a Leading Role.

2003: Directed the action drama feature "Tears of the Sun", which starred Bruce Willis and Monica Belluci; during the filming, a sky-diver hired for stunt work disappeared in the Pacific Ocean and was presumed dead.

QUOTES:

"Tony and Ridley (Scott) definitely influenced me. 'Blade Runner' for Ridley. God, I've watched that so many times. Tony definitely influenced me, even more than I realized it, I just really like Tony's style of filmmaking. I think Tony has a visual sense, as well as a dramatic sense, you know? I remember people used to talk about John Woo and everything, but I would consider myself more like Tony than John Woo."—Fuqua.

Vincent Gallo

BORN: Vincent Gallo, Jr. in Buffalo, New York, 04/11/1961

SOMETIMES CREDITED AS:
Vincent Vito Gallo

NATIONALITY: American

EDUCATION: dropped out of high school at age 16

AWARD: Berlin Film Festival Best Music Award "The Way It Is or Eurydice in the Avenues" 1984

BIOGRAPHY

This gaunt, charismatic player with a mop of curly brown hair (often slicked back), expressive blue eyes and broken Roman nose has emerged as an unlikely leading man for the 1990s. His distinctive looks have also led to a modeling career for Calvin Klein's CK cologne and for Hush Puppies, among others. Gallo's nasal, slightly high-pitched voice also distinguishes him from the standard run-of-the-mill Hollywood types.

Born in Buffalo, NY, Gallo moved to NYC in the late 70s and immediately became embroiled in the "Downtown New Wave" scene. He simultaneously began making Super-8 films (including the 1977 short "If You Feel Froggy, Jump"), painting and sculpting (with showings at galleries in NYC) and pursuing a career as a musician. (Gallo played in several bands such as Jean-Michel Basquiat's Gray and his own Bohack). After developing the hobby of motorcycle racing, Gallo decided to pursue an acting career to gain health insurance. Eric Mitchell not only cast him in "The Way It Is, or Eurydice of the Avenues" (1983) but also tapped him to compose the film's score, which earned Gallo the 1984 Berlin Film Festival Award for Best Music.

But it was not until the 90s that Gallo's acting career truly flourished. He first garnered attention as Johnny Depp's friend, an aspiring actor who sells cars, in Emir Kusturica's "Arizona Dream" (1992) before appearing as the policeman who interrogates Winona Ryder in "The House of the Spirits" (1993). The actor has appeared in three Claire Denis films, including a turn as a US soldier in the made-for-French TV "U.S. Go Home" (1994) and an appearance in the award-winning "Nenette et Boni" (1996). Further displaying his range and versatility, Gallo played a Protestant minister in Rebecca Miller's "Angela" (1995), one of a trio of inept would-be criminals in the fine comedy "Palookaville" (1995) and the volatile younger brother in a crime family whose death is the centerpiece for Abel Ferrara's "The Funeral" (1996). Continuing his busy streak, he was cast as yet another criminal in Kiefer Sutherland's directorial debut "Truth or Consequences, N.M." (1997), had a pivotal role alongside Dermot Mulroney, Mary-Louise Parker and Ellen DeGeneres in Roland Joffe's comedic thriller "Goodbye Lover" (also 1997) and stepped behind the cameras to make his feature writing and directing debut with the semi-autobiographical "Buffalo 66" (1998).

Somewhat of a Renaissance man, Gallo has simultaneously pursued careers in art, music and film. A self-proclaimed hustler and hobbyist, he

chose to act more for its tangible rewards than to fulfill any creative urges, which may explain the uniqueness of his screen presence. A Gallo performance is filled with a mercurial, carnal power. Although he has often appeared in off-beat and little seen roles, there is no denying his abilities. He all but stole "Arizona Dream" from his better-known co-stars (Depp, Faye Dunaway, Lili Taylor and Jerry Lewis). In both "The House of Spirits" and "The Perez Family", Gallo provided a seemingly authentic Latin whereas co-stars like Meryl Streep and Jeremy Irons in the former and Anjelica Huston in the latter appeared miscast. To date, his idiosyncratic screen presence (captured in print by Richard Avedon in the Calvin Klein advertisements) was best displayed with his performances as Russ, the bumbling mastermind, in "Palookaville" and as Johnny, the charming, leftist mobster, in "The Funeral."

COMPANION:

P. J. Harvey. Singer; reportedly dating in 2001 although each claims only to be "good friends"

MILESTONES:

Born and raised in Buffalo, New York

Dropped out of high school at age 16 and moved to NYC to pursue career as a musician

1977: Directed, scored and appeared in the short film "If You Feel Froggy, Jump", filmed during a snowstorm

1978: Worked as an international messenger; reportedly suffered a breakdown during one trip

Played with the bands The Plastics and Gray, the latter included Jean-Michel Basquiat

Learned to speak Italian and began to tell people he was originally from Sicily and that his family lived in the Little Italy section of NYC

1979: Acted on stage in Rome in the Italian-language production "Buffala"

Ran a movie theater headquartered at the Squat Theatre in NYC

Began racing motorcycles

1981: With band Bohack, released album "It Took Several Wives"

1983: Feature acting debut, "The Way It Is or Eurydice of the Avenues"; also composed score

1983: Had first solo art show

Early TV credit, episode of "Miami Vice"

Had role in Claire Denis' short film "Keep It for Yourself"

1990: Acted in "GoodFellas"

1992: Co-starred with Jerry Lewis and Johnny Depp in Emil Kustirica's "Arizona Dream"

1994: Reteamed with Claire Denis on "U.S. Go Home"

1995: Had featured role in Alan Taylor's "Palookaville"

1996: Co-starred with Christopher Walken and Chris Penn in Abel Ferrara's "The Funeral"

1996: Modeled for Calvin Klein; was featured in controversial advertising campaign for fragrance CK1 criticized for glorifying "heroin chic"

1996: Appeared in Claire Denis' "Nenette et Boni"

1996: Formed the band Bunny with actor-musician Lukas Haas; disbanded in 1998; had recorded tracks for an album but project was abandoned; several of the songs were later used on the soundtrack for "Buffalo 66"

1997: Featured in print advertising for Hush Puppies shoes

1998: Feature screenwriting and directorial debut "Buffalo 66"; also acted

1998: Acted in "Goodbye Lover"

1999: Published book of photographs

2001: Released first solo album, "When"

AFFILIATION: Republican

QUOTES:

"I came to New York to be a legend, and within five minutes of realizing I was an interesting kid and other people thought so, I had given myself a nervous breakdown. I was 26 years old before I knew what it was like to have an ordinary day."—Vincent Gallo to Amy Taubin, quoted in "A Hunger Artist", *Village Voice*, October 29, 1996.

"Mr. Gallo seems a study in contradictions: he's a thin-skinned diva who zigzags between childlike honesty about himself and pitiless skewering of others; he's a natural mimic and peculiar polymath (metal working, music, film, politics) and it's sometimes difficult to tell where the real Vincent begins and the performance artist ends."—Phoebe Hoban in "Downtown Actor, Uptown Ambitions" published in *The New York Times*, November 24, 1996.

"I don't want to be an actor; I want to be a movie star. I don't want to be a hip, downtown artist, I want to have a building on Sutton Place. I want my career to be like the game show 'Name That Tune'. I want to get to the top in as few notes as possible. . . . My whole life, my whole career is based on revenge at this point."—Gallo to *The New York Time*, November 24, 1996.

"I haven't bought men's clothes in years . . . They just don't fit."—Gallo in *The New York Times*, November 24, 1996.

"Vince loves to hype himself and he loves to generate his own mystique and he is probably the most exciting person I've ever been involved with."—Alan Taylor, director of "Palookaville"

"All my life I've been kind of a hustler, with no one major commercial success. My next goal is to eliminate that. When I do, I will take over the world. I will be unstoppable."—Gallo somewhat tongue-in-cheek to *Us*, March 1997.

"Artist-model-actor Vincent Gallo just can't stop the controversy. Remember his sexy gauntness in those racy CK perfume ads? Now it comes to light that Gallo . . . has a rather interesting sideline. He casts his penis in plaster and hides the resulting objets d'art in weird, obscure places around the country. Tourists who would like to visit the self-proclaimed Vincent Gallo National Monument can ask Gallo for maps, which are fast becoming collectors' items."—From *Buzz*, March 1997.

On why he opted to take a break from

working as filmmaker, Gallo told *The Observer*, September 29, 2001: "I didn't want to lose my subjectivity and my objectivity about my work. I'm not looking for a career. And I don't need to be regarded. I'm not Harmony Korine ["Gummo"] or Paul Anderson ["Boogie Nights"] or Darren Aronofsky ["Pi, Requiem For a Dream"], who are already working on their chapter in the history of film books. I have the capacity to do lots of different things. I don't feel that I need to repeat myself like that."

DISCOGRAPHY: "It Took Several Wives" Bohack Family Friend Records, 1981; Gallo was a member of the band
"The Way It Is" 1984 original film soundtrack; Gallo composed the score
"When" Vincent Gallo Warp Records, 2001

BIBLIOGRAPHY:
"Gallo 1962–1999" Vincent Gallo; book of photography

Mel Gibson

BORN: Mel Columcille Gerard Gibson in Peekskill, New York, 01/03/1956

NATIONALITY: American

EDUCATION: attended an all-boys Catholic school where he was taunted for his American accent
National Institute of Dramatic Art, Sydney, Australia, 1977; one of his sisters sent in an application on his behalf without his knowledge

AWARDS: Australian Film Institute Award Best Actor "Tim" 1979
Australian Film Institute Award Best Actor "Gallipoli" 1981
People's Choice Award Favorite Motion Picture Actor 1991
NATO/ShoWest Male Star of the Year Award 1992; honored by National Association of Theater Owners
MTV Movie Award Best On-Screen Duo "Lethal Weapon 3" 1993; award shared with Danny Glover
National Board of Review Special Achievement in Filmmaking Award "Braveheart" 1995
Broadcast Film Critics Association Award Best Director "Braveheart" 1995; first annual presentation of award

Golden Globe Award Best Director "Braveheart" 1995
NATO/ShoWest Director of the Year Award 1995; award presented by National Association of Theater Owners
Oscar Best Picture "Braveheart" 1995; award shared with co-producers Alan Ladd Jr. and Bruce Davey
Oscar Best Director "Braveheart" 1995
BAFTA Lloyds Bank Award for Favorite Film "Braveheart" 1995
MTV Movie Award Best Action Sequence "Braveheart" 1996
People's Choice Award Favorite Actor in a Film 1997
People's Choice Award Favorite Motion Picture Star in a Drama 2001
People's Choice Award Favorite Motion Picture Actor 2001
People's Choice Awards Favorite Motion Picture Actor 2003

BIOGRAPHY
Though introduced to American audiences as Australian, the strikingly handsome, blue-eyed Mel Gibson actually hailed from Peekskill, New York. (He and his family had emigrated Down Under in 1968 at the height of the Vietnam War.) After a season onstage with

Sydney's South Australian Theatre Company where he portrayed both Oedipus and Henry IV, he made his name as the leather-clad, post-apocalyptic action hero of George Miller's "Mad Max" and in the radically different "Tim" (both 1979), for which he picked up his first of two Australian Film Institute Awards as Best Actor, playing a retarded handyman in love with Piper Laurie. Peter Weir's World War I drama "Gallipoli" and "Mad Max 2" (both 1981), Miller's transcendent follow-up to "Mad Max" (released in the USA as "The Road Warrior" since American audiences knew nothing of the barely-released earlier movie), established Gibson as an international star. "The Year of Living Dangerously" (1982), Weir's film about the political upheavals of 1960s Indonesia, gave him his first romantic lead opposite Sigourney Weaver and launched him as a sex symbol.

After a turn as a reluctantly mutinous Fletcher Christian opposite Anthony Hopkins' Captain Bligh in "The Bounty", Gibson made an inauspicious American debut in "The River" (both 1984), playing a character so coldly stubborn that few could empathize. The well-made but gloomy "Mrs. Soffel" (also 1984) followed quickly before he returned to Australia to wrap up the "Mad Max" series with "Mad Max Beyond Thunderdome" (1985), a cumbersome satire with less action, a bigger budget, Tina Turner and Max, mostly on foot, looking like a wandering prophet. Gibson then took two years off to concentrate on his family, returning to the screen in "Lethal Weapon" (1987), for which he created perhaps his most popular character, Martin Riggs, an explosive homicide cop paired with the long-suffering Danny Glover. The film propelled Gibson to superstardom, spawned three sequels (to date) and allowed him to incorporate his innate playfulness as part of an unusually rich characterization for a modern action hero. Called at various times "practical joker", "eternal adolescent" and "fun-loving fourth Stooge", Gibson

has remained a "regular guy" who doesn't take himself or his work too seriously and consistently comes across as relaxed and natural.

Gibson sandwiched the meandering "Tequila Sunrise" (1988) and even more disappointing "Bird on a Wire" (1990) around a blockbuster "Lethal Weapon 2" (1989), and his patented swagger could not save the alleged action-comedy "Air America" (1990) from the inadequacy of its script. Next, in a surprising career move, he opted to take his shot at Shakespeare's Melancholy Dane in Franco Zeffirelli's "Hamlet" (1990). While the film was problematic, Gibson turned in a finely rendered portrait of the famed prince in the first project produced by his Icon Productions. He continued in a more sentimental vein with the sudsy "Forever Young" (1992), scored another huge hit with "Lethal Weapon 3" (1993), then made his directorial debut with "The Man Without a Face" (1993), a drama in which he hid his good looks behind the heavy makeup of a burn victim. After this mildly popular effort, Gibson returned to rowdy commercial fare with "Maverick" (1994), teaming for a fourth time with "Lethal Weapon" director Richard Donner for a 90s adaptation of the 60s TV Western-comedy series, which shrewdly parlayed his dashing rogue qualities into more box-office bliss.

Gibson returned to the director's chair for "Braveheart" (1995), a project far bigger than any with which he had been previously involved in any capacity. Clad in a kilt, sporting blue war paint and wielding a big sword, Gibson starred as Sir William Wallace, a 13th-century Scottish nobleman persecuted for his efforts to free Scotland from English rule. Wags dubbed the film "Mad Mac", but the Academy deemed it worthy, voting it five awards including Best Picture and honoring Gibson as Best Director. Later that same year, in addition to providing the speaking voice for John Smith in Disney's "Pocahontas", Gibson made his screen singing debut. His collaboration with Ron Howard, "Ransom" (1996), another box-office hit that earned $35 million its first week, preceded "Conspiracy Theory" (1997), his fifth film with Donner and a surprising commercial dud compared to their previous work, especially with Julia Roberts starring opposite Gibson. The actor-director pair rebounded with "Lethal Weapon 4" (1998), its healthy box office reaffirming Riggs-Murtaugh (in reportedly their last outing) as a bankable team.

Gibson next starred as a murderous thief bent on getting his "Payback" (1999), a loose reworking of the same Donald Westlake novel that had inspired John Boorman's 1967 classic thriller "Point Blank." Playing to Gibson's strengths, the urban Western veered problematically from dark and sinister to comic and whimsical but still managed a respectable box office. His star power could not make Wim Wenders' "The Million Dollar Hotel" (2000) a mainstream success, and though the director's visual skills were on display, the underdeveloped, not very interesting story made it a tough sell at the art-houses. Gibson then joined "popcorn" specialists Dean Devlin and Roland Emmerich for Emmerich's Revolutionary War drama "The Patriot" (also 2000), scripted by Robert Rodat. Essentially a Western, "The Patriot" cast him as a retired "gunslinger", still spooked by his memories of the French and Indian War, who clings fast to his pacifism until his son falls into enemy hands, triggering his course of revenge. After voicing Rocky the Rooster in the animated "Chicken Run", a sort of feathered "Great Escape", he rounded out the busy year as star of Nancy Meyers' romantic comedy "What Women Want" (both 2000).

Aside from making Gibson vehicles, his Icon Productions has produced projects like the Beethoven biopic "Immortal Beloved" (1994, directed by Bernard Rose), the remake of "Leo Tolstoy's Anna Karenina" (1997, also helmed by Rose), the black comedy "Ordinary Decent Criminals" (a fictionalized version of the life of Irish thief Martin Cahill) and the ABC biopic "The Three Stooges" (both 2000).

In 2002, Gibson appeared in the war film "We Were Soldiers," directed by "Pearl Harbor"(2001) scribe Randall Wallace and in "Signs," the much anticipated M. Night Shyamalan movie about crop circles.

FAMILY:

father: Hutton Gibson. Railroad brakeman; born c. 1918; leading figure in a conservative Catholic splinter group, The Alliance for Catholic Traditions; won $21,000 on the Art Fleming-hosted "Jeopardy" in 1968 while waiting out a workman's compensation suit after falling from a train and injuring his back; moved family to Australia soon after, partly because he didn't want his sons drafted into Vietnam War

MILESTONES:

1968: Moved with family to Australia

1976: Stage debut as Romeo (opposite Judy Davis' Juliet) in National Institute of Dramatic Art production of "Romeo and Juliet"

1976: Film debut, "Summer City", playing shy, quiet surfer

1978: Joined South Australian Theater Company; appeared in "Oedipus," "Henry IV" and "Cedoona"

Made TV debut as regular on Australian series, "The Sullivans"

1979: Feature debut as a lead, "Mad Max"; voice dubbed for US release

1979: Played a retarded man opposite Piper Laurie in "Tim"

1979: Appeared onstage alongside Geoffrey Rush in "Waiting for Godot"; during the Australian production, the two shared an apartment for four months

1981: Starred in Peter Weir's engrossing "Gallipoli"; sight of his bare behind more or less made him a sex symbol

1981: Reunited with Miller for "Mad Max 2", released in the USA as "The Road Warrior"

1982: Reteamed with Weir for "The Year of Living Dangerously", playing an Australain journalist in Indonesia

1984: Portrayed Fletcher Christian to Anthony Hopkins' Captain Bligh in the stodgy "The Bounty"

1984: American film debut, "The River", opposite Sissy Spacek

1985: Completed "Mad Max" trilogy with "Mad Max: Beyond Thunderdome"

1987: Starred opposite Danny Glover in "Lethal Weapon"; first film directed by Richard Donner

1989: Reteamed with Donner and Glover for "Lethal Weapon 2"

Formed ICON productions, (formerly known as Gibson Productions)

1990: First film produced by Icon productions, "Hamlet"

1991: Directed and appeared in "Mel Gibson Goes Back to School", an HBO special featuring a discussion on "Hamlet" at an American high school

1992: Reunited with Donner and Glover for "Lethal Weapon 3"

1993: Feature directorial debut, "The Man Without a Face"; also starred

1994: Hosted and sometimes performed in "Rabbit Ears Radio", a children's radio program on Public Radio International

1994: Teamed with Donner on "Maverick", based on the 1960s TV Western

1995: Made screen singing debut as the voice of John Smith in Disney's animated "Pocahontas"

1995: Won Academy Award for directing the epic "Braveheart"; also picked up Best Picture Oscar for producing with Bruce Davey and Alan Ladd Jr.; played leading role of Scotsman William Wallace

1996: Rushed to hospital for emergency appendectomy on March 10 during filming of Ron Howard's "Ransom", which opened later that year to strong box office; did his action scenes for the movie just days after the surgery

1997: Starred opposite Julia Roberts in Donner's "Conspiracy Theory", scripted by Brian Helgeland; despite the star power, it struggled to recoup its investment before ending solidly in the black

1997: Made two uncredited cameos, as the Tattooed Man in Ivan Reitman's abysmal "Father's Day" and as Frances' father in "Fairy Tale-A True Story"

1998: Sixth film to date with Donner, "Lethal Weapon 4"; reportedly pocketed $35 million salary

1999: Played title role in Helgeland's directorial debut, "Payback"; upon viewing Helgeland's cut, he and studio asked the director to reshoot much of the last third of the movie; when Helgeland declined, someone else did the honors, though Gibson told *Empire* (April 1999), "Brian was not fired, his name is still on the film and indeed he is responsible for 80 percent of it . . . "; rumors emerged that Gibson and his mystery director's (former hair dresser Paul Abascol) cut tested worse than Helgeland's

2000: Starred in Wim Wenders' "The Million Dollar Hotel"; premiered at the Berlin Film Festival; released theatrically in the USA in 2001

2000: Executive produced the ABC biopic "The Three Stooges"

2000: Headlined the Revolutionary War saga "The Patriot", essaying a pacifist farmer who must choose sides after his son is captured

2000: Provided the voice for Rocky the rooster in the animated feature "Chicken Run"

2000: Starred as chauvinistic executive who acquires the ability to hear what every female he meets is really thinking in Nancy Meyers' "What Women Want"

2001: Co-created and co-executive produced (with martial arts star Jet Li from "Lethal Weapon 4") movie pilot for proposed TBS action series "Invincible", starring Billy Zane

2002: Had leading role in the Vietnam War–era drama "We Were Soldiers"; was also an executive producer

2002: Moved ICON from Paramount to 20th Century Fox

2002: Starred in the supernatural drama "Signs"

2002: Appeared with Robert Downey Jr. in the musical comedy "The Singing Detective" (lensed 2002)

2002: Served as executive producer of the HBO miniseries "Alexander the Great," based on Mary Renault's historical novels, project slated to air sometime in 2004

2003: Directed the controversial religion feature "The Passion"

AFFILIATION: Roman Catholic

QUOTES:

In 1992, Gibson received the William Shakespeare Award for Classical Theatre (the Will Award) from The Shakespeare Theatre at the Folger in Washington, DC, in recognition of his work on behalf of classical theater.

He reportedly stormed out of the 1996 MTV Movie Awards after the presenters, Ben Stiller and Janeane Garofalo, spoofed "Braveheart" in the opening sequence.

Awarded the Order of Australia medal and honored as the Hasty Pudding Theatricals Man of the Year (Harvard University) in 1997.

On playing "Hamlet": "I didn't have control there. It wasn't just difficult because it was a difficult part—it was difficult because of the work situation. I don't want to name names or anything. I should have done it onstage first. Anyway, long story. Boring, boring . . . making excuses. I'm supposed to know what to do. That's my craft."—Mel Gibson in *Us*, June 1995.

"Americans' first perceptions of Mel Gibson were immediately varied because on the one hand he was a leading man in films like 'The Year of Living Dangerously' and on the other hand was an action hero in a film like 'Road Warrior'. There wasn't one image that had to be torn down and reconstructed to make room for the other. But right away it was clear this was not just another action star. There was something more to him."—Leonard Maltin in *The Hollywood Reporter Mel Gibson Tribute Issue,* March 5, 1996.

In 1999, Gibson donated $640,000 to his alma mater, the National Institute of Dramatic Art in Sydney, Australia on the occasion of its 40th anniversary.

On moving from the USA to Australia as a boy: "It made me observant. Right away I saw there was a difference between them and me. In order to cope and not have a punchup every other day, I tried to be like them. It was good training for an actor."—Gibson to *Daily News,* January 3, 1999.

About pulling rank on director Brian Helgeland on "Payback": "Some changes were required. We asked him if he'd do them. Lots of times. He said no, he wouldn't . . . that he didn't want to compromise his artistic integrity. I, on the other hand, have no problem with artistic integrity.

"As a producer, you have to make decisions based on many different factors, and not everybody's going to be happy. But someone's going to have the casting vote and the final cut . . . It's taken me 20 years to get final cut."—Gibson quoted in *Boston Herald,* February 6, 1999.

"I think violence in the movies gets a bad rap. Over the years I think it's been a handy scapegoat for the inadequacy of the social regime to fix their problems. 'They saw this film and it made them want to go out and shoot people.' Bullshit."—Gibson to *Empire,* April 1999.

"I want to direct, that's the most fun you can have standing up, but if you're going to spend two years of your life with something, you want to make sure it's not horrible.

"It's terrifying, they give you a budget and everyone acts like you know what you're doing. But it's exhilarating at the same time, it's the fear of the unknown and you're actually stepping up to the plate. It's somewhere between frightened and inspired and sometimes those two can feed on each other. They do, in fact. Someone rips ten pages out of your script and you've got to make a change fast and you've got to make the script work, you come up with the answer and you do it fast and you make it work. You need to be up against the wall before you can make those decisions."—Gibson in *Empire*, April 1999.

Terry Gilliam

BORN: in Minneapolis, Minnesota, 11/22/1940

SOMETIMES CREDITED AS:
Jerry Gillian

NATIONALITY: American

CITIZENSHIP: United Kingdom

EDUCATION: Occidental College, Los Angeles, California, political science, 1958–62; edited humor magazine

AWARDS: Cannes Film Festival Special Jury Prize "Monty Python's Meaning of Life" 1983

Los Angeles Film Critics Association Award Best Director "Brazil" 1985

Los Angeles Film Critics Association Award Best Screenplay "Brazil" 1985; shared award with co-writers Tom Stoppard and Charles McKeown

BIOGRAPHY

A successful cartoonist who first met John Cleese while working at *Help!* magazine, Terry Gilliam subsequently became the resident animator with Monty Python's Flying Circus. He also performed with the troupe and wrote several sketches, moving to the big screen with "And Now For Something Completely Different" (1971). After co-directing "Monty Python and the Holy Grail" (1975), he made his solo directing debut with "Jabberwocky" (1976), a grisly medieval interpretation of the Lewis Carroll poem which set the tone for much of his subsequent work. A Terry Gilliam–directed film will

have several hallmarks: fantastic visuals, both in production design and camerawork; a soupcon of the surreal; and strong acting.

Born and raised in Minnesota, Gilliam relocated with his family to L.A. when he was 11. After college, he worked in NYC at HELP!, toiled briefly in advertising in L.A. and finally found his home as an illustrator and animator in London. Gilliam began to contribute animated sequences to such British TV shows as "Marty" and "Do Not Adjust Your Set." Hooking up with Eric Idle and becoming reacquainted with Cleese, they eventually joined together as the performing troupe Monty Python's Flying Circus. After branching out into filmmaking, Gilliam and Pythoner Michael Palin collaborated on the script for "Time Bandits" (1981), a delightfully "adult" children's film that features a group of dwarfs who come to the aid of an English schoolboy, traveling through various epochs and encountering such historical personages as Napoleon and King Agamemnon.

As he moved away from Pythonesque material with "Brazil" (1985), Gilliam encountered critical praise but problems with the Hollywood studio system. He publicly clashed with Universal over the release of the film. The studio balked at the length of this darkly comic look at a futuristic society resulting in two versions, a European cut that ran 142 minutes and an American one that clocked in at 131 minutes. After months of squabbling, the matter was forced when the Los Angeles Film Critics voted their Best Picture, Best Director and Best Screenplay prizes to the unreleased film. At the time of its initial release (and in part because it had become a cause celebre), "Brazil" was a money-maker in its limited venues. Once it opened wider, with little support from the studio, it proved less successful. The studio cut, which runs nearly an hour less, has been aired on American TV, but it lacks Gilliam's trademark fantasy sequences. His vision of an Orwellian future was eventually restored and a director's cut was released in 1998.

Following such a dark tale, "The Adventures of Baron Munchausen" (1988) was a visually stunning spectacle that combined state-of-the-art special effects with a resplendent production design, impeccable cinematography and fantastical costumes. Despite its beauty, there were structural problems with the story—as with much of his work, pacing, particularly in the second half, was uneven, causing the film to flag in spots. Still, John Neville in the title role offered a fine performance. After a three year absence, Gilliam returned to features with another imaginative fable. Working from a strong script (by Richard La Gravenese), he fashioned "The Fisher King" (1991), which featured Jeff Bridges as a callous talk show host who encounters a homeless man (Robin Williams) who used to be a college professor. With several wonderful set pieces, particularly a fantasy set in Grand Central Terminal, the film tied the director's visual flair to a more heart-warming and accessible journey.

"12 Monkeys" (1995) was a return to futuristic fare. In adapting Chris Marker's "La Jetee" as a sci-fi thriller, Gilliam created another eye-catching view of a world to come that was well-acted by Bruce Willis and Brad Pitt. In 1998, he tackled a long-aborning project that had seen many try—and fail—to translate to film: Hunter S Thompson's "Fear and Loathing in Las Vegas." While critics and audiences were divided over just how successful he was, it was clear that Gilliam had come the closest to at least capturing some essence of the spirit of the work. If nothing else, he had once again managed to do what on paper seemed impossible.

MILESTONES:

1951: Moved to L.A.

1962: Moved to NYC after college graduation

1962–1965: Worked as associate editor on *Help!* magazine; also did freelance illustrating

1966: Returned to L.A. to work in advertising

1967: Moved to London

1968: Became resident cartoonist on "We Have Ways of Making You Laugh", a TV series; also created first animated cartoons the show ever aired

1968: Made three short animated films for "Do Not Adjust Your Set"

1969: Joined the comedy troupe "Monty Python's Flying Circus", served as animator, writer and performer

1971: Feature acting debut, also served as animator and co-wrote the screenplay with fellow Monty Python troupe members, "And Now For Something Completely Different"

1972: First commercial animation, an advertising campaign for British Gas

1974: US broadcast debut of "Monty Python's Flying Circus"

1975: Feature debut as a co-director, "Monty Python and the Holy Grail"

1976: Solo directorial debut, "Jabberwocky"; also co-wrote with Charles Alverson

1979: First film as production designer, "Monty Python's Life of Brian"; also co-wrote screenplay, served as animator, and appeared on-screen in a variety of roles

1981: Debut as producer, "Time Bandits"; also directed and shared screenplay credit with Michael Palin

1985: Breakthrough film, "Brazil"; wrote and directed this visually stunning look at a futuristic society

1989: Experienced a box-office disappointment with "The Adventures of Baron Munchausen"

1991: First Hollywood production as director, "The Fisher King"

1995: Directed the futuristic "12 Monkeys", loosely based on Chris Marker's "La Jetee"

1998: Succeeded in bringing to the screen what

was considered an unfilmable book, "Fear and Loathing in Las Vegas"; critics and audiences divided over results

2001: Was subject of documentary "Tilting at Windmills"; screened at Toronto Film Festival

2003: Was the subject (along with his film) of Don Quijote documentary "Lost In Mancha"

QUOTES:

"Acknowledged visionary, former Monty Python member, animator deluxe and cracked mirror of the modern condition, Gilliam also is, depending on who's talking, either the enfant terrible or the guiless manchild of the movies. His films are visually intoxicating, wildly ambitious, personal and at times perplexing. . . .

"—From "Reality Check" by John Anderson, *Newsday,* April 23, 1995.

"I actually go out of my way to make films that are hard to define."—Gilliam quoted in *Entertainment Weekly,* August 25/September 1, 1995.

"I like coming back here [the USA] in short stints. L.A.'s too wrapped up in being Hollywood; all anyone talks about is films and everybody thinks the same thoughts. I don't think I could maintain a unique view without being susceptible to what everybody else thinks." —Gilliam quoted in *Time Out* January 3–10, 1996.

BIBLIOGRAPHY:

"Animations of Mortality" Terry Gilliam, 1978
"Gilliam on Gilliam" Terry Gilliam, 1999

Jean-Luc Godard

BORN: in Paris, France, 12/03/1930

SOMETIMES CREDITED AS:
Hans Lucas

NATIONALITY: French

CITIZENSHIP: Switzerland

EDUCATION: attended school in Nyon, Switzerland
    Lycee Buffon, Paris, France
    Sorbonne, University of Paris, Paris, France, ethnology, 1949

AWARDS: Berlin Film Festival Best Director Award "A Bout de Souffle/Breathless" 1960
    Venice Film Festival Special Jury Prize "Vivre Sa Vie" 1962
    Venice Film Festival Special Jury Prize "La Chinoise" 1967 cited along with Marco Bellocchio's "China is Near"
    Venice Film Festival Golden Lion "Prenom: Carmen" 1983

Honorary Cesar 1987
Special New York Film Critics Circle Award for Lifetime Achievement 1994
Honorary Cesar 1998

BIOGRAPHY

Few filmmakers have had so profound an effect on the development of the art as Jean-Luc Godard, almost certainly the most important filmmaker worldwide to emerge since the end of WWII. From his early days as a critic and thinker in the pages of *Cahiers du Cinema* and elsewhere, through the great age of the New Wave in the 1960s, continuing (with a lesser impact) in the 70s and 80s, Godard has redefined the way we look at film. An essayist and poet of the cinema, he makes the language of film a real part of his narratives.

With a prodigious sense of exploration, Godard has worked his way through no less than four artistic periods since his days as a critic in the 50s: The "New Wave" Godard (still the most influential) lasted from "Breathless" (1959) to "Weekend" (1967). The "Revolutionary"

Godard stretched from "Le Gai savoir" (1968) to "Tout va bien" (1972), encompassing the "Dziga-Vertov" period. Godard the "Videoaste" lasted from the formation of the Sonimage production company with Anne-Marie Mieville in Grenoble through 1978. Finally, the "Contemplative" Godard began with "Sauve qui peut (la vie)", his return to features in 1980, and has extended through "Helas Pour Moi/Woe Is Me" (1993).

Godard's critical examination of international film masters, American auteurs and American genre films in the 50s was paralleled by his own early incursions into the medium. He acted in and produced early short films by fellow critics Eric Rohmer and Jacques Rivette and himself directed a series of shorts: from the documentary "Operation Beton" (1954), through the whimsical "All Boys Are Called Patrick" (1957), to the editing exercise, "Une histoire d'eau" (1958), shot by Truffaut but handed over to Godard after the former had given up on the material. These reciprocal forces, the back-and-forth from production to criticism, led to a series of homages, reinventions and variations which helped us all to understand what film had been—and what it was to become.

In "Breathless", his landmark feature debut, Godard broke with established narrative conventions, spontaneously mixing elements from the detective, comedy and suspense genres. "A Woman Is a Woman" (1961) applied this critical intelligence to the musical genre, as "Alphaville" (1965) did to science fiction. In a fresh, new way, a director was making films that were "about" other films (as well as about themselves), often with very modest resources. "Alphaville", for instance, created a uniquely menacing, futuristic look out of largely contemporary settings. At the same time, Godard was developing the essay form as he began to speak more directly to his audiences. The philosophical discussion Jean Seberg and Jean-Paul Belmondo hold in their bedroom in

"Breathless" was a precursor to more extended ruminations in such films as "Vivre Sa Vie/My Life to Live" (1962), "The Married Woman" (1964) and "Masculin-Feminin" (1966).

With the exception of "A Woman Is a Woman" (his lovesong to then-wife Anna Karina), the subject matter of these films is downbeat and darkly modernist. Godard's couples are alienated both from each other and from their environment; driven by uncertainty and mistrust, surrounded by the crass commercialism of late-20th-century capitalism, they act arbitrarily, often with tragic results. Fleeing the disorder of the city for refuge in nature, as in "Pierrot le fou" (1965), characters still cannot escape death. Language, inherently ambiguous (as discussed by philosopher Brice Parain in "Vivre Sa Vie"), serves as a barrier to communication and precludes love. Even body language fails: in "Contempt" (1963), Godard's cynical satire of mainstream filmmaking, a husband's insecurity makes him suspect his wife's every facial gesture. Prostitution becomes the incessant metaphor.

Godard himself, however, was capable of broader understanding—if his characters couldn't communicate, he himself was getting better at it with every film. He best expressed this positive aspect in "Anticipation," his episode of the portmanteau film "Le Plus vieux metier du monde" (1967). In this parable, a soldier of the "Sovietoamerican" army of the future (Jean-Pierre Leaud) is sent to receive treatment from a "spiritual" prostitute (Anna Karina). Together, they reinvent the kiss (using the one part of the body that can both speak and make love). The authorities declare them dangerous, because "they are making love, progress, and conversation—all at the same time!"

In "Two or Three Things I Know About Her" (1967), considered by some as the greatest of his masterpieces, memorable for such stunning set-pieces as the coffee-cup cosmos and the model city built of consumer goods, Godard himself, the filmmaker/narrator, is a major character, commenting on the dysfunctional bourgeois universe he depicts via a housewife who works part-time on the sly as a prostitute. By "Weekend" (1967), the alienation has become absurd: the married couple openly cheat on each other in a disintegrating world, rendered explicit by endless traffic jams and car crashes. Human dignity and respect are absent from this savage vision of middle-class barbarians and murderous, aimless revolutionaries who become cannibals.

At this point, deciding that there was something fundamentally wrong with the way we lead our modern lives, Godard was ready—like so many of his contemporaries—to turn to political action as a solution. Politics had in fact often been part of the background of the earlier films. "Le petit soldat" (1960), his second film, was actually banned by the government for several years because it dealt with the Algerian situation. "Les Carabiniers" (1963) discussed the politics of war in absurdist terms, with a screenplay co-scripted by one of Godard's key influences, Roberto Rossellini. "Masculin-Feminine" was concerned about the role of youth in contemporary France. "Made in USA" (1966), meanwhile, was a dense and deliberately fragmented attempt at a political suspense film (with references to the Ben Barka affair). "La Chinoise" (1967), meanwhile, one of his more exquisite and fondly remembered films, was a collage portrait, in colorful, pop-art strokes, of the French new left student movement one year before the "events" of May '68. Now it was time to act.

Rejoining his colleagues from *Cahiers du Cinema*, Godard participated in the 1968 demonstrations over the dismissal of Henri Langlois as head of the "Cinematheque Francaise" which for them tied in with the famous nationwide worker strikes and student unrest which came to a head in May. Then, from 1968 through 1972, Godard made 11 films, over half in collaboration with Jean-Pierre Gorin (whose involvement varied from project to project), and most released as signed by the "Dziga-Vertov Group." By invoking the name of one of early Soviet cinema's most inventive filmmakers, Godard and Gorin were, they said, "making political films politically." Although they claimed, "we have no answers, only questions," these films appear to address and support militant issues. Yet, in the end, it's clear Godard and Gorin have more concern with the process of filmmaking than with the process of revolution. Throughout their collaboration, they are obsessed with the job of turning theory into practice. "British Sounds" (1969) is perhaps the most successful of Godard's "revolutionary" experiments, a collection of images and sounds meant to incite discussion about workers, about women (and the female body itself), about students, about revolution. Godard and Gorin went on tour with their films, trying to directly engage their audiences in the dialogue.

The Dziga-Vertov period culminated with two films: "Tout va bien" and "A Letter to Jane" (1972). "Tout va bien", with Yves Montand and Jane Fonda, was one of his more accessible films from this period and meant to summarize something of what the group had learned from their experiments in a commercial movie, complete with international stars. As if in reaction, "Letter to Jane" is an essay about an image of Jane Fonda in Vietnam which had appeared in the magazine "L'Express." A 45-minute monologue by Godard/Gorin, "Letter to Jane" explains much about their theories of images and sounds and how they might relate to politics. Following the line of thinkers whose most influential spokesperson had been Bertolt Brecht, the Dziga-Vertov Group politicized the kind of cinema Godard himself had been creating all along, one which established critical distance and reflection on a film's subject matter through constant disruption of any "invisible" realistic style.

The Dziga-Vertov Group disbanded in 1973. (Gorin moved to California to teach, later turning out a number of bold, engaging films, notably 1979's "Poto and Cabengo".) Godard moved to video, both because it was a better medium for the essays and experimentation he had in mind and because TV had by this time become the best way to communicate with the largest number of people. In 1975, he left Paris for Grenoble, and collaboration with Anne-Marie Mieville, his third wife.

In an alternate life, Godard might have "gone Hollywood." It wasn't for want of trying. Robert Benton and David Newman had approached him in the mid-60s about directing "Bonnie & Clyde." Godard couldn't make a deal with the producers. A while later, again with Benton and Newman, he was set to direct "The Technique of a Political Murder", about Trotsky, for producer Raoul Levy. Levy died unexpectedly, and plans fell apart. Godard was considered as director for Jules Feiffer's "Little Murders" until Elliott Gould realized Godard didn't want to make that movie; he wanted to make a movie about making that movie. In the early 80s he attempted to get an elaborate American production about Bugsy Siegel off the ground. It would have starred Diane Keaton, but it didn't come to pass.

So instead Godard stayed with his small-scale, intimate, idiosyncratic and challenging TV and video work. The main productions of the video period were the two series, "Six Fois Deux/Sur et sous la communication" (1976, ten hours), and "France-Tour-Detour-Deux-Enfants" (1978, six hours). Godard starts with the premise that "video is for those who do not see." These series comprise essays on commonplace, everyday subjects—including family, love, work, communication, and relationships—all as they are presented by the media for mass consumption. With some success, Godard challenges the passivity of TV viewers and their unquestioning acceptance of media messages.

Individual segments of the "Six Fois Deux" series examine the mass media's approach to such subjects as unemployment, farming, the language of images, photo news, relationships,

math, madness and society, and, of course, filmmaking. In separate segments, real people with direct knowledge of each area of inquiry—including a farmer, a filmmaker and a mathematician—personally discuss these topics and their representation in the media.

"France-Tour-Detour-Deux-Enfants" juxtaposes philosophical interviews with two children (ages 9 and 12) from the same family about the meaning of daily activities against images of everyday life with their parents, including watching TV. For the first time, in these projects for the small screen, Godard takes on the role of teacher to share with a much larger audience his understanding of the complex language of film and TV.

In 1975, Godard had released two films— "Numero Deux" (notable not only for its bold sexuality but also for his spare usage of only parts of the frame) and "Comment Ca Va"—which indicated the direction for the future. More fully than ever before he here contemplated his own cinematic history. Starting in 1980, Godard continued the reinvestigation of concerns and themes he had first developed in the 60s. "Sauve qui peut (la vie)" (1980) and "Passion" (1982) give us portraits of emotional confusion mixed with commentary on the problems of filmmaking—a fusion of the 60s and early 70s.

With his next three films, Godard hit his stride again. "First Name: Carmen" (1983) imaginatively retold the old story, with Godard himself playing a role with wry amusement. "Detective" (1985), a challenging comic homage to the genre (dedicated "to John Cassavetes, Edgar G. Ulmer, and Clint Eastwood") brought Godard back with pleasure to his first cinematic love. But it was "Hail Mary" (1985) which really marked Godard's return to theatrical prominence. This modern nativity tale—placing the story of Joseph and Mary in modernist society, rampant with jealousy, loneliness, and divorce—was actually condemned by the Vatican. At the age of 55, Jean-Luc Godard was once again the enfant terrible.

"Hail Mary" evinces the same sort of fresh, exciting—and often infuriating—narrative innovation that made the films of Jean-Luc Godard required viewing for anyone who cared about film in the 60s.

In 1987, the ever-prolific and experimental Godard turned out three more films. His segment of the omnibus feature "Aria" was one of the bolder, funnier exercises, setting Jean-Baptiste Lully's "Armide" in a gymnasium with brooding, nude female workers contemplating the murder of muscle-bound males. "Soigne ta droite" was a docu-essay on French pop group Les Rita Mitsouko, drawing comparisons to his earlier "One Plus One" (1968), which had intercut the Rolling Stones recording "Sympathy for the Devil" with fragments of contemporary English life. "King Lear", meanwhile, marked Godard's English-language and, in some sense, Hollywood debut but unfortunately was not one of his best films of this period. A striking take on the Bard nonetheless, it was shot for Cannon films in Geneva, with Molly Ringwald as Cordelia, Burgess Meredith as Lear, Woody Allen as "Mr. Alien" and stage director Peter Sellars as a bewildered "Will Shakespeare V."

While not a cause celebre, "New Wave" (1990), about big business machinations on a Swiss estate, continued Godard's very personal quest to understand the nature and meaning of the movies. His work seemed to become that of an artist in the twilight of his career, as in "Helas Pour Moi/Woe Is Me" (1993), which reworked the Greek myth of Amphitryon to explore, among other things, the issue of God's role in human lives. His affectionate video "History of the Cinema" and his feature "Germany Year 90 Nine Zero" (both 1991), which revisits both Rossellini's classic "Germany Year Zero" of 1947 and Godard's own "Alphaville", further confirm his singular position in any journeys taken to explore the relationship between cinema and life itself.—Written by Stuart Kauffman

COMPANION:

wife: Anna Karina. Actor; married in March 1961; divorced in 1964; appeared in a number of Godard's early features, including "Le Petit Soldat" (1960), "Vivre Sa Vie" (1962) and others

MILESTONES:

Became naturalized Swiss citizen during WWII

1950: Co-founded *Gazette du Cinema* ; first article published under pseudonym "Hans Lucas"

1950: Film acting debut in "Quadrille" (helped finance; experimental short by Jacques Rivette)

1952–1954: Wrote for *Cahiers du Cinema*

1952: Traveled to North America and South America and began work on first film (never completed)

1954: First short documentary as director "Operation Beton" ("Operation Concrete")

1955: First short fiction film (as Hans Lucas) "Une Femme Coquette"

1956: Wrote film reviews for *Arts*

1957: Briefly worked in the publicity department for 20th Century-Fox in Paris

1957: Hired as press attache for Artistes Associes

1958: First public screening of "Operation beton"

1959: Wrote gossip column "Temps de Paris"

1959: First feature film as director "A Bout de Souffle/ Breathless"; released early 1960

1964: With then-wife Anna Karina, formed Anouchka Films

Television directing debut with "Le Gai Savoir"; never broadcast by its TV producer; released theatrically

1968: Garnered attention for championing Henri Langlois who had been fired as director of the Cinematheque

1967: Directed "Le Weekend", which marked a transitional point in his career; subsequent work was first more politicized (1968–1972) and then more experimental (1973–)

1969: Formed Dziga-Vertov Group (with Jean-Pierre Gorin and others)

1973: Formed Sonimage (with Anne-Marie Mieville), a video production company

1980: Returned to feature films with "Sauve qui peut (la vie)"

1983: Earned international acclaim for "Prenom: Carmen"

1985: Wrote and directed "Je vous salue, Marie/Hail Mary"

1987: Helmed TV commercials for a line of jeans

1987: Directed an odd assortment of ·performers (including Norman Mailer, Woody Allen and Molly Ringwald) in an excessive updating of Shakespeare's "King Lear"

1989: Began a multi-part video project, "Histoire(s) du cinema/History of the Cinema"

1994: Produced, scripted, directed and appeared in the pseudo-biographical "JLG/JLG—Autoportrait de Decembre"

1996: Directed, edited and scripted "Forever Mozart"

Made several videos for TV under the umbrella title "Histoire du cinema"

2000: Commissioned by the Cannes Film Festival. made documentary short "L'Origine du XXieme siecle"

2001: Directed "Eloge d'amour/In Praise of Love"; screened at Cannes

BIBLIOGRAPHY:

"Godard" Richard Roud, 1967

"Focus on Godard" Royal S. Brown (editor), 1972

"Jean-Luc Godard par Jean-Luc Godard" Jean-Luc Godard, 1985; published in USA in 1988 as "Godard on Godard: Critical Writings of Jean-Luc Godard"

"Speaking About Godard" Kaja Silverman and Harun Farocki, 1998, New York University Press

"Jean-Luc Godard: Interviews" David Sterritt (editor), 1998

"The Films of Jean-Luc Godard: Seeing the Invisible" David Sterritt, 1999

"The Cinema Alone: Jean-Luc Godard in the Year 2000" James S. Williams, (editor) 2001

Peter Greenaway

BORN: in Newport, Wales, 04/05/1942

NATIONALITY: English

EDUCATION: Walthamstow College of Art, London, England; met Ian Dury

AWARDS: Chicago Film Festival Hugo "A Walk Through H" 1978

British Film Institute Award "The Falls" 1980

Brussels Film Festival L'Age d'Or "The Falls" 1980

Melbourne Film Festival Sydney Prize "Act of God" 1981; awarded for short film

Chicago Film Festival Hugo Best Documentary "Zandra Rhodes" 1981

Chicago Film Festival Artistic Merit Award "The Belly of an Architect" 1987

Cannes Film Festival Prix de la Meilleure Collaboration Artistique "Drowning By Numbers" 1988

London Film Critics Circle Award British Technical Achievement of the Year "Prospero's Books" 1991

BIOGRAPHY

One of Britain's leading auteurs, Greenaway trained as a painter before spending eleven years, beginning in 1965, as a film editor. During this period he began making short, highly formalist films influenced by structural linguistics, ethnography and philosophy. After shorts such as "Window" (1975), which displayed his fondness for lists (in this case cataloguing all the people who died in a small village by falling out of windows), Greenaway attracted some attention for such vivid medium-length works as "Vertical Features Remake" and the humorous "A Walk through H" (both 1978). He began to garner considerable acclaim on the international festival circuit, and in 1980 made his first feature-length film, a "documentary" set in the future, "The Falls" (1980), chock-full of his trademark riddles and conundrums as he relates the lives of 92 victims of the "Violent Unexplained Event." Greenaway hit the limelight in 1982 with the release of his feature, "The Draughtsman's Contract."

An acclaimed study of 18th-century sexual intrigue set in an English country house, "The Draughtsman's Contract" staked out its director's central concerns with formal symmetries and parallels; each element of the plot was mirrored and repeated several times in order to create an elaborate, baroque structure, which proved popular with critics and public alike. All in all, it was a superb if extremely dry meditation on the construction of perception, desire and of the difference of time past.

Although "Contract" put the English art film back on the map, Greenaway's next three features did not meet with comparable success. "A Zed and Two Noughts" (1985), "The Belly of an Architect" (1987) and "Drowning by Numbers" (1988) are undermined in the eyes of some by their rigid formalism, though they remain intriguing and visually absorbing. "Belly" brought forth fully Greenaway's interest in obsession and its possibly violent manifestations, while "Drowning" kept audiences watching the screen in search of numbers while crazed puns peppered a story of three generations of women, all with the same name, who murdered their husbands by drowning them.

The director returned to a more accessible form with "The Cook, the Thief, His Wife and Her Lover" (1989), a visceral study of haute cuisine, adultery and murder centered on a riveting performance by Michael Gambon as a sadistic, foul-mouthed gangster. Thanks to its relatively conventional narrative and its violent, controversial imagery, "The Cook" brought Greenaway his first substantial recognition in the US. His "Death in the Seine", also released in 1989, was one of Greenaway's fine and pedantic catalogue films, a potently morbid taxonomy of all drowning victims in the Parisian river between 1795 and 1801 that ended up not being bought by British TV as promised.

Greenaway followed with "Prospero's Books" (1991), a film that elicited a great variety of opinion, from claims of the work's near divinity as an intertextual late modernist revision of Shakespeare's "The Tempest" to a view of it as an airless work, a connoisseur's film, jam-packed with visual marginalia and pretense. Here the listing was of the 24 tomes the Bard's wizard brought with him to his island of exile. This prolific period was capped by "Darwin" (1992), a strenuous revision of the biopic genre, and "The Baby of Macon" (1993), another grim semi-satire set in an imaginary court of the Medicis in 17th century and the second part of a historical trilogy that started with "Prospero's Books."

MILESTONES:

Family moved to Essex when Greenaway was two
Raised in Chingford
1964: Exhibited paintings at the Lord's Gallery in England
1965: Began working as film editor (including editing several documentaries for the Central Office of Information)
1966: Directed first film, "Train"
1975: Filmed "Windows"
1978: Edited, directed, scripted, designed, and made maps for own film, "A Walk Through H"
1978: Produced first film (also directed, scripted, and photographed), "Vertical Features Remake"
1980: First feature-length film, the semi-documentary, "The Falls"

1982: First completely fictional feature-length film and first American release, "The Draughtsman's Contract"

1989: Helmed the controversial drama "The Cook, the Thief, His Wife and Her Lover"

1991: Directed John Gielgud in "Prospero's Books", a loose adaptation of Shakespeare's "The Tempest"

1996: Crafted the visually stunning, if emotionally chilly "The Pillow Book"

QUOTES:

Created an Officer of the Order of Arts and Letters by the French government in 1998

There is a website devoted to Greenaway at www.december.org/pg

"Cinema is far too rich and capable a medium to be merely left to the storytellers."—Peter Greenaway (Production notes for "A Zed & Two Noughts")

"Peter Greenaway makes movies that offer viewers little comfort; his plots are not the sort that can be wrapped up with one final, lingering kiss. His films are deeply carnal, but the sexuality he depicts yields little pleasure. And it seems, he delights in filming bodily functions. Yet when the English director insists that his is a 'cinema of esthetics,' one has to agree. Mr. Greenaway designs his movies to be beautiful."—Karrie Jacobs in *The New York Times*, April 21, 1991.

Greenaway has produced several paintings, novels and illustrated books.

"Cinema is more powerful than the other so-called serious arts. We must insure that it contains challenging and provocative ideas." —From *The New York Times*, February 6, 1994.

BIBLIOGRAPHY:

"L'Avant Scene" Peter Greenaway, 1984

"A Zed & Two Noughts" Peter Greenaway, 1985, Faber and Faber

"Being Naked—Playing Dead: The Art of Peter Greenaway" Alan Woods, 1997, Manchester University Press

"The Films of Peter Greenaway" Amy Lawrence

D. W. Griffith

BORN: David Lewelyn Wark Griffith in Oldham County, Kentucky, 01/22/1875

SOMETIMES CREDITED AS:

Gaston Detolignac
Granville Warwick
Irene Sinclair
Lawrence Griffith
M. Gaston de Trolignac
Marquis de Trolignac
Roy Sinclair
Captain Victor Marier

DEATH: in Hollywood, California, 07/23/1948

NATIONALITY: American

AWARDS: Honorary Oscar 1935 for his "distinguished creative achievements as director and producer and his invaluable initiative and lasting contributions to the progress of the motion picture arts"

Directors Guild of America Honorary Life Membership 1938

BIOGRAPHY

David Wark Griffith's achievement is two-fold: he developed for Americans a syntax for expression in the movies, and he showed how the feature film could be a significant commercial and cultural element of American culture. The first achievement is less understood but more important than the second.

Griffith did not enter film with a record as a

successful artist. He was a failure as a play-wright, with but one of his plays actually pro-duced. But because he approached film with the attitude that it was a temporary job, he saw it as an opportunity to experiment, to break the conventions of his era, to develop new means of relating narratives for the screen.

In 1907, when Griffith tried to sell a story to movie producer Edwin S. Porter who signed him on as an actor instead, American movies all too often consisted of series of scenes (orig-inally called views) of events usually taken from the popular press or the stage. Static cam-eras recorded scenes connected by titles and little else. Four years earlier in "The Great Train Robbery," Porter had stumbled onto more elo-quent means of expression—shorter scenes, multiple locations, use of natural landscapes with actors moving through them, even the close-up—but he declined to develop these techniques. In fact when Griffith played the lead in Porter's "Rescued From an Eagle's Next" (1907), the young actor was so carelessly filmed that he was obscured by the edge of the frame. Later that year, Griffith got his chance to direct and he showed an immediate talent for creative use of the frame, as well as developing rhythmic editing to build dramatic tension. Griffith also sought out younger performers who were less bound to the broad style of stage acting and more open to the nuances required for acting before the camera.

From 1907 to 1913, Griffith averaged 2 1/2 films a week, most of them for Biograph, using overlapping schedules and a stock company of actors who rapidly moved from one film to the next, sometimes in the same day. Griffith paid special attention to his actresses, developing a number of important women performers, including Lillian and Dorothy Gish, Mary Pick-ford, Blanche Sweet and Mae Marsh.

In the midst of this whirlwind of produc-tion Griffith was developing new ways of telling stories that were uniquely suited to film. Editing became as important an element as cinematography, most notably in his use of cross-cutting between parallel story lines. This offered opportunities to contrast behavior or social circumstance, as in "A Corner in Wheat", or to develop suspense with a rising tempo of action, as in "The Lonely Villa" (both 1909). Griffith's collaborators in this adventure of inventing film language included not only his cameraman, Billy Bitzer, but also the actors themselves, who were encouraged to suggest mannerisms to enrich their performances.

At this time, filmmakers in other countries, especially France and Denmark, were making comparable discoveries about the importance of editing; often their films were shown in the United States, just as Griffith's Biograph pro-ductions were exported to Europe. This ongoing dialogue has made it nearly impos-sible to clearly define sources of innovation and influences which many historians have consigned solely to Griffith.

In 1913, Griffith broke with the Biograph Company when it declined to let him make feature-length films and the following year he began production on his first feature, "Birth of a Nation" (1915). Its release brought Griffith enormous acclaim and infamy. Audiences were dazzled by the film's sweep and epic power, as well as its intimate moments of pain and joy, but Griffith's embrace of the Ku Klux Klan and his insensitive depiction of black characters stirred up a storm of controversy. Previously relegated to the status of an amusement on the fringes of culture, movies were catapulted by Griffith and his film into social and financial prominence.

Griffith won financial independence with "Birth of a Nation" and almost immediately moved on to another epic, an elaboration on the notion of parallel historical developments, which he would present through cross-cutting across time rather than geography. "Intoler-ance" (1916) was a quartet of stories of man's inhumanity to man which some historians charge was Griffith's compensation for the accusations of racism made against him after "Birth of a Nation." Enormously expensive to produce, the film was nearly as big a box-office flop as "Birth" had been a hit. Its reputation over the years has in some ways surpassed its predecessor, and its influence is apparent in the works of Carl Dreyer, Sergei Eisenstein, Fritz Lang and many other directors.

As great an artistic achievement as "Intolerance" was, it also left Griffith on a permanent financial treadmill, as he sought to pay off his debts with proceeds from future productions. From 1916 to 1931, he made over two dozen more features. At least five of these—"Broken Blossoms" (1919), "Way Down East" (1920), "Orphans of the Storm" (1921), "The White Rose" (1923) and "Isn't Life Wonderful" (1924)—were either commercial or critical successes, but the financial dividends went to Griffith's creditors or producers. On one film, "The Sorrows of Satan" (1926), Griffith's producers inflated the cost of the production by pressuring Griffith to film material he did not need and then recut the film after he had completed it. By the end of the silent era, Griffith was saddled with a reputation for extravagance, which was undeserved, and a Victorian brand of sentimentality, which was an integral part of his personality, although a steadily less compelling component of his films.

Griffith made two sound films, the starched and safe "Abraham Lincoln" (1930) and "The Struggle" (1931). "The Struggle" is a haunting final work, full of melancholy and dread of alcoholism, but also distinguished by superb sequences photographed on New York City streets and an inventive use of sound in factory sequences which revealed Griffith still seeking new ways to narrate stories on film.

Ignored by the industry he played such an important role in creating, Griffith retreated to over a decade of isolation at Hollywood's Knickerbocker Hotel, where he died in 1948. For years, the scurrilous content of "Birth of a Nation" and the unabashed sentiment of many of the other features consigned Griffith to the status of irrelevancy, but in the mid-1960s, a Griffith revival began, with re-appraisal of his early works and acknowlegements of his immense contributions.

MILESTONES:

1896: First theater job as extra with Sarah Bernhardt's company

1897: Stage acting debut with Meffert Stock Company (Louisville)

1906: Published first poem in "Leslie's Weekly"

1906: First play sold "The Fool and the Girl"

1906: Hired by Edison Company (Bronx, NY) as actor

1907: Film acting debut in "Rescued From an Eagle's Nest" (for Edwin S. Porter)

1908: Hired by American Mutoscope and Biograph Company (New York) as actor, writer

1908: Film directing debut with "The Adventures of Dollie"

1911: Directed first two-reeler "Enoch Arden"

1913: Left Biograph; joined Mutual

1913: Directed world's first four-reeler "Judith of Bethulia"

1915: Joined Triangle Corporation; filmed "Birth of a Nation"

Re-released "Judith of Bethulia" in expanded six-reel version entitled "Her Condoned Sin"

1917: Joined Adolph Zukor's Artcraft (pictures released through Famous-Players Lasky—later Paramount)

1919: Formed United Artists (with Charles Chaplin, Douglas Fairbanks and Mary Pickford); released first film for United Artists "Broken Blossoms"

1919: Signed three picture deal with First National

1919: Set up studio complex (Mamaroneck, NY)

1920: Incorporated enterprises into D. W. Griffith Corporation

1924: Last independent production "Isn't Life Wonderful"

1924: Left United Artists; signed with Adolph Zukor for Paramount

1927: Returned to United Artists, signed personal contract with Joseph Schenck

1930: Directed first sound film "Abraham Lincoln"

1931: Directed last film "The Struggle"

1937: Hired by Hal Roach to produce "One Million B.C."

QUOTES:

"He was the first to photograph thought" (Cecil B. DeMille, quoted in *Halliwell's Filmgoer's Companion*); "There is not a man working in movies, nor a man who cares for them, who does not owe Griffith more than he owes anyone else" (James Agee, quoted in *Halliwell's FGC*) The story goes that when an actor once asked him for a raise, Griffith responded, "It's worth a lot more than money to be working for me!" (related in *Halliwell's FGC*)

BIBLIOGRAPHY:

"Star Maker: The Story of D.W. Griffith" Homer Cray, 1959, Duell, Sloan and Pearce; introduction by Mary Pickford

"D.W. Griffith, American Film Master" Iris Barry, 1965, Garland Publishing; with an annotated list of films by Eileen Bowser; bound with Richard Griffith's book, "Samuel Goldwyn, The Producer and His Films"

"The Movies, Mr. Griffith, and Me" Lillian Gish with Ann Pinchot, 1969 Prentice-Hall; autobiography by one of Griffith's most famous discoveries, with considerable reminiscence on their working relationship

"The Man Who Invented Hollywood" D.W. Griffith (edited by James Hart), 1972; based on Griffith's manuscript "D.W. Griffith and the Wolf"

"D.W. Griffith: His Life and Work" Robert M. Henderson, 1972, Oxford University Press

"D.W. Griffith: An American Life" Richard Schickel, 1984, Simon & Schuster

"D.W. Griffith's 'Intolerance': Its Genesis and Its Vision" William M. Drew, 1986

"Family Secrets: The Feature Films of D.W. Griffith" Michael Allen, 1999, Indiana University Press

Christopher Guest

BORN: Christopher Haden-Guest in New York, New York, 02/05/1948

SOMETIMES CREDITED AS:
Baron Haden-Guest Of
Lord Haden-Guest

NATIONALITY: American

EDUCATION: High School of Music and Art, New York, New York
Bard College Annandale-on-Hudson, New York
New York University, New York, New York

AWARD: Emmy Outstanding Writing in a Comedy-Variety or Music Special "Lily Tomlin" 1975/76 shared award with eight writers including Lorne Michaels, Jane Wagner and Lily Tomlin

BIOGRAPHY

A titled Englishman born and raised in New York, an unsettlingly deadpan interview subject capable of passionate and frenetic onscreen portrayals, a successful screenwriter and director who does his best work by allowing his actors to improvise every scene, and seemingly average by all outward appearances despite these at once contradictory and complementary aspects, Christopher Guest has had a long and varied career, achieving cult status for work in such unforgettable pseudo-documentaries as "This is Spinal Tap" (1984) and "Waiting For Guffman" (1997). The son of a British peer (Guest inherited the title when his father died), Guest studied music and drama and began his career as a working actor in New York theater in the late 1960s and early 70s, also working at that time as a contributing writer for the "National Lampoon Radio Show" (eventually creating 59 episodes). In 1973, he earned songwriting credits as well as a featured player spot in "National Lampoon's Lemmings", a successful revue that played at the Village Gate Theatre. It wasn't long before he successfully made the leap to other media.

On the small screen, Guest earned an Emmy as one of the writers for "The Lily Tomlin Special" (ABC, 1975), on which he also performed. He then appeared regularly in sketches on the short-lived ABC variety series "Saturday Night with Howard Cosell" (1975) and moved to episodics with a guest appearance on "All in the Family." Proving his dramatic mettle in longforms like "Billion Dollar Bubble" (NBC, 1977) and "It Happened One Christmas" (ABC, 1977), he next delivered a strong portrayal of Watergate felon Jeb Stuart Magruder in the 1979 CBS miniseries "Blind Ambition." Savvy viewers became more aware of Guest when he joined the cast of NBC's "Saturday Night Live" in 1984, serving as the anchor for the "Weekend Update" segment, creating characters like the trainer for a male synchronized swimming pair in a particularly memorable sketch, and impersonating Dr. Ruth Westheimer, among others. As the 80s progressed, Guest appeared as a guest on comedy specials featuring "SNL" co-stars Martin Short and Billy Crystal, including the HBO productions "Billy Crystal—Don't Get Me Started" (1986) and "I, Martin Short, Goes Hollywood" (1989). With the advent of the 1990s. Guest moved behind the camera, co-producing and directing the premiere of the CBS sitcom "Morton and Hayes" and helming

the TV-movie remake "Attack of the 50 Ft. Woman" (HBO, 1993), starring Daryl Hannah.

While he enjoyed great critical success in later years for his innovative, largely improvisational documentary-style comedy features, Guest's screen career had an uneven start. He debuted as one of the residents in the Oscar-winning black comedy "The Hospital" (1971) and landed his first romantic lead opposite Melanie Mayron in Claudia Weill's "Girlfriends" (1978). Not until Rob Reiner's spoof of rock documentaries "This Is Spinal Tap" did Guest find his footing. Practically stealing the film with an hilarious turn as the pouty guitarist Nigel Tufnel, the co-writer as well as star of the film entered cult film history along with on- and off-screen collaborators Michael McKean and Harry Shearer with this perennial comedy favorite. Reiner later cast the actor as the villainous Count Rugen in "The Princess Bride" (1987) and as a doctor in the military courtroom drama "A Few Good Men" (1992).

Guest moved to the director's chair in 1989 with "The Big Picture" (1989), an insider's look at Hollywood wheeling and dealing filled with good performances and smartly funny jokes. His second effort was "Waiting for Guffman" (1997), in which he cast himself in the central role of a frustrated gay actor unsuccessful in his Off-Broadway pursuits who returns to his home in Missouri to stage a sesquicentennial pageant. Owing a debt to "Spinal Tap", "Guffman" was shot in mock-documentary fashion and affectionately celebrated the American penchant for bad taste. Guest's tour-de-force performance anchored the film, which included incisive bits from Catherine O'Hara, Parker Posey and Fred Willard. His third feature "Almost Heroes" (1998), which followed a bumbling pair of rivals to Lewis and Clark trekking across early-19th-century America, was unfortunately tinged with sadness despite its comic premise as leading actor Chris Farley died before its release. While this stalled at the box office, the 2000 follow-up "Best in Show" proved a critical success and a niche market hit. A sharp and clever comedy set at a dog show, the film followed Guest's successful improvised mockumentary pattern, and reteamed Willard, O'Hara and Posey as well as "SCTV" veteran Eugene Levy, who co-wrote the thematic screenplay outline with Guest. Expecting the most from his players and getting it, "Best in Show" proved even more consistently funny than the riotous "Guffman." From O'Hara and Levy's happily mismatched couple to Willard's alarmingly off-the-cuff announcer, the film celebrated rather than trounced upon its characters quirks, with the same warm sense of humor present in his prior work.

Fondly remembering the explosion of folk music in his New York neighborhood, Guest summoned Eugene Levy as the two began to work on their next project. The result came in the form of the musical comedy "A Mighty Wind" (2003), a feature about a group of folk music have-been's who decides to get together one last time to memorialize a deceased concert promoter.

COMPANION:

wife: Jamie Lee Curtis. Actor; born on November 22, 1958; married on December 18, 1984 at Rob Reiner's home; daughter of actors Tony Curtis and Janet Leigh

MILESTONES:

1966: Made professional acting debut at New Haven's Long Wharf Theater

1967: First teamed up with Michael McKean, playing in a band in New York

1969: Off-Broadway debut, "Little Murders"

1970: Broadway debut, "Room Service"

1971: Feature film debut playing a resident in "The Hospital"

1972: Acted in the short-lived Broadway production "Moonchildren"

1973: Was member of the ensemble, "National Lampoon's Lemmings" at the Village Gate Theatre, NYC

1975: Regular player on the ABC variety series "Saturday Night With Howard Cosell"

1975: Co-wrote and performed in "The Lily Tomlin Special" (ABC)

1977: TV-movie debut, "Billion Dollar Bubble" (NBC)

1977: Made TV episodic debut on "All in the Family" (CBS)

1978: Had first romantic lead opposite Melanie Mayron in "Girlfriends"

1979: Played Jeb Stuart Magruder in CBS miniseries "Blind Ambition"

1980: Appeared with his brother Nicholas alongside the real-life Carradine, Quaid and Keach brothers in Walter Hill's Western "The Long Riders"; played Charlie Ford

1981: Reteamed with Melanie Mayron in "Heartbeeps"

Directed the "Johnny Appleseed" installment of the Showtime series "Faerie Tale Theater"

1984: Co-starred as guitarist Nigel Hufnel and co-wrote "This Is Spinal Tap", Rob Reiner's "mockumentary" about a heavy metal band

1984–1985: Was regular on "Saturday Night Live" (NBC)

1987: Had featured role in Reiner's "The Princess Bride"

1988: Co-starred with Mayron in "Sticky Fingers"

1989: Feature directorial debut, "The Big Picture"

1991: Executive produced CBS sitcom "Morton and Hayes"; also directed premiere episode

1992: Appeared in "A Few Good Men", directed by Reiner

1993: Helmed "Attack of the 50 Ft. Woman", an HBO TV-movie starring Daryl Hannah

1997: Wrote, directed and starred in the cult hit "Waiting for Guffman"

1998: Directed the comedy "Almost Heroes"

2001: Wrote, directed and starred in the dog show-themed comedy "Best in Show"

2003: Co-wrote (with Eugene Levy), directed, and co-starred in "A Mighty Wind"

QUOTES:

"I have no concept of how some people create

a product they think a lot of people will see."—Christopher Guest in *Entertainment Weekly*, February 14, 1997.

Guest on Corky St. Claire, his lovably flamboyant character in "Waiting For Guffman" (from *Venice*, February 1997): "I don't think it was a caricature, but a representation. I think those are different. I make it a point in characters that I do to inhabit these people with a certain viewpoint. I have to like them, and I think, if that happens, then the audience will like them. In the case of Corky St. Claire, his sexuality is not the point of the movie, The point of the movie is that this is who this guy is. People in the town like him. They accept who he is and he is a likable, even loveable character whom they can relate to."

From *Time Out New York*, September 7–14, 2000: Jem Aswad notes: "Your satirical films have been about rock & roll, the film industry, small-town theater and now—dog shows?"

Guest replied: "I guess [the common thread] is a fanaticism that crossed different boundaries in hobbies or professions. I have two dogs and my wife and I used to take them to this dog park near our home. I noticed the behavior of the people more than the dogs, and it evolved from that."

"I don't make movies that make fun of anything. I think if you like the people, that's the important thing. Because if you don't like these people, if they were just to be a one-dimensional parody, then you have no investment emotionally in the end when you're waiting to hear who wins."—Guest on "Best in Show", quoted in *The New York Times*, September 24, 2000.

Christopher Guest on his filmmaking process to *Daily News*, September 24, 2000: "I've put a tremendous amount of trust in these actors to deliver this kind of movie. The actors know what the intention of the scene is, but there are no lines written down, and the first time you hear it and see it on the screen, that's it—that's the first time it was said. I've tried to make all these analogies to what we're doing, mostly with music. Like in jazz—there are no

music stands. Where's the music coming from? They're making it up. And in these films, this is jamming. This is actor jamming."

"Where the clueless subjects of [Robert] Altman's 'Health' and 'Ready to Wear' wander foggily through the director's free-floaring dyspepsia (the last one standing wins the booby prize), Guest's misfits and dreamers enjoy his full hospitality. His humor isn't based on humiliation. When one of the dogs misbehaves and has to be disqualified, it's comic without being cruel. He doesn't dole out punishment by playing nasty tricks on his characters."—*Vanity Fair* 's James Wolcott on Guest, from an October 2000 profile.

Guest on deciding which actors to work with: "These are people who, when you meet them, you immediately know are on your wavelength or whatever you want to call it. Not to say that it's all based on intuition. But if you are in the world of comedy, you can tell immediately if they are sharing a sensibility. And then they're basically in the club. For what I do, it's a small club. I'm not saying it can't expand. It's just that there's not 20,000 people walking around who share that sensibility. It's very specific. You meet them and you immediately recognize something in them. You know instantaneously. Eugene Levy makes me laugh. Why? Here we are again: I don't know."—to Salon.com's Jessica Hundley, October 6, 2000.

DISCOGRAPHY: "Radio Dinner" National Lampoon, MCA, 1972; comedy album with skits and performances by Guest

"Lemmings" National Lampoon Banana/MCA 1973 spoof of "Woodstock" featuring sketch comedy as well as original songs

"Gold Turkey" National Lampoon, Epic, 1975; greatest hits of the "National Lampoon Radio Hour"; Guest has producer, vocals and guitar credits

"Greatest Hits" National Lampoon, Visa, 1978

"Lenny & the Squitones" Lenny & Squiggy, Casablanca, 1980; contributed guitar and

background vocals to this novelty album by "Laverne and Shirley" stars David L Lander and longtime collaborator Michael McKean
"This Is Spinal Tap" Spinal Tap, Polydor, 1984;

had songwriter, vocalist, guitar and mandolin credits in this album by the legendary fictional hard rock band
"Break Like the Wind" Spinal Tap, MCA, 1992

Tomas Gutierrez Alea

BORN: in Havana, Cuba, 12/11/1928

SOMETIMES CREDITED AS:
Tomas Gutierrez Alea

DEATH: in Havana, Cuba, 04/16/1996

NATIONALITY: Cuban

EDUCATION: University of Havana, Havana, Cuba, law, 1950
Centro Sperimentale di Cinematografia Rome, Italy, 1951–53

AWARDS: Melbourne Film Festival Award "Stories of the Revolution" 1961
Karlovy Vary Film Festival Special Jury Prize "Death of a Bureaucrat"
Karlovy Vary Film Festival Special Jury Prize "Memories of Underdevelopment"
Karlovy Vary Film Festival FIPRESCI Prize "Memories of Underdevelopment"
New York Film Festival Chaplin Prize "Memories of Underdevelopment" 1973
National Society of Film Critics Richard and Hinda Rosenthal Foundation Award "Memories of Underdevelopment" 1973; cited "for a film which, although not sufficiently recognized by public attendance has nevertheless been an outstanding cinematic achievement"
Chicago Film Festival Gold Hugo "The Last Supper" 1976
Berlin Film Festival Silver Bear "Strawberry and Chocolate" 1994

BIOGRAPHY

Cuba's greatest and best-known director, Tomas Gutierrez Alea fell in love with cinema at an early age, began as a documentarian much influenced by Italian neo-realism, and fully came into his own as an artist during Fidel Castro's regime. Over the years, he has evinced a fondness for both historical and contemporary fables, invariably politically pointed and satirical, their flights into absurdity showing the influence of Luis Bunuel. An ardent supporter of the revolution which dispatched the despotic Fulgencio Batista and brought Castro to power, Alea has painted a more complex portrait of Cuba in his cinema than the rest of the world has generally been willing to conceive. The documentary impulse has remained, yet it is used to constantly scrutinize contemporary Cuba. Indeed, Alea has made some gutsy critiques of the socioeconomic and political realities of his land, as he ponders the persistence of a petty-bourgeois mentality in a society supposedly dedicated to the plight of the working poor.

Born to a fairly well-off family, Alea was sent to college in Havana to follow in his father's footsteps and become a lawyer. At about the same time he entered school, though, he acquired an 8mm camera and made two short films, "Un fakir" and "La caperucita roja/Little Red Riding Hood" (both 1946). Several years later, he collaborated with fellow student (and future film great) Nestor Almendros on a short Kafka adaptation they named "A Common Confusion" (1950). Upon graduation, Alea journeyed to Italy to study film directing for two years during the crest of neo-realism at the famed Centro Sperimentale de Cinematografia. He returned to Cuba in 1953 and joined the radical "Nuestro Tiempo" cultural society, becoming active in the film section, working as a publicist and aligning himself with Castro's fight against the Batista regime.

In 1955, Alea co-directed with Julio Garcia Espinosa, another society member, the 16mm short "El Megano/The Charcoal Worker", a semi-documentary about exploited workers, acted by nonprofessionals from the locales in which it was shot. The film was seized by Batista's police because of its political content. Soon after the Cuban Revolution in 1959, Alea co-founded (with Santiago Alvarez) the national revolutionary film institute ICAIC ("Instituto del Arte y Industria Cinematografica"). He promptly made a documentary "Este tierra nuestra/This Land of Ours" (1959), full of hope for the new government's plan to help the poor through agrarian reform, and has remained a pillar of the organization ever since.

Alea's diverse creative personality has led him to experiment with a broad range of styles and themes. His first feature, "Stories of the Revolution" (1960), employs a neorealist style to present three dramatic sketches depicting the armed insurrection against Batista. Alea's relatively straightforward approach to film style, however, would change, altered not only through his appropriation of Hollywood and art cinema stylistics but also by his increasingly personal attempts at self-expression. "A Cuban Fight Against the Demons" (1971), for example, the film in which he first worked with regular cinematographer Mario Garcia Joya, comes across as the prelude to a period Alea has described as full of personal and artistic instability as much as it does an aggressive allegorical portrait of church and state corruption. The director's later "Letters from the Park" (1988) is more of a twilight work, exploring the romantic period piece as a scribe meets a diverse cross-section of society via his talents at letter writing. The finest of Alea's historical films, "The Last Supper" (1976) continued to highlight his

versatility, drawing on Afro-Cuban musical motifs and the literary style of magic realism to recreate an 18th-century slave revolt.

Alea has also made several satiric comedies that explore the legacy of bourgeois society in post-revolutionary Cuba. The madcap adventure "The Twelve Chairs" (1962), a film tale also told by Russian filmmakers and by Mel Brooks, satirizes greed and bureaucracy as a lingering post-revolutionary bourgeois, his roguish manservant and a corrupt priest hunt for a chair concealing priceless diamonds. The Hollywoodian black comedy "Death of a Bureaucrat" (1966) cites not only Bunuel but also Mack Sennett and Laurel and Hardy as it criticizes, at an early point in the Castro regime, the administrative muck of the political system. (Alea reused the gallows humor of the bureaucracy connected with burying a corpse for his road picture "Guantanamera", which began to appear at festivals in 1995 and 1996.) In "The Survivors" (1979), an aristocratic family devolves from civilization to savagery; using a metaphor found in many films from poor countries, the family resorts to cannibalism in trying to remain isolated from the Revolution.

The stresses and strains of a revolutionary society were explored in several dramatic works set in contemporary Cuba, among them "Memories of Underdevelopment" (1968) and "Up to a Certain Point" (1984). "Memories", Alea's masterpiece and arguably the best-known Cuban film ever made, brilliantly blends documentary and drama to create an extremely witty yet sensitive portrait of a restless, oversexed, politically uncommitted intellectual as he meanders through the early days of the Revolution. The latter film is, in some ways, a continuation of the former, as documentary filmmakers attempt to examine lingering machismo among dockworkers, eventually discovering that the Revolution's goals for changes in consciousness have succeeded only "up to a certain point".

Alea returned yet again to the nexus between the sexual and the political with the best-known Cuban film of the 90s, "Fresa y Chocolate/Strawberry and Chocolate" (1993). The story of the unusual friendship which develops between a naive believer in Castro's contemporary version of communism and a more experienced, gay critic of the regime was widely praised and just as widely attacked. Some found it atypically gentle for Alea and read its gay lead as a cover-up of Castro's horrifying treatment of homosexuals, while others thought it needlessly provocative in its characterizations; such divergent responses only testify to the complexity typical of Alea's tapestries. In 1994, "Strawberry and Chocolate" became the first Cuban film to receive an Oscar nomination as Best Foreign Film.

Alea has written or co-scripted all his features and, in accordance with ICAIC's collective approach to filmmaking, has served as advisor on two of the institute's most stylistically innovative films: "The Other Francisco", directed by Sergei Giral, and "De cierta manera/One Way or Another" (both 1974), directed by Sara Gomez. Alea has been less active in filmmaking in the 80s and 90s, and Juan Carlos Tabio has co-directed several of the aging master's recent films. He has, though, written a book of film theory, "Dialectica del espectador" (1982), and continued to inspire a new generation of sophisticated and politically committed artists.—Written by David Lugowski

MILESTONES:

1946: Made first amateur short films, "Un fakir" and "La caperucita roja/Little Red Riding Hood", with an 8 mm camera

1950: Collaborated with Nestor Almendros, a fellow student at the University of Havana, on another 8 mm short film, "Una confusion cotidiana/A Common Confusion"

1953: Made first non-amateur short: "El sueno de Juan Bassain/The Dream of Juan Bassin"

1956: Made first documentary short, "El Megano/ The Charcoal Worker", co-directed with Julio

Garcia Espinosa; screened only once before Batista's police force confiscated the print

1956–1959: Wrote regularly for the weekly film news magazine, *Cinerevista*

1959: Co-founded (with Santiago Alvarez) the Instituto Cubano del Arte y Industria Cinematogragicos (ICAIC); made his first film for ICAIC, the documentary "Este tierra nuestra/ This Land of Ours"

1960: Fiction feature directing debut (also writer), the docudrama "Historias de la revolucion/Stories of the Revolution"

1961: Served as war correspondent and documentarian at the Battle of Giron in the Bay of Pigs

1962: First fully fictional feature film, "Las doce sillas/The Twelve Chairs"

1966: First feature to win international acclaim, "Death of a Bureaucrat"

1968: Made his best-remembered and most acclaimed film, "Memories of Underdevelopment"

1971: First collaboration with cinematographer Mario Garcia Joya, "Una pelea cubana contra los demonios/A Cuban Fight Against the Demons"

Made no feature films; worked primarily at Cuba's Film Institute and served as an advisor to other filmmakers on their projects; later claimed the period was one of "a period of instability . . . of personal and artistic confusion"

"Memories of Underdevelopment" finally released in the United States and then later in France

1974: Wrote scenarios for two films which he did not direct, "De cierta manera/One Way or Another" by Sara Gomez, and "El Otro Francisco/The Other Francisco" by Sergio Giral

1976: Returned to feature filmmaking with "La ultima cena/The Last Supper"

1984: First collaboration with Juan Carlos Tabio, "Up to a Certain Point", directed by Alea and written by Alea, Tabio and Serafin Quinones

1985: Supplied the original idea for the film, "Se Permuta/House for Swap", a Cuban production directed by Juan Carlos Tabio

1993: First international co-production, "Strawberries and Chocolate", a Cuban-Mexican-Spanish production co-directed with Juan Carlos Tabio

BIBLIOGRAPHY:
"Dialectica del espectador" Tomas Gutierrez, Alea, 1982; film theory

Lasse Hallstrom

BORN: in Stockholm, Sweden, 06/06/1946

SOMETIMES CREDITED AS:
Lars Hallstrom

NATIONALITY: Swedish

BIOGRAPHY

A popular writer-director of comedies in his native Sweden, Lasse Hallstrom segued to a fairly successful Hollywood career in the early 1990s without abandoning his European sensibilities. Hallstrom has demonstrated an impressive flair for directing actors in general and children in particular. He is attracted to emotional family-related material but deftly avoids sentimentality. Hallstrom gained an international audience with "My Life as a Dog" (1985), an irresistibly bittersweet comedy adapted from Reidar Jonsson's autobiographical novel about the misadventures of a 12-year-old sent to live with relatives in 1950s rural Sweden. When it was released in the US in 1987, the film earned Hallstrom Oscar nominations for Best Director and Best Screenplay (which he co-wrote).

Hallstrom became a filmmaker at age ten with the 8mm ten-minute thriller "The Ghost Thief" (1956). As a high school student, he made a documentary short about his friends' efforts to form a rock band, which was subsequently broadcast on Swedish TV in 1967. After high school, Hallstrom spent ten years making short fillers for Swedish TV—usually writing, shooting and editing his own projects. He then advanced to become the director of an entire TV

program, "Shall We Dance?" (c. 1968). Hallstrom next sought training as a producer, and the ensuing popularity of his many TV projects enabled him to finally make his feature directorial debut. "A Guy and a Gal/En Kille och en Tjej" (1975) was a light romantic comedy that depicted a young couple's relationship. His next project was "ABBA: The Movie" (1977), an enjoyable concert film featuring the Swedish super group. Hallstrom's next three comedies were made under the name Lars Hallstrom and dealt with love, marriage, parenthood and divorce, themes which would continue to preoccupy his work. He also made a sequel to his debut, "Two Guys and a Gal/Tva Killar och en Tjej" (1983).

Hallstrom did not immediately head for Hollywood upon the success of "My Life as a Dog." He helmed two Swedish children's films, "The Children of Bullerby Village/Alla vi barn i Bullerby" (1986) and its sequel "More About the Children of Bullerby Village/Mer om oss barn i Bullerby" (1987), both adapted from the works of Astrid Lindgren (author of the popular "Pippi Longstocking" books).

Hallstrom made his American feature debut as the writer-director of "Once Around" (1991), an uneven family comedy-drama set in Boston, boasting an impressive ensemble including Holly Hunter, Richard Dreyfuss, Danny Aiello and Gena Rowlands. He fared better handling only directing chores on "What's Eating Gilbert Grape" (1993), a quirky, handsome, unsentimental film about an unconventional American family that included a 500-pound mother and a mentally handicapped 18-year-old boy, featuring Johnny Depp, Juliette Lewis and Leonardo DiCaprio. The film was not a box-office success. Hallstrom had slightly better luck with "Something to Talk About" (1995), a semi-feminist comedy-drama written by Callie Khouri of "Thelma and Louise" fame and starring Julia Roberts and Dennis Quaid.

After a four-year absence (during which a dream project to star his second wife Lena Olin collapsed), Hallstrom returned on much surer ground with the exquisite, if slightly sentimental, adaptation of John Irving's mammoth novel "The Cider House Rules" (1999). Working from a screenplay by the author, he crafted an old-fashioned, visually beautiful coming-of-age tale and elicited fine performances from a cast including Tobey Maguire, Charlize Theron, Michael Caine (who netted a Best Supporting Actor Oscar) and Delroy Lindo. Hallstrom received his second Academy Award nomination for directing and saw his somewhat moribund career rebound. "Chocolat" (2000), an adaptation of Joanne Harris' whimsical novel, achieved the right balance of realism and magic and proved enchanting for audiences. Essentially a morality play with a message about tolerance, "Chocolat" examined how an itinerant candy maker (Juliette Binoche) and her conflicts with the mayor (Alfred Molina) affected the lives of the residents of a small French village in the late 1950s. The genial comedy bore the stamp of its director in its warmth and unabashed sentiment tempered by humor. (It also allowed him to direct Olin in the secondary role of a troubled wife who blossoms under the guidance of Binoche's chocolatiere.) Still on a roll, Hallstrom followed with yet another film drawn from a novel, this time, "The Shipping News" (lensed 2001), adapted from Anne Proulx's Pulitzer winner.—Written by David Lugowski

MILESTONES:

Born and raised in Stockholm, Sweden

1956: At age ten, directed first short films, including a three-minute documentary about Gotland Island and the ten-minute thriller "The Ghost Thief"

1967: As a high school student, made a documentary short (about school friends forming a rock band), which was subsequently broadcast on Swedish TV in 1967

Spent about ten years making film inserts, mostly on music groups, for Swedish TV; did much of the shooting and editing

1968: Helmed his first full-length TV program, "Shall We Dance?" (date approximate)

1970: Trained as a TV producer

1972: Began shooting promotional film clips (forerunners of music videos) for the Swedish band ABBA

1975: Feature directorial debut, "A Guy and a Gal/En Kille och en Tjej"

1977: Filmed the documentary performance film, "ABBA: The Movie"

1985: Made first film to gain international recognition, "My Life as a Dog"; received a Best Director Academy Award nomination and shared a Best Adapted Screenplay nod

1988: US TV debut (director, executive producer), "The Big Five", an unsold pilot

1991: American feature debut, as writer-director of "Once Around"

1993: Helmed "What's Eating Gilbert Grape", featuring Johnny Depp and Leonardo DiCaprio

1995: Directed the modestly pleasing romantic comedy "Something to Talk About", starring Julia Roberts

1999: Helmed the feature adaptation of John Irving's novel "The Cider House Rules"; earned Best Director Academy Award nomination

2000: Directed "Chocolat", starring Johnny Depp and Juliette Binoche; wife Lena Olin also featured in cast

2001: Helmed the film adaptation of the award-winning novel "The Shipping News", starring Kevin Spacey

QUOTES:

With his second Oscar nomination for "The Cider House Rules", Hallstrom became the first director to receive nominations as Best Director for both a foreign-language picture (1987's "My Life as a Dog") and an English-language one.

"Television was my film school."—Hallstrom on his training experiences while working in Swedish TV (from the press material for "Once Around")

"Lasse has huge respect for actors. He's extremely collaborative, and he's interested in characters that are multidimensional, that you can act with and take out to an edge and yet are wholly believable. He gets uniformly spectacular performances."—producer Leslie Holleran quoted in *The New York Times*, December 3, 2000.

Curtis Hanson

BORN: in Reno, Nevada, 03/24/1945

SOMETIMES CREDITED AS:
Curtis Hanson
Curtis Lee Hanson

NATIONALITY: American

EDUCATION: dropped out of high school

AWARDS: National Board of Review Award Best Picture "L.A. Confidential" 1997; shared award; Hanson was one of the film's producers

National Board of Review Award Best Director "L.A. Confidential" 1997

New York Film Critics Circle Award Best Picture "L.A. Confidential" 1997 shared award; Hanson was one of the film's producers

New York Film Critics Circle Award Best Director "L.A. Confidential" 1997

New York Film Critics Circle Award Best Screenplay "L.A. Confidential" 1997; shared award with Brian Helgeland

Los Angeles Film Critics Association Award Best Picture "L.A. Confidential" 1997; shared award; Hanson was one of the producers

Los Angeles Film Critics Association Award Best Director "L.A. Confidential" 1997

Los Angeles Film Critics Association Award Best Screenplay "L.A. Confidential" 1997; shared with Brian Helgeland

Boston Society of Film Critics Award Best Picture "L.A. Confidential" 1997; shared award; Hanson was one of the producers

Boston Society of Film Critics Award Best Director "L.A. Confidential" 1997

Boston Society of Film Critics Award Best Screenplay "L.A. Confidential" 1997; shared award with Brian Helgeland

Florida Film Critics Circle Award Best Director "L.A. Confidential" 1997

Florida Film Critics Circle Award Best Screenplay "L.A. Confidential" 1997; shared with Brian Helgeland

Broadcast Film Critics Association Award Best Picture "L.A. Confidential" 1997; shared award

Broadcast Film Critics Association Award Best Adapted Screenplay "L.A. Confidential" 1997; shared award with Brian Helgeland

Society of Texas Film Critics Award Best Adapted Screenplay "L.A. Confidential" 1997; shared award with Brian Helgeland

National Society of Film Critics Award Best Picture "L.A. Confidential" 1997; shared award

National Society of Film Critics Award Best Director "L.A. Confidential" 1997

National Society of Film Critics Award Best Screenplay "L.A. Confidential" 1997; shared award with Brian Helgeland

Film Critics Circle of Australia Award Best Foreign English-Language Film "L.A. Confidential" 1997; shared award

Writers Guild of America Award Best Screenplay Based on Material Previously Produced or Published "L.A. Confidential" 1998; shared award with Brian Helgeland

Golden Satellite Best Motion Picture Screenplay (Adaptation) "L.A. Confidential" 1997; shared award with Brian Helgeland

Chigago Film Critics Award Best Picture "L.A. Confidential" 1997; shared award

Chigago Film Critics Award Best Director "L.A. Confidential" 1997

Chigago Film Critics Award Best Screenplay "L.A. Confidential" 1997; shared with Brian Helgeland

Oscar Best Screenplay Based in Material Previously Produced or Published "L.A. Confidential" 1997; shared award with Brian Helgeland

Australian Film Institute Award Best Foreign Film "L.A. Confidential" 1998

BIOGRAPHY

A former photographer, freelance writer of Hollywood-themed articles and editor of *Cinema* magazine, Curtis Hanson honed his skills in the psychological thriller genre by writing screenplays for low-budget suspensers before establishing himself as a director of high profile thrillers. He debuted as a co-writer on AIP's "The Dunwich Horror" (1970), executive produced by Roger Corman. Hanson became a writer-director with the genuinely unsettling Tab Hunter cult flick "The Arousers/Sweet Kill" (1971, released 1973) and segued to producing as the associate producer (and screenwriter) of "The Silent Partner", a 1978 Canadian flick starring Elliot Gould and Christopher Plummer. With maverick director Samuel Fuller, Hanson also co-wrote the screenplay of the long-unreleased—due to undeserved charges of racism (and consequently overrated in some quarters)—melodrama, "White Dog" (filmed 1982, first theatrical release 1991). He also contributed to the script for the atypical Disney nature film, "Never Cry Wolf" (1983).

After trying his hand producing and/or helming a kids' adventure ("The Little Dragons" 1980) and a teen sex comedy ("Losin' It" 1983, with a young Tom Cruise), Hanson came into his own as a suspense specialist in the late 1980s and early 90s. He wrote and directed "The Bedroom Window" (1989), a surprisingly good Hitchcock homage, and followed up by directing the slick, "Strangers on a Train"-like psychological suspense film "Bad Influence" (1990), starring Rob Lowe and James Spader. Hanson finally enjoyed a runaway box-office success with "The Hand That Rocks the Cradle" (1992), a compelling, expertly acted and cannily directed nanny-from-hell thriller. He advanced to the genre A-list with "The River Wild" (1994), a tense adventure set in the great outdoors that starred Meryl Streep in her action movie debut and featured a top-notch supporting cast including Kevin Bacon and David Strathairn.

Hanson used his new-found clout in Hollywood to get the tricky "L.A. Confidential" (1997) made, its 80 speaking parts and 45 locations demanding the budget of a studio movie. The result was an impeccably crafted, densely plotted, fast-paced tale of police corruption in the City of Angels (c. 1950s) and the best American film noir since Roman Polanski's "Chinatown" (1974). Along with co-writer Brian Helgeland, Hanson faithfully captured the L.A. of James Ellroy's pulp novel, giving great attention to period detail in the background while shooting a contemporary movie focused on the characters and their emotions. Photographed primarily in a naturalistic style that emphasized "practical" lighting whenever possible, "L.A. Confidential" deviated momentarily from its dark palette for some memorable fantasy images contrasting blue with brilliant pink and orange light before reverting to the darkness, carried to powerful extreme in the film's climactic scene. Although it featured relative unknowns Russell Crowe and Guy Pearce, along with the more familiar

Kim Basinger, Danny DeVito and Kevin Spacey, the real star was Los Angeles, growing up before our very eyes.

Hanson's masterful work on "L.A. Confidential" elevated him out of conventional, journeyman thriller and onto Hollywood's A-list of directors-the film also earned him an Oscar nomination, snared a supporting actress trophy for Basinger and made Russell Crowe a major movie star. Rather than plunge into a whirlwind of new commitments, Hanson instead continued to nurture thoughtful, literate material. His next effort was "Wonder Boys" (2000), a film based on author Michael Chabon's acclaimed novel about a college professor and author (Michael Douglas), who has been unable to finish a massive follow-up to his one highly-praised novel, and his quirky relationship with a young, troubled student (Tobey Maguire). Although the story has some wobbly moments and sends some mixed messages, Hanson shot it with flair, style and sensitivity, wresting top-notch performances from Douglas, Maguire and supporting players Robert Downey, Jr., Katie Holmes and Frances McDormand. Hanson next turned his skilled hand a seemingly much more unconventional film: "8 Mile" (2002), a street-level drama played out in the hip-hop world of urban Detroit, starring and loosely based on the life of Grammy-winning rapper Marshall Mathers III, aka Eminem. Adopting a raw, gritty documentary filmmaking style, Hanson was able to garner a compelling, intense from Eminem (in his first on-screen role), as well as strong work from Brittany Murphy, Mekhi Pfifer and his "L.A. Confidential" star Basinger.

MILESTONES:

Grew up in Reseda, California in the San Fernando Valley

Dropped out of high school

Became a photographer and freelance writer of articles about Hollywood

Edited *Cinema* magazine

Interviewed various legendary Hollywood figures including John Ford, Vincente Minnelli, Dalton Trumbo, and William Wellman

Befriended by writer-director-actor John Cassavetes, who invited Hanson to his garage to watch him edit his films

1970: As Curtis Lee Hanson, co-scripted first feature (with Henry Rosenbaum and Ronald Silkosky), "The Dunwich Horror", an AIP thriller executive produced by Roger Corman

1973: Directorial debut, "The Arousers/Sweet Kill" (also wrote screenplay), starring Tab Hunter

1978: Made producing debut as associate producer on "The Silent Partner" (also screenwriter)

1983: Helmed "Losin' It", starring Tom Cruise

1986: TV debut as writer-director of "The Children of Times Square", an ABC TV-movie about a teen runaway

1989: Wrote and directed the surprisingly good homage to Hitchcock, "The Bedroom Window"

1990: Directed "Bad Influence", starring Rob Lowe and James Spader

1992: Helmed the surprise hit thriller, "The Hand That Rocks the Cradle"

1994: Stock soared with commercial success of "The River Wild", starring Meryl Streep

1997: Scored major critical success for directing "L.A. Confidential" (also co-produced and co-wrote with Brian Helgeland); received Oscar nominations for Best Picture, Best Director; won award for Best Adapted Screenplay

2000: Helmed the screen adaptation of Michael Chabon's novel "Wonder Boys", starring Michael Douglas

2002: Directed and produced "8 Mile," a film starring rapper Eminem loosely based on the singer's life

AFFILIATION: Chair, UCLA Film and Television Archives (1999–)

Member, Board of Governors, Academy of Motion Picture Arts and Sciences

QUOTES:

When Hanson got the opportunity to direct his script of "The Bedroom Window", he had to first secure membership in the Directors Guild of America. To this end, he sought the endorsement of three DGA members "whom I admired as filmmakers and as men," he says. His signatories were John Cassavetes, Don Siegel and Sam Fuller.

"They were three directors whose movies and careers meant a lot to me. I felt that the three of them—Cassavetes, the maverick independent; Don Siegel, the consummate studio director; and Sam Fuller, who worked in both worlds—were always able to make original, personal movies," Hanson says. "I hoped that a little of their good fortune would rub off on me."—From the press kit for "The Hand That Rocks the Cradle."

"One of my great joys is that Elliot Gould, with whom I eventually became close, took 'The Silent Partner' and screened it for Hitchcock. The prick didn't invite me, I might add. But he called me immediately afterward saying, 'Hitch loved the movie!' "—Curtis Hanson quoted in *Venice*, September 1997.

"Rather than being a director for hire as I have been on most of my films, 'L.A. Confidential' is that one project where I've been able to cash in the chips I've earned from being lucky enough to have had a couple of financially successful films and saying, 'Okay, now this is the film that I want to make.' It's my most personal movie. Whether it achieves any popular acceptance or not is less important to me. That's not why I made it."—Hanson in *Venice*, September 1997.

Tsui Hark

BORN: in Canton, China, 1951

SOMETIMES CREDITED AS:
Chui Hak
Xu Ke

NATIONALITY: Chinese

EDUCATION: Southern Methodist University, Dallas, Texas; transferred to University of Texas
    University of Texas at Austin, Austin, Texas film, 1972–74

AWARDS: Hong Kong Film Award Best Picture "A Better Tomorrow" 1986; shared award with John Woo
    Hong Kong Film Award Best Director "Once Upon a Time in China" 1991

BIOGRAPHY

Leading figure of the Hong Kong film scene and head of his own production company,

Film Workshop. Hark specializes in kaleidoscopic dramas characterized by frenzied action and a decidedly tongue-in-cheek tone. He is best known in the USA for his complex, breathlessly witty and exciting "Peking Opera Blues" (1986).

COMPANION:
wife: Nansun Shi. Co-founded Film Workshop

MILESTONES:
Born in China
Raised in the Chinese section of Saigon, Vietnam
Made first film at age 10
Sent to Hong Kong to study at age 14
Moved to the USA to attend college in Texas
1974: Moved to NYC; worked with Christine Choy on "From Spikes to Spindles"
1977: Upon return to Hong Kong joined Hong Kong Television Broadcasts Ltd. as director and producer

1979: Feature directing debut (also from story), "The Butterfly Murders"

1982: Made cameo appearance in "Aces to Go Places"

1983: Became established in Hong Kong with "Zu: Warriors from the Magic Mountain"

1983: Acted in and directed "All the Wrong Spies"

1984: Co-formed, with wife Nansun Shi, Film Workshop production company

1987: Produced "A Chinese Ghost Story"

1990: Produced and directed "Swordsman", the first in a series of features

1990: Directed "Once Upon a Time in China", the first in a series of films starring Jet Li

1997: Directed first American feature, "Double Team", starring Jean-Claude Van Damme

1998: Reteamed with Van Damme for "Knock Off"

Renny Harlin

BORN: Renny Lauri Mauritz Harjola Harlin in Riihimaki, Finland, 03/15/1958

NATIONALITY: Finnish

EDUCATION: University of Helsiniki Helsinki, Finland film enrolled in Visual Communications Department

AWARD: Finish Film Board Award Best Short Subject "Hold On" 1982

BIOGRAPHY

A producer and action movie director of the 1990s, Renny Harlin began his career making shorts and documentaries in his native Finland. His "Hold On" won the Finish Film Board Award as Best Short Subject of 1982, and when he moved to the USA in the mid-80s, he crafted "Born American" (1986), bankrolling the first 20 minutes with his own money before acquiring the financing to complete it. Banned in Finland, this rough-and-tumble action movie received little play in the States but attracted the attention of Irwin Yablans who enlisted Harlan to direct "Prison" (1987), a project ideally suited to someone whose father had been a prison doctor. Distribution headaches kept this movie from a wider audience but earned Harlan the chance to direct "Nightmare on Elm Street 4": The Dream Master (1988).

Harlin's "Nightmare" cost a scant $6.5 million and brought in nearly $50 million, prompting eager producers to besiege him in the hope he could wring even more brilliance out of a larger budget. Though one of his biggest bombs followed (1990's decidedly unpopular "The Adventures of Ford Fairlane" starring the obnoxious Andrew "Dice" Clay), Harlan had no time to sulk, immediately plunging ahead on the incredibly successful sequel "Die Hard 2" (1990). Harlin debuted as a producer with the gentle "Rambling Rose" (1991) starring his then-love interest Laura Dern, Diane Ladd and Robert Duvall. This critically acclaimed small film was the first feature from Harlin's production company, Midnight Sun Pictures. He returned to actioners with the high-budget Sylvester Stallone vehicle "Cliffhanger" (1993).

Harlin formed Forge Productions (aka The Forge) with his wife Geena Davis, but to date the efforts of this production company have been lackluster. "Speechless" (1994), which Harlin produced but did not direct, was the best of the fare. A cheerful comedy poking fun at politics and the news media, it depended on the strength of leads Michael Keaton and Davis to overcome the film's unevenness. Nothing could save the disastrous pirate pic "Cutthroat Island" (1995), short of Errol Flynn returning from the dead (and even he would have needed something more than the special effects and stunts to spare). The ridiculous comic-book thriller "The Long Kiss Goodnight" (1996) wasn't much better, and the once happy couple parted in 1997.

COMPANIONS:

Laura Dern, Actor; Harlin produced "Rambling Rose" (1991)

wife: Geena Davis. Actor; married September 18, 1993; separated amicably in April 1997; Davis filed for divorce in August 1997; finalized in 1998

MILESTONES:

Published his own magazine at age nine

Founded production company which made shorts and documentaries at age 20

Completed more than 100 comercials, 10 TV documentaries and many short films by age 23

1982: Made documentary short, "Hold On"

1985: Moved to USA (date approximate)

1986: Privately funded first 20 minutes of his debut feature "Born American" before finding a company to back its completion

1988: Breakthrough directing vehicle, "Nightmare on Elm Street 4: The Dream Master"

Formed production company Midnight Sun Pictures

1990: Directed first big-budget smash "Die Hard 2"

1991: First film as a producer, "Rambling Rose"; directed by Martha Coolidge

1994: Formed Forge Productions with Geena Davis

1995: Helmed "Cutthroat Island", a box-office bomb starring Geena Davis

1996: Directed Davis and Samuel L Jackson in "The Long Kiss Goodnight", which generated little excitement among critics or audiences

2001: Helmed the race car-themed film "Driven"

Mary Harron

BORN: in Canada, 1952

NATIONALITY: Canadian

CITIZENSHIP: United Kingdom

EDUCATION: Oxford University, Oxford, England, English; edited ISIS magazine

BIOGRAPHY

A former reporter of the punk-rock scene whose entree to filmmaking came via British TV documentaries, Mary Harron made the jump to features with the much-awaited "I Shot Andy Warhol" (1996), the story of Valerie Solanas, who in 1968 shot and wounded the art-world legend. A Canadian raised in London, Harron moved to New York in 1976, delighted to leave the stuffiness of her Oxford education behind to work for an alternative film company running its kitchen. She began writing for Legs McNeil's *Punk* magazine and in 1977 penned a lengthy piece for *Village Voice* that explained and explored the London punk scene, introducing what had been a somewhat underground movement to mainstream America. Seemingly a constant presence on pop culture's cutting edge throughout her career, Harron, who participated in and observed the Studio 54 era, the last chapter of the sexual revolution before drugs fell out of favor and AIDS and other STDs prompted more circumspect behavior, remained fascinated by the Warhol "Factory" scene of the late 60s that had so intrigued her as a teenager.

Back in London working as a researcher for the prestigious English arts documentary program "The South Bank Show", Harron was walking to work one day when she passed a used bookstore and found a copy of the *Scum Manifesto* written by Solanas, a lesbian feminist on the fringes of the Warhol circle. Though she began toying with the idea of a documentary on Solanas, she took no immediate action. After hosting "UK Late" (1990), a smart-set talk show, she returned to New York in 1991 to produce segments of "Edge", a PBS documentary series, for awhile sharing an apartment with a pre-drag RuPaul. She showed her proposal for the Solanas documentary to producers Christine Vachon and Tom Kalin, who encouraged her to make a dramatic feature film instead. Eventually, American Playhouse International financed "I Shot Andy Warhol", which attempted to capture the spirit of the artist at his most creative, before his celebrity became greater than his work. Lili Taylor delivered a brilliant portrayal as the delusional Solanas, supported by Stephen Dorff as Candy Darling, Tahnee Welch as Viva and Jared Harris as Warhol. Convincing in its period detail, it debuted at the 1996 Sundance Film Festival and enjoyed great critical success after its release.

Invited by producer Edward Pressman to have a go at adapting Bret Easton Ellis' "American Psycho" (2000), Harron approached the material as a black comedy, believing that the excessive violence in the incendiary novel had blinded people to its satiric look at the 80s and the decadent Wall Street culture which dominated New York City. With Harron attached as director and Christian Bale set to star, "American Psycho" found a home at Lions Gate Films, but when a hot-from-"Titanic" Leonardo DiCaprio expressed interest, she dropped off the project she had nurtured to that point. DiCaprio's case of cold feet led to her and Bale's return. The story of vacuous broker Patrick Bateman, the personification of the yuppie excess who frequently ends his nights of expensive dining, drinking and cocaine snorting with cold-hearted sexual encounters and vicious murders was slapped with an NC-17 rating, reportedly over a sex scene involving Bateman and two prostitutes. "American Psycho" debuted at the Sundance Boasting a supporting cast including Willem Dafoe (the detective pursuing him), Reese Witherspoon (a girlfriend), Jared Leto (his arch rival) and Chloe Sevigny (his secretary) opened to mixed reviews, with most critics praising the acting but questioning the need for the film to be made.

COMPANIONS:

Tony Blair. Politician, British Labour Prime Minister; dated in the 1970s while both were attending Oxford

husband: John Walsh. Producer

MILESTONES:

Grew up in central London

1976: Moved to the East Village in NYC; began writing for *Punk* Magazine; first American journalist to interview The Sex Pistols

1977: Wrote first in-depth article about English punk in the American press for *Village Voice*

Returned to London; worked for five years as a researcher with four of those years doing in-depth research for "The South Bank Show"; began directing segments for TV magazine shows (i.e., "The Late Show")

1990: Hosted "UK Late", a British TV talk show

1991–1992: Returned to New York as producer of PBS' "Edge", a monthly magazine program exploring American pop culture; served as segment producer for "Art Crisis" and "Oliver Stone"; roomed with a pre-drag queen RuPaul

1996: Co-wrote and directed first feature, "I Shot Andy Warhol"; shunned by Warhol pal Lou Reed, leader of the Velvet Undergound, drew solace from the fact that she did have Warhol friends on board, including the Undeground's John Cale who provided the original score

1998: Primetime episodic debut as director, the "Sins of the Fathers" episode of NBC's "Homicide: Life on the Street" (aired in

January); show executive produced by Barry Levinson and Tom Fontana

1998: Helmed "Animal Farm" episode of HBO's "Oz" (aired in August), executive produced by Levinson and Fontana

2000: Co-scripted and helmed the controversial "American Psycho", starring Christian Bale; while shooting in Toronto (substituting for NYC), the film ran into protests from a victim's rights advocacy group led by the mother of one of the two victims of Paul Bernardo and his wife, who allegedly drew inspiration for their atrocities from the Bret Ellis Easton source material; slapped with an NC-17 rating over a sex scene between Bale's character and two women; premiered at the Sundance Film Festival

QUOTES:

"I don't mock my rock 'n roll days, but I realized that a rock writer's career doesn't change much after the age of 22. And I shouldn't be doing the same thing at 40 that I was doing at 22. It took me awhile to get into movies, but I realized it was what I always wanted to do."—Mary Harron in *New York*, February 5, 1996.

"The thing I found difficult is that people here don't understand television experience [in Britain]. There is no independent film, everyone goes to work for English TV.

"People are very patronizing here if you have worked in television. There is a lot of television comedy here, like Roseanne's show, that I admire. And there is also a lot of good writing in crime shows like 'Homicide'. But no one takes television seriously. In terms of survival I would have no problem doing television. But no one understands what I did before. They were short, very stylized films. For example, I did a half-hour film about boredom for Channel Four."—Harron talking with Rose Troche in *Filmmaker*, 1997.

"I had been doing quite well as a journalist during the punk explosion in the late 70s. I did an article anbout the Velvet Underground, the band most closely associated with Warhol's Factory, for *New Musical Express*. And, I also wrote an article about Warhol's influence on pop culture for *Melody Maker*. I actually got to interview Warhol for that piece, as well as peopel in his circle. So, by the time I set out to write my script, I felt pretty comfortable that I knew my story."—Harron quoted in *DGA Magazine*, January 1999.

On "American Psycho" getting slapped with a NC-17 rating for its depiction of the film's star Christian Bale in a three-way sexual encounter with two prostitutes: "The scene is not about sex, but about sex as a transaction, so we made it deliberately banal and distant. That Bateman [Bale's character] is looking at himself in the mirror and not at his partners seems to be an issue for the MPAA, but his expression sums up his frighteningly detatched relationship to the world around him. To me it's one of the most significant scenes in the film and to cut it would cause serious damamge."—From Harron statement, quoted in part by Charles Lyons in *Daily Variety*, January 18, 2000.

Hal Hartley

BORN: Hal Hartley, Jr. in Lindenhurst, New York, 11/03/1959

SOMETIMES CREDITED AS:
Ned Rifle

NATIONALITY: American

EDUCATION: Massachusetts College of Art, Boston, Massachusetts, 1978–79

State University of New York, Purchase, Purchase, New York, film, 1980–84; began reading movie scripts while a student

AWARDS: Sundance Film Festival Waldo Salt

Screenwriting Award "Trust" 1991 tied with Joseph Vasquez for "Hanging with the Homeboys"

Houston International Film Festival Grand Prize Award "Trust" 1991

Cannes Film Festival Screenplay Award "Henry Fool" 1998

BIOGRAPHY

Hal Hartley is a quirky but genuine talent who has made his mark as an award-winning independent filmmaker. His films are modestly scaled, seriocomic portraits of chance encounters between disparate outsiders—characters who typically engage in elliptical exchanges, debating everything from philosophical issues to the workings of internal combustion engines, but don't always learn anything from their discourses or their adventures. Hartley's deft, offbeat comedy is highlighted by circuitous, layered bantering, with punchlines coming late, if at all. The visual correlatives to this non sequitur-laden wit have ranged from a shot of a nun wrestling a policeman to the ground to a camera pan which reveals heavy metal "soundtrack" music to be emanating from the electric guitar of a minor character. Hartley's deadpan, episodic narrative style would seem to betray the influence of Jean-Luc Godard, though his camera is less experimental, his comedy more assimilable and his politics less overt.

Hartley's gallery of indecisive but intelligent characters includes an ex-convict who sets the town talking about what his crime might have been ("The Unbelievable Truth" 1989); a literature professor who spends most of a semester on one paragraph of Dostoyevsky (the PBS project "Surviving Desire" 1992); a manic, bitter electronics whiz who carries a hand-grenade in his pocket ("Trust" 1990); two very different brothers who search for their long-missing radical father ("Simple Men" 1992); and an amnesiac who enlists the aid of a former nun to help him discover his past ("Amateur" 1994).

Some critics have accused the director of making the same film again and again. With "Flirt" (1995), he did just that, depicting three love stories (including one homosexual) utilizing the same dialogue and structure. Moving from New York to Berlin to Tokyo, Hartley examines the essence of love refracted through different characters with ultimately the same results. A flirtatious lover brings about the destruction of his or her own beauty. "Henry Fool" (1997) has been lauded as his best film to date, reiterating his themes of reinvention and the serendipitous experiences that reconstitute relationships.—Written by David Lugowski

MILESTONES:

Raised in Lindenhurst, Long Island, NY

After his mother's death, went to live with various relatives

Left art school in Boston; made eight Super-8 films before enrolling in the film department at SUNY, Purchase

1985: Completed his student thesis film, "Kid"

Began freelancing on commercials and feature films

1989: Made feature directing, screenwriting, producing and editing debut with "The Unbelievable Truth"

1991: Short films, the 10-minute "Ambition" and the 17-minute "Theory of Achievement", broadcast on PBS' "Alive From Off Center"

1992: "Surviving Desire", his first work made expressly for TV, broadcast on "American Playhouse" on PBS

1993: Made short film "Flirt"; later incorporated into the 1995 feature of the same title

1994: Wrote and directed "Amateur"

1995: Helmed the tripartite "Flirt", which incorporated the 1993 short of the same name

1997: Garnered critical acclaim for "Henry Fool"; screened at Cannes where it won the screenplay award

1999: Made the short "The Book of Life"

2000: Directed and wrote and the short "Kimono"

2001: Debut as playwright with "Soon", produced in Los Angeles

2002: Wrote and directed "No Such Thing", an adaptation of "Beauty and the Beast"

AFFILIATION: Roman Catholic

QUOTES:

Hartley has used the pseudonym of Ned Rifle when he composes the scores for his films. Ned Rifle was the name of the hero of his first film "Kid."

"I start the whole creative process with a lot of questions and I usually just wind up with a lot of questions. The questioning is important."—Hal Hartley (*The New York Times*, September 6, 1991).

"The small circle of truly significant American film makers . . . may be gearing up to admit some new members. One candidate is Gus Van Sant. . . . Another is Hal Hartley. . . . Hartley taps into a universe ignored by a Hollywood obsessed with precocious juveniles and expensive extravaganzas. His loners and outsiders are passionate about the idea of love and desire and survival, even while knowing they might very well end up looking ridiculous."—John J. O'Connor (*New York Times*, January 22, 1992).

"Love stories aren't about boys and girls, they are about pain and struggle and fear."—Hartley in *The New York Times Magazine*, August 4, 1996.

"I have found that all incompetence comes from not paying attention, which comes from people doing something that they don't want to do. And doing what you don't want to do means either you have no choice, or you don't think that the moments of your life are worth fighting for."—to *The New York Times Magazine*, August 4, 1996.

Howard Hawks

BORN: Howard Winchester Hawks in Goshen, Indiana, 05/30/1896

DEATH: in Palm Springs, California, 12/26/1977

NATIONALITY: American

EDUCATION: Phillips Exeter Academy, Exeter, New Hampshire

Pasadena High School, Pasadena, California; graduated

Cornell University, Ithaca, New York, mechanical engineering

AWARD: Honorary Oscar 1974 for "a master American filmmaker whose creative efforts hold a distinguished place in world cinema"

BIOGRAPHY

Widely acknowledged as one of the greatest American filmmakers, Hawks pursued a career virtually spanning the Hollywood studio era. In the summers of 1916 and 1917 he had his first experiences with the movies, working in the props department of Famous Players-Lasky during his college vacations. After serving in the armed forces during WWI, Hawks worked as a racecar driver, aviator, and a designer in an aircraft factory—experiences that would later inform both his choice of subjects and his style as a director. He independently produced several films for director Allan Dwan and took a job with the script department of Famous Players-Lasky, where he worked, mostly uncredited, on the scripts of dozens of movies. (He also worked uncredited on the screenplays of all the films he directed.) Hawks wrote his first screenplay, "Tiger Love", in 1924 and directed his first film, "The Road to Glory", in 1925.

Although he made eight films during the silent era (including the exotic melodrama "Fazil" 1928 and the dated but amusing marital farce "Fig Leaves" 1926, which prefigures many of Hawks's later comedies), it was with the coming of sound that Hawks really hit his stride. He used sound expressively, his characters frequently delivering their lines at an unnaturally rapid pace. Indeed, Hawks was one of the few Hollywood directors to employ overlapping sound; as a result, dialogue in many of his films is delivered with the rhythm of machine-gun fire. These staccato bursts of speech reveal a fascination with the American language (made explicit in "Ball of Fire" 1941, with its conflict between Barbara Stanwyck's street slang and Gary Cooper's educated diction) and sustain the breakneck tempo of his comedies (perhaps best exemplified by Cary Grant's and Rosalind Russell's performances in "His Girl Friday" 1940).

Hawks worked well with actors, preferring to let his camera dwell on them rather than to impose his presence through visual style. Katharine Hepburn, Jane Russell and Ann Sheridan gave some of their best performances in Hawks comedies, and Lauren Bacall and Paula Prentiss established their careers under his direction. Cary Grant and John Wayne each enjoyed five of their best roles in Hawks films, with Wayne giving a great performance as the aging yet stubborn rancher Tom Dunson in "Red River" (1948). Hawks once defined a good director as "someone who doesn't annoy you." Consequently, his camerawork is generally more functional than florid. (The repeated motif of the cross in the early "Scarface" (1930, released 1932) is an example of the kind of editorial device that Hawks would soon abandon.) He preferred to position his camera at eye level, where it would best capture the crucial bits of physical business performed by his actors. In Hawks' movies, gestures—as in the way people roll, light and pass cigarettes—become important signifiers of character. According to Andrew Sarris, few other filmmakers have explored the implications of gesture as fully as Hawks. Similarly, with the

exception of the labyrinthine whodunit "The Big Sleep" (1946), the narrative structure of Hawks' films is relatively straightforward. It has often been remarked that in all of his features, not once is there a flashback.

Hawks worked in virtually every genre. He made gangster films ("The Criminal Code" 1930, "Scarface"), war films ("The Dawn Patrol" 1930, "Air Force" 1943), westerns ("Red River", "Rio Bravo" 1959), films noir ("The Big Sleep"), musicals ("Gentlemen Prefer Blondes" 1953), epics ("Land of the Pharaohs" 1955), and science fiction films ("The Thing" 1951, which he produced and, uncredited, partly directed). He is well known for both his sprawling action films ("The Crowd Roars" 1932, "Only Angels Have Wings" 1939) and for his screwball comedies ("Bringing Up Baby" 1938, "Monkey Business" 1952), a genre which some claim begins with his "Twentieth Century" (1934).

Across this generic range, Hawks consistently examined the nature and responsibilities of professionalism—defined as a cluster of values that includes honor, self-esteem and an unswerving devotion to getting a job done in the face of adversity. Hawks's view of such "masculine" professionalism is similar to the idea of "grace under pressure" explored in fiction by his close friend, Ernest Hemingway. (Hawks's memorable "To Have and Have Not" 1944 is, not coincidentally, an adaptation of the Hemingway novel of the same name.) Frequently in Hawks's films, a group of men are isolated from civilization, both physically and spiritually, and must fight against both nature and themselves to achieve their goal. In "Only Angels Have Wings", the men fly mail planes in and out of the Andes; in "Air Force" they work as a unit on a B-17 bomber; in "Red River" the cowhands attempt to drive cattle along the Chisholm Trail; in "The Thing" the soldiers destroy a hostile alien in their isolated post at the North Pole. Removed from civilization, the group defines itself existentially, its purpose only to survive and to succeed. In most of these films conflict arises when a woman—embodying an emotional quality that threatens the stoic nature of Hawksian professionalism—intervenes; inevitably, she must be won over to the masculine point of view.

Hawks' movies would be of minimal interest if their vision were limited to the narrow notions of masculine professionalism offered in the action films. However, as several critics have observed, the moral thrust of the action films is inverted in the comedies, which offer a "feminine" counterweight to their celebration of professionalism. As phrased in Robin Wood's influential study of Hawks, the "Self-Respect and Responsibility" of the action films is undermined by the "Lure of Irresponsibility" in the comedies. In these movies, the female characters are depicted as representing a joyous release and freedom from the constricting and dull responsibilities of professional life. Here, such values as warmth, openness and a sense of humor are celebrated. Perhaps the clearest expression of this alternative view is the end of "Bringing Up Baby", in which Katharine Hepburn's uninhibited, madcap nature causes the ossified world view of paleontologist Cary Grant—symbolized by his reconstructed dinosaur skeleton—to collapse.

This relationship between the comedies and the action films make Hawks one of the most interesting of directors from the perspective of classical auteurism. The meaning of any of the films individually is enhanced by the knowledge of alternatives offered elsewhere in his work. It is no coincidence that in the first issue of "Movie", the influential auteurist journal from Great Britain, dated May 1962, only Hawks and Alfred Hitchcock were honored with the designation of "Great" directors. The significance of Hawks's films is indeed greater, more complex, than their individual meanings. Critical opinion does remain divided: for some, Hawks's films express a male adolescent vision of escape from relationships and responsibility that, as Leslie Fiedler and D.H.

Lawrence have shown, is so pronounced in classic American fiction; for others, his work explores the cultural neurosis that gives rise to the excesses of machismo. While issues of gender, sexual difference and sexual politics continue to dominate cultural criticism, Hawks's work will remain central.

MILESTONES:

1906: Moved to California with family

1917: Began career as prop boy for Famous Players-Lasky

1917: Joined US Army Air Corps as flying instructor

1922: First short film as director and screenwriter (self-financed)

1923: First feature film as producer and writer (story only), "Quicksands"

1924–1926: Ran story department for Famous Players

1926: Moved to Fox, made feature film directing debut with "The Road to Glory"

1930: First sound film, "The Dawn Patrol"

1938: Made first of five films with Cary Grant, "Bringing Up Baby"

1943: Produced first film which he did not direct, the war film "Corvette K-225", directed by Richard Rosson

1948: Made first of five films with John Wayne, "Red River"

1952: Made last of five films with Cary Grant, "Monkey Business"

1970: Directed last film, "Rio Lobo" (also his last film with John Wayne)

BIBLIOGRAPHY:

"Focus on Howard Hawks" Joseph McBride, 1972, Prentice-Hall; critical essays and discussion of Hawks' films

"Howard Hawks: American Artist" Jim Hillier and Peter Wollen, editors, 1997, BFI

"Howard Hawks: The Grey Fox of Hollywood" Todd McCarthy, 1997, Grove Press

BORN: Todd A. Haynes in Encino, California, 01/02/1961

NATIONALITY: American

EDUCATION: Oakwood School California an alternate high school

Simon's Rock of Bard College Great Barrington, Massachusetts

Brown University, Providence, Rhode Island, semiotics, art and film, BA, 1985; attended with Christine Vachon and Barry Ellsworth; graduated with honors

AWARDS: US Film Festival Best Experimental Short "Superstar: The Karen Carpenter Story" 1988

Sundance Film Festival Grand Jury Prize (Dramatic) "Poison" 1991

Cannes Film Festival Artistic Contribution Award "Velvet Goldmine" 1998

New York Film Critics Circle's Awards Best Director "Far From Heaven" 2002

Online Film Critics Society Award Best Original Screenplay "Far From Heaven" 2002

Chicago Film Critics Awards Best Director "Far From Heaven " 2002

Independent Spirit Awards Best Director "Far From Heaven" 2003

Stephen F. Kolzak Award (GLAAD) 2003

BIOGRAPHY

Openly gay, experimental filmmaker Todd Haynes burst upon the scene two years after his graduation from Brown University with his now-infamous 43-minute cult treasure "Superstar: The Karen Carpenter Story" (1987). Seizing upon the inspired gimmick of using Barbie and Ken dolls to sympathetically recount the story of the pop star's death from anorexia, he spent months making miniature dishes, chairs, costumes, Kleenex and Ex-Lax boxes, and Carpenters' records to create the film's intricate, doll-size mise-en-scene. The result was both audacious and accomplished as the dolls seemingly ceased to be dolls leaving the audience weeping for the tragic singer. Unfortunately, Richard Carpenter's enmity for the film (which made him look like a selfish jerk) led to the serving of a "cease and desist" order in 1989 (Haynes had never procured the rights to the Carpenters' music that plays throughout), and despite the director's offer "to only show the film in clinics and schools, with all money going to the Karen Carpenter memorial fund for anorexia research," "Superstar" remains buried, one of the few films in modern America that cannot be seen by the general public.

Haynes' award-winning first feature, "Poison" (1990), intercuts a triptych of stylistically divergent episodes, each set in a world "dying of panicky fright." Shot in the talking-head manner of TV newsmagazines, "Hero" reconstructs the story of a patricide; in "Horror", a parody of 50s B sci-fi flicks, a repressed medical worker isolates a liquid version of the human sex drive which transforms him into a pathetic, pus-oozing ghoul; and "Homo", inspired by the prison writings of Jean Genet, recalls Werner Fassbinder's unrestrainedly gay "Querelle" with its alternating tones of rosy passion and steel-blue brutality. Steeped in obsession, violence and rape, it was not for the faint of heart, prompting walkouts at its 1991 Sundance Film Festival screening and cries of outrage from right-wing critics. Partly funded by a $25,000 NEA post-production grant, "Poison" became a rallying point for both sides in the debate then raging about what constituted "appropriate" use of NEA moneys. Pilloried by the American Family Association as government-sponsored homoerotic filth,

"Poison" established Haynes elsewhere as a socially conscious artist for the AIDS era, despite never addressing the disease directly.

Haynes' return to the short form for the 27-minute comedy-drama "Dottie Gets Spanked" (1993) also marked his first foray into TV with Independent Television Services (ITVS) providing the funding. Airing as part of PBS' "TV Families" in November 1994, the film follows a six-year-old boy's obsession with a Lucille Ball–like TV star and the hostile reaction it engenders in his classmates and his father. When protagonist Steven wins a trip to the set of his Queen of Comedy's show, the filming of an episode in which Dottie gets spanked by an angry husband unleashes a torrent of visual and emotional complications. His already rich fantasy and dream life runs amok with cross-dressing body doubles, mustachioed Dotties and spankings galore. Reviewing its TV debut in the *Village Voice*, Amy Taubman called the short, "an homage to Freud's marvelously intricate essay on infantile sexual development. Like Freud, Haynes understands that sexuality, in its object choices and sadomasochism, is both ambivalent and overdetermined."

The inconclusive final image of "Dottie Gets Spanked" was the precursor of the ambivalence of Haynes' next feature "Safe" (1995). An unconventional, restrained study of a woman (Julianne Moore) suffering from an environmental illness, "Safe" functioned as both a metaphor for the AIDS epidemic as well as for the general malaise of late 20th-century life without giving a concrete clue what the filmmaker was really thinking. When Moore's Carol seeks out an alternative lifestyle as a cure, Haynes presents the New Age retreat she opts for as equally life-denying as the banal suburban existence at the root of her illness. Her character clearly fits the outline of the director's earlier social victims—bombarded by her environment, mold-poured into family constructions and paddled by a series of patriarchs—the latest in his series of plastic dolls. In response to

the confusion surrounding the film, Haynes said, "All I was trying to say is that, in order to live in society, to be part of the world, we have to surrender a wild, unnamable part of ourselves, which often comes out in a self-blaming way . . . When we don't understand something, we blame ourselves . . . "

Haynes took a highly personal look at the British glam rock scene of the early 70s with "Velvet Goldmine" (1998), his biggest and most accessible film yet. Self-consciously structured as a "Citizen Kane"–like investigation into the life and career of a vanished superstar (there's even an extraterrestrial Rosebud—glam rock patron saint Oscar Wilde presented in the cheeky opening minutes as deposited here by alien beings), the film brilliantly reimagines the period as a brave new world of electrifying theatrical and sexual possibility followed by darkness. Though Haynes acknowledges Altman, Scorsese (particularly "The Last Waltz" 1978) and Coppola for its 70s style of filmmaking, "Velvet Goldmine" may resemble the phantasmagoria of Ken Russell more than anything else. Dazzlingly surreal with a vibrant glam-era soundtrack (missing only a representative sampling of David Bowie who refused to release song rights with a movie of his own pending), it puts ordinary period filmmaking and time-capsule musicology to shame. This ambitious step beyond the director's previous work also proved less cohesive and satisfying to his earlier fans.

A revisionist filmmaker whose ouvre consists of clever and insightful reworkings of the tropes of generic filmmaking, Haynes "Far From Heaven" (2002) is a logical extension of the thematic and stylistc elements that have thus far defined his career. While the kitshy "Superstar" and the unabashedly Freudian "Dottie Gets Spanked" critique of the cult of female celebrity and "Poison" and "Safe" underline the sometimes violent and debilitating repercussions of a society obsessed with repressing and containing our most primal sexual drives, "Far From Heaven" revisits, with little nostalgia, the almost forgotten genre of the domestic melodrama. Drawing from the "womens' films" of the 1950s, particularly those of director Douglas Sirk, Haynes' re-imagining of Sirk's "All That Heaven Allows" casts Julianne Moore as a 1957 Connecticut housewife and mother who finds out one day that her idyllic suburban life is a lie once she realizes that her husband is having a homo-sexual affair. Utilizing the genre's propensity for heavy handed symbolism and dramatic mis-en-scene, Haynes explodes the mythical shell of innocence enveloping films from the fifties by exploring the ideological tensions and contradictions concerning gender, sexuality and race that define the melodrama as the quintessential 50s film genre. In doing so, Haynes manages to deconstruct our nostalgic view of an era gone by, while warning us, reminding us, that many of the period's most confining concepts of sexuality and the rigid pursuit of complacency and stability are as alive and volatile today as they were in yester-year's precautionary tales from suburbia.

MILESTONES:

Made student films ("Suicide", "Letter From a Friend", "Sex Shop" and "Assassins: A Film Concerning Rimbaud") prior to moving to NYC

1987: Moved to New York; won underground cult-figure status with featurette, "Superstar: The Karen Carpenter Story"

1987: With Christine Vachon and Barry Ellsworth, formed Apparatus Productions, a non-profit film cooperative which provided resources and money for emerging filmmakers

1989: Served "cease and desist" court order to stop showing "Superstar" by Carpenter estate and A&M Records

1989: Produced short film "He Was Once", directed by Mary Hestand

1990: Wrote and directed first feature, the three-part "Poison" (inspired by the works of Jean Genet and made for approximately $200,000; released in 1991)

1992: Appeared as a phrenology head in Tom Kalin's "Swoon"

1993: Returned to the short form for "Dottie Gets Spanked"; the 27-minute film aired on NYC's Channel 13 in 1994 and throughout the USA on PBS in 1995

1995: Earned critical praise for "Safe", first feature in 35mm; first collaboration with actress Julianne Moore

1997: Contributed additional dialogue to Cindy Sherman's "Office Killer"

1998: Directed "Velvet Goldmine", about 1970s glam-rock; also scripted

2002: Reunited with actress Julianne Moore on "Far From Heaven"; received nominations for both a Golden Globe and an Oscar for Best Screenplay

AFFILIATION: Jewish

Founding member, Gran Fury

Member, AIDS Coalition to Unleash Power (ACT-UP)

QUOTES:

Haynes received a Golden Gate Award for "Superstar" in 1987.

"Mr. Haynes's accomplishment and future are beyond doubt. Like Genet, whose release from a lifelong prison sentence was accomplished with the help of Jean-Paul Sartre and Simone de Beauvoir, Mr. Haynes has gone from being the outlaw creator of "Superstar" to being a praised filmmaker taken up by the intelligentsia. Soon he will probably be eminently acceptable to the mainstream. Who knows yet whether that is Mr. Haynes's blessing or his curse. Meanwhile, there is "Poison", the most iconoclastic little film ever made popular by right-wing politics."—Caryn James in *The New York Times*, April 14, 1991.

"I can't not make films right now that don't deal with illness, I can't. There's just no way. So instead of setting it in the transgressive world of 'Poison', I wanted to put it ['Safe'] about as far away from my reality and my experiences as possible—in a seemingly safe, undisturbed world. So I chose my family's world. I guess in a way, to make myself find the universal, the empathetic, to challenge my own critical instincts."—Haynes quoted by Manohla Dargis in "Endangered Zone: With Safe, Director Todd Haynes Declares His True Independence", *Village Voice*, July 4, 1995.

"Films reflect and instruct us at the same time, and that's strong stuff. So I do delight in the idea that by playing around, tinkering or upsetting that process of identification a little bit, people have to think more about what they're seeing, who's telling then what and why. A viewer has to ask the question: where is this idea coming from? Without losing all the pleasure that's part of the process. . . . I'm always surprised when films of mine which I think are intellectual experiments are received by a wider audience."—Haynes quoted in *Bomb*, c. July 1995.

His feelings on finishing "Velvet Goldmine": "I don't want to touch another film for a few years. I was miserable, and it was largely due to how little money we had and how much I was demanding of myself. I didn't have much fun making the film, and that's sad. It's made me think about the way I work, and what I might want to do differently. Having a real budget would be the first step.

"I don't have a lot of good ways of releasing the enormous tension all directors feel. Often they get rid of it in cruel ways that aren't fair to people around them—I don't like hearing that about directors whose work I love, but I have a feeling they have more fun. When you're a little more sadistic, you get it off your chest."—Todd Haynes, *Sight and Sound*, September 1998.

Amy Heckerling

BORN: in Bronx, New York, 05/07/1954

NATIONALITY: American

EDUCATION: High School of Art and Design, New York, New York

Institute of Film and TV, New York University, New York, New York; made "High Finance" (1975), a prize-winning short starring a young Joel Silver

American Film Institute, Los Angeles, California, directing, 1974; attended on a fellowship; completed a short, "Getting It Over With", submitted for consideration for the Best Short Film Academy Award in 1977

AWARDS: National Society of Film Critics Award Best Screenplay "Clueless" 1995

American Film Institute Franklin J. Schaffner Alumni Medal 1998

BIOGRAPHY
One of the few women directors working regularly in mainstream Hollywood, Amy Heckerling has specialized in amiable character-driven comedies and displayed an eye for acting talent. The New York native worked as a video editor and sound editor before making a name for herself as the helmer of "Fast Times at Ridgemont High" (1982), a superior teen comedy based on writer Cameron Crowe's nonfiction account of his undercover return to high school. The film boasted high energy, a lively rock'n'roll score and a surprising degree of honesty and sensitivity. "Fast Times" also benefited from a fine young cast including Sean Penn, Jennifer Jason Leigh and Judge Reinhold and marked the feature debuts of Eric Stoltz, Anthony Edwards, Forest Whitaker and Nicolas Cage.

This auspicious debut was followed by the less inspired "Johnny Dangerously" (1984), a scattershot spoof of 1930s gangster movies starring

Michael Keaton. Heckerling fared better commercially with the broad antics of "National Lampoon's European Vacation" (1985). Though uneven, this sequel to 1983's "National Lampoon's Vacation" was a box-office hit. No one expected the huge success of her next feature, "Look Who's Talking" (1989). This genial romantic comedy employed the engaging gimmick of broadcasting a baby's thoughts in voice-over, a gag later varied and recycled for two sequels. Heckerling served as writer-director on the first two films and segued to producing with the third. She also made Kirstie Alley into a movie star of sorts and provided the then-former superstar John Travolta with steady work. This unpretentious comedy franchise also generated a fleeting TV series, "Baby Talk" (ABC, 1991–92), for which Heckerling received a creator's credit. Previously, she had worked in TV in the mid-80s as a producer and occasional writer and director on such efforts as "Fast Times" (CBS, 1986), the short-lived TV version of her breakthrough feature, and "Tough Cookies" (CBS, 1986), a cop sitcom.

Following the "Look Who's Talking" trilogy, Heckerling returned to high school to research her next project "Clueless" (1995), a smart satirical look at the lives of affluent Beverly Hills teens. The writer-director hung out with real students so as the capture the nuances of their up-to-date lingo before deploying them in a story that owed much to Jane Austen's novel "Emma." The film opened to generally favorable reviews and a healthy box office, won Heckerling Best Screenplay honors from the National Society of Film Critics, and became a classic in the teen film genre. The spin-off series ("Clueless", 1996–1999) spent a season on ABC before moving to UPN, and Heckerling was credited as creator and executive producer. She also contributed to the sitcom as an occasional writer and director. Her next film project was 1998's "A Night at the Roxbury", which she had a hand in as a producer. Based on unlucky-in-love nightclubbing brothers

from an inane recurring "Saturday Night Live" sketch, the film didn't impress many critics or moviegoers. Heckerling followed up as executive producer of the disappointing "Molly" (1999), an Elisabeth Shue starrer about a developmentally disabled woman.

In 2000, Heckerling seemed poised to reclaim the sleeper glory of "Clueless" with the charming underdog comedy "Loser", a New York University-set feature starring hot tickets Jason Biggs (playing Paul, a sheltered Midwesterner) and Mena Suvari (as Dora, a coed with a crush on her professor). Heckerling was able to draw somewhat on her own experiences with this film, dealing with outcasts in Manhattan as opposed to the beautiful youth of Southern California that had launched ("Fast Times at Ridgemont High") and then solidified ("Clueless") her career.—Written by Kent Greene

COMPANIONS:

husband: Neal Israel. Producer, writer, director; second husband; divorced in 1991

Bronson Pinchot. Actor; engaged as of 1997; separated by fall 1997

Chris Kattan. Actor, comedian; appeared on "Saturday Night Live"; met in 1997 during filming of "A Night at the Roxbury" which Heckerling produced; no longer together

MILESTONES:

Born and raised in NYC

1975: Directed the award-winning short "High Finance", starring Joel Silver

1976: Moved to L.A.

Found work doing video and sound editing

Attended the American Film Institute as a directing fellow; directed the 1977 short "Getting It Over With"

1982: Feature directorial debut, the teen classic "Fast Times at Ridgemont High"

1984: Directed the Michael Keaton gangster comedy "Johnny Dangerously"

1985: Had a cameo acting role in John Landis's "Into the Night"

1985: Helmed the troubled but commercially successful "National Lampoon's European Vacation"

1985: Debuted as a television writer with "Death Benefits", an episode of the CBS comedy anthology series "George Burns Comedy Week"

1986: Served as supervising producer of "Fast Times", the CBS version of the feature; also directed the pilot

1986: Served as supervising producer of "Tough Cookies" (also wrote an episode), a short-lived CBS cop sitcom

1988: Produced "Life on the Flipside", an unsold sitcom pilot

1989: Feature writing debut, "Look Who's Talking", a sleeper hit comedy; also directed

1990: Helmed the successful follow-up "Look Who's Talking Too"

1991–1992: Received a creator's credit on "Baby Talk", a short-lived ABC sitcom loosely derived from "Look Who's Talking"

1993: Feature producing debut as co-producer of "Look Who's Talking Now", the second sequel to the original; also scripted and directed

1995: Was screenwriter and director of "Clueless", the popular and critically acclaimed Beverly Hills–set modern reworking of Jane Austen's "Emma"

Was creator and executive producer of the TV series adaptation "Clueless" (ABC 1996–1997; UPN 1997–1999); also directed and scripted some episodes

1998: Produced "A Night at the Roxbury", a comedy feature based on the club-hopping Bubati brothers from "Saturday Night Live"

1999: Was executive producer of the sentimental and unsuccessful Elisabeth Shue vehicle "Molly"

2000: Helmed the New York City college-set comedy "Loser"

QUOTES:

Amy Heckerling on her inspiration for "Look Who's Talking": I used to look at my daughter in her baby seat and wonder what she was thinking about. I assumed she thought the same way I did. You know, sort of cynical thoughts; not cute, adorable baby thoughts. But her perspective would be without any reference points because she was figuring out everything for the first time.

"Most adults run around intellectualizing and trying to figure out things based on experiences they've had. A baby just has to deal with pure feelings. That's who Mikey is, and he seems to have the adults all figured out."—quoted in the "Look Who's Talking" press notes.

Heckerling on being a woman in the overwhelmingly male dominated field of film directing: "I supposet there's that aspect where people think you have to be tough to make it in a man's world and blah, blah, blah. I live in my own little world, so I don't know what goes on. I have people around me that are tough. If I spent my energy in that place, I wouldn't be able to follow teenagers around and write down dialogue."—quoted in *Rolling Stone*, September 7, 1995.

Amy Heckerling on the alternative lexicon used by the teens in "Fast Times at Ridgemont High" and, more influentially, "Clueless": "People are tired of the same old adjectives, so they make up new ones. They're tired of the old rhythms of speaking, and create a shorthand only they know."—to *Detour*, November 1996.

"People always seem to throw that word, pioneer, at me. Well, when you say that word, I just always think of covered wagons and bonnets."—quoted in *The Hollywood Reporter Women in Film Crystal Awards Special Issue*, June 11, 1999.

"Inside, I'm a teenage boy. I've stayed at an emotional level that keeps me interested in things more mature people don't care about."—quoted in *Fade In*, Summer 2000.

"I have always tried to create a cigarette-free universe in my films. I know it's not realistic, but if the cute, young movie stars are not smoking, maybe it will send a subliminal message. If an actor states that their particular character would smoke, one can argue that their character also goes to the bathroom, but there are some things we're just not going to see. The script is what happens to them between cigarettes."—Heckerling quoted in *Los Angeles Times*, May 7, 2000.

Amy Heckerling answering her own question, "Is the whole teen movie thing coming to an end?": "Probably—only because we're running out of classics to redo. When we get to 'Beowulf' and 'Canterbury Tales' set in high school, you'll know it's over."—quoted in *Los Angeles Times*, May 7, 2000.

Heckerling described working on "National Lampoon's European Vacation" as "a total nightmare" in *Fade In* (Summer 2000). She went on to explain what she learned from the experience: "It prompted me to make a list of

things I'd never do again: 1) Never work with an asshole, 2) never work with material I wasn't happy and secure with, and 3) never work with a crew that has total disdain for Hollywood. After that, I didn't want to be a director for hire and work on other people's scripts. I just wanted to stay home, write, and be with my kid."

In an article in *The Sacramento Bee*, journalist Joe Baltake pointed out the many similarities between Heckerling's "Loser" and Billy Wilder's "The Apartment." Spokespeople for Heckerling dismissed the article claiming that the writer-director did not base her film on the 1960 Oscar-winning Best Picture.

BIBLIOGRAPHY:

"The No-Sex Handbook" Amy Heckerling and Pam Petter; a spoof of how-to books

Werner Herzog

BORN: Werner H. Stipetic in Sachrang, Germany, 09/05/1942

NATIONALITY: German

EDUCATION: Munich University, Munich, Germany

University of Pittsburgh, Pittsburgh, Pennsylvani; attended on scholarship

AWARDS: Cannes Film Festival FIPRESCI Prize "Every Man for Himself and God Against All/The Mystery of Kaspar Hauser" 1975; also known as the International Critics Award

Cannes Film Festival Ecumencial Prize "Every Man for Himself and God Against All/The Mystery of Kaspar Hauser" 1975

Cannes Film Festival Special Jury Prize "Every Man for Himself and God Against All/The Mystery of Kaspar Hauser" 1975

Cannes Film Festival Best Director Award "Fitzcarraldo" 1982

International Documentary Association Award Distinguished Documentary Achievement "Little Dieter Needs to Fly" 1998; cited with Matthew Diamond's "Dancemaker"

BIOGRAPHY

A study in contradictions, Werner Herzog, more than any of his peers, has embodied German history, character and cultural richness in his work, yet unlike those contemporaries (Fassbinder, Wenders, Schlondorff), he has set no significant film in his own country in his own time. Instead, his restless nature has taken him far and wide, and his journeys to the edge have provided the impetus for filmmaking renowned for its physical demands on everyone involved. Though growing up in the shadow of remembered Nazi atrocities prompted him to probe the darker aspects of human behavior, Herzog developed a paradoxical style, its surface realism part of a vision that combined 20th-century Expressionism with 19th-century Romanticism. Unifying these disparate elements was his elevation of the grotesque, first in his lensing of dwarfs and the handicapped and later by casting actors like former mental patient Bruno S. and the willful, manic Klaus Kinski who could convey his ideal of an absurd universe where ugliness triumphs over beauty.

Herzog's genius for self-promotion makes it difficult to sort the fact from the fiction in his own biography. While he definitely traveled extensively as a young man, visiting Greece, Yugoslavia, England and the Sudan, it is less clear (though certainly not inconceivable) whether he worked as a rodeo rider and smuggled arms and TV sets across the Mexican border (as he claims) during his initial forays to the United States. Courting danger in his personal life progressed logically to a preoccupation with authentic experience as the basis for his films, a monomania resulting in his arrest (as a suspected mercenary) and torture in the Cameroon during the making of "Fata Morgana" (1969). The director twice chose the jungles of Peru to infuse arguably his greatest films ("Aguirre, the Wrath of God" 1972 and "Fitzcarraldo" 1982) with their sense of immediacy, and he allegedly threatened to kill Kinski if he left during the filming of the former, whereas the trials of the latter probably made him want to kill himself.

Dismissive of film schools, Herzog considered his apprenticeship complete with his third short, the scathing anti-war satire "The Unprecedented Defense of Fortress Deutschkreuz" (1966). A similar sentiment was also present in his first feature, "Signs of Life" (1968), although the eventual madness of the wounded German soldier sent from Crete to the island of Cos had more to do with the enforced idleness and alien landscape encountered than anything else. The apocalypse of his second feature, "Even Dwarfs Started Small" (1970), which chronicled a day in the life of a prison comprised entirely of dwarfs and midgets, served as a metaphor for the warped nature of mankind. Herzog followed with "Land of Silence and Darkness" (1971), a documentary about a middle-aged deaf and blind woman whose attempts to help her fellow-sufferers underscored the primitive, incommunicable nature of people. As with the community of dwarfs, the flawed handicapped band symbolized the essentially damaged quality of humanity.

Unrelenting in its concentration on filth, disease and brutality, "Aguirre" functions as an allegory of the fascistic personality, invoking both Germany's glorification of the Nazis and America's oppression of Vietnam, not to mention the general reading that a bestiality lingers beneath the facade of civilized conventions. "Aguirre" opens with an extraordinary shot of an almost endless line of conquistadors and slaves making their way down the valley in the jungle and ends with Aguirre (Kinski), his expedition's lone survivor, adrift, raving down the Amazon on a corpse-strewn raft overrun with hundreds of twittering monkeys. In between, the maniacal conquistador, through intimidation and murder, gains control of his party, declares himself the "wrath of God" and sets off to find El Dorado, the legendary Inca city of gold. As the camera circles around the raft, reinforcing a sense of entrapment and doom, the stunning final image conjures a sense of awe, even admiration, for the heroic madman.

"Every Man for Himself and God Against All/The Mystery of Kaspar Hauser" (1975) documented the true story of a 16-year-old boy discovered standing in the town square of Nuremberg in 1828, unable to walk or talk, having been locked away in a dark cellar and deprived of all human contact since birth. Herzog's choice of Bruno S. for the title role was a stroke of genius as the former mental patient's face compellingly expressed the injuries he himself had incurred at the hands of the restrictive machinery of society, establishing the authentic immediacy that was de rigeur for the director's films. Herzog experimented with hypnosis to induce the mass hysteria that overcomes the townspeople of "Heart of Glass" (1976) before reteaming with Bruno S for "Stroszek" (1977), which takes its trio of misfits to Wisconsin and presents the American dream as nightmare. He then let his expressionism run rampant, first in a reverent remake of F. W. Murnau's "Nosferatu" (1978), followed by a film version of Georg Buchner's 1836 play, "Woyzeck" (1979).

"Fitzcarraldo" and its companion piece, "Burden of Dreams" (1983), Les Blank's behind-the-scenes documentary, attest to the danger and extremism of what is ultimately the defining project of Herzog's career. Perhaps the least of the obstacles facing the director was the monumental task of hauling a 320-ton steamboat over a mountain. Finding himself in the middle of a border dispute between Peru and Ecuador, he moved his location. Jack Nicholson backed out before shooting began, his replacement Warren Oates decided against doing it at the last minute and Jason Robards contacted amoebic dysentery halfway through filming, after which Mick Jagger withdrew to prepare for a Rolling Stones concert tour. It remained for Kinski to save the day, and who better to essay the role of the obsessive Irish expatriate who dreams of bringing grand opera to the deep interior of the jungle. In the end, Fitzcarraldo's inability to bend nature to his will parallels Herzog's psychic defeat at the hands of the picture. The director has not returned to the epic scale since, nor has he had a film widely released.

Herzog has not stopped making films, but he is primarily a documentarian these days, often employing his much-loved 360-degree pans in the rendering of his sublime landscapes. Even during his heyday in the 70s, he continued to intersperse amongst his features short works like the 47-minute "The Great Ecstacy of Walter Steiner" (1975) and "La Soufriere" (1976), for which he journeyed to an evacuated Guadeloupe island to photograph the eruption of a volcano which never occurred. He made two highly-acclaimed short films in 1984, "The Ballad of the Little Soldier", which drew protests from pro-Sandanistas that Herzog was in league with the Contras and CIA, and "The Green Glow of the Mountains", full of the exotic scenery that was the backdrop for Reinhold Messner and his partner Hans Kammerlander's mountain climbing heroics in Pakistan. Among his other nonfiction titles are "Herdsman of the Sun" (1988), a record of the sub-Saharan Wodaabe tribe, and "Lessons of Darkness" (1992), a look at the environmental impact of the 1991 Gulf War on Kuwait, which aired on the Discovery Channel. His last film to date was "Dieter Dengler Needs to Fly" (1997).—Written by Greg Senf

MILESTONES:

1954: Parents separated when he was 11; moved to Munich with mother and two brothers (date approximate)

1957: Began submitting film ideas to producers at age 14 (date approximate)

1960: At 17, had a script accepted by a producer, who apparently tore up the contract when he discovered the scenarist was still a teenager (date approximate)

Received prizes for two amateur shorts "Herakles" (1962) and "Spiel im Sand" (1964)

1966: Established Werner Herzog Film produktion

1966: Directed third short, "Die Beispiellose Verteidgung der Festung Deutschkreuz", a savage anti-war satire

1967: Short film, "Letzte Worte/Last Words" won the major prize at the Oberhausen Film Festival

1968: First full length film "Leibenszeichen/ Signs of Life"; won the German National Film award for first feature

1969: Collaborated with Leonard Cohen and Couperin (both providing music) on "Fata Morgana", a sprawling montage of desert footage

1970: Second feature, "Even Dwarfs Started Small", banned in Germany

1972: First collaboration with the actor Klaus

Kinski, "Aguirre, the Wrath of God"; filmed on location in Peru

1975: Chose former mental patient Bruno S for title role of "Every Man for Himself and God Against All/The Mystery of Kaspar Hauser"

1977: Reteamed with Bruno S for "Stroszek"; first collaboration with actress Eva Mattes

1978: Paid homage to F. W. Murnau with reverent remake of the director's 1922 vampire film, "Nosferatu"; Kinski played the good Count

1979: Filmed expressionistic version of Georg Buchner's 1836 play, "Woyzeck", with Kinski in the title role; third and last colaboration with Mattes

1982: Returned to Peru, overcoming obstacles of nightmarish proportions to complete "Fitzcarraldo", starring Kinski

1984: Made two short films, "The Ballad of the Little Soldier" (chronicling the war between the native Miskito Indians of Nicaragua and the Sandanistas) and "The Green Glow of the Mountain"

1988: Last project with Kinski, "Cobra Verde"

1992: Directed "Lessons of Darkness", a 60-minute documentary examining the environmental devastation of the Gulf War in Kuwait in 1991; aired on the Discovery Chanel

1997: Helmed the documentary "Little Dieter Needs to Fly", the true story of Dieter Dengler who moved to the USA and became a Navy pilot who was shot down on his first mission in Vietnam and eventually escaped his captors

1999: Made "My Best Fiend", a documentary on actor Klaus Kinski

1999: Acted in Harmony Korine's Dogma 95 film "Julien Donkey-Boy"

2001: "Invincible" premiered at the Venice Film Festival; released theatrically in USA in 2002

QUOTES:

"I try to make films because I know that I have some sort of vision or insight . . . When I make a film I try to articulate it." For him, "it's the fire" of belief and commitment that makes the film, and goes on: "When I look back at my films I think they all came out of some sort of pain . . . I make films to rid myself of them, like ridding myself of a nightmare." It is not that he wants to "make confessions," only that for him film is "something which has more importance than my private life."—Werner Herzog, quoted in "World Film Directors", Volume Two, edited by John Wakeman

George Roy Hill

BORN: George Roy Hill, Jr. in Minneapolis, Minnesota, 12/20/1922

DEATH: in Manhattan, New York, 12/27/2002

NATIONALITY: American

EDUCATION: Blake High School, Minneapolis, Minnesota, 1939

Yale University, New Haven, Connecticut, music, BA, 1943

Trinity College, Dublin, Ireland, 1946–49; attended on GI Bill; never completed dissertation

AWARDS: British Film Academy Award Best Direction "Butch Cassidy and the Sundance Kid" 1970

Cannes Film Festival Special Jury Prize "Slaughterhouse Five" 1972

Directors Guild of America Award Outstanding Directorial Achievement in Feature Film "The Sting" 1973

Oscar Best Director "The Sting" 1973

BIOGRAPHY

Former Marine pilot George Roy Hill began his career as an actor, debuting with Cyril Cusack's company at the Abbey Theatre in Dublin. He scored a personal success in Strindberg's "The Creditors" (1950) at the Cherry Lane Theatre, before concentrating on writing and directing for American TV in the 1950s. He scripted and acted in his first work for NBC's "Kraft Television Theatre", the autobiographical "My Brother's Keeper" (1953), inspired by his pilot's experience of being "talked down" by a ground controller, and "A Night to Remember" (also for "Kraft"), a drama about the sinking of the Titanic, earned him 1956 Emmy nominations as director and co-author. Hill scored a huge success in his Broadway directing debut, the Pulitzer Prize–winning "Look Homeward, Angel" (1957) and made his feature film debut helming the adaptation of Tennessee Williams' play "Period of Adjustment" (1962), which he had directed on Broadway.

Hill delighted reviewers (though the box office was meager) with "The World of Henry Orient" (1964), starring Peter Sellers, and took his first abortive stab at shepherding a big-budget project, the critical and commercial failure "Hawaii" (1966). His fortunes changed for the better with his first and only movie musical the Roaring Twenties spoof "Thoroughly Modern Millie" (1967), which made a good deal of money and set the stage for his greatest triumphs, two fluid, lightly handled vehicles for the superstar team of Paul Newman and Robert Redford: "Butch Cassidy and the Sundance Kid" (1969) and "The Sting" (1973). The latter earned eight Oscars including Best Picture and one for Hill as Best Director. In between, "Slaughterhouse Five" (1972), adapted from the Kurt Vonnegut novel, won a special jury prize at Cannes but proved uncommercial. Hill also teamed with Redford on "The Great Waldo Pepper" (1975), his hymn to the great aerial stuntman of his boyhood, and with Newman for the hockey burlesque "Slap Shot" (1977).

With "A Little Romance" (1979), Hill returned to the territory he had explored so sensitively in "The World of Henry Orient", that of

adolescent infatuation. Most critics enjoyed the engaging tale of 13-year-olds in love, the gorgeous European locations, the fine acting (including Laurence Olivier's wily old con man) and direction that never wallowed in sentiment, and the public seemed to agree, disregarding the naysayers who dismissed it as a gimmicky product of commercialism. Hill next shocked Hollywood by leaving to teach a class in drama at his alma mater Yale but came back to make "The World According to Garp" (1982), adapted by Steve Tesich from the John Irving novel. Although it couldn't capture Irving's literary imagination, "Garp" offered excellent performances, particularly by Glenn Close (in her film debut) and John Lithgow as a transsexual; both earned Oscar nominations for their work. Hill rounded out his filmmaking career with the unsuccessful thriller "The Little Drummer Girl" (1984) and the mild comedy "Funny Farm" (1988) before returning to academia.

MILESTONES:

Served in World War II as Marine transport pilot

1948: Acting debut in Shaw's "The Devil's Disciple" with Cyril Cusack's repertory company in Dublin

1948: Stage directing debut "Biography" at Gate Theatre in Dublin

Toured USA with Margaret Webster's Shakespeare Repertory Company in early 1950s

Appeared on Broadway in a small part in "Richard II"

1950: Scored considerable personal success as Gustav in Strindberg's "The Creditors" opposite Beatrice Arthur at the Cherry Lane Theatre

Served as a fighter pilot in Korean War, achieved rank of major

1952: Appeared in documentary style drama "Walk East on Beacon Street"

1953: His play, "My Brother's Keeper", performed on "Kraft Television Theatre" (NBC); also acted in it

1956: Nominated for Emmys as director and

co-author of "A Night to Remember" ("Kraft Television Theatre"), a drama about the sinking of the Titanic

1957: Broadway directing debut, the Pulitzer Prize-winning "Look Homeward, Angel", starring Anthony Perkins

1960: Directed Frank Loesser's musical "Greenwillow", again starring Perkins

1962: Film directing debut, adaptation of Tennessee Williams' play "Period of Adjustment", which he had directed on Broadway

Formed independent company, Pan Arts, with his former agent Jerome Hellman

1964: Delighted reviewers with "The World of Henry Orient", starring Peter Sellers; though some maintain it is his beat picture, it did poorly at the box office

1966: Had critical and commercial failure with big-budget "Hawaii", a picture that actually faired better on TV; first collaboration with Julie Andrews

1967: First real moneymaker, the musical "Thoroughly Modern Millie", starring Andrews and Mary Tyler Moore

1969: Scored huge hit with first collaboration with Paul Newman and Robert Redford, "Butch Cassidy and the Sundance Kid", co-produced by Hill and Paul Monash

1972: Co-produced (again with Monash) and directed "Slaughterhouse Five", adapted from the Kurt Vonnegut novel

1975: Reteamed with Newman and Redford and won the Best Director Oscar for "The Sting"

Quit Hollywood after "A Little Romance" (1979) to teach a course in drama at his alma mater Yale

1982: Returned to Hollywood and made "The World According to Garp", adapted by Steve Tesich from the John Irving novel; Hill had cameo as pilot who crashes into Garp's house

1988: Last film to date, "Funny Farm", an easygoing, mildly endearing comedy starring Chevy Chase

Returned to teaching at Yale

AFFILIATION: Catholic

QUOTES:

"He served in the Marines in World War II and Korea, and at sixty still looks like the Marine officer he once was—slender, cold eyes, close-cropped hair . . . His profit participation in "Butch Cassidy" and "The Sting" has made him millions, but he is famous in the movie business for never picking up a check. And his dress can best be described as nondescript, or perhaps janitorial. A producer who once worked with him told me that George bragged that he bought his clothes at an Army surplus store in Santa Monica, where he could get khaki pants for under ten dollars."—John Gregory Dunne, *Esquire*, August 1983

Alfred Hitchcock

BORN: Alfred Joseph Hitchcock in Leytonstone, England, 08/13/1899

SOMETIMES CREDITED AS:
Sir Alfred Hitchcock

DEATH: in Beverly Hills, California, 04/29/1980

NATIONALITY: English

CITIZENSHIP: United States 1955

EDUCATION: St. Ignatius College, London, England, 1908; Catholic school

School of Engineering and Navigation London, England, mechanics, electricity, acoustics, navigation

University of London, London, England, art

AWARDS: New York Film Critics Circle Award Best Director "The Lady Vanishes" 1938

Oscar Best Picture "Rebecca" 1940; Hitchcock was a producer

Golden Globe Award 1957; cited for TV work

Irving G Thalberg Memorial Award 1967; presented by the Academy of Motion Picture Arts and Sciences

Directors Guild of America D. W. Griffith Award 1968

National Board of Review Award Best Director "Topaz" 1969

Cecil B. DeMille Award 1972; presented by the Hollywood Foreign Press Association

American Film Institute Life Achievement Award 1979

BIOGRAPHY

The acknowledged master of the thriller genre he virtually invented, Alfred Hitchcock was also a brilliant technician who deftly blended sex, suspense and humor. He began his filmmaking career in 1919 illustrating title cards for silent films at Paramount's Famous Players—Lasky studio in London. There he learned scripting, editing and art direction, and rose to assistant director in 1922. That year he directed an unfinished film, "No. 13" or "Mrs. Peabody." His first completed film as director was "The Pleasure Garden" (1925), an Anglo-German production filmed in Munich. This experience, plus a stint at Germany's UFA studios as an assistant director, helps account for the Expressionistic character of his films, both in their visual schemes and thematic concerns. "The Lodger" (1926), his breakthrough film, was a prototypical example of the classic Hitchcock plot: an innocent protagonist is falsely accused of a crime and becomes involved in a web of intrigue.

An early example of Hitchcock's technical virtuosity was his creation of "subjective sound" for "Blackmail" (1929), his first sound film. In this story of a woman who stabs an artist to death when he tries to seduce her, Hitchcock emphasized the young woman's anxiety by gradually distorting all but one word—"knife"—of a neighbor's dialogue the morning after the killing. Here and in "Murder" (1930), Hitchcock first made explicit the link between sex and violence.

"The Man Who Knew Too Much" (1934), a commercial and critical success, established a favorite pattern: an investigation of family relationships within a suspenseful story. "The 39 Steps" (1935) showcases a mature Hitchcock; it is a stylish and efficiently told chase film brimming with exciting incidents and memorable characters. Despite their merits, both "The Secret Agent" and "Sabotage" (both 1936) exhibited flaws Hitchcock later acknowledged and learned from. According to his theory, suspense is developed by providing the audience with information denied endangered characters. But to be most effective and cathartic, no harm should come to the innocent—as it does in both of those films. "The Lady Vanishes" (1938), on the other hand, is sleek, exemplary Hitchcock: fast-paced, witty, and magnificently entertaining.

Hitchcock's last British film, "Jamaica Inn" (1939), and his first Hollywood effort, "Rebecca" (1940), were both handsomely mounted though somewhat uncharacteristic works based on novels by Daphne du Maurier. Despite its somewhat muddled narrative, "Foreign Correspondent" (1940) was the first Hollywood film in his recognizable style. "Suspicion" (1941), the story of a woman who thinks her husband is a murderer about to make her his next victim, was an exploration of family dynamics; its introduction of evil into the domestic arena foreshadowed "Shadow of a Doubt" (1943), Hitchcock's early Hollywood masterwork. One of his most disturbing films, "Shadow" was nominally the story of a young woman who learns that a favorite uncle is a murderer, but at heart it is a sobering look at the dark underpinnings of American middle-class life. Fully as horrifying as Uncle Charlie's attempts to murder his niece was her mother's tearful acknowledgment of her loss of identity in becoming a wife and mother. "You know how it is," she says, "you sort of forget you're you. You're your husband's wife." In Hitchcock, evil manifests itself not only in acts of physical violence, but also in the form of psychological, institutionalized and systemic cruelty.

Hitchcock would return to the feminine sacrifice-of-identity theme several times, most immediately with the masterful "Notorious" (1946), a perverse love story about an FBI agent who must send the woman he loves into the arms of a Nazi in order to uncover an espionage ring. Other psychological dramas of the late 1940s were "Spellbound" (1945), "The Paradine Case" (1947), and "Under Capricorn" (1949). Both "Lifeboat" (1944) and "Rope" (1948) were interesting technical excercises: in the former, the object was to tell a film story within the confines of a small boat; in "Rope," Hitchcock sought to make a film that appeared to be a single, unedited shot. "Rope" shared with the more effective "Strangers on a Train" (1951) a villain intent on committing the perfect murder as well as a strong homo-erotic undercurrent.

During his most inspired period, from 1950 to 1960, Hitchcock produced a cycle of memorable films which included minor works such as "I Confess" (1953), the sophisticated thrillers "Dial M for Murder" (1954) and "To Catch a Thief" (1955), a bland remake of "The Man Who Knew Too Much" (1956) and the black comedy "The Trouble with Harry" (1955). He also directed several top-drawer films like "Strangers on a Train" and the troubling early docudrama "The Wrong Man" (1956), a searing critique of the American justice system.

His three unalloyed masterpieces of the period were investigations into the very nature of watching cinema. "Rear Window" (1954) made viewers voyeurs, then had them pay for their pleasure. In its story of a photographer who happens to witness a murder, Hitchcock provocatively probed the relationship between the watcher and the watched, involving, by extension, the viewer of the film. "Vertigo" (1958), as haunting a movie as Hollywood has ever produced, took the lost-feminine-identity theme of "Shadow of a Doubt" and "Notorious" and identified its cause as male fetishism.

"North by Northwest" (1959) is perhaps Hitchcock's most fully realized film. From a script by Ernest Lehman, with a score (as usual) by Bernard Herrmann, and starring Cary Grant and Eva Marie Saint, this quintessential chase movie is full of all the things for which we remember Alfred Hitchcock: ingenious shots, subtle male-female relationships, dramatic score, bright Technicolor, inside jokes, witty symbolism and—above all—masterfully orchestrated suspense.

"Psycho" (1960) is famed for its shower murder sequence—a classic model of shot selection and editing which was startling for its (apparent) nudity, graphic violence and its violation of the narrative convention that makes a protagonist invulnerable. Moreover, the progressive shots of eyes, beginning with an extreme close-up of the killer's peeping eye and ending with the open eye of the murder victim, subtly implied the presence of a third eye—the viewer's.

Later films offered intriguing amplifications of his main themes. "The Birds" (1963) presented evil as an environmental fact of life. "Marnie" (1964), a psychoanalytical thriller along the lines of "Spellbound," showed how a violent, sexually tinged childhood episode turns a woman into a thief, once again associating criminality with violence and sex. Most notable about "Torn Curtain" (1966), an espionage story played against a cold war backdrop, was its extended fight-to-the death scene between the protagonist and a Communist agent in the kitchen of a farm house. In it Hitchcock reversed the movie convention of quick, easy deaths and showed how difficult—and how momentous—the act of killing really is.

Hitchcock's disappointing "Topaz" (1969), an unwieldy, unfocused story set during the Cuban missile crisis, was devoid of his typical narrative economy and wit. He returned to England to produce "Frenzy" (1972), a tale much more in the Hitchcock vein, about an innocent man suspected of being a serial killer. His final film, "Family Plot" (1976), pitted two couples against one another: a pair of professional thieves versus a female psychic and her working-class lover. It was a fitting end to a body of work that demonstrated the eternal symmetry of good and evil.

MILESTONES:

1920: Began career as title designer for London branch of Famous Players—Lasky

Made head of title department

1922: Made assistant director when Famous Players taken over by Michael Balcon's production company

1922: Short film directing debut with "Number 13/Mrs. Peabody" (never completed)

1923: Hired as assistant director by Balcon-Saville-Freedman

1923: First film as assistant director, art director and sole writer "Woman to Woman"

1925: Feature film directing debut with "The Pleasure Garden"

1927: Made the suspense thriller "The Lodger", starring Ivor Novello

1927: Co-wrote (with Alma Reville) and directed, "The Ring"

1929: Directed first British synchronous sound film "Blackmail"; also co-wrote script with Charles Bennet and Benn W. Levy

1930: Set up public relations firm Hitchcock Baker Productions

1932: Wrote and directed the comedy thriller "Number Seventeen"

1934: Helmed "The Man Who Knew Too Much"

1935: Directed the classic "The 39 Steps"

1938: Made "The Lady Vanishes"

1939: Signed by David O. Selznick, moved to Hollywood

1940: American film directing debut with "Rebecca", which won the Best Picture Oscar; received first Academy Award nomination as Best Director

1941: Made the atypical screwball comedy "Mr. and Mrs. Smith"

1941: Directed Joan Fontaine in an Oscar-winning performance in "Suspicion"; first film with Cary Grant

1943: Made "Saboteur" and "Shadow of a Doubt"

1944: Earned second Best Director Oscar nomination with "Lifeboat"

1945: Helmed "Spellbound", the first of three films with Ingrid Bergman; earned third Academy Award nomination as Best Director

1946: Made the classic "Notorious", featuring Bergman and Grant

1948: Initial collaboration with James Stewart, "Rope"

1949: Last film with Ingrid Bergman, "Under Capricorn"

1951: Made "Strangers on a Train", starring Robert Walker and Farley Granger

1953: Helmed "I Confess", starring Montgomery Clift as a priest

1954: Directed Grant and Grace Kelly in "Dial M for Murder"

1954: Teamed Kelly with James Stewart in "Rear Window"; fourth Oscar nomination for Best Director

1955: Third film with Grace Kelly, "To Catch a Thief"; also starred Cary Grant

1955–1962: Hosted and executive produced the anthology series "Alfred Hitchcock Presents" (CBS, 1955–1960; NBC, 1960–1962); also directed 17 episodes

1956: Remade "The Man Who Wasn't There" with James Stewart and Doris Day

Produced the anthology series "Suspicion" (NBC); directed one episode ("Four o'Clock")

1958: Last film with James Stewart, "Vertigo"

1959: Final collaboration with Cary Grant, "North by Northwest"

1960: Directed the classic "Psycho", featuring Anthony Perkins; earned fifth and last Best Director Oscar nomination

1960: Helmed the "Incident at a Corner" episode of "Ford Star Time" (CBS)

Hosted and executive produced "The Alfred Hitchcock Hour" (CBS, 1962–1964; NBC, 1964–1965); also directed the episode entitled "I Saw the Whole Thing"

1963: First of two films with Tippi Hedren, "The Birds"

1964: Second movie with Hedren, "Marnie"

1966: Teamed Julie Andrews and Paul Newman in "Torn Curtain"

1969: Helmed the spy thriller "Topaz"

1972: Directed "Frenzy", about a serial killer

1976: Final feature, "Family Plot"

BIBLIOGRAPHY:

"Hitch: The Life and Times of Alfred Hitchcock" John Russell Taylor, 1978, Pantheon

"Hitchcock" Francois Truffaut, 1967, Simon & Schuster; a series of interviews with Hitchcock conducted by the noted French director

"The Hitchcock Romance" Leslie Brill

"Hitchcock: The Murderous Gaze" William Rothman

"Hitchcock on Hitchcock: Selected Writings and Interviews" edited by Sydney Gottlieb, 1995

"The Dark Side of Genius: The Life of Alfred Hitchcock" Donald Spoto, 1999, Da Capo Press

"Hitchcock's Notebooks: An Authentic and Illustrated Look at the Mind of Alfred Hitchcock" Dan Auiler, 1999, Spike

"Hitchcock Becomed 'Hitchcock': The British Years" Paul M. Jensen, 2000, Midnight Marquee Press

"English Hitchcock" Charles Barr, Cameron & Hollis

"Writing with Hitchcock: The Collaboration of Alfred Hitchcock and John Michael Hayes" Steven DeRosa, 2001, Faber and Faber

Mike Hodges

BORN: Michael Hodges in Bristol, England, 07/29/1932

NATIONALITY: English

EDUCATION: Prior Park College, Bath, England accounting

BIOGRAPHY

British writer-director Mike Hodges honed his craft in television before segueing to the big screen with the gangster melodrama "Get Carter" (1971), starring Michael Caine as a cold-blooded hit man. Dismissed by critics as overly violent at its initial release, the film has come to be regarded as a minor masterpiece and an influence on such disparate movie directors as John Woo, Quentin Tarantino and Guy Ritchie.

Born in Bristol, Hodges originally trained as an accountant but after a requisite stint in the Royal Navy found employment as a teleprompter writer. Exposed to the workings of television, Hodges tried his hand and crafting scripts and sold one. He made the transition to director and producer overseeing segments of the English newsmagazine "World of Action" in the early 1960s. A stint on the arts-themed "Tempo" followed, where he prepared profiles of such notable film personalities as Jean-Luc Godard and Orson Welles. Further honing his craft, Hodges wrote and directed episodes of two thrillers that aired on Thames Television, "Suspect" and "Rumour."

"Get Carter" marked his first feature work and announced a director of impeccable style and a writer capable of conjuring homages to Chandler and Cain. (A measure of the film's influence is its Americanized remake with an all-black cast, "Hit Man" the following year.) Hodges' second film was the loopy comedy "Pulp" (1972), again starring Caine, this time playing a hack writer hired to ghost the memoirs of a Hollywood star (Mickey Rooney). Stylish and off-beat, the film proved a disappointment at the USA box office but it landed its hyphenate a deal in Hollywood. "The Terminal Man" (1974), adapted from Michael Crichton's novel, marked Hodges' debut in the sci-fi/horror genre and was a well-acted thriller about a computer scientist who develops violent characteristics. After penning the second installment of the devil-as-human trilogy, "Damien—Omen II" (1978), he segued to the campy "Flash Gordon" (1980), an eye-popping romp based on the comic strip and movie serials of the 30s and 40s that was better than its advertising campaign would lead one to believe. While it set no records and racked up any awards, "Flash Gordon" proved a cult hit, a guilty pleasure made palatable by its production design and the presence of such actors as Max von Sydow (as Ming the Merciless), Brian Blessed and Timothy Dalton, and the allure of Melody Anderson and Ornella Muti.

Returning to England, Hodges shifted gears considerably to oversee the earnest TV-movie "Squaring the Circle" (1983). Working from Tom Stoppard's above average script, he fashioned a cogent look at the rise of the Solidarity movement in Poland. "Squaring the Circle" received a limited theatrical release in the USA and showed the director at his peak. Hodges was invited to direct the English-language version of Fellini's "And the Ship Sailed On" (also 1983). He stumbled with the laughable "Morons From Outer Space" (1985) and attempted to have his name removed from "A Prayer for the Dying" (1987) after studio interference. A last-minute replacement for Franc Roddam, Hodges had worked with star Mickey Rourke in trying to fashion a character study of a resident Northern Ireland conflicted over the violence surrounding him, but ultimately it was an uneven script and hammy acting by the co-stars as well as the editing that sank the picture. Hodges fared much better with the

intriguing if overlooked "Black Rainbow" (1989) which cast Rosanna Arquette as a medium who foretells the events of a murder. Disenchanted with features, Hodges resumed his small screen career, helming and/or scripting a variety of projects over the next decade. In 1998, he made a triumphant return to the big screen with the film noir "Croupier", featuring a star-making lead turn by Clive Owen. Many critics favorably compared "Croupier" with "Get Carter", particularly as both centered on "meticulous" characters.

MILESTONES:

Raised in Bristol

Served in the Royal Navy

1957: Hired to work as a telepromter writer

Began writing scripts on a freelance basis

Sold teleplay "Some Will Cry Murder"; concentrated on writing full-time

Worked as an editor on the religious TV series "The Sunday Break"

Became a producer and director for "The World in Action" for Granada television

Was producer of the arts program "Tempo", overseeing televised profiles of Jacques Tati, Jean-Luc Godard and Orson Welles, among others

Hired to write, direct and produce "Suspect" and "Rumour" (both for Thames Television)

1971: Feature film directorial debut, "Get Carter", starring Michael Caine; also scripted

1972: Reteamed with Caine as writer and director of "Pulp", with Caine playing an author hired to ghostwrite the autobiography of a Hollywood star (played by Mickey Rooney)

1974: Producing debut with "The Terminal Man", starring George Segal; also wrote and directed

1978: Scripted "Damien—Omen II", the sequel to the hit thriller about the devil born as human

1980: Helmed the campy "Flash Gordon", adapted from the comic books and the 1940s movie serials

1983: Directed the British TV-movie "Squaring the Circle", a drama about the Solidarity movement in Poland written by Tom Stoppard; released theatrically in the USA

1983: Oversaw the English-language version of Fellini's "And the Ship Sailed On"

1983: Helmed the CBS TV-movie "Missing Pieces", starring Elizabeth Montgomery as a reporter tracking her husband's murderers

1987: Directed the thriller "A Prayer for the Dying"; was dissatisfied with studio version and sought to have his name removed from the credits

1989: Last film for close to a decade, "Black Rainbow", a drama about a phony medium who actually "sees" a murder before it is committed

1994: Helmed the two-part TV drama "Dandelion Dead" (aired in USA on PBS' "Masterpiece Theatre")

1998: Returned to feature filmmaking with the character-driven "Croupier", starring Clive Owen

AFFILIATION: Raised Roman Catholic

QUOTES:

"I'm not much of a hustler. But given the way things could have turned out, I'm always astonished that my messages in bottles, as I think of my films, ever got off the ground at all. Astonished, but very happy too."—Mike Hodges quoted in London's *Evening Standard*, June 1999.

Agnieszka Holland

BORN: in Warsaw, Poland, 11/28/1948

NATIONALITY: Polish

EDUCATION: FAMU, Prague, Czechoslovakia, 1966–71; upon her matriculation at age 17, Holland was the youngest student there

AWARDS: Cannes Film Festival FIPRESCI Prize Award "Provincial Actors" 1980

Gdansk Film Festival Grand Prize Award "Fever" 1981

National Board of Review Best Foreign Film "Europa, Europa" 1991 director/screenwriter

New York Film Critics Circle Award Best Foreign Film "Europa, Europa" 1991

Golden Globe Award Best Foreign Film "Europa, Europa" 1991

Boston Society of Film Critics Award Best Foreign Film "Europa, Europa" 1991

BIOGRAPHY

Frequent screenwriter for Andrzej Wajda whose

own films as a director have focused on the lives of the marginal and the doomed. Holland studied filmmaking in Czechoslovakia under Milos Forman and Ivan Passer, returning to Poland in 1972 after police harassment had culminated in a jail sentence. She made her co-directing debut in 1977 with "Screen Tests" and wrote her first screenplay for Wajda, "Without Anaesthesia", in 1978. Two years later her solo feature directing debut, "Provincial Actors", won the FIPRESCI prize at Cannes. After the imposition of martial law in 1981 Holland emigrated to Paris, where she still lives.

Holland's last Polish feature, "A Woman Alone" (1981), chronicles the grim plight of an unmarried mother employed as a letter-carrier. The 1985 West German film "Bitter Harvest", Holland's real breakthrough on the international film scene, reverted to a wartime theme, detailing the relations between a mildly prosperous farmer and the Jewish refugee woman he discovers and shelters. Although her English-language debut film, "To Kill a Priest"

(1988) was considered a career setback, Holland rebounded magnificently with the powerful, acclaimed study of a Jew who masquerades as a Nazi at the height of the Holocaust, "Europa, Europa" (1991). She followed up with another well-received art house item, "Olivier Olivier" (1992), an intriguing story of a child who claims to be a boy who disappeared six years earlier. Holland again explored the world of youth with her first mainstream Hollywood film, an adaptation of the children's classic "The Secret Garden" (1993). Holland followed with another period drama, "Washington Square" (1997) based on the Henry James novel. Formerly married to Czech director Laco Adamik, with whom she has a daughter.—Written by David Lugowski

MILESTONES:

Raised in Poland

Was enrolled at FAMU during the Russian invasion of Czechoslovakia in 1968

1971: Returned to Poland

1977: Feature co-directing debut, "Screen Tests"

1980: Solo feature directing debut, "Provincial Actors"

1981: Immigrated to France

1988: Directed first English-language film, "To Kill a Priest"

1991: Received critical plaudits for helming "Europa, Europa"; received Oscar nomination for Best Adapted Screenplay

1993: Directed first Hollywood film, "The Secret Garden"

1997: Helmed "Washington Square"

Tobe Hooper

BORN: William Tobe Hooper in Austin, Texas, 01/25/1943

NATIONALITY: American

EDUCATION: University of Texas at Austin, Austin, Texas; studied film

BIOGRAPHY

Though he has worked in the horror and dark fantasy genres for more than two decades, producer-writer-director Tobe Hooper's significant contributions can all be traced to just two films: "The Texas Chainsaw Massacre" (1974) and "Poltergeist" (1982). Though produced under very different circumstances—the former was an ultra-low-budget exploitation potboiler while the latter was a major studio spectacular—both films were major commercial successes that reflected the zeitgeist of their day. Surprisingly, neither had quite the salutary effect on Hooper's career as one might have

expected. The filmmaker's current viability, such as it is, has resulted from a canny shift to creating, producing and directing genre projects for the small screen. A popular artist who once helped set trends in entertainment evolved over time into a smooth craftsman striving to ride the wave of his genre's acceptance into the mainstream.

The Austin, Texas native was first bitten by the film bug at age nine upon discovering his father's 8mm camera. By the time he entered his teens, Hooper had completed "The Abyss" (1959), his first short with sound. A number of shorts followed. Hooper's hobby became a job as he broke into professional filmmaking helming commercials and industrial films. In 1968, he gained further exposure directing a PBS documentary on the folk trio "Peter, Paul and Mary." The legacy of coming of age in the 1960s was also conveyed by Hooper's feature bow as producer, director and screenwriter, "Eggshells" (subtitled "An American Freak

Odyssey"). This artsy take on the decline of the Peace Movement garnered a prize at the Atlanta Film Festival but failed to snare a distributor. Hooper turned up before the camera as a supporting player in "The Windsplitter" (1971), another period piece in the "Easy Rider" vein. His breakthrough came with a project whose title belied any interest in peace and love— "The Texas Chainsaw Massacre."

One of the key works in 70s horror cinema, this film was a grueling exercise in nightmarish terror. A group of hapless and notably unpleasant teens run astray of a degenerate family of unemployed slaughterhouse workers with a taste for tourists. Despite its notoriously evocative title, "The Texas Chainsaw Massacre" served its thrills with very little blood but lots of cinematic panache. Even those who dismissed it as sadistic exploitation had to concede its craft. The washed out colors contributed to its raw documentary feel while the overactive camera became an active participant in the mayhem. Generally noted for its emotional intensity and unsettling nihilism, this grisly work of art has garnered praise from Marxist-oriented critics for its jet black satire of class and familial relations. Produced on location in Texas for an exceedingly modest $155,000, the film reportedly grossed as much as $50 million. Due to the vagaries of distribution practices, Hooper received only a fraction of his contractual share of the profits. Nonetheless, he had made a name for himself.

Hooper next entered a period of creative frustration. He completed "Eaten Alive (aka "Death Trap/Legend of the Bayou/Horror Hotel/Starlight Slaughter)" but the producers changed the shape of his conception by recutting the film. Poorly promoted and distributed, the finished film featured stalwart character player Neville Brand as a crazed swamp dweller with a hook hand who feeds tourists to his alligator. Brit culture mag *Time Out* wrote "At its best, the film's lurid tone matches the evocative gloom of the EC horror comics of the 50s, in particular the amazing swamp stories drawn by 'Ghastly' Graham Ingels. Otherwise, it's trite and unconvincing." Hooper was subsequently fired from his next two feature assignments "The Dark" (1979) and "Venom" (1981). In between these twin disappointments, he enjoyed his most trouble-free Hollywood project: a two-part, four-hour TV miniseries based on Stephen King's modern day vampire tale "Salem's Lot" (CBS, 1979). Many fans of the horror novelist still number this among the best King adaptations. The miniseries was re-edited and released theatrically in Europe.

"The Funhouse" (1981), Hooper's stylish concession to the "slasher" movie craze which he helped initiate, also fell victim to studio interference. His fortunes seemed to change when hired by Steven Spielberg to helm a big-budget horror feature "Poltergeist." Set in a Spielbergian suburb, the film told the story of a bourgeois family that manages to fight off the forces of darkness in a crowd-pleasing FX-laden spectacle typical of the top-grossing genre product of the early 80s. While "Poltergeist" brought the ghost story into the modern blockbuster era, it was unfortunately perceived and promoted as a Spielberg picture. Hooper came off seeming like less than a hired hand as reports of Spielberg's daily and active presence on the set emerged from Hollywood. The success of the film should have catapulted its ostensible director onto the A-list but it did not. Dissatisfied by the scripts he was getting, Hooper opted to helm a music video for Brit rocker Billy Idol ("Dancing With Myself").

Hooper entered into an ill-fated three picture deal with Cannon Pictures in 1984, which resulted in a series of flops. The first, the lavishly produced "Lifeforce" (1985), was a tongue-in-cheek evocation of Great Britain's Hammer horror series and the apocalyptic "Quatermass" films. Next up was a well-appointed remake of the 1953 sci-fi classic "Invaders From Mars" (1986). Reviewers deemed it pleasant if pointless and audiences steered clear. Hoping that lightning would strike twice, Hooper shepherded "The Texas Chainsaw Massacre Part 2" (1986) to the screen with disappointing results. Opting for easy gore and outright slapstick, the ill-conceived sequel did not help restore his flagging reputation. Hooper's next outing, "Spontaneous Combustion" (1989) barely made it into the multiplexes before finding its true home on a video store shelf. The Israeli-lensed "Tobe Hooper's Night Terrors" (completed in 1992), an erotic horror flick, failed to receive an American release before arriving in the UK as a 1994 video. Returning to Stephen King country for "The Mangler" (1995), Hooper suffered both critical and commercial neglect.

Fortunately TV had come to welcome dark fantasy in the wake of the success of "The X-Files." Hooper had helmed several telefilms, episodes and specials before signing an exclusive multi-year development deal with Walt Disney TV for his production company Amberson films. He helmed the pilot and another episode of the surreal and cultish UPN suspenser "Nowhere Man" and the pilot for NBC's period UFO drama "Dark Skies." Several other TV projects were in the pipeline as 1996 drew to a close. Hooper was no longer in the front ranks of his field but he remained a trooper.—Written by Kent Greene

MILESTONES:

Began making movies at age nine after discovering his father's 8mm camera

1959: Made first short (with sound), "The Abyss"

1963: Directed short entitled "Heisters"

Directed award-winning short film, "Down Friday Street"

Broke into professional filmmaking via commericals and industrials

1968: Directed a PBS documentary on the folk trio, "Peter, Paul, and Mary"; first produced effort

1969: Feature debut as producer, director and screenwriter, "Eggshells (An American Freak Odyssey)", a story about the decline of the peace movement; won award at the Atlanta Film Festival but failed to find a distributor

1971: Feature acting debut, "The Windsplitter"

1974: Gained notoriety by directing, producing, co-writing (with Kim Hendel), and score composer (with Wayne Bell) the horror/exploitation classic, "The Texas Chainsaw Massacre"; produced on a budget of $155,000, went on to reputedly gross $50 million (reports vary considerably) but, due to complications with distribution, its maker received only a fraction of his contractual share

1976: Completed second feature "Eaten Alive/ Death Trap/Legend of the Bayou/Horror Hotel/ Starlight Slaughter" (directed; wrote story; composed score); had extreme creative differences with the producers who recut the film

1979: Fired as the helmer of a feature entitled "The Dark"; replaced by John Bud Carlos

1979: TV directing debut, directed the well-received CBS miniseries "Salem's Lot", the first TV adaptation of a Stephen King work

1981: Fired as helmer of horror feature "Venom"; replaced by Piers Haggard

1981: Experienced extreme creative differences with producers of "The Funhouse" which he directed

1982: Helmed first big-budget studio feature, "Poltergeist" produced by Steven Spielberg; feature rumored to have been actually co-directed by the overpowering auteur

Dissatisfied with scripts being offered, directed "Dancing With Myself", a music video for recording artist Billy Idol

1984: Signed a three-picture deal with Menahem Golan and Yorum Globus of Cannon Films

1986: First credit as a modelmaker, also provided music, co-produced, and directed, "The Texas Chainsaw Massacre Part 2", a gory yet satirical sequel to his 1974 landmark

1987: TV series directing debut, "Amazing Stories"

1988: Directed the pilot episode ("No More

Mr. Nice Guy") for the syndicated horror anthology series "Freddy's Nightmares"

1989: First screenwriting collaboration with visual effects artist ("Lifeforce" 1985; "The Mangler" 1995) cum writing partner Stephen Brooks, "Spontaneous Combustion" (also directed); released direct-to-video; they also co-scripted "The Mangler" (1995)

1990: TV-movie (as opposed to miniseries) directing debut, "I'm Dangerous Tonight", a supernatural thriller for the USA Network

1991: Directed first TV special, "Haunted Lives . . . True Ghost Stories" for CBS

1993: Directed a segment ("Eye") for the omnibus Showtime telefilm "John Carpenter Presents Body Bags" (also acted)

1995: Signed an exclusive multi-year development deal with Walt Disney TV to create, produce and direct series, movies and miniseries through his Amberson Films

1995: Directed the pilot for UPN's "Nowhere Man", a cultish suspense series

1996: Credited as special visual effects creator on the UPN special "Real Ghosts II" (also directed)

1996: Helmed the two-hour pilot/series premiere of the NBC period sci-fi thriller "Dark Skies"

QUOTES:

Hooper serves as director and partner in Amberson Films, a TV production company.

Hooper sits on the Horror Hall of Fame board of directors.

Hooper received an award from New York Film and Television Festival for his early short film, "Down Friday Street."

A "Texas Chainsaw" video game was marketed in 1982.

Dennis Hopper

BORN: in Dodge City, Kansas, 05/17/1936

SOMETIMES CREDITED AS:
Alan Smithee

NATIONALITY: American

EDUCATION: graduated from high school in San Diego, California

Old Globe Theatre, San Diego, California; won scholarship to attend; instructors were Dorothy McGuire and John Swope

Actors Studio, New York, New York; studied with Lee Strasberg for five years

AWARDS: National Society of Film Critics Special Award "Easy Rider" 1969; cited "as director, co-writer and co-star"

Cannes Film Festival Best New Director Award "Easy Rider" 1969

Venice Film Festival Grand Prize Award "The Last Movie" 1971

National Society of Film Critics Award Best Supporting Actor "Blue Velvet" 1986

Los Angeles Film Critics Association Award Best Actor "Blue Velvet" and "Hoosiers" 1986; both films cited

MTV Movie Award Best Villain "Speed" 1995

BIOGRAPHY

Dennis Hopper's four decade-plus film career as a performer and filmmaker has gained in stature retrospectively due in part to the canny self-promotion and mythicizing that accompanied his remarkable comeback in the 1980s. That his screen debut, "Rebel Without a Cause" (1955), became the stuff of 50s movie legend helped make the case for his significance. Hopper's later critical and commercial success as the director, writer and star (with Peter Fonda) of "Easy Rider"

(1969), one of the zeitgeist films of the 60s, added luster to his story. His subsequent descent into self-indulgence, drugs and alcohol served as a lively cautionary tale about the excesses of 70s Hollywood. Hopper's final transformation in a sober, hard-working, middle-aged character lead provided the necessary upbeat ending for the reactionary 80s.

As "Rebel" became a clarion call for a generation revolting against middle-class American respectability, Hopper himself came to symbolize that revolution, particularly as other actors associated with "Rebel" died. (By 1981, Hopper and Corey Allen were the lone survivors of the film's major players.) His early acting career often cast him in secondary roles, playing sensitive young men, as in "Giant" (1956) and a spate of westerns. His intuitive, improvisatory approach was at odds with many old-time Hollywood professionals; during the making of "From Hell to Texas" (1958), director Henry Hathaway and Hopper reportedly battled through 100-plus takes, an infamous incident that Hopper claimed banned him from major studio productions for eight years. In any event, he was dropped from his Warner Brothers contract. Hopper left Hollywood for NYC where he studied Method acting under Lee Strasberg for five years, worked extensively in TV drama and began a secondary career as a photographer.

Hopper's first starring role came in a little-known gloomy, indie mood piece entitled "Night Tide" (1961; shelved until 1963) that was written and directed by former avant-garde filmmaker Curtis Harrington. He registers growing bewilderment and enchantment as a lonely young sailor smitten with a seaside circus performer who might be a mermaid. Hopper next turned up in "Tarzan and Jane Regained . . . Sort of" (1964), an experimental 16mm film by celebrated pop artist Andy Warhol. A better-behaved Hopper returned to Hollywood where he worked in a Western, the John Wayne–Dean Martin vehicle "The Sons of

Katie Elder" (1965), again helmed by Hathaway. Things proceeded smoothly with Hopper earning positive notices as the weak-willed son of the villain who confesses his father's crimes to a vengeful Wayne. He reteamed with director Harrington playing a doomed astronaut in an entertaining low-budget sci-fi flick entitled "Queen of Blood" (1966).

Hopper enhanced his counter-culture credentials with appearances in Roger Corman's fondly remembered druggy exploitation movie "The Trip" (1967) and Bob Rafelson's "Head" (1968), a zany vehicle for The Monkees, co-scripted by Jack Nicholson. Additional supporting roles in Westerns followed ("Hang 'Em High" 1968; "True Grit" 1969) before his anti-establishment reputation was consolidated by his direction of "Easy Rider." A road movie on motorcycles through reactionary America—a trip in more than one sense—the film featured a notorious psychedelic sequence, shot in a cemetery in New Orleans. Hailed by critics, feted at the Cannes Film Festival as a major new filmmaker, Hopper also found success at home when the low-budget movie was a box-office smash—taking in over $50 million in Hopper's recent estimation. The "Easy Rider" phenomenon sent shockwaves through Hollywood, where dozens of production executives found themselves pink-slipped, and marked the changeover from the Old Guard to the youth culture inside the studios.

The renewed legend of Dennis Hopper proceeded through a documentary self-portrait called "The American Dreamer" (1971) and reached a culmination of sorts in "The Last Movie" (1971), a free-form experimental film shot in Peru about a movie crew making a Western among natives who decide to ape them using real bullets. The film's aspirations were deemed ludicrous, and Hopper was virtually abandoned by critics and other filmmakers. (Of course, the film is now hailed as a masterpiece in some circles.)

For the next 15 years, the often substance-addled Hopper acted mostly in films shot outside the US, where audiences remained loyal to his impervious, impenetrable American swagger. Among his credits were "Mad Dog "(1976), filmed in Australia; "Resurrection" (1979), in Spain; "The American Friend" (1977), directed by Wim Wenders, who initiated the process of Hopper's rehabilitation as a talent, and "White Star" (1981), in West Germany; "Couleur chair" (1977), "The Apprentice Sorcerers" (1977) and "L'Ordre et la Securite du Monde" (1978) in France.

By the late 70s, his drug habits and erratic behavior had virtually sent him into exile, although he reveled in the role of the ugly American. His character in "Apocalypse Now" (1979)—a flipped-out, camera-obsessed journalist—only served to reinforce his reputation. While acting in "Out of the Blue" (1980), a Canadian film shot in the US, Hopper took over direction of the film in mid-production. Though generally ignored some, like the reviewer for London's *Time Out*, found the results edgy and extraordinary. "The teenage [Linda] Manz, in a quite sensational performance under Hopper's direction, embodies the nihilistic ethos of punk in a way that other mainstream projects . . . couldn't begin to achieve."

By this time, Hopper had become an accomplished photographer, and was showing his work in galleries. The breadth of his experience, combined with his bizarre point of view, made his work a unique record of an absurd popular culture.

Hopper's comeback began in earnest with his unnerving appearance as a memorably crazed criminal in "Blue Velvet" (1986). Director David Lynch vociferously defended Hopper's talent against accusations of typecasting. Cast as an alcoholic basketball coach in the bathetic "Hoosiers" (also 1986), the actor seemed to find a perfect vehicle to proclaim "See, I'm clean!" and received a Best Supporting Actor Oscar nomination for his efforts. Ironically, a follow-up film, "River's Edge" (1987),

again featured Hopper as an insane derelict. His rehabilitation seemed complete with his successful direction of "Colors" (1988), a drama about L.A. gang wars, followed by "The Hot Spot" (1990), a film noir for the 90s that featured Don Johnson in an underrated performance as an honorable sleaze in an obscure Texas town full of much worse.

In recent years, Hopper has replaced his old image as a drug-crazed freak with the profile of a regularly employed character lead in film and TV, effortlessly segueing from drama to comedy, from big-budget spectacular to low-budget indies. In 1991 alone, he appeared in Sean Penn's directorial debut, "The Indian Runner", two made-for-cable movies, "Paris Trout" (Showtime) and "Doublecrossed" (HBO), served as an awards show presenter, and participated in two documentaries. In 1993, Hopper turned in four showy feature performances. In "Boiling Point", a lukewarm attempt to recreate a 50s-styled crime flick, Hopper played a rather likeable loser whose desire to stay alive causes many deaths. In "Super Mario Brothers", based on the video game, Hopper is the literally reptilian villain King Koopa. John Dahl's "Red Rock West" found him playing a smarmy psychotic hitman while Tony Scott's "True Romance" gave him one of his favorite scenes of his film career. As the generally sympathetic former cop father of the anti-hero Christian Slater, Hopper gets tortured by gangster Christopher Walken before launching into an unforgettable Quentin Tarantino-scripted speech about the ancestry of Sicilians.

By the mid-1990s, Hopper had become a reliable villain for such special effects-driven blockbusters as "Speed" (1994) and "Waterworld" (1995) while still appearing in such low-profile efforts as the comedy "Search and Destroy", as a late-night cable guru and novelist, and the documentary "Who Is Henry Jaglom?" (both 1995). The nearly 60-year-old Hopper starred in the romantic comedy-drama "Carried Away" (1996) in a change-of-pace "normal" role. He was convincing as a fortysomething school teacher who cares for his invalid mother and juggles a long-term, low-intensity relationship with another teacher (Amy Irving) and a passionate affair with a 17-year-old student (Amy Locane). The aging trooper reported some embarrassment at doing full frontal nudity for this limited release. He subsequently turned up in Julian Schnabel's downtown biopic "Basquiat" (1996), as a European art dealer.

In 1999, Hopper was cast as Hank, the father of Matthew McConaughey's character Ed in the comedy feature, "Edtv". He then portrayed the character Vince Drazen in in the television series "24" (2001), starring Keifer Sutherland as a cop racing through time to prevent the assassination of a popular presidential candidate. In 2002, he joined Vin Diesel and John Malkovich for the Brian Koppelman and David Levien comedy "Knockaround Guys."

COMPANIONS:

wife: Brooke Hayward. Married in 1961; divorced in 1969; daughter of agent-producer Leland Hayward and actor Margaret Sullavan; author of family memoir "Haywire"; had been previously married and had two children by her first husband; later married Peter Duchin

wife: Michelle Phillips. Singer, Actor; married for eight days in 1970

MILESTONES:

Raised on a farm in Dodge City, Kansas, by his grandparents

1949: Moved to San Diego

Had notions about acting transformed by seeing Montgomery Clift in George Stevens' "A Place in the Sun" (1951) and Marlon Brando perform in Elia Kazan's "Viva Zapata" (1952)

After high school acted with the Pasadena Playhouse, California

1955: Film acting debut in "Rebel Without a Cause"

1955: Signed with Warner Bros.

1955: Appeared on first TV show, "Boy in the Storm" on "Medic"

Appeared in two episodes of TV series "Conflict" ("No Man's Road" and "A Question of Loyalty"; both 1957) which were released theatrically abroad

1958: Involved in legendary conflict with director Henry Hathaway on the set of "From Hell to Texas"; reportedly did over 100 takes of a simple scene before giving the requested line reading

1958–1964: Dropped from contract at Warner Bros.; left Hollywood for New York; studied acting with Lee Strasberg for five years; began career as photographer; appeared in Andy Warhol's "Tarzan and Jane Regained . . . Sort Of" (1963)

Starred on Broadway in "Mandingo" with Franchot Tone

Appeared on over 140 TV shows including "The Twilight Zone" and "The Loretta Young Show"

1963: First feature starring role, "Night Tide" (written and directed by Curtis Harrington)

1965: Returned to Hollywood

1969: Feature directing and co-writing debut, "Easy Rider"; also acted; shared Best Original Screenplay Oscar nomination with Peter Fonda and Terry Southern

1971: Credited as co-writer of documentary about himself, "The American Dreamer" (directed by L. M. Kit Carson and Lawrence Schiller)

1971: Made the nearly unwatchable "The Last Movie"

Acted in several low budget, independent films

1979: Won renewed attention for small but showy role in Francis Coppola's "Apocalypse Now"

1986: Acted in controversial role of Frank, a nitrous oxide sniffing thug, in David Lynch's "Blue Velvet"

1986: Earned Best Supporting Actor Oscar nomination for his protrayal of an alcoholic basketball fan in "Hoosiers"

1988: Directed the critically acclaimed feature "Colors", starring Robert Duvall and Sean Penn

Exhibited photography in USA, Tokyo and Europe

1990: Helmed the noir romance "Backtrack"; removed his name after post-production trouble, instead opting to use the DGA moniker, "Alan Smithee"

1991: Acted in Sean Penn's feature directorial debut "The Indian Runner"

1991: Headlined the Showtime movie "Paris Trout"

1994: Performed in the computer game "Hell" (date approximate)

1994: Had villainous role as a mad bomber in the hit film "Speed"

1995: Played the heavy in "Waterworld"

1995: Was the subject of the documentary "Dennis Hopper: L.A. Blues"

1996: Displayed romantic side in a richly realized, change-of-pace characterization of a Midwestern farmer in "Carried Away"

1997: Cast as Mickey Wayne in "The Blackout"

1998: Portrayed Frank Slater in the comedy feature "Meet The Deedles"

1999: Played Matthew McConaughey's father in "Edtv"

2001: Portrayed Victor Drazen in the television series "24"

2002: Co-starred in the sci-fi television series "Flatland"

2002: Cast in the crime comedy "Knockaround Guys"

2003: Starred as Frank in Steve Balderson's thriller feature "Firecracker"

QUOTES:

In a 1996 interview, Hopper revealed that he was suing Peter Fonda, his "Easy Rider" co-star and co-writer, because his old friend supposedly failed to live up to their agreement to share equally in the film's profits.

He had his first museum showing of his paintings in February 2001.

Hopper was invited to participate in the 2002 Whitney Biennial. Twelve of his color photographs were selected for exhibition.

BIBLIOGRAPHY:

"Out of the Sixties" Dennis Hopper, 1988; collection of photographs

"Dennis Hopper: From Method to Madness" J. Hoberman, 1988; Walker Art Center a monograph that accompanied a traveling exhibition of his film work

---

Ron Howard

BORN: Ronald Howard in Duncan, Oklahoma, 03/01/1954

SOMETIMES CREDITED AS:
Ronny Howard

NATIONALITY: American

EDUCATION: Burroughs High School, Burbank, California; classmates included actress Rene Russo

University of Southern California, Los Angeles, California, film; attended briefly; left to pursue career

AWARDS: ShowEast George Eastman Award presented by National Association of Theatre Owners

Directors Guild of America Award Outstanding Directorial Achievement in Feature Film "Apollo 13" 1995

Emmy Outstanding Miniseries "From the Earth to the Moon" 1997/98; shared award

Golden Satellite Best Mini-Series or Motion

Picture Made for Television "From the Earth to the Moon" 1998; shared award

Golden Globe Award Best Mini-Series or Motion Picture Made for Television "From the Earth to the Moon" 1998

Dallas-Fort Worth Film Critics Association Award Best Picture "A Beautiful Mind" 2001

Dallas-Fort Worth Film Critics Association Award Best Director "A Beautiful Mind" 2001

Broadcast Film Critics Association Award Best Picture "A Beautiful Mind" 2001

Broadcast Film Critics Association Award Best Director "A Beautiful Mind" 2001; tied with Baz Luhrmann ("Moulin Rouge!")

Golden Globe Award Best Motion Picture (Drama) "A Beautiful Mind" 2001; shared award

ShoWest Director of the Year Award 2002

Directors Guild of America Award Outstanding Directorial in Feature Film "A Beautiful Mind" 2001

Oscar Best Picture "A Beautiful Mind" 2001; shared with Brian Grazer

Oscar Best Director "A Beautiful Mind" 2001

BIOGRAPHY

A showbiz veteran of over 40 years, Ron Howard experienced great success as a child actor in TV and film, a juvenile lead on the small screen, and a producer-director of successful Hollywood features in his maturity. As a filmmaker, he has proven capable of handling light comic material, special effects sagas, and transgeneric family dramas. The son of actors Rance and Jean Howard and older brother of character actor Clint, he made his first professional appearance at the age of 18 months on stage with his parents in Baltimore, Maryland.

As a child and later teen actor, the cute, red-headed Howard was very much of a "father's son" type: he first gained fame as Opie, the personable son of widowed Sheriff Andy Taylor, on "The Andy Griffith Show" (CBS, 1960–68). He worked in features during breaks in TV production, notably in "The Music Man" (1962) singing "Gary, Indiana" and, the following

year, as the son of another widowed father (Glenn Ford) in "The Courtship of Eddie's Father" (1963). After departing his charmingly rustic TV hometown of Mayberry, North Carolina, Howard embarked on a minor feature career as an actor with a few bright spots, including a major role in "American Graffiti" (1973), the George Lucas–directed landmark comedy-drama of teen life in Southern California in the early 60s. This part led to a long TV gig starring as Richie Cunningham, the all-American-boy-next-door of the popular ABC faux 50s sitcom "Happy Days." Howard essayed Richie regularly for six seasons until 1980 and then made occasional appearances over the series' remaining four years.

On the big screen, Howard fared well in a memorable featured role as the son of a widowed Lauren Bacall who falls under the influence of a moribund John Wayne in "The Shootist" (1976). Otherwise, he appeared mostly in undistinguished Westerns and drive-in fare. Howard made his directing and screenwriting debut at age 23, in the latter arena with "Grand Theft Auto" (1977), a cheapie produced by Roger Corman. After further honing his filmmaking skills on several TV projects, Howard made his mark as a director with his second venture, "Night Shift" (1982), a wacky comedy about two morgue attendants who double as pimps. While "Happy Days" co-star Henry Winkler starred in the movie, it also marked Howard's initial collaboration with several individuals. He and producer Brian Grazer would go on to form a production company while former "Happy Days" screenwriters Lowell Ganz and Babaloo Mandel would team with him on "Splash" (1984), "Gung Ho" (1986) and "Parenthood" (1989) and actor Michael Keaton would star in both "Gung Ho" and "The Paper" (1994).

With his third feature, "Splash", Howard garnered a great deal of attention. A major hit for Disney's then new Touchstone division, this romantic fantasy about a man and a mermaid

(Tom Hanks and Daryl Hannah) proved to be the studio's most successful live-action feature up to that time. Howard enjoyed another hit and directed veteran actor Don Ameche to a Best Supporting Actor Oscar with "Cocoon" (1985), a Spielbergian sci-fi fantasy about old folks who rediscover youthful vigor thanks to alien intervention. On the other hand, "Willow" (1988), a lavish George Lucas–produced fantasy peopled with elves, trolls and a gallant hero, did not find its expected audience. By this point, though, the tone and style of a Howard-directed film was already in place: much as his success as a child actor helped extend the cozy, sweet aura of mainstream film and TV, his features essentially rework old genre formulas, offering plenty of feel-good optimism and playful whimsy to soften the grimmer, more violent edge of contemporary mainstream cinema.

In 1985, Howard and Grazer formed Imagine Films Entertainment and took it public the following year. After a number of very successful features, the dynamic duo felt that Imagine was not paying them their street value, so in 1992, they announced plans to leave Imagine for a joint venture at Universal. This horrified stockholders, who consequently allowed Howard and Grazer to renegotiate their deal so that Imagine lent them money to buy out the company. By 1993, Imagine was a privately-owned entity with Howard and Grazer serving as co-CEOs. Through Imagine, Howard served as a producer on most of his own films as well as the Michael Keaton-vehicle "Clean and Sober" (1988), the comedy "The 'Burbs" (1989), the John Grisham adaptation "The Chamber" (1996) and the period drama "Inventing the Abbots" (1997). Imagine has also made inroads in TV, with Howard and Grazer serving as producers or executive producers of series as varied as sitcoms like "Gung Ho" (ABC, 1986–87, based on the Howard-directed film) and "Hiller and Diller" (ABC, 1997–98), the acclaimed comedy-drama

"Sports Night" (ABC, 1998–2000), and the popular teen drama "Felicity" (The WB, 1998–2002).

In the 1990s, Howard solidified his reputation as a reliable Hollywood genre director, helming several diverse projects including the wholesome ensemble comedy "Parenthood" (as well as producing its sitcom spin-off for NBC in 1990–91), the rousing firefighter drama "Backdraft" (1991) and the historical romantic adventure "Far and Away" (1992). The first two were solid successes while the latter, a would-be epic starring Tom Cruise and Nicole Kidman, was Howard's first critical and commercial disappointment. He received more positive press if not better box office for "The Paper" (1994), a somewhat sentimental comedy-drama about tabloid journalism.

Howard reached new heights at the helm of "Apollo 13" (1995), the based-on-fact drama about a NASA moon mission that encountered difficulties and the efforts of the crew and ground support to avert potential tragedy. Eschewing archival footage, Howard and his team recreated everything in perfect detail, from the interior of the capsule to the command center in Houston to the 1970s decor of the astronaut's homes. With a strong cast that included Tom Hanks, Gary Sinise, Kevin Bacon, Ed Harris and Kathleen Quinlan, "Apollo 13" earned critical kudos and a healthy box office. Indeed, Academy members were suitably impressed and rewarded the film with nine Oscar nominations including Best Picture. Surprisingly, though, Howard was omitted from the Best Director category, an oversight that the Directors Guild of America rectified in part by awarding him its award as Director of the Year.

Howard continued on the space theme, collaborating with Hanks as a producer on the Emmy-winning HBO miniseries "From the Earth to the Moon" (1998), which traced the history of the Apollo missions from their inception in 1961 through the triumphant 1969 moon landing to the end of the project in 1972.

For his next three big screen projects, Howard adapted previously produced material, adding his own spin to the films. "Ransom" (1996) was a remake of a 1956 thriller featuring Mel Gibson and Rene Russo as a wealthy married couple whose son is kidnapped. Somewhat of a departure for Howard, "Ransom" was his first attempt at darker material and if the end results were a mixed bag, it signaled a desire to stretch. "EDtv" (1999), based on the French-Canadian movie "Louis XIX: Roi des Ondes", had the interesting premise of a man being followed by television cameras seven days a week, twenty-four hours a day. Unfortunately, "The Truman Show" (1998) had already been released and proved a hit with audiences. In comparison, Howard's movie was deemed less adventurous, his direction pandering to the lowest common denominator and the script's criticism of contemporary media toothless. The third film, "Dr. Seuss' How the Grinch Stole Christmas" (2000), earned Howard some of the worst notices of his career, yet paradoxically was his biggest hit. Competing with the classic TV cartoon that was also based on the children's book, the film was a grandly produced affair, with spectacular sets, eye-popping costumes and quirky makeup. Howard's film was also graced with the manic energy of Jim Carrey as the green-furred anti-hero. While critics found the effort ponderous, viewers flocked to screenings, pushing its cumulative box-office gross to over $260 million. (Its DVD release netted more than $145 million in its first week of release.)

What would Howard do for an encore? Instead of another remake, he turned his attention to the biopic, a genre in which he had not previously worked, opting to tell the story of mathematician John Forbes Nash Jr. who overcame schizophrenia and won a Nobel Prize. "A Beautiful Mind" (2001) garnered as much controversy as acclaim, though, as many objected to the liberties it took with the facts. Howard and screenwriter Akiva Goldsman conceded that they made a fictionalized account of the

man's life. It also marked another rarity in the director's canon: the film had a single leading role whereas most of his work has been of an ensemble nature. Having received eight Academy Award nominations, one of which was Howard's first as Best Director, it took home four statues, including Best Picture and Best Director.

MILESTONES:

1956: Stage acting debut at 18 months old with parents in "The Seven Year Itch" at the Hilltop Summer Theatre in Baltimore, Maryland; father directed production

1956: Appeared as a baby in "Frontier Woman", featuring his father Rance Howard

Raised in Burbank, California

1958: TV acting debut, "Police Station"

1959: First feature acting role at age four in "The Journey"

1959: TV series debut, playing various characters on the sitcom, "The Many Loves of Dobie Gillis" (CBS)

1960–1968: Portrayed Opie Taylor, the son of Sheriff Andy Taylor, on "The Andy Griffith Show" (CBS)

1962: Had featured role in the big screen adaptation of "The Music Man"

1963: Played Eddie in the feature "The Courtship of Eddie's Father"

1965: Last film role for five years, "Village of the Giants"

Served as co-editor of his high school newspaper

1970: Resumed movie acting career in "Smoke"

1971: Feature debut as director and co-writer at age 23 with "Grand Theft Auto"; also starred

Played Bob Smith on the ABC comedy-drama, "The Smith Family", starring Henry Fonda and Janet Blair

1973: Starred in George Lucas' groundbreaking teen film "American Graffiti"; Cindy Williams was also in the cast

Cast as Richie Cunningham on the long-running ABC sitcom, "Happy Days"; was a regular on the series for six years; left to pursue career as a filmmaker but made occasional appearances when his character "visited"; gradually written out of the show, which continued until 1984

1974: Had dramatic role in the acclaimed TV production "The Migrants" (CBS)

1975: Played title role in the ABC adaptation of "Huckleberry Finn"; his parents and brother played supporting parts

1976: Co-starred with John Wayne in the elegiac Western "The Shootist"

1976: Made uncredited cameo appearance in "The First Nudie Musical", starring Cindy Williams

1978: TV directing and screenwriting debut, "Cotton Candy", an NBC teen comedy movie; co-written with brother Clint

1979: Reprised his role in the less successful sequel "More American Graffiti"

1980: TV producing debut, "Ron Howard's 'Skyward' ", a TV-movie about a paraplegic teen who yearns to pilot her own plane with Bette Davis in featured role; also directed

1980: Cast as a man who honors his brother's wishes by committing a mercy killing and then is tried for murder in the NBC movie "Act of Love"

1980: Feature debut as executive producer, "Leo and Loree"; "Happy Days" co-star Don Most had title role of Leo

1981: Met Brian Grazer

1982: Helmed his breakthrough feature, "Night Shift"; first collaborations with producer Brian Grazer, writers Lowell Ganz and Babaloo Mandel and actor Michael Keaton; "Happy Days" co-star Henry Winkler also starred

1984: Breakthrough feature as director, "Splash", featuring Tom Hanks and Daryl Hannah; scripted by Mandel and Ganz

1985: Moved east with his family to Connecticut at his wife's urging

1985: Founded Imagine Films Entertainment with Brian Grazer; served as co-CEO

1985: Helmed "Cocoon"; actor Don Ameche received a Best Supporting Actor Oscar

1986: Took Imagine Films public

1986: Reprised signature childhood role of Opie Taylor in the NBC reunion movie "Return to Mayberry", executive produced by Andy Griffith

Served as executive producer of the ABC sitcom version of his 1986 feature "Gung Ho", which had starred Michael Keaton

1987: First Imagine production, "Like Father Like Son"

1987: Was an executive producer on the short-lived CBS sitcom "Take Five"

1988: Had box-office misfire with the fantasy "Willow"

1988: Executive produced the TV sequel "Splash Too" (ABC)

1989: Enjoyed hit with the genial comedy "Parenthood"; Dianne Wiest received a Best Supporting Actress Academy Award nomination

1990: Returned to TV series as executive producer of "Parenthood", a short-lived NBC sitcom

1991: Helmed the action thriller "Backdraft", about firefighters with a cast including Robert De Niro, Kurt Russell and Donald Sutherland

1992: Announced that he and Grazer were leaving Imagine for a joint venture at Universal Pictures

1992: Teamed with Tom Cruise and Nicole Kidman on the sweeping period romance "Far and Away"; proved to be a box-office disappointment

1993: Bought out Imagine (with Grazer), making the company private again

1994: Helmed "The Paper", featuring an all-star cast including Michael Keaton, Glenn Close, Robert Duvall and Marisa Tomei

1995: Directed the based-on-fact drama about an aborted NASA mission to the moon, "Apollo 13"; starred Tom Hanks, Ed Harris, Gary Sinise and Kathleen Quinlan; film earned 9 Academy Award nominations including Best Picture but not Best Director; won the DGA Award

1996: Helmed "Ransom", a remake of the 1956 film about a child kidnapping, starring Mel Gibson and Rene Russo

Was an executive producer of the ABC sitcom "Hiller & Diller"

1998: Served as one of the producers of the Emmy-winning HBO series "From the Earth to the Moon"; Tom Hanks was driving force behind the project, serving as executive producer as well as director, screenwriter and co-star

With partner Brian Grazer, was an executive producer of the ABC sitcom "Sports Night"

With Grazer, executive produced the highly-touted drama series "Felicity" (The WB)

1999: Directed the feature comedy "EDtv", starring Matthew McConaughey, a loose remake of a French-Canadian comedy-drama about a man who wins a contest and has his life broadcast 24 hours a day on television

With Grazer and Eddie Murphy, served as executive producer of the animated series "The PJs" (Fox, 1999–2000; The WB, 2000–2001)

2000: Served as executive producer of the short-lived ABC drama "Wonderland", created by Peter Berg

2000: Helmed the live action version of "Dr. Seuss' How the Grinch Stole Christmas", starring Jim Carrey

2000: Renewed Imagine's production deal with Universal through 2005

2001: With Grazer, was an executive producer of the ABC summer series "The Beast"

2001: Provided the character voice of the animated figure Tom Colonic in the mixed media feature "Osmosis Jones"

2001: Directed Russell Crowe in "A Beautiful Mind", a fictionalized biopic of Nobel Prize winner John Forbes Nash who overcame schizophrenia; film received eight Academy Award nominations including two for Howard, Best Picture and Best Director; won four Oscars including Best Picture and Best Director

2002: With Grazer, was a producer of the comedy feature "Stealing Harvard"

QUOTES:

Not to be confused with British actor Ronald Howard, the son of actor-director Leslie Howard.

Three of Howard's four children are named for the places they were conceived: Bryce Dallas in Dallas; Paige Carlyle and Jocelyn Carlyle at the Hotel Carlyle in New York City.—From *Premiere*, April 1991.

"I've always believed that I'd do my best work from age 50 to 65. I told that to my brother Clint about 20 years ago. He looked at me and said, 'That means you're in store for a lot of sh—y movies.' "—Howard quoted in *Entertainment Weekly*, April 1, 1994.

"I've always been involved in sort of pop entertainment. You live with a little bit of frustration that that kind of work is not taken as seriously as other kinds of work. I mean, there's great feedback, but yeah, sure, I was sort of legitimately categorized and types as the all-American guy."—Howard to Bernard Weinraub in *The New York Times*, November 12, 1996.

"Part of my code of life became defined by not fulfilling those cliches for people, which later included not being thrown in jail or being written up as a child actor on the rocks. I consciously wanted to avoid those cliches."—Howard quoted in the *Daily News*, March 21, 1999.

"Well, I would love every review to be glowing and I would like to win every award I can win. But I think I'm treated pretty fairly. I think there are certain people who don't like my stuff. And you just have to understand that."—Howard quoted in *Newsday*, March 24, 1999.

"For a long time, people thought of me as a TV actor dabbling in directing. Then they thought of me as a director who only did comedy . . . Then I started making dramas, and people raised their eyebrows."—Howard quoted in *New York Post*, March 25, 1999.

"I learned to write in order to sign autographs at 5. People were asking me for my autograph on the first season of 'Andy Griffith' and my dad said, 'I guess you'll have to learn to sign your name. Printing won't work.' "—Ron Howard quoted by Stephen Schaefer in *Boston Herald*, March 26, 1999.

"One reason that I became a director was because I felt sort of suffocated at one point in my late teens—"Happy Days" was a number one show at the time, and it was a teenage show to boot, so there was a real pop side to the fan base and the way they would react. That was about as intense as that can be—being uncomfortable to go out Christmas shopping or to Disneyland or to the movies. I was getting ready to have an adult life."—Howard to *Premiere*, April 1999.

"Brian [Grazer]'s a much better producer than I am. . . . Good producers need to roll their sleeves up in a way that I can be kind of timid about. The director in me doesn't want to step on another director's toes, but directors' toes need to a little stomping from time to time. Even mine. I depend on Brian for that with me."—Ron Howard quoted in *Premiere*, April 1999.

"My objective is to reach the point where no script written in this town has my name crossed off as a potential director."—Ron Howard quoted by Peter Bart in *GQ*, May 1999.

"As a director, this film was definitely the biggest challenge I've ever faced. "Apollo 13" was daunting. "Backdraft" was tricky, and I also learned a lot on "Willow", but "The Grinch" had a visual trick in almost every shot. Still, I don't like to be too blatant with those tricks, and I don't like the photography and the sty-

listic choices to overtake and overpower the characters. . . . "—Ron Howard on directing "Dr. Seuss' How the Grinch Stole Christmas" quoted in *American Cinematographer*, November 2000.

"For a long time I was trying to display unexpected range. That was much more of an issue. But in the last four or five years, I kind of worked in all the genres I expect I ever will work in. There was a certain turning point."—Ron Howard to *New York*, December 17, 2001.

"Of course I'm vain, but in my day-to-day living in the East, I'm not encountering people in the business unless I specifically come to work. And I think there's something very liberating about that, being constantly reminded that even if what you're doing is important to you, it's not the be-all and end-all. When you're in L.A., it's the be-all and end-all."—Howard on living on the East Coast to *New York*, December 17, 2001.

"Everybody wants their films to be appreciated and respected at every level," he says. "Of course, I hope 'A Beautiful Mind' is accepted in that way. I wish I'd been nominated and won for 'Apollo 13.' I'd be lying if I didn't say that. But I don't know what factors go into what is an impossible choice to begin with. It's never [comparing] apples to apples anyway—God knows what colors those choices."—Howard on the Oscars, quoted in the *Los Angeles Times*, Janaury 4, 2002.

"Joh Huston directed until he dropped. That's what I wan to do."—Howard quoted in *Premiere*, February 2002.

Albert Hughes

BORN: in Detroit, Michigan, 04/01/1972

SOMETIMES CREDITED AS:
'The Hughes Brothers'

NATIONALITY: American

EDUCATION: Dropped out of high school in 11th grade

Los Angeles City College, Los Angeles, California, filmmaking

AWARD: MTV Movie Award Best Movie "Menace II Society" 1994

BIOGRAPHY

Evincing a greater affinity for the studied "cool" of a Quentin Tarantino than the overt social messages of fellow African-American filmmakers Spike Lee and John Singleton, Hughes transcended the pitfalls of a troubled home life, divorce and welfare to make a striking feature debut as a producer-director, along with his partner and twin brother Allen, with the hyper-realistic morality tale "Menace II Society" (1993). Having studied filmmaking at Los Angeles City College, Albert has defined himself as the more technically-oriented of the pair. Born on April Fool's Day in Detroit to an African-American father and a white Armenian mother, the Hughes twins moved to Pomona, California with their mother when they were aged nine. They became interested in filmmaking as 12-year-olds when their mother lent them a video camera. They never returned the gadget but immediately began churning out their own little movies. When a teacher suggested that they make a "how to" film for an assignment, they complied with "How to Be a Burglar."

The Hughes brothers eventually had their films aired on public access cable where one effort, "The Drive By", snared them an agent. The duo subsequently found themselves directing music videos for such rap artists as Tupac Shakur, Tone-Loc and Digital Underground. They subsequently raised $2.5 million to make their first feature which had its world premiere at the Directors Fortnight in Cannes in 1993. Set in the grim surroundings of South Central Los Angeles and informed by the percussive rhythms and worldview of "gangsta" rap, the gritty, downbeat yet somehow poetic contemporary gangster film went on to earn both respectful reviews and nearly $30 million in domestic box-office receipts. This surprising success allowed them to negotiate themselves out of their commitment to New Line Cinema—which had produced "Menace II Society"—in order to sign a two-picture, three-year deal with Disney's Caravan Productions.

The Hughes brothers were granted a waiver by the Directors Guild of America to take co-credit for directing—the first "brother act" to do so since Jerry and David Zucker (who formed a co-directing trio with Jim Abrahams). Duties were split fairly evenly: Albert dealt with the director of photography, production designer, costume designer and the like, while Allen focused on the actors—especially during rehearsals—and the business aspects. They also make a formidable team when facing the media, shocking and delighting journalists with their playfully irreverent "no-holds-barred" remarks about the state of contemporary Hollywood. (For example, they blithely dismissed Singleton's 1991 feature "Boyz N the Hood" as "an "Afterschool Special" with cussin'.")

The brothers share a love for the work of stylish genre filmmakers like Sergio Leone, Martin Scorsese and Brian De Palma, all of whom are noted for their representations of violence. The Hugheses have endeavored to depict violence in a realistic manner designed to disturb rather than titillate their viewers. Not surprisingly, they were forced to make a number of cuts to "Menace II Society" to avoid the commercially dreaded NC-17 rating.

The Hughes brothers have demonstrated an unusually high concern about the aural qualities of their work, paying great attention to sound design, background scoring and song selection. New Line profited handsomely from the soundtrack for "Menace II Society" while the brothers—who executive produced the album—received nothing extra for the platinum disc. With this slight in mind, they set up Underworld Records, their own rap/rhythm & blues label, at Capitol Records in 1993. Their second feature, the early 1970s-set "Dead Presidents" (1995), also boasted a powerhouse soundtrack of classic R & B hits from the period.

Though misleadingly marketed by Disney as a Black heist picture, "Dead Presidents" was more concerned with the traumas faced by African-American veterans returning home from Vietnam to few economic opportunities. Larenz Tate, so memorable as the murderously nihilistic O-Dog in "Menace", here plays a clean cut, hard-working kid who goes off to war and comes home disillusioned and underemployed. He spirals downward and ends up taking part a poorly planned armored car robbery. The film opened to mixed reviews and disappointing box office.—Written by Kent Greene

FAMILY:

mother: Aida Hughes. Former fast food worker; owner of a vocational rehabilitation company white (Armenian); born in Iran and adopted by a military family; took children and left husband; spent three years on welfare before starting own business; gave the twins their first video camera when they were 12

brother: Allen Hughes. Director, producer; twin; co-directs and produces with Albert

MILESTONES:

1981: Moved to Pomona, California at age nine with brother Allen and mother (date approximate)

1984: Received first video camera at age 12

Began making short films with his brother; when a teacher suggested they make a "how-to" film, they presented "How to Be a Burgler"

Made short films with his brother; some were aired on public access cable TV, one "The Drive By", attracted agents

Co-directed (with his brother Allen) music videos for rap artists KRS-One, Yo-Yo and Digital Underground

Co-directed (with his brother Allen) an episode of "America's Most Wanted"

1993: Feature debut as director, co-producer and story writer (all shared with brother Allen), "Menace II Society"

1993: Allowed to leave commitment with New Line Cinema (which produced "Menace II Society") to sign a two-picture, three-year deal with Caravan Productions; films to be distributed by Disney

1993: With brother, co-founded a rap/R & B record label, Underworld Records

1993: With brother, walked off the set of their Shaquille O'Neal Reebok commercial (aired during the 1994 Super Bowl telecast) over creative differences

1995: Co-directed the taut drama "Dead Presidents"

1996: Brothers signed a four-year, first-look deal with Universal (in April)

1999: With brother, made the documentary "American Pimp"; screened at Sundance

QUOTES:

From "Born II Direct: The Hughes Brothers Interview" by Quendrith Johnson, *DGA Magazine*, Vol. 20, No.3:

[Question:] Coming off something like "Menace II Society" where it really became part of a public dialogue, are you thinking now that you have to keep making films just like that?

Albert: We don't want to be second-guessed by people, as far as saying, "Oh, it's another hood film, who cares?" Or they say, "It's not positive." We're not out to make positive films, or preach and propagandize to the Black community. It's limiting.

From "Born II Direct: The Hughes Brothers Interview" by Quendrith Johnson, *DGA Magazine*, Vol. 20, No.3:

Allen: We're interested in the criminal element, whether it's a gangster, pimp, drug-dealer, whatever. We're interested in the underworld and the underclass. There's too many movies about cops saving the world, which isn't true. There's too many movies about good prevailing over evil, which isn't true either. More times than not, there's evil kicking good's ass. Not that you can't walk away, walk out of a movie feeling good. But we have to figure a way so people aren't walking out all choked up over it. So it's not cheesy.

"They expect that black filmmakers know other black filmmakers," says Allen. "You know what? I can give a fuck about those niggers. I can give a shit about white filmmakers too, unless I like their shit." "I don't want to hang around other filmmakers," adds Albert. "I want to hang around with some regular people."

—From "Hughes's Views" by Martha Frankel in *Movieline*, March 1994.

"You start dealin' with big stars, that's how films are ruined," says Allen. "I don't bring no names up—Sharon Stone. This is Sharon Stone acting," he says, opening his legs. "Tim Allen, is he gonna be the white Cosby? Are we gonna

see a movie every year from this fool? Keanu Reeves is gettin' $7 million [offers]—have you seen this guy ACT?"

—From "The Hugheses: 'Dead' at 22" by Tim Appelo, *Entertainment Weekly*, January 13, 1995.

"Spike Lee, until [cinematographer] Ernest Dickerson left him, was a really good technical director."

—From "The Hughes One-Two Punch" by Sean Mitchell in *Los Angeles Times*, October 1, 1995.

Allen Hughes

BORN: in Detroit, Michigan, 04/01/1972

SOMETIMES CREDITED AS:
"The Hughes Brothers"

NATIONALITY: American

EDUCATION: Dropped out of high school in 11th grade

AWARD: MTV Movie Award Best Movie "Menace II Society" 1994

BIOGRAPHY

Evincing a greater affinity for the studied "cool" of a Quentin Tarantino than the overt social messages of fellow African-American filmmakers Spike Lee and John Singleton, Hughes transcended the pitfalls of a troubled home life, divorce and welfare to make a striking feature debut as a producer-director, along with his partner and twin brother Albert, with the hyper-realistic morality tale "Menace II Society" (1993). A bit more outspoken than his brother in interviews, Allen is also the more actor-oriented half of the team. Born on April Fool's Day in Detroit to an African-American father and a white Armenian mother, the Hughes twins moved to Pomona, California,

with their mother when they were aged nine. They became interested in filmmaking as 12-year-olds when their mother lent them a video camera. They never returned the gadget but immediately began churning out their own little movies. When a teacher suggested that they make a "how to" film for an assignment, they complied with "How to Be a Burglar."

The Hughes brothers eventually had their films aired on public access cable where one effort, "The Drive By", snared them an agent. The duo subsequently found themselves directing music videos for such rap artists as Tupac Shakur, Tone-Loc and Digital Underground. They subsequently raised $2.5 million to make their first feature which had its world premiere at the Directors Fortnight in Cannes in 1993. Set in the grim surroundings of South Central Los Angeles and informed by the percussive rhythms and worldview of "gangsta" rap, the gritty, downbeat yet somehow poetic contemporary gangster film went on to earn both respectful reviews and nearly $30 million in domestic box-office receipts. This surprising success allowed them to negotiate themselves out of their commitment to New Line Cinema—which had produced "Menace II Society"—so as to sign a two-picture, three-year deal with Disney's Caravan Productions.

The Hughes brothers were granted a waiver by the Directors Guild of America to take co-credit for directing—the first "brother act" to do so since Jerry and David Zucker (who formed a co-directing trio with Jim Abrahams). Duties were split fairly evenly: Albert dealt with the director of photography, production designer, costume designer and the like while Allen focused on the actors—especially during rehearsals—and the business aspects. They also make a formidable team when facing the media, shocking and delighting journalists with their playfully irreverent "no-holds-barred" remarks about the state of contemporary Hollywood. (For example, they blithely dismissed Singleton's 1991 feature "Boyz N the Hood" as "an "Afterschool Special" with cussin'.")

The brothers share a love for the work of stylish genre filmmakers like Sergio Leone, Martin Scorsese and Brian De Palma, all of whom are noted for their representations of violence. The Hugheses have endeavored to depict violence in a realistic manner designed to disturb rather than titillate their viewers. Not surprisingly, they were forced to make a number of cuts to "Menace II Society" to avoid the commercially dreaded NC-17 rating.

The Hughes brothers have demonstrated an unusually high concern about the aural qualities of their work, paying great attention to sound design, background scoring and song selection. New Line profited handsomely from the soundtrack for "Menace II Society" while the brothers—who executive produced the album—received nothing extra for the platinum disc. With this slight in mind, they set up Underworld Records, their own rap/rhythm & blues label, at Capitol Records in 1993. Their second feature, the early 1970s-set "Dead Presidents" (1995), also boasted a powerhouse soundtrack of classic rhythm & blues hits from the period.

Though misleadingly marketed by Disney as a Black heist picture, "Dead Presidents" was more concerned with the traumas faced by African American veterans returning home from Vietnam to few economic opportunities. Larenz Tate, so memorable as the murderously nihilistic O-Dog in "Menace", here plays a clean cut, hard-working kid who goes off to war and comes home disillusioned and underemployed. He spirals downward and ends up taking part a poorly planned armored car robbery. The film opened to mixed reviews and disappointing box office.—Written by Kent Greene

FAMILY:

mother: Aida Hughes. Former fast food worker; owner of a vocational rehabilitation company white (Armenian); born in Iran and adopted by a military family; took children and left husband; spent three years on welfare before starting own business; gave the twins their first video camera when they were 12

brother: Albert Hughes. Director, producer; twin; co-directs and produces with Allen

MILESTONES:

1981: At age nine, moved to Pomona, California with brother Albert and mother (date approximate)

1984: Received first video camera at age 12

Began making short films with his brother; when a teacher suggested they make a "how-to" film, they presented "How to Be a Burgler"

Made short films with brother; some were aired on public access cable TV, one "The Drive By", attracted agents

Co-directed (with brother Albert) music videos for rap artists KRS-One, Yo-Yo and Digital Underground

Co-directed (with brother Albert) an episode of "America's Most Wanted"

1993: Feature debut as director, co-producer and story writer (all shared with brother Albert), "Menace II Society"

1993: Allowed to leave commitment with New Line Cinema (which produced "Menace II Society") to sign a two-picture, three-year deal with Caravan Productions; films to be distributed by Disney

1993: With brother, co-founded a rap/R & B record label, Underworld Records

1993: With brother, walked off the set of their Shaquille O'Neal Reebok commercial (aired during the 1994 Super Bowl telecast) over creative differences

1995: Co-helmed "Dead Presidents"

1996: Brothers signed four-year, first-look deal at Universal

1999: With brother Albert, made the documentary "American Pimp"; screened at Sundance

QUOTES:

From "Born II Direct: The Hughes Brothers Interview" by Quendrith Johnson, *DGA Magazine*, Vol. 20, No.3:

[Question:] Coming off something like "Menace II Society" where it really became part of a public dialogue, are you thinking now that you have to keep making films just like that?

Albert: We don't want to be second-guessed by people, as far as saying, "Oh, it's another hood film, who cares?" Or they say, "It's not positive." We're not out to make positive films, or preach and propagandize to the Black community. It's limiting.

From "Born II Direct: The Hughes Brothers Interview" by Quendrith Johnson, *DGA Magazine*, Vol. 20, No.3:

Allen: We're interested in the criminal element, whether it's a gangster, pimp, drugdealer, whatever. We're interested in the underworld and the underclass. There's too many movies about cops saving the world, which isn't true. There's too many movies about good prevailing over evil, which isn't true either. More times than not, there's evil kicking good's ass. Not that you can't walk away, walk out of a movie feeling good. But we have to figure a way so people aren't walking out all choked up over it. So it's not cheesy.

"They expect that black filmmakers know other black filmmakers," says Allen. "You know what? I can give a fuck about those niggers. I can give a shit about white filmmakers too, unless I like their shit." "I don't want to hang around other filmmakers," adds Albert. "I want to hang around with some regular people."

—From "Hughes's Views" by Martha Frankel, *Movieline*, March 1994.

"You start dealin' with big stars, that's how films are ruined," says Allen. "I don't bring no names up—Sharon Stone. This is Sharon Stone acting," he says, opening his his legs. "Tim Allen, is he gonna be the white Cosby? Are we gonna see a movie every year from this fool? Keanu Reeves is gettin' $7 million [offers]— have you seen this guy ACT?"

—From "The Hugheses: 'Dead' at 22" by Tim Appelo, *Entertainment Weekly*, January 13, 1995.

"Spike Lee, until [cinematographer] Ernest Dickerson left him, was a really good technical director."—From "The Hughes One-Two Punch" by Sean Mitchell, *Los Angeles Times*, October 1, 1995.

Howard Hughes

BORN: Howard Robard Hughes, Jr. in Houston, Texas, 12/24/1905

DEATH: in Houston, Texas, 04/05/1976

NATIONALITY: American

EDUCATION: Rice Institute, Houston, Texas; now Rice University

California Institute of Technology, Pasadena, California

BIOGRAPHY

Eccentric entrepreneur who turned to film

production in the early 1920s. In 1930 Hughes launched the career of Jean Harlow—the first of many ingenues he would find and promote—with "Hell's Angels", which he both produced and directed. Following a brief interruption in his film career (during which he embarked on a new trajectory as an airplane designer and pilot), Hughes sparked a furor with the appearance of "The Outlaw (1943), initially withdrawn from theaters thanks to the conspicuous cleavage of Jane Russell.

In 1944 Hughes formed a production company with Preston Sturges, and four years later he obtained a controlling interest in RKO, which he mismanaged from a distance for nearly ten years. Despite the studio's loss of $20 million by 1953 and bankruptcy by 1957, he managed to sell it to a subsidiary of the General Tire Company for a $10 million dollar profit. Hughes was a recluse for the last ten years of his life, managing his business interests from a Las Vegas hotel.

Part of American lore, a Hughes-like character was the central protagonist of the Harold Robbins adaptation, "The Carpetbaggers" (1964), and the actual Hughes was portrayed by Jason Robards in Jonathan Demme's engaging 1980 feature, "Melvin & Howard", and by Dean Stockwell in Francis Ford Coppola's "Tucker" (1988).

COMPANIONS:

Katharine Hepburn. Actor

Norma Shearer. Actor

wife: Terry Moore. Actor; Moore claimed she and Hughes were secretly married and went to court to have herself declared his legal widow; in 2000, Moore made the claim that she never obtained a legal divorce from Hughes and that they therefore committed bigamy in their subsequent remarriages

wife: Jean Peters. Actor; married in 1957; divorced in 1971; last saw him in 1966

MILESTONES:

Assumed management of Hughes Tool Company at age 18

1926: Began investing in Hollywood films aged 20

1926: Debut as producer with "Everybody's Acting"

1930: Debut as producer-director with "Hell's Angels"

1932: Left Hollywood, became co-pilot under assumed name

1935: Designed aircraft, broke world speed record

1937: Broke transcontinental speed record

1938: Flew around world in 91 hours, broke record time

1946: Injured while flying plane he designed

1947: Last formal public appearance

1948: Took over RKO studio and theater chain

1966: Sold TWA holdings

1966: Became recluse; maintained control over $2.5 billion empire

QUOTES:

Awarded the Congressional Medal Awarded by Washington upon return from record breaking flight around the world.

BIBLIOGRAPHY:

"Empire: The Life, Legend and Madness of Howard Hughes" Donald L. Bartlett and James B. Steele, 1979

"The Beauty and the Billionaire" Terry Moore memoir telling of Moore's involvement with and secret marriage to Howard Hughes

"Citizen Hughes" Michael Drosnin, 1986; biography

"Next to Hughes: The Last Years of Howard Hughes's Strange and Tragic Life Chronicled by His Closest Advisor" Robert Maheu and Richard Hack, 1992, HarperTrade

"Howard Hughes: The Secret Life" Charles Higham 1993

"Howard Hughes: The Untold Story" Pat H. Broeske and Peter Harry Brown

"The Passions of Howard Hughes" Terry Moore, 1996

"The Money: The Battle for Howard Hughes's Billions" James R. Phelan and Lewis Chester, 1997, Random House

"Howard Hughes and His Flying Boat" Charles Barton, 1998, Charles A. Barton Inc.

"Hughes: The Private Diaries, Memos and Letters" Richard Hack, 2001, New Millennium Entertainment

John Hughes

BORN: John Hughes, Jr. in Detroit, Michigan, 02/18/1950

SOMETIMES CREDITED AS:
Edmond Dantes
Edmond Dante

NATIONALITY: American

EDUCATION: University of Arizona Tucson, Arizona, art, 1968; dropped out

AWARD: Broadcast Film Critics Association Award Best Family Film "101 Dalmatians" 1996 shared award; Hughes was one of the film's producers

BIOGRAPHY

John Hughes' films are set in the familiar mid-American landscape of well-lit shopping malls, neat two-story houses, and—most especially—locker-lined high school corridors. Peopled by the denizens of middle- and upper-middle-class suburbia, they focus on the discontented teenage children of baby boomers.

A writer and editor for *National Lampoon* magazine, Hughes started in films by writing scripts for two forgettable movies, "National Lampoon's Class Reunion" (1982) and "Nate and Hayes" (1983). These were followed by two family comedy hits of 1983: "National Lampoon's Vacation", which displayed his debt to the magazine's low comedy style, and "Mr. Mom", which revealed his talent for capturing the comic absurdities of the suburban family.

His first film as a writer and director, "Sixteen Candles" (1984), about the heartaches suffered by a young girl (Molly Ringwald) on her 16th birthday, firmly established his command of teenage comedy. "Weird Science" (1985) was a Frankenstein-like fantasy about two lonely high school "nerds" who create the perfect woman for themselves, only to realize that they are better off with girls their own age. "The Breakfast Club" (1985) charted the gradual self-discovery of five high school students serving time in a Saturday detention hall and clearly expressed Hughes' central concern with the perils of coming-of-age. In these early films, and again in the likable "Ferris Bueller's Day Off" (1986), Hughes suggested, cheerfully if unconvincingly, that adolescent woes evaporate once teens recognize their self-worth; by means of a mediator (Ferris for his pal Cameron, Lisa for the two boys in "Weird Science", the "Breakfast Clubbers" for one another), Hughes' high schoolers learn to "fit in" simply by being themselves.

"Pretty in Pink" (1986), written and produced by Hughes and directed by Howard Deutch, was a working-class version of "Sixteen Candles", and the first Hughes film to look at the costs of assimilation rather than seeing it as an end in itself. For the first time, too, Hughes made explicit the class tensions which had been implicit in his earlier films—tensions which become even more central in "Some Kind of Wonderful" (1987, also directed by Deutch for writer-producer Hughes), the culmination of his high school cycle. Here, the middle- to lower-middle-class characters achieve liberation by resisting the snares of the status quo; the rich kids, on the other hand, are trapped in a life of mean-spirited hedonism because of their blind allegiance to a system that fosters petty rivalries and inhumane expectations.

After "Ferris Bueller", Hughes the writer-director tackled life beyond high school. "Planes, Trains and Automobiles" (1987) focused on the misadventures of two traveling businessmen (Steve Martin and John Candy). "She's Having a Baby" (1988) was a vision of what might happen to the couple from "Sixteen Candles" after they get married. "Uncle Buck" (1989) effectively combined Hughes' comic exaggeration with his acute awareness of the problems hiding inside handsome suburban homes. "Home Alone" (1990, written and produced by Hughes, directed by Chris Columbus) took the Hughes focus down to the eight-year-old level and proved a scorching box-office success, as did a sequel, "Home Alone 2: Lost in New York" (1992).

It is easy to dismiss Hughes as a mere "high school humanist." His characters do, however, ask themselves some tough questions, and they do come up with honest answers. "I realized that I took more than I gave," says the young husband at the end of "She's Having a Baby", "that what I was looking for was not to be found but to be made." At his best, Hughes deftly blends comedy and drama, digging beneath the superficial tranquility of suburbia to examine the restive quality of modern American life.

MILESTONES:

Raised in Detroit suburbs

Moved to the Chicago area at age 13

Returned to Chicago after he dropped out of college; took a job in a warehouse; began sending comedians unsolicited jokes, sometimes writing 100 jokes a day (sold some to Rodney Dangerfield)

Joined DDB Needham Worldwide advertising agency; later worked at the Leo Burnett Company in Chicago; during his seven years in advertising worked on Johnson Floor Wax, and the Edge shaving cream commerical that used a credit card to test the closeness of a shave

Wrote full-time for the National Lampoon magazine

1982: First on-screen credit, "National Lampoon Class Reunion"

Signed a film-development deal with Paramount Pictures; wrote original scripts, submitted ideas and doctored scripts; only on-screen credit from this period, "Nate and Hayes" (1983)

1984: Directed first feature, "Sixteen Candles"

Founded his Chicago-based film company, Hughes Entertainment

1992: Co-wrote (with Amy Holden Jones) screenplay for "Beethoven" under the pseudonym Edmond Dante

QUOTES:

Hughes described the genesis of the three "National Lampoon Vacation" films: "These are just simple truths about people and families. I happen to go for the simplest, most ordinary things. The extraordinary doesn't interest me. I'm not interested in psychotics. I'm interested in the person you don't expect to have a story. I like Mr. Everyman."—quoted in *The New York Times* magazine, August 4, 1991.

Hughes "may be the first real auteur of television-style entertainment. He can write funny lines. He comes up with engagingly absurd situations. Yet there is something unnerving about the way he denatures real life."—Film critic Vincent Canby quoted in *The New York Times* magazine, August 4, 1991.

"In 1982, after his script for 'Mr. Mom', was taken out of his control by 20th Century Fox, a slight he recalls—as all others—with bitterness, Hughes decided he had to direct his scripts himself. There was one problem: he had no idea how to do it. He had never even been on a movie set. Logic led him to teen films. Because he didn't know how to move a camera, Hughes decided to write a movie that took place in a single room. And because he feared any experienced actor would know he was a fake, he decided to work with young actors. 'So I thought: "O.K., high-school detention,' " he says, and thus was born 'The Breakfast Club' ... a semi-serious examination of teenage class structure. As it turned out, Hughes wound up directing a second script, 'Sixteen Candles' first."—Bill Carter (*The New York Times* magazine, August 4, 1991).

"There were many satisfactions for John Hughes in the success of "Home Alone", some professional, some intensely personal. For a man, who, on the one hand, often says he has to keep proving himself, and who on the other has a marked antipathy toward official Hollywood and a wide reputation in the film industry as an irascible control freak, "Home Alone" has become a vehicle of validation. 'Nobody will ever say again a Hughes film doesn't open foreign,' Hughes says, armed with reports of further hundreds of millions in international gross receipts."—Bill Carter (*The New York Times* magazine, August 4, 1991).

John Huston

BORN: John Marcellus Huston in Nevada, Missouri, 08/05/1906

DEATH: in Middletown, Rhode Island, 08/28/1987

NATIONALITY: American

CITIZENSHIP: Ireland, 1964

EDUCATION: attended high school in Los Angeles, California until he dropped out aged 15

Smith School of Art, Los Angeles, California

AWARDS: National Board of Review Award Best Screenplay "The Treasure of the Sierra Madre" 1948

New York Film Critics Circle Award Best Director "The Treasure of the Sierra Madre" 1948

Golden Globe Award Best Director "The Treasure of the Sierra Madre" 1948

Writers Guild of America Award Best-Written American Western "The Treasure of the Sierra Madre" 1948

Oscar Best Director "The Treasure of the Sierra Madre" 1948

Oscar Best Screenplay "The Treasure of the Sierra Madre" 1948

National Board of Review Award Best Director "The Asphalt Jungle" 1950

Venice Film Festival Silver Lion Award "Moulin Rouge" 1953; one of six films cited

New York Film Critics Circle Award Best Director "Moby Dick" 1956

National Board of Review Award Best Director "Moby Dick" 1956

Golden Globe Award Best Supporting Actor "The Cardinal" 1963

Writers Guild of America Laurel Award for Achievement 1963

Los Angeles Film Critics Association Career Achievement Award 1979

BAFTA Fellowship 1980; shared with David Attenborough

American Film Institute Life Achievement Award 1983

Directors Guild of America D. W. Griffith Award 1983; for lifetime achievement

New York Film Critics Circle Award Best Director "Prizzi's Honor" 1985

National Society of Film Critics Award Best Director "Prizzi's Honor" 1985

Golden Globe Award Best Director "Prizzi's Honor" 1985

Venice Film Festival Special Golden Lion for Career Achievement 1985; cited with Manuel de Oliveira

Independent Spirit Award Best Director "The Dead" 1987

BIOGRAPHY

In "The Man Who Would Be King" (1975), co-written and directed by John Huston, two rogues, Peachy Carnehan (Michael Caine) and Daniel Dravot (Sean Connery), desert their British army post in India in the 1880s to go adventuring. In a retrospective voice-over, Peachy fondly remembers their encounters with native tribesmen: "At night, we told them stories of our own devising, and they loved them, because we showed them that their dreams could come true."

In the years immediately preceding his death in 1987, John Huston's critical reputation as one of America's leading directors was reestablished with the twin success of "Prizzi's Honor" (1985) and "The Dead" (1987). But it is his earlier films, especially "The Treasure of the Sierra Madre" (1948), "The African Queen" (1951) and "The Maltese Falcon" (1941) which will ultimately be responsible for Huston's place in film history as a teller of imaginative tales of enchantment, quest and loss.

The son of noted stage and screen actor Walter Huston (who would win an Oscar for his role in his son's "The Treasure of the Sierra Madre"), John Huston was a juvenile actor on the vaudeville circuit, a champion boxer, a painter, a leading man on the legitimate stage, a writer and reporter and even a lieutenant in the Mexican cavalry. After an abortive career as a screenwriter in the early 1930s, Huston returned to Hollywood later in the decade and achieved great renown with his contributions to six screenplays written under contract at Warner Bros., including "Jezebel" (1938), "High Sierra" (1941) and "Sergeant York" (1941). Even after he became a director, Huston would continue to contribute substantially to the screenplays of all his films.

Huston made a stunning debut as a director with "The Maltese Falcon." One of the first examples of film noir, this stylistically assured feature revealed his interests in ironic comedy and the motif of the unresolved quest. "The Maltese Falcon" is one of the most influential and enjoyable of the cinema's masterworks.

Huston's wartime filmmaking experiences for the signal corps resulted in equally ground-breaking documentary work, including "The Battle of San Pietro" (1945) and "Let There Be Light" (1945), the latter an account of psychological dysfunction among American GIs which federal authorities withheld from release for many years.

Between 1948 and 1952, Huston produced a succession of important films. "The Treasure of the Sierra Madre" refined the Huston theme of the quest into an archetype and cemented his critical reputation, largely thanks to a series of reviews and articles by James Agee—who would later write the screenplay for "The African Queen." "The Asphalt Jungle" (1950) proved Huston's ability to manipulate simultaneously a variety of characters and stories; the film's sharply drawn milieu and unusual sympathy for its criminal protagonists mark it as among Huston's most compelling works. "The Red Badge of Courage" (1951) began Huston's identification as an adapter of literary classics. This film also marked the first of several visually stylized features which Huston based on specific visual sources. "The Red Badge" took its groupings of figures and sun-bleached tones from Mathew Brady's daguerreotypes of the Civil War; the compositions in "Moby Dick" (1956) emulate scrimshaw carvings from the whaling days it depicts; and "Moulin Rouge" (1952) utilizes a color scheme based on Toulouse-Lautrec's paintings, which are themselves an important part of the film's narrative. This period of maturity and experimentation also saw the production of "The African Queen," an essentially two-character film which underscored Huston's deft control of actors.

Beginning with the disappointing reception accorded his offbeat comic thriller "Beat the Devil" (1953), Huston's reputation suffered a series of setbacks over the next 20 years. A tumultuous personal life mirrored this decline, but Huston continued his dedication to literary adaptations. In 1963, with Otto Preminger's "The Cardinal," Huston began an acting career, appearing in his own and others' films. He provided narration for a multitude of TV shows and documentary films, and appearances in public service campaigns and his outspoken opposition to colorization gained him further public recognition. By the time of his death, Huston's craggy, beautifully ugly face and melodious baritone voice made him one of the few directors of his era as familiar to his public as any of his stars.

"Fat City" (1972), a sorrowful story of the ebbing fortunes of a washed-up boxer, marked the start of Huston's comeback in the critical community. "The Man Who Would Be King," originally planned more than 20 years previous as a vehicle for Bogart and Gable, remains Huston's most fully realized quest narrative. "Wise Blood" (1979), a compelling piece of Southern Gothic based on Flannery O'Connor's novel, similarly represents one of Huston's greatest achievements as an adapter of literature. After the disasters of "Escape to Victory" (1981) and "Annie" (1982), Huston scored another triumph with "Prizzi's Honor", a grim but somehow hilarious and touching comedy of love among mobsters. The film won a supporting actress Oscar for Huston's daughter Anjelica, mirroring father Walter's win for "Treasure of the Sierra Madre."

Huston's final completed film was "The Dead" (1987), another long-cherished literary adaptation, of James Joyce's short story. Huston's son Tony adapted the story and Anjelica was featured in the cast. At the time of his death, he was involved in the production of "Mr. North" (1988) as writer and producer, with his son Danny directing.

FAMILY:

daughter: Anjelica Huston. Actor, director; born on July 8, 1951; mother, Enrica Soma; debut in father's film, "Sinful Davey" (1969) at age 16; later directed by him in the disastrous "A Walk With Love and Death" (1969), "Prizzi's Honor" (1985), for which she earned a Best Supporting Actress Oscar, and "The Dead" (1987)

son: Danny Huston. Director, actor; born on May 14, 1962; mother, Zoe Sallis; designed the main title sequence for Huston's "Under the Volcano" (1984), directed father in the 1990 direct-to-video release "Mr Corbett's Ghost" (shot in 1986) and helmed "Mr. North" (1988), produced and scripted by father

COMPANIONS:

Olivia de Havilland. Actor; had relationship in early 1940s; reunited in the 1950s after her divorce

Marietta Tree. Socialite

wife: Evelyn Keyes. Actor; married in 1946 in Las Vegas; divorced in 1950

wife: Enrica Soma. Born c. 1930; married from 1950 until her death in an auto accident in 1969; separated in 1962; gave birth to daughter Allegra (fathered by a titled Englishman) during separation; mother of Huston's two oldest children, Tony and Anjelica

Maricela Hernandez. Former housekeeper; met c. 1974 when she was 23 years old; the film "The Dead" was dedicated to her

MILESTONES:

1909: Stage acting debut at age three (date approximate)

After parents' separated, moved to Texas with mother

1917: Moved to L.A. for health reasons

Became boxer at age 14, won Amateur Lightweight Boxing Championship in California

Professional stage acting debut at age 19

Moved to Mexico, became calvary officer

1928: Resigned commission

Became reporter with New York *Graphic*

1929: Made acting debut with uncredited appearance in "Hell's Heroes"

Moved to Hollywood in the early 1930s, debut as screenwriter with Samuel Goldwyn on projects like 1932's "Law and Order", "Murder in the Rue Morgue" and "A House Divided"

1932: Left Hollywood

1935: Made contract writer at Warner Bros.

1940: Earned first Academy Award nomination for contributions to script of "Doctor Ehrlich's Magic Bullet"

1941: Co-wrote the biopic "Sergeant York"; shared Academy Award nomination for script

1941: Debut as film director with "The Maltese Falcon"; also scripted; first screen collaboration with Humphrey Bogart; father Walter appeared in small part; received Oscar nomination for screenplay

1942: Became a lieutenant with Signal Corps
Promoted to major
Made several documentaries while in the military including "Report From the Aleutians" (1943) and "Let There Be Light" (1945)

1945: Returned to Hollywood and did uncredited work on the screenplays of "The Killers" and "The Stranger" (both 1946)

1948: Received Oscars as Best Director and for Best Screenply for "The Treasure of the Sierra Madre"; father Walter won Best Supporting Actor Academy Award for same film

1950: Earned dual Oscar nods for writing and directing "The Asphalt Jungle"

1951: Wrote and directed "The African Queen"; garnered two more Academy Award nominations; star Humphrey Bogart received Best Actor Oscar

1952: Garnered yet another Oscar nomination for direction of "Moulin Rouge", the biopic of artist Toulouse-Lautrec

1956: Produced, wrote and directed "Moby Dick", adapted from Herman Melville's classic novel

1957: Earned Academy Award nomination for contributions to script of "Heaven Knows, Mr. Allison"; also directed

1961: Directed "The Misfits", scripted by Arthur Miller and co-starring Clark Gable, Marilyn Monroe and Montgomery Clift

1962: Guided Clift through the title role of "Freud"

1963: Co-starred in "The Cardinal"; received Oscar nomination as Best Supporting Actor

1964: Helmed the screen adaptation of Tennessee Williams' "The Night of the Iguana", featuring Ava Gardner, Richard Burton and Deborah Kerr

1966: Played Noah and provided the voice of God in "The Bible"; also directed

1967: Produced and directed "Reflections in a Golden Eye"

1969: Directed daughter Anjelica in the lead of the medieval romance "A Walk With Love and Death"; also acted

1970: Acted in the camp classic "Myra Breckinridge"

1972: Directed the superb boxing-themed drama "Fat City"

1974: Delivered memorable turn as the nasty Noah Cross in "Chinatown"

1975: Received 13th Academy Award nomination for script of "The Man Who Would Be King", adapted from a Rudyard Kipling story; also directed

1979: Helmed "Wise Blood", adapted from Flannery O'Connor's novel; also acted the role of Hazel's grandfather

1982: Directed first screen musical, the overproduced boxoffice disappointment "Annie", based on the hit Broadway musical

1984: Realized a long-held dream to film "Under the Volcano" with Albert Finney in the lead

1985: Earned final Oscar nomination for the black comedy "Prizzi's Honor"; daughter Anjelica received the Best Supporting Actress statue for her turn as a Mafia princess

1987: Directed last film, "The Dead"; daughter Anjelica offered memorable performance; son Tony wrote the screenplay based on the James Joyce story

1988: Produced and scripted "Mr. North"; had been set to direct but became too ill; son Danny replaced him at the helm

QUOTES:

"The great screenwriter and director John Huston was also a memorable actor and talker. The rumbling, sonorous grandiloquence, the archly raised chin, the massive gaiety, with its suggestion of tricks or outright fraud—there were elements of a ripe, nineteenth-century theatricality in Huston's impish performances and echoes, as well, of florid, speechifying senators and tent preachers saving souls. Huston was not, apparently a very nice man; Polanski caught him at his most purely malevolent in "Chinatown", playing the wealthy and rapacious Noah Cross. But he was one beautiful charmer."—David Denby in his review of "White Hunter, Black Heart" in *New York*, October 1, 1990).

Awarded the Legion of Merit for bravery during WWII.

BIBLIOGRAPHY:

"Fool" John Huston short story, published in H. L. Mencken's *American Mercury Magazine*
"An Open Book" John Huston, 1980, Alfred A. Knopf; autobiography
"John Huston's Filmmaking" Lesley Brill

Peter Jackson

BORN: in New Zealand, 10/31/1961

NATIONALITY: New Zealander

EDUCATION: Kapiti College, Wellington, New Zealand

AWARDS: National Board of Review Award for Special Achievement in Filmmaking "The Lord of the Rings: The Fellowship of the Ring" 2001

Southeastern Film Critics Association Award Best Director "The Lord of the Rings: The Fellowship of the Ring" 2001

Southeastern Film Critics Association Award Best Adapted Screenplay "The Lord of the Rings: The Fellowship of the Ring" 2001; shared with Fran Walsh and Philippa Boyens

Las Vegas Film Critics Society Award Best Director "The Lord of the Rings: The Fellowship of the Ring" 2001

Florida Film Critics Circle Award Best Director "The Lord of the Rings: The Fellowship of the Ring" 2001

American Film Institute Award Movie of the Year "The Lord of the Rings: The Fellowship of the Ring" 2001; shared award with producers Barrie M. Osborne, Fran Walsh and Tim Sanders; initial presentation of the award

Golden Satellite Best Motion Picture (Animated or Mixed Media) "The Lord of the Rings: The Fellowship of the Ring" 2001; shared with producers Barrie M. Osborne and Tim Sanders and Fran Walsh

BAFTA Award Best Film "The Lord of the Rings: The Fellowship of the Ring" 2002

BAFTA David Lean Award for Best Achievement in Direction "The Lord of the Rings: The Fellowship of the Ring" 2002

Las Vegas Film Critics Award Best Director "Lord of The Rings: The Two Towers" 2002

Online Film Critics Society Award Best Director "Lord of the Rings: The Two Towers" 2002

Dallas-Fort Worth Film Critics Awards Best Director "Lord of the Rings: The Two Towers" 2002

BIOGRAPHY

One of the more distinctive directorial voices in the wave of New Zealand cinema which made such an impressive splash in the 1980s and 90s, Jackson was interested in cameras from an early age. When he finally bought a 16mm camera, he decided to make a short science-fiction comedy with it. Over three years later, he completed the feature-length result, "Bad Taste" (1988). Though many might not see past the film's lengthy streams of vomit and blood or what they consider to be the aptness of the film's title, Jackson's feature debut about aliens coming to Earth to hunt for human flesh to stock an outer-space fast food restaurant was not only garishly funny, but also an inventive spin on popular culture and generic conventions.

Jackson's films have an unabashed penchant for the grotesque mixed with a child-like playfulness with the possibilities of cinema. Their tone is humorous, in a manner both campy and celebratory, as well as being genuinely bleak. Unstable psychological states and unhappy family situations mix with extreme yet sometimes cartoonish violence and a satirical, densely referential glance at society and cinema itself. His second feature, "Meet the Feebles" (1990), was another venture into comic horror, but this time people, appropriately for Jackson's emerging style, were replaced with puppets, as a massacre of performers throws suspicion onto one Hilda the Hippo. He stayed with the same genre but once again used live actors for his international breakthrough film, "Dead Alive" (1993, originally titled "Braindead" in New Zealand). It proved so hilarious that its amazing gross-out quotient went down like a smooth custard, yet Jackson's emerging preoccupations with repressive parent-child dynamics and parricide gave the dessert just enough body.

Some saw Jackson's next film, "Heavenly Creatures" (1994), retelling the story of New Zealand's most famous murder case in decades, as both considerably more serious and a real departure for him. It was certainly the former but hardly the latter, as his restless visual stylistics and surprising sympathy for those who commit violence lent depth to a story of two teenage girls whose intense friendship leads to matricide. He and co-scenarist Fran Walsh

received an Oscar nomination for their original screenplay. Jackson followed up with "Jack Brown, Genius" (1995), a comedy about a modern inventor and a medieval monk, and "The Frighteners" (1996), a Michael J. Fox starrer about a psychic investigator. Both films had their moments but seemed like mere breathers coming before the most ambitious undertaking of Jackson's career, a move for which his intriguing combination of the whimsical and the fantastic on the one hand and the potently grim and downbeat on the other seemed well-suited—filming, in what was planned as three motion pictures, J.R.R. Tolkien's landmark mythological novel "The Lord of the Rings" (lensed 1999–2000). Once completed, the ambitious project as scheduled to roll out in installments over three years: "The Fellowship of the Ring" (2001), "The Two Towers" (2002) and "The Return of the King" (2003). The first installment, "The Lord of the Rings: The Fellowship of the Ring", earned praise from critics and audiences for its epic action and skillful take on very complicated material. The film received a near-record 13 Academy Award nominations, including Best Picture, Best Director and Best Adapted Screenplay. The superior special effects in the film also made a lasting impact and elevated the Jackson-backed F/X house WETA Workshop in New Zealand into the upper eschelons of movie magic practitioners. Jackson also re-edited the film, inserting over 30 minutes of unreleased material, for a special DVD version, resulting in an even more entertaining release. The second instalment, "The Two Towers," was released in 2002 to much fanfare, with many critics and moviegoers deeming it an even superior film to the first outing.—Written by David Lugowski

COMPANION:
Frances Walsh. Screenwriter; met c. 1987; wrote "Heavenly Creatures" (1994) with Jackson; worked with him in various capacities on his earlier films

MILESTONES:

Raised in Pukerua Bay, just outside of Wellington, New Zealand

Began making a feature-length vampire film with a Super 8mm camera when he was a teenager

1983: Bought a 16mm camera and decided to test it by making a 10-minute short science-fiction comedy film, "Roast of the Day"; some four years later, the result was Jackson's first feature, "Bad Taste"

1986: Received $5000 grant from the New Zealand Film Commission; quit working as an apprentice photo engraver

1988: Release of first completed feature film, "Bad Taste", which he also produced, starred in, wrote, photographed, edited and did makeup and special effects

1990: First of three consecutive collaborations with producer Jim Booth, "Meet the Feebles"; co-written with Fran Walsh and Stephen Sinclair

1993: Formed WETA, a special effects company

1993: Release of international breakthrough feature, "Dead Alive/Braindead"

1994: Last collaboration with producer Jim Booth, "Heavenly Creatures"; Booth died of cancer on January 4, 1994

1996: Helmed "The Frighteners", a serio-comedic picture starring Michael J. Fox

1999—2000: Directed the trilogy of films based on J.R.R. Tolkein's "The Lord of the Rings"; shot back-to-back; scheduled to be released over a three-year period, "The Fellowship of the Ring" (2001); "The Two Towers" (2002) and "The Return of the King" (2003); received Oscar nominations for Best Picture, Best Director and Best Screenplay for the initial release, "The Lord of the Rings: The Fellowship of the Rings" (2001); received a Golden Globe nomination for Best Director; also received a BAFTA nomination for The David Lean Award for Achievement in Direction

QUOTES:

On December 31, 2001, Jackson was named a Companion of the New Zealand Order of Merit.

"I have an unhealthy interest in the grotesque . . . For a long time I wanted to be (special effects wizard Ray) Harryhausen, and I wanted to be an animator. But I was unable to design or build a monster. I was trying to do my monster, and it all kind of ended up looking like Harryhausen's Cyclops. I was worried that I could never do anything original. It wasn't until I was in my early twenties doing "Bad Taste" that I started to really think I could come up with things that no one has seen before."—Jackson quoted in "Death and the Maidens" by Howard Feinstein, *Village Voice,* November 15, 1994.

"Jackson's . . . forays into over-the-top violence, scatology, and kitsch are a unique blend of Johns Woo and Waters, Jan Svankmajer, and bargain-basement Berlin schlockmeister Jorg Buttgereit ("Nekromantik" 1988). He is preoccupied with mommies and monsters—sometimes even mommie-monsters."—Howard Feinstein in his article, "Death and the Maidens" in *Village Voice,* November 15, 1994.

"I think he is actually a Hobbit himself."—Cate Blanchett, who plays the Elf queen Galadriel in "The Lord of the Rings" on Jackson's passion for the works of Tolkien.

BORN: in Northwood, Middlesex, England, 01/31/1942

DEATH: in London, England, 02/19/1994

NATIONALITY: English

EDUCATION: King's College, University of Cambridge, Cambridge, England, 1963–67; studied history and art history and English

Slade School of Fine Arts, London, England, painting

AWARDS: Peter Stuyvesant Award 1967 awarded given for painting

Los Angeles Film Critics Association Award Best Independent/Experimental Film "The Last of England" 1988 tied with Al Razutis for "Amerika"

BIOGRAPHY

Leading avant-garde British filmmaker whose visually opulent and stylistically adventurous body of work stands in defiant opposition to the established literary and theatrical traditions of his sometimes staid national cinema. With influences ranging from the eccentric writing-directing team Michael Powell & Emeric Pressburger to seminal gay aesthetes Jean Cocteau and Kenneth Anger, Jarman advocated a personal cinema more dedicated to striking imagery and evocative sounds than to the imperatives of narrative and characterization. His comments on one of his strongest films are revealing: " 'The Last of England' works with image and sound, a language which is nearer to poetry than prose. It tells its story quite happily in silent images, in contrast to a word bound cinema."

Like the noted American underground film-maker Anger, Jarman displayed a fascination with violence, homoeroticism, gay representation,

and mythopoeic imagery. Proudly and openly gay, Jarman shared news of his HIV-infection with his public and incorporated his subsequent battles with AIDS into his work, particularly in "The Garden" (1990) and "Blue" (1993). Excavating and reclaiming suppressed gay history was an ongoing project that informed his several unconventional biopics: "Sebastiane" (1975), Jarman's sun-drenched directorial debut about the martyred Christian saint; the unusually accessible and slyly anachronistic "Caravaggio" (1986); the raw and angry modern dress version of Christopher Marlowe's "Edward II" (1991); and the stark and theatrical "Wittgenstein" (1993).

Trained in the fine arts, Jarman began as (and remained) a designer of sets and costumes for ballet and opera. He made his first films (Super-8 shorts) while working as a set designer on Ken Russell's "The Devils" (1971) and "Savage Messiah" (1972). He continued to paint and exhibit his work at London galleries while making his own films which also reflected a painterly concern with composition. Jarman's features, shorts and music videos display an artist's lively interest in contemporary and historical English culture. In "Jubilee" (1978), Queen Elizabeth I is conducted on a tour of a futuristic England in which violence and anarchy hold sway; the film became something of a beacon of the punk movement of the late 1970s. Jarman's take on "The Tempest" (1979) was a typically irreverent and somewhat rambling reworking of Shakespeare's play. The WWI poems of Wilfred Owen, set to the music of Benjamin Britten, shaped "War Requiem" (1988), a powerful essay on the wastes of wars past while commenting on the modern ravages of AIDS.

Jarman's feature about the painter Caravaggio was perhaps his most popular film. This stylishly rendered biopic dramatized the conflicts between the artist's need for patronage, his religious beliefs and his sexuality. Observing that Caravaggio consistently painted St. John as muscle-bound, Jarman suggested that the painter found sexual as well as aesthetic elation with the street thug he used as a model. The director also had fun creating filmic facsimiles of some of the painter's best known works. Curiously, though it undercuts narrative conventions by using anachronisms—typewriters, motorbikes—the film reiterated one of the hoariest cliches of Hollywood biopics like "Lust for Life": i.e. that art is little more than immediately recorded experience, "life" thrown directly onto the canvas; the "process" of artistic creation is surprisingly glossed over.

Like the celebrated American underground filmmaker Stan Brakhage, Jarman was a compulsive film diarist. He chronicled much of his life on Super-8 film and incorporated this footage, blown up to 35mm, into his more personal, non-linear narrative films. Jarman's Super-8 movies of beautiful young men in dramatic landscapes featuring caves, rocks, and water lent a lushly romantic mood to "The Angelic Conversation" (1985), a non-traditional rendering of Shakespeare's sonnets. "The Last of England", a raging, despairing, and emotionally overwhelming vision of Britain as an urban wasteland, intercut shots of Jarman writing in his room with excerpts from home movies shot by the director, his father, and grandfather and surreal tableaux of violence and degradation. Pastoral sequences of Jarman's childhood evince a longing for simpler times for the filmmaker and the nation. Jarman described himself as one of the last generation to remember the "countryside before mechanization intervened and destroyed everything."

Though much of Jarman's work is intensely personal, it was also supremely collaborative. He worked with many of the same people—in front of and behind the camera—on each of his projects. He welcomed and encouraged contributions; significant Liverpool sequences

in "The Last of England" were shot by members of Jarman's crew without his direction. Composer-sound designer Simon Fisher Turner provided powerful scores and/or densely layered soundtracks for "Caravaggio," "The Last of England", "The Garden", "Edward II" and "Blue." Distinguished actor Nigel Terry starred as the tortured Caravaggio and his rich deep voice narrated "The Last of England" and parts of "Blue." Jarman's most important performer was the prodigiously talented Tilda Swinton, whose intensity and unusual beauty graced "The Last of England", "War Requiem", "The Garden", "Edward II", "Wittgenstein", "Blue" and Jarman's segment of "Aria" (1987).

In his last years, Jarman was an outspoken advocate for the rights and dignity of gays and PWAs (Persons with AIDS) but art remained his primary cause. A champion of film art and a dedicated experimentalist, he was a critic of, and at odds with, what he saw as the stifling, repressive commercialism of mainstream cinema. Always struggling for funds, Jarman's first seven features were produced for a combined cost of only $3 million. His final film, "Blue", was his most unconventional—an unchanging field of blue over which we hear voices and sounds. Blind and mortally ill, Jarman remained a visionary film maverick. He authored a number a books including a 1984 autobiography, "Dancing Ledge." Jarman succumbed to AIDS complications at age 52.— Written by Kent Greene

MILESTONES:

Father moved family around frequently; lived in Rome, Venice and Pakistan

Worked on set and costume design for the Royal Ballet

1968: Worked on costume and set design for the Coliseum production of the opera "Don Giovanni"

1971: Set designer on Ken Russell's "The Devils"

1972: Returned to work for the Royal Ballet

1972: Set designer on Ken Russell's "Savage Messiah"

1976: Made feature directorial debut, "Sebastian"

1976: Exhibited in a show of Six British Painters in Houston, Texas

1979: Directed Super-8mm short, "Broken English", a performance film of Marianne Faithful

Directed videos for various musical artists including The Smiths, Bob Geldof and The Pet Shop Boys

1984: Honored with a retrospective of his paintings at the Institute of Contemporary Arts in London

1984: Visited the Soviet Union: returned and made a short film about the experience entitled "Imagining October"

1984: Published his first book, the autobiographical "Dancing Ledge"

1986: Diagnosed as HIV-positive; began keeping a journal

1988: Directed Lawrence Olivier in his final performance, "War Requiem"

1989: Directed the stage show of The Pet Shop Boys World Tour

QUOTES:

"This evening I sit in my apartment high above Charing Cross Road in the debris of my films watching a video of my family's home movies which documents the years 1929 to 1953. There I am in a perpetual Technicolor sunset. 1943, '44, '45, '46. Down below in the street, famished youths eye electric guitars in the music shops. Drunken derelicts jitterbug through the traffic, smack dealers push dirty children in prams which barely conceal the junk. Round the corner Margaret Thatcher's dream children, rich on style, gorge themselves at the Brasserie and spill exhausted into the morning from night clubs. What scenes from what films are left to film in a world of nuclear secrets, the acid and radioactive rain falls as I watch, and the children's children mutate in the debris of hope into multi-colored fungi."
—Derek Jarman, program booklet for "The Last of England."

Jarman on utilizing Super-8 footage transfered to 35mm via video: "It is impossible to tell now if the image on your TV set was generated in Super 8. Blown up to 35mm the quality is something quite new, like stained glass, the film glows with wonderful colors. The video gives you a pallette like a painter, and I find the results beautiful."—Program notes for "The Last of England"

BIBLIOGRAPHY:

"Dancing Ledge" Derek Jarman, 1984; autobiography

"Caravaggio" Derek Jarman, 1986; production chronicle and personal memoir

"The Last of England" Derek Jarman, 1987; constable production chronicle and personal memoir; also published under the title "Kicking the Pricks"

"Queer Edward II" Derek Jarman, 1991; production chronicle and personal memoir

"At Your Own Risk: A Saint's Testament" Derek Jarman, 1992; a distillation of Jarman's philosophy of life and gay sexuality

"Modern Nature" Derek Jarman, 1994; journals covering two years, 1989 and 1990, of the filmmaker's life

"Blue" Derek Jarman

"Smiling in Slow Motion" Derek Jarman (edited by Kevin Collins), 2000; century volume of Jarman's diary entries

"Derek Jarman: A Biography" Tony Peake, 2000; Overlook Press

BORN: in Akron, Ohio, 01/22/1953

NATIONALITY: American

EDUCATION: Cayahoga Falls High School, Cayahoga Falls, Ohio, 1971

Northwestern University, Chicago, Illinois; attended for one year

Columbia University, New York, New York, English, BA, 1975; studied in Paris senior year

Institute of Film and Television, New York University, New York, New York; graduate student, teaching assistant to Nicholas Ray; never finished, using his tuition money to finance his first feature, "Permanent Vacation", shot in ten days for $10,000 and then made short film "New World" which he later expanded into "Stranger Than Paradise"; attended at same time as Spike Lee

AWARDS: Cannes Film Festival Camera d'Or Award "Stranger Than Paradise" 1984

Locarno Film Festival Golden Leopard Award "Stranger Than Paradise" 1984

National Society of Film Critics Award Best Picture "Stranger Than Paradise" 1985

United States (Sundance) Film Festival Special Jury Prize "Stranger Than Paradise" 1985 cited with "The Roommate" and "Brother From Another Planet"

Cannes Film Festival Meilleure Contribution Artistique/Best Artistic Contribution Award "Mystery Train" 1989

Cannes Film Festival Palme d'Or Award Best Short Subject "Coffee and Cigarettes (Somewhere in California)" 1993

Screen International Five Continents Award Best Non-European Film "Dead Man" 1996

BIOGRAPHY

Jim Jarmusch's hip, urban, comic jags arose from the same East Village-New York University explosion that nurtured the relentlessly contemporary films of Susan Seidelman and Spike Lee. His recurring motif is one of narrative as an inevitable byproduct of cultural collision. Jarmusch offers lowlife reflections of post-modernist communication and miscommunication between characters sealed off from one another, their only connection the many-tentacled pop trash culture of America.

In 1971, Jarmusch enrolled at Columbia University in the English literature program. A few months before graduation, on a visit to Paris, he discovered the rich treasures of the Cinematheque Francaise and wound up staying in France for a year. Upon returning to New York City, he enrolled in the graduate film program at New York University, where he became a teaching assistant to director Nicholas Ray. Through Ray's efforts, Jarmusch became a production assistant on Wim Wenders' tribute to Ray, "Lighting Over Water" (1980). After using his NYU tuition money to complete his first feature, "Permanent Vacation" (1980), he began work on a short film, shot over one weekend, that eventually became "Stranger Than Paradise" four years later.

"Stranger Than Paradise" startled audiences with its gritty cool and fresh comic tone, winning the Camera d'Or at Cannes and the Best Film award from the National Society of Film Critics. Jarmusch has referred to his first three feature films as a trilogy. "Stranger Than Paradise," along with "Down By Law" (1986) and "Mystery Train" (1989), take place in a blighted American cultural landscape—from the bleak, wintry moonscape of Ohio and the cracked seaminess of an over-ripe Florida in "Stranger Than Paradise" to the diffuse, cinema-reflected New Orleans in "Down By Law" and the tawdry, clapboard decay of Memphis' "Mystery Train."

In this world, characters make connections by sharing TV dinners, chanting ice cream jingles and revering Elvis Presley.

A Jarmusch film begins with characters who live a robot-like existence, unable to relate or communicate; a typical Jarmusch shot features a character staring off-screen until the screen fades to black or there is a cut to darkness. Into this stultifying atmosphere, another character with a different viewpoint and perspective enters, exposing the shallowness of the enmeshed character's existence. This foreign presence may be a Hungarian visitor ("Stranger Than Paradise"), an Italian tourist ("Down By Law") or Japanese teenagers on a pilgrimage to Graceland ("Mystery Train"). As Jarmusch has explained, "America's a kind of throwaway culture that's a mixture of different cultures. To make a film about America, it seems to me logical to have at least one perspective that's transplanted because ours is a collection of transplanted influences." In this clash lies the basis of Jarmusch's invigorating originality.

Through the course of these three films, Jarmusch's comic vision became more despairing. At the end of "Stranger Than Paradise", two characters still have a hopeful chance of happiness. In "Down By Law", however, two leads are still on the run as another plans for a promising future while in "Mystery Train", the three sets of characters spend the film barely missing each other and, as dawn comes up in Memphis, all race off in different directions. In a world of declining values and lovelessness, the population in Jarmusch's films are all racing off in different directions, seeking their own personal shelters of comfort and familiarity, blanketed by the shrilly blaring music of Screamin' Jay Hawkins and Irma Thomas— recorded voices shouting into a void.

After completing his feature-length trilogy, Jarmusch returned, in a sense, to the short-film format with "Night on Earth" (1991). He had never entirely left that zone of filmmaking, given the segmented quality of his narrative style. (He also continued to shoot short films, like the three completed segments of his ongoing "Coffee and Cigarettes" series.) "Night on Earth" told five separate stories, each centering on the relationship that unfolds between a taxi driver and her or his customer, with episodes set in Los Angeles, New York, Paris, Rome and Helsinki. Critics tended to feel that, as with most anthology films, quality varied from segment to segment, yet the overall effect was quite powerful. Some customary Jarmusch faces peopled his deliberately confined landscapes, and the tone typically veered from side-splittingly funny to quietly poignant, ending on a note of despondency.

Part of the cult fascination with Jarmusch stems not only from his admittedly fascinating films but also from a persona remarkably visible for an independent filmmaker. He has kept quite busy as an actor in independent cinema in parts ranging from cameos to fairly substantial roles. He has appeared in Alex Cox's "Straight to Hell" (1987), Robert Frank and Rudy Wurlitzer's "Candy Mountain" (1987), Mika Kaurismaki's "Helsinki Napoli All Night Long" (1988), Aki Kaurismaki's "Leningrad Cowboys Go America" (1989), Raul Ruiz's "The Golden Boat" (1990), Tom DeCillo's "Johnny Suede" (1992), Alexandre Rockwell's "In the Soup" (1992) and Wayne Wang and Paul Auster's "Blue in the Face" (1995). The presence of the strikingly handsome if odd-looking Jarmusch, with his trademark white pompadour, beestung lips and lanky muscular physique clad in black has lent these films an air of downtown bohemian authenticity.

Jarmusch has, of course, continued to meander along with his own distinctive projects, eschewing the Hollywood establishment for European financing and the attending hands-off policy that allows him to bring his vision uncorrupted to the screen. "Dead Man" (1995), his black-and-white revisionist Western, featured a mix of offbeat younger actors (Johnny Depp, Crispin Glover) and legendarily idiosyncratic faces (John Hurt, Iggy Pop, Robert Mitchum) in its saga of the cultural collision between a Cleveland accountant (Depp) and the West of 1875. Pursued as a murderer by bounty hunters, he befriends a Native American (Gary Farmer) who believes he is the reincarnation of the poet William Blake. Though panned by critics at the time of its release, it has undergone a startling re-evaluation, receiving praise from such quarters as Film Comment which cited "Dead Man" as one of the representative films of the 90s.

Jarmusch's collaboration with Neil Young on "Dead Man" and the subsequent music video "Big Time" (1996) led to "Year of the Horse" (1997), a documentary about Young and his band Crazy Horse. Filmed in Super 8 during the group's 1996 tour (and incorporating some 70s and 80s footage), this ultimate home movie was both a concert film and a revealing look at the daily life of a working band. Jarmusch then returned to features with "Ghost Dog: The Way of the Samurai" (1999), described by the writer-director as a "gangster samurai hip-hop Eastern Western." Starring Forest Whitaker as a Mafia hitman who follows the precepts of the "Hagakure", an early-18th-century Japanese warrior code book of the samurai, "Ghost Dog" possessed Jarmusch's signature zany humor picturing America as a place of crossed cultural wires. It ran afoul of some mainstream critics, however, who abhorred its length and what they felt were incomprehensible plot twists. Its intriguing thematic content underscored by the high-voltage, hip-hop soundtrack composed by The RZA seemed destined to find an audience, perhaps adding new fans to the legion of Jarmusch aficionados.

MILESTONES:

1979: Worked as a production assistant on the epochal Nicholas Ray/Wim Wenders collaboration, "Lightning Over Water"

1980: Provided sound recording for Eric Mitchell's "Underground USA"

1980: Directed, wrote, edited, and composed the music for "Permanent Vacation", his first feature; Tom DiCillo served as director of photography; on its completion, Wenders gave him some leftover film stock which he used for part of "Stranger Than Paradise"

1980: Wrote and directed the short "New World"

1982: Worked as an actor in Lothar Lambert's West German feature "Fraulein Berlin"

1983: Provided sound recording for "Burroughs", a documentary about the writer William S. Burroughs

1984: Directed, wrote, and edited the breakthrough feature "Stranger Than Paradise", an expanded version of his short film "New World"

1985: Helmed the music video "The Lady Don't Mind" by Talking Heads

1986: Worked as a camera operator on Sara Driver's "Sleepwalk"

1986: Directed "Down By Law", starring Roberto Benigni, Tom Waits and John Lurie

1986: Wrote and directed the first in a series of short films titled "Coffee and Cigarettes"; Benigni co-starred with Steven Wright

1988: Wrote and directed the second "Coffee and Cigarettes: Memphis Version", featuring Steve Buscemi, Cinque Lee and Joie Lee

1989: Won acclaim at Cannes for "Mystery Train"

1990–1991: Filmed his 1991 feature "Night on Earth" on location in Los Angeles, New York City, Paris, Rome and Helsinki; project reteamed him with Benigni and Waits who composed music, as well as writing, producing and performing several songs

1990: Helmed "It's Alright with Me", a music video of Waits' single

1992: Reteamed with Waits as director of the music video for "I Don't Wanna Grow Up"

1993: Made third short in the series, "Coffee and Cigarettes: Somewhere in California", featuring Tom Waits and Iggy Pop as themselves; received Cannes Palme d'Or for short films

1995: Wrote and directed the revisionist "Dead Man", a hallucinatory black-and-white period Western starring Johnny Depp as a fugitive befriended by a Native American (Gary Farmer); Neil Young's haunting score greatly enhanced film's atmosphere; Jarmusch subsequently directed the videos for "Dead Man Theme" and for "Big Time", a track from Young's 1996 album "Broken Arrow"

1996: Made cameo appearances in Billy Bob Thornton's feature directing debut, "Sling Blade", and Wayne Wang and Paul Auster's "Blue in the Face"

1997: Helmed the Neil Young concert film "Year of the Horse"

1999: Wrote and directed "Ghost Dog: The Way of the Samurai", about a hit man who finds he's been double-crossed; film featured a highly-charged soundtrack by The RZA (of the Wu-Tang Clan) ; debuted in competition at Cannes

QUOTES:

"Independent filmmaking is a lot like gambling. I could make a lot more money by taking [Hollywood] directing jobs, or giving away control of my films and selling to the highest bidder. But if I'm putting up three years of my life and a lot of work, and you put up the money, we can split the profits, but I keep the negative."—Jim Jarmusch to Variety, December 27, 1989.

"I want the critics to find my films themselves. Most films aren't demanding enough of the audience. I've tried to see this supposed 'new' strain in American movies. Instead, I see the realities like 'Desperately Seeking Susan' and 'Blood Simple'. They're Spielbergian, a play on accepting television language. They don't trust the audience, cutting to a new shot every six or seven seconds. Frankly, I feel the whole situation for making films has gotten worse."—Jarmusch in American Film, October 1986.

"Anytime you make a film, it's not my money I use, so there's business considerations; I'm not naive and not oblivious to them. But they serve the film in the end, rather than the film serving the money. I think maybe that's the basic difference. As soon as the work is there to serve the budget, rather than the budget being there to serve the work, then it's backwards and that's not independent anymore.

"I get to make films the way I want. It would be frustrating if no one would help me finance them. I don't care where the money comes from as long as it doesn't have restrictions with guys in suits telling me how to cast the film and how to cut it and what actors to cast, or what music to use. As long as it's my work then I'm happy. I don't care if that money comes from Universal or if it comes from some independent business guys in, you know, in France, or wherever."—Jarmusch quoted in "Filmmaker Focus" at www.sundancechannel.com.

On censorship: "It's like Oscar Wilde says, paraphrasing him: 'The imagination should be out of bounds to any form of censorship.' Because if you can release things in your imagination you may not have to act on them. For example, sexuality in Scandinavia is probably a hell of a lot more healthy than in America, where it is repressed. I think that there are fewer people there who are raping and abusing others than here. I think if you look at 'gangster rap', which gets constantly harassed, you'll see it's from young brothers comin' out of the streets who have no other way to get out. They get attacked all the time, but you don't see Arnold Schwarzenegger movies attacked in the same way, which are a far more visual form of violence. But I would stick up for those movies, too, because they're strong stories. Look at 'The Iliad'. It is all about very violent war.

"I don't understand that way of thinking, which is a very sneaky way of trying to control us and keep a certain social order by attacking expression. They say, 'The expression is the cause.' No, that's backwards. The expression is a reflection of a history of human-kind. There is something wrong with that suppression. I think that the imagination and expression of the imagination should be protected as a totally free zone. Obviously there are rules. You don't want to have children exposed to certain things, but all cultures protect their children so thay are prepared for life. Even things that are sick and twisted should be permitted to be expressed in some way because thay are an escape valve. It's when these things are repressed that people act out on them. But I don't know. I'm not a sociologist. It's not my job. I don't wave banners around."—Jarmusch quoted in *MovieMaker*, Issue No 37, Volume 7.

"In the past, when I started to write scripts, and ideas came to me from other films or from books, I would shove them away. In this case ['Ghost Dog'] I accepted them. I think it has to do with music, with bebop and hip-hop. Something opened up in me; like when you listen to Charlie Parker and he plays a solo, but then he quotes a standard in his solo, and weaves it in. I think that finally registered for me—and I decided to construct a film where the door was open for things like Jean-Pierre Melville's 'Le Samourai', Seijun Suzuki's 'Branded to Kill', 'Don Quixote', 'Frankenstein',

hip-hop culture . . . a lot of things."—Jarmusch quoted in *Premiere*, February 2000.

"A bunch of old white men have run things so far. That's why I've always been interested in people who don't fit it. I have friends who are in prison, off the grid, living on reservations. I learn more from them, somehow, and I respect them."—Jarmusch to *The New York Times*, February 29, 2000.

"I don't know what 'indie film' means anymore. The term has been usurped as a marketing device. The name is like alternative music—they labeled it to make it mainstream. To me, independent film means that the people making the film love cinema as a beautiful form of expression and make the creative decisions without having market analysis to decide what the audience wants the product to be. After all, the beauty of a film is that when you go into a theater, you enter a world, and you have no idea where it's going to take you. Like a piece of music, it sweeps you along in its own rhythm and its own time."—Jarmusch, quoted in Richard Corliss' review of "Ghost Dog: The Way of the Samurai", in *Time*, March 13, 2000.

Jean-Pierre Jeunet

BORN: in Roanne, France, 1955

SOMETIMES CREDITED AS:
Jeunet & Caro

NATIONALITY: French

AWARDS: Cesar Best Short Subject (Animation) "Le Menage" 1981

Cesar Best Short Subject (Animation) "Foutaises" 1991

Cesar Best First Film "Delicatessen" 1992; shared with Marc Caro

Cesar Best Screenplay "Delicatessen" 1992; shared award

European Film Award Best Director "Amelie" 2001; film also cited as Best Film

European Film People's Choice Award Best Director "Amelie" 2001

San Diego Film Critics Society Award Best Foreign-Language Film "Amelie" 2001

Southeastern Film Critics Association Award Best Foreign-Language Film "Amelie" 2001

Online Film Critics Society Award Best Foreign-Language Film "Amelie" 2001

Dallas-Fort Worth Film Critics Association Award Best Foreign-Language Film "Amelie" 2001

Florida Film Critics Circle Award Best Picture "Amelie" 2001

Florida Film Critics Circle Award Best Foreign Film "Amelie" 2001

Broadcast Film Critics Association Award Best Foreign-Language Film "Amelie" 2001

Lumiere Best Picture "Amelie" 2001

Lumiere Best Screenplay "Amelie" 2001; shared with Guillaume Laurant

Chicago Film Critics Award Best Foreign Language Film "Amelie" 2002

Goya Best European Film "Amelie" 2001

ShoWest International Achievement in Filmmaking Award 2002

BAFTA Award Best Original Screenplay "Amelie" 2002; shared with Guillaume Laurant

Cesar Best Director "Amelie" 2002

Independent Spirit Award Best Foreign Film "Amelie" 2002

BIOGRAPHY

With an eye for meticulous detail and a rakish sense of humor, Jean-Pierre Jeunet and writing and directing partner Marc Caro have teamed together for more than 15 years, first in making short films, TV commercials and music videos, then in scoring international successes with the features "Delicatessen" (1991) and "La Cite des enfants perdu/The City of Lost Children" (1995).

Jeunet had established himself as a filmmaker with the acclaimed shorts "L'Evasion" (1978) and the Cesar-winning "Le menage" (1980). The latter led to a meeting with artist and comic book creator Marc Caro and the duo immediately recognized their kindred spirits. Their first collaboration, "Le Bunker de la derniere rafale/The Last Blast Bunker" (1981), which detailed the rising paranoia among soldiers trapped underground, garnered festival prizes in France. It also marked the beginning of a collaboration that demonstrated a keen visual style and absurdist humor. Jeunet continued to direct music videos and featurettes, including the award-winning "Pas de repos pour Billy Brakko/No Rest for Billy Brakko" (1983) and "Foutaises" (1990).

The initial feature collaboration of Jeunet & Caro was an expansion of Caro's short "La Concierge est dans l'escalier/The Concierge Is in the Stairs" (1987). Set in a post-apocalyptic time when meat is scarce, it focused on an apartment-owning landlord who maims and murders residents of his building to feed the carnivorous appetites of other tenants. The film's storyline was faulted as its weakest point, but critics and audiences responded to the exquisite monochromatic production values. Jeunet & Caro divided responsibilities with the former guiding the actors and the latter coordinating the artistic elements. Jeunet & Caro also set about creating an informal repertory company of actors, as well.

With "La cite des enfants perdu/The City of Lost Children", the duo expanded on their themes. Essentially a hybrid of comic books and fairy tales, the film has several storylines that more or less converge. What drives the plot is a mad scientist who kidnaps young children to harvest their dreams. Striking visuals, including a set design that is both futuristic as well as historical, wild costumes (from fashion designer Jean-Paul Gauthier), moody almost painterly cinematography (by Darius Khondji) and a cast that included established players (Ron Perlman, Daniel Emilfork) and newcomers (Judith Vittet) all combined to create a surreal almost hallucinogenic motion picture. Jeunet managed to elicit strong performances from the cast, notable Vittet, while Caro created the wild world that invoked everything from Dickens to "The Wizard of Oz." While the film was supposed to be suitable for children, some considered it "dark", to which Jeunet and Caro replied that it was no more "dark" than "Pinocchio" or "Bambi."

Jeunet & Caro are noted for painstakingly fine-tuning their work, not rushing their productions and often spending years perfecting story and effects. ("The City of Lost Children" took almost fourteen years to reach the screen.) The international success of "Delicatessen" caught them by surprise and it took them four years to perfect the script for "City of Lost Children." When the latter gained them further attention, it was only a matter of time before

Hollywood beckoned. Caro remained in France, but Jeunet accepted the plum assignment of helming the fourth installment in the "Alien" series, "Alien Resurrection" (1997), which brought Sigourney Weaver's Ripley back to life via cloning to once again do battle.

When his experience in Hollywood proved less felicitous than hoped, Jeunet returned to France and spent several years developing projects. His return to filmmaking (as co-writer and director) was "Amelie" (2001), a highly-praised, whimsical tale of a sheltered young woman who discovers the power to change people's lives through simple means.

MILESTONES:

First met Marc Caro at an animation film festival

1980: With Marc Caro made first short film, "Le Bunker de la derniere rafale/The Last Blast Bunker"

1980–1990: Teamed with Caro to make short films, music videos and TV commercials

1991: Feature directorial debut, "Delicatessen", co-directed with Caro; billed as Jeunet & Caro

1995: Garnered international acclaim with "The City of Lost Children"

1997: First US feature and first solo directorial effort, "Alien Resurrection"

2001: Co-wrote and directed the whimsical French-language feature "Le Fableux destin d'Amelie Poulain"; released internationally as "Amelie"

QUOTES:

"They truly know where they want to go. They have their film entirely in their heads."—Jean-Claude Dreyfus, one of the stars of "The City of Lost Children".

"You step back a little and accept that your film will be full of flaws, and that these flaws become part of the film. There is no perfect movie, ever—it doesn't exist."—Jean-Pierre Jeunet.

Norman Jewison

BORN: Norman Frederick Jewison in Toronto, Ontario, Canada, 07/21/1926

NATIONALITY: Canadian

EDUCATION: Malvern Collegiate Institute, Toronto, Ontario, Canada, 1940–44

Victoria College, University of Toronto, Toronto, Ontario, Canada, BA, 1946–50; received an honor award for writing and directing many college productions

AWARDS: Golden Globe Award Best Motion Picture (Musical or Comedy) "The Russians Are Coming, The Russians Are Coming" 1966

NATO Director of the Year Award 1973; presented by the National Association of Theater Owners

Berlin Film Festival Best Director Award "Moonstruck" 1988

Genie Special Achievement Award 1988 for founding the Canadian Center for Advanced Film Studies

Special Society of Motion Picture and Television Art Directors Award 1998 for "outstanding contribution to cinematic imagery"

Canadian Film Centre Lifetime Achievement Award 1998; initial presentation of biennial prize

Irving G. Thalberg Memorial Award 1998; presented by the Academy of Motion Picture Arts and Sciences

George Eastman Award 1999; presented by NATO/ShowEast

BIOGRAPHY

A consummate craftsman known for eliciting fine performances from his casts, Norman Jewison has addressed important social and political issues throughout his directing and producing career, often making controversial or complicated subjects accessible to mainstream audiences. Like so many of his peers, he got his start in TV, but unlike the ones who made their marks in the live dramas of the day (i.e., Sidney Lumet, Arthur Penn, John Frankenheimer), Jewison's domain was the musical special. After serving in the Navy at the close of WWII and completing college in his native Canada, he moved to London in the early 1950s and finally broke into the business as an actor-writer with the BBC. An invitation to join a television training program at the CBC brought him home, where he rose rapidly and within a few years was directing and producing major variety programs (e.g., "Showtime", "The Big Revue"). CBS took note of his skills and hired him in 1958 to revitalize the live weekly music show "Your Hit Parade", and for the next four years, he solidified his reputation working with such artists as Frank Sinatra, Judy Garland, Danny Kaye and Harry Belafonte.

Disillusioned by the effects of the ratings wars on the quality of TV programming, Jewison relocated from NYC to Hollywood to helm his first Hollywood feature, "40 Pounds of Trouble" (1963), starring Tony Curtis in an updating of the classic "Little Miss Marker" about a selfish casino manager who "adopts" a spunky orphaned waif. The picture did so well that Universal offered a seven-picture contract, and his second film, "The Thrill of It All" (1963, scripted by Carl Reiner), a vehicle for Doris Day and James Garner, became one of the studio's big moneymakers that year. Jewison also banged out "Send Me No Flowers" (1964), which paired Day with Rock Hudson, and reteamed with Reiner and Garner for "The Art of Love" (1965) but was growing tired of the lightweight scripts the studio was offering.

Eager to delve into more serious fare, he found a loophole in his contract and switched to MGM, replacing Sam Peckinpah at the helm of "The Cincinnati Kid" (1965), a tale of professional gamblers starring Steve McQueen, with whom he would also make the sumptuous, no-think entertainment "The Thomas Crown Affair" (1968), a triumph of style over substance which he has called "the only amoral-immoral film I've ever done."

Jewison achieved complete artistic control on "The Russians Are Coming, The Russians Are Coming" (1966) and has enjoyed the coveted final cut on every film since. A farcical take on the Cold War, it featured an all-star cast and scored pre-Glasnost points by emphasizing the shared humanity of Russians and Americans alike, earning its first-time feature producer an Oscar nomination for Best Picture. He followed its success with the gripping, pioneering civil rights drama "In the Heat of the Night" (1967), which boasted the dynamic pairing of Sidney Poitier and Rod Steiger against the claustrophobic, small-town backdrop vividly photographed by Haskell Wexler. Despite losing head-to-head at the box office against "Bonnie and Clyde", it still managed to beat out the competition for Best Picture, in addition to garnering four other Oscars, including one for editor Hal Ashby. Jewison returned to comedy for "Gaily, Gaily" (1969), adapted from Ben Hecht's autobiographical novel of his apprenticeship on a Chicago paper, and though the expensive sets and period flavor evoked nostalgia, he fared better as producer of Ashby's feature directing debut, "The Landlord" (1970).

Jewison's next two movies were adaptations of very successful stage musicals. For the first, "Fiddler on the Roof" (1971), he faced one of the most agonizing casting decisions of his career, turning down both Zero Mostel (who had originated the role of Tevye on Broadway) and his good friend Danny Kaye in favor of little-known Topol. He told the *Los Angeles Times* (March 14, 1999), "I wanted an Israeli actor who didn't speak English very well to play this first-generation Russian Jew. I didn't think it would ring true with a New York Yiddish actor." Filmed on location in Yugoslavia, it received eight Academy Award nominations, including Best Picture and Best Director, earned three, for Best Sound, Best cinematography (Oswald Morris) and Best Musical Scoring (John Williams) and raked in the profits. A similar commercial fate awaited "Jesus Christ Superstar", which he filmed in Israel while managing to simultaneously produce Ted Kotcheff's offbeat Western "Billy Two-Hats" (both 1973), proving his flexibility, if nothing else. The sci-fi drama "Rollerball" (1975) also pointed up his incredible versatility, earning somewhat of a cult following.

Jewison's labor movement picture, "F.I.S.T" (1978), was a giant flop despite the director's careful attention to detail, and when he focused his attention on the legal system, not even a powerhouse performance by Al Pacino could overcome the weak script (by Barry Levinson and Valerie Curtin) of " . . . And Justice for All" (1979), though it performed better commercially than had its predecessor. When he reteamed with Levinson and Curtin for "Best Friends" (1982), the picture failed to meet audience expectations for a Goldie Hawn–Burt Reynolds vehicle, resulting in tepid ticket sales. He finally turned it around with the socially conscious "A Soldier's Story" (1984), adapted from the 1981 Pulitzer Prize–winning play by Charles Fuller. A solid whodunit plus a probing look at racism within blank ranks during WWII, it featured most of its original Negro Ensemble Company cast, including Adolph Caesar in his Oscar-nominated role as the bigoted master sergeant found shot to death on a country road near a Louisiana army base. It also marked Jewison's first collaboration with Denzel Washington, as well as his return to the ranks of Oscar nominees (Best Picture).

"A Soldier's Story" had not completely escaped its theatrical origins but was still a riveting picture. The same cannot be said for Jewison's next two stage-to-film transfers "Agnes of God" (1985) and "Other People's Money" (1991), with neither coming up to the level of its forerunner. In between, however, Jewison enjoyed a mighty box office at the helm of playwright John Patrick Shanley's original screenplay "Moonstruck" (1987), deftly handling the romantic comedy which won Oscars for Best Actress (Cher), Best Supporting Actress (Olympia Dukakis) and Best Screenplay (Shanley). "In Country" (1989), however, despite a fine performance by Bruce Willis as a cynical, shell-shocked recluse and beautifully-handled concluding scenes at the Washington (DC) Vietnam Veterans Memorial, was a disappointing treatment of Bobbie Ann Mason's acclaimed novel. Jewison reemerged from a three-year hiatus with the tepid romantic comedy "Only You" (1994), starring 1993 Oscar-winner Marisa Tomei as a bride-to-be who leaves her groom at the altar to search for her true soul mate (Robert Downey Jr.), followed by the treacly comedy-drama "Bogus" (1996), featuring Whoopi Goldberg and Gerard Depardieu in a story of a young boy's reliance on an imaginary friend to cope with the death of a parent.

Jewison returned to TV as executive producer of the TNT biopic "Geronimo" (1993) and two years later served as an executive producer for Showtime's "Picture Windows" anthology, as well as directing its "Soir Bleu" segment. In Canada, he executive produced Bruce McDonald's feature "Dance Me Outside" (1994) and then shared executive producing responsibilities with McDonald on the Canadian TV series "The Rez" in 1996. The 90s also found him acting in the Canadian picture "Harold Knows Best" (1995), playing a TV director in John Landis' "The Stupids" and appearing as himself in the satirical "Burn, Hollywood, Burn" (1997). On the heels of accepting the prestigious Irving G. Thalberg Memorial Award, he helmed the feature-length

Showtime documentary "Norman Jewison on Comedy in the 20th Century: Funny Is Money" (1999), but the entire decade was just a prelude for "The Hurricane", released in the waning days of the 20th century. Unleashing his social conscience on the film he had wanted to make for 10 years, he masterfully told the story of Reuben "Hurricane" Carter (Denzel Washington), a former middleweight boxing champion unjustly imprisoned 19 years for murders he did not commit. A fabulous tribute to the power of the human spirit, it was arguably Jewison's best film in decades and possibly his best ever.

MILESTONES:

1932: Gave readings of poetry by Robert Service at various Masonic lodge meetings at age six (date approximate)

Served briefly in the Canadian navy at the end of WWII

After college, drove a cab to earn passage to England

1950–1952: Worked in England as actor-writer with BBC (dates approximate)

Returned to Canada to join the CBC's television training program, subsequently working with the network as producer-director

Began working for CBS in NYC, first revitalizing the "Your Hit Parade" show and then staging network specials like "Tonight with Belafonte" and "The Judy Garland Show" (directing and producing the special as well as producing the subsequent series)

1962: Directed first film, "40 Pounds of Trouble"

1963: Based on success of "40 Pounds of Trouble", signed by Universal Studios to a seven-picture deal of which only three were ultimately completed

1965: After directing three "innocuous Hollywood comedies" ("The Thrill of It All" 1963, "Send Me No Flowers" 1964, "The Art of Love" 1965), found loophole in his contract and took over the direction of MGM's "The Cincinnati Kid" from Sam Peckinpah; first collaboration with actor Steve McQueen

1966: First feature producing credit, "The Russians Are Coming, The Russians Are Coming"; also directed; garnered first Oscar nomination for Best Picture; initial collaboration with title designer Pablo Ferro

1967: Helmed Academy Award-winning Best Picture "In the Heat of the Night"; received first Oscar nod for directing; also first collaboration with director of photography Haskell Wexler

1968: Reteamed with McQueen and Wexler for "The Thomas Crown Affair"; checked out that year's Montreal Expo with Wexler and editor Hal Ashby and discovered a short film that introduced multiple screen effects, borrowing the technique for the film; Ferro created and edited the multiple screen effects including the use of 66 images in one frame for the polo sequence, reputedly a first for a 35mm feature

1970: Depressed about the assasinations of the Reverend Martin Luther King and Robert F. Kennedy, moved family to London for eight years

1970: Produced Ashby's feature directing debut, "The Landlord"

1971: First film adaptation of a successful stage musical, produced and directed "Fiddler on the Roof"; film received eight Academy Award nominations including Best Picture and Best Director

1973: Co-wrote screenplay (with Melvyn Bragg), produced and directed the film adaptation of "Jesus Christ Superstar", the Andrew Lloyd Webber–Tim Rice pop opera

1975: Helmed and produced the sci-fi thriller "Rollerball", scripted by William Harrison from his own short story

1979: Teamed with screenwriters Barry Levinson and Valerie Curtin for " . . . And Justice for All", starring Al Pacino

1982: Reteamed with Levinson and Curtin for "Best Friends", a romantic comedy starring Burt Reynolds and Goldie Hawn

1982: Made an officer of the Order of Canada by the Governor-General, the Queen's representative in the Canadian capital of Ottawa; the Order is Canada's highest civilian decoration

1984: Got career back on track with the popular and critical success of "A Soldier's Story", adapted by Charles Fuller from his Pulitzer Prize–winning "A Soldier's Play"; nominated for three Academy Awards including Best Picture; film featured Denzel Washington

1985: Received much less praise for his next stage-to-film adaptation, "Agnes of God"; first feature filmed in his native Canada and initial collaboration with cinematographer Sven Nykvist

1987: Had popular and critical success with the romantic comedy "Moonstruck", receiving Best Picture and Best Director Oscar nominations

Founded Yorktown Productions

1989: Stumbled with "In Country", a poorly executed adaptation of Bobbie Ann Mason's acclaimed novel

1991: Provided Danny De Vito with a great vehicle, "Other People's Money", though the movie lacked the bite of Jerry Sterner's off-Broadway play; third film with Wexler

1993: Produced the TNT biopic "Geronimo"

1994: Teamed with director of photography Sven Nyvist to provide a lush Italian backdrop for the far-fetched "Only You"

1995: Directed "Soir Bleu" segment of Showtime's "Picture Windows" anthology; also served as an executive producer

1996: Missed with pairing of Whoopi Goldberg and Gerard Depardieu in "Bogus"

1996: Played a TV director in John Landis' "The Stupids"

1997: Appeared as himself in "Burn, Hollywood, Burn"

1999: Helmed and executive produced feature-length documentary, "Norman Jewison on Comedy in the 20th Century: Funny Is Money" (Showtime), using the hype surrounding the finale of the wildly successful series "Seinfeld" (NBC) as his launchpad

1999: Produced and directed "Hurricane", starring Denzel Washington as Reuben "Hurricane" Carter, the 1960s world middleweight boxing champion, unjustly convicted of the murder of three white men in a New Jersey bar

2001: Directed the HBO adaptation of the Pulitzer-winning play "Dinner With Friends"

AFFILIATION: Established the Canadian Center for Advanced Film Studies (CCAFS) in 1986

QUOTES:

Jewison became a decorated officer in the Order of Canada in 1982

He received the Lifetime Achievement Award of the Canada-California Chamber of Commerce in 1986.

Named "Filmmaker of the Year" by the Motion Picture Bookers in 1991

Embracing his ancestral occupation of farming, Jewison breeds cattle on his 200-acre farm outside Toronto.

Jewison was originally set to direct the biopic of slain activist Malcolm X until Spike Lee raised objections and eventually assumed the project.

He and his wife market "Norman & Dixie's Maple Syrup Ice Cream"

"My first film, '40 Pounds of Trouble', starring Tony Curtis, launched me as a motion picture director and I have remained in the industry ever since. Every film I make must have a raison d'etre, a reason for being there. As well as being an entertaining story it must have something valid to say about life, that reflects my own private fears or joy. Even though I now know it is a futile and impossible task, I still want to change the world. Well, a little bit!"—Norman Jewison, quoted in "World Film Directors, Volume Two", edited by John Wakeman (New York: The H. W. Wilson Company, 1988)

About Steve McQueen: "He was always looking for a father figure. And I said, 'I'm too young to be your father, but I'll be your older brother. And I'll be the brother that went to college who'll look out for you, OK?' He said, 'You're twisting my melon, man.'

"So he learned to trust me. And on 'Thomas Crown', I knew he wasn't that character, but he desperately had to play it, so he trusted me to guide him. He was absolutely believable. He never acted a day in his life; he just was. There was an honesty about him, and he knew where the camera was."—Jewison to Bill Desowitz in the *Los Angeles Times*, March 14, 1999.

"All my life I've been seeking my own Jewishness. My family is originally from Yorkshire, which was a Jewish stronghold in England. I suspect we might have been assimilated from the 13th century."—Jewison quoted in the *Los Angeles Times*, March 14, 1999.

Roland Joffe

BORN: in London, England, 11/17/1945

NATIONALITY: English

EDUCATION: Manchester University, England, English and drama; graduated

AWARDS: Cannes Film Festival Technique Award "The Mission" 1986

Cannes Film Festival Palme d'Or Award "The Mission" 1986

BIOGRAPHY

The youngest ever director to work at London's National Theatre, Joffe gained directing experience with England's Granada Television before making his big-screen mark in the 1980s with two large-scale, politically oriented spectacles. "The Killing Fields" (1984) was based on the experiences of *New York Times* correspondent Sydney Schanberg and his Cambodian assistant, Dith Pran, before and after the fall of Phnom Penh to the Khmer Rouge in 1975; "The Mission" (1986) focused on political intrigue and exploitation in a Jesuit mission in Brazil in the late 18th century. Both films were visually sumptuous— they earned Chris Menges two Oscars for Best Cinematography—though the lushness and length of each was felt by some critics to lessen their dramatic impact. Joffe's next film, "Fat Man and Little Boy" (1989), about J. Robert Oppenheimer and the Trinity Project which developed

the nuclear bomb, was admittedly flawed but unjustly overlooked. He regained some ground with "City of Joy" (1992), about a dispirited American doctor working amid the poor in India.

MILESTONES:

Joined the Young Vic Theatre after graduation; directed many early productions for its repertory company

Youngest ever director to work at London's National Theater; done while Laurence Olivier was artistic director

Helped form the National Theatre's first touring company

Signed with Granada Television in England; helmed the documentaries "Anne" and "Rope" and the series "Bill Brand" and "The Stars Look Down"

Wrote several "Plays for Today" produced by Tony Garnett, including "The Spongers" and "United Kingdom"

1984: Directed and produced first film, "The Killing Fields"

1991: First American TV producing credit, executive producing the TNT documentary special, "A Taste of Freedom", looking at the life of one family in post–Soviet Russia

1993: Produced first film which he did not direct, "Super Mario Bros."

Signed to produce a half-hour daily series for MTV about people's bedtime habits to be called "Undressed"

BORN: Charles Martin Jones in Spokane, Washington, 09/21/1912

SOMETIMES CREDITED AS:
Chuck M. Jones
Charles M. Jones

DEATH: in Corono del Mar, California, 02/22/2002

NATIONALITY: American

EDUCATION: dropped out of high school

Chouinard Art Institute Pasadena, California enrolled at age 15; graduated; school now called California Institute of the Arts

attended 10 years of night school, studying drawing with Donald Graham

AWARDS: Newsreel Theatre Award best animated cartoon of the year "Old Glory" 1940; Jones reports that "This award was unique in that it was never given before or since and the first award to be won by a cel washer." (Jones was actually the director)

Oscar Best Short Subject (cartoon) "The Dot and the Line" 1965; award shared with Les Goldman, co-producer

Los Angeles Film Critics Association Career Achievement Award 1990; cited with Blake Edwards

Ringling Bros. and Barnum & Bailey Clown College Golden Smile Award 1993; first occurrence of this award

Honorary Oscar 1995 for "the creation of classic cartoons and cartoon characters whose animated lives have brought joy to our real ones for more than half a century"

Directors Guild of America Honorary Life Membership 1996

BIOGRAPHY

With the death of Friz Freleng in 1995, legendary animation producer, director and screenwriter Chuck Jones became the last surviving giant from the golden era of Warner Brothers animation (a period spanning roughly—and arguably—from 1935-59). That such a thoughtful and articulate witness, artist and theoretician has continued to provide information and inspiration as the millennium winds down is an enormous boon to film history and an inspiration to film artists.

Chuck Jones' "children" are not just practitioners of animation; successful live-action directors Steven Spielberg and Joe Dante have paid heartfelt homage to the man and his art in their work. While still a neophyte, Spielberg begged Universal Pictures to pay for forty composite seconds of a Jones-directed Road Runner and Coyote cartoon to use for a particularly poignant scene in his 1974 debut "The Sugarland Express." He subsequently utilized a portion of Jones' "Duck Dodgers in the 24 1/2 Century" (1953) for an important scene in "Close Encounters of the Third Kind." The legendary animation director later served as an uncredited creative assistant on Spielberg's flawed, cartoonish comedy of scale, "1941" (1979). When Jones finally penned his autobiography "Chuck Amuck" in 1989, Spielberg paid a personal tribute by writing the foreword. Dante has displayed his devotion by featuring Jones in cameos in "Gremlins" (1984), "Innerspace" (1987) and "Gremlins 2: The New Batch" (1990). For the latter, Jones also wrote and directed an animated sequence featuring Bugs Bunny.

Jones was the closest thing to an intellectual, self-conscious artist in an industry that was not known for its pretensions. He studied anatomy and drawing during ten years of night school while working as an animator and animation director. Jones began publishing articles on the art of animation as early as 1946. He also gave art classes to his animation crew at Warner Brothers. Whereas such seriousness could have lead to the production of joyless, academic exercises, in the case of Jones, it resulted in some of the funniest yet most rigorously conceptualized cartoons ever produced by the Hollywood studio system. While some could argue that there were other directors at Warner Bros. in the 30s and 40s whose work was at least as wild, original or innovative (namely Tex Avery, Frank Tashlin and Bob Clampett), none could equal Jones' sheer mastery of character animation from the mid-40s through the late 50s. He excelled at designing and posing expressive characters. Jones has been quoted as saying that an animator is "an actor with a pencil." If so, his work revealed him as a master thespian.

A high school dropout, Jones enrolled in the Chouinard Art Institute (later known as the California Institute of the Arts) in Los Angeles at age 15 from which he graduated without feeling secure about his drawing abilities. He found work in a commercial art studio but found himself unsuited to the job. Jones fared better as a cel(luloid)-washer at the Ub Iwerks Studio. He moved up the ranks slightly, successively becoming a cel-painter, cel-inker and in-betweener (assistant animator) before being fired by Iwerks. Jones worked briefly for producers Charles Mintz and Walter Lantz before being rehired by the Iwerks studio. He was soon fired again by Iwerks secretary Dorothy Webster, whom he would marry in 1936. Jones worked variously as a seaman, puppeteer and portrait painter before the future Mrs. Jones obtained him a job as an assistant animator with Leon Schlesinger Productions, the animation unit at Warner Brothers, around 1933. The animation producing team of Hugh Harman and Rudolf Ising (Harman-Ising) had recently departed and Schlesinger was building his own unit.

Jones was promoted to animator in 1934 and worked on several cartoons helmed by Freleng and others before being assigned with Clampett to Avery's unit at Termite Terrace (the nickname for the bungalow on the Warner lot where the animators toiled). This astonishing assemblage of talent first collaborated on the epochal "Golddiggers of '49" (1936), Avery's first cartoon for Warners. With this uneven start, an important new era in cartoon history had begun. Jones and Clampett were briefly loaned out to the faltering Iwerks studio to work as (uncredited) co-directors on two entries in the Gabby Goat series. Soon after their return, Clampett was promoted to director and Jones became his animator. He would graduate to directing himself by 1938 when Tashlin departed Warners.

Jones' early directorial efforts revealed a strong debt to Walt Disney in both style and subject matter. Set in a world where cute was king, these cartoons typically featured a small, quiet character in a large, forbidding environment. Jones' first film, "The Night Watchman" (1938), told the story of a kitten who fills in for his ailing father as the regular night watchman of the house. His first original character of note was Sniffles, a talkative little mouse clad in a porkpie hat and scarf, who debuted in "Naughty but Mice" (1939) and appeared in several more cartoons before being retired in 1947. Other early highlights included an odd series of five cartoons starring Inki, a little stereotyped "African" in his top-knot. These dreamy dialogue-less adventures tended to concern Inki's tumultuous efforts to hunt a lion ("Little Lion Hunter" 1939; "Inki and the Lion" 1941; "Inki and the Mynah Bird" 1943). At unlikely moments, a deadpan and apparently mystical little mynah bird walks through the scene to the musical accompaniment of Mendelssohn's overture to "Fingal's Cave", hopping on odd beats of the music. All in all, some of Jones' early efforts were charming, others were cloying but they tended to be beautifully crafted. It would take him some time to display the sassy irreverence and skillful comic timing that would eventually characterize his best work.

Jones did solid work in the early 40s but he was overshadowed by the blossoming talent of Clampett. This period of stylistic exploration and honing of skills would pay off handsomely later in the decade. Jones also had some outside interests. A dedicated liberal, he became one of the leaders of the historic animators strike at the Walt Disney Studio. Jones also worked evenings without compensation as the director of what would become the first cartoon from UPA (United Productions of America), "Hell Bent for Election" (1944). This was an unapologetic work of advocacy in support of President Franklin Roosevelt's re-election. Significantly, Jones' 1942 cartoon "The Dover Boys" is also considered a major influence on the style, method and timing of what would become the UPA style.

In 1946, the Hollywood Cartoonists' Union won its demand for a 25-percent raise for all its members, who were generally extremely underpaid. This victory resulted in the studios cutting back on production costs and the results were evident in Hollywood cartoons released after 1947 or 1948. The animation became less lavish and fewer characters appeared in a given cartoon. Intriguingly, this cutback seemed to spur Jones to some of the greatest achievements of his career. He had been experimenting with stylized minimalist backgrounds since the early 40s. Moreover, Jones had become increasingly interested in refining movement and paring character animation down to its essentials. He was abetted by some particularly brilliant collaborators including writer Michael Maltese, backgrounds and layout men Maurice Noble and Phil De Guard and such animators as Ken Harris, Abe Levitow, Lloyd Vaughn and Ben Washam. In addition, one cannot discount the invaluable contribution of music supervisor Carl W. Stalling. Allied with such formidable talents, Jones thrived upon the newly imposed restraints.

Jones had directed the second and third appearances of the prototypical Bugs Bunny in "Prest-o Change-o" (1939) and "Elmer's Candid Camera" (1940). Avery would finally crystallize the rabbit's personality later in "A Wild Hare" (1940). Once he had a firm grip on the character (certainly by 1942's "Case of the Missing Hare"), Jones became one of the best helmers of Bugs Bunny. He has said "My Bugs, I think, tended to think out his problems and solve them intellectually, and I insisted upon stronger provocation. Two or three things would happen before he got mad enough—no, he wasn't mad, just the logic would move in— and he'd say, 'Of course, you realize this means war. . . . ' Bugs is a counterrevolutionary, you know. He's not a revolutionary. He's not a Woody Woodpecker, which is how Bob Clampett used him. Clampett's Bugs Bunny did not involve the disciplines we would put in." This marvelous discipline would be reflected in numerous cartoons including "Hare-Raising Hare" (1946) in which Bugs is pitted against a Peter Lorre–like mad scientist and a large, orange-haired, sneaker-clad monster (at one point, the rabbit poses as a chatty manicurist who prattles, "My, I bet you MAHNsters lead INNteresting lives . . . "); "Baby Buggy Bunny" (1954) in which the foundling he takes into his care is actually the notorious gangster Babyface Finster; and "Bully for Bugs" (1953) in which he accidentally burrows into a Spanish bullring ("I knew I shoulda taken that left turn at Albuquerque!") and tangles with an angry bull.

Jones conceived Daffy Duck as a cowardly self-preservationist continually undone by his own greed or selfishness. Jones' trilogy of cartoons starring Bugs Bunny, Daffy Duck and Elmer Fudd—"Rabbit Fire" (1951), "Rabbit Seasoning" (1952) and "Duck! Rabbit! Duck!" (1953)—were masterfully subtle and imaginative examples of character animation as the three very different personalities interacted in a variety of situations involving hunting and whether it was truly rabbit season or duck season. Jones also derived much comic mileage from placing Daffy in wildly incongruous settings such as in "The Scarlet Pumpernickel" (1950), "Duck Dodgers in the 24 1/2 Century" and "Robin Hood Daffy" (1958). This tendency was amplified to a nearly cosmic degree in "Duck Amuck" (1953), a classic example of reflexivity in cinema, in which Daffy is explicitly presented as an animated figure tormented by a (mostly) off-screen animator.

Jones won the studio an Oscar with "For Scent-imental Reasons" (1949) which starred one of his most popular creations, the amorous French skunk Pepe Le Pew. The formula for these cartoons was fairly rigid: a female cat somehow gets a streak of paint drawn down the middle of her back and Pepe mistakes her for another skunk. Immediately smitten with love, he pursues her, totally oblivious of her revulsion for his odor. Jones created an even more minimalist situation for his most successful creation, the Road Runner and Wile E. Coyote series. The formula was totally inflexible. The setting was always the desert; the Coyote would always chase the Road Runner whom he could never catch; the Coyote would always be done in by his own efforts; and the characters could never speak. These cartoons represented the chase film boiled down to its essentials. At their best, they had an absurdist, existential quality. The Coyote's hunger soon ceased to be the primary motivation. Merely chasing the Road Runner was his reason for existence. To further his goal, the hapless canine generally ordered elaborate devices from the ACME Corporation, which invariably betrayed his naive faith in them.

In addition to working with an impressive stable of continuing characters, Jones also excelled at "one-shot" cartoons. The most celebrated example may well be "One Froggy Evening" (1955), an unsettling allegory about a (sometimes) singing frog. Retrospectively christened Michigan J. Frog, this character became the symbol of Warner Brothers' WB Network in the mid-90s.

Many fans and historians believe that Jones achieved his masterpiece with "What's Opera, Doc?" (1957) which miraculously condensed Wagner's 14-hour "Der Ring des Nibelungun" into a classic six-minute cartoon. But what six minutes! This extraordinarily lavish spoof of opera required 106 shots whereas a typical cartoon used about 60. Also a wicked parody of Disney's "Fantasia" (1940), Maurice Noble's monumental designs and melodramatically theatrical color schemes were unlike anything previously seen in a Warner Brothers cartoon. "What's Opera, Doc?" wittily analyzed the long-running battle between Elmer and Bugs and recast it in larger-than-life terms complete with original songs and a hilariously animated ballet. In 1992, the film was justly selected for inclusion in the Library of Congress' National Film Registry.

After the demise of Warner Brothers animation in the early 60s, Jones briefly went to MGM where he produced and directed a memorable series of Tom and Jerry cartoons. He redesigned Jerry (the mouse) and made him even cuter than the Hanna-Barbera original. Jones fared better with Tom (the cat) whom he redesigned into sort of a feline version of Wile E. Coyote. He subsequently kept working through his own production company, Chuck Jones Enterprises, primarily on TV specials (most famously "Dr. Seuss' 'How the Grinch Stole Christmas' ", originally broadcast on CBS in 1966). Jones and his wife co-wrote the screenplay for the UPA animated feature "Gay Purr-ee" (1962), which featured the voices of Judy Garland and Robert Goulet as French cats. He produced, co-wrote and co-directed (with Abe Levitow) the cartoon portion of the film version of Norman Juster's book, "The Phantom Tollbooth" (1969).

After a semi-retirement in which he lectured, led workshops, painted and received numerous awards, tributes and accolades, Jones returned to the business of directing theatrical cartoons. In 1993, he signed a deal with Warner Brothers to produce and direct new animated shorts featuring "classic" as well as possibly new characters. At the age of 82, Jones produced and directed "Chariots of Fur" (1994), a new Road Runner and Wile E. Coyote cartoon that was released with the feature "Richie Rich." He received a star on the Hollywood Walk of Fame the following year. Jones was given an honorary Oscar at the 1996 ceremony for "the creation of classic cartoons and cartoon characters whose animated lives have brought joy to our real ones for more than half a century."—Written by Kent Greene

MILESTONES:
Grew up in Southern California

As a child, worked as an extra in silent movies shot near his home

1930: After art school, found work in a commercial art studio

1931: Hired as a cel-washer by the Ub Iwerks Studio which was then producing Flip the Frog cartoons

Worked successively as a cel painter, cel inker and in-betweener (assistant animator) before being fired by Iwerks

Worked briefly for producers Charles Mintz and subsequently Walter Lantz

Rehired by the Iwerks Studio; soon fired by Iwerks' secretary, Dorothy Webster (whom Jones would marry in 1935)

Worked as a seaman on a large schooner which caught fire

Moved to a "bohemian" section of Los Angeles and worked as a puppeteer and portrait artist ($1 per picture)

1933: Dorothy Webster obtained a job for Jones as an in-betweener at Leon Schlesinger Productions (date approximate)

1934: Promoted to animator

Assigned with animator Bob Clampett to director Tex Avery's unit at the bungalow nicknamed "Termite Terrace" on the Warner Brothers lot

1936: Shared animator credit with Clampett on "Gold Diggers of '49", the first cartoon helmed by Avery at Warner Brothers

Briefly loaned out with Clampett to Iwerks to work as (uncredited) co-directors on two cartoons in the Gabby Goat series

Became Clampett's animator when Clampett was promoted to director

On the recommendation of Harry Bender, Schlesinger's assistant, promoted to director after Frank Tashlin left the studio

1938: Directing debut, "The Night Watchman"

1939: Introduced Sniffles, a cute little mouse, in "Naughty But Mice"; Jones' first original character

1939: Directed "Prest-o Change-o", the second appearance of the prototype Bugs Bunny as a magician's rabbit who bedazzles the Two Curious Puppies

1939: Directed his first cartoon featuring Porky Pig, the patriotic "Old Glory"; marked the character's first appearance in color; notable as the studio's first completely serious cartoon

1940: Directed the third cartoon featuring the prototypical Bugs Bunny, "Elmer's Candid Camera"; most important for its revision of the character of Elmer Fudd

Collaborated with Theodor Geisel (aka Dr. Seuss) on a WWII series of instructional cartoons starring Private Snafu

1941: Became deeply involved in the animators' strike at the Walt Disney studio

1942: Based the staging of his animated short "Conrad the Sailor" on the writings of Soviet filmmaker/theoretician Sergei Eisenstein

1942: Directed "The Dover Boys", an influential Warner Brothers cartoon that influenced the style, method and timing for the acclaimed cartoons to follow from UPA (United Productions of America) in the 1940s and 50s

1944: Working nights without compensation, directed "Hell Bent for Election" in support of Franklin D Roosevelt's re-election; the first full-length UPA short; worked with a crew of other moonlighters

1945: Introduced the amorous French skunk Pepe Le Pew in "Odor-able Kitty"

1946: Began publishing articles on the art of animation (date approximate)

Conducted art classes for his crew

1946: Began his most productive era as a Warner Brothers animation director

1948: Introduced the Little Man from Mars (aka Commander X-2; aka Marvin the Martian) in "Haredevil Hare"

1949: Directed the landmark cartoon "Fast and Furry-ous" which introduced the Road Runner and (subsequently named Wile E.) Coyote, his most successful Warners creations

1949: Directed Pepe Le Pew in "For Scentimental Reasons", the second Warners cartoon to win the Oscar for best animated short subject

1950: Directed and co-scripted (with Friz Freleng) "So Much for So Little", an animated documentary short on the importance of sanitation and health services commissioned by the Public Health Service; first cartoon to win the Oscar for best documentary short subject

1953: Directed one of his most celebrated cartoons, "Duck Amuck", in which Daffy Duck is tormented by a (mostly) off-screen animator

1953: Directed the classic Cold War satire, "Duck Dodgers in the 24 1/2 Century", starring Daffy, Porky and the Little Man from Mars

1954: Directed the only "3-D" Warner Brothers cartoon, "Lumberjack Rabbit"

1954: Left Warners for a period when Jack Warner—thinking that "3-D" would sweep the industry and drive up costs—closed the animation unit

1954: Worked briefly as a gag writer at Walter Lantz Studio

1955: Worked for four months at the Walt Disney Studio after Jack Warner temporarily closed the animation unit at Warner Brothers; worked uncredited on Disney's "Sleeping Beauty"

1955: Directed his most celebrated "one-shot" cartoon, "One Froggy Evening", an unsettling allegory about a singing frog

1957: Directed "What's Opera, Doc?", an acclaimed parodic condensation of Wagner's 14-hour "Der Ring des Nibelungen" into a classic six-minute cartoon

1962: Feature screenwriting debut (with wife Dorothy Webster Jones), wrote screenplay for the UPA feature "Gay Purr-ee"

1962: Established an independent production company, Chuck Jones Enterprises

1963: Formed Tower 12 Productions (with producer Les Goldman)

Hired by MGM to produce a new series of Tom and Jerry cartoons

Tower 12 Productions absorbed by MGM and renamed MGM Animation/Visual Arts Department

1966: Named head of department

1969: Feature debut as producer-director, "The Phantom Tollbooth" (also co-wrote screenplay; directed animated sequences with Abe Levitow)

1970: Named vice president in charge of Children's Programming at ABC

1979: Co-directed (with Phil Monroe) and co-scripted (with Michael Maltese) "The Bugs Bunny/Road-Runner Movie"

1979: Served as an uncredited creative assistant on Steven Spielberg's "1941"

1984: Made a cameo appearance as Mr. Jones in Joe Dante's "Gremlins"

1987: Made a cameo appearance as a supermarket customer in Dante's "Innerspace"

1988: Served as an animation consultant on Robert Zemeckis' "Who Framed Roger Rabbit"

1990: Worked as an animation writer and director for a sequence in Dante's "Gremlins 2: The New Batch" (also made a cameo appearance)

1992: "What's Opera, Doc?" selected for inclusion in the Library of Congress' National Film Registry

1992: Served as animation director on the Robocat sequence of the comedy fantasy "Stay Tuned"

1992: Profiled in the feature-length documentary

"The Magical World of Chuck Jones" directed by George Daugherty and featuring interviews with the likes of Spielberg, Dante, George Lucas, Matt Groening and Friz Freleng

1993: Signed a deal with Warner Bros. to produce and direct animated shorts featuring "classic" (as well as possibly new) Warners characters for theatrical release

1994: Produced and directed "Chariots of Fur", his first short under his deal at Warners (released with the feature "Richie Rich")

1994–1995: Subject of a career retrospective at NYC's American Museum of the Moving Image entitled "Chuck Amuck: The Cartoons of Chuck Jones"

1995: Received a star on the Hollywood Walk of Fame

1995: Served as a creative consultant on the animated title sequence of "Four Rooms", a comedy anthology feature

2000: Created new cartoon character Thomas T. Wolk (aka Timber Wolf) for Warner Bros. Online and the Internet site Entertaindom; with partner Stephen Fossati, created 13 short films featuring the character

2000: Was subject of TV documentary "Chuck Jones: Extremes and In-Betweens, A Life in Animation" (PBS)

QUOTES:

Jones was billed as Charles M. Jones until the mid-1950s.

"These cartoons were never made for children. Nor were they made for adults. They were made for ME."—Chuck Jones, quoted in "Of Mice and Magic: A History of American Animated Cartoons" by Leonard Maltin (NY: Plume, 1987).

"All that I am and all that I hope to be, I owe to Chuck Jones!"—Theodor Geisel aka Dr. Seuss (from a signed drawing included in "Chuck Amuck")

Jones and Dr. Seuss collaborated on two animated TV specials entitled "How the Grinch Stole Christmas" (CBS, 1966) and "Horton Hears a Who" (CBS, 1970) which won the Peabody Award for Television Programming Excellence.

"The difference between what we did at Warner Bros. and what's on Saturday morning is the difference between animation and what I call illustrated radio. For Saturday morning, they make a full radio track and then use as few drawings as possible in front of it."

"The best way to tell the difference is this: if you can turn off the picture and know what's going on, that's illustrated radio. But if you can turn off the sound and know what's going on, that's animation."—Chuck Jones (Quoted in "That's All Folks!: The Art of Warner Bros. Animation" by Steve Scheider (NY: Henry Holt & Co., 1988)

"In 1962 I established my own independent production company, Chuck Jones Enterprises. Chuck Jones Enterprises produced nine half-hour prime-time television specials, all produced, written, and directed by me. They are: "The Cricket in Times Square", "A Very Merry Cricket", and "Yankee Doodle Cricket" (for ABC); three stories from Rudyard Kipling's "The Jungle Book"—"Rikki-Tikki-Tavi", "Mowgli's Brothers" (both of which received the Parents' Choice Awards in 1985) and "The White Seal" (for CBS); two specials populated by some of the classic characters from Warner Bros., "Carnival of the Animals" . . . and "A Connecticut Rabbit in King Arthur's Court" . . . Both were aired on CBS. Also for CBS: "Raggedy Ann and Andy in: The Great Santa Claus Caper", and "The Pumpkin Who Couldn't Smile" . . . "—From "Chuck Amuck" by Chuck Jones (NY: Farrar, Straus & Giroux, 1989)

Jones is a Regents Lecturer at the University of California at La Jolla and Visiting Lecturer at Cambridge University, England, and Guardian Lecturer in England.

Jones has lectured and conducted workshops at Stanford University, the University of Kansas, the University of Iowa, Johns Hopkins, the Universities of California and Nevada, San

Francisco State College, Art Center Ccollege of Design in Pasadena, Cal Arts, USC, UCLA, and many others.

The University of California at Santa Cruz offered an accredited course on the films of Chuck Jones, under the direction of Tim Hunter.

Jones has been honored with a three-day retrospective at London's British Film Institute, twice at the Kennedy Film Center and by the American Film Institute. He has also received tributes in Toronto, Zagreb and Montreal.

"I don't want to criticize. I'm SORRY that people who are as good as Bill Hanna and Joe Barbera once were are not doing the kinds of things they are capable of. I'm sorry that Friz [Freleng] isn't doing the kinds of things he's capable of. I'm sorry I'm not, for that matter, but at least I'm not doing that kind of crap."

—From "Chuck Jones Interviewed" by Joe Adamson in "The American Animated Cartoon:

A Critical Anthology", edited by Gerald Peary and Danny Peary (NY: E.P. Dutton, 1980).

"Perhaps the most accurate remark about me was uttered by Ray Bradbury at his fifty-fifth birthday party. In answer to the usual question: 'What do you want to be when you grow up?' Ray replied: 'I want to be fourteen years old like Chuck Jones.' "

"Perhaps this will be my most apt possible epitaph."

—From "Chuck Amuck" by Chuck Jones.

BIBLIOGRAPHY:

"William, the Backwards Skunk" 1987, Crown; children's book

"Chuck Amuck: The Life and Times of an Animated Cartoonist" Chuck Jones, 1989, Farrar, Straus & Giroux; autobiography; foreward by Steven Spielberg

"Chuck Reducks" Chuck Jones 1996

Spike Jonze

BORN: Adam Spiegel in Rockville, Maryland, 1969

SOMETIMES CREDITED AS:
Richard Koufay

NATIONALITY: American

EDUCATION: attended high school in Bethesda, Maryland

AWARDS: MTV Video Music Award Best Direction "Buddy Holly" 1995; video for single by band Weezer

New York Film Critics Circle Award Best First Film "Being John Malkovich" 1999

Broadcast Film Critics Association Award Breakthrough Performer "Being John Malkovich" and "Three Kings" 1999

Florida Film Critics Circle Award Newcomer

of the Year "Three Kings" (as actor) and "Being John Malkovich" (as director) 1999

Online Film Critics Society Award Best Debut "Being John Malkovich" 1999

Las Vegas Film Critics Society Award Best Newcomer "Being John Malkovich" 1999

Independent Spirit Award Best First Feature—Over $500,000 "Being John Malkovich" 2000; shared award with producers

MTV Movie Award Best New Filmmaker "Being John Malkovich" 2000

London Film Critics' Circle Award Best Director "Being John Malkovich" 2000

MTV Video Music Award Best Direction "Weapon of Choice" 2001; video for single by Fatboy Slim

Grammy Best Short Form Music Video "Weapon of Choice" 2002; shared award

Washington Film Critics Award Best

Director "Adaptation" 2003; tied with Sam Mendes and Denzel Washington

Berlin Film Festival Award Silver Bear "Adaptation" 2003 award given as an overall film runner up

BIOGRAPHY

Spike Jonze quickly established a well-deserved reputation as an exceptional director with a unique vision through his prolific music video work. Responsible for casting the Beastie Boys as 1970s detectives for "Sabotage" and inserting Weezer into an episode of TV's "Happy Days" as a 1950s teen dream band crooning their hit "Buddy Holly", Jonze displayed an ironic sense of humor and an unparalleled fluency in the relatively new genre. His video work led to the related field of commercials, including quirky spots for denim magnates Lee and Levi's, and he would later mark his feature directorial debut with the star-studded strange comedy "Being John Malkovich" (1999). Born Adam Spiegel (heir to the profitable catalog company) and raised in Bethesda, Maryland, BMX (bicycle and motorcross) enthusiast Jonze moved to Los Angeles following high school to work for the magazine *Freestylin'*, where he began to hone his skills as a photographer and became a major player in the scene, particularly known for his breakthrough action photography of skateboarders. As an admirer of teen magazine *Sassy*'s mild subversiveness, and inspired by his experience in publishing, Jonze sought to make his own lifestyle periodical, aimed at teenage boys. The magazine *Dirt* was launched as a brother publication to the then buzzworthy *Sassy*, but didn't go very far. The failure of *Dirt* didn't spell the end for the young entrepreneur, who was busy with his company Girl Skateboards, and working hard as a photographer and video artist, capturing the action of the burgeoning skater scene.

In 1992, Jonze entered the work of music video with a job as co-director of Sonic Youth's "100%." Here the video artist shot raw skateboard footage that was intercut into the video, co-directed by Tamra Davis. He would go on to work with Sonic Youth's Kim Gordon as co-directors of "Cannonball", a "The Red Balloon"-inspired clip for The Breeders' hit, featuring a rolling cannonball that seems to be following the camera. Through Davis (wife of Beastie Boys' Mike D), Jonze met up with the band with whom his work would prove his greatest breakthrough. His inspired clip for "Sabotage" (1994) cast the trio in a campy 1970s cop actioner, the Beasties donning polyester suits, aviator shades and hideous facial hair while they battle the baddies in this faux opening sequence, complete with incorrect credits and an explosive pop-up title. The song was a big hit, due in no small part to its status as an MTV favorite in heavy rotation.

Jonze followed up that same year with Weezer's "Undone (The Sweater Song)", a visually arresting one-take experimental video, filmed with a specialized camera used by Alfred Hitchcock in "Rope." He reteamed with the Beastie Boys for "Sure Shot" before taking up with Weezer again, directing the acclaimed video for their single "Buddy Holly." Jonze dressed the band as clean-cut 50s teen idols, and placed them onstage at Arnold's, the "Happy Days" hangout, with actual footage from the series mixed in with shots of Weezer. This off-the-wall marriage of current music with nostalgia TV (that was itself nostalgic) made the well-executed video one of the most talked about entries in the medium, and the song became an instant hit. "Buddy Holly" walked away with four MTV Video Music Awards in 1995, including Jonze's Best Direction win. He continued to raise the music video bar with conceptually interesting and visually appealing work like Bjork's Hollywood musical-inspired "It's Oh So Quiet" and R.E.M.'s karaoke-like "Crush With Eyeliner", starring Japanese youth posing as the band. He threw out the idea that music video must be a quick changing collage to grab the viewer's short attention span, instead replacing it with a one-image video as in Wax's "California" which included slow-motion footage of a running man on fire.

In 1997, Jonze proved capable of less stylized and more narrative fare, with the bizarre video for Daft Punk's "Da Funk", following an anthropomorphic dog through the city streets, looking for friends and toting a ghetto blaster that plays the song, which acts as background music. That same year he made the senior prom-set "It's All About the Benjamins (Rock Remix)" wherein Puff Daddy's energetic performance incites the previously sleepwalking students to liven up the dance and wreak havoc on the school. Jonze would again break new ground directing and also appearing in the video for Fatboy Slim's dance track "Praise You." He played the choreographer for the fictional Torrence Community Dance Group, a troupe who puts on a show in front of a movie theater one evening. The clip, shot like an amateur tourist home video, features a real audience that gathered, and ends with the unscripted gem of the theater manager angrily turning off the music. In addition to his vast body of impressive music video work, Jonze can count among his credits memorable commercials for Lee Jeans ("Twister", starring Buddy Lee, Man of Action, heroically braving a tornado to save a kitten) and an operating room-set spot for Levi's Wide Leg Jeans, scored with the 80s electropop hit "Tainted Love."

Jonze made his big screen acting debut with a bit part in Allison Anders' "Mi Vida Loca—My Crazy Life" in 1993. He could next be seen with a cameo role as an EMT in the feature "The Game" (1997), but it was in 1999 that he would have his first featured role, playing goofy Desert Storm US soldier Conrad Vig in David O Russell's acclaimed, action-packed dark comedy "Three Kings." While the affable blonde proved a more than capable actor, and had an enjoyably silly screen presence with a squeaky, nasal voice to match, he would make

more of a mark as a director. Before landing on the big screen, Jonze directed segments of the short-lived series "Hi-Octane" (Comedy Central, 1994) starring, produced and written by his future wife Sofia Coppola. Additionally, he created the frenetic title sequence to the short-lived CBS sitcom "Double Rush" (1995) and worked extensively in shorts, from his early 90s skateboard video art to 1995's "Las Nueve Vidas de Paco—'The Chocolate Movie.'" Along with Roman Coppola, he was co-cinematographer of the 1996 short "Bed, Bath and Beyond", directed by Sofia Coppola, Ione Skye and Andrew Durham. In 1998, Jonze's documentary short "Amarillo Morning" screened at Sundance Film Festival. That same year, his work as cinematographer for the concert film of the 1996 Tibetan Freedom Festival entitled "Free Tibet" played on screens. Following an aborted attempt at directing the film adaptation of the beloved children's book "Harold and the Purple Crayon", Jonze landed a development and production deal with Propaganda Films in 1997. He finally made his feature debut with "Being John Malkovich", an appropriately quirky fantasy about a man (John Cusack) who comes upon a room in his office building that leads inside the mind of the titular actor. Being John Malkovich and adopting his perspective becomes an alluring prospect and soon everyone wants in on it. Despite the loopy and abstract concept, the film landed such talent as Cusack, Cameron Diaz, Catherine Keener and Malkovich himself, and quickly created a remarkable advance buzz, supported by rave reviews after its premiere at the Venice Film Festival. Jonze was rewarded for his efforts with an Oscar nomination as Best Director.

Trading on his long-standing relationship with MTV, Jonze made a side-foray into series television in 2000 as a co-creator, writer, performer and executive producer of the controversial cult hit "Jackass" which featured an edgy troupe of fearless street stunt artists led by Johnny Knoxville who engage in all manner of risky real-life adventures—the stupider, grosser and more painful, the better. While "Jackass" took flack for purportedly inspiring teenagers to mimic its stunts with disastrous and occasionally deadly results, it was one of MTV's most popular shows, made a Hollywood star out of Knoxville and spawned a theatrical spin-off, "Jackass: The Movie," in 2002.

On the big screen, Jonze continued to cultivate a close relationship with screenwriter Kaufman, producing his script "Human Nature" in 2001. In 2002 the pair reteamed for the remarkable reality-bending film "Adaptation," which featured Kaufman himself (portrayed by Nicolas Cage) as the central character, a timid, anxiety-ridden screenwriter struggling a to adapt author Susan Orlean's best-selling novel "The Orchid Thief" into a motion picture script. Inspired, loopily funny, artistic and unabashedly eccentric, "Adaptation" was a work of extreme originality, flip-flopping between fact, fiction and fantasy while depicting both Kaufman's angst-ridden life and major plot elements from the book by Orleans (played by Meryl Streep), which chronicled her encounters with real-life Miami orchid thief John Laroche (Chris Cooper).—Written by Jane O'Donnell

COMPANION:

wife: Sofia Coppola. Director, screenwriter, actor, clothing designer; born c. 1971; together as of 1997; announced engagement in 1998; married on June 26, 1999

MILESTONES:

Raised in Bethesda, Maryland

While in high school, met Andy Jenkins and Mark Lewman, publishers of *Freestylin'*, a popular BMX [bicycle motorcross] magazine

After his last high school exam, moved to Los Angeles and joined the *Freestylin'* team as an editorial assistant and began to hone his skills as a photographer

Began shooting photos for the publications *BMX Action* and the short-lived *Homeboy*

1991: With Jenkins and Lewman, launched *Dirt*, a failed, somewhat subversive magazine geared towards teenaged boys, inspired by the thoughtful and unique teenage girl magazine *Sassy*

With skaters Rick Howard and Mike Carroll, founded the company Girl Skateboards

1992: Made music video debut, co-directing Sonic Youth's "100%" with Tamra Davis

1993: Had a bit part in Allison Anders' "Mi Vida Loca—My Crazy Life"

1993: With Sonic Youth's Kim Gordon, directed "The Red Balloon"-inspired video for The Breeders' "Cannonball", featuring a rolling cannonball that follows the camera

Through Tamra Davis (wife of Beastie Boy Mike D) set up a creative collaboration with the Beastie Boys

1994: Outfitted the Beastie Boys with bad suits and obviously fake facial hair for his popular 1970s cop show inspired directorial breakthough "Sabatoge"

1994: Did an experimental one-shot video for Weezer's "Undone (The Sweater Song)", employing a specialized camera last used by Hitchcock in "Rope"

1994: Reteamed with the Beastie Boys for "Sure Shot"

1994: Placed an appropriately dressed Weezer in the middle of an actual scene from the 1950s-set sitcom "Happy Days" (interspersing scenes of the band with footage from the program) in the inspired, award-winning video "Buddy Holly"

1994: With Roman Coppola and Dewey Hicks, directed segments of the short-lived punk rock/fast cars lifestyle series "Hi-Octane", aired on Comedy Central; screened at New York's Low Resolution Film Festival in 1996

1995: Created the frenetic main title sequence for the short-lived CBS sitcom "Double Rush"

1995: Produced, directed and wrote the screenplay for the comedy short "Las Nueve Vidas de Paco—'The Chocolate Movie' "

1995: Continued to make conceptually and

visually interesting videos for artists including Bjork (a 1940s musical-inspired romp for "It's Oh So Quiet"), R.E.M. (young Japanese fans posing as the band, pantomiming "Crush With Eyeliner") and Wax (slow motion footage of a man on fire running for their post-punk "California")

1996: With Roman Coppola, did the cinematography for "Bed, Bath and Beyond", a comedy short co-directed by Ione Skye, Sofia Coppola, and Andrew Durham

1997: Directed Daft Punk's "Da Funk", a music video starring an anthropomorphized dog walking the streets looking for friends with a ghetto blaster in tow

1997: Signed a first-look develpoment and production deal with Propaganda Films for features and TV, with its subsidiary Satellite Films handling commercial and video representation

1997: Had a cameo role in David Fincher's "The Game"

1997: Directed the energetic high school prom-set video for Puff Daddy's "It's All About the Benjamins (Rock Remix)", featuring Jason Schwartzman (cousin of future bride Sofia Coppola) in a cameo role

1998: Directed many memorable commercials, including Lee Jeans' "Twister" spot starring Buddy Lee, man of action saving a kitten in a tornado, and Levi's "ER" inspired promo for their wide leg jeans, featuring an OR rendition of 1980s hit "Tainted Love"

1998: His documentary short "Amarillo by Morning" screened at the Sundance Film Festival

1998: With Roman Coppola, co-directed and starred in the exceptional and compelling video for Fatboy Slim's dance track "Praise You", featuring a group of average-looking people (the fictional Torrance Community Dance Group) dancing in front of a movie theater, shot to look like an amateur documentary

1998: Reteamed with the Beastie Boys for the live version of "Root Down"

1998: Was cinematographer of "Free Tibet", a concert film chronicling the 1996 Tibetan Freedom Concert

1999: Co-starred with George Clooney, Ice Cube and Mark Wahlberg in David O Russell's adventure film "Three Kings"

1999: Feature directorial debut with the odd comedy "Being John Malkovich", starring John Cusack and Cameron Diaz; nominated for a Best Director Academy Award

2000: Directed 13-minute documentary about US presidential candidate Al Gore that was broadcast during the Democratic National Convention

2000: Created and executive produced the MTV series "Jackass"

2001: Helmed the popular music video "Weapon of Choice", performed by Fatboy Slim and featuring actor-dancer Christopher Walken

2001: Produced the film "Human Nature," from a Charlie Kaufman screenplay

2002: Served as a writer, actor and producer on "Jackass: The Movie"

2002: Reteamed with screenwriter Kaufman for "Adaptation"; Received a Golden Globe nomination for Best Director

QUOTES:

Spike Jonze had been set to direct the film adaptation of "Harold & the Purple Crayon", scripted by David O Russell. When the studio pulled the plug on the project, Russell wrote the role of Private Conrad Vig in "Three Kings" especially for Jonze.

Jonze, displaying his notoriously skewed sense of humor, explains why he was offered the job of directing "Ace Ventura: When Nature Calls" (which he turned down): "My stepdad sells juicers to a lot of people in Hollywood and he knew Jim Carrey through his juicing connection. In Hollywood all the big deals are made through juicing."—Quoted in *Entertainment Weekly*, March 17, 1995.

Director Tamra Davis on the possibility of Jonze going Hollywood: "With him there's the

Adam Spiegel side—the businessman, and then there's the Spike side. When Adam Spiegel says make a movie, Spike will probably do it."—Quoted in *Details*, March 1995.

Jonze refuting *Details'* R.J. Smith's allegations that the director's alter ego is Adam Spiegel, heir to the famed catalog company: " 'No! There is no Spiegel thing!' he insists. 'It's all a lie, a product of excellent PR.

'This is my father,' he says, grabbing a CD off a table. 'He's a musician named Wesley Willis.' Spike throws on the CD; a middle-aged black man raves over a cheesy beat. A big smile

crosses Spike's face, and he says apologetically, 'He's very eccentric.' "

"I just told the crew that this was my fourth movie and they were more comfortable."—Jonze on why things went smoothly on his feature directorial debut "Being John Malkovich", quoted in *Rolling Stone*, August 19, 1999.

BIBLIOGRAPHY:

"Skateboarding—The Ultimate Guide to Tricks, Ramps, Gear, Setting Up—And Letting Go!" Kevin Wilkins and Spike Jonze Jonze shot the book's photography

Neil Jordan

BORN: Neil Patrick Jordan in County Sligo, Ireland, 02/25/1950

NATIONALITY: Irish

EDUCATION: University College, National University of Ireland, Dublin, Ireland, literature and history, 1972

AWARDS: Evening Standard Film Award Best Screenplay "The Miracle" 1991

Los Angeles Film Critics Association Award Best Foreign Film "The Crying Game" 1992

New York Film Critics Circle Award Best Screenplay "The Crying Game" 1992

Boston Society of Film Critics Award Best Screenplay "The Crying Game" 1992

Writers Guild of America Award Best Original Screenplay "The Crying Game" 1992

Oscar Best Original Screenplay "The Crying Game" 1992

BAFTA Alexander Korda Award for Outstanding British Film "The Crying Game" 1992

Australian Film Institute Award Best Foreign Film "The Crying Game" 1993

Venice Film Festival Golden Lion Award "Michael Collins" 1996

Berlin Film Festival Silver Bear for Best Director "The Butcher Boy" 1998

BAFTA Award Best Adapted Screenplay "The End of the Affair" 2000

Evening Standard British Film Award Best Screenplay 2000

BIOGRAPHY

Although not a painter like his grandfather, mother and two sisters, Irish filmmaker Neil Jordan inherited the same artistic sensibilities but opted for a camera instead of a brush to create the visually rich canvases of his always complex pictures. He first became established, however, as an acclaimed author of moody, turbulent short stories and novels dealing with passion, sexuality and the changes of the last generation in his native Ireland. On films he has creatively controlled, Jordan has crafted stories that involve unconventional love and the moral issues of violence and death. Elements of whimsy, fantasy, surprise and horror often crop up in his movies, including the political thrillers which stand as some of his finest efforts. At its best, his is a provocative cinema, which, though not as experimental as some would have it, nonetheless combines a stylistic freshness with pensive philosophical, social and sexual dimensions.

After enjoying success with his "Night in Tunisia and Other Stories" and the novel "The Past", Jordan entered films as a script consultant on John Boorman's striking "Excalibur" and soon after saw his screenplay "Traveller" (both 1981) directed in 16mm by Joe Comerford. The first of his political thrillers, it followed a couple forced into an arranged marriage as they embark on a smuggling trip across the border into Southern Ireland. His feature directorial debut. "Angel/Danny Boy" (1982), an intriguing study of a musician possessed with avenging the murder of a mute woman, mined a similar vein and starred Stephen Rea as the first incarnation of a gunman who would appear in subsequent pictures. After giving a haunting, Freudian revamping to the story of Little Red Riding Hood in "The Company of Wolves" (1985), Jordan broke through with "Mona Lisa" (1986), an absorbing tale of obsessive love that transformed the career of little-known character actor Bob Hoskins and garnered the director his first real international recognition.

"Mona Lisa" brought Jordan offers to work in Hollywood, where he quickly encountered studio interference on "High Spirits" (1988), a supernatural comedy distributed in a mutilated version that had little to do with the director's vision. His experience on the remake of "We're No Angels" (1989), which packaged Robert De Niro and Sean Penn in a script by David Mamet, also proved disappointing, so he returned to Ireland to tentatively tackle the subject of mother-son incest in "The Miracle" (1991), based on his award-winning story "Night in Tunisia." In 1992, Jordan's clever mixture of politics and sexual intrigue in "The Crying Game" catapulted an indie designed for art house distribution into a stunning cultural and commercial success. Picking up six Oscar nominations (including a win for Jordan's screenplay) and many critics' awards, it

boasted one of the best-kept plot secrets (regarding sexual identity) in recent film history and also marked the reappearance of the gunman embodied by Rea.

Jordan returned in triumph to Hollywood and with his newly-acquired clout landed the plum, if daunting, assignment of adapting Anne Rice's tricky bestseller "Interview with the Vampire" to the screen. Once he got the cast he wanted (including Brad Pitt, Antonio Banderas and the controversial choice of Tom Cruise to play the vampire Lestat), its collective box-office insurance coupled with the hands-off policy of producer David Geffen and the executive team at Warner Bros. enabled the director to handle his big-budget assignment like an independent. The result garnered mixed if generally favorable reviews and performed quite well at the box office. More impressively, "Interview with the Vampire" also proved thematically consistent with many aspects of Jordan's earlier work, its dank, downbeat tone meshing stylishly and well with its heady sexuality and metaphysical musings.

The financing by Warner Bros. transformed Jordan's most cherished project, gestating for more than a decade, into a reality. The epic story of "Michael Collins" (1996) had frustrated filmmakers for nearly four decades, with individuals from John Ford and John Huston to Robert Redford and Kevin Costner attempting to bring a biopic based on the life of the Irish Republican Army commander-in-chief (and still controversial Irish hero) to the screen. Full of action and period detail, "Collins" drew comparisons to "The Godfather", though there was the inevitable controversy when both English and Irish audiences found fault with its interpretation and condensation of historical facts. Celebrated cinematographer-turned-director Chris Menges volunteered to lens it and provided the rich earth tones and mobile camera work the director's vision demanded. Jordan had wanted Liam Neeson for the title role ever since completing the screenplay in 1983, despite the actor's then low-profile, and Neeson justified this faith, garnering his strongest notices since 1993's "Schindler's List." Jonathan Rhys Meyers' portrayal of Collins' enigmatic assassin continued Jordan's fascination with the gunman.

"The Butcher Boy" (1997) would seem the quintessential indie film, but it too bore the Warner Bros. logo. Adapted from the novel by Patrick McCabe, this harrowing tale of a young boy driven mad by his abusive upbringing was one of the last pre-DreamWorks movies green-lit by Geffen. Featuring an outstanding performance by Eamonn Owens (in his debut) as the disintegrating titular character, this arresting, sometimes hallucinatory (with the controversial Sinead O'Connor appearing as a scatological Virgin Mary) film opened to reviews ranging from gushing to puzzled and did almost no box office. Anticipating the zeitgeist, Jordan correctly assessed that the horror genre was ready for a terrifying film that took itself seriously (i.e., "The Blair Witch Project") and was far more psychologically based (e.g., "The Sixth Sense"). Unfortunately, "In Dreams" (1999), his first collaboration with Geffen at DreamWorks, proved a muddled and overblown affair in its story of a woman (Annette Bening) linked through psychic thoughts to a serial killer (Robert Downey Jr.). That same year saw him tackle the remake of the Graham Greene novel "The End of the Affair" for Columbia Pictures. A love triangle set in wartime England, it starred Ralph Fiennes, Julianne Moore and perennial colleague Rea and offered Jordan the opportunity to intriguingly examine a relationship from two points of view.

COMPANION:

Beverly D'Angelo. actor no longer together; acted in Jordan's "The Miracle" (1991)

MILESTONES:

Grew up in Dublin

Began writing short stories as a teenager

Deterred by high fees from entering National Film School; took a job as a laborer in London

Returned to Dublin and wrote first novel, "The Past"; helped launch theater company for which he also wrote

1974: Co-founded the Irish Writers Co-operative, which helped to publish local authors

1976: Received a grant from the British Arts Council

Wrote three plays for Irish TV, one of which, "Night in Tunisia", based on his collection of stories under the same name, was filmed by Pat O'Connor in 1983 and aired as part of PBS' "Channel Crossings" in 1993

Wrote an Irish TV series based on the life of Sean O'Casey

Played saxophone in an Irish rock band

1981: Hired as creative consultant on John Boorman's "Excalibur"; also shot a documentary on the making of the film

1981: First screenplay credit, "Traveller", shot by director Joe Comerford in 16mm

1982: Feature directorial debut, "Angel/Danny Boy" (first all-Irish feature in many years); initial collaboration with actor Stephen Rea; Chris Menges (only non-Irishman involved) served as director of photography

1985: Teamed for the first time with producer Stephen Woolley on "The Company of Wolves"; Wooley has produced all his subsequent films to date

1986: Enjoyed breakthrough success with "Mona Lisa", starring Bob Hoskins; earned BAFTA nominations for Best Screenplay (co-written with David Leland) and as Best Director

1987: First producing effort, as co-executive producer of the Irish-made "The Courier", directed by Joe Lee and Frank Deasy

1988: Directed first American film, "High Spirits"; also wrote screenplay

1989: Left Hollywood after making second US film, the remake of "We're No Angels"; screenplay by David Mamet, marking first feature for which Jordan did not write script

1990: Helmed the "Miss Otis Regrets/Just One of Those Things" segments of "Red, Hot and Blue" (ABC), a televised variety salute to the music of Cole Porter that also promoted AIDS awareness

1991: Returned to filmmaking in Great Britain with "The Miracle", based on his story "Night in Tunisia"

1992: Had international success with "The Crying Game", starring Stephen Rea and Miranda Richardson; received Oscar for Best Original Screenplay as well a nomination as Best Director

1994: Returned to America to make "Interview with a Vampire", adapted by Anne Rice from her novel; received no writing credit as Writers Guild deemed it Rice's screenplay, though he has claimed "I did quite a bit of work on it"; Rea played a vampire

1996: Helmed the biopic of Irish patriot "Michael Collins", starring Liam Neeson and Aidan Quinn; wrote screenplay in 1983 but was unable to find financing at that time; Rea had supporting role; Menges, who had become established as a director, volunteered to serve as director of photography, his first such assignment in nine years

1997: Co-adapted (with novelist Patrick McCabe from McCabe's novel), executive produced and directed "The Butcher Boy"; Rea played dual role of Mr. Brady and the adult incarnation of the title character

1999: Directed and co-scripted (from Bari Wood's novel "Doll's Eyes") the supernatural thriller "In Dreams", starring Annette Bening and Robert Downey Jr.; Aidan Quinn and Stephen Rea co-starred

1999: Produced (with Woolley), adapted and helmed the remake of Graham Green'e novel "The End of the Affair"; eighth collaboration with Rea, who played the cuckhold husband of Julianne Moore

2001: Directed his own one-act stage play "White Horses" at Dublin's Gate Theater Helmed "Double Down" (lensed 2001)

QUOTES:

"Neil is enigmatic. He's not cut out of a mold that we're used to dealing with in the American film business. He's got a lot of layers to him, and the publicity industry here doesn't know how to deal with that."—producer Art Linson, quoted in *American Film*, January 1990.

Speaking of the restless, antic days of Ireland in the 1960s during which he grew up, Jordan noted in *American Film* (January 1990): "It was a time a lot of us rebelled from, a generation of rebels. We grew up so much with talk of 'The Troubles' and we finally came to realize that 'The Troubles' was unfinished business, and that it would stay unfinished until people began changing their attitudes. The ideal of much of my parents' generation was that Ireland was a kind of pristine Gaelic culture that would be untouched by the outside world—and the Catholic Church did much to enforce this attitude."

"I'm a literary person, and my technique as a film director is an extension of my technique as a writer. I'm aware that the term 'literary' has a pejorative ring to a lot of critics here—they associate it with something like Merchant-Ivory and 'Masterpiece Theater'. But I'm talking about 20th-century literary technique. I can't stand the usual kind of English fiction—you know, 'She was bored with the day's trivialities,' that sort of thing—I decided a long time ago to take the most outrageous chances with narration. I refuse to use devices that would let anyone think they were getting the story too easily—I want to get beneath that level of understanding, stir things up a bit. What's wrong with someone walking around days after they've seen or read something and then realizing, Oh, so THAT'S what that's about? Why does instant gratification in the arts have to be important?"—Jordan quoted in *American Film*, January 1990.

"The validity of the Scorsese comparison is flatly denied by Jordan, partly out of pride, partly out of respect. But the connection is there.

Similar motifs surface in each of their movies. Fetishized women, cheap music, spoiled Catholic imagery. Solitary males reisting the tug of old bonds—the urban neighbourhood in Scorsese, the peasant soil in Jordan.

"The Catholic angle is the most direct link; upfront in Scorsese, religious symbolism creeps into Jordan's films like an insinuating presence. The blades of an unseen police helicopter at the end of 'Angel' scouring the littered earth like a pentecostal wind; distant flames peeping through the legs of a King's Cross whore in 'Mona Lisa'."—Steve Beard in *Arena* magazine, Spring 1991.

"I make no apology [about 'Michael Collins']. 'Yesterday's terrorist is today's statesman.' . . . To me the film shows the attempt of one character who was engaged in warfare and who tried to replace warfare with politics, and that is the continuing story of the relationship between Ireland and Britain, definitely. I don't have to justify that."—Jordan quoted in *Variety*, October 1996.

"Making a film is a strange experience because before the cameras start rolling I've got the entire movie mapped out in my head. The actual shoot is a vast logistical exercise that involves interminable periods of waiting to see what, in a sense, I've already seen. Intellectually it can be draining, but you must stay rigorously focused on your original vision of the film. Making a film involves 2000 voices saying, 'It should be this, it should be that,' and if you listen to them you're screwed."—Jordan to Kristine McKenna in the *Los Angeles Times*, March 29, 1998.

"I don't want to get on this career path of making bigger and bigger movies, which seems to be the logic of the whole industry. I had a bad [big-studio] experience a while ago with [the 1988 Steve Guttenberg–Daryl Hannah ghost comedy] 'High Spirits'. I shouldn't have gotten involved with it. It became a mess. The [studios] seem to do a lot of these huge event movies with young directors. I think they do that because these movies are not so much

directed as made by committee. You've got to make films out of an individual sensibility or there's nothing there."—Jordan quoted in *Entertainment Weekly*, April 24, 1998.

"The fairy-story elelment that Neil brings to his work, even in such realistic films as 'Mona Lisa' is extraordinary. It allows you to read lots of different symbolism and layers into his films that, I think, aren't really in the work of his contemporaries.

"If you look at his second feature, 'Company of Wolves', it obviously wasn't as technically mature as his recent films. But if you look at the ideas and themes ranging through that movie, they're very much the kind of things that Neil is dealing with in 'Butcher Boy' and 'In Dreams' and even 'Interview With the Vampire': stories within stories, the meeting of legend and myth with fact. I personally feel that Neil is one of the few auteurs from Europe who has been able to make films in Hollywood—and certainly not have them turn into Hollywood films."—Producer Stephen Wooley to Bob Strauss of the *Boston Globe*, January 17, 1999.

Remembering his directorial debut on "Angel/Danny Boy": "It was pure, absolute terror. I had no idea that you had to communicate your private thoughts to the 200 people on the set. I was walking up and down a beach with Chris [Menges, the cinematographer], looking for the precise location to do a shot. We'd walk 200 yards to the left, look around and say, 'No, this isn't good.' Then we'd walk back to where we were before, and I'd say, 'No, this isn't good.' I looked up suddenly and saw this enormous procession of vehicles on the promenade above, and everywhere I was walking, they'd follow . . .

"I just shot what I wanted to see, really. And sometimes it was disconcerting for the actors. We would be shooting a dialogue scene with two people, and I'd say, 'I think I want to see a close-up here,' so I'd shoot the close-up of one actor, and not shoot the other one . . . I think literally every foot that I shot ended up on screen."—Jordan quoted in *Premiere*, March 1999.

BIBLIOGRAPHY:

"Night in Tunisia and Other Stories" Neil Jordan, 1976, Co-Op Books; short stories; reprinted by George Braziller in 1980; "Night in Tunisia" won the *Guardian* fiction prize in 1979

"The Past" Neil Jordan, 1979, Jonathan Cape; first novel; reissued by George Braziller

"The Dream of a Beast" Neil Jordan, 1983, Chatto & Windus; second novel; reissued by Random House in 1988

"A Neil Jordan Reader" Neil Jordan, 1993, Vintage Books; stories

"Nightlines" Neil Jordan, 1995, Random House; novel; published in England as "Sunrise with Sea Monster"

"Michael Collins: Screenplay and Film Diary" Neil Jordan, 1996, Vintage Books

Hen Kaige

BORN: in Beijing, China, 08/12/1952

NATIONALITY: Chinese

EDUCATION: Beijing Film Academy Beijing, China 1982; studied in the directing department New York University New York, New York 1987–90

AWARDS: Berlin Film Festival Golden Bear "King of the Children" 1988

Los Angeles Film Critics Association Award Best Foreign Film "Farewell My Concubine" 1993

Cannes Film Festival Palme d'Or "Farewell My Concubine" 1993; shared award with Jane Campion who won with "The Piano"; first Palme d'Or awarded to a Chinese filmmaker or a woman

BIOGRAPHY

The son of a filmmaker from the earlier generation of Chinese socialist realism, Chen Kaige represents the Fifth Generation, filmmakers who attended Beijing Film Institute after the Cultural Revolution. After graduating in 1982, Chen and his classmates began a new wave in Chinese cinema by emphasizing the visual and aural qualities of film rather than traditional dramatic and literary elements. Their films have also been characterized by a strong political commitment which has led to objections from censors and has limited their domestic audience to students and intellectuals. Outside China, however, Chen Kaige and the other Fifth Generation filmmakers have drawn attention from an increasingly wide circle of film sophisticates who have hailed their efforts as the next most important New Wave. Chen has been awarded top festival prizes in Tokyo, Cannes and Berlin.

Chen's first feature, "Huang Tudi/Yellow Earth", was completed in 1983 at a small production unit in southern China. The deceptively simple plot concerns a soldier who comes to a remote village in the spring of 1939 to collect folk songs. Describing revolutionary change and extolling the virtues of communism, the soldier convinces the young bride of an arranged marriage to run away. The girl, however, disappears while crossing a river. Photographed by the famous cinematographer, Zhang Yimou, who later turned director himself with "Red Sorghum" (1987), the film is notable for its exquisite visual imagery and expressive compositions as well as its challenging reexamination of Chinese culture, in this case the repressive ideology of feudalism.

Chen's second film, "Da Yuebing/The Big Parade" (1985), reflects the Fifth Generation filmmakers' sense of history and their political attitude toward the Cultural Revolution. The film relates the experience of an army unit which is compelled to perform arduous exercises in preparation for a brief appearance in a meaningless parade. Chen has called the Cultural Revolution "China's biggest parade."

"King of Children" (1988), his next film, draws heavily on his own life during the years between 1966 and 1976. The hero of the film is sent to work with the peasants (as were Chen and his classmates). Though unprepared for his assignment, the young man is nevertheless directed to teach Maoist ideology to the poor. The film concludes by showing the futility of rote learning whatever the context, be it during the Cultural Revolution or in the contemporary Chinese educational system.

Chen's fourth film, "Life on a String", an official selection in competition at the 1991 Cannes Film Festival, concerns a blind storyteller and his young apprentice who travel from village to village accompanying themselves on the sanxian, a traditional three-stringed instrument.

Chen and the other Fifth Generation filmmakers have brought a new vitality to Chinese cinema that is recognized by film critics around the world. What effect this mounting international attention will have on the official government's assessment of China's new cinema artists remains to be seen. However, if the government's reaction to Chen's fifth feature is any indication, this new generation of film artists will have a long struggle to gain freedom of expression in their native land.

"Farewell My Concubine" (1993) presents an epic portrait of Chinese life that spans from the 1920s to the 70s tracing the homoerotic relationship between two Beijing opera actors. The film's colorful canvas unflinchingly depicts China in the throes of war and peace, military occupation, and the Cultural Revolution. Fearful of political embarrassment, the authorities banned the film in China for a time before finally releasing it in a censored version. "Farewell My Concubine" created a sensation in Western film circles; it shared the Palme d'Or with Jane Campion's "The Piano" at Cannes and screened at the New York Film Festival before opening to enthusiastic reviews. It's critical success has finally prompted recognition of what Chen and other Fifth Generation filmmakers said they set out to do in the early 80s: make Chinese film a recognized, world-class cinema.

FAMILY:
father: Chen Huaikai. Director; directed feature film "Song of Youth"; denounced by Chen, then a Red Guard; placed under house arrest during the Cultural Revolution

MILESTONES:
At age 14 was rounded up and sent to clear forests on a rubber plantation in a remote mountain village in southern Yunnan Province

Worked as a farmer and factory worker in Yunnan for three years during the Cultural Revolution

Denounced his noted filmmaker father

Joined the army to escape the plantation; served for five years

Acted as an aide to the Viet Cong

Returned to Beijing to take the film academy exam

1976: After the Cultural Revolution, enrolled in the Peking Film Academy

Emigrated to USA to teach for a year at NYU's film school and to study in New York (dates approximate)

1993: Film "Farewell My Concubine" banned in his native China

1996: Helmed "Temptress Moon"

1999: Directed the sweeping historical epic "The Emperor and the Assassin"

2002: English-language dirctorial debut "Killing Me Softly", starring Heather Graham

QUOTES:

Chen is the first Chinese director of his generation to have lived abroad for an extended period, to have learned English and begun to assimilate into the international artistic community."—Orville Schell (*The New York Times*, January 27, 1991).

"My experiences abroad make me want to experiment more. I always wanted to teach people through film, to give them a big message. But now what I feel I want to do is more to dream through film, hoping that maybe the film itself will be able to tell more than I can."—Chen Kaige (*The New York Times*, January 27, 1991).

"I don't see the difference between life and art," says Chinese director Chen Kaige. "I believe everyone is playing one role or another."

Chen, 41, knows about role playing. When he was 14, and away at a boy's school for high-ranking Chinese officials, became a member of the Red Guard which was promoting radical change within China in the 1960s. During this turbulent time, Chen publicly denounced his father, a director and former member of the Nationalist Party. He was chosen to be identified as a secret agent. Chen says, "Of course, I knew he wasn't a spy but I still did it." In this period, says Chen, "people were encouraged to hate each other."—Lisa Katzman, "Farewell's Bullhorn in a China shop" (*Daily News*, October 19, 1993).

Member of the Red Guard during the Cultural Revolution.

Tom Kalin

BORN: in Illinois, 1961

NATIONALITY: American

AWARD: IFP Gotham Open Palm Award "Swoon" 1992

BIOGRAPHY

Director, writer, producer, educator, activist, Kalin is a leading light of the "new wave" in gay filmmaking. He started out by writing and directing a variety of short films and videos for the museum circuit, including "Puppets", "Gesicht", "finally destroy us", "News From Home" and "They Are Lost to Vision Altogether". The latter two have been exhibited at numerous international festival venues. Kalin also worked for three years as a producer of AIDS educational materials.

Kalin made his feature debut with "Swoon" (1991), a stylized meditation on the notorious 1924 Leopold and Loeb murder case. The facts of the case—two young, wealthy, gay Jewish men pled guilty to the senseless murder of a 14-year old heir, with defense attorney Clarence Darrow trying to avoid the death penalty by invoking the mitigating circumstance of "sexual perversity"—had provided fuel for two previous screen outings, Alfred Hitchcock's "Rope" (1948) and Richard Fleischer's "Compulsion" (1959). Kalin's more ambivalent version of the story foregrounds the relationship between the pair and incorporates elements of fantasy, as well as pointed anachronisms which highlight the continuing relevance of the case. Photographed in elegant black-and-white, the film suggests visual influences ranging from Calvin Klein ads to Bette Davis film noirs.

MILESTONES:

Worked three years as a producer for *Aidsfilms*, a nonprofit education company that produces prevention information for communities of color

Made the short film "They Are Lost to Vision Altogether", a 13-minute museum circuit video piece about media treatment of AIDS issues

1992: Feature directing debut with "Swoon"

1992: Selected by the American Center as one of seven American artists to produce "Nation", a one-minute spot for broadcast on French and American TV

AFFILIATION: Member, Board of Directors, Independent Features Project

QUOTES:

Kalin has written freelance for "Aperture", "The Village Voice", "Views", "Artforum", and "The Independent."

"I ain't no spokesperson. I am an activist on various levels. I make art at the service of 'the cause.' "Swoon" came out of suppressing certain ways of working during six years of AIDS activism. I think you can be contradictory, lyrical, and didactic—you can make a movie that puts the burden of responsibility on the audience, which "Swoon" does. Art allows you not to draw a conclusion . . . "

(From *QW*, 9/27/92)

"I long for the day," muses Kalin, "when gay subject matter doesn't need to be bracketed by saying it's a gay film. If a gay film means there is an upfront representation of a gay person, then I could claim for gay history the show "Bewitched." I could retroactively claim lots of films as gay, but that would be a little disingenuous."

(From *Premiere*, October 1992)

Kalin is a founding member of Gran Fury, an AIDS activist collective.

Wong Kar-Wai

BORN: in Shanghai, China, 1958

SOMETIMES CREDITED AS:

Wang Jaiwei

Wang Jiawei

Wang Gu Wei

Wong Ga Wai

NATIONALITY: Chinese

EDUCATION: Hong Kong Polytechnic, Hong Kong, graphic design; developed a passion for photography; quit school during second year (1980)

Enrolled in a training program for TV drama production run by Hong Kong Television Broadcasts Ltd (HKTVB) in 1980

AWARDS: Hong Kong Film Award Best Director "Days of Being Wild" 1990

Hong Kong Film Award Best Director "Chungking Express" 1994

Cannes Film Festival Prix de la Mise-en-scene "Happy Together" 1997

European Film Academy Screen International European Film Award "In the Mood for Love" 2000

Cesar Best Foreign Film "In the Mood for Love" 2001

British Independent Film Award Best Foreign Independent Film (Foreign Language) "In the Mood for Love" 2001

New York Film Critics Circle Award Best Foreign Film "In the Mood for Love" 2001

New York Film Critics Online Award Best Foreign Language Film "In the Mood for Love" 2001

BIOGRAPHY

Wong Kar-wai is a rare commodity within the Hong Kong film industry: a maker of "art" films. Moreover, he makes these films with studio backing and all-star casts and some of these projects have even made money. In an entertainment arena dominated by over-the-top actioners, florid melodramas and broad comedies, this is no small achievement. For Wong, genre has merely provided a template through which he works out his ongoing thematic preoccupations such as the transitory nature of experience, the importance of memory, the influence of pop culture and the lasting sting of rejection. His bold stylistic signature—slow-motion action scenes blurred and pixilated by step-printing; huge, distorting close-ups and compacted fight sequences shot from disorienting angles—has tended to overwhelm most conventional generic concerns.

Beloved by critics and the HK acting elite, Wong's films have won him favorable comparisons to master experimentalists Jean-Luc Godard and Alain Resnais in their heyday. His rare genre outings have also been evocative of the work of Sergio Leone and Sam Peckinpah. Called a "poet of time" by BFI's *Sight and Sound*, Wong evinces a greater interest in the poetics of light, mood and texture than with the more prosaic concerns of action or straightforward narrative. Nonetheless, actors—even some of HK's biggest stars (e.g., Maggie Cheung, Tony Leung Chiu-wai, Tony Leung Kar-fai, Leslie Cheung, Brigitte Lin Ching-hsia)—enjoy working with Wong because he encourages improvisation and gives them meaty, unconventional roles (for which they tend to win major awards). Surprisingly, for a purveyor of such an imagistic cinema, Wong first established himself as a writer—initially of TV soap operas.

Born in Shanghai, the five-year-old Wong moved to Hong Kong with his mother in 1963. The rest of the family was to follow. A month later, however, the Cultural Revolution broke out, closing the mainland's borders and trapping his father, elder brother and sister for some years. As the only way to communicate with his detained relatives was through writing, Wong became a regular correspondent. His father also instilled in him a love for Chinese and European literature. Graduating high school, the future filmmaker attended a technical school focusing on graphic design but his true interest was photography. In 1980 during his second year, Wong quit to enroll in a training program for TV drama production run by Sir Run Run Shaw's Hong Kong Television Broadcasts, Ltd. (HKTVB). He soon entered the industry as a production assistant on several dramatic serials. Wong subsequently became an assistant director and later a writer for soaps including

the 1981 thriller serial "Don't Look Now". He left HKTVB in 1982 to pursue a screenwriting career and found considerable success, writing some 50 screenplays—about ten were produced with his name on the credits—in genres running the gamut from action to comedy to melodrama to pornography.

Wong segued to directing with "As Tears Go By" (1989), an idiosyncratic gangster movie punctuated with lots of popular music and fast-paced montages. (Wong also scripted.) The film proudly displays its debts to Martin Scorsese's landmark, "Mean Streets" (1973). A surprise hit, "As Tears Go By" earned nine nominations for Hong Kong Film Awards, an unprecedented number for a directorial debut. This success helped Wong attract major names, like Leslie Cheung, Maggie Cheung, Andy Lau and Tony Leung Chiu-Wai to his next project, "Days of Being Wild" (1991), an ambitiously stylized and experimental look at youthful ennui in 1960s Hong Kong. Though hailed "as some kind of masterpiece" by the likes of *Time Out* (London) film critic Tony Rayns, HK audiences were put off by its slow pacing and indifferent plotting. "Ashes of Time" (1994) was a breathtakingly stark and beautiful rumination on period martial arts movies. The shoot was a difficult one, running behind schedule and over budget. During a two-month break in post-production, Wong, his crew and a few of his stars knocked off a minor masterpiece, "Chungking Express" (1994), a quirky romantic comedy with some crime movie trappings. Wrote Rayns: "This is Godard movies were once like: fast, hand-held, funny and very, very catchy." The film was a great critical and commercial success while the long-awaited "Ashes of Time" proved a box-office disappointment. "Fallen Angels" (1995) marked a return to crime stories that some stateside reviewers found formally appealing but disorienting and inaccessible in its story of the afterhours HK world of a sympathetic hit man (pop star Leon Lai Ming).

"Happy Together" (1997) earned Wong the Cannes Film Festival Best Director Award. Hailed as blending the melancholia and striking visual styles of his earlier efforts, it marked a maturation of the director's style. Essentially a chamber piece exploring the relationship between two gay men from Hong Kong and a heterosexual youth befriended by one, the film was more linear than his earlier efforts and benefited from Christopher Doyle's superb camerawork, creating a distinct and rich look.—Written by Kent Greene

MILESTONES:

1963: At age five, moved from Shanghai to Hong Kong with his mother; the Cultural Revolution broke out a month later, trapping his father, sister and brother on the mainland

Studied graphic design at a technical school but was more interested in photography

1980: Quit school during his second year; enrolled in a training program at HKTVB

Entered the industry as a production assistant on several dramatic serials

Became an assistant director at the station

Started screenwriting for serials including the thriller-soap "Don't Look Now" (1981)

1982: Left HKTVB

1982–1992: Worked as feature screenwriter; wrote around 50 screenplays—ten produced with his name on them—ranging from comedies to melodramas to action to porno

1986: Conceived the plot for "As Tears Go By", his directorial debut, while working on helmer Patrick Tam's "The Final Victory" as a writer

1989: Feature debut as writer-director, "As Tears Go By", a gangster film; received nine nominations for the Hong Kong Film Awards

1991: Wrote and directed "Days of Being Wild", a film set in the youth culture of early 1960s HK, starring several major stars; film was a financial failure

Shot "Chungking Express" during a two-month break in the production of "Ashes of Time" as they were waiting for equipment to re-record the sound

1994: Feature producing debut, executive produced "Chungking Express"

"Chungking Express" selected as the first feature to be released through Rolling Thunder, the specialty distribution label at Miramax created by writer-director Quentin Tarantino and producer Lawrence Bender; released in the USA in 1996

1997: Received Cannes Film Festival Best Director Award for "Happy Together"

2000: Helmed "In the Mood for Love", a period romance set in 1962 Hong Kong

2001: Directed the short "The Follow", one of five film advertisements for BMW shown over the Internet at bmwfilms.com

QUOTES:

" 'I'm fascinated by video,' Wong admits. 'The way it blurs and flattens real life, the way it never looks like you thought it would when you play it back. And so my films, which always deal with memory, start taking on the quality of video—a form of physicalized memory that can be experienced again and again, or recorded over, or screened until it literally falls apart, until it pixilates right in front of you.' "—From "Wong's World" by Gemma Files, *Eye Weekly*, January 25, 1996.

MC: Your film ["As Tears Go By", 1988] is inspired by "Mean Streets." How do you see the relationship between the movie of Scorsese and the society of Hong Kong?

WKW: I think the Italians have a lot of similarities with the Chinese: their values, their sense of friendship, their mob/Mafia, their pasta, their attachment to their mother. When I saw "Mean Streets" for the first time, I was shocked, because I had the idea that the story easily could have happened in Hong Kong.

—From an interview with Wong Kar-wai conducted by Michel Ciment in *Positif*, No 410, April 1995 (freely translated from French by Neil Gouw on the World Wide Web).

"Far and away Wong's zestiest work, 'Chungking Express' is an infectious piece of brightly lit, blithely intoxicating bubblegum cinema. At once a catchy come-on jingle and its own snappy answer-song, the film's flipside pairing of two briefly interknit stories, about jilted cops and their inappropriate rebound choices, rings in the brain with a kind of jukebox magic. Swinging on its characters' haphazard proximities and vamping with an irresistibly vivacious visual wit, it's like a catchier Kieslowski, a hipster's O Henry: melodies merge, harmonies collide, and though its lovers barely meet, they find ways to sail their devotions on a breeze across the divide."—From "Time Pieces: Wong Kar Wai and the Perspective of Memory" by Chuck Stephens, *Film Comment*, vol. 32, no. 1.

"I've never done a costume film. I always think costume films are great fun. You can really be wild. Though in fact it's really hard work. So I find an easy way out: I make everything contemporary, and I sideline things like hierarchy and seniority. Actually costume films are very formalistic. Different social strata have different etiquette, conventions and ways of living. But it's ridiculous to sweat over research on their lifestyles. Because it doesn't matter how you do it, in the end it's all a sham. Even if you got things like sipping tea and eating rice down to their last details, so what? You still don't know if they are real or not."—From Wong Kar-wai's comments on "Ashes of Time" in the *Hong Kong International Film Festival 1995 Catalogue*

"Usually I find that genre conventions get in the way of dealing with certain areas of character psychology, but one of my inspirations for 'Ashes [of Time]' was 'The Searchers'—a film which suggests how you can get inside an apparently opaque protagonist. In Ford's film, I've always been extremely touched by the relationship between the John Wayne character and his sister-in-law, which you see only in the way she passes him a cloth. It must amount to about three seconds of screen time but the hint is enough."—Wong Kar-wai quoted in "Poet of Time" by Tony Rayns, *Sight and Sound*(September 1995).

" . . . Before I start to film a movie, I take a lot of drugs, the time for my interpretations and me to find a single rhythm. Of course, I'm very careful with the number of dosages."—From *Positif*, No 410, April 1995.

BIBLIOGRAPHY:

"Wong Kar-Wai" Jean-Marc Lalanne, David Martinez, Ackbar Abbas and Jimmy Ngai

Lawrence Kasdan

BORN: Lawrence Edward Kasdan in Miami Beach, Florida, 01/14/1949

NATIONALITY: American

EDUCATION: University of Michigan, Ann Arbor, Michigan, English, BA, 1970

University of Michigan, Ann Arbor, Michigan, education, MA, 1972

University of California at Los Angeles, Los Angeles, California, screenwriting; dropped out

AWARDS: Writers Guild of America Award Best-Written Drama Written Directly for the Screen "The Big Chill" 1983; shared award with Barbara Benedek

New York Film Critics Circle Award Best Picture "The Accidental Tourist" 1988; shared award with Charles Okun and Michael Grillo

NATO/ShoWest Director of the Year Award 1992; presented by the National Association of Theatre Owners

Berlin Film Festival Golden Bear "Grand Canyon" 1992

BIOGRAPHY

Unable to find a teaching position after earning an MA in Education from the University of

Michigan, Lawrence Kasdan became an advertising copywriter, a profession he found so loathsome he refused to bring a second child into the world until he escaped it. Still, he labored at it for five years (even picking up a Clio Award along the way), first in Detroit and later in Los Angeles where he tried to interest Hollywood in his screenplays. Although he sold a script ("The Bodyguard") which would not make it to the screen until 1992, his screenplay for "Continental Divide" (1981) caught the eye of Steven Spielberg and led to an introduction to George Lucas who would bring him on board the "Star Wars" trilogy when screenwriter Leigh Brackett died. As a result, Kasdan received screenplay credits on three of the most successful films in motion picture history (his first produced feature "The Empire Strikes Back" 1980, the initial Indiana Jones adventure "Raiders of the Lost Ark" 1981 and "The Return of the Jedi" 1983.)

These colossal hits opened the door for Kasdan to do what he had always wanted to do—direct, and his initial effort seemed to herald the arrival of a major talent. An updated version of Billy Wilder's noir classic "Double Indemnity", "Body Heat" (1981) featured William Hurt and Kathleen Turner as the steamiest screen couple of the early 80s. Peppered with intriguing dialogue and propelled by a tight plot, the film paid homage to the genre without being merely derivative. Along the way, Kasdan demonstrated a knack for subtle characterization, creating a cynical gem that belies his more optimistic work as a Spielberg-Lucas hired pen.

"The Big Chill" (1983) proved more commercially successful, but less satisfying, than his promising debut. Instead of reaching back to the 40s, this time Kasdan covered ground explored by a contemporary film, John Sayles' low-budget "The Return of the Secaucus Seven" (1980). A group of "baby boomers" (played by, among others, Hurt, Glenn Close and Kevin Kline) spend a mournful weekend lamenting their lost innocence, but instead of Sayles' touching character study, Kasdan's film comes off as knee-jerk 60s nostalgia—complete with Motown soundtrack. The film's success paved the way for other Reagan-era films that would romanticize 60s ideals in order to reach that most desirable demographic, the disillusioned hippie.

Politics aside, the most disappointing thing about "The Big Chill" was the two-dimensionality of Kasdan's characters. Similar problems plagued his next feature, the Western saga "Silverado" (1985). Kasdan's early strength, characterization, was now only a memory, as still more hip young actors in flat, underwritten roles paraded through a film that tried too hard to be a parody. "Silverado" suffered from an overly complex narrative, but its real downfall was the film's condescending tone: it ultimately ridicules, rather than satirizes, the Western genre. In the process, Kasdan revealed that writing action pictures and directing them are two different things.

"The Accidental Tourist" (1988), based on Anne Tyler's quirky best-selling novel, returned Kasdan to his original form. Once again the characters were impeccably drawn, and this time his camera, making generous use of the close-up, worked to highlight the brilliant performances offered by Oscar-winner Geena Davis and the reunited Hurt and Turner. Poignant and well-observed, "The Accidental Tourist" is the kind of intelligent, well-crafted work that Kasdan proved himself so capable of producing with "Body Heat."

"Grand Canyon" (1991) was an ambitious but glib attempt to address the issues of class, race and violence as they permeated life in Los Angeles. Co-written by Kasdan and wife Meg, the film received mixed reviews, being dubbed by some critics a "Big Chill for the 90s" and derided by others as mushy, superficial and unconvincing. A considerably worse critical reception greeted "The Bodyguard" (1992), a Kevin Costner–Whitney Houston vehicle directed by Mick Jackson from a script Kasdan had originally written for Steve McQueen in the 70s. Despite the brickbats, the film earned in excess of $120 million, fueled partly by the success of the soundtrack (which included Houston's rendition of "I Will Always Love You") and partly by the on-screen chemistry of the leads.

Kasdan's next venture as auteur, "Wyatt Earp" (1994), starring Costner in the title role, was overly long (3 hours 15 minutes with a special video edition 20 minutes longer than that!), negating the good storytelling that had propelled it for quite awhile, and neither the comic savvy of his stars (Meg Ryan, Kline and Timothy Hutton) nor the striking Paris scenery could save "French Kiss" (1995), a charmless contrivance, which he directed as a hired gun. He made a rare acting appearance as Dr. Green in James L. Brooks' "As Good As It Gets" (1997) and turned up as a producer for "Home Fries" (1998), starring Drew Barrymore, Jake Busey and Shelley Duvall, while the world watched and wondered if he could recover the mastery of his best work.

MILESTONES:

Raised in West Virginia

1972–1975: Worked as advertising copywriter for W. B. Doner and Company in Detroit, MI

Joined Doyle, Dane, Bernbach Advertisers in Los Angeles, CA; wrote and submitted screenplays at the same time

Worked as a freelance screenwriter

1976: Sold first screenplay, "The Bodyguard"; remained unproduced until 1992 when it starred Kevin Costner and Whitney Houston; reportedly written as a Steve McQueen vehicle originally (date approximate)

1980: His screenplay for "Continental Divide" caught the attention of Steven Spielberg who introduced Kasdan to George Lucas; hired by Lucas to work on first screenplay filmed, "The Empire Strikes Back" (which Kasdan took over when screenwriter Leigh Brackett died)

1981: Penned "Raiders of the Lost Ark", the first installment of the Indiana Jones series, for producer Lucas and director Speilberg

1981: Directorial debut, "Body Heat"

1983: With Lucas, co-wrote the third installment of the "Star Wars" series, "The Return of the Jedi"

1983: Executive produced first film "The Big Chill" (also director and co-screenwriter); earned first Academy Award nomination for Best Original Screenplay

1985: Produced first film, "Silverado" (also director and co-writer)

1985: Played Second Detective in John Landis' "Into the Night"

1987: Produced first film that he did not direct or write, "Cross My Heart", directed by Armyan Bernstein

1988: Co-wrote, co-produced and directed "The Accidental Tourist", starring William Hurt, Geena Davis and Kathleen Turner; earned Oscar nominations for Best Picture and Best Adapted Screenplay

1989: Served as executive producer on first film he did not direct or script, "Immediate Family", directed by Jonathan Kaplan

1990: Directed first film that he did not co-write, "I Love You to Death"

1991: Produced, directed and co-wrote (with wife Meg) "Grand Canyon"; received fourth Oscar nomination for Best Original Screenplay

1992: His script for "The Bodyguard" finally produced as vehicle for Costner and Whitney Houston

1994: Produced, directed and co-scripted (with Dan Gordon) "Wyatt Earp", starring Costner in the title role

1995: Stage directing debut, John Patrick Shanley's "Four Dogs and a Bone"

1995: Helmed (only) "French Kiss", starring Meg Ryan (one of the producers), Kevin Kline and Timothy Hutton

1997: Portrayed Dr. Green in James L. Brooks' "As Good As It Gets"

1998: Produced "Home Fries", starring Drew Barrymore, Jake Busey and Shelley Duvall

AFFILIATION: Member, Board of Trustees, American Film Institute

QUOTES:

"Technically, movies have progressed to the point where 50 directors can shoot beautiful movies now, but what there has always been a shortage of—and it's more drastic than ever now—is writing. For the first 40 years of movies writers came out of theater or fiction or journalism. They brought with them classic ideas about character and narrative and dramatic construction. That was for the first 40 years. But for the last 20 years people have come out of television and MTV and out of a disintegrated popular culture, fragmented, and they don't bring with them any literary tradition . . . good writing is about the ambiguity, the complexity of life; there are no easy villains and no easy heroes. Good writing should be disturbing, should raise questions. That's what we tried to do in 'Grand Canyon.' "—Lawrence Kasdan (*New York Times*, January 16, 1992).

Received the Clio Award for his advertising work.

Aki Kaurismaki

BORN: in Finland 04/04/1957

SOMETIMES CREDITED AS:
Aki

NATIONALITY: Finnish

AWARDS: Jussi Award Best First Film "Crime and Punishment" 1983; Finnish film prize

Jussi Award Best First Script "Crime and Punishment" 1983; Finnish film prize

Hong Kong International Film Festival, Special Award "Calamari Union"

Jussi Award Best Finnish Film "Shadows in Paradise" 1986; Finnish film prize

National Society of Film Critics Award Best Foreign Film "Ariel" 1990

Jussi Award Best Director "The Match Factory Girl" 1991; Finnish film prize; film also won awards for best actress, best supporting actor and actress

Cannes Film Festival Grand Jury Prize "The Man Without a Past" 2002

BIOGRAPHY

Young, inventive director who began receiving international recognition in the late 1980s. Kaurismaki's output has ranged from wacky, comic-book style adventures ("Calamari Union" 1985, "Leningrad Cowboys Go America" 1989) to revisionist adaptations of literary classics ("Crime and Punishment" 1983, "Hamlet Goes Business" 1987"), and he has proved himself adept at combining gritty, noir-ish realism with sly, sardonic humor ("Ariel" 1988). Kaurismaki's minimalist style, prolific output and taste for wry melodrama have invited comparisons with filmmakers such as R.W. Fassbinder and Jim Jarmusch.

With his brother Mika ("Rosso" 1985, "Helsinki Napoli All Night Long" 1988), and other directors including Pekka Parikka ("Plainlands" 1988, "The Winter War" 1989), Kaurismaki is at the forefront of a burgeoning new wave of Finnish cinema.

MILESTONES:

1980: First film as screenwriter (also actor), "The Liar"; brother Mika's thesis film

Co-founded Villealfa Filmproductions with brother

1981: Co-directed (with brother) the rock documentary "The Saimaa Gesture" (also the first Villealfa production)

1983: Fiction feature directing and co-writing debut, "Crime and Punishment"

Co-founded Midnight Sun Film Festival in Sodankyla with brother

1999: Helmed the black-and-white silent "Juha"

2002: Directed the award-winning "The Man Without a Past" which he also wrote and produced; received an Oscar nomination for Best Foreign Language Film

QUOTES:

"I have one principle in my life. And that is, physically, to never land my feet in West Coast of United States. Not even as a tourist I go there. I don't like smell of sun(tan) oil so much."—Aki Kaurismaki interviewed in *New York Post*, November 1990.

"First of all, I'd like to thank myself. And then the jury. Thanks."—Kaurismaki's entire acceptance speech for the Grand Jury Prize at the Cannes film festival, 2002.

Elia Kazan

BORN: Elia Kazanjoglou in Kadi-Kev, Constantinople, Turkey, 09/07/1909. Died 09/29/2003

NATIONALITY: Greek

CITIZENSHIP: United States

EDUCATION: Mayfair School, New York, New York

New Rochelle High School, New Rochelle, New York, 1926

Williams College, Williamstown, Massachusetts, 1930

School of Drama, Yale University, New Haven, Connecticut, MFA, 1932

AWARDS: New York Film Critics Circle Award Best Director "Gentleman's Agreement" and "Boomerang" 1947; cited for both films

National Board of Review Award Best Director "Gentleman's Agreement" and "Boomerang" 1947; cited for both films

Golden Globe Award Best Director "Gentleman's Agreement" 1947

Oscar Best Director "Gentleman's Agreement" 1947

Tony Outstanding Director "All My Sons" 1947

Tony Outstanding Director "Death of a Salesman" 1949

Venice Film Festival International Prize "Panic in the Streets" 1950; shared award with Jean Delannoy's "Dieu a besoin des hommes" and Alessandro Blasetti's "Prima Comunione"

New York Film Critics Circle Award Best Director "A Streetcar Named Desire" 1951

Venice Film Festival Special Jury Prize "A Streetcar Named Desire" 1951

Berlin Film Festival International Delegate-Jury Prize of the Berlin Senate "Man on a Tightrope" 1953; award shared with Luigi Zampa's "City on Trial" and Heinosuke Gosho's "Where the Chimneys Are Seen"

New York Film Critics Circle Award Best Director "On the Waterfront" 1954

Venice Film Festival Silver Lion Award "On the Waterfront" 1954; film cited along with Kurosawa's "Seven Samauai," Fellini's "La Strada" and Mizoguchi's "Sansho the Bailiff"

Golden Globe Award Best Director "On the Waterfront" 1954

Directors Guild of America Award Outstanding Directorial Achievement in Feature Film "On the Waterfront" 1954

Oscar Best Director "On the Waterfront" 1954

Golden Globe Award Best Motion Picture (Drama) "East of Eden" 1955; Kazan was the producer

Cannes Film Festival Dramatic Film Award "East of Eden" 1955

Golden Globe Award Best Director "Baby Doll" 1956

Tony Outstanding Play "The Dark at the Top of the Stairs" 1958; co-producer

Tony Outstanding Director "J.B." 1959

Golden Globe Award Best Director "America America" 1963

Kennedy Center Honors Lifetime Achievement Award 1983

Directors Guild of America Honorary Life Membership 1983; cited with Robert Wise

Directors Guild of America D.W. Griffith Award 1987 for lifetime achievement

Berlin Film Festival Honorary Golden Bear 1996 for lifetime achievement

Honorary Oscar 1998; presented "in appreciation of a long, distinguished and unparalleled career during which he has influenced the very nature of filmmaking through his creation of cinematic masterpieces"

BIOGRAPHY

Despite acting in important plays like Clifford Odets' "Waiting for Lefty" and "Golden Boy" and even tackling the movies with roles in "City For Conquest" (1940) and "Blues in the Night" (1941), both helmed by Anatole Litvak, Elia Kazan found he could achieve much greater range by shaping others' acting than by honing his own. The source for his inspired directing was the revolutionary acting technique known as the Method, which he encountered at NYC's influential Group Theatre, and the Greek immigrant who had grown up feeling like an outsider rose to prominence as the preeminent proponent of the Method, first onstage and later in the movies. Kazan's ability to reveal the truth of his characters' behavior made him a favorite of post-war dramatists like Arthur Miller, Tennessee Williams, William Inge and Robert Anderson, whose realistic plays were the finest flowering of the American theater. It wasn't long after his Broadway directing debut with Thornton Wilder's "The Skin of Our Teeth" (1942) that Hollywood came calling, but Kazan refused to renounce the stage for celluloid, electing instead to alternate between the two mediums and experience tremendous success in both arenas.

Recruited by several studios in 1944, Kazan teamed with producer Darryl F. Zanuck at 20th Century Fox, and though he would establish himself as an expert handler of actors and an artist dedicated to addressing contemporary social problems, his early films for Fox are barely recognizable as his, reflecting equal parts Zanuck and Kazan. He made an impressive debut with "A Tree Grows in Brooklyn" (1945), drawing on his immigrant experience to tell the sensitive story of a bright young girl trying to rise above the hardships of tenement life in turn-of-the-century Brooklyn, but he chafed at MGM's interference on his next picture the epic "Sea of Grass" (1947), starring Spencer Tracy and Katharine Hepburn. Kazan saw it as the very essence of America, the pioneers who blazed the trail ultimately displaced by the farmers, the bourgeois and safe people, but MGM had no interest in a picture about class struggles, preferring instead a depiction of the beauteous American landscape. Footage taken without Kazan's involvement found its way into the film, and the director decried the end result as too sweet and entertainment-oriented.

Kazan was back at Fox for the murder-trial thriller "Boomerang" (1947), his reaction to "Sea of Grass" and the whole Hollywood aesthetic that placed mass appeal above all artistic and political concerns. Foreshadowing the neorealism of later more interesting works like "Panic in the Streets" (1950), "On the Waterfront" (1954) and "Wild River" (1960), the picture employed non-actors recruited from its Connecticut locale and focused on psychological developments, rather than plot, for suspense. Zanuck's next assignment for him was "Gentleman's Agreement" (1947), which he squeezed in between two heavily lauded Broadway productions (Miller's "All My Sons" and Williams' "A Streetcar Named Desire") as a moonlighting gig, leaving the editing and post-production to Zanuck. The Fox chief did more than just piece together the raw footage, promoting the film, one of the first Hollywood pictures to deal directly with anti-Semitism, into a must-see event that would win the Best Picture Oscar and earn Kazan a statuette for directing. Although grateful to be swept along in the Academy Award bonanza, Kazan complained "it looked like an illustration for *Cosmopolitan*" and "doesn't get into the parts of anti-Semitism that persist and hurt . . . it's too damn polite, that picture."

Coming post-Holocaust, "Agreement" was a wimpy movie about WASPs. Six million Jews had perished in the death camps, and Hollywood's ground-breaking approach was to watch Gregory Peck pose as a Jew and get refused admittance to hotels. Even less satisfying for Kazan was "Pinky" (1949), which he called a "total dodge . . . a pastiche," completing it for Fox after John Ford left the project. Purportedly another ground-breaker, this time dealing with race relations, "Pinky" cast a Caucasian actress (Jeanne Crain) as a light-skinned black woman at odds with her family and community because she has chosen to pass for white. If Kazan felt compromised in Hollywood, he was enjoying considerable autonomy on the Broadway stage, where he picked up his second Tony Award for directing Miller's "Death of a Salesman" in 1949, as well as renewing his association with Williams ("Camino Real") the same year. He was developing a stable of Method actors like Marlon Brando, Lee J. Cobb and Karl Malden, who would eventually populate the films on which his screen reputation would rest. "Panic in the Streets" marked his passage into a more cinematic phase. Employing many long-shots and a constantly moving camera, as well as adding a wealth of sound effects, he thoroughly exploited his sinister New Orleans locations, bringing a startling noir intensity to back-alley beatings and the pathetic life of small-time crooks.

Kazan won further acclaim as a film director for his memorable adaptation of "A Streetcar Named Desire" (1951), choosing this time only to helm the film version of one of his Broadway successes. Usually, his immersion in the stage production robbed him of any desire to repeat it, but in the case of "Streetcar", he felt that he'd let Brando's Stanley dominate the Broadway production at the expense of Jessica Tandy's Blanche and sought to correct this in the movie. Vivien Leigh replaced Tandy, and she was equal to the challenge of sharing the screen with Brando. Her personal problems at the time—fragile mental state and rocky marriage to Laurence Olivier—gave Kazan a bottomless reservoir to plumb, and he didn't hesitate to goad her into a remarkable, Academy Award–winning performance. "Viva Zapata!" (1952) teamed him with John Steinbeck as screenwriter, telling the story of the grass-roots Mexican revolutionary in a manner that was acceptable to McCarthy era sensibilities. Despite accommodating a repressive national atmosphere, the pair delivered a vibrant film about the Mexican peasant's rise to power and eventual Presidency, featuring Brando in the title role and an Oscar-winning supporting performance by Anthony Quinn.

It was at this point in time that Kazan made the Faustian bargain that saved his career short-term but has effectively black-listed his accomplishments into present day. Renouncing his early involvement with the Communist Party as youthful folly, he "sang" to the House Un-American Activities Committee (reversing his initial resistance to HUAC), naming eight former colleagues (including Odets and actress Paula Strasberg) as dangerous Communist infiltrators. Criticized by many for caving in to the witch hunt, Kazan answered the snubs with "On the Waterfront" (1954), in which dock worker Terry Malloy (Brando) takes the unpopular action of testifying against corrupt labor leaders. Kazan later wrote: "When Brando, at the end, yells . . . 'I'm glad what I done—you hear me?—glad what I done!' that was me saying with identical heat, that I was glad I'd testified as I had." Kazan's detractors saw it as a maddeningly self-serving allegory of recent history, but moviegoers, unconcerned with the ideological debate, responded enthusiastically to an exciting picture of moral awakening, photographed in the gritty, unfamiliar milieu of the Brooklyn and Hoboken docks (complete with real dockworkers). Featuring a superb performance by Brando, supported magnificently by Eva Marie Saint, Lee J. Cobb, Rod Steiger and Karl Malden, the film broke box-office records and won eight Academy Awards, including Best Picture, Best Director and Best Actor.

Kazan's remarkable Broadway run continued throughout the 50s with Anderson's "Tea and Symphony" (1953), Williams' "Cat on a Hot Tin Roof" (1955), Inge's "The Dark at the Top of the Stairs" (1957), Archibald MacLeish's "J.B." (1958) and Williams' "Sweet Bird of Youth" (1959), but his Hollywood reputation had finally caught up (or surpassed) that of his stage work. He had discovered Brando's potential, and he introduced James Dean to a wide audience as the tortured son of Raymond Massey in "East of Eden" (1955), adapted by Paul Osborn from the Steinbeck novel. Recognizing that Dean's Method mumblings (à la Brando) drove Massey to distraction, Kazan stoked the pair's antagonism, capturing their hatred for each other on film. He tapped another Method newcomer (Carroll Baker) for "Baby Doll" (1956), and the same people (namely the Catholic Legion of Decency) who had objected to his suggestive low-angle photographing of Kim Hunter (Stella in "Streetcar") railed against his provocative presentation of Baker. He also drew impressive performances out of neophytes like Andy Griffith ("A Face in the Crowd" 1957) and Natalie Wood and Warren Beatty ("Splendor in the Grass" 1961). In all, Kazan directed 21 Oscar-nominated performances and nine winners.

With the exception of Lincoln Center's inaugural season, Kazan completely abandoned his theater work in the 60s, took up fiction writing and focused his film career on much more personal, independently produced projects. "America, America" (1963) was a critically acclaimed adaptation of his own novel about his family's emigration to the USA. His subsequent efforts, "The Arrangement" (1969, again from his own novel) and "The Visitors" (1972, shot at his home in 16mm), were resounding failures. Kazan made an unexpected return to mainstream filmmaking with Harold Pinter's adaptation of F. Scott Fitzgerald's "The Last Tycoon" (1976), taking over the project abandoned by Mike Nichols. Focusing on the novel's love affair and glamorous settings, he delivered arguably the best feature presentation of Fitzgerald's work, the film benefiting greatly from an outstanding performance by Robert De Niro as the movie producer (based on Irving Thalberg) who is slowly working himself to death. The picture, unfortunately, did no business, and Kazan may have summed it up best: "Harold is a master of understatement, but I think he understated too much in this case."

Kazan the immigrant began his life as an outsider and even when successful remained an outsider. His best work examined the plight of the outsider, and he explained his affinity for Williams, for whom he directed six stage and movie productions over two decades: "What the gay world—then still largely closeted—was to him, my foreignness was to me. We were both outsiders in the straight (or native) society we lived in." It is ironic that many of his most vocal present day detractors were not even born when he testified before HUAC because, despite the hostility Hollywood may have had for him at the height of the McCarthy era, some of its staunchest liberals (Brando, Warren Beatty, Kirk Douglas, Haskell Wexler) willingly worked with the pariah afterwards. Even Arthur Miller reached out to him to direct "After the Fall" in 1964, coming to the conclusion that " . . . If I still felt a certain distaste for Kazan's renouncing his past under duress, I was not at all sure that he should be excluded from a position for which he was superbly qualified by his talent." Kazan's way of prodding actors to dig deep, his channeling of the Method into the cinema stands as his lasting legacy. Long denied lifetime achievement recognition for the sins of his past, he finally received a 1998 Honorary Oscar and with it the tacit forgiveness of an industry which had decided to embrace the unrepentant outsider to its breast before he died.—Written by Greg Senf

FAMILY:

son: Chris Kazan. Screenwriter, novelist, film professor; born in New York City c. 1939; died of cancer on December 14, 1991 in Santa Monica CA; mother, Molly Day Thatcher; wrote and produced "The Visitor" (1972) directed by his father; novels include "Mouth Full of Sugar" (1969) and "The Love Freak"; received BA from Harvard; was an assistant professor of film at Columbia University's School of the Arts; married to Jeneene Harris

son: Nicholas Kazan. Screenwriter, director; mother, Molly Day Thatcher; received Oscar nomination for "Reversal of Fortune" (1990); married to screenwriter Robin Swicord

COMPANION:

wife: Molly Day Thatcher. Filmmaker, photographer; married on December 2, 1932; died in 1963 from a brain aneurysm; worked together with Kazan as members of the anti-fascist filmmaking group Nykino (for New York Camera, using the Russian word for "camera"); were two of the six directors of the famous experimental short, "Pie in the Sky" (1934), in which Kazan also acted

MILESTONES:

1913: After brief stay in Berlin, immigrated to the USA with parents

Raised in New York

1932: Theatrical debut as stage manager and understudy for the Theater Guild production, "The Pure in Heart" in Baltimore, Maryland

1932–1933: Apprenticed with Group Theater

1933: Broadway acting debut, "Men in White"

1934: Film acting debut in the short "Cafe Universal"

1934: Co-directed and acted in the experimental short film, "Pie in the Sky"; wife Molly Day Thatcher also directed a segment

Was a member of the Communist Party

1935: Appeared on Broadway in Group Theatre production of Clifford Odets' "Waiting for Lefty"

1937: Directed short documentary "People of the Cumberland"

1937: Played Eddie Fusseli in the Group Theatre production of Odets' "Golden Boy"

1938: Stage directing debut with "Casey Jones"

1940: Feature film acting debut in "City for Conquest", playing a neighborhood tough-turned-gangster opposite James Cagney

1941: Group Theater folded

1942: Broadway directing debut, Thornton Wilder's "The Skin of Our Teeth"

1945: Feature film directing debut with "A Tree Grows in Brooklyn"

1947: Co-founded (with Cheryl Crawford, Robert Lewis and Lee Strasberg) Actors Studio

1947: Directed seminal Broadway productions of Arthur Miller's "All My Sons" (for which he won his first Tony) and Tennessee Williams' "A Streetcar Named Desire"

1947: Won Best Director Oscar on first-ever nomination for "Gentleman's Agreement"; film also won Best Picture

1949: Helmed the Broadway production of Miller's "Death of a Salesman"; received second Tony Award

1950: "Panic in the Streets" marked his passage to a more ambitiously cinematic phase

1951: Received Oscar nomination as Best Director for "A Streetcar Named Desire"

1952: Directed "Viva Zapata!", written by John Steinbeck and starring Marlon Brando

1952: Testified before the House Un-American Activities Committee and named eight former colleagues (including Odets and actress Paula Strasberg) as dangerous Communist infiltrators

1953: Directed overtly anti-Communist film, "Man on a Tightrope", starring Fredric March

1954: Took home second Oscar as director of "On the Waterfront", written by fellow "name-dropper" Budd Schulberg

1955: Staged the premiere of Tennessee Williams' "Cat on a Hot Tin Roof" on Broadway; exercised much influence over the final draft

1955: Produced first film "East of Eden"; also directed; adapted by Paul Osborn from the Steinbeck novel; picked up fourth Oscar nomination as Best Director

1956: Collaborated with Tennessee Williams on "Baby Doll"

1957: Reunited with Schulberg for "A Face in the Crowd"

1959: Appointed to develop and run the new Lincoln Center Repertory Theater

1959: Received acclaim for producing and directing "J.B.", Archibald MacLeish's retelling of the biblical story of Job

1960: After trying for some time to write a screenplay about the TVA (Tennessee Valley Authority), turned ideas over to Osborn who scripted "Wild River", directed by Kazan

1961: Helmed "Splendor in the Grass" from an Oscar-winning original screenplay by William Inge

1963: Nominated for three Oscars—Best Director, Best Picture (as producer) and Best Screenplay—for "America, America", based on his uncle's life

1964: Directed Miller's "After the Fall" for inaugural season of Lincoln Center Repertory Theater; production starred second wife Barbara Loden playing a thinly disguised Marilyn Monroe

1969: Bombed with "The Arrangement", film version of his own best-selling novel

1972: Accused of union-busting on "The Visitors", a family-affair (son Chris wrote and produced), low-budget picture shot in and around Kazan's home turf of Newton, CT; film reportedly cost $150,000, of which the non-union actors (including James Woods and Steve Railsback) received a total of $1,200; put on "unfair" list of Screen Actors Guild

1976: Directed last feature film to date, "The Last Tycoon", adapted from the unfinished F. Scott Fitzgerald novel by Harold Pinter

1982: Subject of French documentary "Elia Kazan, Outsider"

1988: Published memoirs "Elia Kazan: A Life"

1989: Turned up in a surprising role as Captain of Fishing Boat in foreign film "Sis", directed by Omer Zulfi Livanelli

1995: Subject of documentary "Elia Kazan: A Director's Journey" (AMC), produced by longtime friend Julian Schlossberg

QUOTES:

Kazan's handyman abilities earned him the nickname Gadget—Gadg for short—a handle he has often said he despised for its patronizing tone but which many of his closest friends use to this day as a purely affectionate form of address. Reportedly John Steinbeck told him: "That goddamn name is not you. . . . You're not—or weren't—a handy, friendly adaptable little gadget. You made yourself that way to get along with people, to be accepted, to become invisible . . . "

"I was the first to deal with many difficult subjects in the United States. I read the papers carefully. I get much of my inspiration from them."—Elia Kazan quoted at 1996 Berlin Film Festival in *New York Post*, February 19, 1996.

" . . . I can get along all right with you liking me or disliking me. I'm O.K., I do my work, and that's what I feel is important for an artist—that he does his work in his way with his vision and he doesn't pay a lot of attention to the reaction. And I don't. I never did. . . . On my worst day, when I was being attacked by all sides, I didn't care. I don't live by what people are saying about me. The only way we're ever going to be known is by our work, not by somebody boasting about us.

"You're looking at a man who is essentially content. I'm proud of my films. I think about a dozen of them are very good, and I don't think there are films as good on the subject or feeling. Writing my own work means more to me than I can get out of somebody else's work, and some of the stuff I did turned out all right."—Kazan to *The New York Times*, August 24, 1995.

"For what he's done, he's gone into a hermit's life. The thing is, he did name people, and many careers were destroyed. But you have to remember, this was an era where just ten years before, Japanese citizens, not aliens, had been rounded up and put in concentration camps in this country. We came through a dreadful time. But [Kazan] won't apologize, and he has to live with that. He felt his career would be over unless he did what he did."—Eli Wallach, in *Entertainment Weekly*, March 1998.

"If you can't say what's on your mind in the time it takes to soft-boil an egg, it isn't worth saying."—Elia Kazan quoted by Patricia Bosworth in "Kazan's Choice" in *Vanity Fair*, September 1999.

BIBLIOGRAPHY:
"America, America" Elia Kazan, 1962, Stein and Day; autobiographical novel
"The Arrangement" Elia Kazan, 1968; novel
"Kazan on Kazan: Interviews with Michel Ciment" 1974
"The Assassins" Elia Kazan, 1981; novel
"The Understudy" Elia Kazan, 1986; novel
"Elia Kazan: A Life" Elia Kazan, 1988, Alfred A. Knopf; autobiography
"Beyond the Aegean" Elia Kazan, 1994, Alfred A. Knopf; novel
"The Assassins" Elia Kazan; novel
"Kazan—The Master Discusses His Films— Interviews with Elia Kazan" Jeff Young; 1999

Buster Keaton

BORN: Joseph Frank Keaton in Piqua, Kansas, 10/04/1895

SOMETIMES CREDITED AS:
'The Great Stone Face'

DEATH: in Woodland Hills, California, 02/01/1966

NATIONALITY: American

AWARD: Honorary Oscar 1959 for his unique talents which brought immortal comedies to the screen

BIOGRAPHY
A vaudeville star before the age of ten, Buster Keaton was preparing to make his Broadway debut in 1917 when a meeting with Rosco "Fatty" Arbuckle changed the course of his life and that of the cinema forever. "The Great Stone Face" translated marvelously to the screen, somehow surviving the disasters that came hurtling his way, to eventually become along with Charlie Chaplin and Harold Lloyd one of the most popular comic actors of the Silent Era. Keaton's immediate fascination with the new medium led him to take the camera home, disassembling and reassembling it to more fully understand its operation. If Chaplin's genius was fixing the camera and theatrically framing his Tramp's antics, Keaton created a more cinematic comedy, cleverly using his sense of the American landscape and instinct for interiors to beautifully record his jokes. Arguably the most innovative of the three, he was an early advocate of the moving camera, as well as a pioneer in special effects, and his films viewed today seem far more modern than those of his peers.

By the age of three, Keaton had joined his mother and father in their traveling show, rechristened The Three Keatons, although keeping him working earned the constant scrutiny of the Gerry Society, the turn-of-the-century child labor authorities. Legend has it that the great Harry Houdini, seeing the six-month-old laugh delightedly after taking a tremendous header down a flight of stairs, remarked, "That's some buster your baby took." Myth or not, the nickname stuck, and Houdini took credit for coining it throughout his life. (Other sources indicate it was actor George Pardey who made the comment, the Keatons having not yet met Houdini.) One thing is certain, the Keatons struggled prior to Buster coming on board but became a success soon after he started appearing with them. Tossed about by his father in the most physical of acts, he soon developed a knack for falling coupled with his signature impassivity, a theatrical contrivance—very much in contrast with his off-stage demeanor—which he would maintain throughout his life. Keaton worked with his parents nearly 20 years until his father's excessive drinking led to the break-up of the act.

From his first days before Arbuckle's camera, Keaton understood that film demanded a more subtle acting style than had the stage, and in contrast to his fellow performers' extravagance, he was quiet, controlled, unhurried, economical and accurate. When Arbuckle left to make features for Paramount, Keaton took over the company with Joseph Schenck handling the business end of things as he had for Arbuckle. After appearing in the feature "The Saphead" (1920, on loan to Metro Pictures), Keaton embarked on directing two-reelers, helming 18 in all (plus the three-reel "Day Dreams" 1922) by the time of his feature directing debut, "The Three Ages" (1923), a spoof of D.W. Griffith's "Intolerance" (1916). Perfecting and enriching his craft, Keaton developed recurrent themes in the shorts, which he would transfer to the full-lengths. Starting with "One Week" (1920), he filmed the gag of the do-it-yourself house which

comes crashing down before the comedian's somber gaze, and the house as intricate machine, either ingenious or infernal, became a staple of his shtick, walls collapsing while he remains unscathed, conveniently positioned under open windows.

In "The Playhouse" (1921), a tour de force of special effects unrivaled even to this day, Keaton played every part in a theater: the whole orchestra, the actors, all nine blackface minstrels, both halves of a dance act, and every single member of the audience, young and old, male and female. He was a generous collaborator, sharing directing credit with Eddie Cline on most of the shorts and three features, though Cline graciously conceded that Keaton was responsible for 90 percent of the comic inventions in their films. Working in the same atmosphere of experimentation and absolute artistic control that had characterized Arbuckle's operation, his team developed a sort of anarchic creative style, employing (in addition to houses) all manner of boats, herds of cattle, squads of police and armies of women, among other hostile devices, to imperil the Great Stone Face. Unlike Chaplin's warm comedies, Keaton's humor was cool and aloof, characterized by James Agee as "a freezing whisper not of pathos, but of melancholia." His humorless hero, far from exercising the Tramp's self-pity, exhibited a serene capacity for absorbing frustration and withstanding disasters without ever cracking while seeking a measure of serenity in a world where peace is hard to find.

Despite some delightful gags (i.e., Keaton thrown to an affable lion, manicures its claws), "The Three Ages" did not represent a significant advance over the shorts, but "Our Hospitality" (also 1923), a beautiful period piece, revealed for the first time the artist's love for trains while clearly demonstrating how his work stood apart from the conventions of the period. There was no speeded-up action, which he felt spoiled the timing of the gags, and none of the wild mugging that passed for comic acting of the day. He avoided studio sets, preferring natural locations, kept titles to a minimum and used close-ups sparingly, instead favoring the long-shot, especially as concrete proof that the stunts were real and not some cinematic hocus-pocus. He followed quickly with "Sherlock, Jr." and "The Navigator" (both 1924), assuring his place in film history. More than 60 years before Woody Allen would appropriate the gag by having a movie character step off the screen into life for "The Purple Rose of Cairo" (1985), "Sherlock, Jr." involved a projectionist stepping into and out of the movies he shows upon the screen, becoming subject to the plastic worlds of space and time that Keaton so deftly manipulated in all of his films.

A showcase of clever camerawork, "Sherlock Jr." featured a famous montage sequence which switches him rapidly from a garden to a busy street, to a cliff-edge, to a jungle full of lions, and so on—all without any apparent cuts in his own movements. Keaton remarked, "Every cameraman in the business went to see that picture more than once, trying to figure out how we did some of that." The virtuoso stunts were no less masterful, and Keaton, who did all his own stunts in the film, managed to break his neck in one fall but continued working, discovering the fracture ten years later. For "The Navigator" (co-directed by future Oscar-winning actor Donald Crisp), he provided himself with the biggest prop he could lay his hands on (an ocean liner) and drew from his lifelong joy in creating appealingly crazy mechanical gadgetry. Though his next three films ("Seven Chances" and "Go West" both 1925, and "Battling Butler" 1926) were not up to the standards set by his first features, "Battling Butler" actually out-grossed "The Navigator", and "Seven Chances" boasted time-lapse photography of a puppy growing to become a huge dog, as well as a scene in which Keaton entered a car and promptly exited after the background dissolved to a new location, a bit of movie shorthand greatly appreciated by his audience.

Returning to his love of trains gave Keaton the greatest prop of all for his masterpiece, "The General" (1926). Uncompromising as ever, he refused to use a model for the film's climax, shooting instead (at the unheard of cost of $42,000 for the single take) a real train crashing through a burning bridge, the frame including men on horseback moving on the river bank as proof it was no trick of the camera. Keaton mined history books obtaining " . . . the authenticity and the unassumingly correct composition of a Matthew Brady Civil War photograph", but his streamlined narrative with gags designed to further dramatic action only did not do well at the box office, perhaps because his audience preferred the fancy of his previous work. Deciding to play it safe, he modeled the disappointing "College" (1927) after Lloyd's successful "The Freshman" (1925) but returned to form with the brilliant "Steamboat Bill Jr." (1928), choreographing its phantasmagoric cyclone sequence as if it were ballet. Though he spun, slid, tumbled and eventually gained flight while apparently solid buildings collapsed and vanished magically, the public failed to appreciate his artistry, and the film bombed commercially.

Keaton's undoing came at the hands of his brother-in-law Joseph Schenck who persuaded him to abandon his own studio and join MGM. Chaplin and Lloyd both urged him not to give up his independence, but family pressure (particularly a spendthrift wife) led him to accept $3000 a week for the new arrangement. The studio insisted on completed, plot-heavy scripts in advance, nixing his proven working method of developing a narrative through improvisation, and it wasn't long before he was drinking heavily. Keaton battled for every gag on "The Cameraman" (1928), a film comparable to his pre-MGM features, and made two more comedies that were hits for MGM, his final silent (and by general agreement the last authentic Keaton film), "Spite Marriage" (1929), and the talkie "Free and Easy" (1930), before mediocrity set in. By 1933 both studio and wife had dropped him as a hopeless alcoholic. Within a couple years, he was able to control his drinking and make two-reelers for Poverty Row's Educational until its demise in 1937, but after his final directing projects (three single-reelers for MGM in 1938 and 10 two-reelers for Columbia Pictures), the only work he could consistently obtain (besides the occasional bit part) was as a mostly uncredited gagman.

Agee's *Life* magazine essay ("Comedy's Greatest Era") of September 5, 1949 did much to revive interest in the forgotten Keaton. After a memorable cameo as one of Gloria Swanson's bridge foursome in "Sunset Boulevard" (1950), he acted for the first time with Chaplin in the latter's "Limelight" (1952) and was also working frequently in the new medium of television, often demonstrating the fine art of pie-throwing, though that brand of slapstick had not been a specialty during his heyday. The discovery by actor James Mason, owner of Keaton's former villa, in 1955 of a treasure trove of prints for all his silent features and many of the shorts guaranteed that future generations would know the genius of the "Great Stone Face", and money received for "The Buster Keaton Story" (1957), starring Donald O'Connor, finally ended his perpetual poverty. Two years later, he garnered an honorary Academy Award for "his unique talents which brought immortal comedies to the screen." Happily married to his third wife Eleanor Norris, he lived modestly and worked steadily, earning nearly as much money in the last decade of his life as during his time at the top.

Keaton was pragmatic about his career, having known the ups and downs of show business since childhood. Although temporarily crushed by the impersonal studio system and a first wife only in it for the money, he rose from the depths, scratching by as a trouble-shooter who could come in and find unique solutions to plot problems. Keaton never lost his creativity, only his creative control, and the real loser was a public denied the kind of films he would have made had anyone allowed him to continue. Appearing at the Venice Film Festival of 1965 to a tumultuous reception climaxed Keaton's latter-day fame but also prompted the delighted and touched artist to say afterwards, "Sure it's great—but it's all thirty years too late." Keaton died shortly thereafter but lives on in his films, his art and life splendidly taken up by Kevin Brownlow and David Gill in their two-part TV documentary, "Buster Keaton: A Hard Act to Follow" (PBS, 1987), and addressed again in "Buster Keaton: Genius in Slapshoes" (A&E, 1995).—Written by Greg Senf

MILESTONES:

Made first stage appearance at the age of nine months, crawling into the middle of his father's blackface routine

Joined the family act before the age of three, The Two Keatons becoming The Three Keatons

1900: "Official" professional debut, October 17 at Dockstader's Theatre, Wilmington, Delaware

1900–1917: The Three Keatons traveled widely, appearing all over the USA and becoming headliners in NYC; from the beginning Buster was the star of the act

1909: Keaton family made a brief trip to Europe, during which they played London's Palace

1917: Father's drinking led to break-up of the act

1917: Accepted a part in the Broadway show "The Passing Show of 1917" at $250 a week but broke contract after meeting Rosco "Fatty" Arbuckle and appearing in his first film

1917: First short film as actor, "The Butcher Boy", written and directed by Arbuckle

Drafted into Army and assigned to the 40th Infantry; posted to France

1920: Played a straight role in his first feature, "The Saphead"; made on loan to Metro Pictures

1920: Took over Joseph Schenck's Comique Films (formerly headed by Arbuckle)

1920: First short film as director, "The High Sign" (shelved and not released until 1921)

1920: First released short film as director, "One Week"; co-helmed with Eddie Cline

1921: With Cline, co-wrote and co-directedthe two-reeler "The Playhouse", a special effects tour de force in which he appeared on screen simultaneously nine times, even performing a dance with himself

1922: Comique Films name changed to Buster Keaton Productions (though Schenck still owned it)

1923: Completed first feature comedy, "The Three Ages", a spoof of D.W. Griffith's "Intolerance" (1916)

1924: Released "Sherlock Jr" and "The Navigator"; the former considered by many as one of (if not) his finest films

1926: His best-known film "The General" opened to unfavorable critical response

1928: Last film released under the umbrella of "Buster Keaton Productions", "Steamboat Bill Jr"

1928: Signed contract with MGM

1928: First picture for MGM, "The Cameraman", well up to the standard of his best independent features

1929: Last silent feature, "Spite Marriage"

1929: Made first talking film as actor "The Hollywood Revue of 1929"

Appeared in eight MGM movies, ranging from mediocre to abysmal

1933: MGM contract terminated

1934: Made French film, "Le roi des Champs-Elyses"; never released in USA

1934: Signed contract with Educational Films for two-reelers

1936: Made "Grand Slam Opera", his favorite short for Educational

1937: Educational Films closed down

1937: Signed contract with MGM as gagman only

In the late 30s, a faulty refrigeration system in a film vault destroyed the negatives to all his silent movies

1938: Last directing assignments, three single-reelers for MGM ("Life in Sometown, USA", "Hollywood Handicap", "Streamlined Swing")

1939: Signed contract with Columbia; made 10 shorts over the next two years

1941: Toured USA in detective play, "The Gorilla"

1947: First appearance at Cirque Medrano, Paris (as Malec)

1949: Made TV debut re-enacting a scene from "The Butcher Boy" on "The Ed Wynn Show" (CBS)

1949: James Agee's essay in *Life* sparked renewed interest in silent films, particualrly the work of Keaton, Charlie Chaplin, Harold Lloyd and Harry Langdon

1950: Appeared as himself in Billy Wilder's "Sunset Boulevard"

1952: Acted in Chaplin's "Limelight" (only time the two appeared together)

1955: Met businessman Raymond Rohauer who would pull together a collection of prints of Keaton's silent films

1955: Actor James Mason, then-owner of the villa Keaton had built for former wife Natalie Talmadge in 1925, discovered a cache of film cans in a locked vault in a gardner's shed which contained prints of all of Keaton's silent features and many of his short comedies too, a veritable treasure trove from which Rohauer could begin his work

1956: Appeared in Michael Anderson's "Around the World in 80 Days"

1957: Paramount released "The Buster Keaton Story", starring Donald O'Connor

1959: Awarded a special Oscar for "his unique talents which brought immortal comedies to the screen"

1963: Acted in Stanley Kramer's "It a Mad, Mad, Mad, Mad World"

1965: Received standing ovation as special guest at the Venice Film Festival where "Film", a 22-minute short written for him by Samuel Beckett, premiered

1966: Last film appearances (excluding

archival footage) in Richard Lester's "A Funny Thing Happened on the Way to the Forum" and Luigi Scattini's "War Italian Style" (released in the USA in 1967)

1987: Last film unearthed and restored by Rohaurer (with Kevin Brownlow), the 1921 short "Hard Luck", premiered at London's Palladium

QUOTES:

While his mother gave him the birthname Joseph Frank Keaton, his father later changed it to Joseph Francis Keaton.

When scandal rocked Roscoe "Fatty" Arbuckle's world in 1921, Keaton remained a loyal friend to his mentor. Even though the courts absolved Arbuckle of any wrong-doing in Virginia Rappe's death, Hollywood refused to forgive him, but Keaton stood by him, providing periodic financial support until Arbuckle's death from a heart attack in 1933.

"My old man was an eccentric comic and as soon as I could take care of myself at all on my feet, he had slapshoes on me and big baggy pants. And he'd just start doing gags with me and especially kickin' me clear across the stage or taking me by the back of the neck and throwing me. By the time I got to be around seven or eight years old, we were called 'The Roughest Act That Was Ever in the History of the Stage' "—Buster Keaton.

"We used to get arrested every other week— that is, the old man would get arrested. Once they took me to the mayor of New York City, into his private office, with city physicians . . . and they stripped me to examine for broken bones and bruises. Finding none, the mayor gave me permission to work. The next time it happened, the following year, they sent me to Albany, to the governor of the state."—Buster Keaton (From "The Buster Keaton Myths", by Patricia Eliot Tobias in *Classic Images*)

"One of the first things I noticed was that whenever I smiled or let the audience suspect how much I was enjoying myself they didn't seem to laugh as much as usual. I guess people just never do expect any human mop, dishrag, beanbag, or football to be pleased by what is being done to him. At any rate, it was on purpose that I started looking miserable, humiliated, hounded and haunted, bedeviled, bewildered and at my wit's end."—Buster Keaton.

"I think I have had the happiest and luckiest of lives. Maybe this is because I never expected as much as I got . . . And when the knocks came, I felt it was no surprise. I had always known life was like that, full of uppercuts for the deserving and undeserving alike."—Buster Keaton.

The official website devoted to him can be accessed at www.busterkeaton.com

BIBLIOGRAPHY:

"My Wonderful World of Slapstick" Buster Keaton with Charles Samuels, 1960, Doubleday; memoirs

"Buster Keaton" J.P. Lebel; translated by P.D. Stovin, 1967, Zwemmer Books

"Buster Keaton" David Robinson, 1969, Indiana University Press

"The Silent Clowns" Walter Kerr, 1975, Alfred A. Knopf; has section on Keaton

"Keaton: The Silent Features Up Close" Daniel Moews, 1977, Citadel Press

"The Film Career of Buster Keaton" George Wead and George Lellis, 1997, Regrave Publishing Company

"Keaton: The Man Who Wouldn't Lie Down" Tom Dardis, 1979, Scribner

"The Complete Films of Buster Keaton" Jim Kline, 1993, Citadel Press

"Buster Keaton: A Bio-Bibliography" Joanna Rapf and Gary L. Green, 1995, Greenwood Press

"Buster Keaton: Cut to the Chase" Marion Meade, 1995; biography

"Buster Keaton Remembered" Eleanor Keaton, Jeffrey Vance, and Manoah Bowman, 2001; Harry N. Abrams Inc.

BORN: in Teheran, Iran, 06/22/1940

NATIONALITY: Iranian

EDUCATION: studied art at university

AWARDS: Cannes Film Festival Palme d'Or "Taste of Cherry" 1997; tied with Shohei Imamura's "The Eel"

Boston Society of Film Critics Award Best Foreign Film "Taste of Cherry" 1998

National Society of Film Critics Award Best Foreign Film "Taste of Cherry" 1998

Venice Film Festival Grand Prize "The Wind Will Carry Us" 1999

BIOGRAPHY

Called the grandfather of the Iranian New Wave of Cinema, director Abbas Kiarostami has drawn comparisons to Ingmar Bergman, Michelangelo Antonioni and Jean-Luc Godard, and no less a personage than Japanese auteur Akira Kurosawa considers him the rightful heir to Satyajit Ray's mantle as the greatest living practitioner of social realist filmmaking. His pictures depict a country far different from the medieval Iran of the nightly newscast. Underneath the surface orthodoxy of the present regime beats the heart of Persia—a cosmopolitan culture of long-standing artistic and literary sophistication. Working in the tradition of Italian neo-realism, Kiarostami captures a lyrical but concrete feel for the particulars of place and visual atmosphere and elicits strikingly natural performances from non-actors, blurring the boundaries between fiction and documentary to serve a simple, elegant painterly direction that elevates his stories to the level of poetic allegory.

The former graphic artist and illustrator accepted the invitation (offered partly because of his work designing children's books) to help found the cinema department of the Institute for the Intellectual Development of Children and Young Adults, which would fund his early movies and provide Kiarostami with a stable artistic home. His immersion in films about kids proved particularly fortuitous in the wake of the jihad as the child's world remained an open and fertile ground for metaphor, in contrast to the restrictions placed on other areas of dramatic inquiry. Though his failing marriage ("a revolution going on in my house") precluded his fleeing the country during the revolution of 1978–79, Kiarostami could argue that weathering the storm made him a better filmmaker, and indeed the artists who stayed at home have produced, on the whole, better films than their contemporaries who emigrated.

Kiarostami's first dramatic short, "Bread and Alley" (1970), in which his young protagonist confronts a vicious dog in an alley, demonstrated the esthetic qualities that would distinguish his later films, although he claims naivete led him to choose the difficult subject matter, not realizing how many hours it would take to coax the appropriate reactions from the beast. Once the Islamic Republic decided that a productive, culturally responsible film industry offered more benefits than the reactionary practice of torching cinemas, Kiarostami made his third feature and first since the revolution, "Where Is the Friend's House?" (1987), a simple tale of a rural boy trying to return a friend's notebook after school in order to save him from punishment, encompassing universal geographies of childhood, school, fear and honor. At the time it was winning him fame at Western film festivals, he had no idea it was the cornerstone of the trilogy that would secure his reputation.

After an earthquake devastated the area where he shot "Where Is the Friend's House?",

Kiarostami returned to the region in 1990 to ascertain if his young actors had survived. Tragically, they had not, but he turned this experience into the meditative, documentary-like fiction of "And Life Goes On" (1992), in which a director (played by an actor) and his son drive around the ravaged landscape searching for clues to the young boys' fate. In "Through the Olive Trees" (1994), Kiarostami recreated the making of "And Life Goes On" to serve as the backdrop to a tale of the unrequited love of two bit players, both victims of the quake. Playfully pointing up the artifice of the device, he has the actor portraying the behind-the-scenes director identify himself at the outset as the director, and later an assistant responding to a call from one of the actors brings water on to the set. Another scene shows the director shooting multiple takes, although that repetition enabled Kiarostami to get in an exchange where the Young Man is murmuring to the woman he loves, between the takes.

Kiarostami has also directed intriguing documentaries like "Case No 1, Case No 2" (1979), which so confounded officials of the new Islamic regime that they initially awarded it a prize before banning it, and "Homework" (1990), inspired by the difficulties his son was experiencing at school. His most famous documentary, "Close-Up" (1991), depicted the trial of a poor man (Sabzian) who had gained illicit entree into the upper classes by posing as the famous Iranian director Moshen Makhmalbaf. Kiarostami wryly blends in fiction, persuading Sabzian and the deceived family to reenact certain events that led to the arrest and arranging for the real Makhmalbaf to meet the pretender on the latter's release from prison. At one point the real Makhmalbaf visited the family to impress them in Sabzian's behalf, and the mother said to him when he was leaving: "Mr. Makhmalbaf, the other Mr. Makhmalbaf was more Makhmalbaf than you are." Kiarostami has never more brilliantly invoked his contention that "We can never get close to the truth except by lying."

Kiarostami's "Taste of Cherry" (1997), a lyrical, sun-drenched existential meditation on suicide—an Islamic taboo—ran afoul of the Iranian government which nearly prevented its inclusion at Cannes. When it went on to win the Palme d'Or, the official government reaction was one of icy silence, although his faux pas at the award ceremony caused a scandal at home. In the heat of the moment, Kiarostami disregarded a code of fundamentalist Islamic behavior by kissing presenter Catherine Deneuve on the cheek. His films are not wildly successful in Iran, but he understands the breadth of his increasingly Western audience, saying "I'm happy that only a few people see my films, a select few. It is not realistic to expect this kind of cinema to attract a larger audience." In addition to his own films, Kiarostami wrote the screenplays for Alireza Raisian's "Safar/The Journey" and Jafar Panahi's "Le Ballon blanc/The White Balloon" (both 1995), the latter winning the Camera d'Or at Cannes.—Written by Greg Senf

MILESTONES:

Worked for years doing commercials and graphic design

1969: Invited to help found the cinema department of the Institute for the Intellectual Development of Children and Young Adults in Tehran, Iran

1970: Directed first short film, "Bread and Alley"

1972: First feature, "The Traveler"

1977: Second feature, "The Report"; made outside the Institute's auspices

1979: His 53-minute documentary "Case No 1, Case No 2" condemned highschoolers who ratted on their neighbors; confused officials of the new Islamic regime first gave it an award, then banned it; also made without Institute money

1987: Third dramatic feature and first since the revolution, "Where Is the Friend's House?", told a simple tale of a rural boy trying to return a friend's notebook after school;

eventually became the first film of a trilogy inspired by a 1989 earthquake that devastated the area where it was filmed

1989: Locarno Film Festival screened "Where Is the Friend's House?", introducing him to a European audience

1990: The most famous of his documentaries, "Close-Up", depicted the trial of a poor man who gained illicit entree into the upper classes by posing as a famous film director

1992: Second film of trilogy, "And Life Goes On", was a documentary-like fictional tale of the filmmaker and his son searching to see if his actors had survived the earthquake; won the Rossellini prize at Cannes

1994: Third film of trilogy, "Through the Olive Trees", was his first film to gain major notice in the states

1995: Contributed to two group projects: "A Propos de Nice, La Suite", a tribute to the French filmmaker Jean Vigo who died at age 29, and "Lumiere and Company", featuring 39 international directors' work with the original Lumiere camera and homemade film stock

1995: Wrote the script for former assistant Jafar Panahi's "The White Baloon", which won the Camera d'Or at Cannes

1997: "Ta'm e Guilass/Taste of Cherry" won the Palme d'Or at Cannes

1999: Wrote, directed and edited "The Wind Will Carry Us/Le vent nous emportera"

2000: Exhibit of photographs featured at NYC's Andrea Rosen Gallery

QUOTES:

About why he wears dark glasses inside: "The retina in my left eye has remained open, and no matter what I do it remains open, and it lets too much light in. I have no idea what happened."—Abbas Kiarostami, *Fanfare*, April 6, 1998.

"In 'Through the Olive Trees' we were making a movie about making a movie, but there were moments in the film when we weren't 'doing' anything. I was even sometimes tempted to put a black leader in between the scenes—because I was constantly hunting for scenes in which there was 'nothing happening.' That nothingness I wanted to include in my film. Some places in a movie there should be nothing happening, like in 'Close-Up', where somebody kicks a can (in the street). But I needed that. I needed that nothing there . . .

"So when people tell me 'Your movie slows down here a little bit,' I love that! Because if it doesn't slow down, then I can't lift it again. And that's the problem with American movies: it's all lifting and lifting and lifting."—Abbas Kiarostami in *Film Comment*, July–August 1996.

About ending "And Life Goes On" and "Through the Olive Trees" with elaborately planned shot-sequences, what the French call plans-sequence: "When I use a longshot it distances me from cast and crew, and that affords them an opportunity to submerge themselves into the environment. That's also why I use a telephoto lens and pan with it. It's why I try to avoid tracking shots, because in tracking shots the whole crew stays too close to the actors and makes them self-conscious. It's my experience that when the camera is at a distance from the actors, they feel better, more like themselves, more able to relax into their characters. After the first one or two minutes of a shot-sequence, that's when the performances get interesting."—Kiarostami to *Film Comment*, July-August 1996.

Krzysztof Kieslowski

BORN: in Warsaw, Poland, 06/27/1941

DEATH: in Warsaw, Poland, 03/13/1996

NATIONALITY: Polish

EDUCATION: Lodz State Theatrical and Film, College Poland 1969; directed "Photograph" for TV while still a student

AWARDS: Gdansk Film Festival Award "Personel/The Staff" 1975

Mannheim Film Festival Award "Personel/The Staff" 1975

Gdansk Film Festival Special Jury Prize "Blizna/The Scar" 1976

Gdansk Film Festival Grand Prix "Amator/Camera Buff" 1979

Moscow Film Festival Grand Prize "Amator/Camera Buff" 1979

Chicago Film Festival Grand Prize "Amator/Camera Buff" 1980

Gdansk Film Festival Special Jury Prize "Spokoj/Calm" 1981

Gdansk Film Festival Silver Lion "Przypadek/The Incident" 1987

Cannes Film Festival Special Jury Prize "A Short Film about Killing" 1988

Felix Best Picture "A Short Film About Killing" 1988; first time "Felix" given by the newly formed European Film Society

National Society of Film Critics Award Best Foreign Film "The Double Life of Veronique" 1991

Cannes Film Festival FIRPESCI Prize "The Double Life of Veronique" 1991

Berlin Film Festival Silver Bear for Best Director "White" 1993

Los Angeles Film Critics Association Award Best Foreign Film "Red" 1994

New York Film Critics Circle Award Best Foreign Language Film "Red" 1994

National Society of Film Critics Award Best Foreign Film "Red" 1994

Chicago Film Critics Association Award Best Foriegn Film "Red", "White" and "Blue" 1994 cited for all three films that make up his "Three Colors" trilogy

Chicago Film Critics Association Award Best Foreign Film "The Decalogue" 1996 awarded posthumously

National Board of Review Best Foreign Film "Decalogue" 2000; awarded posthumously; cited with Ang Lee's "Crouching Tiger, Hidden Dragon"

BIOGRAPHY

A leading Polish director whose films are most influenced by those of his countryman Andrzej Wajda, Kieslowski began making documentaries which focused on the cultural, political and economic problems which sparked the emergence of the Solidarity movement. His award-winning 1979 feature, "Camera Buff", a slyly humorous, satirical look at life in a corrupt provincial factory, may have had personal dimensions for Kieslowski as it depicts a filmmaker who exposes himself to both attention and criticism when he progresses from home movies to committed social documentaries. Kieslowski learned firsthand that censorship may ride on the coattails of exposure with "Blind Chance" (1981), which considered three possibilities for Poland's political future as it explored three different outcomes springing from the premise of a student trying to catch a train. "Blind Chance" was unable to include a fourth story in which Poland throws out the Communist Party entirely, and the remaining film, still quite impressive, was banned for over five years before finally being released in 1987.

While the outcome of one "Blind Chance"

story was a blithely apolitical world (the student misses the train, and instead meets a sexy woman with whom he becomes involved), Kieslowski's subsequent "No End" (1984), while not forsaking wit entirely, nonetheless refused to be glibly satirical. The film's hero, a lawyer who represented many Poles oppressed by martial law, is dead at the film's opening.

Kieslowski's films always featured philosophical journeys into the human spirit and a concern for the moral and ethical implications of human action. Fittingly he confirmed his status as a major contemporary director with "Decalogue" (1988), an ambitious series of ten hour-long films funded by Polish TV, telling stories "based" on the Ten Commandments. (In "Decalogue 10", for instance, two brothers, an accountant and a punk rocker, both covet the stamp collection they have inherited from their father.) In the same year, Kieslowski expanded segments five and six into two features, "A Short Film About Killing" and "A Short Film About Love". Partially set, like the rest of the series, on a Warsaw housing estate, "A Short Film About Killing" is a grim and powerful tale drawing formal parallels between the act of murder and the workings of the criminal justice system.

Kieslowski ventured even closer to the realm of the human heart and soul and shifted further away from the political realities of contemporary Poland with his first international co-production, "The Double Life of Veronique" (1991). A more conventional art house item, the film, not surprisingly, gave his career greater international exposure than ever before as it strikingly and intensely paralleled the lives of two very similar women. With his acclaimed trilogy, "Blue" (1993), "White" (1994) and "Red" (1994), based on the tricolor themes of liberty, equality and fraternity, Kieslowski, proffering a densely plotted network of chance meetings and mutually destructive relationships, once again used the alienated female psyche as a vehicle for his recurrent social and metaphysical ruminations. Later in 1994, he announced his retirement from filmmaking. He suffered a heart attack in 1995 and died in March 1996 after undergoing bypass surgery.

MILESTONES:

1969: Short film directing debut, "Z miasta Lodzi/From the City of Lodz"

1973: Feature film writing and directing debut, "Pedestrian Subway"

1990: Contributed a segment to the 11-part anthology drama, "City Life"; each segment had a different director and Kieslowski's contribution was set in Warsaw and entitled "Seven Days a Week"

1991: First international feature co-production, "The Double Life of Veronique", a French-Polish co-production

1993: Began making trilogy of films interrelated thematically; first film, "Blue", followed by "White" and "Red"

1994: Announced retirement from filmmaking at the 1994 Cannes Film Festival

1995: Suffered a heart attack while at vacation home in northern Poland

QUOTES:

"He was a great artist, of great honesty and friendliness"—Polish director Krysztof Zanussi quoted by CNN on learning of Kieslowski's death.

BIBLIOGRAPHY:

"Double Lives, Second Chances: The Cinema of Krzystof Kieslowski" Annette Insdorf, 2000, Talk Miramax/Hyperion

Barbara Kopple

BORN: Barbara J. Kopple in Bear Mountain, New York, 07/30/1946

NATIONALITY: American

EDUCATION: attended college in West Virginia
Northeastern University, Boston, Massachusetts, clincial psychology; did not graduate; decided to return to NY
New School for Social Research, New York, New York; took course in cinema verite

AWARDS: Oscar Best Documentary Feature "Harlan County, USA" 1976
Los Angeles Film Critics Association Special Award 1977; tied with Charles Gary Allison
Oscar Best Documentary Feature "American Dream" 1990
Sundance Film Festival Grand Jury Prize (Documentary) "American Dream" 1991; tied with Jennie Livingston's "Paris Is Burning"
Sundance Film Festival Filmmakers Trophy (Documentary) "American Dream" 1991
Sundance Film Festival Audience Award (Documentary) "American Dream" 1991
International Documentary Award Distinguished Achievement Award "American Dream" 1991
Los Angeles Film Critics Association Award Best Documentary "American Dream" 1991
Directors Guild of America Award Outstanding Directorial Achievement in Documentary "American Dream" 1991
National Society of Film Critics Award Best Documentary "American Dream" 1992
Directors Guild of America Award Outstanding Directorial Achievement in Documentary "Fallen Champ: The Untold Story of Mike Tyson" 1993
American Film Institute Maya Deren Award 1994

CableACE Award Outstanding Sports Information Series "Real Sports with Bryant Gumble" 1996; shared award
Directors Guild of America Award Outstanding Directorial Achievement in Dramatic Series, Night "The Documentary" episode of "Homicide: Life on the Street" 1997
National Board of Review Award Best Documentary "Wild Man Blues" 1998
Broadcast Film Critics Association Award Best Feature Documentary "Wild Man Blues" 1998

BIOGRAPHY
Documentarist whose celebrated films have focused almost exclusively on the struggle of workers to form unions. Kopple began making films in her clinical psychology class while at college in West Virginia and went to live among her coal-mining subjects in Kentucky to film her Oscar-winning debut, "Harlan County, U.S.A." (1976). The film chronicles the miners' violent struggle to join the United Mine Workers union and the effect of the strike on the lives of them and their families. Praised for putting a human face on a political issue, it was one of 25 films chosen by the Library of Congress to be placed on its Film Registry in 1990.

In the late 1970s Kopple began work on her first non-documentary film, a fictionalized account of textile mill worker Crystal Lee Jordan's five-year struggle to unionize the factory where she worked; the project was aborted when it conflicted with Martin Ritt's "Norma Rae" (1979), loosely based on the same incidents. Kopple, however, used much of her research for the 1983 TV film "Keeping On", also about textile mill workers' attempts to organize.

Kopple's second documentary, "American Dream" (1990), which tracks the course of a bitter meat-packers' strike at the Hormel plant in Minnesota, became legendary for the length of time it took to complete. While management in "American Dream" behaves somewhat monolithically, Kopple also uses her omnipresent camera to capture the self-doubts of, and differences between, the striking laborers. Compared to "Harlan County", "American Dream" finds a labor movement badly divided, unsure whether to trust leadership that seems both too charismatic and less than pragmatic. Kopple's film had its world premiere at the 1991 Sundance Film Festival, where it won a special jury prize, the filmmaker's trophy and the audience award as most popular film. It also earned Kopple her second Oscar for best documentary in 1990.

FAMILY:

uncle: Murray Burnett. Playwright; co-author of "Everybody Comes to Rick's", play on which the screenplay for "Casablanca" was based

son: Nicholas Perry. Born c. 1981

MILESTONES:

Raised in Scarsdale, New York

Began making films in a clinical psychology class in college

Worked professionally as an editor, soundwoman and camerawoman on documentary films often for the Maysles brothers

Was camerawoman on a video about the Young Republicans for Nixon at the Republican convention and soundwoman on film about the Year of the Woman at the Democratic convention

1972: Was one of the 18 anonymous directors of "Winter Solider"

1972: Moved to Harlan County in Kentucky to film union struggle at the Brookside mine

1976: Produced and directed documentary, "Harlan County, USA"; film shown at the New York Film Festival; cost $350,000

1978: Announced fictional feature project under the working title, "Crystal Lee", based on Crystal Lee Jordan's struggle to unionize workers in J. P. Stevens textile mill in Roanoke Rapids NC and her gradual politicization over

a five year period; Kopple was to produce and direct; initial script was by Nancy Dowd and Rip Torn had been signed to portray the union organizer; Kopple had researched working conditions when she began a two-week stint as a towel folder in a Southern mill in March 1978, earning $2.25/hour for a ten-hour day

1979: "Crystal Lee" abandoned when Martin Ritt began production on "Norma Rae", loosely based on the same woman and the same mill workers' strike

1979: Co-directed documentary footage of concert film, "No Nukes", with Haskell Wexler

1983: Directed first fiction film and first TV movie, "Keeping On" for PBS's "American Playhouse", which dealt with unionization of textile mill workers in the south

1993: Produced and directed "Fallen Champ: The Untold Story of Mike Tyson," a rare primetime documentary for NBC-TV for which she was given creative control

1998: Earned widespread praise for "Wild Man Blues", a documentary about the 1996 European tour of Woody Allen's jazz band

1998: Executive produced and directed "Friends for Life: Living With AIDS" (The DIsney Channel)

1999: Signed to make fictional feature directorial debut "In the Boom Boom Room", adapted from David Rabe's play

2000: Helmed the documentary "My Generation" Directed documentary set in the Hamptons (lensed 2001) for ABC TV; set to air in 2002

2002: Produced an HBO documentary "American Standoff"

QUOTES:

"My overall goal, is to let people speak and let them be heard, because what they are saying is really important, as important or more important than anything President Bush has to say. It's to film stories about people that you wouldn't ordinarily get to see. To think that these people's stories are going to be shown, that other people will hear them, as a film maker that gives me a tremendous amount of strength to carry on."—Barbara Kopple (quoted in *New York Times*, March 24, 1992).

"I knew there was a poignant story out there about what was happening in Middle America to people who believed in the American dream, the American work ethic, the whole notion of upward mobility, and who were watching those beliefs become unraveled. We had no idea of the kind of, not physical brutality, but mental brutality people would endure to try to keep decent jobs with decent pay, the kinds of things they learned to believe in all their lives."—Barbara Kopple discussing "American Dream" (quoted in *New York Times*, March 24, 1992).

Kopple also produced "Hurricane Irene", a high-definition videotape of an international peace festival filmed in Japan and featuring live performances by Jackson Browne and Peter Gabriel. She also produced and directed "Civil Rights: The Struggle Continues" (c. 1989), a video documentary about the 25th-anniversary activities held in commemoration of the civil rights workers James Chaney, Michael Schwerner and Andrew Goodman slain in Mississippi in 1964.

"Harlan County, USA" was named by Congress to the National Film Registry designating it an American classic (1990).

Stanley Kubrick

BORN: in Bronx, New York, 07/26/1928

DEATH: in Hertfordshire, England, 03/06/1999

NATIONALITY: American

EDUCATION: William H. Taft High School, Bronx, New York, 1946; classmates included singer Eydie Gorme

City College, New York, New York; school now known as City College of the City University of New York

Columbia University, New York, New York; enrolled as a non-matriculating student while working at *Look* magazine

AWARDS: Locarno Film Festival Golden Sail Award "Killer's Kiss" 1959

New York Film Critics Circle Award Best Director "Dr. Strangelove or: How I Learned to Stop Worrying and Love the Bomb" 1964

Writers Guild of America Award Best-Written American Comedy "Dr. Strangelove or: How I Learned to Stop Worrying and Love the Bomb" 1964; shared award

British Film Academy Award Best Film "Dr. Strangelove or: How I Learned to Stop Worrying and Love the Bomb" 1964

British Film Academy Award Best British Film "Dr. Strangelove or: How I Learned to Stop Worrying and Love the Bomb" 1964

British Film Academy United Nations Award "Dr. Strangelove or: How I Learned to Stop Worrying and Love the Bomb" 1964

Oscar Best Special Effects "2001: A Space Odyssey" 1968

New York Film Critics Circle Award Best Motion Picture "A Clockwork Orange" 1971

New York Film Critics Circle Award Best Director "A Clockwork Orange" 1971

National Board of Review Award Best Director "Barry Lyndon" 1975; tied with Robert Altman ("Nashville")

BAFTA Award Best Director "Barry Lyndon" 1975

Directors Guild of America D. W. Griffith Award 1997; 26th recipient of the award established in 1953

Venice Film Festival Golden Lion for Career Achievement 1997

BAFTA Britannia Award 1999; presented posthumously; BAFTA announced that the award would be renamed in Kubrick's honor

BAFTA Academy Fellowship 2000; presented posthumously; Michael Caine was also cited

BIOGRAPHY

One of the most consistently fascinating filmmakers of the last four decades, Stanley Kubrick saw his work praised and damned with equal vigor. Just as his singularly brilliant visual style won him great acclaim, his unconventional sense of narrative often elicited critical scorn. Above all, he remained an unique artist in a medium dominated by repetition and imitation. If his ambitious vision had at times exceeded his capacity to satisfy the demands of mainstream filmmaking, this chink in his armor was perhaps a strength in disguise, and only served to highlight the distinctiveness of Kubrick's cinema.

After some success as a photographer for Look magazine in the late 1940s, the young Kubrick produced and sold several documentaries before attempting a pair of self-financed low-budget features—"Fear and Desire" (1953) and "Killer's Kiss" (1955), which, in scenes like the warehouse finale of the latter, already gave hints of the disturbing images to come. Working with producer James B. Harris, Kubrick was able to graduate to professional cast and crew with his next effort, "The Killing" (1956), a well-paced, assured, cynical drama about a race track heist. At a time when independent filmmakers were still relatively rare, critics justly began to take notice.

"Paths of Glory" (1957) marked Kubrick's emergence as a major director. This WWI saga is a sharp, intelligent, superbly acted indictment of military practice and psychology as well as a powerful piece of filmmaking that synthesized the lessons the director had learned about composition and camera movement. Although his next effort plays today as a more personal effort on producer-star Kirk Douglas's part than it does on Kubrick's, the director showed that he could function within mainstream Hollywood with "Spartacus" (1960), his first—and only—work-for-hire. Critics praised the visual aspects of this widescreen, Technicolor epic a notch above the standard super-spectacle of the 1950s. As he had in "Paths of Glory", Kubrick depicted the "weird disparity" between the aesthetics of warfare and its human consequences.

Kubrick left for England in 1961, searching for greater independence and greater control of his films. He has worked there ever since, developing and producing meticulously crafted yet markedly different films. "Lolita" (1962) was an adaptation of Vladimir Nabokov's controversial novel about a middle-aged man's infatuation with a 12-year-old girl. Though Kubrick has since complained that over-zealous censors kept him from exploring the story in appropriately lubricious detail (two years were even added to Lolita's age), the film stands today as a superb example of understated, double entendre comedy.

The ironic touch displayed in "Lolita" exploded to cosmic proportions with "Dr Strangelove or: How I Learned to Stop Worrying and Love the Bomb" (1964), perhaps the most deliciously satirical comedy of the last three decades. (Ironically, the project began as a serious thriller about the possibility of nuclear Armageddon.) Kubrick's dark laughter at man's penchant for destroying himself reinforced what some reviewers had noted at the time of his overly analytical "The Killing", that he was a "cold" director, and the reputation has followed him to this day.

Despite some moral backlash, the successes of "Lolita" and "Strangelove" earned Kubrick the freedom to choose his own subjects and, more importantly, to exert total control over the filmmaking process, a rare freedom for any director. The first product of this license was the science-fiction classic (and quintessential late 60s "head" movie), "2001: A Space Odyssey"

(1968). Five years in the making, this film redefined the boundaries of the genre and established visual conventions, filmic metaphors and special effects technology that have remained standards for the industry well into the 90s. As visually hypnotic as it was daring in narrative (little dialogue, no final explanations, a time span of eons), "2001" made Kubrick a cultural hero. Despite initial mixed reviews, it has proven to be as stylistically influential as any film released in the last 30 years.

Further cementing his anti-establishment reputation, Kubrick followed "2001" with another futuristic work, "A Clockwork Orange" (1971), adapted from the novel by Anthony Burgess. No critic could take an uncommitted stance toward this film about a violent and amoral punk (played by Malcolm McDowell), whose ruthless behavior is reconditioned by the—equally diabolical—state. Kubrick's camera moved with an audacity unrivaled in contemporary cinema, causing fans to gush unequivocally and detractors to decry what David Thomson called "his reluctance to let a plain or simple shot pass under his name." Anyway you sliced it, there was no denying who was in charge of a Kubrick film.

"Barry Lyndon" (1975) was a bold attempt to bring modern techniques to bear upon a narrative set in the 18th century. Kubrick spent as much technical effort and expertise recreating the lighting and imagery of Thackeray's novel as he had done inventing a future in his two previous films. Although a commercial failure, "Barry Lyndon" fits logically into the Kubrick oeuvre, a dour fable of humanity trapped in the same determinism that had colored his previous work. In that respect he is a latter-day Sophocles, whose characters can never escape their inexorable fate.

Kubrick's adaptation of Stephen King's horror novel "The Shining" (1980), is perhaps his most autobiographical work. He had long ago retreated to his Overlook Hotel (Chilwickbury Manor in Buckinghamshire) just as the writer and his family do in the film. Jack Torrance's isolation is Kubrick's, and by choosing a blocked artist as his main character, he shows his fear at the specter of being unable to create. His typically "cold" analysis may have robbed the film of the trademark terror horror fans expect, but "The Shining" is funny, endlessly interesting and pure Kubrick, with Jack the linear descendant of that ape in "2001", brandishing his bone as weapon.

Kubrick's Vietnam movie, his adaptation of Gustav Hasford's "Full Metal Jacket" (1987), is essentially two movies in one. The first section, Marine basic training on Parris Island that culminates in the suicide of Private Gomer Pyle (Vincent D'Onofrio), is so powerful that it simply overwhelms the second half, where Kubrick's sets and East London locale make a poor substitute for Southeast Asia. Though compelling, well-acted and certainly in keeping with his recurring theme of dehumanization, "Full Metal Jacket" paled in comparison to the tropical splendor of Francis Ford Coppola's "Apocalypse Now" (1979), proving that sometimes, in the interest of verisimilitude, a director needs to go farther than a two-hour drive from home.

The time needed for Kubrick to recharge his creative batteries became increasingly long. Five years passed between "Barry Lyndon" and "The Shining", then seven before "Full Metal Jacket", and more than ten years would pass until Kubrick allowed his next film "Eyes Wide Shut" (1999), starring Tom Cruise and Nicole Kidman, to meet the gaze of the public. True to form, the pedantic filmmaker labored excessively, assigning great importance to each and every image the camera would record, and endlessly reshooting scenes until achieving the exact look he desired. His control over every aspect of his films assured his legacy as a great craftsman, but his isolation and monomaniacal intensity may have obscured his genius. Kubrick once said, "I think that one of the problems with 20th-century art is its preoccupation with subjectivity and originality at the expense of everything else." If he had chosen not to reveal much of himself in his films in order to give us the "everything else", we must accept his enormous gifts while lamenting the high price of obsession.

MILESTONES:

1945: Photograph taken by Kubrick of a newsdealer on the day of President Franklin Roosevelt's death bought by *Look* magazine; Kubrick subsequently hired as a photographer for the magazine and worked there from 1946–1950

1951: First short film as director (also screenwriter, director of photography and producer), the 16-minute documentary "Day of the Fight", about boxer Walter Cartier whom Kubrick had photographed for *Look* magazine

1953: First medium-length film as director (also director of photography), the documentary "The Seafarers"

1953: First feature film as director (also director of photography, editor and producer), "Fear and Desire"

1955: Founded (with James B. Harris) Harris-Kubrick Productions; partnership lasted through "Lolita" (1962)

1956: Scripted first Harris-Kubrick production "The Killing" from Lionel White's thriller "Clean Break"

1957: Adapted (along with Calder Willingham and Jim Thompson) Humphrey Cobb's World War I novel "Paths of Glory", starring Kirk Douglas; as an indictment of war, compared to Lewis Milestone's "All Quiet on the Western Front" and Jean Renoir's "La Grande Illusion"

1957: Signed contract with MGM but released after making no films

1960: Hired by Marlon Brando to direct the Western "One-Eyed Jacks"; left the project after six months; Brando went on to direct (date approximate)

1960: Replaced Anthony Mann as the director of "Spartacus", at the time the most expensive movie ever made in America

1961: Moved to Great Britain, which stood in for America in "Lolita"; based in London ever since

1963: Scripted along with Terry Southern and Peter George from George's novel "Red Alert" the apocalyptic black comedy "Dr Strangelove, or How I Learned to Stop Worrying and Love the Bomb"; also directed, produced and served as special photographic effects designer; Kubrick garnered Academy Award nominations for Best Picture, Best Director and Best Screenplay

1968: Wrote, produced, directed and designed the effects for "2001: A Space Odyssey"; received Oscar for Best Special Effects and nominations as Best Director and for Best Screenplay

1971: Produced, directed and adapted "A Clockwork Orange" from the Anthony Burgess novel; received Academy Award nominations for Best Screenplay and Best Picture and as Best Director

1975: Last feature for five years, "Barry Lyndon"; wrote, produced and directed; again personally nominated for Best Picture, Best Director and Best Screenplay

1980: Returned to features with screen adaptation of Stephen King's "The Shining"

1987: First feature in seven years, "Full Metal Jacket", based on Gustav Hasford's novel "The Short Timers"; shared an Academy Award nomination for Best Screenplay

1996: Announced casting of Tom Cruise and Nicole Kidman in feature "Eyes Wide Shut" and began lensing in November; completed shooting in 1998; film released posthumously in the summer of 1999

2001: "A.I. Artificial Intelligence", a film based on his unproduced screenplay, written and directed by Steven Spielberg released

AFFILIATION: Jewish

QUOTES:

"I'm distrustful in delegating authority, and my distrust is usually well founded."—Stanley Kubrick.

"I tried with only limited success to make the film as real as possible but I was up against a pretty dumb script which was rarely faithful to what is known about Spartacus. If I ever needed convincing of the limits of persuasion a director can have on a film where someone else is the producer and he is merely the highest paid member of the crew, 'Spartacus' provided proof to last a lifetime."—Stanley Kubrick quoted in "World Film Directors" Volume II 1945-1985, edited by John Wakeman (New York: H. W. Wilson Company.)

"There is no doubt that there's a deep emotional relationship between man and his machines, which are his children. The machine is beginning to assert itself in a very profound way, even attracting affection and obsession.

"There is a sexiness to beautiful machines. The smell of a Nikon camera. The feel of an Italian sports car, or a beautiful tape recorder. . . . Man has always worshiped beauty, and I think there's a new kind of beauty afoot in the world."—Stanley Kubrick to *The New York Times* in 1968, at the time of the release of "2001."

"He does not believe in biting the hand that might strangle him."—critic Hollis Alpert.

"He is a brilliant filmmaker, but he does not do well in the final test—as a man."—"A Clockwork Orange" star Malcolm McDowell on Kubrick.

" . . . I think the enemy of the filmmaker is not the intellectual or the member of the mass public, but the kind of middlebrow who has neither the intellectual apparatus to analyze and clearly define what is meant nor the honest emotional reaction of the mass film audience member. And unfortunately, I think that a great many of these people in the middle are occupied in writing about films. I think that it is a monumental presumption on the part of film reviewers to summarize in one terse, witty, clever *Time Magazine* -style paragraph what the intention of the film is. That kind of review is usually very superficial, unless it is a truly bad film, and extremely unfair."—Stanley Kubrick to Robert Emmett Ginna from an unpublished 1960 interview (from *Entertainment Weekly*, April 9, 1999).

"He didn't like stupidity, razzmatazz, celebrity. Stanley refused to accept that drainage of his spirit."—Novelist and friend David Cornwall (aka John Le Carre), quoted in *Newsweek*, March 22, 1999.

"He not only understood humanity, he understood it too well. He had no love of humanity. He was a misanthrope."—Alexander Walker, author of "Stanley Kubrick Directs."

BIBLIOGRAPHY:

"The Making of Kubrick's 2001" Jerome Agel (editor), 1970

"Kubrick" Michel Cimet, 1980

"Stanley Kubrick: A Guide to References and Resources" Wallace Coylee, 1980

"The Films of Stanley Kubrick" Daniel De Vries, 1973

"A Cinema of Loneliness" Robert Philip Kolker, 1980; Kubrick discussed along with other American filmmakers of the 1970s

"Stanley Kubrick: Inside a Film Artist's Maze" Thomas Allen Nelson, 1982

"Stanley Kubrick: A Film Odyssey" Gene D. Philips, 1975

"Stanley Kubrick: A Biography" Vincent LoBrutto, 1996, Donald I. Fine, Inc.

"Perspectives on Stanley Kubrick" Mario Falsetto (editor), 1997, G.K. Hall & Co.

"Stanley Kubrick Directs" Alexander Walker, 1999, W.W. Norton & Co.

"Eyes Wide Open: A Memoir of Stanley Kubrick" Frederic Raphael, 1999, Ballantine

"Kubrick" Michael Herr, 2000, Grove Press

"Kubrick: Inside a Film Artist's Maze" Thomas Allen Nelson, 2000, Indiana University Press

BORN: in Omori, Tokyo, 03/23/1910

DEATH: in Tokyo, Japan, 09/06/1998

NATIONALITY: Japanese

EDUCATION: Morimura Gakuen Japan; primary school

Kuroda Japan primary school; class president; introduced to fine arts by school principal, Seiji Tachikawa

Keika Middle School Japan, 1922–27; graduated; failed course in compulsory military training

Doshusha School of Western Painting, Japan

AWARDS: Ministry of Education Award second prize "Shizuku Nari/All is Quiet" screenplay

Ministry of Education Award first prize "Yuki/Snow" screenplay

Second Place in *Kinema Jumpo*'s best films "Asu o tsukuru hitobito/Those Who Make Tomorrow" 1946

Sixth Place in *Kinema Jumpo*'s best films "Subarashiki nichiyobi/One Wonderful Sunday" 1947

Mainichi Award Best Director "Subarashiki nichiyobi/One Wonderful Sunday" and "Waga seishun ni kuinashi/No Regrets for Our Youth" 1947

First Place in *Kinema Jumpo*'s best films "Yoidori tenshi/Drunken Angel" 1948

Ministry of Education Award "Yoidori tenshi/Drunken Angel" 1948

Mainichi Award Best Picture "Yoidori tenshi/Drunken Angel" 1948

Seventh Place in *Kinema Jumpo*'s best films "Shizukanaru ketto/The Quiet Duel" 1949

Third Place in *Kinema Jumpo*'s best films "Nora inu/Stray Dog" 1949

Motion Picture Art Magazine/Eiga Geijutsu's best films first place "Nora inu/Stray Dog" 1949

Ministry of Education Award "Nora inu/Stray Dog" 1949

Fifth Place in *Kinema Jumpo*'s best films "Rashomon" 1950

Tokyo Motion Picture Reviewers' Club Blue Ribbon "Rashomon" 1950, screenplay

National Board of Review Award Best Foreign Film "Rashomon" 1951

National Board of Review Award Best Director "Rashomon" 1951

First Place in *Kinema Jumpo*'s best films "Ikiru" 1952

Mainichi Film Concours Award Best Picture "Ikiru" 1952

Mainichi Film Concours Award Best Screenplay "Ikiru" 1952

Ministry of Education Award "Ikiru" 1952

Berlin Film Festival Golden Laurel "Ikiru" 1951

Venice Film Festival Silver Lion Award "Shichinin no samurai/Seven Samurai" 1954; award shared with Kazan's "On the Waterfront," Fellini's "La Strada" and Mizoguchi's "Sansho the Bailiff"

Berlin Film Festival International Delegate-Jury Prize of the Berlin Senate "Ikiru" 1954 one of three films cited

Third Place in *Kinema Jumpo*'s best films "Shichinin no samurai/Seven Samurai" 1954

Fourth Place in *Kinema Jumpo*'s best films "Kumonosu-jo/The Throne of Blood" 1957

Tenth Place in *Kinema Jumpo*'s best films "Donzoko" 1957

Second Place in *Kinema Jumpo*'s best films "Kakushi toride no san-akunin/Hidden Fortress" 1958

Berlin Film Festival Silver Bear Best Director "Kakushi toride no san-akunin/Hidden Fortress" 1959

Tokyo Motion Picture Reviewers' Club Blue Ribbon "Kakushi toride no san-akunin/Hidden Fortress" 1959

NHK Network Award "Kakushi toride no san-akunin/Hidden Fortress" 1959

Second Place in *Kinema Jumpo*'s best films "Yojimbo" 1961

Fifth Place in *Kinema Jumpo*'s best films "Tsubaki Sanjuro/Sanjuro" 1962

Venice Film Festival Catholic Film Office Award "Akahige" 1965

First Place in *Kinema Jumpo*'s best films "Akahige/Red Beard" 1965

Tokyo Motion Picture Reviewers' Club Blue Ribbon "Akahige/Red Beard" 1965

Mainichi Concours Award Best Picture "Akahige/Red Beard" 1965

Manila Film Festival Ramon Magsaysay Memorial Award "Akahige/Red Beard" 1965

Seventh Moscow International Film Festival Special Prize "Dodes'kaden" 1971

Fifth Place in *Kinema Jumpo*'s best films "Dersu Uzala" 1975

Federation of International Film Critics Award "Dersu Uzala" 1975

Ninth Moscow International Film Festival Gold Medal "Dersu Uzala" 1975

Order of the Sacred Treasure 1976; given by Japanese government for being a "Person of Cultural Merits;" first given in field

David di Donatello Prize "Dersu Uzala" 1977

European Film Academy 1978; for his "Humanistic Contribution to Society in Film Production"

Cannes Film Festival Palm d'Or "Kagemusha" 1980; co-winner

BAFTA Award Best Foreign Film "Kagemusha" 1980

Cesar Best Foreign Film "Kagemusha" 1981

Cannes Film Festival Special Award 1982; given by the Cannes Film Festival Committee in honor of their 35th anniversary

New York Film Critics Circle Award Best Foreign Film "Ran" 1985

Los Angeles Film Critics Association Award Best Foreign Film "Ran" 1985; tied with Luis Puenzo for "The Official Story"

Los Angeles Film Critics Association Career Achievement Award 1985

National Society of Film Critics Award Best Foreign Film "Ran" 1985

National Board of Review Award Best Director "Ran" 1985

National Board of Review Award Best Foreign Film "Ran" 1985

BAFTA Award Best Film "Ran" 1985

Directors Guild of America Golden Jubilee Special Award 1986 cited with Federico Fellini and the late Oscar Micheaux

Honorary Oscar 1989 "for his cinematic accomplishments that have inspired, delighted, enriched and entertained worldwide audiences and influenced filmmakers throughout the world"

Association of Asian Pacific American Artists Lifetime Achievement Award 1991 also known as the Jimmie Award

Directors Guild of America D. W. Griffith Award 1992 for career achievement

BIOGRAPHY

Akira Kurosawa is unquestionably the best known Japanese filmmaker in the West. This can perhaps be best explained by the fact that he is not so much a Japanese or a Western filmmaker, but that he is a "modern" filmmaker. Like postwar Japan itself, he combines the ancient traditions with a distinctly modern, Western twist.

Kurosawa got his start in films following an education which included study of Western painting, literature and political philosophy. His early films were made under the stringent auspices of the militaristic government then in power and busily engaged in waging the Pacific war. While one can detect aspects of the pro-war ideology in early works like "The Men Who Tread on the Tiger's Tail" (1945) or, more especially, "Sanshiro Sugata" (1943), these films are notable more for stylistic experimentation than pro-war inspiration.

Before he had a chance to mature under these

conditions, though, Kurosawa, like all of Japan, experienced the American occupation. Under its auspices he produced pro-democracy films, the most appealing of which is "No Regrets for Our Youth" (1946), interestingly his only film which has a woman as its primary protagonist. His ability to make films that could please Japanese militarists or American occupiers should not be taken as either cultural schizophrenia or political fence-sitting, for at their best these early films have a minimal value as propaganda, and tend to reveal early glimpses of the major themes which would dominate his cinema. His style, too, is an amalgam, a deft dialectic of the great pictorial traditions of the silent cinema, the dynamism of the Soviet cinema (perhaps embodied in the Japanese-Russian friendship dramatized in his "Dersu Uzala" 1975) and the Golden Age of Hollywood filmmaking (which explains how easily his work has been remade by American directors).

Above all, Kurosawa is a modern filmmaker, portraying (in films from "Drunken Angel" 1948 to "Rhapsody in August" 1991) the ethical and metaphysical dilemmas characteristic of postwar culture, the world of the atomic bomb, which has rendered certainty and dogma absurd. The consistency at the heart of Kurosawa's work is his exploration of the concept of heroism. Whether portraying the world of the wandering swordsman, the intrepid policeman or the civil servant, Kurosawa focuses on men faced with ethical and moral choices. The choice of action suggests that Kurosawa's heroes share the same dilemma as Albert Camus' existential protagonists—Kurosawa did adapt Dostoevsky's existential novel "The Idiot" in 1951 and saw the novelist as a key influence in all his work—but for Kurosawa the choice is to act morally, to work for the betterment of one's fellow men.

Perhaps because Kurosawa experienced the twin devastations of the great Kanto earthquake of 1923 and WWII, his cinema focuses on times of chaos. From the destruction of the glorious Heian court society that surrounds the world of "Rashomon" (1950) to the never-ending destruction of the civil war era of the 16th century that gives "The Seven Samurai" (1954) its dramatic impetus, to the savaged Tokyo in the wake of US bombing raids in "Drunken Angel" (1948), to the ravages of the modern bureaucratic mind-set that pervade "Ikiru" (1952) and "The Bad Sleep Well" (1960): Kurosawa's characters are situated in periods of metaphysical eruption, threatened equally by moral destruction and physical annihilation; in a world of existential alienation in which God is dead and nothing is certain. But it is his hero who, living in a world of moral chaos, in a vacuum of ethical and behavioral standards, nevertheless chooses to act for the public good.

Kurosawa was dubbed "Japan's most Western director" by critic Donald Richie at a time when few Westerners had seen many of the director's films and at a time when the director was in what should have been merely the middle of his career. Richie felt that Kurosawa was Western in the sense of being an original creator, as distinct from doing the more rigidly generic or formulaic work of many Japanese directors during the height of Kurosawa's creativity. And indeed some of the director's best work can be read as "sui generis," drawing upon individual genius such as few filmmakers in the history of world cinema have. "Rashomon," "Ikiru" and "Record of a Living Being" (1955) challenge easy classification and are stunning in their originality of style, theme and setting.

Furthermore, Kurosawa's attractions to the West were apparent in both content and form. His adaptations from Western literature, although not unique in Japanese cinema, are among his finest films, with "Throne of Blood" (1957, from "Macbeth") and "Ran" (1985, from "King Lear") standing among the finest versions of Shakespeare ever put on film. And if Western high culture obviously appealed to him, so did more popular, even pulp forms, as evinced by critically acclaimed adaptations of Dashiell Hammett's "Red Harvest" to fashion "Yojimbo" (1961) and Ed McBain's "King's Ransom" to create the masterful "High and Low" (1962). Of course such borrowings show not only the richness of Kurosawa's thinking and his work but also just how notions of "genius" require a complex understanding of the contexts in which the artist works.

Indeed, for all of the Western adaptations and the attraction to Hollywood and Soviet-style montage, Kurosawa's status as a Japanese filmmaker can never be doubted. If, as has often been remarked, his period films have similarities with Hollywood westerns, they are nevertheless accurately drawn from the turmoil of Japanese history. If he has been attracted to Shakespearean theater, he has equally been drawn to the rarefied world of Japanese Noh drama. And if Kurosawa is a master of dynamic montage, he is equally the master of the Japanese trademarks of the long take and gracefully mobile camera.

Thus to see Kurosawa as somehow a "Western" filmmaker is not only to ignore the traditional bases for much of his style and many of his themes, but to do a disservice to the nature of film style and culture across national boundaries. Kurosawa's cinema may be taken as paradigmatic of the nature of modern changing Japan, of how influences from abroad are adapted, transformed and made new by the genius of the Japanese national character, which remains distinctive yet ever-changing. And if Kurosawa tends to focus on an individual hero, a man forced to choose a mode of behavior and a pattern of action in the modern Western tradition of the loner-hero, it is only in recognition of global culture that increasingly centralizes, bureaucratizes and dehumanizes.

MILESTONES:

1928: Painting accepted by Nitten exhibition

1929: Joined Japan's Proletarian Artists' League in order to study new art movements

1932: Left Artists' League

1936: Answered newspaper ad and was hired by Photo Chemical Laboratory (later Toho Motion Picture Company) as assistant director, worked with mentor Kajiro Yamamoto

1936–1941: Worked way up with Yamamoto's crew from third assistant to chief assistant and B-group second unit director at PCL; also learned editing and dubbing techniques

1941: First screenplay published, "A German at the Daruma Temple"

Wrote seven scripts that won awards but were not filmed and were often censored

1943: Film directing debut with "Sugata Sanshiro/Sanshiro Sugata"

1948: Made first film starring Toshiro Mifune, "Yoidore Tenshi/Drunken Angel"

1950: Directed a film, "Rashomon", which received widespread international acclaim not only for his own films but for much of Japanese cinema as a whole

1959: Gave first press conference; formed, Kurosawa Productions, first independent company run by working director

Co-founded Film Art Association/Eiga Geijutsu Kyokai

Co-founded independent production company, "Yonki no Kai/The Four Musketeers" in the late 1960s

1966: Joseph E. Levine of Embassy Pictures announced the upcoming production of Kurosawa's screenplay "Runaway Train"; differences between Levine and Kurosawa Productions' producer Tetsuro Aoyagi brought project to halt; film was finally made by director Andrei Konchalovsky, working from a re-written version of Kurosawa's original in 1985

1970: Shot first color picture as director, "Dodes'ka-den", in 28 days

1971: Hospitalized in ill health, attempted suicide on December 22

1975: Directed "Dersu Uzala"; received Best Foreign-Language Film Academy Award

1978: Traveled to USA; foreign rights to "Kagemusha" bought by 20th Century Fox

1985: Helmed "Ran", inspired by Shakespeare's

"Macbeth"; nominated for four Oscars including Best Director

1985: Subject of Chris Marker's documentary "AK: Portrait of Akira Kurosawa"

1985: Scripted "Runaway Train", directed by Andrei Konchalovsky

1986: Made Fellow of British Film institute

1989: Awarded honorary Oscar for lifetime achievement

1990: Wrote and directed "Akira Kurosawa's Dreams"

1991: Helmed "Rhapsody in August", featuring Richard Gere; also scripted

1993: Final film, "Madadayo"; released in USA in 2000

QUOTES:

Kurosawa has seen several of his films remade in the West. His epic "Seven Samurai" (1954) was converted into John Sturges's popular Western, "The Magnificent Seven" (1960); "Rashomon" (1950) was "westernized" as "The Outrage" (1964) by director Martin Ritt; Italian director Sergio Leone unofficially borrowed the plot of "Yojimbo" (1961) for his "spaghetti Western" "A Fistful of Dollars" (1964) and

George Lucas has acknowledged the influence of Kurosawa's "The Hidden Fortress" (1958) on his "Star Wars" trilogy.

"When I watch my movies I still find only a few parts which are truly film. I've never made a film where I though that from beginning to end, it was all a film. So I'm still hoping to make one." (*Hollywood Reporter*, 10/2/1992)

Honored at the first London Film Festival together with John Ford, Rene Clair and Vittorio De Sica as the movie directors most contributiong to film and art in 1957.

Received the National Medal with Laurel (together with Charles Chaplin and John Ford) presented by President Tito of Yugoslavia (1973).

Decorated with the French Legion of Honor (c. 1982)

"Rashomon" honored as the "Golden Lion Among Golden Lions" by *La Republicia* newspaper on the anniversary of the Venice Film Festival.

BIBLIOGRAPHY:

"Something Like an Autobiography" Akira Kurosawa, 1982; covers Kurosawa's life up through "Rashomon"

Emir Kusturica

BORN: in Sarajevo, Bosnia-Herzegovina, 11/24/1954

NATIONALITY: Serbian

EDUCATION: FAMU Prague, Czechoslovakia, film direction, 1978; studied under Jiri Menzel; met Vilko Filac, future cinematographer on all of his films through "Underground"

AWARDS: International Student Film Festival Karlovy Vary First Prize "Guernica" 1978

Venice Film Festival Golden Lion "Do You Remember Dolly Bell?" 1981

Cannes Film Festival Palme d'Or "When Father Was Away on Business" 1985

Cannes Film Festival FIPRESCI Prize "When Father Was Away on Business" 1985

Golden Arena Award Best Director "When Father Was Away on Business" 1985; Yugoslavian equivalent of the Oscar; film won a total of five awards

Roberto Rossellini Prize for Lifetime Achievement in Film 1989

Cannes Film Festival Best Director Award "Time of the Gypsies" 1989

Cannes Film Festival Palme d'Or "Underground" 1995

Boston Society of Film Critics Award Best Foreign Film "Underground" 1997

Venice Film Festival Silver Lion for Best Director "Black Cat, White Cat" 1998

BIOGRAPHY

Widely regarded as one of the most innovative filmmakers of his generation, Emir Kusturica twice won the Cannes Film Festival Palme d'Or before the age of 40, and, film for film, it is difficult to think of a more consistently lauded artist than this Bosnian-born director. Possessing the persona of a rock star (he once played bass in the agit-rock band No Smoking and still makes guest appearances with them), he is the antithesis of the Hollywood director, viewing the world as a naif or a dreamer and only helming projects that move him strongly. Though the commerce of movies remains foreign to Kusturica, the opportunity to make a visual statement still drives his work. No fan of the close-up, he always tries to connect one person with what is going on in the midground and background (much like John Frankenheimer), and he has successfully worked with non-actors in the tradition of Italian neo-realism (e.g., Roberto Rossellini). As a result of his unpopular stand regarding the civil war in the former Yugoslavia, however, he finds himself scorned in his own land, literally a director without a country.

While studying under Jiri Menzel at Prague's FAMU, Kusturica met Vilko Filac, his cinematographer of choice on all his films through "Underground" (1995). On the strength of his award-winning diploma film, "Guernica" (1976), he entered TV and helmed two critically acclaimed movies ("The Brides Are Coming" 1978 and "Buffet Titanic" 1979) before making an auspicious feature debut with "Do You Remember Dolly Bell?" (1981), a coming-of-age story set in Sarajevo in the early 1960s, which won the Golden Lion for best first film at the Venice Film Festival. "When Father Was Away on Business" (1985) was an absorbing portrait of provincial life and politics in 50s Yugoslavia, partially seen through the eyes of a six-year-old child and confirmed Kusturica as an international director of note, earning such prizes as the Palme d'Or at Cannes, five Golden Arena awards (the Yugoslavian equivalent of the Oscar) and an Academy Award nomination as Best Foreign-Language Film.

"Time of the Gypsies" (1988) was his first film that did not contain a single frame shot in his beloved Sarajevo. Inspired by a newspaper article about the inter-European trade in young gypsy children, it employed an elliptical, fantastic style influenced by Latin American "magical realism" (i.e., Jorge Luis Borges) and featured non-professional, gypsy actors delivering most of their dialogue in Romany (a language the director barely understood). "Gypsies" brought further critical acclaim earning the Best Director award at the 1989 Cannes Film Festival. Kusturica then embarked on his first English-language film, "Arizona Dream" (1991), starring Johnny Depp, Faye Dunaway and Jerry Lewis. Boasting exceptional performances—one of Dunaway's best in years and one of Lewis' most impressive—the film ran into difficulty finding a US distributor and eventually debuted in theaters (albeit briefly) in 1995.

Kusturica collected his second Palme d'Or, as well as his best American reviews to that time, for "Underground", a film lamenting the death of Yugoslavia and spanning 50 years from the German invasion to the civil war. It also earned him the enmity of his fellow Bosnians. Opening with the ironic but undeniably nostalgic title "Once upon a time there was a country, and its capital was Belgrade," it featured Serb protagonists, causing some to view it as an apologia for Serb leader Slobodan Milosevic's vision of a Serb-dominated Yugoslavia made at a time when a true Bosnian should have been documenting Serbian atrocities against his countrymen. Kusturica's reaction to the criticism was to abandon filmmaking, but he later rescinded his retirement, eventually directing "Black Cat, White Cat" (1998), in which he returned to his passion for gypsy culture. Containing hardly a hint of politics, this prodigiously well-made, frenetic mixture of slapstick and folklore is Kusturica's funniest film yet, brimming with colorful, larger-than-life characters portrayed by a cast that once again included many non-professionals.

MILESTONES:

Began making amateur films in high school

1976: Directed student film, "Guernica"

1978: First TV-movie, "The Brides Are Coming"

1981: Feature directorial debut "Do You Remember Dolly Bell?"; also co-scripted with Muslim poet Abdulah Sidran

Professor of drama at Sarajevo Theater Academy

1985: "When Father Was Away on Business" (scripted by Sidran) won the Palme d'Or at Cannes Film Festival

1987: Co-scripted (with Mladen Mareric) Zlatco Lavanic's "The Magpie Strategy"

1988: Began teaching film directing at Columbia University

1988: Composer Goran Bregovic provided haunting music for "Time of the Gypsies"; co-scripted with Gordon Mihic

1991: Bregovic-Iggy Pop songs were a distinctive feature of his English-language film "Arizona Dream", starring Johnny Depp, Faye Dunaway and Jerry Lewis

1995: Won second Palme d'Or for controversial "Underground"; third and last collaboration with Bregovic

1995: Announced retirement from filmmaking in December

1996: Rescinded retirement; announced he would return to filmmaking in spring 1997 with a comedy to star French actor Daniel Auteil; project eventually abandoned

1998: Helmed "Black Cat, White Cat", once again expressing his passion for gypsy culture; reteamed with screenwriter Gordon Mihic

2000: Signed to make feature acting debut in Patrice Leconte's "La Veuve de St. Pierre" opposite Juliette Binoche

2003: Cast in the comedy feature "The Good Thief"

AFFILIATION: Muslim

QUOTES:

His last name is pronounced KOOS-tah-reet-sah.

"I am a craftsman. I was never going to do business with the movies. I was always starting with my wishes to do something about human beings and about the position of outsiders in every kind of society. I like simple people, people who are ready to sacrifice or who you are ready to sacrifice for. Intellectuals don't mean anything to me."

"I think my artistic motivation might be a little different because I think film is synthesizing different arts, getting together literature with drama, drama with photos. And the main thing that pulls me into cinema is the kind of visual expression you can produce from the beginning to the end. That makes my films a little bit different from current productions you see in America."—Emir Kusturica to *American Film*, c. 1991.

"For me film has to be close to music. If you're not close to music, it's very difficult to believe you could structure a whole film. I don't know any good director who does not have a good ear. If I had a film school, I would always choose people based on whether they at least knew how to whistle, how to fit their vision into a certain musical frame."—Kusturica to *Sight and Sound*, December 1997.

Gregory La Cava

BORN: George Gregory La Cava in Towanda, Pennsylvania, 03/10/1892

SOMETIMES CREDITED AS:
Gregory Lacava

DEATH: in Malibu Beach, California, 03/01/1952

NATIONALITY: American

EDUCATION: Chicago Institute of Art, Chicago, Illinois, painting
   Art Students League of New York, New York, New York

AWARD: New York Film Critics Circle Award Best Director "Stage Door" 1937

BIOGRAPHY

Comedy films have traditionally not received their due from Hollywood, cineastes and academics. There seems to be an erroneous perception that because material is handled in a light fashion, it is without substance. When histories examine the great film directors of the 1930s and 40s, the list of names include well-known figures like Howard Hawks, Preston Sturges, Frank Capra, etc. occasionally at the expense of fine craftsmen like W.S. Van Dyke ("The Thin Man" 1934) and Gregory La Cava. La Cava, in particular, is often overlooked despite directing "My Man Godfrey" (1936), arguably one of the greatest "screwball" comedies. One may assert that he is sometimes neglected because his more dramatic fare is not on the same par with his comedy movies. His own contemporary reputation as "difficult" (stemming in part from his alcoholism) and the fact that he moved from studio to studio undoubtedly figures into this assessment. Still, in examining his oeuvre from the silent comedies through to his less than stellar final output, one can see the sponteneity (he was a proponent of improvisation on set) as well as a subversive social undertone that many have missed.

MILESTONES:

Studied painting at the Chicago Art Institute and the Art Students League in New York City

Because of financial considerations, abandoned art studies and took job as a newspaper reporter in Rochester, New York

Began working as a newspaper cartoonist for the New York *Globe* & and the *Evening World*

1913: Hired as an animator by Barre studios (date approximate)

1915: Appointed editor-in-chief of an animation studio founded by William Randolph Hearst; worked with Walter Lantz on "The Katzenjammmer Kids" and "Silk Hat Harry"

1918–1921: Worked at Bray studio until it discontinued its animation unit

1921: Moved to Los Angeles (date approximate) Hired as a gag writer on one- and two-reelers

1922: First feature, "His Nibs"

Helmed series of All-Star Comedy two-reelers starring Charlie Murray

1924: Returned to feature filmmaking with "Restless Wives" and "The New School Teacher"; wrote screenplay for the latter

1925: Signed to a four-year contract by Famous Players-Lasky Corportation; made 10 silent films, many starring Richard Dix

1926: First film with W. C. Fields, "So's Your Old Man"

1927: Helmed second Fields vehicle, "Running Wild"

1928: Made what is arguably his best silent comedy "Feel My Pulse", with Bebe Daniels

1929: Shot "Saturday's Children" as a silent; film reissued as a partial talkie

1931: Put under contract at RKO; directed "Smart Woman"

1933: Enjoyed a box-office hit with "Gabriel Over the White House" for MGM

1934: Garnered praise for his direction of "The Affairs of Cellini"

1936: Helmed the Claudette Colbert comic vehicle "She Married Her Boss"

1936: Earned first Oscar nomination for Best Director for the screwball comedy "My Man Godfrey"

1937: Received second Best Director Academy

Award nomination for "Stage Door"; first of three films with Ginger Rogers

1940: Co-wrote screenplay (with Allan Scott) and directed "The Primrose Path", featuring a strong performance from Ginger Rogers

Directed Irene Dunne in two films, "Unfinished Business" and "Lady in a Jam"

1947: Last directorial credit, "Living in a Big Way"

1948: Began filming "One Touch of Venus"; reportedly walked off the set after 11 days of shooting and replaced by William A. Seiter

Neil LaBute

BORN: Neil N. LaBute in Detroit, Michigan, 03/19/1961

NATIONALITY: American

EDUCATION: Central Falley High School, Spokane, Washington

Brigham Young University, Provo, Utah theater, BFA, 1985; received academic scholarship

University of Kansas, Lawrence, Kansas, theater and film history, MA

Tisch School of the Arts, New York University, New York, New York; graduated from the Graduate Dramatic Writing Program; met future producing partner Steve Pevner

Brigham Young University, Provo, Utah, theater theory and criticism; attended doctoral program; met Aaron Eckhart in 1991

AWARDS: Sundance Film Festival Filmmakers Trophy (Dramatic) "In the Company of Men" 1997

New York Film Critics Circle Award Best First Film "In the Company of Men" 1997

Society of Texas Film Critics Award Best Original Screenplay "In the Company of Men" 1997

Independent Spirit Award Best First Screenplay "In the Company of Men" 1998

BIOGRAPHY

Playwright Neil LaBute successfully made the transition to features with his assured debut film "In the Company of Men" (1997). A black comedy that explores sexual and corporate politics, the film premiered at the Sundance Film Festival, where it stirred some controversy over its subject matter.

LaBute was born in the Midwest, raised in the Pacific Northwest and attended Brigham Young University as a theater major. The subject matter of his plays caused some consternation on campus; LaBute has not shied away from tackling provocative subjects (e.g., gay bashing) or from bold titles (i.e., "Filthy Talk for Troubled Times"). After graduate work at both the University of Kansas and New York University, the budding playwright received a scholarship to London's Royal Court Theatre. His plays began to receive stagings in the USA in Chicago, L.A. and NYC.

By 1992, LaBute and his family settled in Indiana so he could teach English while continuing to write. Four year later, he began production on "In the Company of Men." Shot in less than two weeks on a budget of $25,000, the film probes in a provocative way the rivalries and psychologies of two mid-level businessmen: the arrogant Chad (LaBute's college chum Aaron

Eckhart) and the mousy Howard (Matt Malloy, who also co-executive produced) who are stuck for six weeks in an unnamed town. Lamenting the state of their love lives, the men hatch a wicked plan to simultaneously seduce and then abandon an unsuspecting female. Targeting a hearing-impaired temporary secretary (Stacy Edwards), the men carry out their plan with surprising and unexpected results. LaBute's strong dialogue and plotting carry the film and allow one to overlook some of its inconsistent production values. Eschewing offers from Hollywood (at least for the moment), LaBute announced his intentions to film one of his plays, "Lepers", again starring Eckhart.

MILESTONES:

Raised in Spokane, Washington

Received literary fellowship to study at the Royal Court Theatre in London

Moved to Chicago

Became established a playwright with such productions as "Filthy Talk for Troubled Times", "Bash" and "A Gaggle of Saints"

1997: Directed debut feature "In the Company of Men," a controversial look at male bonding in a corporate setting

1998: Scripted and helmed second feature, the equally controversial look at marriage and relationships "Your Friends and Neighbors"

1998: With partner Steve Pevner, entered into deals for three films with three production companies

1998: Signed deal with Touchstone TV to develop a TV series for ABC

1999: Made NYC debut as playwright with "bash . . . latter day plays", a series of three one-acts, starring Calista Flockhart, Ron Eldard and Paul Rudd

2000: Helmed the comedy "Nurse Betty"; screened at Cannes

2001: London stage directing debut, helmed production of his own play "The Shape of Things" at Alameida Theater Company

2002: Directed the screen adaptation of A. S. Byatt's novel "Possession"

2002: Wrote and directed the play "The Distance From Here"; premiered at the Alameida Theater in England

AFFILIATION: Mormon

QUOTES:

"Everyone in a relationship has hurt someone or been hurt, usually both. Men are trying to pass off the movie as a fantasy, while women are pretty sure it's a documentary. The truth is somewhere in between."—Neil LaBute on "In the Company of Men", quoted in *Details*, August 1997.

"I'm not sure anything's too sacred to write about. Maybe that is a dangerous way to feel. I think writers are dangerous people. In fact, there's an inherent danger to sitting here with you right now."—Neil LaBute in *Premiere*.

John Landis

BORN: John David Landis in Chicago, Illinois, 08/03/1950

NATIONALITY: American

BIOGRAPHY

Quiet as it's kept, John Landis must be counted among the more important mainstream Hollywood filmmakers to come to prominence in the late 1970s and early 80s. Though enormously successful and influential, Landis rarely turns up in film reference books—an indication of the continuing critical disrespect that greets youth-oriented comedy. Part of the same post-countercultural movement as the laugh-a-minute screenwriting team of Zucker-Abrahams-Zucker, the creative staff of the original "Saturday Night Live" and National Lampoon, Landis translated this liberating sensibility to the big screen with such uproarious features as "The Kentucky Fried Movie" (1977), "National Lampoon's Animal House" (1978) and "The Blues Brothers" (1980).

Flavored with rock'n'roll, rhythm and blues and nonstop movie references, Landis' films reveal him to be as much of a film buff as his contemporary (and fellow Daily Variety "Billion Dollar Director" designee) Steven Spielberg. Natural allies, the two traded off cameos in each other's films—Landis in "1941"; Spielberg in "The Blues Brothers"—before collaborating as producers and segment directors on the ill-fated production of "Twilight Zone—The Movie" (1983). The broad comedy specialist, however, has not found even the qualified critical acceptance of his colleague. Pigeonholed as a vulgarian, Landis has yet to find a "serious" subject (e.g., "Schindler's List") or a universal hit in the manner of "E.T. The Extra-Terrestrial". A faithful adaptation of Mark Twain's satirical masterpiece "A Connecticut Yankee in King Arthur's Court" remains his unrealized dream project.

The standard take on Landis is that he is a solid, sometimes inspired, technician but a sloppy storyteller whose films tend to fall apart in the last reel. His yen for broad physical comedy and ambitious stunts may reflect his former career as a film stuntman. Early efforts like "Kentucky Fried Movie" and "National Lampoon's Animal House" gained Landis a reputation as a prime mover in the modern "comedy of outrage" though they now look surprisingly tame. "The Kentucky Fried Movie" first presented the delirious rapid-fire, hit-or-miss comic technique that Jerry Zucker, Jim Abrahams and David Zucker would further develop in their own "Airplane" and "Naked Gun" movies. Lacking even the patience of

those jittery comic works, the Landis-helmed outing careened from genre to genre in its good-natured parodies. The highlight is "A Fistful of Yen", an extended (and inspired) parody of the Bruce Lee-starrer "Enter the Dragon." "Animal House" offered a gleefully vulgar update of the campus comedy with wildly successful results. Landis counts the "Porky's", "Revenge of the Nerds" and "Police Academy" franchises among his progeny.

In a slight stretch, Landis scored commercially with his ham-handed but accessible approach to social satire in the popular Eddie Murphy vehicles "Trading Places" (1983) and "Coming to America" (1988) but stumbled with his leaden attempt to recreate the character-driven farce of 30s screwball comedy in "Oscar" (1991). More typically, he guided familiar TV faces to big screen success: John Belushi in "Animal House"; Belushi and Dan Aykroyd in the elephantine "The Blues Brothers"; Aykroyd and Chevy Chase in "Spies Like Us" (1985); and Chase, Steve Martin and Martin Short in the amiably silly "Three Amigos!" (1986). In an effort to bolster Eddie Murphy's then-sagging box-office fortunes, Landis directed the underperforming action-oriented sequel, "Beverly Hills Cop III" (1994). Though generally perceived as superior to the second installment, the feature failed to re-establish Murphy's prominence.

Landis deserves credit for his small but significant contribution to modern horror filmmaking. His work provided a bridge between the hard-hitting and arguably subversive horror films of the 70s and the campy horror comedies of the 80s as he provided genuine scares and gore while demonstrating a sharp sense of humor. Abetted by landmark (and subsequently Oscar-winning and much copied) special makeup effects by Rick Baker, alternately poignant and humorous performances from his leads, witty musical cues and his own strong screenplay, Landis gave new life to a stock horror film monster in the impressive horror-comedy "An American Werewolf in London" (1981). Easily his most sustained achievement, the film has acquired the status of a minor genre classic.

Starting out as a mailboy at 20th Century Fox, the 18-year-old Landis made his way to Yugoslavia to work as a production assistant on the Clint Eastwood WWII comedy vehicle "Kelly's Heroes" (1970). That production also marked his screen debut as he played a tall nun. Remaining in Europe, Landis found work as an actor, extra and stunt man in what he has described as "hundreds" of German action movies and Spanish-filmed spaghetti Westerns. Returning to the US, he made his feature debut as a writer-director at age 21 with "Schlock" (shot 1971; released 1973), an affectionate tribute to monster movies, made with $60,000 of his family's money. Clad in a Rick Baker–designed gorilla suit, Landis starred as Schlockthropus, the missing link. The film received very affectionate reviews, the best of his career according to Landis.

In addition to their work on "An American Werewolf in London", Landis and Baker collaborated on what may well be the director's most widely viewed work, the landmark "longform" promotional video for Michael Jackson's song, "Thriller" (1983). The eccentric pop superstar was particularly well-served by Landis as "Thriller" revealed their shared love of special FX, monsters and horror iconography. The short film also playfully (and perhaps prophetically) suggested a dark side to the sexuality of the eternally boyish entertainer. ("I'm not like the other boys," Jackson confided to his date before transforming into the first of the film's several monsters.) The vocal "cameo" of horror star Vincent Price was comparable to the frequent guest appearances that pepper Landis' features. The duo re-teamed for Jackson's lavish video for "Black or White", an improbably controversial work that featured then state-of-the-art "morphing" effects.

Despite the brilliance of much of his career,

Landis' professional and personal reputation may always be marred by his involvement in the tragedy that occurred in 1983 during filming of a sequence of "Twilight Zone—The Movie." Along with his associate producer, unit production manager, helicopter pilot and special FX supervisor, Landis was charged with involuntary manslaughter in the deaths of Vic Morrow and two child actors. The performers were killed when struck by a helicopter which had been hit by debris from an FX explosion during a Vietnam War sequence. All plead not guilty and were acquitted after a highly publicized year-long trial.

Landis has not enjoyed comparable feature success in the 90s. His "The Stupids" (1996) awaited distribution for over a year and was met with mostly negative critical reaction. Instead, Landis has been devoting more of his time to TV as a producer and director, enjoying his greatest success in the medium as the executive producer and occasional director of the ribald movie-mad sitcom "Dream On" (HBO, 1990–96). He also executive produced the first season of the sci-fi parallel universe adventure series "Sliders" (Fox, 1995–96) and became an executive consultant after the series returned from hiatus. Landis also executive produced "Weird Science" (USA, 1994–97) and the TV-movie "Here Come the Munsters" (Fox, 1995).—Written by Kent Greene

MILESTONES:

1950: At age four months, moved with family to Los Angeles

1969: Feature debut at age 18, worked uncredited as a production assistant and played the tallest nun in "Kelly's Heroes" (released 1970), shot in Yugoslavia

Remaining in Europe, worked as an extra and stunt man in "hundreds" of German action movies and Spanish-filmed spaghetti Westerns

Returned to the USA

1971: Feature debut as writer-director at age 21, the monster movie spoof "Schlock"; also starred (in gorilla suit) as the Sclockthropus; first collaboration with makeup effects designer Rick Baker; produced for $60,000 of his family's money (released 1973)

1973: Appeared as an actor in "Battle for the Planet of the Apes"

1975: Appeared as an actor in Paul Bartel's "Death Race 2000"

Reportedly did rewrites on James Bond screenplays for producer Albert Broccoli

1977: Returned to directing when hired by writers Jerry Zucker, Jim Abrahams and David Zucker to helm their screenplay for "Kentucky Fried Movie"

1978: Breakthrough feature as director, "National Lampoon's Animal House"; first collaboration with actor John Belushi

1979: Appeared as an actor in Steven Spielberg's "1941"

1980: Wrote, directed and acted in "The Blues Brothers", then the most expensive—and subsequently the highest-grossing—comedy feature ever made; first collaboration with Dan Aykroyd

1981: Directed, wrote and appeared in the well-received horror comedy "An American Werewolf in London" featuring Oscar-winning makeup effects by Baker

Charged with involuntary manslaughter (along with his associate producer, unit production manager, helicopter pilot and special effects supervisor) after actor Vic Morrow and two (reportedly illegally employed) child actors were accidentally killed on location under his direction; a helicopter was hit by debris from a special FX explosion and crashed into the performers; all plead not guilty and were acquitted after a year-long trial

1983: Feature producing debut (with Spielberg), "Twilight Zone—the Movie"; also directed two segments "Prologue" and "Back There"

1983: Directed Eddie Murphy (their first collaboration) in the comic's breakthrough feature "Trading Places" co-starring Dan Aykroyd

1983: Directed Michael Jackson's landmark "longform" music video, "Thriller"; again collaborating with makeup FX master Baker

1983: Produced the best-selling home video documentary short subject "Making Michael Jackson's 'Thriller' "

1985: TV directing debut, "Disaster at Buzz Creek", an episode of the CBS comedy anthology series "George Burns Comedy Week"

1986: TV producing debut, executive produced "Fuzzbucket", a fantasy telefilm on ABC's "Disney Sunday Movie"

Formed St Clare Entertainment with Robert Weiss and Leslie Belzberg to produce TV series, telefilms and miniseries

1990–1996: Served as executive producer (and occasional director) of the popular ribald HBO sitcom "Dream On"

1991: Directed Michael Jackson's "Black and White" video

1991: Replaced Jack Shoulder as the director of the supernatural romance "Innocent Blood" (released 1992) starring Anne Parillaud and Anthony LaPaglia

Executive produced the spin-off sci-fi teen sitcom "Weird Science" on the USA Network

1995: Served as executive producer for the first season of Fox's sci-fi adventure series "Sliders"; subsequently served as executive consultant

1996: Executive produced (and directed episodes of) the short-lived USA Network sitcom "Campus Cops"

1996: Guest-starred as himself in an episode of the NBC sitcom "Caroline in the City"

AFFILIATION: Member, Board of Directors, American Lung Association of Los Angeles County

QUOTES:

Landis is the Chairman of St. Clare Entertainment.

Landis received the Chevalier of the Order of Arts and Letters from the French government in 1985.

BORN: Friedrich Christian Anton Lang in Vienna, Austria, 12/05/1890

DEATH: in Hollywood, California, 08/02/1976

NATIONALITY: Austrian

CITIZENSHIP: United States 1935

EDUCATION: Volksschule, local primary school

Realschule, 1901; local secondary school; specialized in architecture

Technische Hochshule, architecture, 1908

Vienna Academy of Graphic Arts, art

School of Arts and Crafts, Munich, Germany; art studied under Julius Dietz

Academie Julien, Paris, France

AWARD: Venice Film Festival Special Mention "Hangmen Also Die" 1946; one of eight films cited

BIOGRAPHY

"Human Desire" (1954), made during Fritz Lang's last decade as a film director, begins with an emblematic image: a locomotive rushes forward, swift and dynamic, but locked to the tracks, its path fixed, its destination visible. Like Lang's films the train and the tracks speak of a world of narrowly defined choices. The closing image is even more severe: survivor Glenn Ford departs, his locomotive passing a sign on a bridge. Ford does not see the sign, but we do; abbreviated by intervening beams we suddenly see "The world takes" just before the film ends.

This vision of a hostile universe, constraints on freedom and messages that are missed or misunderstood but always seen by someone, can be found in all of Fritz Lang's films. His work has a consistency and a richness that are unique in world cinema. In Germany, in France, in Hollywood, then in Germany again, Lang built genre worlds for producers and audiences and veiled meditations on human experience for himself.

Lang's vision is that of the outsider. James Baldwin, an outsider himself, catches Lang's "concern, or obsession . . . with the fact and effect of human loneliness, and the ways in which we are all responsible for the creation, and the fate, of the isolated . . . " Born an Austrian, Lang fled his training as an architect for a jaunt through the Middle and Far East, returned to Paris just in time for the beginning of WWI, then fought on the losing side of the war. Recovering from wounds which cost him the sight in his right eye, Lang wrote his first scenarios: a werewolf story which found no buyers, and "Wedding in the Eccentric Club" and "Hilde Warren and Death," which were sold and eventually produced by Joe May. May's deviations from Lang's scripts motivated Lang to become a director himself; his first movie was "Halbblut/The Half-Caste" (1919), a still-lost film about the revenge of a half-Mexican mistress. Later that year he directed the first film of a two-part international thriller called "The Spiders "(1920). Part one, subtitled "The Golden Lake," proved so popular that his producers insisted Lang immediately make part two, "The Diamond Ship." He had been working on another script which he hoped to film, so he reluctantly gave up "The Cabinet of Dr. Caligari" (1919) to Robert Wiene. His contribution to that landmark film nevertheless was crucial: Lang thought up the framing device, in which it is revealed at the story's end that we have been watching a tale told by a madman, thus significantly undercutting the audience's perceptions of the story.

Lang's career in the 1920s was one of

spectacular rise to fame. With each film, he became more assured, garnering critical acclaim as well as a popular following. "Dr. Mabuse the Gambler" (1922), "Die Nibelungen" (1924), "Metropolis" (1927), and "Spies" (1928) are among the greatest silent films produced anywhere. Lang also made a remarkable transition to sound, with "M" (1931), a powerful study of a child murderer pursued by both police and the criminal underworld, but he ran afoul of Nazi authorities with "The Testament of Dr. Mabuse" (1933), whose villains mouthed Nazi propaganda. When the film was banned and Lang was requested to make films for the cause of the Third Reich, he immediately fled Germany, leaving behind most of his personal possessions, as well as his wife, screenwriter Thea von Harbou (who had joined the Nazi party and become an official screenwriter).

Lang made one film in France, then moved on to Hollywood, where he spent the next 20 years working in a variety of genres, mainly thrillers (e.g. "Man Hunt" 1941, "Scarlet Street" 1945, "While the City Sleeps" 1956) and some outstanding westerns ("The Return of Frank James" 1940, "Rancho Notorious" 1952). Tired of warring with insensitive producers, Lang left the US in the mid-1950s to make a film in India and then returned to Germany for his last set of films, including a final chapter in the Dr. Mabuse saga.

The disorienting frame in "Caligari" is an important part of Lang's distinctive vision. His films are punctuated by shifts of viewpoint and discoveries which transform the reactions of his characters—and of his audience. The most obvious of these shifts of viewpoint come in "Caligari" and "The Woman in the Window" (1944), in which the drama is suddenly revealed to be a dream. But they also occur in the "Mabuse" films; in "M", with the policeman mistaken by a burglar for another thief; and in "House By the River" (1950), when a servant is strangled because another maid appears to be responding to her cries for help.

Lang's films are also about contingency, the recognition that extra-personal forces mold our lives, shape our destiny in ways we cannot predict and only somewhat modify. In the two-part film, "Die Nibelungen," Kriemhild is transformed from a secondary figure in the first film ("Siegfried") into a whirlwind of fury in the second ("Kriemhild's Revenge"). Even the characters in the film are shaken by these transformations. The king of the Huns is staggered by Kriemhild's thirst for death; the vengeful underworld in "M" that has captured and tried Peter Lorre is taken aback by Lorre's confession that he "must" rape and murder, that he is something of a spectator to his crimes.

These moments of perception are the foundation of Lang's importance and continuing strength as a filmmaker. They constitute a kind of morality that he never abandoned. In the script for "Liliom" (1934), his French film made after he fled the Nazis, Lang wrote, "If death settled everything it would be too easy . . . Where would justice be if death settled everything?" Thirty years later, playing himself in Jean-Luc Godard's "Contempt" (1963), Lang wrote for his character, "La Mort n'est pas une solution." ("Death is no solution"). Nor does death erase human striving. In "Der Mude Tod/Destiny" (1921) the force of love survives, in "Fury" (1936) the cycle of vengeance is broken, in "Clash By Night" (1952) Barbara Stanwyck chooses responsibility, in "The Big Heat" (1953) Glenn Ford finally turns to the police and ends his vendetta, and in "Human Desire" Ford again leaves the scene of the crime, choosing life over the locus of death.

MILESTONES:

1909: Left home

Served with German army during WWI

1916: Lost vision in right eye; discharged (as lieutenant)

1917: First filmscripts sold "Die Hochzeit im Exzentrikklub/The Wedding in the Eccentric Club" and "Hilde Warren und der Tod/Hilde Warren and Death"

1917: Film acting debut (as "Death") in "Hilde Warren und der Tod/Hilde Warren and Death"

1918: Hired as screenwriter, Decla film company (Berlin)

1919: Film directing debut with "Halbblut/The Half-Caste" (also screenwriter; no longer exists)

1920: Left Decla; signed with Joe May as director for "Das Wandernde Bild/The Wandering Image" (no longer exists)

1920: Left May; returned to Decla (merged to become Decla-Bioscop)

1920: Rights to "Der Mude Tod/Destiny" bought by Douglas Fairbanks

1928: Founded production company Fritz-Lang-Films (released through UFA) Ended association with UFA

1933: Refused work as director of Nazi propaganda films; left Germany for Paris

1934: Left Paris

1934: Hired as director by David O. Selznick, MGM

1935: Became American citizen

1936: Contract with MGM not renewed

1940: First color film and Western as director "The Return of Frank James" (for Fox)

1944: Co-founded production company Diana Productions

1948: Diana Productions went bankrupt

1952: Last Western directed (for RKO) "Rancho Notorious"

1956: Last American film directed "Beyond a Reasonable Doubt"

1960: Last film directed "Die tausend Augen des Dr. Mabuse/The 1000 Eyes of Dr. Mabuse"

1960: Last role as actor in "Le Mepris/ Contempt" (Jean-Luc Godard film; Lang played himself)

QUOTES:

Lang's fourth film "Harakiri" (1919), long thought to have been lost, was uncovered in a Dutch film archive in the 1980s and restored. It was shown in L.A. as part of a 2001 retrospective of the director's work.

BIBLIOGRAPHY:

"Fritz Lang: The Nature of the Beast" Patrick McGilligan, 1996, St. Martin's Press

"The Films of Fritz Lang: Allegories of Vision and Modernity" Tom Gunning, 2000, British Film Institute

David Lean

BORN: David Lean in Croydon, England, 03/25/1908

SOMETIMES CREDITED AS:
Sir David Lean

DEATH: in London, England, 04/16/1991

NATIONALITY: English

EDUCATION: attended a Quaker boarding school in Leighton Park, Reading, where he spent spare time going to the movies

AWARDS: Cannes Film Festival Grand Prix "Brief Encounter" 1946

National Board of Review Award Best Director "The Sound Barrier/Breaking the Sound Barrier" 1952

British Film Academy Award Best Film "The Sound Barrier/Breaking the Sound Barrier" 1952; award shared with co-producer Alexander Korda

British Film Academy Award Best British Film "The Sound Barrier/Breaking the Sound Barrier" 1952; award shared with co-producer Alexander Korda

British Film Academy Award Best British

Film "Hobson's Choice" 1954; award shared with co-producer Alexander Korda

Berlin Film Festival Golden Bear "Hobson's Choice" 1954

New York Film Critics Circle Award Best Director "Summertime" 1955

New York Film Critics Circle Award Best Director "The Bridge on the River Kwai" 1957

Oscar Best Director "The Bridge on the River Kwai" 1957

Golden Globe Award Best Director "The Bridge on the River Kwai" 1957

Directors Guild of America Award Outstanding Directorial Achievement in Feature Film "The Bridge on the River Kwai" 1957

National Board of Review Award Best Director "Lawrence of Arabia" 1962

Oscar Best Director "Lawrence of Arabia" 1962

Golden Globe Award Best Director "Lawrence of Arabia" 1962

Directors Guild of America Award Outstanding Directorial Achievement in Feature Film "Lawrence of Arabia" 1962

Golden Globe Award Best Director "Doctor Zhivago" 1965

L'Ordre des Arts et des Lettres 1968

NATO Distinguished Directorial Achievement Award 1970; presented by the National Association of Theater Owners

Directors Guild of America D. W. Griffith Award 1973; shared with William A. Wellman

Directors Guild of America Honorary Life Membership 1973

National Board of Review Award Best Director "A Passage to India" 1984

New York Film Critics Circle Award Best Director "A Passage to India" 1984

American Film Institute Life Achievement Award 1990; the AFI bent its rules to make Lean the first (and to date only) non-US citizen to receive the honor; also only director to receive the Life Achievement Award who had never made a film in the USA

BIOGRAPHY

The best films of consummate craftsman David Lean are the product of a creative tension between romantic style and realistic content.

Working his way up from clapper-boy to editor's apprentice in the 1930s, Lean edited newsreels and then features. His first outing as a director, with Noel Coward, "In Which We Serve" (1942), was a moving study of wartime England that contrasted the duty to fight with the human sacrifice required to win. Lean's next three films came from Coward's pen: "This Happy Breed" (1944), the story of a London family from 1919 to 1939; the rousingly entertaining "Blithe Spirit" (1945); and the quietly effective "Brief Encounter" (1945), about a bored housewife (Celia Johnson) who almost has an affair with a doctor (Trevor Howard). These were followed by faithful adaptations of "Great Expectations" (1946) and "Oliver Twist" (1948), justly regarded as exemplary translations of Dickens to the screen.

Of his next three films, the semi-documentary "The Sound Barrier" (1952), where he returned to the duty/sacrifice thematics of "In Which We Serve", is most noteworthy. Lean's rollicking version of the stage comedy "Hobson's Choice" (1954), the story of a woman's emancipation from her overbearing father, featured the first in a series of strong, independent women characters that would include Lara in "Dr. Zhivago" (1965), Rosy Ryan in "Ryan's Daughter" (1970) and Miss Quested and Mrs. Moore in "A Passage to India" (1984). "Summertime" (1955), about the Venice affair of a lonely American spinster (Katharine Hepburn), also reprised one of Lean's central themes, the journey as a quest for self-knowledge.

Accordingly, the WWII adventure "The Bridge on the River Kwai" (1957) revolves around the self-delusion of Col. Jock Nicholson (Alec Guinness), leader of the British contingent in a Burmese prisoner-of-war camp. Commercially and critically successful, winning seven Academy Awards including best picture and best director, "Bridge" initiated the cycle of big-budget spectacles that would characterize Lean's later work. Increasingly jaundiced about British assumptions about power in the world, in "Bridge" Lean viewed militarism as an insane but inevitable extension of the strutting male ego, and in "Lawrence of Arabia" (1962) he investigated the psychology of heroism. Starting with a dashing, if eccentric and enigmatic hero (stunningly played by Peter O'Toole), the film gradually peels away his bravado to reveal the confusion beneath.

Lean's next two films, also scripted by Robert Bolt, were love stories. The international success of the lush "Dr. Zhivago", based on the Boris Pasternak novel, may have encouraged him to accentuate his romantic tendency, which he did with disastrous results in "Ryan's Daughter." Partly due to the poor reception of this film, it would be 14 years before Lean would complete his next picture, a splendid adaptation of E.M. Forster's "A Passage to India." Returning to the motif of the journey of self-discovery, reiterating the clumsy damage done by British incursion into the third world, and sharpening the ambiguities of the source novel, Lean succeeded in restoring the romantic/realist tension which had informed his best work.

At its best, Lean's is an elegant style that questions elegance. He is the English benchmark of cinematic technique that mirrors the contradictions of character and society: "The Bridge on the River Kwai" is a wide-screen anti-war statement; "A Passage to India" is a sumptuously photographed critique of colonialism; and "Lawrence of Arabia" is a perfectly made chronicle of human imperfection.

MILESTONES:

Given Kodak Box Brownie camera by uncle at age 12, developed interest in photography

1927: Worked for father's accounting firm at the age of 19 (date approximate)

1927: Began working for Gaumont-British studios as tea-boy, then number-board holder, messenger and camera assistant

1930: Graduated to newsreel editor; then put in charge of Gaumont Sound News

1935: Began cutting feature films with "Escape Me Never"

1942: First film as co-director (with Noel Coward), "In Which We Serve"

1944: First film as solo director and first film as co-adaptor (with Ronald Neame and Anthony Havelock-Allan), "This Happy Breed"

1942–1950: Formed Cineguild with Noel Coward, Ronald Neame 1nd Anthony Havelock-Allan

1974: Subject of British TV documentary, "David Lean: A Life in Film"

1979: TV directing debut: Lean directed and hosted a documentary on explorer Capt. James Cook, "The Story of Cook's Anchor" for New Zealand TV

1991: Production of "Nostromo", his 17th film, halted when Lean became ill with throat cancer (February)

QUOTES:

Lean's films earned 56 Oscar nominations and 28 Oscars. He was nominated as Best Director seven times and won twice.

"He wrote with light and composition until each of his films was the visual equivalent of great novels. His genius rests in the fact that his characters were never diminished by his epic action."—Steven Spielberg in *The Hollywood Reporter*, April 17, 1991.

"David can't wait to finish shooting a picture so he can begin cutting the actors out of it."—Trevor Howard, quoted in Lean's *Variety* obituary, April 22, 1991.

"I had very strong feelings about his work, because I am a longer-is-better kind of guy.... He was willing to let the stories and scenes play out. He liked you to hear information. . . . [His films] are not so plot-oriented, they are like the journeys of people."—Kevin Costner to *New York Post*, April 17, 1991.

"David is sweet—simple and straight—and strong and savage, and he is the best movie director in the world."—Katharine Hepburn in 1989, quoted in Lean's obituary in *The New York Times,* April 17, 1991.

"Lean was a meticulous craftsman noted for technical wizardry, subtle manipulation of emotions, superb production values, authenticity and taste. He was one of the very few directors who edited his own films, and he also adapted or co-adapted half a dozen of them."—Peter B. Flint in Lean's *The New York Times* obituary, April 17, 1991.

Lean left orders that his ashes be strewn over the three areas he loved most: India, Tahiti and Tuscany (where he planned to retire).

Named Commander of the British Empire Award for services to cinema in 1953.

Awarded L'Ordre des Arts et des Lettres in 1968 by the French government

He was an honorary life member of the DGA.

He was made Fellow of the British Film Institute (1983).

He was knighted by Queen Elizabeth II in 1984.

BIBLIOGRAPHY:

"David Lean and His Films" Alain Silver and James Ursini, 1974; reissued in 1992 by Silman-James Press of Los Angeles
"David Lean" Stephen M. Silverman, 1989; Harry N. Abrams Inc. illustrated biography
"David Lean: A Biography" Kevin Brownlow, 1996, St. Martin's Press

Ang Lee

BORN: in Taiwan, 10/23/1954

NATIONALITY: Taiwanese

EDUCATION: Taiwan Academy of Art, Taipei, Taiwan, 1973. studied acting

University of Illinois, Urbana, Illinois, theater, BFA, 1978–82

Institute of Film and Television, New York University, New York, New York, film production, MFA, 1982–84; completed thesis film "Fine Line" in 1984

AWARDS: Golden Harvest Independent Film Festival Best Narrative Film Award "Dim Lake" 1983; Taiwanese film festival

NYU Film Festival Best Director Award "Fine Line" 1985; a 45-minute student film

Asian Pacific Film Festival Best Film Award "Pushing Hands" 1991

Golden Horse Award Best First Feature "Pushing Hands"

Golden Horse Award Special Jury Prize "Pushing Hands" honored for Lee's directing

Berlin Film Festival Golden Bear "The Wedding Banquet" 1993

Seattle International Film Festival Best Director Award "The Wedding Banquet" 1993

Seattle International Film Festival Best Film Award "The Wedding Banquet" 1993; Lee was one of the producers

Golden Horse Award Best Director "The Wedding Banquet" 1993

Golden Horse Award Best Original Screenplay "The Wedding Banquet" 1993; shared award

National Board of Review Award Best Foreign-Language Film "Eat Drink Man Woman" 1994

National Board of Review Award Best Director "Sense and Sensibility" 1995

New York Film Critics Circle Award Best Director "Sense and Sensibility" 1995

Boston Society of Film Critics Award Best Director "Sense and Sensibility" 1995

Berlin Film Festival Golden Bear "Sense and

Sensibility" 1996; first director in 46-year history of festival to receive this award twice

German Film Prize Best Foreign Film "Sense and Sensibility" 1997

National Board of Review Best Foreign Film "Crouching Tiger, Hidden Dragon" 2000; cited with Krysztof Kieslowski's "The Decalogue"

Los Angeles Film Critics Association Award Best Picture "Crouching Tiger, Hidden Dragon" 2000; first time a foreign language film cited in category

Boston Society of Film Critics Award Best Foreign Film "Crouching Tiger, Hidden Dragon" 2000

New York Film Critics Online Award Best Foreign Film "Crouching Tiger, Hidden Dragon" 2000

New York Film Critics Online Award Best Director "Crouching Tiger, Hidden Dragon" 2000

Online Film Critics Society Award Best Foreign Language Film "Crouching Tiger, Hidden Dragon" 2000

Florida Film Critics Circle Award Best Foreign Language Film "Crouching Tiger, Hidden Dragon" 2000

Dallas–Fort Worth Film Critics Association Award Best Foreign Language Film 2000

Southeastern Film Critics Association Award Best Foreign Language Film "Crouching Tiger, Hidden Dragon" 2000

Golden Satellite Best Foreign Language Film "Crouching Tiger, Hidden Dragon" 2000

Phoenix Film Critics Society Award Best Foreign Language Film "Crouching Tiger, Hidden Dragon" 2000; initial presentation of the award

Golden Globe Award Best Foreign Language Film "Crouching Tiger, Hidden Dragon" 2000

Golden Globe Award Best Director "Crouching Tiger, Hidden Dragon" 2000

London Film Critics' Circle Award Best Foreign Language Film "Crouching Tiger, Hidden Dragon" 2000

BAFTA Award Best Film Not in the English Language "Crouching Tiger, Hidden Dragon" 2001

BAFTA David Lean Award for Best Achievement in Direction "Crouching Tiger, Hidden Dragon" 2000

Chicago Film Critics Award Best Foreign-Language Film "Crouching Tiger, Hidden Dragon" 2000

Directors Guild of America Award Outstanding Achievement in Feature Film "Crouching Tiger, Hidden Dragon" 2000

ShoWest International Achievement in Filmmaking Award 2001

Independent Spirit Award Best Feature "Crouching Tiger, Hidden Dragon" 2001; Ang Lee was a producer

Independent Spirit Award Best Director "Crouching Tiger, Hidden Dragon" 2001

Hong Kong Film Award Best Picture "Crouching Tiger, Hidden Dragon" 2001

Hong Kong Film Award Best Director "Crouching Tiger, Hidden Dragon" 2001

Australian Film Institute Award Best Foreign Film "Crouching Tiger, Hidden Dragon" 2001; shared with James Schamus

Gotham Awards Lifetime Achievement 2002

BIOGRAPHY

A New York–based, Taiwan-born independent producer, director and screenwriter, Ang Lee gained international attention with his second feature, "The Wedding Banquet" (1993). Described by one of its producers as "a cross-cultural, gay 'Green Card', comedy of errors," this gentle, observant comedy strove to recreate the plot structure of an old Hollywood screwball comedy while confronting issues of Taiwanese identity. "The Wedding Banquet" became a huge international success: Variety deemed it the most profitable film of 1993 as it yielded a 4,000-percent return on investment. Lee helped put Taiwanese cinema on the international map, especially as "The Wedding Banquet" became the first movie from that country to earn an Academy Award nomination as Best Foreign-Language Film.

After Lee's paternal grandparents were executed for being landowners during the Communist revolution in mainland China, his father, a scholar and school principal, fled to Taiwan. In 1973, Lee surprised his family by heading to Taipei to study acting. Five years later, he moved to the USA to pursue further studies. Following his graduation from the University of Illinois, he headed east to NYU's film school, where he began his moviemaking career. Lee worked in production capacities on student like Spike Lee's "Joe's Bed-Stuy Barber Shop: We Cut Heads" (1982, as assistant to cinematographer Ernest Dickerson). His own shorts, "Dim Lake" (1983) and "Fine Line" (1984) earned prizes and led to representation by the esteemed William Morris Agency. Yet Lee was caught in what can only be termed as "development hell." For five years, he struggled to get various projects off the ground, all the while playing house-husband to his two sons while his wife, microbiologist Janice Lin, was the breadwinner. While he became an accomplished cook of rich Chinese cuisine, his mate researched how such foods contributed to atherosclerosis (hardening of the arteries.)

1990 saw a turning point in Lee's career. He entered two scripts into a national competition in Taiwan and amazingly placed first and second with "Pushing Hands" and "The Wedding Banquet." Both films, along with "Eat Drink Man Woman" (1994), find their central metaphor in food. Taken together, these movies which feature actor Sihung Lung as a patriarch, form what Lee has called his "Father Knows Best" trilogy. 1991's "Pushing Hands" examined the clash of cultures when the father comes to live with his son in America and takes a shine to a Chinese cooking instructor. "The Wedding Banquet" was about a marriage of convenience between a gay man and a Chinese immigrant that was arranged in part to please the man's elderly parents. "Eat Drink Man Woman" (1994), which also picked up an Oscar nomination as Best Foreign-Language Film, told the story of a father—a renowned Taiwanese cook—

and his three daughters as they strive to concoct a recipe for harmonious living. Boasting a more complex screenplay and polished performances, "Eat Drink Man Woman" opened to laudatory reviews and robust box office.

A seemingly unlikely choice to film a classic British novel, Lee was hired to direct "Sense and Sensibility" (1995), his first English-language movie. Adapted from Jane Austen's classic novel and starring Emma Thompson, it earned rave reviews, many of which singled out Lee's nuanced approach to this comedy of manners. In many ways. the film was similar to his earlier work, in that the motion pictures all studies of mores unique to a time and place, the effect of a patriarch on his family and miscommunication. Although the film received seven Oscar nominations, including one for Best Picture, Lee surprisingly did not make the final cut in the Best Director category.

"The Ice Storm" (1997) revolved around a father who watches the collapse of a patriarchal society. Adapted from Rick Moody's novel, the film focused on the societal upheavals in the 1970s (from Nixonian politics to wife-swapping to the burgeoning women's movement), with particular attention to how the interpersonal codes were becoming inverted. With meticulous detail to period, "The Ice Storm" looked at events from the perspectives of both the adults and the teenagers. Featuring a superb ensemble, this mood piece played as a modern Greek tragedy. Lee next undertook perhaps his most ambitious film yet, "Ride With the Devil" (1999), an action-packed post-Civil War–era epic about renegade Confederate soldiers set on the Missouri-Kansas borders. Although based on a Daniel Woodrell's novel "Woe to Love On", the story had its roots in history. To realize the project, the director assembled a cast drawn from a who's who of rising stars, including Jonathan Rhys Meyers, Jewel, Skeet Ulrich and James Caviezel, but its execution provoked a mostly dispassionate response from audiences.

In 2000, Ang Lee saw the realization of a

dream project. He had long harbored the desire to make a film similar to those on which he had been raised while growing up in Taiwan. Returning to his roots, he made his first Chinese-language project in years, "Crouching Tiger, Hidden Dragon", which married two genres—historical romance and martial arts—into an exciting blend. Teaming Hong Kong stars Chow Yun Fat and Michelle Yeoh as mature lovers, utilizing action star Cheng Pei-Pei as a villain, and teaming newcomers Zhang Ziyi and Chang Chen as a younger couple, "Crouching Tiger, Hidden Dragon" had elements to appeal to a mass audience—action for the guys, romance for the gals. Already a hit in Asia when it was released in the USA in late 2000, the movie earned mostly raves and earned a spot on many a critic's Ten Best list, as well as ten Academy Award nominations and the Oscar for Best Foreign Language Film. Lee's next major film was directing the highly anticipated comic adaptation "The Hulk" (2003), which starred Eric Bana and Jennifer Connelly. The high-profile film was met with mixed but generally appreciative responses, with many quarter praising the dark psychological underpinnings of the story while others decried the CGI-created Hulk as too rubbery and cartoony-looking.

MILESTONES:

Born and raised in Taiwan

Failed his national college entrance exams in Taiwan

Did mandatory two-year service in the military

1978: At age 23, moved to USA to attend college

1982: First film job, assistant cameraman on "Joe's Bed-Stuy Barbershop: We Cut Heads", Spike Lee's student thesis film at NYU

1983: Helmed the short "Dim Lake"

1985: Thesis short "Fine Line" won best film and best director at NYU's film festival

Signed five-year contract with William Morris talent agency; spent years trying to develop projects to no avail

1990: Won first and second prizes in the Taiwanese state screenwriting competition for the screenplays for "Pushing Hands" and "The Wedding Banquet"

1992: "Pushing Hands" featured at the Berlin Film Festival in the Panorama; also first collaboration with Good Machine (Ted Hope and James Schamus)

1993: "The Wedding Banquet" became first film from Taiwan to earn a Best Foreign-Language Film Oscar nomination

1994: "Eat Drink Man Woman" also received Academy Award nomination as Best Foreign-Language Film

1995: Directed first full English-language film, "Sense and Sensibility", written and starring Emma Thompson; film received seven Oscar nominations including Best Picture

1997: Earned widespread critical acclaim for "The Ice Storm"

1999: Helmed the post-Civil War-era epic "Ride With the Devil"

2000: Garnered international acclaim with the martial arts romance "Crouching Tiger, Hidden Dragon", which he co-produced and directed; film was nominated for Academy Awards as both Best Picture and Best Foreign Language Film as well as for Best Director; received the Best Foreign-Language Film award

2001: Directed "Chosen", one of five short film advertisements for BMW shown over the Internet at bmwfilms.com

2003: Helmed the feature adaptation of "The Incredible Hulk"

QUOTES:

Lee's "Crouching Tiger, Hidden Dragon" (2000) won the Academy Award as the Best Foreign Language Film.

On "The Ice Storm": "At times I felt like I was making a disaster movie, which is a very 1970s thing, because there is the natural disaster of the ice storm, as well as the human disaster they're all heading towards"—Ang Lee to the London *Times*, February 4. 1998.

"I see a director as a great seducer, who can

organically observe things and try to control them. Maybe I don't have to build it into a dictator situation. I believe a group effort under close control is the best way to work for me."—Ang Lee on his directorial style to *DGA Magazine,* September-October 1997.

"Sense and Sensibility" producer Lindsay Doran described the reaction of that film's cast to *Los Angeles Times,* (October 12, 1997): "[British actors are] used to directors who are either mean and rude or gentle and nice; but having a director who's gentle and nice but also rude was a new experience for them . . . "

Discussing a prominent theme is his work, Ang Lee told *The New York Times* (September 21, 1997): "On the one hand, family is about security and warmth—you cuddle together. On the other hand, family is about restraint. When the social impulse is to be liberated, where does the family go?"

"Movies and my family are the most important things to me. I try to keep them balanced, but my family has made sacrifices for my work. Because movies involve people who put their dreams on my shoulders, it's something larger than my own life. It's a tough balancing act, like that trick where you try to keep plates whirling on poles without dropping them. It's very Chinese!"—Ang Lee quoted in *Interview,* September 1997.

Spike Lee

BORN: Shelton Jackson Lee in Atlanta, Georgia, 03/20/1957

NATIONALITY: American

EDUCATION: John Dewey High School Brooklyn, New York, 1975

Morehouse College, Atlanta, Georgia, communications, BA; met future collaborator Monty Ross

Institute of Film and Television, New York University, New York, New York; first worked with classmate/cinematographer Ernest Dickerson

AWARDS: Student Academy Award "Joe's Bed-Stuy Barbershop: We Cut Heads" 1980

Cannes Film Festival Best New Director Award "She's Gotta Have It" 1986

Los Angeles Film Critics Association New Generation Award "She's Gotta Have It" 1986

Independent Spirit Award Best First Feature "She's Gotta Have It" 1986

Los Angeles Film Critics Association Award Best Film "Do the Right Thing" 1989; award shared with co-producer Monty Ross

Los Angeles Film Critics Association Award Best Director "Do the Right Thing" 1989

Chicago Film Festival Critics Award Best Picture "Do the Right Thing" 1990

Chicago Film Festival Critics Award Best Director "Do the Right Thing" 1990

Chicago Film Critics Association Award Best Picture "Malcolm X" 1992; shared award with Marvin Worth

IFP Gotham Award Filmmaker 1992

Broadcast Film Critics Association Award Best Documentary "Four Little Girls" 1997

Golden Satellite Best Documentary "Four Little Girls" 1997

Las Vegas Film Critics Award William Holden Lifetime Achievement Award 2002

Cesar Award Honorary Career Achievement 2002

BIOGRAPHY

Spike Lee burst onto the movie scene in 1986, immediately establishing himself as one of the most important young American filmmakers and a controversial figure in black culture.

A Brooklynite, a third-generation alumnus

of Atlanta's Morehouse College and a graduate of New York University's film school, Lee won immediate acclaim for his commercial debut, "She's Gotta Have It" (1986). This independently produced, stylish, black-and-white (and partly color) feature did surprising box-office business and garnered critical acclaim at the Cannes Film Festival. Although the film's sharp, witty direction impressed critics, Lee's portrayal of the comic streetwise hustler Mars Blackmon (and his trademark litany, "please, baby, please, baby, please, baby, please, baby") proved to be the most compelling element of the production.

Between film projects Lee directed himself as Mars in an Anita Baker music video ("No One in the World"), a short made for "Saturday Night Live" ("Horn of Plenty") and, most notably, in two Nike Air Jordan television commercials ("Hangtime" and "Cover") in which Mars Blackmon appears with basketball star Michael Jordan.

Television work, in fact, has been a much more frequent outlet for Lee's creative energies, as he battles to make uncompromising yet commercial films about the black experience within Hollywood's white-dominated financing, production and distribution system. Following the success of "She's Gotta Have It", a number of black musical artists, including Miles Davis, Branford Marsalis, Steel Pulse and Grandmaster Flash, have sought Lee to direct their music videos. With a film production team that includes editor Barry Brown and the gifted cinematographer (and neophyte director) Ernest Dickerson, Lee completed not only a number of videos, but also five one-minute spots for MTV, another series of Nike commercials, and ads for Jesse Jackson's campaign in the 1988 New York Presidential primary.

These projects have all supplemented Spike Lee's driving ambition, the production of feature films for his company, 40 Acres and a Mule Filmworks. After the self-described "guerrilla filmmaking" techniques employed to produce the low-budget "She's Gotta Have It", as

well as his earlier NYU thesis film, "Joe's Bed-Stuy Barber Shop: We Cut Heads" (1982), Lee's second feature, "School Daze" (1988), was partly financed by Columbia Pictures. Despite Columbia's underfinancing (Lee was given only a third of the usual Hollywood budget), "School Daze" remained true to his provocative vision. And despite the studio's poor promotion efforts and unenthusiastic reviews, the film grossed more than twice its cost. With an all-black ensemble cast, the film satirically addresses, in the form of a musical-comedy, class and color divisions within the student body at a black college: affluent, light-skinned "gammas" clash with underclass, dark-skinned "jigaboos." In the face of production problems (Morehouse, Lee's alma mater, refused cooperation just before shooting began), "School Daze" was a notable achievement on two counts. Spike Lee became perhaps the first black director given complete control by Hollywood over his film, and "School Daze", as one critic wrote, established that a vehicle which "puts real African American people on the screen" could succeed—redeeming a history of stereotyped screen images by speaking and acting from authentic experience.

Lee's next film, "Do the Right Thing" (1989), enlarged upon his successes on several levels—commercially, artistically and thematically. Based on several real-life racially motivated acts of violence in New York City, Lee's politically charged and polemical drama stirred controversy even before its release. The finished film was widely praised for its exciting and flamboyant visual craftsmanship. Like his other films, "Do the Right Thing" presents a slice-of-life look at a predominantly black environment, in this case a block of Brooklyn's Bedford-Stuyvesant neighborhood. Lee's portrait is both celebratory and critical: the "mise-en-scene", music and dialogue are rich in allusions to African-American cultural history (a deejay's litany of black musical stars mixes with the score written by the director's father, jazz bassist Bill

Lee), and, as in "School Daze", Lee also unflinchingly presents the divisions within the black community by centering the film on a photograph of Malcolm X and Martin Luther King and ending it with seemingly opposing quotations from both men. More importantly, "Do the Right Thing" focuses its tense drama on the interracial violence that occurs between Bed-Stuy's black underclass and the white family that runs the local pizzeria. Climaxing with the killing of a black youth at the hands of white policemen and a fiery street riot, Lee's film offers no resolution for the racial violence which has plagued the city.

In presenting both the inter- and intra-racial problems that have marked recent American history, Spike Lee's films collectively call for an awakening of consciousness. A sleeping character in "Joe's Bed-Stuy Barber Shop" is hailed with the line, "Wake up. The black man has been asleep for 400 years." "School Daze"'s problematic climax features warring factions greeting a sunrise with the cry, "Wake up!" "Do the Right Thing" continues the plea, as the same refrain introduces both the film and Lee's Mookie character.

Lee's next two films failed to live up to the dramatic promise of "Do the Right Thing", though both boasted strong performances, increasingly showy camerawork and colorful, stylized imagery. Inevitably, a critical backlash began to develop against the cannily self-promoting filmmaker.

"Mo' Better Blues" (1990) was Lee's first collaboration with charismatic leading man Denzel Washington, who portrays a self-absorbed jazz trumpeter forced to wake up and open his eyes and heart to the needs of those around him. The film intensified the ongoing criticism of Lee for his shallow characterization of female characters. The director also fielded charges of anti-Semitism for his scathing depiction of a pair of Jewish night club owners. In interviews Lee had decried the inauthenticity of jazz films by white filmmakers—Clint

Eastwood's "Bird" (1988) was a favorite target—claiming that, as the son of a genuine jazz musician, he was better qualified to depict that milieu. Most reviewers, however, deemed the film slight and overlong.

"Jungle Fever" (1991) again courted controversy for its depiction of a lusty affair between a black married professional man and his Italian-American working-class secretary. Despite some powerful scenes and performances, the film is sadly underwritten. The central relationship is neither adequately explained nor realistically depicted, with the film emitting much heat but little illumination on race relations, black self-hatred, or the allure of sex with the other.

Lee's next project would prove to be both his most ambitious and most controversial—indeed, the intensity of the controversy that surrounded "Malcolm X" (1992) even before shooting began made the completed film something of an anti-climax. The press gleefully related tales of Lee intimidating non-black director Norman Jewison into relinquishing the project to him. Lee persuasively argued that only a black filmmaker could tell this story, while some black intellectuals, notably poet/activist Amiri Baraka, publicly doubted that he was the man for the job: Alex Haley's "The Autobiography of Malcolm X" was a revered historical document of a hero more important to black culture than any "Spike Lee Joint." Undaunted, Lee took on the monumental project.

When the film's backers balked at escalating production costs, Lee turned to such black entertainment luminaries as Bill Cosby, Janet Jackson, Tracey Chapman, Oprah Winfrey and Michael Jordan, who gave him the money to complete the film as he envisioned it. The final product was a three-and-a-half hour, surprisingly traditional biopic that swiftly covers a great deal of material before culminating in an emotionally devastating climax. Though a huge production, the film remains "A Spike Lee Joint", encompassing everything from gangster action, flashy costumes and a big dance number, to location shooting in Mecca, with many jaunty directorial flourishes along the way. Most impressive, however, was Denzel Washington's towering performance as the charismatic black Muslim leader. Almost inevitably for a mainstream project about such a complex and controversial figure, "Malcolm X" has its flaws and omissions. Malcolm's early delinquent phase, in particular, is cleaned up for mass consumption. Nor is the extent of his later radicalism, and the controversy it provoked among both whites and blacks, adequately addressed. The Hollywood blockbuster has never been a congenial medium for overtly political filmmaking but, in the final analysis, "Malcolm X" must be viewed as the triumph of Spike Lee's will.

Lee's 1994 film "Crooklyn" was a loosely structured story of a jazz musician, his wife and their children in Brooklyn of the 70s. Packed with the sounds of the seventies, and with little narrative, "Crooklyn" could be viewed as Lee's return to the kind of depictions of neighborhood, family and characters he delivered with such adeptness in "Do The Right Thing" and "She's Gotta Have It". Co-scripted by sister Joie Lee, "Crooklyn", unlike prior Lee-helmed features, emphasized a female protagonist—here the only girl child among the Carmichael's five. Reportedly the film's brightly and loudly nostalgic family romance was only loosely based on the Lees' own youth. Alternately sloppy and shrewd, wise and idiosyncratic, the film met with an extremely mixed critical reception and poor box office.

Lee was reportedly reluctant to direct "Clockers" (1995), a much anticipated adaptation of Richard Price's acclaimed 1991 novel about the world of low-level street crack dealers in Jersey City. He felt that audiences, both black and white, were tired of the spate of grim rap-driven urban crime pictures of the preceding half decade or so. Those in the know had high hopes for "Clockers" as, originally, the august director-star team of Martin Scorsese and Robert De Niro

were attached to the project. Lee came aboard after they bowed out and proceeded to transform Price's screenplay into "A Spike Lee Joint." He shifted the locale to his beloved Brooklyn and rewrote the script to de-emphasize the white cop protagonist's angst in favor of focusing in the African-American victims and dispensers of violence. Working with neophyte feature cinematographer Malik Sayeed, Lee painted a gritty canvas of urban life far more dark and "realistic" (though still highly stylized) than in his previous films. He placed another newcomer, first-time actor Mekhi Phifer, center stage as the tormented young drug dealer Strike. Some reviewers quibbled over Lee's deviations from Price's admired original but many more hailed it as the best work of his career.

FAMILY:

father: Bill Lee. Composer, bassist; born on July 23, 1928; graduated Morehouse College in Atlanta; scored Spike Lee's early films; nickname 'Bleek' used as main character's name in "Mo' Better Blues"; former accompanist to folksinger Leon Bibb in the 1960s; married second wife, Susan Kaplan after Jacquelyn Lee's death; has son, Arnold, born c. 1985; arrested for possession of heroin October 24, 1991

sister: Joie Lee. Actor, screenwriter; born c. 1963; appeared in brother's "She's Gotta Have It", "School Daze", "Do the Right Thing", "Mo' Better Blues"

brother: Cinque Lee. Actor, screenwriter; born Brooklyn c. 1968; videotaped documentary on the making of "Do the Right Thing"

MILESTONES:

Grew up in Brooklyn, New York

Made first student films at NYU (in collaboration with cinematographer Ernest Dickerson), "The Answer" (a ten-minute film about a black screenwriter hired to write and direct a remake of "Birth of a Nation") and "Sarah"

1980: Wrote, produced and directed first medium-length student film (60-minute thesis for NYU) "Joe's Bed-Stuy Barbershop: We Cut Heads"

Founded Forty Acres and a Mule production company

1986: First feature film as director, screenwriter, producer and actor "She's Gotta Have It" (made for approximately $175,000; shot in 12 days)

1987: First book published "She's Gotta Have It: Inside Guerilla Filmmaking" (Simon & Schuster)

Directed music vidoes and Levi 501 ads

Established two annual $5000 grants for minority students at NYU's film school, "Spike Lee Minority Fellowships to Help Second or Third Year Black Students"

1991: Sued by Curtis Brown for money Brown alleged that Lee owed him from when the two men were partners in a production company called Fresh Films, Inc. (in 1984) and Lee was directing and Brown was executive producer of an unfinished film, "The Messenger"

1991: Produced first off-Broadway play, "Folks Remembers a Missing Page"

1992: Formed record label, Forty Acres and a Mule Music Works, a division of Sony; first artists signed: State of Arts, Youssou N'Dour and Lonette McKee

1992: Signed a multi-year contract with Universal Pictures

1997: Signed three-year, first-look production deal with Columbia Pictures

1997: Produced and directed the documentary "4 Little Girls"; earned Oscar nomination

1998: Had first number-one hit with "He Got Game", starring Denzel Washington

1999: Helmed the controversial "Summer of Sam"

2000: Again courted controversy with "Bamboozled", about a TV executive who creates a modern-day minstrel show that becomes a surprise hit TV series

2002: Was director of the documentary "Jim Brown: All American"; produced under the auspices of HBO sports; released theatrically in USA in March

2002: Directed the crime drama "The 25th Hour"

AFFILIATION: Member, Board of Directors, Independent Features Project

QUOTES:

Lee delivered the keynote address at the 1998 Independent Spirit Awards.

"I have the best of both worlds, because I'm an independent filmmaker but I don't have to scrape around for money. I go directly to Hollywood for my financing. It doesn't really mess with my creativity, because I have the final cut and the control over the film that I would have had if I'd raised the money all by myself. Even if I had, I'd still have to go to Hollywood for distribution anyway—there's just no way I'm going to reach the people I want to reach carrying a film can under my arm and going from theater to theater across the country—so why waste two or three years scraping for money? The studios want to make as much money off you as possible, basically just pimp you. Yet it is possible to keep your agenda and make films too."—Spike Lee to *Premiere*, August 1989.

"I'm a filmmaker. I feel that's what I was put on earth to do. But there are certain issues I have opinions about. Film's the most powerful medium in the world. I think I should have been shot if I didn't use this advantage to talk about things that affect us, being a black American today."—Spike Lee quoted in *Newsweek*, October 2, 1989.

"His style is inseparable from his content: he's subverting the conventional ways Hollywood has programmed us to read movies. He doesn't give you good guys and bad guys; he doesn't provide role models and tidy resolutions; his movies don't fall into neat generic categories. In Lee's films, realism and cartoon brush wings, and the narrative flow will suddenly break for a dance, a comic riff, a rant directed straight at the camera. Propelled by music, his rough-edged, seam-showing movies have the urgency of rap, the rhythms of the inner city and the revelations that only an insider can convey."—David Ansen in *Newsweek*, October 2, 1989.

Lee has produced and directed music videos for Public Enemy, Miles Davis, Anita Baker, E.U., Tracy Chapman, Branford Marsalis, Steel Pulse and Phyllis Hyman.

Named honorary co-chairman with NY Gov Mario Cuomo of a plan to preserve the "Negro Burial Ground", a site utilized between 1710 and 1790 (16th century) at downtown New York City.

Lee was interviewed by Anna Deavere Smith as part of "The Filmmaker Series" in *Premiere* (October, 1995).

Smith: Do you think it's important that a black man seem fierce? What if your whole persona was completely different, like "Oh, sweet Spike"—would you still get power?

Lee: Well, I mean, there's two ways to get power. You can ha-ha and chee-chee and roll your eyes and do the bug dance. Or you can say, "Look, I'm not doing that shit." White America, they just want black men to always be smiling. So if you don't do that all the time, then they label you the Angry Black Man. As if we had nothing to be angry about, anyway! I mean, a lot of people's attitude is "Look, you're successful, you have money—what do you have to be angry about?"

Smith: And your answer is?

Lee: "I was one of the lucky ones."

Lee received an honorary degree from Emerson College in 1997.

BIBLIOGRAPHY:

"Five for Five: The Films of Spike Lee" David Lee, 1991; photographic book on his brother's films

"Best Seat in the House" Spike Lee with Ralph Wiley, 1997, Crown; memoir about basketball

Mike Leigh

BORN: in Salford, Lancashire, England, 02/20/1943

NATIONALITY: English

EDUCATION: Salford Grammar School, Salford, England

Royal Academy of Dramatic Art, London, England, 1960–62; directed student production of Pinter's "The Caretaker"; quit because "This was before the Beatles, before the cultural revolution, and the training at the Royal Academy at that time was stultifying"

Camberwell School of Art, London, England, 1963–64

London International School of Film Technique, 1963–64

Central School of Art and Design, London, England, 1964–65

AWARDS: Locarno Film Festival Golden Leopard Award "Bleak Moments" 1972

Chicago Film Festival Golden Hugo Award "Bleak Moments" 1972

George Devine Award 1973

Evening Standard Award Best Comedy "Goose-Pimples" 1981; stage play

London Critics Choice Award Best Comedy "Goose-Pimples" 1981; stage play

People's Prize "Meantime" 1984

National Society of Film Critics Award Best Film "Life Is Sweet" 1991

Cannes Film Festival Best Director Award "Naked" 1993

BAFTA Michael Balcon Award for Outstanding Contribution to Cinema 1995

Cannes Film Festival Palme d'Or "Secrets & Lies" 1996

Los Angeles Film Critics Association Award Best Director "Secrets & Lies" 1996

Boston Society of Film Critics Award Best Director "Secrets & Lies" 1996

London Film Critics Circle Award Best British Director "Secrets & Lies" 1996

Independent Spirit Award Best Foreign Film "Secrets & Lies" 1996

BAFTA Award Best Original Screenplay "Secrets & Lies" 1996

BAFTA Alexander Korda Award for Outstanding British Film "Secrets & Lies" 1996, shared with producer Simon Channing-Williams

Humanitas Prize feature film "Secrets & Lies" 1997

Australian Film Institute Award Best Foreign Film "Secrets & Lies" 1997

New York Film Critics Circle Award Best Director "Topsy-Turvy" 1999

National Society of Film Critics Award Best Director "Topsy-Turvy" 1999

London Film Critics Circle Special Achievement Award 2000

Evening Standard British Film Award Best Film "Topsy-Turvy" 2000

BIOGRAPHY

This stage, TV and film director is noted for his film style—in which the commonplace is often tinged with the extraordinary—has been dubbed "social surrealism," or as he prefers to call it, "heightened realism." A creative force in London's experimental fringe theater since the 1960s, Mike Leigh earned critical acclaim for his numerous TV films investigating the vicissitudes of life among the "proles", notably the 1977 drama, "Abigail's Party."

After making his feature debut with "Bleak Moments" (1971), Leigh took a 17-year hiatus, working exclusively for British stage and TV. He returned to films, winning international attention for "High Hopes" (1988), a grim portrait of Thatcherite London. Leigh's low-key style and his knack for offbeat characterization and warm humor all enrich his surprisingly life-affirming 1991 comedy "Life Is Sweet" about a

dysfunctional working class family. His next effort, "Naked" (1993), was a stark portrait of one man's (David Thewlis) journey into the bowels of his soul. Critically acclaimed in the USA and at the Cannes Film Festival (where he was named Best Director and Thewlis Best Actor), the film was largely panned in England, with most reviewers citing what they saw as the story's misogynistic aspects.

In 1996, Leigh directed what many critics felt was his best film to date, "Secrets & Lies." The winner of the Cannes Film Festival Palme d'Or, it focused on two women, a twentysomething black optometrist adoptee (Marianne Jean-Baptiste) and a heavy-drinking middle-aged working-class white woman (Brenda Blethyn), the former's birth mother. When their lives intersect, the results create familial conflicts and anguish. The film earned five Oscar nominations, including two for Leigh's directions and screenplay. His follow-up "Career Girls" (1997), was thought by some to be a disappointment, particularly in light of the success of "Secret & Lies." A look at female friendship, "Career Girls" delivered on its own merits an off-centered examination of human relationships.

Leigh triumphed with his next major film, "Topsy-Turvy" (1999), inspired by the lives of the operetta writing team of W.S. Gilbert and Arthur Sullivan. Interspersing snippets of production numbers (mostly from "The Mikado"), the film was an aural and visual feast that entranced critics and enchanted audiences. Atypical of Leigh's gritty dramas, "Topsy-Turvy" was a period drama that held contemporary resonance and raised issues about the creation of art.

MILESTONES:

Spent one year as assistant stage manager and bit part actor (in episode of TV series, "Maigret")

1965: Wrote and directed first play, "The Box Play", produced at Midlands Arts Centre, Birmingham

1965–1966: Served as associate director, Midlands Arts Centre Theatre, Birmingham

1966: Formed Dramagraph production company with author David Halliwell to produce Halliwell's play, "Little Malcolm and His Struggle Against the Eunuchs", directed by Leigh (date approximate); company went bankrupt

1966: Acted at the Victora Theater, Stoke-on-Trent

Joined the RSC as an assistant director; directed "Nenaa" for RSC

1972: Wrote and directed first feature film, "Bleak Moments"

1973: Made first TV drama "Hard Labour"

1975: Made series of five "Five Minute Films" (first broadcast in 1982)

1979: Directed and wrote radio play, "Too Much of a Good Thing"

1982: Subject of TV film, "Mike Leigh" Making Plays"

Co-founded with Simon Channing-Williams and Adam Bernstein Imagine Productions, a film, TV and video production House

1991: Commissioned by the London Film Festival to make a new promotional trailer for the event, "Moving Pictures"

1996: Had biggest US hit "Secrets & Lies"

1997: Helmed "Career Girls"

1999: Directed "Topsy-Turvy", a period comedy-drama with music, about the collaboration between W.S. Gilbert & Arthur Sullivan

2002: Wrote and directed "All or Nothing", a contemporary drama about three troubled families in London

AFFILIATION: Jewish

QUOTES:
Created an Officer of the Order of Arts and Letters by the French government in 1998

Leigh "remains a merciless observer of British social types. Leigh has an uncanny gift for creating characters who, even at their most extreme, are such accurate reflections of the way the British think and talk that it comes as a shock to learn that—like the late John Cassavetes—he works without a script."—From Kathleen Carroll's review of "Life Is Sweet" in the *Daily News*, October 25, 1991.

"Much of the '60s ethos survives in the way Leigh arrives at his complex structures—a process that's collaborative, improvisational, and always political. His starting point is unusually an impulse that has not quite jelled into an idea. 'Actors have to agree to doing a work without knowing what it's going to be about or what their part will be," [Leigh explains]. Rehearsals begin as a series of one-on-one conversations, with Leigh urging each actor to describe as many real people as he or she can. Over time Leigh locates one character in each actor's gallery of acquaintances who resonates with characters the other actors have exhumed. Only then does he bring the cast together for improvisations that transform these potential relationships into dramatic material, which in turn evolves into a 'strictly rehearsed and scripted' story."—From *Premiere*, April 1989.

Leigh's theater credits include "Babies Grow Old" (1974), "The Silent Majority" (1974), "Abigail's Party" (1977), "Ecstasy" (1979) and "Smelling a Rat" (1988). His BBC credits include "Hard Labour" (1973), "Home Sweet Home" (1982), "Four Days in July" (1984) and for Channel 4 "Meantime" (1981).

Leigh received the Order of the British Empire in 1993.

BIBLIOGRAPHY:
"The Films of Mike Leigh: Embracing the World" Ray Carney and Leonard Quart, 2000, Cambridge University Press

BORN: Claude Barruck Joseph Lelouch in Paris, France, 10/30/1937

NATIONALITY: French

EDUCATION: College Sainte-Barbe, France, 1953

AWARDS: Oscar Best Writing (Story and Screenplay Written Directly for the Screen) "A Man and a Woman" 1966

Cannes Film Festival Palme d'Or "A Man and a Woman" 1966

Los Angeles Film Critics Association Award Best Foreign Film "And Now My Love" 1975

Cannes Film Festival Technique Award "Les Uns et les autres" 1981

Golden Globe Award Best Foreign Language Film "Les Miserables" 1995

London Film Critics Circle Award Best Foreign Language Film "Les Miserables" 1996

BIOGRAPHY

This French director emerged in the 1960s, scoring a popular international success with the romantic melodrama, "A Man and a Woman" (1966). Despite an early reputation as an "outsider" who combined social criticism with a flashy visual technique, Lelouch rapidly became assimilated into the mainstream of commercial French cinema, remaining prolific throughout three decades and often producing the films of other directors.

Lelouch had spent the earliest years of his childhood hiding from the Nazis alongside his mother. They were captured and sent to the Dachau concentration camp three months before the end of World War II. Both mother and son were liberated and returned to Paris, where they were reunited with Lelouch's father. Lelouch was an indifferent student and he failed his entrance exams into higher education. He

father agreed to finance his cinematic dreams as long as the result showed promise. Traveling with his father, Lelouch made several amateur documentaries, leading to "Le Mal du siecle" (1954), a parody of war as seen through the games at a fair, that won the amateur film division of the Cannes Film Festival.

After making short films while serving in the military, Lelouch established Les Films 13, a production company, and produced, co-wrote, directed and appeared in his first feature "Le Propre de l'homme" (1960). It was a disastrous debut and he spent the next two years making backdrop short films for juke boxes (to run while music was playing) in order to pay off his debts. By 1963, Lelouch was back making films, and in 1966, he won international acclaim with "Un Homme et une femme/A Man and a Woman", which starred Anouk Aimee and Jean-Paul Belmondo as recently widowed people who find each other and love, only to have it all slip away when the woman cannot fully bury her deceased husband. Lelouch won the Oscar for Best Original Screenplay for his work (almost unheard of for a foreign-language film) and landed a ten picture distribution deal with United Artists as well. His subsequent work has never again achieved the international notice of "Un Homme et une femme", but he has been applauded for the spontaneity of his work and the freedom of movement of his style. Lelouch has often operated the camera himself and pioneered the use of compact, light equipment. His films have run the gamut from the well-received "La Bonne annee" (1973), in which a jewel thief and an antique dealer romance, to the disastrous "Another Man, Another Chance" (1977), which starred James Caan and Genevieve Bujold in a story of the romance of an American and a French widow in the Old West. Lelouch reunited Aimee and Belmondo in 1986 in "Un Homme et une femme: Vingt ans deja/A Man and a Woman: 20 Years Later", in which the star-crossed lovers, she now a producer, he now a director, meet again. In 1995, Warner Bros. distributed Lelouch's "Les Miserables", which moved the setting of the Victor Hugo classic to World War II, and starred Belmondo. While it failed to spark at the box office, it received favorable critical notice and earned a Golden Globe Award as Best Foreign Film.

MILESTONES:

Spend WWII in hiding from Nazis; sent to Dachau three months before it was liberated

1954: Short film, "Mal du siecle" won first prize in the amateur division of the Cannes Film Festival

1957–1960: Spent army service making short films

1960: Directed, produced, wrote, and starred in the disastrous "Le Propre de l'homme", his first feature

Made more than 100 short films to be shown as a backdrop in juke boxes

1963: Revived company, Les Films 13

1966: Scored international success with "Un Homme et une femme/A Man and a Woman"

1967: Entered into 10-film distribution deal with United Artists (UA)

1973: Achieved solid international success with "Le Bonne annee"

1977: Made the disastrous English-language "Another Man, Another Chance"

1986: Reprised characters in "Un Homme et une femme: Vingt ans deja/A Man and a Woman: 20 Years Later"

1995: Directed "Les Miserables"

QUOTES:

Lelouch on Lelouch: "I'm a man of the left living in a capitalist context. [My life] is a series of improvisations day to day. I've arrived at a position where I stand in awe neither of criticism nor the critics. Everything had been said about me. Good and bad. So now I can say anything I want . . . I don't make a film in order to be loved, but so that people will come and see it."

Sergio Leone

BORN: in Rome, Italy, 01/03/1921

SOMETIMES CREDITED AS:
Bob Robertson

DEATH: in Rome, Italy, 04/30/1989

NATIONALITY: Italian

EDUCATION: attended law school in Rome

BIOGRAPHY

Began his career as an assistant on numerous Italian productions of the late 1940s and early 50s and came to prominence in the 1960s, when he revitalized the western genre with a series of gritty, semi-satirical homages known as "spaghetti westerns." "The cowboy picture has got lost in psychology," he said; "The West was made by violent uncomplicated men, and it is this strength and simplicity that I try to recapture in my pictures."

Leone's gun-and-sun operas, with their spasmodic violence, striking and insistent use of closeups (often immediately following panoramic establishing shots) and motif-laden Ennio Morricone scores, provided employment for a number of American actors, most notably Lee Van Cleef and Clint Eastwood, who starred as the laconic anti-hero of "A Fistful of Dollars" (1964), "For a Few Dollars More" (1966) and "The Good, the Bad, and the

Ugly" (1966). Leone's last major project was "Once Upon a Time in America" (1984), a bloody tribute to the American gangster film. Though praised at the Cannes Film Festival and across Europe, it was severely cut for US release to an extent which made it almost incomprehensible. Father Vincenzo Leone was a noted silent film director.

MILESTONES:

1948: Acted in Vittorio De Sica's landmark classic of neorealism, "The Bicycle Thief"

1947–1956: Worked as an assistant to Italian and American filmmakers (Mervyn LeRoy, Raoul Walsh, William Wyler) in Italy

Worked as an assistant director on such American productions as "Helen of Troy" (1956), "The Nun's Story", "Ben Hur" (both 1959)

1959: First credit as co-screenwriter, "Nel segno di Roma/Sign of the Gladiator"

1959: Replaced ailing Mario Bonnard as director (also co-screenwriter) on "Last Days of Pompeii" starring Steve Reeves; refused to accept screen credit

1961: Directed first credited feature film, "The Colossus of Rhodes"

Worked as assistant to Robert Aldrich on "Sodom and Gomorrah"

1964: Achieved international success with the first installment in his "Man with No Name" trilogy, "A Fistful of Dollars" (under the pseudonym Bob Robertson), starring Clint Eastwood

1973: Credited with the story idea for "My Name Is Nobody"

Headed his own production company, Rafran Cinematografica

Briefly moved to France in the late 1970s

1984: Last major directorial effort, "Once Upon a Time in America"

BIBLIOGRAPHY:

"Cinema: A Critical Dictionary" Richard Roud (editor) 1980; an interesting entry on Leone discusses the "contradictions" of "the Leone universe"

"Sergio Leone: Something To Do With Death" Christopher Frayling, 2000, Faber and Faber

Richard Lester

BORN: in Philadelphia, Pennsylvania, 01/19/1932

SOMETIMES CREDITED AS:
Dick Lester

NATIONALITY: American

EDUCATION: began grade school aged three
William Penn Charter School, Philadelphia, Pennsylvania, 1947; graduated aged 15
University of Pennsylvania, Philadelphia, Pennsylvania, clinical psychology, BS, 1947–51; member of theatrical groups; composed music for revues; formed jazz combo, The Vocal Group, in senior year

AWARDS: Cannes Film Festival Palme d'Or "The Knack . . . and How To Get It" 1965
MTV Music Video Vanguard Award 1984 cited with The Beatles and David Bowie

BIOGRAPHY
Young American TV director in the 1950s who took a break to travel around Europe, settled in England, and established a career directing some landmarks of 1960s cinema.

Lester's career began with a Peter Sellers collaboration, the short "The Running, Jumping, and Standing Still Film" (1959). He reached major prominence with the Beatles movies, "A Hard Day's Night" (1964) and "Help!" (1965), chronicling the fictional adventures of the pop group in appropriately zany, exuberant style. "The Knack . . . and How To Get It" (1965), from the popular play by Ann Jellicoe, with Michael Crawford and Rita Tushingham, assured his reputation, not only as the chief chronicler of "swinging London" in the 60s, but also as a film stylist whose work has had a profound effect on contemporary film language. Even more than his New Wave contemporaries, Lester freed the camera to join the action, and freed filmmakers from conventions that had become tired and restrictive by that time.

While poorly received at the time, "A Funny Thing Happened On the Way to the Forum" (1966), from the rambunctious musical by Stephen Sondheim and starring a gallery of classic "farceurs" from Zero Mostel to Buster Keaton, remains a classic translation of a rich stage musical—one of few that try to match the moviemaking to the music.

After attempting to apply the same freewheeling style to a more ambitious antiwar subject in "How I Won the War" (1967), Lester returned to America for "Petulia" (1968), an essay on life in these United States set against the background of the Vietnam war, which quickly became a connoisseur's favorite. The story of the breakdown of a marriage set in the hills of San Francisco captured the uneasiness of the times with a haunting metaphor. Back in London, Lester turned to apocalyptic farce with "The Bed-Sitting Room" (1969), a post-nuclear-war idyll which went straight over the heads of audiences the world over who had not yet discovered "Monty Python-s Flying Circus" and couldn't remember "The Goon Show."

Lester sat out the next four years, busying himself with witty TV commercials. When he returned to the big screen with "The Three Musketeers" in 1973, the 60s were long past. His subsequent films, mainly big-budget serial blockbuster productions, have been witty but far more mainstream. But then, so have the times. The Richard Lester of the 60s remains one of the most influential filmmakers of the last 30 years as the anarchic techniques he pioneered have become staples of the contemporary pop video lexicon.

MILESTONES:

Began reading aged three; taught self piano aged 12, became a jazz aficionado

Performed (with The Vocal Group), floor managed and assistant directed at local Philadelphia TV station (WCAU); graduated to director within one year

1954–1955: Moved to Europe as roving newspaper reporter; supported himself as jazz pianist in Europe and North Africa

1955: Moved to Great Britain; wrote TV musical "Curtains for Harry" (broadcast by Associated Rediffusion); had own short-lived TV show, "The Dick Lester Show"; directed "Downbeat," a series of jazz programs for Associated Rediffusion

1956: After marriage, left England, worked in TV in Canada and then Australia; after about a year returned to England and began collaborating (directing, co-writing) with Peter Sellers and Spike Milligan on TV series "Idiot's Weekly, Price Twopence," "A Show Called Fred" and "Son of Fred"

1959: Short film directing debut (also actor), "The Running Jumping & Standing Still Film"

1961: Feature directing debut, "It's Trad, Dad/Ring-a-Ding Rhythm"

1966: US feature directing debut, "A Funny Thing Happened on the Way to the Forum"

1970: Began directing TV commercials in Europe

QUOTES:

In his early work (e.g. "The Dick Lester Show") Lester was credited as Dick Lester.

BIBLIOGRAPHY:

"Getting Away With It: Or, The Further Adventures of the Luckiest Bastard You Ever Saw" Steven Soderbergh and Richard Lester, 2000, Faber and Faber

BORN: in Baltimore, Maryland, 04/06/1942

NATIONALITY: American

EDUCATION: Community College of Baltimore, Baltimore, Maryland
American University, Washington, DC; broadcast journalism worked for a local TV station while a student
studied acting in Los Angeles

AWARDS: Emmy Best Writer in a Comedy-Variety Music Series "The Carol Burnett Show" 1973/74; shared with other writers
Emmy Outstanding Writing in a Comedy-Variety or Music Series "The Carol Burnett Show" 1974/75; shared with other writers
Directors Guild of America Award Best Motion Picture Director "Rain Man" 1988
Oscar Best Director "Rain Man" 1988
Berlin Film Festival Golden Bear "Rain Man" 1989
Writers Guild of America Award Best Screenplay Written Directly for the Screen "Avalon" 1990
George Eastman Award 1991; given by ShowEast at its annual fall exhibitors convention
Los Angeles Film Critics Association Award Best Picture "Bugsy" 1991; award shared with co-producers Warren Beatty and Mark Johnson
Los Angeles Film Critics Association Award Best Director "Bugsy" 1991
Emmy Outstanding Individual Achievement in Directing in a Drama Series "Gone for Goode" (episode of "Homicide: Life on the Street") 1992/93
CableACE Award Dramatic Series "Oz" 1997; shared award; Levinson was an executive producer
ShoWest Director of the Year Award 1998
Berlin Film Festival Silver Bear "Wag the Dog" 1998

Golden Satellite Best Television Series (Drama) "Oz" 1998; shared award
American Comedy Award for Lifetime Achievement 1999
Golden Satellite Best Television Mini-Series "An American Tragedy" 2000
American Cinema Editors Golden Eddie Filmmaker of the Year Award 2002

BIOGRAPHY
Barry Levinson entered the entertainment business as a comic writer and performer, forming a stand-up duo with actor Craig T. Nelson and, with Nelson and Rudy DeLuca, wrote for several TV programs like "The Tim Conway Show" (CBS, 1970) and "The John Byner Comedy Hour" (CBS, 1972). His work on "The Carol Burnett Show" earned him back-to-back Emmy Awards (shared with others) for Outstanding Writing in a Comedy-Variety or Music Series" (1973/74, 1974/75) before he graduated to film work. With Mel Brooks, Levinson co-scripted and appeared in both "Silent Movie" (1976) and "High Anxiety" (1977), providing a memorable turn as the maniacal bellhop in the latter. His next feature project, Norman Jewison's " . . . And Justice for All" (1979), marked the first of five films he would co-write with his first wife Valerie Curtin.

Levinson made an auspicious debut directing his script "Diner" (1982), a semi-autobiographical coming-of-age tale set in late 50s Baltimore. Alternately poignant and hilarious, the film played a large part in promoting the careers of its young stars Mickey Rourke, Steve Guttenberg, Daniel Stern, Kevin Bacon and Ellen Barkin. Levinson demonstrated an understated, non-intrusive style and an ear for ensemble dialogue that would serve him well in subsequent features. His next directorial project, "The Natural" (1984), adapted from Bernard Malamud's 1952 novel and starring Robert Redford as baseball pro Roy Hobbs, received mixed reviews, with some critics finding it inconsistent and sentimental, but nearly all praised the cinematography (Caleb Deschanel) and score (Randy Newman). "Young Sherlock Holmes" (1985) was a mildly charming Steven Spielberg–produced project that turned out to be long on special effects but short on inspiration.

1987 saw the release of two Levinson films, one returning to the autobiographical territory first explored in "Diner" and the other establishing the director's major-league box-office credentials. "Tin Men," set in Baltimore in 1963—several years after the events of "Diner"—followed the misadventures of rival aluminum-siding salesmen. A rich character study, it maintained a fine balance between humor and melancholy, and featured some brilliantly funny dialogue, mostly traded between Richard Dreyfuss and Danny DeVito, the two protagonists. "Good Morning, Vietnam", a commercially successful Robin Williams vehicle, gave its star the chance to tap his improvisational genius in delivering a series of highly effective comic monologues. It earned Williams an Oscar nomination but failed to fully exploit Levinson's talents for ensemble character studies.

Levinson's next feature was "Rain Man" (1988), a finely handled study of the relationship between an autistic "idiot savant" (Dustin Hoffman) and his opportunistic car-salesman brother (Tom Cruise). A huge success at the box office, the film not surprisingly won four Oscars: Best Picture, Best Director (Levinson), Best Actor (Hoffman) and Best Screenplay (Ronald Bass and Barry Morrow). While the central performances garnered most of the critical attention, the director's adept handling of the unorthodox subject-matter with sensitivity and style was central to the film's success. The project had been through at least three other directors and countless re-writes before Levinson finally came on-board two weeks before shooting began. He again returned to Baltimore and for the first time served as producer (in addition to writing

and directing) of "Avalon" (1990), an epic (if curiously deracinated) saga tracing the history of his own family from the point they first arrived in the USA. Critics reacted with measured praise to a work they felt to be overlong and lacking in direction, if ultimately rewarding. That such a personal and uncommercial project could even be produced in the Hollywood of the early 90s bore witness to its director-producer's commitment and vision.

Levinson followed with the lavish "Bugsy" (1991), a stylish if superficial Warren Beatty vehicle centered on gangster Bugsy Siegel and his efforts to establish Las Vegas as a gaming center. While it was critically well received and earned 10 Oscar nominations including Best Picture and Best Director, the film was only a minor financial success. The visual excesses of Levinson's next film, the flop "Toys" (1992), may have contributed to his interest in helming the character-driven "Jimmy Hollywood" (1994), an episodic, anecdotal comedy filmed on a relatively small budget, which also proved a box-office disappointment. In an effort to get his career back on track, Levinson made the commercial, star-driven vehicle "Disclosure" (1994), adapted from Michael Crichton's best-selling thriller by Paul Attanasio. Levinson skillfully orchestrated a suspenseful examination of a new wrinkle on the potential for sexual harassment in the work place. That same year, he made a rare acting appearance in Robert Redford's "Quiz Show", also scripted by Attanasio, playing original "Today" show host Dave Garroway.

Levinson picked up a Best Director Emmy for the pilot episode of the weekly police detective series created by Attanasio, "Homicide: Life on the Street" (NBC, 1993–99), which he produced and shot in his native Baltimore. While the series covered familiar, if not cliched, territory, what was noteworthy was the slightly disorienting hand-held camerawork and story lines spanning several weeks of episodes. His next feature "Sleepers" (1996), which he produced, wrote and directed, received mixed notices and prolonged the controversy that had surrounded the Lorenzo Carcaterra book following its publication the year before as to whether the supposedly true story of institutional abuse was indeed factual. He then continued his association with screenwriter Attanasio, producing the successful wise guys tale "Donnie Brasco" (1997), which also reunited him with Al Pacino.

Barry Levinson has exhibited the courage to take risks turning out remarkably dissimilar movies on his own terms. Though perhaps closest to his autobiographical Baltimore trilogy, he has scored huge hits with intimidating projects like "Rain Man" and "Good Morning, Vietnam", and his few misses have not diminished his bankability. With the David Mamet–scripted "Wag the Dog" (1997), producer-director Levinson delivered a starstudded comedy-drama about the world of politics and TV. He then tackled science fiction for the first time with "Sphere" (1998), a thriller co-scripted by Attanasio starring Dustin Hoffman (in his fourth turn for Levinson), Samuel L. Jackson and Sharon Stone with less than stellar results. Returning to the Baltimore of his youth, Levinson hit pay dirt with "Liberty Heights" (1999), a nostalgic look at coming-of-age in the mid-20th century.

MILESTONES:

Worked as a floor director of a Washington, DC television station

Moved to Los Angeles after graduating from college

Founder and partner, Savan-Levinson-Parker talent agency

Formed comedy duo with actor-friend Craig T. Nelson; wrote comedy with Nelson and Rudy DeLuca; signed by Michael Ovitz

1970: Worked as writer on "The Tim Conway Show"

Worked as writer (with Rudy DeLuca) and performer on "The Carol Burnett Show"

1974: First screenwriting credit (shared with director Michael Miller) on "Street Girls"

1976: Co-writer (with director Mel Brooks and Rudy DeLuca), "Silent Movie"

1977: First film as actor (played bit part of Dennis the bellboy), "High Anxiety"

1979: Co-wrote screenplay for " . . . And Justice for All", the first of five such collaborations with first wife Valerie Curtin; also first screen collaboration with Al Pacino; received first Oscar nomination for Best Screenplay

1982: Feature film directing debut (also writer), "Diner", the first movie in what would become his Baltimore trilogy; won Oscar nomination for its script

1987: Wrote and directed "Tin Men", second film set in the Baltimore of his youth

1988: Won Best Director Oscar for "Rain Man", starring Dustin Hoffman and Tom Cruise

1990: First film as producer (also writer and director), "Avalon"; completed Baltimore trilogy with this ambitious story chronicling his family since their arrival in the USA; nominated for Best Screenplay

Founded Baltimore Picture Company with Mark Johnson

1991: Wrote and directed the acclaimed biopic "Bugsy", starring Warren Beatty; film was nominated as Best Picture and Levinson earned a Best Director nomination

1993–1999: Executive produced (and directed pilot episode) his first TV drama series, "Homicide: Life on the Street", a gritty NBC police procedural set in Baltimore

1994: Played Dave Garroway in Robert Redford's "Quiz Show"

1994: Produced, wrote and directed "Jimmy Hollywood", which did not click with audiences

1996: Received mixed reviews for "Sleepers" (produced, directed and wrote)

1997: Produced the hit "Donnie Brasco"; reteamed him with Al Pacino

1997—Present: Served as one of the executive producers of the acclaimed HBO prison drama "Oz"

1997: David Mamet-scripted "Wag the Dog"

reunited him with Dustin Hoffman and Craig T. Nelson

1998: Produced and directed "Sphere", a sci-fi thriller starring Hoffman, Samuel L. Jackson and Sharon Stone

1998: Merged Baltimore Pictures with Spring Creek Prods. (formed by Paula Weinstein); formed Baltimore Spring Creek Pictures; production company under contract at Warner Bros.

1999: With Fontana served as creator and executive producer of the midseason replacement series "The Beat" (UPN)

1999: Wrote and helmed "Liberty Heights", the fourth of his films set in 1950s Baltimore

2000: Was one of the executive producers of "The Perfect Storm"

2000: Served as an executive producer on the CBS miniseries "An American Tragedy" that focused on the O. J. Simpson murder trial

2000: Directed the Irish-set comedy "An Everlasting Piece"

2001: Produced and directed the crime comedy "Bandits"

2002: With Paula Weinstein, produced "Possession", Neil LaBute's adaptation of the A.S. Byatt novel

2002: With Fontana, served as executive producer of the HBO pilot "Baseball Wives"

2002: Was executive producer (with Paula Weinstein) on "Analyze That"

QUOTES:

Not to be confused with American producer Barry Levinson (born New York City, 1932; died in London, October 23, 1987), active mostly in Europe.

On Warren Beatty's comment that you don't finish a film, you abandon it: "At some point you have to hand it over. It's always tough. 'The Natural' is the only one that plays in my head, because I never really thought I finished it. We were so rushed to get the movie out. The sad thing is, it was supposed to be the first TriStar movie, and they were adamant, saying 'You've got to come out May 15,' or whatever the hell the date was. After we finally turned the thing over, they decided to make 'Where the Boys Are '84' the first TriStar movie. So it was locked and they threw another movie in front of it."— Barry Levinson in *Premiere*, January 1997.

"I'm closest to the Baltimore movies because they are parts of my life and growing up. In many ways, they are the most painful ones to do because you put yourself on the line. Not just in terms of your work but you've invested something that's deeper in terms of your soul. Therefore you're more vulnerable. You get angry if you read something that can attack that. I've always remembered the comment in *Variety* about 'Avalon'—it said the movie has no reason to exist. I said to myself, 'There are 350 movies a year that get made and they don't say it about them. 'Avalon'? That's dealing with a number of issues about the flight to suburbia, the influence of television, the break-up of the family. It has no reason to exist?' I never got over that. It just completely drove me crazy."—Barry Levinson quoted in *San Francisco Examiner*, September 28, 1997.

"As my past has infiltrated my movies through the years, I have been criticized for making some of my characters too Jewish and others not Jewish enough. When 'Diner' came out in 1982, someone complained: 'I didn't know that some of the guys were Jewish until the end of the movie. It should be more clear.' After 'Avalon,' in 1990, people asked, 'Why didn't they celebrate Jewish holidays?' Or, more pointedly, 'They didn't look Jewish enough.' This is difficult to respond to, since my Uncle Ben looked like Harry James. In fact, he once told me that on a trip to New York, he'd gotten great seats in a nightclub because the maitre d' thought he WAS Harry James.

"I had a great uncle who looked like Santa Claus—a Santa who spoke only Yiddish."— From "Barry Levinson: Baltimore, My Baltimore" in *The New York Times*, November 14, 1999.

BORN: in Pittsburgh, Pennsylvania, 07/15/1926

SOMETIMES CREDITED AS:
R. L. Smith
Sheldon Seymour
Gordon Weisenborn
Herschell Lewis
Lewis H. Gordon

NATIONALITY: American

EDUCATION: Northwestern University, Evanston, Illinois, journalism, MA

BIOGRAPHY

Legendary pioneer in the arena of "gore" or "splatter" flicks, Herschell Gordon Lewis moved smartly from the strictures of academia (he had been a literature professor at the University of Mississippi) to the shadowy world of 1950s "nudie" films to the wide open spaces of regional exploitation filmmaking in the 60s and early 70s. He was not a particularly talented filmmaker; indeed the direction, scripting, performances and production values of even his "best" films were often shockingly bad. However Lewis has earned a place in the history of American independent filmmaking for upping the ante on the representation of violence (as well as gratuitous sex) in film while demonstrating that commercial genre fare could be produced on a shoestring totally outside the Hollywood system. Lewis remains the guru of movie gorehounds because his films retain their power to shock. Furthermore, if one can deal with the carnage, they can be screamingly funny.

Lewis is credited with inventing the gore film with "Blood Feast" (1963). Shot in Miami, FL, in "Blood Color", the film told the absurd story of an insane caterer cum author who, obsessed with resurrecting the spirit of the Egyptian princess Ishtar, goes about hacking off parts of female victims to use as courses in a "Blood Feast" in Ishtar's honor. If the acting was as good as Lewis' gore effects, the movie would have been unwatchable. The canny inclusion of several *Playboy* playmates in the cast only served to bolster the box office. "Blood Feast" became a huge success on the drive-in circuit.

Much of Lewis' target audience was based in the rural South. This may help explain the subject matter of his second Florida-lensed horror effort, the genuinely unsettling "Two Thousand Maniacs" (1964). Three vacationing couples from the North get detoured to a small southern town called Pleasant Valley and become special guests of honor at the town's centennial celebration. Unfortunately this entails all manner of grisly torture and murder because the villagers are actually ghosts from the Civil War intent on avenging the destruction of their town by the Union army 100 years before. Filming on a budget of less than $40,000, Lewis demonstrated considerable growth as a filmmaker with some good camerawork. Generally acknowledged as Lewis' best work—as well as his personal favorite—"Two Thousand Maniacs", while quite profitable, did not duplicate the success of "Blood Feast."

Initially Lewis was the only filmmaker making this kind of entertainment but many others soon followed. Lewis did not limit himself to splatter; his subsequent credits include sci-fi ("Monster A Go-Go" 1965), juvenile delinquent dramas ("Just for the Hell of It" 1968), and some that defy easy classification ("Something Weird" 1966–68). He is even reputed to have helmed several cheapie kids' flicks! Lewis often wore several hats on his productions, serving as producer, director, cinematographer, composer and special effects man. A number of his films were released under pseudonyms and some never got north of the Mason-Dixon line. His final horror film, "The Gore-Gore Girls" (1972), which featured Henny Youngman as a nightclub owner whose strippers start meeting horrific fates, was one of the first films to receive an "X" rating for violence.—Written by Kent Greene

MILESTONES:

Worked as a college literature professor at the University of Mississippi

Left teaching to become station manager of WRAC Radio in Racine, Wisconsin

Moved on to manage WKY-TV in Oklahoma City, Oklahoma

Entered filmmaking by creating TV commercials for a Chicago-based advertising agency

1953: Began supplementing income by teaching mass communications at Roosevelt University in Chicago

Became partner in Lewis and Martin Films, a commercial production company co-owned with Martin Schmidhofer

1956: Met David F. Friedman

Worked in 1950s pornography industry producing "nudie" flicks

1960: "Legitimate" feature debut, produced and directed "The Prime Time", a black-and-white melodrama shot in Chicago; also marked Karen Black's film debut

1963: Produced (with David F. Friedman and Stanford S. Kohlberg), directed, lensed, scored and provided special effects for "Blood Feast", a landmark exploitation film considered to be the first "gore" or "splatter" film; shot in Miami, Florida, in "Blood Color"

1964: Directed, scripted, lensed and scored "Two Thousand Maniacs", generally considered his best film; produced by David F. Friedman and shot in St. Cloud, FL, on a budget of less than $40,000; wrote and performed the catchy theme song "The Rebel Yell"

1965: Directed, wrote and lensed "Color Me Blood Red", shot in Florida and produced by Friedman (their final collaboration);

reportedly Lewis and Friedman had a falling out during shooting, the director walked and the producer completed the picture

1965-1967: Took a hiatus from gore films

Made the children's films "Jimmy, The Boy Wonder" and "Santa Visits the Magic Land of Mother Goose"

1965: Purchased an unfinished sci-fi flick entitled "Terror at Halfday", added narration and additional footage and released film as "Monster A Go-Go"; under the pseudonym Sheldon Seymour, served as producer and co-director with Bill Rebane

1967: Made several "sexploitation" films, "Alley Tramp", "Suburban Roulette", "The Girl, the Body, and the Pill" and "Blast-Off Girls"

1972: Produced and directed his final horror film, "The Gore Gore Girls"; one of the first films to receive an X rating for violence

Manufactured and sold limited edition collectors' plates

Served as president of Communicomp, a direct mail advertising agency that was a division of Bozell, Jacobs, Kenyon & Eckhardt, located in Plantation, Florida

Returned to filmmaking as director of "Blood Feast 2: Buffet of Blood" (lensed 2001)

QUOTES:

"The surprisingly witty Lewis is fond of referring to "Blood Feast" as a 'Walt Whitman poem—it's no good, but it's the first of its type and therefore deserves a certain position'."—From "Nightmare Movies: A Critical Guide to Contemporary Horror Films" by Kim Newman (NY: Harmony Books, 1988).

"Lewis had initiated an exploitation-film trend when he switched from Russ Meyer-style "nudie-cuties" to spectacles of unregenerate Grand Guignol, known in the industry as "gore films". . . . "Blood Feast" and its successors featured gruesome murders and eviscerations whose verisimilitude depended mainly on the judicious deployment of animal intestines and whose victims were inevitably half-clad young women. Lewis's films were particularly successful in southern drive-ins but his first critical cult was developed by young French film buffs who had to travel to the more liberal Belgium to see his work. (Told, some years later, that he'd been categorized by *Cahiers du Cinema* as 'a subject for further research,' Lewis riposted, 'That's what they say about cancer.')"—From "Midnight Movies" by J. Hoberman & Jonathan Rosenbaum (New York: Harper & Row, 1983).

Frank Henenlotter's "Basket Case" (1981) is dedicated to Lewis in its end titles.

On the "auteur" theory, Lewis holds strong opinions: "Anybody can aim a camera. That doesn't require any talent at all. You turn it on and you get a picture. To get people to say, 'I want to see that', you have to have a mastery of primitive psychology. I wasn't a director, I just wanted to get people into the theatre."—From *The Independent,* July 19, 2001.

BIBLIOGRAPHY:

"The Businessman's Guide to Advertising and Sales Promotion" Herschell Gordon Lewis

"Amazing Herschell Gordon Lewis, and His World of Exploitation Films" Daniel Krogh

"Herschell Gordon Lewis on the Art of Writing Copy" 1988, Prentice Hall

"Power Copywriting: Dynamic New Communications Techniques to Help You Sell More Products and Services" Herschell Gordon Lewis, 1994, Dartnell Corporation reprint

"Everybody's Guide to Plate Collecting" Margo Lewis and Herschell Gordon Lewis, 1994, Bonus Books

"Open Me Now" Hershell Gordon Lewis, 1995, Bonus Books

"Silver Linings: Selling to the Expanding Mature Market" Herschell Gordon Lewis, 1996, Bonus Books

"The World's Greatest Direct Mail Sales Letters" Herschell Gordon Lewis and Carol Nelson, 1996, N.T.C. Publishing Group

"Selling on the Net" Herschell Gordon Lewis and Robert D. Lewis, 1997, N.T.C. Publishing Group

"Cybertalk That Sells" Herschell Gordon Lewis and Jamie Murphy, 1998, N.T.C. Publishing Group

"How to Write Powerful Fund Raising Letters" Herschell Gordon Lewis, 1998, Precept Press

"Sales Letters That Sizzle" Herschell Gordon Lewis, 1999, N.T.C. Publishing Group

"The Advertising Age Handbook of Advertising" Herschell Gordon Lewis and Carol Nelson, 1999, N.T.C. Publishing Group

"Catalog Copy That Sizzles : All the Hints, Tips, and Tricks of the Trade You'll Ever Need to Write Copy That Sells" Herschell Gordon Lewis, 1999, N.T.C. Publishing Group

"On the Art of Writing Copy: The Best of * Print * Broadcast * Internet * Direct Mail" Herschell Gordon Lewis, 2000, AMACOM

"Herschell Gordon Lewis, Godfather of Gore: The Films" Randy Palmer, 2000, McFarland

"A Taste of Blood: The Films of Herschell Gordon Lewis" Christopher Wayne Curry, 2000, Creation Publication Group; a selection in the Creation Cinema Collection

BORN: Douglas Liman in New York, New York, 1966

NATIONALITY: American

EDUCATION: International Center of Photography, New York, New York, photography; attended while in high school

Brown University, Providence, Rhode Island, 1988; helped to found the school's student-run cable TV station; served as first station manager

School of Cinema—Television, University of Southern California, Los Angeles, California; dropped out

AWARDS: Florida Film Critics Circle Award Newcomer of the Year "Swingers" 1996; tied with Jon Favreau

MTV Movie Award Best New Filmmaker "Swingers" 1997

BIOGRAPHY

This neophyte director scored a hit with his first released feature, the critical hit comedy "Swingers" (1996), on which he did double duty as director of photography. Doug Liman began making short films while still in junior high and studied at NYC's International Center of Photography. While attending Brown, he helped to co-found the student-run cable television station and served as its first station manager. Liman attended the graduate program at USC where he was tapped to helm his first project, the comedy thriller "Getting In/Student Body" (1993). This little seen, direct-to-video release featured a cast of up and coming players (e.g., Stephen Mailer, Matthew Perry, Andrew McCarthy and Christine Baranski) in a tale of a wait-listed med student who bribes those ahead of him only to discover they start turning up dead.

Liman became attached to direct "Swingers"

when its screenwriter Jon Favreau turned down offers from studios who wanted to cast established actors. The director agreed to cast Favreau and his friends (Vince Vaughn, Ron Livingston and Patrick Van Horne) in this comedy about struggling actors amid the L.A. club milieu. Centered around a group of friends trying to snap a heartbroken buddy (Favreau) out of his lovesick funk, the film featured a good bit of swaggering hipness and self-conscious posturing but was strongly grounded in genuine sweetness. Made on a budget of $250,000, the dialogue-propelled "Swingers" was often filmed on locations without permits in a pseudo-documentary style. The result was a film filled with energy and charm that captivated audiences and critics and not only established a cult following, but also jump-started the careers of the featured actors, most notably Vaughn.

Artful, smart and exhilarating, Liman's rapid-paced next effort "Go" (1999) more than lived up to the legacy of the acclaimed "Swingers." A refreshingly optimistic and affirming take on John August's script about young Los Angelenos on the fast track, "Go" was comprised of three separate but related sections, each focusing on different members of the film's talented ensemble of up and comers. Liman showed a rare filmmaker's economy, bringing in this elaborate and energetic ride at well under two hours. Doing double duty as cinematographer, Liman created a look for the film that stylistically captured both the script's vivid spirit and somewhat dark subject matter. The director shot some especially visually arresting scenes, including an Ecstasy-fueled hallucination set in a supermarket, a terrifying neon lit Las Vegas strip car chase and a hazy rave dance floor scene. The film received overwhelmingly positive reviews but box office returns were comparably lackluster. Marketed as a teen movie because of its hip, young cast, the exceptional film was lost in the influx of insipid commercial teen fare.

Following "Go", Liman produced the Sarah Thorp film "See Jane Run" (lensed 1999), starring Clea DuVall and Kevin Corrigan. His next directing project was scheduled to be "3 Days Out", from John Freeman's script about NASA outlaws.

MILESTONES:

Began making short films while in junior high school

Co-founded the student-run cable TV station while attending Brown University; served as first station manager

1993: Feature film directing debut, the direct-to-video release "Getting In/Student Body"

1996: First feature released, "Swingers"; also served as director of photography

1999: Helmed second feature "Go"; also served as director of photography; premiered at the Sundance Film Festival

Produced "See Jane Run", an independent film written and directed by Sarah Thorp and starring Clea DuVall and Kevin Corrigan

AFFILIATION: Chair, Board of Trustees of the National Association of College Broadcasters

QUOTES:

With two friends from Brown University (David Bartis and Liz Hamburg), Liman started the Web site NibbleBox (www.nibblebox.com).

"I think teens are really smart. 'Go' will show you don't have to spoon-feed them garbage and that they can choose to see an original movie."—Doug Liman quoted in *Entertainment Weekly*, April 23, 1999.

"I think there is also a tendency for people who make independent films, they want to make cool movies. This is probably, in terms of psychiatry, the single most likely explanation for that—independent filmmakers want to make cool movies. And part of making a cool movie is to make these dark, edgy, sort of unlikable characters. I don't want to make 'cool' movies, I want to make sweet, uplifting films. To me those are the cool movies, the movies trying not to be cool."—Doug Liman quoted as part of March 1999's Independent Feature Project interview.

Ringo Lam Ling-Tung

BORN: in Hong Kong, 1955

SOMETIMES CREDITED AS:
Lam Ling-Tung

NATIONALITY: Chinese

CITIZENSHIP: Canada, 1981

EDUCATION: York University, Toronto, Ontario, Canada; studied filmmaking for three-and-a-half years; did not graduate

AWARD: Hong Kong Film Award Best Director "City on Fire" 1987

BIOGRAPHY

This leading Hong Kong action filmmaker has kept a lower profile than some of his contemporaries as far as publicity is concerned. Nevertheless, he has helmed some of the key films of the "heroic bloodshed" cycle of HK action movies. The hard-hitting heist film, "City on Fire" (1987) —best known stateside as the unacknowledged but indisputable inspiration for Quentin Tarantino's 1991 debut "Reservoir Dogs"—gave Lam his first major hit and inaugurated a series of features ("Prison on Fire" 1987; "School on Fire" 1988).

Lam's films are noted for the grim realism of their violence and their gritty surfaces. Whereas violence in the films of John Woo is often aestheticized and balletic, similar acts in Lam's world are brutal and brutalizing. In his most extreme work, "Full Contact" (1992), Lam created a more dreamy and stylized environment for the gory confrontation between an honorable gang leader (Chow Yun-fat) and his psychotic gay rival (Simon Yam). Even jaded Hong Kong audiences were frightened away by the level of mayhem on display. As in "City on Fire", Lam made mincemeat of the notion of honor among thieves.

Lam followed in the footsteps of John Woo by making his US directorial debut with a Jean-Claude Van Damme vehicle, "Maximum Risk" (1996). Here the protagonist must take on the identity of a gangster twin that he never knew he had. Reviews were mixed and box office was not up to par but Lam had arrived.

MILESTONES:

1973: Spent a year in an actor's training course in Hong Kong; same class as Chow Yun-fat
1974: Spent six months working as an actor; decided not to pursue it (date approximate)
1974–1976: Worked as a production assistant

Began career as a TV director; decided he did not like it
Studied filmmaking at Toronto's York University; did not graduate
1981: Became a Canadian citizen; returned to Hong Kong
1981: Directorial debut, "Espirit D'Amour"
1987: Produced, directed and wrote story for breakthrough feature, "City on Fire"; first collaboration with Chow Yun-fat
1996: US directorial debut, "Maximum Risk", starring Jean-Claude Van Damme
1997: Returned to HK to direct "Full Alert"
1999: Served as producer of "Simon Sez"
2001: Reunited with Van Damme for "Replicant"

QUOTES:

"I like editing because you feel like God. If I don't like this guy, I can cut him away; if I don't like this shot I can throw it out, You don't need to communicate with too many people. You only tell the editor what you want."—Ringo Lam to Rolanda Chu in *Hong Kong Film Magazine*, Number 4.

Richard Linklater

BORN: Richard Stuart Linklater in Houston, Texas, 07/30/1960

SOMETIMES CREDITED AS:
Rick Linklater

NATIONALITY: American

EDUCATION: Huntsville High School, Huntsville, Texas
Sam Houston State University, Huntsville, Texas; studied literature and drama in college before quitting
University of Texas, Austin, Texas; philosophy audited classes; never officially enrolled

AWARDS: Berlin Film Festival Silver Bear for Best Director "Before Sunrise" 1995
New York Film Critics Circle Award Best Animated Film "Waking Life" 2001
National Society of Film Critics Award Best Experimental Film "Waking Life" 2001

BIOGRAPHY
Houston-born, Huntsville-raised Richard Linklater, a self-taught filmmaker, worked on an offshore oil rig in the Gulf of Mexico before moving to Austin where he founded a film society and started making movies. In 1987 Link-later completed his first film, "It's Impossible to Learn to Plow By Reading Books", and shot his first feature, "Slacker", a comedic look

at then-contemporary youth—post-college lazies, anarchists and neo-beatniks—as they wander around a Texas college campus over a 24-hour period in the summer of 1989. The low-budget film was lauded on the festival circuit in 1990, showcased at the 1991 Sundance Film Festival, and released commercially later that year.

Linklater's second feature, "Dazed and Confused" (1993), demonstrated that he could make a mainstream narrative for a thrifty six million dollars (this relatively paltry budget was still about 250 times greater than that of his previous feature). "Dazed" recounts the lives of a group of high schoolers on the last day of classes in 1976. With its dead-on portrayal of kids driving around aimlessly in search of something to do on this momentous night, the film largely succeeds as an "American Graffiti" for 70s teen drug culture. Linklater's acutely observed coming-of-age comedy serves as a thematic companion piece to "Slacker" and featured a bevy of then-unknown stars including Parker Posey, Jeremy London, Ben Affleck and Matthew McConaughey.

"Before Sunrise" (1995) represented a move in a new direction for the increasingly assured writer-director, with Ethan Hawke and Julie Delpy playing students who meet on a train and spend one romantic night in Vienna. Like his two preceding works, "Before Sunrise" is dialogue-driven, but whereas "Slacker" and "Dazed" were impressionistic compilations of incidents, the later film presented two fully developed characters. Furthermore, Linklater made the city of Vienna into a pivotal character in its own right rather than merely a source of pretty backdrops.

Linklater departed slightly from his dialogue-rich, character-driven prior efforts with the fact-based Western adventure "The Newton Boys" (1998), chronicling the criminal exploits of a little-known band of brothers who were bank and train robbers. Starring McConaughey, Hawke, Vincent D'Onofrio, and Skeet

Ulrich as the four Newtons, the film had a solid cast, a healthy budget and was true to the spirit of co-scripter Claude Stanush's source biography but disappointed many Linklater fans looking for a movie that better bore the director's unique mark.

After a bit of a hiatus, Linklater returned to the film world with gusto in 2001, premiering not one but two experimental works at that year's Sundance Film Festival. "Waking Life" reunited Linklater with "Dazed and Confused" star Wiley Wiggins and had the distinction of being the first known film to be shot with live actors and then animated. With the digital video feature "Tape", Linklater returned to his low-budget roots, this time joined by such big name stars as Hawke, Uma Thurman and Robert Sean Leonard. A real-time feature based on Stephen Barber's edgy one-act play and shot mostly in order thanks to the inexpensive and versatile medium, "Tape" would challenge and broaden independent film in much the same way "Slacker" had a decade earlier.

MILESTONES:

Quit college to work on an offshore oil rig in the Gulf of Mexico

Moved to Austin Texas, co-founded the Austin Film Society in 1985 (with cinematographer Lee Daniel) and began making films

1987: Completed first film, "It's Impossible to Learn to Plow By Reading Books"

1990: Made first feature, "Slacker" (shot in summer 1989)

1993: Wrote and directed first Hollywood feature, "Dazed and Confused"; cast included numerous up and comers including Ben Affleck, Parker Posey, Nicky Katt, Matthew McConaughey, Renee Zellweger, Jason London and Anthony Rapp

1994: Signed a two-year, first-look deal with Castle Rock

1995: First film under the Castle Rock deal, "Before Sunrise", a two-character romance starring Ethan Hawke and Julie Delpy

1995: Appeared in Steven Soderbergh's "The Underneath"

1996: Voiced a character in the animated feature "Beavis and Butt-head Do America"

1997: Helmed the feature adaptation of Eric Bogosian's stage play "subUrbia", featuring Nicky Katt, Parker Posey and Steve Zahn

1998: Directed the based-on-fact "The Newton Boys", about early 20th-century bank-robbing brothers, featuring Ethan Hawke, Matthew McConaughey, Skeet Ulrich and Vincent D'Onofrio

2001: Had two films premiere at Sundance Film Festival: "Waking Life", made with live actors (including Ethan Hawke and Julie Delpy) and then animated; and "Tape", shot digitally and starring Hawke, Uma Thurman and Robert Sean Leonard

2001: Played a cool spy in Robert Rodriguez's children's feature "Spy Kids"

AFFILIATION: Founder, The Austin Texas Film Society (1985–)

QUOTES:

"Ideas and thoughts aren't expensive. As long as your time's not worth anything, it doesn't have to cost a lot."—Richard Linklater quoted in *Entertainment Weekly*, 1991.

"There have been so many bad teenage movies that weren't authentic because no one was telling us their own story. It was just 'let's sell something to the kids'—the whole codification and classification of a generation and the simplistic shorthand that is used to describe it is diametrically opposed to what I want to do."—Linklater on the difference between his "Dazed and Confused" and many other films about teens quoted in *New York Post*, September 27, 1993.

"I like production and I like editing but sometimes I wish the film never had to come out and you never had to worry about whether people will like it."—Linklater to *The Village Voice*, February 7, 1995.

"In 'subUrbia', the challenge was handling material that was definitely more confrontational and inherently more dramatic. In the past, I've tended to diffuse the drama in a story and not make it such a big deal. The characters have been more internal, while in this film they're more external—raising their voices, being more argumentative. I think collaborating with Eric Bogosian really pushed me in that direction."—Linklater to *American Cinematographer*, March 1997.

Linklater on "The Newton Boys": "Every film is a subject that you are attracted to. It's like what you need personally out of a film. I was ready to do a true story. I was ready to work with that bigger canvas. I haven't typically done a lot of action sequences. This is stil a character piece. The action is such a part of the characters.

I really enjoyed planning out all of the shots. For me as a filmmaker, that's the fun stuff. But I just couldn't do a whole acton movie. When I imagine a movie, I imagine characters. I don't imagine all of these action sequences and hanging a narrative within that."—quoted in *Los Angeles Times*, March 26, 1998.

Linklater's Austin Texas Film Society was one of the recipients of the inaugural Directors Guild of America Honors in 1999.

"Some people say that I am not a very good storyteller, but I don't know if I agree with that. I'm just trying to tell a different kind of story and they should all be told differently depending upon what the subject is. Film is all about storytelling, even if the story you are telling isn't particularly narrative."—Linklater to *Filmmaker*, Winter, 2001.

Ken Loach

BORN: Kenneth Loach in Nuneaton, Warwickshire, England, 06/17/1936

SOMETIMES CREDITED AS:
Kenneth Loach
Ken Loach

NATIONALITY: English

EDUCATION: Oxford University Oxford, England law 1957–60 president of Experimental Theatre Club
studied with the BBC Drama Services in the early 1960s

AWARDS: British TV Guild Award Director of the Year "The Coming Out Party" 1965
Italia Festival Prize "Cathy Come Home" 1965
Berlin Film Festival International Critics Prize "Family Life" 1972; cited with Marco Ferreri's "The Audience"
Cannes Film Festival International Critics Prize "Black Jack" 1979; shown out of competition; cited with Pal Gabor's "Angi Vera"
Cannes Film Festival Prix du Cinema Contemporain au Festival International du Film (long metrage) "Looks and Smiles" 1981; cited with "Neige"
Festival dei Popoli Gold Medal Award "Which Side Are You On?" 1984
Cannes Film Festival Jury Prize "Hidden Agenda" 1990
Cannes Film Festival International Critics' Award "Riff-Raff" 1991; film shown out of competition
Felix Best European Film "Riff-Raff" 1991
BAFTA Michael Balcon Award for Outstanding Contribution to Cinema 1993
Cannes Film Festival Jury Prize "Raining Stones" 1993; shared with Hou Hsiao-hsien's "The Puppet Masters"

Berlin Film Festival International Critics Prize "Ladybird, Ladybird" 1994
Cannes Film Festival International Critics Prize "Land and Freedom" 1995
Cesar Best Foreign Film "Land and Freedom" 1996
Venice Film Festival Italian Senate's Gold Medal "Carla's Song" 1996
British Independent Film Award Best Film "My Name Is Joe" 1998
British Independent Film Award Best British Director "My Name Is Joe" 1998

BIOGRAPHY

Like the Italian neo-realists (especially Vittorio De Sica) who served as his inspiration, Ken Loach has acquired a reputation as the leading socially conscious director working in Britain. A quiet, soft-spoken man, he hardly seems the "dean of leftist movie makers" (as he was dubbed by *The New York Times* in June 1998). The son of a working-class factory worker, Loach served in the Royal Air Force, studied law and then worked in theater, first as an understudy and later touring Birmingham in a repertory company. To make ends meet, he picked up work as a teacher.

In the early 1960s, Loach apprenticed as a director at a commercials company before joining the BBC where he graduating to helming episodes of the series "Z-Cars" in 1962. Former actor and committed socialist Tony Garnett was hired by the BBC to serve as producer of a new series "The Wednesday Play." Loach and Garnett worked together closely and pioneered the format of what has been termed "the docu-drama", a mix of techniques employed by the evening news and the fictional film, using location shooting and often casting non-professional actors. Loach first garnered attention for "Up the Junction" (1965), which profiled three impoverished working-class women, and then cemented his reputation with "Cathy Comes Home" (1966), about a couple forced by economic circumstances to live on the streets. The film proved controversial and led to the establishment of Shelter, an advocacy group for the homeless.

Loach moved into features with "Poor Cow" (1967), adapted from Nell Dunn's novel about a shrewish woman, her thieving husband and her criminal lover. Employing a similar cinema-verité style and the leftist principles that infused his TV work, the film was a surprising financial success. Now partnered with Garnett, Loach went on to turn out several stark, socially-conscious films noted for their semi-documentary quality and often performed by well-cast non-professional actors. "Kes" (1969) was a poignant study of a teenaged loner, his pet kestrel falcon and his rebellion against the restrictions of the local Yorkshire school system. Despite initial favorable reaction, the film was held from release until 1970. For much of the next two decades, Loach alternated between television and features. His small screen work included the acclaimed "The Rank and File" (1971), focusing on a strike at a glass manufacturer and the workers' discontent with its union leadership, and the four-part historical drama "Days of Hope" (1975), which traced one family from 1914 to 1926. His film output was, however, light in the 70s and included the psychodrama "Family Life" (1971) and the atypical historical adventure "Black Jack" (1979).

With the rise of Margaret Thatcher, the monies for the kinds of films Loach wanted to direct was not as available. He began to drop the use of dramatizations and began making more conventional documentaries. Loach ran into some problems with "A Question of Leadership" (1981) and the four-part "Questions of Leadership" (filmed in 1984). The former was edited for "balance" while the latter never aired due to legal wranglings by the trade unions over issues of defamation. Even his documentary on a coal miners' strike "Which Side Are You On?"

(1985) was dropped by London Weekend Television which had commissioned the project. It finally aired along with another documentary that was less sympathetic to the miners' plight.

Not that he didn't still make features. "Looks and Smiles" (1981) examined a young man's search for employment while both "Fatherland/Singing the Blues in Red" (1986; released in the USA in 1988), and the highly controversial "Hidden Agenda" (1990) dealt with more overt political themes.

By the 90s. Loach had returned in force to feature work. The comedy/drama "Riff-Raff" (1991) was the first of three films to examine the ramifications of Thatcher's policies on the working-class. "Riff-Raff" looked at union-busting on a construction site whereas "Raining Stones" (1993) followed an unemployed man who was trying to scrape together the money for his daughter's communion dress. The powerful "Ladybird, Ladybird" (1994) was a based-on-fact tale of a single mother exploited by the men in her life, who fights the social service system over custody of her children. In a slight change of pace, Loach handled the diptych "Land and Freedom" (1995), which followed a British man's journey to fight against Franco in the Spanish Civil War, and "Carla's Song" (1996), about the relationship between a Glaswegian bus driver and a Nicaraguan refugee who return to her homeland circa 1987. Both are highly political and both are set primarily out of the United Kingdom. Loach delivered searing indictments of the fractious democratic republicans in the former and the US government and its covert involvement with the Contras in the latter. "My Name Is Joe" (1998) returned the focus to more localized social issues by following an unemployed recovering alcoholic who forges an unlikely relationship with a health worker.

MILESTONES:

Served two years in Royal Air Force as a typist
Professional debut as comedian's understudy
in a revue

Worked intermittently as a teacher

Was a performer and director with a repertory company in Birmingham

1961: Joined BBC as trainee TV director

1962: First TV series directing experience, "Z-Cars", for the BBC

Directed an assortment of stage productions

1965: First film for television, "Up the Junction" directed with Tony Garnett

1966: Won widespread attention for the documentary-like TV drama "Cathy Come Home"

1968: Directed film, "Kes", in first collaboration with writer Barry Hines (released in USA 1970)

1971: Made the semi-documentary "The Rank and File", about a strike by glassworkers

1975: Helmed the multi-part British TV series "Days of Hope"

1979: Wrote and directed the feature "Black Jack", about an 18th Century highwayman

Worked primarily in television during the 1980s, directing only two features, "Looks and Smiles" (1981) and "Fatherland/Singing the Blues in Red" (1986; released in the USA in 1988)

1984: "Questions of Leadership", his four-part TV documentary on the trade-union movement was never broadcast

1990: First feature in four years, "Hidden Agenda", about American human rights activists investigating abuses in Belfast

1991: First of three successive films centered on working-class characters, beginning with "Riff-Raff"; also first collaboration with actor Robert Carlyle (released in the USA in 1993)

1995: Directed "Land and Freedom"

1996: Initial collaboration with screenwriter Paul Laverty, "Carla's Song" (released in the USA in 1998)

1997: Subject of the documentary, "Citizen Ken Loach", directed by Karim Dridi

1998: Second film with Laverty, "My Name Is Joe"; shown at the Cannes Film Festival

2000: Third collaboration with Laverty, "Bread and Roses"

2001: Helmed "The Navigators"; screened at Venice International Film Festival; scheduled to air on Channel 4 in November

QUOTES:

"If one had to choose a battleground, making films is the most effective one."—Ken Loach in the press kit for "Fatherland/Singing the Blues in Red."

"I discovered through the work and humour of the people I met at the time, the strength of working people, which my education had made me immune to. You set academic hurdles and tend to forget where you came from. When you get a little more mature you begin to realize your real loyalties and the real strength of your upbringing."—Ken Loach.

Of Garnett and Loach's technique, "they consciously set out to redefine the content of the material which was customarily slotted into either 'drama' or 'documentary feature.' They ended by forging a dazzling weapon of persuasion by simply effacing the traditional separation between these categories so that it was difficult to be sure which it was that one was viewing. . . . Ideally, they wanted their programmes to be indistinguishable from the items on the television news which preceded them."—Alexander Walker quoted in "World Film Directors, Volume 2."

On the term docudrama: "It's a kind of strange word. It was never a word we used. In the 60s, television drama was very theatrical. It was very much about doing a stage play in a television studio and filming it with electronic cameras. It was very stagey. And what our group tried to do was switch to 16mm, take the camera out on the streets and make drama [there]. That became known as 'docudrama', God help us! But it was never the intention to invent a word for it. It was just to try to put a bit of life into what had become a very kind of moribund form."—Ken Loach, June 1998.

About the lack of financing for his films in the late 1970s and early 1980s, Loach told *The*

New York Times (June 14, 1998): "If the British movie industry at the time had any perception of what I did, it was that I made films in an impenetrable dialect, driven by a kind of hard-line Marxist view, which no one would want to see. And, if they did want to see them, they wouldn't understand them anyway."

Ernst Lubitsch

BORN: in Berlin, Germany, 01/28/1892

DEATH: 11/30/1947

NATIONALITY: German

CITIZENSHIP: United States, 1933

AWARD: Honorary Oscar 1946 for "his distinguished contributions to the art of the motion picture (scroll)"

BIOGRAPHY

Dubbed "a man of pure Cinema" by Alfred Hitchcock, "a prince" by Francois Truffaut and "a giant" by Orson Welles, Ernst Lubitsch is a preeminent figure in the history of cinema. More than a great director of actors and action, Lubitsch added his own personal signature, "the Lubitsch touch," to all his work, a sense of style and grace that has rarely been matched on the screen.

Born the son of a draper, Lubitsch gained prominence at the age of 19 as a member of Max Reinhardt's troupe; by 21, he had begun to create the comic screen persona "Meyer," a slapstick Jewish archetype who became a favorite of German audiences.

The following year, Lubitsch got his first chance to display his filmmaking skills, writing and directing a one-reeler called "Fraulein Seifenschaum/Miss Soapsuds" (1915). Eager to test his own range and gain acceptance as a dramatic actor, Lubitsch wrote and directed "Als Ich Tot War/When I Was Dead" (1916), but the film failed to stir the interest of an audience who loved "Meyer." Stereotyped as an actor, Lubitsch turned his full attention to directing and scored his first major success with "Schuhpalast Pinkus/Shoe Salon Pinkus" (1916).

The first Lubitsch picture to be shown in America was "Die Augen der Mummie Ma/The Eyes of the Mummy" (1918), his first teaming of Pola Negri and Emil Jannings. It was their second film, however, with Lubitsch, "Madame Du Barry/Passion" (1919) which proved to be his first masterwork, as well as a crucial film for the German film industry, as it was the first success of the film's co-producers, the newly formed UFA. With "Madame Du Barry," Lubitsch became known for an unerring ability to "humanize" sumptuous screen spectacles and costume dramas, to give them the warmth that would endear them to the public. In 1923, Lubitsch's career would enter a new phase when Mary Pickford invited him to Hollywood to direct "Rosita."

It was with his next film, "The Marriage Circle" (1924), inspired by Chaplin's "A Woman of Paris," that Lubitsch began to hone his famed "touch." Except for the rare venture into drama ("The Patriot" 1928, "The Man I Killed" 1932), Lubitsch came to specialize in the artfully risque sex farce, where raised eyebrows and closed doors meant everything. After the arrival of sound, Lubitsch's ear for shimmering dialogue and exhilarating musical numbers only enhanced his talent. The director's greatest achievements would begin in 1932 with what is probably his masterpiece, the Art Deco wonder "Trouble in Paradise", and continue with such delights as "Design For

Living" (1933), "The Merry Widow" (1934), "Angel" (1937), "Ninotchka" (1939), "The Shop Around the Corner" (1940), "To Be or Not to Be" (1942), "Heaven Can Wait" (1943) and "Cluny Brown" (1946).

In 1935, Lubitsch was named head of production at Paramount, but his real talent lay in producing and directing motion pictures, not studio administration, and he was relieved of his duties after a year. During production on "That Lady in Ermine" (1948), he died of a heart attack, and the film was completed by Otto Preminger.—Written by David Lugowski

MILESTONES:

1911–1913: Associated with director Max Reinhardt, appearing in his stage productions

1913: Began acting in movies in Germany

1914: Made directorial debut with the short film "Fraulein Seifenschaum"/"Miss Soapsuds"

1922: Moved to USA; put under contract to Mary Pickford

1923: First American film "Rosita", starring Pickford

Gained critical acclaim and popular success in the US with such satirical romantic comedies as "Lady Windemere's Fan" and "So This Is Paris"

1926: Signed contract with Paramount

1927: Helmed the silent "The Student Prince in Old Heidelberg", starring Ramon Navarro and Norma Shearer

1928: Received first Best Director Oscar nomination for "The Patriot"

1929: First sound film, "The Love Parade", his first pairing of Maurice Chevalier and Jeannette MacDonald; garnered second Best Director Oscar nomination

1932: Made the atypical pacifist drama "The Man I Killed"

1933: Became an American citizen

Served as production chief at Paramount

1937: Returned to directing; directed first film in three years, "Angel"

Was briefly with MGM, where he made "Ninotckha" and "The Shop Around the Corner"

1942: Directed the delightful wartime comedy "To Be or Not To Be", teaming Jack Benny and Carole Lombard

1943: Signed contract with Fox

1943: Earned third Best Director Oscar nomination for "Heaven Can Wait"

1946: Completed last film, "Cluny Brown"

1947: Died while working on "That Lady in Ermine" (1948); film completed by Otto Preminger; Lubitsch given screen credit

BIBLIOGRAPHY:

"Lubitsch" Hans Helmut Prinzler and Enno Patalas, 1984, C.J. Bucher Verlag

"The Lubitsch Touch" Herman Weinberg critical appreciation of Lubitsch's career

"Ernst Lubitsch's American Comedy" William Paul critical analysis of Lubitsch's American sound films from "Trouble in Paradise" (1932) through "Cluny Brown" (1946), his last completed film

"Passions and Deceptions: The Early Films of Ernst Lubitsch" Sabine Hake; critical analysis of Lubitsch's films from the early German shorts through his American silent films and several of his US talkies, including "Monte Carlo" (1930) and "Trouble in Paradise" (1932)

BORN: George Walton Lucas, Jr. in Modesto, California, 05/14/1944

NATIONALITY: American

EDUCATION: John Muir School

Downey High School, Downey, California, 1962

Modesto Junior College, Modesto, California, AA, 1964

University of Southern California, Los Angeles, California, film, BFA, 1967; formed Sunrise Productions with Christopher Lewis during senior year

AWARDS: New York Film Critics Circle Award Best Screenplay "American Graffiti" 1973; shared with Gloria Katz and Willard Huyck

National Society of Film Critics Award Best Screenplay "American Graffiti" 1973; shared award with Gloria Katz and Willard Huyck

American Cinema Editors Golden Eddie Award 1991 "for notable and conspicuous contribution to the art and craft of motion pictures."

Irving G. Thalberg Memorial Award 1991; presented by the Academy of Motion Picture Arts and Sciences

MYV Movie Award Best Action Sequence "Star Wars: Episode I—The Phantom Menace" 2000; cited for the pod race

BAFTA Stanley Kubrick Award for Excellence in Film 2001; presented on November 10, 2001 in L.A.

National Board of Review Award Special Award for Visionary Cinematic Achievement 2002

The Vanguard Award Outstanding Achievement in New Media and Technology 2002

Razzie Award Worst Screenplay "Star Wars: Episode II—Attack of the Clones" 2002

BIOGRAPHY

Arguably the most important film innovator working today, George Lucas has continually "pushed the envelope" of filmmaking technology since his early days as a student at USC. Considered a wunderkind by his contemporaries, he had a much harder time communicating his vision to studio executives, whose meddling managed to compromise each of his first three feature directing efforts in some way. The monumental success of "Star Wars" (1977) ushered in the era of the 'blockbuster', which, despite the recent popularity of low-budget, independent films, is still the prevailing mentality powering the Hollywood engine. Though he set the tone and established the expectations influencing studios to devote the bulk of their energy and resources to films designed to blast off into hyperspace and earn spectacular profits, it is doubtful that a film as revolutionary as "Star Wars" was in its day could get made in the current climate.

The son of a Modesto, California retail businessman, Lucas grew up tinkering with cars and dreaming of glory at the race track until a near-fatal auto crash derailed his driving ambitions, forcing him behind the scenes as a mechanic. He had already begun experimenting with both still photography and 8-mm movies when an assignment to help build a racing car introduced him to its owner, distinguished cinematographer Haskell Wexler, with whose encouragement he began to pursue filmmaking seriously. At USC he studied animation, moved to cinematography and excelled at editing, making eight student films ranging from one minute to 25 minutes. As the winner of a Warner Bros. scholarship, he came in contact with Francis Ford Coppola, and the two quickly became allies and close friends, Lucas serving as "general assistant, assistant art director, production aide, general do everything" for Coppola's "The Rain People" (1969). When Coppola opened his American Zoetrope production company (with its ultra modern editing equipment) in a San Francisco warehouse, Lucas was its vice-president.

An expanded version of Lucas' award-winning short "Electronic Labyrinth: THX-1138: 4EB" (1968) was Zoetrope's first film, but Warner Bros., on whom Coppola depended for financial backing, despised "THX-1138" (1971), withdrew their support of Zoetrope and demanded the return of their money already invested, signaling the end of the production company for the time being. Warners did, however, release the picture, cutting five minutes and providing half-hearted promotion, to mixed reviews. Almost universally praised as a "dazzling technical achievement" with "stunning visuals and sound" (Walter Murch provided the sound track), "THX-1138" scored no points with critics for its Orwellian theme of the individual asserting himself against an authoritarian society policed by robots. Though the overall effect was cold and sterile, the zombie characters incapable of stirring sympathy, it was an extremely professional first film, one which its director re-released in 1977 with the missing five minutes restored. THX lives on today as the name of the Lucas company which designs sound for theaters and home entertainment systems.

Wanting to break the industry's conception of him as a "science-fiction guy" with "stainless steel in my veins", Lucas decided to make a crowd-pleasing comedy, proving with "American Graffiti" (1973) that a warm-funny film with an emphasis on personalities was well within his capabilities. His vision was once again at odds with the studios, but Universal finally agreed to make the script (inspired by a conversation with producer Gary Kurtz and written by Lucas with Gloria Katz and Willard Huyck), providing it could be done very cheaply. With Coppola and Kurtz co-producing, Lucas filmed

"Graffiti" for $780,000 in 28 days on location in two small towns near San Francisco, his good friend Wexler taking over the camerawork when the director worked himself into a state of exhaustion. Shooting almost entirely at night, with very low light, they achieved a "curious golden radiance" that would distinguish the picture, but when Universal executives first saw the film at a crowded preview, they hated it, despite the enthusiastic response of the test audience.

The studio brass at Universal felt threatened by Lucas' prodigious talent, and "Graffiti" was so different from the cookie-cutter movies they were comfortable with that it scared them. Coppola pulled out his checkbook at the preview and offered to buy the film, but the executives refused, preferring instead to torment Lucas with a plan to bypass a theatrical release and show it on TV. Considering the nostalgia boom it spawned, it is difficult to understand their fears today, but its reliance on rock "oldies" for its structure seemed hopelessly "B-movie" to them. They did not realize that Lucas was anticipating the zeitgeist, that by setting his film in 1962, he was evoking "the end of a political era, a sociological era, a rock era . . . a warm, secure, uninvolved life." Universal finally relented and released "Graffiti" at the end of the summer (after humiliating Lucas with a four and a half minute cut), and it was an immediate word-of-mouth hit with its target audience, eventually grossing more than $100 million.

It was the last time Lucas would relinquish final cut but not his last war with a studio. Critical respectability and box office success had not made him bankable when pushing his own projects, and he had a difficult time interesting anybody in his proposed live-action comic book with high-tech effects. Three studio chiefs had told him to get lost. Only Alan Ladd Jr. at 20th Century Fox believed in his vision, green-lighting "Star Wars" in 1974 for about $10 million. But Ladd would have a running battle with the Fox board, which insisted it was not commercial right until its blockbuster opening (May 27, 1977) marked a dramatic shift in the culture. With "Star Wars", Lucas drew on his love of racing, creating a two-hour-long image of raw speed that foreshadowed the media-induced state of speed that has become a condition of modern life. Proving himself a master of the long view, he also flabbergasted Fox executives by forgoing his option to receive an additional $500,000 for directing the movie and taking the merchandising and sequel rights instead.

Lucas had wanted to purchase the rights to the "Flash Gordon" comics but found the price prohibitive. Instead, he set about creating his own world, inventing a future that smacked of the past while figuring out a way to strike the archetypal jugular of his audience. In order to come up with his own nonsectarian "Star Wars" mythology, he studied the work of Joseph Campbell, among other sources, took structural elements from many different myths and combined them into an epic story which filled the moral void left by the demise of the traditional Western. He borrowed heavily from film-school canon, drawing inspiration from Kurosawa's "Hidden Fortress" for the lightsabres of the Jedi Knights, Fritz Lang's "Metropolis" for C3PO's look and Leni Riefenstahl's "Triumph of the Will" for the ceremony at the end. Alec Guinness in a way reprised his role from "Lawrence of Arabia", Harrison Ford played Butch Cassidy and Lucas incorporated the references with a childlike naivete into a postmodernist commentary on the history of popular film.

Worn out by the monumental ordeal of coordinating hundreds of cast and crew members, Lucas retired from directing after "Star Wars", retaining control of the script as executive producer and hiring directors like Irvin Kershner ("The Empire Strikes Back" 1980), Richard Marquand ("Return of the Jedi" 1983) and Steven Spielberg (the Indiana Jones trilogy). He poured his fortune into Skywalker Ranch, a secluded,

three-thousand acre, Victorian-style work paradise surrounded by groves of eucalyptus and redwood in Marin County, California, just north of San Francisco, where he forges technological breakthroughs serving the editing and production process. Conceived as a complete filmmaking operation, Skywalker Ranch is headquarters of Lucasfilm, companies with an estimated worth in excess of $5 billion (*Forbes* puts Lucas' personal worth at $2 billion), employing twelve hundred people. One of those companies, Industrial Light & Magic, located 15 inefficient miles away in San Rafael, houses legions of young geeks diligently constructing "polys", the basic elements of computer graphics, in an endless endeavor to produce special effects never seen before.

Lucas' day-to-day activities include the management of the Star Wars story, which is probably the most carefully tended secular story on earth. Everyone in the content-creating galaxy of Star Wars has a copy of 'The Bible', a finite, expanding chronology of all the events that have ever occurred in the Star Wars universe (films, books, CD-ROMs, comic books, et al), maintained by continuity editors. Lucas has the last word on all creative decisions. For example, when Bantam wanted to do the back story of Yoda, guru of 'The Force', the guardian of the tale nixed the notion because he wanted the character to remain a mysterious figure. Taking advantage of the booming interest in his myth, Lucas re-released digitally-enhanced versions of the three "Star Wars" movies in 1997 to a staggering box office. "Star Wars" (the first film) earned $35.9 million its opening weekend on 2,100 screens as opposed to $1.6 million on 43 screens during its 1977 opening. He returned to the director's chair after 20 years to helm "Star Wars: Episode I—The Phantom Menace" (1999). The colossal buzz preceding the prequel's release proved anticlimactic when it finally hit theaters; although the movie generated huge box-office grosses, fans came away somewhat disappointed that despite all of Lucas' breakthroughs in digital technology, he seemed to have lost a step when it came to storytelling and creating characters as iconic and compelling as those in the original trilogy. Despite some canny casting—including Liam Neeson, Ewan MacGregor and Natalie Portman—and many captivating visual elements—such as the climactic lightsaber battle and the demonic look of the villainous Darth Maul—Lucas took heat for the film's mostly lugubrious pace, the weak performance of young actor Jake Lloyd as Anakin Skywalker and particularly for the annonying digitally-created alien Jar Jar Binks. The director was unbowed and, instead of handing off to a new director, proceeded to helm the next installment as well, "Star Wars Episode II: Attack of the Clones" (2002). Though much better received by critics and fans (both casual and diehard), the sequel also suffered from wooden dialogue, a mostly charmless performance by the new Anakin (Hayden Christensen) and a preponderence of computer-generated effects. Fans were pleased by the lessening of the Jar Jar character's role and the new all-digital version of Yoda created for a lightsaber battle. Originally conceived as a cycle of nine movies, Lucas is as yet unsure if the "Star Wars" saga will exceed six, claiming that he will be roughly 80 years old when he might revisit the franchise and doubting that he will have the energy to further it. In 2002 he—along with collaborators Spielberg and Harrison Ford—announced plans to resurrect his second major on-screen enterprise, Indiana Jones, for a fourth and likely final outing. Meanwhile, in 2003 Lucas announced plans to consolidate his film production company, Lucasfilm, his special effects house, Lucas Digital, and video game company, LucasArts Entertainment, under the name Lucasfilm Ltd. As a result, most of the company's 2,000 employees will relocate to the company's planned Digital Arts Center campus at San Francisco's Presidio in 2005.

"I've always had a basic dislike of authority figures, a fear and resentment of grown-ups," Lucas said in "Skywalking", Dale Pollock's

1983 biography, and it is childhood that has remained the source of his magic, burning bright despite his becoming an old-fashioned, paternalistic boss. In a way, "Star Wars" is a metaphor for his own life. He is Luke. Estranged from his father (Darth Vader), he came under the protective influence of Coppola (Obi-Wan), who helped him get his first film made, and as Luke has to contend with the qualities he may have inherited from his father, Lucas cannot deny he has become the successful, fiscally-conservative businessman his father always wanted him to be. He changed movies forever because he saw them through the eyes of a child, jettisoning character and complexity for non-stop action. The concept of an "action beat" every ten minutes to propel a story is one part of the Lucas legacy, coupled with his high tech quest to achieve unparalleled visual effects in filmmaking.
—Written by Greg Senf

COMPANIONS:

wife: Marcia Lucas. Editor; born c. 1945; married in 1969; divorced in 1983; worked on "American Graffiti" and won Oscar for editing "Star Wars"

Linda Ronstadt. Singer; no longer together

MILESTONES:

Won numerous motor racing trophies while a teenager

1962: Badly injured in car crash

1966: Began film career as assistant editor for US Information Agency

1967: Received Grand Prize for Film, National Student Film Festival, for short version of "THX-1138"

1968: Won Warner Bros scholarship; spent six months as observer-administrative assistant to Francis Ford Coppola on "Finian's Rainbow"

1969: Appointed vice-president of Coppola's newly formed American Zoetrope company

1971: Incorporated Lucasfilm Ltd.

1971: Wrote and directed first feature film, "THX-1138"

1973: Formed Star Wars Corp.

1973: Co-produced first feature, "American Graffiti"; also directed and co-wrote; film received five Academy Award nominations including Best Picture, Best Director and Best Original Screenplay

1975: Formed Industrial Light & Magic, a special effects subsidiary of Lucasfilm

1977: Third and last directing assignment before taking 20 year sabbatical, "Star Wars"; film earned 11 Oscar nominations including Best Picture, Best Director and Best Original Screenplay

1980: Formed Sprocket Systems Inc., a research and post-production company

Split off the non-filmmaking sides of Lucasfilm (including ILM, a computer game division and a theater sound systems group), named it LucasArts and gave much of it to his employees in the 1980s

1981: Wrote story and executive produced, "Raiders of the Lost Ark"; first collaboration with director Steven Spielberg

1984: Reteamed with Spielberg for "Indian Jones and the Temple of Doom"; again wrote story and executive produced

1989: Completed trilogy with Spielberg, "Indiana Jones and the Last Crusade", also provided story and served as executive producer

1990–1991: Devoted a year to creating The George Lucas Educational Foundation to provide computer-based technologies for schools to spur learning among teens (date approximate)

1991: Value of the "Star Wars" brand reemerged when Bantam Books published Timothy Zahn's "Heir to the Empire", and it surprisingly soared to No. 1 on *The New York Times* hardcover fiction list

1992: Created and executive produced TV series, "The Young Indiana Jones Chronicles" (ABC)

Executive produced series of "Young Indiana Jones" TV-movies for the Family Channel

1997: Rereleased a digitally enhanced "Star Wars" trilogy

1997: Returned to directing, wrapping principal photography on "Star Wars: Episode I—The Phantom Menace" (released in 1999)

2002: Helmed "Star Wars: Episode II—Attack of the Clones" (filmed in 2000)

2003: Announced plans to consolidate his film production company, his special effects house and video game company under the name Lucasfilm Ltd. and relocate most of the company's 2,000 employees to the company's planned Digital Arts Center campus at San Francisco's Presidio in 2005

QUOTES:

The WEB address for the George Lucas Educational Foundation, established in 1991, is www.glef.org

Lucas won a Special Hugo Award for Science Fiction Achievement, World Science Fiction Society.

"Star Wars" was voted Best Picture of 1977 by the Los Angeles Film Critics Association.

He received an honorary doctorate from USC on May 6, 1994

In 1999, Lucas donated $1.5 million to USC to fund a digital studio to be named in honor of the late Japanese filmmaker Akira Kurosawa.

"You can type this shit, George, but you sure can't say it."—Harrison Ford commenting to Lucas on the quality of his dialogue.

"George Lucas was always the star of the student film festivals then [the 60s]. You'd look through a lot of stuff and fall asleep. But George's films would come on, and they'd be polished and professional, and you'd wonder what in hell he was doing in college."—Steven Spielberg, quoted in "World Film Directors", Volume Two.

"My father provided me with a lot of business principles—a small-town retail-business ethic, and I guess I learned it. It's sort of ironic, because I swore when I was a kid I'd never do what he did. At eighteen, we had this big break, when he wanted me to go into the business and I refused, and I told him, 'There are two things I know for sure. One is that I will end up doing something with cars, whether I'm a racer, a mechanic, or whatever, and, two, that I will never be president of a company.' I guess I got outwitted."—George Lucas quoted by *The New Yorker*, January 6, 1997.

"People say my movies are just like Hollywood movies. And I say, 'I can't help it if Hollywood copies.' "—Lucas quoted in 1999 *Premiere* October 2, 2002.

BIBLIOGRAPHY:

"Skywalking: The Life and Films of George Lucas" Dale Pollack, 1983; biography

"Shadow Moon" George Lucas and Chris Claremont, 1995, Bantam Books

"Shadow Dawn" George Lucas and Chris Claremont, 1996, Bantam Books

"George Lucas: The Creative Impulse: Lucasfilm's First Twenty Years" Charles Champlin, Steven Spielberg and Francis Ford Coppola, 1997, Harry N. Abrams Inc.; revised and updated edition

"Mythmaker: The Life and Work of George Lucas" John Baxter, 1999, Spike

Baz Luhrmann

BORN: Mark Anthony Luhrmann in Sydney, Australia, 09/17/1962

NATIONALITY: Australian

EDUCATION: National Institute of Dramatic Arts, Sydney, Australia; attended in the mid-1980s

AWARDS: Cannes Film Festival Prix de Jeuness "Strictly Ballroom" 1992; also won a Special Mention for the Camera d'Or

Australian Film Institute Award Best Director "Strictly Ballroom" 1992

Australian Film Institute Award Best Screenplay "Strictly Ballroom" 1992; shared award with co-writer Craig Pearce

Berlin Film Festival Alfred Bauer Prize "William Shakespeare's Romeo + Juliet" 1997

BAFTA Award Best Director "William Shakespeare's Romeo + Juliet" 1997

BAFTA Award Best Adapted Screenplay "William Shakespeare's Romeo + Juliet" 1997; shared award with Craig Pearce

Australian Film Institute Byron Kennedy Award 1999; shared with Catherine Martin

National Board of Review Award Best Film

"Moulin Rouge!" 2001; Luhrmann was one of the producers as well as the director

Movieline Visionary Filmmaker Award "Moulin Rouge!" 2001

Broadcast Film Critics Association Award Best Director "Moulin Rouge!" 2001; tied with Ron Howard ("A Beautiful Mind")

Golden Satellite Best Motion Picture (Comedy or Musical) "Moulin Rouge!" 2001; Luhrmann was one of the producers

Golden Satellite Best Director of a Motion Picture "Moulin Rouge!" 2001

Golden Globe Award Best Motion Picture (Musical or Comedy) "Moulin Rouge!" 2001; Luhrmann was a producer

London Film Critics Circle Award Best Film "Moulin Rouge!" 2001

Film Critics Circle of Australia Award Best Director "Moulin Rouge!" 2001

Producers Guild of America Darryl F. Zanuck Producer of the Year in Theatrical Motion Picture "Moulin Rouge!" 2002; shared award

BIOGRAPHY

Considered one of the most innovative directors working at the turn of the 21st century, Australian

Baz Luhrmann had only completed three feature films by 2001 but each was very much a stylized visual treat that found equal measures of detractors as well as champions. The trio of films, "Strictly Ballroom" (1992), "William Shakespeare's Romeo + Juliet" (1996) and "Moulin Rouge!" (2001) all adhere to a specific style developed by Luhrmann and his collaborators that he has dubbed "the Red Curtain". According to the filmmaker, "the Red Curtain" has certain specifics: 1) the audience knows how it will end right from the start; 2) the storyline is thin and simple; 3) the world created in the film is one of heightened reality; and 4) there is to be a specific device driving the story, whether it be dance, iambic pentameter or characters bursting out in song. Technically, Luhrmann keeps his camera constantly moving, employing pans, zooms, close-ups, whatever is best for the particular scene. As he has grown more secure in his position as director (and as the budgets have increased) his camera and editing have merged into a sort of helter-skelter, hellzapoppin' style that manages to blend the emotional and the poetic in ways that appear new and revolutionary.

Although born in Sydney, Australia, Luhrmann spent much of his childhood living in the small rural town of Herron's Creek where his father operated a gas station as well as forays into pig farming and operating the local movie theater. It was there that young Baz (a nickname bestowed by his dad) became enthralled by the power of storytelling. After his parents' divorce, Luhrmann and his siblings settled with their mother in Sydney.

While still in his teens, Luhrmann decided to pursue a career as an actor and landed his first film role alongside Bryan Brown and Judy Davis in "Winter of Our Dreams" (1981), written and directed by John Duigan. A couple of TV roles followed before Luhrmann decided to enroll at the prestigious National Institute of Dramatic Arts (NIDA), an experience that greatly upset him. Having worked as an instinctual actor, Luhrmann found the school's program stifling and the experience more or less put him off performing. During the Australian bicentennial celebrations, he was selected to observe Peter Brook staging "The Mahabarata" and the famed British director offered a simple piece of advice, "get out and do something." Luhrmann had been nurturing an idea for a one-act piece which he called "Strictly Ballroom" and in 1986, he staged a 30-minute version. Having left NIDA, he formed a theater troupe, the Six Years Old Company, which presented a revised and expanded version of "Strictly Ballroom" in 1987 that proved a popular success and toured Australia. Building on his growing reputation, Luhrmann staged "Dance Hall" (1989), which recreated the look and feel of a 1940s establishment on the night that the end of WWII was announced, and earned attention for his progressive "La Boheme" at the Australian Opera, which moved the action to 1950s Paris. (A revival of his staging was filmed in 1993 and aired in the USA on PBS' "Great Performances." He recreated the production on Broadway in 2002.)

In 1992, Luhrmann made the jump to the big screen with a film version of "Strictly Ballroom". Teaming with screenwriters Andrew Bovell and Craig Pearce, he reworked the material into a comic tale of Australian eccentrics obsessed with the world of competitive ballroom dancing and the individual (played by Paul Mercurio) who dared to break tradition by creating his own spontaneous routines. As a director, Luhrmann managed to juggle the multiple storylines in a manner that kept the audience involved, exhibited a flair for staging scenes (mostly via his now trademark moving camera) and demonstrated a grasp of the importance of music in terms of moving the plot forward. A box-office hit in Australia (and winner of eight 1992 Australian Film Institute Awards, including Best Picture and Best Director), "Strictly Ballroom" garnered appreciative critical notices and earned modest returns on its American release.

Twentieth Century Fox took note of Luhrmann and signed him to a three-year, first-look deal which allowed the filmmaker to make his revisionist take on "William Shakespeare's Romeo + Juliet." Set in contemporary Florida, the film starred Leonardo DiCaprio and Claire Danes as the Bard's star-crossed lovers who hail from rival gangster families. Shot in a manner that drew influences from music videos and Hong Kong actioners, "William Shakespeare's Romeo + Juliet" also featured stylized settings (designed by Catherine Martin, whom Luhrmann married in 1997) and a throbbing alternative music soundtrack, but improbably (yet arguably successfully) retained the iambic pentameter of the original play. Although American reviewers were divided over its merits, the film found an audience thanks to its attractive cast and its visual razzle dazzle, raking in more than $45 million in domestic grosses.

Admittedly a slow worker, Luhrmann takes up to three years developing ideas for his films. Once again collaborating with Craig Pearce, he crafted the screenplay for "Moulin Rouge!", a large-scale movie musical set at the end of the 19th Century. Based partly on the Orpheus myth as well as drawing on "La Boheme" and other sources, Luhrmann and his collaborators created the third and most blatant of his "Red Curtain" productions. "Moulin Rouge!" premiered at Cannes to appreciative audiences but a divided critical response. The film's lavish production design, colorful costumes and overblown style appealed to many, while others found fault with the thin plot. Few had quibbles over the stars—Nicole Kidman, Ewan McGregor and Jim Broadbent who did their own singing—and nearly all agreed that, if nothing else, "Moulin Rouge!" helped to revitalize a moribund art form.

MILESTONES:

Raised in the small town of Herron's Creek in New South Wales, Australia until parents' divorce; moved to Sydney after divorce

1981: Appeared opposite Judy Davis in feature film "Winter of Our Dreams"

1982: Had small role in "The Highest Honor—A True Story"

1982: Began working on a stage production about competitive ballroom dancing called "Strictly Ballroom"

1983: Played featured role in the Australian TV docudrama "Kids of the Cross"; last screen acting role

1985: While studying at National Institute of Dramatic Arts, selected to observe director Peter Brook working on the production of "The Mahabarata"

1986: Devised and staged 30-minute theatrical version of "Strictly Ballroom" as well as the musical "Crocodile Creek"

1987: Formed the Six Years Old Company

1988: Staged revised and expanded version of "Strictly Ballroom"; production toured Australia

1989: For the Sydney Festival, staged "Dance Hall" which recreated a 1940s establishment

1990: Directed Puccini's "La Boheme" for the Australian Opera; reset story in 20th-century Paris; production filmed in 1993 for airing on PBS' "Great Performances" in 1994

1990: Staged "Lake Lost", an opera by Felix Meagher

1992: For the Australian Opera, directed "A Midsummer Night's Dream"

1992: Feature debut as director and co-scenarist (with Craig Pearce and Andrew Bovell), "Strictly Ballroom"; premiered at Cannes; film won eight awards from the Australian Film Institute, including Best Picture and Best Director

1993: Served as an advisor to Labour Prime Minister Paul Keating's re-election campaign

1996: Directed and adapted (with Craig Pearce) "William Shakespeare's Romeo + Juliet", featuring Leonardo DiCaprio and Claire Danes; reset the timeless tale in present-day Verona Beach

1996: Established BazMark.Inq. (date approximate)

1998: Produced compilation album, "Baz Luhrmann Presents . . . Something for Everyone"; contained the surprise hit single "Everybody's Free to Wear Sunscreen"

1998: Signed exclusive five-year deal with 20th Century Fox

2001: Helmed the unconventional film musical "Moulin Rouge!", starring Ewan McGregor and Nicole Kidman; also co-wrote script with Craig Pearce; wife Catherine Martin designed the sets and co-designed the costumes

2002: Staged "La Boheme" on Broadway, based on his 1990 Australia Opera production set in 1950s Paris

QUOTES:

Luhrmann's father gave him the nickname "Baz".

His production company is called BazMark Productions.

"Luhrmann, like many first-time directors, is intoxicated with the possibilities of the camera. He uses too many wide-angle shots, in which the characters look like blowfish mugging for the lens, and too many story lines, until we worry we may have lost track of something, but what works is an exuberance that cannot be faked."—From Roger Ebert's review of "Strictly Ballroom" in *The Chicago Sun-Times,* February 26, 1993.

"What Hollywood is about and what the cinema is about is knowing how to make something work. There are now many executives running around that town talking about their next film saying, 'I don't care. I just want it like Romeo and Juliet.'"—Luhrmann on Hollywood's reaction to his film's success in *The Age,* December 24, 1996.

"Let me get this straight. There's a great mythology about this. Peter Brook came to Australia in the bicentenary year. The government spent a million dollars bringing him here so they said they had to let some bright young sparks work with him. So I get the gig and we

sit there in rehearsal from twelve o'clock at night to six in the morning and sleep in the day. I'm like this acolyte. And one day I get my interview with Peter and he says: 'My only advice to you, dear boy, is why are you wasting your time watching me—get out and do something.' I just left."

"At NIDA [National Institute for Dramatic Arts], I did the same thing. That was after NIDA, but at NIDA I was doing the acting course, but at night I would do my own show, and I acted in the original "Strictly Ballroom", so you know, it's not about 'You're not an actor.' There is, I find, too much paid to this craft called acting, this craft called directing. I mean, directors are a sort of recent invention. There is only one craft and that is the craft of telling stories. And that is the real craft—what function you play in that and how you do it and what you use."—Baz Luhrmann quoted in 1996 interview at the now defunct website "MOGUL" (www.mogul.co.nz).

On his propensity for using quick cuts and visual images in his films, Luhrmann told *The Age* (December 24, 1996): "The current generation's mental software for processing story is so much faster and is able to deal with three or four styles in a given moment. That is something inherent in the pop clip."

Ewan McGregor describing working with Luhrmann on "Moulin Rouge!": "It's been a f—in' amazing experience. He seeks perfection, he's so precise, he pushes you and pushes you. And he works like a dog."—quoted in "Bohemian Rhapsody" by David Jenkins in *The Daily Telegraph,* November 13, 2000.

On "Moulin Rouge!", Baz Luhrmann told Paul Fischer in a 2001 interview published at the "Cranky Critic" website (www.cranky-critic.com): "I feel like I've been gearing for this my entire life. . . . As a kid I loved musicals and that idea that you saw an artificial film that made you feel, the fact that all of the audience was involved in the story. To a certain extent, "Strictly Ballroom" and "R[omeo] +J[uliet]" are musicals, so we've just taken a final leap, really, towards a breakout in songs in movie in the use of musicals to tell a story."

Luhrmann described "Moulin Rouge!" to London's *The Sunday Times* (May 6, 2001): "Without an iota of exaggeration, this film—personally, emotionally and creatively—tested me to my outer limit. Simply and easily the most difficult thing I have ever made."

"The third element of Luhrmann's style is, of course, camp and 'Moulin Rouge' . . . is as camp as karaoke. When we met in 1997, I had assumed Baz was gay and was shocked by him telling me he'd just married CM [Catherine Martin], his devoted production designer.

"There is a whole gay sensibility to the work I do," he says today. "You can see it in the films, in the evolution of the work. And that is something that should be there both for CM [Catherine Martin] and me. As I said before, I see all sexual possibilities. We are married and are a real couple but we have never denied ourselves any of the possibilities in life."

So she's bisexual too? "Well, I won't speak for her but I think if you delve into her history, let me put it this way, she has seen all the possibilities in life too."

—From "Rocking With the Legend of Baz" by Andrew Billen in London's *Evening Standard*, May 9, 2001.

On why he stopped acting after attending drama school: "I gave up everything that I had felt instinctively and started to learn all over again, and it killed me. I had a total breakdown. I gave up school eventually and went back to my own thing—basically, imagining and storytelling."—Luhrmann quoted in London's *The Sunday Times*, May 13, 2001.

"This cinema that I've been working on for the past ten years is 'Audience Participation Cinema'. What that means is that the rules of engagement between the audience and the film itself are changed from naturalism. They're quite old rules that are reinvented for now. . . . The first fifteen minutes is what I call 'The wake-up call'

where you go 'Oh my God, what's going on here?'. The next fifteen minutes you either buy the contract or you don't. Seventy-five percent of them are buying the contract. . . . Some people can never sign on to this. . . . It's *Theatrical* cinema. But most are into it . . . "—Luhrmann to Nick Nunziata of www.CHUD.com, June 1, 2001.

"All my films are told in the same language. It's our way of doing movies. They all have a primary myth at the bottom of them, it's very important that you know how the story ends as it begins, they're set in heightened creative worlds, and you have some sort of device whether it's dance, Iambic pentameter, or music to keep the audience constantly alive to the fact they're watching a movie. . . . "

"I'm in a unique position. I have a big circus of creators I work with. We live in Sydney and movies is only one of the things we do. We do operas, we have a record label, theatre, the internet, and we've even done some election campaigns. We decide what to make and we make it on our own schedule. Now when you want to reinvent the musical, it took longer than I thought it would. We're not shooters. In Hollywood it's hyper. You get a couple of million bucks, you shoot your comedy, collect your paycheck and you're out of there. This is our work, our life."—Luhrmann to Nick Nunziata of www.CHUD.com, June 1, 2001.

"Fights? I don't have fights with actors. In absolute honesty, I've never fought with any actor ever. Nicole [Kidman] is no saint. We had crazy mornings. Were there tears? Were there times when I felt this very faint whiff of a desire to murder her? Yes, but if this was a circus highwire act, she walked that wire without a net. I'd love to say we screamed, we yelled, we got into all sorts of theatrics, but I never yelled once at Nicole. And I never yelled at Ewan [McGregor], I would say, "Why are you yelling? What is going on? OK, let's sort this out because whatever happens, you're going to go back in front of that camera and we're going to make a great moment of drama." I understand that anything actors are doing, good or bad, is motivated by fear. I'm not allowed to be frightened—though, of course, I am."—Baz Luhrmann quoted in *Movieline,* June 2001.

"I see myself creating an environment that protects people from the power of fear. I build a wall in Australia, behind which we create. Risk is possible in an environment in which fear is kept at bay. We just cannot hear the sirens calling, the press comment or what the studio thinks, because nobody does know, and all we can know is what's in front of us."—Luhrmann on the House of Iona, a former asylum in Sydney that serves as the headquarters for his company BazMark.Inq., quoted in London's *The Sunday Times,* August 8, 2001.

"All my work tries to push boundaries. Ultimately, I'm reaching out to engage an audience with something."—Luhrmann to the London *Times,* September 4, 2001.

"My early work was 16mm documentaries shot on the streets of Kings Cross, and he was very baroque. He's moved towards a kind of minimalism, whereas as we've moved to our own code, a kind of heightened artifice which is like his early work. But that isn't relevant. What is relevant is that we're sort of heading in the same direction, and there's a mutual admiration there, in the sense that we deal with primary mythology. Whichever way you look at it, the idea of access a direct emotional response through a kind of twisting of simple melodramatic—melodrama is a good word to use, because primary mythology is a basic kind of melodrama. All good, clean stories are melodrama, it's just the set of devices that determines how you show or hide it."—Luhrmann in *The Guardian,* September 7, 2001.

DISCOGRAPHY: "Baz Luhrmann Presents. . . . Something for Everyone" various artists EMD/Capitol 1998 album of compilation music from stage and screen productions directed by Luhrmann; included the hit "Everybody's Free to Wear Sunscreen"

Sidney Lumet

BORN: in Philadelphia, Pennsylvania, 06/25/1924

NATIONALITY: American

EDUCATION: Professional Children's School New York, New York

Columbia University, New York, New York, dramatic literature, 1941–42; dropped out

Actors Studio, New York, New York; joined 1947

AWARDS: Berlin Film Festival Golden Bear "12 Angry Men" 1957

British Film Academy Award Best Director "The Pawnbroker" 1965

Los Angeles Film Critics Association Award Best Director "Dog Day Afternoon" 1975

Los Angeles Film Critics Association Award Best Director "Network" 1976

Golden Globe Award Best Director "Network" 1976

NATO Director of the Year Award 1981; from the National Association of Theater Owners

Venice Film Festival Pasinetti Prize "Prince of the City" 1981

New York Film Critics Circle Award Best Director "Prince of the City" 1981

National Board of Review Award Best Director "The Verdict" 1982

Directors Guild of America Honorary Lifetime Membership 1989

Directors Guild of America D W Griffth Award 1992

National Board of Review Billy Wilder Award for Excellence 1996

Writers Guild of America (East) Evelyn F Burkey Award 1997

IFP Gotham Award Lifetime Achievement

Producers Guild of America Sony New Technology Award 2001

BIOGRAPHY

A product of both the stage and the early days of TV, consummate craftsman Sidney Lumet borrowed from each genre in developing his distinct filmmaking style. From the theater, he learned how to work with actors, earning a reputation as an actor's director and (to date) drawing 18 Oscar-nominated performances from his charges. His high regard for the script and insistence on a rehearsal period before shooting has enabled him to translate classic plays to the screen, including Tennessee Williams' "Orpheus Descending" (released as "The Fugitive Kind" 1960), Arthur Miller's "A View From the Bridge" (1961) and Eugene O'Neill's "Long Day's Journey Into Night" (1962). Television provided him his facility with the camera and a penchant for working quickly, the one habit his detractors decry most. Famous for bringing in his projects on or ahead of schedule (and under budget), Lumet has rarely shot more than four or five takes before moving on to the next setup, causing some to fault his approach as too complacent, even careless.

The son of Baruch Lumet and Eugenia Wermus, veterans of the Yiddish stage, Lumet made his professional debut on radio at age four and his stage debut at the Yiddish Art Theatre at five. For two years during the Depression (1931–32), he played the son in a Yiddish radio serial scripted and directed by his father called "The Rabbi From Brownsville", which also featured his mother as the leading lady and his father in two roles. Lumet first appeared on Broadway in "Dead End" (1935), written by family friend Sidney Kingsley who penned a part especially for him since he was too young to play one of the Dead End Kids. His first important role, Jesus Christ in Max Reinhardt's production of "The Eternal Road" (1937), attracted attention and a string of Broadway parts, including one in "One Third of a Nation" (1939), which became his only film credit as an actor when lensed later that year. Lumet played Jesus as a boy again in Maxwell Anderson's "Journey to Jerusalem" (1940), and his close identification with the character explains why years later he wanted to bring Nikos Kazantzakis' book "The Last Temptation of Christ" to the screen. Unable to secure financing, he dropped his option on it after three years, allowing Martin Scorsese to eventually film it in 1988.

After service in World War II, Lumet returned to the New York stage and, irritated by the pretensions of the Actors Studio, formed his own Off-Broadway acting group, which gave him his first experience directing. In 1950, Lumet's friend Yul Brynner, then a staff director with CBS-TV, invited him to join the network as an assistant director. After his promotion to staff director, he went on to helm about 150 episodes of the series "Danger" between 1951 and 1953 as well as episodes of "I Remember Mama" and "You Are There". In 1953, Lumet began directing original plays for "Playhouse 90", "Kraft Television Theatre" and "Studio One", filming about 200 during TV's "Golden Age" and establishing himself as one of the most prolific and respected directors in the business. He even found time to direct for the theater, staging productions of Shaw's "The Doctor's Dilemma" (1955) and Arch Oboler's "Night of the Auk" (1956). The success of the motion picture "Marty" (1955), originally written and made for TV, paved the way for Lumet's first feature, the small-scale work of social realism "12 Angry Men" (1957), which had already been filmed for television.

With his background, Lumet never envisioned shooting an entire picture in one room as a problem. In fact, he turned it into an advantage, emphasizing the jurors' sense of entrapment by using longer and longer lenses as the movie progressed, so that the ceiling became closer to their heads, the walls closer to their chairs. In addition, he shot the first third of the movie above eye level, the second third at eye level and the final third below eye level so that the ceiling appeared more and more, creating a sense of increasing claustrophobia that raised the tension in the film. Producer Henry Fonda's faith in neophyte Lumet had paid off. Made in 19 days for $343,000, "12 Angry Men" brought Lumet an Oscar nomination for Best Director. He had come to movies fully prepared technically for the task, yet it would take him many years to adjust in terms of scale, filling up a thirty-five-foot screen as opposed to a seventeen-inch piece of glass. This may explain why his early film successes were adapted stage plays, which he shot mostly in the comforting confines of the studio, and why he continued to do some of his best work for the small screen (i.e., his four-hour version of Eugene O'Neill's "The Iceman Cometh", starring Jason Robards).

Lumet's reputation was still far from secure when he achieved a technical triumph in the editing room with his adaptation of Lewis Wallant's novel "The Pawnbroker" (1965). Working with editor Ralph Rosenblum and employing a juxtaposition of images that became known as "subliminal" cutting, Lumet was able to suggest the awakening of concentration camp survivor Sol Nazerman, who is morally numbed by suffering and the guilt he feels as the only member of his family to escape the Holocaust. The reigning wisdom of the time was that the brain could not retain or comprehend an image that lasted less than three frames, one eighth of a second. As Lumet flashed to the horror of Auschwitz, he began with two-frame cuts, repeated as often as he felt necessary for the picture to became clear, and then lengthened the images to four frames, eight frames, sixteen frames, and so on in a mathematical progression until the scene played in its entirety. In this way, he cut back

and forth from the subway car in which Nazerman was riding to the railway car of his subconscious mind that carried his family to the extermination camp. The gradual transition took a minute before the subway car WAS the railway car, leaving Nazerman no escape from his memories. Within a year of the film's release, it seemed all commercials were using the breakthrough technique, and "subliminal" cutting is still a common trick of the trade. Although some critics did not like "The Pawnbroker", Lumet earned the British Academy Award as Best Director.

After generating "The Hill" (1965), a powerful drama of wretched life in a British military prison that starred Sean Connery, Lumet entered a middling phase of his now prominent career. He showed signs of breaking out of his pattern of failure with "The Anderson Tapes" (1971), which reunited him with Connery, then promptly returned to mediocrity with "Child's Play" (1972) and "The Offense" (1973), failed adaptations of stage plays. Just when his career had reached an all-time nadir, Lumet resurrected himself with "Serpico" (1973), the first of four 70s hits that represent the zenith of his career. Sinking his teeth into this story of power and betrayal in the NYC police force, he developed an interest in how the flaws of a criminal justice system negatively impact on democracy. Having found a theme that resonated for him (i.e., loss of innocence in the face of corruption), he would return again and again to the world of cops, lawyers and hoods to explore it. Based on Peter Maas' best-selling biography, "Serpico" starred Al Pacino who dominated the film, vividly presenting his inner personal torment as the idealism of his rookie cop eroded in the face of a stifling, hypocritical bureaucracy. Lumet drew almost universal praise for adeptly combining gritty action and thought-provoking comment in what many consider his finest work.

After momentarily faltering with "Lovin' Molly" (1974), Lumet scored big with the star-studded "Murder on the Orient Express" (1974), the most ambitious British film in years and a thoroughly enjoyable box-office romp. Aided by Paul Dehn's script, Tony Walton's production design and costumes and Geoffrey Unsworth's cinematography, Lumet, along with his above-title players, pulled the period film off to perfection. A number of critics preferred "Dog Day Afternoon" (1975) to "Serpico", finding it richer in characterization and its social implications. The original script by Frank Pierson, based on a true story of three young criminals' disastrous attempt to rob a Brooklyn bank one August afternoon in 1972, began as farce and ended in tragedy. Lumet, in order to let his audience know that this event really happened, used no artificial light, relying instead on natural fluorescence for interiors, and augmenting the light for certain dark scenes just enough to get an exposure. "Dog Day Afternoon" boasted outstanding performances by John Cazale, Charles Durning, Chris Sarandon and James Broderick, but Pacino, as the ringleader, stole the show. In back-to-back phone calls made to his gay lover and wife, shot consecutively without cutting away, he delivered perhaps the most remarkable film acting of his career.

The Lumet juggernaut rolled on with the brilliant satire on television "Network" (1976), his greatest commercial success. Scripted by Paddy Chayefsky, "Network" chronicled the story of fading anchorman Howard Beale's messianic rise in the ratings, denouncing the hypocrisies of his time, and his subsequent fall from grace when his public rantings put off the audience. Despite its popularity, some critics despised it for its crazy preposterousness. Years later, others would accuse it of pretentiousness, both views failing to recognize hyperbole as a necessary ingredient in the tale. While often preachy, hysterical, shrill and bizarre, "Network" also made a compelling statement from within the mad bombast. Outrageous as it all seemed on the surface, the story possessed

more than a kernel of truth, and on certain levels was eerily plausible and predicted many of the coming changes in the industry. Fueled by strong performances from a stellar cast that featured William Holden, Ned Beatty, Peter Finch (in his last screen role), Faye Dunaway and Beatrice Straight, "Network" earned 10 Oscar nominations (including one for Lumet's direction) and went on to win four statutes for Finch, Dunaway, Straight and Chayefsky.

With his next film, the screen version of Peter Shaffer's play "Equus" (1977), Lumet's luck ran out. Although generally admired, particularly for Richard Burton's portrayal of the psychiatrist, it fell well below the standard Lumet had been setting. No one had a good word either for the universally loathed, ill-conceived "The Wiz" (1978), a bomb based on a hit Broadway musical that could have destroyed a lesser career. "Just Tell Me What You Want" (1980), though notable for a fine performance by Alan King, also failed to generate much enthusiasm.

Lumet was back in familiar territory with "Prince of the City" (1981), picking up his first writing credit for the script he penned with Jay Presson Allen. Another story of power and betrayal among NYC cops, this logical progression from "Serpico" told the true story of Bob Leuci, whose undercover work with the Knapp Commission led to 52 indictments and two suicides. Leuci feels he's in complete control and believes he can cooperate without involving his close friends, but once the wheels are in motion, his world comes crashing down around him. To emphasize the cop's increasing sense of alienation, Lumet once again divided his movie into thirds, keeping the background behind him in the first third extremely busy. As the movie develops, there are less and less people in the background until for the last third, there is no one. He is all alone, sleeping in the bed he made for himself. A rewarding experience for Lumet and considered by some a culmination of his work, its sheer ambition doomed it in many eyes. With a nearly three hour running time and a host of characters to keep straight, it made for tedious viewing for some while others applauded its detail.

"The Verdict" (1982), an excellent courtroom drama scripted by David Mamet and buoyed by one of Paul Newman's best screen performances, earned Lumet his fourth Academy Award nomination for Best Director. For this story of a man's redemption, the director wanted as "old" a look as possible, drawing inspiration from a book of Caravaggio's paintings. Polish cinematographer Andrzej Bartkowiak, studying the pictures, pinpointed what the director had in mind as chiaroscuro (a very strong light source, almost always from the side, and on the opposite side, no soft fill light, only shadows) and carried that out in the lighting of the movie. "Daniel" (1983), loosely based on the lives of Julius and Ethel Rosenberg (fictionalized as the Isaacsons), followed the attempts of the Isaacson children to come to terms with their appalling family legacy. Though some critics hated Lumet's bleeding-heart presentation of the condemned couple, most agreed that, despite its flaws, "Daniel" was a provocative, extremely well-made film. After three sub-par films ("Garbo Talks" 1984, "Power" 1986 and "The Morning After" 1986), he returned to form with "Running on Empty" (1988), a quiet and believable tale of 60s radicals still on the run, featuring superb performances from Judd Hirsch, Christine Lahti and most notably River Phoenix.

Lumet returned to the NYC police milieu for "Q & A" (1980), picking up his first solo screenwriting credit adapting the Edward Torres novel. Unfortunately, the gritty, graphic, well-acted story bogged down as it approached its predictable conclusion. He inhabited similar terrain, though less successfully, with "A Stranger Among Us" (1992), which (mis)cast Melanie Griffith as a NYC cop who goes to live among Brooklyn's Hasidic community to uncover a murderer. The farfetched finale made it one of Lumet's least satisfying cop dramas, and it does not really belong alongside "Serpico" or "Prince of the City" as it did not deal with the larger issues of innocence lost and police corruption. He provided a better movie with "Night Falls on Manhattan" (1997), which seemed to pick up where "Prince of the City" left off, depicting the ethical compromises of middle-aged cops who are not inherently bad. Again solo scripted by Lumet, it depicted a compromise with evil at the end, leaving some people cold, but one wonders if it would have sizzled more with another actor instead of Andy Garcia in the lead role. He continued addressing ethical concerns, this time in the medical profession, with "Critical Care" (1997).

Sidney Lumet's virtues have far outweighed his vices in a protean feature directing career now in its fifth decade. For all the visual sloppiness and liberal moralizing, his strong direction of actors, vigorous storytelling and use of the camera to accent his themes have produced a body of work that can not be taken lightly. Refusing to "go Hollywood", he remained in NYC and filmed three out of every four pictures in Gotham, never duplicating locations. The amazing feel for New York that he has transmitted to the screen is certainly an abiding legacy. Perhaps it is hard to reconcile the Lumet of "Serpico" and "Network" with the man who helmed "The Wiz" and "Garbo Talks", but all directors have their flops. Comparing his movies to those of his contemporaries like John Frankenheimer, Arthur Penn and Alan Pakula, one sees how well Lumet stacks up, and when mining the vein of social realism that was an early influence, Lumet has delivered some trenchant pictures no other director could have provided. Though he sometimes disappoints, he continues to entertain, so much so that when he has finally directed his last project, one wonders if anyone will be able to fill his very large shoes. Fortunately, he has preserved his impressions on filmmaking in a book "Making Movies" (1995).—Written by Greg Senf

MILESTONES:

1926: Moved to New York with family

Appeared on stage at age four

1931–1932: Performed in Yiddish radio serial, "The Rabbi from Brownsville", a real Lumet family affair; Baruch Lumet wrote, directed and acted the leading man and grandfather while Eugenia played the leading lady and Sidney, the son; their efforts earned the family $35 per week

1935: Broadway acting debut, Sidney Kingsley's "Dead End"

1938: Acted on Broadway in "Sunup to Sundown", directed by Joseph Losey

1939: Only screen credit as an actor, "One Third of a Nation"; had played in Broadway version earlier in the year

Served in Far East as radar repairman for US Army Signal Corps

1947: Founded own experimental acting group in Greenwich Village; began to direct Off-Broadway

1948: Final Broadway acting performance in "Seeds in the Wind"

1948: Taught acting at High School for the Performing Arts in New York City

1950: Joined CBS-TV as assistant director

1951: Graduated to director as replacement for Yul Brynner

Became leading live TV director, working on such series as "Danger", "You Are There", "Kraft Television Theater" and "Playhouse 90"

Directed such Broadway productions as "The Doctor's Dilemma" (1955), "Caligula" (1960) and "Nowhere to Go but Up" (1962)

1957: Feature film directing debut, "12 Angry Men" (screenplay by Reginald Rose, based on his earlier teleplay); earned Academy Award nomination as Best Director

Formed first production company, Sidney Lumet Productions

1964: First film directed for production company "Fail Safe"

During 1960s and 1970s made a number of British-produced features

1965: Enjoyed commercial success with "The Pawnbroker"; technical breakthrough used to achieve Sol Nazerman's "awakening" came to be called "subliminal" cutting

1965: British directing debut, "The Hill"

1966: First feature as producer (also director; production company), "The Deadly Affair" (Great Britain)

1973: Resurrected career with the huge hit "Serpico", starring Al Pacino

1974: Helmed the star-studded blockbuster "Murder on the Orient Express"

1975: Earned second Oscar nomination for Best Director for "Dog Day Afternoon", starring Pacino

1976: Scored fourth commercial and critical triumph in as many years with the brilliant satire on TV "Network"; received third Best Director Oscar nomination; Faye Dunaway (Best Actress), Peter Finch (Best Actor), Beatrice Straight (Best Supporting Actress) and Paddy Chayefsky (Best Screenplay) all won Oscars

1978: Worst career choice, directing megabomb "The Wiz"; cast then-mother-in-law Lena Horne as Glinda, the good Witch

1980: Formed second production company, LAH Film Group, with screenwriter Jay Presson Allen and producer Burtt Harris; first LAH film, "Just Tell Me What You Want"

1981: Continued fascination with NYC police corruption with "Prince of the City"; first screenwriting credit; earned Academy Award nomination

1982: Received fourth Best Director Oscar nomination for the David Mamet–scripted "The Verdict", starring Paul Newman

1988: Scored modest success with superb, small-scale "Running on Empty"

1990: First film as solo writer (also director), "Q & A"

1995: Wrote primer on filmmaking "Making Movies"

1995: Directed premiere of Cynthia Ozick's play "Blue Light" at Bay Street Theater in Sag Harbor, New York

1996: Directed revised version of Ozick's play (retitled "The Shawl") Off-Off-Broadway

1996: Returned again to the world of power and betrayal among NYC cops, directing "Night Falls on Manhattan"; also received solo screenwritng credit

1997: Released "Critical Care" with a cast that included James Spader, Albert Brooks, Helen Mirren and Anne Bancroft

1999: Helmed unsuccessful remake of John Cassavetes' "Gloria", starring Sharon Stone in role originated by Gena Rowlands

2001: Returned to TV directing for first time in over 40 years at helm of pilot for A&E series "100 Centre Street"; also penned script for first of 13 episodes and served as executive producer of series which ran for two seasons

QUOTES:

Comparing himself to another NYC filmmaker Woody Allen: "The world [Allen is] dealing with is really his own inner world. He is intensely self-involved and trying to figure out, 'why am I an unhappy Jew?' I'm not belittling that. But I, from that kind of New York left wing upbringing, I look at the outside for sources of unhappiness. Whatever I'm contributing to it from my own psyche I don't think is very interesting to anyone, because it's not very interesting to me."—Sidney Lumet in *Daily News,* May 19, 1997.

On a movie he might have made: "Well, I had 'The Last Temptation of Christ', Nikos Kazantzakis' book, under option for about three years, then dropped it. I couldn't get a deal on it anywhere. Then, of course, Marty [Scorsese] did it wonderfully. And all I could think of, with the attacks on Marty, a Catholic fellow, was, 'Thank God I didn't do it!' That's all they needed was a Jew to have directed it. There would have been blood on the street."—Sidney Lumet, *The Hollywood Reporter New York Special Issue,* June 10, 1997.

"My job is to care about and be responsible for every frame of every movie I make. I know that all over the world there are young people borrowing from relatives and saving their allowances to buy their first cameras and put together their first student movies, some of them dreaming of becoming famous and making a fortune. But a few are dreaming of finding out what matters to them, of saying to themselves and to anyone who will listen, 'I care.' A few of them want to make good movies."—Sidney Lumet writing in "Making Movies."

"It's not as if you're kidding anybody, it's out there and it's a stinker, and everybody can see it." Lumet also told Madison magazine: "[Directors] are capable of total self-deception. Especially since there can be 20 other motives for making the movie. Like, you want the money. About a movie, it's not a vision, it's work."—From "Page Six" in *New York Post,* February 23, 1999.

BIBLIOGRAPHY:

"Making Movies" Sidney Lumet, 1995, Vintage Books; memoirs

Ida Lupino

BORN: in Brixton, London, England, 02/04/1918

DEATH: in Burbank, California, 08/03/1995

NATIONALITY: English

CITIZENSHIP: United States 1947

EDUCATION: Clarence House Preparatory and Boarding School, Hove, Sussex

Royal Academy of Dramatic Art, London, England, 1931; entered at age 13

AWARDS: National Board of Review Award Best Acting "High Sierra" and "Ladies in Retirement"

1941 for her work in both films; one of 21 performers cited

National Board of Review Award Best Acting "Moontide" 1943; one of 31 films cited

New York Film Critics Circle Award Best Actress "The Hard Way" 1943

BIOGRAPHY

This extremely talented, intense, British-born artist hailed from a family with theatrical credits going back to the Renaissance. Lupino got her start in films when her youthful-looking mother auditioned for an ingenue role but director Allan Dwan took greater interest in the woman who accompanied her that day—her daughter. Looking slightly older than her almost-15 years, Lupino got the job, dyed her hair platinum blonde (which it would remain for much of the 1930s) and made her debut in "Her First Affaire" (1932), promoted as "the English Jean Harlow."

Moving to Hollywood the following year and eliminating all but slight traces of her British accent, Lupino appeared for the rest of the decade in a series of modest ingenue roles, several of which ("Peter Ibbetson" 1935, "Anything Goes" 1936) gave her at least a slight chance to sparkle. It was not until 1939, though, that she really attracted critical attention as Ronald Colman's tormented Cockney painter's model in "The Light That Failed", a showy supporting role Lupino snagged after vigorously campaigning for the role and auditioning for director William Wellman. Dusky-voiced and dark-haired, with large eyes and a small, slightly angular face, Lupino came into her own playing headstrong, grasping women in a string of Warner Bros. melodramas through the 1940s. Especially memorable roles include a scheming waitress who cracks up in court on the witness stand in "They Drive By Night" (1940); John Garfield's and Humphrey Bogart's romantic interest in, respectively, "The Sea Wolf" and "High Sierra" (both 1941); the austere housekeeper turned murderess in "Ladies

in Retirement" (1941, her favorite role); the ambitious "stage-sister" determined to make her sibling a star in "The Hard Way" (1943); the world-weary nightclub singer in the wonderful sudser "The Man I Love" (1946); and the shy, stuttering woman who shelters an escaped convict in the touching "Deep Valley" (1947).

Combining the nervous energy and, to a lesser extent, the clipped speech patterns of Bette Davis with a toughness characteristic of Barbara Stanwyck, Lupino managed to score an impressive lineup of characterizations at Warners despite the fact that she, Ann Sheridan and other stars were often left to dicker for the roles Davis turned down. Freelancing after 1947, she continued to shine in melodramas including such worthy entries as "Lust for Gold" (1949), "On Dangerous Ground" (1952), "The Big Knife" (1955) and "While the City Sleeps" (1956). The restless actress began to tire of performing in the same types of melodrama she had done for years, though, and, caring more about "develop(ing) talent in others . . . than in my own", Lupino formed a series of production companies and began developing projects. After managing to get several modest films off the ground as producer, she took to directing one herself, the skillfully told story of an unwed mother, "Not Wanted" (1949), when credited director Elmer Clifton had a heart attack after three days shooting. She made her credited directorial debut soon after with "Never Fear" (1949), a semi-documentary styled look at a dancer stricken with polio, an affliction Lupino herself had known as a child.

One of the few women directors to succeed in a male-dominated field, Lupino's seven low-budget feature films have generally attracted less critical attention than fellow director Dorothy Arzner's dozen-plus, partly because Lupino's work, often showing the victimization of women, seemed to some to be "feminist films made from an unfeminist viewpoint." More recent critics dissent, however, finding in her oeuvre compelling portraits of both victims and aggressors wandering through artfully delineated back-street milieus of postwar America. Although perhaps none of her features is an unsung masterpiece, her work is technically very competent (her editing skills being especially notable) and, long before the advent of the TV-movie, dealt with timely, controversial social issues in an intimate, measured manner. Her work includes such films as "Outrage" (1950), an early study of the effects of rape on a young woman, "Hard, Fast and Beautiful" (1951), an entertaining melodrama about an ambitious stage mother in the world of professional tennis, "The Hitchhiker" (1953), a gripping suspense noir, and "The Bigamist" (1953), a deftly handled melodrama which avoids placing the blame too simply on either a man or his two wives.

Reputed to be the young medium's first female helmer, Lupino did most of her subsequent directing for TV, much of it featuring a brand of skillful camerawork that typed her in action drama rather than in the drawing room. She turned out over 100 episodes of such series as "The Untouchables", "The Twilight Zone", "Have Gun, Will Travel", "The Fugitive" and her own show, "Mr. Adams and Eve". During the 60s and 70s, she made occasional TV and feature film acting appearances in "guest star" types of roles. On TV Lupino was the villainous Dr. Cassandra on "Batman." Most notably she was Steve McQueen's oddly youthful mother in Sam Peckinpah's gentle, low-key "Junior Bonner" (1972). Lupino's final acting job was a guest shot on "Charlie's Angels." She was married to actor Louis Hayward (1938–45), executive Collier Young (1948–50), who executive produced "Mr. Adams and Eve" in the late 50s, and actor Howard Duff (1951–73), her co-star in "Mr. Adams and Eve."—Written by David Lugowski

MILESTONES:

1918: Born in London during a German zeppelin bombing

Wrote and produced her first play, "Mademoiselle", at age seven

Suffered from polio as a child

Joined a touring theater company

1932: First film appearance (a bit) in "The Love Race", directed by her uncle, Lupino Lane

1932: Official film acting debut at age 14 in "Her First Affaire", promoted as "the English Jean Harlow"

1933: Went to US under contract to Paramount; tested (unsuccessfully) for "Alice in Wonderland"

1934: US film debut in "Search for Beauty"

1937–1938: Left film acting for about a year after the failure of "Fight for Your Lady"; spent time writing and composing music, including the score for one of her father's shows and a piece, "Aladdin Suite", performed by the Los Angeles Philharmonic

1939: Achieved star status with "The Light That Failed"

1940: Signed contract with Warner Bros.

1941: Reported in "Picturegoer" magazine that "she gave up a contract at $1700 a week rather than play in unsuitable stories"

1946: First film as producer (uncredited co-producer), "Young Widow"

1947: Left Warner Bros.

1947: Formed Arcadia Productions with Benedict Bogeaus; no films produced

1948: First film credited as producer (also first film for own company, Emerald Productions, Inc. which she co-founded with Collier Young and Anson Bond and named after her mother), "The Judge"

1948: Performed her own songs, including "One for My Baby (and One More for the Road)", for her role as a nightclub singer in the film noir, "Road House"

1949: Took over directing "Not Wanted" for an ailing Elmer Clifton; uncredited

1949: Credited feature film directing and co-writing debut, "Never Fear"

1950: Changed name of production company to The Filmakers; took on writer Marvin Wald as another partner

1951: Joined with David Niven, Dick Powell

and Charles Boyer to form Four Star Productions

1951: Reportedly helmed portions of the feature "On Dangerous Ground" while director Nicholas Ray was ill

Appeared on a rotating basis (with David Niven, Charles Boyer and Dick Powell) on "Four Star Playhouse", a CBS-TV dramatic anthology series

Formed Bridget Productions (named after her daughter by Howard Duff)

1956: Acted in last feature films for 13 years, "While the City Sleeps" and "Strange Intruder"

Directed episodes of TV series such as "Have Gun—Will Travel" (the episode "Lady With a Gun" 1959), "Alfred Hitchcock Presents" (ep. "Sybilla" 1960), "The Untouchables" (ep. "Man in the Cooler" 1963) and "The Fugitive" (ep. "The Glass Tightrope" 1963)

Produced, co-starred (opposite then-husband Howard Duff) and directed episodes of the CBS sitcom, "Mr. Adams and Eve"

1966: Directed last feature film, "The Trouble with Angels"

1969: Returned to acting in feature films in "Backtrack"

1982: Appeared in cameo role in only film of the 1980s, "Deadhead Miles"

Health declined; moved to Motion Picture Home

1987: Featured in footage used in "American Lifestyles", a six-part compilation film using material from the "March of Time" newsreels from 1939 to 1950

QUOTES:

Lupino's birth year is open to question: other dates given are 1914, 1916 and 1919.

" 'My father once said to me, 'You're born to be bad,' she recalled. 'And it was true. I made eight films in England before I came to America, and I played a tramp or a slut in all of them.' "—From *The Hollywood Reporter*, August 7, 1995.

"Although she won a best actress award from the New York Film Critics in 1943 for her role as a domineering sister in The Hard Way", she came to view her Hollywood acting career a failure and once referred to herself as 'the poor man's Bette Davis.' "—From *The Hollywood Reporter*, August 7, 1995.

"Her films [as a director] display the obsessions and consistencies of a true auteur. . . . What is most interesting about her films are not her stories of unwed motherhood or the tribulation of career women, but the way in which she uses male actors: particulary in "The Bigamist" and "The Hitchhiker" (both 1953), Lupino was able to reduce the male to the same sort of dangerous, irrational force that women represented in most male-directed examples of Hollywood film noir."—Richard Koszarski in "Hollywood Directors 1914–40" (Oxford University Press, 1976).

"She regarded her own directorial career as an unconventional choice for a woman, and had remarked in an interview that she'd rather be cooking her man's dinner. However, the content and technical virtuosity of her work belie this statement and point to a very wily director who knows the uses of conventionality as a tool."—Barbara Scharres in *The Film Center Gazette* (The School of the Art Institute of Chicago, February 1987).

BIBLIOGRAPHY:

"Queen of the B's: Ida Lupino Behind the Camera" Annette Kuhn, 1995; Kuhn-edited anthology of essays on Lupino's directorial efforts

"Ida Lupino" Jerry Vermilye

"Ida Lupino: A Biography" William Donati, 1996; University of Kentucky Press

BORN: David Keith Lynch in Missoula, Montana, 01/20/1946

NATIONALITY: American

EDUCATION: attended high school in Alexandria, Virginia; graduated in 1964; Jack Fisk was a classmate

Corcoran School of Art, Washington, DC, painting, 1963–64

Boston Museum School, Boston, Massachusetts, 1964–65

Pennsylvania Academy of Fine Arts, Philadelphia, Pennsylvania, 1965–67; attended with Jack Fisk

went with Jack Fisk to study painting in Europe with Oskar Kokoschka; lasted two weeks (1965)

Center for Advanced Film Studies, American Film Institute Los Angeles, California 1970

AWARDS: Cesar Best Foreign Film "The Elephant Man" 1982

Los Angeles Film Critics Association Award Best Director "Blue Velvet" 1986

National Society of Film Critics Award Best Director "Blue Velvet" 1986

Cannes Film Festival Palme d'Or "Wild at Heart" 1990

American Film Institute Franklin J Schaffner Alumni Medal 1991

European Film Award Screen International Award for a Non-European Film "The Straight Story" 1999

British Independent Film Award Best Foreign Independent Film—English Language "The Straight Story" 2000

Cannes Film Festival Best Director Award "Mulholland Drive" 2001 tied with Joel Coen ("The Man Who Wasn't There")

New York Film Critics Circle Award Best Film "Mulholland Dr." 2001

Los Angeles Film Critics Association Award Best Director "Mulholland Dr." 2001

New York Film Critics Online Award Best Picture "Mulholland Dr." 2001

New York Film Critics Online Award Best Director "Mulholland Dr." 2001

New York Film Critics Online Award Best Original Screenplay "Mulholland Dr." 2001

Boston Society of Film Critics Award Best Picture "Mulholland Dr." 2001

Boston Society of Film Critics Award Best Director "Mulholland Dr." 2001

Toronto Film Critics Association Award Best Director "Mulholland Dr." 2001

Online Film Critics Society Award Best Picture "Mulholland Dr." 2001; tied with "Memento"

Online Film Critics Society Award Best Director "Mulholland Dr." 2001

Online Film Critics Society Award Best Original Screenplay "Mulholland Dr." 2001; tied with Alejandro Amenabar ("The Others")

National Society of Film Critics Award Best Picture "Mulholland Dr." 2001

Chicago Film Critics Award Best Picture "Mulholland Dr." 2002

Chicago Film Critics Award Best Director "Mulholland Dr." 2002

Cesar Best Foreign Film "Mulholland Dr." 2002

BIOGRAPHY

Avant-garde director David Lynch has had one of the more unlikely odysseys to film success. Born in Montana, the son of a Department of Agriculture tree scientist, he spent his youth in Idaho, Washington and Alexandria, VA, and found his true vocation while experimenting with "film painting" at Philadelphia's

Pennsylvania Academy of the Fine Arts. On the basis of "The Alphabet" (1968), a five-minute short combining live action and animation, Lynch received a grant from the American Film Institute to make a 34-minute film, "The Grandmother" (1970). Over a five-year period, drawing on his own fears about the confinements of youthful marriage and fatherhood and working in and around the AFI's Center for Advanced Film Studies in Los Angeles, Lynch created his appalling black-and-white meditation on family life, "Eraserhead" (1977), a nightmarish vision packed with grotesque physical deformities and an unlikely quest for spiritual purity, starring Jack Nance in a hair-raising performance, his first of many collaborations with Lynch.

Mel Brooks saw "Eraserhead" and thought Lynch a kindred "madman" who would be the perfect director to film a script Brooks wanted to produce about John Merrick—a man whose exterior was as hideous as his soul was beautiful. Lynch's film about this real person deformed by disease, "The Elephant Man" (1980), employing a visual style reminiscent of "Eraserhead", was an elegy to the freakishness of the human condition disguised as a piece of Victorian morality theater. Exploring familiar territory, Lynch exposed undercurrents of metaphysical anguish and absurdist fear, but the accessible humanity within Merrick's tale made the film a box-office success and earned it eight Academy Award nominations, including Best Director and Best Screenplay nominations for Lynch.

Offered the third "Star Wars" film, "Return of the Jedi", Lynch opted instead to advance his script "Ronnie Rocket" at Francis Coppola's Zoetrope Studios. When this project did not materialize, he waded into deep water with producer Dino De Laurentiis, who owned the rights to Frank Herbert's Byzantine, epic science fiction novel, "Dune." Lynch once described "Dune" (1985), released in a drastically shortened form, as "a garbage compactor. Things are supposed to be mysterious, not confusing." This striking,

underrated, but nevertheless muddled production, incomprehensible without having read the book, was a box-office failure. Feeling like "I had sort of sold myself out," Lynch later forced the removal of his name from the film's credits.

He was back in true form with "Blue Velvet" (1986), a quasi-autobiographical transit through zones of Kafka, Bosch, Bunuel, Capra and Hitchcock that Lynch has described as "The Hardy Boys Go to Hell." In this scatological film noir, composed as if inspired by the ambiance of a nightmarish asylum, collegially handsome Kyle MacLachlan stumbles upon, and is subsumed in, a crucible of child abduction, drug wars, voyeurism, sexual abuse, small town corruption and compulsive souls desperate to find truth in a dimension that seems to be devoid of meaningful questions. Sensuous details mix with a painterly neo-Gothic eye for the bizarre. All is the opposite of what it seems: Neat, placid surfaces cloak macabre "reality" and the outwardly horrible is ultimately the most benign. Malignant impulses fester deep within people and things. Dennis Hopper's manic performance as Frank catapults that character into the stratosphere of cinema psychos. The surreal conclusion gives the audience pause—where does the dream end and the temporal world begin?

Though "Wild at Heart" (1990), adapted from a novel by future collaborator Barry Gifford, won the prestigious Palme d'Or at Cannes, it met with critical disfavor at home. Reviewers found this "road" movie's impassioned scenes of brain bashing and decapitation all but unbearable, despite strong performances by Nicolas Cage and Laura Dern on their trek through Hell (or is it Oz?). He faired far better with his first entry to network programming, ABC's groundbreaking "Twin Peaks" (1990–91). This creation of Lynch and screenwriter-author Mark Frost depicted a community's intricate web of secret sex, violence and horror, unearthed by murder and revealed through the investigation of FBI agent Dale

Cooper (MacLachlan) how evil can get passed from troubled heart to troubled heart. Though it had run its course before finally leaving the air, the sensation of its first several weeks demonstrated that network TV could produce an audacious and cutting-edge work of culture, paving the way for quirky shows like "Northern Exposure", "Picket Fences" and "The X-Files."

Lynch miscalculated when he returned to "Twin Peaks" terrain for the feature "Twin Peaks: Fire Walk With Me" (1992). Critics savaged it, audiences hissed at Cannes and US moviegoers stayed away, proving beyond a shadow of a doubt that the "Twin Peaks" time had come and gone. Lynch had changed film and changed TV, but success had made him more uncompromising. His characters had always inhabited the outer fringes of society and mind, but in his best-received work, though he delivered something magnificent and terrible, he would pull back from the horror and restore some semblance of order. His unabated vision is just too much to bear for all but the most devout Lynchophile.

Take for example his unrestrained "Lost Highway" (1997), co-written with Gifford, the final moments of which are nothing but chaos and fear. Whatever the movie is about, Lynch refused to make it a neat package for spoon-feeding, preferring to leave room for each individual viewer to dream and have a different take. Characters change (or do they?), and the plot goes off in a different direction (or does it?). Who or what is that Mystery Man played by Robert Blake (who agreed to the role without having a clue as to what it was about)? Perhaps the point is that there is no point. At the end of the 20th century, we live in a world that is not always comprehensible or correctable. In Gifford's words: "We went out on a limb with this thing and just let everything out. When you do that, people don't generally like this sort of stuff, so you know you're going to get slapped around to some extent."

Lynch demonstrated his brilliance with "Premonitions Following an Evil Deed", his contribution to the "Lumiere and Company" (1995) project, providing perhaps the most inventive use of the restored Lumiere camera and home-made film stock from among the 39 participating directors. There is no denying his originality, but the courage shown in allowing his art to grow increasingly darker and more difficult could impact negatively on his future as a filmmaker.

Never one to play it safe, Lynch confounded expectations when he directed "The Straight Story" (1999), a based on fact drama about an elderly man who rode a tractor several hundred miles in order to reconcile with his estranged brother. In lead Richard Farnsworth, the director found the perfect embodiment of sincerity. That same year, Lynch attempted another foray in TV series with the pilot "Mulholland Dr.", but the suits at ABC found the material too dark and odd for mainstream consumption. Even maverick cable channels like HBO passed on the show, but producer Alain Sarde was sufficiently impressed to offer to bankroll additional footage allowing Lynch to make a feature film that premiered at Cannes in 2001. A dystopian look at the price of the pursuit of fame in Hollywood, "Mulholland Dr." was meant to echo Billy Wilder's 1950 masterpiece "Sunset Boulevard." Many of the typical Lynchian touches could be found, with creepy villains, oddball secondary characters and a mid-film switch that echoed "Lost Highway" but which was here more effective. Lynch shared the Cannes Best Director Award and the film opened to universal critical acclaim, although audiences tended to be somewhat confused and confounded by the piece. Despite earning numerous prizes from critics' groups, "Mulholland Dr." did not fare well with the more conservative members of the Motion Picture Academy. Lynch received the film's sole nomination for Best Director, almost insuring he would not win.

As a filmmaker, Lynch revels in his power to stimulate, understanding full well that his visceral, often oblique images may frustrate and even antagonize audiences. Though his work is full of abstractions, it is still, in large part, about the old-fashioned conflict between "good and evil", something on which movie-goers can certainly hang their hat. Lynch has said that "finding love in hell" is a theme in all his movies, and as he casts about for future projects, one wonders if he can be true to his terrible vision without alienating the people who go see his movies.—Written by Greg Senf

MILESTONES:

As a child, lived in Sandpointe and Boise, Idaho, Spokane, Washington, and Alexandria, Virginia

Worked as shop assistant, engineer, janitor, newspaper deliverer, in between studies

1966: First film, a one-minute color animated loop entitled "Six Men Getting Sick", shown on three skull-shaped screens (based on Lynch's head) to the accompaniment of a siren (date approximate)

1967: Made short film combining animation and live action, "The Alphabet," as entry in Pennsylvania Academy contest

1970: Made first short live-action film, "The Grandmother"; given grants totalling $5,000 by American Film Institute (completed film for $7,200)

1971: Began working on first feature, "Eraser-head"; first feature collaboration with cine-matographer Frederick Elmes and with actor Jack Nance

1977: "Eraserhead" released

1980: Earned first Oscar nomination as Best Director for "The Elephant Man"; also nomi-nated for Best Adapted Screenplay (co-written with Eric Bergren and Christopher DeVore)

1983–1992: Creator and illustrator of syndi-cated comic strip "The Angriest Dog in the World"

1984: First project with actor Kyle MacLachlan, "Dune"; feeling like "I had sort of sold myself out," Lynch later forced the removal of his name from the film's credits

1987: Wrote and presented documentary on dadaist cinema, "Ruth roses and revolver," for British TV series "Arena"

1987: Won acclaim (and second Best Director Oscar nomination) for the controversial "Blue Velvet"

Produced and wrote for singers Julee Cruise and Koko Taylor (songs used in his films "Blue Velvet" and "Wild at Heart")

1989: Composed musical work "Industrial Symphony No. 1" with Angelo Badalamenti; performed at the Brooklyn Academy of Music in November; made video in 1990

1990: "Wild at Heart" won the prestigious Palme d'Or Award at Cannes but met with critical disfavor at home; last feature collabo-ration (to date) with Frederick Elmes

1990: Directed TV commercials for the per-fumes Opium and Obsession

Creator/director of popular TV series, "Twin Peaks" (ABC)

1991: Directed the music video for Chris Isaak's song "Wicked Game"; song featured on the soundtrack to "Wild at Heart"

1991: Executive producer for "The Cabinet of Dr. Ramirez"

1992: Returned to "Twin Peaks" land with fea-ture "Twin Peaks: Fire Walk With Me" (also co-executive producer); wrote 11 songs

1992: Served as creator, executive producer and director of the premiere of ABC's short-lived (six episodes) "On the Air"

1993: Made television commercials for Gio, the perfume by Armani (1992), for a coffee drink Coca-Cola markets in Japan (1993) and for Alka-Seltzer Plus (1993); also directed a teaser-trailer used to market Michael Jackson's "Dangerous" album

1993: Was creator, executive producer and director of "Blackout" and Tricks" episodes of HBO's "Hotel Room"

1994: Executive produced "Nadja" (and played a small part as Morgue Attendant)

1994: "Presented" the documentary "Crumb", an extraordinarily intimate portrait of underground comic artist Robert Crumb, directed by Terry Zwigoff

1997: Ran off the road with "Lost Highway", a great-looking but senseless, overlong post-modern hybrid of film noir and "The Twilight Zone"

1997: Helmed TV commercial for the home pregnancy test Clear Blue Easy

1999: Directed the atypically based-on-fact "The Straight Story", about a man who drove a tractor from Iowa to Wisconsin to reunite with his estranged brother

1999: Made the pilot "Mulholland Drive" for ABC TV; series not picked up; Lynch received additional funding from StudioCanal and shot more footage, creating a feature film that premiered at Cannes in 2001 where it shared the Best Director trophy; released theatrically in fall 2001

QUOTES:

Lynch launched a members-only web site at www.davidlynch.com in December 2001.

He served as president of the jury at the 2002 Cannes Film Festival.

When Lynch was a child, his father used to drive him into the deep woods, drop him off, then go to his job as a scientist for the Forest Service. He would leave young David completely alone, surrounded, as the filmmaker once told *Time* magazine, by "the most beautiful forests, where the trees are very tall and shafts of sunlight come down in the mountain stream and the rainbow trout leap out."

Lynch's interest in furniture making started at an early age, when he hung around his father's wood shop, learning how to use tools and mastering the fundamentals of building. Though he often built furniture for his movies, his first professional efforts at marketing his furniture came in the early 1990s when he sold a tiny espresso table (priced at $600) through Skankworld, a vintage furniture store in Los Angeles. He showed his attractive Club Table, an effective marraige of wood and steel which comes with special recessed areas to hold drinks, at the prestigious Salone Del Mobile in Milan and has an agreement with a Swiss Company to produce his pieces on a limited basis.

About the failure of "Wild at Heart" and "Twin Peaks: Fire Walk With Me": "When you love something and feel you've done it correctly, then negative criticism doesn't hurt so bad. I love those movies. But in order to say you're successful, a film has to make quite a lot of money, and I haven't really done that. If I was successful in that way, I'd be . . . I don't know, making pictures maybe more within the system."—David Lynch to *Rolling Stone*, March 6, 1997.

BIBLIOGRAPHY:

"Images" Hyperion; book of film stills as well as photographs of Lynch's other art work

Adrian Lyne

BORN: in Peterborough, England, 03/04/1941

NATIONALITY: English

EDUCATION: Highgate School, London, England; father taught there

BIOGRAPHY

Flashy film stylist Adrian Lyne began as a successful director of British TV commercials and short films before making his first feature, "Foxes" (1980), a dark gritty look at four young girls growing up fast in the San Fernando Valley. He scored a huge hit with "Flashdance" (1983)—dismissed by some as an extended rock-video with breaks for dialogue—proving such a musical could still be commercially viable. Though "9 1/2 Weeks" (1986) and "Fatal Attraction" (1987) elicited charges of misogyny (their stylish editing and glamorous imagery made emotional and physical violence towards women look attractive and justified), the latter solidified Lyne's reputation as a bankable director, doing incredible business ($157 million in North America alone) and spawning a profitable sub-genre of the thriller: Women from Hell (e.g., "Single White Female" 1992, "The Hand that Rocks the Cradle" 1992, "The Crush" 1993). Lyne even pandered to the tastes of his audience, dumping the film's more subtle and intriguing original ending in favor of a more vigilante one replete with Rambo-style retribution that would satisfy the stated preference of the survey groups.

The ambitious change of pace of Lyne's next project confounded Hollywood. "Jacob's Ladder" (1990) provided a dark, unsettling look at the emotional turmoil of a Vietnam veteran (Tim Robbins) but received mixed reviews and generated tepid response at the box office. Taking the hint, Lyne opted for good grosses, returning to the more commercial material of "Indecent Proposal" (1993), a glossy examination of how the sexes look at relationships and money, starring Robert Redford, Woody Harrelson and Demi Moore. His reputation as a commercial filmmaker who feeds the moviegoers what they crave rankled him, however, and Lyne set out to make an artistic statement with his remake of Vladimir Nabokov's literary classic "Lolita" (1997). Having adored the book since his initial reading in his mid-twenties, he remained much more faithful to it than had Stanley Kubrick in his 1962 adaptation (though reports say he failed to capture its humor), but viewers in the USA may never get to judge his achievement. Because it depicts a minor engaging in sexual intercourse with an adult, no distributor has been willing to challenge the Child Pornography Act of 1996 by releasing it.

MILESTONES:

Directed numerous commercials for British TV

1971: His first film short, the 10-minute "The Table", debuted at the London Film festival

1974: Second film, the 40-minute "Mr Smith" about a man looking for a reason to live and not finding one, received excellent reviews; also showcased at the London Film Festival

1980: Directed first feature, "Foxes", a look at the friendship among four teenage girls growing up fast in the San Fernando Valley

1983: Scored a huge commercial success with "Flashdance"; detractors derided it as little more than an extended rock video

1986: Savaged by American critics, "9 1/2 Weeks" became a huge hit abroad when showed in its uncensored entirety

1987: "Fatal Attraction" struck powerful chord with audiences, becoming one of the year's most successful films; received Best Director Oscar nomination

1990: Faltered with "Jacob's Ladder", a tale of a haunted Vietnam vet; his first film not to make money

1993: Returned to the winner's column with "Indecent Proposal"

1997: Release of remake of Vladimir Nabokov's "Lolita" blocked in the USA due to the Child Pornography Act of 1996

QUOTES:

"If I were doing a movie about a 13-year girl getting chopped up by cannibals, there'd be no problem."—Adrian Lyne to a reporter prior to filming "Lolita"

BORN: in Ottawa, Illinois, 11/30/1943

SOMETIMES CREDITED AS:
David Whitney

NATIONALITY: American

EDUCATION: St. Stephen's Episcopal School, Westlake, Texas, prep school; was star football player

Harvard University, Cambridge, Massachusetts, philosophy, BA, 1966

Magdalen College, Oxford University, Oxford, England; attended as a Rhodes scholar; left without completing thesis

Center for Advanced Film Studies, American Film Institute, Los Angeles, California, 1969–71

AWARDS: New York Film Critics Circle Award Best Director "Days of Heaven" 1978

National Society of Film Critics Award Best Director "Days of Heaven" 1978

Cannes Film Festival Best Director Award "Days of Heaven" 1979

New York Film Critics Circle Award Best Director "The Thin Red Line" 1998

Golden Satellite Best Director "The Thin Red Line" 1998

Chicago Film Critics Award Best Director "The Thin Red Line" 1998

Berlin Film Festival Golden Bear "The Thin Red Line" 1999

American Film Institute Franklin J. Schaffner Alumni Medal 2000

BIOGRAPHY

Terrence Malick was one of the most meticulous and original American filmmakers to emerge in the 1970s. Unlike other equally gifted directors who came of age contemporaneously (e.g., Martin Scorsese, Francis Ford Coppola, Steven Spielberg), he seemingly disappeared from features for close to two decades. Yet, Malick's legacy assured he would be ranked as more than a cult figure.

An intensely private individual, Malick rarely granted interviews and issued conflicting information about his upbringing and vital statistics. (Sources vary widely over the place and year of his birth.) This son of an oil company executive was raised in Oklahoma and Texas and spent several summers working as a farm hand. He graduated from Harvard with a degree in philosophy and received a Rhodes scholarship to Oxford, although he dropped out before completing his thesis. When he returned to the USA, Malick worked for a time as a journalist, publishing articles in *Life*, *Newsweek* and *The New Yorker*.

In 1968, Malick received an appointment as a lecturer in philosophy at the Massachusetts Institute of Technology. Before the year was out, he had decided that teaching was not his forte. Instead, he enrolled in the first class at the American Film Institute's Center for Advanced Studies and began his film career. While still studying at the AFI, Malick began to work as a script doctor and rewrite man. He did uncredited work on Jack Nicholson's official directorial debut "Drive, He Said" (1971) and spent several weeks honing the script for "Dead Right" to star Marlon Brando. (The latter eventually became the Clint Eastwood vehicle "Dirty Harry" in 1971.) That same year, Malick sold his first script, "Deadhead Miles", a virtually plotless film that traces a rogue trucker (Alan Arkin) and his adventures on the highways. Directed by Vernon Zimmerman and owing a debt to other road movies like "Easy Rider" and Monte Hellman's "Two-Lane Blacktop", the episodic film which was shot in 1972 played more as an in-joke (especially with the casting of such veterans as Ida Lupino and George Raft in cameo roles). Held from release for nearly a decade, it received festival screenings in 1982 and then was again shelved by the studio. Malick's contributions are difficult to measure as allegedly Zimmerman had a hand in the script. The final film's uneven narrative structure and trite dialog were hardly precursors of Malick's output.

For his thesis film at AFI, Malick wrote, directed and produced the short "Lanton Mills" (1971), an oddball comedy about two modern-day Texas cowboys (Warren Oates and Harry Dean Stanton) who turn to bank robbing. Malick expanded on this theme, for his first theatrically released feature, the comedic Western "Pocket Money" (1972), directed by Stuart Rosenberg. This film was also the initial offering of First Artists, the production company formed by Barbra Streisand, Sidney Poitier, Steve McQueen and Paul Newman, who toplined with Lee Marvin. Working from the novel "Jim Kane", Malick fashioned another episodic story that centered on a modern-day cowboy (Newman) and his sidekick (Marvin) who cross paths with crooked cattlemen. Critical reaction was tepid at best, although some praised Malick's quirky script.

Deciding to forego studio involvement, Malick chose the then-novel way to independently produce his directorial debut, raising the money by selling limited partnerships to small investors. Using a non-union crew and without a distribution agreement, he began shooting "Badlands" (1973). Inspired by the real-life figures of Charles Starkweather and Carol Fugate, "Badlands" traced the murder spree of a twentysomething spree killer and his teenaged girlfriend in the 1950s, well-played by Martin Sheen and Sissy Spacek. Malick's film is on the continuum that reaches from Nicholas Ray's "They Live by Night" (1949) to Arthur Penn's "Bonnie and Clyde" through to Oliver Stone's "Natural Born Killers" (1994); a "lovers-on-the-run" scenario. Malick's take is singular, though;

his is starkly beautiful, almost dreamlike and he utilizes what became his signature, voice-over narration by a young woman. Spacek's flat-toned, detached vocals are in contrast to the screen images and the result was widely praised. Both Sheen and Spacek were lauded for their portrayals. (Malick himself appears in one scene as an architect with bad timing.) Warner Bros. distributed the film, but the writer director wisely retained control over the copyright.

Five years passed before Malick was behind the cameras again, although in the interim he co-wrote the crime drama "The Gravy Train" (1974), employing the pseudonym "David Whitney." "Days of Heaven" (1978), however, was Malick's masterwork. Again the plot revolved around a young couple on the run in a period piece that employed a young female narrator. Partly what sets "Days of Heaven" apart, though, is the expert camera work of Nestor Almendros (with an assist from Haskell Wexler) and the production designs of Jack Fisk (art direction) and Patricia Norris (costumes). Linda Manz's world-weary vocals offered a perfect counterpoint to the screen images. Richard Gere and Brooke Adams portrayed the central lovers who leave Chicago after a confrontation with his boss. Arriving in Texas, they find work on a farm and their lives become intimate entangled with that of the owner (Sam Shepard), eventually with tragic consequences. The motion picture is filled with gorgeous, eye-popping set pieces that recalled the art work of Millet and Wyeth and the early silents work of Murnau, Sjostrom, Lang and Griffith, notably a nocturnal sequence when the fields are set afire to combat an invasion of locusts. Malick tapped a variety of primeval sources to create his allegorical storyline; both mythic and biblical in its intent, "Days of Heaven" can be read as a meditation on the fall of man.

After achieving this high point, Malick virtually disappeared for nearly two decades. Reports were that he went to live in Paris and later in Texas. There were rumors to the effect that he kept a hand in the film business by doing uncredited script rewrites while others claimed that he had returned to teaching. As he prefers to maintain his privacy, Malick himself developed a somewhat mythic reputation. Whatever the truth, he emerged in 1997 with a script for a new screen version of James Jones' novel "The Thin Red Line" (previously filmed in 1964). Malick reportedly spent a decade carefully crafting his adaptation. The film, expected to be released in 1998, went before the cameras in June 1997 with a cast that was a virtual who's who of Hollywood, including veterans Sean Penn, Woody Harrelson, John Cusack and Nick Nolte and relative newcomers like Jim Caviezel, Dash Mihok, Arie Verveen and John C. Reilly.—Written by Ted Murphy

MILESTONES:

Raised in Waco and Austin, Texas and Bartlesville, Oklahoma

Worked as journalist in mid-1960s; writings published in *Newsweek, Time* and *The New Yorker*

1968–1969: Was lecturer in philosophy at Massachusetts Institute of Technology

1970: Did uncredited work on the screenplay for "Drive, He Said"

1970: First produced screenplay, "Deadhead Miles"; film was shelved until 1982 release

1971: Wrote, directed and acted in short film, "Lanton Mills"

1971: Reportedly worked on script for "Dirty Harry" under the title "Dead Right"

1972: First film theatrically released with a screenplay by Malick, "Pocket Money", directed by Stuart Rosenberg; also played small role

1973: Feature producing and directing debut, "Badlands"; also scripted and acted in a bit part

1974: Co-wrote script for "The Gravy Train" with Bill Kerr; credited under the pseudonym David Whitney

1976: Wrote and directed "Days of Heaven"; spent two years editing film which was released in 1978

Moved to Paris for several years

Returned to the USA and settled in Texas

1998: Wrote and directed first film in twenty years, "The Thin Red Line"

Louis Malle

BORN: in Thumeries, France, 10/30/1932

DEATH: in Beverly Hills, California, 11/23/1995

NATIONALITY: French

EDUCATION: Jesuit College at Fontainebleau, Fontainebleau, France was the locale for his 1987 auto-biopic, "Goodbye, Children"

Institut d'Etudes Politiques, Sorbonne, University of Paris, Paris, France, political science

Institut des Hautes Etudes Cinematographiques, Paris, France, 1950–53

College des Carmes

AWARDS: Cannes Film Festival Palme d'Or "The Silent World" 1956; Malle co-directed with Jacques-Yves Cousteau

Oscar Best Documentary Feature "The Silent World" 1956

Prix Louis Delluc Best Feature "Ascenseur Pour l'Echafaud/ Elevator to the Gallows/Frantic" 1957

Venice Film Festival Special Jury Prize "The Lovers" 1958

Venice Film Festival Special Jury Prize "The Fire Within" 1963; cited along with Igor Talankin's "Introduction to Life"

Grand Prix du Cinema Francais Best Film "Viva Maria" 1965

Melbourne Film Festival Grand Prix "Calcutta" 1970; documentary

British Film Academy Award Best Film "Lacombe, Lucien" 1974; producer and director; award shared with executive producer Claude Nedjar

British Film Academy United Nations Award Best Film "Lacombe, Lucien" 1974; producer and director; award shared with executive producer Claude Nedjar

Venice Film Festival Golden Lion "Atlantic City" 1980 co-winner with John Cassevetes' "Gloria"

National Society of Film Critics Award Best Director "Atlantic City" 1981

BAFTA Award Best Director "Atlantic City" 1981

Los Angeles Film Critics Association Award Best Foreign Film "Au Revoir, Les Enfants" 1987

Venice Film Festival Golden Lion "Au Revoir, Les Enfants" 1987

Cesar Best Film "Au Revoir les enfants" 1988

Cesar Best Director "Au Revoir les enfants" 1988

Cesar Best Screenplay "Au Revoir les enfants" 1988

BIOGRAPHY

One of the most consistently innovative filmmakers of his generation, Louis Malle has rarely received the critical attention his work deserves. Unlike the other directors most often associated with the French New Wave—Truffaut, Godard, Rohmer, Chabrol—Malle did not contribute criticism to *Cahiers du Cinema*; unlike those filmmakers, he came from a privileged background, as an heir to the Beghin sugar fortune. His work is not easily evaluated according to the tenets of the auteur theory promoted by these critics-turned-filmmakers, who emphasized consistently recognizable stylistic or thematic traits in directors' work. From undersea documentaries to "films noirs", from exposes on poverty to extended dinner conversations, Louis Malle's work could hardly be more diverse.

A graduate of IDHEC (the French government's prestigious filmmaking school), Malle began his career working with Jacques Cousteau on "Le Monde du silence" (1955) and assisting Robert Bresson on "A Condemned Man Escapes" (1956). His first feature was a stylish commercial thriller, "Elevator to the Gallows" (1957). International recognition came the next year with "The Lovers", a study of upper-class ennui which featured a dazzling performance by Jeanne Moreau and which, due to its sexual frankness, was the first of Malle's films to generate scandal. Others include "Zazie dans le metro" (1960), the story of a foul-mouthed pre-teenager; "The Fire Within" (1963), a masterful study of mental disintegration; "Murmur of the Heart" (1971), a light, comic tale of incest; and "Lacombe Lucien" (1974), whose opportunistic protagonist sets out to become a hero of the Resistance but learns the fine art of political collaboration under the Nazis.

Malle also produced an impressive body of documentary filmmaking, beginning with his collaboration with Cousteau. In 1969 he released "Calcutta," an extended expose of the city's incredible poverty and overpopulation; this was followed by a 6-hour series of documentary films, "Phantom India" (1969), shown originally on French TV. "Place de la Republique" (1973) featured confrontational remarks by passers-by at this Parisian intersection, and "Humain trop humain" (1973) explored, without recourse to narration, the dehumanizing effects of assembly-line manufacture.

In 1978 Malle returned to provocative fictional subjects with "Pretty Baby", a tale of child prostitution in WWI-era New Orleans, starring Brooke Shields and Keith Carradine. Two outstanding American films followed: "Atlantic City" (1980), involving a has-been gangster (Burt Lancaster) and a city in transition, and "My Dinner with Andre" (1981), a lengthy conversation between playwright Wallace Shawn and director Andre Gregory. "Au Revoir les enfants" (1987) marked Malle's professional return to France. An explicitly autobiographical work about boyhood friendships and betrayal during the German Occupation, it is perhaps his most successful film in terms of public and critical response. He helmed the slight but diverting comedy "May Fools" (1990) set in the French countryside in 1968 as the students rioted in Paris, and then collaborated again with actor Wallace Shawn and director Andre Gregory on what was to be his last film, "Vanya on 42nd Street" (1994). The feature depicts a troupe of actors rehearsing Chekhov's "Uncle Vanya" (translated by David Mamet) in the dilapidated New Amsterdam Theater in NYC. Malle was married to actress Candice Bergen from 1980 until his death from lymphoma in 1995.

COMPANIONS:
Susan Sarandon. Actor; together in the 1970s

wife: Candice Bergen. Actor; second wife; married in 1980; survived him

MILESTONES:

1954: Directorial debut doing underwater sequences, "The House on the Waterfront"

1954: Began working with Jacques Cousteau as assistant director, "Calypso cap au sud"

1957: Feature film directing debut and screenplay adaptation, "Elevator to the Gallows"

1958: Directed and scripted breakthrough film, "The Lovers"

1978: US feature film debut, "Pretty Baby"

1995: Diagnosed with an invasive lymphoma that broke down his immune system and attacked his brain

BIBLIOGRAPHY:
"Louis Malle par Louis Malle" Louis Malle, 1978

David Mamet

BORN: David Alan Mamet in Chicago, Illinois, 11/30/1947

SOMETIMES CREDITED AS:
Richard Weisz

NATIONALITY: American

EDUCATION: Goddard College, Plainfield, Vermont, English, BA, 1969; spent junior year in off-campus study program at the Neighborhood Playhouse in New York

The Neigborhood Playhouse School of the Theatre, New York, New York, 1967–68

AWARDS: OBIE Award Best New American Play "Sexual Perversity in Chicago" and "American Buffalo" 1975/76; two plays cited

New York Drama Critics Circle Award Best American Play "American Buffalo" 1976/77

OBIE Award Best New American Play

"Edmond" 1982/83; award shared with Harry Kondoleon and Tina Howe

OBIE Award Playwriting "Edmond" 1982/83

Society of West End Theatres (SWET) Award Best Play "Glengary Glen Ross" 1982/83

Pulitzer Prize in Drama "Glengarry Glen Ross" 1984

New York Drama Critics Circle Award Best American Play "Glengarry Glen Ross" 1983/84

Joseph Dintenfass Award "Glengarry Glen Ross" 1984

London Film Critics Circle Award Screenwriter of the Year "Homicide" 1991

OBIE Award Best Play "The Cryptogram" 1994/95

Florida Film Critics Circle Award Best Screenplay "State and Main" 2000

BIOGRAPHY

David Mamet is a leading American playwright whose spare, gritty, often scatological work reflects the rhythms of Harold Pinter and the tough attitudes of his native Chicago. Noted for his strong male characters and their macho posturings, Mamet's knack for creating low-key yet highly charged verbal confrontations in a male-dominated world has consistently made his work fodder for discussion and deconstruction. Beginning in the mid-1970s, he enjoyed a number of stage successes like "American Buffalo" (1975–76), the story of three small time con men, and "A Life in the Theatre" (1977), which explored the relationship between two actors, one old, the other young. He made an impressive film debut with his first produced screenplay "The Postman Always Rings Twice" (1981), adapted from the novel by James M. Cain and directed by Bob Rafelson. Despite his prolific output for the cinema, Mamet has also continued to write regularly for the stage, winning OBIE Awards for "Edmond" (1982–83) and "The Cryptogram" (1994–95) and returning to Broadway in 1997 with "The Old Neighborhood."

His meticulously crafted script for Sidney Lumet's "The Verdict" (1982) starred Paul Newman as a Boston lawyer on the skids and earned Mamet an Academy Award nomination. He scripted Brian De Palma's "The Untouchables" (1987), a blockbuster update of the well-remembered TV series, and made his directorial debut helming his own script "House of Games" (1987), an engrossing study of confidence trickery starring his then-wife Lindsay Crouse and Joe Mantegna. He also wrote and directed the whimsical comedy "Things Change" (1989), teaming Mantegna and Don Ameche, and the uneven but occasionally gripping police thriller "Homicide" (1991), also starring Mantegna.

Mamet has seen two of his plays filmed for PBS' "Great Performances", "A Life in the Theatre" (1979) and his adaptation of Chekhov's "Uncle Vanya" (1991), both directed by longtime friend Gregory Mosher. He made his debut as executive producer for an HBO Showcase presentation of "Lip Service", his friend William H Macy's directorial debut, and also served as executive producer for the TNT movie version of "A Life in the Theatre", again directed by Mosher. Mamet adapted for "TNT Screenworks" his early play "The Water Engine" (1992) and played a small role in it, wrote the Showtime short "Texan", directed by Treat Williams, and helmed the HBO Special "Ricky Jay and His 52 Assistants" (1996), which he had directed for the stage two years earlier.

Mamet has transformed his plays to features with varying results. He adapted his 1984 Pulitzer Prize-winning play "Glengarry Glen Ross", a visceral look inside a gritty Chicago real estate office, into an acclaimed 1992 film directed by James Foley and starring Al Pacino and Jack Lemmon. Louis Malle used Mamet's translation of Chekhov's "Uncle Vanya" to great effect in "Vanya on 42nd Street" (1994), reuniting the "My Dinner With Andre" team, Andre Gregory and Wallace Shawn, as members of a company rehearsing the play-within-the-movie. The screen version of "Oleanna" (1994), which Mamet also directed and featured his wife Rebecca Pidgeon and William H. Macy, suffered from too much staginess and dramatic obviousness. Michael Corrente's "American Buffalo" (1996) was also hampered by a similar fate, despite the presence of Dustin Hoffman and Dennis Franz in pivotal roles.

1997 was a banner year for Mamet, and though American audiences could not see Adrian Lyne's "Lolita", which Mamet helped rewrite, there was no shortage of him on the big screen. His scripts powered two major releases, Lee Tamahori's adventure thriller "The Edge", pitting Anthony Hopkins and Alec Baldwin against the Arctic wilds and a hungry bear, and Barry Levinson's star-studded "Wag the Dog", a comedy-drama about politics placing Hollywood firmly in bed with Washington. With "The Spanish Prisoner", Mamet finally delivered on his promise as a director. Adapted from his 1985 stage play, this independent sleight-of-hand thriller echoed the tone of his earlier "House of Games" and kept audiences off-balance throughout with its devilishly clever series of reversals.

In addition to his stage and film work, Mamet has published a number of books, including several volumes of essays, two novels and a book of poems.

COMPANION:

wife: Rebecca Pidgeon. Actor, singer; married on September 22, 1991 in Gloucester, Massachusetts; born on October 25, 1965 in Cambridge, Massachusetts and raised in Edinburgh, Scotland; converted to Judaism and had a bat mitzvah since marrying

MILESTONES:

Lived with mother in the Chicago suburbs for two years from age 13 to 15 after parents' divorce

Appeared as a soda jerk in a weekly local TV variety show that dealt with Jewish themes and issues

Worked in community theater and worked as a busboy in the Second City improvisational comedy troupe's home base

1970: First play, "Lakeboat", produced in Marlboro, VT

1971–1976: Founded Chicago's St Nicholas Theatre Company at age 24; served as artistic director

1973: Drove a cab, worked at *Oui* magazine, waited tables and worked as an assistant office manager for a real estate business in Chicago

1975: Double bill of plays first produced Off-Broadway, "Sexual Perversity in Chicago" and "Duck Variations"

1975: First play produced on Broadway, "American Buffalo"

Was lecturer in drama at the University of Chicago

Taught at the Yale Drama School

1978: Appointed artistic director and playwright-in-residence at Goodman Theatre in Chicago

1979: First script for TV, adaptation of his play "A Life in the Theatre" (PBS); later remade for TNT in 1993

1981: Scripted first feature, "The Postman Always Rings Twice"

1982: Screenplay for "The Verdict" earned Oscar nomination

1983: His play "Glengarry Glen Ross" premiered in England; won the 1984 Pulitzer Prize in Drama

1985: Founded the Atlantic Theatre Company (traveling company based in New York) with William H Macy and Gregory Mosher as a summer workshop in Vermont for his NYU students

1985: Debuted "The Spanish Prisoner" at Chicago's Goodman Theatre

1987: Feature acting debut, "Black Widow"

1987: Debut as a feature director, "House of Games"; also scripted from his original story

1987: Wrote the screenplay for Brian De Palma's big screen version of "The Untouchables"

1988: Earned Tony nomination for "Speed-the-Plow", which featured Ron Silver and Madonna

1992: Wrote screen adaptation of "Glengarry Glen Ross"

1992: Had controversial Off-Broadway hit with "Oleanna", which examined sexual politics and political correctness; also directed

1992: Adapted "The Water Engine" for TNT; also appeared in bit part

1994: Published first novel, "The Village"

1994: Staged the Off-Broadway production of "Ricky Jay & His 52 Assistants"

1994: Scripted the Treat Williams-directed short "Texan", aired on Showtime's "Directed By" series

1994: Provided the adaptation of "Uncle Vanya" that was the basis for Louis Malle's art-house success "Vanya on 42nd Street"

1996: Directed HBO special "Ricky Jay & His 52 Assistants"

1996: Wrote screenplay adaptation of "American Buffalo"

1996: Directed HBO special "Ricky Jay & His 52 Assistants", based on his Off-Broadway staging

1997: Provided screenplays for Lee Tamahori's "The Edge" and Barry Levinson's "Wag the Dog"; shared credit on the latter with Hilary Henkin; also shared Oscar nomination for Best Adapted Screenplay

1997: Wrote and directed "The Spanish Prisoner", based on his play of the same name

1997: Returned to Broadway with "The Old Neighborhood"

1998: Co-wrote the action film "Ronin"; used pseudonym Richard Weisz

1999: Adapted and directed film remake of Terrence Rattigan's "The Winslow Boy"

1999: Penned the play "Boston Marriage" about a lesbian couple (played by Felicity Huffman and Rebecca Pidgeon); premiered at American Repertory Theatre in Cambridge, Massachusetts

1999: Agreed to serve for one-year as a contributor to *Premiere* magazine

2000: Wrote and directed the comedy film "State and Main"

2000: Began contributing cartoons to *Boston* magazine; feature called "Dammit, Mamet!"

AFFILIATION: Jewish

QUOTES:

"I'm a writer, trying to work from day to day and tell a story. As far as reaching people, I don't think it's the wrfiter's job to reach people. It's the writer's job to write."—David Mamet to *Daily News*, November 2, 1994.

"When I'm making a movie, I'm just about as happy as I can be. I'm playing doll house with my best friends."—Mamet quoted in *The New Yorker, November 17, 1997.*

"They call a movie 'art house' until they find out people like it, in which case it's mainstream. Art house just means no one wants to release it very widely."—Mamet to *The Hollywood Reporter*, November 11, 2000.

BIBLIOGRAPHY:

"Lone Canoe" David Mamet, 1979, musical book

"Warm and Cold" David Mamet, 1984, Solo; children's book with illustrations by Donald Sultan

"Writing in Restaurants" David Mamet, 1986, Viking; essays, speeches and articles

"The Owl" David Mamet with Lindsay Crouse, 1987' Kipling; juvenile

"Some Freaks" David Mamet, 1989, Viking; essays

"The Hero Pony" David Mamet, 1991; poetry

"On Directing Film" David Mamet, 1992, Faber and Faber; essays based on the series of classes at Columbia University

"The Cabin: Reminiscences and Diversions" David Mamet, 1993, Vintage Books; essays

"The Village" David Mamet, 1994, Little, Brown; novel

"Passover" David Mamet, 1995, St. Martin's Press

"Make-Believe Town: Essays and Remembrances" David Mamet, 1996, Little, Brown

"The Old Religion: A Novel" David Mamet, 1997, Free Press; fictional account of the Leo Frank trial

"True and False: Heresy and Common Sense for the Actor" David Mamet, 1997, Pantheon; essays on acting

"3 Uses of the Knife: On the Nature and Purpose of Drama (The Columbia Lectures on American Culture)" David Mamet, 1998, Columbia University Press

"Bar Mitzvah" David Mamet, 1999, Little, Brown; illustrations by Donald Sultan

"Jafsie and John Henry" David Mamet, 1999, Free Press

"The Chinaman" David Mamet, 1999, Overlook Press

"Henrietta" David Mamet, 1999, Houghton Mifflin; children's book; illustrated by Elizabeth Dahlie

"Wilson: A Consideration of the Sources" David Mamet, 2000, Faber and Faber; novel about US President Woodrow Wilson and his wife Edith Bolling Galt; published in United Kingdom; published in the USA in 2001

James Mangold

BORN: James Allen Mangold, 12/16/1963

SOMETIMES CREDITED AS:
James Allen Mangold

NATIONALITY: American

EDUCATION: California Institute of the Arts, Valencia, California, acting and film, BFA, 1985; studied with Alexander Mackendrick
  Columbia University, New York, New York, film, MFA, 1991

AWARD: Sundance Film Festival Special Jury Prize (Dramatic) "Heavy" 1995; tied with Matthew Harrison's "Rhythm Thief"

BIOGRAPHY
The brief but already impressive career of screenwriter-director James Mangold offers a cautionary tale about how the quick fulfillment of a young filmmaker's dream can easily became a nightmare. Amazingly, the second act is of even greater interest.

The son of respected artists, Mangold began making his own short live-action and animated films as early as age 11. He earned his BFA at the Disney-subsidized CalArts, attending both the Acting and Film Schools and studying closely under the celebrated filmmaker Alexander Mackendrick ("The Man in the White Suit"; "The Sweet Smell of Success"). He also wrote and directed four short student films including the award-winning "Barn"(1985).

The story goes that on the Monday following his 1985 graduation, Mangold was packing his bags in his dorm room preparing to go home to a summer job in a photo shop in the Hudson Valley (NY) town from which he hailed. In short order, he received phone calls from three very high-powered entertainment figures: Michael Eisner, the then new chairman and CEO of Walt Disney Productions, Barry Diller then-head of Twentieth-Century Fox and Jeff Berg, chairman of International Creative Management. All had seen his student work and all had offers. With Berg as his agent, Mangold signed a one-year contract with Disney. His Hollywood career had officially begun.

Unfortunately, Mangold got on the bad side of Walt Disney Studios chairman Jeffrey Katzenberg over a minor deal point that Berg had negotiated into his contract granting him an assistant. As a result, Katzenberg never fully accepted the new recruit into the Disney "family." Mangold scripted a Disney TV-movie, "Deacon Street Deer", and was assigned to direct. The studio, however, found his interpretation too dark and replaced him with veteran TV director, Jackie Cooper. Mangold next co-wrote one of the studio's less impressive animated features "Oliver & Company" (released 1988). This was back in the time before the Disney animation renaissance so it was hardly a plum assignment. When his year was up, he found himself adrift in Los Angeles.

Mangold scared up a few jobs, writing trailers for cheesy genre movies, scripting a Will Vinton animated children's special (which would later win an Emmy) and contemplated writing a novel. Fearing he'd end up a minor TV director, Mangold confounded his friends by moving to NYC and enrolling in Columbia's MFA program in Film. His experience won him advanced standing and, two years later, one of five places in Milos Forman's advanced writing and directing workshop where he developed the script for what would be his feature directorial debut.

Mangold wrote and directed several well-received shorts while at Columbia including "Victor" (1991), a 30-minute silent film, and "Tree/Line", a documentary about his mother, artist Sylvia Mangold Plimack, that accompanied her museum show.

The project that begin its genesis at Columbia, "Heavy", was screened at the 1995 Sundance Film Festival and won its maker Special Jury Recognition for Directing. The deliberately paced character-driven story concerned an overweight pizza maker (Pruitt Taylor Vince) emotionally stuck in a life dominated by his mother/boss (Shelley Winters) until a beautiful young college drop-out (Liv Tyler) enters his life. The film received a limited release in 1996 and garnered generally respectful reviews.

Mangold's second feature project was "Cop Land" (1997), a low-budget ($15 million) independent feature with A-list stars (including Sylvester Stallone, Robert De Niro) about a suburban sheriff who learns of corruption within the NYPD. The stars were so impressed by Mangold's screenplay that they deferred their usual salaries and worked for scale. In retrospect, Mangold decided that Katzenberg had done him a great favor by saving him from a standard studio career.—Written by Kent Greene

MILESTONES:

Raised in the Hudson Valley, New York area

1974: Began making animated and live action films at age 11 (date approximate)

While attending CalArts, performed in and directed many plays

Wrote and directed four short films

1985: His short film "Barn" earned him an agent and a one-year contract with Walt Disney Studios

1986: Credited as James Allen Mangold, wrote teleplay for "The Deacon Street Deer"; fired as the project's director because his approach was deemed too dark; the film aired as a "Disney Sunday Movie" on ABC

Assigned to co-write the screenplay for "Oliver & Company", the 27th animated Disney feature

1986–1989: Remained in Los Angeles after his Disney contract ended; wrote trailers for Cannon Pictures films; scripted "The Claymation Easter Special" (aired on CBS in 1982) for animator-producer Will Vinton (dates approximate)

1988: Feature screenwriting debut on Disney animated film "Oliver & Company" (re-released in 1996)

1989: Moved to NYC

Was awarded advanced standing at Columbia University's Masters Program in Film

1991: Wrote and directed "Victor", a 30-minute silent film which was screened at The London Film Festival, The Kennedy Center in Washington, DC

Directed "Tree/Line", a documentary about his mother, artist Sylvia Plimack Mangold, that accompanied her museum show

1991: Was one of five candidates selected by Milos Forman for his advanced writing and directing workshop at Columbia; developed the screenplay for his feature directorial debut "Heavy" at this seminar

1994: Developed the screenplay for "Cop Land" at the Sundance Filmmaker's Lab

1995: Feature directorial debut, "Heavy" (also wrote); film was distributed in 1996

1997: Helmed "Cop Land", starring Sylvester Stallone and Robert De Niro

1999: Directed and contributed to the screenplay of "Girl, Interrupted"

2000: Signed to develop a series version of "Cop Land" reportedly for HBO

2001: Directed and received screenwriting credit on the time-traveling romantic comedy "Kate & Leopold"

Helmed the thriller "I.D." (lensed 2002)

QUOTES:

Mangold's 1991 short film "Victor" was awarded the Silver Prize at the Chicago International Film Festival and the Grand Prize at the Humboldt Film Festival.

The Mangold-scripted children's special "The Claymation Easter Special" (CBS, 1992) won the Emmy for Best Animated Special.

Joseph L. Mankiewicz

BORN: Joseph Leo Mankiewicz in Wilkes-Barre, Pennsylvania, 02/11/1909

SOMETIMES CREDITED AS:
Joseph Mankiewicz

DEATH: in Bedford, New York, 02/05/1993

NATIONALITY: American

EDUCATION: P.S. 64, New York, New York
   Stuyvesant High School, New York, New York
   Columbia University, New York, New York
English, 1928; classmate was future director Chester Erskine

AWARDS: National Board of Review Award Best American Film "Fury" 1936; one of ten films cited
   National Board of Review Award Best American Film "Three Comrades" 1938; one of ten films cited
   Writers Guild of America Award Best-Written American Comedy "A Letter to Three Wives" 1949
   Directors Guild of America Award Outstanding Directorial Achievement in Feature Film "A Letter to Three Wives" 1948/49
   Oscar Best Director "A Letter to Three Wives" 1949
   Oscar Best Screenplay "A Letter to Three Wives" 1949
   Writers Guild of America Award Best-Written American Comedy "All About Eve" 1950

New York Film Critics Circle Award Best Director "All About Eve" 1950
   Golden Globe Award Best Screenplay "All About Eve" 1950
   Directors Guild of America Award Outstanding Directorial Achievement in Feature Film "All About Eve" 1950/51
   Oscar Best Director "All About Eve" 1950
   Oscar Best Screenplay "All About Eve" 1950
   Writers Guild of America Laurel Award for Achievement 1962
   Directors Guild of America Honorary Life Membership 1981
   Directors Guild of America D. W. Griffith Award 1986

BIOGRAPHY

Like his brother Herman, Mankiewicz first made his mark in films as a scenarist, after a stint as a foreign correspondent in Berlin. In 1928, Mankiewicz secured a $60-a-week writing contract at Paramount. He wrote intertitles and in 1931 co-wrote the script of the acclaimed boy and his dog story, "Skippy." He began producing for MGM in 1936, overseeing such fine projects as Fritz Lang's "Fury" (1936), Frank Borzage's "Three Comrades" (1938), George Cukor's "The Philadelphia Story" (1940) and George Stevens's "Woman of the Year" (1942). Louis B. Mayer allegedly told him he had to produce before he could direct, but in 1943 with no directorial assignments in sight, Mankiewicz switched over to Fox, co-writing and producing "The Keys of the Kingdom" (1944). His directorial debut came in 1946, with the Gothic melodrama "Drag-onwyck" followed by directing three films written by Philip Dunne, including "The Ghost and Mrs. Muir." He returned to writing with the classic, "A Letter to Three Wives" (1948), building a reputation as one of Hollywood's more literary directors. The staginess of some of Mankiewicz's films is more than compensated for by the urbanity and wit of his screenplays and his brilliant handling of actors; "A Letter to Three Wives", "House of Strangers" (1949), "All About Eve" (1950) and "Julius Caesar" (1953) are all superb examples of his art. In 1951, he returned to New York, and remained there for the rest of his life. Before the disaster of "Cleopatra," Mankiewicz would direct and write "The Barefoot Contessa" (1954), "The Quiet American" (1958), an adaptation of Graham Greene's novel that was one of Mankiewicz's personal favorites, and "Suddenly, Last Summer" (1959). Mankiewicz took over the direction of "Cleopatra" (1963) from Rouben Mamoulian; despite his attempts to salvage the film, it proved to be one of Hollywood's most expensive flops, and dealt a serious blow to his directing career, reportedly costing a then-record sum of $40 million. The final film he completed was the cross and doublecross murder yarn, "Sleuth" (1972) that was produced independently. While failing to recapture the sublime effervescence of Mankiewicz's seminal and delightful work of the 1940s and 50s, it still succeeded as a sophisticated showpiece for stars Michael Caine and Laurence Olivier. Mankiewicz's son Tom is a screenwriter ("Superman" 1978, "The Man with the Golden Gun" 1974).

MILESTONES:

1928: Moved to Hollywood

1929: Played a bit part as a reporter in the feature film, "Woman Trap"

1933: Was a co-founder of the Screen Writer's Guild

Became a producer; worked at MGM

1946: Directed first film, "Dragonwyck"

1961–1963: Career harmed by the costly, scandal-ridden and prolonged filming of "Cleopatra"

1963: Was one of five filmmakers (along with Carl Foreman, Jean-Luc Godard, Akira Kurosawa and Elia Kazan) interviewed in the documentary short, "The Directors"

Appeared in the feature documentaries "George Stevens: A Filmmaker's Journey" (1985), "50 Years of Action" (1986), and "Hello Actors Studio" (1987)

Anthony Mann

BORN: Emil Anton Bundsmann in San Diego, California, 06/30/1906

SOMETIMES CREDITED AS:
Anton Bundsmann
Anton Mann

DEATH: in Berlin, Germany, 04/29/1967

NATIONALITY: American

EDUCATION: Central High School, New York; fellow student of Dore Schary

BIOGRAPHY

New York actor who went to Hollywood in the early 1940s and, after making a series of skillful and enjoyable B-films ("Dr. Broadway" 1942, "The Great Flamarion" 1945), eventually emerged as one of the leading directors of his day. Beginning with "Desperate" (1947), Mann directed a cycle of taut films noirs that displayed an immaculate visual style and introduced one of the director's favorite themes: the intelligent, thoughtful man who is driven to violence. Of these films, "T-Men", "Raw Deal" (both 1948) and "Border Incident" (1949) stand out.

Mann then turned to Westerns, making a number of films that are often cited as among the genre's highest achievements. Classics such as "Winchester '73" (1950), "Bend of the River" and "The Naked Spur" (both 1952) are noted for their well-crafted screenplays (often by Borden Chase), effective use of landscape and gritty violence. Starring in all three of these

was James Stewart, who also appeared in several of the director's non-Western movies, notably "The Glenn Miller Story" (1953).

Mann's final films were sprawling, big-budget productions such as "El Cid" (1961) and "The Fall of the Roman Empire" (1964), which remain among the more intelligent and absorbing period spectacles Hollywood has produced. He died during the filming of the spy thriller "A Dandy in Aspic" (1968), which was completed by the film's star, Laurence Harvey. Married to actress Sarita Montiel from 1956 to 1963.

Michael Mann

BORN: Michael K Mann in Chicago, Illinois, 02/05/1943

NATIONALITY: American

EDUCATION: University of Wisconsin, Madison, Madison, Wisconsin, English literature

London Film School, London, England, MA, 1967

AWARDS: Cannes Film Festival Jury Prize "Jaunpuri" 1971; short

Directors Guild of America Award TV Special "The Jericho Mile" 1979

Emmy Outstanding Writing in a Limited Series or Special "The Jericho Mile" 1978/79; shared award with Patrick J Nolan

Emmy Outstanding Miniseries "Drug Wars: The Camarena Story 1989/90; served as co-executive producer

National Board of Review Freedom of Expression Award "The Insider" 1999

Los Angeles Film Critics Association Award Best Picture "The Insider" 1999; shared award; Mann was one of the film's producers

Golden Satellite Best Motion Picture

(Drama) "The Insider" 1999; Mann was one of the film's producers

Golden Satellite Best Director "The Insider" 1999

Writers Guild of America Paul Selvin Award 2000; shared with Eric Roth

Humanitas Prize feature film "The Insider" 2000; award shared with Eric Roth

BIOGRAPHY

Entering the American entertainment industry as a TV cop show writer in the 1970s, Michael Mann went on to become one of Hollywood's leading stylists of the 80s and 90s, enjoying success on the small and large screens alike. Despite not helming any episodes of "Miami Vice" (NBC, 1984–89), he was (as executive producer) the man responsible for the proliferation of pastel colors in men's clothing that series heralded. ("It was somewhat annoying to find myself an arbiter of taste," Mann remarked to *The New York Times*, December 24, 1995.) As for his features, he had the rare distinction of being nearly equally lauded for his richly textured screenplays, strong female characters and skillful handling of performers as for his complex camera movements, meticulous compositions and slick, shadowy imagery. Though he has worked his atmospheric magic on an oddball WWII-era supernatural tale ("The Keep" 1983), a classic pre-Revolutionary War costume drama ("The Last of the Mohicans" 1992) and the best film about investigative journalism since "All the President's Men" ("The Insider" 1999), Mann remains best known as a crime specialist and a major practitioner of the contemporary film noir, with the critically-lauded "Thief" (1981), "Manhunter" (1986) and "Heat" (1995) complementing his TV work.

The Chicago-born Mann became interested in filmmaking after taking a film history course while working toward an undergraduate degree in English literature at the University of Wisconsin at Madison. In England he earned an MA at the London Film School in 1967, found work in an advertising agency and became a director of commercials and documentaries. Returning to the USA in 1971, he moved to Los Angeles where he eventually began writing teleplays for "Police Story" (NBC), "Starsky and Hutch" and "Vega$" (both ABC) and later worked uncredited on the screenplay for "Straight Time" (1978) before graduating to the director's chair with "The Jericho Mile" (ABC, 1979), an Emmy-winning TV-movie released theatrically abroad. Inspirational yet gritty, this thoughtful story (co-scripted by Mann) starred Peter Strauss as a convicted killer under a life sentence who, determined to become the world's fastest runner, aims for a spot on the US Olympic team. Mann then made his feature film debut as an executive producer-writer-director with "Thief", described by Brit culture magazine *Time Out* as "a philosophical thriller filled with modernist cool." The film featured an outstanding central performance by James Caan as a professional thief who initially believes that he can control his own destiny, a superb supporting cast, hi-tech visuals and a classic electronic score by Tangerine Dream.

After the commercial and critical failure of

"The Keep", a wildly uneven exercise that attempted to graft German Expressionist techniques on a bizarre story that straddled the horror and war genres, Mann returned to TV, overseeing the cultural phenomenon of "Miami Vice." Legend has it that Mann developed the series based on a brief memo by a network exec requesting "MTV cops." He filled the bill by crafting a terminally hip show featuring slick action sequences, driving musical scores (courtesy of Jan Hammer) and detectives dressed in expensive designer clothes. Once deemed cutting edge, "Miami Vice" did not age well and failed in syndication where it looked as hopelessly dated as "Dragnet." Some critics greatly preferred his less successful effort "Crime Story" (NBC, 1986–88), a would-be epic initially set in 1960s Chicago but concluding its run in the awesomely glitzy environment of "Casino"-era Las Vegas. After "Miami Vice" petered out, Mann executive produced, scripted and directed "L.A. Takedown" (NBC, 1989), a TV-movie pilot which failed to get picked up but provided the foundation for his 1995 feature "Heat." He returned to TV briefly in the early 90s, executive producing two popular docudrama miniseries, the Emmy-winning "Drug Wars: The Camarena Story" (NBC, 1990) and it sequel "Drug Wars: The Cocaine Cartel" (NBC, 1992).

Returning to the big screen, Mann took a more hands-on approach with his subsequent features, opting to produce rather than executive produce "Manhunter", a grim and disturbing psychological thriller that marked the screen debut of the celebrated cannibalistic psychiatrist Dr. Hannibal Lecter. Though quite violent, the carnage was more implied than shown, and the picture remains unfairly neglected, largely because its Lecter (Brian Cox) is less spectacular than Anthony Hopkins in "The Silence of the Lambs" (1991). The movie focused on a FBI agent (William Petersen) with a useful but troubling knack for getting inside the heads of the serial killers he hunts and was

Mann's first collaboration with director of photography Dante Spinotti, responsible for the lush cinematography of all the director's subsequent features. He followed with a thoughtfully revisionist adaptation (which he co-wrote) of James Fenimore Cooper's novel "The Last of the Mohicans", oscillating between the sweep of historical fiction and the smaller canvass of its love story. This epic romantic adventure featured galvanizing battle scenes, a typically rousing score (by Randy Edelman) and a charismatic central performance by Daniel Day-Lewis, proving he could be a Hollywood action star.

Mann staked out more familiar territory with "Heat", an absorbing crime drama promoted for its landmark teaming of two American acting titans, Robert De Niro and Al Pacino. (These master thespians had previously graced 1974's "The Godfather, Part II" but had no scenes together.) The former played a driven, supremely controlled professional thief while the latter was an equally dedicated detective with a messy personal life. Much more than a cat-and-mouse outing, "Heat" boasted a wealth of novelistic detail in its screenplay, virtuosic action set pieces and a generally high level of acting in a cast of 70 speaking parts, garnering mostly good reviews for the director, though a few holdouts decried it as an overly long triumph of style over substance. Mann mined recent history for his next project, "The Insider", picking the brain of fellow Wisconsin grad Lowell Bergman (played by Pacino), an investigative journalist in the middle of the brouhaha over CBS' 1995 refusal to air a "60 Minutes" segment featuring Brown & Williamson research scientist-turned-whistleblower Jeffrey Wigand (Russell Crowe). Though "The Insider" sometimes played fast and loose with historical accuracy, its broad strokes essentially told the emotional truth of how one man's damning information presented skillfully through a free press exposed big tobacco's tissue of lies, earning Mann the

best reviews yet of his distinguished career. He also picked up three Academy Award nominations for Best Picture, Best Screenplay and Best Director.

Mann returned to the big screen two years later with "Ali" (2001), the biopic of boxer Muhammad Ali, tracing the decade between the champion's defeat of Sonny Liston in 1964 and his comeback fight in Zaire against George Foreman in 1974. Casting singer-turned-actor Will Smith in the title role, the film didn't always focus on its title character which was one of its flaws. Still, it enjoyed a profitable opening and a mostly positive critical reception.

MILESTONES:

Became interested in directing after taking a film history class at college

1965–1971: In England, worked for advertising agency and as director of documentary films and commercials

1971: Returned to the USA and moved to Los Angeles

Began writing for primetime TV crime dramas including "Starsky and Hutch" (ABC) and "Police Story" (NBC)

1978: Scripted the TV-movie pilot for "Vega$"; also wrote for the subsequent series (ABC, 1978–1981)

1978: Feature debut, uncredited screenwriter on the crime drama "Straight Time"

1979: TV directorial debut, the ABC drama "The Jericho Mile"; also co-wrote Emmy award-winning screenplay with Patrick J. Nolan

1981: Feature debut as executive producer-director-writer, "Thief", starring James Caan

TV producing debut, executive producing influential "MTV-styled" cop series "Miami Vice" on NBC

Executive produced 1960s-set cop series "Crime Story" for NBC; also provided story for eight episodes

1986: First film project as executive producer without directing, "Band of the Hand", an actioner helmed by "Starsky and Hutch" star Paul Michael Glaser

1986: First feature credit as producer, "Manhunter"; also directed and scripted; first collaboration with director of photography Dante Spinotti; film introduced character of Hannibal Lecter (played by Brian Cox)

1987: Episodic TV directing debut, "The King in a Cage", an episode of "Crime Story" broadcast March 6th

1989: Sole story credit for "Freefall", a Latin American-set "Miami Vice" episode broadcast on May 21

1989: Executive produced, scripted and directed "L.A. Takedown" (NBC), a failed TV-movie pilot that provided a number of plot elements later expanded in the 1995 feature "Heat"

1990: TV miniseries producing debut (executive producer), "Drug Wars: The Camarena Story", an NBC crime docudrama; also provided story; project won an Emmy

1992: Executive produced "Drug Wars: The Cocaine Cartel", an NBC miniseries sequel

1992: Co-wrote, directed and served as producer on the remake of "The Last of the Mohicans", starring Daniel Day-Lewis; reteamed with Spinotti

1995: Helmed the highly-anticipated, although slightly disappointing first screen pairing of Al Pacino and Robert De Niro in "Heat"; produced and scripted as well; again reteamed with Spinotti

1999: Reteamed with Pacino for "The Insider", the based-on-fact story of tobacco industry whistleblower Jeffery Wigand; Pacino was cast as "60 Minutes" producer Lowell Bergman; produced and co-scripted (with Eric Roth); fourth feature with Spinotti; received Oscar nominations for Best Picture, Best Director and Best Screenplay

2001: Directed "Ali", a biopic of boxer Muhammed Ali starring Will Smith; also scripted with Eric Roth

AFFILIATION: Jewish

QUOTES:

"[Mann] has a certain anger. Not like a nasty thing but like this boiling pot in your stomach. He takes a hard line on everything and knows what he wants. He's not one of these guys who makes up his mind in the cutting room."—James Caan, star of "Thief", quoted in *The New York Times*, December 24, 1995.

"As interesting as I found L.A. before I shot the film ["Heat"], I find it even more exciting now. Because of the way it's laid out, lots of people move through self-imposed cultural ghettos that track through different parts of the city's topography. When you're shooting in Wilmington in South Central, L.A.'s a very different place than when you're shooting in the Alps; it's like the East L.A. version of Beirut. Lots of preconceptions about L.A. turn out to be false. The reality—the Mexican-black-Cambodian neighborhoods, the culture of South Central—is much more interesting. It's a culturally complex, commercial-industrial conurbation, and that's what turned me on."—Michael Mann to Graham Fuller in *Interview*, December 1995.

"Could I have worked under a system where there were Draconian controls on my creativity, meaning budget, time, script choices, etc.? Definitely not. I would have fared poorly under the old studio system that guys like Howard Hawks did so well in. I cannot just make a film and walk away from it. I need that creative intimacy, and quite frankly, the control to execute my vision, on all my projects."—Mann quoted in *DGA Magazine*, November 1999.

BORN: Christian Francois Bouche-Villeneuve in Neuilly-sur-Seine, France, 07/29/1921

NATIONALITY: French

AWARDS: Prix Jean Vigo "La Jetee"

Cannes Film Festival FIPRESCI Prize "Le Joli Mai" 1963

Venice Film Festival Award for Best First Film "Le Joli Mai" 1963; cited along with Jorn Donner's "A Sunday in September"

National Society of Film Critics Special Award "Battle of Chile" 1978

Cesar Best Short Film (Documentary) "Junkopia" 1983

BIOGRAPHY

Chris Marker is essentially an audio-visual poet and essayist whose (mainly) nonfiction films are characterized by the use of static images, evocative sound tracks and strong, literate commentary. A prolific writer and still photographer as well, Marker has a directorial perspective which has always been that of the alien in foreign territory, his films travel diaries with political overtones.

Marker's early life is shrouded in some mystery, much of it perpetrated by the filmmaker himself (e.g. born in France, Marker has been known to claim himself as a native of Outer Mongolia). During WWII, he served as a resistance fighter during the occupation of France; some accounts claim he also joined the US Army. As a novelist and critic, he authored an important study of dramatist Jean Giradoux, with whom Marker shares a talent for the abstract narrative devices of existentialist theater.

In the early 1950s, Marker turned to documentary filmmaking, bringing his radical politics to bear on a variety of subjects, many shot outside of France. In 1952, he made his first film, a 16mm short, "Olympia 52", depicting the Olympic Games in Finland. He later won attention with "Sunday in Peking" (1956), "Letter from Siberia" (1957) and "Cuba Si!" (1961). Marker has also been a motivator of, and collaborator on, a number of politically inspired films such as Patricio Guzman's powerful and ambitious "The Battle of Chile" (1976, which he co-produced) and the 1967 pro-North Vietnam compilation, "Loin du Vietnam/Far From Vietnam." On this polemical documentary anthology, Marker's collaborators included the likes of Jean-Luc Godard, Joris Ivens, Claude Lelouch and Agnes Varda, among others.

Marker's best-known work, however, is the fictional "La Jetee/The Pier" (completed 1962, released 1964), a haunting time-travel parable which consists—except for one short, and very beautiful, sequence of a woman waking up—of a series of still images accompanied by voice-over narration. Considered an important milestone in the history of science-fiction cinema, "La Jetee" also self-consciously explores the philosophical implications of understanding the world through film and, indeed, the boundaries of what can be considered cinema. Marker's film quickly became a cult classic, so much so that, over three decades after its making, Hollywood produced an interesting feature-length adaptation, "12 Monkeys" (1995).

Like "La Jetee", "Le Joli Mai" (1963), Marker's memorable study of Paris during a time of political turmoil, evinces a preoccupation with the manipulation of time and the paradox of memory. Marker is attempting in these films to do away with conventional storytelling techniques, creating an almost incantatory experience of movement in space and time. It is in this sense that his work comes closest to that of his friend and sometime collaborator, Alain Resnais, with whom he has worked on films including "Loin du Vietnam"; "Night and Fog" (1955), Resnais' landmark study of the Holocaust and its aftermath; and the controversial "Les Statues meurent aussi" (1953). The latter film, exploring the decline of Black art as a result of African cultures having contact with Western civilization, was banned by French censors until 1965.

In 1966, Marker established SLON ("Societe de Lancement des Oeuvres Nouvelles"), a Marxist-inspired arts collective which gave increased impetus to cinema verite documentary. Originally established specifically for the production of "Loin du Vietnam", Marker revived the enterprise in the light of the nationwide upheavals attending the worker and student strikes in France in May of 1968, and SLON continued well into the 70s producing collectively authored agit-prop material. "Junkopia", a 1981 short shot at Emeryville beach near San Francisco, reflects Marker's continued use of verite techniques in its recording of a spontaneous creation of "found art" sculpture. Unlike proponents of the "direct cinema" school, however, Marker has always played the role of catalyst—some would say "agent provocateur"—in interviewing his on-camera subjects.

Among other explorations of notable subjects, Marker's 1985 film, "A.K.", is a fascinating portrait of master filmmaker Akira Kurosawa; it is typical of Marker that his film should be a behind-the-scenes look at Kurosawa while the Japanese director was filming his epic "Ran." Marker later made another film portrait with "The Last Bolshevik" (1993), his tribute to Alexander Medvedkin, the Soviet filmmaker who was behind the so-called "film trains" (mobile film studios) of the 30s. Marker's most important and accomplished film of his later years, though, has probably been "Sans Soleil/Sunless" (1982). A complexly fragmented, endlessly reflexive and often wryly witty look at life around

the globe, the film's form, based on a series of letters, seems almost a portrait of Marker himself, a globe-trotting cameraman who writes constantly, both with his pen and with his camera.—Written by David Lugowski

MILESTONES:

Served as a resistance fighter for France during WWII

Worked for the publishing house Editions deu Seuil in the 1950s; among other work he edited a series of books, "Petite planete"

1950: Began working on the documentary short, "Les statues meurent aussi", with filmmaker Alain Resnais; was not completed until 1953

1952: Completed his first film, the documentary short, "Olympia 52", which he also co-photographed and for which he provided the commentary

1962: Made his most famous film and his only fictional film, "La Jetee/The Pier"

1966: Formed a production company, Slon, also often designated SLON, especially for the making of the episodic documentary collaboration, "Loin du Vietnam/Far From Vietnam"; Marker collaborated on the screenplay and producing responsibilities, and was also an editorial supervisor (uncredited); the film's various segments were directed by Jean-Luc Godard, Alain Resnais, William Klein, Joris Ivens, Agnes Varda, Claude Lelouch and Ruy Guerra

1968: Revived SLON after the famous nationwide student and worker strikes in France in May in order to distribute and produce agitprop material

1976: Co-produced, and also collaborated on the screenplay for, the ambitious two-part political film, "The Battle of Chile", a Chilean-Cuban production directed by Patricio Guzman

1995: Marker's film "La Jetee" adapted for the Hollywood-made feature-length film, "12 Monkeys"

1995: Commissioned by the Wexner Center for the Arts at Ohio State University to create an installation commemorating the centenary of the motion picture; created "Silent Movie" consisting of five monitors on which random scenes played to random selections of music

BIBLIOGRAPHY:

"Veillee de l'homme et de sa liberte" Chris Marker 1949 play

"Le Coeur net" Chris Marker 1950 novel

"Giradoux par lui-meme" Chris Marker 1952 literary criticism; a study of the French playwright and author Jean Giradoux

"Coreennes" Chris Marker 1962 photographs

"Commentaires" Chris Marker 1962 collection of Marker's writings on film

"Commentaires II" Chris Marker 1967 a second volume of Marker's writings on the cinema

"Le Depays" Chris Marker 1982

Garry Marshall

BORN: Garry Kent Marscharelli in Bronx, New York, 11/13/1934

SOMETIMES CREDITED AS:

Garry K. Marshall

NATIONALITY: American

EDUCATION: DeWitt Clinton High School, Bronx, New York, 1952

Medill School of Journalism, Northwestern University, Evanston, Illinois, 1956

AWARDS: American Comedy Award for Lifetime Achievement—Male 1990

Publicists Guild of America Motion Picture Showmanship Award 1992

Producers Guild of America David Susskind Television Lifetime Achievement Award 1998

BIOGRAPHY

Born and raised in the Bronx, future Hollywood producer, director, writer and sometime actor Garry Marshall grew up just across the Grand Concourse from where Carl Reiner and his son Rob (later husband to Marshall's younger sister Penny) lived. Responsible for a string of small and large screen hits that have made him one of the industry's biggest names, he began his career in NYC as a copy boy and sports reporter for the

Daily News while also moonlighting as a gag writer for such stand-up talents as Phil Foster and Joey Bishop. A drummer in his own successful jazz band and an ineffectual stand-up comic, Marshall made his TV acting debut with a recurring role in the long-running "George Burns and Gracie Allen Show" (CBS, 1950–58) and since then has contributed frequent cameos, plus the occasional larger part, to both film and TV projects. In 1960 Jack Paar hired him to write material for the original "Tonight Show", and in 1962, Joey Bishop, who had gotten his own TV show, brought Marshall out to Hollywood to work with him.

Marshall began a long-standing collaboration with Jerry Belson, writing episodes for such legendary sitcoms as "The Danny Thomas Show" (ABC), "The Lucy Show" (CBS) and "The Dick Van Dyke Show" (CBS, created by the elder Reiner), as well as for the dramatic adventure series "I Spy" (NBC). They also worked on several primetime specials and created and produced the short-lived NBC sitcom "Hey, Landlord" (1966–67) before developing Neil Simon's Broadway hit "The Odd Couple" into the long-running sitcom (1970–75) starring Jack Klugman and Tony Randall as network TV's first all-male household. Marshall also gave baby sister Penny her first acting job in a recurring role on the series as Klugman's secretary. Though not considered an unqualified success during its initial five-year run, it later achieved its classic status in reruns. With Belson, he also dipped his toe into feature waters for the first time, producing and scripting "How Sweet it Is" (1968), starring James Garner and Debbie Reynolds.

Independent of Belson, Marshall anticipated the zeitgeist and developed "Happy Days" (1974-84), flagship for the 50s nostalgia craze and one of TV's longest running and highest rated series. More cartoon than sitcom, the show started modestly and built in popularity until the 1976-77 season when it became television's number one program. Viewing the era though the rose-tinted glasses of the 70s, it made a major star out of one of its supporting actors, Henry Winkler, whose greasy-haired dropout Arthur 'Fonzie' Fonzarelli (a.k.a. The Fonz') provided an edgy counterpoint to the show's innocent teenagers (i.e., Ron Howard, Anson Williams) and helped make the series a hit. The Smithsonian Institute's 1980 announcement that it would enshrine the Fonz's leather jacket confirmed Winkler's iconic status, an amazing cultural phenomenon for the actor who had risen all the way from fifth billing to top billing with Howard's departure that year.

Marshall spun-off two successful ABC sitcoms from "Happy Days", "Laverne and Shirley" (1976-83), about two zany roommates—one played by Marshall's sister Penny—who like the "Happy Days" bunch lived in 50s Milwaukee (and worked for a brewery), and "Mork and Mindy" (1978-82), which made Robin Williams an overnight star as Mork, the space alien who arrives on Earth to study life on the primitive planet. Propelled by the laughs that their characters and situations generated, the three shows had no planned, deeper messages, and Marshall's decision to make broad entertainments concentrating more on amusement than enlightenment received tremendous validation the week of January 18, 1979, when no fewer than four of Neilsen's top five series were his: "Laverne and Shirley" (1), "Happy Days" (2), "Mork & Mindy" (3) and NBC's "Angie" (5). The "Happy Days" franchise would spawn one final series, "Joanie Loves Chachi" (ABC, 1982-83), but by then his attention had wandered to a new arena.

Marshall parlayed his triple threat TV career—writer, director, producer—into feature film directing, debuting with "Young Doctors in Love" (1982), an all-star comedy that didn't quite hit the mark. His directorial outings during the 80s included well-received movies like the coming-of-age teen movie "The Flamingo Kid" (1984, starring Matt Dillon), the Goldie Hawn–Kurt Russell comedy "Overboard" (1987), and the Bette Midler soaper "Beaches", but he hit big box office pay dirt with the highly popular "Pretty Woman" (1990), which not only revived Richard Gere's sagging career and made Julia Roberts a star, but also became one of Disney's highest grossing live-action features. Next, critics almost unanimously hailed Marshall's affecting direction of Al Pacino and Michelle Pfeiffer as two lonely people finding each other in "Frankie and Johnny" (1991), but his follow-up project, an adaptation of Anne Rice's erotic novel "Exit To Eden" (1994), which he co-produced and directed, was a timid tease and an unqualified flop.

Marshall professes a lifelong fondness for the theater, and his first stab at playwriting, "Shelves", ran for four weeks in Chicago's Pheasant Run Playhouse. Subsequently, "The Roast" (1980), which he co-wrote with partner Belson, lasted four days on Broadway, but he had better luck with "Wrong Turn at Lungfish" (1993), co-written with "A League of Their Own" screenwriter Lowell Ganz, which enjoyed regional exposure in Los Angeles and at Chicago's Steppenwolf Theatre before its off-Broadway run at NYC's Promenade Theatre (a production helmed by Marshall). His plans to build a theater got sidetracked in the mid-80s

("I pretty much lost the money I made in TV"), but the success of "Pretty Woman" got the ball rolling again, culminating in the opening of Burbank's 120-seat Falcon Theatre (named after a "gang" he used to hang with during his Bronx teenage days) in 1997.

Ironically, Marshall achieved a more prominent public profile for his recurring role on the popular CBS sitcom "Murphy Brown" from 1993–98 than for all his many successes "off-camera." He also acted in sister Penny's "A League of Their Own" (1992) and executive produced and starred in the Showtime movie "The Twilight of the Golds" (1997, adapted from the play by Jonathan Tolins), not to mention making cameo appearances in "Hocus Pocus" (1993), "Soulmates" (1996) and "With Friends Like These . . . " (1998). As for feature directing, Marshall was finding "Pretty Woman" a very tough act to duplicate. "Dear God" (1996), after getting off to a promising start, lost its conviction, and despite strong performances by leads Juliette Lewis and Giovanni Ribisi, in "The Other Sister" (1999), the cloying sweetness of that romantic comedy about two mentally challenged people who fall in love seemed better suited to the small screen. Marshall hoped to recapture some long-ago magic by reteaming with Roberts and Gere in "Runaway Bride" (also 1999) in a romantic comedy about a woman who has left four men at the altar and the intrepid reporter who succumbs to her charms while investigating her story.

FAMILY:

father: Tony Marshall. Producer, director of industrial films; received credit as producer on many of son's projects beginning with "The Odd Couple" (1970–1975); once worked as an usher at the legendary Loews Paradise movie theater in the Bronx with Leonard Goldenstein, who went on to become the head of ABC-TV; died on July 12, 1999 at age 93

mother: Marjorie Irene Marshall. Dance instructor; ran a tap dance school called The Cellar in the basement of their Bronx apartment building; when she died in 1983, the family funded a $1 million building to Northwestern University in her honor, called the Marjorie Ward Marshall Dance Studio

sister: Penny Marshall. Director, actor; born on October 15, 1942; got first break on "The Odd Couple", produced by Garry; later starred in "Laverne and Shirley"

sister: Ronelle Marshall. Producer; began as casting consultant on "Happy Days", eventually receiving credit as associate producer and producer on the series; executive produced ABC's "Joanie Loves Chachi" (1982–83); produced ABC's long-running "Step By Step" (1991–1998); acted in brother's "Dear God" (1996)

MILESTONES:

Joined the army in late 1950s and served in Korea; wrote for *Stars and Stripes* and the *Seoul News* ; served as production chief for the Armed Forces Radio Network

Played drums with own jazz group

Worked as sports reporter for NYC's *Daily News*

Made TV series debut in recurring role on "The George Burns and Gracie Allen Show" (CBS, 1950–1958)

1960: Hired as writer for "The Tonight Show" (NBC), starring Jack Paar

1962: Brought to Hollywood to write for "The Joey Bishop Show" (NBC)

With partner Jerry Belson wrote episodes for sitcoms like "The Danny Thomas Show" (ABC), "The Lucy Show" and "The Dick Van Dyke Show" (both CBS)

1964: TV special writing debut (with Belson), "Think Pretty" (NBC)

1965–1968: Was writer for NBC series, "I Spy"

Created and produced (with Belson) the short-lived NBC sitcom "Hey, Landlord"; Quincy Jones supplied the music; Sally Field and Jack Albertson played recurring characters

1968: Made screenwriting debut with the romantic comedy "How Sweet It Is", starring James Garner and Debbie Reynolds;

produced and scripted with Belson; helmed by veteran TV director Jerry Paris

1968: Feature film acting debut, "Psych-Out"

1970: Co-wrote (with Belson) "The Grasshopper", also directed by Paris

Enjoyed first series success as creator and executive producer (with Belson) of "The Odd Couple" (ABC); sister Penny joined show from 1971–1975 in part of Myrna Turner

1972: TV-movie debut as producer, "Evil Roy Slade" (NBC), directed by Paris and co-written with Belson

1972: Wrote and produced the ABC pilot "Love and the Happy Days", which aired as part of "Love, American Style"; future "Happy Days" cast members Ron Howard, Marion Ross and Anson Williams were on board, but Harold Gould played the father; Jackie Coogan portrayed Uncle Harold

Was creator and executive producer of the NBC comedy "The Little People/The Brian Keith Show"

1973: Debut as playwright with "Shelves", mounted at an Illinois dinner theater

Created and executive produced the long-running ABC sitcom "Happy Days"

Was creator and executive producer of successful "Happy Days" spin-off, "Laverne and Shirley" (ABC), starring sister Penny as Laverne

1977: Directed episodes of "Blansky's Beauties" (ABC); also executive produced

Executive produced ABC's "Mork and Mindy"; also directed episodes of the hit series; show was another spin-off from "Happy Days"

1980: Co-wrote (with Jerry Belson) the play, "The Roast"; open and closed on Broadway after four performances

1982: Feature directorial debut, "Young Doctors in Love"

1984: Co-wrote and directed the charming "The Flamingo Kid"

1985: Played a casino owner in Albert Brooks' "Lost in America"

1986: Acted in sister Penny's feature directorial debut, "Jumpin' Jack Flash"

1987: Directed "Overboard", starring Kurt Russell and Goldie Hawn

1988: Helmed the soap operish "Beaches", starring Bette Midler; initial collaboration with director of photography Dante Spinotti

1990: Directed "Pretty Woman", one of Disney's highest grossing live-action films (with over $400 million worldwide); film propelled Julia Roberts to superstardom and revitalized Richard Gere's moribund career

1992: Acted in "A League of Their Own", directed by sister Penny Marshall; script by Lowell Ganz and Babaloo Mandel

1993: With Lowell Ganz, co-wrote the play "Wrong Turn at Lungfish"; opened Off-Broadway after successful runs in Los Angeles and at Chicago's Steppenwolf Theatre; NYC production starred George C Scott, Jamie Gertz and Tony Danza and was panned by *The New York Times* theater critic Frank Rich

Played recurring role as network boss Stan Lansing on popular CBS sitcom "Murphy Brown"

1997: Executive produced and starred in Showtime movie "The Twilight of the Golds", based on the play by Jonathan Tolins

1997: Became a theater proprietor, opening the new Falcon Theatre in Burbank, California, where he could "hide from Frank Rich"

1998: Inducted into the Bronx Hall of Fame

1999: Helmed and co-scripted "The Other Sister", the story of two mentally challenged people who fall in love and fight for independence from their families; third collaboration with Spinotti

1999: Portrayed a smarmy studio executive in "This Space Between Us"

1999: Executive produced and directed the Showtime documentary "Garry Marshall on Marriage in the 20th Century: In Search of the Happy Ending"

1999: Reteamed with Gere and Roberts as director of "The Runaway Bride"; ninth film with actor Hector Elizondo

1999: Directed stage production of "Crimes of the Heart" at his Falcon Theater in Los Angeles

QUOTES:

According to the press notes for "Exit to Eden", Marshall's TV series and performers have received 16 Emmy nominations and won seven; and nominations for nine Golden Globe awards, winning four.

Marshall received a star on The Hollywood Walk of Fame in 1983.

He was inducted into the Television Hall of Fame in 1997

"We were always taught on the old "Dick Van Dyke Show" to write everything. Dick Van Dyke was very funny, so Jerry Belson and I wrote once: Dick's going to a wedding, and he puts his cummerbund on funny. And Carl Reiner said, 'What is this? Puts his cummerbund on funny? What are we paying you for? I could get a guy off the street to write, Puts his cummerbund on funny. You've got to tell me how.' "

"Comedy is a very mystical thing to a lot of people. For me, it's not so mystical. It's very hard. You can't use your imagination. Imagination will get you maybe two ideas, and then you go sell shoes. You always have a comedy eye; you're always looking. You're always saying, I'll remember that. And then you learn, truthfully, to steal other people's lives. Don't steal other people's material, though; just things that appear in their everyday lives. Lenny Bruce put it best: Pain plus time equals humor. When you're going through pain, it ain't funny, but if you give it a little time, it will become humor."—Garry Marshall, quoted in *American Film*, April 1990.

About growing up in the Bronx: "You get your sense of humor from where you grew up. Everybody has a sense of hunmor in the Bronx.

"Those friendships were solid. Nobody had any money, nobody was anybody, nobody's father was anybody. It was all based on pure friendship, and that's why I love the Bronx."

"A lot of my work is based on the interactions of the kids on my block. Fonzie (the character played by Henry Winkler on 'Happy Days') was built around three characters here. Laverne and Shirley were based on the girls in the area who would punch you. I always liked stories about overcoming adversity and being heralded for doing something good on a small scale."—Garry Marshall to Jennifer Tung, in *New York Post*, March 2, 1999.

BIBLIOGRAPHY:

"Wake Me When It's Funny" Gary Marshall and Lori Marshall, 1995; Adams Media; autobiography

Penny Marshall

BORN: Carole Penny Marscharelli in Bronx, New York, 10/15/1942

NATIONALITY: American

EDUCATION: Walton High School, Bronx, New York, 1960

University of New Mexico, Albuquerque, New Mexico, math and psychology, 1961–64

studied acting with Harvey Lembeck and Jeff Corey

AWARDS: Women in Film Crystal Award 1991

American Comedy Award for Lifetime Achievement—Female 1992

BIOGRAPHY

A TV veteran from a showbiz family whose directing career started as an acting career, Marshall had her first major continuing role as Jack Klugman's secretary Myrna Turner on her brother Garry's first hit series, "The Odd Couple" (ABC, 1970-75). With her pretty/ugly looks, whiny voice and brilliant comic timing,

Marshall was akin to a modern Patsy Kelly or Polly Moran. Her next series was as Paul Sand's sister-in-law on "Friends and Lovers" (CBS, 1974–1975), then came the role that made her a star—Laverne DeFazio in the hit sitcom "Laverne and Shirley" (ABC, 1976–1983). First introduced on an episode of "Happy Days", Marshall's Laverne was spun-off to her own sitcom produced by brother Garry and sometimes directed by Penny herself. The show was a lowbrow but often hilarious tale of two blue-collar pals (Marshall and Cindy Williams) in late 1950s Milwaukee. Marshall also appeared in a handful of TV-movies, beginning with a bit part in "The Feminist and the Fuzz" (ABC, 1971). Her first starring part was in "Wives" (CBS, 1975), and she co-starred with husband Rob Reiner in "More Than Friends" (ABC, 1978) and John Ritter in "Love Thy Neighbor" (ABC, 1984).

Marshall's film acting career never really took off. She played small parts in "How Sweet It Is" (her 1968 debut), Steven Spielberg's "1941" (1979) and did delicious cameos in "The Hard Way" (1991), "Hocus Pocus" (1993) and "Get Shorty" (1995).

Marshall began to segue to directing with an episode of the fleeting TV sitcom "Working Stiffs" in 1979. Her first feature helming assignment came when she was called in as a replacement director on the Whoopi Goldberg comedy, "Jumpin' Jack Flash" (1986). While that film was not the most promising debut, "Big" (1988) quickly established Marshall as one of the most effective comic directors in Hollywood. She deftly handled the whimsical and the warm-hearted elements of the age-switching comedy, eliciting a particularly charming and credible performance from Tom Hanks. Marshall also displayed a shrewd understanding of her audience: "Big" allowed many to bare their nostalgia for their ostensibly innocent American childhoods, and untapped emotion that lay buried somewhere under double-breasted suits and the self-centered 80s work ethic.

After this critical and box-office success,

Marshall turned to a more sobering topic with her Oscar-nominated psychological hospital drama, "Awakenings" (1990), a somewhat sleepy version of the Oliver Sacks book. Marshall again proved her skill with handling talented actors, vis-a-vis Robert De Niro's aphasiac. Her TV work of the same period included directing segments of the comedy-variety program, "The Tracey Ullman Show" (Fox, 1987–90), and directing the premiere episode of "A League of Their Own" (CBS, 1993), a failed spin-off of her 1992 hit film.

By the time she had directed the feature, "A League of Their Own", Marshall was one of the most bankable directors around, and by default, the most famous woman film director working currently. "League" was the bubbly tale of an all-female baseball team during World War II. It re-teamed her with Hanks as an alcoholic manager and featured Geena Davis, Lori Petty, Rosie O'Donnell and Madonna among the players.

Marshall produced the little-seen Jason Priestley vehicle "Calendar Girl" and the pallid "Getting Away with Murder" (1996). She returned to the director's chair with "Renaissance Man/By the Book" (1994), an amiable comedy starring Danny DeVito as an ad man turned English teacher at an Army base who, as might be expected, inspires the recruits to take learning seriously. Just in time for Christmas 1996, Marshall helmed the heartwarming romance "The Preacher's Wife" (a loose remake of 1947's "The Bishop's Wife"), starring Denzel Washington and Whitney Houston. It was perhaps the first time a white woman directed a big-budget, all-black movie. In 2001 she returned to the director's chair with the bittersweet comedy "Riding in Cars With Boys."

FAMILY:
father: Tony Marscharelli. Producer, director of industrial films; born in 1906; producer of "Laverne and Shirley" (1976–83); died on July 12, 1999 at age 93

mother: Marjorie Irene Marscharelli. Dance instructor; died of Alzheimer's disease in 1983

brother: Garry Marshall. Producer, director; born 1934; producer of TV series, "The Odd Couple" and "Laverne and Shirley"

COMPANIONS:

husband: Michael Henry. Football player; met while Marshall was a student at the University of New Mexico; biological father of Tracy Reiner; divorced 1966

husband: Rob Reiner. Director, actor; second husband; married April 10, 1971; divorced c. 1980

MILESTONES:

Competed on and won "Ted Mack's Amateur Hour" with friends at age 14

Performed as teenager on "The Jackie Gleason Show"

Played one season of summer stock in Durango, CO in the mid-1960s

1967–1968: Made TV debut on "The Danny Thomas Hour"

1968: Appeared in films "How Sweet It Is" and "The Savage Seven"

1970–1975: Played recurring role of Myrna Turner on the ABC sitcom, "The Odd Couple"

1977: Starred as Laverne opposite Cindy Williams on the ABC sitcom "Laverne and Shirley"

1979: TV directing debut, an episode of the sitcom "Working Stiffs"

1982: Directed episodes of "Laverne and Shirley" toward the end of its run (date approximate)

Asked by Paramount to direct feature film, "The Joy of Sex" starring John Belushi; Belushi was then found dead and the film was made by Martha Coolidge in 1984

1986: Feature directorial debut, "Jumpin' Jack Flash", a Whoopi Goldberg comedy vehicle

1988: Directed Tom Hanks to his first Oscar nomination in "Big"

1990: Feature executive producing debut, "Awakenings"; film earned a Best Picture Oscar nomination

1992: Helmed "A League of Their Own", about the women's baseball league; film starred Geena Davis and Hanks and featured Rosie O'Donnell and Madonna in supporting roles

1994: Suffered what may have been a heart attack

1995: Began appearing with Rosie O'Donnell in a series of TV commercials for K-Mart

1996: Signed three-year, first-look deal with Universal Pictures

1996: Helmed "The Preacher's Wife", a remake of the 1942 film "The Bishop's Wife"; Marshall's version starred Denzel Washington, Whitney Houston and Courtney B Vance

2001: Directed the comedy-drama "Riding in Cars With Boys", starring Drew Barrymore

QUOTES:

"Hollywood's top three directors today are Meathead, Opie and Laverne."—comic Bill Maher.

"I've been married. I have a child and a grandson. I'm very happy to watch a video at home with a friend rather than do dinner. I have a good support system of friends and family."—Penny Marshall to *People*, December 23, 1996.

"I was a tomboy, basically. I looked like a coconut [with] an overbite. You know how guys describe women as 'beautiful' or 'they have a good personality?' I was the one with the good personality. But I'm okay about it. I'm a grandmother now—I'm waiting to wear muumuus . . . The good thing about directing is you can get as old and funny looking as you want and not worry about it."—Penny Marshall, quoted in New York's *Daily News*, May 31, 1994.

"By all accounts, including her own, Marshall carries off her responsibilities as a director through the power of understatement. 'I administer in a very odd way—begging, whatever. But it gets done.' The main problem she sees for a woman directing a film is that 'girls cry.' "—Sean Mitchell in *Los Angeles Times*, December 16, 1990.

Marshall, whose real first name is Carole, was named after actress Carole Lombard, who died the year before she was born.

BORN: Robert Marshall in Madison, Wisconsin, 10/17/1960

NATIONALITY: American

EDUCATION: Carnegie-Mellon University Pittsburgh, Pennsylvania 1982

AWARDS: Emmy Outstanding Choreography "Annie" 1999/00

American Choreography Award Outstanding Achievement in Television—Variety or Special "Annie" 2000

Dora Mavor Moore Award Outstanding Choreography in a Play or Musical "Cabaret" 2000

National Board of Review Award Best Directorial Debut "Chicago" 2002

Directors Guild of America Outstanding Directorial Achievement in Motion Pictures "Chicago" 2002

BIOGRAPHY

Initially renowned as a brilliant choreographer for stage, screen and television, Rob Marshall made the rare transition to film director with his 2002 big-screen adaptation of the 1972 John Kander and Fred Ebb stage musical "Chicago," which became a smashing critical and commercial phenomenon and secured his place among Hollywood's A-list helmers.

Marshall first began making home movies as a youth with his sisters, including a parody of "The Brady Bunch" well before it was en vogue, but dance proved to be his true calling, beginning as a performer and eventually rising to become a dance captain, a choreographer and ultimately a director after he graduated from Carnegie-Mellon University, appearing in shows such as "Cats" and "Zorba." His first choreographic effort on Broadway had him providing additional choreography for "The Kiss of the Spider Woman" (1993)—with music and lyrics by Kander & Ebb and book by Terrence Mann—working with legendary director Hal Prince, choreographer Vincent Patterson and star Chita Rivera. Prince subsequently tapped Marshall to lay down the dance moves for a revival of "Company" (1995), which closed after 60 performances, and production of "The Petrified Prince" at the Public Theater.

Marshall's next big moment came when he choreographed the Tony-award-winning Broadway production of "She Loves Me" (1993), which earned him an Olivier nomination when the show ran in London; and he won major acclaim for his choreography of the 1994 Broadway revival of "Damn Yankees" starring Victor Garber and Bebe Neuwirth, as well the show's subsequent national tour with Jerry Lewis and the London production, which resulted in a second Olivier nomination. Marshall's dance touch also graced the smash 1996 revival of "A Funny Thing Happened on the Way to the Forum" starring Nathan Lane and, later, Whoopi Goldberg; the 1995 stage production of Blake Edwards' "Victor/Victoria" starring Julie Andrews; and an off-Broadway revival of Steven Sondheim's "Roundabout."

Marshall's string of successes on stage attracted the attention of Hollywood, and he was soon tapped to choreograph the dance sequences in lavish musical television productions such as the CBS telepic "Mrs. Santa Claus" (1996) starring Angela Lansbury; ABC's successful all-star TV version of "Rogers & Hammerstein's Cinderella" (1997) starring Brandy Norwood, Whitney Houston, Whoopi Goldberg and Jason Alexander, for which he also did the musical staging; and the Tim Robbins–directed "The Cradle Will Rock" (1998), which told the true story of the government injunction against Marc Blitzstein's 1937 musical of the same name.

Back on Broadway in 1998, Marshall made his directorial debut by co-directing (with Sam Mendes) and choreographing the wildly popular revival of Kander and Ebbs' sensation "Cabaret" starring Alan Cumming as the Master of Ceremonies and Natasha Richardson as Sally Bowles. That show won just about every award imaginable, including the Tony, the Drama Desk Award and the Outer-Critics Circle Award. That same year he also helmed the Tony-winning Broadway run of Neil Simon's "Little Me" starring Faith Prince and Martin Short, and "Promises, Promises" for the City Center Encores! series.

Marshall made a major splash on the small screen with Disney and ABC's ratings-grabbing television adaptation of "Annie" (1999) with Kathy Bates, Victor Garber, Alan Cumming and Kristin Chenoweth, which marked Marshall's first professional foray behind the camera as a director and became the most-viewed TV movie of that year. The Peabody-award winning broadcast also resulted in Marshall winning his own Emmys for best directing and best choreography, and a Director's Guild of America Award nomination.

Hollywood strongly beckoned and, after replacing the original director on the Broadway musical "Suessical" (which he did uncredited, working with the show's choreographer, his sister and former assistant Kathleen) in 2000, he began meeting with movie studio executives looking for his first feature film project. A meeting at Miramax—studio head Harvey Weinstein's children obsessively watched and re-watched "Annie"—in which he was supposed to discuss directing a big-screen version of "Rent" instead found the director pitching a long-dreamed-of ambition, putting "Chicago" on film. Marshall had earlier directed a well-received Los Angeles production of the musical starring Bebe Neuwirth in 1992 which had

earned him a Dramalogue Award. Though there had been several failed efforts to bring the project to the screen since the 1980s involving a revolving door full of talents ranging from Bob Fosse, Larry Gelbart, Nicholas Hytner, Goldie Hawn, Madonna and a pre-"Moulin Rouge" Nicole Kidman, Marshall believed he had the concept that would allow contemporary filmgoers to embrace the inherent unreality of the movie musical: he would keep the music sequences theatrical and showy by making them imaginary figments unfolding in the head of the delusional lead character, Roxie Hart. Miramax agreed and greenlit the film, even before the surprise success of director Baz Luhrmann's "Moulin Rouge" (2001), and Marshall set to work crafting a script with writer-director Bill Condon that veered between fantasy and reality.

Marshall also cannily cast major stars who were proven box office draws—Renee Zellweger, Catherine Zeta-Jones and Richard Gere—but were not known for their musical talents; nevertheless, they had the chops to pull off the demanding numbers. He also populated the supporting roles with highly unconventional choices, including Queen Latifah, John C. Reilly, Taye Diggs and Lucy Liu, which amped up the curiosity factor. But no gimmicks could beat Marshall's remarkably assured direction and whip-smart style, made all the more impressive by the director's grueling three-month, seven-day-a-week schedule. The result was a revelation: a potent, energetic, engaging and highly original film that captured the electricity of Broadway-style dance without sacrificing a theatrical sensibility for cinematic realism. Miramax's risky gamble and Marshall's back-breaking efforts proved fruitful when the film was released in 2002 to gushing critical accolades and strong box office receipts, a ride which resulted in several major awards nominations for Marshall, including an Academy Award nomination, a Directors Guild of America nod and a Golden Globe nomination.

MILESTONES:

began career as a Broadway dancer

1992: Directed production of "Chicago" starring Bebe Neuwirth in Los Angeles; won a Dramalogue Award

1993: Provided additional choreography for "Kiss of the Spider Woman" on Broadway

1993: Choreographed the Broadway production of "She Loves Me"

1994: Choreographed the revival of "Damn Yankees" starring future collaborators Victor Garber and Bebe Neuwirth

1995: Choreographed the stage production of "Victor/Victoria"

1996: Choreographed the revival of "A Funny Thing Happened On the Way to the Forum"

1996: Oversaw the dance sequences in the CBS TV movie "Mrs. Santa Claus"

1997: Choreographed ABC's TV version of "Rogers & Hammerstein's Cinderella"

1998: Provided the dance numbers for director Tim Robbins' "The Cradle Will Rock"

1998: Directorial debut on Broadway (co-directing with Sam Mendes) with revival of "Cabaret"

1999: Television directorial debut with "Wonderful World of Disney's" adapatation of the musical "Annie"; won Emmys for best directing and best choreography

2000: Uncredited directing on the Broadway show "Suessical"

2002: Directed the screen adaptation of the musical "Chicago" starring Renee Zellweger, Catherine Zeta-Jones and Richard Gere; received nominations for a BAFTA and an Oscar for his achievement in directing

QUOTES:

"He is just so nice and gentle and decent . . . And he treats every beat like a universe of meaning that has to connect to something in you."—Gere in *Entertainment Weekly*, February 2003.

Albert Maysles

BORN: Albert H. Maysles in Boston, Massachusetts, 11/26/1926

NATIONALITY: American

EDUCATION: Brookline High School, Brookline, Massachusetts

Syracuse University, Syracuse, New York, psychology, BA

Boston University Graduate School of Arts and Science, Boston, Massachusetts, psychology, MA, 1953

AWARDS: Emmy Outstanding Individual Achievement in Classical Music/Dance Programming "Vladimir Horowitz: The Last Romantic" 1986/87 award shared with David Maysles

Sundance Film Festival Excellence in Cinematography (Documentary) Award "Christo in Paris" 1991; shared with brother David

International Documentary Association Distinguished Achievement Award "Soldiers of Music: Rostropovich Returns to Russia" 1991; one of five documentaries honored

Emmy Outstanding Individual Achievement in Informational Programming-Directing "Soldiers of Music: Rostropovich Returns to Russia" 1990/91; award shared with Peter Gelb, Susan Froemke and Bob Eisenhardt

CableACE Award Documentary Special "Abortion: Desperate Choices: America Undercover" 1992; shared award

CableACE Award Directing, Documentary Special "Abortion: Desperate Choices: America Undercover" 1992; shared award with Deborah Dickinson and Susan Froemke

International Documentary Association Career Achievement Award 1994

CableACE Award Directing, Documentary Special "Letting Go: A Hospice Journey" 1996; shared with Deborah Dickson and Susan Froemke

American Society of Cinematographers President's Award 1998

Sundance Film Festival Excellence in Cinematography Award (Documentary) "LaLee's Kin: The Legacy of Cotton" 2001

BIOGRAPHY

With his brother David, Albert Maysles became one of the chief exponents of the "direct cinema" school of documentary filmmaking. The brothers began working as a team in 1957, each having previously been involved in film in very different ways—Albert making a documentary on Soviet mental institutions and David working as production assistant on two Marilyn Monroe movies. The Maysles brothers designed their own portable equipment to help in their goal of capturing the raw, spontaneous flow of experience, without intruding into the situations being filmed and were influenced by Robert Drew and Richard Leacock, with whom they had worked on "Primary" (1960).

Born and raised in Massachusetts, this son of Russian Jewish immigrants developed a childhood interest in photography. After receiving his MA in psychology, Maysles traveled to Russia and shot photographs inside mental hospitals. Although he was unsuccessful in selling those pictures, he did manage to obtain a movie camera from CBS the following year and on a return visit shot his first documentary "Psychiatry in Russia" (1955). While no network would touch the finished product, he did find an outlet at Boston's public television station WGBH which aired the documentary. He and his brother David shot footage of a student revolt in Poland which aired on NBC in 1957. Shortly thereafter, the brothers met Pennebaker who in turn introduced them to Drew and Leacock.

After "Primary", the Maysles were selected by Grenada Television to shoot the US arrival of a new rock'n'roll band, resulting in "What's Happening! The Beatles in the USA" (1964). Although there was interest in studio distribution, the band's contract to make "A Hard Day's Night" precluded any widespread showings. CBS purchased a shortened version and aired it with narration provided by Carol Burnett. Often collaborating with Charlotte Zwerin, the Maysles brothers produced one of their best-known works in 1968. "Salesman", a look at door-to-door bible sellers in Boston, which for various reasons also did not gain widespread exposure until a 1994 airing on PBS. "Gimme Shelter" (1970), on the other hand, garnered much controversy. This record of a Rolling Stones concert stirred much debate over its capturing of the knifing death of one of the concertgoers. The moral issues raised by the filmmaker's "detached observer" status were hotly debated. A similar fate befell "Grey Gardens" (1976), their portrait of the Beales, a mother-daughter living in seclusion in a run-down East Hampton mansion. A pathetic but human look at two women who share their living space with a multitude of felines, the film is a fascinating depiction of co-dependence and resentment with particular emphasis on the mother-daughter dynamic. At the time of its release, "Grey Gardens" divided critics, some of whom praised it as one of the year's best films while others found it tasteless and exploitative.

The brothers received their sole Oscar nomination in 1973 for the first of several collaborations with the artist Christo. "Christo's Valley Curtain" (1973) explored the artist's hanging a nine-ton orange nylon fabric in Rifle Gap, Colorado which was destroyed by nature after a day. Without explaining the why of Christo, the film documents the project. Similarly, the others in the series "Running Fence" (1978), "Islands" (1986), "Christo in Paris" (1990) and "Umbrellas" (1995) all merely show the artist at work.

In the 1980s, Maysles turned his attentions to profiling classical musicians like Seiji Ozawa and Vladimir Horowitz. After David's death in 1987, he partnered with Susan Froemke and embarked on a series of made-for-cable documentaries, including "Abortion: Desperate Choices" (HBO, 1992) and "Letting Go: A Hospice Journey" (HBO, 1996). More recently, he chronicled the development of the Los Angeles Center in "Concert of Wills: Making the Getty Center" (1997).

MILESTONES:

Raised in Brookline, Massachusetts

At age seven, purchased first still camera

Worked as salesman

During WWII, served with Army tank corps; after discharge enrolled in college

1952–1955: Taught psychology at Boston University

1955: Went to USSR to study mental health care; began making films

1955: First film (made solo), "Psychiatry in Russia"; attempted to sell film to networks; eventually aired on WGBH the public television station in Boston

1957: First film made with brother David, "Youth of Poland"

1959: Co-shot D.A. Pennebaker's "Opening in Moscow"

With Pennebaker, Richard Leacock and David Maysles, became member of Drew Associates (founded by Robert Drew)

1960: Co-directed "Primary", an examination of the Democratic campaign for president

Formed Maysles Films, Inc.

1962: First Maysles Brothers collaboration with Charlotte Zwerin and first Maysles Films, Inc. production, "Showman"

1964: Made the documentary short "What's Happening! The Beatles in the U.S.A./The Beatles: The First U.S. Visit"; could not be released theatrically; aired on CBS with narration by Carol Burnett

1964: Photographed Godard's segment ("Montparnasse et Levallois") of omnibus feature, "Paris vu par . . ./Six in Paris"

1969: "Salesman", a portrait of bible sellers in Boston, was withheld from audiences for 25 years; aired on PBS' "POV" in 1994

1970: Garnered widespread acclaim for "Gimme Shelter"; co-directed and co-shot with brother David

1973: Shared Academy Award nomination for "Christo's Valley Curtain"; also first of several film collaborations with the artist Christo

1974: Worked as cinematographer on Leon Gast's documentary "When We Were Kings", about the Muhammed Ali-George Forman 'Rumble in the Jungle'; film not released until 1996

In early 1980s, worked on film profiles of musicians Seiji Ozawa and Vladimir Horowitz; earned Emmy Award for "Vladimir Horowitz: The Last Romantic"

1990: Last feature collaboration with brother David, "Christo in Paris"; released three years after David's death

1992: Co-directed the award-winning "Abortion: Desperate Choices", an HBO documentary; also served as a producer

1994: Filmed "Conversations With the Rolling Stones" (broadcast on VH-1)

1996: Produced, shot and co-directed the award-winning HBO documentary "Letting Go: A Hospice Journey"

1997: Co-directed with Susan Froemke and Bob Eisenhardt the documentary "Concert of Wills: Making the Getty Center"

2001: With Froemke and Deborah Dickson, worked on "LaLee's Kin: The Legacy of Cotton"; premiered at Sundance before airing on HBO

2001: Profiled directors Martin Scorsese, Wes Anderson, Robert Duvall and Jane Campion in the TV specials "With the Filmmaker: Portraits by Albert Maysles" (PBS)

AFFILIATION: Jewish

QUOTES:

"People sense—from the way you handle the camera, even the way you introduce yourself— if you're going to intrude on them or hurt them. They sense when you are really paying attention. To attend means to wait. That perfectly describes what we do."—Albert Maysles quoted in *The New York Times*, February 13, 1994.

"As a child, I didn't speak. It wasn't a deformity. I was just extremely quiet. No one knew if I was broght or dumb, so I had to repeat kindergarten. But my personality made me an avid listener,

which served me well."—Albert Mayseles quoted in *American Cinematographer*, January 1998.

"We couldn't have made all of those films without each other. There was no sibling rivalry because we weren't in competitive roles. We worked as a filming team, with me behind the camera. David also took control of postproduction, and we both found stories and made decisions. But above all, we held ourselves subservient to our subjects and the quality of our films."—Maysles in *American Cinematographer*, January 1998.

Deepa Mehta

BORN: in Amritsar, India, 1949

SOMETIMES CREDITED AS:
Deepa Mehta Saltzman
Deepa Metha Saltzman

NATIONALITY: Indian

CITIZENSHIP: Canada

EDUCATION: University of New Delhi New Delhi, India, philosophy, BA, 1973; met future husband while attending

AWARD: Canadian Film Award Documentary Under 30 Minutes "At 99: A Portrait of Louise Tandy Murch" 1975; shared with then-husband Paul Saltzman

BIOGRAPHY

The two predominant themes in the work of writer-director Deepa Mehta are 1) the transcendence of age differentials and cultural barriers and 2) passion in its various guises. Drawing on her own status as a woman whose identity straddles two disparate worlds, her native India and her adopted homeland of Canada, this gifted filmmaker sheds new light

on the seemingly banal topics of friendship and history. In a handful of films, Mehta has emerged as a potent voice in world cinema.

The daughter of a film distributor, Mehta was raised in Delhi, India along with her brother, photojournalist Dilip Mehta. While obtaining her degree in philosophy at the University of New Delhi, she met Canadian Paul Saltzman, whom she married. In 1973, they settled in Toronto where she broke into the film industry as a scriptwriter for children's movies. Mehta learned as she went, starting as a writer and editor on documentaries (many made in tandem with her then-husband under their production banner Sunrise Films) before stepping behind the camera to make the documentary short "At 99: A Portrait of Louise Tandy Murch" in 1975. Several other documentaries, including one on her brother "Travelling Light: The Photojournalism of Dilip Mehta" (1988), followed, as well as the occasional small screen assignment (e.g., the Canadian-produced "The Twin" 1988).

Mehta moved into fictional films with 1991's "Sam & Me", about the unlikely friendship between an Indian hired to look after an elderly Jewish man, establishing a central motif in the director's work: overcoming obstacles to form a bond. The Muslim immigrant and the Hebraic man grow to trust and enjoy one another's company despite the growing objections from their communities. Material that easily could have devolved into maudlin claptrap was tempered by Mehta's levelheaded direction and writing. While it depicts the Indian immigrant striving to maintain his integrity, the film also examines the closed mindset of communities banding together by culture. Although it flirts with melodrama, "Sam & Me" showcased an intriguing directorial voice. "Camilla" (1994), Mehta's second feature, was almost a distaff remake of her first, this time with Hollywood stars Jessica Tandy and Bridget Fonda as an elderly violinist befriended by a much-younger musical aspirant. Despite the presence of such luminaries, the film received a limited release, yet it also exhibited the director's capability with actors.

Between her first two features, Mehta received a big career boost when George Lucas tapped her to helm the "Benares, January 1910" segment of the ABC series "The Young Indiana Jones Chronicles" in 1992. She was invited back in 1996 to handle the Greece segments of the TV-movie "Young Indiana Jones: Travels With Father" (The Family Channel). By this point, Mehta had begun working on the script for a proposed trilogy. Newly divorced, she wrote and directed "Fire" (1996), a beautifully realized portrait of friendship and love between two unhappily married Indian women, a newlywed in an arranged marriage and her older sister-in-law. Mehta has said she set out to make a film "about the intolerance in class, culture and identity" and she more than succeeded. Some, however, found the film one-sided with the male characters depicted as boors and chauvinists while the lesbian aspect to the women's relationship upset religious leaders around the world. (Theaters showing the film in India were firebombed.) Seen as a feminist tract by its harsher critics, "Fire" upset many males as it challenged society's patriarchal norms by allowing its female characters degrees of choice.

No less controversial was her follow-up "Earth" (1998), based on Bapsi Sidhwa's semi-autobiographical novel "Cracking India", set on the eve of the 1947 independence of India and the subsequent creation of Pakistan, a little explored historical period that resulted in the deaths of more than a million people and the displacement of some 12 million more. As filtered through the eyes of a Parsee child, the story unfolded to examine issues of nationalism, religious fervor, friendship and betrayal. While the historical events provided a dramatic background, center stage was a love triangle between a Hindu nursemaid and two Muslims, a masseur and an ice candy vendor. Mehta wrote and directed an intimate epic that demonstrated the horrors of separatism and ethnic cleansing that had a universal resonance. She had announced plans for the third installment in her trilogy "Water", which would focus on a child bride widowed by age seven, but filming was suspended due to local protests in India. Additionally, Mehta was developing "A Girl in the Paperbag" with Nastassja Kinski and Eric Stoltz attached as co-stars.

MILESTONES:

Raised in Delhi, India

1973: Emigrated to Canada

Early work in the movie industry, writing scripts for children's films

With then-husband Paul Saltzman and brother Dilip, co-founded Sunrise Films Ltd.

1974: Scripted and edited the documentary "The Bakery", directed by Saltzman

1975: Directorial debut with the documentary short "At 99: A Portrait of Louise Tandy Murch"

1986: Directed documentary about her brother, "Travelling Light: The Photojournalism of Dilip Mehta"

1988: With Norma Bailey and Daniele J Suissa, co-directed "Martha, Ruth & Edie"; also produced; credited as Deepa Mehta Saltzman

1988: Helmed an episode of the Canadian TV series "The Twin"; also acted in a separate episode

1988–1989: Directed four episodes of the TV series "Danger Bay"

1991: First fictional feature "Sam & Me"; also co-produced

1992: Directed "Benares, January 1910", an episode of "The Young Indiana Jones Chronicles" (ABC)

1994: Helmed second feature "Camilla", a character study co-starring Jessica Tandy, Bridget Fonda and Hume Cronyn

1996: With Michael Schultz, credited as director of "Young Indiana Jones: Travels With Father", a telefilm aired on The Family Channel

1996: Scripted, co-produced and directed "Fire", the first in a proposed trilogy of films named after elements; film generated controversy as it depicted the growing relationship between an Indian woman and her sister-in-law; initial collaboration with actress Nandita Das; film provoked a firestorm of controversy when it played in India as more than 2000 members of the Shiv Sena, a reactionary faction of the government's majority Hindu Nationalist Party protested the film with firebombs

1998: Co-produced, wrote and directed "Earth", the second film in her trilogy, detailing the 1947 partition of India and Pakistan filtered through the eyes of a crippled Parsee child; based on the semi-autobiographical novel "Cracking India" by Bapsi Sidhwa; film co-starred Aamir Khan, Nandita Das and Rahul Khanna

2000: Attempted to complete her trilogy filming "Water"; project put on hold when shooting was suspended because of local protests in India

AFFILIATION: Hindu

QUOTES:

"I wrote ["Fire"] at the end of my own 14-year marriage to a white Canadian. I had always thought of myself as a liberated, emancipated woman, but when we married I never questioned the idea that I would follow him. I was a good, obedient wife. To give up went against everuthing I had been taught about being a woman. To be divorced questioned my deepest ideas of self-worth."—Deepa Mehta quoted in *Sydney Morning Herald*, August 15, 1997.

"When I was growing up, sometimes we had a lot of money and sometimes we didn't, depending on how well my father's films did. He always used to say to me, 'There are two things in life you never know—when you're going to die and how a film is doing to do.' "—Deepa Mehta to Diane Taylor in "Lesbian Sisters, Freaky In-laws and Pervy Men. This is Indian Life as Deepa Mehta Knows It", from *The Guardian*, November 13, 1998.

"I'm really tired of 'exotic' India. It just doesn't exist anymore. The othe extreme is an Indian with a begging bowl. And in between, there are 350 million people who are not unlike the people in the West."—Mehta quoted in *New York*, August 25, 1997.

"I'm not really Indian, I'm not really Canadian. I'm a bit of both or a lot of one and a lot of the other. But I feel lost. I don't know where I belong."—Deep Mehta quoted in *Toronto Sun*, September 11, 1998.

"Reading a Deepa Mehta script is like watching the movie itself."—Indian actor Rahul Khanna, co-star of "Earth", quoted at www.indiabollywood.com/profiles/deepa-mehta.htm

"The partition of India was like a Holocaust for us and I grew up hearing many stories about this terrible event. Naturally I was attracted to this subject.

"I have my own theory about why there has been such a silence about this tragedy by western filmmakers, and it is just a theory. I think it is bound up with a number of attitudes that prevail in the western countries about India. Obviously I am not including everybody in this generalisation, there are many exceptions, but there are several conceptions that prevail in the west about India. There is firstly the spiritual India—a place where you go and find nirvana. Secondly, there is the conception that India is entirely poverty stricken, with a permanent kind of begging bowl attitude. There is the India of Maharajas, princes and queens, and the India that comes from nostalgia for the Raj. And there is always the prevailing pressure that people should feel superior to some other place: look how bad India is with all the beggars, aren't we lucky to be better off.

"It is uncomfortable and difficult for some filmmakers to produce works that destroy these perceptions. India brings specifically fixed images in many western minds, and the minute you start de-exoticising that, you have you deal with Indians as real people, and there is a pressure not to do that.

"Finally, there are many dark political questions about partition that the British establishment doesn't want brought to light. When you know the real history of partition and the responsibility that lands in the laps of the British, obviously you understand why it is a very uncomfortable subject for them. Generally the response there has been to romanticize Gandhi and Lord Mountbatten. This is done to such a degree that I find it quite nauseous."—

Mehta quoted on World Socialist Web Site (www.wsws.org)

"There are a quite a number but there is one group of great masters. There is Satyajit Ray whose work has played an enormous part in my appreciation for the cinema. I regard him as one of the most lyrical and humanist filmmakers of the century. I also admire Mizoguchi, Ozu, Vittorio de Sica, as great masters.

"There are three contemporary directors that immediately come to mind whom I enjoy and am inspired by. I think Emir Kusturica is brilliant, and one of my favourite films of all time is 'Time of the Gypsies'. I like the fact that he doesn't flee from an emotion, he embraces it fully. He doesn't seem to give a damn about how his films will be perceived. If he wants to be irreverent he will be. I like the use of music in his films, I love the heart of his films and they always carry a very strong political message. I also like Pedro Almadovar very much— I like his black humour—and I like Peter Weir, because he has managed to keep his integrity as a director while making his films very accessible. That I admire enormously. I am sure I could go on at length."

—Deepa Mehta quoted on the World Socialist Web Sit (www.wsws.org)

Georges Melies

BORN: Marie-Georges-Jean Melies in Paris, France, 12/08/1861

SOMETIMES CREDITED AS:
Geo. Smile

DEATH: 01/21/1938

NATIONALITY: French

EDUCATION: Lycee Imperial, Paris, France

Lycee Louis-le-Grand, France, 1870–80, graduated

Ecole des Beaux Arts, Paris, France

BIOGRAPHY
One of the visionary pioneers of the cinema, Georges Melies was born to a boot manufacturer and passed through adolescence exhibiting two talents: for drawing and for making cardboard Punch & Judy shows. During his military service he was stationed

near the home of Robert Houdin, the magician whose optical illusions had captivated Melies as a child, and whose theater he would eventually attend but after he escaped from his family job as overseer of factory machinery.

When the Lumiere brothers unveiled their Cinematographe in public on December 28, 1895, Melies was not only present, but clearly the most affected member of the audience. Frustrated when the Lumieres would not sell him the machine, he sought out R.W. Paul and his Animatographe in London. Melies then built his own camera-projector and was able to present his first film screening on April 4, 1896.

Melies began by screening the films of others, mainly those made on the Edison Kinetoscope, but within months he was showing his own works; these were apparently one-reel views, usually consisting of one shot lasting sixty seconds. Although Melies is often credited with inventing the narrative film by relating stories as opposed to simply depicting landscapes or single events, this is not strictly true; many of the Lumiere brothers' films were also much more than simple, static views. Melies signal contribution to the cinema was to combine his experience as a magician and theater owner with the new invention of motion pictures in order to present spectacles of a kind not possible in the live theater.

Within nine months, Melies had increased the length of the filmed entertainment (his last film of 1896 consisted of three, three-minute reels) and was making regular use of previously unimaginable special effects, such as making performers disappear by stopping his camera in mid-shot. As the year ended he was also completing a glass-walled studio where he could make films without fear of elements.

From 1897 to 1904 Melies made hundreds of films, the great majority now lost. The scores of prints which survive show why his contemporaries were both initially impressed, and ultimately bored. Melies regarded the story in

his films to be mere "thread intended to link the 'effect' . . . I was appealing to the spectator's eyes alone." Falling to develop any consistent ideas, his entertainment consisted only of a succession of magical tableaux peopled by Melies (who often dressed as the conjurer or the devil) and young women recruited from the theaters of Paris, performing against flat, painted backdrops. Melies' own resources and interest in these films apparently began to dwindle after 1905, party due to competition from other filmmakers and rising costs, partly because of the growing industrialization of the French film industry, and partly due to his wish to continue presenting live programs at the Theatre Robert Houdin. By 1911 he had ceased independent distribution; but the time France entered WWI in 1914 his career as a producer-director had ended. His best-known surviving works are "A Trip to the Moon" (1902), "The Melomaniac" (1903), "An Impossible Voyage" (1904) and "The Conquest of the Pole" (1912), his last year of production.

Jean-Pierre Melville

BORN: Jean-Pierre Grumbach in Paris, France, 10/20/1917

SOMETIMES CREDITED AS:
Jean Pierre Melville

DEATH: 08/01/1973
NATIONALITY: French

EDUCATION: Lycee de Condorcet France
    Lycee de Michelet France
    Lycee de Charlemagne France

BIOGRAPHY
Director whose economical production methods were a major influence on the French New Wave. Forced to work outside France's studio system, Melville set up his own production company in 1946 and two years later turned out his first feature, "Le Silence de la mer", beginning his long-term association with cameraman Henri Decae. Melville's adaptation of Jean Cocteau's novel, "Les Enfants Terrible" (1950), is considered among the finest film renderings of a literary work; other notable films include "Bob le flambeur" (1955), a homage to American film noir, and "Leon Morin, Pretre" (1961), which saw Jean-Paul Belmondo in a surprisingly effective role as a priest. Much of Melville's output reflected his passion for American culture (he took his name from that of novelist Herman Melville) and, especially, for Hollywood movies of the hard-boiled style.

Sam Mendes

BORN: Samuel Alexander Mendes in Redding, England, 08/01/1965

NATIONALITY: British

EDUCATION: Magdalen College School, Oxford, England
    Peterhouse College, University of Cambridge, Cambridge, England, 1987

AWARDS: London Critics' Circle Award Most Promising Newcomer 1989; tied with actress Julia Ormond
    London Critics' Circle Award Best Director "The Glass Menagerie" 1995
    Los Angeles Film Critics Association Award Best Director "American Beauty" 1999
    Broadcast Film Critics Association Award Best Director "American Beauty" 1999
    Florida Film Critics Circle Award Best Director "American Beauty" 1999
    Online Film Critics Society Award Best Director "American Beauty" 1999
    Dallas-Fort Worth Film Critics Association Award Best Director "American Beauty" 1999
    Golden Globe Award Best Director "American Beauty" 1999
    London Film Critics Circle Award Director of the Year "American Beauty" 2000
    Directors Guild of America Award Outstanding Directorial Achievement in Feature Film "American Beauty" 1999
    Oscar Best Director "American Beauty" 1999
    Lumiere Best Foreign Film "American Beauty" 2000
    Dora Mavor Moore Award Outstanding Direction of a Musical "Cabaret" 2000

Washington Film Critics Award Best Director "Road To Perdition" 2003; tied with Denzel Washington and Spike Jonze

Laurence Olivier Award Best Director (stage) "Twelfth Night" and "Uncle Vanya" 2003

Laurence Olivier Award Best Revival "Twelfth Night" and "Uncle Vanya" 2003

Laurence Olivier Award Special Achievement Award for his 10-year-tenure at London's Donmar Warehouse Theater 2003

ShoWest Director of the Year 2003

BIOGRAPHY

Hot on the heels of his successful in your face Broadway staging of "Cabaret" (1998), innovative and iconoclastic British stage director Sam Mendes made the leap to features with his 1999 debut "American Beauty." In 1990, at only 25 years old, Mendes began directing for the Royal Shakespeare Company, his credits including "Troilus and Cressida" with Ralph Fiennes and "The Alchemist" (both 1991). The prolific director additionally took on Sean O'Casey's "The Plough and the Stars" at the Old Vic Theatre and "The Sea" for the National Theatre Company that same year. He next directed "The Rise and Fall of Little Voice", Jim Cartwright's play that showcased Jane Horrocks' remarkable vocal abilities in the role of a young woman who isolates herself from her cruel mother and the outside world by retreating into old records and giving note perfect impersonations of legendary singers including Judy Garland, Sarah Vaughan and Marilyn Monroe. Mendes' spare staging of the play made for a powerful performance, but caused difficulties for film director Mark Herman when the play was later adapted into a 1998 feature starring Horrocks, Brenda Blethyn and Michael Caine. (At one time Mendes was attached to direct but the end of his off-screen relationship with Horrocks led to his withdrawal.)

In 1992, Mendes was named artistic director of the Donmar Warehouse, one of London's leading nonprofit studio theaters and what would become the breeding ground for some of the most exciting productions to appear on the British stage. One of his first projects in his new capacity was "Assassins", Stephen Sondheim's unusual musical about the personalities responsible for the murders of US presidents. While his work at the Donmar was extensive (including "Richard III"), the director did not work there exclusively. His 1993 effort "The Tempest" was produced by the Royal Shakespeare Company while his 1994 staging of Harold Pinter's "The Birthday Party" played at the Lyttleton Theatre for the National Theatre Company. That same year, his "Oliver!" debuted at the London Palladium, and four years later earned the distinction of having the longest run of any show produced at that theater.

Mendes moved away from musicals briefly with an inspired 1996 take on the Tennessee Williams classic "The Glass Menagerie." This Donmar production relied more on the original text, including the scenic specifications, than the many legendary past productions had, with Mendes casting actors closer to the age of Williams' characters. He elicited fine work from Claire Skinner as Laura, Ben Chaplin as Tom and especially Zoe Wanamaker as Amanda, resulting in a more contemporary, less literal take on the play that made for a particularly moving theatrical experience while underlining the original's timelessness. The successful 1995 revival of Sondheim's "Company" met with largely positive notices, and Mendes broke new ground by casting the impressive Adrian Lester in the lead role, marking the first time a black actor starred in a Sondheim musical. The director updated George Furth's original book, changing this look at 1970 New York society, marriage and relationships to a present day examination of the same. He followed up with another American musical, this time an original entitled "The Fix", a darkly comedic look at modern politics, that met with somewhat mixed reviews. Many critics found its exploration of image versus ideas in late-20th-century United States unevenly staged with heavy-handed delivery.

Mendes' revival of Kander & Ebb's "Cabaret" debuted at the Donmar Warehouse in 1994, starring Alan Cumming as the Emcee and Jane Horrocks as Sally Bowles. The daring environmental production was seedier and more unsettling than the legendary Broadway run starring Joel Grey (who reprised his role in the 1972 film). Mendes made his Broadway directing debut in 1998 when the production was reprised, winning most major theater awards in its premiere season and subsequently enjoying a long run. The production, performed in a space meant to recreate the atmosphere of a real Berlin cabaret was at once grand and claustrophobic, giving even those familiar with the play the feeling that anything could happen. Mendes and fellow stager Rob Marshall (who also choreographed) stressed the dimensionality of the characters and their situations, making them both likable and abhorrent, resulting in less cartoonish and more frighteningly realistic portrayals of the political and social unrest of the time. Theatergoers flocked to see the critically acclaimed musical even after its Tony-winning stars Natasha Richardson and Alan Cumming departed the production. The director had another New York success when his overwhelmingly acclaimed "Othello" had a limited run at the Brooklyn Academy of Music. Mendes' returned to Broadway with "The Blue Room", an adaptation of "La Ronde" penned by David Hare. The play, originally produced at the Donmar Warehouse, received a great deal of press in Britain over a brief nude scene by co-star Nicole Kidman. New York audiences were less impressed, finding the play to be well-paced and skillfully directed but lacking the punch that would warrant the surrounding hype.

Movie audiences were treated to Mendes' work in 1999 when he made his cinematic debut with "American Beauty", a brave and moving darkly comedic look at a man (Kevin Spacey) in the midst of a self-destructive mid-life crisis, and the effect it has on his relationship with his controlling wife (Annette Bening) and teenaged daughter (Thora Birch). Mendes' assured debut earned him numerous accolades including a Best Director Oscar.

Mendes next project was the lofty and somber "Road to Perdition" starring Tom Hanks with Jude Law and Paul Newman both giving excellent supporting roles. It was the story of a son and father's journey after the father's connection to the Irish mafia caused his wife and other son to be killed. While the appearance of the film and the acting of the leads was praised, many critics felt Mendes's directing to be somewhat self-conscious and hollow. But while "Perdition" was not fully embraced by moviegoers, Mendes continued to be a considerable force on the legitimate stage in 2003, directed heralded London productions of Shakespeare's "Twelfth Night" and Chekov's "Uncle Vanya", which later went to Broadway and collecting an unprecedented trio of prestigious Lawrence Olivier Awards (the British equivalent of Broadways' Tonys) in the same year, for Best Director, Best Revival and a special achievement award for his 10-year-tenure with London's tiny Donmar Warehouse Theater.—Written by Jane O'Donnell

COMPANIONS:

Jane Horrocks. Actor; together c. 1992–1995

Cameron Diaz. Actor; no longer together

Calista Flockhart. Actor; reportedly dated in late spring and summer 1999

Rachel Weisz. Actor; dated on and off from c. 1999 to c. 2001

Kate Winslet. Actor; announced relationship in November 2001

MILESTONES:

Raised in London

1987: Was artistic director of Minerva Studio Theatre in Chichester, England

1990: Began directing at the Royal Shakespeare Company (RSC)

1991: Helmed "The Plough and the Stars" at the Old Vic Theatre

1991: Directed Ralph Fiennes in "Troilus and Cressida" for the RSC

1991: Staged the RSC production of "The Alchemist"

1991: Helmed "The Sea" produced by Britain's National Theatre Company

1992: "The Rise and Fall of Little Voice", directed by Mendes and starring Jane Horrocks debuted at the Lyttleton Theatre

1992: Became artistic director of the Donmar Warehouse, a leading nonprofit studio theater in London

1992: Directed the Stephen Sondheim–John Weidman musical "Assassins" at Donmar

1993: Produced and directed "Richard III" at Donmar Warehouse

1993: Directed the Royal Shakespeare Company's production of "The Tempest"

1994: Staged Harold Pinter's "The Birthday Party" at the National Theatre Company's Lyttelton Theatre

1994: Produced and directed an environmental production of "Cabaret" for the Donmar, starring Alan Cumming and Jane Horrocks

1994: His revival of "Oliver!" opened at the London Palladium, setting a record four years later as the theater's longest-running production

1996: Directed acclaimed London revival of the Sondheim musical "Company"

1996: Staged a well-received version of "The Glass Menagerie" featuring Zoe Wanamaker and Ben Chaplin

1997: Flopped at the Donmar with new American musical, "The Fix"

1998: Made Broadway directing debut with revival of "Cabaret" with Cumming repeating his London role; shared Tony nomination with co-stager Rob Marshall

1998: Staged widely acclaimed sellout London production of "Othello" which also had a brief engagement at the Brooklyn Academy of Music (BAM)

1998: Directed David Hare's "The Blue Room", an adaptation of "La Ronde", starring Nicole Kidman and Iain Glen; opened to raves in London and transferred to Broadway

1999: Made feature directorial debut with the black comedy "American Beauty" starring Kevin Spacey and Annette Bening; received Best Director Academy Award

1999: Staged the workshop production of the long-awaited Sondheim-Weidman show "Wise Guys", starring Nathan Lane and Victor Garber; withdrew after it was decided not to move the show to Broadway

2000: Formed Donmar Films, with partial backing from DreamWorks

2000: Returned to stage directing with "To the Green Fields and Beyond", starring Dougray Scott and Ray Winstone

2001: In November, announced plans to leave position as artistic director of the Donmar Warehouse in December 2002

2002: Helmed second feature "The Road to Perdition," starring Tom Hanks

2003: MAde theater history when he became the first triple winner at Britain's prestigious Laurence Olivier awards

AFFILIATION: Jewish

QUOTES:

In June 2000. he was made Commander of the Order of the British Empire in the Queen's birthday honors.

"If you shout in the theater, people think you've gone a bit mad. But if you raise your voice on a film set, people just work a bit harder."—Sam Mendes quoted in *Premiere*, September 1999

"I love America. I like being there, the culture of movies. There are problems as there are in any society but I'm not anti-American. I love NY particularly; L.A. is an acquired taste which

I haven't yet acquired. (laughs)."—Mendes to Andrew L Urban at www.urbancinefile.com/au

"Confidence is the key when it comes to directing," says Mendes. "To some degree, it's a con trick. There's always a part of you that doubts some part of what you're doing, but it's crucial that that's not available to the people you're working with." A friend says:

"His power is in manipulation. He'll allow you time to come to the conclusion that he had in mind all along."—From the London *Times*, February 20, 2000.

"To me all great movies have tension. You pull a wire tight at the beginning of a film and you don't relese it."—Mendes to *Premiere* Magazine, August 2002.

Russ Meyer

BORN: Russell Albion Meyer in Oakland, California, 03/21/1922

SOMETIMES CREDITED AS:
B. Callum

NATIONALITY: American

BIOGRAPHY

WWII newsreel photographer who snapped centerfolds for *Playboy* before turning out his first "skin flicks" in the 1950s. "The Immoral Mr. Teas" (1959) marked the first of a series of soft-core sex romps featuring Meyer's now notorious trademarks: a predilection for oversized breasts; high-speed, disjointed camerawork; anarchic humor; and overblown violence. The huge commercial success of "Vixen" (1968) led to Meyer being invited by 20th Century-Fox to direct such spectacles as "Beyond the Valley of the Dolls" (1970), which was scripted by film critic Roger Ebert. After a ten-year hiatus, Meyer announced his return to film directing—again with an Ebert-scripted project—in July 1990, but nothing came of it.

COMPANIONS:
wife: Eve Meyer. Model, actor; married in 1952; divorced in 1970; died in plane crash in 1977
wife: Edy Williams. Actor; married in 1970; divorced
Kitten Natividad. Actor; no longer together

Debra Angela Masson. Born c. 1960; together since 1985; assaulted Meyer in 1998 when he reportedly refused to give her $50,000; sentenced to three years' probation and told to attend 104 meetings of A.A. as well as undergo one year of counseling for domestic abuse

MILESTONES:
Was a combat photographer during World War II
Worked in industrial film in the San Francisco area
1955: Was a still photographer for "Guys and Dolls"
1956: Worked as a still photographer on "Giant"
Shot pin-ups for *Playboy*
1959: Directed first feature, "The Immortal Mr. Teas"; the film cost $24,000 and grossed $1 million
1961: Helmed "Eve and the Handyman", starring then-wife Eve Meyer; also directed the erotic anthology "Eroticon"
1963: Directed the erotic feature "Heavenly Bodies"
1965: Helmed the cult classic "Faster, Pussycat! Kill! Kill!" starring Tura Satana as one of a trio of buxom brutes wreaking havoc on a desert road trip
1967: Had producer, director, editor, director of photography and story credits for the erotic melodrama "Good Morning, and

Goodbye!", a story about a wealthy farmer and his dissatisfied young wife

1969: Was director, producer, screenwriter and editor of the menage a trois feature "Cherry, Harry and Raquel"

Signed deal with 20th Century Fox

1970: Directed the psychedelic sex romp "Beyond the Valley of the Dolls", scripted by Roger Ebert

1973: Was producer, director, screenwriter and second unit camera operator for the campy adventure "Blacksnake!"

1974: Produced, directed, wrote and was cinematographer of "Super Vixens"

1976: Directed, produced and edited the erotic comedy "Up!"

1979: Helmed his last feature to date, "Beneath the Valley of the Ultravixens"; was also producer, screenwriter and featured in a cameo role

1987: Had a cameo as a video salesman in a Jon Landis-directed segment of the 1987 comedy anthology "Amazon Women on the Moon"

QUOTES:

"He understood that sex was fun. His women had an exuberance and vitality you rarely see in film anymore."—controversial feminist author Camille Paglia on Russ Meyer, quoted in *Entertainment Weekly*, April 5, 1996.

"I love big-breasted women with wasp waists. I love them with big cleavages. I love the perspiration between their cleavages. . . . "
—Russ Meyer quoted in the London *Times*, May 23, 1999.

BIBLIOGRAPHY:

"A Clean Breast: The Life & Loves of Russ Meyer" Adolf Schwartz, 1992

"Russ Meyer—The Life and Films" David K. Frasier 1990, McFarland; "a biography and a comprehensive, illustrated and annotated filmography and bibliography"—from publisher's catalogue

Oscar Micheaux

BORN: in Metropolis, Illinois, 01/02/1884

DEATH: in North Carolina, 04/01/1951

NATIONALITY: American

AWARD: Directors Guild of America Golden Jubilee Special Award 1986; awarded posthumously; cited with Akira Kurosawa and Federico Fellini

BIOGRAPHY

The most prolific black—if not independent—filmmaker in American cinema, Oscar Micheaux wrote, produced and directed nearly forty feature-length films between 1919 and 1948. Despite his importance to black cinema, Micheaux remains an enigmatic and ignored figure; few of his films have survived. In addition, his controversial racial beliefs and technically inferior films make him difficult to interpolate within mainstream film history.

The fifth child in a family of eleven, Micheaux worked as a shoeshine boy, farm laborer and Pullman porter until 1904, when he purchased a homestead in South Dakota. Within nine years, he had expanded his holdings to 500 acres and also written, published and distributed the first of ten semi-autobiographical novels, "The Conquest" (1913).

In 1918, the Lincoln Film Company in Nebraska—one of the first all-black companies that arose in response to D.W. Griffith's "The Birth of a Nation" (1915)—offered to film Micheaux's 1917 novel, "The Homesteader." But when Lincoln refused to produce the film on the scale that he desired, Micheaux responded by founding his own production company and shooting the work himself in the abandoned Selig studio in Chicago. The film opened in Chicago in 1919.

Micheaux worked successfully and prolifically throughout the next decade, largely thanks to the promotional techniques he had developed in selling his own novels. With script in hand he would tour ghetto theaters across the nation, soliciting advances from owners and thus circumventing the cash-flow and distribution problems that limited other all-black companies to producing only one or two pictures.

When the advent of sound (with its attendant high costs), Hollywood's move into the production of all-black musicals and the Depression combined to bring about the demise of independent black cinema in the early 1930s, Micheaux alone survived. (He did declare bankruptcy in 1928, forcing him thereafter to depend increasingly on white backers.) He released his first "talkie," "The Exile", in 1931.

The increasing controversy surrounding Micheaux's films, especially "God's Step Children" (1938), and his unsuccessful attempts to imitate Hollywood genre movies brought his career to a halt in 1940. He staged a disastrous comeback in 1948 with "The Betrayal" and died three years later while on a promotional tour of the South.

Micheaux offered audiences a black version of Hollywood fare, complete with actors typecast as the "black Valentino" or the "sepia Mae West." But because he operated under financial and technical restraints, his films were poorly lighted and edited. Non-professional actors were used, and scenes were often shot in one take, leading to inevitable "flubs." Micheaux incorporated these limitations into a unique style that added a self-conscious element to his films: errors were included "to give the audience a laugh," continuity defied expectation, and narrative was often abandoned in favor of sheer excess.

Above all, Micheaux saw his films as "propaganda" designed to "uplift the race." In the 1930s, however, black critics and audiences rejected his message as racially ambivalent. His bourgeois ideology of the "self-made man" found expression in all-black casts in which the light-skinned blacks succeeded, while the rest were blamed for their own oppression. Nevertheless, his films represented a radical departure from Hollywood's portrayal of blacks as servants and brought diverse images of ghetto life and related social issues to the screen for the first time.

MILESTONES:

Lived in Chicago in the early 1900s

Became sole black man to obtain a land claim in Gregory, South Dakota; obtained 500 acres of land and worked as a homesteader

1908: Wrote first novel "The Conquest"

1916: Approached by Noble and George Johnson who wanted to purchase screen rights to one of his novels, "The Homesteader"

1919: Feature directorial debut with film version of "The Homesteader"; first full-length feature produced by an American black

1925: Directed Paul Robeson in "Body and Soul"

1931: First talking film, "The Exile"

1948: Made last film, "The Betrayal"

QUOTES:

Only 10 of the 43 films (27 silents and 16 talkies) Micheaux made are commercially available; the majority have been classified as "lost." Prints of two silents, "Within Our Gates" (1919) and "The Symbol of the Unconquered" (1920), were discovered and restored in the late 1990s.

"I think of Micheaux as the Black Pioneer of American film—not because he was a black man, or because in his youth he pioneered the American West, or because he was the greatest figure in "race" movies and an unjustly ignored force in early American cinema. Micheaux is America's Black Pioneer in the way that Andre

Breton was Surrealism's Black Pope. His movies throw our history and movies into an alien and startling disarray"—J. Hoberman in "Bad Movies"—6–10–02 Time.com

BIBLIOGRAPHY:

"The Conquest: The Story of a Negro Pioneer" Oscar Micheaux, 1913

"The Homesteader: A Novel" Oscar Micheaux, 1917; reworking of "The Conquest"

"The Wind From Nowhere" Oscar Micheaux; novel

"The Case of Mrs. Wingate" Oscar Micheaux, 1945

"The Story of Dorothy Standfield" Oscar Micheaux, 1946

"Masquerade: A Historical History" Oscar Micheaux, 1947; novel

"Black Novelist as White Racist: The Myth of Black Inferiority in the Novels of Oscar Micheaux" Joseph A. Young, 1989, Greenwood Press

"Oscar Micheaux: A Biography: Dakota Homesteader, Author, Pioneer Film Maker" Betti Carol VanEpps-Taylor, 1999, Mariah Press

"Writing Himself into History: Oscar Micheaux, His Silent Films, and His Audiences" Pearl Bowser and Louise Spence, 2000, Rutgers University Press

"Straight Lick: The Cinema of Oscar Micheaux" J. Ronald Green, 2000, Indiana University Press

Anthony Minghella

BORN: in Ryde, Isle of Wight, England, 01/06/1954

NATIONALITY: English

EDUCATION: University of Hull, Hull, Yorkshire, England, English and drama, BA, 1975

AWARDS: Plays and Players London Theatre Critics Award Most Promising Playwright "A Little Like Drowning" 1984

Plays and Players London Theatre Critics Award Best Play "Made in Bangkok" 1986; awarded by the London Theater Critics

Evening Standard Award Most Promising New Writer "Truly, Madly, Deeply" 1991

BAFTA Award Best Original Screenplay "Truly, Madly, Deeply" 1991

Australian Film Institute Award Best Foriegn Film "Truly, Madly, Deeply" 1992; initial presentation of the award

Society of Texas Film Critics Award Best Adapted Screenplay "The English Patient" 1996

Broadcast Film Critics Association Award Best Director "The English Patient" 1996

Broadcast Film Critics Association Award Best Screenplay "The English Patient" 1996

Golden Satellite Best Motion Picture Screenplay (Adaptation) "The English Patient" 1996; initial presentation of the award

Directors Guild of America Award Outstanding Directorial Achievement in Feature Film "The English Patient" 1996

Oscar Best Director "The English Patient" 1996

BAFTA Award Best Film "The English Patient" 1996 shared award with producer Saul Zaentz

BAFTA Award Best Adapted Screenplay "The English Patient" 1996

National Board of Review Award Best Director "The Talented Mr. Ripley" 1999

ShoWest Director of the Year 2000

BIOGRAPHY

Anthony Minghella grew up as the child of Italian immigrants living on the Isle of Wight in Great Britain, so it is hardly surprising that the dominant theme of the outsider is found in the handful of films he has written and directed in the 1990s. From the woman haunted by her dead lover in "Truly, Madly, Deeply" (1990) to the scarred titular character in "The English Patient" (1996) to the charming psychopath in "The Talented Mr. Ripley" (1999), each of the main characters in a Minghella film is a foreigner in a landscape that is both wondrous and threatening.

As a youngster, Minghella assisted his parents in the operation of their ice cream franchise but harbored dreams of a career as a writer. Despite his family's initial objection, he persevered and attended the University of Hull where he majored in English and drama. Also interested in music, Minghella wrote songs and it was an attempt to create a showcase for some of his ditties that led him to pursue a writing career. At the same time, he began directing for the stage while supporting himself as an academic at his alma mater. With the 1981 success of his play "Whale Music", his career began in earnest with commissions for radio and television plays coming in as supplements to his theatrical ventures. The West End production of his examination of the exploitation of women in Thailand, "Made in Bangkok", brought further notice and a citation for Best Play from the London Critics' Circle.

Although he penned several episodes of the popular mystery series "Inspector Morse", Minghella began to truly come into his own as a screenwriter when he was tapped by Jim Henson to script segments of the children's fantasy "The Storyteller" (NBC, 1987–88). Among his beguiling entries in the series were "Hans, the Hedgehog", "Fearnot" and "The Luck Child" and the series' Emmy Award win owed considerably to his light but thoughtful touch. (Several "lost" episodes dealing with Greek myths were aired in the USA on the cable network HBO in 1997.) Minghella continued his association with the Muppet creator when "The Storyteller" was folded into "The Jim Henson Hour" (NBC, 1989). That same year, he penned "Living with Dinosaurs" which

aired on British TV and featured Juliet Stevenson. Impressed with the actress' range and talent, Minghella penned "Truly, Madly, Deeply" expressly for her, assuming the director's chair and making an auspicious debut. This modestly budgeted film about a bereaved woman (Stevenson) who literally wills her dead lover (Alan Rickman) back to life echoed the themes of his work for Henson while exhibiting his growing interest in depicting the outsider. Despite its coy premise, the film transcends via its strong script and fine performances.

Hollywood inevitably beckoned and after working on drafts of the William Hurt vehicle "The Doctor" (1991), Minghella tackled his first studio film, "Mr. Wonderful" (1993). Working from a script by Amy Schor and Amy Polon, he fashioned a whimsical romantic comedy about a man (Matt Dillon) who falls back in love with his ex-wife (Annabella Sciorra) while trying to fix her up with another man. Although the box-office results were disappointing, the director's reputation for character development was duly noted. While he perhaps seemed an appropriate choice to tackle the screenplay adaptation of Michael Ondaatje's dense but poetic novel "The English Patient" (1996), Minghella was hardly the obvious choice to direct. Managing to forge a cogent script from what some felt was unfilmable fiction, he crafted a movie that combined the sweep and grandeur of a David Lean epic (complete with appropriately gorgeous desert cinematography by John Seale) with the romantic intimacy of a Frank Borzage drama (embodied by the actors Ralph Fiennes, Kristin Scott Thomas and Juliette Binoche). "The English Patient", which centered on a Hungarian man burned beyond recognition and was thus a dual alien, integrated several storylines told via flashbacks and memories and tapped into an audience looking for a literate love story. Backed by Miramax, the film earned an impressive 12 Academy Award nominations and took home nine statues, including Best Picture and one for Minghella as Best Director. (Ironically, his greatest achievement, the script, lost to Billy Bob Thornton's "Sling Blade".)

Although he could have had his pick of follow-up projects, Minghella decided to direct a project on which he had originally be tapped to write. Prior to lensing "The English Patient", he had begun adapting Patricia Highsmith's novel "The Talented Mr. Ripley", following the exploits of another outsider who covets the life of a wealthy playboy enough to consider murder. Having spent so long nurturing the script and tweaking Highsmith's original story (previously filmed in 1960 by Rene Clement as "Plein Soleil/Purple Noon"), Minghella did not to relinquish control to another director. After considering numerous performers for the pivotal title role, he settled on rising talent Matt Damon. Rounding out the cast were Gwyneth Paltrow, Cate Blanchett and Jude Law. Again, the writer-director made a well-acted "intimate epic" filmed against a dazzling background (Seale once again served as cinematographer). Although some fans of the book carped over the changes (i.e., Blanchett's character does not appear in the novel, Jack Davenport's plays a lesser role), most reviews were respectful if not overly praising. Minghella forged ahead, penning the adaptation of another popular novel, "Cold Mountain" (in development as of 2000), which followed the struggle of a wounded Confederate soldier attempting to return to his wife during the American Civil War.

MILESTONES:

Raised on the Isle of Wight

1975: Made stage directing debut with own play "Mobius the Stripper" in Hull, England

1976–1981: Was lecturer in drama at University of Hull

1981: Enjoyed modest success with play "Whale Music"

1983: Wrote teleplays for the British series "Studio"

1986: Earned notice for his West End debut,

"Made in Bangkok", about the exploitation of women in Thailand

1986: Scripted the British teleplay "What If It's Raining?"

Wrote for the English TV series, "Inspector Morse"

Wrote for the series "The Storyteller" (NBC), produced by Jim Henson; some episodes not previously aired on the USA debuted on HBO in 1997; debuted with award-winning episode "Hans My Hedgehog"

1988: Penned the BBC radio play "Cigarettes and Chocolate"

1989: Wrote for "The Jim Henson Hour" (NBC)

1989: Scripted the British TV-movie "Living with Dinosaurs", starring Juliet Stevenson

1990: Feature directorial debut, "Truly, Madly, Deeply"; also scripted; reunited with Juliet Stevenson; shown at the London Film Festival; released theatrically worldwide in 1991

Wrote draft of "The Doctor", directed by Randa Haines; did not receive final screen credit

1993: First American film, "Mr. Wonderful", featuring Matt Dillon

1996: International breakthrough feature, "The English Patient"; film received 12 Academy Award nominations and won nine, including Best Picture and Best Director

1999: Adapted and directed "The Talented Mr. Ripley", a based on a Patricia Highsmith novel; material had been been previously filmed by Rene Clement in 1960 as "Plein Soleil/Purple Noon"

2000: Became partner with Sydney Pollack in Mirage Enterprises

Wrote screenplay and directed feature adaptation of Charles Frazier's Civil War-era novel "Cold Mountain" (lensed 2002)

QUOTES:

Made a Commander of the Order of the British Empire in June 2001.

"I directed before I wrote. When I was a student, I was directing. I had no thoughts of becoming a writer. My thoughts were about how to make music, how to direct music, how to be involved as a musician and a director in the theater and film, or something. I had written a series of songs that I wanted to lace together into some event to direct, and in lacing together, I found myself writing scenes. And what happened was I found something in that process which really intrigued me, and almost accidentally found myself writing for a living. And the thing that I would say without any hesitation is I'm a writer who directs. I think it would be tragic for me if I didn't direct another film; I think it would be impossible for me to stop writing."—Anthony Minghella quoted in *Written By*, March 1997.

"I made a pact with John Seale, the cinematographer, and production designer Stuart Craig that we would never invest in the landscape. There is no shot in the film ["The English Patient"] which begins on some gorgeous scenery or bit of architecture. We were interested only in that activity generated by character which requires you to look beyond an elbow or a neck."—Anthony Minghella quoted in the London *Times*, March 3, 1997.

On his screenplay for "The English Patient", Minghella told the London *Times* (March 3, 1997): "The camera is so prosaic that the film required a full frame, a much denser architecture than the novel. I suppose there's a certain literalness to the way I've done the screenplay—although, in relation to other screenplays, it's wild."

"Yes, we weren't keen at first [on Minghella's decision to pursue a career in the arts and not to work in the ice cream business], his mother was horrified, but how could we have anticipated what would happen."—Edward Minghella (Anthony's father) to the London *Times*, March 26, 1997.

"The advantage I have when I walk on a set with my own writing is that I know every beat and impulse and nuance of it because it's come directly through me, and so there's nothing I don't know about the screenplay. It means I'm free to let go of it completely."—Minghella to *DGA Magazine*, May–June 1997.

"I was trained as an academic, but my instincts as a writer are unintellectual. There's nothing 'from the head' when I go to make movies. I'm interested in emotional journeys rather than theoretical ones. 'The Talented Mr. Ripley', for instance, is very influenced by Italian filmmakers like Fellini, De Sica, the Taviani brothers and Rossellini, whose movies have an enormous spirit of humanity that doesn't judge, doesn't simplify. I love that, and I think that like them, 'Ripley' has an operatic edge to it—it's naked, raw and emotional."—Minghella quoted in *Movieline*, December 1999–January 2000.

Stephen Rebello: . . . Have you found yourself surprised, delighted, bemused by what projects were offered you?

Anthony Minghella: No, because I knew what I was going to do next. I'm not really in the marketplace for the kind of opportunities which accrue to directors who have some success. I'm not for hire. There's nobody and nothing in "The English Patient" I didn't want in it, and it was made entirely the way I wanted, If it didn't work, it was my problem. I fell entirely the same about "Ripley." I'll stand passionately by the result.

—From *Movieline*, December 1999–January 2000.

"He's the infra-red end of the spectrum of collaboration. Ultra-violet is someone like Milos Forman, who has a team of editors and tells them how to make every cut. Anthony gives me freedom and responsibility. But he asks for advice from everyone on the picture. He even asked Miramax and Paramount! He listens to everyone, and when people really think you're listening they'll give you strange and valuable ideas. But when we're editing it's just the two of us. There is no other stage after us, and really what I feel we're doing is completing the script-writing process."—editor

Walter Murch on working with Anthony Minghella to David Thomson in *The New York Times*, December 19, 1999.

On why he had to direct "The Talented Mr. Ripley" for which he wrote the screenplay before directing "The English Patient", Minghella told Eric Harrison of the *Los Angeles Times* (December 19, 1999): "I felt such a profound connection with the material that I couldn't bear the thought of somebody else doing it."

Vincente Minnelli

BORN: Lester Anthony Minnelli in Chicago, Illinois, 02/28/1903

DEATH: in Beverly Hills, California, 07/25/1986

NATIONALITY: American

EDUCATION: left school aged 16

AWARDS: Golden Globe Award Best Director "Gigi" 1958

Director's Guild of America Award Best Director "Gigi" 1958

Oscar Best Director "Gigi" 1958

BIOGRAPHY

Vincente Minnelli directed some of the most celebrated entertainments in cinema history, including "Meet Me in St. Louis" (1944), "Father of the Bride" (1950), "An American in Paris" (1951), "The Bad and the Beautiful" (1952), "The Band Wagon" (1953), "Lust for Life" (1956) and "Gigi" (1958). Nevertheless, serious commentary on his work has, until recently, been sparse, partly because of the "glossy" nature of his films. Minnelli's first jobs in show business were as costume and set designer; the sophistication he would bring to the American stage and film musical was always redolent of "Vogue" or "Vanity Fair," and it is no accident that he once directed a charming comedy entitled "Designing Woman" (1957). Even one of his dramatic films, "The Cobweb" (1955), involves neurotic tensions that begin to break out in a psychiatric clinic when new drapes are selected for the common room.

Minnelli was born into a theatrical family; his parents and his uncle operated a tent show that toured the Midwest. As a young man he became a costume and set designer for the Balaban and Katz theater chain in Chicago and in 1931 he moved to New York, where he worked for Radio City Music Hall, eventually graduating in 1935 to directing Broadway musicals. After a brief, abortive stay as a producer at Paramount in the late thirties, he was brought permanently to Hollywood in 1940 by producer Arthur Freed, who was assembling his own unit at MGM. Under Freed's sponsorship, he directed his first film, the underrated all-black musical "Cabin in the Sky" (1943). Minnelli remained at MGM for two decades, specializing in musicals, domestic comedies, and melodramas. Minnelli kept files on different styles of painting, and he liked to run through them for inspiration. He particularly admired the surrealists and was among the first Hollywood directors to appropriate their motifs. He was not, however, a painterly filmmaker. He loved flamboyant color, costume, and decor, but he never allowed those elements to freeze into static compositions. A master of changing patterns and complex movements, he filled his pictures with swooping crane shots, swirling patterns of fabric and light, with a skillful orchestration of background detail. A sensitive director of actors, he elicited some of the best performances from such diverse players as Judy Garland (his wife from 1945–51 and mother of his daughter, Liza Minnelli), Spencer Tracy and Kirk Douglas.

The imagination or one of its surrogates, such as show business or dreaming, was Minnelli's favorite subject. His central female characters live in fantasy worlds, finding happiness only when they exchange dreams for artifice; his leading men usually play writers, painters, or performers, and if they are not artistic types by profession they tend to be dandies or sensitive youths. By the same token, his films generally take place in studio-manufactured settings, where the boundaries between fantasy and everyday life are blurred. Even when his films are set in small-town America, they tend to burst into remarkable dream-like passages, such as the Halloween sequence in "Meet Me in St. Louis," the berserk carnival in "Some Came Running" (1958) and the mythic boar hunt in "Home From the Hill" (1960). The ultimate tribute to Minnelli is that few directors in the history of Hollywood have made so many consistently enjoyable, diverse films.

FAMILY:
father: Vincent Minnelli. Musical conductor
daughter: Liza Minnelli. Singer, actor; born on March 12, 1946; mother, Judy Garland; appeared in father's 1976 film "A Matter of Time"

COMPANIONS:
wife: Judy Garland. Actor, singer; married in 1945; divorced in 1951; directed her in four films including "Meet Me in St. Louis" (1944)

BIBLIOGRAPHY:
"I Remember It Well" Vincente Minnelli, 1974

Hayao Miyazaki

BORN: in Tokyo, Japan, 01/05/1941

SOMETIMES CREDITED AS:
Telecom

NATIONALITY: Japanese

EDUCATION: Omiya Elementary School, Tokyo, Japan
Eifuku Elementary School, Tokyo, Japan
Omiya Junior High School, Tokyo, Japan 1956
Toyotama High School, Tokyo, Japan 1959
Gakushuin University Tokyo, Japan; politcal science and economics 1963

AWARDS: Japanese Academy Award Best Picture "Princess Mononoke" 1997 first animated film ever to receive the award
Berlin Film Festival Golden Bear "Sen to Chihiro no Kamikakushi/Spirited Away" 2002 tied with Paul Greengrass' "Bloody Sunday"
Oscar Best Animated Feature Film 'Sen to Chihiro no Kamikakushi/Spirited Away" 2002

BIOGRAPHY
Long acknowledged as the preeminent animator and director in Japan, Hayao Miyazaki remained a cult figure to American devotees of "manga" (Japanese comic books) and "anime" (Japanese animated features) until the 1999 US release of his undisputed masterwork "Princess Mononoke" (1997). Acquired by Miramax and redubbed into English using a script by Neal Gaiman and the vocal talents of actors like Billy Bob Thornton, Claire Danes, Billy Crudup and Minnie Driver, "Princess Mononoke" introduced the richly crafted animation and superb storytelling to mainstream audiences. The film was deemed too violent for

young children used to Disney cartoons filled with cheery anthropomorphic sidekicks and sing-along musical scores but their older siblings and parents could marvel at the detailed set pieces and enjoy the three-dimensional characters, who were neither true blue heroes nor all black villains. Miyazaki's anime classic explored big themes like man versus nature and good versus evil but they were couched in mythology and memorable visuals.

Born in Tokyo in January 1941, Hayao Miyazaki spent his formative years in the capital city. His father's family owned an airplane parts factory and that small matter had a great impact on the future filmmaker in developing his particularly unique animation style. A Miyazaki feature often contains aerial shots that swoop and soar which in turn are contrasted by segments of quietude and intimacy which serve to heighten the fantastical elements of the tales. During his childhood, his mother was confined to bed with spinal tuberculosis and Miyazaki later paid her homage in "My Neighbor Totoro" (1988), which focused on two sisters whose mother has been hospitalized.

From his earliest childhood, Miyazaki was fascinated by drawing, particularly models of airplanes but when it came to sketching people, he was less than successful. Rather than pursue his hobby, he enrolled as a political science and economics major at Gakushuin University. But his desire to draw finally won out and following his matriculation, Miyazaki landed work at Toei Animation, where he served an apprenticeship before being assigned to work as an in-betweener on the 1963 feature "Wan Wan Chushingura/Watchdog Bow Wow" and the TV series "Okami Shonen Ken/Wolf Boy Ken" (1963–65). The latter marked his first collaboration with Isao Takahata with whom he would later collaborate before forming Studio GHIBLI together in 1985. The pair worked together as animator (Miyazaki) and director (Takahata) on such varied projects as the TV series "Hassuru Panchi/Hustle

Punch" (1965–66) and the feature "Taiyo no Ouji—Horus no Diboken/Prince of the Sun—The Great Adventure of Horus/Little Norse Prince Valiant" (1968).

In the 70s, Miyazaki left Toei and joined Takahata at A-Pro and then moved to Zuiyo Pictures, all the while dividing his attentions between features and TV. As the decade waned, he moved into the director's chair for 16 episodes of the series "Mirai Shonen Konan/Conan, The Boy in Future" (1978), also assisting in character design and development. In 1980, Miyazaki joined Telecom as an animation instructor and used the company's name as a pseudonym when he helmed two episodes of the series "Rupan Sansei—Cagliostro no Shiro/Lupin III: Castle of Cagliostro." While he was originally set to make his feature directorial debut with "Ritoru Nimo/Little Nemo" in 1982, he left the project during pre-production. That year, he created his initial manga entry "Kaze no Tani no Nausicaa/Nausicaa of the Valley of the Wind", which became the basis for his first film in 1984.

"Nausicaa of the Valley of the Wind" contains the archetypes of all of the animator's future work: a smart heroine, swooping sequences that recreate the experience of flying, ecological themes, and dilemma and characters that are neither all villainous or all heroic. This film's story, set in a post-apocalyptic future, concerns a princess attempting to protect her subjects from two larger warring powers, in the process aiding in diffusing an potential ecological disaster. A critical and commercial success in Japan, "Nausicaa" gave Miyazaki the resources to co-found his own animation studio (Studio GHIBLI) under whose auspices his second film "Tenkuu no Shiro Rapyuta/Laputa: The Castle in the Sky" (1986) was produced. Again working as screenwriter and director, Miyazaki crafted a fanciful tale of a mysterious girl who literally falls from the sky into a bleak industrial town. Notable for its delicate, almost watercolor-like backgrounds and its spectacular flying sequences, the film proved popular in his native land.

Miyazaki moved away from the timeless to the 1950s of his childhood for his next feature "Tonari no Totoro/My Neighbor Totoro" (1988), In what many see as a tribute to his mother, he tells the tale of two young girls (whose own mother has been hospitalized) who discover a magical world in an abandoned house. Episodic and leisurely paced, "My Neighbor Totoro" again featured the animator's trademarked attention to detail, with gorgeous renderings of the Japanese countryside. (A dubbed-in-English version opened briefly in 1993 but US viewers, still primed on viewing Disney-style cartoons, were less than embracing.) The similarly conceived "Majo no Takkyubin/Kiki's Delivery Service" (1989), about a young witch who opens a flying delivery service in a seaside town, also suffered from a lack of a strong story. Nevertheless, the elaborate flying sequences as well as the detailed depiction of the backgrounds, replete with crowds, served as compensation. ("Kiki's Delivery Service" was also dubbed into English and released direct-to-video in the USA in 1998). Airborne sequences also played important roles in the story of "Kurenai no Buta/Porco Rosso" (1992), which followed a WWI Italian flying ace (who happened to be a talking pig!) who abandons the military during the rise of Fascism in favor of becoming a bounty hunter. Capitalizing on Miyazaki's long-held interest in aviation and mixing in some of his political views, it perhaps ranks as one of his most personal films.

Before tackling his anime masterpiece, "Mononoke Hime/Princess Mononoke", Miyazaki crafted TV advertisements and produced and wrote "Mimi wo Sumaseba/Whisper of the Heart" (1995), adapted from a manga by Aoi Hiragi and directed by Yoshifumi Kondo. By the time "Princess Mononoke" became the second highest-grossing film in Japan (behind "Titanic"), the tide had shifted in the USA.

Aficionados of anime had grown beyond a cult, fueled in part by bootlegs and dubbed versions of "Akira" (1989) and "Ghost in the Shell" (1995) as well as a revival of interest in the 60s animated series "Astro Boy" and "Speed Racer" had primed audiences. In addition, Disney faced challenges on the animation front from Warner Bros. (e.g., "The Iron Giant" 1999) and DreamWorks ("The Prince of Egypt" 1998), among others. A certain sophistication had become the norm creating a more hospitable atmosphere for Miyazaki's work.

Because of his painstaking attention to detail, the animator has suffered eyestrain over the years, and there had been rumors floated that "Princess Mononoke" would be his last film. (He later announced plans to make another film, although he would play a less active role in the more detail-heavy aspects of the work.) Perhaps stemming from the fact that it took some 20 years from initial inspiration (originally as more of a "Beauty and the Beast"–like story) to its final incarnation which tells of "the conflict between the ancient land of primeval forests and animistic gods and the then-emerging modern industrial civilization, which was a product of Japan's contact with the outside world." Without being preachy, Miyazaki posits a delicate balance between nature and industrial progress and show the effects if that balance tips too far in favor of one over the other. While his message may not to be for everyone, there was no denying the power of his images.—Written by Ted Murphy

MILESTONES:

Raised in Tokyo, Japan

1963: Hired to work as an in-betweener at Toei Douga; worked on the TV series "Okami Shonen Ken/Wolf Boy Ken" and the feature "Wan Wan Chushingura/ Watchdog Bow Wow"

1965–1968: Spent three years working on the animated feature "Prince of the Son", directed by Isao Takahata

1971: Left Toei Douga to join Takahata at A-Pro

Accompanied Yukata Fujioka to Sweden in vain attempt to secure rights to "Pippi Longstocking"

Directed or co-directed episodes of the animated TV series "Lupin III"

1973: Left A-Pro and joined Zuiyo Productions

1973: Visited Switzerland as research for "Heidi: Girl of the Alps"

1975: Traveled to Italy and Argentina for inspiration for "Three Thousand Miles in Search of Mother"

1980: Became chief instructor for animators at Telecom; used company name as pseudonym on some TV directing assignments

1982: Launched the manga serial "Nausicaa of the Valley of the Wind" in the magazine "Animage"; completed in 1984

1984: Wrote, directed and storyboarded the anime feature version of "Nausicaa of the Valley of the Wind"; after being edited, released in USA as "Warriors of the Wind" in 1986

1985: Founded Studio GHIBLI

1986: Wrote, designed and directed "Tenku no shiro Laputa/Laputa: Castle in the Sky"

1988: Designed, wrote and directed "Tonari no Totoro/My Neighbor Totoro"; an English-language dubbed version was released in the USA in 1993

1989: Produced, wrote and directed the anime "Majo no takkyubin/Kiki's Delivery Service"; dubbed English version released direct-to-video in the USA in 1998

1991: Served as producer on Takahata's "Omohide poro poro/Only Yesterday"

1992: Crafted the WWII-era romance "Porco Rosso/The Crimson Pig", about a fighter pilot who is turned into a pig

1995: Produced and scripted "Mimi wo sumaseba/Whisper of the Heart", directed by Yohifumi Kondo

1995: Directed and provided story for the rock duo Chage & Ake's music video "On Your Mark"

1997: Wrote and directed the anime "Mononoke Hime/Princess Mononoke"; Disney and Miramax purchased US distribution rights

and spent two-years preparing English-dubbed version featuring an all-star cast led by Billy Crudup, Claire Danes and Minnie Driver and released in 1999

2001: Enjoyed a box-office hit in Japan with the anime feature "Sen to Chihiro no Kamikakushi/Spirited Away"; reportedly his last feature film

AFFILIATION: Marxist (until the late 1980s)

QUOTES:

"When an idea for a project is formed, there are always market considerations—this might appeal to a certain age group, and so on. But its never the way you would expect it. Sometimes in the beginning a predictable age group will come, but the end result might be another: middle-aged men, young women, whatever. You can never be sure."—Miyazaki to Philip Brophy posted at "The Black, The White" (www.electricrain.net/NihonSun/Black&White/Interview/html)

"I'm completely baffled by the popularity of my work in America. I think it must prove that for all our superficial differences, we humans have a great deal in common."—Hayao Miyazaki through a translator to *Los Angeles Times*, October 24, 1999.

"From a pure filmmaking standpoint, hs staging, his cutting, his action scenes are some of the best ever put on film, whether animated or not."—American animator John Lasseter quoted in *The New York Times*, October 21, 1999.

"My own work has been influenced by so many different factors and films: All artists take their place in the continuing cycle of influencing and being influenced.

"In some ways, the history of art represents a great relay race, with each runner transforming the baton as he carries it. At some point, I'll be ready to hand the baton on to the next generation—if they wish to receive it."—Miyazaki quoted in *Los Angeles Times*, October 25. 1999.

"I think that if you are very genuine in doing films for young children, you must aim for their heads, not deciding for them what will be too much for them to handle. What we found was that children actually understood the movie and what we were trying to say more than the adults."—Hayao Miyazaki quoted in *The New York Times*, October 21, 1999.

"I've come to the point where I just can't make a movie without addressing the problem of humanity as part of an ecosystem."—Miyazaki quoted in *Film Comment*, November-December 1998.

Kenji Mizoguchi

BORN: in Tokyo, Japan, 05/16/1898

DEATH: in Kyoto, Japan, 08/24/1956

NATIONALITY: Japanese

EDUCATION: Aohashi Western Painting Research Institute Tokyo, Japan

AWARDS: Venice Film Festival International Prize "The Life of Oharu" 1952; one of three movies cited

Venice Film Festival Silver Lion Award "Ugetsu" 1953; one of six movies cited

Venice Film Festival Silver Lion Award "Sansho the Bailiff" 1954; award shared with Kazan's "On the Waterfront," Kurosawa's "Seven Samurai" and Fellini's "La Strada"

BIOGRAPHY

Mizoguchi's life spanned the most important years of the development of the Japanese cinema. Although he made over 85 films in a career that stretched over 30 years, over 50 of them have been lost, primarily through studio fires, the ravages of war or poor preservation methods. Those that remain include leftist-inspired "tendency films", literary adaptations, historical dramas, proto-feminist critiques, Meiji-period pieces and—from the later stage of his career—works of a more transcendental and symphonic nature.

Although there are relatively few connecting threads in Mizoguchi's varied oeuvre, one

common theme is a sympathy for the exploited and marginalized members of society, whether they be women, traveling artists, feudal servants or slaves. While often turning the camera away from moments of extreme violence, Mizoguchi rarely turned away from difficult social themes. His films have been praised for the way in which they harmonize seeming opposites—light and shadow, harshness and beauty, societal pulls and individual needs.

Mizoguchi grew up in the rougher "shita-machi" (downtown) area of Tokyo, but subsequently moved to the more genteel city of Kyoto following the 1923 Kanto earthquake. The unusual degree of empathy he felt toward women was undoubtedly influenced by his having seen both his older sister, Suzu, and his mother suffer from his father's callous treatment of them. Mizoguchi's father undoubtedly influenced the director's portrayal of the male characters in his films, who tend to be self-serving and manipulative. Similarly, his depiction of women, which had been cool and objective in early films like "Sisters of the Gion" and "Osaka Elegy" (both 1936), became much less so following the onset of his wife's madness due to syphilis in 1941.

Mizoguchi's training as a painter is apparent in the exquisite pictorial quality of his films, especially in the subtle treatment of light and in his asymmetrical composition (common to the Japanese visual arts in general). Stylistically, he is best known for his elegant use of the long take ("one scene, one shot") which was inspired by his love for the theater, by his respect for the integrity of an actor's performance and by the Japanese horizontal picture scroll ("emakimono") in which the eye gazes at each section in turn, but then moves on in an irreversible forward progression. This technique causes the viewer to vacillate between a sense of involvement in the characters on the screen, and a sense of distance which invites objective contemplation.

As a director, Mizoguchi was known as a perfectionist; the demands he made on his cast and staff are legendary. This perfectionism was tied in with his desire to immerse his actors in as perfect a setting as possible, in order to help them forget their daily existence and thus draw out of them their best performances. He attracted a loyal group of collaborators including screenwriter Yoshikata Yoda, cameraman Kazuo Miyagawa, art director Hiroshi Mizutani, music director Fumio Hayasaka and actress Kinuyo Tanaka.

Mizoguchi earned international renown when his films "The Life of Oharu" (1952), "Ugetsu Monogatari" (1953) and "Sansho the Bailiff" (1954) won top prizes at the Venice Film Festivals of those respective years. He died a few years later, in 1956, with the script for his next work, "Osaka Story", at his bedside. The film was subsequently realized by director Kozaburo Yoshimura.

Michael Moore

BORN: in Davison, Michigan, 1954

NATIONALITY: American

EDUCATION: St. Paul's Seminary, Saginaw, Michigan; left in second year after deciding he was not suited for priesthood

University of Michigan, Flint, Michigan, 1976; founded alternative school newspaper, *The Flint Voice*

AWARDS: New York Film Critics Circle Award Best Documentary "Roger & Me" 1989

Los Angeles Film Critics Association Award Best Documentary "Roger & Me" 1989; director and producer

Emmy Outstanding Informational Series "TV Nation" 1995

Boston Society of Film Critics Award Best Documentary "The Big One" 1998

Online Film Critics Award Best Documentary "The Big One" 1998

Cannes Film Festival Special 55th Anniversary prize "Bowling for Columbine" 2002; first documentary to be allowed into the competition in 50 years; only award to receive a unanimous decision from the festival jury

Writers Guild of America Award Best Original Screenplay "Bowling for Columbine 2002

Oscar Best Documentary Feature "Bowling for Columbine" 2002

Independent Spirit Awards Best Documentary "Bowling for Columbine" 2003

BIOGRAPHY

Guerrila documentarian and anti-corporate gadfly Michael Moore wields a Swiftian satirical sword in his multi-media battle against contemporary robber barons, for whom "enough" is a dirty word. Raised in working-class Flint, Michigan, the tall, burly, bespectacled filmmaker had never made more than $17,000 dollars a year when the highly profitable documentary "Roger and Me" (1989) introduced his affable manner, comforting girth and omnipresent baseball cap (usually the Detroit Tigers), catapulting the "lefty" journalist to millionaire celebrity status. Prior to that, Moore had become one of the first 18-year-olds elected to public office when he won a seat on the local school board in 1972 and went on to found and edit *The Flint Voice* (later *The Michigan Voice*). He had also served as a commentator on National Public Radio's "All Things Considered" and had a brief stint as executive editor of *Mother Jones* magazine before making his feature debut as the producer, director, writer, narrator and on-screen interviewer of "Roger and Me."

It took the self-styled Robin Hood with a camera three years and $250,000 to complete this darkly ironic film, following Moore's inspired attempts to track down General Motors chairman Roger Smith and show him how factory closings had impacted the Flint economy. (Warner Bros. acquired it for $3 million, including $25,000 for Flint's homeless families.) Along the way, he made a co-star of Sheriff's Deputy Fred Ross, who, with cool efficiency, traveled around the town proclaimed by *Money* magazine "the worst place to live in the country," pounding on doors and evicting families from their homes. Moore savagely exposed the heartlessness of the Reagan 80s, lampooning such establishment lackeys as the Reverend Robert Schuller ("Tough times don't last, tough people do") and Anita Bryant (singing a buck-up rendition of "You'll Never Walk Alone") who arrive to offer lip service as balm for the disenfranchised of Flint. Of course, there were the charges he tampered with chronology (Pauline Kael said he "improvises his own version of history" and uses "leftism as a superior attitude"), but he concocted with his non-objective cinema-verite a bit of "alternative" propaganda so entertaining it can only reside on Comedy shelves in video stores.

Following the success of "Roger and Me", Moore established the Center for Alternative Media, a foundation devoted to supporting independent filmmakers and social action groups. He also made a short "sequel", "Pets or Meat: The Return to Flint" (1992), revisiting Bunny Lady Rhonda Britto from "Roger and Me", before venturing into TV with a summer replacement series—the irreverent "TV Nation" (NBC, 1994). Working with three partners (Columbia TriStar TV, the BBC, and NBC), Moore served as executive producer and anchor, as well as writing, directing and reporting segments of the left-leaning newsmag which earned the 1995 Emmy as Outstanding Informational Series. Despite critical acclaim, "TV Nation", which also aired in England. remained merely a summer replacement, and though Fox revived the series in the summer of 1995, that network also chose not to pick it up for the regular season. Moore's merry band of troublemakers included Janeane Garofalo, Steven Wright and investigative reporter Crackers the Corporate Crime Chicken, opining on such subjects as pets on Prozac, a real-estate broker pushing houses along a toxic dump site, a day with Dr. Death (Jack Kevorkian) and Avon ladies in the Amazon.

Moore segued into fiction films with "Canadian Bacon" (1995), a fanciful political satire in which the USA declares war on its northern neighbor, and though the writer-director claimed it tested badly because audiences were reluctant to laugh at or laugh with the late comic John Candy in his final screen appearance, critics almost universally panned it for its dearth of yucks. The one-man insurrection rebounded nicely with a return to guerrilla tactics for "The Big One", pointing out in true killjoy fashion that, despite the much-ballyhooed economic boom of the 90s, there were people all across the nation suffering labor pains resulting from the capricious decisions of their employers. On the 47-city book tour promoting his best-selling 1996 book "Downsize This! Random Threats from an Unarmed American", Moore journeyed to Centralia, Illinois, where a good year at the Payday candy bar factory (a $20 million dollar profit) had enabled ownership to sell the company, resulting in the plant's closing, prompting Moore to say, "In other words, if the workers had done a lousy job, and the plant only made

$100,000 dollars in profit . . . " and the manager finished his sentence: "They'd have had to keep it open."

The rabble-rousing Moore had great fun writing checks like the one for 80 cents ("The first hours wage for a Mexican worker") he tried to present to Johnson Products of Milwaukee along with a Downsizer of the Year Award. There was a $100 check for Pat Buchanan's presidential campaign from Abortionists for Buchanan and checks from Satan Worshippers for Dole, Pedophiles for Free Trade (Perot) and Hemp Growers for Clinton, but the big coup of "The Big One" was his on-camera corralling of Nike CEO Phil Knight. Unlike Roger Smith, who had consistently dodged the dogged Moore, Knight welcomed the pesky miscreant with open arms, then, amazingly enough, spoke with more candor than business savvy about his company's use of cheap Indonesian labor (some workers as young as 14) to manufacture its trendy sneakers. Nike's attempt at damage control after the "horse was out of the barn" did not move Moore to remove the CEO's imprudent comments, though a deal could have been struck if Knight had acceded to the filmmaker's request that he build a factory in Flint. Knight, however, remained true to his original statement that "Flint's not on our radar screen."

Moore next turned up on TV with "The Awful Truth" (Bravo, 1999–), claiming: "I loved 'TV Nation', but 'The Awful Truth' is the show that we always wanted to do but could never get past the censors." Crackers the Corporate Crime-Fighting Chicken also returned, and the humor was darker than ever. For one segment, he invited the employees of an HMO that denied a transplant to a sick man to attend the man's funeral—before his death, so thoroughly embarrassing the company [Humana] that it reconsidered in the man's favor. Other stunts included leading a merry bunch of carolers—sans voice boxes due to laryngeal cancer—to the homes and offices of tobacco executives and

attempts to give Bill Gates a weed-wacker and some Martha Stewart sheets for the multi-billionaire's new $60 million house, not to mention trying to find a date for Hillary Clinton once she is "officially free" in 2001. Moore's brand of satire may even be more popular in England where Channel 4, who had first seen the merit of "Roger and Me" but had delayed sending a promised 20,000 pounds to edit it, wasted no time outbidding the BBC to commission the uncensored 12-part series.

In 2002, Moore produced the documentary "Bowling for Columbine," a characteristically sardonic examination of America's gun-obsessed culture. Moore received a special Award at the Cannes Film Festival for his film (which marked the first time a documentary was allowed into the festival in 50 years) as well as an Academy Award for Best Documentary Feature.

MILESTONES:

1972: Became one of the first 18-year-olds in the country elected to public office when he won a seat on his local school board

1976: Founded a crisis intervention center

1976–1986: At age 22, founded and edited an alternative newspaper *The Flint Voice* (later *The Michigan Voice*)

Was producer and host of a weekly radio show, "Radio Free Flint"

1985: Appeared as a commentator on National Public Radio's "All Things Considered"

1986: Appointed executive editor of *Mother Jones,* one of the largest circulation political magazines in the USA

1986: Fired from *Mother Jones* for refusing to run a particular article

1986: Started production company, Dog Eat Dog Films

Worked as a principal interviewer and production coordinator on "Blood in the Face" (originally titled "Right Thinking"), a documentary feature about modern white supremacist organization directed by Anne

Bohlen, Kevin Rafferty, and James Ridgeway (released 1991)

Won a "modest" settlement in his wrongful discharge suit againt *Mother Jones*

Spent three years preparing his filmmaking debut, "Roger and Me"; budgeted at $260,000

1989: Paid an estimated $3 million by Warner Bros for the acquisition of "Roger and Me", including $25,000 for homeless families affected by the closing of General Motors

1989: Feature debut as producer, director, screenwriter, on-screen interviewer, and narrator of "Roger and Me", a darkly humorous documentary

1991: Wrote the forward to Ben Hamper's well-reviewed collection of essays, "Rivethead: Tales from the Assemblyline"

1992: Produced, directed, scripted and appeared in the documentary short "Pets or Meat: The Return to Flint", a sequel to "Roger and Me"

1992: TV debut, directing and appearing in a segment of "Rock the Vote", a Fox variety special designed to get young people to register to vote

1994: Served as creator, executive producer, director, writer and correspondent for NBC's "TV Nation", an irreverent, opinionated, magazine show; aired during the summer

1995: "TV Nation" revived by Fox TV for the summer season

1995: Feature fiction writing-directing debut, the disappointing "Canadian Bacon", John Candy's last film

1998: Directed documentary satire of corporate America, "The Big One"

Wrote and executive produced the CBS comedy pilot "Better Days" (filmed in 1998), starring James Belushi and Chris Elliott as laid-off Wisconsin auto workers

1999: Appeared in cameo role in Ron Howard's "EDTV"

1999: Executive produced and appeared in the newsmagazine "The Awful Truth"; made for Britain's Channel 4 and aired in the USA on Bravo

2000: Had acting role in Nora Ephron's "Lucky Numbers"

2002: Published "Stupid White Men . . . and Other Sorry Excuses for the State of the Nation!" which became a *New York Times* Bestseller

2002: Examined American's gun culture in the award-winning documentary "Bowling for Columbine"

2002: Signed a $3 million book deal with Time Warner Book Group

AFFILIATION: Founder, Center for Alternative Media. Moore used the profits from "Roger and Me" to create this foundation dedicated to the support of independent filmmakers and social action groups.

QUOTES:

Michael Moore stands 6'3".

Moore has published articles in *The Columbia Journalism Review, Newsday, The Nation, Los Angeles Times* and *Detroit Free Press.*

His website address is www.michael-moore.com

Among Moore's other targets was literary agent Lucianne Goldberg who was involved in the Monica Lewinsky–Linda Tripp–Bill Clinton scandal. Moore created a website (www.iseelucy .com) which pointed a camera at Goldberg's NYC apartment. In retaliation, she put up signs espousing support of tabloid publications like *The National Enquirer* and *The Star.*

Moore on the irony of NBC, a subsidiary of General Motors, allowing him to have his own anti-Establishment, left-leaning TV show:

"It's been proven over 40 years of TV that networks will put on anything if they believe it'll get an audience. . . . I'm just the opposite extreme of 'Manimal' or 'ALF'."—From *Entertainment Weekly,* July 15, 1994.

"The thing that has surprised me the most is that people whom you would consider fellow travelers in the left-of-center political end of the spectrum are usually the ones who will attack you the most. Like, where's our Bob Dole? Who's our barracuda who's gonna fight for US? Now that I'm doing interviews for 'TV Nation' people have been asking me to describe myself politically. My politics come from Flint, Michigan, from my family, who are workers. Whatever I believe in and care about was formed in that kind of upbringing. As far as dealing with success on a personal level, I've done that by maintaining the same friends and relationships I've had for the past decade or two. You know, I'm still in the same relationship I was in thirteen years ago."—Michael Moore quoted in "The Moore, the Merrier" by Karen Duffy, *Interview*, September 1994.

"Why is it that during this time of great economic recovery, families are being evicted, and 68 percent of the kids in the Flint school district are still eligible for federal lunch programs, which means they live below the poverty level? On the surface things look good, but if you peel back the layers, personal bankruptcies are at an all-time high, there are 40 million people without health care. The one-third who are doing really well right now are doing it on the backs of the other two-thirds, and that's the story which is not being written."—Moore to *The Boston Globe*, April 5, 1998.

About his not pulling punches to please the "suits": "Look, I didn't have any of this till I was 35 years old. I enjoyed my life back in Flint a great deal. I could go back to doing what I was doing and be very happy.

"Once you truly believe that, they can never have you. They can never own you, and they know that."—Moore to *New York Post*, April 7, 1998.

"I think the root cause is that we, as Americans, were founded in fear and greed. There were two sets of Europeans that came here, one set came here out of fear of being religiously persecuted in Northern Europe. The other, the Southern Europeans, came here motivated purely by greed to see what the riches were—the wealth that was here, the natural resources, whatever, the gold—and to then steal it and take it back [to their countries]. And the Northern Europeans quickly joined in on that, too. Once the Pilgrims started settling, the British and Dutch realized there was quite a bit of bounty here—and the French. So I think we had our start in a really ugly way . . . "—Moore on the root cause of gun violence.

BIBLIOGRAPHY:

"Downsize This! Random Threats From an Unarmed American" Michael Moore, 1996

"Adventures in a TV Nation" Michael Moore with Kathleen Glynn, 1998, HarperCollins; published by Boxtree in England; paperback published by HarperPerrenial Library

"Stupid White Men and Other Excuses for the State of the Union" Michael Moore, Reagan-Books; was originally scheduled to be shipped the second week of September; after the terrorist attacks on September 11, book held in warehouse and released later

Errol Morris

BORN: in Hewlett, New York, 02/05/1948

NATIONALITY: American

EDUCATION: Putney School, Putney, Vermont; studied the cello

University of Wisconsin, history, BA, 1969; accepted to Princeton graduate program, did not attend

University of California at Berkeley, Berkeley, California, philosophy, MA

AWARDS: Edgar Allan Poe Award for Motion Pictures "The Thin Blue Line" 1989

Golden Horse Award "The Thin Blue Line" 1989 Taiwanese equivalent of the Academy Award

New York Film Critics Circle Award Best Documentary "The Thin Blue Line" 1988

Sundance Film Festival Grand Jury Prize (Documentary) "A Brief History of Time" 1992 shared award with "Finding Christa" (Camille Billops, James Hatch)

Sundance Film Festival Filmmakers Trophy (Documentary) "A Brief History of Time" 1992

Seattle International Film Festival Best Documentary Prize "A Brief History of Time" 1992

IFP Gotham Filmmaker Award 1997

National Board of Review Award Best Documentary "Fast, Cheap & Out of Control" 1997

New York Film Critics Circle Award Best Nonfiction Film "Fast, Cheap & Out of Control" 1997

Boston Society of Film Critics Award Best Documentary "Fast, Cheap & Out of Control" 1997

Society of Texas Film Critics Award Best Documentary "Fast, Cheap & Out of Control" 1997

Florida Film Critics Circle Award Best Documentary "Fast, Cheap & Out of Control" 1997

National Society of Film Critics Award Best Nonfiction Film "Fast, Cheap & Out of Control" 1997

Independent Spirit Award Best Documentary "Fast, Cheap & Out of Control" 1998 tied with Danielle Gardner's "Soul in the Hole"

BIOGRAPHY

The innovative documentary filmmaker Errol Morris made two off-beat, critically-acclaimed studies (1978's "Gates of Heaven", about pet cemeteries, and 1981's "Vernon, Florida", about small-town American eccentrics) before achieving his breakthrough with the feature-length "The Thin Blue Line" (1988). The film was an unsettling investigation into the case of Randall Adams, a Texas man who claimed he had been wrongfully convicted of murder. It mixed oddly deadpan interviews, stylized recreations of conflicting accounts of the crime and alienating close-ups of documents and objects both centrally- and tangentially-related to the case, all underpinned by a driving, hypnotic score provided by composer Philip Glass. "The Thin Blue Line" was influential in securing the ultimate overturning of Adams' conviction.

Although his narrative feature debut, the Robert Redford-produced "The Dark Wind" (1991), based on the Tony Hillerman novel, went straight to video, he scored big with his next movie, "A Brief History of Time" (1992). Made for NBC, the film documented wheelchair-bound, British scientist Stephen H. Hawking and his courageous battle with Lou Gehrig's disease. Unable to talk, Hawking typed his words onto a keyboard enabling a computer to speak for him, and, undaunted by his physical limitations, kept his razor-sharp intellect attuned to the cutting edge of science. Philip Glass once again provided the score.

Many have compared "The Thin Blue Line" with Truman Capote's "In Cold Blood" and Norman Mailer's "The Executioner's Song", both nonfiction works about killers, but Morris, making a film, not writing a book, found himself in uncharted waters with his murder investigation/movie: "It took over my life. I'm still obsessed by it." A remarkable, one-of-a-kind movie, it helped set an innocent man free and stands as a monument to the relentless pursuit of the truth. Morris has described himself as a new kind of hyphenate, a director-detective, and has carved out a niche for himself by telling the stories of unique individuals in his distinctive voice.

"Fast, Cheap & Out of Control" (1997), a contemporary meditation on the myth of Sisyphus, profiled four esoteric professionals: a topiary gardener, a lion tamer, a robot scientist and a mole-rat photographer. On the surface an unrelated group, but Morris discovers surprising links among them. The two former are practitioners of idiosyncratic dying arts while the latter two reflect what may come to pass—a world pre-programmed by instinct only. While the helmer lets the audience draw its own conclusions, the film is a singular, cerebral and original look at four unique individuals.—Written by Greg Senf

MILESTONES:

Worked as consultant to Werner Herzog and Volker Schlondorff; Herzog had said he would eat his shoe if Morris ever finished "Gates of Heaven" and made good on his bet, the preparation and consumption of appetizing boot documented in Les Blank's short "Werner Eats His Shoe"

1978: Directed first film, "Gates of Heaven", a documentary about two California pet cemeteries

1981: Completed second documentary, "Vernon, Florida", an account of an eccentric American town; shown on PBS in 1983

1988: Achieved major breakthrough as filmmaker with "The Thin Blue Line"; film led to release of its subject, the unjustly imprisoned inmate Randall Dale Adams

1991: Narrative feature directorial debut "The Dark Wind", based on a best-selling Tony Hillerman novel and produced by Robert Redford, released directly on video

1992: Directed "A Brief History of Time" for NBC-TV about British scientist Stephen H. Hawking; based on Hawking's best-selling book of same title.

1997: Profiled four esoteric professionals in "Fast, Cheap and Out of Control"

QUOTES:

Awarded a MacArthur Foundation "genius" grant.

Paul Morrissey

BORN: in New York, New York, 02/23/1938

NATIONALITY: American

EDUCATION: Fordham University, New York, New York

BIOGRAPHY

Often overlooked as an independent filmmaker because of his association with Andy Warhol, Paul Morrissey was instrumental in enhancing the celebrity of that pop icon, while his own fame fell victim to the success of his myth-making. The Fordham University graduate had made several short films prior to meeting Warhol who remarked, "Your films are great. They are in focus! Why not come help me make a movie?" Warhol had already made the epically monotonous "Empire" (1964), in which the camera stares at the Empire State Building for eight hours, among his experi-

ments in the inane. Morrissey brought camera movement and editing to the Warhol pictures, as well as the camp, satire and 'social realism' that made the films appeal to a wider circle. Though Warhol liked to operate the camera, he withdrew from the filmmaking process after Valerie Solanas shot him on June 3, 1968, leaving the field wide open for Morrissey to enjoy unprecedented freedom as a director, though Warhol's "brand name" continued to "present" the product. He has described the shooting in interviews as "an ill wind that blew somebody some good."

One day in 1967, while Morrissey and Warhol were shooting "The Loves of Ondine" (1967), Joe Dallesandro walked in through the open door of the Greenwich Village apartment and ended up in the movie. It was the beginning of a long collaboration between Morrissey and Dallesandro, who as the enigmatic, often naked star of a trilogy of films at the center of the Morrissey oeuvre "forever changed male sexuality in the cinema," according to director John Waters. Morrissey had already found a formula for working improvisationally with young, untrained actors, and now he had his Brando, the quiet, eye of the storm around whom he could spin dramatic lunacy. In "Flesh" (1968), which would go on to make $2 million on its meager $1500 budget, Dallesandro was a male hustler turning tricks to pay for his wife's girlfriend's abortion. In "Trash" (1970), Morrissey's enduring commercial hit re-released in 2000, the actor was a drug addict unable to perform sexually despite numerous opportunities, whereas "Heat" (1972), which marked the director's transition to traditional linear storylines, cast him as a washed-up child star preying on Sylvia Miles à la "Sunset Boulevard." In all, Dallesandro radiated a sort of passive virility (to go with the beefcake) attractive to both women and gay men.

Though Morrissey worked with producers Carlo Ponti, Andy Braunsberg and Jean-Pierre Rassam on two Gothic horror spoofs "Flesh for Frankenstein" (1973) and "Blood for Dracula" (1974) in Europe. Warhol got the credit when distributors called them "Andy Warhol's Frankenstein" and "Andy Warhol's Dracula." Both starred German actor Udo Kier opposite Dallesandro and both made money, but "Frankenstein" with its severed heads and hands galore (plus an X rating) made more money than any of Morrissey's previous films, while "Dracula" was the better, more poetic picture. Kier's Old World Baron was at the other end of the spectrum from Dallesandro, whose howlingly funny Jersey accent cut an incongruous swath through the European accents around him, but the premise of "Dracula" presented an even better gag. Kier's sickly Count, who must feast on the blood of virgins ("where-gins") to survive, keeps getting beaten to the bed by the hunky Dallesandro. Morrissey abandoned improvisation when he realized his actors were having trouble acting spontaneously in front of

the biggest crew he had ever used and would never return to it. Instead, he brought a secretary to the set to record his "off-the-cuff" dialogue for the cast to quickly memorize before going before the cameras.

Morrissey's association with Warhol was over, and he struggled in the absence of the Warhol "branding." Despite the comic input of Dudley Moore and Peter Cook, "The Hound of the Baskervilles" (1978) fell flat, and of his next five films, only two, "Mixed Blood" (1985) and "Spike of Bensonhurst" (1988, his last film to date and arguably his most mainstream confection), received timely releases. "Retired" from filmmaking because he refuses to give up the control he has always had over his product, by the late 90s, Morrissey was finally emerging from Warhol's shadow as more and more people recognized him as a true "independent." One of the oddest ducks to work at the Warhol "Factory", he was the conservative businessman of the group, putting in his nine hours a day to generate revenue throughout his time there. Ironically, this man who saw his work labeled as "obscene, vulgar and profane" was a Ronald Reagan Republican, but he was just faithfully recording the times. Having anticipated the tenets of Dogma 95 by about 30 years, it is little wonder that Danish filmmaker Lars von Trier's company has a project in development with Morrissey about a man who tries to make it look like he's having sex with children in order to make a name for himself in the fashion business.—Written by Greg Senf

MILESTONES:

While working at an insurance office job in Manhattan was inspired to make movies by critic-filmmaker Jonas Mekas' Monday evening programs at an Off-Broadway theater

Made own short films in the 1960s, including "Ancient History" (1961), a five-minute "rearranged newsreel", and "Taylor Mead Dances" (1963), a 14-minute profile of underground "superstar" Taylor dancing with wild abandon at the Second City nightclub

Introduced to Andy Warhol through mutual friend, poet Gerard Malanga

Managed the celebrity of Warhol, using the "underground" films to raise the artist's profile and ultimately the price of his art; put Warhol on the lecture circuit, allegedly going back and forth across the country the first year with a Warhol impersonator, owing to Warhol's fear of speaking in public; discovered Nico and the Velvet Underground and signed them to a management agreement and was instrumental in the production and selling (to Verve Records) of their first album; also served as the first editor of *Interview* magazine until he turned it over to Bob Colacello who worked as editor from 1970–1982

1965: First Warhol film on which he considers he had input in the direction, "My Hustler", his third or fourth project with Warhol; convinced Warhol that a panning camera produced footage superior to that captured by a fixed camera, putting an end to Warhol's use of the fixed camera

1968: Wrote, directed and shot "Flesh", the first in a trilogy; all three films starred Joe Dallesandro and were produced by Warhol; in London in 1969, an entire audience was arrested for watching the "pornographic" picture

1968: Edited, executive produced and shot Warhol's "Lonesome Cowboys", filmed in Tucson, Arizona; the two-and-a-half days in Arizona brought the budget to a whopping $5000

1969: Made cameo appearance as a party guest in the mainstream film "Midnight Cowboy"

1970: Wrote, directed, shot and edited "Trash", the second part of the trilogy; filmed for $3000; re-released in 2000

1971: Helmed "Women in Revolt", a transvestite take-off on 1950s women's prison movies

1972: Wrote and directed the final segment of trilogy, "Heat", a campy reworking of "Sunset Boulevard" with Dallesandro cast opposite Sylvia Miles as the faded star; also served as cinematographer; filmed for $6000 over three weeks in Los Angeles

Wrote and directed the horror films "Andy Warhol's Dracula/Blood for Dracula" and "Andy Warhol's Frankenstein/Flesh for Frankenstein"; first pictures working with a full studio crew; the original credits read "Andy Warhol presents a Carlo Ponti, Andy Braunsberg, Jean-Pierre Rassam Production", but distributors simply changed the billing in the ads, making it seem like the "presenter" had more to do with the films, when in reality Warhol did not see them until they were complete

1978: Directed "The Hound of the Baskervilles"; also co-scripted with Dudley Moore and Peter Cook

1981: Made cameo appearance as a party guest in "Rich and Famous"

1982: Helmed "Forty Deuce" about a teenage hustler (Kevin Bacon) who tries to frame a client for murder; based on the play by Alan Browne; released in 1996

1984: Co-scripted (with Browne) and directed "Mixed Blood", a black comedy of rival drug gangs in Greenwich Village's "alphabet city"

1985: Helmed and co-scripted (with Mathieu Carriere) "Beethoven's Nephew"; released in 1988

1988: Wrote and directed "Spike of Bensonhurst", arguably his most mainstream movie, which drew favorable comparison to that year's "Married to the Mob" along with criticism for its ethnic stereotypes and "politically incorrect" humor

1989: "Retired" from film directing

1990: Appeared in Chuck Workman's documentary "Superstar: The Life and Times of Andy Warhol"

1993: Featured in the documentary "Jonas in the Desert", about avante-garde filmmaker Jonas Mekas

1994: Appeared in "Nico Icon", a documentary

about the heroin-addicted heroine of the Velvet Underground

1997: Interviewed for the documentary portrait of the early works of John Waters "Divine Trash"

AFFILIATION: Roman Catholic

QUOTES:

"I just chose to find story material in people who led idiotic lives, doing their own thing. I was making fun of people who accepted the hippie life of sex and drugs and rock 'n' roll."—Paul Morrissey to William Grimes in *The New York Times*, December 26, 1995.

"Andy not only did not try to put direction in, he was incapable of it. He didn't even think in sentences, only disconnected nouns and fragments. He would say 'bathtub', then 'It's outdoors', then 'Viva's in it'. For him, that was a scene."—Morrissey in *The New York Times*, December 26, 1995.

"Andy brought the camera and film, I loaded the camera and set the lights, he operated the camera until the 35 minute reels ran out. I gradually began to choose the performers in front of the camera and make more and more suggestions as to what they should improvise about, and in what tone of voice to do it in. I tried to make sure all the performers understood that nothing 'dramatic' was wanted. I deliberately wanted to avoid the phony acting-class improvisations that were just becoming fashionable . . . two or three actors beginning slowly, finding something they could argue about, then raising their voices and escalating their dialogue to shouting matches wherein their 'sincere' and 'profound' emotions were supposed to be revealed . . . In order to avoid this agonized style of performing I never used anyone who informed me they were 'studying acting', even though New York was then, and remains, the acting capitol of the world."—quoted in the 1997 Stockholm Film Festival Catalogue.

"I have always felt that if filmmaking is ever to have any direct connection to the filmmaker himself it is essential that one person be in full charge of all the possible mistakes and possible choices. Few filmmakers get this opportunity, and I will always be grateful to producers like Andy Warhol and others who had the common sense to let me make my own films. I was spoiled from the very beginning by producers like this. In America such freedom is really unknown. When I felt that I no longer had the possibility of fully controlling the films, I chose instead to stop making them."—Morrissey in the 1997 Stockholm Film Festival Catalogue.

"Every movie I ever made says the same thing. They all find comedy in people trying to live their lives without any rules. They are a record of the period, but without any overt messages. And I think that confuses people.

"A movie should only be concerned with characters, not some big moral, although it's always underneath. I just thought the idea of people doing whatever they want was a great subject for films. The characters may be losers, but they're all kind of likable. I can't imagine putting unlikable characters in a movie. As to why their lives are so messed up, well that's for the audience to figure out."—Paul Morrissey quoted in *The New York Times*, February 27, 2000.

"Paul is very straight and narrow. But he's not moralistic. That's why we got along so well. And that's why his fans run the gamut from A to Z, from old ladies to gay liberals."—Holly Woodlawn to *The New York Times*, February 27, 2000.

"Without institutionalized religion as the basis, a society can't exist. All the sensible values of a solid education and a moral foundation have been flushed down the liberal toilet in order to sell sex, drugs, and rock'n'roll."—Morrissey to Maurice Yacowar, quoted in Gary Morris' "Slapstick Realist: Paul Morrissey."

"Cool is something fashionable, and fashion is frivolous. But now in the absence of any other standards, there's only fashion. There's nothing else but what's cool. This is a pagan planet, and anybody who speaks up for anything religious is ridiculed. But when you take away standards, you can't have stories. A game played with no rules is not worth playing. Today people live with no rules—so their life is not worth living."—Morrissey quoted in *Boston Phoenix*, February 21, 1999.

Jonathan Mostow

BORN: Jonathan C. Mostow, 11/28/1961

SOMETIMES CREDITED AS:
Jon Mostow

NATIONALITY: American

EDUCATION: Harvard University, Cambridge, Massachusetts, BA; began making films
American Repertory Theatre, New York, New York
The Lee Strasberg Theatre Institute, New York, New York

BIOGRAPHY

A director and screenwriter who quickly established himself as a purveyor of action-oriented films that have a deeper psychological investigative base, Jonathan Mostow made his feature debut with 1997's "Breakdown." This taut thriller, with Kurt Russell as a man whose wife seems to have vanished in the desert, proved to be a surprise box-office hit. Mostow went on to co-found a production company with former executive Hal Lieberman and signed a four-year deal with Universal.

A graduate of Harvard, Mostow also trained at the American Repertory Company and NYC's Lee Strasberg Institute. He helmed several short films and documentaries as well as music videos before making his first feature, the direct-to-video release "Beverly Hills Bodysnatchers" (1989) which owed a passing debt to "Re-Animator" (1985) as both dealt with attempts to bring people back from the dead. Mostow landed the Showtime film "Flight of the Black Angel" (1991), about a colonel who trains fighter pilots and his troubled protege who wants to attack the local population. Subsequently, he spent several years developing "Breakdown" and "The Game" (1997), penning an early draft of the latter with the hope of directing. Instead David Fincher landed the assignment behind the camera and Mostow was relegated to an executive producer credit. Mostow and Michael Douglas (who starred in "The Game") were to collaborate on a WWII-era submarine film "U-571" (2000) but Douglas pulled out due to scheduling conflicts. Instead, the director assembled a cast of established players (Harvey Keitel, Bill Paxton, Matthew McConaughey) and rising talent (Jack Noseworthy, Matthew Settle, Thomas Guiry) and helmed a taut thriller about an attempt by the USA to intercept a German U-boat carrying a coding device. Based on fact (although it really involved British forces, not Americans), "U-571" was a throwback to the enjoyable popcorn movies popular during the 1940s and 50s. Mostow once again demonstrated a talent for building and maintaining suspense and taking the audience on a rollercoaster ride.

MILESTONES:

Raised in Woodbridge, Connecticut

Moved to L.A. after graduating Harvard; screened 11-minute thesis film for Michael Eisner

1989: Made first film "Beverly Hills Bodysnatchers"; released direct-to-video

Directed music videos for Alicia Bridges and Leon Patillo

1991: Directed "Flight of the Black Angel"; aired on Showtime

1997: Feature film directorial debut with "Breakdown"; also scripted

1997: Formed Mostow/Lieberman Productions with Hal Lieberman; company signed production deal with Universal

1997: Was executive producer of "The Game"; had written an early draft of the film which he had hoped to direct

1998: Directed episode 12 "Le Voyage Dans la Lune", of the HBO series "From the Earth to the Moon"

2000: Co-wrote and directed the WWII thriller "U-571"

Helmed the sequel "Terminator 3: The Rise of the Machines" (lensed 2002)

QUOTES:

"What I love about Hollywood is that there's a great equalizer at work here. No one gave me a break because I had an Ivy League diploma. What people care about is: Do you have a script that I can buy, or an idea for a movie that makes sense? That to me is very American; it's just that, instead of inventing something in your workshop, you're sitting in your kitchen with a typewriter writing a screenplay. And you can go from obscurity to an Academy Award in one shot."—Jonathan Mostow to Michael Sragow at Salon.com, May 4, 2000.

F. W. Murnau

BORN: Friedrich Wilhelm Plumpe in Bielefeld, Westphalia, Germany, 12/28/1888

SOMETIMES CREDITED AS:
Peter Murglie
Friedrich Wilhelm Murnau

DEATH: in Santa Barbara, California, 03/11/1931

NATIONALITY: German

EDUCATION: University of Heidelberg, Heidelberg, Germany, literature and art history
 University of Berlin, Berlin, Germany, philology

BIOGRAPHY

Called "the greatest poet the screen has ever known" by French film theorist (and director) Alexandre Astruc, German director F.W. Murnau did more than any of his contemporaries to liberate the cinema from theatrical and literary conventions, achieving a seamless narrative fluency by freeing the camera to discover uniquely varied perspectives for the new visual medium. Criticized for facile, underdeveloped characters, Murnau was more painter (or even composer) than novelist, his art more concerned with mood and rhythm than whether his characters were highly individualized. He was a master chiaroscurist, brilliantly orchestrating a world moving between lightness and shadows. Rejecting the rigid expressionism prevailing in Germany, he happily went on location to service the look of his pictures. Rather than obsessing over angles for a fixed camera, he made his camera soar, and because of his innovative skill with the moving camera became known as the Great Impressionist, obliterating the boundaries between the real and the unreal.

 Born Friedrich Wilhelm Plumpe, the tall, handsome, melancholic actor took the name Murnau (from a small town in Bavaria) for his stage debut with Max Reinhardt's Deutches Theatre and later worked with Reinhardt as an assistant director before World War I interrupted his career. Serving first in the infantry on the Eastern front, he graduated to the air force and survived seven crashes before losing his way in the fog and landing in neutral Switzerland, where he remained interned for the duration of the hostilities. Swiss authorities did, however, allow him to act in and direct theatrical productions, as well as to assist in the compilation of propaganda films for the German Embassy in Bern. That latter experience helped convince Murnau that his future lay in directing moving pictures. Back in Berlin after the war, he formed a production company (Murnau Veidt Filmgesellschaft) with the actor Conrad Veidt and other colleagues from his Reinhardt days, quickly turning out his first feature "Der Knabe in Blau/The Boy in Blue" (1919), a Gothic melodrama inspired by the Gainsborough painting.

Murnau and his associates proceeded to the more ambitious "Satanas" (also 1919), a three-episode film modeled after D.W. Griffith's "Intolerance" (1916), in which Lucifer (Veidt) contemptuously manipulates human affairs in Egypt, Renaissance Italy and revolutionary Russia. Scripted by Robert Wiene (director of "The Cabinet of Dr. Caligari" 1919), it teamed Murnau for the first of nine times with cinematographer Karl Freund. "Der Bucklige und die Tanzerin/The Hunchback and the Dancer" (1920) marked his initial collaboration (of seven) with scriptwriter Carl Mayer (co-author of "Dr Caligari"), a key figure of the German silent cinema and perhaps the first writer to think wholly in cinematic terms. Those films and the intriguing "Der Januskoph/The Janus Head" (1920), based without acknowledgment on Robert Louis Stevenson's "Dr. Jekyll and Mr. Hyde" and starring Veidt in the dual role, are part of the director's "lost" oeuvre. In fact, of his total output of 21 films, only 12 have survived, the earliest being "Der Gang in Die Nacht/The Gang in the Night" (1920).

From the little known about the "missing movies", Murnau's gift for producing stunning visuals was firmly in place, but his first extant picture exhibits a naturalism normally associated with Scandinavia (he himself was of Swedish descent and Mayer had adapted the picture from a play by Harriet Bloch, a frequent writer for the Danish cinema). This naturalistic influence would continue to temper the extreme German expressionism characterized by absolute studio control over a thoroughly composed and designed cinema displaying a strict sense of narrative structure and moral certainty. His films may have lacked the dogmatic self-confidence (in message) of his fellow German directors, but he made up for that with his own brand of courage filming his first masterpiece, "Nosferatu" (1922). Most German horror films of the period emulated the studio-bound style of "Dr. Caligari" and its distorted expressionistic sets, but Murnau filmed his unauthorized version (and most macabre of all film versions) of the "Dracula" story on location, in rugged mountain landscapes and on northern streets, proving he could photograph the real world and yet invest it with a variety of poetic, imaginative and subjective qualities.

Murnau made three films with Fritz Lang's wife Thea von Harbou as scenarist, "Phantom" (1922, based on a novel by Gerhart Hauptmann), "Die Austreibung/The Expulsion" (1923, adapted from a play by Gerhart's brother Karl and the last of his lost films) and "Die Finanzen des Grossherzogs/The Finances of the Grand Duke" (1923, his sole attempt at an original comedy). "Phantom", due possibly to the influence of von Harbou, conforms more closely to the expressionistic conventions of the day than any other surviving Murnau film, its most striking sequences refracted through the distorting prism of the protagonist's crazed perception. On the other hand, "The Finances of the Grand Duke", a lumbering farce filmed on the Dalmatian coast and performed by most of the cast at a high level of misplaced energy, exposed both Murnau and von Harbou as ill-equipped for comedy. Also during this period between masterpieces, "Der Brennende Acker/The Burning Earth" (1922) represented a primitive mining of a theme he would refine later in "Faust" (1926), "Sunrise" (1927) and "Tabu" (1931): individuals cut themselves off from some form of primal innocence (i.e., the country life), releasing dark, infernal forces as they experience forbidden emotional and physical depths.

Murnau's next effort, "Der Letzte Mann/The Last Laugh" (1924), reuniting him with Mayer and Freund, was arguably his most complete realization of a preconceived ideal and firmly established his reputation internationally. Shot entirely in the studio (with sets by Robert Herlith and Walter Rohrig), the film attained an unprecedented degree of camera mobility and camera subjectivity, telling the story purely in visual terms and dispensing with unnecessary inter-titles. Mounting the camera on a bicycle, fixing it to his stomach, hurling it through the air attached to a scaffolding and moving it forward on a rubber-wheeled trolley of his own design were some of the methods Freund employed to translate the ideas of Murnau and Mayer to film, transforming the camera into a "living narrative instrument, as lean and eloquent as the prose of Hemingway at his best." The simple tale of a pompous hotel doorman (Emil Jannings) reduced to lavatory attendant revolutionized motion picture photography all over the world with its new camera-thinking and led in due course to the director's departure for Hollywood.

Murnau would make two more German films, "Tartuffe" and "Faust" (both 1926), allowing the former's picturesque elements of costume and set design to thoroughly dominate his version of the Moliere play at the expense of the characters. His addition of a modern-day prologue and epilogue further hamstrung the project, so that despite its sumptuous look, it had a very un-Moliere feel about it. He fared better with "Faust", which of all his films has aroused the most violently divergent critical opinions. At times the film superbly measures up to the metaphysical

nature of its theme, particularly in its prologue in heaven, described by Lotte Eisner as "the most remarkable and poignant images the German chiaroscuro ever created," and in the ingenious photographing of Mephistopheles' flight over the town bearing the curse of the black plague, an effect requiring Emil Jannings to hang suspended for three hours, his black cape billowing from the force of three electric fans, as soot, ejected from a propeller, enveloped the miniature village below. Though it unwisely drew from Gounod as well as from Marlowe and Goethe, the film's greatest weakness lay in its uniformly deplorable casting.

William Fox brought Murnau to the United States and granted him an unprecedented degree of artistic control over his first project, "Sunrise" (1927), often referred to as the most German film ever made in Hollywood (and certainly one of the most beautiful). Director and designer (Rochus Gliese) took full advantage of their carte blanche, constructing hugely elaborate country and city sets (covering 20 acres of studio lot) around which the camera prowled and glided even more relentlessly than in "The Last Laugh". Mayer provided the script, adapted from Hermann Sudermann's "A Trip to Tilsit", emphasizing the archetypal, mythic nature of the three main characters by calling them simply The Man (George O'Brien), The Wife (Janet Gaynor) and The Woman from the City (Margaret Livingston). Infatuated by The Woman from the City, The Man (at her urging) plans to murder his wife and make it seem an accidental drowning. He cannot go through with it, but his wife guesses his intentions and flees, forcing him to pursue and win back her love. The film is a perfect marriage of naturalistic acting with a pictorially expressionistic dream landscape that was seemingly real and unreal at the same time.

"Sunrise" was an artistic triumph (Robert Sherwood called it "the most important picture in the history of movies"), winning three Academy Awards (Best Actress, Best

Cinematography and for "artistic quality of production"), but at the box-office, it failed to recoup its investment. Consequently, Fox mucked with Murnau's two subsequent pictures, releasing them in forms very different from the director's original intentions. Mayer's script for "Four Devils" (1928), adapted from a novel by Hermann Bang, had one of the two male acrobats seduced by a vamp to the despair of his female partner and the couple tragically falling to their deaths at picture's end. In the studio-imposed happy ending, the female acrobat falls alone, sustaining minor injuries, and her partner begs for forgiveness. The director then bought an Oregon farm (with studio money) to shoot the proposed "Our Daily Bread" on location, and though there exists an 88-minute silent version that is pure Murnau, featuring a breathtakingly romantic tracking shot through the ripe wheat, the film (renamed "City Girl" 1930) that finally opened to poor business was little more than an hour and included footage shot by either William K. Howard or 'Buddy' Erickson.

Disgusted and disillusioned with Fox, Murnau broke his contract and teamed with documentarian Robert Flaherty to make a movie in Tahiti, signing a contract with the newly established Colorart company. When Colorart went bankrupt, Murnau financed "Tabu" (1931) out of his own pocket, giving him final say over the film's content, and Flaherty, losing the battle of artistic wills, left the picture amicably, later securing money from Paramount (who would distribute it) for its completion and the commission of an original score. Though Flaherty received credit as co-writer and co-director, "Tabu" is the realization of Murnau's desire to impose a fictional (not a documentary) plot and European cultural values on the Polynesian material. Director loosed his camera on his new-found paradise, the simple plot sometimes lost amidst the idyllic landscape, but always fate lurked behind each pleasing frame. When Matahi runs away

with his love Reri, a sacred virgin, their attempt to cheat the gods goes for naught, ending in Matahi's tragic drowning.

"Tabu", executed independent of Hollywood control, proved the sole box-office hit of Murnau's American career, but the great director did not live to see its success. A week prior to its opening, he had driven up the coast from Los Angeles in a hired Rolls Royce, choosing his driver more for his appealing looks than his driving ability. Murnau had always viewed America as a promised land of sorts, where he could practice his homosexuality without fear of Germany's punitive penal code. Ironically, it was his predilection for a pretty face that doomed him to an early death as the car crashed, killing only him among its passengers. Murnau was about to embark on a 10-year contract with Paramount where he might have done more for American film than did his fellow countrymen Lang or Lubitsch. Dead at the age of 42, he would never direct a 'talkie', but all the same, his contributions to the cinema are formidable. His stories may have been simple, his characters generic Everypersons, but the sheer visual elegance of his films bordered on the magical and greatly advanced the vocabulary of the medium. Because of his revolutionary freeing of the camera, the modern cinema could be said to begin with Murnau.—Written by Greg Senf

MILESTONES:

1896: Moved with family to Kassel, Germany at age seven (date approximate)

1908: Joined Max Reinhardt's Deutsches Theatre company on part-time basis while still attending college

1909: Stage debut for Reinhardt in "Das Mirakel", using the stage name Murnau (after a small town in Bavaria) for the first time

After college graduation, joined Reinhardt full-time as actor and assistant director

1914: Joined the Army when WWI broke out; first served as a driver on the Eastern front of battle; after service in the infantry, joined the air force, surviving seven crashes

1917: Plane accidentally landed in Switzerland due to fog; was interned in Andermatt; subsequently worked as an actor there in plays staged in Bern and Zurich; directed a play, "Marignano"; also made propaganda compilation films for German Embassy in Bern

1919: Co-founded (with Conrad Veidt and others) production company Murnau Veidt Filmgesellschaft; made film directing debut with company's first production, "Der Knabe in Blau/The Blue Boy"

1919: First film in collaboration with cinematographer Karl Freund, "Satanas"

1920: First film in collaboration with screenwriter Carl Mayer, "Der Bucklige und die Tanzerin/The Hunchback and the Dancer"

1920: Earliest surviving film, "Der Gang in die Nacht/Journey in the Night", starring Veidt

1922: Directed the film generally regarded as his first masterpiece, "Nosferatu"

1923: Sole original comedy as director, "Die Finanzen des Grossherzogs/The Finances of the Grand Duke"

Hired by UFA in the mid-1920s

1924: Appeared in the film "Der Film im Film", directed by Friedrich Porges

1924: Co-wrote the screenplay for "Komodie des Herzens" with film's director Rochus Gliese; script credited onscreen to 'Peter Murglie'

1924: Received considerable international acclaim for his landmark film, "Der letzte Mann/The Last Laugh" (first film for UFA)

1926: Last German film, UFA's "Faust"

1926: Immigrated to USA (Hollywood) after he was signed by William Fox to a four-year contract

1927: Directed first American film. "Sunrise/Sunrise: A Story of Two Humans"; received special Academy Award for artistic merit, arguably the first recipient of the Best Picture Oscar as the award won by "Wings" was voted by the public

1929: Last film for Fox, "City Girl"

1931: Co-directed and co-wrote last film "Tabu" (with Robert Flaherty; Murnau killed a week before premiere)

1958: "Sunrise" voted in a *Cahiers Du Cinema* poll as "the most beautiful film there is"

1970: Was the subject of the French-made TV production, "Cineastes de notre temps: Murnau/Cineastes of Our Times: F.W. Murnau", directed by Alexandre Astruc

1988: Was the subject of another made-for-TV film, "Phantombilder", directed by Frieda Grafe and Enno Patalas

2000: Portrayed by John Malkovich in the speculative feature "Shadow of the Vampire"

QUOTES:

"When I think I shall have to leave all this I already suffer all the agony of going. I am bewitched by the place . . . Sometimes I wish I were at home. But I am never 'at home' anywhere—I feel this more and more the older I get—not in any country nor in any house with anybody."—F.W. Murnau writing to his mother, reprinted in "World Film Directors, Volume I" edited by John Wakeman (New York: The H.W. Wilson Company, 1987).

Shortly before his death, a fortune teller Murnau was in the habit of consulting told the director he would be with his mother on April 5, a date which was not in keeping with his plans. However, after the March 11 auto accident that claimed his life, his remains travelled by ship to Germany, arriving in Germany on April 4. The woman who gave him life claimed them the following day, April 5, 1931.—From "The Motion Picture Guide, Volume X" (Chicago: CineBooks Inc., 1986).

Anticipating Alexandre Astruc's "camera-stylo": "The camera is the director's pencil. It should have the greatest possible mobility in order to record the most fleeting harmony of atmosphere. It is important that the mechanical factor should not stand between the spectator and the film."—F.W. Murnau, reprinted in "A Biographical Dictionary of Film" by

David Thompson (New York: Alfred A. Knopf, 1994).

"Of all the great personalities of the cinema, Murnau was the most German. He was a Westphalian, reserved, severe on himself, severe on others, severe for the cause. He could show himself outwardly grim, but inside he was like a boy, profoundly kind. Of all the great directors, he was the one who had the strongest character, rejecting any form of compromise, incorruptible. He was a pioneer, an explorer, he fertilized everything he touched and was always years in advance. Never envious, always modest. And always alone."—Emil Jannings' written tribute to Murnau, reprinted in "The Great German Films" by Frederick W. Ott (Secaucus, New Jersey: The Citadel Press, 1986).

BIBLIOGRAPHY:

"Nosferatu" Jim Shephard, 1998, Alfred A. Knopf; novel; fictionalized account of Murnau's life

Dan Myrick

BORN: in Sarasota, Florida, 1963

NATIONALITY: American

EDUCATION: University of Central Florid,a Orlando, Florida, film, BA

AWARDS: Florida Film Critics Circle Golden Orange Award for "Outstanding Contribution to Film" "The Blair Witch Project" 1999

Independent Spirit Award Best First Feature— Under $500,000 "The Blair Witch Project" 2000; shared award

BIOGRAPHY

After slaving years on the edges of the Industry as an award-winning video and commercial director, Daniel Myrick struck filmmaking gold as one-half of the genius behind "The Blair Witch Project" (1999). From the beginning, he and his partner Eduardo Sanchez strove for the ultimate in realism, but the secret to their success lay in trusting the results of their guerilla filmmaking and allowing it to stand by itself rather than frame it with 1940s-style newsreel and TV documentary devices as they had originally intended. "I was scared shitless to just let it go, as is," recalled Myrick in the *Village Voice* (July 20, 1999). "Think about it. It's Hi-8 video, as raw as you can get. Are people going to look at over 80 minutes of shaky-cam? I'm thinking, 'It'll never play in a theater.'" It was the rawness though, the amateurish home-movies feel coupled with completely naturalistic performances from the actors, that resonated with audiences and made "Blair Witch" the year's sleeper success.

The Myrick-Sanchez plan for scaring audiences was nothing short of brilliant. Hire three no-name actors with improvisational skills, give them a crash course in filmmaking, send them back-packing into the woods for eight days and then terrorize them while they record it all on 16mm and video. Equipping the actors with Global Positioning System (GPS) handsets enabled the directors to know where they were at all times and lead them to specific locations where preconceived parts of the story would play out. The filmmakers left flagged baskets for the actors, containing fresh film, video, batteries and directing notes, all written in the first person for that character's eyes only. Myrick and Sanchez also left food for the actors, but increasingly less as the shoot went on, since the harried group was running out of food in the story. Heather Donahue told the *Village Voice* (July 20, 1999), "I have not had a Power Bar since, and I probably never will again" but also insisted she would "do it again in a heartbeat," citing the built-in challenges of the conceptual piece.

The filmmakers distilled the 20 hours shot by their actors, much of which Myrick admits was "pretty boring," into the compelling narrative which first worked its disturbing magic at a midnight screening at Sundance, effectively blurring the line between what is real and what is fake. Add to that a website (www.blairwitch.com), which made no attempt to present their Blair Witch mythology as fiction, and you can understand why the filmmakers received countless e-mails and calls asking if it was true. Inspired by the old "In Search Of" TV show with Leonard Nimoy and such classics as "The Legend of Bigfoot", they had laid it on thick and people had bought into it. According to Myrick (*Empire*, November 1999): "We're still trying to acclimatise to the idea that we're filmmakers who make money. We're still thinking that next year we may be scraping around for industrial videos again." Meanwhile, with a supernatural drama series pilot in the works for Fox, not to mention a proposed comedy feature and all the Blair Witch backstory offers in the way of prequels (if not sequels), Myrick may indeed have left industrials behind forever.

MILESTONES:

Grew up in Sarasota, Florida

1990: Met Eduardo Sanchez while both were students at the University of Central Florida's film school; worked on the abortive "Fortune" (a film about a witch) with Sanchez while there, among other projects

Worked with Sanchez and fellow University of Central Florida film school alumnus Gregg Hale on "Black Chapters", a "Twilight Zone"-style trilogy of short movies

1992: Won Alamo award for music video at the Fort Lauderdale Film Festival

1993: Established the Filmmaker's Alliance at Universal Studios in Orlando

1995: Earned the national Charlie award for

work on a documentary about the Bolles School (a K-12 preparatory school located in Jacksonville, Florida)

1997: Commissioned to write and direct the award-winning trailer for the Florida Film Festival

1997: Recruited by indie film guru John Pierson to work first as a cinematographer, then as an editor on segments of his series "Split Screen" (Independent Film Channel)

1997: With Sanchez and Hale founded Haxan (from the 1920s Swedish documentary "Haxan: Witchcraft Through the Ages"), a company which initially made ads and industrial films; later that year fellow UCF alumni Mike Monello and Robin Cowie rounded out the Haxan 5 crew

1997: Eight-minute trailer for the Myrick-Sanchez brainchild, "The Blair Witch Project", shown on "Split Screen" and presented as fact, not fiction, capped first season of series; another "Blair Witch" segment appeared on the first episode of the second season of Pierson's "Split Screen"

1999: "The Blair Witch Project" debuted at a midnight showing at the Sundance Film Festival and received the festival's first distribution deal just hours later from Artisan Entertainment which purchased the worldwide rights to the movie, including sequels, for just over $1 million, a figure that left rivals laughing, although Artisan would enjoy the last laugh

1999: In concert with the widespread release of the picture, the Sci-fi Channel broadcast "The Curse of the Blair Witch", a mock TV documentary originally intended to frame the "found" footage as part of the feature film; rejected from the final cut (but not abandoned) when filmmakers decided to construct entire movie from the "found" footage

Signed to co-direct and co-write (with Sanchez) "Heart of Love"

2000: Produced the pilot for "Freaky Links", a supernatural drama series developed by Haxan for Fox

QUOTES:

The three principal actors shot every single frame of the movie's completed footage, a motion picture first.

The website and general hype was so convincing that the Internet Movie Database originally listed the "Blair Witch" stars as deceased.

"In the contracts the actors signed, we told them we were going to scare them. We told them, 'Don't sign this if you have heart problems, because we're going to subject you to psychological techniques that are used in a lot of military scenarios—you know, immersive scenarios.' It was a survival school approach."— Daniel Myrick to Michael O'Sullivan in *The Washington Post*, July 11, 1999.

"Ed and I came up with an outline, just an infrastructure, of this world we created for them to go to for the days that they were out there. So we had it pretty detailed hour for hour, day to day, what was going to happen for us, but the actors didn't know. We gave them what they needed to know to get to the next rendezvous point, but if they came to a store or something like that, they didn't know who was an actor in the store and who wasn't."—Myrick quoted in *Detour* magazine, August 1999.

"Whether it's folklore your grandfather told you or a movie, the best ideas are the simplest. 'Jaws' affected me for a year and what is it? A monster in the water. We've all heard bumps in the night; we all have our own bogeyman. Everyone knows what it feels like to say, 'I know where I am.' and then, 'Holy shit. Where am I?' Y2K fear is like that right now. People are thinking, Will my computer shut down? Will my bank crash? And on a bigger level it's: Should I buy a gun? Is there going to be civil unrest? It's affecting everybody in the same place. None of us knows what's waiting around the corner until the clock ticks over."—Myrick to Elizabeth Weitzman in *Interview*, October 1999.

"Were we sitting around in our jacuzzis while all this was going on? No. It was a 24-7 shoot for us. In some respects we were working a lot harder than they [the actors] were. We were the Blair Witch. We had to get up at three in the morning and run round their tent. We had to build all the stickmen that were hanging from the trees. We had to hike through the woods to drop off directing notes. Then we'd review Heather's [Donahue] video tapes at the end of the day to see how it was reading on camera. We really didn't know what we were getting into. We theorised about shooting it this way and we had a pretty detailed blueprint but no one really knew what was going to happen. That's part of the beauty of 'Blair Witch'—we discovered the movie in the editing suite."— Myrick quoted in *Empire*, November 1999.

Mira Nair

BORN: in Bhubaneshwar, Orissa, India, 1957

NATIONALITY: Indian

EDUCATION: attended Irish Catholic Missionary school in Simla

Delhi University Delhi, India, Indian sociology; joined amateur theater group; toured with group

Harvard University Cambridge, Massachusetts, theater, 1979; enrolled in 1976; awarded full scholarship

AWARDS: American Film Festival Best Documentary Prize "India Cabaret" 1985

Cannes Film Festival Camera d'Or "Salaam Bombay!" 1988

Cannes Film Festival Prix du Publique "Salaam Bombay!" 1988

Los Angeles Film Critics Association New

Generation Award "Salaam Bombay!" 1988; director

Venice Film Festival Golden Lion "Monsoon Wedding" 2001; Nair became the first female director to take the top award

BIOGRAPHY

Born in a small Indian town and educated at Harvard, Mira Nair describes her life as having been spent "between two worlds". Primarily concerned with telling the stories of people on the margins of society, she has made four non-fiction films examining aspects of Indian life, winning best documentary prize at the American Film Festival for "India Cabaret" (1985), a controversial portrait of strippers in a Bombay nightclub.

Nair's highly acclaimed first feature, "Salaam Bombay!" (1988), was a riveting and uncompromising tale of urban street life in the tradition of Bunuel's "Los Olvidados" and Hector Babenco's "Pixote." "Salaam Bombay!" featured fine performances from non-professional child actors and won both the Camera d'Or (for best first feature) and the Prix du Publique (for most popular entry) at Cannes. She followed up with "Mississippi Masala" (1992), a winning interracial romance set in the American South and starring Denzel Washington and Sarita Choudhury. Nair is now divorced from her first husband, Mitch Epstein, who was co-producer and production designer of both features.

MILESTONES:

Spent first fifteen years of her life in Orissa, a delta area in eastern India

Acted for amateur theater company, directed by Barry John (who later worked with her when he directed the children's workshop preceding the shooting of "Salaam Bombay"!") In Delhi for three years

1976: Offered scholarship by Cambridge University; turned it down in favor of Harvard

1976: Moved to USA to study at Harvard

1979: Made first film, "Jama Masjid/Street Journal," as student thesis at Harvard

1988: Directed first feature, "Salaam Bombay!"; nominated for the Best Foreign-Language Film Academy Award

1992: Helmed the romance "Mississippi Masala", starring Sarita Choudhury and Denzel Washington

1995: Directed "The Perez Family", featuring Anjelica Huston and Alfred Molina

1997: Helmed "Kama Sutra: A Tale of Love", a semi-controversial feature due to its sexual content; Sarita Choudhury and Naveen Andrews co-starred

1999: Produced and co-directed (with Adam Bartos) the documentary "The Laughing Club of India"

2001: Premiered feature "Monsoon Wedding" in India; directed film about a family whose secrets are revealed in the days just before a wedding; screened at Venice Film Festival

2002: Directed the HBO movie "Hysterical Blindness", starring Uma Thurman and Juliette Lewis; screened at Sundance

QUOTES:

"If I were to find a common thread in my work, I would have to admit that I have always been drawn to stories of people who live on the margins of society—on the edge, or outside, learning the language of being in-between, always dealing with the question: what, and where, is home? These concerns are, of course, inextricably linked with my personal history as well, since I have spent most of the past 12 years living between two worlds."—Mira Nair (quoted in public relations material for "Mississippi Masala" 1991)

Nair's documentaries include "Jama Masjid Street Journal" (1979); "So Far From India" (1982), the story of a subway newsstand worker in Manhattan and his pregnant who awaits his return in India; and "India Cabaret" (1985).

BORN: Timothy Blake Nelson in Tulsa, Oklahoma, 05/11/1964

SOMETIMES CREDITED AS:
Tim Nelson

NATIONALITY: American

EDUCATION: Brown University, Providence, Rhode Island, classics, 1986; received the Workman-Driscoll Award for Excellence in Classical Studies
The Juilliard School, New York, New York, drama, 1990

BIOGRAPHY

A playwright who has adapted his works for the big screen and proven a skilled screenwriter and director as well as a engaging onscreen performer, Tim Blake Nelson is a remarkably multitalented creative force, equally adept at absurdist comedy and soul-stirring drama. The gangly, dark-haired performer's early credits on the sketch comedy series "The Unnaturals" (HA! and CTV) earned him CableACE Award nominations for both his writing and performing. The HBO miniseries "Hardcore TV" (1993) showcased his uncommon comedy as well, and in 1995, when John Leguizamo debuted on Fox with the sketch comedy show "House of Buggin", Nelson was a guest on the series. An early screen credit as Julie Kavner's comic pal David in the comedy-drama "This Is My Life" (1992) marked Nelson's feature debut, and the actor went on to play a detective in Hal Hartley's "Amateur" (1994) and had a small role in the preteen comedy "Heavyweights" (1995) before taking a featured role in the ABC miniseries "Larry McMurtry's Dead Man's Walk" in 1996.

While at times Nelson's career saw him with such odd roles as that of a cockroach in the insect-infested MTV Films production "Joe's Apartment" (1996), his stirring stage work seemed his true creative focus. He performed in such productions as "Mad Forrest" (1992), "An Imaginary Life" (1993) and "Troilus and Cressida" (1995) and in 1996 Nelson's own play "The Grey Zone" was produced. Eliciting both horror and raves from critics and audiences, "The Grey Zone" (an allusion to an unclear moral ground) was an unsettling but ultimately sympathetic and human look at the Jewish enablers at Auschwitz, based upon Primo Levi's assertion that merely surviving in that atmosphere is to be a collaborator. In 2002, "The Grey Zone" made it to the big screen, directed and written by the playwright, following Nelson's stage-to-screen success "Eye of God" (1997), a widely acclaimed, Sundance-screened drama that echoed the strong themes of life and death from the play while bringing a truly fresh and evocative visual approach to the material. Nelson returned to acting that year, playing an FBI techie in the crime drama "Donnie Brasco." 1998 saw him take on the role of Private Tillis in Terrence Malick's stirring war film "The Thin Red Line." Nelson directed the dialogue-driven short "Kansas" in 1998, the same year that his prison-set one-act play "Andarko" was staged in NYC starring David Patrick Kelly.

On the strength of the 1997 Sundance showing of "Eye of God", Nelson was tapped to direct "O", a prep school-set update of "Othello." Lensed in 1999, the film promised to bring an edge that was missing in the spate of contemporary teen updates of Shakespeare, but the drama, starring hot up-and-comers Josh Hartnett, Mekhi Phifer and Julia Stiles was mishandled by Miramax, and began looking elsewhere for distribution in the fall of 2000 before being scheduled for a spring 2001 opening. In the meantime, audiences could catch Nelson in another adaptation of the Bard's classics, with a featured role in the 2000 update of "Hamlet" starring Ethan Hawke as the haunted prince. That same year he was heralded for his co-starring performance alongside John Turturro and George Clooney, playing a trio of escaped convicts in the Depression-era south in "O Brother, Where Art Thou?", the Coen brother's update of "The Odyssey". Nelson brought irresistible charm and dignity to his portrayal of Delmar, the more wide-eyed and dimwitted of the group, showing him as an unspoiled innocent rather than a babbling idiot.

After winning audiences' affection in "O Brother," Nelson continued to essay a series of offbeat characters in both high- and low-profile films, including independent director Finn Taylor's quirky "Cherish," Miguel Arteta's sensitive "The Good Girl" and Steven Spielberg's sci-fi opus "Minority Report." But Nelson also effectively switched gears as a filmmaker, adapting his own play and directing the film version of "The Grey Zone."—Written by Jane O'Donnell

MILESTONES:

Raised in Tulsa, Oklahoma

1990–1991: Was writer and performer on the sketch comedy show "The Unnaturals" (HA! TV Comedy Network and CTV: The Comedy Network)

1992: Appeared in the Off-Broadway staging of Caryl Churchill's play "Mad Forrest" alongside Calista Flockhart and Juilliard classmate Jake Weber

1992: Acted in Nora Ephron's comedy-drama "This Is My Life", playing Dennis, a comedian compatriot of Julie Kavner's Dottie

1993: Appeared in episodes of HBO's sketch comedy "Hardcore TV"

1993: Featured in the stage production "An Imaginary Life" at Playwrights Horizons in New York City

1994: Played a detective in Hal Hartley's "Amateur"

1995: Starred as Thersites in the Delacourt Theater production of "Troilus and Cressida"

1995: Made guest appearance on John Leguizamo's short-lived comedy-variety show "House of Buggin' "

1996: Was featured in the ABC miniseries "Larry McMurtry's Dead Man's Walk"

1996: "The Grey Zone", a disturbing drama chronicling Nazi horror, produced at New York City's Manhattan Class Company (MCC) Theater; third play and first to be produced in NYC

1997: Wrote and directed the acclaimed independent drama "Eye of God", based on his own play

1997: Was an FBI technician in the crime thriller "Donnie Brasco"

1998: Wrote and directed the short "Kansas"

1998: His prison-set drama "Andarko" staged at MCC in NYC, starring David Patrick Kelly

1998: Played Private Tillis in Terrence Malick's adaptation of "The Thin Red Line"

2000: Had small role in a modern feature adaptation of "Hamlet", directed by Michael Almereyda

2000: Co-starred with George Clooney and John Turturro as an escapted con in the Coen Brothers 1930s-set "O Brother, Where Art Thou?"

2001: Directed the prep school-set "Othello" update "O" (filmed in 1999)

2001: Adapted the screenplay of his play "The Grey Zone" for the big screen; also directed and edited; released theatrically in USA in 2002

2002: Appeared as the unlikely love interest in the quirky independent film "Cherish"

2002: Co-starred the critically hailed Jennifer Aniston–starrer "The Good Girl"

2002: Had a small but notable part in Steven Spielberg's "Minority Report"

Starred alongside David Arquette and Emily Mortimer in "A Foreign Affair" (lensed 2001–2002)

AFFILIATION: Jewish

QUOTES:

"You have a color here, a color there. Certain colors are echoed, certain colors appear only once, and if you've done your job as a writer and director, it's coherent in the end."—Nelson to the *Brown Alumni Magazine*, March 1998.

Tim Blake Nelson on what he learned about filmmaking from Terrence Malick: "I was with a man who seemed to be screaming in his gentle, quiet, and completely unpretentious manner, that nothing would ever be more important in my life as a filmmaker than simply directing and editing the films I'd make. Whatever existed outside those two realms was politics and ego, both of which are usually destructive. While I have neither the temperment nor the temerity to shun as much of the world as Terry does, I learned an incredible amount from this man, and, in the best ways, more of it concerned being a good human being than being a good director."—quoted in "Year in the Life", a 1998 feature on filmmakers at Sundance.com.

"I have a cold aesthetic. I don't like schmaltz."—Nelson to *Time*, January 15, 2001.

Andrew Niccol

BORN: in New Zealand, 1964

NATIONALITY: New Zealander

AWARDS: Online Film Critics Society Award Best Original Screenplay "The Truman Show" 1998

BAFTA Award Best Screenplay (Original) "The Truman Show" 1999

BIOGRAPHY

New Zealand–born screenwriter-director Andrew Niccol began his career in London, successfully directing TV commercials before moving to Los Angeles in order to make films "longer than 60 seconds." He interested high-powered producer Scott Rudin in his "The Truman Show" (1998) script, but Rudin was not willing to gamble on a rookie director, particularly when Jim Carrey came aboard, swelling the budget to about $60 million. Peter Weir helmed instead, bringing a complementary vision which lightened the material somewhat, and the clever satire, which followed a cheerful insurance man (Carrey) as he slowly realizes that all the people in his life are just actors in a TV show, opened to critical raves. Since the deal for "Truman" came together slowly, Niccol actually made his screenwriting

and directing debut with "Gattaca" (1997), a superb, well-acted sci-fi movie that raised issues of genetic engineering in a totalitarian environment, focusing on Vincent (Ethan Hawke), an genetically imperfect man who assumes the identity of a crippled superior (Jude Law) willing to sell his DNA. Niccol added a murder mystery and a romance (with Uma Thurman) to the mix and created a believable futuristic society that was undermined by a slightly muddled conclusion. On the heels of his success, he negotiated a two-year production deal with DreamWorks SKG to write, direct and produce projects under the banner of Niccol Productions.

MILESTONES:

Raised in New Zealand

Moved to London

Began career directing TV commercials in England

1997: Feature directorial debut, "Gattaca"; also scripted

1998: Scripted the acclaimed "The Truman Show"; received Oscar nomination

1998: Formed Niccol Productions

1999: Received $2 million from New Line Cinema for script "River Road"; attached as director

2001: Made controversial decision to use a computer-generated leading lady opposite Al Pacino in "Simone"

QUOTES:

"We have this strange relationship with television. In Los Angeles recently, there was a man who died on the freeway and it was televised. I think in many people's minds they're hoping for a violent, fiery outcome. In this case, it just happened to be a little too violent."

"From Truman's point of view, I guess I like the idea of questioning the authenticity of our lives. I would love for people coming out of the theater to look twice at whoever they're with."—Andrew Niccol in *The New York Times*, May 28, 1998.

Mike Nichols

BORN: Michael Igor Peschkowsky in Berlin, Germany, 11/06/1931

NATIONALITY: German

EDUCATION: Dalton School, New York, New York; classmates included Buck Henry

Walden School New York, New York 1948 progressive high school

University of Chicago, Chicago, Illinois 1950–53; became interested in acting; met author Susan Sontag at registration; later met Elaine May through Paul Sills; dropped out of school in 1953

studied acting with Lee Strasberg in 1954

AWARDS: Grammy Best Comedy Performance "An Evening With Mike Nichols and Elaine May" 1961; shared with Elaine May

Tony Director (Dramatic) "Barefoot in the Park" 1964

Tony Director (Dramatic) "Luv" and "The Odd Couple" 1965; award won for both plays

Outer Critics Circle Award Citation for Directing 1966

Oscar Best Director "The Graduate" 1967

Directors Guild of America Award Outstanding Directorial Achievement in Feature Film "The Graduate" 1967

Golden Globe Award Best Director "The Graduate" 1967

New York Film Critics Circle Award Best Director "The Graduate" 1967

British Film Academy Award Best Director "The Graduate" 1968

Tony Director (Dramatic) "Plaza Suite" 1968

Special Outer Critics Circle Award "Plaza Suite" 1969

Tony Director (Dramatic) "The Prisoner of Second Avenue" 1972

Drama Desk Award Outstanding Director of a Play "Comedians" 1977; tied with Alan Schneider ("A Texas Trilogy")

Tony Best Musical "Annie" 1977; producer; shared award

Tony Director of a Play "The Real Thing" 1984

American Comedy Award for Lifetime Achievement 1994

Directors Guild of America Honors Filmmaker Award 2000

Humanitas Prize PBS/Cable (90 minutes or longer) "Wit" 2001; shared with Emma Thompson

Emmy Outstanding Made for Television Movie "Wit" 2000/01; shared award; Nichols was one of the executive producers as well as the director and co-author of the screenplay adaptation

Emmy Outstanding Directing for a Miniseries, Movie or Special "Wit" 2000/01

National Board of Review Award Best Film Made for Cable TV "Wit" 2001; shared award; Nichols was one of the executive producers

BIOGRAPHY

As a child, he was a refugee from Nazi Germany. By age 12, he had been certified as a genius. In his late twenties, he was half of a popular comedy act. By his late thirties, he was an acclaimed and award-winning director of stage and screen. As the 20th century gave way to the 21st, Mike Nichols was celebrated as a show business legend who still had some of his best work before him.

Born in Berlin in 1931, Nichols (born as Michael Igor Peschowsky) emigrated with his brother Robert to the USA in 1939. Sent to live with his doctor father, he and his sibling were soon placed with an English-speaking family and it wasn't until his mother arrived in NYC in 1941 that the family was reunited, despite his parents' stormy marriage. The untimely death of his father from leukemia the following year meant the family slipped into poverty. From an early age—when he had a bad reaction to a defective vaccination for whooping cough and was left permanently hairless—Nichols felt "different." Since he barely spoke English when he arrived in the USA, matters were further complicated. Despite being certified as a genius, he proved a lackluster student and drifted until 1948 when he attended the second performance of "A Streetcar Named Desire" and felt he had found his metier.

Decamping to the University of Chicago, he finally enjoyed the feeling of fitting in. Among the many in whose circle he moved were intellectuals like Susan Sontag and Heyward Ehrlich and theatrical types including Edward Asner, Severn Darden, Barbara Harris, Zohra Lampert and Eugene Troobnick. By his sophomore year, Nichols was directing and acting in plays when he was introduced to a woman who would change his life—Elaine May.

Although they had been introduced, Nichols and May did not begin their partnership in earnest until 1955 after he had dropped out of college and briefly studied Method acting with Lee Strasberg. He joined the relatively new Compass Players in Chicago, an improvisatory troupe among whose founders were Paul Sills and Elaine May. Although she was comfortable performing with others in the group, Nichols only managed to be funny when he was partnered with her. The duo shared that ineffable thing called "chemistry" and onstage they continued to challenge one another and enjoyed displaying not only their verbal wit but also their intellects. Over the next several years, until the pair underwent a bitter break-up in the early 1960s, Nichols and May enjoyed success as the premiere comedy duo of the time. The culmination of the pair's collaboration was the Broadway production "An Evening with Nichols and May" (1960) which led to a Grammy-winning recording. The strain of performing together, though, began to take its toll and when in 1962, the play "A Matter of Position"—which she wrote and directed and in which he starred—failed in Philadelphia, so did their partnership and friendship.

Feeling abandoned and without moorings, Nichols was unsure what to do next. When he was offered a chance to stage the Broadway-bound Neil Simon play "Nobody Loves Me" (later retitled "Barefoot in the Park"), he accepted. With a cast including Elizabeth Ashley, Robert Redford, Mildred Natwick and Kurt Kaznar, the light romantic comedy became a hit. Nichols earned the first of his (to date) six Tony Awards and marked the beginning of a long collaboration between playwright and director. The next year, they perhaps reached the apotheosis of their working relationship with "The Odd Couple", but also included "Plaza Suite" (1967), "The Prisoner of Second Avenue" (1968) and the short-lived "Fools" (1981). Except for the latter, Nichols earned a Tony for each of the others as well as for his staging of Tom Stoppard's "The Real Thing" in 1984.

Having honed his craft on stage, Nichols

moved to the big screen when screen goddess Elizabeth Taylor handpicked him to direct the film adaptation of Edward Albee's blistering portrait of a marriage, "Who's Afraid of Virginia Woolf?" (1966). Although he clashed with studio head Jack Warner (who wanted it made it color), Nichols shot the film in stark black and white and occasionally used handheld shots to intensify the dramatic tension. Because the movie tackled difficult subjects including adultery and alcoholism, Warner was concerned that the Catholic League of Decency would condemn it, but the director wasn't above using some pressure courtesy of his friendship with former First Lady Jacqueline Kennedy to obtain the League's blessing. "Who's Afraid of Virginia Woolf?" became a box-office and critical success and went on to earn a near record 13 Academy Award nominations, including those for each of the four actors as well as for Best Director.

While Nichols lost the Oscar on his first bid, he captured the statue with his sophomore film, "The Graduate" (1967), which spoke to the members of a disaffected generation by giving life to otherwise inchoate feelings of alienation and frustration. With Dustin Hoffman in the lead ably supported by Anne Bancroft and Katharine Ross as the women in his life and a score by Paul Simon, "The Graduate" became one of the seminal films of the 60s and, along with "Bonnie and Clyde" (1967) and "Easy Rider" (1969), ushered in a cycle of youth-oriented motion pictures that rejuvenated a moribund American film industry hurt by the splintering of the studio system.

Now at a place in his career where he could do almost anything, Nichols opted to adapt Joseph Heller's complex cult novel "Catch-22." The overly-detailed 1970 feature, however, has to be ranked as a noble failure. Critics felt that Nichols' somewhat sentimentalization of the darkly comic absurdity found in the book undermined the film. While it was beautifully shot (by cinematographer David Watkin) and well acted, "Catch-22" kept the audience at bay

with a cerebral remoteness. Nichols obviously was taking a risk, but it was that didn't work.

A similar fate befell his next effort, "Carnal Knowledge" (1971), a trenchant exploration of sexual politics that solidified Jack Nicholson's star status, proved Candice Bergen was more than a pretty face and renewed the sagging acting career of Ann-Margret. It didn't help his film career that his next two project, the George C. Scott vehicle "The Day of the Dolphin" (1973) and the period comedy "The Fortune" (1975), with Warren Beatty, Jack Nicholson and Stockard Channing, didn't exactly impress audiences or critics. Indeed, two weeks into shooting "Bogart Slept Here" from a Neil Simon script in 1975, Nichols pulled the plug on the project and left Hollywood for nearly a decade. (Although he did spend some of the period attempting to jump-start a film version of "A Chorus Line".)

He first turned his attentions to the small screen, serving as an executive producer on the acclaimed, award-winning drama "Family" (ABC, 1976–80) and then returned to Broadway directing Trevor Griffiths' play "Comedians" (1976) and serving as one of the producers of the Tony-winning hit musical "Annie" (1977). He enjoyed another stage success at the helm of "The Gin Game" (1977) but stumbled a bit with the comedies "Lunch Hour" (1980) and the aforementioned "Fools".

In 1983, Nichols returned to features with the biopic "Silkwood", that not only served as a commentary on the plight of women in a male-dominated culture, but also depicted how anyone could be dehumanized by a complex system, whether it be the government or big business. "Silkwood" not only restored Nichols to the ranks of top directors in Hollywood, it also refreshed the career of singer-actress Cher (who played a supporting role as a lesbian), catapulted Kurt Russell to the ranks of leading men and further demonstrated the seemingly endless talents of star Meryl Streep.

Reuniting with both Streep and Nicholson, he helmed "Heartburn" (1986), an adaptation of Nora Ephron's caustic roman-a-clef about her failed marriage, that once again explored the impact of sexual politics. His follow-up, 1988's "Working Girl" satirized the same idea within a corporate setting. His adaptation of Carrie Fisher's semi-autobiographical "Postcards From the Edge" (1990) also looked at how women coped in business, but this time the industry examined was movie making. Although it garnered respectful reviews, the bloom was beginning to fade on his career.

In the early 90s, Nichols suffered box-office disappointments with "Regarding Henry" (1991) and "Wolf" (1994), despite high profile leads Harrison Ford and Jack Nicholson, respectively. The former was a somewhat sappy look at a venal corporate lawyer whose life is changed after a shooting, while the latter was a metaphoric character study of the male libido embodied by a man literally turning into a beast. In his first overt reteaming with Elaine May (she reportedly has worked as a script doctor on each of his films since they reconciled in the 1970s), Nichols enjoyed a hit with "The Birdcage" (1996), an Americanized remake of the popular French farce "La Cage aux folles." While some gay and lesbian groups were not particularly pleased by what were thought to be stereotypical depictions of homosexual characters, the movie allowed Robin Williams and Nathan Lane to cut loose and give larger-than-life portrayals as a long-standing couple whose lives are upturned when Williams' son visits with his conservative fiancee and her family.

Instead of capitalizing on this success, though, Nichols made the daring decision to return to stage acting in the 1996 London production of Wallace Shawn's play "The Designated Mourner" which was preserved on film and released theatrically the following year. Somewhat static and talky, the movie at least allows audiences a rare opportunity to see Nichols tackle a dramatic role. When he did resume his directorial career, it was with the feature adaptation of the controversial political

roman-a-clef "Primary Colors" (1998). Original choice Tom Hanks passed on the project in part over concerns on how the lead character—a presidential candidate closely modeled on Bill Clinton—was depicted. John Travolta, though, had no qualms and accepted the role. While the movie was accomplished, it suffered from a case of poor timing. Released when the American presidency was in crisis over the Chief Executive's sexual liaison with a White House intern, "Primary Colors" had the feeling of being yesterday's news. Elaine May's script was sharp but overshadowed by the unfolding history and Nichols' direction seemed curiously muted and uneven. "What Planet Are You From?" (2000), an unfunny comedy about an alien who arrives to find a willing female to bear his spawn, was even more of a disappointment and quickly was relegated to cable outlets and video store shelves. Nichols roared back, though, by collaborating with "Primary Colors" lead Emma Thompson on a small screen adaptation of the Pulitzer-winning drama "Wit" (HBO, 2001). Focusing on an uptight, sardonic professor who contracts terminal cancer, the film version was a brilliantly acted ensemble piece, anchored by Thompson's luminous performance. Nichols served as co-executive producer, co-author of the teleplay (with Thompson) and director and earned Emmy Awards for his direction and as producer of the Outstanding Made for Television Movie. A remarkable achievement for any medium, "Wit" demonstrated that when given the right material, Nichols could still rise to the occasion. So anticipation runs high for his next project, the six-part HBO adaptation of Tony Kushner's charged epic "Angels in America" (lensed 2002). With a stellar cast led by Al Pacino, Meryl Streep and Emma Thompson, the completed film would undoubtedly be among the most highly anticipated TV presentations of the year.—Written by Ted Murphy

COMPANIONS:

Elaine May. Actor, writer, director; met in 1954

while both were living in Chicago; had brief romance before forming their famous on-stage partnership

wife: Diane Sawyer. Anchorwoman, journalist; born on December 22, 1945; married on April 29, 1988 in New York

MILESTONES:

Born in Berlin

1936: At age four, had a bad reaction to a defective whopping-cough vaccine that left him permanently denuded

1939: Sent with brother to USA to live with father who had arrived in NYC in 1938

1939: Placed by father with an English-speaking family

1943: Certified as a "genius" at age 12 (date approximate)

1948: As a 16-year-old, attended a performance of the Broadway play "A Streetcar Named Desire" and decided he had to "be around theatre"

While attending the University of Chicago, directed first stage play, a student production of "Purgatory", featuring Edward Asner

1954: After dropping out of college, moved to NYC to study acting with Lee Strasberg; returned to Chicago after just about a year

1955–1957: With Elaine May, Alan Arkin, Barbara Harris and Paul Sills, formed improvisational group The Compass Players (later Second City)

Formed a comedy trio with May and Shelley Berman

1958: Was fired from The Compass at May's insistance

1958: With May, began appearing in nightclubs in NYC; appeared on "The Steve Allen Show" and later "Omnibus"

1959: TV debut as panelist on "Laugh Line"

1960: Made Broadway debut in "An Evening with Mike Nichols and Elaine May"; reportedly the pair began to experience difficulties which occasionally spilled over into their performances

1962: Had lead in May's stage play "A Matter of Position"; closed out of town in Philadelphia; following the failure of the production, the pair ended their professional and personal relationship for many years

1962: Staged "The World of Jules Feiffer" in New Jersey; Stephen Sondheim contributed the music

1962: Was one of the writers for the variety special "Julie and Carol at Carnegie Hall" (CBS), featuring Julie Andrews and Carol Burnett

1963: Directed first Broadway play, "Barefoot in the Park" (originally titled "Nobody Loves Me" during its tryout at the Bucks County Playhouse); won first Tony Award

1965: Enjoyed two stage successes with "Luv" and Simon's "The Odd Couple", earning second Tony Award for direction of both

1966: Feature film directing debut, "Who's Afraid of Virginia Woolf?"; received first Academy Award nomination as Best Director

1967: Earned Best Director Oscar for "The Graduate"

1968: Reunited with Simon on "Plaza Suite"; picked up Tony Award

1970: Directed the screen adaptation of Joseph Heller's comic novel "Catch-22"

1971: Feature producing debut, "Carnal Knowledge"; also directed

1972: Was director of the Neil Simon play "The Prisoner of Second Avenue"; won Tony Award

1973: Helmed "The Day of the Dolphin"

1975: Directed "The Fortune", teaming Jack Nicholson and Warren Beatty

1975: Left film directing for a period after closing down the set of the Neil Simon-scripted "Bogart Slept Here"

Executive produced the ABC drama series "Family"

1977: Produced first stage musical, "Annie", the Tony-winning Best Musical adapted from the comic strip

1977: Staged the Pulitzer-winning two-character comedy-drama "The Gin Game", starring Jessica Tandy and Hume Cronyn

1980: Returned to stage acting as George in "Who's Afraid of Virginia Woolf?" at the Long Wharf Theatre in New Haven, Connecticut (opposite Elaine May as Martha)

1980: Directed the concert film "Gilda Live"

1983: Picked up third Best Director Oscar nomination for "Silkwood", starring Meryl Streep

1984: Staged Tom Stoppard's play "The Real Thing"; won Tony Award

1984: Produced and served as production supervisor on the one-person show "Whoopi Goldberg"

1986: Executive produced "The Long Shot", helmed by Paul Bartel

1986: Reteamed with Streep and Nicholson for "Heartburn", adapted from Nora Ephron's roman-a-clef

1988: Served as executive producer of the short-lived ABC sitcom "The Thorns"

1988: Received fourth Academy Award nomination for Best Director for the screen comedy "Working Girl"

1988: With Paul Sills and George Morrison, founded the New Actors Workshop

1988: Staged a revival of Beckett's "Waiting for Godot" with Steve Martin, Robin Williams and Bill Irwin in leading roles

1990: Third film with Streep, "Postcards From the Edge"

1991: Directed Harrison Ford in "Regarding Henry"

1992: Last Broadway directorial assigment to date, "Death and the Maiden", starring Glenn Close, Gene Hackman and Richard Dreyfuss

1993: As one of the producers, shared Best Picture Oscar nomination for "The Remains of the Day"

1994: Reunited with Jack Nicholson for "Wolf"

1996: First film collaboration with Elaine May, "The Birdcage", a loose remake of "La cage aux folles", teaming Robin Williams and Nathan Lane

1996: London stage acting debut, "The Designated Mourner", by Wallace Shawn

1997: Film acting debut, reprised role in David Hare's film of "The Designated Mourner"

1998: Again teamed with May, helming her script for the film version of the political satire "Primary Colors"

1999: Honored with a tribute by the Film Society of Lincoln Center (May 3)

2000: Produced and directed "What Planet Are You From?"

2001: Helmed the HBO adaptation of the Pulitzer-winning play "Wit", starring Emma Thompson, with whom he co-wrote the script; also executive produced; premiered at Berlin Film Festival; earned Emmy awards for direction and as co-executive producer

2001: Returned to stage directing, helming "The Seagull" in NYC's Central Park

Directed the HBO adaptation of Tony Kushner's epic "Angels in America" (lensed 2002)

QUOTES:

Nichols formed Icarus Productions.

When he won the Emmy Award in 2001, he joined the ranks of a select few who have won all four of the major entertainment awards in competition. The others are Mel Brooks, Rita Moreno, Marvin Hamlisch, Helen Hayes, Sir John Gielgud and Audrey Hepburn.

Presented with the 2002 National Medal of Arts by US President George Bush.

"In the late '80s, Nichols had a crise de conscience, triggered, he says, by a severe depression brought on by Halcion . . . He would begin to feel he was subject to some vague retribution 'for having escaped, for no particular reason the Holocaust . . . ' He considers the 'art film' or 'auteur' period of the '60s and '70s an aberration, a dead end. He points out that movies have always been a popular medium . . . Do we really want to hear Bach on the harmonica? Wouldn't we prefer 'Oh! Susanna'?"— From *Premiere*, March 1994.

"I never worked with anyone in my life— nor will I work with anyone as good as Mike Nichols."—playwright Neil Simon.

"He appears to defer to you, then in the end he gets exactly what he wants. He conspires with you rather than directs you, to get your best."—Richard Burton.

"A joke is like an orgasm. It has no politics."—Mike Nichols

"I was standing right behind Marilyn Monroe when she sang 'Happy Birthday' [to President John F. Kennedy in 1962] She had been sewed into her dress. And as she stepped up on the thing, it split. I could see her *ass*. In this sort of flesh-colored-to-begin-with dress. So I have a very clear memory of that.

"There was a party after that show and we made some Bobby jokes, and [Bobby Kennedy] was very pissed. He said, 'I'm going to look into your tax returns.' And then we were on the dance floor, and he and Marilyn danced past us, having met that night. And I actually heard her say—it's so bizarre—I heard her say, 'I like you, Bobby.' And he said, 'I like you, too, Marilyn.' Who would write this dialogue for the night they met? And I heard it! I was Zelig! You don't know that history is being made when it's being made."—Nichols quoted in *New York*, March 2, 1998.

"I am drawn to the mystery of marriage. You can never know what the contract is between two people, and that is a very strong subject. I think it may be *my* subject. The few intimate scens that there are in ["Primary Colors"] are very powerful. They are clues to a mystery that can't be solved. If you've ever known a couple where the husband is a great philanderer, you'll recognize that no one ever knows what the wife thinks about it, or how much she knows. It cannot be known. All that's known is that in some way, to some extent, she is a participant."—Nichols to *Empire*, November 1998.

On his relationship with Elaine May, Mike Nichols was quoted in the *Los Angeles Times* (March 15, 1998): "She has all my references. She's the person to whom I have to explain nothing. In the '50s, we were two hot, head-strong adolescents. Now we're two infinitely courteous, almost Japanese diplomats."

"As a director, my job is, and always has been, divided into a number of things: dealing with the crew, the money and the studio, and the marketing and publicity. These are all different jobs that have to be learned and done as well as possible. The celebrity part rarely touches a director."—Mike Nichols to Brendan Lemon in *Interview*, April 1998.

About why he cannot live in Los Angeles, Nichols was quoted by Peter Applebome in *The New York Times* (April 25, 1999) as saying: "There's a virus I have no protection against if I'm there: How am I perceived? And you can do whatever you like, put towels at the bottom of the door, not read the trades, which I have not done in 35 years. if you're there long enough, you will think, 'But how am I perceived?' If you're vulnerable to the virus, you've got to stay away from the matrix."

"He always pushed with agents—I speak for us all: more money, more power, more billing. Eventually the demands became cruel. Artists in the theater should not take from each other things that are not necessary.

. . . "He's ruthless when he wants to be, maybe even when he doesn't want to be. He doesn't let anything stand in his way."—agent Robert Lantz quoted in the February 21 & 28, 2000 *The New Yorker* profile by John Lahr.

"My father wasn't too crazy about me. I loved him anyway. One of the things I regretted for a long time was that he died before he could see that he would be proud of me. I was actually more what he wished for than he thought."—Mike Nichols quoted by John Lahr in a profile published in *The New Yorker* February 21 & 28, 2000 and collected in the 2001 book "Show Time: *New Yorker* Profiles."

"He's not as generous to himself as he deserves to be. He's got a voice in him that's very harsh, and unnecessarily so."—Annette Bening quoted in a profile of Nichols written by John Lahr first published in *The New Yorker* (February 21 & 28, 2000) and later collected in "Show and Tell: *New Yorker* Profiles", published in 2001.

Christopher Nolan

BORN: in England 1970

NATIONALITY: British

CITIZENSHIP: United Kingdom
United States

EDUCATION: University College London, England English

AWARDS: Sundance Film Festival Waldo Salt Screenwriting Award "Memento" 2001

London Film Critics' Circle Award Best British Screenplay "Memento" 2000

British Independent Film Award Best Foreign Independent Film (English Language) "Memento" 2001

Los Angeles Film Critics Association Award Best Screenplay "Memento" 2001

Boston Society of Film Critics Award Best Screenplay "Memento" 2001

Toronto Film Critics Association Award Best Film "Memento" 2001

Toronto Film Critics Association Award Best Screenplay "Memento" 2001

Southeastern Film Critics Association Award Best Picture "Memento" 2001

Southeastern Film Critics Association Award Best Original Screenplay "Memento" 2001; awarded despite the fact the film is based on a short story

Las Vegas Film Critics Society Award Best Picture "Memento" 2001

Las Vegas Film Critics Society Award Best Screenplay (Original or Adapted) "Memento" 2001

Online Film Critics Society Award Best Picture "Memento" 2001; tied with "Mulholland Dr."

Online Film Critics Society Award Best Adapted Screenplay "Memento" 2001

Online Film Critics Society Award Breakthrough Filmmaker "Memento" 2001

Dallas-Fort Worth Film Critics Association Russell Smith Award "Memento" 2001

Florida Film Critics Circle Award Best Screenplay "Memento" 2001

American Film Institute Award Screenwriter of the Year "Memento" 2001; initial presentation of the award

Broadcast Film Critics Association Award Best Screenplay "Memento" 2001

Chicago Film Critics Award Best Screenplay "Memento" 2002

Independent Spirit Award Best Feature "Memento" 2002

Independent Spirit Award Best Director "Memento" 2002

Independent Spirit Award Best Screenplay "Memento" 2002

MTV Movie Awards Best New Filmmaker 2002

BIOGRAPHY

Like many future filmmakers, British-born Christopher Nolan began making amateur movies at an early age, playing around with a Super-8mm camera that belonged to his father. When his family relocated to Chicago for three years during his formative years, this child of a British father and American mother traded tips on movie making with pals Roko and Adrian Belic (who in 1998 premiered their documentary "Genghis Blues"). While an undergraduate at University College in London, Nolan saw his short "Tarantella" air in the USA on PBS in 1989. By the mid-90s, he had hooked up with Jeremy Theobold who appeared in the shorts "Larceny" and "Doodlebug." Theobold would go on to produce and star in Nolan's feature directorial debut, "Following" (1998). Serving as director, co-producer, co-editor and cinematographer, he inverted some of the conventions of the film noir to recount the tale of a blocked writer (Theobold) who spends his days stalking strangers in the hopes of jump-starting his imagination. Then, one of his "victims" turns the tables and invites the scribe to join in a series of petty thefts. Juggling time via flashbacks and flash forwards, Nolan established a key signature of his work in which chronology takes a back seat to character. Critics found much that was admirable in Nolan's first feature, although most felt it was a marginal achievement, at best.

Nolan took a giant leap forward with his second film, "Memento" (2000), working from an unpublished short story by his brother Jonathan. An intriguing skewering of the conventions of film noir, "Memento" centers on a man with "anterograde amnesia", a condition that does not allow him to form new memories, who is seeking the man who raped and murdered his wife. While the heart of the piece was a conventional revenge drama, the story unfolded in an intriguing manner—backwards, with bits of additional information added each time. Fascinating and complex, "Memento" earned great acclaim when it opened in Europe in fall 2000 and at its US premiere at the 2001 Sundance Film Festival where Nolan picked up the Waldo Salt Screenwriting Award. The film also earned him numerous citations from critics' groups. Despite the fact that the idea for the story originated with his brother's fiction, Nolan's screenplay was deemed an original for the purposes of Academy Award consideration, in part because the film had premiered in both Great Britain and the USA before the short story was published in the March 2001 issue of *Esquire*. Capitalizing on his success, Nolan directed the English-language remake of the 1997 Norwegian crime thriller "Insomnia" (2002), starring three previous Academy Award winners, Al Pacino, Robin Williams and Hilary Swank. The critical response to the film was mixed: while some labeled the thriller as an early Oscar contender and heaped praise on Williams' smart, controlled performance, others found the film a lackluster sophomore follow-up to the bravura efforts of "Memento." Nevertheless, Warner Brothers, which produced "Insomnia," was still confident enough in Nolan's talents to tap him to direct its long-aborning effort to revive the all-but-defunt "Batman" franchise after various other incarnations failed to make it into production.

FAMILY:
brother: Jonathan Nolan. Author; wrote short story upon which "Memento" (2000) was based

COMPANION:
wife: Emma Thomas. Producer

MILESTONES:
Began making short films at age seven
Spent three years of his youth living in Chicago; made early films with Roko and Adrian Belic (the future Oscar nominees for the documentary "Genghis Blues")
1989: Made short "Tarantella" which received airing on PBS in USA
1996: Short film "Larceny" screened at the Cambridge Film Festival; Jeremy Theobald made acting debut
Collaborated with Theobald on the short "Doodlebug"
1998: Feature directorial debut, "Following"; Theobald starred and served as one of the producers
2000: Helmed second feature, the acclaimed thriller "Memento", adapted from a story by his brother
2002: Directed the English-language remake of "Insomnia"
Tapped to direct a revival of Warner Bros. superhero franchise "Batman" (deal announced 2003)

QUOTES:

"I'm interested in films that you want to come back to multiple times."—Christopher Nolan quoted in *Daily Variety,* January 17, 2001.

In response to a query about the problems of adapting a short story as a film, Nolan told Will McKenzie of www.6degrees.co.uk (October 2000): "Well I think the problems in the case of a highly conceptual piece of material is to come up with a story that can hold the attention for a couple of hours without losing the simplicity. It is a very simple concept and it's very challenging to create a two-hour story where every-thing keeps on coming back to that concept. Very often the temptation as a filmmaker is to take the concept of the story and go somewhere different. I tried to take the story that was an organic expansion of the concept. That was the biggest challenge."

"I get annoyed when I see films and I end up questioning where the camera has been placed. When I shoot a film, I want to know in every shot whose point of view we're seeing."—Christopher Nolan, quoted in the *Daily Varsity* (www.varsity.cam.ca.uk), October 19, 2000.

Phillip Noyce

BORN: in Griffith, New South Wales, Australia, 04/27/1950

NATIONALITY: Australian

EDUCATION: Australian Film Television and Radio School, Sydney, Australia, 1973; year-long program; made the short, "Castor and Pollux"

AWARDS: Australian Film Institute Award Best Short Film "Castor and Pollux" 1973

Australian Film Institute Award Best Original Screenplay "Newsfront" 1978

Australian Film Institute Award Best Director "Newsfront" 1978

Australian Film Institute Award Best Film "Newsfront" 1978

National Board of Review Award Best Director "The Quiet American" and "Rabbit-Proof Fence" 2002

BIOGRAPHY

Leading Australian filmmaker turned mainstream Hollywood director, Noyce began making short films and documentaries in the late 1960s and gained attention when he won the Australian Film Industry (AFI) award for best short film. He directed documentary short subjects for Film Australia while working on his first feature, "Backroads" (1977). Noyce became a prominent director in the Australian film industry when his feature "Newsfront" (1978), which he also co-wrote, garnered three AFI awards for Best Feature, Director, and Original Screenplay.

Noyce's next feature, "Heatwave" (1981), starring a then-unknown Judy Davis, was another critical success. He continued to make films in Australia until Hollywood beckoned, after seeing his accomplished work on "Dead Calm" (1989). Produced by George Miller, this seagoing thriller starred Sam Neill, Nicole Kidman, and Billy Zane. Noyce made an inauspicious American debut with "Blind Fury" (1989), starring Rutger Hauer as a blind Vietnam vet who is improbably adept with swords and other low-tech tools for maiming. Noyce rebounded with a major popular success, "Patriot Games" (1992). Starring Harrison Ford, this was the second installment of the Jack Ryan franchise derived from Tom Clancy's immensely popular espionage novels. Noyce followed up with "Sliver" (1993), a routine psychosexual thriller with Sharon Stone, and rejoined the Ford money train, directing the

"Patriot Games" follow-up "Clear and Present Danger" (1994). In 1997, he steered Val Kilmer and Elisabeth Shue in the big screen remake of "The Saint" and had a mild hit with the thriller "Bone Collector" (1998) starring Denzel Washington and Angelina Jolie. But Noyce grew restless as a journeyman director of Hollywood fare and turned his attentions back to his more independent roots, a gambit that paid off handsomely in 2002 when two of his films were released nearly simultaneously. He received tremendous critical praise for his screen adaptation of Graham Greene's "The Quiet American," which starred Brendan Fraser and, in a performance that generated terrific awards buzz, Michael Caine. Equally well-received was "Rabbit-Proof Fence," the true story of the epic journey of three Aboriginal girls in 1930s Australia.

MILESTONES:

1967: Made first short-film at age 17, "Better to Reign In Hell"

Worked at Film Australia, directing short documentaries

1975: First feature credit, as assistant director, "The Golden Cage"

1976: Credited as 2nd assistant director on the feature, "Let the Balloon Go"

1977: Feature directorial debut, "Backroads" (also producer and screenwriter)

1980: Became the part-time manager of the Sydney Filmmaker's Co-operative

Directed and co-wrote the ten-hour Australian mini-series, "Cowra Breakout"

1986: American TV debut, "The Curse"

1989: American feature debut, "Blind Fury"

1989: Major breakthrough as director of the sleeper hit "Dead Calm"

1992: Directed his first Jack Ryan film based on the books by Tom Clancy, "Patriot Games"; the first film with Harrison Ford in the lead role

1993: Directed the voyeuristic thriller "Silver" starring Sharon Stone

1994: Helmed second Tom Clancy film "Clear and Present Danger," again with Ford

1997: Directed update of the pulp hero "The Saint" starring Val Kilmer

1998: Directed the little-seen thriller "The Repair Shop"

1999: Helmed "The Bone Collector" with Denzel Washington

2002: Directed "Rabbit-Proof Fence," a true story of Australian Aboriginal girls set in the 1930s; received National Board of Review Award as Best Director; also for "The Quiet American"

2002: Directed film adaptation of Graham Greene's "The Quiet American," starring Michael Caine and Brendan Fraser; received National Board of Review Award as Best Director; also for "Rabbit-Proof Fence"

Manoel de Oliveira

BORN: Manoel Candido Pinto de Oliveira in Oporto, Portugal, 12/12/1908

SOMETIMES CREDITED AS:

Manoel de Oliveira

NATIONALITY: Portuguese

EDUCATION: Colegio Universal Oporto, Portugal; primary school

Colegio de la Guardia, Galicia, Spain; quit before graduating

studied acting with Rino Lupo in Porto

AWARDS: Siena Film Festival Grand Prix "Acto da primavera" 1963

International Centre for the Defense of the Arts and Literature in the Cinema (CIDALC) Gold Medal 1980

Venice Film Festival Special Golden Lion for

Career Achievement 1985; cited with John Huston

Cannes Film Festival Special FIPRESCI Prize 1990 awarded for his body of work

Venice Film Festival Special Jury Prize "La divina comedia" 1991

Luchino Visconti Award 1994

European Film Academy FIPRESCI Prize "Viagem ao principio do mundo/Voyage to the Begining of the World" 1997

Cannes Film Festival Jury Prize "A Carta/The Letter" 1999

BIOGRAPHY

This preeminent Portuguese filmmaker began his career as an actor and documentary filmmaker in the 1920s and turned to fictional works in 1942. When his first feature, the brilliantly photographed children's film "Aniki-Bo" failed to find an audience, he retreated for close to 15 years before returning to moviemaking. By the time, Oliveira began to receive worldwide attention as a prominent director, he was already in his 60s. Thirty years later, he was still making accomplished films that captivated critics and audiences.

The son of a prominent businessman, Manoel de Oliveira spent part of his youth engaging in athletic pursuits. By the age of 17, he had dropped out of school and had begun working in the family business, all the while pursuing leisure time activities as varied as racing cars (which he continued to do until 1940) and the cinema. Strongly influenced by Soviet filmmakers as well as the French impressionists (especially Jean Vigo), German expressionists (such as Walther Ruttmann) and American pioneers like D.W. Griffith, Oliveira began his film career at age 19 when he worked on an uncompleted film about Portugal's participation in World War I. Over the next two years, he acted in "Fatima Milagrosa" (1928), directed by his acting teacher Rino Lupo and collaborated with painter Ventura Porfirio on another unrealized animated motion picture.

Over the next three years, Oliveira worked on his first silent documentary, "Douro, Faima Fluvial/Hard Labor on the River Douro" (1931), establishing a pattern of working as writer, editor, producer and director.

Over the course of the 1930s, Oliveira devoted his energies to several abortive features and produced only a handful of forgettable documentaries (e.g., "Estautuas de Lisbon/Statues of Lisbon" 1932). He also had a substantial role in Portugal's premiere all-sound feature "A Cancao de Lisbon/Song of Lisbon" (1934). By the time the 40s rolled around, Oliveira was at work on his first feature, "Aniki-Bobo" (1942), which combined elements of French poetic realism with what came to be regarded as Italian neorealism. The film, however, proved unsuccessful in his homeland, partly due to its location shooting and its frank depiction of street urchins. (Several Portuguese critics deemed it immoral). Perhaps ironically, these qualities were exactly what drew praise from foreign critics. Nearly forty years later, partly from repeated airings on Portuguese television, "Aniki-Bobo" became one of the most popular films in the country.

After the devastating reception of "Aniki-Bobo", Oliveira retreated to the life of a gentleman farmer while not wholeheartedly abandoning scriptwriting. It took 14 years and a sojourn to Germany to study color techniques, however, before he was able to secure financing for his first color film "O Pintor e a Cidade/The Painter and the City" (1956), a documentary set in his birthplace of Oporto. By contrasting photographic shots of the city with the paintings of artist Antonio Cruz, Oliveira crafted what one critic called a "philosophical essay in film language about the behavior of the human being in a town." The filmmaker followed with the near silent "O Pao/Bread" (1959), which traced the production of loaves from the wheatfields through to the consumer.

1963 marked the beginning of Oliveira's worldwide acclaim. That year's superb "Acto da

Primavera/The Passion of Jesus", ostensibly a documentary of a staging of a Passion Play that Oliveira framed in a political context. Some theorists have posited that "Acto da Primavera" coupled with the same year's short "A Caca/The Hunt", which centered on attempts by a hunting party to rescue on of its members who has fallen into a bog, as reflective of the director's views on heaven and hell. Certainly the former possesses a certain spiritual dimension while the latter was originally meant to be a discourse on violence (although censorship forced him to adopt a more hopeful resolution). The pair of films brought him further attention from outside his homeland (Oliveira was the subject of retrospectives at the 1964 Locarno Film Festival and at the Paris Cinematheque the following year) but also marked the beginning of an eight-year hiatus in filmmaking.

At the age of 63, Oliveira was asked to join a filmmaking cooperative comprised mostly of members of the New Portuguese cinema. He turned out what has come to be called his "Quartet of Frustrated Loves", which began with "O Passado e o Presente/Past and Present" (1971), a satirical look at marriage among the upper classes that many praised for its visual inventiveness (with a great debt to Bunuel) and aural wonders. "Benilde ou a Virgem Mae/Bernilde: Virgin and Mother" (1975) was based on a play by long-time associate Jose Regio that examined the predicament of a deeply religious young woman who mysteriously becomes pregnant. Oliveira stumbled in a major way with the third entry in his tetrology, "Amor de Perdicao/Ill-Fated Love" (1978) which was originally made as a four-part television presentation of Camilo Castello Branco's popular novel. Loosely inspired by "Romeo and Juliet" and unsuccessfully acted by amateurs, the production unfolded at a glacial pace and critics and audiences rejected it. It took the director four years to return to grace with what many consider one of his finest films, "Francesca" (1981). Adapted from a romance novel about an Englishwoman torn between Castello Branco and his friend Jose Augusto, "Francesca" contained highly imaginative, theatrical tableaux and literate dialogue. He concluded the quartet in 1992 with "O Dia do Desepero/The Day of Despair", an examination of the last years in the life of Castello Branco.

In between, Oliveira cast a backward glance and crafted the autobiographical "Memorias e Confissoes/Memories and Confessions" (1982), which after its completion he deemed was too personal to be released until after his death. Instead, he returned to the documentary form for "Lisboa Cultural/Cultural Lisbon" (1983) and "Nice a propos de Jean Vigo" (1984), which featured his eldest son in an examination of the city of Nice and its thriving Portuguese community. Also in 1983, Oliveira began working on his epic nearly seven-hour adaptation of Paul Claudel's 1929 verse drama "The Satin Slipper/Sapato de Cetim/Le Soulier de satin". Divided into four parts, this ambitious historical drama, shot on a $12 million dollar budget, inaugurated a new theme in the director's oeuvre, theatrical cinema. As he explained at the time, "Theater is the representation of life; cinema is the representation of life, not of theater. Theater and cinema are the same thing with different possibilities." Critics praised "The Satin Slipper" when it premiered at the 1985 Venice Film Festival, citing its visual splendor, humor and craftsmanship.

Building on those themes, Oliveira next filmed "Mon cas/My Case" (1986), another four-part piece that incorporated a one-act by Jose Regio performed three times, once with sound, another silently with a voice-over reading from Samuel Beckett and lastly with a reversed sound track. The fourth section drew on the biblical story of Job. Highly stylized, the film had little appeal beyond those interested in charting the director's career, Undaunted, the director tackled filmed opera in "Os Canibais/The Canibals" (1988), a triangular romance that contained fascinating tableaux but which left viewers a bit put off.

As the 90s progressed, Oliveira continued to work at a time when many of his contemporaries were either dead, too infirm to work or retired. The tireless director continued to make at least one film per year, some more successful than others. "The Valley of Abraham" (1993) was a cleverly conceived homage to Flaubert's "Madame Bovary" while "The Convent/O Convento" (1995) marked his first time using an International cast of "name" actors (in this case John Malkovich and Catherine Deneuve). Stylistically, "The Convent" which was essentially the Faust tale recast with an academic, seemed more accessible than much of his other work, but it also was replete with his sparing use of camera movement and closeups. For some, his work leaned to the old-fashioned while to his devotees, it provided an intelligent and often humorous viewpoint. The cerebral chamber piece "Party" (1996) did little to win him new admirers but "Journey to the Beginning of the World" (1997) improved his profile, partly because his semi-autobiographical film featured the final screen performance of Marcello Mastroianni playing a thinly-veiled version of the director. Even after achieving this career high and approaching his 90th birthday, Oliveira continued to work, turning out the tripartite omnibus "Inquietude/Anxiety" (1998) and "A Carta/The Letter/La Lettre" (1999), a modern-day adaptation of "La Princess de Cleves", about a woman (the luminous Chiara Mastroianni) striving to maintain her "good name" by avoiding an affair with a pop singer. While there was something quaint and decidedly anachronistic about the main character's dilemma, the director managed to package the proceedings beautifully.

MILESTONES:

While growing up, competed as a gymnast and athlete

1925: Joined father's business aged 17 (date approximate)

Competed as a race car driver in Portugal and Brazil up until 1940

1927: With others attempted—but failed—to make a film about Portugal's participation in WWI

1928: Acting debut in the silent "Fatima Milagrosa", directed by Rino Lupo

1929: Worked with painter Ventura Porfirio on an animated film that was eventually abandoned

1931: Filmmaking debut as director, editor and scenarist with the documentary "Douro, faina fluvial/Hard Labor on the River Douro"; re-released 1934 with a score by Luis de Freitas Branco

1933: Acted in "A cancao de Lisboa/Song of Lisbon"; Portugese's first full sound film

During the 1930s, made shorts and documentaries; also worked on various projects that for many reasons were never completed

1942: Feature film writing and directing debut, the children's film "Aniki-Bobo"; at the time of its release was called "immoral" by many critics and proved a box office failure; inthe 1980s thanks to repeated showings on Portuguese television, it had become one of the country's most popular films

1943–1955: Supported family by farming; wrote various scripts but no film projects came to fruition

1955: Traveled to Germany to study color film techniques

1956: First film in 14 years, "O pintor e a cidade/The Painter and the City", a 45-minute documentary which contrasted photographic images of the city of Oporto with native painter Antonio Cruz's canvasses; served as writer, director, editor, producer and cameraman

1959: Wrote, directed and produced "O pao/Bread", a documentary commissioned by Portugal's National Federation of Industrial Millers; also edited and served as cameraman

1963: Filmed a Passion Play in northeastern Portugal for the documentary "Acto da primavera/The Passion of Jesus"

1963: Helmed the fictional short "A Caca/The Hunt"

1964: Retrospective of film work at Locarno

1964: Last film on which he served as cameraman, the short "As pinturas do meu irmao Julio/My Brother Julio's Paintings" (filmed in 1959), a collaboration with poet Jose Regio and his painter brother Julio

1971: At age 63, made return to fiction films with "O passado e o presente/Past and Present"

1975: Directed "Benilde ou a Virgem Mae/Benilde: Virgin and Mother", based on a play by Jose Regio

1978: Made "Amor de Perdicao/Ill-Fated Love", a loose adaptation of "Romeo and Juliet"; first feature to receive widespread festival screenings

1981: "Francesca", based on the novel "Fanny Owen", selected for the Directors' Fortnight at the Cannes Film Festival

1981: Appeared in Joao Botelho's "I, the Other/Conversa acabada"

1982: Made the autobiographical "Memorias e confissoes/Memories and Confession", based on his family history; decided the film should not be released until after his death

1985: Wrote and directed the nearly seven-hour "Sapato de cetim/The Silk Slipper", an adaptation of Paul Claudel's 1929 verse drama "Le Soulier de satin"; spent two years making the film

1986: Adapted another Regio play as "Mon cas/My Case"; selected as opening night presentation at the Venice Film Festival

1987: Debut as playwright, "De Produndis", based on a story by Agustina Bessa Luis and poems by Jose Regio

1988: Edited, wrote and directed "Os Canibas/The Cannibals", an opera about a love triangle

1991: Wrote, directed and edited "The Divine Comedy", a drama set in an insane asylum

1992: Made biographical drama about Camilo Castelo Branco, "O dia do desespero/The Day of Despair"

1993: Using Flaubert's "Madame Bovary" as inspiration, wrote, edited and directed "Vale Abraao/The Valley of Abraham"

1995: Teamed Catherine Denueve and John Malkovich in the drama "The Convent"

1996: Wrote and directed "Party", starring Michel Piccoli as an aging Don Juan

1997: Made semi-autobiographical feature "Viagem ao principio do mundo/Voyage to the Beginning of the World", in which Marcello Mastroianni played a filmmaker named Manoel reminiscing about his childhood

1999: At age 90, modernized "La Princess de Cleves" as "A Carta/La lettre/The Letter", starring Chiara Mastroianni as a woman struggling to retain her virtue in contemporary society

QUOTES:

"Artists always steal from life and the masters they had . . . Art is like a tree which spreads its different branches. Each artist adds a leaf, a little personal touch which is not, however, independent of all roots, whether it be history itself, those of nations or that of personal itineraries through life's fiction, feelings or men's reactions. That is why I am particularly conscious of that which is historical, whether it be based on history itself, on culture, or history of art, the artistic evolution of fiction, which is also a way of saying what is the way of life, what the different periods mean, and ways of being in the world.

"The richest writer is the biggest thief. " —Manoel Oliveira.

Nagisa Oshima

BORN: in Kyoto, Japan, 03/31/1932

NATIONALITY: Japanese

EDUCATION: University of Kyoto, Kyoto, Japan, law and political history; vice-president of university student association

AWARD: Cannes Film Festival Direction Award "Empire of Passion" 1978

BIOGRAPHY

Nagisa Oshima's career extends from the initiation of the "Nuberu bagu" (New Wave) movement in Japanese cinema in the late 1950s and early 1960s, to the contemporary use of cinema and television to express paradoxes in modern society.

After an early involvement with the student protest movement in Kyoto, Oshima rose rapidly in the Shochiku company from the status of apprentice in 1954 to that of director. By 1960, he had grown disillusioned with the traditional studio production policies and broke away from Shochiku to form his own independent production company, Sozosha, in 1965. With other Japanese New Wave filmmakers like Masahiro Shinoda, Shohei Imamura and Yoshishige Yoshida, Oshima reacted against the humanistic style and subject matter of directors like Yasujiro Ozu, Kenji Mizoguchi and Akira Kurosawa, as well as against established left-wing political movements.

Oshima has been primarily concerned with depicting the contradictions and tensions of postwar Japanese society. His films tend to expose contemporary Japanese materialism, while also examining what it means to be Japanese in the face of rapid industrialization and Westernization. Many of Oshima's earlier films, such as "Ai To Kibo No Machi/A Town of Love and Hope" (1959) and "Taiyo No Hakaba/The Sun's Burial" (1960), feature rebellious, underprivileged youths in anti-heroic roles. The film for which he is probably best known in the West, "Ai No Corrida/In the Realm of the Senses" (1976), centers on an obsessive sexual relationship. Like several other Oshima works, it gains additional power by being based on an actual incident.

Other important Oshima films include "Koshikei/Death by Hanging" (1968), an examination of the prejudicial treatment of Koreans in Japan; "Shonen/Boy" (1969), which deals with the cruel use of a child for extortion purposes, and with the child's subsequent escapist fantasies; "Tokyo Senso Sengo Hiwa/The Man Who Left His Will on Film" (1970), about another ongoing concern of Oshima's, the art of filmmaking itself; and "Gishiki/The Ceremony" (1971), which presents a microcosmic view of Japanese postwar history through the lives of one wealthy family.

In recent years, Oshima has repeatedly turned to sources outside Japan for the production of his films. This was the case with "Realm of the Senses" (1976), "Merry Christmas, Mr. Lawrence" (1983), and "Max mon amour" (1987). It is less well known in the West that Oshima has also been a prolific documentarian, film theorist and television personality. He is the host of a long-running television talk show, "The School for Wives", in which female participants (kept anonymous by a distorting glass) present their personal problems, to which he responds from off screen.

MILESTONES:

1954: Joined Shochiku film company as assistant director at Ofune Studios
Assisted directors including Masaki Kobayashi and Hideo Oba

1956: Began writing film criticism for various publications

1959: First film as director and screenwriter, "A Town of Love and Hope"

1960: Left Shochiku after company withdrew "Night and Fog in Japan" from release for fear of inciting political unrest

1965: Formed independent production company, "Sozosha" ("Creation") with wife, actress Akiko Koyama; first film, "Pleasures of the Flesh"

1976: First international co-production, "Empire of the Senses" (banned by US customs as "obscene" one day before scheduled screening at New York Film Festival)

1986: First film produced entirely outside Japan, "Max, My Love"

1996: Suffered stroke

1999: Returned to filmmaking after 12-year absence to helm "Gohatto/Forbidden/Taboo", dealing with homosexuality among a group of samurai; screened at Cannes in 2000

BIBLIOGRAPHY:

"The Films of Oshima Nagisa: Images of a Japanese Iconoclast" Maureen Turim 1998 University of California Press

Frank Oz

BORN: Frank Richard Oznowicz in Hereford, England, 05/25/1944

NATIONALITY: English

EDUCATION: Oakland City College, Oakland, California, 1962; enrolled to study journalism

AWARDS: Daytime Emmy Individual Achievement in Children's Programming "Sesame Street" 1973/74; shared award

Daytime Emmy Outstanding Individual Achievement in Children's Programming "Sesame Street" 1975/76; shared award with Jim Henson, Jerry Nelson, Carroll Spinney, and Richard Hunt

Emmy Outstanding Comedy Variety or Music Series "The Muppet Show" 1977/78; shared award with David Lazar, Jim Henson, Jerry Nelson, Richard Hunt, and Dave Goelz

Daytime Emmy Individual Achievement in Children's Programming "Sesame Street" 1978/79

American Comedy Award for Lifetime Achievement 1998

Art Directors Guild Cinematic Imagery Award 2002

BIOGRAPHY

Emmy-winner Frank Oz originally found fame for giving voice and life to such widely-loved synthetic creations as Fozzie Bear, Miss Piggy and Yoda. He has since gained recognition as a multi-talented director of comedies and children's fare. A longtime associate of Muppet creator Jim Henson, Oz's professional career took off on the celebrated children's educational series, "Sesame Street" (PBS, 1969–), where he operated and aurally embodied such kiddie icons as Grover and The Cookie Monster. While holding on to his day job, Oz followed Henson to evening TV for "The Muppet Show" (syndicated, 1976–81). Whereas "Sesame Street" targeted youngsters and stressed multi-culturalism, the ABCs and 1–2–3s, "The Muppet Show" courted older kids and adults by providing visual gags for the tots and verbal jabs and awful puns for the elders. Henson once credited Oz for "much of what's funny about the Muppets," but the best comedy emerged from the interplay between the exuberant Oz and the more subdued Henson.

Oz broke into features with "The Muppet Movie" (1979), which presented an excellent showcase for his prodigious skills as a puppeteer and voice artist. This paved the way for his vocal star turn as Yoda, the beloved 300-year-old midget mystic of "The Empire Strikes Back" (1980), "Return of the Jedi" (1983) and the untitled "Star Wars" prequel (scheduled for release in 1999). Despite success outside his collaboration with Henson, Oz remained loyal to the Muppets, staying involved both in front and behind the camera on their subsequent projects, although he could always find time for an acting cameo in the films of his director friend John Landis. Beginning with his role as a corrections officer in "The Blues Brothers" (1980), he appeared in "An American Werewolf in London" (1981), "Trading Places" (1983), "Spies Like Us" (1985), "Innocent Blood" (1992) and "Blues Brothers 2000" (1998).

Oz made his feature directorial debut co-directing with his mentor Henson "The Dark Crystal" (1982), an uneven fantasy adventure starring unfamiliar Muppets of a larger and less cute variety, then helmed solo "The Muppets Take Manhattan" (1984), which he also co-wrote (and in which Landis provided a cameo). With the musical remake "Little Shop of Horrors" (1986), adapted from the Off-Broadway hit, Oz proved himself an able director of live action with an assured sense of comedic timing. This also marked his first collaboration with comic actor Steve Martin; their subsequent projects would include "Dirty Rotten Scoundrels", a 1988 remake of the 1964 Marlon Brando/David Niven comedy "Bedtime Story", and "Housesitter" (1992), a light comedy with Goldie Hawn.

Oz returned to kids' stuff as director of the engagingly old-fashioned "The Indian in the Cupboard" (1995). Adapted from an acclaimed best-selling children's novel by Melissa Mathison, the sensitively rendered film told the story of a boy who learns a series of life lessons after discovering that an old cupboard can bring his toys to life. Following Henson's death in 1990, Oz debuted as executive producer on "The Muppet Christmas Carol" (1992), directed by Henson's son Brian, and served in the same capacity for Brian Henson's "Muppet Treasure Island" (1996), providing his trademark voices of Miss Piggy, Fozzie Bear and Sam Eagle for both. He then directed the highly successful "coming out" comedy hit "In & Out" (1997), starring Kevin Kline and Tom Selleck.

MILESTONES:

Born to parents whose hobby was the art of puppetry, began putting on his own shows by age of 12

Moved with family to Oakland, CA

1963: Recruited by Jim Henson at a West Coast convention of puppeteers

1969: First notable collaboration with Jim Henson, "Sesame Street" (PBS)

1976–1981: Created many voices for the syndicated "The Muppet Show"

1979: First feature, credited for voices, song performer and as creative consultant, "The Muppet Movie"

1980: Feature acting debut, "The Blues Brothers"

1980: Provided the voice of Yoda in "The Empire Strikes Back"

1981: First feature as producer, "The Great Muppet Caper"

1982: Feature directing debut, co-directed (with Jim Henson) "The Dark Crystal"

1984: First screenplay credit and solo directorial debut, "The Muppets Take Manhattan"; also puppeteer and voice of Miss Piggy, Fozzie Bear and Animal

1986: First non-Muppet feature directing assignment, the musical "Little Shop of Horrors"

1992: Debut as executive producer, "The Muppet Christmas Carol"

1993: Signed a two-year deal with Limelight Entertainment to direct commercials

1996: Puppeteer and provided voice characterizations for ABC's short-lived "Muppets Tonight!"

1996: Executive produced and performed in "Muppet Treasure Island", directed by Henson's son Brian

1997: Directed "In & Out", starring Kevin Kline

1998: Reprised his role as a corrections officer for John Landis' "Blues Brothers 2000"

1999: Once again operated the Yoda puppet and provided his voice for the "Star Wars" prequel "Episode I—The Phantom Menace"

2001: Directed the drama "The Score", starring Robert De Niro, Marlon Brando and Edward Norton

AFFILIATION: Vice president of Henson Associates

QUOTES:
In May 1999, Oz received the John C. Zacharis Memorial Award from Emerson College in Boston, Massachusetts

On the Henson legacy: "Something said at Jim's memorial was that he made good guys interesting. It's always the bad guys who are interesting. Jim's were good guys, but they were weird—just the irreverent joy he created was amazing."—Frank Oz in *Los Angeles Times*, September 14, 1997.

"In one rehearsal, I was working as Miss Piggy with Jim, who was doing Kermit, and the script called for her to slap him. Instead of a slap, I gave him a funny karate hit. Somehow, that hit crystallized her character for me—the coyness hiding the aggression; the conflict of that love with her desire for a career; her hunger for a glamour image; her tremendous out-and-out ego."—Frank Oz quoted in the obituary of Jim Henson in *The New York Times*, May 17, 1990.

Yasujiro Ozu

BORN: in Tokyo, Japan, 12/12/1903

DEATH: 12/11/1963

NATIONALITY: Japanese

EDUCATION: Uji-Yamada Middle School, Japan; entered Uji-Yamada Middle School aged 16, expelled from dormitory aged 17
   Waseda University Japan

AWARDS: Third Place in *Kinema Jumpo*'s Best Films "Ojosan/Young Miss" 1930; film now lost
   Third Place in *Kinema Jumpo*'s Best Films "Tokyo no gassho/Tokyo chorus" 1931
   First Place in *Kinema Jumpo*'s Best Films "Umarete wa mita keredo/I Was Born, But . . . " 1932

First Place in *Kinema Jumpo*'s Best Films "Dekigokoro/Passing Fancy" 1933
   First Place in *Kinema Jumpo*'s Best Films "Ukigusa monogatari/A Story of Floating Weeds" 1934
   First Place in *Kinema Jumpo*'s Best Films "Toda-ke no kyodai/The Brothers and Sisters of the Toda Family" 1940
   First Place in *Kinema Jumpo*'s Best Films "Banshun/Late Spring" 1950
   First Place in *Kinema Jumpo*'s Best Films "Bakusho/Early Summer" 1951

BIOGRAPHY
Few filmmakers outside the avant-garde have developed a personal style as rigorous as Yasujiro Ozu. While his films are in a sense experimental, he worked exclusively in the mainstream Japanese film industry, making extraordinary

movies about quite ordinary events. His early films include a ghost story, a thriller, and a period piece, but Ozu is best known and admired for his portraits of everyday family life shot in what one critic has called a most "unreasonable style."

Ozu's early fascination with cinema soon turned into an obsession; as a student he reportedly went to great lengths to skip school and watch movies, usually Hollywood fare. His own filmmaking career began with his entry in 1923 into the newly formed Shochiku Studios, where he worked as an assistant cameraman and an assistant director. He directed his first film in 1927, and over the next four years directed twenty-one more.

The years 1931 to 1940 saw some of his greatest films, and he received the Best Film award from Kinema Jumpo three consecutive times, for "I Was Born, But . . . " (1932), "Passing Fancy" (1933) and "A Story of Floating Weeds" (1934). During the war, he directed two relatively successful films before being sent to Singapore to make propaganda pictures. There, he had the opportunity to screen captured prints of American films; later he would comment: "Watching "Fantasia" made me suspect that we were going to lose the war. These guys look like trouble, I thought."

Upon his return to Japan, he directed several unexceptional films before returning to form with "Late Spring" (1949). From this point onward, Ozu scaled down his output to about one film a year, while maintaining the high standards he had set during the thirties.

The most distinctive aspect of Ozu cinema is its self-imposed restraint. The elements of his unique style were in place by the mid-1930s and are deceptively easy to list. They represent a range of "unreasonable" choices, which the director continually refined (or reduced) throughout his career. Ozu's signature feature is his camera placement, which is usually (but not always) close to the ground. Its position is actually proportional: the height can change, as long as it stays lower than the object being shot.

Ozu also developed a curious form of transition, which various critics have labeled "pillow shots" or "curtain shots." Between scenes, he would always place carefully framed shots of the surroundings to signal changes in setting, as well as for less obvious reasons. Basically a hybrid of the cutaway and placing shots, these transitions were considered unusual for extended length; they sometimes seem motivated more by graphic composition and pacing than by the demands of the narrative.

Ozu's most radical departure from classical style was his use of 360-degree space. By convention, Hollywood style dictates that the camera should stay within a 180-degree space to one side of the action. This is to provide proper "screen direction" and a sense of homogenous space. Ozu's camera, on the other hand, orbits around the characters. Furthermore, this 360-degree space is broken down into multiples of 45 degrees, into which the camera angles generally fall. This produces a number of unusual effects, but Ozu's stories are so engrossing that they don't disrupt the story.

One effect of jumping over the 180-degree stage line is that actors facing each other seem to look off in the same direction. Ozu's response to this was to place characters in identical positions between (as well as within) shots. He favored a sitting position with the actor's body "torqued" to face the camera. Frustrated actors found their bodies treated as objects to be carefully manipulated within the frame, their lines to be delivered with a minimum of emotion and movement.

Ozu pushed this "graphic matching" between shots to notorious extremes: it is not unusual to see props such as beer bottles moved across tables or closer to the camera to preserve their size and screen position from shot to shot. Any effects that interfered with composition were cast away; Ozu never used a zoom and only one dissolve (in "Life of an Office Worker," 1929). He also subordinated camera movement to composition; he never used pans because they disturbed his framing. The few Ozu tracking shots were designed to maintain a static composition (by moving along a road with a character, for example). When Ozu began shooting in color (with "Higanbana," 1958), he did away with camera movement altogether.

While Ozu's films are not flashy, they are exceedingly complex. An essay this brief cannot begin to suggest the extent to which all these stylistic features are systematically choreographed. The permutations of form and variation become so minute they are visible only on close, multiple viewings.

The motives for Ozu's style have been the subject of rigorous debate. Because he was thought "too Japanese" for foreigners to accept or understand, for many years his films were not exported. When critics in the West finally discovered his work, his "unreasonable style" was usually explained in thematic, anthropomorphic and even religious terms. His low camera, for example, was described as the point of view of a child, a dog, a god or a person sitting Japanese style. Some critics attempted to explain the Ozu style through questionable comparisons to Zen Buddhism. Marxist critic Noel Burch, on the other hand, felt Ozu exemplified a rejection of Hollywood style and its ideological baggage. To date, the most convincing explanation has been offered by Kristin Thompson and David Bordwell, who suggest that in Ozu's cinema questions of style may be detached from theme and narrative. Ozu's films feature a playful, overt narration in which stylistic features do not have to mean anything and can be appreciated for their own sake.

Despite their restraint, Ozu's films, with their families in the throes of marriage and death, are among the most touching of melodramas. As important and influential as Ozu was, no other filmmaker has ever adopted his style, leaving his 53 films quite unique in the history of cinema. Ironically, the influence of Ozu's visual style may be more readily noticeable in a number of non-Japanese filmmakers, including Wayne Wang, Jim Jarmusch and Wim Wenders, who called Ozu's films "a sacred treasure of the cinema."

MILESTONES:

1924: Joined Shochiku company as assistant cameraman

1926: Hired as assistant director to Tadamoto Okubo

1927: Film directing debut with "Zange no Yaiba/The Sword of Penitence" (based on US film "Kick-In;" first collobaration with screenwriter Kogo Noda)

1936: First sound film as director "Hitori musuko/The Only Son"

1937–1939: Served as infantry corporal in China during Sino-Japanese War

1943: Sent to Singapore to make propaganda films (never made any)

1958: Color-film directing debut with "Higanbana/Equinox Flower"

1962: Last film as director "Samma no aji/An Autumn Afternoon"

BIBLIOGRAPHY:

"Transcendental Style in Film: Ozu, Bresson, Dreyer" Paul Schrader

BORN: Alan William Parker in Islington, England, 02/14/1944

SOMETIMES CREDITED AS:
Sir Alan Parker

NATIONALITY: English

EDUCATION: Owen's School Islington, England, 1960

AWARDS: International Emmy Award Best Director "The Evacuees" 1975

BAFTA Award Best Screenplay "Bugsy Malone" 1976

BAFTA Award Best Direction "Midnight Express" 1978

British Press Guild Award Best Documentary "A Turnip Head's Guide to British Cinema" 1984

Cannes Film Festival Special Jury Prize "Birdy" 1985

BAFTA Michael Balcon Award for Outstanding Contribution to Cinema 1985; cited with Alan Marshall

National Board of Review Award Best Director "Mississippi Burning" 1988

Berlin Film Festival Silver Bear "Mississippi Burning" 1988

Tokyo International Film Festival Best Director Award "The Commitments" 1991

BAFTA Award Best Film "The Commitments" 1991

BAFTA Award Best Director "The Commitments" 1991

Golden Satellite Best Motion Picture (Musical or Comedy) "Evita" 1996; shared award with co-producers Robert Stigwood and Andrew Vajna; initial presentation of award

Golden Globe Award Best Motion Picture (Musical or Comedy) "Evita" 1996; shared award with co-producers Robert Stigwood and Andrew Vajna

Cineam Expo Lifetime Achievement Award 1999

BIOGRAPHY

From his humble beginnings as an office boy at age 19, Alan Parker worked his way up in the advertising business and began his career in earnest when he and partner Alan Marshall founded a production company to make industrial films and commercials. Between 1969 and 1978, Parker churned out over 500 television commercials, winning every major industry award, while also being cited as an important influence on both fashion and film style of that time. He adeptly used lighting, and his sense of drama as a feature film director has seemed to come as much from his early need to convey a message in 30 seconds as from a sense of pictorial grace.

In 1973, Parker wrote and directed a 50-minute film, "No Hard Feelings", which the BBC bought and eventually aired several years later. "The Evacuees" (1975), his first film produced for the BBC, brought attention from the theatrical marketplace. The following year, he and producer David Puttnam collaborated on Parker's debut as a writer-director, "Bugsy Malone", a musical spoof of gangster films with an all-children cast. His second feature, the powerful "Midnight Express" (1978) was based on the true story of an American arrested in Turkey for drug smuggling and earned six Oscar nominations, including one for Parker. (It won for the awards for Best Adapted Screenplay and Best Score.)

Parker followed the popular and stylish musical "Fame" (1980), his first US-produced feature, with arguably his most personal film "Shoot the Moon" (1981), a sensitively detailed examination of the disintegration of a marriage. The quirky, touching "Birdy" (1984) and the controversial "Angel Heart" (1987) solidified his reputation as a highly visual storyteller whose palette made use of the soundtrack as well as strong imagery. "Mississippi Burning" (1988), a glossy recreation of a famous civil rights murder case was praised for its fine performances (particularly by Gene Hackman as a veteran FBI man), but drew fire for its glib reworking of history. Plunging into farce, Parker directed Anthony Hopkins in "The Road to Wellville" (1994), a send-up of American health fadist John Kellogg. Parker also produced and wrote the screenplay based on T. Coraghessan Boyle's novel, but the colorful casting and spectacular cinematography was pretty much wasted on this uneven romp.

Among his contemporaries, Parker is the only director courageous enough to return again and again to the movie musical. Of course, good reviews build confidence, and critics have been generous with their praise of his efforts. The charming idea of casting kids in a gangster movie struck a responsive chord in most and "Bugsy Malone" also profited from an astonishingly assured performance from a 13-year-old Jodie Foster. His insights into talented young people and his ability to tell their stories in dozens of vignettes as opposed to a conventional linear plot helped insure the success of "Fame", and in "Pink Floyd—The Wall" (1982), he transformed a best-selling rock album into one of the great modern musicals. Visually stunning in its wide array of images that included animated sequences by cartoonist Gerald Scarfe, this movie appealed to a much wider audience than just rock 'n' roll fans. "The Commitments" (1991) for all its high energy and great soul music fell a bit short of the mark established by his other musicals, and though his "Evita" (1996) was epic, lavish and fascinating, the MTV-style editing diluted the inherent power of the material and worked against the integrity of Madonna's titular performance.

Always fiercely independent, Parker has often lambasted the British film establishment and film critics. No stranger to controversy, he took on the ratings board of the MPAA and personally challenged their "X" rating of "Angel Heart." Parker has also authored a compilation of satirical cartoons, "Hares in the Gate" (1982), and in 1984 produced "A Turnip Head's Guide to British Cinema", a sarcastic documentary which ridiculed the critical mentality, a film that delighted his filmmaking contemporaries as well as his four children, whom he has cited as his chief inspiration.—Written by Greg Senf

MILESTONES:

First worked as office boy for *Hospital Equipment News*

1963: After graduating from high school, joined advertising agency as an office boy at age 19 (date approximate)

After working at various agencies and progressing to writing copy, landed at Collet, Dickinson and Pearce; while there met David Puttnam and Alan Marshall; also worked with Ridley Scott and Adrian Lyne

1966: At urging of Puttnam, went to work on first feature film script; eventually made as "Melody" (1972), Puttnam's producing debut

1968: Television commercial directing debut

1969–1978: Directed nearly 500 TV commercials in London

1970: Formed own production company, The Alan Parker Film Company, with Alan Marshall

1973: Medium-length film writing and directing debut, "No Hard Feelings" (50 mins); independently produced (Parker invested his own 30,000 pounds), it was subsequently bought by the BBC, and aired in 1976

1975: TV-movie directing debut, "The Evacuees" (BBC-produced)

1976: Feature film directing debut (also writer), "Bugsy Malone"

1977: Published novel, "Puddles in the Lane"

1978: Directed the international hit "Midnight Express"; won Oscar nomination as Best Director

1980: First US-produced feature, "Fame"

1982: Published collection of cartoons, "Hares in the Gate"

1982: Expanded the themes of the bestselling rock concept album in the film version of "Pink Floyd—The Wall"; employed innovative animation techniques

1984: Scored big at Cannes Film Festival with "Birdy"

1987: Personally challenged the ratings board of the MPAA for their "X" rating of "Angel Heart"

1988: Helmed the civil rights drama "Mississippi Burning"; film received seven Academy Award nominations including one for Parker's direction

1991: Returned to movie musical format with "The Commitments", an upbeat story of poor North Dublin kids who form a band to play American soul music

1994: Wrote, produced and directed "The Road to Wellville", a sendup of health fadist John Kellogg

1996: Film version of Andrew Lloyd Webber and Tim Rice's "Evita" opened to mixed reviews

1997: Signed first-look producing deal with PolyGram (May)

1997: Appointed as chair of the British Film Institute (BFI)

2000: Became head of the Film Council, which oversees funding allotted to the British Film Commission, the Arts Council's Film Lottery panel, the British Film Institute and British Screen Finance

AFFILIATION: Founding member and Vice-Chairman, Directors Guild of Great Britain
  Chair, British Film Institute (1997–1999)
  Chair, Film Council of Great Britain (1999–)

QUOTES:

Awarded knighthood by Queen Elizabeth II in the New Year's Eve honors 2001.

" . . . film is a collaborative art form, I quite like working with a lot of people as long as there is one singular vision. In that respect, you have to be quite tough, egocentric about it. I wanted to be a writer. I never ever wanted to be a director when I started. To me, writing was the most important thing and that is a very singular occupation . . . I suppose the beauty of film is that you do get to reach a very wide audience. The language of film is pretty universal . . . It's quite exciting for me to know that's how I can communicate to people."—Alan Parker, quoted in *Location Update*, 1988.

"I'd direct another musical, though maybe not immediately. But you know, no one's ever been able to persuade Andrew [Lloyd Webber] to do an original score for a musical film. Now that I have an in, maybe he'll do it for me one day."—Alan Parker quoted in *Los Angeles Times*, December 24, 1996.

BIBLIOGRAPHY:
"Puddles in the Lane" Alan Parker, 1977; novel
"Hare in the Garden" Alan Parker, 1983; book of cartoons

Pier Paolo Pasolini

BORN: in Bologna, Italy, 03/05/1922

DEATH: in Ostia, Italy, 11/02/1975

NATIONALITY: Italian

EDUCATION: University of Bologna, Bologna, Italy

AWARDS: Venice Film Festival Special Jury Prize "Il Vangelo Secondo Matteo" 1964; cited along with Kozintsev's "Hamlet"

Venice Film Festival Catholic Film Office Award "Il Vangelo Secondo Matteo" 1964

Cannes Film Festival, Special Jury Prize "One Thousand and One Nights" 1974

BIOGRAPHY

Pier Paolo Pasolini considered himself first and foremost a poet. But his poetic vision was of people who lived on the edge of society or outside the law, a vision that carried over into his filmmaking.

The son of a committed Fascist officer, he graduated from the university in his hometown of Bologna and in rebellion against his father's political beliefs turned to communism. Conscripted for the army, he was taken prisoner by German forces following the Italian surrender to the Allies. He escaped and hid out with his family; being on the run and hiding out would become recurrent themes in his life and work.

In 1947 Pasolini became secretary of the communist party cell at Casarsa. Two years later, after he was accused of corrupting minors and fired from the Casarsa school where he taught, he moved to Rome with his beloved mother. Though he was an avowed atheist, communist and homosexual, he had great respect for his mother's simple beliefs, a respect which probably played a role in the

making of his most celebrated film, "Il Vangelo Secondo Matteo/The Gospel According to St. Matthew", which won the special jury prize at the 1964 Venice Film Festival.

During the early 1950s, Pasolini was indicted for obscenity for his first novel, "Ragazzi di Vita." Though he continued writing fiction and poetry, he began to turn to film scripts as well, working under Federico Fellini on "Le Notti di Cabiria" (1956). His first film as a director was "Accatone" (1961), based on his own novel of a low-life crook and pimp in the slums of Rome. Two years later, he was back in trouble with the law when he was prosecuted for vilification of the Church for directing the "La Ricotta" segment of the anthology film "RoGoPag." Other Pasolini films of the 1960s included "Teorema" (1968), an allegory with Terence Stamp, and "Medea" (1970), with opera diva Maria Callas.

In the 70s Pasolini embarked on a series of films based on ribald classical literary works such as "The Decameron" (1971) and "The Canterbury Tales" (1972). His last film was the controversial "Salo" (1975): subtitled "The 120 Days of Sodom." This allegory of Fascist Italy was filled with savage violence, sadomasochism and a variety of other sexual depravities.

On November 2, 1975, Pasolini was murdered in a manner bizarre enough to come out of one of his films. He was bludgeoned to death near a soccer field by a 17-year old boy, who was later arrested for speeding in Pasolini's Alfa Romeo. The killer claimed Pasolini had made sexual advances to him.

Regarded abroad as one of the foremost filmmakers of his generation, Pasolini, was also, according to Susan Sontag, "indisputably the most remarkable figure to have emerged in Italian arts and letters since the Second World War." His personal vision was of a world of violence and sexuality, ranging from the shanty towns and city streets of contemporary Rome to the moral fantasies of Boccaccio and the Arabian Nights. His films are portraits of outsiders in violent struggle with their society, much of that concern reflecting his own inner turmoil.

MILESTONES:

1954: First film as screenwriter, "La donna del Fiume"

1961: Feature film directing debut, "Accatone"

BIBLIOGRAPHY:

"Una vita violenta/A Violent Life" Pier Paolo Pasolini, novel

"Pasolini Requiem" Barth David Schwartz, 1992; reissued in paperback in 1992 by Vintage

"Petrolio" Pier Paolo Pasolini, 1997, Pantheon; unfinished novel (translated from the Italian)

"Pasolini: Forms of Subjectivity" Robert S. C. Gordon, 1997, Clarendon Press

Alexander Payne

BORN: Constantine Alexander Payne in Omaha, Nebraska, 1961

NATIONALITY: American

EDUCATION: Creighton Prepatory School, Omaha, Nebraska; Jesuit-run, all-male Catholic high school

Stanford University Stanford, California history and Spanish literature, BA

University of California at Los Angeles, Los Angeles, California, film, directing, MFA; enrolled in 1984

AWARDS: Los Angeles Film Critics Association New Generation Award 1999; shared with Jim Taylor

New York Film Critics Circle Award Best Screenplay "Election" 1999; shared with Jim Taylor

Florida Film Critics Circle Award Best Screenplay "Election" 1999; shared with Jim Taylor

Online Film Critics Society Award Best Adapted Screenplay "Election" 1999

Writers Guild of America Award Best Screenplay Based on Material Previously Produced or Published "Election" 2000; shared with Jim Taylor

Independent Spirit Award Best Director "Election" 2000

Independent Spirit Award Best Screenplay "Election" 2000; shared with Jim Taylor

Los Angeles Film Critics Association Awards Best Screenplay "About Schmidt" 2002; shared with Jim Taylor

Golden Globe Award Best Screenplay "About Schmidt" 2002; shared with Jim Taylor

BIOGRAPHY

Writer-director Alexander Payne has shown a remarkably interesting vision with his first two films, "Citizen Ruth" (1996) and "Election" (1999). With the former, he examined the gravely serious issue of reproductive rights, an unlikely subject for a comedy, and turned out a smart satire. In the latter, he used a seemingly inconsequential high school presidential race to plumb the darkest recesses of human nature. Of Greek ancestry, Payne (the family name was Anglicized from Papadopoulos) was born in Omaha, Nebraska, the Midwestern city which would serve as setting for many of his projects. His journey to filmmaking began in the early 1960s when his father, who owned a restaurant, received an 8mm camera from Kraft Foods as a bonus for being a good customer. Although only six years old, Payne began making films. He studied history and Spanish literature at Stanford University before going on to UCLA's film school, where his hour-long thesis film "The Passion of Martin" (1989) earned him rave reviews and industry attention. The story of an alienated still photographer who falls in love, "The Passion of Martin" secured Payne a spot at the Sundance Film Festival and landed him a position at Universal Pictures. While the film worked the festival circuit, Payne wrote the unproduced script "The Coward" for Universal and completed several shorts produced by Propaganda Films and screened on the Playboy Channel. By now the buzz surrounding his student film was fading and the director was no longer a hot commodity, but he turned down a job directing 1994's "Romeo Is Bleeding" nonetheless, believing it to be a weak script.

In 1992, Payne and then roommate Jim Taylor took an interest in the increasingly heated abortion debate. Noting the myriad possibilities for a film exploring the personalities behind the opposing sides, the two collaborated on the script that would become the celebrated satire "Citizen Ruth." Laura Dern was cast as the titular dim drifter addicted to chemical inhalants who ends up pregnant. Faced with Ruth's vagrancy, unapologetic drug use and pregnancy, a judge charges her with felony child endangerment, with the condition that she can be cleared if she agrees to terminate her pregnancy. The case grabs the attention of the pro-life camp who seeks to "save" Ruth and her unborn child, with Ruth later "rescued" by pro-choice activists, both camps looking to use the conflicted glue-sniffer to send a message. A slyly satirical, yet balanced look at the abortion debate, "Citizen Ruth" skewered both sides' hypocrisy with skillful even-handedness, turning the movie into a statement about personal freedom rather than taking a position on reproductive rights. Winning rave notices from critics, the film was touted for its offbeat humor as well as its courageous unconventionality.

Payne and Taylor reteamed to pen "Election", an adaptation of Tom Perrotta's satirical novel inspired by the 1992 presidential campaign, shifting the setting from Perrotta's New Jersey to Payne's own hometown of Omaha. Mixing seasoned professionals like Matthew Broderick as teacher Jim McAllister and Reese Witherspoon as the ruthlessly ambitious Tracy Flick with newcomers Jessica Campbell as the high-minded and lovelorn Tammy Metzler and Omaha find Chris Klein as her sweetly benign jock brother Paul, Payne constructed a proficient cast that capably pulled off his three-dimensional characterizations. Using a high school election run by a maniacally over-achieving candidate, an affable football hero forced into the race by the strangely obsessed McAllister and his charismatic revenge-minded younger sister, Payne painted a picture less about politics than the universally significant dark side of human nature and the mutable role of ethics in society. Released by MTV Films and Paramount and marketed as a teen movie because of its high school setting, "Election" was by far one of the smartest and most transcendent youth-oriented film in recent memory.

Passionate about filmmaking, and interested in exploring less chartered genres like the modern western, Payne would no doubt continue to turn out well-made and thought provoking above average fare well into the new millennium. His next film with Jim Taylor, "About Schmidt" (2002), delivered on the promise of his earlier efforts, depicting yet another normal, average American—not a typical movie hero or even an antihero—in the form of 66-year-old Warren Schmidt (Jack Nicholson), a man who, after the death of his distant wife of 42 years, sets out on a journey to find his daughter (Hope Davis), who's about to marry into a family of boobs. Although rife with comedic moments, the film also charted serious territory unflinchingly and generated intense critical fanfare.—Written by Jane O'Donnell

MILESTONES:

1984: Enrolled as a graduate film student at

UCLA after considering attending New York's Columbia School of Journalism

1989: Student film "The Passion of Martin" screened at Sundance Film Festival

Landed a job at Universal Pictures; while in the studio's employ, wrote unproduced scripts

Completed several shorts for Propaganda Films, aired on the Playboy Channel

Roomed in Los Angeles with frequent collaborator Jim Taylor

1992: Turned down chance to direct "Romeo Is Bleeding" (released in 1994); began writing "Meet Ruth Stoops"

1996: Made feature debut as screenwriter (co-written with Taylor) and director with acclaimed satire "Citizen Ruth/Meet Ruth Stoops"; premiered in competition at the Sundance Film Festival

1999: Helmed and co-wrote (along with Taylor) second feature "Election", a critically successful dark comedy starring Matthew Broderick and Reese Witherspoon

1999: Signed to $1 million deal to write and direct "Sideways" for Artisan Entertainment

2001: With Taylor contributed to the script of "Jurassic Park 3"

2002: Directed "About Schmidt", with Jack Nicholson; received a Golden Globe nomination for Best Director

AFFILIATION: Greek Orthodox

QUOTES:

"I like satire and comedy based in painful experience. Humor and satire allow distance by asking you to take a step back and look at the situation as if it is in a fishbowl, which can perhaps give people a certain objective perspective on things."—Alexander Payne quoted in press material for "Citizen Ruth."

When asked how his parents felt about his choice to pursue a career in filmmaking, Payne was quoted: "For them, I'm the lawyer who never was. My older brother is a doctor. You know for them law, medicine and business were good professions. They never discouraged me regarding filmmaking, but they didn't encourage me either. I felt strongly about what I was doing and they trusted my judgment, but when I was struggling for a living after graduating from UCLA, they kept offering me money to enroll in law school."—in "Meet Alexander Payne" by Dan Georgakas, *The Greek American*, January 18, 1997.

Payne was an altar boy at the local Orthodox Church when he was growing up. Because of his Greek heritage, he requested that "Citizen Ruth" have its European debut at the Thessaloniki Film Festival.

Payne on using his hometown of Omaha, Nebraska as a filming location: "No one raises an eyebrow when Spike Lee and Woody Allen and Martin Scorsese shoot in New York or Tarantino shoots in L.A. If you're from an out-of-the-way place like Omaha, it's 'Why do you want to shoot there?' But if you have deep roots and it means something to you, you want to use that."—Quoted in the *Los Angeles Times*, February 1, 1998.

"I feel personally responsible for the future of American cinema. Me personally. But so should you."—Payne quoted in *Spliced Online*, April 16, 1999.

"The most heinous shift in American films is that they reinforce good things like 'couples' and 'relationships'. I think films have to have a little danger and should go further in terms of questioning things—maybe everything we know is wrong, maybe we are all profoundly fucked up, and what can we do about it?"—Payne quoted in *L.A. Weekly*, April 23–29, 1999.

BORN: David Samuel Peckinpah in Fresno, California, 02/21/1925

DEATH: in Inglewood, California, 12/28/1984

NATIONALITY: American

EDUCATION: Fresno High School, Fresno, California; was member of football team

San Rafael Military Academy, transferred there for his senior year

California State University, Fresno, California, drama, BA, 1949; met Marie Selland there and changed major to drama

University of Southern California, Los Angeles, California, drama, MA, 1950; for master's thesis, wrote adaptation of a one-act play by Tennessee Williams which he filmed (movie was destroyed)

BIOGRAPHY

Sam Peckinpah was a paradox who both cultivated and disdained his own legend as one of Hollywood's most difficult directors, his often violent films evoked strong responses and varied, almost contradictory, readings. Born to a California legal clan, Peckinpah served in the Marine Corps and earned a master's degree from U.S.C. in 1950. He spent his early career as a theater and television director before becoming an assistant on five films to director Don Siegel, famed for his hard-bitten action films (Peckinpah even played a small part in Siegel's "Invasion of the Body Snatchers," 1956). Peckinpah soon became associated with the western genre, writing and directing episodes of "Gunsmoke," "The Rifleman," "The Westerner" and other TV series. His 1957 script on the legend of Billy the Kid eventually became, without his participation and with many changes, Marlon Brando's eccentric "One-Eyed Jacks" (1961).

Peckinpah's first film as a director, "The Deadly Companions" (1961), plus "Ride the High Country" (1962), "Major Dundee" (1965), "The Wild Bunch" (1969) and "Pat Garrett and Billy the Kid" (1973) form an arc in the stylistic span of outlaw mythology; among other accomplishments, they raised to the level of perverse sacrament the male gesture of mutual respect that supersedes fear of death. His "semi-westerns," "The Ballad of Cable Hogue" (1970) and the director's personal favorite, the lovely and atypically gentle "Junior Bonner" (1972), extended his theme of the demise of a noble way of life in the face of a modern world. "The Getaway" (1972) and "Convoy" (1978) put contemporary antiheroes ahead of as well as outside the law.

Perhaps his most controversial film was "Straw Dogs" (1971); the inevitable brutality of its protagonist, ostensibly a man of reason, offers a metaphor on the ancient bent of the human psyche vis-a-vis personal territory and blood rites. "Bring Me the Head of Alfredo Garcia" (1974), reputedly autobiographical, was a psychodrama refracted through a tequila haze, a saga of a loner/artiste who reaps the grotesque wages of sin on a desperate trek of atonement. Peckinpah's distrust of policymakers was reflected in "The Killer Elite" (1975) and his last film, "The Osterman Weekend," (1983), both essays on vicious tactics and dissolute friendship in the CIA. "Cross of Iron" (1977), Peckinpah's largest production, is a fiercely edited view of World War II slaughter where the Wehrmacht wear the patented scars of his honorable killers.

Few directors have had more conflict with studio heads and producers than Peckinpah. Feuds over the content and final cuts of "Major Dundee" (after which Peckinpah was blacklisted for three years), "The Wild Bunch" and "Pat Garrett" are the stuff of Hollywood legend. Critical response to his work has often been as violent as the films themselves, with Peckinpah frequently berated for demeaning women and excessively glorifying male exploits. On an aesthetic level, Peckinpah is celebrated for his slow motion furies, first employed in a 1963 entry of TV's "Dick Powell Theater" called "The Losers," exercised to startling effect in "The Wild Bunch", but somewhat overused in subsequent work. "Cathartic violence" was a term that seemed coined to define his iconoclastic postures. In Peckinpah's Conradian scheme that mixes nobility with tragedy, all are guilty to some degree and all have their reasons. His work typically exists on a skewed moral plane between eras and cultures, with ambiguous quests for identity and redemption undertaken by hopelessly lost outcasts and enemies. He vividly defines the thin line between internal conflict and external action, and, perhaps most importantly, the violent displacement of a false code of honor (and law itself) by another more enduring and devout.

As thorny as his relationships with producers and executives were, Peckinpah could inspire extraordinary loyalty among actors and technicians. An ensemble of notable Peckinpah players would include David Warner, Warren Oates, L.Q. Jones, Strother Martin, James Coburn, Kris Kristofferson and Ben Johnson. Peckinpah also enjoyed repeated and fruitful collaborations with cinematographers Lucien Ballard and John Coquillon and composer Jerry Fielding.

MILESTONES:

1943: Enlisted in the Marines; sent to China in 1945 and began studies of Zen

1950–1951: Began career as director-producer in residence at the Huntington Park Civic Theatre for a year and a half

Joined KLAC-TV in Los Angeles as a stagehand, propman and floor-sweeper; stayed two years; lost job after row with studio executive (dates approximate)

1953: Hired by CBS as an assistant editor on basis of short films he had made on his own time at KLAC

1954: First job in the film industry; hired by Walter Wanger as third assistant casting director (gopher) at Allied Artists; first assignment on Don Siegal's "Riot in Cell Block 11" (date approximate)

Worked as "dialogue director" (in reality personal assistant to Don Siegal) on "Private Hell 36" (1954), "An Annapolis Story" (1955), "Invasion of the Body Snatchers" and "Crime in the Streets" (both 1956)

Worked as dialogue director on some of Jacques Tourneur's films for Allied Artists

Wrote first scripts for TV series, "Gunsmoke" (most were adaptations of "Gunsmoke" radio scripts)

1957: Sold first original feature script, ("The Authentic Death of Hendry Jones" (later in altered form it was filmed by Marlon Brando as "One-Eyed Jacks")

1958: Directed first TV episode, "The Knife Fighter" on series "Broken Arrow"

1958: Reworked an original script rejected by "Gunsmoke"; sold to Dick Powelll at Four Star Productions as "The Sharpshooter" (1958) which served as pilot for series, "The Rifleman" (also directed four episodes)

1958: Debut as TV producer on NBC series, "The Westerner" (also directed five episodes and co-wrote four)

1961: Directed first feature film, "The Deadly Companions"

Returned to TV as producer-director of two hour-long films for "The Dick Powell Theatre" ("Pericles on 31st St Street" 1962 and "The Losers" 1963)

1963: Joined Walt Disney Productions as writer-director; left after disagreement with producer (date approximate)

1967: Taught writing and directing at UCLA

1983: Directed final film, "The Osterman Weekend"

QUOTES:

At his memorial service in 1985, an actor told the crowd, "You can tell this is a Peckinpah production. We got started late and nobody knows what's happening."—quoted in *Vanity Fair*, December 1991.

BIBLIOGRAPHY:

"Crucified Heroes: The Films of Sam Peckinpah" Terence Butler, 1979

"Peckinpah" Garner Simmons

"Bloody Sam" Marshall Fine, 1991, Donald I. Fine, Inc.

"Peckinpah: The Western Films—A Reconsideration" Paul Seydor, 1997, University of Illinois Press

Kimberly Peirce

BORN: Kimberley A. Peirce in Harrisburg, Pennsylvania 07/25/1969

SOMETIMES CREDITED AS:
Kim Peirce
Kimberly Ane Peirce

NATIONALITY: American

EDUCATION: University of Chicago, Chicago, Illinois, Japanese and English literature, BA

School of the Arts, Columbia University, New York, New York, film, MFA

AWARDS: Boston Society of Film Critics Award Best New Filmmaker "Boys Don't Cry" 1999

Las Vegas Film Critics Society Award Best Director "Boys Don't Cry" 1999

Las Vegas Film Critics Society Award Best Adapted Screenplay "Boys Don't Cry" 1999; shared with Andy Bienen

BIOGRAPHY

Director Kimberly Peirce made her feature film debut with 1999's acclaimed "Boys Don't Cry", a fact-based dramatization of the events leading up to the tragic murder of Teena Brandon, a Nebraskan teenage girl living convincingly and happily as a young man. Skillfully written and artfully shot, Peirce's evocative first effort was further strengthened by impressive performances by Chloe Sevigny, Peter Sarsgaard, Brendon Sexton III, and a

remarkable turn by Hillary Swank as Brandon. The filmmaker heard about the Teena Brandon story while attending Columbia University as a graduate film student and switched her thesis project to this compelling subject from her original similarly themed focus, a spy drama following a woman posing as a man during the Civil War. Fascinated by Brandon's story, Peirce went to Falls City, Nebraska, the town where the drama unfolded, did extensive research and attended the trial of the two men accused of the murders. In 1995, she made a short film on the subject featuring Anna Grace as Brandon; it received an Astrea Production Grant which helped fund the cost of developing the project into a full-length feature. The resulting screenplay (then titled "Take It Like a Man"), co-written by Peirce, was picked up for workshopping at the Filmmaker's Lab of the Sundance Institute in 1997. Upon its release, "Boys Don't Cry" became one of the most talked about and acclaimed independent features of the year, and the fledgling director was applauded for her success in creating a moving but non-sensational modern American tragedy.

Considering herself not unlike Brandon in terms of her drifting nature and search for a comfortable identity, Peirce grew up in various locales within the United States. While attending the University of Chicago, she ran out of money and subsequently moved to Japan to work as an English instructor. She returned to the USA and the university after earning enough money, and also was able to tour Southeast Asia, a trip that yielded photographic work as well as providing creative inspiration. The aspiring filmmaker went on to earn an MFA at Columbia, and made the most of her time at that university, working on numerous short films and forming valuable creative alliances. Peirce made her directorial debut with the 16mm short "The Last Good Breath" (1993), screened to acclaim at various festivals. The following year she was involved in the production of the shorts "Greetings From Africa" and "Miss Ruby's House". Peirce additionally served as an editor on the 16mm animated film "Anastasia and the Queen of Hearts" (1995).

MILESTONES:

Moved around frequently while growing up, lived in Pennsylvania, Florida, Puerto Rico and Chicago

Worked in Japan as an English teacher and a model to fund her undergraduate education

1993: Made directorial debut with the experimental 16-minute short "The Last Good Breath", screened on the festival circuit

1994: Was working on a script about a female spy posing as a man in the midst of the Civil War when she learned of the Teena Brandon incident and switched her thesis subject

1994: Was assistant editor of Cheryl Dunye's short "Greetings From Africa" and worked on and appeared in Lisa Collins' short "Miss Ruby's House"

1995: Edited Shawn Atkins' experimental 16mm animated film "Anastasia and the Queen of Hearts"

1995: Made short film based on the Brandon murder while a student at Columbia; film was nominated for the university's Princess Grace Award and received an Astrea Production Grant

1997: Chosen to participate in the Filmmaker's Lab at the Sundance Institute to work on "Boys Don't Cry" (then titled "Take It Like a Man")

1999: Feature directorial debut, "Boys Don't Cry"; also co-wrote with Andy Bienen

QUOTES:

Peirce on necessarily toning down the violence in "Boys Don't Cry": "By its nature, the film reduced the reality Brandon faced. The real story is a kind of horror that I think few people will ever know"—From *Los Angeles Times*, September 12, 1999.

Director/screenwriter Kimberly Peirce on her "Boys Don't Cry" filmmaking approach: "This story had been covered so sensationalistically, and people were making Brandon into an icon, so I knew that what I needed to do was enter as deeply as possible into his character. And I thought that the heart of that was actually to be inside of his desire. I didn't want to reduce it to questions like 'Was he a lesbian?' or 'Which came first, wanting to be with women or wanting to dress like a boy?' I wanted to be deeply inside his experience, and that's why I chose a lot of close-ups, that's why the color is saturated, that's why you start the movie in his bedroom [with him] looking at himself in the mirror—that's like the birth of Brandon . . . What I really wanted to do was bring the audience in and allow them to enter into a pretty epic tragedy, but on a really, really human level [in order to] bring Brandon to life. And to see the world as he saw it."—quoted in *Filmmaker*, Fall 1999.

Advice to other new filmmakers, from Kimberly Peirce: "I would just say to people [reading this], just stick with it. If it matters to you it's going to matter to other people eventually. Financiers don't make scripts until they're ready. And everybody says 'People don't understand my script'. But I think it's that the script is not ready. And if you just rewrite and tell the story with more clarity, it will get made." —quoted in *Filmmaker*, Fall 1999.

Peirce on working with a studio on post-production for "Boys Don't Cry", granted financing for an additional twenty-two weeks of editing after being picked up by Fox Searchlight:

"Twenty-two weeks of editing is the only way that I found that movie. That movie needed to be screened and tested and screened and tested, and that's why I collaborated with the studio. The studio would give me notes, and some of them were great. Some I disagreed with, and I learned that in response to one page of notes, you write ten pages of a memo. You absolutely justify every single thing that you're doing." —quoted in *Indiewire*'s coverage of the 1999 New York Film Festival, October 1, 1999.

"I identified with Teena. Probably the re-telling of Teena's search for family was about my own search for a family. And her drifting reflected my own moving around. Making her-self into the fantasy she had of herself is some-thing I related to as a filmmaker. I make sense of my own life by what I write about and what I make movies about. This film is very autobio-graphical, really. I used myself to understand my characters more deeply."—Peirce on "Boys Don't Cry", quoted in *Moviemaker*, December 1999.

Arthur Penn

BORN: in Philadelphia, Pennsylvania, 09/27/1922

NATIONALITY: American

EDUCATION: Olney High School, Philadel-phia, Pennsylvania

Black Mountain College, Ashville, North Carolina, 1947–49; also taught acting

University of Perugia, Perugia, Italy

University of Florence, Florence, Italy

Actors Studio, Los Angeles, California

studied acting with Michael Chekhov

AWARD: Tony Director (Play) "The Miracle Worker" 1960

BIOGRAPHY

Arthur Penn has proved himself a true triple threat during his career, achieving extraordinary success as a director of live television dramas, Broadway plays and feature films. Like Sidney Lumet and John Frankenheimer, he owes a huge debt to the crucible of TV's "Golden Age", but it is Elia Kazan he resembles most in his sympathy for actors, the flights of fancy he allows and the incredible range of expression he elicits. Penn understands the poetry of close camera work, acknowledging that words are to the theater

what actions are for film ("A look, a simple look, will do it"), his use of lighting and sound are stylistically and intellectually sophisticated, but it is his themes, rather than his style, which propel his pictures. No other director during the volatile 1960s had his fingers so securely on America's pulse, and audiences responded enthusiastically to his exploration of the rela-tionship between outsiders and mainstream society, his sympathies lying invariably with the outcasts, though he rarely presented them as blameless victims.

Penn's initial interest in theater lay in its technical side (lighting, building scenery, etc.), but he also acted in high school plays and got his first chance to direct at Philadelphia's ama-teur Neighborhood Playhouse. While in the Army at Fort Jackson, South Carolina, he formed a small theater group, meeting Fred Coe who would later produce much of Penn's tele-vision and theater work, as well as his first two feature films. After attending Black Mountain College in North Carolina and studying litera-ture in Italy for two years, he landed the job of third floor manager for NBC-TV's "Colgate Comedy Hour", working his way up to assistant director and moving with the show when it relo-cated to Los Angeles. Coe then lured him back to NYC to direct a live dramatic series called

"Gulf Playhouse: 1st Person" (NBC), and he also worked as a writer and director for NBC's "Philco Television Playhouse" before switching to CBS where he served as producer and director for the prestigious "Playhouse 90." While there, he came in contact with the writer William Gibson, helming his teleplay, "The Miracle Worker" in 1957.

Penn had made an inauspicious Broadway debut as director of "The Lovers", a play which closed after four performances in 1956, but he fared much better with his second effort, Gibson's "Two for the Seesaw" (1957), starring Henry Fonda and Anne Bancroft which ran for 750 performances. He would enjoy incredible good fortune over the next two years on the Great White Way, beginning with "The Miracle Worker", for which he won the Tony as Best Director, and followed quickly with Lillian Hellman's "Toys in the Attic", "An Evening with Mike Nichols and Elaine May" and Tad Mosel's "All the Way Home", earning the reputation as "the most gifted director since Kazan." As a favor to Coe, Penn directed his first film, "The Left Handed Gun" (1958), a psychological interpretation of the legend of Billy the Kid (Paul Newman) based on Gore Vidal's television play. Received with indifference in the USA, the film won a Grand Prix at the Brussels Film Festival, but more importantly, it identified several themes which would recur throughout Penn's work: the dichotomy of father-son relationships; the function of myth in reconciling reality; the arbitrary nature of violence; and the outcast as reflection of society.

Infuriated that Warner Bros. had edited the picture against his intentions, Penn waited four years before choosing to adapt "The Miracle Worker" (1962), the play he had successfully directed for television and on Broadway. Though to some extent hampered by its stage origins, it was still a powerful and emotionally compelling film, featuring superlative acting from Oscar-winners Anne Bancroft as Annie Sullivan, the teacher bearing civilization's message, and Patty Duke as Helen Keller, the noble savage restrained by culture. For his efforts, Penn received his first Academy Award nomination as Best Director, but the success would be short-lived. During the 1962–63 Broadway season, in contrast with his earlier run of luck, he directed three flops in a row, and one week into the shooting of "The Train" (1963), producer-star Burt Lancaster replaced him at the helm with John Frankenheimer, a director more to his liking.

The bitterness and sense of persecution left their mark on Penn's next film, "Mickey One" (1965), a determined excursion into European existentialism, but still an intriguing commentary on an America beset by conspiracy. Deeply noir in tone, the fragmented, elliptical tale of a nightclub comic (Warren Beatty) on the run from mobsters exhibited the influence of French New Wave directors, especially Truffaut and Godard, whose work Penn greatly admired. Serving as his own producer, the director had complete control for the first time and though the film does retain a strong cult following, this "allegory of a man's trip through purgatory" bewildered most critics at the time and did poorly at the box office. "The Chase" (1966) focused on the tensions that ignite into violence in a small Texas town when one of its citizens, an escaped convict (Robert Redford), makes his way home. A logical progression, "The Chase" showed what happens when the law steps aside and leaves the arena to outlaws and depraved citizens, the killing of the convict at the end echoing the shooting of Lee Harvey Oswald.

The failure of "Mickey One" had forced Penn to relinquish final cut on "The Chase", and the director was deeply dissatisfied with the released version. In the theater, however, his luck had changed first with "Golden Boy" (1964), a musical version of Odets' play, and later with the thriller "Wait Until Dark" (1966). Penn might have abandoned the cinema altogether had Warren Beatty not persuaded him to direct "Bonnie and Clyde" (1967), a complex, romantic myth based on the real Barrow Gang of the American Depression-era. Arguably his finest film, it was also, without doubt, one of the most significant and influential American films of the decade, receiving 10 Academy Award nominations, including his second as Best Director. His startling juxtaposition of comedy and mayhem encouraged audiences to sympathize with the charismatic criminals, but for all the exhilarating fun, Bonnie and Clyde were clearly doomed by their shallowness and intellectual limitations. The famous prolonged riddling of their bodies with bullets at the movie's finale was a poetry of slow motion that enhanced through its very excess the mythical impact of their deaths.

Penn's next two films sustained the theme of the outcast's relationship with conventional society. "Alice's Restaurant" (1969), for which he received his third Oscar nomination, portrays a metaphorical death of 60s idealism in its story about a commune of hippies. Despite always working closely with his writers, the director for the first time took screenwriting credit (shared with Venable Herndon). His most informal film in its openness to improvisation, it revealed with great sympathetic insight the essential weaknesses and inadequacies of the hippie movement. "Little Big Man" (1970) attacked the myths of the American West in a sometimes lyric, often brutal story told in flashback by a 121-year-old man (Dustin Hoffman) who claims he is the only white survivor of Custer's Last Stand. The shadow of the Vietnam War (though disguised by historical analogy) hung over this film as it had for "Alice's Restaurant", and Penn alternated humor and violence to debunk conventional romanticism, presenting the West as merely another arena for the establishment of personal and political advantage.

"Little Big Man" was Penn's last great film. Immediately following, he underwent a personal and psychological crisis from which some say he never completely emerged artistically. However, his return to filmmaking, "Night Moves" (1975), is an underrated noirish detective story soured by the disillusion and malaise of the Watergate era, and "The Missouri Breaks" (1976), a bomb in its day, demonstrates a mature, beautifully composed visual style and features a wonderfully eccentric performance by Marlon Brando. Of his later films, the Steve Tesich-scripted "Four Friends" (1981) showed the most promise, returning to the turbulent 60s, with which the director so closely identified, as a setting for self-discovery. "Targets" (1985) was a mess, "Penn and Teller Get Killed" (1989) was barely released, and Penn is living proof that a great director can go cold. He has maintained a close connection to the theater as President of the Actors Studio, and though "Inside", his 1996 Showtime outing didn't lead to more work, he has not given up on the cinema, hoping to direct a film version of "Sly Fox", the adaptation of Ben Johnson's "Volpone" which he staged on Broadway in 1976.—Written by Greg Senf

MILESTONES:

Moved with his mother and older brother Irving to NYC following his parents' divorce; between the ages of eight and ten attended at least 12 different grammar schools

Returned to Philadelphia to live with his father when he was 14

Worked for local radio station in Philadelphia

1943–1945: Served in US Army during WWII

Formed dramatic group in Fort Jackson, South Carolina while in military service; met future associate, producer Fred Coe

1945: Joined US Army's Soldier Show Company (headed by Joshua Logan, members included Mickey Rooney and Paddy Chayefsky)

Spent two years studying literature at Italian colleges

1951: Began working at NBC-TV in NYC as floor manager on "Colgate Comedy Hour"; worked his way up to assitant director, moving to Los Angeles when show relocated there

1953: Invited to New York by Fred Coe to direct NBC's "Gulf Playhouse: 1st Person" (date approximate)

Began writing and directing TV dramas for "Philco Television Playhouse" (NBC)

1955: Staged a production of James Leo Herlihy's "Blue Denim" for summer stock company in Westport, Connecticut

1956: Moved to CBS, where he directed for "Playhouse 90"

1956: Made inauspicious Broadway debut, directing "The Lovers", which closed after four days

1957: Helmed William Gibson's "The Miracle Worker" for "Playhouse 90"

1958: Directed Gibson's "Two for the Seesaw" on Broadway; starred Henry Fonda and Anne Bancroft

1958: Feature directorial debut, "The Left-Handed Gun"; produced by Coe

1960: Won a Tony as director of the Broadway version of "The Miracle Worker", starring Bancroft and Patty Duke

1962: Adapted "The Miracle Worker" to the big screen; again with Bancroft and Duke; earned first Oscar nomination as Best Director; Coe produced

1965: Produced and directed "Mickey One", starring Warren Beatty

1966: Deeply dissatisfied with the editing of "The Chase", vowed he would not "give an inch" in the future

1967: Earned second Oscar nomination for "Bonnie and Clyde", starring Beatty (who also produced), Faye Dunaway and Gene Hackman; first of six collaborations with editor Dede Allen

1969: Co-wrote (with Venable Herndon) and directed "Alice's Restaurant"; received third Academy Award nomination for Best Director

1970: Presented view of the American West where the Indians were the good guys in "Little Big Man"

Did no work in theater or television for five years; sole contribution to film was one section of the eight-director documentary on the 1972 Munich Olympics, "Visions of Eight" (1973); his segment, "The Highest", dealt with pole-vaulting

1975: Returned to features with "Night Moves", featuring Hackman

1976: Helmed "Sly Fox" on Broadway, starring George C. Scott

1977: Returned to Broadway as director of "Golda", starring Anne Bancroft

1981: Produced and directed "Four Friends", from an autobiographical script by Steve Tesich

1985: Third film with Hackman, "Target"

1987: Directed Ron Silver and Dianne Wiest in "Hunting Cockroaches" for NYC's Manhattan Theatre Club

1989: Last feature film (to date), "Penn and Teller Get Killed"

1995: Contributed to the omnibus project "Lumiere and Company"

1996: Helmed "Inside", a Showtime TV movie exposing the excesses of apartheid in South Africa

2000: In fall, became an executive producer on NBC's "Law & Order"

2002: Returned to stage directing with "Fortune's Fool", starring Alan Bates and Frank Langella

AFFILIATION: President, The Actors Studio (to 2000)

QUOTES:

"I would say that the only people who really interest me are the outcasts from society. The people who are not outcasts—either psychologically, emotionally, or physically—seem to me good material for selling breakfast food, but they're not material for films. What I'm really trying to say through the figure of the outcast is that society has its mirror in its outcasts. A society would be wise to pay attention to the people who do not belong if it wants to find out what its configuration is and where it's failing."—Arthur Penn, quoted in "World Film Directors, Volume Two", edited by John Wakeman.

D.A. Pennebaker

BORN: Donn Alan Pennebaker in Evanston, Illinois, 07/15/1925

SOMETIMES CREDITED AS: "Penny"

NATIONALITY: American

EDUCATION: Yale University, New Haven, Connecticut, engineering, 1947; interrupted college to serve as an engineer in the Naval Air Corps during World War II

AWARD: Special IFP Gotham Award Documentary 1992

BIOGRAPHY

One of the founding fathers of "direct cinema", American filmmaker's adopted name of choice for "cinema verite", and perhaps it's best known practitioner during the 1960s and early 70s, Pennebaker helped construct a style of storytelling and an attitude toward his subjects (often political figures or entertainers) that influenced a generation of nonfiction filmmakers. He is a proponent of a cinema which favors the filming reality in as unobtrusive a manner as possible, usually without narration. "You don't necessarily need a script or actors to tell a compelling tale," he has declared. "Finding a person at a key moment in his life and rendering the truth as you see it—that's the truest form of drama."

This former engineer, advertising copywriter and painter began making films in the early 50s after falling under the influence of experimental filmmaker Francis Thompson. Pennebaker's first film, "Daybreak Express" (1953), combined his documentary and experimental impulses in a five-minute portrait of the soon-to-be-demolished Third Avenue elevated subway in NYC set to Duke Ellington's music.

Pennebaker later established himself as a member of Drew Associates, which included major documentarians Richard Leacock and Albert Maysles. Robert Drew and Leacock were the two major guiding sensibilities of this extraordinary team. Hired to make documentaries for "Living Camera" (Syndicated, 1959–64), a TV series produced by Time-Life, these "filmakers" (as they named their equipment-sharing film co-op) collaborated on ten documentaries which chronicled a crucial day, week, or month in the lives of both famous and unknown subjects. They also produced projects for the ABC News "Closeup" series. Their most memorable work includes "Primary" (1960), a landmark political documentary focused on the 1960 Democratic primary contest between candidates John Kennedy and Hubert Humphrey in Wisconsin; "Adventures on the New Frontier" (1961), shot in the White House during the early weeks of the Kennedy Administration; "The Chair" (the events took place in July 1962 but it was not broadcast in the USA until October 1964 due to lack of network sponsorship), a powerful story of a condemned man and his lawyers' feverish attempts to get his death sentence commuted; and "Crisis: Behind a Presidential Commitment" (1963), a controversial chronicle of JFK and Attorney General Robert Kennedy's successful conflict with Alabama governor George Wallace over school desegregation.

Pennebaker and Leacock left Drew Associates in 1963 and formed Leacock-Pennebaker, Inc. Though they were partners, the two documentarians worked separately for the most part. Pennebaker went on to direct a short film entitled "Timothy Leary's Wedding Day/You're Nobody Till Somebody Loves You" (1964) and

"Elizabeth and Mary" (1965), a deeply moving account of "a day in the life" of a pair of twin ten-year-old sisters, one of whom is blind and mentally handicapped. He became famous with the release of "Don't Look Back" (1967) which documented Bob Dylan's first tour of England in 1965. That film's celebrated "Subterranean Homesick Blues" sequence, with Dylan standing in an alley accompanying his song with cardboard-sign "flash cards," is often cited as the first rock video. (Incidentally, Beat poet Allen Ginsberg does a walk-on cameo.) Pennebaker's "Monterey Pop" (1968), the first major rock concert feature, cemented his reputation as the foremost chronicler of 60s youth culture—particularly through its music. He would often return to the world of show business in subsequent features, shorts, and TV specials including "Original Cast Album: Company" (1970), "Ziggy Stardust and the Spiders From Mars" (1973) and "Dance Black America" (1985).

Pennebaker served as the director of photography on three semi-experimental films directed by Norman Mailer, "Beyond the Law" (1968), "Wild 90" (1969) and "Maidstone" (1970). He also completed and edited "One PM" (1971), a film begun by Jean-Luc Godard.

Pennebaker faded from prominence during the 70s. His company faltered after a disastrous foray into foreign film distribution and he had to work on other people's projects to pay off debts. Pennebaker hooked up with experimental filmmaker turned documentarian Chris Hegedus in 1976. She began as his editor, salvaging an abandoned film project depicting a 1971 debate between Norman Mailer and a group of feminist writers to make "Town Bloody Hall" (1979). Hegedus received credits as a co-director, co-writer, and editor. The pair married in 1982 and went on to collaborate on various music-oriented projects throughout the second half of the 80s. Pennebaker made a triumphant comeback with "The War Room" (1993), a fascinating political documentary set during the last months of the 1992 presidential campaign.

Hailed as a return to form, the film focused on the masterminds of Arkansas governor Bill Clinton's successful presidential bid—James Carville and George Stephanopoulos. He followed with a warts and all look at the out-of-town tryout of the stage comedy "Moon Over Buffalo" (featuring Carol Burnett and Philip Bosco) in "Moon Over Broadway" (1998).— Written by Kent Greene

MILESTONES:

1947: Moved to New York City after graduating from Yale

Worked as an advertising copy writer

Started Electronics Enginering, the company that developed the first computerized airline reservation system

Sold Electronics Engineering

Met experimental filmmaker Francis Thompson; was inspired to become a filmmaker

1953: Made first film, "Daybreak Express", a five-minute portrait of NYC's now defunct Third Avenue elevated subway set to Duke Ellington's music

Began making industrial films

1959: Joined Richard Leacock and others in Filmakers, an equipment-sharing film cooperative

1959: Joined Robert Drew's Drew Associates for "Living Camera", the TV documentary series produced by Time-Life

Worked on ten TV documentaries, each intended to chronicle a crucial day, week, or month in the lives of both famous and unknown subjects

1960: Co-directed (with Richard Leacock, Albert Maysles, Robert Drew, and Terence Macartney-Filgate) the landmark political documentary, "Primary", about the 1960 Democratic primary contest between candidates John Kennedy and Hubert Humphrey in Wisconsin

Was involved with "Adventures on the New Frontier", an ABC documentary shot in the White House during the early weeks of the Kennedy Administration

1963: Collaborated on "Crisis", a chronicle of Robert Kennedy's successful battle with Alabama governor George Wallace over school desegregation

1963: Left Drew Associates and formed Leacock-Pennebaker, Inc. with Richard Leacock

1967: Produced, shot and directed the landmark feature-length pop artist portrait, "Don't Look Back", about Bob Dylan's 1965 English tour; the film's cardboard-sign sequence for Dylan's "Subterranean Homesick Blues" is often cited as the first rock video

1969: Co-directed (with James Desmond, Barry Feinstein, Albert Maysles, Roger Murphy, Richard Leacock and Nick Proferes) the first major rock concert film, "Monterey Pop"

Served as director of photography on three films directed by Norman Mailer: "Beyond the Law" (1968), "Wild 90" (1969) and "Maidstone" (1970)

1970: With Leacock, directed "Original Cast Album: Company", a look at the grueling 15-hour marathon recording session of the landmark Stephen Sondheim stage musical

1973: Shot the strange concert film "Ziggy Stardust and the Spiders From Mars" featuring David Bowie in his alternative persona

1979: First collaboration with editor, producer, and future wife Chris Hegedus on "Town Bloody Hall", a record of a 1971 debate between Norman Mailer and a group of feminist writers

1980: With Hegedus, directed "Elliott Carter", a profile of the influential modern composer

1986: Profiled rock star Jimi Hendrix in "Jimi Plays Monterey"; not released theatrically until 1989

1989: Made "Depeche Mode 101", a nonfiction look at the British rock band's US tour

1992: Co-directed "Branford Marsalis: The Music Tells You", a look at the influential jazz musician

1993: Garnered critical praise for "The War Room", a behind-the-scenes look at the 1992 US Presidential campaign of Bill Clinton

1998: Undertook a look at the making of a stage play by following the out-of-town tryout of the comedy "Moon Over Buffalo" in the documentary "Moon Over Broadway"

2001: Served as a producer on "Startup.com", co-directed by Chris Hegedus

QUOTES:

"Yet today, at 68, D.A. Pennebaker has proved himself to be much more than just "still alive." That night in Little Rock, while Carville watched Bush's convention speech on TV, he permitted Pennebaker to film him and Hegedus to wire him for sound; his beady eyes and alertly cocked head allowed a brief smile when Bush cracked an Elvis joke. Then Carville and communications director George Stephanopoulos continued to grant them sporadic access to Command Central through election day. (Carville remembers Stephanopoulos saying, "If the Kennedys let him into the White House, I don't know why we can't let him in the War Room!) The resulting movie, "The War Room"—selected for the New York Film Festival and opening in several cities beginning the day after election day—is a historical treasure and reasserts Pennebaker's mastery much in the way "The Player" did for Robert Altman."— David Handelman, "In the Line of Fire" in *Vogue*, November 1993.

"Primary" (1960) selected for inclusion in the Library of Congress' National Film Registry in 1990.

BORN: in Emden, Germany 03/14/1941

NATIONALITY: German

EDUCATION: Johanneum School Hamburg, Germany 1953–60

studied acting in private schools in Hamburg and Berlin

German Film and Television Academy Berlin, Germany 1966–70

AWARDS: Bavarian Film Award Best Direction "Das Boot" 1982

ShoWest Director of the Year 2001

BIOGRAPHY

Growing up in the wake of World War II, talented German director Wolfgang Petersen developed a passion for all things American and by the age of 11 had decided that making movies (to his mind an essentially American art form) was what he wanted to do with his life. Initially drawn to the films of John Ford for their clear presentation of good and evil (in contrast to the messy Europe of the day), he went on to immerse himself in the directors of the French Nouvelle Vague, especially Francois Truffaut, whom he cites as his most important influence, though he is quick to add "there's nothing German, or even particularly European about my films." (*Los Angeles Times*, July 6, 1993) After beginning as an actor and director in Hamburg theater during the 1960s, he enrolled in film school and shortly after graduating made his directorial debut for German TV with "I Will Kill You, Wolf" (1970). He also helmed six 100-minute TV dramas, all with separate stories and casts, for a series of thrillers entitled "Tatort/Scene of the Crime" that greatly enhanced his reputation.

Petersen moved to features with "One of Us Two" (1973), the story of a student who blackmails one of his professors. It, like his next picture, the controversial homosexual love story "Consequences" (1977), starred Jurgen Prochnow, an actor with whom he had worked on "Tatort." After shooting the chess thriller "Black and White Like Night and Day" (1978), he reteamed with Prochnow as the "old man" of "Das Boot" (1981), at the time the most expensive German film ever made (about $12 million). Based on war correspondent Lothar-Guenther Buchheim's bestseller, it authentically recreated a single mission aboard a German U-boat during World War II while remaining faithful to the anti-war point-of-view of the book. With the odds stacked against them, the crew descends to the depths, taking the audience on a suspense-filled ride to the bottom of the ocean that culminates in a surprise ending back at their port of origin. "Das Boot" won international acclaim and (surprisingly for a subtitled film) was a hit in the USA where it earned Petersen Oscar nominations for Best Director and Best Adapted Screenplay.

After the success of "Das Boot", Petersen moved toward Hollywood filmmaking with the German-American co-production of a charming Capra-style fairy tale "The Neverending Story" (1984), dubbed by some critics as "the neverending movie." Carrying a price tag of $27 million, his first English-language picture became the highest grosser in German box office history and would be the director's most successful "Hollywood" film for nearly a decade. Neither his sci-fi adventure "Enemy Mine" (1985) nor his Hitchcockian thriller "Shattered" (1991) scored well with critics and audiences, but Petersen rebounded with the taut, suspenseful "In the Line of Fire" (1993), which pitted Clint Eastwood's aging Secret Service Man against John Malkovich's bitter CIA operative-turned-would-be presidential assassin. His status boosted by its $100 million-plus gross, he followed with "Outbreak" (1995), a thriller about the race to stop the spread of a deadly virus. Despite a fine star turn by Dustin Hoffman and support from the likes of Rene Russo, Morgan Freeman and Kevin Spacey, "Outbreak" fell far short commercially of the mark set by "In the Line of Fire."

Returning to the film that made him, Petersen supervised the director's cut of "Das Boot", re-released to critical acclaim in 1997. Drawing on the additional footage available from the five-hour epic made simultaneously for German TV, he expanded the 128 minutes of the original US release to his definitive feature-length of 210 minutes. Later that year, he teamed with box-office champ Harrison Ford as a US President unafraid to fight in order to wrest "Air Force One" (1997) away from the Kazakhstani terrorists who have hijacked the plane. The summer blockbuster reunited him with old friend Prochnow in a silent cameo as a fascist general captured by commandos during the prologue and reinforced Petersen's box-office clout by taking in more than $170 million domestically. It was then back to the sea to recreate "The Perfect Storm" (2000), the best-selling nonfiction work by Sebastian Junger that told the story of a doomed fishing vessel caught in a storm of unmatched ferocity. The digital effects of Industrial Light & Magic notwithstanding, critics remained divided regarding the film's merits, many pointing the finger at the unsympathetic lead character played by George Clooney. While some felt the vessel faced rough weather in recouping its $140 million budget, the film's opening week grosses of more than $40 million seemed to indicate otherwise.

MILESTONES:

Began career as assistant director at Ernst Deutsch Theater, Hamburg; also acted

1961: Directed first play

1970: German TV directorial debut, "I Will Kill You, Wolf"

1971–1976: Directed six episodes of German series "Tatort/Crime Scene"; first met and worked with actor Jurgen Prochnow on this series

1973: Feature directorial debut, "Einer von uns Beiden/One or the Other", the story of a student who blackmails one of his professors; won the German National Film Prize as Best New Director; Prochnow acted in picture, re-released in 1979 and picked up by Lufthansa airlines to show on its cross-Atlantic flights

1977: First feature as a screenwriter (also director), "The Consequence", a controversial homosexual love story starring Prochnow; banned in parts of Germany

1978: Helmed "Black and White Like Night and Days", a thriller set in the world of championship chess starring Bruno Ganz

1981: Won international acclaim with "Das Boot", at the time the most expensive German film ever made (about $12 million); received Best Director and Best Adapted Screenplay Oscar nominations, giving him the distinction of being the first director of a German film to receive a directing nod; scripted from the haunting memoirs of war correspondent Lothar-Gunther Buchheim; simultaneously created a five-hour epic for German TV

1984: Helmed and co-scripted "The Neverending Story", a partly American-financed project filmed in Munich's Bavarian Studios; first English-language film

1985: American directorial debut, "Enemy Mine" (also filmed at Bavarian Studios)

1987: Moved to California

Worked on a project with Kathleen Turner that dissolved when the actress became pregnant

1991: Directed, wrote and produced the stylish thriller "Shattered", adapted from Richard Neely's novel "The Plastic Warriors"; first association with producing partner Gail Katz (who co-produced); had planned to film this story prior to "Das Boot"

1993: Enjoyed hit with American debut as an executive producer, "In the Line of Fire", starring Clint Eastwood; also directed; first film made with the full cooperation of the Secret Service

1995: Directed "Outbreak", a thriller about a deadly virus running amok; despite the Ebola hysteria of that year, the picture stumbled at the box office compared with "In the Line of Fire", though it did more than make back its money; with Katz served as one of film's producers; first collaboration with German cinematographer Michael Ballhaus

1997: Supervised the director's cut of "Das Boot", re-released theatrically to enormous acclaim; enhancement included redesigned and re-recorded sound bringing it up to digital standards of the day, as well as a restored negative, reprinted onto the improved color-rich film stock available

1997: Had huge box-office success with the summer thriller "Air Force One"; served as one of the film's producers (as did Katz) and also directed; picture reunited him with Prochnow; second film with Ballhaus

1997: Executive produced Jon Avnet's "Red Corner"

1999: Executive produced Jon Turteltaub's "Instinct" and produced Chris Columbus' "Bicentennial Man"

2000: Helmed the film adaptation of the nonfiction best-seller "The Perfect Storm"; seventh producing collaboration with Katz

Returned to TV as executive producer of two-part, $12 million adaptation of "The Ring", based on Wagner's "Das Niebelungenlied"

2000: Formed Red Cliff Prods.

2001: Served as one of the executive producers of the CBS fall drama "The Agency"

QUOTES:

Petersen and Gail Katz's production company is Radiant Productions.

"I grew up in the 'fifties. The Americans came to Germany and they were like people from Mars. It was like a new vision with the most positive messages. I was a kid, 7 or 8, in Hamburg. And the American ships came in one morning and it was like a vision, like out of 'Close Encounters of the Third Kind'. We had no money, and these big shiny ships came in, and the troops on the ships began throwing down chewing gum and oranges and bananas. It was like gifts from heaven. I fell in love with America then and there."—Wolfgang Petersen to Bernard Weinraub in *The New York Times*, July 6, 1993.

"Even the thought of directing Clint [Eastwood] made me sweat. Coming from Europe, coming from Germany, I was awed by Eastwood. He's even more of a legend there than he is here. To have him say, 'We want you to direct this script' is very intimidating.

"But Clint, from the first day, said he would not interfere. And he never did. I've worked with a lot of actors and he was probably the easiest. There were no star things, no ego problems. And he has the power—he could have done that—but he never did."—Petersen in *The New York Times*, July 6, 1993.

"I've always aspired to work in the manner of David Lean, who had a great talent for combining the excitement of a large-scale visual experience, with very concentrrated, intimate character studies. I'm not interested in wall-to-wall action—I want to be touched and moved—but that doesn't mean the characters have to sit in the kitchen all the time and talk. This is, after all, a visual medium."—Petersen to *Los Angeles Times*, July 4, 1993.

On the director's cut of "Das Boot": "I always thought that even though the film version I delivered worked well it would be wonderful to one day go back and cut my own ideal version—to ask what is the best way for me to tell the story of 'Das Boot' based purley on creative rather than commercial considerations . . .

"My vision for 'Das Boot' was always to show the gritty and terrible reality of war, and to combine it with a highly entertaining story and fast-paced action style that would pull audiences into the experience of these young men out there. This cut represents my ideal version of that experience. Thanks to new technology, the film now comes even closer to revealing the shocking realities of life in a U-boat—the way it sounded, the way it felt, the way it affected people so strongly—and I think that this new cut will be even more shocking and affecting for audiences."—Petersen, quoted on dasboot.com.

Roman Polanski

BORN: Raimund Polanski in Paris, France, 08/18/1933

SOMETIMES CREDITED AS:
Romek Polanski

NATIONALITY: Polish

EDUCATION: Lodz Film School, Lodz, Poland, 1954–59

AWARDS: Venice Film Festival Critics' Prize Award "Knife in the Water" 1962

British Film Academy Award Best Direction "Chinatown" 1974

Golden Globe Award Best Director "Chinatown" 1974

Los Angeles Film Critics Association Award Best Director "Tess" 1980

Cesar Best Director "Tess" 1980

European Film Award European Acvhievement in Cinema 1999; cited with Antonio Banderas

Cannes Film Festival Palm d'Or "The Pianist" 2002

National Society Of Film Critics Best Picture "The Pianist" 2002

National Society of Film Critics Best Director "The Pianist" 2002

BAFTA The David Lean Award for Achievement in Direction "Pianist" 2002

BAFTA Best Film "Pianist" 2002 shared with Robert Benmussa and Alain Sarde

Oscar Best Director "Pianist" 2002

BIOGRAPHY
This internationally renowned filmmaker has become as notorious for his tumultuous life as for his sometimes darkly funny but deeply disquieting psychological dramas, jet black comedies and tough-minded period films. After a childhood stained with Nazi atrocities, Polanski began his film career first as a juvenile actor and later as a neophyte director in Poland. He went on to establish his reputation with several films shot in England before finding his artistic and commercial apotheosis in Hollywood. The European expatriate also found Southern California to be a place of shocking violence and profound personal tragedy. Polanski fled the US to escape the consequences of a sex scandal. He continued to make films in exile albeit with less frequency and smaller budgets. Though still controversial, Polanski continues to be numbered among the world's great directors.

Roman Polanski was born in Paris of Polish-Jewish parents. At the age of three, he and his family returned to Krakow in his father's native Poland. As a seven-year-old, Polanski witnessed the Nazis sealing the Krakow ghetto where his family lived. The youngster soon became an active participant in smuggling runs in and out of the ghetto. While on these missions, Polanski would sneak into outlying movie theaters. The following year, his parents were taken to a Nazi concentration camp, where his pregnant mother was gassed shortly after arrival. Polanski only narrowly avoided capture when his father pushed him through a gap in a wall as the Nazis approached. Some of these horrifying events would later be recreated by Steven Spielberg in "Schindler's List" (1993). During the long genesis of that film's screenplay, Spielberg reportedly approached Polanski on several occasions about directing the film. However, with several friends and relatives among the Krakow Jews whom Schindler saved from the camps, Polanski found the material too personal and painful.

Growing up in war-torn Poland, the young Polanski found solace in trips to the cinema and in acting in radio dramas, on stage and in films. His early screen acting credits included work with famed Polish director Andrzej Wajda. In 1954, he was accepted to an intensive five-year program at the Lodz Film School. One of his student films, "Two Men and a Wardrobe" (1958), won five international awards, including a Bronze Medal at the Brussels World's Fair. In 1962, Polanski directed his first feature-length film, "Knife in the Water." Poorly received by Polish state officials and some domestic critics, the film was a sensation in the West, was awarded the Critics' Prize at the Venice Film Festival and won an Academy Award nomination as Best Foreign Film.

Polanski moved to England to make his next three films: "Repulsion" (1965), a psychological horror story of a young woman's mental disintegration; "Cul-de-Sac" (1966), a dark comedy of mobsters and a mismatched couple set in an isolated castle; and a Hammer horror parody, "Dance of the Vampires/The Fearless Vampire Killers, or Pardon Me But Your Teeth Are in My Neck" (1967), in which Polanski co-starred with American actress Sharon Tate. He and Tate married in 1968, the year that also marked Polanski's American film debut with "Rosemary's Baby", an enormously successful adaptation of Ira Levin's tale of gynecological horror. The following summer, Polanski's new-found success was dealt a shattering blow when the eight-months pregnant Tate and three of Polanski's friends were murdered by members of the Charles Manson cult. His next film, "Macbeth"

(1971), was a brutally realistic adaptation of the violent Shakespeare tragedy that was interpreted by some critics as the filmmaker's cathartic response to the Manson slayings. Polanski himself, however, downplayed the link between the film and the tragic murders.

In 1974, Polanski was back in Hollywood for his greatest triumph, "Chinatown", a tale of greed, corruption and incest set in 1930s Los Angeles. The director made a memorable impression on-screen, too, as the cocky gangster who slices Jack Nicholson's nose. Two years later, Polanski undertook his most arduous acting role, directing himself as the lead in "The Tenant." This profoundly unsettling but darkly comic portrait of a gradual descent into madness featured Polanski as a man who unravels after moving into the apartment of a woman who had committed suicide.

In 1977, Polanski was arrested in California on charges of unlawful sexual intercourse with a thirteen-year-old girl. He spent forty-two days under psychiatric observation in Chino, CA in compliance with a plea bargain. The judge subsequently wavered and—before further criminal proceedings could get underway—Polanski fled the United States. He made his next film, "Tess" (1979), in France. This acclaimed version of the Thomas Hardy novel "Tess of the d'Urbervilles" told the story of a beautiful country girl (Nastassja Kinski) who is systematically seduced by an older man. In 1981, he returned to Poland to direct and star in a stage production of "Amadeus."

Polanski's next film to achieve some degree of critical and commercial success was the suspenseful yet dreamy "Frantic" (1988), featuring Harrison Ford as an American in Paris searching for his missing wife (Betty Buckley). Also lensed in Paris was "Bitter Moon" (released abroad in 1992 but not in the US until 1994), which depicted a boat journey that for an upright Englishman (Hugh Grant) becomes a tortuous and dank voyage into the narrative of a wheelchair-bound would-be Henry Miller played by Peter

Coyote. "Bitter Moon" also starred Polanski's wife Emmanuelle Seigner as the femme fatale destroyer/victim of the writer, 20 years her senior. This has encouraged critics, who were variously wowed, perplexed and repelled by the film, to read it as a refracted autobiography. It was obviously another variation on the director's preoccupation with psychic and sexual decay.

Polanski's "Death and the Maiden" (1994) was a widely acclaimed film adaptation of Chilean playwright Ariel Dorfman's three character political allegory. Set in an unidentified South American country, the story follows a human-rights attorney (Stuart Wilson) who becomes stranded on a highway when his car breaks down. A kind doctor (Ben Kingsley) gives him a ride home where his wife (Sigourney Weaver) awaits. The wife immediately recognizes the doctor's voice as belonging to the man who supervised her torture under the previous regime. She takes him hostage, confronts him with her charges and puts him on trial before her lawyer husband. Even more claustrophobic than the play, the film powerfully considered issues of guilt and innocence and boasted powerhouse performances. After a four-year hiatus Polanksi returned in 2000 with the thriller "The Ninth Gate," as director and one of the screenwriters, an adaptation of a French horror novel in which Johnny Depp plays a rare book collector seeking a manuscript featuring artwork created by Satan himself. That film did little to enhance or detract from the director's resume, but his next major work, 2002's "The Pianist," re-established Polanksi as a top-flight auteur. Working from the true story of acclaimed Polish composer Wladyslaw Szpilman, who narrowly escaped a roundup that sent his family to a Nazi death camp and struggled to survive until he was able to reclaim his artistic mastery, Polanski also drew on his own vivid recollections of escaping the Holocaust. The result was a triumphant, complex masterwork that moved audiences and critics worldwide and resulted in a new appreciation of the director's gifts, even as he still worked in European exile following his flight from the U.S. decades earlier. Even after "The Pianist" received a wealth of awards including an Oscar as Best Director for Polanski—the director, who had previously had a deal to dismiss the charges denied by the Los Angeles district attorney, announced that he had no plans to try to return to America to collect his accolades.

Polanski has had a minor but interesting career as an actor since childhood. At age 21, he won a featured role in Andrzej Wajda's first full-length film, "A Generation" (1954). Polanski would subsequently appear in Wajda's "Lotna" (1959), "Innocent Sorcerers" (1960) and "Samson" (1961). In addition to acting in many of his own shorts and features, Polanski had character parts and cameos in a number of European films. He was the charming but lethal Soviet gangster in the direct-to-video romantic thriller "Back in the U.S.S.R." (1992), appeared in a scripted role as himself in Michel Blanc's comedy-drama "Grosse Fatigue" (1994) and shone in a tour-de-force character lead opposite Gerard Depardieu in Giuseppe Tornatore's claustrophobic cat-and-mouse drama "A Pure Formality" (1994; released in the USA in 1995). In the latter, Polanski more than held his own against the French superstar, playing a "Columbo"-like inspector with fascistic undertones who interrogates a celebrated writer suspected of murder.

As an artist who exerts tremendous control over his films, often co-writing the screenplays and sometimes acting in them, Polanski instills his work with a uniquely personal worldview. His recurring themes are violence and victimization, isolation and alienation, and a profound sense of the absurd. The relationship between Polanski's personal life and his work has received a great deal of attention. While there are some strong parallels, focusing on this relationship has unfortunately tended to overshadow the surprising diversity of his films and eclipse his achievements as a filmmaker.

FAMILY:

mother: Bula Polanski. Russian; half Jewish; left her first husband to marry Ryszard Polanski in 1932; gassed to death (while four months pregnant) in Auschwitz concentration camp during WWII

COMPANIONS:

wife: Sharon Tate. Actor; born in 1943; married in January 1968; met while acting in Polanski's "The Fearless Vampire Killers" (1967); murdered by the Charles Manson clan in August 1969; was eight months pregnant at time of death

Nastassja Kinski. Actor; born in 1960; began relationship with Polanski at age 15; appeared in a photo spread in an issue of French *Vogue* guest edited by Polanski; starred in "Tess" (1979)

MILESTONES:

1933: Born in Paris, France

1936: At age three, moved with his parents to his father's native Krakow, Poland

1940: As a seven-year-old, witnessed the Nazi's sealing off the Krakow ghetto where he and family lived

Participated in smuggling runs by slipping out of the ghetto through secret passageways (date approximate)

Sneaked into the outlying movie houses to watch Aryan romances

1941: Parents taken to Nazi concentration camp when Polanski was eight (mother killed at Auschwitz); Roman avoided capture after his father pushed him through a gap in the wall sealing the ghetto (date aproximate)

1944: Returned to Krakow at age 11; reunited with father (date approximate)

1945: Began acting in radio shows at age 12

1946: Set up by his father in his own apartment at age 13 (date approximate)

1947: Made stage debut at age 14

Became a celebrity on Krakow radio, usually playing street tough kids considerably younger than his actual age

1954: Began acting in films and making documentaries

1954: Won a featured role in Andrzej Wajda's first full-length film "A Generation"; first collaboration with the director

Accepted into the rigorous four-year training program at the national film school in Lodz; began making short films

1960–1961: Moved to Paris

Met future frequent screenwriting collaborator Gerard Brach

1962: Directed first feature, "Knife in the Water"

1964: First collaboration with Brach, co-screenwriter of "Amsterdam" sequence of the international omnibus feature, "Les plus belles escroqueries du monde" (also directed)

1965: Moved to London to direct "Repulsion"

1968: Moved to Hollywood to write and direct his US debut "Rosemary's Baby"

1969: Second wife Sharon Tate, her eight-month-old fetus, and four others murdered by the Charles Manson "family"

1976: Served as guest editor for the Christmas issue of French *Vogue*; featured Nastassja Kinski in a photo layout taken in the Seychelles Islands

1977: Reportedly approached by *Vogue Hommes* to produce a layout on the theme of "young girls of the world"

1977: Arrested for having sex with a thirteen-year-old girl he was auditioning for the *Vogue* photo layout

1977: Indicted on six criminal counts including "unlawful sexual intercourse", "rape by use of drugs", committing a "lewd and lascivious act" on a child, and "sodomy"

1978: Accepting a plea bargain, plead guilty to one charge of "unlawful sexual intercourse"; served 42 days under psychiatric evaluation in the Chino State Psychiatric Prison

1978: Fled the US upon learning that the judge had changed his mind and planned to sentence him to additional jail time unless he agreed to be deported

1993: Settled out of court in a civil suit with his accuser; part of the agreement stipulated that he could not discuss or write about the incident

1996: Directed first music video for Italian rock singer Vasco Rossi

1996: Announced as director of "The Double" with John Travolta attached as star; Travolta left project nine days before the start of principal photography; left project shortly thereafter as well

1996: Returned to the theater as director of the Paris production of "Master Class"

1997: Staged the musical "Dance of the Vampires", based on "The Fearless Vampire Killers", in Vienna

2000: Returned to features as director of the supernatural thriller "The Ninth Gate"

2002: Returned to acting, starring in "Zemsta/The Vengeance", directed by Andrzej Wajda

2002: Directed "The Pianist," a true story about a Jewish piano player who survived the Warsaw ghetto; won top prize at Cannes

QUOTES:

In 2003 at the height of Polanksi's noteriety for directing "The Pianist," Samantha Geimer, the alleged victim in Polanksi's statutory rape case when she was 13, claimed in an op-ed piece in the *Los Angeles Times* that the director fled to France because the judge in the case reneged on a plea bargain struck by both parties that limited Polanski's punishment to the 40 days he had already spent incarcerated awaiting trial. "Who wouldn't think about running when facing a 50-year sentence from a judge who was clearly more interested in his own reputation than a fair judgment?," Geimer wrote. She also indicated that she believed his film work should be judged on its own merits:

"I believe that Mr. Polanski and his film should be honored according to the quality of the work. What he does for a living and how good he is at it, have nothing to do with me or what he did to me," said Geimer, describing herself as a happily married mother of three.

"'[Polanski] would be excommunicated by Hollywood because his wife had the bad taste to be murdered in the papers,' his friend Jack Nicolson said later."—From "Profile: Artist in Exile" by Lawrence Weshler, *The New Yorker,* December 5, 1994.

"When Sharon died, the press said the most terrible things about us—that it was connected to black magic, that it had something to do with the type of movies I had always made. They just lie and lie and lie, but when they print it, then people think it's true. When they found out that Manson was behind it, then they changed their song. But they were relentless. And when the trouble happened with the girl, it was like everyone said, 'We were right about him, he's crazy, that's why his wife got killed.' "—Polanski quoted in "Roman Holiday" by Martha Frankel, *Movieline,* January/February 1995.

"As for the ending [of "Chinatown"], [screenwriter Robert] Towne, in his original version, had had the Faye Dunaway character killing her father [and incestuous tormentor], the creepy John Huston character, before he could get his hands on the barely pubescent child whom he had sired upon her and whom she was desperately endeavoring to protect. Instead, Polanski had the Faye Dunaway character herself getting gruesomely killed right in front of the child, whom the Huston character now enveloped in his oily embrace, leading her away as Jack Nicholson's detective character looked on ineffectually and a police pal muttered, 'Forget it, Jake, it's Chinatown.' "—From "Profile: Artist in Exile" by Lawrence Weshler in *The New Yorker,* December 5, 1994.

"When Polanski discusses the violence that occurs in his films, he often asserts that, far from being a sensationalist, he is a pure realist; and certainly he is one of the few directors around who have experienced at first hand such a sheer amount and so many varieties of violence."—From "Profile: Artist in Exile" by Lawrence Weshler in *The New Yorker,* December 5, 1994.

Polanski served as president of the 44th Annual Cannes Film Festival committee in 1991.

"I have a friend who worked for Polanski on "Repulsion." For years after he kept the director's picture pasted inside one of his shoes, 'So every time I took a step I'd crush the wretched dwarf.' Roman Polanski has no problem playing the prick. He can also play a smarmy civil servant or a sentimental fool aching to be victimized. Terrorized children—Polanski eluded the Nazis—pick up useful tricks. If he hadn't needed to control things, he could've been an actor of Ben Kingsley's

stature."—From Georgia Brown's review of "A Pure Formality" in *Village Voice* May 30, 1995.

"I miss the efficiency of the studios, I miss the big machine, I know how to operate it. It has great inertia this machine, but if you know how to use it, you can do alot of interesting things."
—Polanski's response when asked if he misses working in America, *Village Voice,* April 19, 1994.

Polanski was supposed to direct "The Double" in 1996. Conflicts with star John Travolta led to Travolta's leaving the film days before shooting was to begin. Polanski eventually left the project as well.

BIBLIOGRAPHY:

"The Roman Polanski Story" Thomas Kiernan
  1980 Delilah/Grove Press

"Roman" Roman Polanski 1984 autobiography

Sydney Pollack

BORN: in Lafayette, Indiana, 07/01/1934

NATIONALITY: American

EDUCATION: graduated from high school, 1952
  The Neigborhood Playhouse School of the Theatre, New York, New York, 1952–54; awarded fellowship; studied with Sanford Meisner, then taught there afterwards, serving as Meisner's assistant until 1960

AWARDS: Emmy Outstanding Directorial Achievement in Drama "The Game" 1965/66
  New York Film Critics Circle Award Best Director "Tootsie" 1982
  NATO Director of the Year Award 1983; presented by the National Association of Theater Owners
  Oscar Best Picture "Out of Africa" 1985; producer of film
  Oscar Best Director "Out of Africa" 1985
  John Huston Award for Artists Rights 2000

BIOGRAPHY
A curly-haired, six-footer usually clad in jeans and boots, Sydney Pollack is an engaging, enthusiastic and unpretentious man who has consistently elicited fine performances from Hollywood stars, including Robert Redford, Jane Fonda, Dustin Hoffman, Barbra Streisand, Paul Newman and Burt Lancaster. His affinity for actors stems from his years at NYC's Neighborhood Playhouse, where he studied with Sanford Meisner and stayed on at Meisner's request as an acting teacher, developing the nurturing qualities that have made him an "actor's director". As a performer, Pollack worked Off-Broadway with Zero Mostel and Sylvia Miles in "A Stone for Danny Fisher" (1954) and followed with his Broadway debut in Christopher Fry's "The Dark Is Light Enough" (1955). But it was a role in a "Playhouse 90" production of "For Whom the Bell Tolls", directed by John Frankenheimer, that changed his life forever,

Working as dialogue coach on Frankenheimer's first feature ("The Young Savages" 1961) led to a lasting relationship with its star Burt Lancaster, who encouraged Pollack to pursue directing and opened doors by introducing him to heavy-hitter Lew Wasserman. Although he considered his first attempt behind the camera (an episode of the syndicated "Shotgun Slade") a bust, Pollack apprenticed to an editor, experimented with still photography and ran countless movies to bridge the gap between what he didn't know and needed to learn. The next five years offered him a tremendous opportunity to grow as a director as he helmed more than 80 shows for the small screen, including 15 episodes of the popular "Ben Casey" series. He also made his feature film debut as an actor in Denis Sanders' "War Hunt" (1962), making the acquaintance of another player appearing on the big screen for the first time, Robert Redford.

Pollack's first feature, "The Slender Thread" (1965), spotlighted Anne Bancroft as a suicidal woman and Sidney Poitier as a crisis center worker trying to keep her on the telephone while emergency services track her down. This taut black-and-white drama, shot on location in Seattle, opened with an aerial shot, and his next film, "This Property Is Condemned" (1966), starring Redford in the first of his seven collaborations (to date) helmed by Pollack, also exhibited two effective examples of this device, which became a director's trademark. Two more pictures ("The Scalphunters" 1968, "Castle Keep" 1969) preceded his first major success (and initial credit as producer), "They Shoot Horses, Don't They?" (also 1969), a harrowing drama set during a Depression-era dance marathon. Although criticized for toning down the harsher, more abrasive qualities of the Horace McCoy novel, it did earn Gig Young an Oscar as Best Supporting Actor and Pollack a nomination for Best Director.

Pollack reteamed with Redford for "Jeremiah Johnson" (1972), but the film did not make near the commercial splash of "The Way We Were" (1973), an old-fashioned love story pairing Redford and Barbra Streisand. Although critics and audiences both maligned the Japanese gangster film "The Yakuza", starring Robert Mitchum, "Three Days of the Condor" (both 1975), which cast Redford as the on-the-run surviving member of a massacred US intelligence office, registered well with moviegoers while garnering mixed reviews. After another misstep ("Bobby Deerfield" 1976), Pollack returned to a winning formula with "The Electric Horseman" (1979), a romantic comedy about a modern-day cowboy and a reporter that matched Redford with Jane Fonda. He then enjoyed a huge commercial and critical success directing the breakthrough gender-bending comedy "Tootsie" (1982), in which he also acted, delivering a memorable performance in his small role as agent to an intransigent actor played by Dustin Hoffman (who insisted that Pollack play the part). The film earned a Best Supporting Actress Oscar for Jessica Lange, another feather in his cap as an actor's director.

Pollack's career reached a zenith of sorts with "Out of Africa" (1985), the sumptuous biopic of writer Isak Dinesen (Meryl Streep) which focused on her love affair with Denys Finch Hatton (Redford) and featured exquisite photography by David Watkins and a rich score by John Barry. Pollack won two Oscars as producer and director (out of the seven the picture received), but as resounding as the accolades were for his triumphant trip to Africa, the howls that greeted his next effort, "Havana" (1990), were equally loud. Overly reminiscent of "Casablanca" and loaded with bad dialogue, this meandering tale of the last days of Battista's Cuba failed to give Redford (in his last teaming to date with Pollack) a consistent, believable character. The anticipated heat between the star and romantic interest Lena Olin sputtered due to a lack of screen chemistry and the pair's lackluster, abbreviated sex scenes. The pillorying left Pollack shaken and made him particularly cautious in selecting his next directorial assignment, the adaptation of John Grisham's best-selling "The Firm" (1993), which, much to his relief, did boffo box office.

Since forming Mirage Enterprises in 1985, Pollack has frequently produced (or executive produced) other directors' successful projects, including "Bright Lights, Big City" (1988), "The Fabulous Baker Boys" (1989), "Presumed Innocent" (1990), "Dead Again" (1991), "Searching for Bobby Fischer" (1993), the Oscar-nominated "Sense and Sensibility" and his own pallid remake of "Sabrina" (both 1995). He has also devoted more time to acting in recent years, receiving kudos for his major supporting performance in Woody Allen's "Husbands and Wives" (1992) as a New York professional who leaves his wife (Judy Davis) of many years and appearing that same year in both Robert Altman's "The Player" and Robert Zemeckis' "Death Becomes Her." Pollack has done a little bit of everything recently, acting in Stanley Kubrick's "Eyes Wide Shut", directing "Random Hearts" and producing "Up at the Villa" (all 1999).

MILESTONES:

Grew up in South Bend, Indiana

1954–1960: Beginning at age 19, assisted Sanford Meisner and taught acting at Neighborhood Playhouse for six years (dates approximate)

1954: Off-Broadway acting debut in "A Stone for Danny Fisher", starring Zero Mostel and Sylvia Miles

1955: Broadway acting debut in Christopher Fry's "Dark Is Light Enough", with Tyrone Power, Katharine Cornell and Christopher Plummer

Served in US Army

Taught drama at NYU

Acted on TV in a "Playhouse 90" production of "For Whom the Bell Tolls" directed by John Frankenheimer

1961: Served as Dialogue coach for Franken-

heimer's "The Young Savages" starring Burt Lancaster

Urged to pursue a career in directing by Lancaster

Introduced to agent-turned-movie mogul Lew Wasserman

Moved to L.A. with his wife

First TV directing assignment, an episode of "Shotgun Slade", a syndicated half-hour Western series

Directed for various TV series including "Alfred Hitchcock Presents", "The Defenders", "Ben Casey", and "The Bob Hope Chrysler Theatre" (dates approximate)

1962: Feature film acting debut, "War Hunt"; also Robert Redford's debut

1963: Served as voice dubbing supervisor of the American version of Luchino Visconti's "Il Gattopardo/The Leopard" (at Burt Lancaster's request)

1964: "Chrysler Theatre" telecast of his "Two Is the Number", starring Shelley Winters, won International TV Festival Award in Monte Carlo

1965: Directed first feature, "The Slender Thread", starring Sidney Poitier and Anne Bancroft

1966: First of seven movies directing Redford, "This Property Is Condemned"

1969: "They Shoot Horses, Don't They?" won First Prizes at the Belgium and Yugoslavian Film Festivals; received the Moscow Film Festival's Special Jury Prize; Pollack's first producing credit; received first Best Director Academy Award nomination

1972: "Jeremiah Johnson", starrig Redford, won American Heritage Award for Best Western, Yugoslavian Film Festival Award and *Parents* magazine Award

1975: "Three Days of the Condor" (again with Redford) won the David Di Donatello Prize in Taormina, Sicily and the Edgar Allen Poe Mystery Writers Award

1980: Participated in American Legion Seminar with James Woods

1981: Became executive director (with Lee Strasberg) of the Actors Studio in L.A.

1982: First feature acting appearance in 20 years as Dustin Hoffman's agent George Fields in "Tootsie", directed and produced by Pollack; Hoffman insisted he play the role; earned Best Director and Best Picture Academy Award nominations

1983: Agreed to work with Nova film production company as creative consultant; venture organized by Columbia, HBO and CBS

1985: Picked up two Oscars, one as producer (Best Picture), and one as Best Director for "Out of Africa", co-starring Redford and Meryl Streep

1985: Formed production company, Mirage Productions Inc.

1986: Served as jury president at 39th Cannes Film Festival

1989: Split with Mark Rosenberg as partners in Mirage Productions Inc. after three years; company renamed Mirage Enterprises

1989: Sued by producer Richard Roth for over $1 million after being excluded from production of "Havana" (when Pollack decided to produce and direct himself) on which he had worked for 15 years (when project was known as "The New Orleans Story"); released in 1990, it was his last picture (to date) directing Redford

1992: Acted in three films released the same year, Woody Allen's "Husbands and Wives", "Death Becomes Her" (uncredited), and "The Player"

1993: Directed and produced "The Firm", the first movie adapted from a John Grisham novel

1995: Remade Billy Wilder's "Sabrina" (1954), starring Harrison Ford, Julia Ormond and Greg Kinnear

Replaced Harvey Keitel, acting in Stanley Kubrick's "Eyes Wide Shut" (lensing completed in 1998; film released in 1999)

1998: Executive produced "Poodle Springs", an HBO movie adapted from the Robert B. Parker novel based on an unfinished manuscript by Raymond Chandler

1999: Directed "Random Hearts", a failed romance teaming Kristin Scott Thomas and Harrison Ford

1999: Executive produced "The Talented Mr. Ripley", written and directed by Anthony Minghella

2000: Was one of the executive producers of "Up at the Villa", starring Kristin Scott Thomas

2000: Joined by Minghella as a full partner in Mirage Enterprises

2000—Present: Had occasional recurring role on the NBC sitcom "Will & Grace"

Served as one of the producer on the remake of "The Quiet Man" (lensed 2001)

QUOTES:

Pollack broke his hip in January 2000.

"If you get the recipe for Coca-Cola down, the rest of it is just marketing. They're now trying to do that with movies, and it's not going to work, because you re-invent the art form every time you make a movie. You can't sell them like other products. Marketing costs have skyrocketed . . . and this marketing thing will get a picture open, but it won't do anything beyond that.

"Look, I thought 'Havana' was a good movie. I didn't do anything different on 'Havana' than I did on 'Out of Africa' . . . But the people [moviegoers] didn't like it. If I could control that . . . I'd make nothing but hits, retire and sell the recipe . . . It doesn't work like that."—Sydney Pollack quoted in USA Today, June 30, 1993.

"I have two different careers here. I have a career as a director where I produce my own films and I also own and run Mirage, and that has a different life. I can make tiny films there. If we don't make a film a year, it doesn't matter. We've done 12 films in the 12 years I've had the company, which is a tidy number of films.

"I am looking for a small film to direct, but everyone thinks of me as being a major director who spends a lot of money making big movies with the Hollywood stars."—Pollack to Screen International, June 13–19, 1997.

BORN: Michael Latham Powell in Bekesbourne, Kent, England, 09/30/1905

DEATH: in Avening, Gloucestershire, England, 02/19/1990

NATIONALITY: English

EDUCATION: King's School Canterbury, England; attended until 1918

Dulwich College, England; began studies in 1918, taking the place of his deceased older brother

AWARDS: Cannes Film Festival Special Award Originality of Lyrical Adaptation to Film "Tales of Hoffman" 1951; shared award with Emeric Pressburger

Venice Film Festival Golden Lion for Career Achievement 1982

BIOGRAPHY

Michael Powell's introduction to the film business came at 20, when, with the assistance of his father, he secured a job with Rex Ingram's film unit based in Nice, France. In the late 1920s, Powell worked at Elstree Studios for Harry Lachman and Alfred Hitchcock. During the early 30s, Powell cut his directorial teeth on a number of forgettable, low-budget "quota quickies" for independent production companies in England.

In 1938, after making "The Edge of the World" (1937), a personal exploration of man's battle with nature on an isolated island off the coast of Scotland, Powell was brought together with German scriptwriter Emric Pressburger to develop "The Spy in Black" (1939) as a vehicle for Conrad Veidt. Powell made two more films without Pressburger, including co-directing "The Thief of Bagdad" (1940), a

remarkable fantasy film, before forming a partnership with Pressburger in their own production company, the Archers.

Some of the most notable Powell-Pressburger achievements include "The Life and Death of Colonel Blimp" (1944), a satiric view of the British military that incurred the wrath of Winston Churchill, "A Canterbury Tale" (1944) and "I Know Where I'm Going" (1945), lyrical, often romantic, but sharp films which were, according to Powell, "a crusade against materialism"; "A Matter of Life and Death" (1945, known as "Stairway to Heaven" in the US), an epic but thoughtful fantasy film; "Black Narcissus" (1947), one of the most gorgeous films ever shot in color; and the lush "The Red Shoes" (1948), Archers' most prestigious effort and still cited as the best ballet story ever made.

Preoccupied with technique, Powell strove to achieve what he called "the unity of art". The essence of Powell's visual style and his attitude toward art and life, are best displayed in "Black Narcissus" (1947) and "The Tales of Hoffmann" (1951). "Black Narcissus" chronicles the failure of a group of Anglican nuns to establish a mission in the Himalayan mountains. Powell shot virtually all of the film in a studio to maintain complete control over color, setting and atmosphere in service to the film's complex character's and theme. With its constant undercurrent of repressed sexuality and the mystical power of nature, the film also reveals Powell's paganistic philosophy. Finally, for the film's dramatic climax, Powell first used what he called "composed film": Brian Easdale wrote the music for the scene before the dramatic action was plotted out and measured with a stop watch; the sequence was then shot and edited to mirror the rhythms of the music. "The Tales of Hoffmann," an eccentric, astonishingly expressionistic ballet-opera version of

Jacques Offenbach's last work, stands as Powell's most magnificent attempt to fuse the arts into film form. Perhaps its only rival in this context is Disney's worthy but uneven and often overrated "Fantasia."

After Powell and Pressburger dissolved their partnership in 1956, Powell's most notorious work was the controversial "Peeping Tom" (1960). This brilliant, endlessly self-reflexive film is the story of a killer who stalks his female victims with a spear-and-mirror-equipped camera, to film them as they watch themselves die. Critical attacks on "Peeping Tom" were so vicious and extreme that they virtually terminated Powell's career. This uniquely unsettling film has since been revived and praised by Martin Scorsese, among others, as one of the great movies about the psychology of filmmaking and film viewing.

Although he is now acknowledged as one of England's foremost filmmakers, Michael Powell paid an enormous price for cultivating his personal vision within the context of a national cinema almost totally at odds with his artistic concerns. His emphasis on the bold uses of imagery and color has inspired a whole generation of filmmakers, including Ken Russell, Nicolas Roeg, John Boorman and Derek Jarman.

MILESTONES:

Raised in Canterbury, England and the South of France

1922–1925: Worked as a bank clerk

1925: Became an assistant to director and producer Rex Ingram

1928: Was the stills photographer on Alfred Hitchcock's "Champagne"

1928: Worked as a film cutter on "A Knight in London"

1930: Debut as scenarist, the "quota quickie" feature "Caste"

1931: Feature directorial debut, "Two Crowded Hours"

1937: Helmed "The Edge of the World", about residents of one of the remote islands in the North Sea; caught attention of Alexander Korda; also appeared in opening scenes as a British tourist alongside wife Frances "Frankie" Reidy

1939: Alexander Korda offered contract to direct "The Spy in Black"; initial teaming with frequent collaborator Emeric Pressburger

1940: Was one of the many directors on "The Thief of Bagdad"

1940: First co-directing credit with Pressburger, "Contraband"

1942: With Pressburger, established the production company The Archers

1942: Shared Oscar nomination with Emeric Pressburger for the screenplay of " . . . One of Our Aircraft Is Missing"

1943: First Archers production in color, "The Life and Death of Colonel Blimp"; engendered controversy for its use of color during wartime rationing; also elicited the scorn of Prime Minister Winston Churchill, who didn't like its critique of British stuffiness while the country was in the midst of WWII

1946: With Pressburger, co-directed, co-wrote and co-produced the unconventional "A Matter of Life and Death/Stairway to Heaven", which mixed fantasy elements with a dramatic story of a pilot who survives a crash through the mistake of an angel and then must plead his case to a heavenly tribunal

1947: Co-produced (through The Archers), co-wrote and co-directed "Black Narcissus"; film won Academy Awards for for Best Color Cinematography and Best Color Art Direction

1948: Made one of the most famous of the Archers Productions, "The Red Shoes", about a ballerina torn between two men; film received five Academy Award nominations including Best Picture

1950: With Pressburger, crafted the remake "The Elusive Pimpernel", starring David Niven; film was originally intended as a musical but the production numbers were dropped

Difficulties in getting work in Britain due to

"Peeping Tom", directs episodes of "Espionage" and "The Defenders" for TV

1960: Produced and directed the controversial film "Peeping Tom"; at time of its release was nearly universally panned; has since been re-evaluated as a masterpiece

Following the ill-fated reaction to "Peeping Tom", had difficulty in obtaining work in Britain; began helming episodes of the TV series "Espionage" and "The Defenders"

1966: Produced and directed "They're a Weird Mob", a comedy written by Pressburger (under the pen name Richard Imrie)

1984: Marries film editor Thelma Schoonmaker

1986: First edition of his autobiography, "A Life in Movies"

1979: Published novel "A Waiting Game"

1981: Served as senior director in residence at Zoetrope Studios

1995: Second volume of memoirs, "Million Dollar Movie", published posthumously

BIBLIOGRAPHY:

"200,000 Feet on Foula" Michael Powell, 1939; based on the film "The Edge of the World"

"A Waiting Game" Michael Powell, 1979; novel

"A Life in Movies" Michael Powell, 1987; autobiography

"Million Dollar Movie" Michael Powell, 1995, Random House; autobiography; published posthumously

Otto Preminger

BORN: Otto Ludwig Preminger in Austria, 12/05/1906

DEATH: in New York, New York, 04/23/1986

NATIONALITY: Austrian

CITIZENSHIP: United States, 1943

EDUCATION: University of Vienna, law, LLD, 1928; earned degree after flunking once

AWARDS: Golden Globe Award Best Motion Picture (Musical/Comedy) "Carmen Jones" 1954

Locarno Film Festival Critic's Grand Prize Best Film "Carmen Jones" 1955; one of two films cited

Golden Globe Award Best Motion Picture (Drama) "The Cardinal" 1963

BIOGRAPHY

Former assistant to German stage producer Max Reinhardt who began his directing career with the 1935 Broadway melodrama, "Lible."

Preminger then directed a couple of B films at 20th Century Fox before a dispute with Darryl F. Zanuck temporarily halted his behind-the-camera career. When he found himself in demand as an actor—Preminger's stern features and Viennese accent made him the perfect screen Nazi—he used this new popularity to maneuver his way back into the director's chair. Preminger made his breakthrough with the critical and commercial smash, "Laura" (1944), on which he took over the direction from Rouben Mamoulian. His subsequent work at Fox was disappointing and he began independently producing his own films, through his Carlyle Productions company, in the early 1950s. Preminger soon earned a reputation for turning out controversial works which broached previously taboo subjects such as drug addiction ("The Man With the Golden Arm" 1955).

A skilled technician who lacked any consistently discernable style, Preminger's career encompassed polished successes including "Anatomy of a Murder" (1959), "Exodus" (1960), "Advise and Consent" (1961) and

"Bunny Lake is Missing" (1965), alongside notable flops such as "Saint Joan" (1957) and "Rosebud" (1975). Father, by stripper Gypsy Rose Lee, of producer-screenwriter Eric Lee Preminger and brother of agent-turned-producer Ingo Preminger.

COMPANIONS:

wife: Marion Mill. Actor; married in 1932; divorced in the late 1940s; hired Preminger to represent her in the only legal case he ever handled; Preminger then cast her in the stage production of "The Front Page" which he directed (1931); became a well-known New York and Hollywood hostess

Gypsy Rose Lee. Ecdysiast, entertainer; mother of Erik Lee Preminger

wife: Mary Gardner. Model; married in 1951; divorced in 1958

Dorothy Dandridge. Actor, singer

wife: Patricia Hope Bryce. Fashion coordinator; married in 1958; was fashion coordinator on Preminger's film "Bonjour Tristesse" (1957); mother of Preminger's twin son and daughter

MILESTONES:

Acting debut at age 12, the only child among adults at a poetry reading

Apprenticed at Max Reinhardt's Theater, Josefstadt in Vienna

Stage debut as Lysander in "A Midsummer Night's Dream" at Josefstadt Theater (not directed by Reinhardt) at age 17

1925: Joined German theater in Aussig (now in Czechoslavakia) where he also made his directorial debut with a production of Klabund's "Kreiderkreis/The Chalk Circle"

Returned to Vienna to launch theater of his own, the Komedia and two years later, the Schauspielhaus while simultaneously studying law at the University of Vienna

1931: Returned to the Josefstadt as an assistant director

1931: Handled only law case, a breach-of-contract suit brought by a nightclub owner against actress Marion Mill (whom he represented); Preminger then cast Mill in "The Front Page" which he was directing and married her the following year

1931: Directed first film, "Die Grosse Liebe/The Great Love"

1932–1933: Took over as director of the Josefstadt when Reinhardt went into semi-retirement

1935: Invited by Joseph M Schenck to work for his newly merged 20th Century Fox in Hollywood

1935: Directed first Broadway play, "Libel"

1936: Directed first Hollywood film, "Under Your Spell"

After falling out with Darryl F. Zanuck, returned to New York and directed seven plays

1941: Made Broadway acting debut (replacing another actor) in Clare Boothe Luce's play, "Margin for Error" (also directed)

1942: Returned to Hollywood as an actor, playing a Nazi officer in "The Pied Piper"

1943: Hired to recreate his role in "Margin for Error" in film version, Preminger offered to direct and star for only an actor's fee; resulted in a contract with 20th Century Fox to act, direct and produce

1944: Hired as producer, he also replaced Rouben Mamoulian as director on film noir classic "Laura"

1951: Returned to the Broadway stage to direct "Four Twelves Are Forty-Eight" and "The Moon Is Blue"

1953: Became an independent producer; first film project, "The Moon Is Blue" became first film refused Production Code seal of approval when Preminger refused to delete the words "virgin" "pregnant", "mistress" and "seduction" from the script of the film

1979: Directed last film, "The Human Factor"

QUOTES:

Preminger's "narrative lines are strewn with deceptive counterpaths, shifting viewpoints, and ambiguous characters who perpetually slip out of static categories and moral definitions . . . Preminger frequently mystifies the spectator who is looking for a fixed moral reference."—Richard Roud ("Cinema": A Critical Dictionary")

Writing about Preminger's 20th Century-Fox film noir classics of the late 1940s, Jean-Pierre Coursodon wrote in "American Directors": [They are] "not only thematically similar, they look alike, and generate the same kind of atmosphere. . . . The fluidity of the camerawork is the concrete expression of his attitutde to his material. The camera unobtrusively but relentlessly follows the characters around in medium shots and long boom or dolly shots, so as to integrate them to the surroundings. Preminger's vision is a global one, he strives to capture the whole, not details—hence the paucity of close-up and reaction shots in his films. . . . This stylistic option is consistent with Preminger's unfailingly objective attitude toward characters and situations. . . . If the harmony of form and content, expression and intention, is the mark of 'classic' art, Preminger is one of the great classics of the American film."

In his autobiography, Preminger explains the discrepancy in his birth date and place: "One set of documents lists Vienna as my birthplace but another set . . . places my birth at my great-grandfather's farm some distance away. One records that I was born on the fifth of December, 1906, the other exactly one year earlier."

BIBLIOGRAPHY:

"Preminger: An Autobiography" Otto Preminger, 1977, Doubleday

"All I Want is Everything" Mariom Mill Preminger, 1957

"The Cinema of Otto Preminger" Gerald Pratley, 1971

Sam Raimi

BORN: Samuel Marshall Raimi in Royal Oak, Michigan, 10/23/1959

SOMETIMES CREDITED AS:
Sam M. Raimi

NATIONALITY: American

EDUCATION: Michigan State University, East Lansing, Michigan; founded Society of Creative Filmmaking with brother Ivan and roommate Robert Tapert; sponsored 1st All-Student US film festival; dropped out to form Renaissance Motion Pictures

AWARD: George Pal Memorial Award 2001; presented at the Saturn Awards

BIOGRAPHY
This movie-mad maker of two over-the-top modern horror film favorites—"The Evil Dead" (filmed in 1979; released in 1983) and "Evil Dead 2: Dead By Dawn" (1987)—subsequently diversified into TV where he quietly became a major auteur of fantastic entertainment, executive producing the syndicated phenomena "Hercules: The Legendary Journeys" and "Xena: Warrior Princess" (both debuted in 1995). Raimi also executive produced the critically acclaimed cult favorite "American Gothic" (CBS, 1995–96). Back on the big screen, he oversaw the US debut of celebrated Hong Kong action filmmaker John Woo as an executive producer on the superior Jean-Claude Van Damme vehicle "Hard Target" (1993). Raimi finally graduated to big-budget filmmaking ($30 million) and "A-list" stars (Sharon Stone, Gene Hackman, Leonardo DiCaprio) as a "hired gun" helmer on the exceedingly stylish Western spoof "The Quick and the Dead" (1995).

Raimi first gained critical success at the 1983 Cannes Film Festival with "The Evil Dead", a kinetic exercise in outrageously gory but deadly serious horror which went on to become an international cult favorite. He delivered an even bloodier yet hilariously cartoonish sequel, "Evil Dead 2: Dead By Dawn" (1987), which confirmed his taste for camera pyrotechnics, slapstick comedy and gruesome surrealism. Raimi took his first stab mainstream filmmaking with 1990's "Darkman." A stylish, witty transposition of the comic-book aesthetic to the screen, "Darkman" also paid satiric tribute to the Universal horror features of the 1930s; it was a success at the box-office and introduced a wider audience to Raimi's work. One can only imagine what HE would have done with "Batman"!

Raimi's roots as a filmmaker go back to his childhood, when he made 8mm fantasy adventure shorts, and to his college days, when he formed creative partnerships which have lasted through five feature films. At Michigan State University, Raimi founded the Society of Creative Filmmaking with brother Ivan, who later co-scripted "Darkman" (1990) and "Army of Darkness" (1993), and actor Robert Tapert, who has produced all Raimi's features to date. He left school to form Renaissance Pictures with Tapert and another student performer, Bruce Campbell, who has appeared in all of his films, notably as Ash in the "Evil Dead" stories. Raimi has also been associated with the Coen Brothers; producer Ethan was an assistant editor on "The Evil Dead", both brothers scripted "Crime Wave" (1985) and Raimi co-wrote "The Hudsucker Proxy" (1993), a Capraesque period comedy, with the duo. After a three-year hiatus, he returned to the director's chair with the more mainstream "A Simple Plan" (1998), mixing his trademark humor with more detailed characterizations. The result was not to everyone's taste but marked a significant step in his development as a director. He continued with the big-budgeted, baseball-themed Kevin Costner vehicle "For the Love of the Game" (1999).

Raimi has become increasingly active as a character player in films and TV, often in projects by his cronies, with credits including John Landis' "Spies Like Us" (1985), the Coens' "Miller's Crossing" (1990) and "Indian Summer" (1993). The latter won him some positive notices for playing the assistant of camp director Alan Arkin in this nostalgic character-driven comedy. On TV, he may have been most widely seen in a supporting role as a hapless lackey of a diabolical Jamey Sheridan in the popular miniseries "Stephen King's 'The Stand'" (ABC, 1994).—Written by Kent Greene

MILESTONES:

Raised in Franklin, Michigan

Given 8mm movie camera by father as a child; made numerous amateur short films

Met future collaborators Bruce Campbell, Scott Spiegel and John Cameron in junior high school

1978–1979: Founded and served as president of Michigan State University Society for Creative Filmmaking

1979: With college roommate Robert Tapert and childhood buddy Bruce Campbell co-founded Renaissance Motion Pictures in Ferndale, Michigan; served as vice president

Directed and co-wrote the short, "Within the Woods", served as a precursor to "The Evil Dead"

1979: Wrote and directed first feature, "The Evil Dead" (released in 1983)

1985: First film appearance, in "Spies Like Us"

1987: Feature producing debut, executive produced sequel "Evil Dead 2: Dead By Dawn" (also directed and co-scripted with Scott Spiegel)

1989: Served as an executive producer on "Easy Wheels", a direct-to-video action comedy; also reportedly co-wrote screenplay under a pseudonym

1990: First studio feature, directed, wrote story

and co-scripted (with Chuck Pfarrer, Ivan Raimi, Daniel Goldin, and Joshua Goldin) "Darkman"

1993: TV acting debut, appeared in "Journey to the Center of the Earth", an unsold TV-movie pilot

1993: First relatively substantial film supporting role, played flunky of camp director Alan Arkin in "Indian Summer"

1993: Served as an executive producer on the Jean-Claude Van Damme vehicle "Hard Target"; marked the US directorial debut of celebrated Hong Kong director John Woo

1994: Debut as a TV producer, creator and writer, executive produced, created and provided story for "Mantis", a Fox superhero TV-movie pilot (also acted uncredited)

1994: Collaborated with Van Damme again as the executive producer of "Timecop"

1994: Executive produced the syndicated TV-movie "Hercules and the Amazon Women", the first in a series of five telefilms produced under the umbrella title "The Legendary Journeys of Hercules" as part of the "Action Pack" series

1994: TV miniseries acting debut, played Bobby Terry, hapless bad guy in ABC's "Stephen King's 'The Stand' "

TV series debut, created and executive produced "M.A.N.T.I.S." a Fox superhero series with a black protagonist

1995: First feature assignment as a director without also scripting and first "big" budget production ($30 million) the parodic Western "The Quick and the Dead", starring Sharon Stone

Executive produced the immensely popular syndicated action fantasy series "Hercules: The Legendary Journeys"

1995: Credited as executive producer and "based on characters by" for "Darkman II: The Return of Durant", a direct-to-video sequel; received the same credits on the subsequent video sequel "Darkman III: Die Darkman Die" (1996)

Executive produced the hugely successful syndicated spin-off series "Xena: Warrior Princess"

Executive produced the cultish supernatural drama series "American Gothic"

Executive produced the spin-off Fox series "Young Hercules"

1998: Returned to features as director of "A Simple Plan"

1999: Helmed the Kevin Costner baseball-themed "For the Love of the Game"

2000: Directed the thriller "The Gift" with Cate Blanchett playing a psychic who becomes embroiled in a local murder

2002: Helmed the feature version of the Marvel comic "Spider-Man", with Tobey Maguire in the lead

QUOTES:

In 1999, Raimi was named the sixth recipient of the Beatrice Wood Film Award

See also the biography of Bruce Campbell for more information on the early horror films.

Yvonne Rainer

BORN: Yvonne V Rainer in San Francisco, California, 11/24/1934

NATIONALITY: American

AWARDS: Los Angeles Film Critics Association Award Best Independent/Experimental Film "Journeys to Berlin 1971" 1980; tied with Joel De Mott in "Demon Lover Diary"

American Film Institute Maya Deren Award 1988

Sundance Film Festival Filmmakers Trophy (Dramatic) "Privilege" 1990

BIOGRAPHY

A noted modern dance choreographer of the 1960s (she co-founded the influential Judson Dance Theater in 1962), the openly lesbian Yvonne Rainer turned her attention to feature films in the early 70s, subsequently emerging as a critically lauded practitioner of politically challenging, avant-garde cinema.

Rainer began integrating slides and short films into her dance work as early as 1968, and made her feature debut with "Lives of Performers" (1972), an outgrowth of her dance background. A politically committed artist, her film work evolved away from the influences of the so-called American avant-garde (materialist, structuralist films) to concern itself not only with the film medium, but with its modes of representation (of gender, race, class, etc.). Rainer's films break with the illusionism of Hollywood, disrupting the story, relying heavily on verbal language, and dealing most often with power relations (particularly between the sexes). Her use of Brechtian distancing effects (e.g. extended voice-overs, combining documentary with enacted footage) is comparable to the work of Jean-Luc Godard.

Collage-like, multi-layered and theoretically-aware, Rainer's "The Man Who Envied Women" (1985), is perhaps her most ambitious film, dealing with psychoanalytic and narrative theory, aging, US policy in Central America and New York's housing crisis, while quoting substantially from such major thinkers as Michel Foucault, Frederic Jameson and Julia Kristeva. Her "Privilege" (1990) focused on a group of women facing menopause while "Fast Trip, Long Drop" (1993) profiled the HIV-positive activist and filmmaker Gregg Bordowitz as he dealt with his homosexual and Jewish identities and the political dimension of the AIDS crisis. In 1996, Rainer directed "*Murder* and Murder", a meditation on the sexual politics of a late in life affair between two women.— Written by Stuart Kauffman

MILESTONES:

1957: Began studying modern dance in New York

1960: Began choreographing own pieces

1962: Co-founder of the Judson Dance Theater, New York

Many presentations of choreography in both US and Europe

1968: Began integrating short films into dance pieces

1969: Broadway debut

1972: Feature writing and directing debut (also co-editor; performer), "Lives of Performers"

1975: Began concentrating exclusively on filmmaking

1976: Appeared in Rosa Von Praunheim's "Underground and Emigrants"

1980: Recorded voice-over narration for Laura Mulvey and Peter Wollen's "Amy!"

1985: First film to achieve general theatrical release in the USA, "The Man Who Envied Women"

1990: Produced, wrote, directed and edited "Privilege", which explored the effects of menopause on women

1996: Wrote, directed, produced and edited "Murder and Murder", a non-narrative exploration of topics ranging from ageism to lesbian sexuality to breast cancer

2000: Choreographed a new dance piece for Mikhail Baryshnikov's White Oak Dance Project

QUOTES:

Rainer received a MacArthur Foundation "genius" award in 1990.

BIBLIOGRAPHY:

"Yvonne Rainer: Work 1961–1973" 1974, Nova Scotia College of Art and Design/New York University Press

"The Films of Yvonne Rainer" 1989; Indiana University Press films scripts and critical essays by Ruby Rich, B. de Lauretis, et al.

"Radical Juxtaposition: The Films of Yvonne Rainer" Shelley Green, 1994, Scarecrow Press

BORN: Harold Allen Ramis in Chicago, Illinois, 11/21/1944

NATIONALITY: American

EDUCATION: Senn High School, Chicago, Illinois

Washington University, St Louis, Missouri, BA, 1966

AWARDS: ACTRA Award Best Writing-Variety "SCTV Network" 1978; shared award; presented by the Academy of Canadian Television and Radio Artists

Earle Grey Award 1995; presented to the cast of "SCTV"

BIOGRAPHY

This versatile comic talent wrote for Chicago's renowned Second City troupe and the National Lampoon radio show before co-scripting the antic fraternity house romp, "National Lampoon's Animal House" (1978). Harold Ramis worked as a mental ward orderly and wrote jokes for *Playboy* before starting his show business career. He teamed with John Belushi, Gilda Radner, and Bill Murray on "The National Lampoon Show," but when it came time to organize The Not Ready For Prime Time Players for NBC's "Saturday Night Live" in 1975, he was not asked to join the company by Lorne Michaels. Instead, he applied his comic abilities to the scripts for "Animal House" and the similar "Meatballs" (1979), both of which employed "SNL" cast members (John Belushi and Bill Murray, respectively). Ramis has frequently teamed with comedian Rodney Dangerfield (e.g., TV specials and 1991's animated "Rover Dangerfield"), producer-director Ivan Reitman and especially Murray. Ramis moved to the director's chair with "Caddyshack"

(1980, featuring both Dangerfield and Murray), followed by "Stripes" (1981), a Murray vehicle produced by Reitman. Working with Dan Aykroyd, he shaped the script for the comic blockbuster "Ghostbusters" (1984), which Reitman helmed and which featured Aykroyd, Murray, Ramis and Ernie Hudson as parapsychologists out to rid Manhattan of bizarre apparitions. The inevitable 1989 sequel, "Ghostbusters II", though proved less enchanting and less successful.

Throughout the late 1980s, the lanky, curly-haired bespectacled Ramis carved a secondary career as a character player, making appearances as Diane Keaton's live-in lover who leaves with she takes in a child in "Baby Boom" (1987) and offered a somewhat dramatic turn as Mark Harmon's former childhood buddy in "Stealing Home" (1988). Returning behind the camera, he had a surprise hit with the genial romantic comedy "Groundhog Day" (1993), wherein Bill Murray essayed a weatherman doomed to relive a February 2 over and over until he got it right. "Stuart Saves His Family" (1995), based on a sketch from "Saturday Night Live", however, proved less impressive to audiences, although it had a few amusing moments, many provided by writer-star Al Franken. "Multiplicity" (1996) offered a plethora of Michael Keatons as the actor played a harried businessman who allows himself to be cloned. After a cameo as Jack Nicholson's psychiatrist in "As Good As It Gets" (1997), Ramis tackled "Analyze This" (1999) which had Billy Crystal playing shrink to a mob boss (Robert De Niro).

MILESTONES:

1968–1970: Served as associate editor of *Playboy* magazine

Was writer for Second City improvisational theater troupe in Chicago

Became writer and performer with National Lampoon Radio Show in NYC

1975: Co-wrote "The National Lampoon Show", a stage show produced off-off-Broadway

Acted in and served as head writer for the syndicated "SCTV Network"

1978: First film as co-screenwriter, "National Lampoon's Animal House"

1980: First film as director "Caddyshack"; also marked initial onscreen appearance

1981: First significant acting role in "Stripes"

1982: Produced and appeared in " The Rodney Dangerfield Show: It Ain't Easy Bein' Me" (ABC)

1984: Had biggest hit as star and co-writer of "Ghostbusters"

1987: Executive produced and narrated "Will Rogers: Look Back in Laughter" (HBO)

1989: Reprised role in and co-wrote sequel "Ghostbusters II"

1993: Directed pal Bill Murray in "Groundhog Day"; also produced and scripted

1995: Helmed "Stuart Saves His Family", based on a sketch written by Al Franken for "Saturday Night Live"

1996: Produced and directed "Multiplicity", starring Michael Keaton

1997: Made cameo appearance as a psychiatrist treating Jack Nicholson in "As Good As It Gets"

1999: Helmed "Analyze This", which teamed Billy Crystal and Robert De Niro

Brett Ratner

BORN: in Miami, Florida, 1970

NATIONALITY: American

EDUCATION: Attended Miami Beach Senior High School
Tisch School of the Arts, New York University, New York, New York; enrolled at age 16

AWARD: MTV Video Award Best Video From a Film Madonna's "Beautiful Stranger" from the "Austin Powers: The Spy Who Shagged Me" soundtrack 1999

BIOGRAPHY

A precocious youngster growing up in Miami, Florida, director Brett Ratner channeled his energy into becoming one of the hottest young directors of his time. After spending his childhood enthusiastically filming his friends with a camcorder, yet not-so-enthusiastically doing his schoolwork, Ratner was accepted to NYU, a school he chose primarily because it was

Martin Scorsese's alma mater, at the age of 16. He was required to pitch his burgeoning directing skills as worthy of admittance to the prestigious Tisch School of the Arts at NYU due to his lackluster academic record (after being initially rejected he begged the dean to view his films to keep him from "living on my mom's couch in Miami the rest of my life."). NYU was impressed enough to let Ratner enroll, despite being the youngest member of his class.

His senior year at NYU, Ratner applied for dozens of scholarships to help fund his senior project. He was granted only one, from Steven Spielberg's production company, Amblin Entertainment. The project was a documentary about a child star made famous by appearing in Underwood lunch meat commercials. Ratner received considerable attention for his film, titled "Whatever Happened to Mason Reese" and through his friendship with hip-hop entrepreneur Russell Simmons, began directing videos.

Over the next decade, Ratner made more than

100 videos, working with the industry's hottest stars including Wu Tang Clan, Jay Z, D'Angelo, Puff Daddy, Mariah Carey and Madonna. His break into features came when the original director of "Money Talks" dropped out of the project and Ratner was brought in. He made an impressive debut with this film which revitalized Charlie Sheen's career and also starred Chris Tucker, Heather Locklear and Paul Sorvino.

Ratner's next project was directing Chris Tucker and Jackie Chan in a unique fish-out-of-water/buddy comedy, "Rush Hour" (1998). Suddenly, and quite unexpectedly, Ratner was a hot director. "Rush Hour"(1998) would end up earning $250 million worldwide and was New Line Cinema's highest grossing film up to that date. The careers of Chris Tucker and Jackie Chan also took off and plans were immediately made for a sequel. Expectations were high for the second installment of this action-comedy series, which paired the high-pitched, wise-cracking Tucker with the naively hyper martial arts master Chan. But no one could have predicted the success of "Rush Hour 2" (2001) which had the highest opening comedy weekend box office gross (on a non-holiday) in history. Ratner was now established as formidable directing talent and had just only reached his 31st birthday.

In between the "Rush Hour" movies, Ratner sought a departure from urban and action comedies. After a fair amount of convincing on his part, Ratner was taken on board to direct "The Family Man" (2000), starring Nicolas Cage and Tea Leoni. The film, a "It's A Wonderful Life" tale of what-might-have-been, had modest success with the box office and critics. However, the phenomenal success of "Rush Hour 2" left no question where Ratner's strength as a director laid. He landed the much-coveted director's job on "Red Dragon" (lensed 2002), the prequel to "Silence of the Lambs" (1991) starring Anthony Hopkins and Edward Norton along with Emily Watson and Harvey Keitel. In addition, "Rush Hour 3" (lensing

2003) is expected to be yet another smash hit for this fortunate young director. At the end of 2002 Ratner was demonstrating his potential versatility juggling two disparate, long-aborning projects: Warner Bros.' much-delayed update of the "Superman" franchise and a self-described Robert Altman–style character drama set against the backdrop of the Rolling Stones' 40th anniversary tour.—Written by Anna Lotto

COMPANION:

Rebecca Gayheart. actor directed her in the short "What Ever Happened to Mason Reese?"; together from c. 1989 to summer 1999; reportedly reconciled in 2001

MILESTONES:

1978: Made his first "movie" at eight years old with a camcorder

Attended schools in Miami where he was a lackluster student

1986: Moved to New York to enter NYU at the age of 16

1987: Met fellow NYU student Russell Simmons who hired Ratner to direct a music video featuring Run DMC

1989: Received scholarship from Steven Spielberg's company Amblin Entertainment his senior year to fund his thesis project

1990: Produced senior film "Whatever Happened to Mason Reese" and received several student awards

1990: Through his friend and now up-and-coming rap producer Russell Simmons, Ratner began directing music videos; directed videos for Heavy D, Jodeci, Mariah Carey, Mary J. Blige and Madonna among others

1997: Moved to Los Angeles and landed his first feature directing job with "Money Talks" starring Charlie Sheen and Chris Tucker

1998: Directed Chris Tucker and Jackie Chan in the smash hit "Rush Hour"

1999: Directed under-achieving drama "The Family Man" starring Nicolas Cage and Tea Leoni

2001: Directed sequel "Rush Hour 2," a record-breaking box office hit

2002: Directed "Red Dragon," prequel to "Silence of the Lambs" (1991)

2002: Signed on to direct "Rush Hour 3"

2002: named as director of Warner Bros. "Superman" revival

AFFILIATION: Jewish

Board of Directors, Chrysalis Foundation

QUOTES:

Had small acting part in "Black and White," a 1999 feature about a group of inter-racial teens in New York City; played himself

" . . . I just cried. I knew I had to make this movie. I never would have been interested in making a romantic comedy before this."—Brett Ratner on reading the script for "The Family Man" (dvdfile.com: In The Director's Chair, July 10, 2001)

Campaigned, unsuccessfully, to direct a James Bond movie

"That's why I go to universities all around the county and I speak to students and I tell them how I did "Rush Hour" and what the process was. Once you hear someone talk about it and hear the experience that they went through, it becomes easier. So that's something that I love doing for other people because it was the way that I learned how to make movies."—Brett Ratner (Directorsworld.com, January 8, 2001)

"I think the fans of 'Rush Hour' are going to see the movie, and they're going to be happy. They're going to be pleased. This is a good movie. Nobody did it just to get rich."—Brett Ratner on "Rush Hour 2," shortly before it opened as a record-breaking box office Smash (Audiencemag.com, July 2001)

Nicholas Ray

BORN: Raymond Nicholas Kienzle in Galesville, Wisconsin, 08/07/1911

DEATH: in New York, New York, 06/16/1979

NATIONALITY: American

EDUCATION: University of Chicago, Chicago, Illinois; won scholarship due to a radio play he wrote; stayed one year

University of Wisconsin, Madison, Wisconsin; stayed one year

won scholarship to study at Frank Lloyd Wright's artistic colony at Taliesin, studying architecture, music, sculpture, philosophy, and theater

BIOGRAPHY

"I'm a stranger here myself," is the epigram

most closely associated with Nicholas Ray. The phrase is spoken by the title character in Ray's "Johnny Guitar" (1954) and is also a concise expression of Ray's relationship to the Hollywood studio system and of his central concerns as a filmmaker.

Prior to becoming a film director, Ray studied architecture with Frank Lloyd Wright and then worked with Elia Kazan and John Houseman on stage projects. His film directing debut, produced by Houseman, was "They Live By Night" (1948), a convincing version of the now-familiar lovers-on-the-run-from-the-law theme. This was followed by two middling melodramas, "A Woman's Secret" and "Knock on Any Door" (both 1949). The latter made a forceful social statement about juvenile delinquency, but its emphasis on polemics rather than drama blunted the overall effect. The film starred Humphrey Bogart, who returned for Ray's next production, "In a Lonely Place" (1950), among the best work ever done by both star and director.

Ray was already concentrating on disaffected loners—individuals who, by choice or fate, could not be integrated into society's mainstream. "In a Lonely Place" explored the life of an asocial screenwriter suspected of murder. Ray extracted Bogart's most passionate performance, placing it in a spare, direct framework. "In a Lonely Place" is not only one of the best movies about Hollywood and the fallacy of romance but also a bitter parable about the postwar condition. It remains a very contemporary motion picture.

"On Dangerous Ground" (1951) starred Robert Ryan as a disillusioned city cop infected with the violence which surrounds him. Ray's careening camera served as an apt metaphor for the instability of an atomized urban existence. Despite the studio-imposed happy ending, with Ryan returning to the blind Ida Lupino in a bleak rural landscape, the film's evocation of the paralyzing angst of modern life could not be evaded. Alienated protagonists populated Ray's films of the early 1950s—Robert Mitchum's ex-rodeo star searching for home and security in "The Lusty Men" (1952); Joan Crawford as the embattled saloon owner in the uniquely baroque, woman-dominated Western, "Johnny Guitar" (1954); and of course, James Dean—along with Natalie Wood and Sal Mineo—in "Rebel Without a Cause" (1955).

It was in "Rebel" that Ray's allegiance with the marginalized was most evident and most sympathetic. The teenagers in the story are at the mercy of a society that demands conformity and saps individuality. Integration or destruction are the only options available and, though Dean and Wood are reintegrated into society by film's end, Ray makes it clear that this action is tantamount to a slow death.

In "Bigger Than Life" (1956) James Mason plays a teacher whose addiction to cortisone

leads to neuroses that foreground a number of the era's dominant concerns—conformity, consumption, education and religion. The film is not only excellent drama, but, like most Ray movies, it is also an important social document. Furthermore, "Bigger Than Life," like "Rebel," demonstrated that Ray was one of the few directors to use CinemaScope in an accomplished way. His time with Frank Lloyd Wright had given him a keen sense of space and horizontal line.

Ray's films had been largely taken for granted in his native country until the critics of *Cahiers du Cinema* embarked upon a concerted process of deification. In its wake, such films as "Party Girl" (1958), once dismissed as lurid, were suddenly respected for their stylistic and thematic flamboyance and complexity. Concurrent with the spread of the Ray cult to the USA in the early 1960s, the director's output underwent a significant change, as he undertook two period epics, "King of Kings" (1961) and "55 Days at Peking" (1963). Though both films featured Ray flourishes, they lacked the intensity of his earlier, more emotionally compact works.

Ray subsequently abandoned Hollywood and spent some time in Europe before returning to the States in the late 1960s to take a job teaching film at New York State University at Binghampton. A unique collaborative project with his students resulted, usually known as "You Can't Go Home Again" (1973). Ray's increasingly poor health limited his activities to several cameo appearances in films of other directors; he himself was the subject of his last directorial effort, in collaboration with Wim Wenders, "Lighting Over Water" (1980), about the final months of Ray's battle with cancer. It was a difficult but fitting epitaph, as the director (like so many of his characters) was shown searching for peace and a sense of place.

COMPANION:
wife: Gloria Grahame. actor married in 1948; divorced in 1952; later married Ray's son Anthony (by a previous marriage); directed

by Ray in "A Woman's Secret" (1949) and "In a Lonely Place" (1950)

MILESTONES:

1932: Moved to New York

1935: Played lead role in Elia Kazan's first play as director, "The Young Go First"

Worked as producer of CBS radio show, "Back Where I Come From"

Produced propaganda broadcasts for Voice of America during WWII

1945: Began movie career as assistant director on Elia Kazan's "A Tree Grows in Brooklyn"

1948: First film as director, "They Live By Night"

1963: Last film for over 15 years, the historical epic, "55 Days at Peking"

1979: Last film, "Lightning Over Water", co-directed with Wim Wenders, about the last days of his (Ray's) life

Satyajit Ray

BORN: in Calcutta, India, 05/02/1921

DEATH: in Calcutta, India, 04/23/1992

NATIONALITY: Indian

EDUCATION: Ballygunj Government School, Calcutta, India

Presidency College, University of Calcutta, Calcutta, India, science and economics, BA, 1936–40; graduated with honors at age 19

Santiniketan University, India, art history, 1940–42

AWARDS: Cannes Film Festival Prix du Document Humaine "Pather Panchali" 1956

San Francisco Film Festival Best Director Award "Pather Panchali" 1957

San Francisco Film Festival Best Film Award "Pather Panchali" 1957

Venice Film Festival Golden Lion Award "Aparajito" 1957

San Francisco Film Festival Best Director Award "Aparajito" 1958

Berlin Film Festival Best Director Award "Mahanager/The Big City" 1964

Berlin Film Festival Best Director Award "Charulata/The Lonely Wife" 1965

Berlin Film Festival Jury Tribute 1966

India Film Critics Award Best Film "Shatranj ke Khilari" 1977

Honorary Oscar 1991 in recognition of "rare mastery of the art of motion pictures, and of his profound humanitarian outlook, which has had an indelible influence on filmmakers and audiences throughout the world"

San Francisco Film Festival Akira Kurosawa Lifetime Achievement Award 1992

New Delhi National Film Festival Award Best Indian Film "Agantuk/The Stranger" 1992

New Delhi National Film Festival Award Best Director "Agantuk/The Stranger" 1992

BIOGRAPHY

Satyajit Ray, India's only internationally renowned filmmaker, was born into a family prominent in Bengali arts and letters for fifteen generations. In 1940, after receiving his degree in science and economics, he attended Rabindranath Tagore's "world university" in rural Santiniketan. Tagore, the dominant figure in India's cultural renaissance, had a strong influence on Ray, whose humanist films reaffirm his Bengali heritage within a modern context.

In 1942, Ray returned to Calcutta, where he spent the next ten years as layout artist and art director for a British-run advertising agency. In his spare time he wrote film scenarios, among them an adaptation of Tagore's novel, "Ghare Baire," which producers rejected when Ray refused to make changes. With India's independence in 1947, Ray co-founded Calcutta's first film society with Chidananda Das Gupta and wrote articles calling for a new cinema.

His reputation as a graphic artist brought offers to illustrate books, including an abridged edition of Bibhuti Bhusan Banerjee's classic novel, "Pather Panchali," in 1946. After an influential encounter with Jean Renoir in Calcutta in 1949 and a business trip to London in 1950, where he saw Vittorio De Sica's "The Bicycle Thief "(1948), Ray set out to script and direct "Pather Panchali." The film, shot on location on weekends, failed to attract backers and could not be completed until a request from the Museum of Modern Art in New York to include it in their Indian art exhibit led the West Bengal government—in an unprecedented move—to provide funds.

"Pather Panchali" (1956) won several international awards and established Ray as a world-class director, as well as being a box-office hit at home. Artistic and financial success gave Ray total control over his subsequent films; in his numerous functions—writer, director, casting director, composer (since 1961) and cinematographer (since 1963)—he was able to continue Tagore's example in theater of welding the arts into a unified entity. Two sequels also based on the novel ("Aparajito" 1957, "The World of Apu" 1959) completed the acclaimed "Apu" trilogy, whose slow-paced realism broke with the song-and-dance melodramas of Indian cinema. Using long takes and reaction shots, slow camera movements, and—in "Kanchanjangha" (1962)—real-time narrative, Ray allows the meticulous accumulation of details to reveal the inner lives and humanity of diverse Bengali characters.

In 1961, Ray revived "Sandesh," a children's magazine founded by his grandfather, to which he continued to contribute illustrations, verses and stories throughout his life.

Beginning in 1969, he also made four popular children's films which contain an unobtrusive yet distinct political awareness. Earlier in his career, Ray was criticized by Indian critics for failing to deal with Calcutta's immediate social problems. And although he defended his humanist (versus ideological) approach, "Pratidwandi" (1971) signaled a shift toward political themes. In the 1970s, Ray's films acquired a bitter tone and deviated from his usual classical style, with the abrupt use of montage, jump cuts and flashbacks.

Ray's "Ghaire Baire/The Home and the World" (1984) was a return to his first screen adaptation. While shooting, he suffered two heart attacks and his son, Sandip, completed the project from his father's detailed instructions. Ray continued to write prolifically, completing 13 half-hour TV screenplays to be directed by Sandip, and returned to directing in 1989 with an adaptation of Ibsen's "Enemy of the People". In 1992, the year of his death, Ray was awarded an honorary Oscar for "his rare mastery of the art of motion pictures, and for his profound humanitarian outlook, which has had an indelible influence on filmmakers and audiences throughout the world."

MILESTONES:

1942–1952: Worked for D.J. Keymer & Co., British-run advertising agency; began as layout artist, worked his way up to senior art director

1947: Founded Calcutta's first film society with Chidananda Das Gupta

1956: Wrote, produced and directed first feature, "Pather Panchali"

1992: Received lifetime achievement honorary Oscar on March 16 at a Calcutta hospital where he had been admitted with chest pains and respiratory problems a few weeks earlier

QUOTES:

"Not to have seen the films of Satyajit Ray would mean existing in the world without seeing the sun or the moon."—Akira Kurosawa quoted in *The New York Times*, February 21, 1992.

"Ray's productions were virtually one-man shows. He wrote the screenplay, cast the parts, designed the costumes, scored the music, directed, mixed and edited the final package.

Originally a graphic artist, he also sketched the advertisements."—From *New York Post* obituary, April 24, 1992.

Given the Gem of India Award (1992), the highest civilian honor in India.

Robert Redford

BORN: Charles Robert Redford, Jr. in Santa Monica, California, 08/18/1936

NATIONALITY: American

EDUCATION: University of Colorado, Boulder, Colorado; attended on baseball scholarship; had an alcohol abuse problem which interfered with his sporting performance; left in 1957 to travel in Europe

Pratt Institute, Brooklyn, New York, art, 1958

American Academy of Dramatic Arts, New York, New York

AWARDS: Theatre World Award "Sunday in New York" 1962

Golden Globe Award Most Promising Newcomer-Male "Inside Daisy Clover" 1965

British Film Academy Award Best Actor "Tell Them Willie Boy Is Here" and "Butch Cassidy and the Sundance Kid" 1970; cited for both films

Golden Globe Award World Film Favorite—Male 1974

Golden Globe Award World Film Favorite—Male 1976

Golden Globe Award World Film Favorite—Male 1977

National Board of Review Award Best Director "Ordinary People" 1980

Golden Globe Award Best Director "Ordinary People" 1981

Directors Guild of America Award Outstanding Directorial Achievement in Feature Film "Ordinary People" 1980

Oscar Best Director "Ordinary People" 1980

Cecil B. DeMille Award 1994; lifetime achievement award presented by the Hollywood Foreign Press Association

New York Film Critics Circle Award Best Picture "Quiz Show" 1994; shared award with fellow producers Michael Jacobs, Julian Krainin, Michael Nozik

Screen Actors Guild Life Achievement Award 1995

Honorary Oscar 2001; statuette; award citation read: "Robert Redford—Actor, Director, Producer, Creator of Sundance, inspiration to independent and innovative filmmakers everywhere"

BIOGRAPHY

Once, according to screenwriter William Goldman, Robert Redford was described as "just another California blond—throw a stick at Malibu, you'll hit six of him." It is unlikely, however, that any of the six would combine Redford's charm, intelligence, talent and looks. He attended the University of Colorado on a baseball scholarship but dropped out in 1957 to spend a year traveling and painting in Europe. Back in the States, he studied theatrical design and acting in New York.

In the late 1950s and early 60s, Redford appeared on scores of television shows, including as a "stooge" on the quiz show "Play Your Hunch." Among his early appearances were "The Twilight Zone", "Alfred Hitchcock Presents" (in three different episodes), "Maverick",

"Naked City", "Route 66" and "Dr. Kildare." He won critical praise for "In the Presence of Mine Enemies", an episode of "Playhouse 90" (CBS, 1960) and earned an Emmy nomination as Best Supporting Actor for his performance in "The Voice of Charlie Pont" (ABC, 1962). Redford had made his Broadway debut in a small role in "Tall Story" (1959), following up with the shows "The Highest Tree" (1959) and "Sunday in New York" (1961). He enjoyed his biggest Broadway success as the stuffy newlywed husband of Elizabeth Ashley in Neil Simon's "Barefoot in the Park" (1963).

Redford made his screen debut in "War Hunt" (1962), co-starring with Tom Skerritt and Sydney Pollack in an anti-war film set during the Korean conflict. After his Broadway success, he began to be cast in larger feature roles. He was a bisexual movie star who marries starlet Natalie Wood in "Inside Daisy Clover" (1965) and reteamed with her for Pollack's "This Property Is Condemned" (1966), again as her lover. The same year saw his first teaming with Jane Fonda (Arthur Penn's pallid "The Chase", in which he was a fugitive on the run). Fonda and Redford were paired to better effect in the big screen version of "Barefoot in the Park" (1967) and were again co-stars in Pollack's "The Electric Horseman" (1979).

Redford—already concerned about his blond male starlet image—turned down roles in "Who's Afraid of Virginia Woolf?" and "The Graduate", holding out for the phenomenal popular success, George Roy Hill's "Butch Cassidy and the Sundance Kid" (1969), with Paul Newman. This film made him a bankable star and cemented his screen image as an intelligent, reliable, sometimes sardonic good guy. As so often happens, his next few films—while not all artistic losses—were hardly hits at the box office. "Downhill Racer" (1969), on which he served as executive producer, was an interesting look at the world of competitive skiing, but "Tell Them Willie Boy is Here" (1969), "Little Fauss and Big Halsey" (1970), "The Hot

Rock" (1972) and the underrated outdoors drama "Jeremiah Johnson" (both 1972) did little to forward Redford's stardom. His next real success came with the incisive political satire "The Candidate" (1972), which traded on his Golden Boy image to skewer Watergate-era Washington.

The year 1973 was a huge one for Redford, who starred in the high-profile "The Way We Were" and "The Sting." The former teamed him with a glowing Barbra Streisand in a successful "through-the-years" romance, the latter reteamed him with Newman in a crime comedy. About the first film, Redford joked, "nice Jewish girl gets nice blond WASP", and about the second, "nice Jewish BOY gets nice blond WASP." Already, Redford was known for bringing out the best in his co-stars; his frequent pairings with Newman, Wood and Fonda worked superbly; and actresses such as Streisand, Faye Dunaway, Meryl Streep and Michelle Pfeiffer were rarely so relaxed or sensual as when playing opposite him.

During the years 1974–76, exhibitors voted Redford Hollywood's top box-office name; his hits included the glossy but impressive-looking "The Great Gatsby" (1974), "The Great Waldo Pepper" and "Three Days of the Condor" (both 1975). Another popular and acclaimed film, Alan J. Pakula's "All the President's Men" (1976), was a landmark film for Redford. Not only was he the executive producer and co-star, but the film's serious subject matter, the Watergate scandal, also reflected the actor's off screen concerns for political causes.

In 1980, Redford's first outing as a director, "Ordinary People", a drama about the slow disintegration of a middle-class family, won him an Oscar. Redford managed to get a powerful dramatic performance out of America's Sweetheart, Mary Tyler Moore, as well as superb work from Donald Sutherland and Timothy Hutton. His second stint behind the camera would not be for another eight years with "The Milagro Beanfield War" (1988), a well-crafted (though not terribly popular) screen version of John Nichols' acclaimed novel of the Southwest. Other directorial projects have included the highly successful period family drama "A River Runs Through It" (1992), based on Norman McLean's novella, and the intelligent expose "Quiz Show" (1994). Working with noted cinematographer Michael Ballhaus and a strong cast that featured John Turturro and Ralph Fiennes, Redford's directorial finesse had critics talking.

Besides his directing (and producing) duties, Redford did not stop acting as he entered middle age. He made a fine romantic lead opposite Meryl Streep in Sydney Pollack's Oscar-winning "Out of Africa" (1985); although many critics complained that his portrayal of Isak Dinesen's lover wasn't particularly realistic, Redford's characterization was more substantial than the ghostly figure of Dinesen's book. After the box-office disaster of "Havana" (1990), he turned in amiable performances in the computer caper "Sneakers" (1992), the silly sex drama "Indecent Proposal" (1993), with Demi Moore, and opposite Michelle Pfeiffer in the newsroom romance "Up Close and Personal" (1996). His good looks had weathered considerably after years in the Utah sun and wind, but with kind lenses he could still romance Moore and Pfeiffer. Continuing in the romantic vein, Redford directed and starred opposite Kristin Scott Thomas in a strong adaptation of Nicholas Evans' novel "The Horse Whisperer" (1998). Like other Redford-directed films, this one featured a strong cast in a drama that centered around a troubled family. His follow-up behind the camera, "The Legend of Bagger Vance" (2000), though, suffered from an overly earnest approach and a miscalculated performance from star Will Smith as a black caddy with seemingly mystical powers. Redford next returned to acting playing an aging CIA agent whose protege becomes a hostage in "The Spy Game" (2001). Since founding the nonprofit Sundance

Institute in Park City, Utah, in 1981, Redford has been actively involved in every aspect of that body. Through its various workshop programs and the popular Film Festival, Sundance has provided much-needed support for independent film production. In 1995, Redford signed a deal with Showtime to start up a 24-hour cable TV channel devoted to independent films. The Sundance Channel premiered on February 29, 1996.

MILESTONES:

1957: After leaving college worked as a carpenter, shop assistant and oil field worker

1957–1958: Traveled to Europe and lived in Paris and Florence

1958: TV debut, "Perry Mason" (CBS)

1959: Made Broadway debut in a small role in the comedy, "Tall Story"

1960: Had breakthrough TV role playing a Nazi soldier opposite Charles Laughton in "In the Presence of Mine Enemies", the final installment of CBS' "Playhouse 90"

1961: First major role on Broadway, "Sunday in New York"

1961: Bought Utah ranch which eventually became home of Sundance Film Festival

1962: Made film acting debut in "War Hunt"; Sydney Pollack co-starred

1963: Received Emmy nomination for supporting role in "The Voice of Charlie Pont", aired on "Alcoa Premiere" (ABC)

1965: First film with Natalie Wood, "Inside Daisy Clover"; portrayed a bisexual movie star

1966: Initial screen teaming with Jane Fonda in "The Chase"

1966: Reteamed with Natalie Wood in "This Property Is Condemned"; directed by Sydney Pollack

1967: Recreated stage role of uptight newlywed Paul Bratter in film version of "Barefoot in the Park" opposite Jane Fonda

1969: Breakthrough screen role as Harry Longbaugh aka The Sundance Kid in "Butch Cassidy and the Sundance Kid", co-starring Paul

Newman; directed by George Roy Hill and scripted by William Goldman

Formed Wildwood International (later Wildwood Enterprises)

1969: First film produced under Wildwood banner, "Downhill Racer"

1972: Played a jewel thief in the comedy "The Hot Rock", scripted by William Goldman

1972: Starred as a frontiersman in "Jeremiah Johnson", directed by Sydney Pollack

1972: Cast as a Kennedyesque politician in "The Candidate", scripted by Oscar-winner Jeremy Larner

1973: Starred opposite Barbra Streisand in the romantic drama "The Way We Were", helmed by Sydney Pollack

1973: Reteamed with Paul Newman and director George Roy Hill for the period caper comedy "The Sting"; received Best Actor Oscar nomination

1973: First made exhibitors' annual poll of top ten boxoffice stars; placed 5th

Placed first in boxoffice poll three years in a row

1974: Tapped to star as F. Scott Fitzgerald's anti-hero Jay Gatsby in the lavish film remake "The Great Gatsby"

1975: Reunited with director George Roy Hill and screenwriter William Goldman for the period comedy-drama "The Great Waldo Pepper"; played a barnstorming pilot

1976: Portrayed *Washington Post* journalist Bob Woodward (to Dustin Hoffman's Carl Bernstein) in the political drama "All the President's Men", written by William Goldman

1977: Placed 5th in annual exhibitors' boxoffice poll

1979: Reteamed with Jane Fonda in the romantic comedy "The Electric Horseman"

1980: Featured directorial debut, "Ordinary People"; movie won four Academy Awards including Best Picture and Best Director

1980: Founded Sundance Institute and its film and theater development lab

Returned to the box office top ten in 1980 (placing 2nd) and in 1984 (placing 7th)

1983: Founded Institute for Resource Management, an environmental organization

1984: Starred as baseball player Roy Hobbs in the screen adaptation of "The Natural"

1985: Portrayed Denys Finch Hatton, a British adventurer who romances author Isak Dinesen (Meryl Streep) in the Oscar-winning Best Picture "Out of Africa"; Sydney Pollack directed

1986: Returned to screen comedy as a lawyer in "Legal Eagles"

1987: Served as executive producer on "Promised Land", which was fostered by the Sundance Institute

1988: Helmed second film, "The Milagro Beanfield War"

1989: Formally assumed control of the US Film Festival and renamed it the Sundance Film Festival

1990: Experienced boxoffice failure with the big-budget romance "Havana", helmed by Pollack

1992: Executive produced and narrated the documentary "Incident at Ogala", directed by Michael Apted

1992: Directed third feature, the adaptation of Norman MacLean's autobiographical novella "A River Runs Through It"; also produced and did uncredited narration

1993: Starred opposite Demi Moore and Woody Harrelson as a wealthy man who offers $1 million to a couple for one night with the wife in "Indecent Proposal"

1993: Executive produced Steven Soderbergh's underrated "King of the Hill"

Formed second production company, South Fork Films, to produce modestly-budgeted films

1994: Helmed the period drama "Quiz Show", about the 1950s TV quiz show scandals; film received four Academy Award nominations including Best Picture and Best Director

1995: Signed with the Showtime Networks to form The Sundance Film Channel, a 24-hour pay cable station featuring independent films

1996: Played a veteran newsman who mentors and romances an rising talent (Michelle Pfeiffer) in "Up Close and Personal"

1996: Served as executive producer of Edward Burns' second film "She's the One"

1997: Announced formation of Sundance Cinemas, a chain of movie theaters that will only show independent films; venture is a joint effort with GC Cos. which operates the General Cinema movie theaters

1998: Executive produced Edward Burns' "No Looking Back"

1998: Directed himself for the first time in "The Horse Whisperer"; also produced

1998: Served as a producer on "A Civil Action"

2000: Executive produced the well-received festival-screened "How to Kill Your Neighbor's Dog"

2000: Directed sixth motion picture, "The Legend of Bagger Vance", a period drama about a Southern golfer and his mysterious caddy

2001: Had leading role in "The Last Castle"

2001: Co-starred with Brad Pitt in "Spy Game"

AFFILIATION: Raised Christian Scientist

QUOTES:

"Hollywood is a formula industry. It's all about business and profit, and that's why they're always looking at a formula for guaranteed success. You can't make $100 million on a small black-and-white love story or anything that tells about our lives and the diversity out there."—Robert Redford quoted in *USA Today*, May 8, 1995.

"Bob is a minimalist; he withholds, he never seduces his audience but makes them come to him."—film director Sydney Pollack to *Los Angeles Times*, December 9, 1990.

Redford on his transition from sports to art while in college: It had to do with "defining a lot of emotional stuff that was never formed right. For some people it's therapy. Maybe it is for all of us. For me it was anger and finding a place to put my disappointment and frustration with a lot of things. I was a mess. I was somewhat in trouble socially. I lost my (basketball) scholarship pretty quick after I discovered drinking. When I left (college) and got into art, that got me out . . . finding my place in the world had a lot to do with acting."—quoted in *Los Angeles Times*, December 9, 1990.

He received an honorary LHD from the University of Colorado (1987).

He was honored with the 1996 National Medal of Freedom from the National Endowment for the Arts.

BIBLIOGRAPHY:

"The Films of Robert Redford" James Spada, 1977, Citadel Press

"Robert Redford" David Downing, 1982, W.H. Allen & Co.

"Robert Redford" Bruce Crowther, 1985, Spellmount

Carl Reiner

BORN: in Bronx, New York, 03/20/1922

NATIONALITY: American

EDUCATION: WPA Dramatic Workshop, New York, New York; Reiner learned of the free class through his brother Charles

School of Foreign Service, Georgetown University, Washington, DC, 1943

AWARDS: Emmy Best Supporting Performance by an Actor "Caesar's Hour" 1956

Emmy Best Continuing Supporting Performance by an Actor in a Dramatic or Comedy Series "Caesar's Hour" 1957

Emmy Outstanding Writing Achievement in Comedy "The Dick Van Dyke Show" 1961/62

Emmy Outstanding Humor Program "The Dick Van Dyke Show" 1962/63; Reiner was executive producer of the series

Emmy Outstanding Writing Achievement in Comedy "The Dick Van Dyke Show" 1962/63

Emmy Outstanding Comedy Program "The Dick Van Dyke Show" 1962/63; Reiner was executive producer of the series

Emmy Outstanding Writing Achievement in Comedy or Variety "The Dick Van Dyke Show" 1963/64; award shared with Bill Persky and Sam Denoff

Emmy Outstanding Program Achievements in Entertainment "The Dick Van Dyke Show" 1964/65; one of four winners in the category; Reiner was executive producer of the series

Emmy Outstanding Comedy Series "The Dick Van Dyke Show" 1965/66; Reiner was executive producer of the series

Emmy Outstanding Variety Special "The Sid Caesar, Imogene Coca, Carl Reiner, Howard Morris Special" 1966/67; star

Emmy Outstanding Writing Achievement in Variety "The Sid Caesar, Imogene Coca, Carl Reiner, Howard Morris Special" 1966/67; co-winner with Mel Brooks, Sam Denoff, Bill Persky and Mel Tolkin

American Comedy Award for Lifetime Achievement-Male 1992

Emmy Outstanding Guest Actor in a Comedy Series "Mad About You" 1994/95; episode entitled "The Alan Brady Show"; Reiner recreated his Alan Brady character from "The Dick Van Dyke Show"

Grammy Spoken Comedy Album "The 2000 Year Old Man in the Year 2000" 1999; shared with Mel Brooks

Kennedy Center Mark Twain Prize for Humor 2000; third recipient

BIOGRAPHY

A quadruple-threat master of comedy, Reiner parlayed his wry sense of humor and ironic delivery into a long career as a comedian, writer, director, producer and sometime raconteur, a "veritable conglomerate of comedy" as he has been called. After entertaining the troops in the South Pacific with Major Maurice Evans's Special Service Unit during World War II, he appeared in the Broadway revues "Call Me Mister", "Inside U.S.A." and "Alive and Kicking" in the late 1940s before turning to television as writer and performer on Sid Caesar's classic "Your Show of Shows" (1950–54) and later "Caesar's Hour" (1954–57).

By the late 1950s Reiner had appeared as panelist and host of numerous TV quiz programs, had created the inspired "2000-Year-Old Man" sketch with Mel Brooks and made his screen acting debut in "Happy Anniversary" (1959). In 1960 he wrote and created a TV pilot, "Head of the Family" in which he starred as a TV comedy writer, Rob Petrie. The network didn't pick up the series, but the following year, recast and retitled "The Dick Van Dyke

Show", it went on to become a popular, long-running (1961–66) comedy hit; Reiner won numerous Emmys as head writer of the behind-the-scenes show business sitcom and also played Alan Brady, the egotistical star of the TV show for whom Dick Van Dyke worked.

After writing two screenplays ("The Thrill of It All" 1963 and "The Art of Love" 1965) for director Norman Jewison, Reiner made an impressive directorial debut with an adaptation of his autobiographical novel and stage play, "Enter Laughing" (1967). He has subsequently made several offbeat comedy gems including "Where's Poppa?" (1970) and box-office hits such as "Oh, God" (1977). He has directed four films starring Steve Martin ("The Jerk" 1979, "Dead Men Don't Wear Plaid" 1982, "The Man With Two Brains" 1983, "All of Me" 1984). Most inventive when working from his own screenplays, Reiner has also directed "Summer Rental" (1985), "Summer School" (1987) and "Sibling Rivalry" (1990) from scripts by others.

FAMILY:

brother: Charles Reiner. Died on February 28, 2001 at age 82; Reiner always credited his brother for his career because his brother told him about an acting class sponsored by the Works Public Administration

son: Rob Reiner. Director, Actor; born March 6, 1945

son: Lucas Reiner. Director, writer, actor; born c. 1960; directorial debut, "The Spirit of '76" (1990)

MILESTONES:

Raised in the Bronx, New York

1942–1946: Served in the US Army; performed with Major Maurice Evans' Special Services Unit in armed services tour of the South Pacific

1947: Broadway acting debut in "Call Me Mister"

Appeared on Broadway in "Inside U.S.A."

TV acting debut as series regular, "The Photographer" on the comedy series "The Fashion Story" (ABC)

1949: Was featured in Broadway musical "Alive and Kicking"

1949: Had regular role on the CBS variety show "The Fifty-Fourth Street Revue"

1950: Joined "Your Show of Shows" (NBC) as a performer and writer; first met Mel Brooks

1950: With Mel Brooks, began performing routine of the 2000-year-old man in the writers' room at "Your Show of Shows"; eventually did the routine at parties

Was regular on "Caesar's Hour" (NBC); won first two Emmy Awards in 1956 and 1957

1958: Published first novel, the autobiographical "Enter Laughing"

Emceed TV quiz show, "Keep Talking"

1959: Film acting debut, "Happy Anniversary"

Appeared as panelist on TV show, "Take a Good Look" (NBC)

1960: Released comedy album "2,000 Years with Carl Reiner & Mel Brooks"; earned Grammy nomination

1960: Wrote and starred in pilot for proposed series called "Head of the Family" (CBS); played Rob Petrie, a TV writer who commutes from his Westchester home to NYC

1961: Issued follow-up album "2,000 and One Years with Carl Reiner and Mel Brooks"; also earned Grammy nomination

At suggestion of producer Sheldon Leonard, rewrote and recast "Head of the Family"; Dick Van Dyke hired to play Rob Petrie and series was retitled "The Dick Van Dyke Show"; served as writer and producer on the series; also made appearances as TV star Alan Brady; won pilot, "Head of the Family" which he wrote; a single episode aired (in July 1960); producer Sheldon Leonard refilmed the episode with a new cast including Dick Van Dyke as Rob Petrie, retitled show, "The Dick Van Dyke Show" and hired Reiner as the real head writer of the series; Reiner also appeared as Alan Brady on series; won seven Emmy Awards for penning episodes and as producer of the show

1963: Wrote first screenplay for "The Thrill of It All", starring Doris Day

1963: Appeared as regular on "The Art Linkletter Show" (NBC)

1963: Had supporting role in "It's a Mad, Mad, Mad, Mad World"

1966: Made feature film directorial debut with "Enter Laughing", based on his novel; also made producing debut and wrote the screenplay

1976: Returned to TV to play Mr. Angel on short-lived series, "Good Heavens"

1980: Broadway directing debut, "The Roast"

QUOTES:

Inducted into the Academy of Television Arts and Sciences' Hall of Fame in 1998.

DISCOGRAPHY:
"2,000 Years with Carl Reiner & Mel Brooks" 1960 earned Grammy nomination for Best Comedy Recording
"2,000 and One Years with Carl Reiner & Mel Brooks" 1961 earned Grammy nomination
"The 2000 Year Old Man in the Year 2000: The Album" Carl Reiner and Mel Brooks, Rhino 1997; Grammy winner

BIBLIOGRAPHY:

"Enter Laughing" Carl Reiner, 1958, Simon & Schuster; autobiographical novel; was turned into a play in 1964 by Joseph Stein and a short-lived 1976 musical called "So Long, 174th Street" with a book by Stein and a score by Stan Daniels

"The 2000 Year Old Man" Carl Reiner and Mel Brooks, 1981, Warner Books

"All Kinds of Love" Carl Reiner, 1993, Birch Lane Press; novel

"Continue Laughing" Carl Reiner, 1995, Birch Lane Press; sequel to "Enter Laughing"

"The 2,000 Year Old Man in the Year 2000: How to Not Die and Other Good Tips" Carl Reiner and Mel Brooks, 1997, HarperCollins

"How Paul Robeson Saved My Life and Other Stories" Carl Reiner, 1999, Cliff Street Books; short stories

Rob Reiner

BORN: Robert Reiner in Bronx, New York, 03/06/1945

NATIONALITY: American

EDUCATION: University of California at Los Angeles, Los Angeles, California

AWARDS: Emmy Best Supporting Actor in a Comedy Series "All in the Family" 1973/74

Emmy Best Supporting Actor in a Comedy Series "All in the Family" 1977/78

MTV Movie Award Best Movie "A Few Good Men" 1993

American Cinematheque Award 1994

Honorary People's Choice Award 1997 "special achievement tribute for his thirty years in television and film"

American Comedy Award for Lifetime Achievement 1997

BIOGRAPHY

The son of quadruple-threat master of comedy Carl Reiner, Rob Reiner grew up in the same Bronx neighborhood as his future wife Penny Marshall and followed a path much like his father's en route to his own success, performing stand-up comedy and writing for TV shows like "Romp" (ABC, 1968) and "The Summer Smothers Brother Show" (CBS, 1968). After appearing in two films directed by his father ("Enter Laughing" 1967; "Where's Poppa?" 1970), the prematurely balding, heavy-set actor made his TV debut as a "motorcycle hood" on "The Partridge Family" (ABC) in 1970. Fame came knocking the following year when Norman Lear cast him as Mike 'Meathead' Stivic, Archie Bunker's liberal son-in-law (and straight man), on the classic 1970s series "All in the Family" (CBS). The ground-breaking show weathered initial resistance to its blunt, outrageous humor, and Reiner stayed on from 1971–78, winning two Emmy Awards (a paltry sum when compared with his father's ten) before leaving to pursue his own projects.

Reiner created, executive produced, and wrote for several short-lived TV series and acted in four forgettable films before making an hilarious feature directing (and screenwriting) debut with "This Is Spinal Tap" (1984), a mock "rockumentary" that parodied filmmakers' reverence for rock stars. Featuring himself as film director "Martin DiBergi", a wicked spoof of Martin Scorsese in "The Last Waltz" (1978), the satire received universally good reviews, yet when he had ventured out into the executive suites of Hollywood asking for the chance to helm it, his 'Meathead' persona had prevented people from taking him seriously. Fortunately, Lear saved the day, supplying the money to finance not only "Spinal Tap" but subsequent films as well. Though "The Sure Thing" (1986) was utterly predictable, Reiner's less distinctive but pleasant follow-up to "Spinal Tap" was an amiable teen road movie that evoked screwball comedies of old, setting the tone for his sharply funny, ostensibly adult feel-good fare to come.

"Stand By Me" (1986), one of Reiner's best films, marked his first collaboration with Stephen King, whose non-horror novella "The Body" served as its basis. Narrated by Richard Dreyfuss and boasting superb, fresh young faces like Wil Wheaton, River Phoenix and Kiefer Sutherland, the film offered an affectionate slice of 50s Americana in its story of four boys who set out on a search for the body of a dead teenager and learn powerful life lessons along the way. He continued establishing his reputation as one of Hollywood's most reliable, consistently commercial directors with his producing debut, "The Princess Bride"

(1987), a quirky fairy tale and comic swashbuckler demonstrating his versatility within yet another genre. Reiner co-founded Castle Rock Entertainment that year, going on to score his biggest hit yet with the romantic comedy "When Harry Met Sally . . . " (1989) while attracting the wrath of some reviewers who accused him of pilfering Woody Allen's Manhattan sensibilities, a ridiculous criticism to aim at a native New Yorker. Turning again to King, he translated the author's "Misery" to the screen in 1990, providing a tour de force, Oscar-winning role for Kathy Bates.

Reiner's first collaboration with writer Aaron Sorkin brought him his only Oscar nomination (Best Picture) to date as one of the producers of the slick military courtroom drama "A Few Good Men" (1992), adapted from Sorkin's play. Resorting for the first time to a superstar cast (i.e., Tom Cruise, Jack Nicholson, Demi Moore), the director effectively expanded the story for movie retelling and elicited top-notch performances across the board from his talent, though the convenient breakdown of the crusty Nicholson at the film's climax was only one of the contrivances that rang false. The blockbuster marked the end of a stunning run of luck that had seen him helm his first seven pictures without having a stinker among them. Next up was the disastrous "North" (1994), a fable about a kid (Elijah Wood) who divorces his parents and a picture so wrong-headed it earned zero stars from film critic Roger Ebert as "one of the most unpleasant, contrived, artificial, cloying experiences I have ever had at the movies."

Reiner recovered his dignity with "The American President" (1995), a Capraesque romantic comedy scripted by Sorkin about a widowed president (Michael Douglas) smitten by a luminous lobbyist (Annette Bening). A smart script and fine acting from both the leads and a stellar supporting cast (including Richard Dreyfuss, Michael J. Fox and Martin Sheen) helped propel the starry-eyed affair past the considerable gaps in credibility. He followed with "Ghosts of Mississippi" (1996), based on the true story of the long-delayed conviction of a Southern racist for the murder of civil rights activist Medgar Evers. Whoopi Goldberg delivered an excellent portrayal as Evers' widow, and James Woods was even better as the wily, aging murderer Brian De La Beckwith. Unfortunately, the high-minded movie suffered from Hollywood revisionism and a lack of edge that might have enabled it to be the uplifting hymn to justice to which it had aspired. Meanwhile, if Castle Rock wasn't exactly enjoying smashes with Reiner's features, the company, jointly purchased with New Line Cinema by Turner Broadcasting in 1993 for $650 million, could point with pride to the fabulous success of NBC's "Seinfeld" (1989–98), which had emerged from its stable.

Reiner stepped out from behind the camera to play his first feature role in ten years in "Throw Momma from the Train" (1987), and as his directorial output slowed during the 90s, he worked with increasing frequency as an actor. He oozed flattery on the strung-out Meryl Streep in Mike Nichols' "Postcards from the Edge" (1990) before asking her to take a drug test and also appeared in Nichols' "Regarding Henry" (1991) and "Primary Colors" (1998). He popped up in his brother Lucas Reiner's directing debut, "The Spirit of '76" (1990), and played Tom Hanks' best friend in Nora Ephron's "Sleepless in Seattle" (1993), not to mention surfacing in her "Mixed Nuts", Woody Allen's "Bullets Over Broadway" (both 1994) and Hugh Wilson's popular "First Wives' Club" (1996). Terrific as a villainous network executive in Ron Howard's "EdTV", he turned up as himself in Albert Brooks' "The Muse" and then acted for the first time in a picture he directed, portraying Bruce Willis' best friend in "The Story of Us" (all 1999), a technically proficient vehicle that did little to dispel the notion that his most recent directorial efforts have lacked

the freshness and unpredictability of his earlier work. After a lengthy hiatus in which he worked seriously to promote his political agenda regarding child care, Reiner returned behind the camera as the director and (uncredited) co-writer of the 2003 romantic comedy "Alex & Emma," which paired Luke Wilson as a blocked writer with a deadline opposite sassy stenographer Kate Hudson. The film took serious critical blows, mostly suggestions that the director wasn't able to recreate the light, airy tone his own earlier romantic comedy efforts. That same year, Reiner also stepped before the cameras, playing himself as a major Hollywood player who holds the professional fate of David Spade's grown kid actor in "Dickie Roberts: Former Child Star."

FAMILY:

father: Carl Reiner. Actor, writer, director, producer; born on March 20, 1923; directed Reiner in "Enter Laughing" (1966) and "Where's Poppa?" (1970)

mother: Estelle Reiner. Actor, entertainer; had a memorable cameo in the deli scene in "When Harry Met Sally . . . " (1989)

sister: Sylvia Reiner.

brother: Lucas Reiner. Director; born c. 1960; made directorial debut with "The Spirit of '76" (1990), in which Reiner had a cameo

step-daughter: Tracy Reiner. Actor; daughter of Penny Marshall and Michael Henry; raised by Reiner and adopted his name; has appeared in films directed by mother, Reiner and others

COMPANIONS:

wife: Penny Marshall. Actor, director; born on October 15, 1942; married on April 10, 1971; divorced c. 1980

Elizabeth McGovern. Actor; together in the late 1980s

wife: Michelle Singer. Photographer; married in May 1989; met on the set of "When Harry Met Sally"

MILESTONES:

Worked in regional theater and with improvisational comedy troupes

1966: First appearance in a film, "Enter Laughing", directed by father Carl Reiner

1968: TV writing debut, the ABC special "Romp", followed by "The Summer Smothers Brothers Show" (CBS)

1970: Played first major film role in his second feature the teen drama "Halls of Anger"

1970: Reteamed with father for "Where's Poppa?"

1970: TV acting debut in "The Partridge Family" (ABC)

1971–1978: First role as a regular on a TV series, as Michael Stivic (aka 'Meathead') on the ground-breaking CBS sitcom "All in the Family", for which he also wrote occasionally; won Emmy Awards in 1974 and 1978 as Best Supporting Actor in a Comedy Series

1972: Wrote for the short-lived ABC sitcom "The Super"

1974: First TV producing and directing credits, in collaboration with Phil Mishkin, on the CBS sitcom pilot "Sonny Boy"

1978: First TV series as creator and executive producer (in collaboration with Mishkin), the short-lived ABC sitcom "Free Country", for which he also wrote and in which he starred as Lithuanian immigrant Joseph Bresner

1978: Executive produced and wrote (with Mishkin) first TV-movie, "More Than Friends" (ABC), in which he co-starred opposite Penny Marshall in a romantic comedy based on their own courtship

1980: Broadway acting debut in his father's play "The Roast"

1984: First feature film as director and first screenplay credit, "This is Spinal Tap", for which he also wrote several songs and acted; first feature collaboration with Billy Crystal (had previously acted with him in the ABC comedy special "The TV Show" 1979)

1986: Initial collaboration with producer Andrew Scheinman, "The Sure Thing"

1986: Helmed the coming-of-age tale "Stand By Me", adapted from a Stephen King novella; produced by Scheinman

1987: First film as producer, "The Princess Bride"; also directed; initial collaboration with William Goldman who adapted his novel of the same name; Scheinman produced and Crystal contributed a cameo

1987: First feature acting role in ten years, "Throw Momma From the Train", Danny DeVito's directorial debut, starring Crystal and DeVito

1987: Formed Castle Rock Entertainment (named for a fictional Maine town that appears in Stephen King's work) with partners Alan Horn, Glenn Padnick, Scheinman and Martin Shafer

1989: Scored box office hit with the romantic comedy "When Harry Met Sally . . . ", written by Nora Ephron and starring Crystal and Meg Ryan

1990: Acted with father in time-travel comedy "The Spirit of '76", directed by brother Lucas Reiner

1990: Directed Kathy Bates to a Best Actress Oscar in "Misery", an adaptation of a Stephen King novel which reteamed him with Goldman

Hosted regular TV installments of the "Showtime 30-minute Movie"

1990: First feature collaboration with Mike Nichols, appearing in "Postcards From the Edge" as a movie producer

1991: Created (in collaboration with Phil Mishkin) and executive produced the short-lived CBS sitcom "Morton & Hayes"

1991: Acted in Nichols' "Regarding Henry"

1992: Helmed the screen adaptation of Aaron Sorkin's Broadway play "A Few Good Men"; film received a Best Picture Oscar nomination

1993: Castle Rock Entertainment (as well as New Line Cinema) purchased by the Turner Broadcasting System for $650 million

1993: Played Tom Hanks' friend in Ephron's "Sleepless in Seattle"

1994: Helmed the misfire "North"; first collaboration with Bruce Willis

1994: Acted in Woody Allen's "Bullets Over Broadway" and in Ephron's "Mixed Nuts"

1995: Reteamed with Sorkin, directing the romantic comedy "The American President"

1995: Played a radio shrink in "Bye, Bye Love"

1996: Directed the civil rights drama "Ghosts of Mississippi"; co-star James Woods earned a Best Supporting Actor Academy Award nomination

1998: Acted in the political satire "Primary Colors", directed by Nichols and scripted by Elaine May

1999: Appointed by California Governor Gray Davis to serve without salary as chairman of the nine-member state Children and Families First Commission

1999: Made cameo appearance as himself in Albert Brooks' Hollywood comedy "The Muse"

1999: Acted in and directed "The Story of Us", a comedy-drama about a troubled marriage starring Michelle Pfeiffer and Willis

1999: Honored with a star on the Hollywood Walk of Fame (October 12); star is located next to his father's

2001: Voice was used for a small part in "The Majestic"

2003: Served as the director and co-writer of the feature "Alex and Emma"; also played the character Wirtschafter

AFFILIATION: Democrat

Chair, California Children and Families' First Commission

QUOTES:
Some sources list 1947 as the year of Mr. Reiner's birth.

Frank Capra III had worked as first assistant director on three Reiner films prior to co-producing "Ghosts of Mississippi" (1996) and executive producing "The Story of Us" (1999). He also served as first assistant director on both pictures as well.

Reiner was honored with a Friars Club Celebrity Roast in October 2000.

"As an actor I was always more aware of everybody else onstage, or if I was doing 'All in the Family', I was aware of where all the cameras were, where the other actors were, the audience. I was always more interested in the script and in the structure of the script than I was in my performance. Which is not such a great way to approach your acting job."—Rob Reiner quoted in *Los Angeles Times*, November 25, 1990

In 1998, Reiner championed a successful California ballot initiative, Proposition 10, which resulted in a 50-cent tax on cigarettes going to early educational programs for children.

Ivan Reitman

BORN: in Komarmo, Czechoslovakia, 10/26/1946

NATIONALITY: Czech

CITIZENSHIP: Canada

EDUCATION: McMaster University, Hamilton, Ontario, Canada; music, BMus; 1969

AWARDS: NATO/ShoWest Director of the Year Award 1984; honored by the National Association of Theater Owners

Genie Golden Reel Award 1982

Genie Special Achievement 1985

BIOGRAPHY
Although he received less personal publicity than his box-office powerhouse contemporaries

George Lucas and Steven Spielberg, Reitman had a comparable impact on filmmaking trends of the late 1970s and 80s. When the demographics of moviegoers shifted to favor teens, these visionary showmen more than understood their target audience—they molded it with their own distinctive tastes and obsessions. What Lucas and Spielberg did for fantasy adventure, Reitman did for comedy. He took the kind of quasi-disreputable material once geared to teens in second-string low budget fare, made it mainstream and big budget, and reaped megabucks. While one may quibble about the artistic merit of some of his product, no one can deny its impact.

Reitman began his career as a stage and TV producer and turned out his first feature film in 1971. Among his initial low-budget Canadian productions were two striking early horror films directed by David Cronenberg, "They Came from Within" (1975) and "Rabid" (1977). As a producer and/or director, Reitman played a significant role in the film careers of several Second City (Chicago and Toronto-based) performers who first gained fame on "Saturday Night Live"—Bill Murray, Dan Aykroyd, and John Belushi. Aykroyd was featured in "Greed", a Reitman-produced variety show for Canadian TV. Murray made a big splash on screen in the Reitman-directed "Meatballs" (1979) and "Stripes" (1981). Both actors also appeared in his blockbuster comedy "Ghostbusters" (1984), Reitman's biggest commercial success to date. John Belushi's all-too-brief movie stardom, meanwhile, was initiated by his riotous performance in the Reitman-produced "National Lampoon's Animal House" (John Landis, 1978).

"Animal House" marked the beginning of a fruitful collaboration between Reitman and Harold Ramis, who scripted that frat war comedy. Ramis also worked on the films "Stripes" (as screenwriter and actor), "Ghostbusters" (as screenwriter and actor) and "Ghostbusters II" (as screenwriter and actor). Reitman also tried to soften the image of Arnold Schwarzenegger by directing him in the comedy "Twins" (1988), teaming him with the diminuitive Danny DeVito, and by producing "Kindergarten Cop" (1990). Similarly but considerably less successfully, Reitman produced "Stop! or My Mom Will Shoot" (Roger Spottiswoode, 1992) for Sylvester Stallone.

Until John Hughes' "Home Alone" (1990) supplanted it, Reitman's outsized supernatural spoof was the highest grossing comedy in movie history. The quirky "Ghostbusters" mythos quickly became part of 80s popular culture, yielding a hit single, tons of merchandise, a long-running cartoon series (on which he served as executive consultant), "The Real Ghostbusters" (1986–88) which evolved into "Slimer! and the Real Ghostbusters" (1988–91), and the inevitable sequel, "Ghostbusters II" (1989, directed by Reitman).

Reitman scored a surprise hit as the executive producer of "Beethoven" (Brian Levant, 1992), a canine comedy starring the deadpan Charles Grodin. He returned to directing after a three-year hiatus with "Dave" (1993), a political satire starring the talented cast of Kevin Kline, Sigourney Weaver, Frank Langella, Ben Kingsley, and Grodin. As a modern variation on Twain's "The Prince and the Pauper", it suggested Akira Kurosawa's "Kagemusha" (1980) as directed by Frank Capra. The director fared less well with his follow-up comedies. "Junior" (1994) reteamed Schwarzenegger and DeVito in an improbable story of a male scientist (Schwarzenegger) who becomes pregnant while "Father's Day" (1997) teamed Robin Williams and Billy Crystal in an Americanized version of a French farce about two men searching for a runaway teen they both think they fathered. He next teamed Harrison Ford and Anne Heche for the romantic comedy, "Six Days, Seven Nights" (1998).

Reitman's other credits as a director include "Cannibal Girls" (1972) and "Legal Eagles" (1986), with Debra Winger and Robert Redford, while his producing credits include the animated "Heavy Metal" (1981) and the Howard Stern biopic "Private Parts" (1997).

MILESTONES:

1951: Fled Czechoslovakia with family and relocated to Canada

Began career as theater and TV producer in Canada

Produced live variety show, "Greed," for Canadian TV (starred Dan Aykroyd)

1971: Directed and produced first feature film, "Foxy Lady"

Produced "Spellbound" for the Toronto stage

Produced "The Magic Show", a popular Broadway show starring Doug Henning which he developed from "Spellbound"

Produced "The National Lampoon Show" for Off-Broadway and the subsequent year-long tour

1974: Produced "They Came From Within/

Shivers/The Parasite Murders", David Cronenberg's feature directorial debut

1978: First collaboration with Harold Ramis, "National Lampoon's Animal House"

1979: Directed "Meatballs"; first collaboration with Bill Murray

1979: Executive produced "Delta House", the ABC-TV spinoff of "Animal House"

1988: Produced and directed "Twins" starring Arnold Schwarzenegger and Danny DeVito; Schwarzenegger's first lead in a comedy

1997: Received star on Hollywood Walk of Fame (May 5)

1998: Entered into a five-year partnership with Thomas Pollock and PolyGram Filmed Entertainment to form a production company

Jean Renoir

BORN: in Montmartre, Paris, 09/15/1894

DEATH: in Hollywood, California, 02/12/1979

NATIONALITY: French

EDUCATION: College Saint-Croix, Neuilly, France; entered at age seven, first time in school

Ecole Sainte-Marie de Monceau; attended as a result of running away from College Saint-Croix several times

Ecole Massena, Nice, France

University of Aix-en-Provence; mathematics and philosophy BA 1913

AWARDS: Venice Biennale International Jury Cup Award "La Grande Illusion/Grand Illusion" 1937; award created for "La Grande Illusion"

New York Film Critics Circle Award Best Foreign Film "La Grande Illusion/Grand Illusion" 1938

National Board of Review Best Director "The Southerner" 1945

Venice Film Festival Best Film Award "The Southerner" 1946

Venice Film Festival International Prize "The River" 1951; one of three films cited

Brussels World Fair Award "La Grande Illusion/Grand Illusion" 1958; named fifth best movie ever

National Society of Film Critics Special Award 1974

Honorary Oscar 1974 for "a genius who, with grace, responsibility and enviable devotion through silent film, sound film, feature, documentary and television, has won the world's admiration"

BIOGRAPHY

Renoir is arguably the greatest artist that the cinema has ever known, simply because he was able to work effectively in virtually all genres without sacrificing his individuality or bowing to public or commercial conventions. Although the son of the famed impressionist painter Auguste Renoir, his visual sensibility was entirely his own, and the technical facility that marks his films is the result of long and assiduous study.

Renoir's first serious interest in cinema developed during a period of recuperation after he had been wounded by a stray bullet while serving with the Alpine infantry in 1915. His first active involvement came in 1924, when money raised by the sale of some of his father's paintings (Auguste Renoir had died in 1919) allowed him to began production on "Catherine/Une Vie sans joie" in 1924. Renoir provided the screenplay and Albert Dieudonne the direction; Renoir's young wife Andree Madeleine Heuchling, a former model of his father's, was the star, with her name changed to Catherine Hessling for billing purposes. Renoir's first film as director, "La Fille de l'eau," was shot in 1924, with Renoir also functioning as producer and art director and Catherine Hessling again starring. Anticipating Jean Vigo's "L'Atalante" (1934), the film's plot centered on a young woman who lives and works on a river boat. It's modest success led Renoir to plunge, somewhat impulsively, into the direction of "Nana" (1926), an adaptation from the Zola novel which now looks uncharacteristically stagebound.

Nearly bankrupt, Renoir had to take out a loan to finance his next film, "Charleston" (1927), a 24-minute fantasy that featured Hessling teaching the popular title dance in costumes that were as brief as possible. After it attained only limited success, Renoir accepted a straight commercial directing job on "Marquitta" (1927).

Renoir's next significant film was "Tire-au-Flanc" (1928), a military comedy that Francois Truffaut would later call a visual "tour de force" and which marked the director's first collaboration with actor Michel Simon. The working relationship between Renoir and Hessling, meanwhile, had taken its toll; the couple separated in 1930, though Hessling continued to appear in Renoir's films through "Crime et chatiment/Crime and Punishment" (1935).

To prove that he understood the new medium of the sound film, Renoir directed a down-and-dirty comedy based on a farce by Georges Feydeau, "On Purge Bebe" (1931). The film was shot on a very brief schedule, with Renoir apparently letting the camera run for as long as possible during each take, in order to work around the clumsy sound-on-disc recording apparatus. He also inserted a number of instances of mild "blue humor" (for example, the sound of a toilet heard flushing off-screen). Perhaps because he had aimed so resolutely for commercial success, Renoir's first talkie was a huge hit, allowing him to rush into production on his first major sound film, "La Chienne/The Bitch" (1931). This was the first of his films to be edited by Marguerite Mathieu, with whom Renoir became romantically involved at this time and who would later take the name Marguerite Renoir, though the couple never married. It was on this film, too, that Renoir developed his early strategy of sound shooting. In the face of objections from his producers down to his sound technicians, he insisted on using only natural sync-sound, recorded for the most part in actual locations. He also made extensive use of a moving camera, particularly in one sequence where the camera "waltzes" around the dance floor, keeping perfect time with the actors.

Renoir next directed his brother Pierre in "La Nuit du carrefour/Night at the Crossroads" (1932), a brilliant but little-seen detective film based on one of Georges Simenon's Inspector Maigret novels. He followed it with the delightful comedy, "Boudu sauve des eaux/Boudu Saved From Drowning" (1932). The film uses Renoir's by now polished on-location sync-sound shooting technique to tell the tale of Boudu (Michel Simon), a bum who is fished out of the Seine after a suicide attempt by a well-meaning bourgeois bookseller, Lestingois (Charles Granval). Taken into the Lestingois household, Boudu wreaks havoc until he escapes during a boating accident, free to wander again. The charm and invention of this beautiful film make it one of the glories of the early sound cinema. (It was remade in 1986 by director Paul Mazursky as "Down and Out in Beverly Hills.")

With the critical and popular success of "Boudu," Renoir embarked upon a project reminiscent of "Nana." "Madame Bovary" (1934) starred Pierre Renoir as Charles Bovary and Valentine Tessier as Emma Bovary. The first cut of the film ran three hours and thirty minutes, but it was eventually trimmed to two hours. Still, the film met with little commercial success; undeterred, Renoir began shooting "Toni" (1934) almost entirely on location in Martigues, using non-professional actors in most of the roles. "Toni" thus presages the Italian Neorealist movement by more than a decade, and in following his inherent bent for "naturalism," Renoir created a beautiful and tragic film which is now recognized as one of his finest works. Nevertheless, the film met with little public or critical favor, a pattern which was becoming increasingly familiar.

Renoir's next film, "The Crime of Monsieur Lange" (1936), marked the director's only collaboration with writer Jacques Prevert, and gave ample evidence of the director's increasing politicization. Marked by beautiful, fluid, yet carefully precise camera work, as well as the excellent ensemble acting of the Groupe Octobre, "The Crime of Monsieur Lange" is one of Renoir's finest and most accessible films. It was followed by "La Vie est a nous/People of France" (1936), a political tract which bears a striking resemblance to Godard's 16mm "cine tracts" of the late 1960s and early 70s. Initially withheld by the censor, the film enjoyed a limited release in the US in 1937 but was not shown to the paying French public until 1969, as a result of the student riots in France the previous May.

Renoir was now nearing the end of his first great stage of directorial activity, and in rapid succession he created a series of unforgettable films: "Une Partie de compagne/A Day in the Country "(1936), based on a short story by Guy de Maupassant, completed in the face of considerable production difficulties, and not released in France until 1946 and the USA in 1950; "Les Bas fonds/The Lower Depths" (1936), an adaptation of the Maxim Gorky play; "La Grande Illusion/Grand Illusion" (1937), one of the best known and beloved films of all time, as compelling an anti-war document as has ever been created; "La Marseillaise" (1938), an examination of the events of the French Revolution, characteristically reduced to human scale, despite impressive production values; "La Bete humaine/The Human Beast" (1938), an adaptation of Zola's novel (remade by Fritz Lang in 1954 as "Human Desire"); and finally, "La Regle du jeu/The Rules of the Game" (1939), now universally recognized as the director's masterwork, although, amazingly enough, it was reviled upon its initial release. This astutely observed tale of romance among the aristocrats and working class during a sporting weekend in the country was a complete box-office failure on its initial release. The film was withdrawn after a brief run and not revived until 1945, and later 1948—and then only in a mutilated version which gave no sense of the original. It was not until 1965 that the "definitive" version of the film was painfully reconstructed from various archival materials.

Renoir spent much of 1939 in Rome, teaching at the Centro Sperimental di Cinematografia. He co-wrote, with Carl Koch and Luchino Visconti, a screen version of "La Tosca" and began production on it in the spring of 1940, only to be interrupted by Italy's entry into WWII. Koch completed the film, and Renoir returned to France.

In 1940, however, Renoir came to America at the behest of documentarian Robert Flaherty. His "American period" would be marked by a number of uneven films, but saw the production of at least two of great beauty and accomplishment. Renoir enjoyed modest success with his first American film, "Swamp

Water" (1941), starring Dana Andrews, Walter Huston, John Carradine and Walter Brennan and filmed on location in Georgia. Meanwhile, however, his admirers in France had turned on him. At a crucial moment in his country's history, they complained, the director had "gone Hollywood." Disregarding the controversy for the moment, Renoir signed to shoot a Deanna Durbin musical, then abandoned the project nearly two-thirds of the way through shooting.

This misadventure was followed by "This Land Is Mine" (1943), a story of the French resistance shot entirely on studio sets, starring Charles Laughton, Kent Smith, George Sanders and Maureen O'Hara. The film did acceptable business in the US, but received a truly hostile reception in France. Renoir attempted to make amends with a 20-minute short, "Salute to France" (1944), which was produced by the Office of War Information from a script by Philip Dunne, Renoir and Burgess Meredith, who also acted in the film. Kurt Weill supplied the music for this well-intentioned effort, which did nothing to salvage Renoir's reputation at home, although it was well received in the US.

Renoir's next film was an independent production, "The Southerner" (1945), starring Zachary Scott, Betty Field, J. Carrol Naish and Percy Kilbride. Working with his old associate Eugene Lourie as set designer, Robert Aldrich as assistant director and William Faulkner as dialogue consultant, Renoir created one of his most satisfying American films, a tale of the trials and tribulations of an Southern cotton farmer. "The Southerner" received the best contemporary critical notices of any of its director's American efforts.

"The Diary of a Chambermaid" (1946) was a curious choice for Renoir, and the result was a highly uneven film. The cast included Paulette Goddard, Burgess Meredith (who also co-produced and co-authored the screenplay), Hurd Hatfield, Reginald Owen, Judith Anderson, Irene Ryan and Francis Lederer. Shot on severely stylized studio sets, the film is overtly theatrical and eschews almost entirely the style Renoir had so carefully developed in his early sound films of the 1930s.

Renoir's last American film, "The Woman on the Beach" (1947), was directed for RKO. He originally developed the idea for the film with producer Val Lewton, justly famous for his series of horror films for RKO in the 1940s. However, Lewton left the production before shooting commenced and the film was substantially cut before its release. At least two versions now circulate; the most complete edition begins with a long undersea nightmare sequence reminiscent of "La Fille de L'eau," in which the film's protagonists, Robert Ryan and Joan Bennett, encounter each other at the bottom of the ocean. Jacques Rivette, Manny Farber and other critics have hailed the film as a masterpiece. Mutilated as it is, it displays a maturity of vision equal to the precise grace of "The Rules of the Game" or "The Crime of Monsieur Lange." In truncated versions running as short as 71 minutes, the film is only a fragment of what it might have been, but Rivette has aptly compared it to Erich von Stroheim's "Greed" (1925).

Renoir's third and final period as a director begins with "The River" (1950), an independently produced film based on Rumer Godden's novel. Shot entirely in Calcutta, it won first prize at the Venice Film Festival in 1951. This relaxed and contemplative coming-of-age story, beautifully photographed in Technicolor, represents a return to the naturalism of Renoir's early work. "Le Carosse d'or/The Golden Coach" (1952) shares with "Diary of a Chambermaid" an intense interest in theatrical film style, and gave Anna Magnani one of her greatest roles as Camilla, the fiery diva of a traveling theater troupe. Though Eric Rohmer has called "Le Carosse d'or" "the 'open sesame' of all of Renoir's work," the film was not well received upon its initial release.

Renoir was unable to find backing for another film until "French Cancan" (1954, sometimes known in the US as "Only the French Can"), his first made in France in over 15 years. This valentine to the Moulin Rouge met with great public success and featured a number of French music hall performers in cameo roles, including a very brief appearance by Edith Piaf. "Elena et les hommes/Paris Does Strange Things" (1956) starred Ingrid Bergman, Jean Marais and Mel Ferrer in another, lightweight love letter to a bygone age.

"Le Testament du Dr. Cordelier" (1959), though not regarded as one of Renoir's finest works, has him using multiple cameras for the first time, blocking the film as though it were a stage play in the manner now routinely used by TV sitcoms. Based on "Dr. Jekyll & Mr. Hyde," the film stars Jean-Louis Barrault as Dr. Cordelier and his mad alter ego, Opale, and is shot in stark black-and-white, in contrast to the lush coloring of Renoir's other film of this final period.

"Le Dejeuner sur l'herbe/Picnic on the Grass" (1959) followed, a topical fantasy film which has much in common with "Une Partie de campagne." Shot in delicious pastel colors, the film is at once ephemeral and melancholic, as if the director were acknowledging his bewilderment in the face of the "civilizing" forces of modern society. "Le Caporal epingle/The Elusive Corporal "(1962) is a return to the drabness of "Le Testament du Dr. Cordelier"; it recalls "La Grande Illusion" in its WWII tale of the numerous escape attempts of a corporal (Jean-Pierre Cassel) who is incarcerated in a series of German prison camps.

In 1968, Renoir appeared in and directed a short film, "La Direction d'acteur par Jean Renoir" which shows him directing the actress Gisele Braunberger in a scene from a Rumer Godden novel, "Breakfast with Nicolaides." Shot in a half-day, the film's direction credit is sometimes given to Ms. Braunberger. The following year, Renoir directed his last feature, "Le Petit Theatre de Jean Renoir", which was released in 1971. Jeanne Moreau is featured in four sketches which Renoir wrote, directed and narrated for French TV; when released theatrically in the US, it was warmly received, even though it was far from the director's most accomplished work.

At last, the public had caught up with Jean Renoir. "The Rules of the Game" had long since been reconstituted and enshrined as one of the greatest films of all time, and its director was pleased to accept an honorary Oscar in 1975 for his lifetime achievement in the cinema. The year before, Renoir had completed his memoirs, "Ma Vie et mes Films/My Life and My Films", which contain valuable insights into the director's method of scripting, direction and his ability to retain a sense of "self" in a highly commercial and competitive industry. In 1977, Renoir received his final major honor, the French Legion of Honor.

MILESTONES:

Enlisted in Chasseurs Alpins, served in WW I as second lieutenant and with Flying Corps as pilot

1924: First film as producer, writer, actor and co-director "Catherine/Un Vie sans joie"

1924: Sole directing debut with "La Fille de l'eau"

1925: Opened art gallery

1926: Directed first Franco-German collaboration "Nana"

1929: Last silent film as director "Le Bled"

1931: Sound-film directing debut with "On purge Bebe"

Artistic advisor, Theatre de la Liberte

1937: "La Grande Illusion" banned in Italy, Germany and Belgium

1938: Co-founded production company, La Nouvelle Edition Francaise to film "Les Caprices de Marianne;" bankrupt after one film

1939: "La Regle du jeu/The Rules of the Game" banned in Paris (ban reimposed during German occupation)

1940: Immigrated to US via Algiers, Casablanca and Lisbon

1946: "Un Partie de Campagne/A Day in the Country" released (shot 1936)

1941: Signed as director for one year by Darryl F. Zanuck at Fox

1941: Ended Fox contract

1942: Signed long-term contract with Universal; asked for release after few days

1947: Last US film as director (for RKO) "The Woman on the Beach"

Contract with RKO ended; co-founded Film Group production company (with Burgess Meredith); folded before any films were made late 1940s

1951: First color film as director "The River"

1954: Stage directing debut with "Julius Caesar" (2,000th anniversary of Caesar's discovery of Arles, France where play was staged)

1955: Debut as playwright with "Orvet" (also directed; Paris)

1959: Television directing debut with "Le Testament du Docteur Cordelier/Experiment in Evil"

BIBLIOGRAPHY:

"Renoir/Renoir My Father" Jean Renoir, 1962; biography

"Les Cahier du Capitaine Georges" Jean Renoir, 1966; novel

"Ma vie et ses films" Jean Renoir, 1974; semi-autobiography

"Le Coeur a l'aise" Jean Renoir, 1978; novel

"Le Crime de l'anglais" Jean Renoir, 1979; novel

"Geneveive" Jean Renoir, 1979; novel

"Jean Renoir: Projections of Paradise" Ronald Bergan, 1995; Overlook Press

Alain Resnais

BORN: in Vannes, France, 06/03/1922

NATIONALITY: French

EDUCATION: College St. Francois Xavier, Vannes, France; left due to chronic asthma

studied acting with Rene Simon from 1940–42

Institut des Hautes Etudes Cinematographiques, Paris, France, 1943–44

Cinematheque Francaise, Paris, France; Henri Langlois introduced a whole generation of future filmmakers to the masterpieces of world cinema, screening up to six movies a day

AWARDS: Cannes Film Festival International Critics Prize "Hiroshima, Mon Amour" 1959 shared award with Margot Benacerraf's "Araya"

Venice Film Festival Golden Lion "Last Year at Marienbad" 1961

Cannes Film Festival International Critics Prize "La guerre est finie" 1966; shared award with Volker Schlondorff's "Young Torless"

Cesar Best Director "Providence" 1978

Cannes Film Festival FIPRESCI Prize "Mon Oncle d'Amerique" 1980

Cannes Film Festival Special Jury Prize "Mon oncle d'Amerique" 1980

Venice Film Festival Pasinetti Italian Critics Prize "I Want To Go Home" 1989

Cesar Best Director "Smoking/No Smoking" 1994

Berlin Film Festival Outstanding Single Achievement Award "Smoking" and "No Smoking" 1994; companion films often given the joint title "Smoking/No Smoking"

Venice Film Festival Golden Lion for Lifetime Achievement 1995

Prix Louis Delluc Best French Film "On Connait la chanson/Same Old Song" 1997

Berlin Film Festival Silver Bear for Lifetime Achievement 1998

BIOGRAPHY

Arguably the single most important director to emerge from the French New Wave, Alain

Resnais fed his early imagination a varied diet of popular movies, pulp fiction, Proust, Katherine Mansfield and comic books, retaining throughout his career the ability to bridge the gap between high and low culture in his films. He began making 16mm documentary "art" shorts in the late 1940s, visiting the works of Hans Hartnung, Felix Labisse, Henri Goetz and Max Ernst, among others, but it was his more ambitious "Van Gogh" (1948) which finally succeeded in truly drawing the observer into the artist's world. The film impressed producer Pierre Braunberger sufficiently that he requested Resnais film a 35mm version which earned the 1949 Best Short Subject Oscar. With "Guernica" (1950), a short directed in collaboration with Robert Hessen, the former editor took his filmmaking one step farther, employing the montage techniques he had gradually been mastering to create a passionate protest against war that is at the same time an affirmation of faith in humanity and the possibility of love.

Resnais' most memorable documentary is the 31-minute "Nuit et brouillard/Night and Fog" (1956), a disturbing excursion into the world of Nazi concentration camps, in which he first revealed his preoccupation with the theme of memory and a visual style emphasizing probing camera tracking. Called by then-critic Francois Truffaut the greatest film ever made, it carefully juxtaposed black-and-white stills and newsreel footage depicting the obscenities that once transpired with restless color tracking shots of the post-war locations of those crimes. The poetic refrain of the narrator—"Who is responsible?"—forces viewers to confront the Holocaust as a continuing potentiality. The endless stacks and corridors of the Bibliotheque National in Resnais' subsequent "Toute la memoire du monde" (1956), his lyrical documentary about the great library, lent themselves particularly well to long tracking shots, and "Le Chant du styrene/The Styrene Song" (1958), which traced plastic back to its primeval beginnings, allowed him to experiment with editing to increase the feeling of speed for its own exciting sake.

Considered by many the first masterpiece of the French New Wave, Resnais' debut feature, "Hiroshima, Mon Amour" (1959), won the International Critics Prize at the same Cannes Film Festival that named Francois Truffaut best director for "The 400 Blows." Expanding on the stylistic experiments begun with "Night and Fog", this collaboration with screenwriter Marguerite Duras detailed the affair between a Japanese man and a French actress who had come to Hiroshima to make a film about the atomic holocaust. Particularly notable is the long opening sequence which combines the images of the nude, intertwined lovers with horrific documentary footage of the aftermath of the bombing. Resnais' montage allows him to travel from one place to another and from the "present" to a variety of past times, marrying the private moments of the two principals with the very public tragedy of Hiroshima. In addition to its revolutionary editing, the film was also innovative in its elevation of sound as a vital component independent and often contrapuntal to the visual images.

Setting out to capture the "stream of consciousness" technique of the modern novel, Resnais conceived a completely plotless narrative that was a subjective recreation of the past in the memory of the protagonist for his next film, "L'Annee derniere a Marienbad/Last Year at Marienbad" (1961), scripted by Alain Robbe-Grillet. An expressionist exercise in the manipulation of time and memory, "Marienbad" placed three characters, enigmatically named A, X and M, within the endless corridors and grounds of a huge castle resort, where they may or may not have previously met. Throughout the film, the camera lovingly and sensuously dollies through the corridors to reveal the physical realities of the castle's objects and geometrically choreographed movements of characters, who act more like automatons than people—even though (in one of the most famous images from the film) they have shadows, whereas the trees and gardens do not. The intellectually absorbing, visually exciting but puzzling picture was a staggering success at the box office.

Though the characters of "Muriel" (1963) are more fully developed than in Resnais' earlier films, his first color feature was still, despite its commercial failure, a triumph of style over content. Abandoning his tracking camera for a static, fragmented feel, he overcame the problem of assembling a huge number of shots by allowing the sound belonging to one cut to overlap briefly into the next—a technique so widely imitated it has become commonplace. Concretely grounded in one family's moral dilemmas within the context of the Algerian War, "Muriel" offered emotional relationships typical of Resnais, stronger when remembered or invented than they are in the present tense. "La Guerre est finie/The War is Over" (1966), however, boasted loves scenes that were the very antithesis of his norm—lush, sensual, and trying to compensate for the cerebral emphasis elsewhere. Its "flash forwards" not withstanding, the popular story of an aging revolutionary in contemporary France was far more orthodox and accessible than its predecessors, its simple structure dictated by the direct and strongly motivated personality of the hero.

"Je t'aime, je t'aime" (1968), one of Resnais' rarely screened films, continued his interest in time and memory, its love story including the science-fiction element of a time machine in which the leading character becomes trapped. Taking a real editor's joy in intercutting shots from various arbitrary time periods in his protagonist's mundane life, Resnais came as close to creating the condition of dreaming and unconsciousness as is possible in cinema, but the effect, though exhilarating, was a little too abstract for the mainstream. Financial difficulties prevented him from completing a film for six years, so he made certain to stack the deck

in his favor for "Stavisky" (1974), the story of the disreputable financier whose fall toppled a French government. The 1930s setting exploited the art-deco nostalgia of the time, its Stephen Sondheim score became a best-selling LP and Jean-Paul Belmondo's acceptance of the lead role guaranteed financial backing and box-office success.

Resnais moved into an English-language medium for "Providence" (1977), a film exploring the workings of the creative process (Resnais' creative processes in particular) and featuring a stellar cast including John Gielgud, Dirk Bogarde, Elaine Stritch and Ellen Burstyn. Contrasting the author's (Gielgud) imagined thoughts about his family with real-life encounters, Resnais and screenwriter David Mercer provided a primarily intellectual construction that Gielgud ultimately transcended with some of his best film acting, but the success accorded the film internationally eluded it in the USA. Returning to his native language, Resnais teamed with scenarist Jean Gruault for "Mon Oncle d'Amerique/My Uncle in America" (1980), their first of three films together. This provocative, humorous expansion of biologist Henri Laborit's theories on the human condition intercut the stories of three people suffering from stress with footage from a lecture about the effects of frustration on rats, and though director and screenwriter continued their deconstructionism with "La Vie est un roman/Life Is a Bed of Roses" (1983), its commercial failure may have influenced the virtually linear narrative of their third effort, "L'Amour à mort/Love Unto Death" (1984).

If there has always been a struggle within Resnais between artistic aspirations and the more conventionally dramatic, a devotion to character and feeling has won out in his later work. "Melo" (1987), adapted from a 1929 stage play about a romantic triangle, the companion films "Smoking" and "No Smoking" (1993, often referred to as one film "Smoking/No Smoking"), based on Alan Ayckbourn's "Intimate

Exchanges", and "On connait la chanson/Same Old Song" (1997), all eschew the fancy camerawork and editing of his ground-breaking films to concentrate on the invisible, deterministic forces affecting human relationships. For many who long for him to repeat his earlier work, this exploration of a theatrical cinema may seem ridiculous and sentimental, but for those who felt his more bravura technical efforts sacrificed warmth and anecdote, this growth of the mature artist is a welcome departure. Considered an auteur despite his reliance on collaborating screenwriters, Resnais has consistently adhered to strategies of fragmented point-of-view and multiple temporality and has significantly advanced film's ability to express the vagaries of the human mind.

MILESTONES:

Began making amatuer films as a teenager in the 1930s; father had given him an 8mm camera at the age of 12, and he screened his movies in an attic outfitted with "real wooden theatre seats"

1939: Moved to Paris

Acted during the last part of World War II with Les Arlequins, a classsical theater troupe

1946: Returned to Paris, where he made his first adult film, a 16mm silent short called "Schema d'une identification"; no known prints are extant

1947: Worked as assistant editor on Nicole Vedres' prize-winning compilation film "Paris 1900"

1947: Embarked on a series of short 16mm documentaries attempting to take "paintings out of the dusty setting of museums"

1948: Made a film more ambitious than his other art films, the 16mm short "Van Gogh"; remade in 35mm at producer Pierre Braunberger's invitation; that version won the 1949 Oscar for Best Short Subject (Two reel)

1950: Directed "Guernica" in collaboration with Robert Hessens; employed the montage techniques he had gradually been mastering to create a passionate protest against war that is also an affirmation of faith in humanity and the possibility of love

1954: Co-edited Agnes Varda's first feature film, "Le pointe courte"

Received the Prix Vigo for "Les Statues meurent aussi" (1953) and "Nuit et brouillard/Night and Fog" (1956); the latter, generally considered the finest of Resnais' short films, was a meditation on the Nazi death camps, alternating restless color tracking shots of the camps as they appeared post-war with black-and-white stills or newsroom footage showing the atrocities

1958: Last short, "Le Chant du styrene/The Styrene Song"

1959: Made first feature, "Hiroshima, Mon Amour", considered the first masterpiece of the French New Wave

1961: Created an even bigger stir with his second film, "L'Annee derniere a Marienbad/ Last Year at Marienbad", the very model of the modern avant-garde in narrative film, along with Antonioni's "L'Avventura"

1963: First color feature, "Muriel"

1966: Helmed "La Guerre est finie/The War Is Over", scripted by Jorge Semprun

1968: Last film for six years, "Je t'aime, je t'aime"

1974: Returned to filmmaking with "Stavisky", a box office and critical success scripted by Semprun and starring Jean-Paul Belmondo as the disreputable international financier who brought down a French government; featured a musical score by Stephen Sondheim

1977: First English-language film, "Providence"; rather cooly received in the USA, it garnered seven Cesars and international praise as "one of the great films of our time"

1980: Achieved an unqualified commercial success with "Mon oncle d'Amerique/My Uncle in America"; first of three collaborations with scenarist Jean Grualt (also "La Vie est un roman/Life Is a Bed of Roses" 1983 and "L'Amour a mort/Love Unto Death" 1984)

THE HOLLYWOOD.COM GUIDE TO FILM DIRECTORS

1993: Continuing a threatricality begun with "Melo" (1986), adapted "Intimate Exchanges" by Alan Ayckbourn for the diptych "Smoking/No Smoking", two 2-hour movies that could be viewed in any order; pared the 16 different endings of the original plays down to 12 in the two films

1997: "On connait la chanson/Same Old Song" won the Prix Louis Delluc as Best French Film

QUOTES:

"I never dreamed of being a film director when I was young, but when I saw the first Ginger Rogers/Fred Astaire dance numbers (or maybe it was even before, with Dick Powell and Ruby Keeler), I suddenly had a strong, even violent, desire to make films. Those dance numbers had a kind of sensual movement which really took hold of me, and I remember thinking I would like to make films which had the same effect upon people, that I wondered if I could find the equivalent of that exhilaration."
—Alain Resnais, quoted in David Thomson's "A Biographical Dictionary of Film"

"I like it when I can see that a film has a specific form—when it's not just a documantary slice of life. Even if the form is hidden, I like it when I can see that by working on it, you can get at an underlying structure that will make the film hold together. I like composers such as Alban Berg, who in "Lulu" and "Wozzeck" is working with fixed forms—they're not always visible in the presentation, but they provide an internal tension. It makes for hidden scaffolding and that's what I need to work with."
—Resnais, quoted in *Sight and Sound*, c. 1993.

Leni Riefenstahl

BORN: Helene Berta Amalie Riefenstahl in Berlin, Germany, 08/22/1902

DEATH: in Poecking, Bavaria, Germany, 09/08/2003

NATIONALITY: German

EDUCATION: Mary Wigmann School for Dance, Dresden, Germany; studied Russian ballet Jutta Klamt School for Dance, Berlin, Germany

AWARDS: German National Film Prize Award "Triumph of the Will" 1935; awarded by Joseph Goebbels

Paris World Exhibition Grand Prize Award "Triumph of the Will" 1937

German National Film Prize Award "Olympia" 1938

Venice Film Festival Grand Prize Award "Olympia" 1938

International Olympics Committee Award Diploma for the Gold Medal "Olympia" 1939

Art Directors Club Gold Medal "The Last of the Nuba" 1969

BIOGRAPHY

An undeniably brilliant filmmaker whose celebration of the Nazi Party in "Triumph of the Will" (1935) would prevent her from pursuing a post-World War II directing career, Leni Riefenstahl began as a dancer under the aegis of Max Reinhardt but happened to see one of Arnold Fanck's "mountain films" while convalescing from a career-ending knee injury. Her enthusiasm for this distinctively German genre, deemed analogous to the American Western, led her to become the only female member of his team, skiing and climbing as the star of a series of popular films, magnificently photographed on location and celebrating the most dramatic and grandiose kinds of beauty. Embodying an inflated spirit of heroic idealism, which went hand in hand with the growing Nazi fervor, Fanck pictures like "Peaks of Destiny" (1926), "The Big Leap" (1927), "The White Hell of Piz Palu" (1929) and "Avalanche" (1930) presented her as an intense naif, aspiring to the purity of the mountains, her incredible vitality a symbol of the new Germany.

Riefenstahl learned the fundamentals of mise-en-scene and the value of aerial shooting, among other film techniques, from Fanck, often finding herself involved in the camera work and collaborating with the directorial crew. She formed her own production company, Leni Riefenstahl Studio Films, in 1931 and made her directing and co-writing (with Hungarian film theorist Bela Belazs) debut, "The Blue Light" (1932), her personal favorite among her films and one that in hindsight seems to prefigure her artistic tragedy. Based on a folk tale about a mysterious blue light in the Italian Dolomites that lured young climbers to their death, it starred the director as Junta, an innocent child of nature thought to be a witch by local villagers for her ability to reach the light and survive. A visiting painter follows her to its source, discovers a grotto of precious crystals and reveals the secret to the villagers, who greedily remove the treasure. Climbing again, but without the crystals to guide her, Junta falls to her death. The director would have preferred to make the picture in the studio, but a shortage of funds obliged her to film on location and persuade the Dolomite peasants to appear as themselves (anticipating the methods of neo-realism by twenty years).

"The Blue Light" brought Riefenstahl critical acclaim and the attention of Adolf Hitler who invited her to shoot a documentary about the Nazi Party's annual rally at Nuremberg in 1933. "Victory of Faith" (1934), withdrawn after Hitler's purge of party leadership that year, never received a public viewing but earned her a return trip to Nuremberg for the next year's revelries,

resulting in the extraordinary "Triumph of the Will", arguably the most honest and compelling fruit of the fascist temperament. Riefenstahl has admitted that the carefully-orchestrated spectacle was stage-managed for her cameras, raising concerns that the filming process had actually shaped the rally and given it meaning, but her repeated claims that her effort was purely documentary, a work for hire, rings hollow since the film's mythos blatantly manipulates the viewer. Perhaps she knew only one way to tell the story with her background in the mountain films, but Hitler's arrival by air, through the endless vistas of clouds, evoked a god's descent to earth, setting the idolatrous tone for the entire movie. Her stirring assault on the pagan heartstrings, using all the tricks at her disposal (effective camera angles, moving shots and masterful editing), made it almost impossible to maintain perspective. Whether intended or not, it is the finest example of a propaganda film in the history of the medium.

The sheer relentless certainty of "Triumph of the Will", its utter lack of uncomposed shots, its refusal to risk any threat to visual order condemned Riefenstahl in the eyes of the world as an agent of the demagoguery, but she was hardly a cog in the propaganda machine of Joseph Goebbels, who was bitterly jealous of her success and influence with Hitler. She clearly had her own agenda and artist's integrity when, in defiance of Goebbels' orders to play down the accomplishments of "non-Aryan" athletes during the 1936 Berlin Olympics, she gave special prominence to the dominance of black American track star Jesse Owens in the most ambitious of her films, "Olympia" (1938), a two-part record of the games. Employing a team of 45 cameramen, Riefenstahl mounted cameras on steel towers, lifted them on balloons (prefiguring the blimp shots of today's sporting events), sunk them in trenches, floated them on rafts, and for the famous diving sequences had a cameraman specially trained as a diver to take the underwater shots. After the games were over, she spent a year and a half editing the 200 hours of film down to four hours of some of the most dazzling footage ever brought to the screen. A hymn of praise to physical strength and beauty (and to Hitler and his entourage), it struck many to be just as openly fascistic as "Triumph of the Will", but it remains a masterpiece undimmed by time, unsurpassed as a study of physical motion. A trimmed-down, propaganda-free version appeared in 1948 under the title "Kings of the Olympics."

When WWII began, she served briefly as a war correspondent, following the advancing German Army into Poland with a camera team, a fact that would come back to bite her later. (A damning photograph of Riefenstahl watching a massacre of Polish civilians in 1939 surfaced in the early 50s, published in a German illustrated weekly. During a 1952 inquiry in a West Berlin denazification court, requested by her, witnesses supported her claim that she had come upon the atrocity and tried to stop it at some risk to herself.) Refusing Goebbels' invitation to make propaganda films, she returned to the tradition of "The Blue Light", working on a non-musical version of Eugen d'Albert's opera "Tiefland", which starred the director as a poor girl ensnared by a powerful lowlander but rescued by a highland shepherd. An atmospheric and visually poetic drama, "Tiefland" was an affirmation of faith in simple people living close to nature. If she had finally recognized Nazi criminality and was attempting to recover her innocence through the project, she would discover there was no escaping the pervasive evil. Riefenstahl recruited gypsies from a concentration camp to dance with her in the opening scenes, unaware that their final destination would be Auschwitz. Goebbels stonewalled her on state financing, and there were constant interruptions during filming. She finally finished it in 1944 (apparently at the Barrandov Studios in Prague) but did not complete the editing for nearly a decade, releasing it in 1954.

Though Riefenstahl was never a member of the Nazi Party, her two great documentaries served Nazi ideology exceedingly well, and her technical virtuosity—use of automatic and hand-held cameras, jump-cuts and impressionistic sound effects—influenced later German newsreels and films by the German Army Propaganda Companies, many of whose members had worked as part of her "Olympia" team. For her contributions to the Third Reich, she spent nearly four years in American and French internment camps after the war, but the worst was yet to come. With the exception of "Tiefland" (which was already in the can) and the aborted "Black Cargo", a documentary about the slave trade in Africa, Riefenstahl has never made another film, her inability to raise financing leading her to a career as a still photographer instead. She would win acclaim for her pictures of the Mesakin Nuba tribe of the Sudan, cover the 1972 Munich Olympics for the London *Times* and was still going strong in her 90s, scuba diving and working on a deep-sea video reflecting her fascination with underwater themes. Indeed, timed to coincide with her 100th birthday was the release of "Underwater Impressions" (2002), a 45-minute film drawn from footage shot while scuba diving between 1974 and 2000.

Riefenstahl's talent was her tragedy. The directors of more politically objectionable films, like Veit Harlan, maker of the notorious "Jew Suss", went back to work in the postwar German film industry, but the genius that had finally won her the support of the traditionally anti-feminist Nazis may have alienated her from the male hierarchy of the modern Germany. There is no question of her political naivete during the Nazi years. The Berlin film critic Lotte Eisner reported how Riefenstahl once invited her to a luncheon with Hitler, despite the fact that the Nazi press had condemned her as a "Jewish Bolshevik", and one should never forget that she shot "Triumph of the Will", revealing her naked admiration for the Fuhrer, a year before the promulgation of the racial laws and four years before the Kristallnacht pogrom. She is fond of quoting a pro-Hitler comment allegedly made by Winston Churchill in the mid-30s, arguing that if Churchill could not foresee the horrors to come, how could she?

The Riefenstahl case addresses the relationship of art and accountability. For her part, she has claimed, "If an artist dedicates himself totally to his work, he cannot think politically," but where does a statement like that leave us? Ray Muller, director of "The Wonderful, Horrible Life of Leni Riefenstahl" (1995) observed, "I believe that she was purposefully blind not to look in the direction that would get her into trouble." She made her Faustian bargain with devils and rode the wave of opportunity, making two masterpieces that will forever be lauded for their artistry and condemned for their content, but when ol' Scratch called in the chits, she paid handsomely, relegated to her own little Hell on earth, separated from her first love, filmmaking.

She was able to reclaim a portion of her career in the 1960s when she lived with and photographed the Nuba, an African tribe she grew to adore, resulting in a critically acclaimed portrait of the tribespeople. She wrote three books, mainly photographic essays documenting the vanishing beauty of African people and cultures, from 1972 to 1997—possibly her best defense of accusations of harboring a racist philosophy—and she also learned to live with her infamous past. "I've never laughed so much as I did when living with the Nuba. I became reconciled with myself," she said. She next turned to underwater photography, diving in the Maldives, the Indian Ocean, the Red Sea, and off Papua New Guinea. She learned to dive when she was 72, lying about her age by 20 years to gain admittance to a class. Yet still her past haunted her: as late as 2002, Riefenstahl was investigated for Holocaust denial after she said she did not know that gypsies taken from concentration camps to be used as extras in one of her wartime films later died in the camps. Authorities eventually dropped the case, saying her comments did not rise to a prosecutable level. Despite the suspicions that hounded her, she was not embittered, defensive old woman, but rather a vigorous, soft-spoken and courteous nonagenarian who at age 1000 assembled a lengthy collection of underwater footage into one last documentary film, "Impressions Under Water" (2002), providing a fitting coda for her remarkable life. Prior to her death in 2003 at age 101, she said she hoped to be remembered simply as "an industrious woman who has worked very hard her whole life and has received much acknowledgment." —Written by Greg Senf

MILESTONES:

Raised in Berlin

Attracted attention of Max Reinhardt, who sent her on a tour of Europe in a program of modern dances of her own creation

1924: Knee injury ended her dancing career

1926: Signed contract with Arnold Fanck, playing a dancer turned climber in "Peaks of Destiny/The Holy Mountain"; co-starred opposite Luis Trenker

1927: Reteamed with Fanck and Trenker for "The Great Leap"

1929: Most popular mountain film with Fanck, "The White Hell of Piz Palu"

1930: First talkie, Fanck's "Avalanche"

1931: Founded own production company, Leni Riefenstahl Studio Films

1932: Film directing debut with "The Blue Light" (co-wrote with Bela Balazs)

1932: Met Adolf Hitler

1933: Last film with Fanck, "S.O.S. Iceberg"

1933: Appointed by Hitler as "film expert to the National Socialist Party"

1934: Asked by Hitler to film Nuremberg Nazi party rally, resulting in "Triumph of the Will" (1935)

1935: Made short documentary, "Day of Freedom", to celebrate the Wehrmacht (German army)

1936: Filmed Olympic Games in Berlin

1938: "Olympia", using footage of the 1936 Olympics released on Hitler's birthday (April 20)

1938: Made first trip to USA to promote "Olympia"; film did not find a US distributor

1939: Worked briefly as a war correspondent; followed advancing German army into Poland with a camera team

1940: Refused Goebbels' invitation to make propaganda films and began work on a non-musical version of Eugen d'Albert's opera "Tiefland"

1945–1948: Detained in American and French internment camps, undergoing denazification

1948: Trimmed-down (to an hour-and-a-half), propaganda-free version of "Olympia" released as "King of the Olympics"

1952: In response to a published picture of her watching the massacre of Polish civilians by German troops in 1939, requested an inquiry in a West Berlin denazification court; witnesses supported her claim that she had tried to end the atrocity at some risk to herself; incident had led her to withdraw from all war-oriented filmmaking

1954: Completed editing on and released "Tiefland" (shot between 1940 and 1944), her last film for almost 50 years

1955: Hollywood jury voted "Olympia" one of the ten finest motion pictures of all time

1956: Traveled to Africa to begin work on "Black Cargo", a documentary on the modern slave trade made on behalf of the London Anti-Slave Society; project came to an end after her serious injury in a car accident in Kenya; film ruined by incorrect laboratory procedures

Ostracized and denied a chance to continue filmmaking, turned to still photography

1962: Returned to Africa (the southern Sudan) to film and photograph the Mesakin Nuba tribe, living among them and recording their daily lives, their ceremonies and their athletic contests

1972: Commissioned by the London *Times* to photograph the Munich Olympics

1974: Honored at Telluride (Colorado) Film Festival; festival picketed by anti-Nazi groups

1974: Learned scuba diving; began taking a series of underwater photographs

1993: Subject of Ray Muller's documentary, "The Wonderful, Horrible Life of Leni Riefenstahl"

1995: Appeared as herself in "The Night of the Film-makers"

1997: First exhibit of her photography in postwar Germany (Hamburg); pointedly, there were no stills from "Triumph of the Will"

2000: Was injured in a plane crash in the Sudan; broke several ribs; was on visit attempting to reconnect with Nuba tribespeople she had met on previous visits

2002: Released first film in almost 50 years, "Underwater Impressions"; a 45-minute compilation of footage shot during scuba dives made between 1974 and 2000; release timed to coincide with her 100th birthday

QUOTES:

"I was thinking of this: in 'The Blue Light', I played the role of a child of nature who, on the nights of the full moon, climbed to the blue light, the image of an ideal, an aspiration dreamed of, a thing to which each being, above all when young, ardently desires to attain. Well, when her dream is destroyed Junta dies. I spoke of that as my destiny. For that is what was accomplished, much later, in me, after the war when everything collapsed on us, when I was deprived of all possibility of creatng. For art, creation—this is my life, and I was deprived of it. My life became a tissue of rumors and accusations through which I had to beat a path; they all revealed to be false, but for twenty years they deprived me of my creation. I tried to write, but what I wanted to do was make films.

"I tried to make films, but I couldn't. Everything was reduced to nothingness . . . at that moment I was dead."—Leni Riefenstahl, 1964 quote reprinted in Thomson's *A Biographical Dictionary Of Film*

BIBLIOGRAPHY:

"Behind the Scenes of the Reich Party Congress" Leni Riefenstahl, 1935

"Beauty in the Olympic Struggle" Leni Riefenstahl, 1937

"The Last of the Nuba" Leni Riefenstahl, 1968

"The People of Kau" Leni Riefenstahl, 1976

"Coral Gardens" Leni Riefenstahl, 1978

"Leni Riefenstahl and 'Olympia' " Cooper C. Graham, 1986, Scarecrow Press

"Leni Riefenstahl, A Memoir" Leni Riefenstahl, 1993, St. Martin's Press

"A Portrait of Leni Riefenstahl" Audrey Salkeld, 1996; biography; published in England

Marlon Riggs

BORN: Marlon Troy Riggs in Texas, 02/03/1957

DEATH: in Oakland, California, 04/05/1994

NATIONALITY: American

EDUCATION: Harvard University, Cambridge, Massachusetts, BA

University of California at Berkeley, Berkeley, California, MA, 1982

AWARDS: Emmy "Ethnic Notions: Portraits of Prejudice"

Peabody Award "Color Adjustment"

Los Angeles Film Critics Association Award Best Independent/Experimental Film "Tongues Untied" 1990

Sundance Film Festival Filmmakers Trophy (Documentary) "Black Is . . . Black Ain't" 1995

American Film Institute Maya Deren Award 1992

BIOGRAPHY

Fiercely proud black gay filmmaker, teacher, writer and activist, one of the most distinctive, inventive voices in documentary and experimental video of the 1980s and 90s.

Beginning to make documentaries in 1982 after finishing a master's degree at UC, Berkeley, Riggs first gained attention with an award-winning made-for-TV documentary, "Ethnic Notions: Portraits of Prejudice" (1987). "Ethnic Notions" focused particularly on the construction of what is connoted by contemporary African-American identity. Riggs points out how deeply routed strategies in American culture, specifically the creation of stereotypes, have fueled anti-black sentiment on both local and national levels. He continued such investigations in "Color Adjustment" (1991), his important, reflexive documentary on the history of black representation in mainstream TV. Here Riggs potently critiqued both the more obviously racist traditions of portraying humble and/or stupid people of African descent as well as more recent, blandly liberal yet compromised attempts to speak to the diversity of contemporary black life. Interviews and footage are regularly punctuated with the question, "Is this a positive image?", as the film ultimately suggests that issues of representation and racism are more complex than has generally been acknowledged, and that the problem of mass media imaging cannot be reduced to a dichotomy of "good image" vs. "bad image." Probably Riggs' best-known, most important and most controversial work, though, is his landmark "Tongues Untied" (1989), a bold mixed-mode work which combined documentary with political essay, memoir, satire, and performance pieces including poetry and dance. Riggs angrily suggests that contemporary identity politics wants him to be either black or gay, but not both at the same time. Furthermore, Riggs examines both the homophobia of the black community and the racism of queer folk. Highlights of the video include the hilarious lesson in "Snap!thology", the means of communication and commentary via finger-snapping used especially among gay men of color, and the problematic yet deliberately provocative final catchphrase, "Black men loving black men is the revolutionary act." Highly acclaimed in many quarters, and the work that confirmed Riggs' status in experimental film and video circles, "Tongues Untied" became a site of struggle between gay activists and other liberal groups on the one hand and conservative religious and political organizations on the other with respect to both airings on PBS stations nationwide and its status as a work supported by a $5,000 grant from the National Endowment of the Arts. Footage from the film—especially scenes of nudity or representations of queer subcultures such as drag and SM—has in fact been recycled without copyright permission in the lobbying films and advertisement of anti-gay movements nationwide.

Other films Riggs made were less ambitious than "Tongues Untied" but continued with his interests in articulating the lives of black gay men and arguing for the importance of their perspective. "Non, je ne regrette rien/No Regrets" (1992) was a relatively simple short film which again used music and poetry, this time to examine more specifically the lives of black gay men living with HIV or full-blown AIDS. Some of the film's most powerful moments, however, came in the form of interviewed disclosures from a variety of men living with the disease. "Anthem" (1992), meanwhile, was a more experimental short film which again used explicit imagery in forcefully arguing for the validity of the black gay man as an American citizen, most memorably with shots of black gay male couples embracing before the American flag as the national anthem is played. Riggs was also an educator of note, becoming one of the youngest people ever to receive tenure in the arts and humanities at the University of California at Berkeley.—Written by David Lugowski

MILESTONES:

1982: Began making documentary films after graduating from Harvard

1987: Gained prominence with his made-for-TV documentary, "Ethnic Notions: Portraits of Prejudice"

1994: Was working on "Black Is . . . Black Ain't" at the time of his death

Guy Ritchie

BORN: Guy Stuart Ritchie in Hatfield, Hertfordshire, England, 1968

NATIONALITY: English

EDUCATION: Stanbridge Earls School, Romsey, Hampshire, England; expelled from private preparatory school for allegedly snorting speed on sports day; last in a series of more than 10 schools, both public and private

received a GCSE (General Certificate of Secondary Education) in film studies

AWARDS: Tokyo International Film Festival Best Director "Lock, Stock and Two Smoking Barrels" 1998

BAFTA Orange Audience Award "Lock, Stock and Two Smoking Barrels" 1999

MTV Movie Award Best New Filmmaker "Lock, Stock and Two Smoking Barrels" 1999

BIOGRAPHY

Though he may have enjoyed cultivating his image as a boy from the wrong side of the tracks, British filmmaker Guy Ritchie was actually the son of successful advertising executive John Ritchie and, after his parents divorced, spent much of his youth at the 17th-century home of his baronet stepfather, Sir Michael Leighton. His dyslexia made school a tough proposition, and he managed only a GCSE (General Certificate of Secondary Education) in film studies, knocking about as a laborer until finally setting his sights on a filmmaking career at age 25. Beginning as a film runner, he branched into directing music videos, doing "20 videos back to back, really crappy ones with sort of German rave bands" his first year. He may have abhorred the music, but he learned a lot about the camera and moved on to helm a couple commercials before directing a 20-minute short, "The Hard Case" (1995). When it aired on Channel 4, it caught the eye of Sting, whose wife Trudie Styler would serve as an executive producer of his 1998 feature directing debut, "Lock, Stock and Two Smoking Barrels." (Sting would make a cameo appearance.)

Possessing style to spare, Ritchie's glamorization of the tawdry world of East End crooks became one of that year's biggest home-grown successes in the United Kingdom, second only to "Sliding Doors", starring Gwyneth Paltrow. Though it didn't fare as well in the USA, it was not for lack of humor or plot twists that kept the clever caper movie from running out of steam in the final act. Ritchie scripted some wonderful characters with Damon Runyonesque names like Hatchet Harry (P.H. Moriarty), Barry the Baptist (Harry's "muscle" played by the late bare knuckles champion Lenny McLean) and Big Chris, a deadpan hitman essayed with panache by British soccer bad boy Vinnie Jones. He also wisely chose to play some of the most vicious acts of violence off camera, showing the ramifications while effectively distancing the viewer from the bloodshed. His accomplished first picture made him one of the hottest young directors around and earned Sony's backing for his second film, "Snatch" (2000), a return to the same colorful gangland milieu that featured Brad Pitt. Ritchie also co-scripted and produced that year's "Lock, Stock and Four Stolen Hooves", the pilot for the seven-part British TV series version of "Lock, Stock and Two Smoking Barrels" (for Channel 4).

Once Ritchie married and fathered a son with the decade-older multimedia megastar Madonna, an on-screen collaboration seemed inevitable. The couple started with baby steps, teaming for the stylish music video for her hit song "What It Feels Like for a Girl" and, later, the fast-paced and funny short film "Star", part of a five-episode series of car-oriented vignettes featured on the website for automaker BMW. The married duo finally hit the big screen together in 2002 when Ritchie directed his wife in the romantic comedy "Swept Away", a remake of Lina Wertmuller's 1974 Italian film of the same title, in which Madonna plays a spoiled rich woman marooned on a deserted island with a spirited sailor (Adriano Gainnini).

COMPANIONS:

Rebecca Green. Born c. 1974; daughter of British tycoon Michael Green; her parents reportedly financed "The Hard Case", his short film that became his calling card for "Lock, Stock and Two Smoking Barrels"

wife: Madonna. Singer, actor; involved from c. 1999; met through Trudie Styler, wife of pop star Sting and an executive producer on "Lock, Stock and Two Smoking Barrels"; previously married to actor Sean Penn; has daughter with former beau Carlos Leon; mother of Ritchie's son Rocco; married on December 22, 2000 in Scotland

MILESTONES:

Split time between Fulham and Hatfield until parents divorced

Following parents' divorce, spent much of his youth at Loton Park, the 17th-century home of his baronet stepfather, Sir Michael Leighton

After washing out of Standbridge Earls School at age 15, worked at Island Records

Began working construction jobs at age 17

1993: Got job as a runner for Soho film producers (date approximate)

Directed about 20 music videos as well as a few commercials

1995: Made 20-minute short film, "The Hard Case"

1998: Debut feature as writer-director, "Lock, Stock and Two Smoking Barrels"; first film with producing partner, Matthew Vaughn; a friend of Ritchie's had aroused Vaughn's interest by lying that he had collaborated with playwright Peter Shaffer on the "Lock, Stock" script

2000: Co-wrote and produced "Lock, Stock and Four Stolen Hooves", the pilot for seven-part British TV series "Lock, Stock and Two Smoking Barrels", based on the feature; aired on Channel 4

2000: Arrested May 17 for alledgedly assaulting a man outside the $2.7 million mansion he was renting with his girlfriend Madonna, who was five months pregnant at the time

2000: Follow-up feature, "Snatch", with much of the "Lock, Stock" cast (i.e., Jason Flemying, Vinnie Jones, Jason Statham) and Brad Pitt, released in Britain; on the strength of his debut, Sony committed to film without reading a script; co-produced with Vaughn

2001: Helmed Madonna's music video "What It Feels Like for a Girl"

2001: Directed "Star", one of five short film advertisements for BMW shown over the Internet at bmwfilms.com; Madonna had featured role

2002: Directed "Swept Away", a remake of the Italian film starring Madonna

QUOTES:

About getting "Lock, Stock and Two Smoking Barrels" made: "Financing was extremely difficult. We very nearly gave up, because we got the money pulled from us four days before shooting, and that was a blow I was hardly capable of bearing. Especially after all the other blows that we'd had running up to that period. So we got left with 200-grand's worth of debts and everyone hated us, you know, and we couldn't show our faces in public for a month. We got shat on from a great height, and consequently all the people who'd been working for us out of the goodness of their hearts and without payment got shat on as well. But we finally got it together."—Guy Ritchie to *Neon*, January 1999.

"There's nothing I enjoy more than a good story about a villain; people on the wrong side of the law are highly entertaining. Maybe it's because they're not conforming; they're doing what we're all sensibly scared to do. The whole job of intimidation is when to be funny and when not. These guys are actors; they know how to put on a show."—Ritchie quoted in *Los Angeles Times*, January 23, 1999.

"I think English filmmaking has always been a bit up its own ass. It traditionally has just lacked entertainment. Apart from people like David Lean, I think English filmmaking has always been better-suited for the TV rather than the cinema—and I wanted to spice things up a bit."—Guy Ritchie to Juan Morales in *Detour*, March 1999.

"I wanted to make a film that would appeal to the blue-collar man. In London we call it 'the man on the terraces', for the cheap row of seats at a football game. I worked on building sites and found their humor electrically sharp.

"The established filmmakers patronize these guys, but they're very sophisticated in their humor. So I wanted to make something complicated that would stand up to scrutiny but appeal to the working man.

"I know a lot of villains and policemen who liked it, and then it crossed over to the intelligentsia."—Ritchie to Stephen Schaefer in *Boston Herald*, March 14, 1999.

On the press' coverage of him: "The only thing that really pisses me off is that so much of this stuff is lazy. There was no journalism involved. Everyone just copied everyone else. Once they'd done the 'Cockney Toff' angle, they got stuck. There was nowhere else for them to go. And people copy each other's mistakes. They just go on and on uncorrected. I mean, I've never claimed that I 'lived in the East End for 30 years'. Before you know it, there's a profile of your whole life that is largely fictional. I'm not losing any sleep over it one way or the other."—Ritchie

to Neil Norman in London's *Evening Standard*, May 22, 2000.

"I'd like to say I don't care what critics think, but they insidiously manage to work their way into your psyche . . . "—Ritchie *Movieline* October 2002.

"It made communication on the set that much more efficient because you'd have dinner with her and you could talk about something . . . then you wake up in the morning and you can talk and before you knew it when you go on the set you knew exactly what you were doing. It's all about communication, filmmaking . . . " —Ritchie on working with his wife, Madonna.

Jacques Rivette

BORN: Pierre Louis Rivette in Rouen, France, 03/01/1928

NATIONALITY: French

EDUCATION: Lycee Corneille, Rouen, France

AWARDS: Cannes Film Festival Grand Prix "La Belle Noiseuse" 1991

Los Angeles Film Critics Association Award Best Foreign Film "La Belle Noiseuse" 1991

BIOGRAPHY

Although Francois Truffaut has written that the New Wave began "thanks to Rivette," the films of this masterful French director are not well known. Rivette, like his *Cahiers Du Cinema* colleagues Truffaut, Jean-Luc Godard, Claude Chabrol and Eric Rohmer, did graduate to filmmaking but, like Rohmer, was something of a late bloomer as a director. He made two shorts ("Aux quatre coins" 1949 and "Le Quadrille" 1950, starring Jean-Luc Godard); in the mid-1950s he served as an assistant to Jean Renoir and Jacques Becker; and in 1958 he was, along with Chabrol, the first of the five to begin

production on a feature-length film. Without the financial benefit of a producer, Rivette took to the streets with his friends, a 16mm camera, and film stock purchased on borrowed money. It was only, however, after the commercial success of Truffaut's "The 400 Blows", Resnais' "Hiroshima, mon amour" and Godard's "Breathless" that the resulting film, the elusive, intellectual, and somewhat lengthy (135 minutes) "Paris nous appartient", saw its release in 1960.

In retrospect, Rivette's debut sketched out the path which all his subsequent films would follow; "Paris Nous Appartient" was a monumental undertaking for the critic-turned-director, with some 30 actors (including Chabrol, Godard and Jacques Demy), almost as many locations, and an impenetrably labyrinthine narrative.

His next film, the considerably more commercial "La Religieuse" (1965), was an adaptation of the Diderot novel which Rivette had staged in 1963. The least characteristic of all his features, it was also his first and only commercial success, becoming a "success de scandale" when the government blocked its release for a year.

Rivette's true talents first made themselves

visible during the fruitful period, 1968–74. During this time he directed the 4-hour "L'Amour fou" (1968), the now legendary 13-hour "Out 1" (made for French TV in 1971 but never broadcast; edited to a 4-hour feature and retitled "Out 1: Spectre," 1972), and the 3-hour "Celine and Julie Go Boating" (1973), his most entertaining and widely seen picture. In these three films, Rivette began to construct what has come to be called his "House of Fiction"—an enigmatic filmmaking style influenced by the work of Louis Feuillade and involving improvisation, ellipsis and considerable narrative experimentation.

Unfortunately, Rivette seems to have no place in contemporary cinema. On the one hand, his work is considered too inaccessible for theatrical distribution; on the other, although his revolutionary theories have influenced figures such as Jean-Marie Straub & Danielle Huillet and Chantal Akerman, he is deemed too commercial to be accepted by the underground cinema; he still employs a narrative and uses "name" actors such as Jean-Pierre Leaud, Juliet Berto, Anna Karina and Maria Schneider.

Since "Celine and Julie," Rivette's career has been as mysterious as one of his plots. In 1976 he received an offer to make a series of four films, "Les Filles du feu." "Duelle" (1976), the first entry, received such negative response that the second, "Noroit" (1976)—which some critics call his greatest picture—was held from release. The final two installments (one of which was due to star Leslie Caron and Albert Finney) were never filmed. The 1980s proved no kinder. He made five films, but only one of them, 1984's "Love on the Ground", opened in the US (it received disastrous reviews). The 90s, though, did witness the successful American release of his haunting four-hour meditation on the artistic vocation, "La Belle noiseuse" (1991). Although he continued to be an innovative and challenging artist, Rivette failed to find the type of audience that contributed to the commercial success of his New Wave compatriots.

MILESTONES:

Moved to Paris in late 1940s; began voraciously consuming films at the Cinematheque Francaise, alongside other future New Wavers Jean-Luc Godard, Claude Chabrol, Francois Truffaut and Eric Rohmer; began reviewing films for the *Gazette du Cinema*

1949: Amatuer short film directing debut, "Aux quatre coins" (20 min, silent, 16 mm)

1950: Made second short film, "Le quadrille", which starred Godard

1952: Began writing for *Cahiers Du Cinema* upon its founding, along with Godard, Chabrol et al.

1956: Directed first 35mm film, "Le coup du berger" (28 min.)

1957: Without a producer, began shooting first feature, "Paris nous appartient/Paris Belongs to Us" (also the first feature begun by a member of the New Wave proper); released 1961

1963–1965: Served as editor-in-chief of *Cahiers du Cinema*

1971: Completed the 13-hour film for French TV, "Out One," which was never broadcast (the following year it was released in a four-hour version, edited down by Rivette)

1976: Made first two ("Duelle" and "Noroit") of planned four-film series "Les filles du feu"; subsequent two films cancelled

1993: Rewowrked footage shot (but much of it not used) for "La Belle Noiseuse" into another, considerably different, feature film, "Divertimento"

BORN: in New Mexico, 1957

SOMETIMES CREDITED AS:
M. Jay Roach

NATIONALITY: American

EDUCATION: Stanford University, Stanford, California, BA
   University of Southern California, Los Angeles, California, film production, MFA

AWARD: People's Choice Award Favorite Comedy Motion Picture "Meet the Parents" 2001

BIOGRAPHY

Jay Roach made his feature directorial debut with the "Austin Powers: International Man of Mystery" (1997), which united the suave glamour of a James Bond film with the sharp silliness of a Peter Sellers vehicle. A fun summer movie, it received decent reviews and box office returns, but proved a greater success on home video, where it became a big seller and repeatedly viewed cult classic. Written by and starring comedic actor Mike Myers, the film opened with a truly inspired musical romp on a swinging 60s Carnaby Street, introducing popular ladies man Austin Powers (Myers), a fashion photographer with a sideline as a secret agent. After a thirty-year deep freeze Powers finds himself thawed out in the 1990s, a time with a cautious climate entirely different from the groovy free love haven he is accustomed to. It is a world which nevertheless needs this bumbling spy's aid against perennial archvillain Dr. Evil (also played by Myers), a comparably out-of-touch cryogenics experiment. Roach employed much of the jumpy stylistic editing so popular in 60s cinema and also used appropriately garish Technicolor hues in scenery and costumes. The quick

and sometimes unsteady pace of the cartoonish "Austin Powers" at once parodied and celebrated movie effects of yore, particularly those so routinely practiced in the self-consciously hip swinging spy films of that era.

The New Mexico native who trained at USC was tapped to helm the 1999 time travel follow-up, "Austin Powers II: The Spy Who Shagged Me", where secret agent Powers returns to the 1960s only to find that the square sensibilities of his adopted 1990s world have affected his attitude and diminished his appeal. Similar in theme and style to its predecessor, this film was an even more over-the-top affair, super stylized, unabashedly mad and just behind "Star Wars: Episode I—The Phantom Menace" as an eagerly awaited summer film. Released that same year to much less hype was "Mystery, Alaska", also directed by Roach. This compelling story of a quietly scandalous small town and its local hockey team's face off with the New York Rangers was both penned and produced by David E. Kelley. Starring Russell Crowe and Mary McCormack, the film was poignantly funny, atmospheric and understated, a far cry from Roach's outrageous "Austin Powers" work, proving the director's versatility.

Roach's reputation as an agile director made him a pretty hot Hollywood property, with 1999 developing projects including a film adaptation of *MAD* magazine's popular "Spy vs. Spy" comic strip and the Universal/Dreamworks comedy "Meet the Parents." Most promising was his proposed film adaptation of Douglas Adams' popular comedic sci-fi adventure novel "The Hitchhiker's Guide to the Galaxy" (already adapted into a BBC radio series and a PBS miniseries). Starting with source material already held as a cult favorite, and working closely with novelist Adams doing double duty as executive producer and screenwriter, Roach's vision promised to maintain the novel's integrity. The film would no doubt win over genre fans, and hoped to capture a wider audience.—Written by Jane O'Donnell

COMPANION:

wife: Susanna Hoffs. Musician, actor; born c. 1969; formerly with the group The Bangles

MILESTONES:

While at USC, student film "Asleep at the Wheel" was nominated for a student Academy Award

1991: Served as consultant to director Jessi Wells on the feature "Zoo Radio"

1993: Worked with producer Pen Densham as co-producer and writer of the short-lived CBS sci-fi series "Space Rangers"

1993: Was co-producer of the Fox TV-movie "Lifepod", a sci-fi remake of Alfred Hitchcock's "Lifeboat"

1994: Wrote the story for the feature film "Blown Away", co-produced by Densham

1996: Produced "The Empty Mirror", a psychodrama examining Adolf Hitler; also worked as second unit director (released theatrically in 1999)

1997: Feature directorial debut, the zany hit spoof "Austin Powers: International Man of Mystery", starring Mike Myers

1999: Helmed the sequel "Austin Powers II: The Spy Who Shagged Me"

1999: Directed "Mystery, Alaska", a hockey-themed film starring Russell Crowe and Mary McCormack

2000: Enjoyed success with "Meet the Parents", a comedy starring Robert De Niro and Ben Stiller

Attached to direct the film adaptation of Douglas Adams' popular comic sci-fi novel "The Hitchhiker's Guide to the Galaxy"

Alain Robbe-Grillet

BORN: in Brest, France, 08/18/1922

NATIONALITY: French

EDUCATION: Institut National Agronomique, France, 1944

AWARDS: Feneon Prize "Les Gnomes" 1954 literary award

Prix des Critiques "Le Voyeur" 1955 literary award

Prix Louis Delluc "L'Immortelle" 1963

BIOGRAPHY

A leading figure of the French Nouveau Roman ("New Novel") movement of the late 1950s, Robbe-Grillet wrote the screenplay for Alain Resnais' labyrinthine "Last Year at Marienbad" (1961) which incorporated many of the characteristic features of his novels: an undermining of chronological and narrative structure; an "objective" style supposedly free from authorial involvement; an investigation of the nature of memory and repetition; and a stylized eroticism. The film remains a landmark of European art cinema. Robbe-Grillet made his directorial debut with "L'Immortelle" (1963) and continued to navigate similar thematic and stylistic terrain, though to decreasingly innovative and successful effect. His introduction to the published screenplay of "Last Year at Marienbad" raised interesting theoretical questions on the differences between the novel and the film as media.

COMPANION:

wife: Catherine Robbe-Grillet. Married in October 1957; appeared in "Trans-Europ-Express"

MILESTONES:

1945–1948: Served as charge de mission at Institut National des Statistiques

Was agricultural engineer with the Institut des Fruits et Agrumes Coloniaux; worked in Morocco, French Guinea, Martinique and Guadeloupe

1954—Present: Served as literary advisor to Editions de Minuit, Paris

1961: First screenplay, "Last Year at Marienbad"

1963: Made directorial debut with "L'Immortelle"; also scripted

1966: With wife, appeared in "Trans-Europ-Express"; also directed and scripted

1983: Directed last feature to date, "La belle captive/The Beautiful Prisoner"

QUOTES:

Named an Officer of the Order of Merit

Named Chevalier in the Legion of Honor

Tim Robbins

BORN: Timothy Francis Robbins in West Covina, California, 10/16/1958

NATIONALITY: American

EDUCATION: Stuyvesant High School, New York, New York, 1976

State University of New York, Plattsburgh, Plattsburgh, New York; transferred to UCLA

University of California at Los Angeles, Los Angeles, California, theater; graduated with honors

studied with French actor Georges Bigot at Theatre du Soleil after graduation from college

AWARDS: Cannes Film Festival Best Actor Award "The Player" 1992

Golden Globe Award Best Actor in a Motion Picture (Musical or Comedy) "The Player" 1992

Berlin Film Festival Ecumenical Jury Prize "Dead Man Walking" 1996

Berlin Film Festival Prize of Guild of German Art House Cinemas "Dead Man Walking" 1996

Humanitas Prize feature film "Dead Man Walking" 1996

CableACE Award Best Entertainment-Cultural Documentary Special "The Typewriter, the Rifle and the Movie Camera" 1996; shared award; Robbins served as executive producer

Sundance Film Festival Piper-Heidsieck Tribute to Vision Award 1997

National Board of Review Special Achievement in Filmmaking Prize "Cradle Will Rock" 1999

BIOGRAPHY

The son of folk-singer Gil Robbins, actor-writer-director Tim Robbins came of age on the LSD-drenched streets of NYC's Greenwich Village, caught between 60s psychedelia and the Pope. "My parents were by no stretch of the imagination bohemians or hippies or anything like that. We were Catholics, and I grew up in a very structured, rigid environment. I mean, they were open-minded, yes—but I went to Catholic school." Robbins longed to play first base for the New York Mets, relishing their surprising 1969 World Championship, but at the age of 12 he followed his older sister on a less conventional path, catching the acting bug with the Theater for the New City, an avant-garde company that performed on city streets. Following his graduation (with honors) from UCLA, he co-founded The Actors' Gang (serving as artistic director until 1997) and was soon co-writing (with Adam Simon) original pieces for the Gang, culminating in a satire of Christian fundamentalism, "Carnage", which played Off-Broadway at the New York Shakespeare Festival in 1989.

The lanky Robbins made his TV debut opposite Helen Hunt in the movie "Quarterback Princess" (CBS, 1983) and landed a small role in a Martin Scorsese–directed episode of Steven Spielberg's "Amazing Stories" entitled "Mirror, Mirror" (NBC, 1986). Following his feature debut in "No Small Affair" (1984), he delivered a memorable turn as the show tune-singing driver in Rob Reiner's "The Sure Thing" (1985), cultivating a lasting association with that film's star John Cusack, before showing up on the periphery of the blockbuster "Top Guns" (1986). His first lead, ominously, was in the notorious flop "Howard the Duck" (also 1986), but the lucky actor survived it to work again, playing Jodie Foster's former boyfriend who protects her from a twisted John Turturro in the unheralded, eccentric, early-60s civil rights drama "Five Corners" (1987), scripted by John Patrick Shanley. He also reteamed with Cusack as a reluctant video director for "Tapeheads" (1988), a picture which marked his first songwriting credit.

The turning point in his career—and life— was also the fulfillment of a lifelong dream. His role as the goofy, garter-wearing 'Nuke' LaLoosh, the baseball innocent coached by Kevin Costner and Susan Sarandon in Ron Shelton's "Bull Durham" (also 1988), allowed him to show off his pitching prowess, throwing a fastball clocked at the very respectable major-league speed of 85 miles per hour ("But I had absolutely no control"). Robbins met Sarandon at the audition in Los Angeles, and the pair began a relationship during filming that has endured to date. If the film had one downside, it was in creating a misconception of him as a sort of male bimbo, an image he would eventually dispel after marking time with "Miss Firecracker" and Terry Jones' comedy "Eric the Viking" (both 1989) and stealing the show from the manic Robin Williams in "Cadillac Man" (1990). He broke through once again as a tormented Vietnam veteran in the spooky "Jacob's Ladder" (1990) and then played the first of his self-styled "trilogy of assholes", the racist boss in Spike Lee's "Jungle Fever" (1991).

With his soft, unthreatening looks and easy manner, Robbins can make a killer seem sympathetic, which he managed to do in Robert Altman's "The Player" (1992), As insecure studio executive Griffin Mill, a modern-day Faust, he smiled calmly while his colleagues dropped like flies and he climbed over their Armani-clad corpses to the top of the back-lot heap. His deceptively wicked performance earned best actor awards from both Cannes and the Golden Globes. Starring in his feature directorial/screenwriting debut, the "mockumentary" "Bob Roberts" (1992), he portrayed a right-wing, folk-singing senatorial candidate, spouting sound-bite local yokelisms and creating a frighteningly real portrait of a perfectly respectable, profoundly crooked politician ("That was probably the work I'm most proud of"). Reteaming with Altman for "Short Cuts" (1993), a resetting of Raymond Carver's collection of short stories, Robbins provided much of the humor with his somewhat caricatured portrayal of an egocentric Los Angeles cop. However, his third film with Altman, the fashion industry comedy "Ready to Wear (Pret-a-Porter)" (1994), earned the director some of the most scathing reviews of his career.

In 1994, Robbins let his gawky charm work overtime as an idealistic bumpkin who unwittingly becomes a corporate stooge in the Coen brothers' stab at mainstream accessibility, "The Hudsucker Proxy", and also tried his hand at a romantic lead (to mixed reviews) opposite Meg Ryan in "I.Q.", but in "The Shawshank Redemption" he gave a low-key and exquisitely modulated performance that was easily his best of the year. His tour-de-force portrayal of the mild-mannered, unjustly imprisoned banker, coupled with that of Morgan Freeman playing the seasoned lifer who befriends him, significantly elevated the well-crafted but overly long and somewhat predictable jailhouse drama adapted from a novella by Stephen King.

Chaos, the production company Robbins formed in 1993 bore its first fruit with the death penalty drama "Dead Man Walking" (1995). For this true story, the sophomore director used the same director of photography (Roger Deakins) who had so effectively captured prison life for "The Shawshank Redemption." Sarandon played a nun acting as spiritual counselor to a death row murderer (Sean Penn) and took home the Best Actress Oscar. Though the film was ostensibly a plea against the death penalty, Robbins' treatment of the subject matter was so even-handed that many capital punishment advocates believed the director was in their camp. For his efforts, he garnered a well-deserved Best Director Academy Award nomination and proved that his relationship with Sarandon could easily survive "six horrible days" incurred during filming.

Just as people were thinking he was too serious, Robbins crossed them up with his next acting project, starring opposite Martin Lawrence in the buddy-pic "Nothing to Lose" (1997). As a hotshot advertising executive gone 'round the bend, he turned the tables on Lawrence's carjacker by taking him hostage. Unfortunately, audiences found "Nothing to Lose" nothing to laugh at, and the Steve Oedekerk film fizzled at the box office. After an 18-month hiatus to concentrate on fatherhood, Robbins was back on the screen in 1999, contributing a cameo as the President in "Austin Powers II: The Spy Who Shagged Me" and once again exploring his dark side in "Arlington Road", a thriller echoing the Oklahoma City bombing and raising hard questions about domestic terrorism.

Robbins came by his political conscience honestly enough, inheriting it from his peace and civil-rights activist father. He remembered his sister getting arrested for protesting the Vietnam War and his parents telling him, "It took courage for your sister to do this." In keeping with his sense of social responsibility, his third time in the director's chair, "Cradle Will

Rock" (1999), resulted in his most ambitious film to date, a deeply felt homage to a time when passionate commitment, not dreams of profit or celebrity, drove artistic activity. Taking the Federal Theater's polemical 1936 musical drama "The Cradle Will Rock" as a starting point, Robbins evoked the dynamic cultural landscape during a tumultuous and exciting period. Though it may have erred in its tendency toward caricature when portraying certain famous individuals, "Cradle Will Rock" was that rare Hollywood-backed venture, a $32 million picture about committed people and a testament to Robbins' will to make movies that ran counter to the mainstream. After the triumph—artistically if not commercially—of "Cradle," Robbins eased into a succession of character roles in mid-level movies, playing an astronaut in Brian de Palma's "Mission to Mars" (2000), a Bill Gates-esque software manufacturer in the thriller "Antitrust" (2001) and a scientist who discovers a feral man in the off-kilter comedy "Human Nature" (2002). He also reassumed the reigns at the Actors' Gang, returning as artistic director in 2001 and spearheading a renewed, ambitious production schedule that frequently employed his many talents: he directed a new production of "Mephisto," starred with Helen Hunt in the Los Angeles production of the 9/11-themed play "The Guys" and saw a revival of "Alagazam," a play he co-wrote with Adam Simon. When he returned to acting on the big screen in a mainstream project—Jonathan Demme's "Charade" remake "The Truth About Charlie" (2002)—it was also as a supporting player, stepping into the calculating role of Mr. Bartholomew, in which he freely and gleefully borrowed from Walter Matthau's original characterization, defying Demme's edict not to reference the original film.

FAMILY:

father: Gil Robbins. Folk singer, publishing executive; ran the Gaslight, a nightclub and cafe; member of the folk group The Highwaymen, joining them one year after their 1961 Number 1 hit "Michael" (aka "Michael Row Your Boat Ashore"); acted in son's "Bob Roberts", "Dead Man Walking" and "Cradle Will Rock"

COMPANION:

Susan Sarandon. Actor; co-starred in "Bull Durham" (1988); also appeared in the Robbins-directed "Bob Roberts" (1992) and won an Oscar under his direction for "Dead Men Walking" (1995)

MILESTONES:

1960: Family moved to Greenwich Village in NYC

1967: First acting experience at age nine, playing St. Peter in Catholic school play (date approximate)

1970: Joined the Theater for the New City by age 12 (date approximate)

1981: Co-founded with a group of fellow UCLA students and (until 1997) served as artistic director of The Actors' Gang, a theater troupe based in Los Angeles

1983: Made TV-movie debut in CBS' "Quarterback Princess"

1984: Film acting debut, "No Small Affair"

1985: Wrote and filmed an early version of "Bob Roberts" for NBC's "Saturday Night Live"

1985: Played Joseph Cotton in TV-movie "Malice in Wonderland" (CBS)

1986: First feature lead in the disastrous "Howard the Duck", produced and disowned by George Lucas

1988: Breakthrough role as 'Nuke' LaLoosh in Ron Shelton's baseball comedy "Bull Durham", which introduced him to significant other Susan Sarandon

1988: Acted opposite John Cusack in the energetic but pretentious "Tapeheads"; also wrote the song "Repave Amerika", which would later find its way into "Bob Roberts"

1989: First time headlining a feature as the

eponymous "Erik the Viking", directed by Terry Jones

1989: Co-wrote and directed The Actors Gang in "Carnage" at NYC's New York Shakespeare Festival, Public Theater

1990: Played crazed, simple-minded cuckholded husband who takes everyone hostage in a car dealership in "Cadillac Man", starring Robin Williams

1990: Starred as the troubled Vietnam veteran of the underrated "Jacob's Ladder"

1992: Solidified standing as a leading actor in Hollywood playing the murderous Hollywood excutive in Robert Altman's satirical "The Player"; first of three films with Altman

1992: Borrowed Altman's director of photography, Jean Lepine, for feature directorial debut, "Bob Roberts"; starred as titular character; also wrote the script and all the songs (a nod to his father Gil)

1992: First radio play, "Mayhem: The Invasion" for L.A. Theater Works

1993: Formed Chaos Productions

1993: Reteamed with Altman for "Short Cuts"

1994: Made third film with Altman "Ready to Wear (Pret-a-Porter)"

1994: Changed production company name from Chaos to Havoc Inc.

1994: Was perfectly cast as the wide-eyed patsy of the Coen brothers' extravagant "The Hudsucker Proxy"

1994: Delivered a tour de force performance in "The Shawshank Redemption", based on a novella by Stephen King

1995: Earned Oscar nomination as Best Director for "Dead Man Walking", which won Sarandon the Best Actress Oscar

1996: Executive produced, hosted, narrated and served as interviewer for "The Typewriter, the Rifle and the Movie Camera", the Independent Film Channel's documentary on iconoclastic filmmaker Sam Fuller

1997: Played a hotshot advertising executive who goes on a rampage in Steve Oedekerk's "Nothing to Lose"

1999: Contributed cameo as the President in "Austin Powers II: The Spy Who Shagged Me"

1999: Starred opposite Jeff Bridges in "Arlington Road", a thriller echoing the Oklahoma City bombing and raising hard questions about domestic terrorism

1999: Directed "Cradle Will Rock"; marked his fifth collaboration with Cusack; Sarandon portrayed Margherita Sarfatti, Mussolini's emissary and former mistress

2000: Acted in Brian De Palma's "Mission to Mars"

2001: Portrayed a billionaire software manufacturer in the thriller "Antitrust"

2001: Teamed with Patricia Arquette as a scientist who discovers a feral man in "Human Nature"; premiered at Cannes; released theatrically in USA in 2002

2001: Resumed position as artistic director of the Actors' Gang Theater; directed new production of "Mephisto"

2002: Directed the CBS TV pilot "Queens Supreme"

2002: Acted opposite Helen Hunt in the Actors' Gang's Los Angeles production of the 9/11–themed two-person play "The Guys"

2002: Co-starred in the action thriller "The Truth About Charlie"

cast in director Clint Eastwood's psychological thriller "Mystic River"

AFFILIATION: Raised Roman Catholic

QUOTES:

Robbins and Sarandon created a controversy at the 1993 Oscar ceremony by chiding the government on its treatment of HIV-positive Haitian immigrants.

About the fallout from the 1993 Oscars: "What I found really interesting is that in all the times I've protested something in a Republican administration, I've never caught the hell that I've caught protesting against a Democratic administration. And I don't want to say it isn't a coincidence or anything, but I've been audited twice during the Clinton administration. You fill in the blanks."—Tim Robbins quoted in *US*, June 1997.

On getting movies made: "There is always a test of wills, always a point where you have to face down the devil and say, 'Do I want to make this movie, because no one is making it easy?'

"It's never easy, no matter who you are. Even Martin Scorsese has trouble putting his films together. There is always someone who will find a way to humiliate you or make you work for less or question your motives or find some fault with your movie or say: 'There's no commerciality in this project . . .'

"You have to realise that doing what you love to do invovlves a certain amount of challenge and a lot of obstacles that will be placed in your path. That's good in a way, I suppose, because it means you have to examine yourself and the project and see whether you really want to go through with it. I try to keep a sense of humour about it, I really do."—Robbins to Martyn Palmer in the London *Times*, November 13, 1997.

"If an actor doesn't surprise me, I won't work with him again. They've got to show me something I could never think up myself. But what really amazed me was Tim's restraint as a director in 'Dead Man Walking'. A lot of guys are facile at showing off. But he hid. To do that, you have to have your ego in the right place. I can't do that. It was masterful."—Robert Altman quoted in *Us*, June 1997.

Robert Rodriguez

BORN: Robert Anthony Rodriguez in San Antonio, Texas, 06/20/1968

NATIONALITY: American

EDUCATION: University of Texas at Austin, Austin, Texas; film and communications; did not graduate; returned to school to complete a BA degree in communications after "El Mariachi" (1993)

AWARDS: Sundance Film Festival Audience Award (Best Feature) "El Mariachi" 1993 presented by the 5000 attendees of the Sundance Film Festival

Independent Spirit Award Best First Feature "El Mariachi" 1993

BIOGRAPHY

This Texas-based Mexican-American filmmaker burst upon the indie scene with a miraculous $7000 (shooting cost) action film geared for the Mexican Spanish-language video market. Touted as the cheapest film ever released by a studio, "El Mariachi" (1993) was a galvanizing send-up of Mexican action films, American Westerns and tough anti-hero movies informed by such auteurs as Sergio Leone and Sam Peckinpah. It told the fast-moving story of a mariachi musician who arrives in a Mexican border town at the same time as a hitman. Violent complications ensue after they accidentally switch guitar cases. On the strength (and economy) of this first feature, Rodriguez snared representation by ICM and a two-year development deal with Columbia Pictures.

Columbia also picked up the several hundred thousand dollar tab for completing a final edit (on film rather than video), redubbing the sound and dialogue in Dolby stereo and blowing it up to 35mm. "El Mariachi" did only

modest business at the box office—perhaps due to insufficient marketing to the Spanish-speaking action audience—but it provided a wake-up call to an often profligate industry.

Rodriguez began making Super 8 movies as a 13 year-old, using his large family—five sisters and four brothers—as a stock company. Though a born filmmaker, he was initially rejected by the film program at the University of Texas at Austin. Undaunted, Rodriguez continued with borrowed equipment and little money, making over 30 short films. He compiled a number of these for "Austin Stories", a video anthology of three vignettes starring his younger siblings, which won Rodriguez several awards and admission to film school. There he made his first 16mm short, "Bedhead" (1991), a remarkable eight-minute-long calling card film about a little girl who uses her newfound telekinetic powers to enact revenge on her obnoxious older brother. The film racked up awards at 14 film festivals.

During his 1991 summer break from college, Rodriguez spent a month in a research hospital as a test subject for a new cholesterol drug. He was paid $3000 for his trouble and emerged with the script for "El Mariachi." Rodriguez acquired another $4000 from a friend before he began his 14-day shoot in a Mexican border town using mostly amateur actors. He would return to that same town several years later to film the sequel "Desperado" (1995).

In between, Rodriguez ventured into TV to helm, script, edit and provide a song for "Road-racers" (1994), an outstanding installment of "Rebel Highway", Showtime's stylish series of low-budget remakes of the 1950s drive-in fare produced by American International Pictures. The filmmaker's first work in 35mm, "Road-racers" was a story about teen rebellion in the most general sense. Its true subject matter was smoking cigarettes in a cool 1950s fashion. Rodriguez also used this TV-movie as an unofficial audition reel for his leading lady Salma Hayek whom he wanted to cast in "Desperado" opposite Antonio Banderas' mariachi.

Budgeted at a thrifty $6 million (with only $3.3 million going into the actual production), "Desperado" proved to be a superior action entry with style to spare. Intensely charismatic leads, delightful cameos and a killer score by Los Lobos aided immensely but the bulk of the credit had to go to the gifted producer-writer-director-editor. Hollywood took notice.

Rodriguez went on to direct a segment of the anthology film "Four Rooms" (1995). Most critics praised his section which reteamed Banderas and Salma Hayek. Hayek also co-starred in his vampire flick "From Dusk Till Dawn" (1996), which featured Quentin Tarantino and George Clooney as brothers caught in a border town inhabited by night creatures. Rodriguez also enjoyed a popular (although critically-derided) success with the teen horror flick "The Faculty" (1998), written by Kevin Williamson. Drawing on films like "Alien" and "Scream", "The Faculty" was an updated take on the old chestnut "Invasion of the Body Snatchers" wherein the teachers and other authority figures were overtaken by beings from outer space leaving a group of students to fight to save the world.

After a hiatus, Rodriguez returned to features with "Spy Kids" (2001), a family film about a family of espionage agents headed by Antonio Banderas and Carla Gugino. Working from his own script for the first time in more than five years, he crafted a gentle spoof of the James Bond features that had cross-generational appeal thanks to its smart script, lavish, gadget-heavy production design and terrific performances. The film was so widely viewed and loved that preparations for a sequel were made. In 2002, "Spy Kids 2: The Island Of Lost Dreams" was released. The film reunited the Cortez family (Banderas, Gugino, Vega and Sabara) as spies who once again set out to save the world—

which they did, returning again for the final Rodriguez-helmed instalment, "Spy Kids 3-d: Game Over" (2003). After firmly establishing his ability to create highly successful and entertaining mainstream studio fare, Rodriguez next returned to his roots with the El Mariachi sequel "Once Upon a Time in Mexico" (2003), a true tour de force for the filmmaker, who wrote, production designed, edited, scored and shot the film on a Sony 24-frames-per-second digital high-definition camera. The film was another rousing and popular venture, with Rodriguez demonstrating a remarkably fresh, fluid and riveting directorial style while also paying homage to his influences like director Sergio Leone. —Written by Kent Greene

MILESTONES:

1982: Began making films at age 13 (date approximate)

Initially rejected by the film program at the University of Texas at Austin

Continued making Super 8 movies outside of school

Completed nearly 30 short narrative films with borrowed equipment and very little money

Featured his youngest siblings in "Austin Stories", an award-winning video anthology which helped him gain admission to film school

Made first 16mm short at the University of Texas at Austin

Starting writing and drawing a daily comic strip entitled "Los Hooligans", featuring characters inspired by his younger siblings, which ran for three years in the *Daily Texan* newspaper

Directed an eight-minute long short entitled "Bedhead," starring four of his nine siblings

Won prizes at 14 film festivals with his short film, "Bedhead"

1991: During his summer break from college, volunteered to spend a month in a research hospital as a test subject for a new cholesterol drug

1991: Wrote screenplay for "El Mariachi" while in hospital

1991: Shot (in two weeks), sound-recorded (in Spanish for the Mexican home video market), edited (on video) and directed "El Mariachi", his first feature

Completed the film from script through an electronic final edit for $7000, using the $3000 hospital pay and $4000 from a friend

Sent a trailer for "El Mariachi" to an agent at International Creative Management (ICM) to get feedback on his work

1992: Signed with ICM's Robert Newman, who sent tapes of the film to all the major studios

1992: Signed a two-year writing-directing deal with Columbia Pictures, which also agreed to release "El Mariachi"

Columbia paid to re-edit "El Mariachi" on film

1993: "El Mariachi" released by Columbia in Spanish with subtitles; one of the cheapest films ever released by a studio

1994: TV debut, scripted, directed, edited and wrote a song for "Roadracers", a TV-movie remake of a 1959 American International Pictures production, broadcast as part of Showtime's "Rebel Highway" series

1995: Produced, wrote, edited and directed "Desperado", starring Antonio Banderas and Salma Hayek

1995: Helmed "The Misbehavers" segment of "Four Rooms"

1996: Edited and directed the vampire-themed "From Dusk Till Dawn", written by and starring Quentin Tarantino

1998: Directed and edited the teen horror thriller "The Faculty", scripted by Kevin Williamson

2001: Reteamed with Banderas for "Spy Kids"; served as writer-director

2002: Reteamed with the cast of "Spy Kids" to film "Spy Kids 2: The Island Of Lost Dreams"

2003: Again collaborated with Banderas on "Once Upon a Time in Mexico" a sequel to "Desperado"

QUOTES:

Erroneously called "Richard Rodriguez" in a February 1, 1993 *The New York Times* article entitled "The Winners and Losers at Sundance."

Rodriguez's short "Bedhead" won numerous film festival prizes including first place at the Atlanta Film and Video Competition, the Marin County Film Festival, the 11th Annual Edison Black Maria Film Festival, the Charlotte Film Festival and the ninth annual 3rd Coast Film Festival. It also won awards at the Melbourne International Film Festival and at the Fine Arts Film and Video Competition.

" . . . A key detail somehow got overlooked in most of the press coverage after 'El Mariachi' hit theaters in early 1993: The ending of this fairy tale wasn't nearly so happy as most people assumed.

" 'El Mariachi' wound up grossing 'only about $1.8 million', producer [Bill] Borden says. 'Now, if you look at it in terms of percentages—the movie only cost $7000, and then Columbia put a couple of hundred thousand into finishing it, bringing it up to 35mm and re-dubbing it so you could release it in big theaters. Well, you know, to invest a couple of hundred thousand dollars into a movie that returned $1.8 million was not such a bad investment. . . . But the reality of that investment is it didn't make them any money. Because by the time you put in the cost of (prints and advertising), and flying Robert around for all the publicity trips and all that stuff, it was a break-even proposition.' "—From "Cranking Up the Volume" by Joe Leydon, *Los Angeles Times Calendar*, November 27, 1994.

The press release for Showtime's "Rebel Highway" series, for which the precocious film-maker directed an outstanding installment entitled "Roadracers", states that "Rodriguez has also been honored for additional short film and video works and has won several awards for cartooning, including two prestigious Columbia University Awards, one for "Los Hooligans" and one for political cartooning. Rodriguez, who began making films at age 13, is completing studies in communications at the University of Texas at Austin."

"My feeling is, your first impulse is almost always the best one. So you make a decision and you stick with it, instead of trying to make everything perfect. I don't want my movies to be perfect. Perfect is the enemy of creativity. Art should be flawed."—Rodriguez to *The New York Times*, July 29, 2002.

BIBLIOGRAPHY:

"Rebel Without a Crew" Robert Rodriguez, reprinted in paperback in 1996

Nicolas Roeg

BORN: Nicolas Jack Roeg in London, England, 08/15/1928

NATIONALITY: English

EDUCATION: Mercers School, London, England

AWARDS: Cannes Film Festival Technical Award "Insignificance" 1985

British Independent Film Lifetime Achievement Award 1999

BIOGRAPHY

Nicolas Roeg started working in the film industry at the age of 19 at the Marylebone Studio, where he was a tea-boy and assisted in the dubbing of French films. Roeg then went to work for MGM's London studios, where he slowly moved his way up the ladder to become a camera operator. He did second-unit photography for "Lawrence of Arabia" (1962) and finally became a director of photography on such films as "The Caretaker" (1963), "Fahrenheit 451" (1966), "Far From the Madding Crowd" (1967) and "Petulia" (1968).

In 1968, Roeg co-directed "Performance" with screenwriter Donald Cammell, but Warner Bros. was so dismayed with the film that they initially refused to release it. (The plot involved two characters—James Fox as a gangster on the run and Mick Jagger as a reclusive rock singer—whose identities merge.) When "Performance" was finally released in 1970, reactions were hardly tepid; critic Richard Schickel called it "the most disgusting, the most completely worthless film I have seen since I began reviewing." The film postulates the frightening concept that individualized, integrated personality is a fiction; it remains one of the most boldly experimental features made within the commercial confines of the English film industry.

With "Walkabout" (1971), Roeg transformed a didactic children's novel about a teenaged girl and her young brother lost in the Australian outback into a film about missed opportunities and different ways of seeing the world. "Don't Look Now" (1973), perhaps his most carefully structured work, is also about perception and perspective and can even be analyzed as a self-reflexive work about how we watch films. Roeg's visionary philosophy and his disavowal of traditional narrative conventions reached their most extreme form in "The Man Who Fell to Earth" (1976), in which he attempted, in his words, "to push the structure of film grammar into a different area . . . by taking away the crutch of time which the audience holds on to." Unlike his previous films, where ambiguities can be best understood through multiple viewings and careful analysis of correspondences, "The Man Who Fell to Earth" can't be fully grasped because Roeg refuses to give his viewers all the necessary information; it is his most open-ended work.

"Bad Timing" (1980) and the rarely

screened "Eureka" (produced 1983, released 1985) both reflect the director's concerns with convoluted narrative, the merging of disparate identities and the "interconnectedness" of all things, in a style characterized by frenzied editing and shifting camera angles. Like many of Roeg's subsequent films, they starred his wife, actress Theresa Russell.

After "Eureka," Roeg seemed to be moving away from some of these themes and techniques, perhaps finding it increasingly difficult to balance his unique personal vision with the overriding commercial considerations of the 1980s. "Insignificance" (1985), "Castaway" (1986), "Track 29" (1987) and "The Witches" (1990) pale in comparison to his early, ground-breaking films.

FAMILY:

son: Luc Roeg. Producer, agent; born c. 1962; mother Susan Stephen; made hundreds of music videos during the 1980s; associate producer of "Un Ballo in Maschera" segment of "Aria" (1987) directed by father; produced first film "Big Time" (1988); also produced "Let Him Have It" (1991); producer of "Two Deaths" (1992) directed by father; became head of independent films at the London office of William Morris in 1998

MILESTONES:

Served as projectionist for army unit during WWII

1947: Began working at London's Marylebone Studio as dubber and assistant editor

1950: Moved to MGM's London studios as clapper boy, assistant to camera crew

1960: First work as second-unit photographer

1961: Debut as director of photography with "On Information Received"

1963: First earned recognition as dop with Roger Corman's "The Masque of the Red Death"

1970: First film as co-director (with Donald Cammell), "Performance"

1971: First film as solo director, "Walkabout"

1973: Helmed the cult classic thriller "Don't Look Now", starring Donald Sutherland and Julie Christie

1980: First collaboration with actress Theresa Russell, "Bad Timing: A Sensual Obsession"

1989: TV directorial debut for "Sweet Bird of Youth"

1990: Directed the satirical "The Witches", featuring Anjelica Huston

1992: Helmed episode of the US TV series "The Young Indiana Jones Chronicles"

1996: Directed the TNT biblical movie "Samson and Delilah"

1999: At the Cannes Film Festival, announced plans to direct the feature "Night Train", based on Martin Amis' novel

BIBLIOGRAPHY:

"Nicholas Roeg" Neil Feineman, 1979, Twayne

"The Films of Nicolas Roeg—Myth And Mind" John Izod, 1992, St. Martin's Press

"Fragile Geometry—The Films, Philosophy and Misadventures of Nicolas Roeg" Joseph Lanza, 1989, Performing Arts Journal Publications

"Nicolas Roeg Film By Film" Scott Salwolke, 1993, McFarland

"The Films of Nicolas Roeg" Neil Sinyard, 1991

Eric Rohmer

BORN: Jean-Marie Maurice Scherer in Nancy, France, 04/04/1920

SOMETIMES CREDITED AS:
Jean-Marie Maurice Scherer
Gilbert Cordier

NATIONALITY: French

AWARDS: Berlin Film Festival Silver Bear Best Feature "La Collectionneuse/The Collector" 1968

Cannes Film Festival Max Ophuls Award "Ma nuit chez Maud/My Night at Maud's" 1969

San Sebastian Film Festival Award "Claire's Knee" 1970

New York Film Critics Circle Award Best Screenplay "My Night at Maud's" 1970

National Society of Film Critics Award Best Screenplay "My Night at Maud's" 1970

Prix Louis Delluc "Claire's Knee" 1970

National Board of Review Award Best Foreign Film "Claire's Knee" 1971

Cannes Film Festival Special Jury Award "The Marquise of O" 1976

Berlin Film Festival Silver Bear for Best Direction "Pauline at the Beach" 1983

Venice Film Festival Golden Lion Award "Le Rayon Vert" 1986

Venice Film Festival Best Screenplay Award "Autumn Tale" 1998

Las Vegas Film Critics Society Award Best Foreign Film "Autumn Tale" 1999

National Society of Film Critics Award Best Foreign Film "Autumn Tale" 1999

Venice Film Festival Golden Lion for Career Achievement 2001

BIOGRAPHY

Along with Francois Truffaut, Jean-Luc Godard, Jacques Rivette and Claude Chabrol, Eric Rohmer was one of the founding contributors to the influential film magazine, *Cahiers du Cinema*, where he also served as editor from 1956 to 1963. Born Jean-Marie Scherer, he had written a novel during the Occupation under the name Gilbert Cordier and went on to write film criticism in the 1950s under the name Eric Rohmer. Among his critical writings were a monograph on Alfred Hitchcock (co-written by Chabrol) and a dissertation on F.W. Murnau, whose "rich imagination" he expressly admires.

Rohmer tested his own talent in short films through the 1950s, abandoning his first feature, "Les Petites filles modeles", in 1952. Chabrol's company produced Rohmer's first feature, "La Signe du lion" (1960), but it was hardly a revolutionary manifesto in terms of cinematic language. Indeed, Rohmer took a more literary, philosophical turn in his art, conceiving his "Six Moral Tales," not as the moralistic fables implied in the English translation, but as stories which, as Rohmer describes them, "deal less with what people do than with what is going on in their minds while they're doing it. A cinema of thoughts rather than actions."

The first two of the six "Tales" films, "La Boulangere de Monceau" (1962) and "La Carriere de Suzanne" (1963), were minor efforts, but the third, "My Night at Maud's" (1969), a talkative chamber drama dealing with ethics, religion and hypocrisy, was a surprise hit that garnered Rohmer an Oscar nomination for best screenplay. The fourth to be released in the series (but third to be filmed) was "La Collectionneuse" (1967). Though not as successful as "Maud," it is nevertheless an engaging tale about a young woman "collecting" one-night-stands. "Claire's Knee" (1970) and "Chloe in the Afternoon" (1972) completed the cycle and established Rohmer, and his cameraman Nestor Almendros, as creators of a unique cinematic world firmly rooted in ethical concerns and suffused by the director's devout Catholicism.

In the mid-1970s, Rohmer turned to literary adaptations and historical subjects with "The Marquise of O" (1975), a well-received tale of unrestrained passion; "Perceval le Gallois" (1978), his interpretation of medieval codes of gallantry; and a TV film, "Catherine de Heilbronn."

For the 1980s Rohmer embarked on a new series of six films, "Comedies and Proverbs," launched by "The Aviator's Wife" (1980). These droll, intimate stories, set in ever-shifting contemporary French society, revolve around quirky characters whose emotional problems almost overwhelm them but who finally discover the resources for survival. "Le Rayon vert/Summer" (1986) is about a young girl on vacation hoping for a romantic revelation without compromise. She struggles idealistically against a companion's more relaxed approach, until at the end she is rewarded with the indescribably beautiful, ephemeral "green ray" of a perfect sunset. This fragile study of youthful yearning and confusion won the Golden Lion prize at the Venice Film Festival.

"Quatre aventures de Reinette et Mirabelle/Four Adventures of Reinette and Mirabelle" (1987) was a fine successor to Rohmer's morality tale tradition, depicting a winning innocent Provincial and her more worldly cosmopolitan counterpart (although they both seem sunny and innocent), and their various engagements together.

"Conte de printemps/Tale of Springtime" (1990) and its companion film "Conte d'hiver/A Winter's Tale" (1992) received accolades in what is projected to be a quartet of season-related films. "Tale of Springtime" mined a wealth of philosophical and emotional resonance from what seemed like grounds for romantic comedy, as a young woman tries to match her father with an older friend she recently made. "A Winter's Tale" featured both a hairdresser who hopes for a near-magical reuniting with the missing father of her daughter and delicate allusions to the Shakespeare play of the same name.

Youth continues to be the preoccupation of this aging director, although his attention is focused on the struggle to grow up—or, at least, to behave that way. This focus has broadened Rohmer's audience, yet he still makes talky, spare, low-budget films with unknown actors and little background music, preferring to shoot in sequence at the place and during the season of the narrative. In 1987, when the Montreal Film Festival honored him for his entire "Comedies and Proverbs" series, he announced, "I'm lucky to have practically complete independence, which is rare. That's because I make films in which there is no waste." An elegant simplicity is his achievement.

MILESTONES:

Began career as teacher in Clermont-Ferrand

Moved to Paris, worked as freelance journalist

1946: Published novel under pseudonym Gilbert Cordier

1948: Began writing film criticism

1950: Made first short film, "Journal d'un scelerat" (16 mm)

1951: Made first 35 mm film, "Presentation", starring Jean-Luc Godard (12 min.)

1951: Joined staff of *Cahiers du Cinema*

1952: Began work on uncompleted feature, "Les Petites Filles Modeles"

1956: Promoted to editor of *Cahiers du Cinema*

1959: First feature released, "Sign of Leo"

1962: Began series of six "Moral Tales" with "La Boulangere de Monceau" (16 mm., black-and-white, 16 min.)

1980: Began series of "Comedies and Proverbs" with "The Aviator's Wife"

BIBLIOGRAPHY:

"Hitchcock" Claude Chabrol and Eric Rohmer 1957

George A. Romero

BORN: George Andrew Romero in New York, New York, 02/04/1940

SOMETIMES CREDITED AS:
George Romero

NATIONALITY: American

EDUCATION: Carnegie-Mellon University, Pittsburgh, Pennsylvania, art, theater and design

AWARD: United States Film Festival Special Jury Prize "Martin" 1978; cited with Eagle Pennell's "The Whole Shootin' Match"

BIOGRAPHY

This Pittsburgh-based independent filmmaker was a pivotal figure in the development of the contemporary horror film. Beginning with his first feature, "Night of the Living Dead" (1968), Romero not only upped the ante on explicit screen violence and gore but also offered an often satirical critique of American society that reflected the cultural upheavals of the late 1960s and early 70s. Ethnically and sexually integrated, pro-feminist, gay-friendly, anti-macho and skeptical about capitalism, his work represents the progressive wing of a sometimes reactionary genre. In Romero's films, the source of the horror can be found, more often than not, deep in the heart of the bourgeois family.

Inspired by Michael Powell and Emeric Pressburger's "Tales of Hoffmann" (1951), Romero made 8mm shorts, industrial films and commercials before co-writing, editing, shooting and directing his first feature, "Night of the Flesh Eaters." Produced for $114,000 and renamed "Night of the Living Dead" (1968) by its distributor, the film became a landmark cult film and a significant social document. A stark parable of the American family consuming itself, the film's influences encompassed the EC horror comics of the 1950s, the cheapie gore exploitation flicks of Hershell Gordon Lewis, Hitchcock's "The Birds" (1963) and Rod Serling's talky allegorical dramas. Its intense scenes of violence—low-tech but convincing—which still have power to shock. Shot with a handheld camera in grainy high contrast black-and-white, "Night" could be a cinema-verite documentary of a nightmare.

Romero made several more low-budget privately financed features in his beloved Pittsburgh before securing his cult status with two remarkable films: "Martin" (1978) and "Dawn of the Dead" (1979). The former, Romero's favorite, was a lyrical, poignant, and deeply disturbing tale of a shy quiet boy who is convinced that he is a vampire. Produced by his partner, Richard Rubinstein, "Martin" was Romero's first project for their company, Laurel Entertainment. It also began an important collaboration with Tom Savini, a brilliant special makeup effects designer who provided cheap but astonishing gore effects for many of Romero's subsequent features. Their next project, the expansive sequel "Dawn of the Dead", was primarily set in a deserted suburban shopping mall where a hardy band of survivors are beset by zombies, bikers and their own personal demons. A powerful apocalyptic action film leavened with pitch black comedy, "Dawn" critiqued bourgeois culture, consumerism and machismo while spraying the screen with outrageous comic-book carnage. This classic of the horror film became one of the most profitable indies in US film history.

Romero continued to do interesting work for much of the the 80s. A rare respite from things gruesome, "Knightriders" (1981) was a quirky, leisurely paced take on Arthurian legend. Ed Harris functions as King Arthur for a traveling band that stages medieval fairs with "knights" jousting on motorcycles. Clearly a personal film, "Knightriders" can be viewed as an allegory about working as an independent filmmaker. Scripted by Stephen King, "Creepshow" (1982) was a more blunt and commercial work featuring higher production values and a cast of seasoned professionals. This smart and boldly stylized homage to EC horror comics also contained a sly critique of patriarchy. "Day of the Dead" (1985), the ostensible conclusion to the "Living Dead" trilogy, was brutally undermined by last-minute budget cuts but still emerged as Romero's strongest horror film of the decade. Claustrophobic, talky, progressive and amazingly bloody, "Day" was Romero's last film as a director for Laurel Entertainment.

While still a partner at Laurel, Romero also worked in TV as the creator, co-executive producer and occasional writer of "Tales from the Dark Side." The thematic and stylistic concerns of "Creepshow" helped shape the early episodes. Frequent Spike Lee collaborator Ernest Dickerson photographed the first season of this visually striking low-budget syndicated horror/fantasy series.

Romero's first project as a journeyman writer-director was the uneven psychological thriller, "Monkey Shines: An Experiment in Fear" (1988), which was marred by a studio-imposed happy ending. For his next feature, "Two Evil Eyes" (1990), Romero and the celebrated Italian horror filmmaker Dario Argento each wrote and directed a story inspired by Edgar Allan Poe. Released widely in Europe, the film barely opened in the US before being shunted off to the video stores. Romero fared better with the medium budget Stephen King adaptation, "The Dark Half" (1993), garnering enthusiastic reviews and lackluster box office. Hailed as a return to form for the horror master, this well-crafted film featured a strong dual performance by Timothy Hutton. "The Dark Half" numbers among the most thoughtful of the films made from King's works.—Written by Kent Greene

MILESTONES:

Borrowed an 8-mm Revere camera from a wealthy uncle

1954: Arrested at age 14 for throwing a flaming dummy off a Bronx rooftop while filming "The Man From the Meteor"

Won a Future Scientists of America Award for "Earthbottom", a geology documentary produced as a high school science project

1958: Spent the summer before college working as a grip on Alfred Hitchcock's "North by Northwest"

1963: Founded Latent Image (commercial/industrial production company) in Pittsburgh

Worked extensively in TV

1968: First feature film as director, "Night of the Living Dead"

1970: Honored by the Museum of Modern Art as the subject of their "Cineprobe" series on June 16, 1970

Co-founded Laurel Entertainment with Richard P. Rubinstein

1974: Began directing episodes of a TV series produced by Laurel entitled "The Winners" about famous sports figures

1978: First feature collaboration with producer Richard Rubinstein and special makeup effects artist Tom Savini, "Martin"

1982: First collaboration with Stephen King, "Creepshow"

1983: First TV teleplay, "Trick or Treat", the pilot for "Tales From the Darkside"

Debut as TV executive producer/writer, "Tales From the Darkside" (also created)

1987: First feature screenplay that he did not direct, "Creepshow 2"

Left Laurel Entertainment to work independently in mid-1980s

1990: First feature credit as executive producer on the remake/sequel "Night of the Living Dead" (also wrote screenplay)

AFFILIATION: Member of the Board of Directors of The Horror Hall of Fame.

QUOTES:

In a radio interview on WBAI in New York City, Romero stated that "The Dark Half" was his fifth attempt to bring a Stephen King novel to the screen after thwarted efforts with "Salem's Lot", "The Stand", "It", and "Pet Sematary". He was involved at the development stage but failed to snare the directing assignments due to scheduling conflicts or other complications.

"Until the Supreme Court establishes clearcut guidelines for the pornography of violence, 'Night of the Living Dead' will serve nicely as an outer-limit definition by example. . . . This film casts serious aspersions on the integrity of its makers, distrib Walter Reade, the film industry as a whole and exhibs who book the pic, as well as raising doubts about the future of the regional cinema movement and the moral health of filmgoers who cheerfully opt for unrelieved sadism."—From *Variety* (October 16, 1968) quoted in "Midnight Movies" by J. Hoberman & Jonathan Rosenbaum (New York: Harper & Row, 1983)

"Well, let's face it, we're dealing with a fantasy premise, but deep down inside we were all serious filmmakers and somewhat disappointed because we had to resort to horror for our first film. I mean, everyone would like to do the great American film, but we found ourselves making a horror film. Once we adapted to that for openers, we then tried to make the best, most realistic horror film that we could on the money we had available."—Russell Streiner, producer and cast member ("Johnny") of "Night of the Living Dead", quoted in "Nightmare Movies: A Critical Guide to Contemporary Horror Films" by Kim Newman (New York: Harmony Books, 1988)

ROMERO: . . . I'm very unhappy with some of my work. I don't think I have yet made a film where I've had the money or time to execute it exactly the way I would want to execute it. I'd like to do that sometime.

WIATER: Is there any film that still stands out as perhaps coming closest to your initial vision?

ROMERO: Strangely, a little film I made called "Martin", which was a $275,000 production, comes closest in terms of the finished product to what my conception was going in. That's because all of us were working on that out of dedication. It was one of those little films that we went out with nine people and made a movie. It didn't matter if we had to shoot at night, we shot at night. We were just there to get the movie done. I had the most freedom on that film that I've had on any of the other ones.

—George A. Romero interviewed in Stanley Wiater's "Dark Visions" (New York: Avon Books, 1992).

" . . . On the surface, I was doing popular genre stuff, but I always feel when there's no linear thread underneath it all. Fantasy has always been used as a parable, as sociopolical criticism: "Alice in Wonderland", "Gulliver's Travels" . . . I love the Japanese Godzilla films. They're not scary at all, but as a phenomenon born out of the war, the bomb, they say more to me than "Hiroshima Mon Amour." So I insist on having that underbelly.

"When I write a script, that's what I think about first. After I have it in my head, I can write the script in two weeks, because the surface doesn't matter: the characters can behave any way you want them to. But you have to know where you're going."—George Romero quoted in "Morning Becomes Romero" by Dan Yakir in *Film Comment,* May/June 1979.

" . . . In the Sixties we used to sit around in coffee shops and talk and solve all the problems of society and the filmmakers did it in their movies. We don't do that anymore. Films are still critical of society, but this criticism has taken the form of parables communicated through the fantasy film. I do it in very broad strokes, with a comic-book type humor and extreme staging and a very pedantic kind of structure. But the socio-political parable is to me like a handshake with the audience. I don't think I'm saying anything new; it's a wink and should be taken as such."—George Romero quoted in "Morning Becomes Romero" by Dan Yakir in *Film Comment*, May/June 1979.

From Romero's shooting script for "Dawn of the Dead": "Stores of every type offer gaudy displays of consumer items . . . at either end of the concourse, like the main altars at each end of a cathedral, stand the mammoth two-story department stores, great symbols of a consumer society . . . They appear as an archaeological discovery, revealing the Gods and customs of a civilization now gone."

"It is perhaps the lingering intellectual distrust of the horror genre that has prevented George Romero's 'Living Dead' trilogy from receiving recognition for what it undoubtedly is: one of the most remarkable and audacious achievements of modern American cinema. Now that it has been completed by "Day of the Dead" one can see it clearly for what it always promised to be: the most uncompromising radical critique of contemporary America that is possible within the terms and conditions of a popular 'entertainment' cinema."—Robin Wood from "The Woman's Nightmare: Masculinity in 'Day of the Dead' ", in *Cineaction!*, August 1986.

Gary Ross

BORN: Gary A. Ross in Los Angeles, California, 11/03/1956

NATIONALITY: American

EDUCATION: University of Pennsylvania, Philadelphia, Pennsylvania, writing; dropped out after three years and went to work on a fishing boat in Seattle, Washington

AWARDS: Writers Guild of America Paul Selvin Award 1994

Golden Satellite Best Motion Picture Screenplay (Original) "Pleasantville" 1998

Producers Guild of America Golden Laurel Vision Award Artistic Achievement in Film "Pleasantville" 1998

BIOGRAPHY
This son of Hollywood screenwriter Arthur Ross initially wrote fiction but eventually followed in his father's footsteps, scoring a megahit with his first produced feature script. "Big" (1988), co-written and co-produced with Anne Spielberg, recounted the story of a young boy

who wakes up one morning—BIG—and must navigate the world in a man's body. The writers shared an Oscar nomination for Best Original Screenplay and Ross netted a second nod for his first solo effort, "Dave" (1993), about a look-alike who steps in after the US President has a heart attack. Gary Ross has proven his ability to tap the zeitgeist and create gentle, somewhat exaggerated scripts which revolve around mistaken identities and subversion of the status quo by an outsider who often is pretending to be something other than his or her true self.

The apotheosis of this scenario was his feature directorial debut "Pleasantville" (1998), a Capraesque fable in which two 90s teens find themselves transported into the homogenized, black-and-white world of 50s television. Like the main characters in his previous efforts, the pair both upset and embellish the society in which they find themselves, bringing muchneeded change that comes at a price. When Ross naively hit upon the concept of making a movie that began in black-and-white and gradually turned to color (a metaphor for coming alive), he had no idea of the technical expertise required to make it work. 1,700 special effects and $40 million later and after a post-production period spanning more than a year, the finished film opened to generally praiseworthy reviews. For his part, though, the director said, "I'm dying to do a movie that doesn't have any special effects in it. That would be a walk in the park."

It would be five years before Ross would step behind the camera again—although he kept busy with uncredited rewriting chores on films such as "Inspector Gadget" (1999), "Kangaroo Jack" (2003) and "Just Married" (2003)—this time in an attempt to film writer Laura Hillenbrand's bestselling nonfiction book "Seabiscuit" (2003), about the real-life 1920s-era racehorse who became an unlikely champion and an American folk hero of his day. Reteaming with past collaborators Tobey Maguire and William H. Macy as well as top-line performers Jeff Bridges and Chris Cooper, Ross assembled an inspirational, often moving and beautifully photographed version of the historical events, although his desire to capture as much of the book's historical information led to intentionally shorthanded and brisk scenes that often avoided plumbing the characters' genuine emotional depths.

FAMILY:

father: Arthur Ross. Screenwriter; wrote "Creature From the Black Lagoon" (1954), "The Great Race" (1965); earned an Oscar nomination for "Brubaker" (1980); blacklisted during the McCarthy era; founded the Hollywood branch of the Committee for a Sane Nuclear Policy in the late 1950s

MILESTONES:

1984: Feature acting debut, "Crackers"

1984: First produced script, a segment of HBO's horror anthology, "The Hitchhiker"

1988: With Anne Spielberg, co-scripted and co-produced "Big"; received Best Original Screenplay Academy Award nomination

1992: Collaborated on the screenplay for Fred Schepisi's "Mr. Baseball"

1993: Picked up second Oscar nomination for solo screenwriting effort, the comedy "Dave"

1994: Contributed to the screenplay for "Lassie"

1994: Reportedly did uncredited work on the screenplay for "The Flintstones"

1997: Was one of the producers of "Trial and Error"

1998: Feature directorial debut, "Pleasantville"; also wrote and produced

1999: Did draft of screenplay for "Mr. Gadget"

2003: Wrote, Produced and Directed the drama "Seabiscuit"

QUOTES:

An outspoken liberal who has written speeches for Michael Dukakis and Bill Clinton, Ross made no secret of modeling the heartless president in "Dave" after Ronald Reagan.

"Bob Dole wanted to build a bridge to the past, and many people are in love with a past that I don't think ever existed—one that was devoid of conflict or poverty or strife. As a culture, there's a need to do that now, to mythologize. It's like telling ourselves big, 3-D lies because we don't want to face the consequences of what a big society is."—Gary Ross to *Los Angeles Times*, September 20, 1998.

BORN: in Rome, Italy, 05/08/1906

DEATH: 06/04/1977

NATIONALITY: Italian

AWARDS: Cannes Film Festival Grand Prix Award "Open City" 1946; one of eleven films cited

Venice Film Festival Special Mention "Paisan" 1946; one of eight films cited

National Board of Review Award Best Foreign-Language Film "Open City" 1946

New York Film Critics Circle Award Best Foreign Film "Open City" 1946

Locarno Film Festival Critic's Grand Prize Best Film "Germany, Year 2000" 1948

National Board of Review Award Best Film "Paisan" 1948

National Board of Review Award Best Director "Paisan" 1948

New York Film Critics Circle Award Best Foreign Film "Paisan" 1948

Venice Film Festival International Prize "Europa 51" 1952; cited with John Ford's "The Quiet Man" and Kenji Mizoguchi's "The Life of Oharu"

Venice Film Festival Golden Lion Award "Il General Della Rovere" 1959; tied with Mario Monicelli's "The Great War"

Venice Film Festival Catholic Film Office Award "Il General della Rovere" 1959

Venice Film Festival International Film Critics Prize "Il General della Rovere" 1959

BIOGRAPHY

Often identified with the constrictive "neorealist" label, Roberto Rossellini stands as one of the greatest directors in the history of Italian film: the man responsible for the postwar rebirth of Italian cinema and one of the few truly great humanists (along with Jean Renoir) to work in the medium.

Born into a bourgeois Roman family, Rossellini spent his formative years under Mussolini's fascist fist and, by his early 30s, had drifted into filmmaking—a common pattern amongst the idle Italian rich. He worked with his friend, producer Vittorio Mussolini, the son of "Il Duce", on the script for "Luciano Serra Pilota" (1938), a propaganda film which showed some early marks of a neorealist style. After directing a handful of pictures under the official government banner, Rossellini, the stereotypically apolitical Roman, made an indelible mark on world cinema in 1945 with "Open City." Despite a lukewarm response in Italy, the film was a sensation in France and the US with its raw, near-documentary style: grainy black-and-white photography, amateur performers and real locations. These were elements that audiences had not previously seen in feature films, and "Open City" was hailed as bringing a new kind of realism, "neorealism," to the screen.

While his two subsequent films—"Paisan" (1946, one of his greatest achievements) and "Germany, Year Zero" (1947)—bore the hallmarks of the neorealist style, Rossellini drew increasing critical fire for his use of melodrama (especially through his brother Renzo's musical scores) and Hollywood narrative conventions. He had never been a strict neorealist, however. His aim was to understand rather than recreate reality, sometimes for an expressly pedagogical function (witness his masterful and unusual "The Flowers of St. Francis" 1948), and he incorporated other expressionistic elements into nearly all his work. These elements are particularly evident in films such as the underappreciated "Fear" (1954), with its psychologically based visuals, but had already been partially present in "Open City."

In 1949, Rossellini further challenged the film community's expectations by forming a creative and personal—not to mention scandalous—union with one of Hollywood's greatest stars, Ingrid Bergman. Beginning with "Stromboli" (1949), the pair collaborated over a six-year period on seven films, all of which proved disastrous with both critics and public. (Several years later, however, writers for *Cahiers du Cinema* were hailing "Voyage in Italy" [1953] as a masterpiece, and its influence is readily apparent in films by French New Wave directors.) By 1958, the two had separated, following revelations of Rossellini's affair with Indian screenwriter Somali Das Gupta. Rossellini's documentary "India" (1958) was a box-office failure, although its critical reputation remains high. Commercial success finally returned with "General Della Rovere" (1959), a wartime Resistance story, which also marked a return to the familiar neorealist style; Rossellini would later see the film as a retread of the ideas and forms of his previous successes.

By 1964, Rossellini had been canonized by numerous critics, as well as fellow filmmakers like Jean-Luc Godard and Bernardo Bertolucci (in the latter's "Before the Revolution" 1964, a character declares, "One cannot live without Rossellini!"). Concerned chiefly with the state of cinema and its function as an artistic and educational tool, Rossellini decided to remove himself from the commercial arena. Viewing himself as a craftsman and not an artist, he devoted his creative energies to TV films on science and history: the five-hour "L'Ete del Ferro/The Age of Iron" (1964), the twelve-hour "Lotta Dell'Uomo per la Sua Sopravvivenza/ Man's Struggle for Survival" (1967) and the six-hour "Atti Degli Apostoli/ The Acts of the Apostles" (1968), as well as biographies of Socrates, Blaise Pascal, Augustine of Hippo, Descartes, Jesus and Louis XIV.

Only the latter," The Rise of Louis XIV" (1966), has received its due acclaim, chiefly because it is one of the few to have been screened theatrically.

FAMILY:

brother: Renzo Rossellini. Composer; scored many of his brother's films; born in 1908; died in 1982

son: Renzino Rossellini. Mother, Marcella de Marquis

son: Romano Rossellini. Deceased; mother, Marcella de Marquis

son: Roberto Ingmar Rossellini. Businessman; born on 1950; mother, Ingrid Bergman

daughter: Isabella Rossellini. Actor, model; born on June 18, 1952; twin of Ingrid; mother, Ingrid Bergman

daughter: Ingrid Isotta Aborne. Professor; born on June 18, 1952; twin sister of Isabella Rossellini; studied for doctorate in Italian literature at Columbia

COMPANIONS:

wife: Marcella De Marquis. Marriage annulled; mother of Renzino and Romano

Anna Magnani. Actor; separated in 1949

wife: Ingrid Bergman. Actor; married in 1950; marriage annulled in 1957

wife: Somali Das Gupta. Screenwriter; divorced; one son together; Indian

MILESTONES:

1934: Began working in film industry as editor, dubber, screenwriter (date approximate)

1937–1938: Made amateur film, "Prelude a l'apres-midi d'un faune" (banned by Italian censors)

1938: First screen credit as writer of "Luciano Serra, Pilota" (also directed some sequences)

1941: First feature as director, "La Nave Bianca/The White Ship" (expanded from original documentary form)

1945: Made breakthrough film, "Roma, Citta Aperta/Rome, Open City"

1949: Made first film with Ingrid Bergman, "Stromboli"

1954: Made last film with Ingrid Bergman, "La paura/Fear"

1977: Directed last film, "The Messiah"

1985: Posthumously appeared in Jonas Mekas' experimental compilation of sketches, "He Stands in a Desert Counting the Seconds of His Life"

BIBLIOGRAPHY:
"Roberto Rossellini" Patrice Hovald, 1958

"Roberto Rossellini" Massimo Mida, 1961

"Roberto Rossellini" Mario Verdone, 1963

"Roberto Rossellini" Jose Luis Guarner (translated by Elizabeth Cameron), 1970

"Roberto Rossellini: The War Trilogy" Roberto Rosselini, 1973, Garland Publishing; his war trilogy consists of "Rome, Open City" (1945), "Paisan" (1946), and "Germany Year Zero" (1947)

"The Adventures of Roberto Rossellini" Tag Gallagher, 1998, Da Capo Press

Alan Rudolph

BORN: Alan Steven Rudolph in Los Angeles, California, 12/18/1943

NATIONALITY: American

EDUCATION: University of California at Los Angeles, Los Angeles, California; business studies

Assistant Directors Training Program, Directors Guild of America, Los Angeles, California, 1967

AWARDS: Berlin Film Festival Golden Bear Best Screenplay "Buffalo Bill and the Indians, or Sitting Bull's History Lesson" 1976

Los Angeles Film Critics Association New Generation Award "Choose Me" 1984; writer and director

BIOGRAPHY

The son of director Oscar Rudolph, writer-director Alan Rudolph followed in the footsteps of mentor Robert Altman, embracing a similar kind of ensemble picture while pursuing his own personal, less satiric, more human vision. Despised by mainstream Hollywood, he has managed to stay true to his idiosyncratic muse and remain in the game despite never having had a breakthrough commercial success. Rudolph's dialogue has a snappy, flirtatious quality, and his distinctive "pan-and-zoom" style allows audiences to experience performances that are not built from cut to cut. It is not unusual for a Rudolph film to contain four or five shots that are as long as six or seven minutes, unheard of in this era of high-tech editing. Actors who like working with him because he lets them get into real-life rhythms wave their usual salaries, enabling him to adhere to ridiculously low budgets, and he frequently reteams with his talent, knowing that subsequent collaborations will only be richer.

Growing up around the film industry, Rudolph made a screen appearance in his father's "The Rocket Man" (1954), a campy fantasy co-scripted by comedian Lenny Bruce. He would later quit college to continue learning about filmmaking by watching studio people work and considers his days at his father's side his version of film school. He did eventually enter the Directors Guild training program for assistant directors, drawing inspiration from TV directors Joseph Sargent and Leo Penn before meeting Altman. By 1970, Rudolph had made several short films set to rock-and-roll hits—an early indication of his concern with musical themes and desire to use music as an inspirational element for his screenplays. Following his virtually forgotten (until its appearance on video) first feature, the pretentious horror flick "Premonition" (1972), he worked as an assistant director on three Altman films: "The Long Goodbye" (1973), "California Split" (1974) and "Nashville" (1975). He also co-wrote the script for Altman's "Buffalo Bill and the Indians, or Sitting Bull's History Lesson" (1976), and Altman, in turn, produced Rudolph's first "official" feature, "Welcome to L.A." (1976).

"Welcome to L.A." boasted a name cast thanks to Altman's involvement, including Keith Carradine, Sally Kellerman and Geraldine Chaplin, among others, and offered an ironic view of laid-back L.A. hustling, though its dark sensibility was not appreciated in all quarters. In his second film, "Remember My Name" (1978), which he still considered his finest as of 1994, Rudolph gave Chaplin full rein to create an enigmatic character study of a woman released from prison to haunt the man who has abandoned her. The director also underlined the film's sense of menace with a soundtrack featuring celebrated blues singer Alberta Hunter. His first work-for-hire, "Roadie" (1980), a look at life on the road for pop performers, abandoned laid-back stylishness for funky, chaotic comedy and marked the beginning of Rudolph's long association with producer Carolyn Pfeiffer. Though he had received acclaim early on as an important new 'auteur', the studio behind his second work-for-hire, the political thriller "Endangered Species" (1982), remained unimpressed, locking him out of the editing room during the film's post-production. The resulting impersonal quality would repeat itself in his subsequent forays as hired-gun on "Songwriter" (1984) and "Made in Heaven" (1987).

The provocative and bizarre "Return Engagement" (1983), a documentary of the debates between 60s counterculture guru Dr Timothy Leary and Watergate conspirator G Gordon Liddy, helped Rudolph acquire financing for his next "personal" film, "Choose Me" (1984). Inspired by soul singer Teddy Pendergrass' song of the same name, it moodily mused on the convoluted romantic entanglements of a bar owner and her lovelorn patrons, including a radio talk show hostess called Dr. Love, and was his biggest (big being a relative term here) hit to that time. By his next film, "Trouble in Mind" (1985), Rudolph had gathered a following dedicated to his meditations on love and loneliness in peculiar settings, this time a town called Rain City in an unspecified dystopian future. The Rudolph brew had also come to mean cryptic performances by, typically, Chaplin, Carradine and Genevieve Bujold, and a whimsical absurdity that could sometimes sabotage narrative flow. 1990's "Love at Large", starring Tom Berenger, Elizabeth Perkins and Anne Archer, despite its appealing mix of parody and sobriety, suffered from this problem to some extent, while his follow-up, "Mortal Thoughts" (1991), could have used more of it.

"The Moderns" (1988) marked the realization of a long-cherished project, a story of an American artist in 1920s Paris who witnesses the transformation of "art" into a commodity. The film deftly satirized an era of art history and high culture whose reputation has enjoyed great reverence. It mixed fictional characters with historical figures such as Gertrude Stein, who sums up Rudolph's approach in one line: "I'm not interested in the abnormal; the normal is so much more simply complicated." He again tackled material close to his heart in "Mrs. Parker and the Vicious Circle" (1994), creating a finely tuned tribute to the celebrated writers and artists that comprised the legendary Algonquin Round Table of the 1920s. Dismissing the notion that the two are companion pieces, Rudolph told DGA News (October-November 1994): " 'The Moderns' was intentionally a dream movie, there was no reality . . . ['Mrs. Parker'] is the first time I made a film based on a reality other than my own invented one." Altman rejoined him as producer on the high-profile project, and noteworthy performances from Jennifer Jason Leigh as celebrated wit Dorothy Parker and Campbell Scott as humorist Robert Benchley elicited positive buzz, if mixed reviews. Its poor performance at the box office, however, reduced Rudolph's stock around Hollywood to a career nadir.

Expert at making Montreal stand in for Paris and New York in his previous two films, Rudolph let it be itself for "Afterglow" (1997), a look at marriage and infidelity most similar to the director's "Choose Me" in its noirish meditation on loneliness and the elusiveness of love. The "unwashed soap opera" is an alternately giddy and sorrowful fable (Nick Nolte's character's name is Lucky Mann) about two married couples whose lives intersect with a shuffling of partners. By the end, there's a hint the original couples may be reunited, but Rudolph, ever the master of the ambiguous ending, is loathe to wrap things up neatly. Having adapted Kurt Vonnegut's "Breakfast of Champions" for Altman during the middle 70s, he was finally able to make the 1999 film himself with the help of Bruce Willis, who came aboard as Dwayne Hoover, the successful car salesman who underneath the bright smile and slick threads is falling apart. Though Rudolph would seem an ideal choice for the material, his failure to capture the satiric spirit of the book seemed to reinforce the notion it was unfilmable, with only Nolte's juicy turn as a paranoid lingerie-lover rising to the required comic level. Nolte was back as the pompous Senator Avery in Rudolph's slapstick gangster pic "Trixie" (2000), which starred Emily Watson as the titular security guard who earnestly tackles a murder case with dreams of glory.

MILESTONES:

1954: First film appearance, "Rocket Man", directed by his father Oscar Rudolph

Given a camera by his older brother; made over 200 short films

Worked at odd jobs for various Hollywood studios

1967: Entered Directors Guild of America assistant director's training program

1972: First film as director, screenwriter and co-producer, "Premonition", executive produced by his father

1973: First collaboration with Robert Altman, as an assistant director on "The Long Goodbye"; would also assist Altman on "California Split" (1974) and "Nashville" (1975)

1976: First film as director to achieve significant theatrical release, "Welcome to L.A."; also wrote screenplay; produced by Altman; inaugurated collaborations with actors Keith Carradine and Geraldine Chaplin, though he knew both from working on Altman films

1976: With Altman, co-wrote the screenplay for "Buffalo Bill and the Indians, or Sitting Bull's History Lesson"

1978: Provided stunning vehicle for Geraldine Chaplin as a woman returning from prison bent on disrupting her ex-husband's life in "Remember My Name", produced by Altman; there were only six prints of the movie, of which reportedly none is extant

1980: First film with producer Carolyn Pfeiffer and first film as director-for-hire, "Roadie"

1982: Helmed and co-wrote (with John Binder) "Endangered Species", a conspiracy thriller inspired by real-life cattle mutilations in the Midwest

1983: Directed the feature-length documentary, "Return Engagement", featuring Timothy Leary and G. Gordon Liddy

1984: Scored critically with "Choose Me", an evocative use of L.A. locations starring Genevieve Bujold, Carradine and Lesley Ann Warren; also wrote and directed that year's "Songwriter" (first film with Kris Kristofferson), starring Willie Nelson

1985: Set his noirish melodrama "Trouble in Mind" in the not-too-distant future; picture reteamed him with Kristofferson, playing an idealistic ex-cop fresh from a stint in jail; cast also included Carradine and Bujold; first collaboration with director of photography Toyomichi Kurita

1987: Helmed the misfire about reincarnation, "Made in Heaven"

1988: Recovered his director's aplomb for "The Moderns", a strikingly visual look at 1920s Paris of the Lost Generation; originally set to shoot picture in late 1970s with Mick Jagger in the role eventually played by John Lone; sixth and last film produced by Pfeiffer (the last four with producing partner David Blocker); featured Kevin O'Connor (in first of three turns for Rudolph) as the best-ever Ernest Hemingway on screen; second film with Kurita; last film to date with Chaplin

1990: Appeared as himself in the documentary feature "Hollywood Mavericks"

1991: First collaboration with actors Bruce Willis and Glenne Headly, "Mortal Thoughts", co-produced by Demi Moore (who also acted); hired the day before shooting commenced, delivered arguably his most mainstream entertainment, though Columbia, which purchased it after the success of "Ghost" (Moore) and "Die Hard II" (Willis), hated it and wanted to reshoot it so that the pair had a love story; both Willis and Moore stood behind the version as filmed

1992: Appeared as himself in Altman's "The Player"

1994: Provided a nice look into the world of the Algonquin Hotel's Round Table of writers with "Mrs. Parker and the Vicious Circle", produced by Altman; Carradine, in his fifth film for the director, portrayed Will Rogers; the director's first foray into a fact-based reality

1997: First collaboration with actor Nick Nolte (though both appeared as themselves in "The Player"), "Afterglow", produced by Altman; reteamed with Kurita; picture cost less to make than Nolte's regular Hollywood salary

1999: Did his best to capture the grandness of Kurt Vonnegut's satiric vision of American greed and commercialism in "Breakfast of Champions"; had originally written screenplay for Altman shortly after novel's publication in 1973; picture reteamed him with Nolte, Willis and Headly; produced by Blocker and Willis' brother David; six-week shoot was director's shortest schedule since "Choose Me"

2000: Reunited with Nolte for "Trixie", produced by Altman; first film with Lesley Ann Warren in 16 years

2001: Helmed "Speaking of Sex"

Directed "The Secret Lives of Dentists" (lensed 2002)

QUOTES:

Named by the 1985 Toronto Film Festival as one of ten filmmakers whose work would shape the next decade of cinema. He was the only American on the list.

Rudolph credits TV directors Joseph Sargent and Leo Penn as inspirations: "They had a sense of romance that I had hoped I would get from directors, but which I found from no one else until I worked with [Robert] Altman." —From *DGA News*, October-November 1994.

About working for studios: "I've been asked to do quite a few things, and the money was always interesting, but I didn't think I could do it or work with certain people. I might have if I hadn't had such bad experiences with some of my earlier films [as a studio hire], which I came out of with a brutal reminder of how something wonderful can be destroyed. I would think I made a pretty good movie and then all the knives would start flashing and what came out the other end was a film that wasn't anyone's vision.

"The thing with those films is that I was always broke. Every time I'd do something for the studios, there would be a paycheck which was more than I'd ever experienced. I was literally checkerboarding my way through the rent. I'd go broke and then do a picture for a studio to pay the rent. But it wasn't worth it, I could see that. No matter how often you play Faust, you're going to get a bad review some way."—Alan Rudolph in *DGA News*, October–November 1994.

"I don't have much knowledge in anything else, so I've basically been making the same film for 20 years. It's very fertile ground, and I just seem interested in the dance that people do together when they don't know the music and they don't know the steps. I'm always interested in taking a stab at this love thing, which just seems endless

"A lot of people resist my movies, they really don't like them. I really couldn't figure it out until I began to understand that my films require the audience's participation on an emotional level. You have to basically bring yourself, and a lot of people won't do that.

"The point isn't to strive to be original. My movies aren't made for mass audiences, and I guess I'm not really interested in mass audiences. The masses will take care of themselves. I'm interested in the individual in the audience."—to *Boston Globe*, January 1, 1998.

"I tell you what, movies have become currency. It's that good news, bad news thing. The good news is that you can make a movie just about anywhere with anyone for any amount of money, and someone might pay attention. The bad news is that everything's been co-opted. The so-called independent movement is basically a label and a sales pitch. All the independent distributors are owned by the major studios, which means its stuff for one decimal point less. I think filmmakers are in the best and worst of times right now. They should be encouraged to be original and true, but that's not what's happening."—Rudolph quoted in *Chicago Tribune*, January 23, 1998.

"The truth is, the first film I made with real actors, 'Welcome to L.A.', was the most audacious film I'll ever make, because I didn't know the difference. I had written the script for [Robert Altman's] 'Buffalo Bill and the Indians.' 'Buffalo Bill' was at the time a pretty high-budget film, maybe $7 million. Had Paul Newman, all that. So we're in Calgary, the day before shooting, and all those terrific United Artists guys like Arthur Krim and Eric Pleskow

fly up to have a big production meeting with Bob. He wants me to be in on the meeting. Bob's sitting there and says, 'OK, let's make a proposition. Our picture costs $7 million. For less than $1 million more, we'll make another movie. Alan will write and direct, and we'll get a lot of stars.' They say OK. Later, Bob said, 'Hey, you better write something.' So I made 'Welcome to L.A.' It wasn't conventional, but I had no frame of reference."—quoted in *Filmmaker*, Winter 1998.

"No one has ever come up to me and asked, 'what do you want to do next?' If I stopped generating [projects] myself, I would just be another statistic."—Rudolph quoted in *Screen International*, November 14–November 20, 1997.

"One of the greatest rejections I ever got was when a foolish agent thought he could send 'Afterglow' to a studio, and the studio guy turned down the script. He said, 'We don't want to make this, it's just about people.' The real truth is I know my films are never going to cost very much money because I can't get very much money to do them, so I restrict the scope before I start writing. On 'Choose Me' I was the mouse on the rotating wheel for a new company, Island Alive, and I'd just done a documentary for them, 'Return Engagement', that had worked out. They said, 'That was good, let's do another one.' And I said, 'I want to do a real movie.' I wish I had the napkin, because it was truly a napkin deal. I was sitting there with Chris Blackwell and Carolyn Pfeiffer and they said, 'How much would a movie cost?' And I figured out we could do it for $639,000. They said, 'OK, that's the budget.'"—quoted in *Sight and Sound*, June 1998.

BORN: in Puerto Montt, Chile, 07/25/1941

SOMETIMES CREDITED AS:
Raul Ruiz

NATIONALITY: Chilean

CITIZENSHIP: France 1996

EDUCATION: University of Chile, theology and law; left to write full-time after receiving a Rockefeller grant in 1962
studied film under Fernando Birri in Santa Fe, Argentina, in 1964
University of Iowa, Iowa City, Iowa; took creative writing classes

AWARDS: Cesar Best Short Film (Fiction) "Colloque de chiens" 1980
Berlin Film Festival Silver Bear for Lifetime Contribution to the Art of Cinema 1997

BIOGRAPHY

Rising to international prominence in the early 1980s, Raul Ruiz has proved one of the most exciting and innovative filmmakers of recent years, providing more intellectual fun and artistic experimentation, shot for shot, than any filmmaker since Jean-Luc Godard. Slashing his way through celluloid with machete-sharp sounds and images, Ruiz is a guerrilla who uncompromisingly assaults the preconceptions of film art. This frightfully prolific figure—he has made over 50 films in twenty years—does not adhere to any one style of filmmaking. He has worked in 35mm, 16mm and video, for theatrical release and for European TV, and on documentary and fiction features.

Ruiz's career began in the avant-garde theater where, from 1956 to 1962, he wrote over 100 plays. Although he never directed any of these productions, he did dabble in filmmaking in 1960 and 1964 with two short, unfinished films. In 1968, with the release of his first completed feature, "Tres tristes tigres," Ruiz, along with Miguel Littin and Aldo Francia, was placed in the forefront of Chilean film. A committed leftist who supported the Marxist government of Salvador Allende, Ruiz was forced to flee his country during the fascist coup of 1973. Living in exile in Paris since that time, he has found a forum for his ideas in European TV. His first great European success came with "The Hypothesis of the Stolen Painting" (1978); a puzzling black-and-white film adapted from a novel by Pierre Klossowski, constructed in a "tableaux vivants" style that tells the enigmatic story of a missing 19th-century painting.

Influenced by the fabulist tradition that runs through much Latin American literature (Gabriel Garcia Marquez, Jorge Luis Borges, and Alfonso Reyes have all been cited as influences), Ruiz is a poet of fantastic images whose films slip effortlessly from reality to imagination and back again. A manipulator of wild, intellectual games in which the rules are forever changing, Ruiz's techniques are as varied as film itself—a collection of odd Wellesian angles and close-ups, bewildering p.o.v. shots, dazzling colors, and labyrinthine narratives which weave and dodge the viewer's grasp with every shot. As original as Ruiz is, one can tell much about him by the diversity of his influences; in addition to adapting Klossowski, he has been inspired by Franz Kafka ("La Colonia Penal" 1971 is a Chilean reworking of "The Penal Colony"), Racine ("Berenice" 1984), Calderon ("Memory of Appearances: Life Is a Dream" 1986), Shakespeare ("Richard III" 1986), Robert Louis Stevenson ("Treasure Island" 1985), Orson Welles (whose "F For

Fake" is a precursor of "The Hypothesis of the Stolen Painting "1978), and Hollywood B movies (Roger Corman was executive producer on "The Territory" 1983). Like Godard (whom Ruiz names as an early influence and who also owes a debt to B films), Ruiz makes no differentiation between the "high art" of Racine or Calderon and the "low art" of Roger Corman.

Unfortunately, only a handful of Ruiz's films are available for viewing in the USA, and it is on these few films that his reputation here is built. The few works that are available, however, bear witness to the genius that informs his entire body of work.

MILESTONES:

Worked in Chile as TV news editor and soap screenwriter

Became associated with other future directors such as Miguel Littin, Pedro Chaskel, Aldo Francia, etc.

1968: Made first completed feature film, "Tres tigres tristes/Three Sad Tigers"

1970: After election of Allende, began working with state film agency, Chile Films

1973: Fled Chile after overthrow of Allende; moved to Germany

1974: Settled in Paris

1985: Appointed co-director of Maison de Culture, Le Havre, France

1991: Shot first feature in US, "The Golden Boat"

QUOTES:

Ruiz received the 1997 National Art Award presented biennially by the Chilean government which included $25,000 cash and a yearly pension of $1,200 a month.

David O. Russell

BORN: in New York, 1958

NATIONALITY: American

EDUCATION: Amherst College Amherst, Massachusetts BA 1981

AWARDS: Sundance Film Festival Audience Award (Dramatic) "Spanking the Monkey" 1994

Independent Spirit Award Best First Feature "Spanking the Monkey" 1994

Independent Spirit Award Best Screenplay "Spanking the Monkey" 1994

Boston Society of Film Critics Award Best Director "Three Kings" 1999

BIOGRAPHY

David O. Russell stirred controversy with his first full-length feature, "Spanking the Monkey" (1994), which he wrote, directed and executive

produced for $80,000. The film was a black comedy about a dysfunctional family, but the scene that made eyebrows perk and some lose their breath was the one in which a young man is sexually intimate with his mother. The film won the Audience Award at the Sundance Film Festival in 1994, and two Independent Spirit Awards in 1995 after it was released by Fine Line.

Russell neither attended film school, nor did he set out to become a filmmaker; rather he was a political organizer and literacy teacher. But an urge to tell stories led him to make three short films, the documentary "Boston to Panama" (1985), "Bingo Inferno" (1987), which was screened at the Sundance Film Festival, and "Hairway to the Stars" (1990), about beauticians. Russell then wrote the script for "Spanking the Monkey" (1994). New Line Cinema offered him $1 million to produce and direct the film if he could find an acceptable star to play the mother. Instead, Russell raised the funds on his own and cast the relatively unknown Alberta Watson and Jeremy Davies, although he married New Line executive Janet Grillo. His wrote and directed his second feature, "Flirting With Disaster" (1996), another dark comedy about an adoptee (Ben Stiller) on a quest to find his biological parents. Three years passed before Russell returned to the helmer's chair, this time guiding George Clooney and Mark Wahlberg through their paces in the action adventure "Three Kings" (1999).

MILESTONES:

Raised in Larchmont, New York

After graduating from Amherst, worked as a political organizer and literacy teacher

Returned to NYC; worked as bartender for catering company while writing screenplays

1985: First short film, "Boston to Pananma"

1987: Made second short film, "Bingo Inferno"

1990: Produced, wrote and directed the short film, "Hairway to the Stars"

1994: Release of first feature film, "Spanking the Monkey"

1996: Second film, "Flirting With Disaster" released

1999: Directed the adventure-themed "Three Kings", starring George Clooney, Mark Wahlberg and Ice Cube

QUOTES:

"I don't think the parents of our generation were very interested in their kids. I think they were interested in what their kids represented in terms of potential and kudos and achievements."—David O. Russell in *Filmmaker*, Summer 1994.

"When you're outside there in the cold, you think, 'If I only had a deal at New Line, things would be great.' Well, we had a deal at New Line and it didn't solve any of our problems. You just get a whole set of other problems, and we didn't solve them. That's why we're back on the street."—Russell in *Filmmaker*, Summer 1994.

"All those great seventies movies. That's my guiding vision as a filmmaker. The seventies was a strange window in which Hollywood had stars, they were commercial, yet they were very original and very subversive"—Russell in *New York* magazine, April 29, 1996.

Ken Russell

BORN: Henry Kenneth Alfred Russell in Southampton, England, 07/03/1927

NATIONALITY: English

EDUCATION: Pangbourne Nautical College, Pangbourne, England, 1941–44

Walthamstow Art School, London, England, photography, 1949; met future wife Shirley Kingdon

International Ballet School, London, England, 1950; won scholarship but proved inept and was asked to leave shortly after enrolling

AWARDS: National Board of Review Award Best Director "The Devils" and "The Boy Friend" 1971

Cannes Film Festival Technique Award "Mahler" 1974

BIOGRAPHY

Known primarily for his exploration of sexual themes and his stylistic excesses, controversial British director Ken Russell first found himself artistically as a still photographer, contributing to such publications as *Picture Post* and ILLUS-TRATED, after ineffectual forays into the ballet and theatrical worlds. He converted to

Catholicism while shooting his first film, "Peepshow" (1956), then made "Amelia and the Angel" (1957) with the aid of the Catholic Film Institute, followed by "Lourdes" (1958), a conventional documentary about the legendary shrine. The latter two projects earned him a job replacing John Schlesinger as director of the BBC-TV arts program "Monitor", and he began by making a series of 15-minute shorts on subjects like pop art and folk dancing before immersing himself in the biographical documentary and revolutionizing the genre. Early works introducing living artists—the poet John Betjeman, the humorist Spike Milligan, the choreographer John Cranko, and others—finally gave way to exposes of dead artists.

Russell was ingenious in subverting BBC restrictions, gradually transforming the boring little factual accounts that relied solely on photographs and old newsreels to evocative longer films using real actors to impersonate historical figures. He made giant strides with "Prokofiev" (1961) and really broke through with the visually gorgeous "Elgar" (1962), an extraordinarily successful film on British composer Edward Elgar which made him famous overnight and led to his first opportunity to direct a feature. When "French Dressing" (1964) flopped, Russell continued opening up his BBC biopics, showing how artists like Bartok, Debussy and Isadora Duncan "transcended real problems and weaknesses in creating great art." He sandwiched "Dante's Inferno" (1967), a 90-minute study of Dante Gabriel Rossetti (Oliver Reed) which made more use of fantasy than its predecessors, and "Song of Summer" (1968), an account of the last years of British composer Frederick Delius (considered by many the finest of his TV films), around his second feature, "Billion Dollar Brain" (also 1967), a critically-acclaimed box office failure.

Russell's career took off again with the commercial and critical success of his next picture, a fine period evocation of D.H. Lawrence's "Women in Love" (1969). Noted for its bold erotic sensibility, particularly in the famous nude wrestling scene between Reed and Alan Bates, the film garnered an Oscar for actress Glenda Jackson, establishing her as a major star of the 70s. His last film for the BBC, "The Dance of the Seven Veils: A Comic Strip in Seven Episodes" (1970), which presented Richard Strauss as an egomaniac and a crypto-Nazi, conducting "Der Rosenkavalier" waltzes while SS men torture a Jew, drew howls of protest condemning his tasteless brutality. Although he would work the rest of his career almost entirely in the cinema, Russell's passion for music, art and biography pursued so relentlessly as a documentarian have remained at the forefront of his feature filmmaking. He has continually courted controversy as a purveyor of what his detractors have called "cultural pornography" and "visual madness," while his admirers have praised his visual flair, reveled in his excesses and compared him with Fellini.

Russell demonstrated considerable range with the three films he directed in 1971. "The Music Lovers", a self-indulgent and factually dubious account of Tchaikovsky focusing on the composer's homosexuality, struck many viewers as inappropriate. With "The Devils", based on the John Whiting play and Aldous Huxley novel "The Devils of Loudon", he once again played fast and loose with history and fashioned a relentlessly grotesque melodrama of 17th-century demonic possession, ending in the burning at the stake of the Christ-like Father Grandier (Reed), a sexually liberated priest whose ethics had brought him into conflict with the political ambitions of Cardinal Richelieu and the Catholic Church. Decried by Catholic officials for its "perverted marriage of sex, violence and blasphemy," "The Devils" featured exceptional cinematography, period costuming and art direction (and a fiery finale not for the squeamish). Russell's finale that year, "The Boy Friend", was an extreme change of pace, allowing the director to successfully rise to the challenge of making a musical on a budget of less than $2 million that looked as if it had cost ten times that amount. For many not enamored of his stylistic excess, it remains the best-liked of his films.

It was at this peak of his career that Russell decided to film "Savage Messiah" (1972), an adaptation of the H. S. Ede biography of sculptor Henri Gaudier-Brzeska, which had inspired him at an extremely low point during his early career as a failed dancer and actor. Investing his own money, he shot a restrained, convincing, impressive "portrait of an artist as a young man" that is often ignored amid the more flamboyant representatives of his oeuvre. Russell followed with "Mahler" (1973), an energetic and gorgeous biopic of the tormented life of the turn-of-the-century composer which (though one of his best films) did not receive nearly the warm reception of "Tommy" (1975), a virtually guaranteed success because of The Who's popularity and its all-star cast (including Ann-Margret, Reed, Elton John and Tina Turner). With "Lisztomania" (also 1975), the director embarked on one of his most outlandish extravaganzas, a so-called biography of Franz Liszt whose wrapper should bear the warning: "For Russell devotees only! All others BEWARE!" His career reached a low with the commercial failure of "Valentino" (1977), a typically excessive, visually flamboyant Ken Russell "biography", offering little insight into the silent film star and an awkward performance by ballet star Rudolph Nureyev in the title role.

The box-office success of Russell's "Altered States" (1980) once again made him bankable, and though most critics savaged his follow-up, "Crimes of Passion" (1984), as "sleazy tripe" or "lewd for the sake of being lewd", it was a watchable mess featuring fine performances by Kathleen Turner as a fashion designer-hooker and Anthony Perkins, the mad, street-corner preacher bent on saving her. The two films served as prototypes for later Russell films. "Altered States" drew comparisons to "The

Wolfman" and "Dr. Jekyll and Mr. Hyde" and paved the way for the director to mine the "horror" vein in "Gothic" (1986), a tale depicting a night in 1816 that inspired Mary Shelley ("Frankenstein") and Dr. Polidori ("The Vampyre") to write their classics, and "Lair of the White Worm" (1988), adapted from a Bram Stoker ("Dracula") novel. He revisited D. H. Lawrence with his adaptation of "The Rainbow" (1989), a prequel to "Women in Love" with Jackson appearing as the mother of her character from the first film, delivering a restrained feature filled with many beautiful and striking moments. "Whore/If You Can't Say It, Just See It" (1991), returned to the "Crimes of Passion" territory of sordid sex and prostitutes, with a very broad, even funny portrayal by Theresa Russell (no relation to the director) in the lead.

Russell returned to Lawrence a third time for "Lady Chatterley" (1993), a BBC miniseries based on the author's "Lady Chatterley's Lover." Most recently, he directed The Movie Channel's "Dogboys" (1998) and completed "Mindbender" (lensed c. 1996), an as yet unreleased biopic about the psychic Uri Geller.

His first wife, the costume designer Shirley Kingdon (a.k.a. Shirley Russell), was instrumental to the look of his early movies working on seven of his features, as well as the BBC documentaries. His second wife, screenwriter Vivien Jolly, collaborated with him on several projects, including "The Rainbow" and the script for a proposed film adaptation of Edith Wharton's "The House of Mirth." Like him or hate him, there is no confusing Ken Russell's work with anyone else's. Since courting the British establishment with "Elgar", he has consciously refused to make movies in the genteel tradition, preferring instead to shock his viewers. At his worst, Russell's movies are self-indulgent travesties, but at his best, the pictures are visually exciting and intelligent. His reputation for excess not withstanding, Russell is an important director whose legacy as a filmmaker revolves around his biographies, stretching the form from the strictly factual through the controversial "biased" documentaries to those that represent some of his best work.—Written by Greg Senf

MILESTONES:

1945: Entered Merchant Navy; released due to nervous breakdown

1946–1948: Served with Royal Air Force

Worked with British Dance Theatre, London Theatre Ballet, Ny Norsk Ballet, and in provincial repertory theater

Worked as freelance still photographer

1956: Made first amateur short film, "Peepshow"

1959: Began working as director for the BBC arts series "Monitor"

1962: Secured permission to use actors in "Elgar" on condition that they appeared only in long shot and spoke no dialogue

1964: First feature film as director, "French Dressing"

1965: Worked with actor Oliver Reed on "The Debussy Film"; got around BBC restrictions on using actors to represent historical figures by building the picture around a group of actors making a film about Debussy

1967: Cast Reed as Dante Gabriel Rosetti in "Dante's Inferno"

1970: Gained international attention with film "Women in Love"; Reed portrayed rich young mine owner Gerald Crich; first of five features with actress Glenda Jackson who won an Oscar for her performance; film garnered controversy over its nude male wrestling scene

1971: First feature as producer, "The Music Lovers"; also directed; second film with Jackson

1971: First screenplay credit, "The Devils", adapted from the John Whiting play based on Aldous Huxley's "The Devils of Loudon"; also directed and produced; Reed starred as Father Urbain Grandier

1972: Filmed "Savage Messiah", adapted from the H. S. Ede biography of the sculptor Henri

Gaudier-Brzeska from which he had drawn great strength at a low point in his life

1975: Commercial hit at the helm of The Who's "Tommy"; last feature (to date) with Reed

1980: Returned to the winner's column with "Altered States", although screenwriter Paddy Chayefsky disowned the final film which was based on a Chayefsky novel

Began to direct stage operas in 1980s; directed in England, Australia, Italy and Greece

1986: Directed highbrow horror film "Gothic", filled with trademark hallucinatory visuals

1988: Made feature acting debut in "Salome's Last Dance"; also directed

1989: Second Lawrence adaptation, "The Rainbow"; fifth and last (to date) feature with Jackson

1990: Directed first US TV production, "Dusk Before Fireworks" segment of "Women and Men: Stories of Seduction" (HBO)

1991: Last feature to date, "Whore"

1991: Second assignment for HBO, directing "Prisoner of Honor", a movie about a turn of the century anti-Semitic French army officer who challenges the massive government coverup in the imprisonment of Alfred Dreyfus

1993: Returned to the work of Lawrence, directing four-part miniseries "Lady Chatterly" (BBC), adapted from "Lady Chatterly's Lover"

1994: Contributed 27-minute "The Insatiable Mrs Kirsch" to executive producer Regina Ziegler's six-part "Erotic Tales"

1998: Directed The Movie Channel's "Dogboys"

2000: Made short film "Lion's Mouth"; screened on the Internet

AFFILIATION: Roman Catholic; converted when he married Shirley Kingdon

QUOTES:

Asked about the weirdest place he had ever vomited: "A coal bucket in Upper Norwood . . .

I'd just been to a press showing of my first feature film, "French Dressing", and I didn't know that it wasn't good form to go. I was asked not to as it was a press showing but after the film I just talked to the only person who would talk to me, the film critic of *The Bombay Times*, who loved it. All the rest universally condemned it. I was so upset. It was a sherry party so I got drunk on sherry. I remember tottering along Regent Street and collapsing in a doorway of what used to be a bank. I was moved on by a policeman so I stumbled down to Green Park and slept until it was dark. Then I got a 74 bus home to Upper Norwood and collapsed on the bed where I said to my wife at the time, 'I think I'm going to throw up!' and she convenietly brought a coal bucket over and I did. So that's the end of that. I never listened to the critics again."—Ken Russell in *Empire*, November 1997

"I've never had final cut on any of my films. Kubrick does on his films, but I can't think of anybody else. You get three cuts and three previews, and then they take over and chop it up. I'm told that the version of "The Devils" now out on video is the longest version. I haven't looked at it yet, but it's certainly longer than the version Warner Bros. had out before. When the film first came out, it did pretty well in Britain, ran for years in Italy, but was pretty well cut to shreds in America. (They cut out every scene that had pubic hair in it and it ended up about 15 minutes shorter)."—Russell to *Sight and Sound*, October 1997

BIBLIOGRAPHY:

"Ken Russell" Gene D. Phillips, 1979, Twayne

"Altered States: The Autobiography of Ken Russell" Ken Russell, 1991, Bantam Books

"The Lion Roars: Ken Russell on Film", 1993, Faber and Faber

"Mike and Gaby's Space Gospel" Ken Russell, 2000, Little Brown; novel

"Directing Film: From Pitch to Premiere" Ken Russell, 2000

Nancy Savoca

BORN: in Bronx, New York, 1960

NATIONALITY: American

EDUCATION: Queens College, Flushing, New York, attended briefly

New York University, New York, New York, film, 1982; wrote and directed two award-winning short films, "Renata" and "Bad Timing"

AWARDS: NYU Film Festival Haig P. Manoogian Award for Overall Excellence in Filmmaking "Renata" and "Bad Timing" student films

Sundance Film Festival Grand Jury Award (Dramatic) "True Love" 1989

BIOGRAPHY

The daughter of Sicilian and Argentine immigrants, writer-director Nancy Savoca graduated from the film school at New York University where she received the Haig P. Manoogian Award for overall excellence for her short films "Renata" and "Bad Timing". Her earliest professional experience came as an assistant auditor on two Jonathan Demme–directed pictures ("Something Wild" 1986, "Married to the Mob" 1988) and as a production assistant to John Sayles ("Brother From Another Planet" 1984). Sayles, in turn, provided funding for her feature directing and co-screenwriting debut, "True Love" (1989), an incisive comedy about Italian-American courtship and marriage rituals in the Bronx. Hailed by both Janet Maslin and Vincent Canby of *The New York Times* as one of the best films of the year, "True Love" subsequently was purchased and released by MGM-UA and its accompanying soundtrack on RCA records boasted two Top 40 hits on the BILLBOARD charts. Its success enabled Savoca to make her only Hollywood film to date, "Dogfight" (1991), although she has taken all her projects to the studios first before going the independent route. Filmed for $8 million (eight times the budget of "True Love"), "Dogfight" told the story of a young Vietnam-bound soldier (River Phoenix) and the wallflower waitress (Lili Taylor) whom he takes to a mean-spirited contest for the ugliest date. The film received favorable reviews but a poor box-office reception but further demonstrated the director's flair and facility with actors.

Savoca returned to the compromise world of independents with "Household Saints" (1993), a bittersweet tale of three generations of Italian-American women which received glowing reviews in many quarters and a healthy (if modest) box office. Featuring stellar work from Taylor (as a religious fanatic), Tracey Ullman and Vincent D'Onofrio (as Taylor's mismatched parents) and veteran Judith Malina as D'Onofrio's mother, this adaptation of Francine Prose's novel proved a strong depiction of Italian-Americans in NYC. Like many an indie, the project faced monetary problems; Savoca has said: "I can tell you this: that we could not have made 'Household Saints' for a dollar less than we did. We shaved the budget and shaved the budget and finally we went back to the investors and we said: 'If we make this budget any smaller you're gonna get a movie that's unreleasable.' "

Although she had contributed a short film for the syndicated children's series "The Great Spacecoaster" in the early 80s, Savoca spent her time during her third and fourth features really getting her feet wet in TV, directing a 1995 episode of "Murder One" (ABC) for Steven Bochco and the unsold ABC series pilot "Dark Eyes" (1995), starring Kelly McGillis as a female cop assigned to a special task force. She also directed the "1952" and "1974" segments (and wrote all three) of "If These Walls Could Talk" (1997), HBO's tripartite movie focusing on the issue of reproductive choices. Borrowing from her own experiences as a mother of three, Savoca then tackled the legend of the modern-day superwoman in "The 24 Hour Woman" (1999), revealing with great humanity how everything comes with a price. Starring Rosie Perez as a TV producer whose pregnancy, birth and child-raising become the focus of her quirky talk show, the film rang true to the merciless gauntlet endured by working mothers, and though some found the tone wearying, others appreciated its Darwinian message about motherhood and delighted in its send-up of daytime TV.

FAMILY:
son: Kenneth Guay. Born in January 1989 while "True Love" was enjoying its Sundance success; named after producer Kenneth Utt (a producing associate of family friend Jonathan Demme)

MILESTONES:
Raised in the Bronx
Worked as a script reader for a small film distribution company
1984: Worked with husband as volunteer on production of John Sayles' "The Brother From Another Planet"; Sayles would later invest money in her feature directing debut
1985: Shot a nine-minute trailer for "True Love"
1986: Worked as assistant auditor on Jonathan Demme's "Something Wild"
1988: Hired by Demme for "Married to the Mob", this time credited as production auditor assistant
1989: Directed and co-wrote first feature, "True Love"
1991: Helmed second film, "Dogfight", a period romance starring Lili Taylor and River Phoenix

1993: Reteamed with Lili Taylor for "Household Saints"; co-wrote screenplay and directed

1995: TV directing debut, the ABC special "Dark Eyes"

1995: Helmed an episode of the ABC legal drama "Murder One"

1997: Directed the "1952" and "1974" segments of the HBO movie dealing with women's reproductive rights, "If These Walls Could Talk", which became the then-highest rated original movie in HBO history; scripted all three segments

1998: Feted as a "New York trailblazer" at the New York Women's Film Festival

Honored by the Los Angeles chapter of the advocacy organization Women in Film & Television (WIFT)

1999: Returned to features as co-writer and director of "The 24 Hour Woman"; premiered at the Sundance Film Festival

Penned the teleplay for "The Dusty Springfield Story", to be produced for VH1 by MADGUY Productions

QUOTES:

"I'm not a real man expert, I think women can get together and talk about what goes on . . . I don't know what happens—men either know less about what goes on, or they're confused."—Savoca on her ability to understand women and not men, from *Premiere*, October 1993.

"I'm better as a director [than a writer], 'cause it's easier for me to get my ideas across to the people I'm working with than to write them down."—Savoca to *Interview*, September 1993.

"Whenever you meet independent filmmakers you're always asking 'Who financed your movie'?"—Savoca in *Filmmaker*, Autumn 1993.

On why she turned down the chance to direct "Wayne's World": "I wasn't hip enough to get it. You just can't take on anything. You've really got to love what you're doing. I could convince myself that I really like the project, that I could do big-budget things and actually

do a little inroading on the woman director thing, but the problem is I've also got to convince a cast of actors that I love being there.

"I've got enough energy in me to argue with executives over all the changes I want. There's so much that goes into making a movie, and it's almost a two-year process, so I have to really in some way believe that I'm doing the greatest movie on Earth—which I've always felt every time I've gone out and made my movies. Whether other people agree or not, I feel like I'm doing something great. And that's why I get up in the morning. But it's different if you take something for a paycheck."—From *The Washington Post*, February 28, 1999

About how her collaboration with husband Richard Guay works: "The easy answer is to say that I am the creative one who works with actors, and he is the producer trying to figure out how to get the money. Except that we have this writer thing. In the writing phase, it is up for grabs creatively, but once we get into production, we pretty much respect each other's territory.

"And also, since he's so different from me, I get another point of view that I trust . . . His approach is like the polar opposite of how I would approach it, and sometimes therein lies the answer. If things are getting convoluted, I go to him because he is a clear thinker. I could take a scene on for 80 pages and never be able to get out of it. Rich will say, 'The scene ends here.' In 'Household Saints', the novel was something like 235 pages, and the script was longer, and he just came in and cut it."—From *Filmmaker*, February–April 1999.

BORN: John Thomas Sayles in Schenectady, New York, 09/28/1950

NATIONALITY: American

EDUCATION: Mount Pleasant High School, Schenectady, New York; won letters in baseball, track, basketball and football

Williams College, Williamstown, Massachusetts, psychology, 1972; also studied film and creative writing and began acting

AWARDS: O. Henry Award "I-80 Nebraska" 1975 short story award

Los Angeles Film Critics Association Award Best Screenplay "Return of the Secaucus Seven" 1980

United States Film Festival Special Jury Prize "Return of the Secaucus Seven" 1981 cited with "The Day After Trinity" and "The War at Home"

Sundance Film Festival Special Jury Prize "Brother From Another Planet" 1985 cited with "The Roommate" and "Stranger Than Paradise"

Tokyo International Film Festival Grand Prix Award "City of Hope" 1991 prize won by film as best film

London Film Critics Circle Special Award 1991 "for service to American independent cinema"

Society of Texas Film Critics Award Best Director "Lone Star" 1996

Society of Texas Film Critics Award Best Original Screenplay "Lone Star" 1996

IFP Gotham Award Filmmaker 1996

Golden Satellite Best Motion Picture Screenplay (Original) "Lone Star" 1996; tied with "The People vs. Larry Flynt"; initial presentation of the award

Writers Guild of America Laurel Award for Career Achievement 1997

BIOGRAPHY

In an era when last year's indie wunderkind is too often this year's studio sellout, screenwriter-director John Sayles stands apart, his rugged self-reliance a beacon to aspiring filmmakers wishing to make complex pictures that say something. His limited experience within the studio system (1983's "Baby, It's You" for Paramount; 1988's "Eight Men Out" at Orion) convinced him that easing the financial burden was not worth the resultant loss of artistic freedom; subsequently he has steered his own path, working in Hollywood only as script doctor or screenwriter for hire. Between assignments, Sayles has become America's most celebrated independent filmmaker, one who has not repeated himself, moving from one distinct subject matter to the next. Though his visual style has often seemed secondary to his literary concerns, his command of the camera has grown, thanks in part to collaborations with the likes of such esteemed directors of photography as Haskell Wexler and Robert Richardson.

After acting in school plays and summer stock while at Williams College, Sayles embarked on a career as a fiction writer, submitting stories to magazines and supporting himself as an orderly, day laborer and meat packer. His two novels, "Pride of the Bimbos" (1975) and "Union Dues" (1977), and his short story anthology, "The Anarchist's Convention" (1979), received critical acclaim for their honest characterizations and authentic use of dialect, although they did not meet with financial success. Interested in writing for film, Sayles adapted Eliot Asinof's "Eight Men Out" and, using it as a sample of his work, found a place with Roger Corman's New World Pictures, where he penned Joe Dante's "Piranha" (1978), Lewis Teague's "The Lady in Red" (1979) and Jimmy Murakami's "Battle Beyond the Stars" (1980). He also scripted two witty genre send-ups in 1981, "The Howling", reteaming him with Teague, and "Alligator", directed by Dante.

Taking $60,000 earned from screenwriting, Sayles directed his first feature, "Return of the Secaucus Seven" (1980), a witty, poignant look at a reunion of 1960s activists on the verge of adulthood. Praised as a more authentic and charming portrait of the same territory explored in the more commercially successful "The Big Chill" (1983), the film used few sets, unknown actors, sparse camera movement and little action, but it won the Best Screenplay award from the Los Angeles Film Critics. Sayles turned in a winning performance as Howie, setting a precedent for acting in many of his subsequent films, and David Strathairn, a familiar face from the Sayles repertory company, made his feature debut. He followed with "Lianna" (1982), a daring yet subtle examination of the changes a married woman undergoes following her discovery that she is a lesbian. Alternately praised for its sensitivity and derided as exploitative, the low-budget film ($300,000) contained another good role (as a film professor) for the director and helped him obtain Paramount's backing for his next project.

"Baby, It's You", the story of a doomed high-school romance between a college-bound Jewish girl (Rosanna Arquette) and a working class Italian youth (Vincent Spano), however, suffered from the studio's involvement (and later abandonment). The uncharacteristically frothy departure for Sayles was his least successful feature. He dropped out of the Directors Guild as he couldn't afford to remain in the union as an independent. "If I was going to do 'Brother From Another Planet' (1984) for $400,000, a production manager, first assistant director, and second assistant director"—all jobs required by the guild—"were going to cost me a third of my budget." The prestigious MacArthur Foundation "genius grant" which came his way in 1983 provided him with a tax-free yearly stipend of $30,000 over a five-year period and greatly facilitated the making of "Brother", an unlikely story of a mute, black alien (Joe Morton) adrift in Harlem. "Every month this check would arrive that would pay the rent and the bill for renting the editing machine. I always walk a tightrope financially, but this was like having a net."

Finished screenplays for two pet projects, "Matewan" and "Eight Men Out", had long languished due to their perceived commercial inviability. Sayles finally made the former in 1987, exploring the personal and political dimensions of union making and breaking in the West Virginia coal mines of the 1920s. A complex study of individual integrity and community solidarity, the film, typically for Sayles, is largely dialogue-driven—although the director succeeded, with the help of Appalachian locations, Wexler's cinematography and Mason Daring's lively bluegrass soundtrack, in creating an evocative setting for his narrative. His ambitious "Eight Men Out", an account of the 1919 scandal that rocked the baseball world, examined the controversy through the eyes of individual ball players, each having complex reasons for agreeing or refusing to throw the World Series. Sayles (aided by director of photography Robert Richardson) relied even more on visuals, using impressionistic lighting and scrupulous production design to help capture this period of American history. Though it was an Orion film, the studio's sole provision was that he keep it under two hours, a feat the director claims to have accomplished by having the actors talk fast.

Sayles continued to forge his own distinctive path in the 90s. "City of Hope" (1991) was a somber study of life in a mid-sized contemporary American town, weaving together several storylines to create a bleakly complex picture of corruption and decay. "Passion Fish" (1992), about the relationship between a paralyzed former TV soap star and her live-in nurse, earned praise for its central performances by

Mary McDonnell and Alfre Woodard while garnering Sayles his first Oscar nomination for Best Original Screenplay. "The Secret of Roan Inish" (1994), reteamed him with Wexler and was a real change of pace, as it was filmed on location in the wild western islands of Ireland. Adapted from Rosalie Frye's novella "The Secret of Ron More Skerry", the story centered around a girl living with her grandparents in County Donegal and incorporated mystical and whimsical elements unusual for the writer-director, which he handled superbly.

Sayles, whose films had consistently scored with the critics but performed meagerly at the box office, registered his biggest commercial breakthrough with the gritty "Lone Star" (1996), earning a second Oscar nomination for his original screenplay. Mainstream audiences responded enthusiastically to the richly textured, thoroughly engrossing drama that featured a strong ensemble cast including Kris Kristofferson, Chris Cooper, Elizabeth Pena, Frances McDormand, Joe Morton and rising star Matthew McConaughey. Its story followed a Texas sheriff (Cooper) trying to unravel the life and death of his father (McConaughey) who had been sheriff of the Texas border town 15 years earlier. For several scenes, Sayles moved his camera from a long shot in the past to a close-up in the present, allowing both eras to exist simultaneously in the same tracking shot, a device that proved quite eloquent in his hands. Unfortunately, his next film "Men With Guns" (1998) did not fare as well commercially, its lack of name actors and Spanish dialogue dooming it to the fate of so much of his previous work.

Sayles' contributions to other media are less well-publicized, but in addition to his novels, he has written two one-act plays, "New Hope for the Dead" and "Turnbuckle", which he directed in NYC's Boat Basin Theatre in 1981. He helmed three popular Bruce Springsteen videos, and his TV work began with "A Perfect Match" (CBS, 1980), for which he wrote the screenplay. Sayles created the 1989 pilot and

was creative consultant on the highly acclaimed but short-lived series "Shannon's Deal" (NBC, 1990–91), about a disillusioned Philadelphia lawyer scraping by on small cases in his own small walkup practice. He also wrote and acted in the Vietnam vet drama "Unnatural Causes" (NBC, 1986), played a baseball player on "Mathnet: The Case of the Unnatural" (PBS, 1992) and turned up on the documentaries "Naked Hollywood" (A&E, 1991) and "Baseball" (PBS, 1994).

MILESTONES:

Acted and directed with Eastern Slope Playhouse, North Conway, New Hampshire

1975: Publication of first novel, "Pride of the Bimbos"

1978: First screenwriting assignment, Joe Dante's "Piranha" (for Roger Corman); also played small unbilled role

1978: Directed first film, "Return of the Secaucus Seven"; also wrote, edited and acted; film shot in 25 days on budget of $60,000; completed and released in 1980

1980: TV debut as screenwriter on "A Perfect Match" (CBS)

1982: Wrote and directed lesbian coming-of-age tale, "Lianna"

1983: Worked within studio system (at Paramount) to ease the financial burden of making "Baby, It's You"

1984: Played one of the Men in Black (with frequent Sayles repertory actor David Strathairn) sent to hunt down "The Brother from Another Planet" (Joe Morton); also wrote and directed

1986: TV acting debut, in "Unnatural Causes"; also scripted

1987: First collaboration with cinematographer Haskell Wexler, "Matewan"

1988: Told the story of baseball's "Black Sox" scandal with "Eight Men Out"; played the role of sportswriter Ring Lardner; second attempt to compromise with studio system (this time Orion) convinced him it wasn't worth curtailing his artistic freedom; first collaboration with director of photography Robert Richardson

1990–1991: Created TV series "Shannon's Deal"; also scripted episodes and wrote lyrics; prominent jazz musicians Wynton Marsalis (who wrote the theme), Dave Grusin, Chick Corea and Lee Ritenour contributed to the score

1991: Reteamed with Richardson and received almost universally good reviews for "City of Hope"

1992: Received first Oscar nomination for Best Original Screenplay, "Passion Fish"

1994: Reteamed with Wexler for "The Secret of Roan Inish"; Sayles' first foreign location

1996: Earned second Oscar nomination for Best Original Screenplay for big commercial breakthrough, "Lone Star"

1998: Wrote and directed "Men With Guns", a pet project of his put temporarily on hold prior to filming "Lone Star"; Spanish dialogue and lack of big names in the principle roles made it a tough sell; filmed in Mexico

1999: Third collaboration with Wexler, "Limbo"; also seventh role for David Strathairn

2000: Served as executive producer on the Sundance prize winner "Girlfight", directed by Karyn Kusama

2002: Wrote and directed "Sunshine State"

QUOTES:

In 1983, Sayles received a 'genius grant' from the MacArthur Foundation receiving $30,000 tax-free over a five-year period.

The three Bruce Springsteen videos he has directed are "Born in the USA", "I'm On Fire" and "Glory Days."

"When you're making something with a lot of story lines, a lot of actors, and all these technical problems, and its very ambitious for the budget, you're juggling a lot of things. Anytime you've worked with an actor before, you can eliminate a question mark. That's just that much emotional energy and time that you don't have

to spend working something out with an actor. You know, I've worked with Chris Cooper a couple of times and I know he can take care of himself. Poor Chris! So many of his scenes in 'Lone Star' involve asking for information. He's so consistent and such a deep actor; we could come to him with only two hours left in the day and say, 'Okay. now we're going to do your angle,' and he wouldn't feel panicked. He would have been doing good stuff with the other actors all day, but he still had what he needed left." —John Sayles in *Filmmaker*, 1996.

"If I had $200 million I'd probably find something more useful to put it into than movies, but if they told me I had to make a movie with the money, then I would probably make about 20 movies with it." —Sayles to *Daily News*, March 4, 1998.

"There are movies which are just 'movie movies,' where the references in the movies are to other movies, where the behavior is a kind of movie behavior, and that's fine because that's the universe you're being asked to enter. Then there are movies on the other side of the continuum which are a little bit more like what goes on in life and is recognizable human behavior, and the references are to things that happen in real life, not to things which happen in movies.

"Ours are way over on that side. Even if there's a fantasy element, they still have their feet planted firmly on the ground of what happens in the world." —John Sayles, quoted in *The Boston Globe*, March 8, 1998.

"One of the problems with my movies is that it's often hard to say what they're about in less than two sentences. I think that makes them more interesting, but much harder to sell." —Sayles in *American Cinematographer*, March 1998

Sayles is often referred to as the father of modern indie cinema.

"I feel like so often you see women in films presented in this language of film that we've seen forever. They're inaccurate potraits, but we're so used to seeing them that we accept them. And John's movie is not like that"

—Maggie Gyllenhaal on loving John Sayles' work. *Interview* November 2002

BIBLIOGRAPHY:

"Pride of the Bimbos" John Sayles, 1975, Atlantic/Little, Brown; novel

"Union Dues" John Sayles, 1977, Atlantic/Little, Brown; novel; partial basis for film "Matewan"; won a National Book Award nomination

"The Anarchists' Convention" John Sayles, 1979, Atlantic/Little, Brown; stories

"Thinking in Pictures: The Making of the Movie Matewan" John Sayles, 1987, Houghton Mifflin; non-fiction

"Sayles on Sayles" John Sayles and Gavin Smith, 1998, Faber and Faber

"Los Gusanos" John Sayles, 1991, Harper-Collins; novel written partly in Spanish

"John Sayles: An Unauthorized Biography" Gerry Molyneaux, 2000, Renaissance Books

Joel Schumacher

BORN: in New York, New York, 08/29/1939

NATIONALITY: American

EDUCATION: Fashion Institute of Technology, New York, New York; attended briefly in his late teens

Parsons School of Design, New York, New York; attended on scholarship; graduated with honors

AWARDS: NATO/ShoWest Director of the Year Award 1997; presented by the National Association of Theater Owners

ShowEast Award of Excellence in Filmmaking 1999

BIOGRAPHY

Previous work experience as a window display artist and fashion designer provided an appropriate foundation for the films of Joel Schumacher. Amiably shallow, slickly produced and filled to overflowing with glossy images and beautiful people, these films are a triumph of fashion over substance. At their best, they are tasty Hollywood confections. At their worst, they're just movie junk food. But they usually go down easy.

After entering the industry as a costume designer, Schumacher wrote screenplays for "Car Wash" (1976), a modest ethnic comedy, "Sparkle" (1976), an old-fashioned Black musical and "The Wiz" (1978), the notorious musical flop. Schumacher made his feature directorial debut with "The Incredible Shrinking Woman" (1981) starring Lily Tomlin. Though not all reviewers were convinced by the film's feminist aspects, many were struck by its striking design sense and peculiar color scheme. Most of his subsequent output has been mainstream Hollywood fare: "brat pack" vehicles including "St. Elmo's Fire" (1985) and two well-done entries, "The Lost Boys" (1987) and "Flatliners" (1990); "Cousins" (1989), a saccharine romantic comedy derived from the popular French film, "Cousin, Cousine" (1975); and "Dying Young" (1991), a glossy weeper starring Julia Roberts and Campbell Scott.

"Falling Down" (1993) presented an opportunity for an ambitious change of pace. A bespectacled Michael Douglas wore a severe crew cut as the "Last Angry White Man" cutting a violent swath across the sweltering streets of south central Los Angeles. What could have been a "Taxi Driver" for the 90s became, under Schumacher's soothing hands, sort of a "Travis Bickle Lite." Less filling and less unsettling than a serious film, very little is at stake in this attractively photographed, well-acted, and remarkably innocuous vigilante movie. It was the number one film of its opening weekend but soon fizzled. Schumacher chose a more conventional follow-up: a slick legal thriller adapted from a bestseller and boasting a respected cast. Adapted from the John Grisham novel, "The Client" (1994) starred Susan Sarandon, Tommy Lee Jones and promising newcomer Brad Renfro as a street smart 11-year-old who knows too much about a mob-related assassination. The film was a solid success that won Sarandon an Oscar nomination for Best Actress.

Schumacher has also worked in TV with limited success. He honed his directing skills on TV-movies and ventured into producing with pilots and short-lived series. Schumacher even played a part in Drew Barrymore's aggressive comeback campaign by casting her in his fleeting (but some say fabulous) primetime soap, "2000 Malibu Road" (1992), which he executive produced and directed the pilot and the three subsequent episodes.

Fans were surprised to learn that smooth operator Schumacher was selected to replace confirmed eccentric Tim Burton as the helmer of the heretofore surefire "Batman" series. Significantly, neither filmmaker previously possessed a reputation for adventure acumen. Schumacher was handed Warner Brothers' biggest asset because of his reputation as a stylist who gets his films completed on time and under budget. He is also known for his ability to work with major stars under trying circumstances. While still a blockbuster, Burton's "Batman Returns" (1992) was deemed a commercial disappointment. Worse still, some parents found it too disturbing for the kiddies. Schumacher's assignment was to make a lighter and more fun "Batman" movie that would help keep the franchise alive. He would only accept if his friend Burton approved. He did.

The new helmer was aided in his mission by a new star, Val Kilmer (replacing the departing Michael Keaton), a tough and buffed Robin (Chris O'Donnell), and two accomplished scene-stealers as villains. The superhot Jim Carrey was cast as The Riddler and the seemingly ubiquitous Tommy Lee Jones played Two-Face. Budgeted at $80 million, with another $20 million for promotion, "Batman Forever" (1995) rode a massive wave of hype and anticipation as one of the blockbusters to beat in the summer of 1995. The former costume designer and set decorator was afforded an opportunity to flex those old muscles again on a massive scale. Even more lavish and art directed than its illustrious predecessors (it boasted a 62-person design crew), the film abandoned the somber tones of the Burton films in favor of vivid comic-book colors. Batman and Robin's costumes were also revised from earlier incarnations to give them a pumped up body-conscious look complete with nipples and codpieces, Schumacher innovations both. Audiences (and many reviewers) embraced the new model thereby affording Schumacher his biggest hit up to that point in his career. Warner Bros.' Batman franchise seemed alive and well until the fourth installment "Batman & Robin" (1997), with George Clooney now assuming the cape, proved to be a loud and confusing mishmash. Critics and fans were disappointed and plans for a fifth segment were temporarily scuttled.

Schumacher's version of "The Client" had so impressed John Grisham that the author personally selected Schumacher to helm "A Time to Kill" (1996). Adapted from Grisham's first (and many feel best) novel, the film centers on the effects of a murder trial on the residents of a small Southern town. Schumacher selected the virtually unknown Matthew McConaughey to play the leading role of a crusading lawyer and surrounded the novice with veterans Samuel L. Jackson (as the murder suspect), Sandra Bullock (as a law student), Donald Sutherland (as the lawyer's mentor) and Kevin Spacey (as the prosecuting attorney). Critics raved about the performances and Schumacher's sensitive handling of the racially-charged story.—Written by Kent Greene

MILESTONES:

Grew up an only child in Long Island City in Queens, NY

Father died while Schumacher was a young child; mother supported by selling dresses

1948: Began drinking at nine-years-old (date approximate)

Built puppet theaters to perform at parties

Volunteered to dress neighborhood store windows while working for a local butcher

Briefly attended the Fashion Institute of Technology in New York, NY

1954: Left home at 15-years-old (date approximate)

1954: Claiming to be 18, worked at Macy's selling men's gloves (date approximate)

Worked as a window dresser for Macy's, Lord & Taylor and Saks

Moved to Miami where he became heavily involved with life in the fast lane

Worked as design and display artist for Henri Bendel's department store in NYC

Attended the Parsons School of Design on scholarship

Worked as fashion designer

Helped run a popular trendy boutique called Paraphernalia on the Upper East Side of NYC; associated with the likes of Andy Warhol and Edie Sedgwick

1970: Stopped taking drugs

Joined Revlon as designer of clothing and packaging

Worked on TV commercials

1971: Talked his way into a trial job as costume designer on Frank Perry's "Play It As It Lays"

Moved to L.A.

1973: Worked as costume designer on three features: "Blume in Love," "The Last of Sheila," "Sleeper"

1974: First TV credit, as production designer on Curtis Harrington's TV-movie, "Killer Bees", starring Gloria Swanson

1974: TV-movie co-writing and directing debut, "The Virginia Hill Story"

1976: First feature as screenwriter, "Sparkle"

1981: Feature directing debut, "The Incredible Shrinking Woman"

1983: First TV credit as executive producer, the unsold CBS pilot, "Now We're Cookin'" (also scripted)

1985: Executive produced his first TV series, "Code Name: Foxfire", a short-lived adventure series for NBC

1990: First film on which he had right of final cut, "Flatliners"

1994: First adaptation of a John Grisham novel, "The Client"

1995: Chosen to direct the third installment of the Batman series "Batman Forever"

1996: Helmed the feature adaptation of Grisham's first novel "A Time to Kill"

1997: The fourth installment in the series and second directed by Schumacher, "Batman & Robin" received negative reviews and essentially killed off the franchise

1999: Directed Robert De Niro and Philip Seymour Hoffman in "Flawless"; also wrote script

2000: Helmed the acclaimed Vietnam-era drama "Tigerland"

2002: Directed the action comedy "Bad Company", featuring Chris Rock and Anthony Hopkins

2002: Hand-picked Colin Farrell to star in his thriller suspense feature "Phone Booth"

QUOTES:

When Mr. Schumacher approached her (actress Susan Sarandon who subsequently starred in "The Client") about starring in the thriller, he shot straight for the heart. During lunch at a packed restaurant in Ms. Sarandon's Chelsea neighborhood in New York, he had flowers sent to the table and then, to her astonishment, got down on the floor. "I just couldn't imagine making the movie without her," he says. "I thought, 'I've got to do something really dramatic.' So I took her hand and I proposed. I said,

'I can't live without you. Come and marry me on the screen for four months.' "—From *The New York Times*, July 17, 1994.

Sarandon was both embarrassed and charmed by Schumacher's public display of wretched excess. Yet as someone who covets candor in personal transactions, Sarandon was more beguiled by the rest of Schumacher's rap, which he says went something like this: "I've got a lot to learn as a director, but I can cast a movie better than anyone. You'll be cast well. You'll be treated with respect. And you'll have a lot of fun."—From

"Why They All Want Susan" by Gene Seymour, *New York Newsday: Fanfare*, July 17, 1994.

" . . . The director's work has also been criticized for being more flashy than substantive. Asked about this, his voice drops. 'If you ask people to leave their homes, spend a lot of money on a movie, buy that terrible popcorn and those diluted sodas,' he said, 'you'd better tell them, a story and entertain them. There's absolutely nothing wrong about that.' "—From "Visual Flair, A Hip Sensibility And a Past" by Bernard Weinraub, *The New York Times*, June 11, 1995.

Martin Scorsese

BORN: in Flushing, New York, 11/17/1942

NATIONALITY: American

EDUCATION: attended Catholic grade school
   entered junior seminary at age 14; expelled
   Cardinal Hayes High School, Bronx, New York; transferred from junior seminary
   New York University, New York, New York, English, BS, 1964; directed first short film, "What's a Nice Girl Like You Doing in a Place Like This?" (1963)
   New York University, New York, New York, film, MA, 1966

AWARDS: Cannes Film Festival Palme d'Or "Taxi Driver" 1976
   Cannes Film Festival International Grand Prix "Taxi Driver" 1976
   Los Angeles Film Critics Association New Generation Award 1976; tied with Jodie Foster
   National Society of Film Critics Award Best Director "Taxi Driver" 1976
   National Society of Film Critics Award Best Director "Raging Bull" 1980
   Independent Spirit Award Best Director "After Hours" 1985; tied with Joel Coen for "Blood Simple"

Cannes Film Festival Best Director Award "After Hours" 1986
   Venice Film Festival Best Director Award "GoodFellas" 1990
   Los Angeles Film Critics Association Award Best Director "GoodFellas" 1990
   New York Film Critics Circle Award Best Director "GoodFellas" 1990
   National Society of Film Critics Award Best Director "GoodFellas" 1990
   BAFTA Award Best Director "GoodFellas" 1990
   BAFTA Award Best Screenplay (Adapted) "GoodFellas" 1990; shared with Nicholas Pileggi
   National Board of Review Award Best Director "The Age of Innocence" 1993
   Independent Feature Project (IPF) Gotham Award 1993; awarded for lifetime achievement
   BAFTA Britannia Award 1993 annual award
   American Society of Cinematographers Board of Governors Award 1995
   Venice Film Festival Golden Lion Award for Lifetime Achievement 1995
   ShowEast Cecil B. DeMille Award 1995 for lifetime achievement; presented by the National Association of Theater Owners (NATO)
   John Huston Award for Artists Rights 1996;

third recipient; cited for his work in film preservation; presented by the Artists Rights Foundation

American Film Institute Life Achievement Award 1997

National Board of Review Billy Wilder Award 1998

Directors Guild of America Honors Filmmaker Award 1999; initial presentation

Honorary Cesar 2000

Special David di Donatello Prize 2001

National Board of Review William K. Everson Award for Film History "Il Mio Viaggo in Italia/My Voyage to Italy" 2001

National Society of Film Critics Film Heritage Award "My Voyage to Italy/Il Mio Viaggio in Italia" 2001

Golden Globe Award Best Director "Gangs of New York" 2002

Directors Guild of America Life Achievement Award 2002

BIOGRAPHY

One of the most prominent and influential filmmakers of the latter half of the Twentieth century, Martin Scorsese generally roots his films in his own experience, exploring his Italian-American heritage and examining themes built around religious or social sin and redemption. While he has not enjoyed the kind of mainstream marketplace success of many of his contemporaries, Scorsese has directed numerous critically acclaimed features.

The one-time seminary student studied filmmaking at NYU and shot a handful of short films while obtaining his degrees. In 1967, his first feature, "Who's That Knocking at My Door?" was shown at the Chicago Film Festival but failed to find a distributor. While teaching at NYU, Scorsese aided fellow student Michael Wadleigh in the editing of the Oscar-winning documentary "Woodstock" (1969). Producer Joseph Brenner agreed to distribute Scorsese's first film if it included a gratuitous sex scene, which he dutifully added. "Who's

That Knocking at My Door?", a semi-autobiographical look at an Italian-American Catholic (played by Harvey Keitel) who deals with women as either virgins or whores, opened to critical praise.

Roger Corman tapped Scorsese to direct the Depression-era allegory "Boxcar Bertha" (1972), a film which parallels the story of Christ and Mary Magdalene. Featuring Barbara Hershey and David Carradine, the film introduced a favorite theme of the director's: that of the "sinner" who temporarily falls from grace only to be finally, if ambiguously, redeemed. The following year, Scorsese broke through with "Mean Streets", his autobiographical tale of a group of young hoods living and dying in NYC (although ironically, the film was shot in Los Angeles). Again Harvey Keitel was the director's screen alter ego with Robert De Niro as his unstable friend Johnny Boy. A stylish and richly realized character piece, "Mean Streets" marked the beginning of one of the most productive and important star-director pairings in film history. In De Niro, Scorsese found the perfect vehicle to channel rage tempered with humanity.

As a follow-up, though, Scorsese attempted a "woman's picture", the feminist "Alice Doesn't Live Here Anymore" (1974). Reportedly lead Ellen Burstyn had asked Francis Ford Coppola for recommendations on directors and he gave her only one name: Scorsese's. When they met, Burstyn asked the director what he knew about women and he reputedly replied, "Nothing, but I'd like to learn." Evoking the styles of such famed "women's directors" as Douglas Sirk and George Cukor, "Alice" was a critical and box-office success that netted its star a Best Actress Oscar and spawned a long-running CBS sitcom. Scorsese was on much more familiar ground with the testosterone-laden "Taxi Driver" (1976). An iconographic street opera penned by Paul Schrader, it not only gave De Niro a tour-de-force role as the unstable Vietnam veteran turned vigilante Travis Bickle, the film also melded the themes of Scorsese's early works.

The two female characters are literally a whore and a golden girl, treated oppositely by Bickle who is the epitome of the sinner in need of redemption. The film garnered its share of controversy at its release mostly because of its bloody finale—a sustained, hallucinatory, brilliantly staged set piece of carnage built around Jodie Foster's teenage prostitute.

With "New York, New York" (1977), Scorsese set out initially to create a nostalgic look at the movie musical but during filming shaped the story around the dark relationship between a musician (De Niro) and his deteriorating relationship with a band singer (Liza Minnelli, whose character was deemed to be loosely based on her own mother, Judy Garland). The overall result was an uneven film that audiences, expecting an affectionate musical, found too depressing.

After the box-office failure of "New York, New York", Scorsese triumphed with what is considered his masterpiece, "Raging Bull" (1976). Drawn from the autobiography of boxer Jake La Motta, the film is a no-holds-barred look at the rise and fall of a champion. The literate script co-written by Scorsese and Mardik Martin afforded Robert De Niro with the role of his career. Shot in black-and-white (except for the "home movie" sequences) and expertly edited by longtime collaborator Thelma Schoonmaker, the film earned eight Academy Award nominations, including Best Picture and Best Director. (De Niro and Schoonmaker took home statues.)

Scorsese continued to examine the effects of fame in the underrated "The King of Comedy" (1983), which cast De Niro as an obsessed fan and Jerry Lewis as the talk show host object of his attentions. The director attempted to film a dream project, "The Last Temptation of Christ", but Paramount withdrew funding at the last minute, In reaction, Scorsese made "After Hours" (1985), a relatively small black comedy set on the mean streets of New York during one night. He moved on to Chicago for "The Color

of Money" (1986), a sequel to 1961's "The Hustler", with Paul Newman reprising his role of pool shark 'Fast' Eddie Felsen and Tom Cruise as his protege. After several false starts, Scorsese was finally able to realize his vision and film "The Last Temptation of Christ" (1988). Based on the novel by Nikos Kazantzakis, the film depicted a very human spiritual leader who was a social outcast, wavering between good and evil, battling the desires of the flesh and ultimately choosing a path to redemption. It was the culmination of Scorsese's filmic theses. As written by Paul Schrader and interpreted by Willem Dafoe, this Christ suggested a "Messiah on the Verge of a Nervous Breakdown." Although superbly shot, using exotic locations and a galvanizing world music score by Peter Gabriel, the film somehow lacked the emotional power and cohesion of Scorsese's earlier, smaller-scale productions. Clearly an intensely personal project for Scorsese and Schrader, the film generated controversy, with religious forces accusing the film of blasphemy, causing some theater and video chains to refuse to carry the film.

Adapted from Nicholas Pileggi's book "Wiseguys", about small-time gangster-turned-Federal witness Henry Hill, "GoodFellas" (1990) marked a return to classic Scorsese form and content. The film captures both the undeniable excitement as well as the tawdry, daily details of life on the fringes of 'the Mob', pushing audience manipulation to the extreme by juxtaposing moments of graphic violence with scenes of high humor. The film boasts superb camerawork, including several extended tracking shots, and consummate performances from De Niro, Ray Liotta, Joe Pesci and Lorraine Bracco. Some critics rank "GoodFellas" among Scorsese's finest achievements; others found it a less challenging retread of "Mean Streets", superior entertainment but not a work of art.

"Cape Fear" (1991) was another matter. The result was a slick, pretentious and excessive remake of the compact and powerful 1962 original which teamed Gregory Peck and Robert

Mitchum. The performances, as to be expected, were strong (notably Nick Nolte and Juliette Lewis) and the camerawork and editing were impressive. De Niro's central performance was showy and over-the-top in contrast to Mitchum in the original. Additionally, the film's climactic scenes were more suitable to low-budget horror films than typical of Scorsese's other work. Nonetheless, the film was the biggest hit of the director's career to date.

"The Age of Innocence" (1993), based on Edith Wharton's Pulitzer Prize–winning novel, seemed unlikely offerings from the director as it was a subtle drama of manners set among the high society of 19th-century New York. Using a careening camera, sumptuous color and decor to convey the characters' repression, Scorsese turned to such masters as James Whale, William Wyler, Max Ophuls and Luchino Visconti for inspiration and his completed film earned respectful reviews and a healthy box office. He was back in typical fashion with "Casino" (1995), set in the 70s and 80s and again focusing on 'the Mob', this time transposed to Las Vegas. Filled with iconic images, "Casino" was a flawed allegory of America's loss of innocence and most reviewers felt it simply raised the same issues (which had been covered to better effect) in "GoodFellas."

Again defying categorization, Scorsese turned his attentions to another unlikely subject, the Dalai Lama. "Kundun" (1997) was a biopic as only Scorsese could direct. The story of a proponent of non-violence, it moves the audience into the world of Tibet. Filled with gorgeous saffrons and deep maroons, "Kundun" was a visual and aural feast (the Philip Glass score was among its best components). The sequences covering the Dalai Lama's early life and training were compelling, but the director and screenwriter Melissa Mathison seemed at a loss as how to end their film. Following on the heels of another similar-themed feature (the Brad Pitt vehicle "Seven Years in Tibet"), "Kundun" struggled at the box office despite critical kudos.

Scorsese next directed Nicolas Cage in the morbid drama "Bringing Out the Dead" (1999). He spent the next few years working on a long-awaited opus, "The Gangs of New York", the story of the New York immigrant riots of the late 19th century. Starring Leonardo DiCaprio and Daniel Day-Lewis, the movie went through a series of set-backs, budget problems and a year-long release delay as Scorsese reportedly wrangled with Miramax head Harvey Weinstein over various details before its fall 2002 release. "Gangs" was given its due as a mighty achievement, lavishly staged and photographed and featuring a powerhouse performance from Day-Lewis, but while some critics and audiences marveled at the world that the director created, there was some dissatisfaction with the story, which was not as urgent and engrossing as Scorsese's previous top-shelf fare. Nevertheless, with his relationship with Miramax repaired by the time of the film's release, Weinstein began stumping for an Academy Award nomination for the director with one of Weinstein's famously shrewd award campaigns and the results were fruitful: not only did Scorses take home the Golden Globe award as Best Director of a drama, he also scored an Oscar nomination for "Gangs."

FAMILY:

father: Luciano Charles Scorsese. Garment worker, actor; Sicilian-American; worked for 40 years as a pants presser; appeared as himself in Scorsese's "Italianamerican" and acted in small roles in a number of his son's films as well as Brian DePalma's "Wise Guys"; also served as a wardrobe consultant; consultant to Francis Coppola on "The Godfather, Part III"; died after a lengthy illness at age 80 on August 23, 1993; married to Scorsese's mother for 60 years

mother: Catherine Scorsese. Garment worker, actor; Sicilian-American; appeared as herself in Scorsese's "Italianamerican"; has played small roles in several of her son's films, including "Mean Streets" and "GoodFellas", as well as films directed by others ("Moonstruck" 1987, "The Godfather Part III" 1990); published "The Scorsese Family Cookbook"; died January 6, 1997 from complications from Alzheimer's disease

COMPANIONS:

wife: Isabella Rossellini. Actor, model; married on September 29, 1979; divorced in 1983; daughter of Ingrid Bergman and Roberto Rossellini

wife: Barbara De Fina. Producer; married in February 1985; separated during 1991; began association with Scorsese when she worked as post production supervisor on "The King of Comedy" (1983); executive produced "GoodFellas" (1990) and continued working with him on "The Age of Innocence" (1993) after their separation; divorced

Ileana Douglas. Actor; born c. 1964; granddaughter of actor Melvyn Douglas and Congresswoman/actress Helen Gahagan Douglas; hired to scream in "The Last Temptation of Christ" (1988); appeared in "New York Stories" (1989), "GoodFellas" (1990) and "Cape Fear" (1991); no longer together

wife: Helen S. Morris. Book editor; works at Random House; married on July 22, 1999; her second marriage

MILESTONES:

1963: Made first short film while at NYU, "What's a Nice Girl Like You Doing in a Place Like This?"

1966: First feature as director and writer, "Who's That Knocking at My Door?"

1967–1968: While in Europe, wrote dialogue for the American version of Pim de la Parra's Dutch thriller "Obsessions"; also made six-minute film, "The Big Shave," with the support of the Belgian Cinematheque

1968: Hired as director of "The Honeymoon Killers" but replaced after one week

Taught film at NYU

1969: "Who's That Knocking at My Door?" released with added nude scene; alternately titled "J.R.", "Bring on the Dancing Girls" and "I Call First"

1970: First documentary as director, "Street Scenes"

1971: First feature as co-producer, Francois Reichenbach's "Medicine Ball Caravan"

Commercial feature directing debut (for producer Roger Corman), "Boxcar Bertha"

Fired from NYU for missing classes while filming "Mean Streets"

1973: First cameo appearance, "Mean Streets"; also breakthrough as director

1974: Helmed the "woman's" picture, "Alice Doesn't Live Here Anymore", starring Ellen Burstyn

1976: Played an important one-scene supporting role in "Taxi Driver", which he also directed

1977: Helmed the nostalgic movie musical "New York, New York", which teamed Robert De Niro and Liza Minnelli

1977: Stage directing debut, "The Act" starring Minnelli

1980: Directed what many critics have proclaimed the best film of the 1980s, "Raging Bull"; earned first Best Director Oscar nomination

1983: Helmed "The King of Comedy", a darkly humorous portrait of an unhinged aspiring comic played by De Niro

1985: Directed the comedy "After Hours"

1986: Helmed "The Color of Money", a sequel to "The Hustler" with Paul Newman reprising his role as 'Fast Eddie' Felsen

1987: Directed first music video, "BAD", starring Michael Jackson and scripted by Richard Price

1988: Directed the controversial "The Last Temptation of Christ"; earned a Best Director Oscar nomination

1990: Helmed and co-wrote "GoodFellas", based on Nicholas Pileggi's non-fiction "Wiseguy"; film earned six Oscar nominations including Best Picture, Best Director and Best Adapted Screenplay

1990: Signed a six-picture film production deal with Universal; first film completed under deal, "Cape Fear" (1991)

1992: Formed film preservation and distribution company Martin Scorsese Presents

1993: Co-scripted (with Jay Cocks) and directed the elegant adaptation of Edith Wharton's "The Age of Innocence"; nominated for a Best Adapted Screenplay Academy Award

1997: Directed the biopic of the Dalai Lama, "Kundun"

1998: Served as president of the Cannes Film Festival Jury

1999: Helmed "Bringing Out the Dead"

2000: Created the Turner Classic Movies (TCM) three-part documentary "A Personal Journey with Martin Scorsese Through American Movies"

2000: Co-produced the film "Smiling Fish and Goat on Fire" (filmed in 1998)

2000: Directed "Il Dolce Cinema", a documentary about the Italian cinema through the 1970s; shown at the Venice Film Festival in September

2001: Made "My Voyage to Italy/Il Mio Viaggio in Italia", a four-hour-plus history of Italian cinema; screened at the New York Film Festival and released for one-week Oscar qualifying run; aired on TCM in 2002

2002: Was executive producer of "Rain", a drama directed by Katherine Lindberg that was screened at the Sundance Film Festival

2002: Executive produced "Deuces Wild", starring Matt Dillon and Deborah Harry

2002: Directed Leonardo DiCaprio in the period drama "Gangs of New York"; received nominations for a BAFTA and an Oscar for his achievement in directing

2003: Served as executive producer of the PBS series "The Blues", a six-part history of blues music with episodes directed by Spike Lee and Wim Wenders, among others

2003: Received a Star on the Hollywood Walk of Fame (February 28, 2003)

AFFILIATION: Co-founder, The Film Foundation

QUOTES:
Scorsese suffers from chronic asthma

He was honored with a Congressional Arts Caucus Award for his vision in making and preserving movies in 1991.

Scorsese received a honorary doctorate from New York University in 1992.

Honored by the Film Society of Lincoln Center in 1998

He received the Torch of Liberty Award from the ACLU in 1999. There was some controversy over the award as the ACLU had defended the Hollywood Ten during the 1950s McCarthy era and Scorsese had championed the honoring of Elia Kazan (who "named names") at the 1999 Academy Awards.

"Once we're thrown into the middle of the characters' world, and we start to feel comfortable with them, they hopefully become less strange and different to us—whether it's Nicky [Santoro, played by Joe Pesci] or the Dalai Lama."—Martin Scorsese quoted in *American Cinematographer,* February 1998.

On "Kundun": "Basically, it's the story of a little boy, and we only see what he sees; that's why it's the perfect Disney movie."—Scorsese in *Interview,* January 1998.

"I would love to be able to—and this ego speaking—grow as a filmmaker. Which means that I have to assume I had something as a filmmaker to start with, and I'm not sure about that anymore. Some of my films are very strong, I think. I'll sign them any day. But I wonder if I had any place to go to begin with. I know I had it with 'Mean Streets', I'll tell you that. I honestly don't think I had enough money or time to execute it the way I wanted to, but the force of the actors blasted through it. The other stuff? I don't know. . . . I *would* like my pictures to speak to people in the future, and to mean something to them. And I'm trying like hell, but it's very hard in this marketplace."—Scorsese in *Interview,* January 1998

Question: "What do you think people's biggest misconception about you is?

Scorcese: "Because of the movies I make, they get nervous, because they think of me as difficult and angry. I AM difficult and angry [laughs], but they don't expect a sense of humor. And the only thing that gets me through is a sense of humor. . . . "

—From "Good Fella" in *Time Out New York,* December 24, 1997–January 8, 1998

Made a chevalier in the French Legion of Honor in 1998.

BIBLIOGRAPHY:

"Scorsese on Scorsese" Martin Scorsese, 1989, Faber and Faber; interviews, stills and sketches

"Martin Scorsese and Michael Cimino" Michael Bliss, 1985, Scarecrow Press

"Martin Scorsese: A Journey" Mary Pat Kelly, 1991, Thunder's Mouth Press; an oral history of the filmmaker's career comprised of interviews with Scorsese, his co-workers and actors

"A Personal Journey With Martin Scorsese Through American Movies" Martin Scorsese and Michael Henry Wilson, 1997, Hyperion/Mirimax

"A Director's Diary: The Making of 'Kundun' " Martin Scorsese, 1998, Random House

"Martin Scorsese Interviews" Peter Brunette, editor, 1999, University of Mississippi Press

Ridley Scott

BORN: in South Shields Northumberland, England, 11/30/1937

NATIONALITY: English

EDUCATION: West Hartlepool College of Art, Hartlepool, England

Royal College of Art London, England; art and film graduated with 1st-class honors; won one-year scholarship to USA; contemporaries included David Hockney

AWARDS: Cannes Film Festival Best First Film Award "The Duellists" 1977

London Film Critics Circle Award Director of the Year "Thelma & Louise" 1991; film also won Film of the Year and earned Susan Sarandon the Actress of the Year award

Broadcast Film Critics Association Award Best TV Movie "RKO 281" 1999; shared award; tied with "Tuesdays With Morrie"

Golden Globe Award Best Mini-Series or Motion Picture Made for Television "RKO 281" 1999

BIOGRAPHY

When moviegoers see the credit "A Ridley Scott Film" they know they are in for something special. No matter what, the film will be visually spectacular, transporting them to a palpable, richly detailed setting, whether it be Napoleonic France ("The Duellists" 1977), outer space ("Alien" 1979) or ancient Rome ("Gladiator" 2000). A former art director, Scott clearly has an affinity for the "look" of his films, and he often collaborates with top cinematographers, costume designers and production designers to achieve his vision. Some critics have carped that this attention to the visual often comes at the expense of well-rounded characters or coherent stories but others have countered that the distinctive styles work to advance the storytelling and enhance the themes of Scott's films.

Born and raised in Northumberland, England, Scott showed an affinity for graphic design and painting and enrolled at the West Hartlepool College of Art. While attending the Royal Academy of Art, he branched out into filmmaking with the short "Boy on a Bicycle," which featured his younger brother Tony and their father. After completing his schooling, Scott secured a position at BBC Television as a set decorator and moved up the ranks to become a production designer. In 1966, he segued to directing, helming episodes of the popular docudrama "Z Cars" before branching out into commercial production. In a roughly ten year period, Scott helmed more than 2,000 advertisements marking him as one of the most prolific commercial makers. Having tackled those challenges, it was only natural that he would set his sights on the big screen.

Five years in the making, from conception to financing to production, "The Duellists" marked his initial foray into feature films. Several reviewers complained that the piece was little more than carefully composed tableaux that rarely illuminated the human aspects of its central characters. One might argue the same about Stanley Kubrick's contemporaneous "Barry Lyndon" (1975), which like "The Duellists" was a triumph of style over substance. Both were visually appealing with museum quality period recreations and a somewhat inert dramatic arc. While critics embraced Kubrick's work (because it was Kubrick), they were more dismissive of Scott who had yet to become established.

Four years later, though, Scott would move to the forefront of contemporary filmmakers with "Alien", a stylishly influential stomach-churning sci-fi thriller. Drawing on the work of surrealist H.R. Giger and French comic book artist Moebius (Jean Giraud), the director and his design team crafted a stunning looking, completely believable futuristic world. In Sigourney Weaver's tenacious Ellen Ripley, Scott also found the first of several strong female characters that peppered his oeuvre.

"Alien" proved a box-office hit and spawned three sequels.

Applying the same sense of detail to the equally futuristic world of Los Angeles in 2019 in "Blade Runner" (1982), Scott delineated a bleak version of an over-populated, media-saturated metropolis. Based on a sci-fi tome by Philip K Dick, the film focused on a bounty hunter (Harrison Ford) tracking a gang of outlaw androids searching for their maker. In its initial release, "Blade Runner" was praised for its visual style but Ford's wooden, cliched voice-over and tacked on happy ending disappointed many. Over time, though, Scott has tinkered with the film, re-editing and integrating previously unused footage. By the time of the 1993 release of the "director's cut", "Blade Runner" had developed a cult following and has earned the reputation as a minor classic in the genre, although it remains problematic structurally (a fault of the screenplay by Hampton Fancher and David Webb Peoples).

With "Legend" (1985), Scott stumbled badly. Essentially a fairy tale, the movie was overshadowed by its striking production design and undermined by a dark, almost bleak tone. Instead of coming away from the film cheering for its romantic leads Tom Cruise and Mia Sara, audiences left recalling Tim Curry's malevolent Prince of Darkness. Switching gears to helm "Someone to Watch Over Me" (1987), a more straightforward romantic suspense thriller, Scott employed Hitchcockian flourishes in lieu of pyrotechnic special effects, allowing the stellar acting of leads Tom Berenger and Mimi Rogers to carry the piece. Audiences, however, were left unimpressed and stayed away. With "Black Rain" (1989), he was back in the winner's column, scoring his biggest box-office success since "Alien." A police corruption thriller set in NYC and Japan and starring Michael Douglas, "Black Rain" also suffered from an inconsistent subplot though.

That was a warm-up for his first hit of the 90s, "Thelma and Louise" (1991), a distaff road picture that earned both critical praise and audience support. Relying on the conventions of the male-buddy film Scott, screenwriter Callie Khouri and stars Susan Sarandon and Geena Davis engendered controversy and angered (mostly male) and delighted (mainly female) viewers by allowing two women to take charge and act out center stage. Hollywood finally embraced Scott by bestowing a Best Director Academy Award nomination. His subsequent outing, however, "1492: The Conquest of Paradise" (1992) may have looked great on paper but the unwieldy international cast failed to breath life into the costume drama.

It took Scott four years to return to the director's chair, this time at the helm of "White Squall", a based-on-fact tale of a floating prep school. Although it featured an attractive male cast of up and comers (i.e., Ethan Embry, Jeremy Sisto, Ryan Phillippe) supporting veteran Jeff Bridges and several nicely staged set pieces (including a dynamic storm at sea), "White Squall" proved a disappointment. Similarly, his follow-up "G.I. Jane" (1997), with Demi Moore as a recruit determined to make the cut as the first female Navy SEAL, confounded. While it was appealing to have a strong central female character, the weak script again defeated the overall effort. Scott finally found the proper mix with "Gladiator", a throwback to the sword and sandal epics of the late 50s and early 60s. Again transporting audiences to a meticulous recreation of a foreign world, Scott and company enjoyed widespread critical kudos and a healthy box office.

He segued to "Hannibal" (2001), the long-awaited sequel to 1991's "The Silence of the Lambs." While much had been made over Thomas Harris' original story, significant changes were reportedly made in the script to make the film more palatable to audiences. Oscar-winner Anthony Hopkins was on board re-creating Hannibal Lecter, but Julianne Moore stepped in to replace Jodie Foster as FBI agent Clarice Starling. As with any Scott-directed film, "Hannibal" was a triumph of the visual.

Scott then tackled another potentially controversial topic in "Black Hawk Down" (2001), which examined the events of a US humanitarian mission in Somalia that went horribly wrong, resulting in the deaths of several US soldiers and hundred of Somalis. Scott once again employed his trademark ability to place the audience in the midst of the action and while the character development in the story was somewhat lacking, there was no denying his achievement. Indeed, both the DGA and the Motion Picture Academy included him on the shortlist as one of the five nominees for Best Director of 2001. Scott next tackled a more scaled-down, human-level story when he took the helm of "Matchstick Men" (2003), directing Nicolas Cage as a quirk-addled conman who unites with the teen daughter he never knew.

In addition to his directorial and producing efforts, Scott is also the Co-Chairman of Mill Film, one of the largest digital production and post-production houses in London. Founded in 1987, it boasts involvement in the visual effects of such features as "Shakespeare in Love", "Babe: Pig in the City", "Pitch Black", "Cats & Dogs", "Harry Potter and the Sorcerer's Stone", "Lara Croft: Tomb Raider" and dozens more. Mill Film was recognized with an Academy Award for their visual effects on Scott's "Gladiator." He is also Co-Chairman of Pinewood-Shepperton Holdings, Ltd., a London facility where "Alien" was filmed and that provides 42 stages, backlots and locations plus award-winning post-production and support services. The Scott brothers (as part of a consortium) purchased Shepperton Studios in 1995, which merged with Pinewood Studios in 2001.

In recognition of his contribution to the arts, Scott was awarded knighthood in January 2003.

FAMILY:

brother: Tony Scott. Director; born on June 21, 1944

MILESTONES:

First short film, "Boy on Bicycle" shot during attendence at Royal College of Art; starred brother Tony and their father

Spent one year in USA on scholarship from Royal College of Art; worked at Time-Life, Inc., with Richard Leacock and D. A. Pennebaker

Joined BBC-TV as production designer; soon promoted to director

1966: Directed episodes of "Z Cars", a popular crime docudrama series

Formed Ridley Scott Associates, a commercial production company; directed over 2,000 commercials in ten years; served as managing director

1977: Feature directorial debut, the period drama "The Duellists"

1979: Directed the stylish and thrilling sci-fi actioner "Alien"

1982: Helmed first American feature, the sci-fi themed "Blade Runner"; dismissed by audiences at the time, film has become something of a minor genre classic

1985: Stumbled with the fantasy "Legend", starring Tom Cruise; film was critical and box-office disappointment

1987: Executive produced "Someone to Watch Over Me", a rather conventional but visually stylish romantic thriller; also directed

With brother Tony, co-founded RSA USA, a commercial production house

1989: Helmed the intriguing thriller "Black Rain", about two NYC cops who must escort members of the Yakuza back to Japan

1991: Produced and directed the acclaimed, controversial "Thelma & Louise"; earned Best Director Oscar nomination

1992: Helmed "1492: The Conquest of Paradise" with a miscast Gerard Depardieu as Christopher Columbus

1994: Served as producer only on "Monkey Trouble" and the remake of "The Browning Version" helmed by Mike Figgis

Formed film production company Scott Free with brother Tony

1995: With Tony, purchased London's Shepperton Studios from Panavision subsidiary Lee International

1996: Executive produced and directed "White Squall", a based on fact tale of a prep school aboard a brigantine

1997: Directed Demi Moore in "G.I. Jane"

1998: Was one of the producers of "Clay Pigeons", helmed by David Dobkin

1999: Served as exicutive producer of the acclaimed HBO original movie "RKO 281", about the making of "Citizen Kane"

2000: Produced "Where the Money Is", a modest caper film enlivened by the casting of Paul Newman and Linda Fiorentino

2000: Directed the box-office smash "Gladiator", a drama set in ancient Rome starring Russell Crowe as a former general forced into slavery and a life as a gladiator; film received 12 Oscar nominations, including one for Best Director; it won five awards including Best Picture

2001: Helmed "Hannibal", the long-awaited sequel to "The Silence of the Lambs"

2001: Directed the fact-based drama "Black Hawk Down", about the 1993 US raid on Somalia; received Best Director Academy Award nomination

QUOTES:

Scott chairs a production company with his brother Tony called Scott Free.

Scott's commercial work has been recognized at Cannes, Venice and by the New York Art Directors' Club.

Since the 1990s, Ridley Scott has enjoyed a secondary career as a producer of such efforts as the 1994 remake of "The Browning Version", "Clay Pigeons" (1998), the acclaimed HBO drama "RKO 281" (1999) and the Paul Newman vehicle "Where the Money Is" (2000).

In 2002, the Scott brothers along with Michael Grade announced plans to construct a state-of-the-art "megastudio" in Toronto.

According to the announced plans, construction would begin in March 2003 with an anticipated opening in spring 2004.

" . . . I've never had a problem with strong females. I'm still very much involved in advertising. I've got two companies, and over the past years, the best guys got the jobs of running them—and they both happened to be female. I just seem to find females in general carry intuition that's more accurate than men's. . . . I've never really had a problem dealing with and losing arguments to women. In regards to dealing with the roles they play in my films, it's always been fun really—enjoyable."—Ridley Scott quoted in *BuzzWeekly*, August 22–28, 1997.

"I'm so heavily oriented visually that the way I make films is second nature to me. In preparing a film a lot of directors delegate, in terms of the visual side of things, leave it to other people, and concentrate on the actors and the script; I like to concentrate on everything. I do all my own location hunting; for "G.I. Jane" I must have seen over 30 military camps and operational bases, and I find that kind of thing absolutely invaluable. Not only do you see everything, you meet people, officers, soldiers in the ranks. It's all an educational process, and that's essential."—Ridley Scott quoted in the London *Times*, November 8, 1997.

"I'm only competitive with myself."—Scott quoted in the London *Times*, November 8, 1997.

"Most people never tell you the truth. I'll show [brother] Tony a cut of my film, even before the studio sees it. Or vice versa. And then he'll give me 30 pages of notes. But it's always good to be able to bounce things off someone."—Scott to the London *Times*, November 8, 1997.

On his interest in the military, Scott told *Empire* (December 1997): "I am interested in that arena. It's pretty sick, I suppose, because in the end they are killers. But they serve their purpose, and there are arguments for and against. But there is war. There's an argument for the presence of real power; the fact that there has been no third world war. Others will argue that that's just a matter of time. But I think not. I think there is an argument for a deterrent."

"What I do is create worlds. Whether it's historical or futuristic, creating a world is the most attractive thing to me about filmmaking because everything goes—it's a matter of drawing up your own rule book and sticking to it."—Ridley Scott to *Los Angeles Times Calendar*, April 23, 2000.

"Over the years, I've learned to pay attention to material to the extent that I now understand that story and characters are the most important thing in any movie. The audience must identify with someone in a film and go on a journey with them. That's called escapism. I don't care if it's the stupidest mainstream movie or a really smart movie—it's got to communicate."—Ridley Scott quoted in *Los Angeles Times Calendar*, April 23, 2000.

On the revised impression of "Blade Runner", now thought to be one of the 1970s most influential films, Scott told Stephen Rebello of *Movieline* (May 2000): "Revenge isn't really sweet when it comes too many years later. As you mature, you realize all the more that the key audience member you must make truly happy is yourself. I'm always sufficiently pragmatic now by the end of the of a film to sit back, stare at it and go, 'That works' or 'Not a bad patch-up, despite a few errors here and there.' Beyond that, you need luck in everything. Why do people got for a film in a huge way when you look at it and go, 'Well, it's OK but it doesn't warrant a giant reaction.' Certain movies just color people's imaginations and you can't predict that."

Susan Seidelman

BORN: in Huntingdon Valley, Pennsylvania, 12/11/1952

NATIONALITY: American

EDUCATION: Drexel Institute of Technology, Philadelphia, Pennsylvania, BA

Institute of Film and TV, New York University, New York, New York, MFA, made directing debut with 28-minute student film, "And You Act Like One Too" (won Student Academy Award and was featured in Whitney Museum's "New Directors" series)

BIOGRAPHY

In an arid comedy landscape, the films of Susan Seidelman seem like a teeming oasis. Her relentlessly contemporary features are knowing satires that examine contemporary issues of fame, self-fulfillment and relations between the sexes.

Seidelman grew up in a middle-class Philadelphia suburb and studied graphic design at Drexel University and film at New York University. Her satiric flair earned student film awards for her shorts, "And You Act Like One Too," "Deficit" and "Yours Truly, Andrea G. Stern". On the strength of these productions she managed to raise $80,000 to make her first feature, "Smithereens" (1982), the story of a selfish hustler (Susan Berman) with ambitions to become the manager of a punk rock band. The success of "Smithereens" in America and Europe brought her the attention of the major studios and the chance to direct "Desperately Seeking Susan" (1985), a hit comedy of an identity mix-up between a New Jersey housewife (Rosanna Arquette) and a downtown New York rocker (Madonna).

Seidelman's next three films gathered some critical support but were less successful at the box-office. "Making Mr. Right" (1987) focused on a savvy public relations expert and her attempts to promote an android astronaut (John Malkovich). "Cookie" (1989) was the comic story of a mob hood (Peter Falk) and his wacky daughter (Emily Lloyd). With "She-Devil" (1989), Seidelman explored the vengeance a dumpy housewife (Roseanne Barr) wreaks on her romantic rival (Meryl Streep), but the film, despite its admirably feminist intentions, was less of a critical—or popular—success than some of Seidelman's earlier efforts.

MILESTONES:

Worked at UHF TV station in Philadelphia

1982: Directed first feature, "Smithereens" (first independent American feature to be accepted into competition at Cannes Film Festival

1985: Breakthrough feature, "Desperately Seeking Susan"

Made several short films, including the documentary "Confessions of a Suburban Girl" (1992) and the fantasy "The Dutch Master", both of which she also wrote

BORN: in Ziguenchor, Casamance, Senegal, 01/01/1923

NATIONALITY: Senegalese

EDUCATION: studied for seven years at a Quran (Muslim) school
Ecole de Ceramique, Marsassoum, France
VGIK Moscow, Russia, 1961; studied under Mark Donskoi

AWARDS: Jean Vigo Award "Black Girl" 1966
International Critics Award "The Money Order" 1968
Tashkent Festival Soviet Directors Award "The Money Order" 1968
Atlanta Film Festival Best Foreign Film Award "The Money Order" 1968
Moscow Film Festival Silver Medal Award "Emitai" 1971

BIOGRAPHY

The first film director from an African country to achieve international recognition, Ousmane Sembene remains the major figure in the rise of an independent post-colonial African cinema. Sembene's roots were not, as might be expected, in the educated elite. After working as a mechanic and bricklayer, he joined the Free French forces in 1942, serving in Africa and France. In 1946, he returned to Dakar, where he participated in the great railway strike of 1947. The next year he returned to France, where he worked in a Citroen factory in Paris, and then, for ten years, on the dock in Marseilles. During this time Sembene became very active in trade union struggles and began an extraordinarily successful writing career. His first novel, "Le Docker Noir," was published in 1956 to critical acclaim. Since then, he has produced a number of works which have

placed him in the foreground of the international literary scene.

Long an avid filmgoer, Sembene became aware that to reach a mass audience of workers and preliterate Africans outside urban centers, cinema was a more effective vehicle than the written word. In 1961, he traveled to Moscow to study film at VGIK and then to work at the Gorky Studios. Upon his return to Senegal, Sembene turned his attention to filmmaking and, after two short films, he wrote and directed his first feature, "Black Girl" (1965). Received with great enthusiasm at a number of international film festivals, it also won the prestigious Jean Vigo Prize for its director.

Shot in a simple, quasi-documentary style probably influenced by the French New Wave, "Black Girl" tells the tragic story of a young Senegalese woman working as a maid for an affluent French family on the Riviera, focusing on her sense of isolation and growing despair. Her country may have been "decolonized," but she is still a colonial—a non-person in the colonizers' world. Sembene's next film, "Mandabi/The Money Order" (1968), marked a sharp departure. Based on his novel of the same name and shot in color in two language versions—French and Wolof, the main dialect of Senegal— "Mandabi" is a trenchant and often delightfully witty satire of the new bourgeoisie, torn between outmoded patriarchal traditions and an uncaring, rapacious and inefficient bureaucracy.

"Emitai" (1971) records the struggle of the Diola people of the Casamance region of Senegal (where Sembene grew up) against the French authorities during WWII. Shot in Diola dialect and French from an original script, "Emitai" offers a respectful but unromanticized depiction of an ancient tribal culture, while highlighting the role of women in the struggle against colonialist oppression. In "Xala" (1974),

Sembene again takes on the native bourgeoisie, this time in the person of a rich, partially Westernized Moslem businessman afflicted by "xala" (impotence) on the night of his wedding to a much younger third wife. "Ceddo" (1977), considered by many to be Sembene's masterpiece, departs from the director's customary realist approach, documenting the struggle over the last centuries of an unspecified African society against the incursions of Islam and European colonialism. Featuring a strong female central character, "Ceddo" is a powerful evocation of the African experience.

MILESTONES:

1940–1944: With Free French Army's Senegalese sharpshooters

Worked in France as docker and in automobile factory

Began painting and publishing poetry

1956: Published first novel, "The Black Docker"

Studied film in Moscow and worked at Gorky Film Studios with Sergei Gerasimov

1963: Made first film (unreleased documentary) for the government of Mali

1963: Made first short fiction film, "Cart Owner"

1966: Directed first feature, "Black Girl"

1968: First film in Wolof (native Sengalese tongue) "The Money Order/Mandabi"

1972: Founded Wolof monthly magazine, *Kaddu*

1974: Scripted and directed "Xala"

1977: Wrote, directed and appeared in "Ceddo"; film was banned in Senegal

1987: First film in a decade, co-directed and wrote "Camp de Thiaroye", about the slaughter of African war veterans at the hands of the French

1992: Produced, directed and wrote "Guelwaar", which focused on an accidental body swap of a Muslim and a Catholic at a morgue

2000: Returned to filmmaking after eight year absence with "Faat-Kine"

AFFILIATION: Member of the French Communist Party from 1950–60.

BIBLIOGRAPHY:

"The Cinema of Ousemane Sembene, a Pioneer of Black African Film" Francoise Pfaff, 1984, Greenwood Press

"A Call to Action: The Films of Ousemane Sembene" Sheila Petty (editor), 1996, Praeger

Tom Shadyac

BORN: 1959

NATIONALITY: American

EDUCATION: University of Virginia, Charlottesville, Virginia, BA

University of California at Los Angeles, Los Angeles, California, film, MFA, 1989; directed short film "Tom, Dick and Harry"

BIOGRAPHY

Tom Shadyac meandered in Hollywood as a comedy gag writer and occasional actor for more than a decade before hitting pay dirt as the co-writer and director of "Ace Ventura: Pet Detective", the 1994 feature film that confirmed that Jim Carrey as one of the biggest stars in Hollywood.

It didn't do too badly for Shadyac either, who had arrived in Hollywood in 1983 and became what has been said to be the youngest gag writer ever on Bob Hope's staff. During the 80s, he occasionally won acting roles—on such series as "Magnum, P.I." and "Trapper John, M.D." and in the feature film, "Jocks" (1986). He attended the graduate school of UCLA, earning an MA in 1989. Armed with his degree and a short film called "Tom, Dick and Harry", Shadyac successfully began working as a writer, first doing rewrites for two George Carlin TV-movies on Fox, "Working Trash" and "Fraternity Girl" (both 1990). In 1991, he was given the chance to direct, resulting in "Frankenstein: The College Years" (Fox), which did well with the audience.

Also a stand-up comedian, Shadyac had become friendly with Carrey and the duo collaborated on the ribald, raucous "Ace Ventura", which Shadyac directed and co-wrote. The result grossed more than $200 million worldwide. In 1996, Eddie Murphy looked to Shadyac to helped give a new boost to his sagging career with the remake of "The Nutty Professor", which garnered positive notices and a healthy box office. Carrey and Shadyac reteamed for "Liar, Liar" (1997), about a lawyer forced to tell the truth as a result of his son's birthday wish. The film earned positive critical notices, particularly for Carrey (who was coming off the disastrous "The Cable Guy") and Shadyac's sure-footed direction. It also proved to be another box-office hit, passing the $100 million mark in just over two weeks.

MILESTONES:
Raised in Falls Church, Virginia

1983: Moved to L.A.
Became youngest staff joke writer ever for Bob Hope at age 23
1986: Appeared as actor in feature film "Jocks"
Made short film "Tom, Dick and Harry" while enrolled at UCLA film school
1991: Directed Fox TV-movie "Frankenstein: The College Years"
1994: Co-wrote and directed "Ace Ventura: Pet Detective"
Formed Shady Acres Productions
1996: Directed and co-wrote the remake of "The Nutty Professor", starring Eddie Murphy
1998: Helmed the box office hit "Patch Adams"
Formed 333 Music Group
1999: Signed three-year first-look agreement with Universal
2000: Directed and executive produced proposed pilot for an ABC sitcom starring Brett Butler, tentatively titled "Homecoming Queen"
2002: Directed "Dragonfly"

QUOTES:
"They say never work with animals and children. I've got about 50 animals AND Jim Carrey [in 'Ace Ventura']. That pretty much says its, don't you think?"—Tom Shadyac in press kit for "Ace Ventura: Pet Detective"

Jim Sheridan

BORN: in Dublin, Ireland, 1949

NATIONALITY: Irish

EDUCATION: University College, Dublin, Ireland; studied acting

New York University, New York, New York, film, 1981, studied at the Institute of Film and TV at the Tisch School of the Arts

AWARDS: Edinburgh Festival Fringe Award Best Play "Spike in the First World War" 1983

Berlin Film Festival Golden Bear "In the Name of the Father" 1993; awarded for best picture; top prize of the festival

David di Donatello Prize Best Foreign Film "In the Name of the Father" 1994

Goya Best European Film "The Boxer" 1999

BIOGRAPHY

Acomplished director/playwright of the Dublin and New York stage turned filmmaker. Sheridan had eight plays produced including the highly regarded "Spike in the First World War" (1983). "My Left Foot" (1989), his feature debut, was based on the life of writer-painter Christy Brown who was challenged by cerebral palsy. Bolstered by Daniel Day-Lewis' Oscar-winning performance, the film earned international praise, resulting in a flood of offers from Hollywood for the neophyte director. Sheridan, however, chose to remain in Ireland where he wrote and directed "The Field" (1990). Featuring a tour-de-force performance by Richard Harris as a farmer who vigilantly defends his land from an American real estate developer, the film solidified Sheridan's reputation as an "actor's director."

Sheridan has continued to work in Ireland, writing the screenplay for Mike Newell's "Into the West" (1992), a delicate yet rousing "fairy tale" about two gypsy children who go on the lam with a possibly mystical white horse. He reteamed with Day-Lewis for "In the Name of the Father" (1993) to tell the story of Gerry Conlon. Conlon was thought to be the leader of the Guilford Four, a group wrongly prosecuted and imprisoned for 15 years for an IRA bombing. The film elicited condemnation in Great Britain where Sheridan, Day-Lewis and co-star Emma Thompson were accused of making an anti-English film. By contrast, it received glowing notices in the U.S. where some critics likened the pairing of Sheridan and Day-Lewis to that of Scorsese and De Niro.

MILESTONES:

Raised in Dublin, Ireland

Contracted scarlet fever at age seven and nearly died

Formed "Children's T" theater company after graduating from college

1976–1980: Founded (and served as the artistic director) the Project Arts Centre in Dublin

1981: Moved to Canada

1981: Moved to New York

1981: Enrolled at NYU's Tisch School of the Arts

Artistic director of New York's Irish Arts Centre

Worked as a cab driver while serving as artistic director of the Irish Arts Centre

Wrote a biography of Irish boxing champion Barry McGuigan

1989: Film directing and screenwriting debut, "My Left Foot"

Started production company, Hell's Kitchen Productions; partnered with Arthur Lappin

1993: Feature debut as a producer, "In the Name of the Father", starring Daniel Day-Lewis

1996: Wrote and produced the IRA-themed drama "Some Mother's Son"

1997: Reteamed with Day-Lewis for "The Boxer"; wrote, produced and directed the character study

1999: Served as producer on "Agnes Browne", helmed by Anjelica Huston

2000: Was executive producer of "Borstal Boy", a biopic of Irish author Brendan Behan

Produced, wrote and directed the semi-autobiographical drama "East of Harlem" (lensed 2001)

QUOTES:

"Hollywood is like being at a party where, while I'm telling you a story, you're looking over my shoulder. People here are always playing to somebody else out there—a mass, consensus. Even actors here don't talk to the person in the scene with them—they want the mass endorsement as the validation." —Sheridan's take on the Hollywood system (from *Movieline*, 12/93)

"I'm totally aware that sometimes a lack of humor in a movie gives you the feeling that you're trapped in a bar with a guy who's ranting on and on while you're going, 'Jesus, take a break so I can go to the toilet', It comes out of an urgency to tell the story. I am kind of extreme. But there's so many people in the film world being so well-rewarded for always giving audiences what they want."—Sheridan on his type of films as opposed to Hollywood (from *Movieline*, 12/93)

"It's a kind of symbiotic relationship. I almost feel that I'm writing what he's feeling. I have to concede to him a small degree of mad-ness when I'm directing him, because, after all, he's the inspiration for a bit of it in me." —Sheridan on his relationship with Daniel Day-Lewis, (from *The Daily News*, 12/28/93)

Sheridan opened a restaurant in Dublin with singers Bono and Gavin Friday called Mr. Pussy's Cafe de Luxe in 1994.

M. Night Shyamalan

BORN: Manoj Nelliyattu Shyamalan in Pondicherry, India, 08/06/1970

NATIONALITY: Indian

CITIZENSHIP: United States

EDUCATION: Waldron Academy, Philadelphia, Pennsylvania; a private Catholic school; school name later changed to Waldron Mercy; Shyamalan filmed "Wide Awake" there

Episcopal Academy, Philadelphia, Pennsylvania; was a National Merit Scholar

Tisch School of the Arts, New York University, New York, New York, film, 1993

AWARD: Golden Satellite Best Motion Picture Screenplay (Original) "The Sixth Sense" 1999

BIOGRAPHY

Despite his making amateur movies from the age of 10, M. Night Shyamalan was being groomed for a medical career by his cardiologist father and obstetrician mother. When it came time for college, the Indian-born, Philadelphia-bred aspiring Spielberg opted to attend NYU's film school rather than Penn's premed program. While his parents may have suffered some consternation, it all worked out in the end, particularly by 1999 when Shyamalan had written and directed one of the year's biggest and most surprising hits, the supernatural thriller "The Sixth Sense."

While attending NYU, the future filmmaker was determined to develop a catholic aesthetic by taking liberal arts courses. Less interested in creating a distinct visual style, he concentrated on creating rounded characters whose behavior is rooted in reality. As part of his degree requirements, Shyamalan completed several screenplays (including one which became his second produced film, 1997's "Wide Awake"). In fact, while still an undergraduate, he was attempting to put together a deal to direct that film but negotiations broke down. Instead, he turned to another idea which eventually became "Praying With Anger" (1992), a film about an Indian American who travels to Madras to explore his roots. Shyamalan took on the leading role as well as producing, writing and directing chores. Made for a reported budget of $750,000, it debuted at the Toronto Film Festival to mostly negative reviews which effectively killed a national release. One of the few particularly positive reviews appeared in *Daily Variety* (September 22, 1992) which deemed the film "an impressively self-assured triple-threat debut".

Undeterred, Shyamalan pressed on, selling the script "Labor of Love", about a widower and his devotion to his late wife, to Fox with the guarantee that he would direct. The studio eventually balked on his helming the project relegating it to development hell. In 1995, he sold "Wide Awake" to Miramax on the condition he direct the film and that it would be shot in

Philadelphia. Focusing on a ten-year-old Catholic schoolboy who embarks on a spiritual mission questioning whether his dead grandfather is being cared for by God, the script attracted well-known names like Denis Leary, Dana Delany, Robert Loggia and Rosie O'Donnell (as a nun!). Most reviewers, however, found the screenplay too coy and contrived. A few appreciated Shyamalan's earnestness but audiences stayed away and "Wide Awake" quickly was relegated to the video shelves.

While working on a 1997 rewrite of the script for a combined live action-animated version of the E. B. White children's classic "Stuart Little" (1999), Shyamalan also drafted the original script for "The Sixth Sense", a tidy thriller about a clairvoyant boy that became a summer blockbuster in part because of a twist ending that drew audiences back for multiple viewings. The film offered Bruce Willis a fine showcase but young Haley Joel Osment emerged as the real star. The movie's success and six Oscar nominations, including Best Picture, Best Director and Best Original Screenplay undoubtedly served as a balm for his previous failures. It also helped that he picked up a record $5 million for his next script, the suspense thriller with supernatural overtones "Unbreakable" (2000), and another $5 million as director of the project. Clearly Shyamalan had made the right choice when he opted not to become a doctor.

"Unbreakable" was released to eager audiences in 2000 and was quickly panned by critics. Shyamalan had failed to live up to the expectations set by "The Sixth Sense" but one can't help but wonder if all the pressure led to the deflated feeling of "Unbreakable." Shyamalan sought to correct his record with the intriguing Sci-fi thriller "Signs" in 2002. Mel Gibson starred as a reverend in a small town in Pennsylvania whose farm begins producing mysterious crop circles.

MILESTONES:

With family moved from India to Penn Valley, Pennsylvania

1980: Began making film at age 10 (date approximate)

1986: By age 16, had completed 45th short film (date approximate)

1992: Feature film debut as writer, director and star of "Praying With Anger", filmed in Madras, India in 1992

1993–1994: Wrote screenplay for "Labor of Love"; sold to Fox for $750,000; attached to direct; when studio reportedly reneged on his directing the film, project was shelved

1995: Sold the script for "Wide Awake" to Miramax for $250,000 on condition he direct film in Philadelphia; lensed in 1996 and released in 1997

1997: Hired to rewrite script for "Stuart Little" (1999)

1999: Breakthrough film, "The Sixth Sense", starring Bruce Willis and Haley Joel Osment; wrote and directed and made cameo appearance as a doctor; also played small role; received Academy Award nominations as Best Director and for Best Original Screenplay

2000: Reportedly received $5 million to write and $5 million to direct the thriller "Unbreakable", starring Willis and Samuel L. Jackson; made cameo appearance as a drug dealer

2002: Wrote and directed the supernatural thriller "Signs," starring Mel Gibson and Joaquin Phoenix

2003: Reunited with Joaquin Phoenix for the horror feature "The Woods", for which he served as writer and director

AFFILIATION: Hindu

QUOTES:

His last name is pronounced SHAH-ma-lawn.

"My biggest fear in life is to be average."
—M. Night Shyamalan quoted in *Philadelphia Inquirer Magazine,* March 8, 1999.

"I'm not a big spiritual guy. But I think that what it is, is the remnants of my being Indian. I've seen a lot of spiritual people and cultures.

The Hindu culture is very spiritual. And I almost take it for granted—that that's a part of my life. I think that's what's infusing the movies."—Shyamalan quoted in *Fade In*, Volume 5, Number 2, Summer 1999.

"To call me an Indian filmmaker is a misrepresentation. My wife loves the Bollywood movies but they go against my philosophy of film-making because they're just made for an Indian audience. I want to make movies everyone wants to see, movies for the whole world."—M. Night Shyamalan quoted in London's *Evening Standard*, November 5, 1999.

Brad Silberling

BORN: Bradley Mitchell Silberling, 09/08/1963

SOMETIMES CREDITED AS:
Bradley Silberling

NATIONALITY: American

EDUCATION: University of California at Santa Barbara, Santa Barbara, California, BA, 1984

University of California at Los Angeles, Los Angeles, California, film, MA, 1987

BIOGRAPHY

This son of successful TV producer and production executive Robert Silberling was already working in the entertainment industry while attending UCLA Film School. Silberling was a production assistant on the CBS Schoolbreak Special "Little Miss Perfect" in 1986, then completed his studies in 1987. A film he wrote, directed and edited called "Repairs" won notice at Universal and he was signed to a development contract with the studio. Little came of that effort, but Steven Bochco hired Silberling to direct episodes of his series, including "L.A. Law," "Cop Rock," "Doogie Howser, MD," and "Civil Wars." In 1992, Silberling directed the short-lived Fox sitcom "Great Scott", also serving as its supervising producer. He later helmed episodes of "Brooklyn Bridge" for Gary David Goldberg, which caught the attention of Steven Spielberg who hired Silberling to direct "Casper" (1995), an Amblin' Entertainment

production based on the "Friendly Ghost" comic strip character. The result was a hit film that grossed more than $100 million domestically, vaulting its director onto the A-list. His follow-up was "City of Angels" (1998), loosely inspired by Wim Wenders' "Wings of Desire" (1987). Silberling chose to concentrate on the romantic interplay between an angel (played by Nicolas Cage) and the woman (Meg Ryan) he was sent to watch over.

In 1989, Silberling and young actress Rebecca Schaeffer were romantically involved when she was murdered by a fanatic admirer. Silberling hosted the tearful memorial service held at the Warners Ranch. He later married actress Amy Brenneman, whom he met on the set of "NYPD Blue". Together, they founded the Cornerstone Theatre Co. in Los Angeles and in 1999, Brenneman created and starred in the hit series "Judging Amy" which Silberling directed.

In 2002, Silberling produced and directed his first script, "Moonlight Mile." This deeply personal drama was Silberling's response to the tragedy of Rebecca Schaeffer's death. "Moonlight Mile" is the story of a young man (Jake Gyllenhaal) whose fiance dies and how his relationship with her parents (whom he is living with) unfolds. The script was shopped around extensively before being taken on by Disney, perhaps because the studios were wary of such a personal and powerful story or as Silberling commented: "There is such a fear of any story that has death as a backdrop, even as a catalyst,"

COMPANIONS:

Rebecca Schaeffer. Actor; was Silberling's girl-friend at the time of her 1989 murder by an obsessed fan

wife: Amy Brenneman. Actor; met on set of "NYPD Blue"; married September 30, 1995

MILESTONES:

1986: Worked as production assistant on CBS Schoolbreak Special "Little Miss Perfect"

1987: Wrote, directed and edited independent film, "Repairs"; lead to deal with Universal Studios

1987–1994: Directed episodes of such TV series as "L.A. Law", "Brooklyn Brige", "Doogie Howser, MD", "NYPD Blue"

1992: Was supervising producer and director of Fox sitcom "Great Scott"

1995: Feature directorial debut, "Casper"

1998: Helmed the successful "City of Angels", a loose Americanized remake of Wim Wender's "Wings of Desire"

Formed Reveal Entertainment

1998: Signed production agreement with DreamWorks

1999: Directed pilot of "Judging Amy", starring wife Amy Brenneman in role reportedly based in part on her own mother

2002: Wrote first feature, which he also directed and produced. "Moonlight Mile" starred Dustin Hoffman and Susan Sarandon as parents who grieve their dead daughter by taking in her fiance

Bryan Singer

BORN: 1966

NATIONALITY: American

EDUCATION: West Windsor-Plainsboro Regional High School, South, Plainsboro, New Jersey; classmates included Christopher McQuarrie

School of Visual Arts, New York, New York, left after two years

School of Cinema—Television, University of Southern California, Los Angeles, California, critical studies, BA, 1989

AWARDS: Sundance Film Festival Award Grand Jury Prize "Public Access" 1993; tied with "Ruby in Paradise" directed by Victor Nunez

Seattle Film Festival Best Director Award "The Usual Suspects" 1995

Society of Texas Film Critics Award Best Director "The Usual Suspects" 1995

Saturn Award Best Director "X-Men" 2001

BIOGRAPHY

Bryan Singer took a leap toward a lengthy career as a director with the 1995 release of "The Usual Suspects," a film noir-cum-actioner with numerous, intriguing plot twists and an impeccable cast. With a script by Singer's childhood friend Christopher McQuarrie, "The Usual Suspects" earned positive reviews and a healthy box office, as well as Academy Awards for McQuarrie and supporting actor Kevin Spacey.

Singer is, in his own words, a self-taught director that happens to specialize in dark movies about characters who are never what they seem. He studied for two years at the School of Visual Arts in NYC, but was rejected by the USC film school. Instead, he moved to L.A. and enrolled at USC majoring in critical studies, for which he has said he is now grateful as it gave him time to screen hundreds of films. Singer and McQuarrie made "Public Access", the story of a mysterious man who turns a small town against itself through his cable TV show in

1992 and entered the film in the 1993 Sundance Film Festival. It was named co-winner of the Grand Jury Prize and Singer became sought after by the Hollywood power elite, although the film itself received little notice after the Festival. Gramercy Pictures was willing to back Singer on "The Usual Suspects", considered one of the "independent finds" of 1995, which he brought in not only on time, but under budget.

Singer followed up his initial successes with "Apt Pupil" (1998), a powerful and moving drama that explored the nature of evil. The young auteur based his disturbing movie on Stephen King's novella of the same name, having convinced the writer that he could turn the seemingly unfilmable material into a movie. Previous attempts by other filmmakers had failed to bring to the big screen King's story of a bright teen who blackmails a war criminal into regaling him with memories of Nazi atrocities. King was initially reluctant to let another director take control of his work, but that was before Singer sent him a copy of the yet-to-be-released "Usual Suspects." King reportedly loved the flick and optioned "Apt Pupil" to Singer for one dollar, trusting that his story was in good hands. Although "Apt Pupil" received respectable notices—and its stars Ian McKellen, Brad Renfro and Bruce Davison raves—Singer's achievement was marred by a series of lawsuits alleging that he and crew members inappropriately forced underage boys to appear nude in a brief shower scene. Although the Los Angeles County District Attorney's office found no evidence of criminal wrongdoing, the boys and their parents launched civil suits against the director, that (to date) have yet to be resolved.

For his next project, Singer reunited with McQuarrie, McKellen and Davison for the special effects-laden "X-Men" (2000). Based on the Marvel Comic book series, the hotly anticipated flick chronicled the adventures of a group of disenfranchised, unlikely and reluctant superheroes and marked Singer's first foray into the world of directing big-budget studio pictures. Asked by a journalist from the *DGA Magazine* (November 1998) why he insists on having "A Bryan Singer Film" appear in his movies' credits, the man who produced as well as directed his first three movies replied that he wanted audiences to associate his name with "dark, interesting" entertainment of "a certain level of quality." Mission accomplished.—Written by Karen Butler

MILESTONES:

Raised in Princeton Junction, New Jersey

1979: Began making films at age 13; some films (including "Lion's Den") featured actor Ethan Hawke (date approximate)

1993: Feature directing debut "Public Access"; also co-scripted with childhood pal Christopher McQuarrie

1995: Produced and directed labyrinthine crime thriller "The Usual Suspects", written by McQuarrie

1997: Helmed "Apt Pupil", an adaptation of a Stephen King novella; first collaboration with actors Ian McKellen and Bruce Davison; another childhood friend Brandon Boyce scripted

2000: Re-teamed with McKellen and Davison for the feature version of the dark, comic-book adventure "X-Men"

2003: Helmed the sequel "X2"; also worked on screenplay

AFFILIATION: Raised Jewish

QUOTES:

"While there are apparent similarities to Quentin Tarantino, Singer sings a more melodic, less irritating tune. He derides the celebration of violence—because his mother doesn't like it. If Tarantino is the personfication of 90s pop culture—Eddie Haskell doing Elvis backed by four guys with big guns—Singer is Ricky Nelson with a bullet."—Tom Christie in *Details*, September 1995.

"I wanted to take the crime drama genre and twist it a bit. Everyone's got a piece of the puzzle, everyone thinks they know something, but they don't. I like the idea of things not always being what they seem."—Singer on "The Usual Suspects" in the *Los Angeles Times*, January 27, 1995.

"Bryan Singer's got ice water in his blood."—Stephen King.

"Perception as a whole has always interested me. The idea that behind every face, There's a thousand faces. Beneath the placid veneer of middle America, there lies terrors. Everything is much more complex than we like to think it is. Which is why Kurt Dussander ("Apt Pupil") interests me, which is why Keyser Soze ("The Usual Suspects") interests me. It's almost a trick on the audience, people think there's a purposeful goodness to this character and then he turns evil. The audience is confused, 'I invested myself in this character as a hero, and now I don't understand'. Well, that's your problem; that's what you wanted to see".—Singer to *MovieMaker*, November-December 1998

Singer told *The New York Times* (July 9, 2000) that he was inspired to become a director after watching a TV profile of Steven Spielberg: "He was this Jewish kid like me, he lived in New Jersey for awhile, he had a drawer full of 8-millimeter movies too when he was young. And I thought, I make all these films for fun and I take all these photographs and why don't I do this for a living, just like Steven Spielberg?

"I remember walking home to my house in the middle of the night feeling like, wow, if nothing else I've decided what I want to do with my life. Even if I weren't successful I knew I would always make films."

John Singleton

BORN: John Daniel Singleton in Los Angeles, California, 01/06/1968

NATIONALITY: American

EDUCATION: School of Cinema-Television, University of Southern California, Los Angeles, California, film writing, 1986–90; received Black Alumni Association scholarship, Robert Riskin Writing Award and—two years in a row—Jack Nicholson Writing Award

AWARDS: Los Angeles Film Critics Association New Generation Award "Boyz N The Hood" 1991

New York Film Critics Circle Award Best New Director "Boyz N the Hood" 1991

NAACP Image Award Outstanding Film "Boyz N the Hood" 1991

NATO/ShoWest Award Directorial Debut of the Year "Boyz N the Hood" 1992

NATO/ShoWest Award Screenwriter of the Year "Boyz N the Hood" 1992

MTV Movie Award Best New Filmmaker Award "Boyz N the Hood" 1992

BIOGRAPHY

This African-American director won several awards as a film student at USC which in turn led to a contract with the powerful Creative Artists Agency. John Singleton's assured directorial debut "Boyz N the Hood" (1991) received major studio backing, a $6 million budget and a showcase at the 1991 Cannes Film Festival. An urgent, powerful coming-of-age tale, the film found a spark of hope amid its bleak, violence-ridden South Central Los Angeles setting and became one of the top-grossing features ever made by a black film-maker. Almost unanimously praised by the critics, the film earned Oscar nominations for Best Original Screenplay and Best Director. The latter nomination made history as Singleton became not only the first black but also the youngest filmmaker cited in the category.

As a follow-up, Singleton helmed the 1992 Michael Jackson video "Remember the Time", featuring Jackson, Eddie Murphy, Iman and Magic Johnson in an Egyptian setting. His second feature "Poetic Justice" (1993) was a modern romance set in turbulent South Central L.A. that paired singers-turned-actors Janet Jackson and Tupac Shakur. While the film received a warm reception at the box office, critics were less than enthusiastic. "Higher Learning" (1995), which charted relations on a multi-racial college campus, did over $13 million at the box office its opening weekend and eventually earned close to $39 million. As with "Boys N the Hood", both films examined contemporary relationships set against everyday violence and while each started out strongly, the endings seemed forced and disjointed.

For the first time in his career, Singleton was a director-for-hire on his next project, the true story of a nearly all-black town on the Florida panhandle that was destroyed by white rednecks in 1923. While anticipated as an important film of substance, "Rosewood" (1997) was virtually overlooked by all audiences at the box office, an ironic twist in a year that also saw the release of the bigger-budgeted "Amistad", another based-on-fact but little known story. Singleton then turned his attention to his loose remake of "Shaft" (2000), which garnered much ink in the press over lead Samuel L. Jackson's confrontations with producer Scott Rudin and screenwriter Richard Price. His follow-up was the much more personal "Baby Boy" (2001), which could be seen as a companion piece to his debut film, as it focused on a young black man who fails to live up to his potential. Taking actor-model Tyrese, the star of "Baby Boy," with him, Singleton next jumped aboard to helm "2 Fast, 2 Furious," the critically panned high-octane 2003 sequel to the sleeper thriller "The Fast and the Furious."

As a director, he has been attached to the proposed—but heretofore never realized—screen version of August Wilson's play "Fences", which was acquired by Eddie Murphy. Singleton, unlike other film directors who came into prominence in the late 80s and 90s and seem driven to put themselves on the screen, has kept a low public profile. He did have bit parts, however, in "Boyz N the Hood" (as a letter carrier) and "Beverly Hills Cop III" (1994, as a firefighter).

COMPANION:

Tyra Banks. Model; no longer together

MILESTONES:

Raised in South Central Los Angeles

Signed with Creative Artists Agency while still studying at USC

1991: Wrote and directed (also has bit part as a mailman) first feature, "Boyz N the Hood"

1991: Became the first black director and the youngest filmmaker to receive Academy Award nomination for Best Direction

1992: Directed the Michael Jackson music video, "Remember the Time"

1993: Helmed second feature, "Poetic Justice"

1994: Can be sighted in bit role of a fire fighter in "Beverly Hills Cop III"

1995: Signed two-year, first-look deal with Universal; disolved partnership after eight months in July 1996

1995: Produced, wrote and directed "Higher Learning"

1997: Directed "Rosewood"

1997: Signed exclusive eighteen month development deal with Warner Bros. TV; co-created and directed pilot for proposed series "Crash"

2000: Directed loose remake of "Shaft" with Samuel L. Jackson in the title role

2001: Helmed "Baby Boy", a coming-of-age story of a 20-year-old street hustler with two children by two different women

2003: Directed the sequel "2 Fast and 2 Furious"

QUOTES:

Singleton was inspired to make films by the motion picture, "Star Wars" (1977). "When I was in high school, somebody told me that the film business was controlled by literary properties, i.e., screenplays. After I heard that I knew that I had to learn how to write, so I did." —John Singleton quoted in the press kit for "Boyz N The Hood" (1991).

"Real acceptance comes when you make a good film and its gets widely accepted as a good film. It's not about the novelty. Of course, there's a lot of new black filmmakers now, but I ain't no fucking novelty. I'm in it for the long haul."—John Singleton to *Rolling Stone*, September 5, 1991.

"In the late Sixties and early Seventies, everybody was asking questions of themselves and the society around them. So we had films that were serious and tackled issues, and it was profitable to do that because that was in vogue. Then in the Eighties we were told, 'Don't worry, be happy' by our government, and cinema reflected that. Now, they're still trying to tell us that, but we know we've got a lot of problems. Thought went out of vogue in the Eighties, but I think it's coming back."—Singleton in *Rolling Stone*, September 5, 1991.

He received the USC Black Alumni Association's Eme Award (1992).

Douglas Sirk

BORN: Claus Detlev Sierk in Hamburg, Germany, 04/26/1900

SOMETIMES CREDITED AS:
Detlef Sierck

DEATH: in Lugano, Switzerland, 01/14/1987

NATIONALITY: Danish

EDUCATION: Naval Academy, Germany
Munich University, Munich, Germany
Jena University, Germany
University of Hamburg, Hamburg, Germany
attended Albert Einstein's talks on his theory of relativity

BIOGRAPHY

Best known for his Hollywood melodramas of the 1950s, Douglas Sirk first achieved success in post-WWI Germany, as a theater director. Under the name Claus Detlef Sierck, he directed for the stage from 1922 to 1937, emphasizing the work of such classic playwrights as Moliere, Ibsen,

Shaw and Shakespeare. In 1934 he was hired by UFA, which released his first feature film, " 'T was een April/It Was in April", in 1935. Despite his great success, Sirk left Germany in 1937 because of his opposition to the policies of the Third Reich. After a brief stay in France and Holland, where he worked on several scripts and produced two films, Sirk was invited to America to remake "Zu Neuen Ufern/To New Shores" (1937), one of his most successful German films featuring the great star Zarah Leander.

In Hollywood, after several years of aborted projects, Sirk directed his first American feature, "Hitler's Madman" (1943). His early work in Hollywood remains largely undistinguished, although Sirk devotees insist that, like his later, more important films, it contains ironic critiques of American culture. "Lured" (1947) and "Sleep, My Love" (1948) stand out in this period as atypical but competent thrillers.

Sirk's great period was during his association with Universal-International studios, beginning in 1951 and continuing until his retirement from filmmaking in 1959, and particularly with producers Albert Zugsmith and Ross Hunter. The series of melodramas he made for Universal struck a responsive chord with audiences; among the best-remembered are "Magnificent Obsession" (1954), "All That Heaven Allows" (1956), "Written on the Wind" (1956), "A Time to Love and a Time to Die" (1958) and "Imitation of Life" (1959). During its release, "Imitation of Life" became Universal's most commercially successful picture. Yet it also proved to be Sirk's last film: either because of ill health, a distaste for American culture or both, Sirk retired from filmmaking and returned to Europe, living in Switzerland and Germany until his death.

Largely considered merely a director of competent melodramas by critics in North America, Sirk's career was redefined by British criticism in the early 1970s. He became the subject of essays in theoretical film journals such as *Screen* and was given a retrospective at the 1972 Edinburgh Film Festival, along with an accompanying critical anthology. Such Sirk remarks as, "The angles are a director's thoughts. The lighting is his philosophy" endeared him to a new generation of film critics viewing Sirk as a socially conscious artist who criticized Eisenhower America from within mainstream filmmaking.

Sirk's style hinges on a highly developed sense of irony, employing subtle parody, cliche and stylization. At one time Sirk was seen as a filmmaker who simply employed conventional Hollywood rhetoric, but his style is now regarded as a form of Brechtian distancing that drew the viewer's attention to the methods and purposes of Hollywood illusionism. The world of Sirk's melodramas is extremely lavish and artificial, the colors of walls, cars, costumes and flowers harmonizing into a constructed aesthetic unity, providing a comment on the oppressive world of the American bourgeoisie. The false lake, a studio interior in "Written on the Wind", for example, is presented as "obviously" false, an editorial comment on

the self-deceptive, romanticized imagination that Marylee Hadley (Dorothy Malone) brings to the past. Sirk is renowned for his thematic use of mirrors, shadows and glass, as in the opening shot of "Imitation of Life": behind the credits, chunks of glass, supposedly diamonds, slowly fill the frame from top to bottom, an ironic comment, like the film's very title, about the nature of its own appeal. Later, more obviously political filmmakers like Rainer Werner Fassbinder have been influenced by Sirk's American melodramas, which have been offered as models of ideological critique that may also pass as simple entertainment.

MILESTONES:

Born to Danish parents in Hamburg; raised in Denmark; moved to Germany as teenager to study art and drama

Became stage producer and director

1934: Switched to film work after Nazi rise to power (films were less subject to Nazi scrutiny)

1935: Debut as feature director

1937: Immigrated to USA

1959: Retired; returned to Germany

BIBLIOGRAPHY:

"Sirk on Sirk" Douglas Sirk, 1973; book-length interview

BORN: Kevin Patrick Smith in Highlands, New Jersey, 08/02/1970

NATIONALITY: American

EDUCATION: Henry Hudson High School, Highlands, New Jersey
The New School for Social Research, New York, New York, creative writing, 1988–89; dropped out after one year
Vancouver Film School Vancouver, British Columbia, Canada, film, 1990; left after four months

AWARDS: Sundance Film Festival Filmmakers Trophy (Dramatic) "Clerks" 1994; shared with Rose Troche's "Go Fish"
Cannes Film Festival Prix de la Jeunesse "Clerks" 1994
Independent Spirit Award Best Screenplay "Chasing Amy" 1998

BIOGRAPHY

Bearded, wearing glasses and a perennial long wool coat on top of shorts and a shirt, Kevin Smith became the idol of aspiring filmmakers everywhere when his independent feature "Clerks" (1994)—made for $27,575—won art prizes and a contract with the Creative Artists Agency (CAA). Raised in New Jersey, Smith had dropped out of The New School for Social Research's creative writing program when the school administration called his parents to complain their son was throwing water balloons from his dorm window. Seeing an ad in the *Village Voice* for the Vancouver Film School, he matriculated for four months before dropping out once again. Unsure of his next move, Smith took a job as a clerk at a convenience store in Leonardo, NJ.

In 1991, he saw "Slacker", Richard Linklater's

comedy about shiftless youth. Inspired by both the feature and the possibility of low-budget moviemaking, Smith contacted former film school classmate Scott Mosier. In late 1992, Smith wrote the script for "Clerks", a somewhat plotless slice-of-life look at life from behind the counter at a convenience store. With Smith directing, Mosier producing and moneys raised from Smith's former college tuition fund, the sale of his extensive personal comic collection, plus loans from Mosier's parents and credit cards, the duo made "Clerks" in 21 nights, filming in the very Quick Stop in which Smith was working by day. A screening at the Independent Feature Film Market conjured a buzz for their efforts, and "Clerks" went on to become the toast of the Sundance Film Festival in January 1994, sharing the Filmmaker's Trophy with Rose Troche's "Go Fish."

The quirky "Clerks" earned Smith an agent at Hollywood's CAA powerhouse and a distribution deal with Harvey and Bob Weinstein of Miramax. More acclaim and awards followed at the Cannes Film Festival, but the MPAA ratings board determination that it should receive an 'NC-17' for language delayed the commercial release of the film. Enlisting Harvard law professor and noted attorney Allen Dershowitz in their cause, Smith and Mosier appealed the decision, and the film eventually got its 'R' rating and a release in late 1994. Playing in a limited number of theaters, many of them art-houses, "Clerks" grossed more than $1 million and garnered critical acclaim. By then, Smith was already at work on his next effort, "Mallrats" (1995), a look at youth at a mall over the course of a weekend. Funded by distributor Gramercy for $5.8 million, "Mallrats" earned lukewarm critical notices and an anemic box office.

Returning to his indie routes, Smith made the critically-acclaimed "Chasing Amy" for

$250,000. The film, about the unlikely relationship between a bisexual woman and a comic book writer, grossed $12 million for Miramax and spelled redemption for the filmmaker. He and Mosier also urged the Weinsteins to buy the Ben Affleck–Matt Damon script for "Good Will Hunting" (both 1997) from Castle Rock for $800,000 and shared co-executive producing credit for what became Miramax's highest grossing picture (as of 1998). Smith merged his passions for film and comics when he wrote a screenplay for "Superman Lives" which Tim Burton was assigned to direct. Conflicts with Warner Bros. and Burton, however, relegated it to the trash heap. Smith put his career as a writer of comics firmly on track with the debut of "Clerks (the Comic)" in 1998 and his collaboration on Marvel Comics' "Daredevil". He departed from the boy-girl relationship format of his previous movies for "Dogma" (1999), a pro-God satire about two fallen angels trying to re-enter Heaven starred Damon and Affleck and featured George Carlin, Chris Rock, Salma Hayek and Bud Cort, among others.

COMPANIONS:

Joey Lauren Adams. Actor; together from c. 1995 to 1997; appeared in "Mallrats" and "Chasing Amy"

wife: Jennifer Schwalbach. Journalist; born c. 1970; married on April 25, 1999 by a Catholic monk at Skywalker Ranch in California

MILESTONES:

1991: Saw "Slacker", Richard Linklater's film about shiftless youth; inspired to make a film of his own

1992: Wrote script for "Clerks"

1994: "Clerks" was the hit of the Sundance Film Festival; Miramax acquired distribution rights
Formed production company, View Askew

1995: Second feature, "Mallrats", released by Gramercy; first affiliation with actor Ben Affleck

1996: Signed deal with Carsey-Werner Productions to develop TV sitcom; deal fell apart

when Jason Lee (star of "Mallrats") decided he didn't want to do a sitcom

1996: First producing credit (as executive producer) on a movie he did not direct, "Drawing Flies"

1997: Received Independent Spirit Award for Best Screenplay for "Chasing Amy", starring Affleck, Lee and then-girlfriend Joey Lauren Adams; Matt Damon played a small role

1997: Received co-executive producing credit on "Good Will Hunting" for his help getting the Damon-Affleck script made

1998: "Clerks (the Comic Book)" debuted, offering the continuing adventures of super slackers Dante and Randal

1998: Rewrote screenplay for straight-to-video "Overnight Delivery"

1999: Directed "Dogma", featuring Damon and Affleck; Smith played Silent Bob, "fourpeating" the role he portrayed in his three previous directorial efforts

2000: Executive produced, wrote and voiced character of Silent Bob on the animated "Clerks" (ABC)

2001: Helmed and co-starred in "Jay and Silent Bob Strike Back"

AFFILIATION: Roman Catholic

QUOTES:

Not to be confused with New Zealand actor Kevin Smith.

Smith owns the comics store Jay & Silent Bob's Secret Stash in Red Bank, New Jersey. The success of "Clerks" enabled him to buy back the "hawked" collection which had helped finance its making.

His website is www.viewaskew.com.

Smith has written a series of comics "Jay & Silent Bob" (based on characters from his films) and "Clerks. (The Comic Book)" as well as teaming with artist Joe Quesada for six issues of Marvel Comics' "Daredevil." (Source: Entertainment Weekly, February 20–27, 1998.)

"Talk is cheap. Production values can

come from unlikely sources, such as great dialogue. Special effects and amazing sets are not necessary. Get a strong script. If you're working on your first indie film, you're going to be forgiven for a lot. Don't bang your head against the wall getting it exactly right. Errors you see as blinding other people won't pick up at all."—Smith in *The Hollywood Reporter*, Independent Producers Special Issue, August 1995.

"Smith cracked up audiences during Q & A sessions after screenings, and charmed reporters. He demonstrated as much talent for dealing with media as Spike Lee and Quentin Tarantino. Smith's outrageous wit, warmth, self-deprecation and singular dress (wool trench coat with shorts) give him a unique and winning presence."—From *Los Angeles Times*, January 6, 1995.

Steven Soderbergh

BORN: Steven Andrew Soderbergh in Atlanta, Georgia, 01/14/1963

SOMETIMES CREDITED AS:
Peter Andrews

NATIONALITY: American

EDUCATION: took an animation course at Louisiana State University at age 13
 graduated from high school in 1980

AWARDS: Cannes Film Festival Palme d'Or Award "sex, lies and videotape" 1989
 Sundance Film Festival Audience Award (Dramatic) "sex, lies and videotape" 1989
 Independent Spirit Award Best Director "sex, lies and videotape" 1989
 National Society of Film Critics Award Best Director "Out of Sight" 1998
 National Board of Review Best Director "Erin Brockovich" and "Traffic" 2000; cited for work on both films
 New York Film Critics Award Best Director "Traffic" and "Erin Brockovich" 2000; cited for both films
 Los Angeles Film Critics Association Award Best Director "Erin Brockovich" and "Traffic" 2000; cited for both films
 Broadcast Film Critics Association Award

Best Director "Erin Brockovich" and "Traffic" 2000; cited for both films
 Toronto Film Critics Association Award Best Director "Traffic" 2000
 Las Vegas Film Critics Award Best Director "Erin Brockovich" and "Traffic" 2000; cited for both films
 Florida Film Critics Circle Award Best Director "Traffic" and "Erin Brockovich" 2000
 National Society of Film Critics Award Best Director "Traffic" 2000
 Dallas-Fort Worth Film Critics Association Award Best Director "Traffic" 2000
 Southeastern Film Critics Association Award Best Director "Traffic" 2000
 Golden Satellite Best Director "Traffic" 2000
 Phoenix Film Critics Society Award Best Director "Traffic" 2000; initial presentation of the award
 Chicago Film Critics Award Best Director "Traffic" 2000
 Oscar Best Director "Traffic" 2000

BIOGRAPHY
There are those who credit Steven Soderbergh with creating the late 20th-century boom in independent filmmaking. Certainly there had been other directors working outside the studio system for many, many years, but after his small art-house film "sex, lies

and videotape" won the 1989 Palme d'Or at Cannes, a flood of other indie moviemakers followed in his wake. (The role played by the Sundance Film Festival also cannot be overlooked.) Still, as the new millennium dawned, it was perhaps ironic that this stalwart non-Hollywood director had crossed over and become the darling of the mainstream and a prime contender for Oscar glory.

Born in Atlanta, Soderbergh spent his prime formative years in Baton Rouge, Louisiana where his father served as Dean of the College of Education at Louisiana State University (LSU). As a teenager, he cut his teeth making short Super-8mm films with equipment borrowed from LSU film students. Skipping college, Soderbergh endured a frustrating spell in Hollywood. To support himself, he worked as a game show scorer and cue card holder and eventually as a freelance film editor. Returning home, he further developed his craft and made several Super 8-shorts, including "Rapid Eye Movement" (about his time in Los Angeles) and "Winston", about sexual deception. His first break came in 1986 when the rock group Yes enlisted him to shoot concert footage which he eventually shaped into the Grammy-nominated video "9012Live."

Soderbergh's first feature project was the finely crafted, low-budget ($1.2 million) drama, "sex, lies and videotape." Using events that occurred when he was 24 years old, the writer-director molded the piece into the modern film equivalent of a morality play, a small-scale drama of sexual intrigue and mendacity. After galvanizing the United States Film Festival (the forerunner of Sundance), "sex, lies and videotape" scored a double triumph at Cannes, winning the Palme d'Or for Soderbergh and the Best Actor award for James Spader. With the requisite buzz, the film opened in late summer and proved a box-office hit, later earning an Oscar nomination for its screenplay and establishing Soderbergh as one of the most promising young filmmakers of his generation.

His subsequent films have been an artistically mixed bag and it took nearly a decade before he had a success equal to his first effort. Soderbergh's almost inevitably disappointing follow-up was "Kafka" (1991), an interesting if muddled existential thriller starring Jeremy Irons as the prince of paranoia. Mostly shot in black-and-white and evocative of German Expressionism, "Kafka" failed in its story development, with its crucial conflict unfolding slowly and murkily.

Soderbergh rebounded from his sophomore slump with another study in emotional isolation, "King of the Hill" (1993), a sensitively wrought underappreciated gem that followed a Depression-era boy coping with poverty and neglect. The director developed another variation on the same theme with "The Underneath" (1995), a remake of Robert Siodmak's 1949 film noir "Criss Cross." This heavily stylized film (the director attempted to use a chromatic palette to cue the audience), intricately told in fragmented scenes that include flashbacks and flash forwards, won some critical support but audiences generally agreed with the reviewers who felt the film lacked substance. Soderbergh scripted but did not direct the inferior English-language version of the Danish thriller "Nightwatch" (1997).

Finding himself in a rut after "The Underneath" and feeling the need for a refresher course in the joys of indie filmmaking, Soderbergh trekked home to Baton Rouge and shot "Schizopolis" (1997) for $250,000, employing used equipment, a bare-bones crew and casting himself in a dual lead role. Adding an element of psychodrama, he also cast his ex-wife, actress Betsy Brantley, in scenes that wickedly parodied their disintegrated five-year marriage. While editing "Schizopolis" in Baton Rouge, he took ten days to shoot "Gray's Anatomy" (1997), creating the most cinematic of the filmed Spalding Gray monologues. Batteries recharged, he returned to mainstream movies, directing the adaptation of Elmore Leonard's novel "Out of Sight" (1998), starring George Clooney and Jennifer Lopez, which received glowing reviews and was a surprise winner of several end-of-the-year critics' prizes.

Now on a creative role, Soderbergh tackled "The Limey" (1999), a revenge drama about a British ex-con who travels to L.A. to avenge his daughter's death. Casting established stars like Terence Stamp and Peter Fonda in leading roles, the director tapped into their iconic screen presences which lent an extra layer to the story. (He even used clips of Stamp in Ken Loach's "Poor Cow" (1967) as flashbacks.) Soderbergh's visual panache and strong handle on the material took what could have been a run-of-the-mill gangster story and elevated to a work of art.

His immediate follow-up, the highly commercial "Erin Brockovich" (2000), would on the surface seem to be an atypical project, yet the film's theme of the outsider runs through much of his work. Toplined by star Julia Roberts, impeccably acted by Albert Finney, Marg Helgenberger and others, and following a more linear story narrative, "Erin Brockovich" became the director's most successful picture, grossing over $125 million. For that achievement alone, Soderbergh would have been lauded but he also directed and shot "Traffic" in 2000. "Traffic", based on a 1989 British miniseries, was something of a cross between the director's commercial films and his experimental ones. Acting as his own director of photography (but taking the credit as Peter Andrews), Soderbergh shot each of the film's three major storylines in a different color scheme. The sprawling film—there were 110 speaking roles alone—traced the war on drugs from all sides—the justice department, the suppliers and the users—and was a critical triumph and a box-office success. This one-two punch brought Soderbergh numerous end-of-the-year prizes and sparked talk of his becoming the first director since Michael Curtiz in 1938 to receive dual Academy Award nominations. In taking home the Oscar for "Traffic", the indie king had finally made it to the mainstream. If further evidence were needed, his next project was the all-star remake of "Ocean's Eleven" (2001), featuring George Clooney, Julia Roberts, Brad Pitt and Matt Damon. In 2002, Soderbergh took a different approach to his craft and directed the non-narrative "Full Frontal" starring Julia Roberts. The film was shot in 18 days and features guerilla-style camera work and encouraged improvisation from the actors.

COMPANIONS:

wife: Betsy Brantley. Actor; met while he was doing preliminary casting for "The Last Ship"; has acted in such films as "Another Country" (1984), "The Princess Bride" (1987) and "Havana" (1990); sister of journalist-screenwriter Duncan Brantley; divorced

Laura Bickford. Producer; dated; no longer together; produced "Traffic" (2000); was Soderbergh's date to the 2001 Academy Awards

wife: Jules Asner. TV reporter; dating as of summer 2001; married on May 10, 2003

MILESTONES:

Moved with family to Texas when he was three months old; later lived in Pennsylvania and in Charlottesville, Virginia before settling in Baton Rouge, Louisiana

1978: At age 15, made short film titled "Janitor"

First completed project was an Ex-Lax commercial

1980: Moved to Los Angeles after graduating high school

In Los Angeles worked as an editor on TV show, "Games People Play" (canceled after six months); took odd jobs as cue-card holder and game-show scorekeeper until employed as freelance editor for Showtime

Returned to Baton Rouge; worked as coin-changer in a video arcade while making Super-8 shorts, including "Rapid Eye Movement" (about waiting for his big Hollywood break)

Worked at a video production house in Louisiana

Began directing videos for local bands in Louisiana

1986: First professional video directing assignment with "9012LIVE", made for rock group "Yes", based on concert performances promoting their album "90125"; video premiered on MTV and was later nominated for a Grammy for Best Music Video, Long Form

Made "Winston", a short about sexual deception that prefigured "sex, lies and videotape", for $7,500

1989: Feature film directing debut, "sex, lies and videotape"; also wrote and edited; film was shot for $1.2 million; Soderbergh was paid $37,000 for his services; won Cannes Film Festival Palme d'Or; garnered Oscar nomination for Best Original Screenplay

After several unsatisfactory screenplay drafts, abandoned "The Last Ship", a post-nuclear-war story set on a destroyer and made "Kafka" instead

1993: Made TV directorial debut with "The Quiet Room", an episode of the Showtime film noir anthology series, "Fallen Angels"

1993: Crafted the tender, underappreciated gem "King of the Hill", based on A. E. Hotchner's autobiographical novel about depression-era St Louis

1995: Remade Robert Siodmark's 1949 film noir "Criss Cross" as "The Underneath"

1996: Returned to Baton Rouge to shoot "Schizopolis" (released in 1997), starring himself opposite his ex-wife Betsy Brantley

1997: Directed "Gray's Anatomy", reuniting him with Spalding Gray who had acted in "King of the Hill"

1998: Helmed "Out of Sight", an adaptation of an Elmore Leonard novel co-starring George Clooney and Jennifer Lopez

1999: Directed "The Limey", starring Terrence Stamp as a man seeking information about and revenge for his daughter's death; incorporated scenes of Stamp from "Poor Cow" directed by Ken Loach as flashbacks

With Clooney, formed Section Eight, a production company

2000: Directed Julia Roberts in the based-on-fact drama "Erin Brockovich", about a woman who was instrumental in a class action lawsuit over poisoned drinking water

2000: Helmed "Traffic", a feature based on the British miniseries "Traffik"; also served as director of photography (credited as Peter Andrews)

2001: Became first filmmaker since Michael Curtiz in 1938 to receive dual Academy Award nominations for Best Director for both "Erin Brockovich" and "Traffic"; won award for "Traffic"

2001: Reteamed with George Clooney on the remake of "Ocean's Eleven"

2002: Reteamed with Julia Roberts in an "unofficial" sequel to "sex, lies and videotape" (1989), a non-narrative film

QUOTES:

Soderbergh became only the second person in the history of the Directors Guild of America Awards to be nominated for more than one film in the same year when he was tapped for a pair of 2000 releases, "Erin Brockovich" and "Traffic." The first man so honored was Francis Ford Coppola in 1974 when he was nominated for "The Conversation" and "The Godfather, Part II" (for which he won the prize).

On the similarities between Soderbergh and the lead character of Graham in "sex, lies and videotape", actor James Spader told writer Terri Minski: "We never talked about it. But there would be days when I'd get out of wardrobe and come to the set, and we'd be wearing the same thing."—From *Rolling Stone*, May 18, 1989.

"There's a certain way I like to work. It goes—this is the script, this is the budget, this is the schedule. Assuming these things stay as they are, I want to be left alone."—Steven Soderbergh quoted in "The Road Less Traveled" by David Gritten in the *Los Angeles Times Calendar*, November 25, 1990.

When asked what it was like directing and acting opposite his ex-wife in "Schizopolis": "I highly recommend it. I think everybody must have thought I was insane while we were making the movie. But, when you think, 'It's just life. Why shy away from it?' In terms of my work, I'm always looking for the stupid thing to do, the thing that makes you think, 'Why would anyone put themselves through that?' It was very therapeutic. It really was like standing on the bow of a ship in a bad storm. It required an enormous amount of equilibrium."—Steven Soderbergh to the *Village Voice*, April 1, 1997.

"People assume they know what it means for a director to be true to himself, which they don't. America has no shortage of auteurs. What we have is a shortage of films being made by smart filmmakers that open in 4,000 theaters. I don't understand why a filmmaker should be penalized for working in the mainstream. Why not give the big money to the most interesting filmmakers instead of putting them in quarantine, where, in order for them to do something interesting, they have to do it for a million bucks?"—Soderbergh quoted in *The New York Times*, June 21, 1998.

In your book, "Getting Away With It," you have some pretty tough words for movie critics, calling them "parasitic," questioning their legitimacy and so on. Have the recent awards from the New York Film Critics Circle changed those opinions?

No. I think what I was referring to at that point was whether or not, in the current structure of how movies are made and sold, they have the kind of role that they used to have. There was a time when I think critics had a more significant and integral role in what was happening with movies. But the business has changed so much that you could argue that's not true anymore. When you can find somebody somewhere to call every film a masterpiece, then it's gotten out of hand.

Also, the number of serious critics who are allowed and/or encouraged to write at length and seriously about movies is diminished, which is sad. I didn't always agree with Pauline Kael, but I sure loved reading her stuff because she was incredibly bright and knew a lot about a lot of things, not just movies. There aren't many like that anymore.

Yet, by strict definition, critics are parasitic in the sense that they can't exist without the artist. The artist has to create something that is then commented on. It's great when a group of critics gets together and gives you an award like that. But the bottom line is, it doesn't make me any better at my job, which is all I think about when I get up in the morning. You have to give such awards their proper weight.—From Stephen Lemons' interview with Soderbergh on Salon.com (December 20, 2000).

"I try to strike a balance between design and life."—Steven Soderbergh explaining his directorial style to Aleksandrs Rozens of Reuters, December 28, 2000.

On his direction of actors, Soderbergh told Stephen Rebello of *Movieline* (December 2000/January 2001): "What I always want to do is find the best version of them. It's not that I want to glamorize them, it's just that I'm pretty good at minimizing whatever weaknesses they have. My gut instinct about that is pretty good, from how to pitch a performance tonally to how to frame, light and cut them. That's my job.

" . . . A lot of directors don't like actors. They don't want to talk to them, don't know how to talk to them. Some directors who work that way make good films. But I'm very impressed by what actors do. You cannot describe the kind of exposure that standing in front of a camera with a crew around means. There's no control and the rejection is very personal. I'm very sympathetic toward actors because I have a sense of what that's like. Naked doesn't begin to describe it. I have enormous respect for people who want to do it, and for people who do it well. It's a career I wouldn't wish on a lot of people—the worst."

Asked by Anthony Kaufman of Indiwire.com (January 3, 2001) about serving as his own director of photography on "Traffic", Soderbergh replied: "It is [relentless]. But it's so satisfying. Because you're getting what you want all day. I certainly underestimated the restorative value of being able to leave the set for 5 minutes, which you cannot do when you are your own cinematographer. Literally. I couldn't go to the bathroom until lunchtime. Because I had to sit there and make sure things we're going. Or we were shooting. Most of our day was spent shooting. The lion's share of the film is shot with available light, so we showed up early, ready to shoot. But in this case, it felt so organic that it didn't really feel like I was doing another job. It felt very much like when I was making my short films. It was a very stripped down crew. It was really just: Let's show up and shoot."

"I'm no longer a control freak. The implementation of whatever aesthetic I choose for each film is as considered and systematic as it used to be, but I have a completely different way of doing it now. I used to be a perfectionist but it was the wrong kind of perfection. And I no longer think perfection is interesting—by definition it's not lifelike. On the set, it's really about refining your sense of what's important within a scene, and within the context of the film. You train yourself to start gravitating toward it, like a metal detector, and you let the other stuff roll down your back."—Soderbergh to Dennis Lim in "Both Sides Now", from *Village Voice,* January 3–9, 2001.

On his approach to casting actors, Soderbergh told Ben Thompson of London's *The Daily Telegraph* (January 6, 2001): "I think most of them want to find that area in which they can have a little bit of wiggle room—somewhere they can be interesting movie stars—but a lot of them don't get the opportunity. Maybe they're not encouraged by their handlers or their studios, and then a little bit of pressure builds up and you end up with someone making a horrifically wrong-headed choice."

"I don't think I've ever felt on the inside. It may have looked that way—and in some ways my awareness that it looks that way just makes the sensation even stranger—but to me it's always felt like everyone else is having all the fun."—Steven Soderbergh quoted in "The Director Who Came in From the Cold" by Ben Thompson in *The Daily Telegraph,* January 6, 2001.

"'Traffic' links back to the political cinema of the Sixties and Seventies. In its combination of radical form and content, it is reminiscent of 'Medium Cool' and, most of all, 'The Battle of Algier'. Like Pontecorvo's revolutionary classic, 'Traffic' has both a broad scope and a sharp immediacy. With other filmmakers, these comparisons would be speculative, but Soderbergh is the biggest film buff among current American directors, a man who actually described 'The Limey' as 'Alain Resnais directing "Get Carter."'"—From "What a Lucky Soderbergh" by Mark Morris in *The Observer,* January 7, 2001.

BIBLIOGRAPHY:

"Getting Away With It: Or, The Further Adventures of the Luckiest Bastard You Ever Saw" Steven Soderbergh and Richard Lester, 2000, Faber and Faber

BORN: in Newark, New Jersey, 10/15/1959

NATIONALITY: American

EDUCATION: attended a succession of religious, public and private schools
Yale College, Yale University, New Haven, Connecticut, English 1981
New York University, New York, New York, film, 1985

AWARDS: Sundance Film Festival Grand Jury Prize (Dramatic) "Welcome to the Dollhouse" 1996
Berlin Film Festival Cicae Prize of International Federation of Art Cinemas "Welcome to the Dollhouse" 1996 shared award with "Chinese Chocolate" (directed by Yan Cui and Qi Chang) and "To Have (or Not)" (directed by Laetitia Masson)
Cannes Film Festival FIPRESCI Prize "Happiness" 1998
British Independent Film Award Best Foreign Independent Film—English Language "Happiness" 1999

BIOGRAPHY

The strange film career of writer-director Todd Solondz, responsible for "Welcome to the Dollhouse" (1995), a heartbreaking yet hilarious chronicle of junior high school life, has provided some quirky twists to the standard Hollywood success story. Born in Newark and raised in suburban New Jersey, the eight-year-old future filmmaker wanted to become a rabbi. This desire propelled him through a succession of religious, public and private schools. Having decided against the ecclesiastical life, Solondz eventually landed among the decidedly humanistic literary set, studying English at Yale College.

Though he was unhappy academically, Solondz received an invaluable education through myriad campus screenings that exposed him to the glories of cinema's past. Inspired, Solondz headed west to Los Angeles where he worked as a messenger at the Writers Guild while writing screenplays. He acquired an agent on the strength of his first script but the agent disliked his second. Tiring of the scene, Solondz returned to NYC where he enrolled in NYU's highly regarded film school. There he made several promising short films, most notably, "Schatt's Last Shot" (1985), a 12-minute comedy. On the strength of this little movie, Solondz won a high-powered agent with International Creative Management Inc. At age 26, he found himself with highly coveted three-picture deals at both Columbia and 20th Century Fox. Solondz was living the young filmmaker's dream until it soon became a bit of a nightmare.

Solondz found himself with no creative control over his first project, "Fear, Anxiety and Depression" (1989). He wrote, directed and starred in this poorly received, barely released would-be comedy about struggling twenty-somethings trying to make it in the trendy "downtown" NYC art scene. As writer Ira Ellis, Solondz plays a character so desperate that he sends his latest play to his idol Samuel Beckett in hopes of a collaboration. The filmmaker found the experience so dispiriting that he decided to leave Hollywood. Solondz returned to NYC where he failed to get accepted by the Peace Corps. Instead, he accepted a job as a teacher of English as a Second Language to newly arrived Russian immigrants, an experience he has described as deeply rewarding.

School lay-offs were looming on the horizon when a lawyer friend of Solondz's announced that she could raise financing for a feature. He remembered the screenplay he had written right after the debacle of "Fear, Anxiety and Depression." That script became "Welcome to the Dollhouse." This story of an 11-year-old bespectacled doormat of a girl who faces abuse at every front won the hearts of reviewers and audiences and introduced a cast of talented newcomers, including Heather Matarazzo, Brendan Sexton III and Eric Mabius. Hailed for its realism, emotional truth and unsentimental humor, the elegantly composed low-budget film won Solondz (who also produced) major prizes at the Berlin and Sundance Film Festivals.

Solondz followed up with the controversial but widely well-received "Happiness" (1998). Both exceptionally funny and wildly disturbing, "Happiness" caused quite a stir following its award-winning Cannes debut, and was subsequently dropped by October Films when Universal Pictures and parent company Seagram's forbade the subsidiary to distribute it, citing moral outrage. An ensemble film focusing on the lives of three sisters and the people with whom they interconnect, "Happiness" included among its characters an obscene phone caller, a murderer and a pedophile, all portrayed in an irreverently sympathetic light, highlighted by the cast's wonderful performances, including the especially memorable Dylan Baker, Phillip Seymour Hoffman and Jane Adams. While quite unsettling, most would agree that Solondz's work (finally released by a specially formed distribution annex of the independent production company Good Machine) was more morally exploratory than bankrupt, but the controversy did buy the film and the director a great deal of press, undoubtedly bringing in moviegoers who may not have otherwise seen this remarkable film.—Written by Kent Greene

MILESTONES:

Moved with family from Newark to suburban New Jersey in the 1960s

1968: At age eight, briefly entertained the idea of becoming a rabbi (date approximate); subsequently attended a succession of religious, public and private schools

Moved to Los Angeles; worked as a messenger at the Writers Guild while writing screenplays

Won an agent on the strength of his first script; agent disliked his second script

Returned to NYC; enrolled at NYU

1984: Wrote and directed first student short, "Feelings", at NYU

1984: Wrote and directed "Babysitter", another NYU student short

1985: Wrote and directed his breakthrough 12-minute student film, "Schatt's Last Shot"

1986: TV debut, made "How I Became a Leading Artistic Figure in New York City's East Village Cultural Landscape", a short made for NBC's "Saturday Night Live"

Signed with International Creative Management Inc.

Received three-picture deals at both Columbia and Fox

1988: Feature acting debut, bit part as "The Zany Reporter" in Jonathan Demme's "Married to the Mob"

1989: Featured as an interview subject on "SST: Screen, Stage, Television", an ABC documentary special about show business stories

1989: Wrote, directed and starred in debut feature, "Fear, Anxiety, and Depression", a critical and commercial flop

Wrote screenplay for "Welcome to the Dollhouse"

Quit Hollywood; returned to NYC

Rejected by the Peace Corps

Took a job as a teacher of ESL (English as a Second Language) to new Russian immigrants

Learned that a lawyer friend could raise financing for a low-budget indie

1994: Returned to feature filmmaking as producer, writer and director of "Welcome to the Dollhouse"; shown at Toronto International Film Festival in September 1995; acquired for distribution that fall by Sony Classics; screened to acclaim at Sundance Film Festival in January 1996; released theatrically in March 1996

1997: Made cameo appearance as a bus passenger in James L. Brooks' "As Good As It Gets"

1998: Engendered controversy with "Happiness", a searing character study of three sisters and the men and women in their lives; October Films was forced by its parent companies to drop its distribution of the film because of some of the subject matter; producers Ted Hope and James Schamus formed Good Machine Releasing to oversee distribution

2001: Premiered fourth feature "Storytelling" at Cannes; released theatrically in USA in 2002

QUOTES:

"He looks like Woody Allen, sounds like E.T., and thinks like Harvey Weinstein."—unidentified Hollywood agent describing Solondz, quoted in *The Hollywood Reporter*, June 3, 1996.

Solondz on Universal's refusal (on the grounds of moral outrage) to release "Happiness" through its subsidiary October Films: "It's not based on morality; I don't think they've ever operated on that basis. Universal considered how large an audience there is for a movie like this and is it worth all the flak for a movie that is going to make so little money? If the movie somehow made $50 million, I'm sure they would reconsider."—From *USA Today*, October 21, 1998.

"Sometimes I've been accused of a certain kind of misanthropy, but I don't think that's fair or accurate. I think it's only by accepting and embracing people for all their flaws and foibles that one can, in fact, really embrace all of who we are."—Solondz quoted in *Boston Herald*, October 26, 1998.

Barry Sonnenfeld

BORN: in New York, New York, 04/01/1953

NATIONALITY: American

EDUCATION: P. S. 173, New York, New York; elementary school

Eleanor Roosevelt Junior High School, New York, New York; Sonnefeld has referred to his attendance as "the worst three years of my life; I was beaten up every day"

High School of Music and Art, New York, New York; he has called his high school experience "the three best years of my life"; played French horn and eventually made it into the all-city orchestra

New York University, New York, New York, political science; attended NYU's Bronx campus for three years while living at home

Hampshire College, Amherst, Massachusetts, BA

Institute of Film and Television, New York University, New York, New York, MFA, 1978

AWARD: Daytime Emmy Outstanding Achievement in Single Camera Photography "Out of Step" 1984/85

BIOGRAPHY

Loud, brash, outspoken and highly strung, Barry Sonnenfeld embodies everything expected of a Hollywood director, and yet this man described by colleague Ethan Coen to *Newsweek* as "an urban neurotic" is also meek and nebbishy, adjectives hardly invoking images of Orson Welles, Alfred Hitchcock or John Huston. Go figure how this only child of overprotective Jewish parents ("My mother said if I went to what she called 'sleep-away school'—what others call 'college'—she would commit suicide") could grow up to have his finger on the pulse of what is hip and cool, but that is exactly the case for this A-list director whose sterling reputation attracts high caliber talent anxious to work with him. Although he did not know fellow NYU classmate Joel Coen while they were in school together, Sonnenfeld met Joel and his brother Ethan later, making his mark as director of photography for their darkly comic film noir feature debut, "Blood Simple" (1984), the beginning of a successful collaboration that encompassed the wacky hellzapoppin camerawork of "Raising Arizona" (1987) and the somber hues of the gangster pastiche, "Miller's Crossing" (1990).

Drawn particularly, if not exclusively, to comedy in his assignments as a cinematographer, Sonnenfeld performed lensing chores on Danny DeVito's "Throw Momma from the Train" (1987), Rob Reiner's "When Harry Met Sally . . . " and Penny Marshall's "Big" (both 1988) before earning his first feature credit as a second unit director while shooting Reiner's wintry "Misery" (1990). Sonnenfeld then segued to the director's chair with "The Addams Family" (1991), an ornately stylish film adaptation of Charles Addams' cartoons (also inspiration for the classic 60s sitcom), which, despite repetitious humor and a throwaway plot, earned over $110 million at the box-office. He followed-up by directing a typical Michael J. Fox romantic comedy vehicle, "For Love or Money" (1993), which garnered little attention from press or public, before helming a superior sequel (though not a bigger money-maker), "Addams Family Values" (1993). Bolstered by sharp ensemble playing (with young Christina Ricci a standout), this effort was more consistent, thanks to somewhat more coherent screenplay from playwright-turned-screenwriter Paul Rudnick.

Sonnenfeld had played a key role in developing "Forrest Gump" (1994), suggesting that the fat, strong Gump of Winston Groom's novel be a lanky, fast guy on-screen; commissioning Eric Roth's script; and bringing Tom Hanks, a friend since "Big", on board before deciding to make "Addams Family Values" instead. Though he regretted his choice for some time, his career didn't suffer as he immediately enjoyed his first critical hit with "Get Shorty" (1995), a humorous, literate and well-nuanced Elmore Leonard adaptation boasting a dream cast including John Travolta, Danny DeVito, Gene Hackman and Rene Russo. Here the director proved he could make a mainstream movie that relied more on acting and dialogue than gimmickry without compromising his love of blacker-than-black humor. Sonnenfeld executive produced, as well as portrayed a doorman, losing out in his battle with his editor who insisted that the doorman footage not be cut. He also managed to helm some commercials, including the first batch of Duracell ads featuring the mean-spirited, battery-powered Puttermans. Duracell defanged the Puttermans for subsequent ads, prompting Sonnenfeld to say: "I was saddened to see how quickly they gave up on being a little darker. They chickened out."

Sonnenfeld delivered the biggest blockbuster of 1997, the ultra-hip sci-fi comedy "Men in Black", accomplishing what Tim Burton had failed to do with the campy "Mars Attacks!" (1996)—a close encounter of the truly funny kind. Immediately after coming on board, the director had requested a rewrite, setting most of the action in New York City and patterning it not after classic sci-fi but on "The French Connection" (1971). Instead of Gene Hackman as Popeye Doyle with a guy up against the bathroom wall, he gave the audience Tommy Lee Jones interrogating an alien "stoolie" in the guise of a dog. Drawing from the popular urban legend that aliens are here among us, Sonnenfeld teamed with multiple Oscar-winner Rick Baker to design the alien puppetry, but the best gag of all was the screen that kept tabs on registered aliens who qualify as celebrities, showing the likes of infomercial guru Tony Robbins, Newt Gingrich, Sylvester

Stallone, psychic friend Dionne Warwick, ILM chief George Lucas and Steven Spielberg (who would allow it only if Lucas said OK, too). Sadly, Sonnenfeld couldn't get permission from everyone on his alien wish list. "I wanted Michael Jackson very badly. He wouldn't do it . . . None of the real aliens would."

Back in Elmore Leonard country, Sonnenfeld executive produced Steven Soderbergh's underrated "Out of Sight" (1998) and executive produced (the series) and directed the highest-rated network pilot premiering in the summer in four years, ABC's "Maximum Bob", which he had originally considered doing as a feature before opting for the expanded format seven episodes afforded. He also executive produced ABC's ill-fated remake of "Fantasy Island" (1998–99), inserting Malcolm McDowell into the role of Rourke to take advantage of the actor's dangerous, edgy charm and make the character more controlling ("like the devil") than depicted originally by Ricardo Montelban. "Television all looks the same . . . I want to take something that is banal and put my own absurdist twist on it." Also, one of the executive producers for UPN's "Secret Agent Man" (2000), Sonnenfeld had by no means renounced the large screen in favor of the small, though, ironically enough, the inspiration for his next feature was the classic 60s Western series "Wild Wild West" (CBS, 1965–70). Reteaming with Will Smith as an 1800s James Bond, Sonnenfeld announced, "We will absolutely address the fact that this time, our lead character is a black man during this period in time. It's a concept we're embracing a lot." Professing that the movie would be bigger than "Men in Black" ("We've got an 80-foot tarantula in this movie"), he hoped audiences would agree and deem it the "cool" movie of the summer. It wasn't.

MILESTONES:

Grew up in NYC's Washington Heights
Upon graduation from Hampshire College

worked in photo lab in New York; then returned to college (NYU) for graduate film studies
After graduating, claims to have served as cinematographer on at least nine pornographic films shot over a 22-day period
Shot corporate films and documentaries
1982: Was cinematographer on the hour-long documentary, "In Our Water", about water pollution in New Jersey (shown on PBS' "Frontline")
1984: First feature film as director of photography, Joel Coen's "Blood Simple"; first of a series of collaborations with the Coen brothers; had shot the trailer that enabled the Coens to raise money for the project
1984: First TV credit as director of photography, "Out of Step", an "ABC Afterschool Special"; won a Daytime Emmy
1985: Shot first TV miniseries "Doubletake" (CBS)
1986: Provided "additional projection camera" for Laurie Anderson's experimental concert film "Home of the Brave"
1986: First TV-movie as cinematographer, "Welcome Home, Bobby" (CBS)
1987: Reteamed with the Coens as cinematographer of "Raising Arizona"
1988: First film with director Rob Reiner, "When Harry Met Sally . . . "
1990: Last project to date with the Coens, "Miller's Crossing"
1990: Second time as director of photography for Reiner, "Misery"
1991: Directorial debut, "The Addams Family"
1993: Feature producing debut (as co-producer), "For Love or Money"; also directed
1994: Helmed sequel, "Addams Family Values"
1995: Signed two-year deal with Walt Disney Company; formed own eponymous production company
1995: Directed "Get Shorty"; marked first work on an adaptation of an Elmore Leonard novel; script by Scott Frank; also played small role as Doorman
1997: Helmed the summer blockbuster sci-fi

comedy "Men in Black", teaming Tommy Lee Jones and Will Smith

1998: Executive produced "Out of Sight", directed by Steven Soderbergh and scripted by Frank; based on Leonard's novel

1998: Served as an executive producer for the series and director of the pilot of "Maximum Bob", an ABC summer series based on another Leonard book

1998–1999: Served as executive producer of the ABC series remake "Fantasy Island"

1999: Directed the feature version of the 1960s TV series "Wild Wild West", starring Will Smith and Kevin Kline

1999: Uninjured when the Gulfstream II jet on which he was the lone passenger crash-landed at Van Nuys, California airport

2000: Was one of the executive producers of "Secret Agent Man" (UPN)

2000: In July, terminated film producing partnership with Barry Josephson; TV deal unaffected

2001: Served as executive producer and occasional director of the Fox midseason replacement series "The Tick"

QUOTES:

Sonnenfeld was the cinematographer on a commercial for Nike entitled "Dog" which won a 1989 Clio award.

"With the Coens, I used to throw up a lot. I threw up, like, 18 times on 'Blood Simple' from being nervous. Well, the first time was because I was filming Danny Hedaya vomiting after getting kicked in the groin by Fran McDormand. And I'm a sympathetic vomiter. If I see, smell or hear vomiting, I will vomit. So when Danny was vomiting, I was vomiting while operating the camera. On the second take, Joel suggested that the soundman point the microphone at me, because my vomiting sounded better than Hedaya's."—Barry Sonnenfeld, quoted in *Time Out New York*, June 26–July 3, 1997.

About his relationship with Sony Pictures Entertainment (SPE) president of worldwide marketing Robert Levin: "Bob rings up and says, 'It has all worked out well. I just wanted to let you know that I feel very close to you because my middle name is Barry.' And I said: 'You know, Bob, that's so weird because my penis' name is Bob.' There was this long silence on the end of the phone line. Silence. Silence. Silence. Then Bob said, 'You know what Barry, I have just decided that your penis' name is Bob and not that you're telling me to go f**k myself.' We've got on fine ever since."—Sonnenfeld, quoted in *Screen International*, August 1, 1997.

On his brush with death as passenger of a jet that crashed: "We were coming in for a landing, and we came down so late in the runway. It's almost a life-changing thing. You have enough time to scream. They were desperately looking for things to hit so they would slow down. That's when I got really scared. . . .

"I thought it was strangely calm until I saw the fuel pouring out of the plane and onto the engine. . . .

"No one was hurt, but I hope that someday the NTSB gives me back my suit jacket and my various pieces of luggage. . . .

"The weird thing is that I hate to fly, and the quote that I give people is that every time I get off a plane, I view it as a failed suicide attempt. The sad news for Warner and Disney is that I'm not going to take any of these rented jets."—Sonnenfeld to Dan Cox of *Daily Variety*, February 17, 1999

BORN: in New Orleans, Louisiana, 12/02/1945

NATIONALITY: American

EDUCATION: University of California at Los Angeles, Los Angeles, California, film, MFA
American Film Institute, Los Angeles, California

AWARD: Sundance Film Festival Freedom of Expression Award "The Decline of Western Civilization, Part III" 1998

BIOGRAPHY

A figure of some note in 1980s fringe independent filmmaking, Spheeris found substantial mainstream success in the 90s helming high-profile adaptations of TV sketches, old sitcoms and other pop culture artifacts. She worked as a film editor before forming her own company, Rock 'n' Reel, through which she produced and directed short promotional films for the music industry—sort of proto-rock videos. Spheeris worked on two of comic Lily Tomlin's 70s TV specials, where her colleagues included Richard Pryor and Lorne Michaels, and went on to produce seven comedy shorts directed by Albert Brooks for the early "Saturday Night Live". Spheeris broke into features as the producer of Brooks' "Real Life" (1979), a clever send-up of PBS's "An American Family", and other works of "cinema verite."

Spheeris established her reputation as the producer, director and screenwriter of "The Decline of Western Civilization" (1981), a knowing, humorous but clear-eyed record of the late 70s L.A. punk rock scene. The film was well received critically and commercially. Serving as just the director, she followed up with "The Decline of Western Civilization Part II, The Metal Years" (1988), a quasi-sequel which documented the mid-80s heavy metal phenomenon. In between these two nonfiction works, Spheeris wrote and/or directed a series of youth-oriented narrative films which, despite cultish appeal, were generally poorly received critically and did little business.

Spheeris' first fiction film, "Suburbia/The Wild Side" (1983), a drama about alienated suburban teens, was dismissed by "Leonard Maltin's Movie and Video Guide 1995" as a "poorly staged, perfectly awful drama" whose message was lost amid "gratuitous violence". In sharp contrast, Geoff Andrew of London's *Time Out* praises the film for its "manifest sincerity" and how it "combines intelligent social comment with the conventions of the teens-in-revolt exploiter." Spheeris revisited similar territory for her next feature directing assignment, "The Boys Next Door" (1985), starring Maxwell Caulfield and Charlie Sheen as a pair of hopeless and desperate high schoolers who go on a motiveless murder spree. She lightened up with two comedies, "Hollywood Vice Squad" (1986) and "Dudes" (1987), and made some inroads into TV as the story editor for much of the second season of the hit sitcom "Roseanne" (ABC, 1989–90).

Spheeris joined Hollywood's big leagues helming the surprise comedy blockbuster "Wayne's World" (1992) based on "Saturday Night Live" sketches featuring Mike Myers and Dana Carvey as nerds with their own public access cable show. A considerably more benign variation on the filmmaker's typical milieu, the film grossed over $120 million domestically. Spheeris wandered a bit further afield to produce and direct "The Beverly Hillbillies" (1993), a popular if critically derided adaptation of the 60s sitcom. She provided the story and screenplay as well as directed "The Little Rascals" (1994), an update of the beloved comedy shorts of yore, which fared well at the box office. Spheeris also directed the comedy "Black Sheep" (1996) starring Chris Farley as the brother of a political candidate (Tim Matheson).

MILESTONES:

1945–1952: Spent her first seven years traveling around the American South and Midwest with her father's carnival, Magic Empire Shows (date approximate)

Worked as a waitress for 12 years; one employer was the International House of Pancakes

Worked as film editor before forming own company, Rock 'n' Reel; produced and directed promotional films for the music industry

Worked on two Lily Tomlin specials in the 1970s; first professional association with writer (and future "Saturday Night Live" producer) Lorne Michaels

Produced seven short films directed by Albert Brooks for "Saturday Night Live"

1979: First feature as producer, Albert Brooks' documentary spoof, "Real Life"

1981: Produced, directed, wrote screenplay and provided additional photography for "The Decline of Western Civilization", an acclaimed documentary feature about the LA punk scene

1984: Directed first narrative feature, "Suburbia"

1986: Provided the screenplay for "Summer Camp Nightmare/The Butterfly Revolution"

1988: Directed the quasi-sequel documentary, "The Decline of Western Civilization Part II, The Metal Years"

1989: Worked in the recording industry as an A&R exec, a high-profile talent scout; signed her first band—Grave Danger—to MCA Records

1989: TV directing debut, "Thunder and Mud",

a cable pay-per-view special featuring female mud wrestling set to LA-based rock bands

Joined the staff of the hit sitcom "Roseanne" during its second season to serve as story editor

1989: Co-directed "Decade", an MTV special about 1980s trends

1990: Feature acting debut, "Wedding Band"

1991: TV fiction directing debut, "Prison Stories: Women on the Inside" on "HBO Showcase"; directed the segment entitled "New Chicks"

1991: Network TV directing debut, "Visitors From the Unknown", a CBS reality-based special about extraterrestrial encounters

1992: Directed her commercial breakthrough, the surprise blockbuster comedy, "Wayne's World", from the popular "SNL" sketches

1993: Created, executive produced, directed the pilot and sometimes provided the story for "Danger Theatre", a short-lived Fox Adventure spoof

QUOTES:

" 'If the only three films I made were "Wayne's World", "Beverly Hillbillies" and "The Little Rascals", then I would probably have some guilt about a lack of originality and creativity . . . But you can't forget I also did these other things that were so weird I couldn't get a job in Hollywood for 20 years.' "

"She admits her appearance didn't help. 'I had every color hair. I had the weirdest clothes. I was freaky visually. It changed for me when somebody said 'Do you really need all that attention?' And I went 'oh.' . . . Once I figured it out I didn't need it anymore. . . . I enjoy life so much more fading into the crowd.' "

—From "Penelope Spheeris' Wayward Road to 'Rascals' " by Susan Spillman, USA Today, August 25, 1994.

BORN: Steven Allan Spielberg in Cincinnati, Ohio, 12/18/1946

NATIONALITY: American

EDUCATION: Saratoga High School; Spielberg first experienced anti-Semitism

California State College, Long Beach, California, English, BA, 1970; not accepted to University of Southern California's film department, chose Cal State as alternative; made five films there; school now California State University

AWARDS: National Society of Film Critics Award Best Director "E.T. The Extra-Terrestrial" 1982

Los Angeles Film Critics Association Award Best Film "E.T. The Extra-Terrestrial" 1982; shared award with co-producer Kathleen Kennedy

Los Angeles Film Critics Association Award Best Director "E.T. The Extra-Terrestrial" 1982

Directors Guild of America Award Outstanding Directorial Achievement in Feature Film "The Color Purple" 1985

Eastman Kodak Second Century Award 1987; initial presentation of the award; shared honors with actor Burt Reynolds

Irving G. Thalberg Memorial Award 1987; honored for career achievement by the Academy of Motion Picture Arts and Sciences

National Board of Review Award Best Director "Empire of the Sun" 1988

Daytime Emmy Outstanding Animated Program "Steven Spielberg Presents Tiny Toon Adventures" 1990/91; shared award; Spielberg was executive producer

Daytime Emmy Outstanding Animated Program "Steven Spielberg Presents Tiny Toon Adventures'" 1992/93; shared award; Spielberg was executive producer

Venice Film Festival Golden Lion Career Achievement Award 1993; awarded at the 50th Venice Film Festival

Peabody Award "Steven Spielberg Presents Animaniacs" 1993

National Board of Review Award Best Picture "Schindler's List" 1993; shared award with Gerald R. Molen and Branko Lustig

Los Angeles Film Critics Association Award Best Picture "Schindler's List" 1993; shared award with Gerald R. Molen and Branko Lustig

New York Film Critics Circle Award Best Picture "Schindler's List" 1993; shared award with Gerald R. Molen and Branko Lustig

National Society of Film Critics Award Best Director "Schindler's List" 1993

National Society of Film Critics Award Best Picture "Schindler's List" 1993; shared award with Gerald R. Molen and Branko Lustig

Golden Globe Award Best Picture (Drama) "Schindler's List" 1993; shared award with Gerald R. Molen and Branko Lustig

Directors Guild of America Award Outstanding Directorial Achievement in Feature Film "Schindler's List" 1993

Golden Globe Award Best Director "Schindler's List" 1993

Oscar Best Picture "Schindler's List" 1993; shared award with Gerald R. Molen and Branko Lustig

Oscar Best Director "Schindler's List" 1993

BAFTA Award Best Film "Schindler's List" 1993; shared award with Gerald R. Molen and Branko Lustig

BAFTA Award Best Director "Schindler's List" 1993

American Society of Cinematographers Board of Governors Award 1994

American Film Institute Life Achievement Award 1995; youngest person to receive this award

John Huston Award for Artists Rights 1995; second recipient; cited for his work in the area of film preservation; presented by the Artists Rights foundation

Honorary Cesar 1995

Daytime Emmy Outstanding Animated Children's Program "Steven Spielberg Presents Animaniacs" 1995/96; shared award; Spielberg is executive producer

Emmy Outstanding Animated Program "Steven Spielberg Presents A Pinky & The Brain Christmas Special" 1995/96; executive producer; award shared with senior producer Tom Ruegger, producer-director-writer Peter Hastings and producer-director Rusty Mills

Daytime Emmy Outstanding Special Class/Animated Program "Steven Spielberg Presents Freakazoid!" 1996/97; shared award; Spielberg was executive producer

Daytime Emmy Outstanding Children's Animated Program "Steven Spielberg Presents Animaniacs" 1996/97; shared award

Producers Guild of America Kodak Vision Award for Theatrical "Amistad" 1997; shared with Debbie Allen and Colin Wilson

Los Angeles Film Critics Association Award Best Picture "Saving Private Ryan" 1998

Los Angeles Film Critics Association Award Best Director "Saving Private Ryan" 1998

New York Film Critics Circle Award Best Picture "Saving Private Ryan" 1998

Toronto Film Critics Association Award Best Picture "Saving Private Ryan" 1998

Toronto Film Critics Association Award Best Director "Saving Private Ryan" 1998

Broadcast Film Critics Association Award Best Director "Saving Private Ryan" 1998

Online Film Critics Society Award Best Picture "Saving Private Ryan" 1998

Online Film Critics Society Award Best Director "Saving Private Ryan" 1998

Producers Guild of America Milestone Award 1998

Dallas-Fort Worth Film Critics Association Award Best Picture "Saving Private Ryan" 1998

Dallas-Fort Worth Film Critics Association Best Director "Saving Private Ryan" 1998

Golden Globe Award Best Picture (Drama) "Saving Private Ryan" 1998; shared award

Golden Globe Award Best Director "Saving Private Ryan" 1998

Chicago Film Critics Award Best Picture "Saving Private Ryan" 1998; shared award

Producers Guild of America Darryl F. Zanuck Award for Theatrical Motion Picture "Saving Private Ryan" 1998

Directors Guild of America Award Outstanding Directorial Achievement in Feature Film "Saving Private Ryan" 1998

Oscar Best Director "Saving Private Ryan" 1998

Nastri d'Argento Best Foreign Director "Saving Private Ryan" 1998

Daytime Emmy Outstanding Special Class/Animated Program "Steven Spielberg Presents Pinky and the Brain" 1998/99; shared award

NAACP Vanguard Award 2000

Directors Guild of America Lifetime Achievement Award 2000; formerly known as the D. W. Griffith Award

BAFTA Stanley Kubrick Britannia Award 2000

Daytime Emmy Outstanding Children's Animated Program "Steven Spielberg Presents Pinky, Elmira and the Brain" 1999/2000; shared award

National Board of Review Billy Wilder Award for Excellence in Direction 2001

American Film Institute Award Movie or Mini-Series of the Year "Band of Brothers" 2001; shared with Tom Hanks; initial presentation of the award

Golden Globe Award Best Mini-Series or Motion Picture Made for Television "Band of Brothers" 2001; shared award

Producers Guild of America David L. Wolper Producer of the Year Award in Longform Television Award "Band of Brothers" 2002; shared award

ShoWest Lifetime Achievement Award 2002

BIOGRAPHY

Arguably the most important figure to emerge from the creative ferment of Hollywood cinema in the 1970s, Steven Spielberg has changed the way movies are made and about what they are made. He is perhaps the Western world's most famous living filmmaker; three movies he directed ("E.T. the Extra-Terrestrial" 1981; "Jurassic Park" 1993; "Jaws" 1975) are among the top ten highest grossing films of all time. His former production company, Amblin Entertainment, was also responsible for such hits as "Gremlins" (1984), "Back to the Future" (1985) and "Who Framed Roger Rabbit" (1988). Spielberg has succeeded in combining the intimacy of a personal vision with the epic requirements of the modern commercial block-buster, but his astonishing success invalidated his acceptance as an artist for many years. Marketplace issues aside, Spielberg certainly travels in august creative company: like Orson Welles, he has been celebrated and penalized for precocity; like Alfred Hitchcock, he has been alternately praised and damned as a master of emotional manipulation; and like Frank Capra, he has been criticized for shameless sentimentality. Spielberg's most important spiritual predecessor, however, is Walt Disney, another creative individual who made himself into a brand name while attending to the serious business of making "frivolous" entertainments.

Several Spielberg films have become landmarks in the development of special effects, both in their visual and aural aspects. This filmmaker, however, is no technocrat nor does he display a serious intellectual interest in science fiction. Spielberg utilizes elements of sci-fi and fantasy but tends to eschew heavy ideas in favor of sublime feelings, such as childlike awe and trust. Indeed, his work has decisively influenced the emphasis in late 20th-century sci-fi filmmaking on the sensibility of youth and they succeed in spite of blatant sentimentality through the director's masterful use of emotionally potent visual imagery. If nothing else, Spielberg possesses an uncanny knack for eliciting and manipulating audience response.

Unlike many of his contemporaries, Spielberg did not attend a major university film program. Largely self-taught, at age 16, he fashioned his first film "Firelight", a two-hour science fiction movie, that a local movie house in Phoenix, AZ, consented to run for one evening. His short film, "Amblin'" (1969) impressed executives at the television unit of Universal Studios and Spielberg was hired, making his debut directing the formidable Joan Crawford in the TV-movie pilot for Rod Serling's "Night Gallery" (NBC, 1969). He went on to hone his craft helming episodes of such weekly series as "Columbo" and "Marcus Welby, M.D." as well as three TV-movies. One telefilm, "Duel" (ABC, 1972), about a salesman (Dennis Weaver) pursued by a giant diesel truck whose driver is never seen, was released theatrically in Europe, where it enjoyed both critical and commercial success.

Spielberg's first theatrical film, "The Sugarland Express" (1974) was based on the true story of a lumpen Texas woman and her escaped convict husband fighting to regain custody of their baby. The film anticipates the emphasis on family in Spielberg's subsequent work; his choreographed car chases and deft handling of suspense and comedy marked him as a director to watch. Poorly marketed, this entertaining and poignant feature failed at the box office. Spielberg's second, "Jaws", however, helped usher in the modern age of movie blockbusters. This troubled production—a neophyte director and a disgruntled crew with a malfunctioning automated shark—emerged as a classic adventure yarn that propelled Spielberg to the A-list of Hollywood directors.

His transcendent follow-up, "Close Encounters of the Third Kind" (1977), revealed the first flowering of his cinematic interest in the world of childhood, an affinity shared with the late Francois Truffaut, who played the head scientist in the film. Though initially terrifying, the alien creatures in this revisionist work resemble strange and wondrous children, presenting a more benign representation than the monstrous conquerors of 50s sci-fi films. These beings offer the promise of life beyond the restrictions of middle-class conventions. When Richard Dreyfuss boards the mother ship for unknown adventures, it is the film's final grandiloquent embrace of the possible.

Riding high after two back-to-back blockbusters, Spielberg attempted a colossal big-budget comedy. "1941" (1979) was a loud, sprawling and wildly uneven film about paranoia in a small California town after the attack on Pearl Harbor. Though it ultimately turned a profit, the film was perceived as a huge and indulgent flop. Spielberg next chose to work under the watchful eye of a tough producer, George Lucas, and fashioned what would turn out to be one of his signature films, "Raiders of the Lost Ark" (1981). The movie introduced the world to Indiana Jones (played by Harrison Ford), the celebrated archeologist and intrepid adventurer that became the most popular screen hero since James Bond and spawned two sequels. During the production, Spielberg was so wearied by the rigors of location shooting that he would relax by concocting a story for a little personal film to feature a couple of kids and a lost alien. This set the stage for "E.T. The Extra-Terrestrial"—the work for which Spielberg may well be best remembered. An instant classic, this emotionally overwhelming film transformed its maker's career.

In most Spielberg films, anything that threatens the family and its routine existence is evil. In "Jaws", the normally safe harbor of a public beach is threatened by a great white shark. The heroes of "The Sugarland Express" and the Indiana Jones trilogy are transported from normal life to a world of exciting adventure though, in the former, the consequences are tragic. As a young filmmaker, Spielberg seemed to prefer the child's world of harmless adventure (c.f., "E.T.") to the violence and hardships of the real world. Significantly, Spielberg presented WWII through the eyes of a youthful protagonist in "Empire of the Sun" (1987), a transitional work, and he oversaw an Oedipal fantasy as the producer of "Back to the Future", in which a son remakes his parents from nerds into successful yuppies.

The Lucas collaborations—"Indiana Jones and the Temple of Doom" (1984), in particular—have aspects that some find embarrassingly racist, imperialist, and misogynistic. Even his affecting adaptation of Alice Walker's novel "The Color Purple" (1985), although dealing with racism, wife-beating and lesbianism, recreates the air of an old-fashioned Disney film. That Spielberg co-produced and co-wrote "Poltergeist" (1982) and took over directing the film when Tobe Hooper was incapacitated is significant, for it presents the dark underside of suburbia that is only hinted at in his own films.

There was a marked shift in Spielberg's artistic and commercial concerns beginning in the mid-80s, as he began devoting more time to producing. With the notable exception of the continuing Indiana Jones franchise, the projects he chose to direct were departures from his usual material. After "The Color Purple" and "Empire of the Sun", he directed Always" (1989), his first romantic feature in which he also dealt with issues of emotional commitment, loss, and mortality. Even "Indiana Jones and the Last Crusade" (1989) broke new ground, shifting the locale to Europe and the emphasis to Jones' family dynamics. While the action sequences were largely uninspired, the spiky father-son banter between Harrison Ford and Sean Connery was the film's highlight.

Through Amblin, Spielberg continued to oversee the production of a series of popular escapist fantasies, animated features and conventional genre films into the 90s. He even diversified into TV with the fantasy anthology series, "Amazing Stories" (NBC, 1985–87), which he executive produced and provided with many of its stories. Though lavishly produced and often dealing with Spielberg's characteristic themes, too many of the episodes were slight and unsatisfying, although at least one, "Family Dog," an animated outing with director Tim Burton, was spun off into its own 1993 series. He achieved far greater success with such children's animated series as "Tiny Toon Adventures" (syndicated, 1990–95) which attempted to resurrect the style and sensibility of classic Warner Brothers animation, the knowingly retro "Steven Spielberg Presents Animaniacs" (Fox, 1993–95; The WB, 1995–1998) and its spin-off "Steven Spielberg Presents Pinky and the Brain" (The WB, 1995–1998); along with "Freakazoid" (1995–1997) and the short-lived "Toonsylvania" (1998). Spielberg's involvement with high-quality retro animation stemmed back to his stint producing the 1988 film "Who Framed Roger Rabbit?" which pioneered effects techonology that allowed live action characters to interact with animated creations.

On the big screen, "Hook" (1991) was Spielberg's long-awaited return to fantasy material. A lavish yet quirky update of the Peter Pan story, the film displayed its maker's increased concern with the responsibilities of parenting, the therapeutic aspects of regression and preparing for death. Budgeted at over $60 million, the film garnered mixed reviews and decently impressive box office but—due to an unprecedented deal brokered by Creative Artists Agency wherein Spielberg and his stars, Dustin Hoffman, Robin Williams, and Julia Roberts split a huge cut of worldwide revenues up front—failed to make much money for its studio.

The Spielberg of the 90s again made directing a top priority, lending his name to various Amblin products while leaving producing chores to others. "Jurassic Park", a $70 million adaptation of Michael Crichton's dinosaur disaster novel, represented a return to the kind of muscular adventure that served Spielberg so well in the past. The film was a special effects breakthrough and boasted awesome action

sequences though the characters were unusually shallow. Intriguingly, Spielberg did relatively little publicity for one of the most aggressively marketed films in history. He had juggled post-production work on "Jurassic Park" in Paris—with George Lucas reportedly lending a hand stateside—with filming his long-awaited WWII Holocaust drama, "Schindler's List" (1993) in Poland.

Filmed in black-and-white, without big stars and few slick stylistics, this bleak version of Thomas Keneally's Booker Prize–winning novel (based on a true story) marked a dramatic change-of-pace for this purveyor of warm WASP visions. For once, he went against his instincts and made an impressively restrained, documentarian drama of Jewish suffering that built to a shattering yet life-affirming conclusion. The resulting film earned Spielberg the most respectful notices of his career. Spielberg was now widely hailed as one of the masters of world cinema. (That the film, which earned seven Oscars including Best Picture and Best Director, also grossed over $100 million domestically didn't hurt either.)

As an encore, he returned to familiar ground with the inevitable sequel "The Lost World: Jurassic Park" (1997) which merely rehashed the story of the far superior original. Spielberg then tackled the tricky historical drama "Amistad" (also 1997), based on a true story of a mutiny on a slave ship that spawned a legal battle in the USA. Meticulously staged, the film was noted for its depiction of the Middle Passage, a harrowing portrayal of the conditions of slavery. The following year, Spielberg returned to WWII for one of his most acclaimed films, "Saving Private Ryan." A nearly three-hour fictionalized look at a unit sent to locate the sole survivor of four brothers serving in the military. the film earned praise for its no-holds-barred depiction of the battlefield, although the characters bordered on cliche. Critics anointed the picture one of the year's best on its release in July and it subsequently earned over $200 million at the box office and received 11 Academy Award nominations. Although favored to take home the Best Picture award, it didn't, but Spielberg was crowned with a Best Director statue.

In the fall of 1994, Spielberg, recording mogul David Geffen and former Disney production head Jeffrey Katzenberg formed a new multimedia entertainment company, christened DreamWorks SKG, which would produce live-action and animated features, TV programs, recordings and interactive computer software in a relatively cost efficient manner. According to Spielberg, DreamWorks would grant its filmmakers "moral rights" to protect the original versions of their films after release. The studio also decided to give its animators and screenwriters contracts that guarantee them a share of a given film's success in defiance of the standard creative bookkeeping for the industry. Spielberg oversaw the design of the studio's physical plant, laid out like a college campus on the old Howard Hughes aircraft site near the wetlands of Playa Vista, California. The game plan was that Spielberg would oversee the production of live-action features, Katzenberg would direct the state-of-the-art animation division, and Geffen would head SKG's independent recording label. The fledgling studio's first small screen efforts met with limited success; only the Michael J. Fox vehicle "Spin City" (ABC, 1996–2002) was a hit. Other efforts like "Champs" (ABC, 1996), a male-bonding comedy, and the overly-familiar police drama "High Incident" (ABC, 1996–97) came and went quickly. Even DreamWorks' first major feature "The Peacemaker" (1997), a nuclear war thriller, enjoyed only a modest box office, but the studio eventually came into its own with hits such as "Saving Private Ryan," "Shrek," "The Ring," "Gladiator," "Galaxy Quest," "American Beauty," "A Beautiful Mind," "Meet the Parents" and "Minority Report," which company produced and/or co-produced with other studios.

Spielberg was also not without success on televison, being one of the executive producer of the smash hit medical drama "ER" (1994–) created by Chrichton, and the hugely-rated Sci-Fi channel miniseries "Taken" (2002). His most impressive accomplishment on the small screen was the HBO mini-series "Band of Brothers" (2001), based on historian Stephen Ambrose's book about Easy Company, the 506th Regiment of the 101st Airborne Division, U.S. Army. Spielberg produced the powerful 10-episode series with Tom Hanks, and "Band of Brothers" earned a multitude of Emmys along with critical and popular acclaim.

But moviemaking with himself behind the camera remained the director's primary passion, and he continued to explore the boundaries of his talents within a commercial context. Although he was unable to fully integrate his own crowd-pleasing filmmaking sensibilities with the more bleak and philosophical viewpoint of one of his idol, director Stanley Kubrick, when he elected to make "A.I. Artificial Intelligence" (2001), a Pinocchio-like sci-fi fable Kubrick had mused over for over a decade, the film was a noble failure, with several arresting moments, eye-popping visuals and fine performances from Haley Joel Osment and Jude Law. But Spielberg returned to top blockbuster form when he adapted Phillip K. Dick's sci-fi novella "Minority Report" (2002) and tapped Tom Cruise, one of the biggest movie stars on the planet at the time, to star. A fast-paced, intense and compelling thriller, "Minority Report" was Spielberg's leanest and meanest film in years, despite its abundant sci-fi trappings, and showed that the director still stood head-and-shoulders above the new wave of video-game style directors of similar action-adventure fare. The director followed that artistic and commercial triumph with yet another impressive achievement that same year, helming "Catch Me If You Can," the true-life story of con man Frank Abagnale, Jr. (Leonardo DiCaprio), the youngest person ever to make the FBI's Most Wanted list. Not only did Spielberg flawlessly recreate-on both a realistic and nostalgic level-the 1960s setting and coax DiCaprio's most charming and mature performance to date, he cannily cast his close collaborator Hanks against type as the downtrodden, schleppy FBI agent who doggedly pursues the con artist.

Spielberg's success also allowed him to pursue numerous philanthropic and cultural pursuits. He refused to accept any earnings from "Schindler's List"—calling it "blood money"—and channeled those millions into the Righteous Persons Foundation, which has granted money to a range of projects that impact on modern Jewish life. He also served as chairman for the Survivors of the Shoah Visual History Foundation, an ambitious project devoted to filming interviews with Holocaust survivors. Back in the entertainment world, Spielberg lent his name and clout to several organizations devoted to film preservation and artists' rights. The once awkward outsider has become the ultimate insider, generally considered as one of the most powerful individuals in Hollywood.

FAMILY:

father: Arnold Spielberg. Electrical engineer; lost relatives in the Holocaust; involved in the early development of computers; born c. 1918; divorced from Spielberg's mother; remarried on April 6, 1997

mother: Leah Adler. Former concert pianist; restaurateur had four children with Arnold (Steven the youngest); married to second husband, Bernie Adler; they own a kosher dairy restaurant called The Milky Way on Pico Boulevard in Los Angeles

COMPANIONS:

Margot Kidder. Actor; had relationship in the early 1970s

Sarah Miles. Actor; had relationship in the early 1970s; Miles reportedly became pregnant and chose to have an abortion

wife: Amy Irving. Actor; had on-again, off-again relationship from the late 1970s; married on November 27, 1985 in Santa Fe, New Mexico; divorced in 1989

Holly Hunter. Actor; had relationship c. 1989

wife: Kate Capshaw. Actor; married on October 12, 1991 at Spielberg's East Hampton, Long Island, New York estate; converted from Episcopalianism to Judaism c. 1993 after more than a year of study with an Orthodox rabbi

MILESTONES:

Made first 8mm (3 1/2 min.) Film while in grade school; set up a tree-planting business to pay for film and equipment while in teens

1960: Won first contest with 40-minute war film, "Escape to Nowhere" at age 13

1962: Made first amateur 8mm feature film, "Firelight" at age 16; father hired local theater to screen film

1968: Professional debut with 24-minute short, "Amblin' " (shown at Atlanta Film Festival)

1968: Signed to seven-year contract as TV director with Universal-MCA

1969: TV directing debut with the "Eyes" episode of the anthology series "Night Gallery"; segment starred Joan Crawford

1971: First feature-length film for TV, "Duel" (ABC)

1973: Wrote story for feature film, "Ace Eli and Rodger of the Skies"

1974: Feature directorial debut, "The Sugarland Express"

1975: Breakthrough feature film, the summer blockbuster "Jaws"; also first collaboration with actor Richard Dreyfuss; film brought in 100 days over schedule (and comparably over budget); reportedly the first director to do so

1977: Reteamed with Dreyfuss on the sci-fi classic "Close Encounters of the Third Kind"; received first Best Director Oscar nomination

1978: First feature as executive producer, Robert Zemeckis's "I Wanna Hold Your Hand"

1979: Had rare flop with the large-scale comedy "1941"

1980: Made a cameo appearance as the Cook County Clerk at the end of John Landis's "The Blues Brothers"

1981: First collaboration with executive producer George Lucas; first collaboration with actor Harrison Ford, "Raiders of the Lost Ark"; garnnered second Best Director Academy Award nomination

1982: First film as producer, "Poltergeist", helmed by Tobe Hooper

1982: Helmed the blockbuster "E.T. the Extra-Terrestrial"; also served as one of the producers; became the top-grossing movie of all time pulling in $399 million in its initial release; earned third Best Director Oscar nomination as well as a Best Picture nod; re-released on 20th anniversary in March 2002 with minor changes and enhanced digital effects

1983: Helmed the "Kick the Can" segment of "Twilight Zone—The Movie"

1984: Directed the sequel "Indiana Jones and the Temple of Doom"

1984: Formed production company, Amblin Entertainment

1985: First TV series as executive producer, "Amazing Stories" (NBC)

1985: Produced and directed "The Color Purple", adapted from Alice Walker's novel; movie received 11 Academy Award nominations including Best Picture, but not one for Best Director

1986: Executive produced first animated feature, "An American Tail"

1987: Made the underrated WWII drama "Empire of the Sun", which featured a young Christian Bale in his debut

1989: TV acting debut as himself in a segment of "The Tracey Ullman Show" (Fox)

1989: Served as a founding member and VP of the Artists Rights Foundation

1989: Directed the second sequel "Indiana Jones and the Last Crusade"

1989: Stumbled a bit with the romance "Always", a remake of the 1943 feature "A Guy Named Joe"; third film with Richard Dreyfuss

1991: Helmed the lavish "Peter Pan" update "Hook" starring Robin Williams as a grown-up Peter and Dustin Hoffman as the title character

1992: With wife Kate Capshaw, co-hosted "Shattered Lullabies", a documentary on high infant mortality rates in the USA, broadcast on Lifetime as an episode of "Your Family Matters"

1992: Signed a one-year deal to produce "seaQuest DSV" a 22-episode series, a joint effort between Universal and Amblin Entertainment

1993: Directed his most commercially successful feature, "Jurassic Park"; film outgrossed "E.T." to become the top movie of all time (to that date)

1993: Co-produced and directed his most critically acclaimed feature, "Schindler's List"; first feature shot in black-and-white; won Best Director Oscar as well as the Best Picture award

1994: Formed the Survivors of the Shoah Visual History Foundation to videotape the testimonies of Holocaust survivors

1994: Invested in a CD-ROM company Knowledge Adventure; participated in the creation of five titles

1994: Announced, along with mogul David Geffen and former Disney executive Jeffrey Katzenberg, the formation of DreamWorks SKG, a multimedia entertainment company for the production of live-action and animated features, TV programming, music and interactive software

1995: Announced that DreamWorks SKG would grant their filmmakers "moral rights" to protect the original versions of their films after release

1996: "Champs", an ABC sitcom from executive producer Gary David Goldberg, became the first DreamWorks TV series (only lasted for a month)

1996: Received story credit on the premiere

episode of "High Incident", an ABC cop drama, the first hour-long dramatic series from DreamWorks; reportedly was highly involved with production, even personally choosing each cast member, and operating a camera during portions of the pilot

1997: Helmed the sequel "The Lost World: Jurassic Park"

1997: "Amistad", a film based on a real-life 19th-century legal case involving slaves who staged a mutiny on the ship carrying them to North America, was subject of some controversy; author Barbara Chase-Riboud claimed that the film's script was based in part on her book; subsequent threats of lawsuits and articles tainted film's release

1998: Bounced back with the acclaimed WWII story "Saving Private Ryan", starring Tom Hanks; earned second Best Director Academy Award

2001: Returned to filmmaking with "A.I. Artificial Intelligence", based on a story by the late Stanley Kubrick; also wrote screenplay

2001: With Hanks, produced the HBO WWII miniseries "Band of Brothers"

2002: With the Survivors of the Shoah Visual History Foundation, served as presenter of "Broken Silence", a series of five documentaries about Holocaust survivors; aired on Cinemax

2002: Served as a co-executive producer on Woody Allen's "Hollywood Ending"

2002: Was an executive producer of "The Tuxedo", starring Jackie Chan

2002: Directed the sci-fi thriller "Minority Report", starring Tom Cruise and Colin Farrell

2002: Executive produced the hit Sci-Fi Channel miniseries "Taken"

2002: Reunited with Tom Hanks who co-starred as an FBI agent pursuing the first teenager ever to make the Ten Most Wanted list in "Catch Me If You Can", starring Leonardo DiCaprio

2003: Received star of the Hollywood Walk of Fame (January 10, 2003)

AFFILIATION: Jewish

Vice President and Founding Member, Artists Rights Foundation

Chairman, Survivors of the Shoah Visual History Foundation

Founder, Righteous Persons Foundation

Member, Board of Trustees, University of Southern California

Member, Board of Trustees, American Film Institute

Co-founder (with Kate Capshaw and others) of Children's Action Network

Chair, Starbright Pediatric Network (aka Starbright Foundation)

QUOTES:

During a routine physical in February 2000, Spielberg's doctor discovered "an irregularity" that resulted in the director having to undergo surgery to remove one of his kidneys.

He was the owner of a sandwich shop in L.A. called Dive! While that outlet closed in 1999, a branch is Las Vegas remained open.

"I never felt comfortable with myself, because I was never part of the majority," Steven Spielberg said. "I always felt awkward and shy and on the outside of the momentum of my friends' lives. I was never on the inside of that. I was always on the outside.

"I felt like an alien. I always felt like I never belonged to any group that I wanted to belong to. Unlike Woody Allen, you know, I WANTED to become a member of the country club." —From "We Can't Just Sit Back And Hope" by Dotson Rader, *Parade Magazine*, March 27, 1994.

Received an honorary doctorate from USC May 6, 1994.

"Spielbergian images suffuse the planet's collective consciousness."—Nancy Griffin in her article "Manchild in the Promised Land" in *Premiere*, June 1989.

"Along with Scorsese, Spielberg shepherded the restoration of the Columbia Pictures classic (David Lean's "Lawrence of Arabia" 1962). Shortly after Dawn Steel inherited the top job at the studio from David Puttnam, Spielberg says, he marched into her office and said, 'You have to do this or I'll never make a picture for Columbia again.' When he viewed 'Lawrence' in all its original glory, it 'made me feel like going back to film school. One of the most intimidating things for anybody who takes himself seriously as a filmmaker is to sit in that theater and realize that so many of us have so far to go before we're able to recreate seven moments in a masterwork like that.' "—From "Manchild in the Promised Land" by Nancy Griffin in *Premiere*, June 1989.

"[Director Sidney] Lumet says, 'I just feel he is the most brilliant purely cinematic talent that I have seen. He is a thrilling, thrilling moviemaker.' He scoffs at Spielberg's detractors' judgment that he can't cut it with grown-up material. 'I'm sorry. That's bullshit,' says Lumet. 'Spielberg's talent is so rich, it's going to take him a lifetime to explore; he could go in so many directions.' "—From "Manchild in the Promised Land" by Nancy Griffin in *Premiere*, June 1989.

"After the final crescendo, when the last galloping rider has disappeared from the screen, he says softly, 'I'm going to miss looking into Harrison's eyes through the shadow of his fedora.' "—Spielberg remarking at the end of the scoring for "Indiana Jones and the Last Crusade" in "Manchild in the Promised Land" by Nancy Griffin in *Premiere*, June 1989.

" 'Schindler's List' brings a preeminent pop mastermind together with a story that demands the deepest reserves of courage and passion. Rising brilliantly to the challenge of this material and displaying an electrifying creative intelligence, Mr. Spielberg has made sure that neither he nor the Holocaust will ever be thought of in the same way again. With every frame, he demonstrates the power of the film maker to distill complex events into fiercely indelible images."—Janet Maslin, "Imagining the Holocaust to Remember It" in *The New York Times*, December 15, 1993.

"Its one identifiable Spielberg trademark is its total command of cinema; what's new is a seriousness of purpose and level of filmmaking fury not seen since the director's early works."—Mike Clark, " 'Schindler's List' is Spielberg's Triumph" from *USA Today*, December 15, 1993.

"Schindler is also a touchingly obvious projection of Spielberg's own dreams of posterity, a man remembered above all for being a good boss, for being truly loved by his employees (the film is dedicated to Steve Ross, the late Time Warner chairman who was Spielberg's mentor). As Schindler says, he is a man who has made more money than anyone could spend in a lifetime, yet in making that money he has touched people's lives in a meaningful way—Schindler by drawing up his list, Spielberg by filming it. In Spielberg's happily capitalist world, profit motive is not the enemy of humanism but its spur."—Dave Kehr, "A Spielberg Check-'List' " (review of "Schindler's List"), *Daily News*, December 15, 1993.

"Spielberg was far more collaborative than I ever imagined he would be. He really wanted ideas and encouraged people to give their input. Everyone had told me he shoots fast and that was so true—it makes your head spin. I had also been told he is very technical, which I didn't find at all. He was far more of an actor's director."—Jude Law to *The Daily Telegraph*, February 17, 2001.

Awarded The Order of the Smile in 1993 by the older children of Poland for being a role model and hero; previous recipient was the Pope.

The Righteous Persons Foundation was established with Spielberg's earnings from "Schindler's List" to fund projects which impact on modern Jewish life (e.g. "to engage Jewish youth, to support the arts, to promote tolerance and to strengthen the commitment to social justice"). As of fall 1995, the foundation had made 30 grants totaling nearly $10 million. The organization projected to distribute more than $40 million over its first decade of existence.

Received an honorary doctorate from New York University in 1996.

Anonymously purchased Clark Gable's 1934 Oscar for a record $550,000 then donated it to the Academy of Motion Picture Arts and Sciences.

In April 1999, he donated $500,000 to USC's Robert Zemeckis Center for Digital Arts.

Spielberg received the Defense Department Public Service Award on August 11, 1999

In January 2001, he recevied an honorary knighthood from Queen Elizabeth II for his extraordinary contributions to the entertainment industry.

"I don't think that 'Jaws' would do as well today as it did in 1975, because people would not wait so long to see the shark. Or they'd say there's too much time between the first attack and the second attack. Which is too bad. We have an audience now that isn't patient with us. They've been tought, by people like me, to be impatient with people like me."—Spielberg to *The New York Times*, June, 16, 2002.

Received an honorary doctrate degree from Yale University in 2002

BIBLIOGRAPHY:

"Spielberg: The Man, the Movies, the Mythology" Frank Sanello, 1996

"Steven Spielberg" Elizabeth Ferber, 1997 Chelsea House Publishers; children's book

"Steven Spielberg: A Biography" Joseph McBride, 1997, Simon & Schuster

"Steven Spielberg" John Baxter, 1997, Harper-Collins

George Stevens

BORN: in Oakland, California, 12/18/1904

DEATH: in Paris, France, 03/08/1975

NATIONALITY: American

EDUCATION: attended high school in Lonoma, California; 1918–1919; dropped out to join parents' theatrical troupe

AWARDS: New York Film Critics Circle Award Best Director "The More the Merrier" 1943

Golden Globe Award Best Motion Picture (Drama) "A Place in the Sun" 1951

Directors Guild of America Award Outstanding Directorial Achievement in Feature Film "A Place in the Sun" 1951

Oscar Best Director "A Place in the Sun" 1951

National Board of Review Award Best Director "Shame" 1953

Irving G. Thalberg Memorial Award 1953; presented by the Academy of Motion Picture Arts and Sciences

Directors Guild of America Award Outstanding Directorial Achievement in Feature Film "Giant" 1956

Oscar Best Director "Giant" 1956

Golden Globe Award Best Film Promoting International Understanding "The Diary of Anne Frank" 1959

Directors Guild of America D. W. Griffith Award 1960 for lifetime career achievement

BIOGRAPHY

Leading Hollywood craftsman, responsible for some fine films of the 1930s and 40s, but whose later output tended toward the over-ambitious and excessive.

The son of performers, Stevens entered films at age 17 as a cameraman and later worked for the Hal Roach company, where he directed his first shorts. He joined RKO in 1934 and proceeded to churn out a series of crafty comedies and light musicals, scoring his first major success with "Alice Adams" (1935), which was followed by the Astaire-Rogers classic "Swing Time" (1936), the action-packed "Gunga Din" and the brilliantly realized debut pairing of Katharine Hepburn and Spencer Tracy, "Woman of the Year" (1941).

After heading the Army Signal Corps Special Motion Picture Unit during WWII, Stevens re-entered civilian life in 1945 and hit his peak with "I Remember Mama" (1948) and "A Place in the Sun" (1951). His subsequent work, including "Shane" (1953) and "Giant" (1956), strove for epic status but came off as overblown and excessive. Stevens's final effort, "The Only Game in Town" (1970), was a refreshing, if flawed, return to his earlier, more modest, style.

Son George Stevens, Jr., is a producer who made a well-received documentary on his father, "George Stevens, Filmmaker" (1984), served as chief of the United States Information Service's motion picture division from 1962–67 and was named the first head of the American Film Institute in 1977.

MILESTONES:

1909: First appearance on stage at Alcazar Theater in San Francisco in "Sappho"

1920–1921: Became actor and stage manager for father's theatrical company

1921: Moved to Hollywood; began working as assistant and second cameraman

1924: First film as cameraman, "The White Sheep"

1927: Joined Hal Roach as cameraman and scriptwriter for Laurel and Hardy, Our Gang, and Harry Langdon comedy shorts

Directed first two-reel comedies for Roach

1930: First film as director, "Ladies Past"

1932: Directed shorts for Universal and RKO

1933: Directed first feature film, "The Cohens and the Kellys in Trouble"

1938: Producing debut, "Vivacious Lady"

1943: Joined US Army Signal Corps and became head of Special Motion Pictures Unit

1945: Formed Liberty Films with William Wyler, Frank Capra and Samuel J. Briskin

QUOTES:

Awarded a citation from General Eisenhower for filming such important war events as D-Day and the freeing of inmates at Dachau (1945)

BIBLIOGRAPHY:

"George Stevens: An American Romantic" Donald Richie, 1971, Garland Publishing

---

Ben Stiller

BORN: Benjamin E. Stiller in New York, New York, 11/30/1965

NATIONALITY: American

EDUCATION: University of California at Los Angeles, Los Angeles, California, film, 1983–84; attended for nine months

AWARDS: Emmy Best Writing in a Variety or Music Program "The Ben Stiller Show" 1992/93; shared award with Judd Apatow,

Robert Cohen, Brent Forrester, Jeff Kahn, Bruce Kirschbaum, Bob Odenkirk, Sultan Pepper and Sino Stamatopoulos

MTV Movie Award Best Fight "There's Something About Mary" 1999; shared with Puffy the Dog

American Comedy Award Funniest Male Performer in a Motion Picture "Meet the Parents" 2001

MTV Movie Award Best Comedic Performance "Meet the Parents" 2001

BIOGRAPHY

Trying to cast the lead role of Mel Coplin, an adoptee searching for his biological parents in the wake of his own son's birth in the comedy "Flirting With Disaster" (1996), writer-director David O. Russell knew what he wanted: "a young Dustin Hoffman type, who was kind of urban, kind of smart and ethnic." Ben Stiller, the only son of the venerable husband-and-wife comedy team of Jerry Stiller and Anne Meara, convinced Russell that he could fill the bill. Increasingly busy before and behind the camera, the curly-haired, quirkily handsome actor-writer-director seemed well poised to become the poster boy for Generation X era comedy—regardless of his stated discomfort with such a designation. With decisive roles played by nepotism, "Saturday Night Live" and MTV, Ben Stiller's swift career trajectory may be somewhat paradigmatic to those for whom the name "Barrymore" evokes "Drew" before "John" or "Lionel."

Stiller utilized his connections to land his first professional acting job in the 1985 Lincoln Center revival of John Guare's dark comedy "The House of Blue Leaves" (his mother was in the original production) after two years of struggling. During its run, he made a short comic film with the play's cast (which ended up airing on "Saturday Night Live"). In 1987, Stiller reprised the role of the son, Ronnie Shaughnessy, a would-be papal assassin, for the play's PBS "American Playhouse" production. In that same very productive year, he also made his film acting debut in Steven Spielberg's "Empire of the Sun" and his TV writing and acting debut in a ten-minute short parody of Martin Scorsese's "The Color of Money" for NBC's "Saturday Night Live", in which he offered a devastating caricature of Tom Cruise. He subsequently remained as a featured player and apprentice writer on "SNL" for about a year. (Stiller reportedly left due to creative frustration; the show had limited interest in him directing film clips.)

In 1989, he was given his own half-hour comedy/variety show on MTV entitled "The Ben Stiller Show." A prototype to his more elaborate network effort, the series suffered from music video interruptions and the lack of proper format that would have allowed Stiller to showcase his considerable talents. He also continued working in films, playing supporting roles in such diverse misfires and mediocrities as "Hot Pursuit" (1987, with his father), "Fresh Horses" (1988), "That's Adequate" (1989, with his parents and sister Amy), "Next of Kin" (1989), the Bette Midler weeper "Stella" (1990) and "Highway to Hell" (1992, another family get-together).

A career turning point came when Fox TV signed him for "The Ben Stiller Show" (1992–93), a sketch comedy program with an emphasis on pop culture parodies. An inspired spoof combining "The Munsters" and "Cape Fear" to create "Cape Munster" (which featured Stiller skillfully evoking a hybrid of Robert De Niro and Eddie Munster) was fairly emblematic of the show's irreverent sensibility. Other sketches, featuring skewerings of Bruce Springsteen and Tom Cruise, The Pig-Latin Lover, the amusement park Oliver Stoneland and the evil sock-puppet Skank made the show one of the hippest and funniest on TV, but it was canceled in its first season. Nevertheless, Stiller shared a writing Emmy for his efforts.

Stiller segued to the big screen as a filmmaker making his feature directorial bow with "Reality Bites" (1994), an old-fashioned romance marketed as a "Generation X" comedy. Co-starred with Winona Ryder and Ethan Hawke, he played a neurotic, workaholic music TV exec who occupies one point in the love triangle. The film received some positive notices—especially for Ryder's performance—and Stiller was commended for his skill with actors but his command of narrative storytelling was deemed shaky in some quarters. In any event, the ostensible target audiences largely steered clear.

Though it still remains too early to make any sweeping generalizations about Stiller's screen persona, one may note that, in his choices, he has eschewed conventional romantic leads in favor of problematic eccentrics. Though occasionally (and from certain angles) quite handsome on camera, Stiller has tended to undercut or lampoon his looks. As a sketch performer, he delighted in mocking such presumed studs as Cruise and U2's Bono. A not atypical film role had him playing an obnoxious fitness guru, the baddie, in the inferior Disney comedy "Heavyweights" (1995). This project was notable for reuniting him with Judd Apatow, here a producer-writer and formerly Stiller's collaborator on his Fox series.

Stiller returned to the director's chair for (and played a small role in) "The Cable Guy" (1996). Though budgeted at a formidable $40 million (half of which went to its ascendant star), this Jim Carrey vehicle dared to offer a change-of-pace as the rubber-faced comic played a darker, more menacing variation of his usual persona. Though the film has its share of admirers, "The Cable Guy" proved to be the first flop of Carrey's career as a superstar and stalled Stiller's behind-the-scenes work.

Also in 1996, Stiller enjoyed a solid arthouse success with the starring role in "Flirting with Disaster", a rare straightforward romantic lead. He also brought manic energy to his portrayal of a conceptual artist with designs on Sarah Jessica Parker in the unsuccessful romantic comedy "If Lucy Fell." He finished out the year with a (shrewdly?) uncredited turn in fellow "SNL" alum Adam Sandler's feature vehicle "Happy Gilmore", as the smarmy operator of a nursing home.

1998, however, proved to be Stiller's breakout year as a performer. He began with an understated turn as the partner of a reclusive investigator in "Zero Effect", directed by Jake Kasdan. On the heels of that comic portrayal, he played a nebbish haunted by his high school prom date who hires a private detective to track her down in the Farrelly brothers' low-brow surprise blockbuster "There's Something About Mary". Ironically, he was not the studio's first choice for the role and had to fight for it. But he proved to be perfect, willing to go to any lengths for the part. He captured the awkwardness of a gawky teenager (especially when he caught his private parts in his zipper on the night of the prom) and the odd, forlorn adult version of the same character. As an actor, he was willing to undertake potentially embarrassing scenes and mine them for their humor. Applying a similar technique to dramatic material, Stiller essayed a weaselly college professor who embarks on an affair with his best friend's wife in Neil LaBute's "Your Friends and Neighbors" and capped the year with an all-out tour de force portraying drug-addicted screenwriter Jerry Stahl in "Permanent Midnight."

Stiller was next featured alongside longtime friend Janeane Garofalo in "Mystery Men" (1999), a disappointing comedy centered around a band of off-kilter superheroes. He rebounded the following year with a starring role in the oddly charming sleeper romance "Keeping the Faith", playing a rabbi who finds himself falling for the same childhood friend (Jenna Elfman) his best friend (Edward Norton as a Catholic priest) is also in love with. That same year he had a bona fide box-office hit with "Meet the Parents", starring as a man driven to desperation by the overprotective and overbearing father (Robert De Niro) of his would-be fiancée (Teri Polo). The feel-bad brand of slapstick comedy connected with a large audience, and Stiller proved not only as lovable a loser as he had in "There's Something About Mary", but a worthy screen partner of De Niro. Acting turns in the independents "The Suburbans" and the aptly named "The Independent" rounded out 2000 for the actor.

Stiller returned to the big screen in 2001 as a director and actor, helming and starring in the often riotous though somewhat poorly received "Zoolander", a send-up of the modeling world at once smart and silly. Released shortly after the tragic events of September 11th, the film lost some of its comedic steam but would find life as a cult favorite. He reteamed with his "Zoolander" nemesis and frequent co-star Owen Wilson in "The Royal Tenenbaums", a masterful seriocomedy co-written by Wilson and director Wes Anderson and starring Gene Hackman, Anjelica Huston, Gwyneth Paltrow, Stiller and Luke Wilson as a family with great potential that slowly falls apart as they separate. Stiller's portrayal of anxiety-plagued, rage-ridden, red Adidas warm-up suit-garbed widower Chas featured some of the film's most honestly moving moments and garnered the performer critical accolades.

In 2002, after a cameo in Jake Kasdan's comedy "Orange County", Stiller appeared onscreen in "Run Ronnie Run", a feature adaptation of a popular sketch from the off-kilter HBO comedy series "Mr. Show Starring Bob and David". He next co-starred with Drew Barrymore in "The Duplex" (2003), a black comedy about the lengths one will go to in order to rent the perfect apartment in New York City directed by Danny DeVito.

FAMILY:

father: Jerry Stiller. Actor, writer, comedian; born in 1927; married Anne Meara on September 14, 1954; half of comedy team of Stiller and Meara; recalled for playing recurring role of Frank Constanza on "Seinfeld"

mother: Anne Meara. Actor, comedian, playwright, screenwriter; born in 1929; married Jerry Stiller on September 14, 1954; half of husband-wife comedy team Stiller and Meara; directed by son in "Reality Bites"

COMPANIONS:

Janeane Garofalo. Actor, comic; had brief relationship in the early 1990s

Jeanne Tripplehorn. Actor; had on-again, off-again relationship for several years; reportedly engaged at one time; no longer together

Amanda Peet. Actor; dated briefly in 1998

Claire Forlani. Actor; dated c. 1998–99

wife: Christine Taylor. Actor; began dating as of June 1999; became engaged in fall 1999; married in Kauai, Hawaii on May 13, 2000

MILESTONES:

1975: Acting debut in a guest spot on his mother's series "Kate McShane" (CBS)

1976: Began making Super 8 films at age 10 (date approximate)

1985: Broadway debut in the Lincoln Center revival of John Guare's "The House of Blue Leaves"

1987: Feature acting debut in Steven Spielberg's "Empire of the Sun"

1987: Made a 10-minute short spoof of "The Color of Money" and sold it "Saturday Night Live" (SNL)

1987: Became featured player on "SNL"

1987: TV acting debut (as an adult) in PBS' "American Playhouse" production of "The House of Blue Leaves"

1989: Starred, created and wrote "The Ben Stiller Show" for MTV; series lasted 13 episodes

1992: Starred, created, wrote and directed segments of "The Ben Stiller Show" (Fox)

1994: Feature directorial debut, "Reality Bites"

1995: Reruns (and one first-run episode) of "The Ben Stiller Show" aired on Comedy Central

1996: Starred in art-house hit comedy "Flirting with Disaster"

1996: Helmed the mainstream commercially "disappointing" Jim Carrey vehicle "The Cable Guy"; first film with Owen Wilson

1997: Signed to exclusive contract by Fox; deal called for Stiller to establish a production company (Red House Productions) with Fox 2000 division

1998: Starred opposite Cameron Diaz in the mainstream low-brow blockbuster "There's Something About Mary"

1998: Took supporting role of a weasely

college drama professor in "Your Friends and Neighbors"

1998: Offered strong dramatic turn as a heroin-abusing screenwriter in "Permanent Midnight", based on the memoir of Jerry Stahl; Owen Wilson also appeared

1999: Starred alongside Janeane Garofalo in the superhero comedy "Mystery Men"

2000: Played a rabbi in love with the same woman (Jenna Elfman) as his priest pal (Edward Norton) in "Keeping the Faith"

2000: Co-starred with Robert De Niro in the box-office smash "Meet the Parents"; Owen Wilson had supporting role

2001: Directed and starred in "Zoolander", based on a vacuous male model character he introduced on VH-1; Owen Wilson played a rival male model

2001: Portrayed the eldest child in a family of geniuses in "The Royal Tenenbaums"; Owen Wilson co-wrote screenplay with director Wes Anderson and co-starred as a family friend

2002: Made cameo appearance as a firefighter in "Orange County", directed by Jake Kasdan

2002: Appeared in the comedy feature "Run Ronnie Run"

2003: Starred opposite Drew Barrymore in "The Duplex," directed by Danny De Vito

QUOTES:

According to "Jews Who Rock", a book by Guy Oseary, Stiller was once a drummer in a band called Capital Punishment.

"You know what SUCKS? The focus groups. Seeing your movie broken down into numbers takes the heart out of what you're doing—it becomes PERCENTAGES. As a filmmaker who wants to work in the studio system, I found myself wanting to IMPROVE those numbers. [But] after a certain point, a filmmaker shouldn't be pushed to get the score up like an SAT score. All of a sudden it was like I was back in high school saying 'No, wait I KNOW I can get a better score on this test!' "—Stiller on

directing "Reality Bites," quoted in *Movieline*, March 1994.

"I think this whole celebrity world is weird anyway. Weird and funny and kind of pathetic and yet so ripe for parody. There's a sense here in L.A. that everybody's aware of everybody all the time. It's funny but we choose it. People who are here want to be here, including me." —Stiller, quoted in *Interview*, April 1996.

"I don't think it's ever easy to be funny. I find it easy to amuse myself with a certain sort of cynical, dark humor that tends toward the meaner side, like my character in 'Happy Gilmore.' Those kinds of characters come easily to me. I'm just not a naturally cheery person. I'm naturally moody. I know that from people who spend a lot of time with me."—Ben Stiller, quoted in *Interview*, April 1996.

"I never thought I was funny."—Stiller to Janeane Garofalo in *The New York Times Magazine*, December 28, 1997.

"I've never really felt like a funny, funny guy. I've never really felt like Mr. Life of the Party. People who know me know that I'm not the most gregarious person. I'm trying to open myself up more. I've realized in the last few years that my state of mind affects how I live my life."—Ben Stiller quoted in "His Journey From Nerdy New York Kid to Hip Hollywood Royalty Proves There's Something About Ben Stiller" by Chris Mundy in *Rolling Stone*, November 12, 1998.

"I think the Farrelly brothers (and David O. Russell when I did 'Flirting With Disaster') see me as a reactive guy. If you have a guy doing something really funny, I like to contribute on some level by being the straight person, that's about subtelty and not having to do anything except 'be', and that's a real challenge. It's amazing what is picked up by the camera. . . ." —Stiller to *Empire*, October 1998.

"What most people don't know is that Ben has his own demons; he's got pain for days, and he really tapped into that. As Ben once said, 'The reason I don't do drugs is that I would like them too much.' Which I can relate to. I just have a different story."—Jerry Stahl, whom Stiller portrayed in "Permanent Midnight", quoted in *Premiere*, November 1998.

"In 'Permanent Midnight', I identified with my character's alienation. I connected with his feelings of self-loathing, of being unable to embrace who he was or bond with other people."—Stiller quoted in *The New York Times*, September 20, 1998.

"I see Ben as the conscience of his generation, and a messenger of all its excesses. I follow his career like I follow the path of a hurricane."—Jerry Stiller on his son, quoted in *The New York Times*, September 20, 1998.

"I do have anger. Rage and anxiety are kind of a funny mix because they're fighting against each other, and I definitely cop to that." —Stiller to *Los Angeles Times*, September 9, 2001.

"When I was a kid, I didn't fantasize about being a comedy star. I was thinking, wouldn't it be great to be Gene Hackman in 'The Poseidon Adventure'? My specific goal was to be a director and make all different kinds of movies. 'There's Something About Mary?', 'Meet the Parents', I didn't fantasize about being that guy."—Stiller to *GQ*, September 2001.

Stiller on parallels between the world "Zoolander" occupies and Hollywood: "I've met a few male models and they remind me of actors because there are some actors who don't take what they do seriously at all, but there are others who think they're God's gift to humanity. Also, acting and modeling aren't very masculine professions. That's why I like directing more, because to me it feels like a job you can feel comfortable doing. Not that I'm a macho guy at all, but sometimes it can be a little strange being the guy who has the make-up put on. Sometimes, you want to take more responsibility for yourself.—to *The Times* of London, November 25, 2001.

In the wake of the attacks on September 11, Stiller cancelled his appearance as host of the season opener of "Saturday Night Live". Answering producer Lorne Michaels' snipe, "I thought he was a New Yorker", Stiller told *Details* (December 2001): "I don't need to defend myself as a New Yorker. I grew up here. I'm not Canadian."

"Did I say that I wanted to stretch? You know, I like doing comedies, and I think that comedy is challenging. For whatever reason, the comedies are the best opportunities I've been offered.

"I don't really have a burning desire to go off and be taken really seriously as an actor. You know, I don't have a master plan in that way. I just want to do what I enjoy doing and hopefully not do the same thing over and over again."—Stiller to *Chicago Sun-Times*, December 22, 2001.

BIBLIOGRAPHY:

"Feel This Book" Janeane Garofalo and Ben Stiller, 1999; parody of self-help books

Oliver Stone

BORN: in New York, New York, 09/15/1946

SOMETIMES CREDITED AS:
Minh Duc

NATIONALITY: American

EDUCATION: The Hill School, New York, New York

Yale University, New Haven, Connecticut; dropped out in 1965

Tisch School of the Arts, New York University, New York, New York, film, BFA, 1971; tutored by Martin Scorsese

AWARDS: Golden Globe Award Best Screenplay "Midnight Express" 1978

Writers Guild of America Award Best-Written

Drama Adapted from Another Medium "Midnight Express" 1978

Oscar Best Screenplay Adaptation "Midnight Express" 1978

Directors Guild of America Award Outstanding Directorial Achievement in Feature Film "Platoon" 1986

Oscar Best Director "Platoon" 1986

Independent Spirit Award Best Director "Platoon" 1986

Independent Spirit Award Best Screenplay "Platoon" 1986

Berlin Film Festival Best Director Award "Platoon" 1987

BAFTA Award Best Director "Platoon" 1987

Directors Guild of America Award Outstanding Directorial Achievement in Feature Film "Born on the Fourth of July" 1989

Golden Globe Award Best Director "Born on the Fourth of July" 1989

Oscar Best Director "Born on the Fourth of July" 1989

Golden Globe Award Best Director "JFK" 1991

Berlin Film Festival Golden Camera/40th Anniversary Prize 1990

Gold Reel Award 1992; presented to special friends of the Independent Feature Project/West

Writers Guild Foundation Career Achievement Award 1993; given annually for excellence in writing

Venice Film Festival Special Jury Prize "Natural Born Killers" 1994

Emmy Outstanding Made for Television Movie "Indictment: The McMartin Trial" 1994/95; producer; award shared with Janet Yang, Abby Mann and Diana Pokorny

Chicago Film Critics Award Best Director "Nixon" 1995

National Board of Review Freedom of Expression Award "The People vs. Larry Flynt" 1996; shared award with Milos Forman

Golden Satellite Best Mini-Series or Television Movie "The Day Reagan Was Shot" 2001; shared award; Stone was executive producer

BIOGRAPHY

Since the mid-1970s, Stone has evolved from a respected screenwriter of major features and director of modest genre fare to become one of the most honored, best known and most controversial filmmakers working in modern Hollywood. Impressively, Stone has made his name and fortune from "difficult" political subjects—the Vietnam War, the Kennedy assassination, US involvement in El Salvador—which, in other hands, generally fail to ignite the box office. Stone is also a successful producer, overseeing such diverse projects as Barbet Schroeder's "Reversal of Fortune", Kathryn Bigelow's "Blue Steel (both 1990) and Wayne Wang's "The Joy Luck Club" (1993). He also executive produced "Wild Palms" (ABC, 1993), a popular, paranoid sci-fi miniseries.

Stone first gained acclaim as a writer, winning an Oscar, a Writers Guild Award and a Golden Globe for his screenplay for "Midnight Express" (1978). Prior to that, at age 25, he wrote, directed and edited "Seizure" (1974), a stylish, low-budget ($150,000) Canadian horror film starring Jonathan Frid (of "Dark Shadows" fame). An intriguing cast failed to compensate for the incoherence of the screenplay about a novelist, his family and friends, who are bedeviled by what may be the writer's nightmares given flesh; the film has nonetheless acquired a small cult following. Stone returned to horror for his next directing assignment—"The Hand" (1981), a retread of "The Beast with Five Fingers" (1946), starring Michael Caine as a cartoonist who loses his hand in an accident. His life becomes further complicated when his missing member goes on a murder spree. Stone's screenwriting jobs were somewhat more respectable genre films, including "Conan the Barbarian" (1982), co-written with director John Milius; Brian De Palma's "Scarface" (1983); and "Year of the Dragon" (1985), co-written with director Michael Cimino. While these films have their admirers, each to varying degrees reflects criticisms that would plague much of Stone's work as a director—charges of racism (particularly toward Asians), excessive violence and the marginalization of female characters.

With the release of "Salvador" (1986), Stone was off and running to achieve his current status as one of Hollywood's most forceful directors, tackling social and political themes with evident skill and commitment, as well as generous doses of bombast. His films were often heavy-handed, a bit simplistic, and masculinist, but they moved people with their big emotions and powerhouse imagery. Stone received a second Oscar and a Directors Guild Award for "Platoon" (1986), one of the starkest treatments of the Vietnam war to reach American screens, and brought a similarly uncompromising gaze to bear on the world of high finance in "Wall Street" (1987), the street where his own father plied his trade as a stockbroker. "Born on the Fourth of July" (1989), meanwhile, based on the true story of Vietnam veteran Ron Kovic and featuring Tom Cruise in his first "heavyweight" dramatic role, earned Stone a second DGA Award and Oscar for directorial achievement. The film depicted Kovic's evolution from naive gung-ho kid to frightened soldier to embittered paraplegic to committed anti-war activist.

Stone's most ambitious and controversial work was "JFK" (1991), a dramatization of the attempts by New Orleans D.A. Jim Garrison (Kevin Costner) to uncover a conspiracy behind the assassination of President John F. Kennedy. A substantial artistic achievement which weaves volumes of theories and hypotheses into a narrative peppered with colorful cameo performances, the film led to Congress' opening of the classified files relating to the shooting, as well as providing armies of conspiracy theorists with ammunition for their views. Stone reached a new level of notoriety with the release of "JFK"; no longer just a filmmaker, he was a political figure. As such, Stone was variously attacked and applauded by politicians, editorial writers and newspaper columnists across the country.

Stone returned to Vietnam for "Heaven and Earth" (1993), but this story was told from an Asian female perspective. Based on two autobiographical books by Le Ly Hayslip, "When Heaven and Earth Changed Places" and "Child of War, Woman of Peace", this was the continent-spanning story of how the war impacted upon the life of one young woman in Vietnam and back in the States with her American husband. Some saw the film as an atonement for the narrow "American male" point of view expressed in the first two installments of Stone's unplanned Vietnam trilogy. In any event, the film was greeted by mixed reviews and lukewarm box office.

Stone actively courted controversy again with "Natural Born Killers" (1994), a project that harkened back to his early pulp fictions. The original story by hotshot writer-director Quentin Tarantino was overwhelmed by Stone's hallucinogenic vision of two lovers (Woody Harrelson and Juliette Lewis) who become media darlings due to a spectacular murder spree. Taking inspiration from music videos, commercials and other media, "Natural Born Killers" launched a sensory assault with an ultra-cool soundtrack, rapid-fire montages, various film stocks, animated sequences and sharply observed TV parodies. Audiences and reviewers alike were sharply divided over the film's merits but it opened to brisk box office.

Stone returned to politics and history with his massive, controversial, near Shakespearean study of the 37th President of the United States, "Nixon" (1995). Clocking in at over three hours, filled with visual gimmicks (flashbacks, black and white footage, varying film stock) and layered in pop psychology, "Nixon" (played by Anthony Hopkins) attempts to capture the essence of the man, but fails to truly humanize him. Nonetheless, there were critics who hailed "Nixon" as a masterpiece and most reviewers agreed that Stone elicited strong performances from the ensemble (including Joan Allen as Pat Nixon, James Woods as H.R. Haldeman, and E.G. Marshall as John Mitchell).—Written by Kent Greene

MILESTONES:

1965–1966: Taught English, math, history and geography at Free Pacific Institute, in the Chinese district of Saigon, South Vietnam

Served in combat in Vietnam in US infantry

Wounded before Tet Offensive, received Bronze Star for combat gallantry and Purple Heart with Oak Leaf Cluster

1968: Returned to USA

1970: First feature credit, providing photography for documentary compilation, "Street Scenes"

1970: Directed a short student film entitled "Last Year in Vietnam"

1971: Worked as a NYC cab driver

1974: Feature writing and directorial debut, "Seizure"

1978: Wrote the award-winning screenplay adaptation for "Midnight Express"

1981: Made feature acting debut as a bum in "The Hand" (also wrote screenplay and directed)

1986: First gained prominence as a filmmaker with the success of "Salvador"; feature debut as producer (also wrote and directed)

1990: Produced "Reversal of Fortune", directed by Barbet Schroeder

1992: Subject of a Showtime TV documentary, "Olvier Stone: Inside Out" by Joel Sucher and Steven Fischler, broadcast March 19

Formed feature production company, Ixtlan Productions

1991: Feature debut as executive producer, "Iron Maze", directed by Hiroaki Yoshida

1993: Appeared as himself in the political comedy, "Dave"

1993: First TV credit as executive producer, "Wild Palms", a sci-fi miniseries

1996: Received Star Number 2063 on the Hollywood Walk of Fame on March 15

1999: Agreed to undergo drug rehab and plead no contest to charges of drunk driving and possession of a controlled substance; arrested on June 9; entered plea in August

1999: Helmed the football-themed drama "Any Given Sunday"

2001: Served as executive producer of the Showtime movie "The Day Reagan Was Shot"

QUOTES:

Stone was awarded France's Order of Arts and Letters (1992).

Stone was presented with the "Director of the Decade" Award by the Chicago International Film Festival (1992).

In June 1999, Stone was arrested for DWI. When the police stopped him, they reportedly also discovered hashish in the car.

"In 1992, three years after Stone optioned (Le Ly) Hayslip's first book, and after they had spent weeks visiting her mother's house in Ky La, she took Stone to her master, a Buddhist monk in California, who put the lapsed Catholic through a soul cleansing ritual called Quy Y and gave him a Buddhist name, Minh Duc, which, a shock to his foes, means 'virtue and brilliance'.—From "The Road to 'Heaven and Earth' " by Jack Mathews, *Los Angeles Times Calendar,* December 23, 1993.

Describing his then upcoming project, a $30 million satire entitled "Natural Born Killers", Oliver Stone made the following comparisons:

"It's in the vein of 'Scarface' . . . because of its large-scale portrait of criminality. It deals with the death penalty and the prison system in passing. It's [also] a slumming road picture in the vein of 'Salvador'. It's violence in the media and the American way of death. It's Peckinpah meets Kubrick, not that I'm that good, but if I was, it would be somewhere in that zone."

—"Stone Giving Berth to Tarantino 'Killers'", *Daily Variety,* March 19, 1993.

From "Oliver Stone's Killer Instinct", an *Interview* piece by Graham Fuller:

GF: Did you know instantly that Tarantino's script would have to be reworked?

OS: I felt it was a brilliant script but I did not know enough about the killers from reading it. Quentin warned me, "You can never make these killers real. The movie's about the media, not about them." That was his caveat. I didn't quite agree with it. I wanted to know why they killed and to draw their lives into the history of violence in this century, which is why I have bits and pieces of arcana junking up their minds.

From "Oliver Stone's Killer Instinct", an *Interview* piece by Graham Fuller:

GF: You pack it all in there in that closing montage: the Menendez trial, Tonya, Waco, Lorena Bobbitt, O.J. Simpson. OS: Tragedy has become the new soap opera, and it hasn't enhanced our ability to empathize at all. Instead, it's made us callous. The concept of television as gladiator game, as spectacle, has densensitized the audience and made our society "the Great Yawn," as Octavio Paz called it. Unsatiated, insensitive to pain, needing more and more—because nothing shocks anymore. . . .

"I wanted to have fun," [Stone] said. "And I really wanted to do a combination of a road movie, like "Bonnie and Clyde", and "Easy Rider", and a prison film, like "The Great Escape" and "Papillon."

"It's such an outrageous story," he said. "And in the time between optioning the film and making it, tremendous things have happened on America's landscape." Mr. Stone

insisted that some of his other films, such as "Scarface", "J.F.K." and "Platoon", were far more violent than "Natural Born Killers". Those earlier films, he said, were realistic, while his current one is not.

"There's not a gruesome scene in the film," he said, making a point that's highly debatable.

"It's a love-it-or-hate-it movie," he said.

No one is likely to argue with that.

—From "How a Movie Satire Turned Into Reality" by Bernard Weinraub in *The New York Times*, August 16, 1994.

"I would imagine that if Oliver Stone showed his movie to a thousand people and a thousand people didn't exactly get the point that he was trying to make, he would think he failed. To me the best thing about him is his energy. But his biggest problem is that his obviousness cancels out his energy and his energy pumps up his obviousness. He's Stanley Kramer with style."—Quentin Tarantino's take on Stone (From *Premiere*, November 1994)

BIBLIOGRAPHY:

"Stone" James Riordan, 1995, biography

"Nixon: An Oliver Stone Film" Eric Hamburg (editor), 1995, Cinema Books

"A Child's Night Dreams" Oliver Stone, 1997, St. Martin's Press novel; written before returning to Vietnam as a soldier c. 1966

"Oliver Stone's USA: Film, History, Controversy" Robert Brent Toplin (editor), 2000, University of Kansas Press

Barbra Streisand

BORN: Barbara Joan Streisand in Brooklyn, New York, 04/24/1942

NATIONALITY: American

EDUCATION: Erasmus Hall High School Brooklyn, New York, 1959; honor student

AWARDS: New York Drama Critics Circle Award "I Can Get It For You Wholesale" 1962

Grammy Album of the Year (Other Than Classical) "The Barbra Streisand Album" 1963

Grammy Best Vocal Performance—Female "The Barbra Streisand Album" 1963

Grammy Best Vocal Performance—Female "People" 1964

Emmy Outstanding Individual Achievement in Entertainment—Actors and Performers "My Name Is Barbra" 1964/65; one of five performers cited

Grammy Best Vocal Performance-Female "My Name Is Barbra" 1965

London Critics Musical Award 1966

Oscar Best Actress "Funny Girl" 1968; tied with Katharine Hepburn, who won for "The Lion in Winter"; only the second time in Oscar history that two performers have tied for an award

Golden Globe Award Best Actress in a Comedy or Musical Motion Picture "Funny Girl" 1968

NATO Star of the Year Award 1968; presented by the National Association of Theater Owners

Golden Globe Award World Film Favorite—Female 1969

Golden Globe Award World Film Favorite—Female 1970

Special Tony 1970 award as "Best Actress of the Decade"

Golden Globe Award World Film Favorite-Female 1974

People's Choice Award Favorite Female Musical Performer 1975; tied with Olivia Newton-John

People's Choice Award Favorite Motion Picture Actress 1975

Golden Globe Award Best Motion Picture-Musical/Comedy "A Star is Born" 1976; executive producer

Golden Globe Award Best Actress-Musical/Comedy "A Star is Born" 1976

Golden Globe Award Best Original Song "Evergreen" (from "A Star is Born") 1976 award shared with Paul Williams

Oscar Best Original Song "Evergreen" (from "A Star is Born") 1976; award shared with Paul Williams

Golden Globe Award World Film Favorite—Female 1977

American Guild of Variety Artists Georgie Award 1977

Grammy Song of the Year "Evergreen" 1977; shared with co-writer Paul Williams; tied with Joe Brooks' "You Light Up My Life"

Grammy Best Pop Vocal Performance-Female "Love Theme From 'A Star Is Born' (Evergreen)" 1977

People's Choice Award Favorite Motion Picture Actress 1977

People's Choice Award Favorite Motion Picture Actress 1978

Grammy Best Pop Performance By a Duo or Group with Vocal "Guilty" 1980; shared with Barry Gibb

American Music Award Pop/Rock Female Vocalist 1980

People's Choice Award Favorite All-Around Female Performer 1984; tied with Barbara Mandrell

Golden Globe Award Best Motion Picture—Musical or Comedy "Yentl" 1984 producer

Golden Globe Award Best Director "Yentl" 1984

Women in Film Crystal Award 1984

Grammy Best Pop Vocal Performance—Female "The Broadway Album" 1987

People's Choice Award Favorite All-Time Musical Star 1988

NATO/ShoWest Star of the Decade Award 1988; presented by the National Association of Theater Owners

Grammy Legend Award 1992

CableACE Award Best Performance in a Music Special or Series "Barbra Streisand The Concert" 1994

Directors Guild of America Award Musical/Variety Special "Barbra Streisand, The Concert" 1994; shared with Dwight Hemion

Emmy Outstanding Individual Performance in a Variety or Music Program "Barbra Streisand, The Concert" 1994/95

Emmy Outstanding Variety, Music or Comedy Special "Barbra Streisand, The Concert" 1994/95; co-producer with Dwight Hemion

The Recording Academy Lifetime Achievement Award 1995

ShowEast Filmmaker of the Year Award 1996; presented by the National Association of Theater Owners

Cecil B. DeMille Award 2000; presented by the Hollywood Foreign Press Association

American Film Institute Life Achievement Award 2001; first female director to be so honored

Daytime Emmy Outstanding Special Class Special "Reel Models: The First Women of Film" 2000/01; Streisand was both host and one of the executive producers

Emmy Outstanding Individual Performance in a Variety or Music Program "Barbra Streisand: Timeless" 2000/01

BIOGRAPHY

This multi-talented performer shot to fame when she conquered Broadway with her galvanizing stage presence in the musicals, "I Can Get It for You Wholesale" (1962) and "Funny Girl" (1964), in the latter as the gawky but gifted Fanny Brice. Streisand next powered a number of popular albums ("My Name Is Barbra") and award-winning TV specials ("Barbra Streisand: A Happening in Central Park"; "My Name Is Barbra", which was based on her hit album and won five Emmys) before moving into films. Equally magnetic on the big screen, Streisand patented a brash, loquacious, aggressively optimistic screen persona, starring in musicals before moving on to, and proving herself more than capable in, screwball comedies and romances.

Compensating for her angular, prominent features (which she has often played up self-mockingly in films as her "imperfect" beauty) with unbounded energy and immense talent, Streisand won an Oscar for her first film, William Wyler's adaptation of "Funny Girl" (1968), in which she recreated her successful stage role of comedian Fanny Brice. She subsequently turned several mediocre movies into box-office successes, and appeared in such enjoyably old-fashioned films as the farcical "What's Up, Doc?" (1972) and the sudsy "The Way We Were" (1973), making her the biggest female box-office star of the 1970s.

Increasingly criticized for her sometimes megalomaniac tendencies, Streisand responded by noting that healthy ambition in men has often been seen as unattractive pushiness in women. She also branched out into producing (starting with 1976's "A Star is Born") and then directing (beginning with 1983's "Yentl", which she also wrote). She has since produced most of her own occasional film vehicles and continued to enjoy considerable chart success with her albums and show-stopping singles through the early 80s, ranging from the theme songs of "The Way We Were" and "The Main Event", to "Guilty", "A Woman in Love", and a disco-flavored duet with Donna Summer, "Enough Is Enough."

"Yentl", the story of a Jewish girl who disguises herself as a boy in order to pursue an education, garnered Streisand generally respectful but mixed reviews from critics. In general they liked her handling of actors and obvious sincerity and attention to detail, but carped at the many indulgent musical monologues and routine visual style.

After another producing effort and larger-than-life star performance as a woman on trial who is considered "Nuts" (1987), Streisand directed a second film, "The Prince of Tides" (1991), based on Pat Conroy's best-selling novel. Both critical and popular response to Streisand's sensitive directorial work were notably improved, dismay being largely reserved in some corners for Streisand's glamorized appearance and performance as a sympathetic psychiatrist. The film received seven Oscar nominations among both acting and technical categories, including one for Best Picture. The lack of a nomination for Streisand as director caused a mild stir in the entertainment community, but she blithely continued with other directorial projects, AIDS and Democratic

Party activism, and a very well-received compilation of songs associated with her career.

1994 marked a rare return to live concert singing for Streisand with an incredibly popular multi-city tour which found her charisma and her singing voice both in mint condition. She also produced, directed and starred in "The Mirror Has Two Faces" (1996), a remake of a 1958 French film of the same name directed by Andre Cayatte and starring Michele Morgan. The usual stories about Streisand's perfectionism surrounded the lengthy production, complete with changes of cast and crew. Advance buzz, though, was also generally favorable in its retelling of the story of a plain woman whose marriage is rocked when she undergoes a transformation.

Streisand was formerly married to her "I Can Get It For You Wholeseale" co-star Elliot Gould; their son is actor Jason Gould, who played her son in "The Prince of Tides."—Written by David Lugowski

COMPANIONS:
husband: Elliot Gould. Actor; married on March 21, 1963; divorced in 1971

Ryan O'Neal. Actor; co-starred together in "What's Up, Doc?" and "The Main Event"

Jon Peters. Producer, executive, former hairdresser; formerly married to Lesley Ann Warren

Don Johnson. Actor, singer; no longer together

James Newton Howard. Composer; scored "Prince of the Tides"; separated 1991

Liam Neeson. Actor; dated briefly

Richard Baskin. No longer together

husband: James Brolin. Actor; met at a dinner party on July 1, 1996; announced engagement in May 1997; married at her Malibu home on July 1, 1998

MILESTONES:
1960: Stage acting debut in "The Insect Comedy"

1960: Won a singing contest at The Lion, a small Greenwich Village club; led to engagements at Bon Soir and the Blue Angel

1961: Made TV debut as guest on "The Tonight Show", guest hosted by Orson Bean

1961: Off-Broadway debut in the revue "Another Evening with Harry Stoones"; also featured was Dom DeLuise

1962: Broadway debut as the secretary Miss Marmelstein in "I Can Get It For You Wholesale"; received Tony nomination

1962: Put under contract by Columbia Records in October

1963: Released first solo album

1964: Breakthrough stage role, Fanny Brice in "Funny Girl"; received second Tony nomination

1966: Made London stage debut reprising her Broadway success in "Funny Girl"

1968: Film debut in director William Wyler's adaptation of "Funny Girl"; tied with Katharine Hepburn for the Best Actress Academy Award

1969: Starred in the overblown film version of "Hello, Dolly!", directed by Gene Kelly; ironically Carol Channing who originated the role won the 1964 Tony Award beating out Streisand in "Funny Girl"

1972: Formed Barwood Films; first Barwood-produced film, "Up the Sandbox"

1972: Delivered a fine comic turn in the modern screwball "What's Up, Doc?"; first screen teaming with Ryan O'Neal

1973: Had big success teamed with Robert Redford in "The Way We Were"; also sang the theme song; earned second Best Actress Oscar nomination

1974: Reprised role of Fanny Brice in the sequel "Funny Lady"

1976: First film as executive producer, "A Star Is Born"; also starred and composed some of the songs; received second Oscar for the song "Evergreen", making her the first female composer ever to receive an Academy Award; song co-written with Paul Williams

1979: Produced first film, "The Main Event" (with Jon Peters); reteamed on screen with Ryan O'Neal

1983: Feature directorial and screenwriting

(co-writer) debut, "Yentl"; also produced and starred in title role of a woman who poses as a boy to study the Talmud

1985: "The Broadway Album" returned her to her theatrical roots

1987: Starred as an upper-class woman forced into prostitution who is accused of murdering one of her clients in "Nuts", adapted from the Broadway play; also served as producer and composer

1991: Helmed second film, the Oscar-nominated Best Picture "The Prince of Tides"; also starred and served as a producer; film received a total of eight Academy Award nominations, but was not nominated for its direction

1993: Released "Back to Broadway", a second recording of theater music

1993: Donated her 24-acre, $15 million estate to the Santa Monica Mountains Conservancy; to be named the Streisand Center for Conservancy Studies

1993: Received a reported $12 million for two concerts in Las Vegas

1994: Went on a landmark multi-city concert tour; included her first live New York performances since "A Happening in Central Park" in 1967; concerts were taped and aired first on HBO and in a slightly revised form on CBS

1995: Served as an executive producer on the Emmy-winning TV-movie "Serving in Silence: The Margarethe Cammermeyer Story", starring Glenn Close

1996: Helmed third film "The Mirror Has Two Faces", also starred, produced and contributed to the music score

1998: Served as an executive producer of the NBC TV-movie "The Long Island Incident"

1999—2000: Went on a "farewell" concert tour, culminating in concerts in Las Vegas on New Year's Eve 1999 and New Year's Day 2000; videotaped and aired as a 2001 Fox special "Barbra Streisand—Timeless"

2000: Hosted the award-winning AMC special "Reel Models: The First Women of Film"; also served as executive producer

2000: Executive produced the Showtime original movie "Frankie and Hazel", directed by JoBeth Williams

2000: Was executive producer of a series of PBS specials aired under the umbrella title "The Living Century"

2001: Served as executive producer of the Lifetime lesbian-themed movie "What Makes a Family"

2001: Was executive producer of the Showtime original "Varian's War"

AFFILIATION: Founder, The Streisand Foundation

QUOTES:

In 1997, with the success of "Higher Ground", she became the top female singer with the most multi-platinum albums.

Received the National Medal of Arts from US President Bill Clinton (2000).

"Barbra Streisand is a Marie Antoinette, because she's unaware of the facts of common existence. It's the danger of believing you're larger than life. Nobody is bigger than life." —ex-husband Elliot Gould to *The Daily Telegraph*, March 1999.

"I am a nice person. I care about my driver having lunch, you know."—Streisand in *Movieline* November 2002

DISCOGRAPHY: "Pins and Needles" Barbra Streisand, Columbia, 1962

"I Can Get It for You Wholesale" Columbia, 1962; original Broadway cast recording featuring Streisand as Miss Marmelstein

"The Barbra Streisand Album" Barbra Streisand, Columbia, 1963

"The Second Barbra Streisand Album" Barbra Streisand, Columbia, 1963

"Funny Girl" Capitol, 1964; original Broadway cast recording; Streisand played Fanny Brice

"Barbra Streisand: The Third Album" Barbra Streisand, Columbia, 1964

"People" Barbra Streisand, Columbia, 1964

"My Name Is Barbra" Barbra Streisand, Columbia, 1965

"My Name Is Barbra, Two . . . " Barbra Streisand, Columbia, 1965

"Color Me Barbra" Barbra Streisand, Columbia, 1966

"Je m'appelle Barbra" Barbra Streisand, 1966

"Harold Arlen and Barbra Streisand—Harold Sings Arlen (with Friend)" Harold Arlen and Barbra Streisand, Columbia, 1966; Arlen and Streisand singing songs composer Arlen created during his career

"Simply Streisand" Barbra Streisand, Columbia, 1967

"A Christmas Album" Barbra Streisand, Columbia, 1967

"Funny Girl" 1968; original motion picture soundtrack; Streisand reprised her stage role as Fanny Brice and won an Oscar as Best Actress

"A Happening in Central Park" Barbra Streisand, Columbia, 1968

"What About Today?" Barbra Streisand, Columbia, 1969

"Hello, Dolly!" 1969; original motion picture soundtrack; Streisand played title role of Dolly Gallagher Levi

"On a Clear Day You Can See Forever" Columbia, 1970; original motion picture soundtrack; Streisand played Daisy

"Barbra Streisand's Greatest Hits" Barbra Streisand, Columbia, 1970

"The Owl and the Pussycat" 1971; original motion picture soundtrack

"Stoney End" Barbra Streisand, Columbia, 1971

"Barbra Joan Streisand" Barbra Streisand, Columbia, 1972

"Barbra Streisand: Live Concert at the Forum" Barbra Streisand, Columbia, 1972

"Barbra Streisand . . . And Other Musical Instruments" Barbra Streisand, Columbia, 1973; soundtrack to acclaimed TV special

"The Way We Were" 1974; soundtrack album for the feature film of the same name

"The Way We Were" Barbra Streisand, Columbia, 1974

"Butterfly" Barbra Streisand, Columbia, 1974

"Funny Lady" 1975; original motion picture soundtrack to sequel to "Funny Girl"; Streisand once again played Fanny Brice

"Lazy Afternoon" Barbra Streisand, Columbia, 1975

"A Star Is Born" Columbia, 1976; original motion picture soundtrack; Streisand also co-wrote several songs included on the album including the Oscar-winning "Evergreen"

"Classical Barbra" Barbra Streisand, Columbia, 1977

"Streisand Superman" Barbra Streisand, Columbia, 1977

"The Stars Salute Israel at 30" Columbia, 1978; Streisand contributed vocals

"Songbird" Barbra Streisand, Columbia, 1978

"Barbra Streisand's Greatest Hits" Barbra Streisand, Columbia, 1978

"The Main Event" 1979; original motion picture soundtrack

"Wet" Barbra Streisand, Columbia, 1979

"Guilty" Barbra Streisand and Barry Gibb, Columbia, 1980

"Memories" Barbra Streisand, Columbia, 1981

"Yentl" Barbra Streisand, Columbia, 1983; original soundtrack for the film of the same name

"Emotion" Barbra Streisand, Columbia, 1984

"The Broadway Album" Barbara Streisand, Columbia, 1985

"One Voice" Barbra Streisand, Columbia, 1986

"Till I Loved You" Barbra Streisand, Columbia, 1988

"A Collection: Greatest Hits . . . And More" Barbra Streisand, 1989

"Just for the Record . . . " Barbra Streisand, 1991; four-disc compilation of her entire recording career

"Back to Broadway" Barbra Streisand, Columbia, 1993

"Barbra—The Concert" Barbra Streisand, Columbia, 1994

"Higher Ground" Barbra Streisand, Columbia, 1997

"A Love Like Ours" Barbra Streisand, Columbia, 1999

"Timeless—Live in Concert" Barbra Streisand, 2000

"Christmas Memories" Barbra Streisand, Columbia, 2001

BIBLIOGRAPHY:

"Barbra: The First Decade—The Films and Career of Barbra Streisand" James Spada, 1974, Lyle Stuart

"Streisand: The Woman and the Legend" James Spada and Christopher Nickens, 1983, Pocket Books

"Barbra Streisand: The Woman, the Myth, the Music" Shaun Considine, 1985, Delacorte

"Barbra: The Second Decade—The Films and Career of Barbra Streisand" Karen Swenson, 1985, Lyle Stuart

"Streisand: Her Life" James Spada, 1995, Crown

"Streisand" Anne Edwards, 1997, Little, Brown; biography

Preston Sturges

BORN: Edmund Preston Biden in Chicago, Illinois, 08/29/1898

DEATH: in New York, New York, 08/06/1959

NATIONALITY: American

EDUCATION: Dr Coulter's Harvard School, Chicago, Illinois, 1905

Lycee Janson de Sailly, Paris, France, 1907

Ecole des Roches, Normandy, France

La Villa, Lausanne, Switzerland

also attended schools in Berlin and Dresden, Germany

School of Military Aeronautics, Austin, Texas, 1917

AWARDS: Oscar Best Original Screenplay "The Great McGinty" 1940

Writers Guild of America Laurel Award for Achievement 1974; awarded posthumously

BIOGRAPHY

Preston Sturges ranks as one of the American cinema's most gifted and talented screenwriters and directors. His writings featured astringent dialogue that was both cosmopolitan and jargonistic. Sturges also excelled in staging scenes with razor-sharp wit but was willing to include broad slapstick. As Terrence Rafferty put it, "he was one of the true wild men of movie comedy, a legitimate successor to the improvisatory gagmen of the silent era. . . . "

Born on August 29, 1898, Edmund Preston Biden spent his early childhood shuttling between his native Chicago (where his adoptive father, Solomon Sturges, lived) and Europe. His iconoclastic mother, born Mary Dempsey but known as Mary Desti, would bring her son with her as she journeyed throughout the Continent with dancer Isadora Duncan. At her urging, Sturges would dress in a Greek tunic while attending school in Chicago. After she separated from her second husband, Desti enrolled her son in series of boarding schools in France, Germany and Switzerland. Having such a colorful figure as a mother affected him and how he viewed women and he clearly inherited her originality. As he was once quoted, "My mother was in no sense a liar, nor even intentionally unacquainted with the truth . . . as she knew it. She was, however, endowed with such a rich and powerful imagination that anything she had said three times, she believed fervently. Often, twice was enough." Sturges himself went on to demonstrate his own brand of inventiveness and often modeled characters in his scripts on both Solomon Sturges and Mary Desti.

By 1914, the teenaged Sturges was working at Maison Desti, his mother's cosmetics shop in Deauville, France. Sent back to America when World War I erupted, the youngster briefly worked back stage for one of Duncan's New York engagements and then assumed responsibilities for the New York branch of Maison Desti. When the USA joined the war, Sturges served in the US Army Signal Corps, although he never saw action. Following his discharge, he returned to the cosmetics business. An amateur inventor, Sturges developed a "kiss-proof" lipstick but he had to relinquish management of the business to his mother when she returned home.

After the failure of his first marriage and the break-up of a relationship with an actress who told him their relationship was merely fodder for her art, Sturges turned to playwriting, basing his first effort on his last romantic relationship. "The Guinea Pig" was produced at the Provincetown (MA) Playhouse and then transferred to Broadway in January 1929 where it ran for some 16 weeks. Although a modest success, it paled in comparison with his second play "Strictly Dishonorable" (1929) which proved to be a smash despite the stock market crash. His next three stage efforts, however, proved disappointing failures and took a financial toll as Sturges invested his own money in them. By then, he had made inroads in the motion picture business. In 1929, Paramount Pictures tapped him to write dialogue for the film version of two plays, one of which "The Big Pond" (1930), possesses traces of what would become Sturges' hallmarks: a love-triangle, a sense of fate, a character of a business tycoon and the use of puns and misunderstandings. Universal put him under contract to pen an adaptation of "The Invisible Man" in 1932. Changing the setting to Central Europe, he fashioned a highly-praised screenplay, but director James Whale wanted to remain more faithful to H. G. Wells and brought in another writer forcing Universal to drop the

writer's option. Sturges subsequently sold to Fox (in a then-groundbreaking move of a mixture of cash and a percentage of the gross profit) an original screenplay based on stories told to him by his second wife about her grandfather, C. W. Post. "The Power and the Glory" (1933), directed by William K. Howard, was the tale of a railroad tycoon (Spencer Tracy) told in a non-linear fashion dubbed "narratage". Sturges used flashbacks with narration in the film which was critically well-received but not a box-office success. Interestingly, "The Power and the Glory" has been seen as a precursor of what most feel is the greatest American film ever made, Orson Welles' 1941 masterpiece "Citizen Kane."

Having been allowed on the set during shooting, Sturges noted the treatment of the director by the studio, cast and crew. Coming from the theater where the writer was the most important figure, he was reluctant to give up that power. After finishing out the 1930s as a screenwriter, penning such interesting efforts as the biopic "Diamond Jim" (1935), the screwball comedy "Easy Living" (1937) and the period drama "If I Were King" (1938), he struck a deal with Paramount to direct an early original script of his, "The Great McGinty."

Sturges became one of the first writer-directors in the studio system, paving the way for John Huston and the multitudes that have followed. Much of his reputation rests on the eight films he made in the period between 1940 and 1944. Targeting a system that he felt stressed material success and moral hypocrisy, Sturges lobbed his comedic grenades by inverting the standards of popular romantic comedies, including mistaken identities, the fickleness of fate and the repetition of events. "The Great McGinty" (1940) satirized the American political system by showing how a disreputable type could rise to become mayor and then governor, only to be brought down by his truth-telling wife. The film, which brought Sturges an Oscar for its screenplay, made his reputation as a comedic director. He also began associations with several actors (e.g., William Demarest, Harry Rosenthal, Robert Warwick) who went on to form an unofficial "stock company", appearing in several of his films. Also in 1940, the studio released "Christmas in July", which skewered big business, advertising and the conspicuous consumer. "The Lady Eve" (1941) is perhaps Sturges' best picture, a complex romantic comedy about a bumbling snake hunter (Henry Fonda) who becomes the prey of a cool, sexy con artist (Barbara Stanwyck). Fonda and Stanwyck enjoy a shipboard romance but he rejects her when he learns of her unsavory past. In order to win her man, Stanwyck reinvents herself as a British noblewoman. In one of the most memorable set pieces in films, Stanwyck takes a moment on their honeymoon to regale her new husband with a list of every love affair she has ever had. As the scene progresses and Fonda's jealousy increases, Sturges skillfully employs the soundtrack as a counterpoint: the train enters tunnels with its wheels clacking and whistle blowing, a storm develops and the score swells. Marvelously acted, "The Lady Eve" was a hit for Paramount and boosted the stock of all involved.

Paramount gave Sturges free rein with his next films. "Sullivan's Travels" (1941) is perhaps his most personal, focusing on a comedy film director (Joel McCrea) who wants to make more meaningful motion pictures. Determined to experience poverty first-hand, he sets off as a hobo with an aspiring actress (Veronica Lake) in tow. For a comic piece, this film has a dark undertone but the ultimate moral is that people don't want to be reminded of their situations, they want escapism. As Sullivan says near the end of the picture, "There's a lot to be said for making people laugh." In 1942, Sturges wrote and directed "The Palm Beach Story", a satire of business and greed about a woman (Claudette Colbert) who leaves her inventor husband (McCrea) for a millionaire

(Rudy Vallee). When McCrea arrives in Florida, he is pursued by Vallee's sister (Mary Astor) with unpredictable results. The film owes much to the French farces that captivated a youthful Sturges.

After stumbling somewhat with "The Great Moment" (lensed in 1942; released in 1944), a somber biography of the inventor of anesthesia that employed some of the flashback techniques of "The Power and the Glory", Sturges hit his stride with two comedies set in small-town America: "The Miracle of Morgan's Creek" and "Hail the Conquering Hero" (both 1944). The former took on marriage, motherhood, religion, patriotism and politics as it focused on Trudy Kockenlocker (Betty Hutton), the daughter of a local constable who finds herself pregnant after a rowdy evening and later gives birth to sextuplets. The latter satirizes the American need for hero worship as a reject from the Marines fakes war service and is welcomed home in triumph, only to be later unmasked. Sturges received two 1944 Academy Award nominations in the same category (Best Original Screenplay) for these films.

In retrospect, it seems foolish but Sturges terminated his contract with Paramount partly because he craved more independence, The studio relented, despite the fact his films were successful. Sturges then entered into an ill-advised partnership with Howard Hughes, forming the California Pictures Corporation. His first film under this new agreement was to be a comeback for silent screen star Harold Lloyd. "The Sin of Harold Diddlebock/Mad Wednesday" (1947) attempted to present Lloyd's character from 1925's "The Freshman" as a bookkeeper who loses his job and embarks on a series of adventures. A mixed bag, there are moments of brilliance (usually featuring Lloyd) but there are also dull spots. Even before the film was released, problems between Hughes and Sturges ensued. Max Ophuls had originally been hired to direct "Vendetta" but Hughes was displeased with his work and handed the film over to Sturges who in turn failed to make Hughes happy. Sturges was fired from "Vendetta" (which went through a string of directors with Mel Ferrer finally ending up with the credit in its 1950 release) and their partnership was dissolved. Hughes released "The Sin of Harold Diddlebock" briefly in 1947 but quickly withdrew it. A revised, recut version, now titled "Mad Wednesday" was released in 1950 but met with a mixed reception.

Daryl F. Zanuck offered a haven to Sturges at 20th Century Fox and the writer-director responded with his last major film "Unfaithfully Yours" (1948), a black comedy about a famous conductor who suspects his wife of adultery. Sturges employed a technique of telling the same story in a multiple manner, using two fantasy sequences in which the conductor (Rex Harrison) plots revenge on his cheating wife before the same events unfold in reality, with the maestro contemplating murder. "Unfaithfully Yours" was not appreciated in its time but has since acquired a following. Hoping to fashion a hit for Fox, Sturges undertook the Western spoof "The Beautiful Blonde From Bashful Bend" (1949), featuring Betty Grable as a saloon singer mistaken for a schoolmarm. His only film made in color, it was a box-office failure in its initial release and all but ended Sturges' Hollywood career.

Over the next decade, Sturges wrote several scripts that went unproduced, acted in "Paris Holiday" (1958) and made one last film, 1956's "The French They Are a Funny Race/Les Carnets du Major Thompson", a marital comedy about a stuffy British military officer and the repercussions of wedding to a French-woman. Despite several abortive attempts, he was unable to get a film project made. In 1958, he was hired to direct the Broadway play "The Golden Fleece" but was fired when one of the producers announced he was taking over the show. Sturges had struck a deal with a publisher for his memoirs and settled into NYC's Algonquin Hotel to write but the project was left unfinished by his death on August 6, 1959 of a heart attack. His widow subsequently assembled the material and published the book under the title "Preston Sturges on Preston Sturges" in 1990. In 1998, MGM announced that it was polishing one of Sturges' unproduced screenplays, "Mr. Big and Littleville", with Michael Douglas attached as star.—Written by Ted Murphy

COMPANION:

wife: Anne Margaret Nagle. Lawyer, former actor; married on August 15, 1951; mother of Sturges' two younger sons

MILESTONES:

Raised in Europe and the USA

1914: Managed Maison Desti, his mother's cosmetic shop in Deauville, France

1914: Returned to the USA at the outbreak of WWII

1915: Managed Maison Desti in NYC

1917–1918: Served in Air Corps; wrote and drew weekly comic strip "Toot and His Loot" for camp newspaper

1920: Invented "kiss-proof" lipstick

1927: Began writing plays after a bout of appendicitis

1928: First play, "The Guinea Pig" produced in Provincetown, Massachusetts

1929: "The Guinea Pig" opened to a 16-week run on Broadway in January

1929: Had success with second play, "Strictly Dishonorable"

1929: Wrote first screenplays, "The Big Pond" and "Fast and Loose", for Paramount Pictures in Astoria, Queens

1930: Had flop with play "Recapture"

1932: Moved to Hollywood to work on script of "The Invisible Man" for Universal in September; studio dropped their option when assigned director disliked his script

1933: Wrote script for "The Great McGinty"

1934: Script for "Fanny" written for Universal shelved due to objections of censors

1935: Founded Sturges Engineering Company, a manufacturer of vibrationless diesel engines

1936: With Ted Snyder, opens restaurant Snyder's (closed in 1938)

1936: Signed two-year contract with Paramount

1938: Loaned to MGM

1939: Sold rights to "The Great McGinty" to Paramount for $10 in return for studio agreeing to allow him to direct the film

1940: Film directing debut, "The Great McGinty"; received Academy Award for Best Original Screenplay

1940: Made uncredited acting appearance in "Christmas in July"

1940: Opened first restaurant, The Players, in L.A.

1941: "The Lady Eve", starring Henry Fonda and Barbara Stanwyck, and "Sullivan's Travels", with Joel McCrea and Veronica Lake, released

1942: Appeared as himself in "Star Spangled Rhythm"

1943: Ended contract with Paramount

1944: Earned two Oscar nominations for Best Original Screenplay in the same year for "Hail the Conquering Hero" and "The Miracle of Morgan's Creek"

1944: With Howard Hughes, formed California Pictures Corporation (Cal-Pix)

1946: While filming "Vendetta", Hughes dissolved partnership; replaced as director; Mel Ferrer received final screen credit

1947: Put under contract by 20th Century Fox

1955: Directed last film, "Les Carnets du Major Thompson/The French, They Are a Funny Race"

1950: Wrote book for the stage musical "Make a Wish", based on his 1934 screenplay "The Good Fairy"

1955: Directed last film, "Les Carnets du Major Thompson/The French, They Are a Funny Race"

1956: Last produced screenplay (to date) "The Birds and the Bees"

1958: Final screen appearance, acted in "Paris Holiday"

1990: Subject of award-winning documentary "Preston Sturges: Rise & Fall of an American Dreamer" (aired on PBS)

1998: MGM announced plans to make film from original unproduced screenplay "Mr. Big and Littleville"

QUOTES:

There is an official website at www.preston-sturges.com

He was the subject of an award-winning 1990 documentary "Preston Sturges: The Rise and Fall of an American Dreamer"

"The underlying cynicism of Sturges is appealing because he keeps wanting to level his people but he can't. He reveals our foolishness, our hypocrisy, our self-involvement, but he does it in a way that says: 'We are all like this. I am one of you.' He connects us by it, as opposed to separating us."—filmmaker Ron Shelton quoted in *The New York Times*, July 19, 1998.

"Sturges wasn't a deep-dish artist; he wasn't really even a satirist—more a playful, inspired manipulator of low comedy, slapstick, verbal irony and, when the occasion arose, the odd cynical joke about social realities."—Terrence Rafferty writing in *GQ*, August 1998.

BIBLIOGRAPHY:

"Between Flops: A Biography of Preston Sturges" James Curtis

"Intrepid Laughter: Preston Sturges and the Movies" Andrew Dickos, 1985

"Five Screenplays by Preston Sturges" 1985, University of California Press

"Preston Sturges by Preston Sturges" Sandy Sturges, editor, 1990; unfinished autobiography edited by his widow

"Madcap: The Life of Preston Sturges" Donald Spoto, 1990

"Christmas in July: The Life & Art of Preston Sturges" Diane Jacobs, 1992, University of California Press

"Four More Screenplays by Preston Sturges" 1995, University of California Press

"Preston Sturges's Vision of America: Critical Analyses of Fourteen Films" Jay Rozgonyi, 1995, McFarland

"Three More Screenplays by Preston Sturges" 1998, University of California Press

Istvan Szabo

BORN: in Budapest, Hungary, 02/18/1938

NATIONALITY: Hungarian

EDUCATION: Academy for Theater and Film Art, Budapest, Hungary, directing, 1956–61; graduated; made diploma film "Konzert/ Concert"

AWARDS: Hungarian Critics Prize "Konzert/ Concert" 1962

Amsterdam Academy Prize "Konzert/Concert" 1963

Oberhausen Film Festival Prize "Konzert/Concert" 1963; Diploma of the Volkhochschuljury

Cannes Film Festival Diploma Award "Te/You" 1963

Tours Festival Grand Prize "Te/You" 1963

San Francisco Film Festival Best Short Fiction Feature Award "Te/You" 1963

Locarno Film Festival Silver Sail "Almodozasok Kora/The Age of Daydreaming" 1965

Moscow Film Festival Main Prize "Apa/Father" 1967

Locarno Film Festival Critics Grand Prize "Apa/Father" 1967; one of two films cited

Oberhausen Film Festival Main Prize "Alom a hazrol/Dream About a House" 1972; short film

Locarno Film Festival Golden Leopard Award "Tuzolto Utca 25/25 Fireman's Street" 1974

Atlanta Film Festival Best Foreign Film Award "25 Fireman's Street" 1974

Oberhausen Film Festival Grand Prize "Varos terkep/City Map" 1977

Berlin Film Festival Silver Bear "Bizalom/ Confidence" 1980

Cannes Film Festival FIPRESCI Prize "Mephisto" 1981

Cannes Film Festival Jury Prize "Oberst Redl/Colonel Redl" 1985

Felix Best Screenplay "Sweet Emma, Dear Bobe" 1992

European Film Award European Screenwriters "Sunshine" 1999; shared with co-writer Israel Horowitz

BIOGRAPHY

Istvan Szabo has emerged as one of the most important Hungarian filmmakers of the 20th century. The Central European experience, from the Austro-Hungarian Empire to the Warsaw Pact, is the key to the content of his films as well as their symbolic structure. There may even be an implied metaphor in a film like "Colonel Redl" (1985) between the complex social atmosphere and political issues in the old imperial dynasty and the modern people's republic. His output perhaps reached a culmination in 1999 with the epic "Sunshine", which followed the rise and fall of a Jewish Hungarian family from the late 19th century to the mid-1960s.

In Szabo's films, the illusory hopes and dreadful realities of the past are always presented in the most immediate human terms, whether the fanciful imaginings of a son for a dead parent in "Apa/Father" (1966), the memory of Nazi deportations in "25 Fireman's Street" (1974), the failed 1956 rebellion of "Szerelmesfilm/Love Film" (1970) or the memory of betrayal by a lover to one's enemies in "Bizalom/Confidence" (1979).

Szabo's use of symbols and devices can be bewilderingly complex, as in "25 Fireman's

Street," or exceedingly droll, as in "Budapest Tales" (1976), where a tram is set working again by a group of displaced people at the war's close. In this allegory of socialist reconstruction, tyranny and deceit rival heroism and honesty in an effort to reach Budapest.

Szabo was catapulted to international success and fame in 1979 when "Confidence" won the Silver Bear at the Berlin Festival and a Best Foreign-Language Film Oscar nomination. His work in the 1970s moved away from the youthful influences of the French New Wave—his first features owed much to Francois Truffaut and Jean-Luc Godard—toward the more darker approach of an Alain Resnais. Szabo solidified his worldwide reputation with the Oscar-winning "Mephisto" (1981's Best Foreign-Language Film) which starred Austrian Klaus Maria Brandauer and featured Hungarian and Polish performers. "Mephisto" chronicled the moral quandary and professional success of an actor befriended by a high-ranking Nazi, modeled after Hermann Goering, whose wide powers extend to the Prussian State Theater. A disturbingly likable careerist, the actor ends his marriage to a leftist, yet can give work to a Jewish employee and insult a Nazi colleague. Still, he stages an Aryan "Hamlet" and ends an affair with a dancer because of her one African parent. At the film's close, it is clear that despite his success and celebrity, he is no match for his ruthless patron.

For his next film, Szabo delved deeper into the past and the twilight of the Austro-Hungarian Empire. The figure in a celebrated pre-WWI espionage case and the subject of a novel and play, "Colonel Redl" may also be Szabo's metaphor for contemporary Communist relations. Again, Brandauer starred as the professional army officer who is caught up in the swirl of ethnic hatreds, class prejudices and dynastic intrigue. Internally driven by homosexual impulses and fears of his provincial origins, Redl is lured into the kind of counter-espionage trap he has used on others. Once more, Szabo's film was among the five competing for the

Academy Award for Best Foreign-Language Film (although it did not earn the final statue).

Szabo's "Hanussen" (1988), completed a trilogy on similar themes that encompassed "Mephisto" and "Colonel Redl", and it, too received a Best Foreign-Language Film Academy Award nomination. Based on the experiences of a clairvoyant famous in pre-Nazi Berlin, the film attempted to portray its main character as a mixture of conscious showman and tormented mystic (Brandauer) who ends up a political victim. Due to either inadequate scripting or acting, "Hanussen" did not enjoy the success of the director's earlier work.

Szabo made his English-language debut with a romantic drama, "Meeting Venus", about the politics of art that was meant as commentary on the late century push for reunification in Europe. Eschewing his usual flashbacks and dream sequences, the director opted for a straightforward approach in detailing the relationship between a Hungarian conductor (played by the French-born Niels Arestrup) and a Swedish diva (the American Glenn Close, whose singing was dubbed by New Zealander Kiri Te Kanawa).

His follow-up "Sweet Emma, Dear Bobe—Sketches, Nude", competed at the 1992 Berlin Film Festival. receiving high marks as a stylistic return to his earlier work. Despite its bleak settings in post-Communist Hungary, the film treated the central love story with sensuality. The culmination of his career to date, though, is undoubtedly "Sunshine/A Taste of Sunshine", a three-hour generational drama about a middle-class Jewish family whose fortunes are tied to an herbal remedy. Encapsulating experience from the waning days of the Austro-Hungarian Empire through two world wars, the film restated a favorite Szabo theme of assimilation versus persecution. While somewhat old-fashioned in its sweeping grandeur, some critics carped over plot points and the casting of Ralph Fiennes in three central roles (a man, his son and grandson). Szabo, who lost his own father when he was a child, was perhaps overcompensating by focusing on these patriarchs. In attempting to perhaps personalize man's inhumanity to man, one's search for identity and the symbolic use of names (the family, originally Sonnenschein is Magyarized to Sors), and the universal call for tolerance in a civilized society, Szabo faltered slightly. More than one review criticized the screenplay for focusing on too much minutia at the expense of more important historical details. Still, despite its flaws, "Sunshine" provided much to admire, from Lajos Koltai's cinematography to the performances of a stellar cast (including Fiennes, Rosemary Harris, Rachel Weisz, James Frain, William Hurt).

MILESTONES:

Born and raised in Budapest

1961: First short film as director, the thesis film "Konzert/Concert"

Joined Bela Balazs Studio as assistant after graduation

Helmed the shorts "Variaciok egy temara/Variations Upon a Theme" (1961) and "Te/You" (1963)

1964: First feature-length film, "Almodozasok Kora/The Age of Daydreaming"; film starred Andras Balint

1966: Directed second feature, "Apa/Father"

1970: Helmed first color film "Szerelmesfilm/Love Film", an unofficial sequel to "Apa"

1973: Moved into darker, more experimental works by crafting a film with a building as its central character, "Tuzolto utea 25/25 Fireman's Street"

1974: First TV film, "Premiere"

1976: Helmed the modern allegory "Budapest Tales/Budapesti mesek"

Lectured at Academy for Theatre and Film Art

1979: Breakthrough feature "Bizalom/Confidence"; garnered international attention and festival awards; first of six films with director of photography Lajos Koltai; earned a 1980 Oscar nomination for Best Foreign-Language Film

1979: Directed "The Green Bird" for German television

1981: Adapted (with screenwriter Peter Dobai) the roman-a-clef "Mephisto" for German television; focused on an actor who finds a mentor in a top Nazi general; first film with Klaus Maria Brandauer; earned the Best Foreign-Language Film Academy Award

1985: Directed "Colonel Redl", based on espionage scandal in Austrian army just prior to WWI and on John Osbourne's play "A Patriot for Me"; received Best Foreign-Language Film Oscar nomination

1988: Third collaboration with Brandauer, "Hanussen" also received Best Foreign-Language Film Academy Award nomination

1991: English-language debut, "Meeting Venus", starring Glenn Close

1999: Received widespread acclaim for the English-language "Sunshine/A Taste of Sunshine"; screened at Toronto Film Festival

AFFILIATION: Born Jewish; family converted to Roman Catholicism in 1944

QUOTES:

"My actual theme is always a human characteristic which becomes fateful because of the age. My aim is to portray a human feeling, to show the moment of catharsis which, if possible know it's about them, clarifies matters for them and fills them with positive energies."—Istvan Szabo.

"This is my aim as director—to leave a mark, a lsting mark on people's memory, with the help of images—trying to avoid cheap methods, because that would unfortunately be too easy."—Istvan Szabo.

"After many years of working as a film-maker, suddenly I realise all my films are describing different aspects of the same problem. Looking back over 10 or 12 feature films. I know that I have a line and this line is about fighting for the feeling of security. The questions are always the same—how to find myself, how to find a safe life, how to be accepted by the society that the character would like to live in."—Szabo to *Daily Telegraph*, April 26, 2000.

BORN: in New Zealand, 1951

NATIONALITY: New Zealander

AWARD: Australian Film Institute Palace/AFI Members Award Best Foreign Film "Once Were Warriors" 1995

BIOGRAPHY

"Once Were Warriors" was one of only three feature films made specifically by and for New Zealand in 1994, but despite its $1.4 million budget, it created an international sensation with its tale of a dysfunctional Maori family and its charting of the decline of the indigenous people of New Zealand. As a result, its director, Lee Tamahori, who is, himself of mixed Maori and European descent, was plucked by Hollywood to direct major motion pictures. Tamahori began his film career as a boom operator in the late 70s, then, in the early 80s, was an assistant director on numerous New Zealand feature films. The first of these, Geoff Murphy's "Utu" (1982), also dealt with Maori culture. But it was as a TV commercial director, beginning in the mid-80s, that Tamahori began to attract international notice. During a ten-year period, Tamahori directed more than 100 commercials, including spots for Mobius in the USA, and was particularly acclaimed for his storytelling style. The chance to direct "Once Were Warriors" (1994) came as a result of his renown in TV commercials, and the film, about an abusive father and his family dealing with being social outcasts in New Zealand, attracted enough critical acclaim that soon Hollywood called. His first studio picture, 1996's "Muholland Falls," was a stylishly crafted noir thriller with an unfortunately mediocre story involving the Los Angeles Police Department's notoriois Hat Squad of the 1950s. Tamahori's next film was the crackerjack survival thriller "The Edge" (1997) which combined a tidy sheltered-man-against-nature tale with the director's visual panache and winning performances from Anthony Hopkins, Alec Baldwin and even Bart the Bear, Hollywood's premiere ursine actor. "Along Came a Spider" (2001) was a less challenging but bigger-grossing effort, as it was a prequel of sorts to the hit thriller "Kiss the Girls" and again starred Morgan Freeman as novelist James Patterson's detective Alec Cross.

Tamahori next took on an even more iconic hero from fiction and film: Bond, James Bond. In 2002 the director helmed the 20th instalment of the 007 franchise, "Die Another Day," in which he cleverly paid tribute to the film's precursors in several visual homages, illicited the best performance yet from star Pierce Brosnan, turned Oscar-winner Halle Berry into an action hero-style Bond Girl and generally updated the franchise for the 21st century.

MILESTONES:

Began working in film industry in late 1970s as boom operator

1982: Worked as assistant director on "Utu"

1984: Began directing TV commercials (date approximate)

1994: Made feature film directorial debut with "Once Were Warriors"

1996: Made Hollywood directing debut with "Mulholland Falls"

1997: Helmed the thriller "The Edge"

2000: Directed episode of "The Sopranos" titled "Toodle-Fucking-Oo"

2001: Directed the film adaptation of James Patterson's thriller "Along Came a Spider"

2002: Helmed "Die Another Day", the 20th James Bond feature starring Pierce Brosnan and Halle Berry

Signed to direct "The Guide" with Berry in the lead role

QUOTES:

"I've always admired films that make you reel out of the theatre and you have to go to a bar and get a drink. I want to make one that makes people stand up and makes the hairs on the back of their necks stand up."—Lee Tamahori.

Quentin Tarantino

BORN: Quentin Jerome Tarantino in Knoxville, Tennessee, 03/27/1963

NATIONALITY: American

EDUCATION: dropped out of high school after ninth grade

AWARDS: Cannes Film Festival Palme d'Or "Pulp Fiction" 1994

National Board of Review Award Best Director "Pulp Fiction" 1994

Los Angeles Film Critics Association Award Best Director "Pulp Fiction" 1994

Los Angeles Film Critics Association Award Best Screenplay "Pulp Fiction" 1994; based on stories by Tarantino and Roger Avary

New York Film Critics Circle Award Best Director "Pulp Fiction" 1994

New York Film Critics Circle Award Best Screenplay "Pulp Fiction" 1994; from stories by Tarantino and Roger Avary; shared award with Avary

Boston Society of Film Critics Award Best Director "Pulp Fiction" 1994

Boston Society of Film Critics Award Best Screenplay "Pulp Fiction" 1994; from stories by Tarantino and Roger Avary

Society of Texas Film Critics Award Best Director "Pulp Fiction" 1994

Society of Texas Film Critics Award Best Screenplay "Pulp Fiction" 1994; from stories by Tarantino and Roger Avary

National Society of Film Critics Award Best Director "Pulp Fiction" 1994

National Society of Film Critics Award Best Screenplay "Pulp Fiction" 1994; from stories by Tarantino and Roger Avary; shared award with Roger Avary

Chicago Film Critics Association Award Best Director "Pulp Fiction" 1994

Chicago Film Critics Association Award Best Screenplay "Pulp Fiction" 1994; award shared with Roger Avary

Golden Globe Award Best Screenplay "Pulp Fiction" 1994 shared award with Roger Avary

Independent Spirit Award Best Director "Pulp Fiction" 1994

Independent Spirit Award Best Screenplay "Pulp Fiction" 1994; from stories by Tarantino and Roger Avary; shared award with Roger Avary

Oscar Best Screenplay Written Directly for the Screen "Pulp Fiction" 1994; from stories by Tarantino and Roger Avary

BAFTA Award Best Original Screenplay "Pulp Fiction" 1994; shared with Roger Avary

MTV Movie Award Best Movie "Pulp Fiction" 1995

BIOGRAPHY

The relatively young career of Quentin Tarantino instantly became the stuff of Hollywood legend. His improbable story incorporates plot elements previously encountered in earlier "boy wonder" lore (e.g., the youthful adventures of Orson Welles and Steven Spielberg) but, much like this unlikely celebrity's rapid-fire vocal delivery, the pace has been greatly accelerated. As of 1998, Tarantino, who also has acted in several features, had helmed only three features and a segment of a poorly received omnibus film. While this output is somewhat impressive for a four-year span, it would hardly seem to justify the three book-length studies of the filmmaker that were published in late 1995. Of course, winning the Oscar, Golden Globe and numerous critics' awards for Best Original Screenplay for "Pulp Fiction" (1994) only added to his luster. Not bad for a high school dropout who picked up much of his film education while working as a video store clerk.

For better or worse, the entertainment press has selected Tarantino as the symbol of a new generation of young directors of popular films. Hailed by VARIETY as "the videostore generation of filmmakers", these would-be auteurs learned what they know about moviemaking and film history by watching tapes on TV and not at film school. A minimum wage job behind a video store counter became a road to a treasure trove of cinematic expression—particularly if one worked, as Tarantino did, at a well-stocked outfit like Video Archives in Manhattan Beach. Cinephiles rather than cineastes, these young buffs tended to have rather catholic if idiosyncratic tastes. One can see influences of everything from arcane Hong Kong action titles to French New Wave classics in Tarantino's work.

Tarantino and his mother left Knoxville, TN, when he was two years old and settled in Los Angeles. After leaving school, he held a succession of odd jobs before finding his niche at Video Archives where, for five years, he regaled customers, including many low-profile industry players, with his passionate opinions and recommendations. There Tarantino first met the film school-trained Roger Avary, his future collaborator on the screenplays for "Reservoir Dogs" (1992), "True Romance" (1993) and "Pulp Fiction" (although the exact nature of their work together remains in dispute).

The pair were hired by producer John Langley, a regular customer who was impressed by the duo's film knowledge, to work as production assistants on a Dolph Lundgren exercise video. This led to work at Cinetel Productions, where they hooked up with producer Lawrence Bender and finished their screenplay for "Dogs." "The Tarantino Story" kicked into high gear with the release of this acclaimed feature debut as writer-director-actor. A brutally violent yet elegantly written crime drama originally budgeted for a mere $35,000, the production grew to $1.5 million when Harvey Keitel became enamored of the script and agreed to star. The result, a cleverly structured and stylized caper with themes of masculinity, loyalty and betrayal, benefited greatly from top notch tough-guy performances from a superior ensemble that also included Tim Roth, Steve Buscemi and Michael Madsen. It premiered at the 1992 Sundance Film Festival and was pointedly snubbed by the jury. Nonetheless, Tarantino was courted by the industry and lionized by some as the next Martin Scorsese, albeit with liberal sprinklings of Samuel Fuller and John Woo.

Tarantino continued in this vein with the screenplay for "True Romance", a gleefully adolescent daydream fueled by pop culture, violence and testosterone. Slickly directed by Tony Scott, the film offered grandstanding performances and a glossy commercial sheen that rendered the ample violence less distressing than that in "Dogs." "Natural Born Killers", also penned during the same burst of creativity, was helmed with a heavy hand by Oliver Stone, who had the script extensively rewritten, consigning Tarantino to a story credit. Consequently, Stone took the kudos and brickbats that the controversial film eventually generated.

Tarantino returned to the director's chair for "Pulp Fiction", marking a return to a familiar urban landscape characterized by themes of trust, betrayal, and inhabited by gangsters given to low-level postulating. Boasting another A-list cast including Bruce Willis, John Travolta, Samuel L. Jackson, Uma Thurman and Christopher Walken, the film premiered to acclaim and some controversy at the 1994 Cannes Film Festival where it received the Palme d'Or. It went on to surprising box-office success, grossing over $100 million domestically. "Pulp" made Tarantino the toast of Tinseltown and resuscitated the commercial and critical fortunes of Travolta, whose career management became a well-publicized sideline for the red-hot young filmmaker.

After taking home well over a dozen major awards for "Pulp Fiction", Tarantino was all but omnipresent in late 1994 and 1995. As an actor, he had began popping up in small roles in independent features ("Sleep With Me" and "Somebody to Love", both 1994) but was now being cast in low and medium budget studio pictures. He was the lead in the disastrous comic fantasy "Destiny Turns on the Radio" and did an enjoyable turn as a hapless drug dealer in Robert Rodriguez's "Desperado" (both 1995). Segueing to TV, Tarantino did a guest shot on Margaret Cho's ABC sitcom "All-American Girl" and directed a flashy installment of the hit NBC medical drama "ER."

Tarantino and Bender expanded their production company A Band Apart (taken from "Bande a Part", the original French title of Jean-Luc Godard's 1964 classic "Band of Outsiders") to include A Band Apart Commercials and Rolling Thunder. The latter was a specialty distribution label under Miramax Pictures designed to acquire, distribute and market four films per year. The emphasis would be on visceral, exploitation-tinged genre movies. The first acquisition was a quirky Hong Kong import, Wong Kar-Wai's "Chungking Express" (1994; released in the USA in 1996), an exquisitely stylized romantic comedy in police drama drag.

As a filmmaker, Tarantino returned to the screen to executive produce "Four Rooms" (1995), a poorly received comedy anthology, for which he also wrote, directed and starred in one segment. He fared better as executive producer, scripter and co-star of Rodriguez's "From Dusk Till Dawn" (1996), a moody, violent crime flick transformed halfway through into a gory special effects-laden vampire movie. The reviews were mixed but box office was brisk. Still in demand as an actor, Tarantino played an unsympathetic version of himself as "QT" in Spike Lee's sex comedy "Girl 6" (1996).

For his long-awaited follow-up feature, Tarantino adapted Elmore Leonard's novel "Rum Punch" and turned it into "Jackie Brown" (1997), a vehicle for actress Pam Grier. Those expecting "Pulp Fiction 2" were disappointed slightly, but the auteur fashioned a textured, satisfying story about a flight attendant (Grier) who conspires with a bail bondsman (Robert Forster) to take down a gun dealer (Samuel L. Jackson). While some critics carped over the film's length, most were enthralled with the script and the casting.

A great interview subject, Tarantino has quickly cultivated an intriguing public persona. He enjoys dual status as the "film geek who made good" and the reigning avatar of postmodern "cool." The latter quality is conveyed by the playful hipster tone of his protagonists, their retro clothing, a mastery of pop culture allusions and killer soundtracks. Eventually, the mere fact that Tarantino liked a particular film or performer became a marketable selling point.—Written by Kent Greene

COMPANIONS:

Allison Anders. Director; no longer together
Margaret Cho. Actor, comic; no longer together
Mira Sorvino. Actor; together from c. January 1996 to February 1998

MILESTONES:

1965: Moved, with mother, from Knoxville, Tennessee to Los Angeles (date approximate)
Raised in Los Angeles
Dropped out of high school at age 15 after ninth grade
Began studying acting
Began making (unfinished) first film, "My Best Friend's Birthday", from a screenplay co-written with Craig Hamann; they both co-starred
1985–1990: Spent five years working at Video Archives, a well-stocked video store in suburban Los Angeles; co-worker was future writing collaborator Roger Avary (dates approximate)
Hired with Avary as production assistants for a

Dolph Lundgren video after impressing John Langley—producer of Fox-TV's "Cops" and a regular customer at Video Archives—with their film knowledge

Working at Cinetel Productions, met future producer Lawrence Bender and finished script for "Reservoir Dogs"

1990: TV acting debut as an Elvis impersonator in an episode of "The Golden Girls"

1990: Commissioned to write a screenplay based on a 6-page story by Robert Kurtzman (co-founder of the special effects makeup company KNB Effects); eventually became "From Dusk Till Dawn"; was paid $1500 and offered free makeup effects on his "Reservoir Dogs"

1991: Co-founded A Band Apart Productions with producer Bender to make "Pulp Fiction" and subsequent projects

1992: Feature debut, co-wrote (with Avary), directed and acted in "Reservoir Dogs"

1992: Met future collaborator writer-director Robert Rodriguez at the Toronto Film Festival

1993: First film as screenwriter only, "True Romance", directed by Tony Scott

1994: Made career transforming feature, "Pulp Fiction"; directed, co-wrote and acted in

1994: Received strong notices for performance in "Sleep With Me"

1994: Played a cameo as a fast-talking bartender in Alexandre Rockwell's "Somebody to Love"

1994: Received story credit for Oliver Stone's "Natural Born Killers"

1994: First film as producer only, executive produced "Killing Zoe", Avary's debut as a writer-director

1994: Subject of profile, "Quentin Tarantino: Hollywood's Boy Wonder" on BBC-TV's "Omnibus" series

1995: With producer Bender, set up Rolling Thunder, a specialty distribution label under Miramax Pictures, designed to acquire, distribute and market four films a year

1995: With Bender, launched A Band Apart Commercials, a commercial production house under the Miramax banner

1995: Did a guest shot on the ABC sitcom "All-American Girl"

1995: Played first feature lead, Johnny Destiny in "Destiny Turns on the Radio", a romantic comedy-adventure

1995: TV directing debut, "Motherhood", an episode of the hit NBC medical drama "ER"

1995: Did an uncredited rewrite on Tony Scott's "Crimson Tide"

1995: First collaboration with writer-director Rodriguez, played a small role in "Desperado"

1996: Had earliest screenplay, "My Best Friend's Birthday", acquired by a number of old associates including former manager of seven years Cathryn James and "Natural Born Killers" producers Don Murphy and Jane Hamsher; rewrite assigned to Avary and the original co-writer Craig Hamann

1997: With Lawrence Bender, formed A Band Apart Records to market and distribute recordings made on Madonna's Maverick label

1997: Sued for $5 million by producer Don Murphy after Tarantino assaulted Murphy

1997: Wrote and directed "Jackie Brown", adapted from the Elmore Leonard novel "Rum Punch"; tailored leading role for actress Pam Grier

1998: Starred on stage opposite Marisa Tomei in a revival of "Wait Until Dark"

2000: Had featured role in "Little Nicky", starring Adam Sandler

2002: Played recurring role in episodes of the popular ABC drama series "Alias"

Wrote script "Kill Bill" for actress Uma Thurman; was scheduled to direct in 2001 but postponed after Thurman became pregnant; went before the cameras in 2002; released 2003

QUOTES:

From review of "Sleep With Me" by Todd McCarthy, *Daily Variety,* May 16, 1994: "But the extent to which energy and drama have been missing from the film is almost embarrassingly revealed by the strong final party. A hilarious recurring riff by helmer Quentin Tarantino, in which he delivers a convoluted but coherent interpretation of "Top Gun" as a gay film, packs more punch than anything else in the picture. . . . "

From review of "Pulp Fiction" by Todd McCarthy, *Daily Variety* May 23, 1994: "A spectacularly entertaining piece of pop culture, "Pulp Fiction" is the "American Graffitti" of violent crime pictures . . . Tarantino positions himself as the Preston Sturges of crimeland, putting the most incongruous words and thoughts into the mouths of lowdown, amoral characters."

While attending a screening for "Pulp Fiction" Tarantino allegedly stood up in the front row and asked the audience who among them liked his earlier films, "Reservoir Dogs" and "True Romance". After many hands were raised, he asked who liked "The Remains of the Day"; those who responded were told to "Get the f—k out of this theater."—From *Daily News,* June 26, 1994.

"Watching 'Pulp Fiction', you don't just get engrossed in what's happening on screen. You get intoxicated by it—high on the rediscovery of how pleasurable a movie can be. I'm not sure I've ever encountered a filmmaker who combined discipline and control with sheer wild-ass joy the way Tarantino does. For 2 hours and 35 minutes, we're drawn into the lives of violently impassioned underworld characters—hit men, drug dealers, lethal vamps—who become figments of fury and grace and desire. We're caught up in dialogue of such fiendishly elaborate wit it suggests a Martin Scorsese film written by Preston Sturges, in plot twists—they're closer to zigzags—that are like whims bubbling up from the director's unconscious. 'Pulp Fiction' is the work of a new-style punk virtuoso. It is, quite simply, the most exhilarating piece of filmmaking to come along in the nearly five years I've been writing." —From Owen Gleiberman's review of "Pulp Fiction", *Entertainment Weekly,* October 14, 1994.

Tarantino's nomination for Outstanding Directorial Achievement by the Directors Guild of America for "Pulp Fiction" made him the first American-born non-DGA member to be so honored.

As a guest on PBS' "Charlie Rose" (from c. 1994 around the time of the release of "Pulp Fiction"; rebroadcast on August 25, 1995), Tarantino revealed the titles of his three favorite films: "Rio Bravo" (Howard Hawks, 1959); "Taxi Driver" (Martin Scorsese, 1976); and "Blow Out" (Brian DePalma, 1981).

From "Take Cover! Tarantino Forms Rolling Thunder" by Kirk Honeycutt, *The Hollywood Reporter,* July 14, 1995: Tarantino said he is patterning Rolling Thunder on World Northal, a US distribution company that released most of the major kung fu movies in the 1970s. "I want dynamic, visceral films that are exploitation in nature. It says something that the most dynamic, in-your-face foreign movie currently in release is 'Belle de Jour'," Tarantino said, referring to Miramax's recent release of Luis Bunuel's 1967 classic.

Tarantino said he and Bender intend to estabish two theaters in both New York and Los Angeles where Rolling Thunder films will open initially and—depending on a film's success—will go out to other cities later. He said that Hong Kong kung fu films would be released with new subtitles he would supervise in the New York and L.A. houses, but would be released in dubbed versions in urban areas to attract black and Latino audiences.

From "Take Cover! Tarantino Forms Rolling Thunder" by Kirk Honeycutt, *The Hollywood Reporter,* July 14, 1995: The logo for Rolling Thunder, which Tarantino described as "the image of a big bloody hook swooping down," is being designed by Robert Rodriguez, who is currently directing "From Dusk Till Dawn", a vampire thriller starring and written by Tarantino. The label's name refers to the title of a 1977 American International Pictures revenge melodrama about a Vietnam vet whose family is murdered and whose hand is forced down a garbage disposal, causing him to wear a hook for the rest of the movie.

"It's one of my favorite movies," Tarantino said.

"Reflecting on the cost of fame, he told *Details*, "Since designers starting sending me free stuff to wear, it's kind of taken the fun out of shopping." Even worse, he complains to *Us*, "I'd like to hang out with Warren Beatty. I don't have the time." —From "Talking Movies: Tarantino's Trajectory" by Anna Scotti, *Buzz* (April 1996).

BIBLIOGRAPHY:

"Quentin Tarantino: Shooting From the Hip" Wensley Clarkson, 1995, Overlook Press; biography

"Quentin Tarantino: The Cinema of Cool" Jeff Dawson, 1995, Applause Books; biography

"Quentin Tarantino: The Man and His Movies" Jami Bernard, 1995, HarperPerennial paperback; biography

Andrei Tarkovsky

BORN: in Laovrazhe, Ivanov, USSR, 04/04/1932

SOMETIMES CREDITED AS:
Andrei Tarkovski

DEATH: in Paris, France, 12/29/1986

NATIONALITY: Russian

EDUCATION: Soviet School of Music
Institute of Oriental Languages Arabic 1952 marks year of enrollment
VGIK Moscow, Russia 1956–60 graduated; studied under Mikhail Romm; graduate film entitled "The Steamroller and the Violin" (1960)

AWARDS: Venice Film Festival Golden Lion "Ivan's Childhood" 1962
Cannes Film Festival International Critics Prize "Andrei Rublev" 1969
Cannes Film Festival Special Jury Prize "Solaris" 1972
Cannes Film Festival Grand Prix du Cinema de Creation "Nostalgia" 1983
Cannes Film Festival FIPRESCI Prize "Nostalgia" 1983
Cannes Film Festival Special Jury Prize "The Sacrifice" 1986

BIOGRAPHY
Distinguished Soviet director whose austerely poetic, deeply personal films made him one of the most treasured artists of his generation.

Tarkovsky followed his prize-winning short diploma piece, "The Steamroller and the Violin" (1960), with a lyrical feature debut "My Name is Ivan/Ivan's Childhood" (1962). The film portrays a young boy's espionage activities with the Partisans during WWII and was awarded top honors at the Venice Film Festival. Tarkovsky followed it with the epic, allegorical "Andrei Roublev" (1966).

Over three years in the making, "Andrei Roublev" follows the life of a 15th-century icon painter as he loses faith in society, god and art, finally achieving spiritual revitalization in the famous, concluding bell-making scene. Shelved for several years for its references to the plight of the contemporary Soviet artist, the film was released to wide acclaim in the West in 1969. Like most of Tarkovsky's work, it is a slow-moving, sumptuously textured canvas with a richly emotional climax.

Most of Tarkovsky's subsequent films deal in some degree with the other-worldly; in "Solaris" (1971), a space-traveler's fantasies are conjured into reality; "Stalker" (1979) takes place in "the zone," a mysterious, forbidden wasteland; and "The Sacrifice" (1986) unfolds in the final hours before a nuclear armageddon. "The Mirror" (1974), an intensely personal, multi-layered aural and visual poem, recalls an artist's youth in the Soviet Union during WWII. Tarkovsky's real-life mother plays the mother of the artist and his father, the esteemed poet Arseniy Tarkovsky, reads his own works on the soundtrack.

Tarkovsky began working outside the USSR in the early 1980s, making "Nostalgia" (which he himself described as "tedious") in Italy in 1983. He then employed several members of Ingmar Bergman's filmmaking team, including actor Erland Josephson and cinematographer Sven Nykvist, to make "The Sacrifice" (1986) in Sweden. Josephson plays a celebrated, retired artist/intellectual who can only avert a worldwide holocaust by making a supreme personal sacrifice. Visually sumptuous and extremely slow-paced (the opening shot is nearly ten minutes long), the film is a supreme summation of what Tarkovsky considered his most crucial concern: "the absence in our culture of room for spiritual existence." "The

Sacrifice" won a Special Jury Prize at Cannes in the same year that Tarkovsky died of lung cancer in Paris at age 54.—Written by Stuart Kauffman

MILESTONES:

1959: Directed first short, "There Will Be No Leave Today"

1962: Debut as feature film director, "Ivan's Childhood"

1966: "Andrei Rublev" banned by Soviet authorities (was shown in Cannes, 1969 but not released in Soviet Union until 1971)

1983: Shot first film out of Soviet Union, "Nostalgia" (in Italy)

1984: Defected to the West (July)

BIBLIOGRAPHY:

"Andrej Tarkovkij" A. Frezzato, 1977, published in Italy

Jacques Tati

BORN: in Le Pecq, France, 10/09/1908

SOMETIMES CREDITED AS:
Jacques Tatischeff

DEATH: 11/05/1982

NATIONALITY: French

EDUCATION: Lycee Inernational St. Germain-en-Laye, France

sent to trade school to learn picture framing and conservation; left after one year

attended college of arts and engineering, 1924

AWARDS: Venice Film Festival Best Script Award "Jour de Fete" 1949

Grand Prix du Cinema Francais "Jour de Fete" 1949

Cannes Film Festival International Critics Prize "Les vacances de M. Hulot/Mr. Hulot's Holiday" 1953

Prix Louis Delluc "Les vacances de M. Hulot/Mr. Hulot's Holiday" 1953

Cannes Film Festival Special Jury Prize "Mon oncle/My Uncle" 1958

New York Film Critics Circle Award Best Foreign Film "Mon oncle"/My Uncle 1958

Prix Melies Best Foreign Film "Mon oncle"/My Uncle 1958

Grand Prix National des Arts et des Lettres in Cinema 1979

Honorary Cesar 1977 cited with Henri Langlois

BIOGRAPHY

Jacques Tati is a chess master of modern film comedy, a creator of complex comic structures in which gag constructions and audience expectations become pawns on his cinematic board. The recurring figure in these games is Monsieur Hulot (played by the director), a blank-faced comic cipher garbed in a crumbled raincoat and ill-fitting trousers, an ever-present pipe muffling any words he may say, an umbrella clutched in indecisive hands. His determinedly irresolute stride across Tati's expansive canvases is the unlikely spark that sets the comic machinery afire. On the basis of a mere four features ("Mr. Hulot's Holiday" 1953; "Mon Oncle" 1958; "Playtime" 1967; and "Traffic" 1971) over a 20-year period, Tati managed to reshape slapstick comedy, turning it into an intellectual parlor game.

Tati began performing in French music halls and cafes as a pantomimist and impersonator. In 1931, he filmed a comedy short, "Oscar, Champion de Tennis," but it was never completed. Following were a number of short films which anticipated his later features in their use of natural and mechanical sounds—"On Demande une brute" (1934), "Gai dimanche" (1935), and "Soigne ton gauche" (1936). After WWII, Tati appeared in the features "Sylvie et le Fantome" (1945) and "Le Diable au corps" (1946). In his short film, "L'Ecole de facteurs" (1947), Tati created the character of Francois the postman, a character he would play himself in his first self-directed feature, "Jour de Fete" (1948). "Jour" used the riffing gag structure Tati would explore more fully in his later features, plus creative sound as a source for gags.

Unhappy with the Francois character, Tati sought a persona with a more universal appeal. With Monsieur Hulot, Tati found his cosmic archetype: a zero who creates comic anarchy in his wake. In "Mr. Hulot's Holiday", Tati applies Hulot to the gag structures of "Jour de Fete." "Mon Oncle" deals with the tension between Hulot's old world sensibilities and the new world of modern mechanization and consumerism. "Playtime", Tati's masterpiece, released in 70mm and stereophonic sound, examines the disappearance of humanity within the maze-like confines of post-industrial society. "Traffic" portrays the anthropomorphism of automobiles and the mechanization of human beings.

Tati's cold, crisp examinations are a result of his re-inventing film comedy structures. Hulot has no purpose except to ignite the gag machinery. He is never the center of a gag sequence and frequently disappears from the gag situation once the perpetual motion machine takes hold. (In one sequence in "Playtime," Hulot appears merely as a reflection in a glass window.) Once the gag machinery begins, Tati subverts the punchline by either delaying it or ignoring it altogether. The result creates a tension for audience expectations: will the punchline continue to be prolonged or simply demolished? Tati does not allow his audience to identify with the main character in the scene; as a result, the subject of the shot becomes everything that appears within the frame. A Tati film is characterized by a tangled texture (especially on his densely packed soundtracks) that requires many viewings to unravel.

This complexity was Tati's commercial undoing; because of the prolonged preparations required to plan his films, Tati lost his audience. The nine-year gap between "Mon Oncle" and "Playtime" crippled the momentum of his career, and after the extravagances of "Playtime," Tati never recovered financially. When "Traffic" was released, it seemed a throwback to his films before "Playtime" and was a financial failure. In 1974, Tati released his final film, "Parade," a low-budget celebration of pantomime recalling his shorts from the thirties.

Although Tati influenced filmmakers as diverse as Jerry Lewis and Robert Altman, his career seems in a way to be both the beginning and the end of a comic tradition. Nevertheless, Tati's structural experiments did breathe life for a time into a moribund form.

MILESTONES:

1924: Apprenticed to Spiller's, a British picture-framer, in London (date approximate)

Worked briefly as professional rugby player

1924–1930: Worked as amateur entertainer, performing sports-related pantomimes in London

1931: Returned to France and became professional cabaret and music hall entertainer

1932: Experiments as filmmaker—writing, directing and starring in short, "Oscar, champion de tennis"

1934: Major recognition on stage at the Ritz on bill with Maurice Chevalier

1938: Debut as producer, "Retour a la terre" (also starred)

1946: Directorial debut, short "L'Ecole des facteurs"

1949: Directed and starred in first feature film, "Jour de fete/The Big Day"

1961: Created play, "Jour de fete a Olympia", based on "Jour de fete"

1971: After failure of "Traffic," creditors seized Tati's assets, impounding all his previous features

1973: Directed first program for Swedish TV, "Parade"

1977: Paris distributor paid off Tati's $1.6 million debt and re-released impounded features

QUOTES:
Made Commandeur des Arts et des Lettres

Julie Taymor

BORN: in Boston, Massachusetts, 12/15/1952

NATIONALITY: American

EDUCATION: Julia Portman's Theatre Workshop, Boston, Massachusetts

Newton High School, Newton, Massachusetts, 1969; graduated at age 16

L'Ecole Mimet Theatre, Paris, France; studied mime with Jacques LeCoq

Oberlin College, Oberlin, Ohio, folklore and mythology, BA, 1974; member of Phi Beta Kappa

HB Studio, New York, New York, acting; studied for one year during college; school was previously named Herbert Berghof Studio

AWARDS: Joseph Maharam Design Award "The Haggadah" 1980

Joseph Maharam Award "Tirai" 1981

Special OBIE Award 1984/85; presented for "visual magic"

OBIE Award Direction "Juan Darien, A Carnival Mass" 1987/88

Outer Critics Circle Award Outstanding Director of a Musical "The Lion King" 1998

Outer Critics Circle Award Outstanding Costume Design "The Lion King" 1998

Drama Desk Award Outstanding Director of a Musical "The Lion King" 1998

Drama Desk Award Outstanding Costume Design "The Lion King" 1998

Drama Desk Award Outstanding Puppet Design "The Lion King" 1998; shared award with Michael Curry

Tony Director of a Musical "The Lion King" 1998; first woman ever to win award for directing a musical

Tony Costume Designer "The Lion King" 1998

Boston Theatre Critics Association Elliot Norton Award for Sustained Excellence 1998

Grammy Musical Show Album "The Lion King" 1999; shared award

Evening Standard Award Theatrical Event "The Lion King" 1999; initial presentation

Olivier Award Best Costume Design "The Lion King" 2000

Dora Mavor Moore Award Outstanding Costume Design "The Lion King" 2000

L.A. Ovation Award Director (Musical) "The Lion King" 2001

L.A. Ovation Award Costumes (Large production) "The Lion King" 2001

BIOGRAPHY

One of the most cerebral and experimental of theatrical directors and designers, whose fusion of folklore, puppetry and intellectually demanding themes made her a favorite of those with a taste for the cutting edge, Julie Taymor worked almost exclusively in the world of the not-for-profit theater before bringing her downtown sensibility uptown as director of "The Lion King" (1997), Disney's remarkable marriage of art and commerce at Broadway's New Amsterdam Theater. The media giant's deep pockets enabled her to experiment with new kinds of puppetry, to sculpt, to build and to test, resulting in what *The New York Times* called "the most memorable, moving and original theatrical extravaganza in years." Disney did not compromise Taymor's distinctive Indonesian-influenced minimalist style of mixing live actors, puppets, shadows and masks, and she picked up two Tony Awards (directing and costumes) for her first exposure to mainstream audiences, drawing comparisons to such legends as Bob Fosse, Michael Bennett and Harold Prince.

Taymor's theatrical roots run deep. The Newton, MA native's backyard performances for family and friends at age seven led to her playing Cinderella (despite preferring the wicked step-sisters), among other roles, with the Boston Children's Theater. Her first exposure to Asian theater came while visiting Sri Lanka and India on a cultural exchange program at 15. She also studied mime in Paris before beginning her folklore and mythology studies at Oberlin College, where she joined Herbert Blau's experimental theater company, which included teaching assistant Bill Irwin. After graduation, Taymor went to Indonesia for four years, courtesy of Watson and Ford Foundation fellowships, and developed a mask-dance troupe, Teatr Loh, living with one of the actors in a small compound with a dirt floor and no running water, electricity, or telephone. The tensions she witnessed as a slow-moving individualistic culture confronted the fast pace of consumer-driven change inspired her first major theater work, "Way of Snow", performed by an international company of actors, musicians, dancers and puppeteers.

Taymor designed her first US production, "The Odyssey" (1979), at the Baltimore Stage, then received her first NYC acclaim as production designer for Elizabeth Swados' "The Haggadah" (1980), creating a giant seder tablecloth that billowed up, Peking Opera-style, to become the Red Sea, not to mention life-size puppet rabbis debating Passover scholarship, and alarmingly graphic plague effects projected through Plexiglas shadow puppets. A mutual friend sent composer Elliot Goldenthal to see the show, calling it "just as grotesque" as his own work, and Taymor and he soon become companions, as well as co-creators of "Liberty's Taken" (1985), an irreverent look at the American Revolution, produced in Boston and featuring a bobbing-wooden-heads-on-wheels device to satirize the morality legislating Boston Committee of Safety. There are tentative plans to make movies out of two Goldenthal-Taymor collaborations, their mask-and-puppet adaptation of Thomas Mann's fantastical novella "Transposed Heads" (1986) and "Juan Darien, A Carnival Mass" (1988), which Lincoln Center revived in 1996, giving Taymor her first Broadway credit.

As visually rich as it was musically complex, "Juan Darien" blended rain forest rhythms, the Latin Mass and Day of the Dead imagery to tell the story of an orphaned jaguar cub, nursed to health and, miraculously, into the human form of a boy, Juan Darien, by a woman who lost her own son to a plague. Combining elaborate costumes and various forms of puppetry—from the Japanese bunraku style of large, eerily life-like wooden figures manipulated by black-clad puppeteers to simple hand puppets à la Punch and Judy—"Juan Darien" follows the boy's life up to his flogging and crucifixion and resurrection in jaguar form. All the human characters but one (Juan) wore masks designed by Taymor, haunting oversize heads reminiscent of primitive art and tribal carvings. Her staging resembled a kind of theater-cinema, suggesting the three-dimensional equivalent of pans, tracking shots, and close-ups as full-scale characters and sets shifted to miniatures that turned and moved through stage-space. It was genius, pure and simple, but a little overwhelming for the Lincoln Center membership audience.

Disney, hewing to the artistic high road, gambled that Taymor's genius could sell tickets, and she, for her part, preserved the essence of "The Lion King" franchise characters, while placing her distinctive stamp on them. A soft, furry, bland animal story was anathema to her, so she created puppets and masks with a sharp-edged, rough-hewn look that continued her trademark obscuring of the lines between actor and puppet and costume. Cable-operated masks hang over the actors playing the lions like headdresses, suggesting ancient religious masks, but when the lions turn aggressive, the masks lower smoothly to cover the actors' faces. One low-tech to high-effect sequence involves the brilliant sea of savanna that as it grows reveals the actors underneath, wearing tables of savanna-like hats, but her masterstroke was to create life-size animal puppets operated by actors in full view of the audience. A giraffe, for instance, is actually an actor wearing a cone-like giraffe neck and head—balanced on arm and leg stilts. It was this idea of the "duality of the puppet and the actor" that sold Disney, and the company did not balk at her changing male monkey Rafiki into a female baboon-cum-shaman, allowing a darker tone to underscore lion cub Simba's journey to adulthood, and merging South African music with Elton John's pop tunes.

Taymor took a story that everybody knew (the 1994 film grossed more than $450 million worldwide) and elevated it to a theatrical event that will play for years. This is in stark contrast to all her other work that enjoyed only limited runs, like her 1992 staging of Stravinsky's opera "Oedipus Rex" (conducted by Seiji Ozawa) in Japan, employing a cast of 120, which played only two days, or her 1993 production in Florence, Italy of Mozart's "The Magic Flute", running fewer than a dozen performances. Besieged with opportunities since her incredible success, Taymor, whose only prior work for the screen was a hallucinatory short film for PBS ("Fool's Fire" 1992), made her feature directing debut with an adaptation of Shakespeare's "Titus Andronicus" (lensed 1998), based on her bloody 1994 stage version at NYC's Theatre for a New Audience. Taymor's artsy, edgy and avant garde take on Shakespeare's early drama, complete with music video-style editing and cinematography, was definitely a lightning rod for discussion, with some praising its ingenuity and daring and others offended by its goriness and lack of reverence for the source material. She attempted to launch a film version of "The Magic Flute" but the project languished in development. Her next directorial effort, the biopic "Frida" for star and producer Salma Hayek, was deemed far more conventional, albeit visual arresting, and the tamer Taymor disappointed many aficionados who admired her earlier boldness and daring. On the horizon is a long-discussed exploration of "Grendel", a proposed opera in collaboration with Goldenthal based on John Gardner's novel about Beowulf from the monster's point of view, and "The Flying Dutchman," a modern-day film adaptation of Wagner's opera.—Written by Greg Senf

COMPANION:

Elliot Goldenthal. Composer; first met c. 1980; have worked together on a number of productions; born c. 1954; nominated for Academy Awards for his scoring of "Interview with a Vampire" and "Michael Collins"

MILESTONES:

Raised in Newton, Massachusetts, where she began performing backyard theater for her family at the age of seven

Performed as a child with the Boston Children's Theatre; played Cinderella, among other roles

1968: Lived in Sri Lanka as part of an exchange program when she was 15; traveled to India (date approximate)

Spent part of her senior year in high school studying mime in Paris

While in college, spent part of a year studying acting in NYC

Acted with several theater companies in NYC including the Open Theatre and Bread and Puppet Theater

Joined Herbert Blau's experimental theater company Kraken, headquartered at Oberlin; fellow actors included Bill Irwin; company disbanded c. 1974

1974: Received a Watson Traveling Fellowship to study in Asia

1974: Visited Indonesia; remained there rather than travel through Asia

While in Indonesia, formed Teatr Loh with partial funding from the Ford Foundation

1976: First interdisciplinary stage production, "Way of Snow", combined elements of Eskimo, Indonesian and American culture; incorporated masks, shadow puppets, and Javanese-style rod puppets that Taymor carved herself from a cotton tree outside her house

Created second show "Tirai"

1979: Returned to the USA (date approximate)

1979: Designed first US stage production, "The Odyssey" at Baltimore Stage

1980: Received acclaim in NYC for her designs for Elizabeth Swados' stage production "The Haggadah"

1980: Worked on "Black Elk Lives"

1984: Provided visual concept and designed puppets for the American Repertory Theatre's staging of "The King Stag"

1985: Directed and co-wrote (with Eliot Goldenthal) "Liberty's Taken", an irreverent look at the American Revolution, produced in Boston

1986: Staged production of Shakespeare's "The Tempest"; character of Ariel was represented by a Japanese bunraku puppet; recreated staging in 1987 and 1992

1986: Directed "The Transposed Heads", a collaboration with Goldenthal at the American Musical Theatre Festival; also co-adapted

1988: With Goldenthal, created "Juan Darien, A Carnival Mass"; produced Off-Broadway; Taymor designed, directed and co-wrote the show

1992: TV debut as director, producer and writer, "Fool's Fire", an adaptation of Edgar Allen Poe's story "Hopfrog" produced for PBS' "American Playhouse"

1992: Directed Stravinsky's opera "Oedipus Rex" in Japan, featuring a 70-person orchestra and a cast of 120, including legendary diva Jessye Norman (conducted by Seiji Ozawa); production recreated for PBS in 1993

1993: Staged Mozart's "The Magic Flute" (conducted by Zubin Mehta) in Florence, Italy

1994: Directed Shakespeare's "Titus Andronicus" at the Theatre for a New Audience

1995: Had Off-Broadway critical success with "The Green Bird", created in collaboration with Goldenthal

1996: "Juan Darien" revived and played on Broadway; received Tony nomination as Best Musical; Taymor nominated as Best Director of a Musical and Best Scenic Designer

1997: Designed, contributed to the book and score and staged the Broadway version of Disney's "The Lion King"; show received 11 Tony Award nominations including Best Musical, Best Book, Best Score, Best Director of a Musical and Best Costume Designer; won six Tony Awards including Best Musical, Best Director and Best Cosutme Designer

1999: Feature directorial debut with "Titus", an adaptation of Shakespeare's tragedy "Titus Andronicus" co-starring Anthony Hopkins and Jessica Lange

2002: Directed second feature. "Frida", a biopic of Mexican artist Frida Kahlo, starring Salma Hayek

QUOTES:

Taymor received a Guggenheim Fellowship in 1990 and a MacArthur Foundation "genius" grant in 1991.

Her production of Stravinsky's "Oedipus Rex" won 1992's International Classical Music Award for best opera prodution.

Received an honorary degree from Columbia University in 1999

"We have a ways to go in understanding the power of puppetry, Our problem is for too long we have thought of puppets as being for children,"—Julie Taymor in *The New York Times*, July 2, 1991.

"Julie is uncategorizable as an artist." —Stephen Sondheim in *The New York Times* magazine, March 22, 1992.

To those who would say a mainstreaming of her talent can only mean dilution: "You don't have to sell out. It's easier for me to work with Disney now than 15 years ago. I have enough history now. I have a track record. This is what I do, and if you don't want what I do, get somebody else.

"I studied folklore and mythology in college, and that's the same territory Disney has been traipsing in."—Julie Taymor to *USA Today*, July 28, 1997.

About her creations for "The Lion King": "I want the people to be aware of both the puppet and the actor. I don't want to upstage the puppet, but I also want people to see the actor, too. That way they can watch it on different levels. They can focus on the puppet or they can focus on the actor or they can focus on the way both of them are working together."—Taymor in *The New York Times*, October 14, 1997.

With masks, "you have to abstract the essence of the character in one fell swoop. One face has to cover all the expressions—tenderness, sorrow, fear and anger."—Julie Taymor quoted by *USA Today*, November 14, 1997.

Recalling a meeting with Michael Eisner of Disney: "I said, 'Now, Michael, if you hide the wheels, what you'll have is traditional puppet theater. But the audience knows that's pretend, so why not let them in on how it's done? The magic is showing how one actor can make seven gazelles leap through the air.' "—Taymor in *Daily News*, November 11, 1997.

BIBLIOGRAPHY:

"Julie Taymor: Playing with Fire: Theater, Opera, Film" Eileen Blumenthal, 1996, Harry N. Abrams Inc.

Andre Techine

BORN: in Valence d'Agen, France 03/13/1943

NATIONALITY: French

AWARDS: Cannes Film Festival Direction Award "Rendez-vous" 1985

Cesar Best Director "Les Roseaux sauvages/ Wild Reeds" 1995

Cesar Best Screenplay "Les Roseaux sauvages/ Wild Reeds" 1995 shared award with Gilles Taurand and Olivier Massart

New York Film Critics Circle Award Best Foreign Film "Wild Reeds" 1995

Los Angles Film Critics Circle Award Best Foreign Language Film "Wild Reeds" 1995

National Society of Film Critics Award Best Foreign Language Film "Wild Reeds" 1995

Boston Society of Film Critics Award Best

Foreign Language Film "Ma Saison Preferee/My Favorite Season" 1996

BIOGRAPHY

Wide-eyed country boy Andre Techine relocated to Paris from his provincial hometown in southwest France at the age of 19 and, though he did not gain admittance to his country's top film school, was soon writing movie reviews for the prestigious *Cahiers du Cinema*. He made his directorial debut with "Pauline s'en va" (1969) and followed with "Souvenirs d'en France" (1976), while providing screenplays for other directors (i.e., Liliane Dekermadec's "Aloise" 1975). He demonstrated his flair for richly textured, atmospheric storytelling with the aptly titled thriller "Barocco" (1977), starring Gerard Depardieu and Isabelle Adjani, but faltered somewhat with the sluggish, well-crafted "The Bronte Sisters" (1978)—worthwhile mainly for the superlative performances of Isabelle Huppert, Marie-France Pisier and Adjani, as well as the sole dramatic outing of literary theorist Roland Barthes (a fan of Techine's) in the role of William Thackery. The director himself has said: "I think my first films were too theoretical. They were too inspired by cinema, and not by real life."

"Hotel des Ameriques/Hotel of the Americas" (1981) marked the first time Techine let his actors improvise, a practice he has continued ever since, adjusting his scripts to accommodate the new material. It was also his first time directing Catherine Deneuve, and three films later, having played unglamorous, matronly roles to stretch her repertoire, she was still enthusiastic about working with him: "There are some directors who are more feminine than others, like Techine, like Truffaut. They are an exceptional gift to actresses." Juliette Binoche found that out as the star of "Rendez-Vous" (1985), a stylishly engrossing tale of obsessive sexuality which earned him the Cannes Festival Best Direction Award. Binoche was outstanding in her first lead role as an innocent provincial girl who arrives in Paris to pursue a career in the theater. Given the

choice of the apparently virginal Wadeck Stanczak and his seedy roommate Lambert Wilson (playing an actor in a sex show), she opts to indulge her hedonistic impulses with the fascinating, repelling Wilson, his eventual demise profoundly maturing the once carefree girl.

Techine's poignant coming-of-age saga "Les Roseaux sauvages/Wild Reeds" (1994) earned him Cesars for his direction and screenplay and took honors as Best Picture. His first film released in the USA (in 1995) and his most autobiographical picture to date (the sensitive Francois discovering he is gay clearly an alter ego for the helmer) centered on the inner turmoil of a trio of youngsters at a provincial boarding school in 1962 and evoked the effect the Algerian War had on rural France. As Francois' platonic best friend Maite, Elodie Bouchez was nothing short of a revelation, garnering a Cesar as Most Promising Newcomer—Female. For his next two features released in the USA, Techine guided Deneuve to her most self-revelatory performances in years. "Ma Saison preferee/My Favorite Season" (1993, released in USA in April 1996) cast her and Daniel Auteuil as estranged siblings forced together by the decline of their ailing mother, while "Les Voleurs/Thieves" (1996), using the crime genre as a starting point, paired them in a "Rashomon"-style exploration of family and amorous ties. Techine's "Alice and Martin" (1998), a haunting love story between two emotionally damaged outsiders, reteamed him with Binoche, whose subtly nuanced performance as she moved from insecurity to almost obsessive purpose lent a dignity to her character that was the abiding memory of the film.

MILESTONES:

1962: Moved to Paris from home in southwest France at the age of 19 (date approximate)

Failed to gain admittance to France's top film school

Began writing movie reviews for the prestigious magazine *Cahiers du Cinema*

1969: Directorial debut, "Pauline s'en va"

1973: Made uncredited acting appearance in Jean Eustache's "The Mother and the Whore"

1975: Co-wrote (with director) the screenplay for Liliane Dekermadec's "Aloise"; first association with Isabelle Huppert

1976: Scripted and helmed "Barocco", starring Gerard Depardieu and Isabelle Adjani

1978: Directed "The Bronte Sisters", starring Adjani (as Emily), Huppert (as Anne) and Marie-France Pisier (as Charlotte); co-wrote script with Pascal Bonitzer and Jean Gruault

1982: First film with Catherine Deneuve, "Hotel des Ameriques/Hotel of the Americas"

1985: Won the Cannes Festival Best Direction Award for "Rendez-Vous", starring Juliette Binoche; co-wrote screenplay with *Cahiers du Cinema* critic Olivier Assayas

1986: Reteamed with Deneuve for "Le Lieu de crime/The Scene of the Crime"; second screenplay collaboration with Bonitzer

1993: First film with actor Daniel Auteuil, "Ma saison preferee/My Favorite Season"; also co-starred Deneuve; film released in USA in 1996

1994: Scored big hit with "Les Roseaux sauvages/Wild Reeds", winning Cesars for direction and screenplay; first film released in USA

1996: Reteamed with Deneuve and Auteuil for "Les Voleurs/Thieves"; fifth screenplay on which Techine shared credit with Bonitzer

1998: Reteamed with Binoche for "Alice and Martin" (released in the USA in 1999)

QUOTES:

His last name is pronounced TESH-ee-nay

Techine served on the jury at the 1999 Cannes Film Festival

"Films were my only opening to the world. They were my only possibiltiy of escaping my family environment and my boarding school. It was probably dangerous because, through movies, I learned how the world works and how human relations work. But it was magical, and I was determined to follow the thread of that magic . . .

"I never know how each film will end. When I'm filming, I shoot each scene as if it were a short film. It's only when I edit that I worry about the narrative. My objective is to tell a story, but that's the final thing I do."
—Andre Techine quoted in *The New York Times*, December 30, 1996

Giuseppe Tornatore

BORN: in Bagheria, Sicily, Italy, 05/27/1956

SOMETIMES CREDITED AS:
Guiseppe Tornatore
Salvatore Giuseppe Tornatore

NATIONALITY: Italian

AWARDS: Salerno Film Festival Best Documentary Award "Le minoranza etniche in Sicilia/Ethnic Minorities in Sicily" 1982

Cannes Film Festival Special Jury Prize "Cinema Paradiso" 1989

BAFTA Award Best Screenplay "Cinema Paradiso" 1990

BAFTA Award Best Film Not in English "Cinema Paradiso" 1990; shared with Franco Cristaldi

Venice Film Festival Special Jury Prize "The Star Maker" 1995; award shared with Joao Cesar Monteiro for "A Comedia de Deus"

David Di Donatello Prize Best Director "Star Maker" 1996

Nastri d'Argento Best Director "The Legend of the Pianist on the Ocean" 1998

Nastri d'Argento Best Screenplay "The Legend of the Pianist on the Ocean" 1998

David Di Donatello Prize Best Director "The Legend of the Pianist on the Ocean"

BIOGRAPHY

Sicilian-born Giuseppe Tornatore proved a prodigy of sorts, beginning his career as a prize-winning still photographer. While in his mid-teens, he began directing, first for the stage and then by making the short film "Il Carretto/The Wagon." Eventually Tornatore caught the attention of RAI television and was hired to hem documentaries and TV-movies. In 1982, he garnered attention for his documentary "Ethnic Minorities in Sicily," which picked up a prize at the Salerno Film Festival. He shifted to fictional features co-writing the script to 1983's "Centro Giorni a Palermo/A Hundred Days in Palermo." Three years later, he debuted his first full-length feature as director, "Il Camorrista/The Professor/The Cammora Murder" (1986), a drama about a journalist who runs afoul of gangsters.

As he began to earn notoriety, Tornatore caught the attention of producer Franco Castaldi who nurtured what became the director's breakthrough film. When "Nuevo Cinema Paradiso" opened in Rome in 1988, it met with a less than stellar reception. The director, who favors long takes, worked under Castaldi's prodding and guidance, to cut and reshape the material. The new version debuted at the 1989 Cannes Film Festival where it was met with high praise and picked up a Special Jury Prize. A sentimental but powerful paean to the power of the movies set in Tornatore's hometown, "Cinema Paradiso" depicted the odd friendship between a movie-loving boy and the projectionist at the local theater. Audiences around the world responded positively, particularly to its tour de force final sequence of censored clips, and the film went on to win numerous awards and prizes including the 1989 Academy Award as Best Foreign-Language Film. "Stanno Tutti Bene/Everybody's Fine"

(1990) proved a slightly disappointing follow-up, however. Trafficking in the director's now trademarked sentimental style, the movie revolved around an aging widower (well played by Marcello Mastroianni) who decides to visit his children and learns that each has been lying to him about their lives. While the intriguing premise of depicting a parent's aspirations for his children offered great potential, Tornatore tended to dilute its power by focusing more on the landscapes of his travels and "Everybody's Fine" was deemed a failure. After contributing a segment to the anthology film "La Domenica Specialmente/Especially on Sunday" (1991), the filmmaker returned to his native area to teach aesthetics at the University of Palermo. Resuming his film career in 1994, Tornatore wrote, directed and edited the fascinating, if eccentric, thriller "Una Pura Formalita/A Pure Formality." Dropping his usual sentimentality, he instead focused on a cat-and-mouse game of interrogation between a police inspector (Roman Polanski) and a suspected murderer (Gerard Depardieu). While the setting was mostly held to a poorly lit room in the local police station, the director managed to make the proceedings interesting not only through his expert editing and fluid camera movement but also by eliciting strong performances from his two leads.

Slipping back into his usual style, Tornatore next fashioned "L'Uomo delle Stelle/The Star Maker" (1995), what many see as a companion piece to "Cinema Paradiso." Returning to the Sicily of the 1950s, the titular character is a con man who preys on the hopes and dreams of villagers by pretending to be a talent scout. Complications ensue when an aspiring actress stows away in his van and the pair embark on a romance. Ravishingly photographed by Dante Spinotti and featuring a lovely score by Ennio Morricone, Despite some mixed reviews (which felt the film was more travelogue than compelling drama), it earned a 1995 Oscar nomination for Best Foreign-Language Film.

For his next major film, Tornatore turned to a one-man stage monologue for inspiration. A modern fable about a musical prodigy who spends his entire life on board the ship on which he was born, "The Legend of 1900/La Leggenda del Pianista sull'Oceano/The Legend of the Pianist on the Ocean" (1998) marked Tornatore's first English-language film. Lushly scored by Morricone and starring Tim Roth as the adult musician, it debuted in Italy with a running time of nearly three hours. Critics hailed several of the set pieces (most notably a piano duel between Roth's character and Jelly Roll Morton, played by Clarence Williams III) but felt the overall narrative was too slight to handle the epic-like treatment afforded. Even in its US debut in 1999, with nearly an hour cut and a new title ("The Legend of 1900"), many still felt the simple story was overblown.

MILESTONES:

Won awards from various Italian photography magazines

1972: Directed two stage plays, "Bella Vita" and "L'Arte della Commedia"

1972: Made first short film, "Il Carretto/The Wagon" (date approximate)

1978–1985: Served as president of CLCT Cooperative

1979: Hired by RAI Television where he directed such films as "Diario di Guttuso" and "Brancati and Sciascia"

1982: Garnered attention with the documentary "Ethnic Minorities in Sicily"

1983: Co-screenwriting debut, "Centro giorni a Palermo/A Hundred Days in Palermo"; also served as second unit director; film produced by CLCT Cooperative

1986: Feature film directorial debut, "Il Camorrista/The Professor"; also penned screenplay

1988: Wrote and directed second film, "Cinema Paradiso"; opened theatrically in Rome; after editing and reshaping, shown in competition at the 1989 Cannes Film Festival; garnered the 1989 Best Foreign-Language Film Academy Award; marked initial collaborations with producer Franco Cristaldi and composer Ennio Morricone

1990: Wrote and directed the comedy "Stanno tutti bene/Everybody's Fine", starring Marcello Mastroianni; shown in competition at the Cannes Film Festival

Taught aesthetics at the University of Palermo

1994: Wrote and directed fourth film, "Una pura formalita/A Pure Formality", starring Gerard Depardieu and Roman Polanski

1995: "L'Uomo delle stelle/The Star Maker", a companion piece to "Cinema Paradiso", earned a Best Foreign-Language Film Academy Award nomination

1998: Helmed first English-language feature "The Legend of the Pianist on the Ocean" (released in USA in 1999 as "The Legend of 1900"); also wrote script based on the monologue "Novacentro" by Italian novelist Alessandro Barrico; Ennio Morricone provided the lush score

Robert Towne

BORN: Robert Bertram Schwartz in Los Angeles, California, 11/23/1934

SOMETIMES CREDITED AS:
Edward Wain
P. H. Vazak

NATIONALITY: American

EDUCATION: Chadwick School, Palos Verde, California

Pomona College, Claremont, California, literature and philosophy studied acting with Jeff Corey, where he met Jack Nicholson and Roger Corman in 1958

AWARDS: Writers Guild of America Award Best-Written Drama Written Directly for the Screen "Chinatown" 1974

British Film Academy Award Best Screenplay "Chinatown" and "The Last Detail" 1974 cited for both films

Golden Globe Award Best Screenplay "Chinatown" 1974

Oscar Best Original Story and Screenplay "Chinatown" 1974

National Society of Film Critics Award Best Screenplay "Shampoo" 1975 shared award with Warren Beatty

Writers Guild of America Award Best-Written Comedy Written Directly for the Screen "Shampoo" 1975 shared award with Warren Beatty

Writers Guild of America Screen Laurel Award 1997

BIOGRAPHY

Despite four Oscar-nominated screenplays, California native Robert Towne owes much of his reputation to his prowess as a pinch hitter, earning considerable respect as one of Hollywood's preeminent script doctors. Entering the business under the aegis of legendary schlockmeister Roger Corman—who discovered Jack Nicholson and him in Jeff Corey's acting class in the late 1950s—he scripted (and sometimes acted in) low-budget curiosities like "The Last Woman on Earth" (1960) and "The Tomb of Ligeia" (1965). He also wrote episodes for TV series like "The Outer Limits" and "The Man from U.N.C.L.E." before graduating to "special consultant" status for his contributions to Robert Benton and David Newman's scenario for "Bonnie and Clyde" (1967), directed by Arthur Penn. His uncredited work for Francis Ford Coppola on "The Godfather" (1972) earned him words of thanks during Coppola's acceptance speech for his Oscar-winning

screenplay, and he would even rewrite two-time Academy Award-winner William Goldman ("Marathon Man" 1976).

After acting in friend Nicholson's directorial debut, "Drive, He Said", and doctoring "Cisco Pike" (both 1971) and "The New Centurions" (1972), from which he walked, Towne established himself with three Oscar-nominated scripts, two for Nicholson ("The Last Detail" 1973, "Chinatown" 1974) and one ("Shampoo" 1975) for "Bonnie and Clyde" star Warren Beatty (who shared screenwriting credit). They exhibited his deft command of narrative structure and natural dialogue in the service of a warm, untidy humanism and a special love of southern California. Towne took home a statue for the best of them, "Chinatown", a flat-out masterpiece considered by many the finest screenplay of the last 30 years, although director Roman Polanski won out in the battle over whose ending eventually got made. A magnificent portrait of a Los Angeles coming of age in the 30s, "Chinatown" is one of the most-studied scripts of all time, but the writer invariably breathes drama, subtlety and depth of character into all his work, credited or not.

Towne made an impressive directorial debut with "Personal Best" (1982), a character study of a lesbian athlete, but his ugly battle with its producer David Geffen ultimately cost him a chance to helm his pet project, "Greystroke: The Legend of Tarzan" (1984), providing the bitterest disappointment of his career. Extremely displeased with the final result, he took his credit as P. H. Vazak (his dog's name), and when the screenplay received an Oscar nomination, his dog became the first canine ever to be so honored. Towne's second directing assignment, the slick romantic thriller "Tequila Sunrise" (1988), fared better with audiences than with critics, but the studio's refusal to allow him to shoot his ending may have contributed to its overall tepid reception. His friendships with Nicholson and Beatty both soured on the final collaboration with each, although Nicholson giving him the boot as director of "The Two Jakes" (1990) hurt far worse than "Love Affair" (1994), his first failure with Beatty (again as co-writer) after doctoring successes like "The Parallax View" (1974), "Heaven Can Wait" (1978) and "Reds" (1981).

Towne's new best friend is superstar Tom Cruise, with whom he first worked on "Days of Thunder" (1990). He then co-wrote the script for "The Firm" (1993), a huge hit for Cruise adapted from John Grisham's best-selling novel, and later co-scripted Brian De Palma's "Mission: Impossible" (1996) for its producer-star. Cruise had originally planned to star as Steve Prefontaine in "Without Limits" (1998), another pet project the writer had been developing for some time, but pulled out thinking the public would not accept him (a family man in his 30s) in the scenes where 'Pre' is a teenager. Instead, the actor threw his support behind it as producer (along with partner Paula Wagner), insuring that it got made with Towne at the helm, despite the presence of a competing movie at Disney about the same famous distance runner. In a way, "Without Limits" is Towne's story: Prefontaine's passion for running is the writer's passion for the movies, and the runner's failure at the 1972 Olympic Games a metaphor for the low points of Towne's career that followed his incredible success of the 70s.

MILESTONES:

Raised in the gated community of Rolling Hills, California

Moved to Los Angeles in the early 1950s

Worked as a tuna fisherman while in college

1960: First screenwriting credit (as Edward Wain), Roger Corman's "The Last Woman on Earth"; also acting debut (billed as Edward Wain)

1962–1963: Wrote four episodes for "The Lloyd Bridges Show" (CBS)

1964: Wrote episodes for "The Outer Limits" (ABC), "Breaking Point" (ABC), "The Man

from U.N.C.L.E." (NBC) and "The Richard Boone Show" (NBC)

1967: Was member of Warren Beatty's production staff and made uncredited contributions to screenplay of "Bonnie and Clyde"; credited as special consultant

1968: Co-scripted (with Sam Peckinpah) "Villa Rides", directed by Buzz Kulik

1971: First feature collaboration with friend Jack Nicholson, acting in Nicholson's directing debut, "Drive, He Said"

1972: Scripted one scene (where the mantle passes from Brando to Pacino) in Francis Ford Coppola's "The Godfather"

1973: Received first Oscar nomination for his adaptation of Darryl Ponicson's novel, "The Last Detail", directed by Hal Ashby; first feature collaboration with Nicholson as actor

1974: Won Oscar for original screenplay for Roman Polanski's "Chinatown", starring Nicholson

1975: Co-wrote (with Beatty) "Shampoo", directed by Ashby; earned third screenwriting Oscar nomination in as many years

1975: With Paul Schrader, co-wrote "The Yakuza", directed by Sydney Pollack

1977: Contributed uncredited "script-doctoring" to "Marathon Man", rewriting William Goldman (a master himself)

1982: Film producing and directing debut, "Personal Best"

1984: Took screenwriting credit for "Greystoke: The Legend of Tarzan, Lord of the Apes" as P. H. Vazak (his dog's name); had orinally intended to direct film, but fallout from his war with David Geffen on "Personal Best" led Warner Bros. to give the helm to Hugh Hudson; shared Oscar nomination with other credited writer Michael Austin

1987: Portrayed Stan in James Toback's "The Pick-up Artist"

1987: Executive produced "The Bedroom Window", directed by Curtis Harrington

1988: Second film as writer-director, "Tequila Sunrise"

1990: Scripted "Chinatown" sequel "The Two Jakes"; originally supposed to direct but replaced by Nicholson; friendship did not survive the flap

1990: First association with Tom Cruise, "Days of Thunder"; co-wrote story with Cruise, then executed the screenplay

1993: Collaborated with David Rabe and David Rayfiel on screenplay for "The Firm", adapted from the John Grisham novel; starred Cruise and directed by Sydney Pollack

1994: Second screenwriting collaboration with Beatty, the disastrous remake "Love Affair"

1996: Co-wrote "Mission: Impossible" with David Koepp for producer-star Cruise

1998: Third film as writer-director, "Without Limits", produced by Cruise and Paula Wagner; second film in as many years about legendary runner Steve Prefontaine; co-wrote with Kenny Moore, former University of Oregon and 1972 Olympic teammate of Prefontaine

QUOTES:

"The movies started changing with 'Superman'. The stars became Sly Stallone, Arnold Schwarzenegger, Indiana Jones. It's a need for heroes. When we feel we can't do much of anything right, build a car or a TV set, we want someone who can change events, who can do it for us. The characters I write about are men who control events far, far less than events control them. My characters get caught, they try even though they don't prevail or even significantly influence events. These guys muddle through."—Robert Towne quoted in *The New York Times*, November 27, 1990.

"There are no novels or plays I'm itching to write and there never have been. I love movies. I think movies best communicate whatever I have to say and show; or to put it another way, when what you want to show is what you have to say, you are pretty much stuck with movies as a way of saying it."—Towne in *Esquire*, July 1991.

"Working on 'Personal Best' was a great experience for me. And though the film was not a commercial success, it certainly got a lot of good critical attention and has had a long and honorable life in terms of being a sort of reference point in films. As for 'Tequila Sunrise', it was doomed from the beginning, when I was prevented from doing a script in which the hero is killed. That just twisted everything. Had that movie ended with Mel Gibson's death, the way it had been written, I think it would have been better reviewed and more commercially successful."—Robert Towne to *Premiere*, April 1998.

On giving the scene he wrote to Marlon Brando in "The Godfather": "He was in his makeup chair and he said, 'Read it to me.' 'Read it to you?' 'Yeah.' 'Both parts?' 'Yeah.' That immediately pissed me off, because I thought, 'Well, this fucker's got to know that's an intimidating thing to do to anybody.' I made up my mind about one thing: I ain't gonna read this well. Acting for Brando is one mistake I'm not gonna make. I read it and he said, 'Read it again.' Then he did something that only Tom Cruise has ever done since—he took that scene apart, line by line, pause by pause, word by word. He wanted to know absolutely everything in my head that I could tell him about."—From *Movieline*, October 1998.

About his differences with director Roman Polanski regarding the ending of "Chinatown": "Roman and I have been much misunderstood about this. We both agreed that it ended darkly. The only difference was I felt it was too melodramatic to end it his way. The way I had it figured was just about as dark, but Roman felt he needed that finale. I was wrong and he was right. Roman is one of the most gifted filmmakers of all time. As the years have gone by, I see that he taught me more than anybody. The best working relationship I ever had was with him. By far. He's a giant."—From *Movieline*, October 1998.

Robert Townsend

BORN: in Chicago, Illinois, 02/06/1957

NATIONALITY: American

EDUCATION: William Patterson College, Wayne, New Jersey

Illinois State University, Normal, Illinois

Hunter College, New York, New York

Negro Ensemble Company, New York, New York acting

Second City Comedy Workshop, Chicago, Illinois

studied acting with Stella Adler

BIOGRAPHY

Multi-talented figure who graduated from stand-up comedy to film, making his screen acting debut in Paul Mazursky's "Willie and Phil" (1980) and contributing a fine dramatic performance in "A Soldier's Story" (1984).

Frustrated at the dearth of significant screen roles for blacks, Townsend scraped together some $100,000 (putting most of it on his assortment of credit cards) to produce, direct, write and star in his witty lampoon of the travails of an aspiring minority actor, "Hollywood Shuffle" (1987). His subsequent credits include Eddie Murphy's concert movie, "Raw" (1987), several cable TV comedy shows and "The Five Heartbeats" (1991), a somewhat old-fashioned show biz comedy-drama about a rhythm and blues singing group set in the 1960s.

In interviews, Townsend has decried the anger and negativism that he believes characterizes too much of contemporary black filmmaking. Raised in inner-city Chicago, he sought escape through the films of Frank Capra. This sunny sensibility in the face of adversity characterized "The Meteor Man" (1993), an urban fairy tale about a mild mannered school teacher who is transformed into a crime-fighting superhero. The film contained no profanity or explicit violence—and fizzled at the box office.

Townsend returned to series TV in 1993 with the short-lived variety series "Townsend Television" (Fox). He scored slightly better with his next effort, the likeable yet unspectacular sitcom "The Parent 'Hood" (1995–99) on the fledgling The WB network. Townsend (who also co-executive produced) played a college professor coping with raising four children in Manhattan.

MILESTONES:

Worked with Experimental Black Actors Guild in Chicago at age 16

1974: Film debut (bit part) in "Cooley High"

Stand-up comic with Second City and at NY's Improvisation

1979: New York stage debut in "Take It from the Top" at the Henry Street Settlement

1979: Early TV movie appearance in the CBS docudrama, "Women at West Point"

1980: Film acting debut in "Willie and Phil"

1987: First film as director-writer-producer "Hollywood Shuffle" (also star)

1990: Purchased Hollywood Professional School and renamed it Tinsel Townsend Studios to turn into a mini-studio (date approximate)

1993: Executive produced, hosted, and wrote for "Townsend Television", a variety series on Fox

1995–1999: Co-starred in and co-executive produced "The Parent 'Hood" (The WB)

1998: Hosted the syndicated weekly series "Mowtown Live"

2000: Directed the NBC biopic "The Little Richard Story"

2000: Helmed the TV biopic "The Natalie Cole Story" (NBC)

2001: Was director of the MTV special "Carmen: A Hip Hopera"

QUOTES:

"I didn't want to put my name on anything that would suggest to my audience that I was selling out. Hollywood grinds out dispossable movies geared for one good weekend before they die. As Costner showed us, if you want quality roles, you have to create them yourself. . . . " Studios are justifiably nervous when a comedian tries to get serious. History is full of horror stories about those that failed. But I'm still a baby creatively. I refuse to be put in a box. This wasn't going to be "Hollywood Shuffle" with music."—Robert Townsend on "The Five Heartbeats" (*Los Angeles Times*, March 29, 1991)

"Some of the things that these black film makers, writers, directors do, if a white person did it, they would be crucified. I'm supposed to look up at the screen and go: 'Oh, it's a black person exploiting me. Oh, as long as it's black-on-black exploitation, I'm cool with that.'

"What it does is keep everybody in slavery. All it says to the kids in those neighborhoods is that you're not going to make it. You're going to die. Why peddle that?"

—From "His Caped Crusade" by Sherryl Connelly in *Daily News*, August 4, 1993.

Rose Troche

BORN: in Chicago, Illinois, 1964

NATIONALITY: American

EDUCATION: University of Illinois Urbana, Illinois

AWARDS: Sundance Film Festival Filmmakers Trophy (Dramatic) "Go Fish" 1994; shared with Kevin Smith's "Clerks"

IFP Gotham Open Palm Award "Go Fish" 1994

BIOGRAPHY

Filmmaker whose feature debut "Go Fish" (1994), a 16mm romantic comedy set in the lesbian community of Chicago's Wicker Park, was the hit of the Sundance Film Festival and was the first of the features there to gain a distributor. Troche had made short films and worked in video in the years preceding "Go Fish", which was shot over 1991 and 1992 and wrapped with the financial intervention of independent producers Christine Vachon and Tom Kalin.

"Go Fish" starred Troche's co-writer and co-producer Guinevere Turner, whose search for romance brings about countless frustrations, quips, awkward interactions and finally love itself with a rather unexpected object choice. The feature proved to be a deft comedy which keenly explored the very idea of community as it portrayed contemporary urban lesbian culture. Its stylistic pleasures were based on its roots in low-budget and video filmmaking, its occasional forays into overt political questions balanced with small revelations possessing the charm and insight of good gossip.

It took several years, but Troche delivered an impressive follow-up feature, "Bedrooms & Hallways" (1998), a frothy romantic comedy that married elements of Noel Coward's "Design for Living" and Arthur Schnitzler's "Reigen/La Ronde". Instead of modern lesbians, Troche opted to focus on a British gay man whose 30th birthday causes him to reflect on his life. A comic examination of gender and sexual identity and attraction, "Bedrooms & Hallways" proved popular on the festival circuit before First Run Features picked it up for domestic distribution. Troche exhibited a strong command of the material, a flair for visual stylings and a gentle hand in guiding her ensemble cast which included Kevin

McKidd as the protagonist, James Purefoy as the object of his affection and Tom Hollander as McKidd's flamboyant flatmate.

MILESTONES:

1994: Feature film directorial, producing and screenwriting debut, "Go Fish"

1997: Appeared as herself in "Pride Divide"

1998: Directed the romantic comedy "Bedrooms and Hallways", starring Kevin McKidd

2001: Wrote and directed "The Safety of Objects"; screened at Toronto Film Festival

QUOTES:

"Back when we were casting, I thought if I could make a genderless movie, that's something I would so love to do. As we go into the next century, can we please leave some of our identity politics back here? Cinema is so that's one thing it should do. Films are out different reasons, but a movie like 'Bedrooms & Hallways' happens to be out there for a similar reason to, I think, 'The Object of My Affection', which is to further an understanding and to loosen a grip on what is right and what is wrong and say that these things are understandable. Can we not treat them as being so different any more?"— Rose Troche to Andrew L Urban at Urban Cinefile (www.urbancinefile.com.au)

Francois Truffaut

BORN: in Paris, France, 02/06/1932

DEATH: in Neuilly-sur-Seine, France, 10/21/1984

NATIONALITY: French

EDUCATION: Lycee Rollin dropped out at age 14

AWARDS: Cannes Film Festival Best Director Award "The 400 Blows" 1959

Cannes Film Festival Catholic Film Office Award "The 400 Blows" 1959

National Society of Film Critics Award Best Director "Stolen Kisses" 1969

Prix Louis Delluc "Stolen Kisses" 1969

National Board of Review Award Best Director "The Wild Child" 1970

National Society of Film Critics Award Best Director "Day for Night" 1973

New York Film Critics Circle Award Best Director "Day for Night" 1973

British Film Academy Award Best Director "Day for Night" 1973

New York Film Critics Circle Award Best Screenwriting "The Story of Adele H." 1975; shared award with Jean Grault and Suzanne Schiffman

Cesar Best Director "Le dernier metro/The Last Metro" 1981

Cesar Best Screenplay "Le dernier metro/The Last Metro" 1981; shared with Suzanne Schiffman

Los Angeles Film Critics Association Special Prize 1984; for "his extraordinary contribution to world cinema" (awarded posthumously); cited along with Andrew Sarris

BIOGRAPHY

Influential film critic, leading New Wave director and heir to the humanistic cinematic tradition of Jean Renoir, Francois Truffaut made films that reflected his three professed passions: a love of cinema, an interest in male-female relationships and a fascination with children.

After a troubled childhood, Truffaut joined the French army, deserted and was sentenced to a prison term. Critic Andre Bazin helped secure his release and encouraged his interest in film. In Bazin's influential journal, *Cahier du Cinema*,

Truffaut published "Une Certaine Tendance du Cinema Francais" ("A Certain Tendency in French Cinema") in 1954, proposing what came to be known as the auteur theory. A reaction against the bloated "Tradition of Quality" cinema in France, the article was a plea for a more personal cinema and an informal manifesto for the New Wave, which had not yet broken on the shores of French film.

As a filmmaker, Truffaut began by making shorts ("Une Visite" 1954, "Les Mistons" 1957) and working as an assistant to Roberto Rossellini. In 1959 he completed his first feature-length film, the semi-autobiographical childhood story "The 400 Blows", about a troubled adolescent, Antoine Doinel. Truffaut went on to chronicle Doinel's youth and young adulthood in the "Antoine and Colette" episode of "Love at Twenty" (1962), "Stolen Kisses" (1968), "Bed and Board" (1970) and "Love on the Run" (1979), all films featuring the same actor, Jean-Pierre Leaud, as Antoine.

Two diverging strains characterize most of Truffaut's work from the early 1960s on. On the one hand, the director celebrated life in the humanistic tradition of Jean Renoir. These films include that masterwork of 60s cinema, "Jules and Jim" (1961), which defined the modern romantic triangle for a generation—it is the bittersweet story, not of Jules and Jim, the two men, but of Catherine (Jeanne Moreau), the woman who dominates their lives and is free, at least, to choose; "The Wild Child" (1970), an essay in signs and meaning in which Truffaut himself starred as the historical Dr. Jean Itard, obsessed with understanding how to establish human communication with a boy raised outside of society; the ebullient "Such a Gorgeous Kid Like Me" (1972); "Day For Night" (1973), an exuberant celebration of the joy of filmmaking, the ultimate communal art; the joyous depiction of childhood, "Small Change" (1975); the celebration of women and love in "The Man Who Loved Women" (1977); and the gentle thriller "Confidentially Yours" (1982).

On the other hand, many of Truffaut's films are fatalistic or even cynical, displaying a Hitchcockian fascination with life's darker side. This group includes "The Bride Wore Black" (1967), his most explicit homage to Hitchcock, scored by the master's regular composer, Bernard Herrmann; "Two English Girls" (1971), about a writer (Leaud) and his affairs with two sisters; "The Story of Adele H." (1975), one of the most harrowing examinations of unrequited love ever filmed; "The Green Room" (1978), about the love of death; and "The Woman Next Door" (1981).

Yet another group of films reflect an uneasy balance of these two divergent tendencies, as in his anatomy of adultery, "The Soft Skin" (1964); the romantic but brooding "Mississippi Mermaid" (1968), which Truffaut described as being about "degradation, by love"; and "The Last Metro" (1980).

"I want a film I watch to express either the joy of making cinema or the anguish of making cinema," Truffaut once said. "I am not interested in all the films that don't vibrate." In 1976, Truffaut accepted the invitation of the wildly successful young American director Steven Spielberg to star in "Close Encounters of the Third Kind" as the scientist in search of communication with extra-terrestrials. His stoic portrait in that film is an emblem of Truffaut's . . . pain; the arduous difficulty a born outsider encounters in communicating. This pain suffuses his lesser films, and cramps them, but it also lurks never far from the heart of his great films. It's what makes them "vibrate."

Always concerned with the process as well as the product of his profession, Truffaut maintained his role as critic and commentator throughout his filmmaking career, as proud of his books as he was of his films. Among his publications is a book-length interview with Hitchcock, "Hitchcock-Truffaut" (1967), a perennial critical classic which he revised in 1983, shortly before his death. His critical essays were collected in "Les Films de ma Vie"

(1975) and his letters—posthumously—in "Francois Truffaut Correspondance" (1990), with a foreword by Jean-Luc Godard.

Truffaut died—dramatically, arbitrarily—of a brain tumor in the American Hospital in Neuilly in 1984. He is the father of Laura Truffaut (born 1959) and Eva Truffaut (born 1961), both of whom appeared in their father's film "L'Argent de Poche" (1975) and whose mother is his first wife, Madeleine Morgenstern; and of Josephine (born 1983), whose mother is Fanny Ardant.

MILESTONES:

Lived with grandmother until eight years of age; quit school at 14 and worked as messenger, then as sales clerk; joined Paris cine-clubs

1948: With Robert Lachenay formed own cine-club, Cercle Cinemane

1949: Hired as reporter at "Elle" (date approximate)

1950: Published first film article in "Bulletin of the Latin Quarter Cine-Club"

1950: First film appearance (a bit part) in Rene Clement's "Le Chateau De Verre"

1951: Became film critic for Andre Bazin's "Cahiers du Cinema"

1951–1952: Served in National Service from which he deserted, was caught and dishonorably discharged

1953: Employed by the Service Cinematographique of the Ministry of Agriculture; fired after few months

1954: Began directing amateur 16mm shorts with "Une viste"

1956: Appeared as himself in the short film, "Le Coup de Berger", directed by Jacques Rivette

Worked as assistant to Roberto Rossellini on three of his unreleased films

1957: Directed first short film, "Les Mistons"

1958: Founded own film company, Les Films du Carrosse (named after Jean Renoir's film, "Le Carrose d'Or")

1959: Feature film directing debut with "Les Quatre Cents Coups/The 400 Blows"

1959: Wrote original story and appeared in Jean-Luc Godard's "A bout de souffle/Breathless"

1968: With Godard and Lelouche helped organized protests over dismissal of Henri Langlois, head of Cinematheque Francaise; instigated shutting down of Cannes Festival that year

1970: Played first major acting role in a feature, "L'enfant sauvage/The Wild Child", which he also directed

1977: American film acting debut, "Close Encounters of the Third Kind"

1978: Last acting role in a feature film, "La Chambre Verte/The Green Room", which he also directed

1983: Directed last film, "Vivement Dimanche/Confidentially Yours"

1983: Hospitalized with cerebral hemorrhage

QUOTES:

"If you like, you could call my cinema one of compromise in that I think constantly about the public, but not one of concessions, since I never put in a comic effect that I haven't laughed at, nor a sad one that hasn't moved me."—Francois Truffaut (in Georges Sadoul's "Dictionary of Film Makers")

BIBLIOGRAPHY:

"The Films of My Life" Francois Truffaut, 1973; anthology of Truffaut's film criticism

BORN: Tom Tykwer in Wuppertal, Germany, 1965

NATIONALITY: German

EDUCATION: graduated high school with an average of 3.6 (out of 6 with 1 being the best mark)

AWARDS: German Film Prize in Gold Best Director "Run Lola Run" 1999

Florida Film Critics Circle Award Best Foreign Film "Run Lola Run" 1999

Online Film Critics Society Award Best Foreign Film "Run Lola Run" 1999

Dallas-Fort Worth Film Critics Association Award Best Foreign-Language Film "Run Lola Run" 1999

Independent Spirit Award Best Foreign Film "Run Lola Run" 2000

BIOGRAPHY

Hailed as German Cinema's bright new hope, Tom Tykwer has quickly made a name for himself abroad as a fresh visualist with an energetic and passionate cinematic style. For his breakthrough film, the international success "Run Lola Run" (1999) and his follow-up feature "The Princess and the Warrior" (2001), Tykwer has enjoyed early comparisons to the late Polish auteur Krzysztof Kieslowski for his stylistic explorations of the effects of chance and choice on the human condition.

Tykwer's love for the cinematic arts began at the young age of 11, when he directed his first film with a Super-8 camera. A cinefile seemingly from birth, Tykwer's earliest jobs were at repertory cinemas, where he would lock himself into the theater overnight so that he could repeatedly watch the featured shows without interruption. After a brief stint in the Frankfurt military, Tykwer moved to Berlin to take over programming at the Moviemento Theater.

In 1993, Tykwer made his feature debut with the "Deadly Maria." The dark thriller earned the young director honors from the German Camera Association. He went on to write and direct the romantic feature "Wintersleepers" in 1997, but international recognition for his burgeoning talent would have to wait until the release of "Run Lola Run" in 1999.

"Run Lola Run" introduced the world to Tykwer's artistic eye and it also introduced Tykwer to future love interest, Franka Potente, who would go on to benefit greatly from the film's universal and international appeal. From the film's opening moments, Tykwer took the viewer of "Run Lola Run" on a frantic race through the crowded city streets of Germany, breaking cinematic rules and altering linear time, shifting states of emotion and meaning in the name of breathless forward momentum. The theme of the film is simple: protagonist Lola has only twenty minutes to raise enough cash to save her boyfriend from the unkind hands of local criminals. Tykwer's execution, however, is a multi-layered exploration of causality and coincidence, offering various scenarios in which Lola's task is met with numerous obstacles and completed with varying amounts of success. The film went on to become Tykwer's best to date as well as Germany's top German film of the year. The film's release internationally was just as successful and the film ranks as one of the largest-grossing foreign films to be distributed in the United States.

Set in his hometown, Wuppertal, Tykwer once again returned to the themes of chance and coincidence in his brain-teasing 2001 thriller "The Princess and the Warrior." As metaphysical in content as it is mathematic in structure, the film succeeds as a romantic, if not surreal, fairy tale about a nurse in a mental ward (Franka Potente) whose life is saved by Bodo (Benno Furmann), a criminal on the lam. Scene by scene since their chance encounter, an elaborate thematic equation is built on ever-widening circles of connection between Sisi and Benno that showcase well Tykwer's storytelling skills. More speculative than speedy, Tykwer's follow up to "Run Lola Run" received critical praise though the film's box offices sales were relatively mild.

When Krzysztof Kieslowski died of a heart attack in 1996, he left behind fragments of a project called "Heaven." This final work was meant to be the first part of a trilogy that was to continue with "Hell" and "Purgatory." The script, co-written by his collaborator Krzystof Piesieweicz, was a thriller about a woman named Philippa who is forced to take the law ino her own hands when she is suspected of being part of a terrorist organization. On the lam, she falls in love with Filippo, a police officer who was to be her captor. Though in preproduction with "The Princess and the Warrior" when the script was presented to his film collaborative, X Filme, Tykwer only needed one read-through to know that this would be his next endeavor. Released in 2002, starring Cate Blanchett and Giovanni Ribisi, the film's end result is an engaging and visually thrilling melding of two cinematic visions, preserving Kieslowski's rigourous explorations of the human condition in the fresh, passionate and energetic style that is quickly becoming the trademark of a young director on the rise.

COMPANION:

Franka Potente. Actor; starred in "Run Lola Run"

MILESTONES:

1976: Made his first Super 8 film at the age of eleven-years-old

Volunteered his time as a substitute for the compulsory military service in Frankfurt

1988: Relocated to Berlin and worked as a pro-grammar at the Moviemento Theater

1991: Presented his first short film to the Hof Film Festival

1993: Presented his first feature film "Deadly Maria"

1994: Founded the production company X-Filme Creative Pool with Stefan Arndt, later joined by Wolfgang Becker and Dani Levy

1996: Co-wrote the feature film "Life Is All You Get"

1997: Released "Wintersleepers" in Germany

1998: Directed the successful feature "Run Lola Run" in Germany; film becomes most successful German film of the year in his native country

1999: "Run Lola Run" is released in America, enjoying sensational reviews for both its direction and the performance of its young star, Franka Potente

2001: Directed "The Princess and the Warrior," again casting Franka Potente in the lead role.

2002: Directed "Heaven" starring Cate Blanchett

QUOTES:

Name is pronounced "tick-ver"

BORN: Liv Johanne Ullman in Tokyo, Japan, 12/16/1939

NATIONALITY: Norwegian

EDUCATION: Webber-Douglas Academy of Dramatic Art London, England studied acting for eight months when she was 17

AWARDS: National Board of Review Award Best Actress "Hour of the Wolf" and "Shame" 1968 for work in both films

New York Society of Film Critics Award Best Actress "Hour of the Wolf" 1968

New York Society of Film Critics Award Best Actress "Shame" 1968

Golden Globe Award Best Actress-Drama "The Emigrants" 1972 Swedish production

New York Film Critics Circle Award Best Actress "Cries and Whispers", "The Emigrants" 1972 cited for both films

National Society of Film Critics Award Best Actress "The New Land" 1973

National Board of Review Award Best Actress "The New Land" 1973

National Society of Film Critics Award Best Actress "Scenes From a Marriage" 1974

New York Film Critics Circle Award Best Actress "Scenes From a Marriage" 1974

New York Film Critics Circle Award Best Actress "Face to Face" 1976

Los Angeles Film Critics Association Award Best Actress "Face to Face" 1976

National Board of Review Award Best Actress "Face to Face" 1976

Outer Critics Circle Award Outstanding Actress-Play "Anna Christie" 1977

David di Donatello Prize Best Actress "Moscow Adieu" 1987

BIOGRAPHY

Possessing one of the most expressive faces in cinema history, Liv Ullmann will forever be associated with the work of her mentor Ingmar Bergman. She was his muse, his female alter ego inspiring him to look deeply into himself. More than any other Bergman actress, she embodied his core themes of anguish, loss and failure, and the nine films they made over 12 years represent the director at his peak, exploring his most private concerns. Throughout their collaboration, Bergman photographed Ullmann extensively in close-up, trusting her honesty completely, and the camera's proximity never intimidated the superb parade of emotions emanating from her luminous blue eyes and softly rounded features. Their professional life survived the dissolution of their private life, and years after she played her last role for him, Bergman asked her to interpret his autobiographical screenplay "Private Confessions" (1997) and allowed her to put her personal stamp on it as director, adding a new dynamic to their artistic relationship.

Born to Norwegian parents in Japan, Ullmann moved from Tokyo to Toronto, Canada at the outbreak of World War II and then to Norway following her father's death. She acquired eight months of acting training in London prior to making her stage debut in a Norwegian production of "The Diary of Anne Frank" (1957) and also appeared in her first film ("Fools in the Mountains") that year. She followed her success in the provinces with success in the capital city of Oslo, becoming a member of the Norwegian National Theatre Company, and continued acting in Norwegian films until Bergman introduced her to a wider audience in "Persona" (1966), the director's landmark take on reality versus art and the larger issues of life and death. Chosen for her remarkable resemblance to co-star Bibi

Andersson, Ullmann played an actress whose breakdown has made her mute, and Andersson was the voluble nurse trying to coax her to speak again. Without words, she relied solely on facial and body gestures to tell her tale of alienation, and the lack of text was far from limiting as her questioning, sometimes impenetrable looks poignantly projected her traumatized rejection of the world. And yet . . . her silence becomes a form of power. In the movie's most famous shot, the women's faces fuse into one, symbolizing Andersson's incorporation into the now stronger Ullmann.

While mentor and muse fought their demons as best they could, their art flourished with "Hour of the Wolf" (her first film with actors Max von Sydow and Erland Josephson) and "Shame" (both 1968) and "The Passion of Anna" (1970). The collaboration continued long after the actress had packed up and returned to Norway with their child, perhaps reaching its fullest flowering in "Scenes From a Marriage" (1973), a passionate, probing look into the disintegration of a marriage and the relationship that follows. Ullmann and Josephson were outstanding as the couple in this intimate, often painful slice of art imitating life, originally made as six 50-minute TV episodes and edited into feature-length by writer-director Bergman. She also enjoyed great success during this period in two films directed by Jan Troell, "The Emigrants" (1971) and its sequel "The New Land" (1973), earning the first of two Best Actress Oscar nominations for the former. The films told the tale of Ullmann, husband von Sydow and fellow Swedes who fled their famine-ravaged homeland in the mid-1800s to try their luck in America. She and von Sydow would return to the same era later for "The Ox" (1991), the directorial debut of longtime Bergman cinematographer Sven Nykvist, only this time portraying the plight of those who stayed behind.

Ullmann earned her second Best Actress Academy Award nomination for Bergman's "Face to Face" (1976), but their association was winding down. Only "The Serpent's Egg" (1977) and "Autumn Sonata" (1978) remained, although she has expressed regret at not acting in his swan song "Fanny and Alexander" (1983), her refusal angering him greatly at the time. By then, she had made her Broadway debut in "A Doll's House" (1975) and returned to the Great White Way as Eugene O'Neill's "Anna Christie" in 1977, a part fellow Scandinavian Greta Garbo had played in the 1930 film. Later that year, she also published the first installment of her autobiography, "Changes", and was the subject of a documentary ("A Look at Liv"). At the height of her worldwide popularity, she even made her Broadway musical debut in the Richard Rodgers–Martin Charnin adaptation of "I Remember Mama" (1979), an experience that perhaps eased the embarrassment of warbling Bacharach-David in her disastrous American feature debut, the 1973 musical remake of "Lost Horizon." In 1980, she began her long-standing association with UNICEF as its goodwill ambassador and two years later was back on Broadway as Mrs. Alving in Ibsen's "Ghosts."

Ullmann made a smooth transition to middle-aged roles, and two of her more notable films of the 80s were "Gaby—A True Story" (1987, as the wealthy mother of a girl who becomes a celebrated writer despite her severe cerebral palsy) and "The Rose Garden" (1989, defending Maximillian Schell against charges of having been a Nazi). She also began a second career as a director and screenwriter with the "Parting" segment of the anthology feature "Love" (1981) and in the 90s devoted increasing time to this new passion, starting with her feature debut, "Sofie" (1992), the story of a young Jew in 19th Century Copenhagen. She enlisted Nykvist as her cameraman for her sophomore effort, "Kristin Lavransdatter" (1995), an adaptation of Sigrid Undset's epic novel of 14th century Norway, and had him back on board for "Private Confessions"

(1997). Though her filmmaking style owes much to Bergman (she too favors the close-up), "Private Confessions" (despite being shot by Nykvist) does not especially look like a Bergman film. Screenwriter and director argued over a few things in the rough cut, but in the end he embraced her choices, which included playing up the religious angle a bit more than he might have. Obviously their reteaming was tonic for both, and Ullmann embarked on her second interpretation of Bergman at the helm of his autobiographical "Faithless" (2000).—Written by Greg Senf

MILESTONES:

Family moved from Japan to Canada at the outbreak of WWII

Moved to Norway from Toronto after death of father

1957: Made stage debut in title role, "The Diary of Anne Frank" at Stavanger, Norway

1957: Film debut, "Fools in the Mountain"

1960: Became a member of the Norwegian National Theater Company

1966: Swedish film debut, Ingmar Bergman's "Persona"; starred opposite Bibi Andersson

1968: Initial collaboration with actors Erland Josephson and Max von Sydow, Bergman's "Hour of the Wolf"

1969: Reteamed with Bergman, Andersson and Josephson for "The Passion of Anna"

1972: Received a Best Actress Oscar nomination for Jan Troell's "The Emigrants"; starred opposite von Sydow

1973: Reprised her "Emigrants" role for Troell's "The New Land", again opposite von Sydow

1973: Offered an outstanding performance in Bergman's "Scenes from a Marriage", mining the breakup of her own five-year relationship with the director for the part; third film with Andersson; fourth with Josephson; originally made for Swedish TV

1973: US film debut, the ill-fated musical remake of "Lost Horizon"; also sang in film

1974: Following in Greta Garbo's footsteps,

played Queen Christina in Anthony Harvey's "The Abdication"

1975: American stage debut in New York Shakespeare Festival revival of Henrik Ibsen's "A Doll's House"

1976: Earned second Best Actress Oscar nomination for Bergman's "Face to Face"; starred opposite Josephson

1977: Played title role of Eugene O'Neill's "Anna Christie" on Broadway; Garbo had played part in 1930 movie

1977: Subject of a feature-length documentary, "A Look at Liv"

1978: Ninth and last film acting for Bergman, "Autumn Sonata"; played Ingrid Bergman's daughter

1979: Broadway musical debut in Richard Rodgers' "I Remember Mama"

1979: Acted in "Great Performances" (PBS) presentation of "The Human Voice", a monologue during which a despondent and desperate woman tries vainly to communicate on the telephone with her former lover; Ingrid Bergman had played it for a 1967 ABC telecast

1980: Played widow seduced by husband's lover in Harvey's "Richard's Things", sripted by Frederic Raphael from his novel

1980: Appointed goodwill ambassador of UNICEF

1981: First screenplay credit and debut as a director with the "Parting" segment of the anthology feature "Love"

1982: Returned to Broadway in Ibsen's "Ghosts"

1984: Acted in the Oscar-winning (Best Foreign Film) "Dangerous Moves"

1987: Headlined Luis Mandoki's "Gaby—A True Story", playing the title character's mother

1989: Portrayed an attorney who defends Maximillian Schell against charges of having been a Nazi in "The Rose Garden"

1991: Appeared along with von Sydow and Josephson in "The Ox", the feature directorial debut of Bergman's longtime cinematographer Sven Nykvist

1992: Starred opposite Michael York in "The Long Shadow", feature directing debut of another famous cinematographer, Vilmos Zsigmond

1992: Feature directorial debut, "Sofie", a Bergmanesque tale of a young Jew in late 19th-century Copenhagen; based on the novel "Mendel Philipsen and Sons" by Henri Nathansens; Josephson acted in film; also co-scripted

1994: Fourth film acting with Andersson, "Dromspel", based on August Strindberg's "A Dream Play"; Josephson also in film

1995: Contributed to "Lumiere and Company"

1995: Sophomore effort behind the camera, "Kristin Lavransdatter"; also wrote script, adapting Sigrid Undset's epic novel of 14th Century Norway for which the author received the 1928 Nobel Prize and may have inspired parts of "Gone With the Wind"; reportedly the most expensive film ever produced in Norway; original cut ran three hours, but Ullmann whittled it down to two hours and twenty-one minutes in response to criticism of its excessive length; became that country's "Titanic", seen at least once by more than half the population; Nykvist was director of photography; tenth collaboration with Josephson

1996: Reteamed with Bergman who requested she helm his screenplay "Private Confessions", a continuation of his autobiographical films that began with "Fanny and Alexander" (1983) and included Billie August's "The Best Intentions" and son Daniel Bergman's "Sunday's Children" (both 1992); miniseries version aired first on Swedish TV in December; released theatrically in Europe in 1997 and in the USA in January 1999; Nykvist served as director of photography; von Sydow was featured in cast

2000: Directed "Faithless", an autobiographical script by Bergman; Erland Josephson hired to portray Ingmar Bergman

QUOTES:

Took a year off from acting to tour Europe as goodwill ambassador for the United Nations Children's Fund (1980–81)

Received the Dag Hammarskjold award (1986)

Presented the Order of St. Olav (also known as the Peer Gynt Award) by the King of Norway

Ullmann served as president of the jury at the 2001 Cannes Film Festival (stepping in for a previously announced Jodie Foster who withdrew over scheduling conflicts).

"I prefer acting on stage. If you're surrounded by good people and have a wonderful set and good lighting and a director who really has a vision, then I prefer the stage. But, so often this is not so and you are carrying the load of, maybe, some actors who are going in another direction, a director who didn't do his homework and a set that you can't act on. And I'm getting more and more impatient with that! First of all, I work very badly in these surroundings. I'm not challenged by them and I feel I can't waste my time anymore. With film, even though you're not in control because they can cut you out and they can use ghastly light and so on, at least you know the moment the camera is on you. Then you can give whatever you have and you can give it to that camera—which is your audience—and in a way, you are more in charge. And if it's a bad thing, you don't have to repeat the performance every day as you have to on stage."—Liv Ullmann, from interview with John Weitz

About her feature debut in Bergman's "Persona": "Luckily, the part he gave me was a silent person. I was Norwegian, I couldn't even have tried to speak Swedish, I was probably too scared to talk at all. But I did recognize him somehow, and I knew that I was him. That was my great understanding at 25. I didn't really understand my part, because I was playing someone 40 years old. But I knew I was Ingmar, and my instinct explained it for me."—Liv Ullmann quoted in *The New York Times*, January 3, 1999.

On her relationship with Bergman: "We were walking on this stony beach and he said, 'I have to tell you, this night I had a dream we were painfully connected.' You know, I more or less fell in love with that. I mean, Ingmar Bergman is painfully connected to me?"

"Well, I regretted it and went back to Norway, and he came to Norway and got me back to Sweden. And then I became pregnant, and I left him again. Then he asked me to come back; he had written a film for a pregnant woman. So I went back, and that was 'Hour of the Wolf'. We never married. I moved to Faro, where I lived for five years. It was there we did 'Shame', and then 'The Passion of Anna', but that was toward the end. And then it was over, that part, and I took my child and went back to Norway."—Ullmann to *The New York Times*, January 3, 1999.

She is currently honorary chair of the Women's Commission for Refugee Women and Children. "We work only for women and children because so many of the laws are written by men and for men. We have visited refugee camps, written books, articles, speeches—and really changed laws." Atlantic Monthly Press has just put out "Letter to My Grandchild", edited by Ullmann, in which more than 30 prominent world figures contribute letters to real or imagined grandchildren expressing their hope for the future.—From *Time Out New York*, January 7–14, 1999.

BIBLIOGRAPHY:

"Changing" Liv Ullmann, 1977; autobiography

"Without Make-up: Liv Ullmann—A Photo Biography" David E. Outerbridge, 1979, William Morrow

"Choices" Liv Ullmann, 1984; second volume of autobiography

"Letter to My Grandchild" Liv Ullmann, editor, 1998, Atlantic Monthly Press

Melvin Van Peebles

BORN: Melvin Peebles in Chicago, Illinois, 08/21/1932

NATIONALITY: American

EDUCATION: Ohio Wesleyan University Delaware, Ohio BA, 1953

West Virginia State College

attended graduate school in Holland; studied astronomy

AWARDS: Drama Desk Award Most Promising Book "Ain't Supposed to Die a Natural Death" 1972

Humanitas Prize childrens live-action "The Day They Came To Arrest The Book" 1987

Vivian Robinson Audelco Recognition Pioneer Award 1998

BIOGRAPHY

The cinema is just one medium in which the multi-talented Melvin Van Peebles has distinguished himself. After serving a stint in the US Air Force, he lived in Mexico where he worked as a portrait painter in the mid-1950s. Van Peebles made his first short films ("Sunlight" and "Three Pickup Men for Herrick", 1958) while working in a San Francisco post office. He went on to live in Holland and France and earned his living as a crime reporter in Paris where he also began writing French language novels. Van Peebles made his feature debut adapting his novel, "La Permission/The Story of a Three-Day Pass" (1967); the story of a romance between an American Negro soldier and a French girl, it was selected as the French entry in the 1968 San Francisco Film Festival. Some American reviewers embraced the picture as a promising directorial debut.

Choosing between various offers from American studios, Van Peebles returned to the US to direct and score a hilarious, sharp-edged comedy, "Watermelon Man" (1970), about a white bigot (played by comedian Godfrey Cambridge in whiteface) who one day wakes up black. Though still a crowd-pleaser, some contemporary reviewers deemed it a one-joke movie that was too broadly played. The year before, Van Peebles had recorded his first album, "Br'er Soul", which has been subsequently cited as a precursor to rap music.

Van Peebles independently produced, directed, wrote, scored and starred in his best known film, the tough, controversial "Sweet Sweetback's Baadasssss Song" (1971). A violent, frenzied, and exceedingly stylized tale of a black superstud on the run from the police, "Sweetback" cost $500,000 to make (including $50,000 borrowed from Bill Cosby) and grossed over $14 million. Opening to mixed reviews ranging from adoration from the hipsters to cautious condemnation from both the black and non-black critical establishment, the film's reputation has only grown with time. "Dedicated to all the Brothers and Sisters who have had enough of the Man", "Sweet Sweetback's Baadasssss Song" is an art film in the guise of an exploitation flick. Van Peebles favored gritty zoom photography, multiple exposures and hallucinatory colors. It has been hailed as one of the first films to define an African-American esthetic. In any event, it certainly helped to usher in the edgy "Blaxploitation" movies of the 70s and established Van Peebles as a folk hero.

After having worked in three vastly different styles of filmmaking (European art, American studio, independent), Van Peebles moved on to other interests. He shone on the musical stage in the 70s with "Ain't Supposed to Die a Natural Death" and "Don't Play Us Cheap" (a 1972 film version languished on the shelf for 18 years), which contributed to the growing black presence on Broadway. Van Peebles segued to TV,

scripting and composing the title song for a TV-movie pilot for MTM Enterprises entitled "Just an Old Sweet Song" (CBS, 1976). Cicely Tyson and Robert Hooks starred in this drama about a Detroit family that is strongly affected by a two-week vacation down South. He reworked the project into an hour-long special entitled "Down Home" (CBS, 1978) which replaced Tyson with Madge Sinclair but again failed to get picked up. In between, Van Peebles wrote the screenplay for "Greased Lightning" (1977), a low-budget biopic starring Richard Pryor as Wendell Scott, the first black racecar driver.

Van Peebles' experience in the arts taught him that often the most challenging aspect of creation was financing a given project. With this in mind, he tried his hand at commodities trading where he enjoyed success in the 80s. He even authored a financial self-help guide entitled "Bold Money: A New Way to Play the Options Market" (1986).

Van Peebles' son Mario worked as a model and first gained celebrity as an actor in films and TV. He starred as "Sonny Spoon" (NBC, 1988), a quirky short-lived detective series from producer Steven J. Cannell. The show afforded the elder Van Peebles his first gig as a recurring character on a TV series as he played Spoon's bartender father Mel. Van Peebles again collaborated with his son (who scripted, co-produced and starred) on "Identity Crisis" (1989), his first feature helming effort in 17 years. A broad farce about a young straight black American rapper who gets reincarnated in the same body with a gay white French fashion designer, the film bombed commercially and critically. Van Peebles played a supporting role in the mostly black Western "Posse" (1993), directed by his son.

Van Peebles returned to the spotlight with "Panther" (1995), a fictionalized chronicle of the rise of the black Panther Party for Self Defense, which he produced with Mario (who directed), scripted (from his unpublished novel) and appeared in a small role. The modestly budgeted feature opened to mixed reviews, disappointing box office and blistering attacks from both the political left and right. Controversy arose from the many liberties the film took with the historical record for dramatic purposes.

Though none of his subsequent work has had a comparable impact to "Sweetback", Van Peebles has remained visible as an actor in a variety of film and TV projects. He has become an iconic presence in films by a younger generation of black filmmakers. His relatively brief film career is less important for its artistic finesse than for the fact that his grittier-than-Hollywood portraits of black America somehow made it through the system. In 1990, New York's Museum of Modern Art held a retrospective of his works.—Written by Kent Greene

FAMILY:
son: Mario Van Peebles. Actor; eldest child

MILESTONES:
Served as a navigator and bombardier in the US Air Force Stategic Air Command for three years

1957: Lived in Mexico where he worked as a portrait painter (date approximate)

1958: Made short films, "Sunlight" and "Three Pick-Up Men for Herrick" while earning living as cable car grip and post office employee in San Francisco

Lived in Holland and France; in Paris, worked as crime reporter and began writing novels (in French)

1964: Debut as stage writer, lyricist and composer, "Harlem Party" (first produced in Belgium)

1968: Feature film directing debut, "La Permission/ The Story of a Three-Day Pass" (also writer, co-composer with Mickey Baker)

1969: Recorded first album, "Br'er Soul"

1970: First US feature as director, "Watermelon Man" (also co-composer)

1971: Directed, scripted, edited, scored, financed and starred (his feature acting debut) in the controversial exploitation cum art film, "Sweet Sweetback's Baadasssss Song"

1972: Broadway debut as producer, director, writer, "Don't Play Us Cheap"

1972: Produced, directed, wrote screenplay adaptation, edited, scored, and wrote songs for "Don't Play Us Cheap", the film version of his Broadway show; except for benefit screenings in 1972, shelved for 18 years

1976: TV writing debut, scripted and wrote title song for the TV-movie pilot, "Just an Old Sweet Song", for MTM Enterprises

1977: Wrote the screenplay for "Greased Lightning", a biopic starring Richard Pryor as Wendell Scott, the first black racecar driver

1978: Reworked "Just an Old Sweet Song" into an hour-long pilot entitled "Down Home" for MTM

1979: TV acting debut, "The Sophisticated Gents" (also scripted, associate produced and wrote the song "Greased Lightning); shelved for two years and aired in 1981

1983: Worked on Wall Street as options trader on the American Stock Exchange in the 1980s (formed own municipal bonds firm in 1987)

Music video directing debut, "Funky Beat"

1987: Wrote the teleplay for "The Day They Came to Arrest the Book", a presentation of "CBS Schoolbreak Specials", based on Nat Hentoff's young adult novel

1988: Played the recurring role of Mel, the bartender father of Mario Van Peebles on the quirky detective series, "Sonny Spoon"

1989: Provided the voice of Louis Armstrong for "Satchmo: The Life of Louis Armstrong", a presentation of PBS's "American Masters"

1989: Returned to feature directing after 17 years to helm "Identity Crisis", a broad farce scripted by and starring Mario Van Peebles (also edited and acted)

1990: Directed an installment of "The Big Room/Carry a Big Schtick", a stand-up comic's showcase on Ha! TV Comedy Network

1993: Directed by his son as an actor in "Posse", a largely black Western

1994: Produced, directed, scripted, edited and scored "Vrooom, Vrooom, Vrooom", a German-produced erotic fantasy short

1995: Produced (with Mario Van Peebles), scripted (from his unpublished novel) and appeared in "Panther", a controversial fiction film about the rise of the black Panther Party for Self Defense

DISCOGRAPHY: "Br'er Soul" Melvin Van Peebles, 1969

BIBLIOGRAPHY:

"Un ours pour le F.B.I" Melvin Van Peebles, 1964; Buchet-Chastel novel published in France; published as "A Bear for the F.B.I." by Trident in the USA, 1968

"Un Americain en enfer Melvin Van Peebles, 1965; Editions Denoel novel, translated as "The True American: A Folk Fable" and published in USA by Doubleday, 1976

"Le Chinois du XIV" Melvin Van Peebles, 1966; Le Gadenet short stories

"La Fete a Harlem" Melvin Van Peebles, 1967; J. Martineau novel adapted from his play "Harlem Party"; translated a "Don't Play Us Cheap: A Harlem Party" and published in US by Bantam, 1973

"The Big Heart" Melvin Van Peebles, 1967; photo essay

"La Permission" Melvin Van Peebles, 1967; J. Martineau novel, basis for Van Peebles' first film "The Story of a Three-Day Pass"

"The Making of Sweet Sweetback's Baadasssss Song" Melvin Van Peebles, 1972, Lancer Books

Gus Van Sant

BORN: Gus Van Sant, Jr. in Louisville, Kentucky, 07/24/1952

SOMETIMES CREDITED AS:
Gus Van Sant, Jr.

NATIONALITY: American

EDUCATION: Catlin Gabel School, Portland, Oregon; a private, progressive high school

Rhode Island School of Design, Providence, Rhode Island, film and painting, BFA, 1976

AWARDS: Los Angeles Film Critics Association Award Best Independent/Experimental Film "Mala Noche" 1987

New York Film Critics Circle Award Best Screenplay "Drugstore Cowboy" 1989; award shared with Daniel Yost

National Society of Film Critics Award Best Picture "Drugstore Cowboy" 1989

National Society of Film Critics Award Best Screenplay "Drugstore Cowboy" 1989

National Society of Film Critics Award Best Director "Drugstore Cowboy" 1989

Independent Spirit Award Best Screenplay "Drugstore Cowboy" 1989

Los Angeles Film Critics Association Award Best Screenplay "Drugstore Cowboy" 1989 award shared with Daniel Yost

Independent Spirit Award Best Screenplay "My Own Private Idaho" 1991

Berlin Film Festival German Film Guild Prize "Finding Forrester" 2001

BIOGRAPHY

Van Sant's poetic yet clear-eyed excursions through America's seamy, skid row underbelly have yielded some of the more potent independent films of the late 1980s and early 90s. "I guess I'm interested in sociopathic people," he has stated, "in life and in my movies." With art school training in painting as well as film, Van Sant worked in commercials before entering the film industry by making small personal films that played the festival circuit, notably in highbrow gay and lesbian venues. Openly gay, he has dealt unflinchingly with homosexual and other marginalized subcultures without being particularly concerned about providing positive role models.

Van Sant's first feature was "Mala Noche" (1986), a dreamy black-and-white rumination on the doomed relationship between a teen Mexican migrant worker and a liquor-store clerk. Made for about $25,000, the film won a Los Angeles Film Critics Award as the best independent/experimental film of 1987. "Drugstore Cowboy" (1989) chronicled the exploits of a rootless druggie (Matt Dillon) and his "crew" who survive by robbing West Coast pharmacies. Lyrically shot, and boasting superb performances from Dillon and co-star Kelly Lynch, the film marked Van Sant as a director of considerable promise.

Van Sant's 1991 feature, "My Own Private Idaho", based on his first original screenplay, starred River Phoenix as a narcoleptic male prostitute whose search for home and family takes him from Portland, OR, to such disparate locales as Idaho and Italy. Keanu Reeves plays his well-heeled companion of the streets and son of the local mayor who, like Shakespeare's Prince Hal, goes slumming amongst the low-lifes before reclaiming his place in society. Unified by poetic visual imagery, the film combines a less than entirely successful contemporary retelling of the Bard's "Henry IV" with a harsh, unsentimental and nonjudgmental look at the lives of hustlers.

The trades buzzed that Van Sant would make his Hollywood studio debut as the helmer of "The Mayor of Castro Street", based on Randy Shilts' book about San Francisco's assassinated, openly gay city supervisor Harvey Milk. Oliver Stone was set to produce and Robin Williams reportedly wanted the lead.

The project eventually fell apart due to the creative differences between Van Sant and Stone over the screenplay.

Van Sant returned to familiar territory—another indie road picture centering on an outsider (budgeted at $7.5 million), "Even Cowgirls Get the Blues" (1994). Adapted from Tom Robbins' 1976 cult novel about a young woman whose outsized thumbs make her a formidable hitchhiker, "Cowgirls" was highly anticipated after the attention-getting success of the writer-director's preceding two features. The film was reportedly rushed through editing to be ready for the international film festivals. After "underwhelming" audience response at the 1994 Toronto Film Festival opening night screening, "Cowgirls" was returned to the editing room for extensive recutting. (Van Sant has denied the rumors that reshooting was required.) Nonetheless, the final product was deemed a tedious bore, top heavy with would-be quirky characters. It fizzled with both critics and audiences.

The debacle of "Even Cowgirls Get the Blues" could have derailed Van Sant's career had he not already committed to helming "To Die For" (1995), his first major studio project, before the release of "Cowgirls." The medium budget satire also marked the first time Van Sant directed a film without receiving a screenplay credit. Scripted by Hollywood veteran Buck Henry, "To Die For" was inspired by the true story of a high-school teacher who seduced her teenage lover into murdering her husband. A modest commercial success, the film was a critical hit for everyone involved, particularly its star Nicole Kidman who portrayed the media-obsessed careerist who romances Joaquin Phoenix into murdering Matt Dillon. Some demurred from the consensus, dismissing the critique of American media as facile and Kidman's characterization as misogynistic. However, most were impressed by Van Sant's empathetic handling of the alienated teen characters.

That same year, Van Sant served as executive producer on one of the more controversial films of 1995—Larry Clark's "Kids", a 'verite'-styled drama about the sex and drug habits of a group of middle-class Manhattan teens. Some found the work profound, while others found it profoundly troubling for its "exploitive" use of young actors (though the filmmakers maintain that all actors shown simulating drug-taking and copulation were at least 18). Van Sant's favored cinematographer Eric Edwards ("Mala Noche", "Drugstore Cowboy", "My Own Private Idaho") lensed the visually striking feature.

As a follow-up, Van Sant returned to the director's chair to guide "Good Will Hunting" (1997), about an underachiever (Matt Damon) on the road to self-destruction who finds unlikely aid from several people, including a therapist (Robin Williams) and his best friend (Ben Affleck). Written by Damon and Affleck, the film is well-crafted, but somewhat predictable. Van Sant's sure-handed direction and authentic sense of place (it is set in Cambridge, MA) overcome whatever deficiencies and he elicited strong performances from the cast. While "Good Will Hunting" might seem an unlikely choice for the director, its themes of outsiders struggling to connect to the mainstream place it squarely in his oeuvre. The feature's success moved Van Sant toward mainstream Hollywood.

Since 1984, Van Sant has been making an annual, autobiographical short film that he ultimately plans to assemble into a cinematic diary; Van Sant also paints, plays guitar and writes for his own Portland rock band, "Destroy All Blondes."—Written by Kent Greene

MILESTONES:

Moved extensively around the country with his parents as a child before settling in Darien, Connecticut

1967: Had a summer advertising job on NYC's Madison Ave at age 16

1968: As an art student, discovered the work of Andy Warhol; inspired to start making films (date approximate)

Shot his first painterly, animated films with an 8 millimeter Kodak

Family moved to Portland, OR, when Van Sant was 17

Collaborated with future cinematographer Eric Edwards (who later worked on "Mala Noche", "Drugstore Cowboy" and "My Own Private Idaho") on high-school film project, "The Happy Organ", his first sound film, a 20-minute black-and-white movie about a brother and sister who go on a weekend trip on which she is struck and killed by a car

1976: After college graduation, moved to Hollywood where he worked as an assistant to Ken Shapiro ("Groove Tube"), working on comedy scripts

1978: Received credit for the sound on the comedy film, "Property"

Feature film directing debut, "Alice in Hollywood" (which he later cut to featurette length), an attempted screwball comedy about a girl who comes to Los Angeles to become a star, winds up destitute on Hollywood Blvd. and then lands a role on a TV show; never released

Moved in with parents who had returned to Darien, CT and worked for his father in a New Jersey warehouse

1981–1983: Moved to New York; created commercials for a Madison Avenue advertising firm

1983: Settled back in Portland, OR, where he has written and directed films, commercials and music videos and briefly taught film production at the Oregon Art Institute

Short film, "The Discipline of D.E." debuted at the New York Film Festival

1985: First widely acclaimed feature, "Mala Noche" (released theatrically 1989; 16 millimeter, black-and-white film made for $25,000 from his savings account); also wrote, edited, produced and performed the song "Morir por tu amor" (English version)

1989: First film with a sizable budget, "Drugstore Cowboy", made for between $4 and $7 million; also his first feature in color

Made rare TV appearance interviewed by film critic Charles Champlin on "Champlin on Film" on Bravo

1991: First original feature film screenplay, "My Own Private Idaho" (also directed)

1992: First directed for TV with the short, "Thanksgiving Prayer", a segment of the PBS compilation special, "American Flash Cards"

1993: Signed a contract with The Gap to film commercials

1993: Started a band in Portland, OR, with Mike Parker and Scott Green, the two ex-hustlers who inspired the leads in "My Own Private Idaho"

1995: First film as executive producer, Larry Clark's "Kids"

1995: Directed first film he did not write, "To Die For"

1997: Helmed the mainstream drama "Good Will Hunting"; received first Best Director Academy Award nomination

1998: Signed to make a color version of "Psycho" using Joseph Stefano's original script

QUOTES:

"He has used 'Hollywood' actors, but he keeps them shabby, quiet, and unglamorous—and he helps them be better than any system has alloed: Matt Dillon in 'Drugstore Cowboy' and River Phoenix in '[My Own Private] Idaho'. Van Sant is gay, gritty, and arty all at the same time. There is no trace of camp or swishiness: he is determined on heartfelt feelings and commonplace tragedy. He has a great eye, and an even better sense of adjacency—not quite cutting, but a feeling for cut-up simultaneity."—David Thomson, "A Biographical Dictionary of Film."

Van Sant won second place as Best Director and "My Own Private Idaho" came in second as Best Picture in the 1991 New York Film Critics Circle Awards. River Phoenix also came in second as Best Actor for "My Private Idaho."

"I've tried to be as intimate with film as the written word is. There are all these little metaphors about how the clouds look like mushrooms. Or a writer can talk about the color of the sky for a paragraph. But how to do that in film was my big problem—how to take that imagery into a theater and have it be accessible, or, at least, watchable."—Gus Van Sant (*The New York Times* magazine, September 15, 1991).

" 'He's got a real voyeuristic side to him; he's tricky that way,' says Matt Dillon. 'He's always got this look on his face like there's some private little joke in the back of his mind.' His films share that sensibility: they're filled with off-balance images and quirky jokes—not standard gag lines, but wry turns that take a moment to sink in. . . . The jokes hang in the air before the payoff kicks in—and so do the movies themselves. Like the film maker, they don't give much away on the surface; they hold their secrets closely."—Thomas J. Meyer (*The New York Times* magazine, September 15, 1991).

"When he was a child, dreaming of making movies, Van Sant suspected that his reserved nature might preclude his chosen career. 'I thought that film makers were really gregarious partiers who were able to convince everybody to be in their movies because they were just social butterflies. . . . So I thought it really wasn't a good job for me.' As it turns out, his films have done the talking for him."—Thomas J. Meyer (*The New York Times* magazine, September 15, 1991).

"Since he came to film making by way of painting, Van Sant is obsessed with controlling the cinematic frame; his films rely as much on the ability of pictures themselves to tell stories as on narrative structure.

"The films are punctuated with close-up images shot at odd angles: the grille of a car with clouds rushing over head; the edge of a pack of gum; the printing on the top of a light bulb . . . The close shots yield moments that are at once anchoring and unsettling, giving the audience an intimate link to the setting, but showing it from an eccentric point of view.

"The director also encourages surprises in the filming process by being so prepared that there's room for accidents. He puts great time and effort into rehearsing scenes and having actors assume their roles off camera, so that when the time comes to shoot, they're able to go with the impulse of the moment."

—Thomas J Meyer (*The New York Times* magazine, September 15, 1991)

BIBLIOGRAPHY:
"Pink" Gus Van Sant, 1997, Doubleday/Nan Talese; novel

Agnes Varda

BORN: in Brussels, Belgium, 05/30/1928

NATIONALITY: Belgian

EDUCATION: College de Sete, France
Lycee Victor Duruy, Paris, France
Sorbonne, University of Paris, Paris, France, literature, BA
Ecole du Louvre, Paris, France, art history; studied to become museum curator
Ecole de Vaugirard Paris, France; studied at night school

AWARDS: Prix Melies "Cleo de 5 a 7/Cleo from 5 to 7" 1961
Prix Louis Delluc "Le Bonheur" 1966
Cesar Best Short Film (Documentary) "Ulysse" 1984
Los Angeles Film Critics Association Award Best Foreign Film "Vagabond" 1986; director
European Film Academy Award European Documentary "Les Glaneurs et la glaneuse/The Gleaners and I" 2000
Prix Melies "Les Glaneurs et la glanuese/The Gleaners and I" 2000
Honorary Cesar 2001
New York Film Critics Circle Award Best Non-Fiction Film "The Gleaners and I" 2001
Los Angeles Film Critics Association Award Best Documentary "The Gleaners and I" 2001
New York Film Critics Online Award Best Documentary "The Gleaners and I" 2001

National Society of Film Critics Award Best Non-Fiction Film "The Gleaners and I" 2001

BIOGRAPHY

Agnes Varda is often called the "grandmother of the New Wave." Although not a member of the *Cahiers du cinema* critical fraternity which formed the core of this movement, the Belgian-born Varda completed her first feature, "La Pointe Courte," in 1954, five years before the New Wave's first films. With almost no academic or technical knowledge of film (though she had been a still photographer for Jean Vilar's Theatre National Populaire), Varda told two parallel tales (a structure inspired by William Faulkner's "Wild Palms"): the jagged romance of a young married couple and the struggles of the fishermen in the village of La Pointe Courte. Critic Georges Sadoul called this work "certainly the first film of the Nouvelle Vague" and it set the tone for Varda's career to come, combining fiction with documentary and also, in its debt to Faulkner, illustrating Varda's desire to expand the language of film. "I had the feeling," she said later, "that the cinema was not free, above all in its form, and that annoyed me. I wanted to make a film exactly as one writes a novel."

Unfortunately for Varda, "La Pointe Courte" (which was edited by Alain Resnais, who initially refused to work on it because Varda's techniques were close to those which he was developing) would be the only feature she would make in the

1950s. Although she lit the fuse under the New Wave, it was not until the explosive feature debuts of her male counterparts that Varda received another opportunity to direct a feature, "Cleo From 5 to 7" (1961), which established her as a significant talent on the international film scene. In "Cleo," the story of two hours of a woman's life as she waits to hear if she has cancer, we witness the emergence of a great Varda theme, borrowed from Simone de Beauvoir: "One isn't born a woman, one becomes one."

From her first film to her most recent projects, Varda has shown a strong connection to the Earth, becoming a kind of cinematic Mother Nature, whose characters have been personifications of wood and iron ("La Pointe Courte"), sickly trees ("Vagabond," 1985), animals ("Les Creatures," 1966) and food ("Apple" of "One Sings, The Other Doesn't" 1977). The world of Agnes Varda is one expansive Garden of Eden, where characters can live without the human burden of morality or sin, whether that world is the French Riviera (the short "Du cote de la cote" 1958), the city ("Cleo from 5 to 7"), or the country ("Le Bonheur," 1965; "Les Creatures," "Vagabond"). Varda knows that this Eden is a mythical place which exists only in the minds of her main characters and for this reason, her films also contain contrasting elements: troubled characters (the struggling fishermen of "La Pointe Courte" or the suicidal wife of "Le Bonheur") or less picturesque surroundings (the frozen landscape of "Vagabond").

Although Varda's initial impact on cinema was a powerful one, by the mid-1960s her career as a commercial filmmaker began to wane. After the improvisational and obscure "Lions Love" (1969), about an avant-garde woman director who goes to Hollywood, Varda completed only one more fictional commercial feature over the next fifteen years—the epic feminist tale of womanhood and motherhood, "One Sings, the Other Doesn't." She remained active by directing numerous shorts and documentaries, but much of her work went unseen or unnoticed.

It was not until the mid-80s that Varda reemerged in the commercial realm. While "Kung Fu Master!" (1987) was a misnamed and rather tentative story of the abortive romance between a middle-aged woman (Jane Birkin) and a 14 year-old video game buff (played by Varda's son Mathieu), "Vagabond," a documentary-style feature about a young French female wanderer, was arguably her best work to date. It dealt with all her major concerns: the independence of women, the coexistence with nature, the need for freedom, the acceptance of chance, the cyclical nature of birth and death, the personification of nature, and the seamless blending of documentary and fiction. Sadly the illness and death of Varda's husband, filmmaker Jacques Demy, helped to inspire her affectionate docu-valentine to his youth in "Jacquot/Jacquot de Nantes" (1992).

COMPANION:

husband: Jacques Demy. Director; together from 1959; married from 1962 until his death on October 27, 1990 at age 59; made such films as "Lola" (1961) and "The Umbrellas of Cherbourg" (1964)

MILESTONES:

Grew up in her mother's home town of Sete in France

1947: While a student, became photographer for Theater Festival of Avignon

1951–1961: Hired by Jean Vilar to be official photographer for Theatre National Populaire

Recevied photojournalism assignments which took her all over Europe during the 1950s

1954: Debut as screenwriter, director and producer with "La pointe courte"

Directed two documentary travelogues commissioned by the French Tourist Office, "O saisons, o chateaux" and "Du cote de la Cote"

1977: Founded Cine-Tamaris, a production company, to produce "One Sings, the Other Doesn't"

QUOTES:

"In my films I always wanted to make people see deeply. I don't want to show things, but to give people the desire to see."—Agnes Varda (from Sadoul's "Dictionary of Film Makers").

Gore Verbinski

BORN: Gregor Verbinski in Tennessee, 1964

NATIONALITY: American

EDUCATION: University of California at Los Angeles, Los Angeles, California, 1987

BIOGRAPHY

Well-versed in crafting stylish, glossy images and particularly adept at creating suspense, film director Gore Verbinski made short films and worked on award-winning advertising campaigns (he won four Clio awards and one Cannes advertising Silver Lion, and was best known for creating the Budweiser Frogs) before moving into features. His feature directing debut was the cartoony, high-volume family comedy "Mouse Hunt" for Disney in 1997, followed by "The Mexican" with Julia Roberts and Brad Pitt in 2001, an awkward road romance that failed to delvier the sparks expected with its star combo. Verbinski then gained greater acclaim and exposure after venturing into thrillers with the suspenseful, popular and critically hailed "The Ring" in 2002, a film which solidified his future and made a true movie star out of Naomi Watts. His next project, "Pirates of the Caribbean: The Curse of the Black Pearl" (2003), was based on the beloved Disney theme park ride. and while receiving mixed reviews it definitely scored points for its stylized spooks and swash-buckling and a comedic tour-de-force performance from star Johnny Depp.

MILESTONES:

Born in Tennessee

Family moved to San Diego, California

As a teenager, began shooting 8mm films with his friends

In the late 1980s, after college, directed music videos for alternative bands like L7

1993: Began helming commercial advertisements

1995: Directed the popular Budweiser campaign featuring belching frogs

1996: Wrote and directed the short film, "The Ritual"

1998: Feature film debut as director, "Mouse Hunt"

2001: Helmed second feature, "The Mexican"

QUOTES:

Verbinski won four Clio awards for his commercials work.

Michael Verhoeven

BORN: in Berlin, Germany, 07/13/1938

NATIONALITY: German

EDUCATION: graduated medical school in 1969

AWARD: Berlin Film Festival Best Director Award "Das Schreckliche Madchen/The Nasty Girl" 1990

BIOGRAPHY

Physician turned filmmaker who has dissected historical and political issues such as the Vietnam war ("O.K." 1970), unemployment ("Plenty to Eat on a Silver Platter" 1976), pollution ("Killing Cars" 1984) and German amnesia about its Nazi past ("The Nasty Girl" 1989). "O.K.", about the rape of a Vietnamese girl by American soldiers, is based on the same incident which inspired Brian De Palma's "Casualties of War" (1989); the splendid "The Nasty Girl" earned Verhoeven his first significant recognition in the USA. Verhoeven's father was German director-actor Paul Verhoeven, not to be confused with the Dutch director Paul Verhoeven of "Total Recall" and "Basic Instinct" fame.

FAMILY:

father: Paul Verhoeven. actor, director deceased; after WWII, appointed head of State Theater in Munich; not to be confused with Dutch director of the same name

MILESTONES:

1950: Began acting in theater and film when in teens

Directed three feature films while attending medical school

Practiced medicine for four years before becoming full-time filmmaker

1967: Wrote first feature film, "Paarungen"

Paul Verhoeven

BORN: in Amsterdam, The Netherlands, 07/18/1938

NATIONALITY: Dutch

EDUCATION: University of Leiden, Leiden, The Netherlands, mathematics and physics, PhD; studied for six years

AWARDS: Los Angeles Film Critics Association Award Best Foreign Film "Soldier of Orange" 1979

Los Angeles Film Critics Association Award Best Foreign Film "The Fourth Man" 1984; director

Toronto Film Festival International Press Award "The Fourth Man" 1984; director

Avoriaz Festival Prize of the Jury "The Fourth Man" 1984

BIOGRAPHY

Well into his forties before moving to America to work, Dutch-born director Paul Verhoeven has thrived in the world of big budgets, exercising his lurid imagination and tremendous appetite for sex and violence to become a master of modern sensation. His first three Hollywood films were authentic smash hits, beginning with the explicit brutality of "RoboCop" (1987), continuing through the gasp-making action of "Total Recall" (1990) to the viscerally explosive and controversial "Basic Instinct" (1992). Then came "Showgirls" (1995), a sort of topless "All About Eve", which was such a bomb that it has enjoyed a rebirth as a camp classic. Verhoeven was even sport enough to show up and give a speech at the Golden Raspberry Foundation's annual 'Razzie' awards (where the film received seven prizes) commenting that the experience "helped a lot to get rid of that unpleasant feeling of being hurt." Perhaps "Showgirls" was just the tonic to stave off complacency because he rebounded with the turbo-charged sci-fi actioner "Starship Troopers" (1997), raising the standard for spaceship battle effects while offering a disturbing political subtext.

Verhoeven spent his childhood in the Nazi-occupied Netherlands, and the wartime visions of fire in the sky and death became imprinted on the future filmmaker's consciousness. Though he earned a doctorate in mathematics and physics at the University of Leiden, he put his heart in film, having feasted on action-packed American fare since his youth, as well as enjoying a passing fascination with the French New Wave and the films of Fellini. Verhoeven had directed a series of shorts before service in the Royal Dutch Navy film corps forever turned him from the academic life. After first making documentaries for Dutch TV, he moved into fiction, gaining attention for the medieval series "Floris", starring Rutger Hauer. His feature debut came in 1971 with "Business Is Business", but it was "Turkish Delight" (1973), Oscar-nominated for Best Foreign Film, which established his credentials. The erotic, satirical study of a marriage between a sculptor (Hauer) and a middle-class girl (Monique van de Ven) scored at the domestic and international box office, although some saw the seeds of pornography in this early art-house success.

Verhoeven fashioned his varied Dutch oeuvre working with several valued collaborators:

Rob Houwer produced his first four features, screenwriter Gerard Soeteman wrote or co-scripted all his pictures through his first English-language film ("Flesh + Blood" 1985) and Jan de Bont was the cinematographer of choice before Jost Vacano joined the team for "Soldier of Orange" (1979). (Though de Bont would collaborate on three more films with Verhoeven, he would replace Vacano for only "Basic Instinct" among the director's first five Hollywood films.) "Keetje Tippel" (1975), the follow-up to "Turkish Delight", again starred Hauer and van de Ven who played a poor-but-determined young woman who struggles against all odds (even becoming a prostitute) to climb the social ladder in 19th-century Amsterdam. With "Soldier of Orange", Verhoeven delivered a rousing World War II story with plenty of action, reminiscent of US war films of the late 1940s and 50s. Hauer came into his own as the handsome aristocrat who reluctantly joins the Dutch Resistance, and Jeroen Krabbe, in his first of three performances for the director, pushed Hauer for acting honors, dying at the hands of the Nazis after exacting his measure of revenge.

For "Spetters" (1980), a gritty look at a teenage motorcycle gang, Verhoeven and Soeteman returned to formula: squeezing in as much sex as possible without crossing into hardcore, relieved by quick action so the audience never feels like a voyeur. Though both Hauer and Krabbe were present in small roles, Renee Soutendijk stole the film as the little sexpot who will sleep with anyone to advance her career in the fish-and-chips business, setting the stage for her starring role as a scissors-wielding hairdresser in the psycho-sexual thriller "The Fourth Man" (1982). Castration-anxiety abounded in the film, and whether Soutendijk has murdered three husbands or not, she definitely messes up the mind of gay writer Krabbe when he tries to investigate. Though it generated little critical enthusiasm in Holland, it garnered the greatest international attention yet for the director, leading to "Flesh + Blood", a rowdy swashbuckler set in 16th-century Europe. Possessing plenty of its promised titular gore, it paired Hauer with Jennifer Jason Leigh but scored points only for its sheer audacity.

Verhoeven went to Hollywood and teamed with producer Jon Davison, screenwriter Ed Neumeier and special effects guru Phil Tippett on "RoboCop." For his first stab at science fiction, he had envisioned the future in the tradition of "Blade Runner", but the paltry budget was enough only for the very necessary RoboCop costume and the fantastic stop-motion animation of opponent ED-209. Jettisoning his elaborate production design, Verhoeven shot it straight in Dallas (standing in for a not so futuristic Detroit), and turned the film into a heavy-metal comedy with more than a few caustic things to say about the progressive dehumanization of civilization. The success of "RoboCop" ensured there would be more than enough money for the sci-fi summer blockbuster "Total Recall", a big, loud comic book of a movie adapted from Philip K. Dick's "We Can Remember It for You Wholesale." Although the project had languished in developmental hell for 10 years with different directors, Arnold Schwarzenegger's box-office clout finally got it off the ground, and Verhoeven fashioned an ambiguous twist to make Dick proud. Does Arnold really go to Mars, destroy the dictatorship and save the world? Or does he just dream it?

Sharon Stone had played Arnold's wife in "Total Recall", and though she was not the director's first choice for the role of kinky murder suspect Catherine Trammell in "Basic Instinct", she nailed it with her brazenly sexual and cold-blooded portrayal. Audacious, erotic and larger-than-life, "Basic Instinct" falls short of its vastly superior prototype "The Fourth Man", but it still kept audiences guessing to the final shot. The sexual tension Verhoeven managed to get on screen was a by-product of his own unconsummated love-hate relationship with Stone. As he explained to *Movieline*

(October 1995): "Everything I felt and everything she felt for me is in the movie. It was not consumed in bed. That's the victory. It was translated to art." Screenwriter Joe Eszterhas, happy to bask in the box office glow of "Basic Instinct", wasted no time, however, breaking ranks from "Showgirls" to publicly denounce it, causing the director to question his character.

Reuniting with his "RoboCop" team, Verhoeven roared back into Hollywood favor with the sci-fi blockbuster "Starship Troopers", about a highly-trained force sent to fight an invasion of insect-like aliens. The resounding failure of "Showgirls" did not prevent him from getting $100 million to make what is essentially a war movie, characterized by screenwriter Neumeier as " 'Full Metal Jacket' meets 'Them!' in the style of 'RoboCop'." Very little of that big budget went to its cast of relative unknowns, including Dina Meyer, Denise Richards, Jake Busey and Casper Van Dien, but what the film lacked in star power, it made up in fire power, featuring 500 digital special effects shots of bugs, explosions and flames, as well as the "old-fashioned technique" of using miniature models for the spaceships. In all, more than 250 artists and technicians worked under the skilled supervision of Tippett. Accustomed to courting controversy, Verhoeven refused to make a mere popcorn movie and drew on his genuinely subversive streak to depict the good guy humanoids as fresh-faced fascists. After a three-year absence, Verhoeven returned to the big screen with the sci-fi tinged "The Hollow Man" (2000), focusing on a trio of scientists (two men and a woman) who discover a potion for invisibility. When one of the males consumes it, he begins to stalk the others who have begun a love affair. Boasting a cast headed by Kevin Bacon, Elisabeth Shue (who injured her foot causing shooting delays) and Josh Brolin, it allowed Verhoeven to once again combine eroticism, thrills and special effects.

MILESTONES:

Directed shorts like "A Lizard Too Much" (1960) and "Let's Have a Party" (1963, which he also produced) before military service

1964–1966: Served as an officer in the Royal Dutch Navy film corps, making documentaries like "Het Korps Mariniers/The Royal Dutch Marine Corps" (1965)

Directed Dutch TV documentaries such as "Mussert" (1968), a profile of a notorious Dutch quisling who collaborated with the Nazis in WWII

1969: Gained recognition for directing Dutch TV series, "Floris", a medieval adventure starring Rutger Hauer

1971: Feature film directorial debut, "Wat Zien ik/Business is Business"; first collaboration with screenwriter Gerard Soeteman and producer Rob Houwer

1973: Acted in "Oh Jonathan, Oh Jonathan"

1973: Breakthrough film "Turkish Delight", starring Hauer; received Oscar nomination as Best Foreign Film; written by Soeteman and produced by Houwer

1975: Second feature with Hauer, "Keetje Tippel"; written by Soeteman and produced by Houwer

1979: First feature as screenwriter (with Soeteman and Kees Holierhoek), "Soldier of Orange"; also directed; Hauer starred as a handsome hero of the Dutch resistance; first association with cinematographer Jost Vacano; produced by Houwer

1980: First film with Renee Soutendijk starring opposite Hauer, "Spetters"; written by Soeteman

1984: Reteamed with Soutendijk (as a femme fatale) for noirish "The Fourth Man"; scripted by Soeteman

1985: US debut (co-produced with the Netherlands), "Flesh + Blood"; also scripted with Soeteman; fifth and last feature to date with Hauer

1987: Delivered sharp, slick action package with first Hollywood movie "RoboCop", a grim look into the not-too-distant future

1990: Helmed "Total Recall", another sci-fi film featuring his trademark over-the-top violence; first feature with Sharon Stone

1992: Scored hit with "Basic Instinct", his first collaboration with screenwriter Joe Eszterhas; film starred Stone as a bisexual femme fatale

1995: Bombed with "Showgirls", the first mainstream Hollywood film released with an NC-17 rating; second teaming with Eszterhas

1997: Returned to sci-fi with "Starship Troopers"; reteamed with screenwriter Edward Neumeier, special-effects wizard Phil Tippett and producer Jon Davison, having worked with all on "RoboCop"; sixth collaboration with director of photography Vacano

2000: Directed the sci-fi tinged thriller "The Hollow Man", co-scripted by William Goldman; production delayed when leading lady Elisabeth Shue tore an Achilles tendon

QUOTES:

"Many people were born into a violent environment, of course, but I always had the need to communicate my feelings about it. I like looking at violence, sure. But in real life I've never used my hands to touch a human being in a violent way."—Paul Verhoeven to The London *Times,* January 7, 1996.

"If it's only straight entertainment, I get bored. If it's only sending people out of the theater two hours later as empty as they came in, basically I couldn't do that. I need to see something in a movie that appeals to me from an existensial point of view. That doesn't mean that that's the primary objective of the movies I made, but I need it for myself. It's a simple question of survival: I'm not able to spend one and a half years on a movie if I don't feel it has meaning to me in some way."—Verhoeven, to Dan Persons for *Cinefantastique,* June 1967.

"I was only six when the Nazis arrived. It

sounds strange, but as a filmmaker I love the imagery of what I saw as a child when Holland was occupied. Rocket launchers and tanks were across the street from my house. One day a group of Dutch Nazi sympathizers threw me up against a wall and put a gun to my head. I peed my pants. That part I didn't love so much. But it was very emotional, to say the least.

"When I was a child, there was bombing all the time. You would look up in the sky and see fire. I don't think you can ever erase that image from your brain. When the starship explodes in ["Starship Troopers"], it's based on what I saw as child looking up in the sky. It was Allies' planes bombing the German planes. I'd see them catch on fire and fall close to my house. Then the kids would go looking for the dead pilot the next day."—Verhoeven, quoted in the *Chicago Sun-Times*, November 2, 1997.

About "Showgirls": "I think that movie would have been better served by insisting that it was not a peep show and that it would not give you an erection. In fact, you'd probably be impotent for the rest of your life because you thought sex was so awful. That's more the movie, isn't it? It's more a study of evil or the use of sex as a tool to get anywhere you want to be, than a movie to make you horny."—Verhoeven, to Jeff Dawson, *Empire*, February 1998.

On the cryptofascist world of the humanoids in "Starship Troopers": "If you think this is an ideal society, then what's the price we have to pay for that? That's why we show the news item with people getting caught in the morning, tried in the afternoon and executed in the evening. The movie seduces you into thinking this is fine, but later you realize you might have identified with a system that contains fascist ideology. The ambiguity isn't in the enemy but in ourselves. That's the real political context of the movie."—Verhoeven, quoted in *Time Out New York*, November 13–20, 1997.

Dziga Vertov

BORN: Denis Arkadievitch Kaufman in Bialystok, Poland, 01/02/1896

DEATH: 02/12/1954

NATIONALITY: Polish

EDUCATION: Bialystok Music Conservatory attended medical school in St. Petersburg, 1916–17

BIOGRAPHY

Dziga Vertov was born as Denis Abramovich (later changed to Arkadievich) Kaufman to a Jewish book-dealer's family. His younger brothers, renowned Soviet documentary filmmaker Mikhail Kaufman and cameraman Boris Kaufman, would later establish their own niches in film history. As a child he studied piano and violin, and at the age of ten began to write poetry; Vertov's films would reflect these early interests.

After WWI started the Kaufman family fled to Moscow. In 1916, Vertov enrolled in Petrograd Psychoneurological Institute. For his studies of human perception, he recorded and edited natural sounds in his "Laboratory of Hearing," trying to create new sound effects by means of rhythmic grouping of phonetic units. Familiar with the Russian Futurist movement, he took on the pseudonym "Dziga Vertov" (loosely translated as "spinning top"). In 1918 Mikhail Koltstov, who headed Moscow Film Committee's newsreel section, hired Vertov as his assistant. Among Vertov's colleagues were Lev Kuleshov, who was conducting his legendary montage experiments, and Eduard Tisse, Eisenstein's future cameraman. Vertov would recall later that they were most strongly influenced by Griffith's "Intolerance."

Vertov began to edit documentary footage and soon was appointed editor of "Kinonedelya," the first Soviet weekly newsreel. His first film as a director was "The Anniversary of the Revolution" (1919), followed by two shorts, "Battle of Tsaritsyn" (1920) and "The Agit-Train VTSIK" (1921), and the thirteen-reel "History of Civil War" (1922). In editing those documentaries, Vertov was discovering the possibilities of montage. He began joining pieces of film without regard for chronology or location to achieve an expressiveness which would politically engage the viewers.

In 1919, Vertov and his future wife, the talented film editor Elisaveta Svilova, plus several other young filmmakers created a group called "Kinoks" ("kino-oki," meaning cinema-eyes). In 1922 they were joined by Mikhail Kaufman, who had just returned from the civil war. From 1922 to 1923 Vertov, Kaufman, and Svilova published a number of manifestos in avant-garde journals which clarified the Kinoks' positions vis-a-vis other leftist groups. The Kinoks rejected "staged" cinema with its stars, plots, props and studio shooting. They insisted that the cinema of the future be the cinema of fact: newsreels recording the real world, "life caught unawares." Vertov proclaimed the primacy of camera ("Kino-Eye") over the human eye. The camera lens was a machine that could be perfected infinitely to grasp the world in its entirety and organize visual chaos into a coherent, objective picture. At the same time Vertov emphasized that his Kino-Eye principle was a method of "communist" deciphering of the world. For Vertov there was no contradiction here; as a true believer he considered Marxism the only objective and scientific tool of analysis and even called a series of the 23 newsreels he directed between 1922 and 1925 "Kino-Pravda," "pravda" being not only the Russian word for the truth but also the title of the official party newspaper.

Nevertheless, Vertov's films weren't mere propaganda. Created from documentary footage, they represented an intricate blend of art and rhetoric, achieved with a sophistication that, among Vertov's contemporaries, would be rivaled only by Leni Riefenstahl. Vertov's achievement was also his tragedy. He considered his films documentaries, but they also strongly reflected his personal, highly emotional poetic vision of Soviet reality, a vision he maintained throughout his life. As early as the mid-1920s Vertov was arousing suspicion from party authorities with his utopian and ecstatic cine-tracts and his pioneering techniques, including slow and reverse motion, "candid camera" tricks, bizarre angles, shooting in motion, split screens and multiple superimpositions, the inventive use of still photography, constructivist graphics, animation and most importantly rapid montage that sometimes consisted of only several frames. All these advances also left the masses indifferent. Among filmmakers Vertov acquired the reputation of an eccentric, an extremist who rejected everything in cinema except for the Kinoks' work. Fortunately Vertov, like Eisenstein, received the support of the influential European avant-garde. His feature-length "Kino-Eye—Life Caught Unawares" (1924) was awarded a silver medal and honorary diploma at the World Exhibit in Paris, and that success led to two more films commissioned by Moscow: "Stride, Soviet!" and "A Sixth of the World" (both 1926).

By now, the central authorities were fed up with Vertov's formal experimenting, and they refused to support his most ambitious project, "The Man With a Movie Camera" (1929). To make the film, Vertov had to accept the invitation of the film studio VUFKU in the Ukraine, where he moved with Svilova and Kaufman. These changes resulted in the collapse of the Kinoks group and by the time the project was finally realized there were already several similar "city symphonies" completed by such innovative filmmakers as Alberto Cavalcanti (in Paris), Mikhail Kaufman (in Moscow) and Walter Ruttman (in Berlin). Then too, Vertov's youngest brother Boris Kaufman, who lived in France, was about to start shooting "A Propos de Nice" for Jean Vigo. However, Vertov's film was significantly different from its brethren: its goal was not only to present a mosaic of the life of a city (a combination of Kiev, Moscow and Odessa) by use of the most advanced cinematic means, but also to engage spectators in theoretical discourse on the relationship between film and reality, on the nature of cinematic language and human perception.

In so doing Vertov was at least 30 years ahead of his time: his ideas of the self-reflective cinema, of the viewer identifying himself with the filmmaking process, would reemerge only at the end of the fifties in the work of Chris Marker, Jean-Luc Godard, Michael Snow and Stan Brakhage. But in 1929, when "The Man With a Movie Camera" was publicly released, it was too obscure, even for Eisenstein. Mikhail Kaufman was also dissatisfied by the final version of the film and it marked the end of his collaboration with Vertov.

In the transition to sound Vertov outstripped Eisenstein and most of the other silent cinema masters. He was prepared for the sound revolution because of his early experiments with noise recording, and in "A Sixth of the World" he had even discovered substitutes for the human voice: by using various prints in his intertitles and by rhythmically alternating the phrases with images, Vertov achieved the illusion of off-screen narration. His first sound picture, "Enthusiasm: Donbass Symphony" (1931), was an instant success abroad; Chaplin wrote that he had never imagined that industrial sounds could be organized in such a beautiful way and named "Enthusiasm" the best film of the year. Yet at home it was widely ridiculed as cacophony, in spite of its ideological fervor. Vertov's next film, "Three Songs of Lenin" (1934), made in commemoration of the tenth

anniversary of Lenin's death, had to wait six months for its official release, allegedly because it had failed to emphasize the "important role" of Stalin in the Russian Revolution. Subsequently, the proper footage was added. In spite of these complications, the film turned out to be a popular success both at home and abroad. Even those who had little reason to adore Lenin couldn't help praising the overall elegance of its structure, the elegiac fluidity of montage, the lyrical inner monologue and the highly expressive and technologically innovative synchronous-sound shots of people talking.

In spite of such success, by the end of the 1930s Vertov was deprived of any serious independent work. He was not persecuted, like many of his avant-garde friends; he lived for almost 20 years in obscurity, editing conventional newsreels, the same kind of films he had once proven so capable of transforming into art.

Six years after his death, French documentary filmmakers Jean Rouch and Edgar Morin adopted Vertov's theory and practice into their method of Cinema-Verite. In recent years Vertov's heritage of poetic documentary has influenced many young filmmakers all over the world. In 1962 the first Soviet monograph on Vertov was published, followed by "Dziga Vertov: Articles, Diaries, Projects," which was published in English as "Kino-Eye, The Writings of Dziga Vertov." In 1984, in commemoration of the 30th anniversary of Vertov's death, three New York organizations—Anthology Film Archives, the Collective for Living Cinema and Joseph Papp's Film at the Public—mounted the first American retrospective of Vertov's work, with panels and lectures by leading Vertov scholars and screenings of films by Vertov's contemporaries and his followers from all over the world.

MILESTONES:

1914–1916: Wrote poems, stories, essays and novels and began using name Dziga Vertov (literally, whirling or spinning top)

1915: Moved to Moscow with family after German invasion of Poland

1918: Worked as editor (and then senior editor) of the Moscow Film Committee's "Kino-nedelya/Cinema Week", a regular newsreel service

1919: Completed first long documentary compilation, "Godoushchine revolyutsii/Anniversary of the Revolution"

1919: Published Kinoks-Revolution manifesto

1922: Introduced theory of Kino-Glaz

1922: Created screen magazine, "Kino-Pravda"

1931: First sound film, "Enthusiasm/Symphony of the Donabas"

1937: Directed last personal film, "Lullaby"

Worked for newsreel, "Novosti Dnia/News of the Day"

BIBLIOGRAPHY:

"Kino-Eye" Dziga Vertov (translated by Kevin O'Brien and edited by Annette Michelson) 1984 University of California Press

Charles Vidor

BORN: in Budapest, Hungary, 07/27/1900

DEATH: in Vienna, Austria, 06/05/1959

NATIONALITY: Hungarian

EDUCATION: University of Budapest, Budapest, Hungary; civil engineering

University of Berlin, Berlin, Germany; civil engineering

BIOGRAPHY

Editor and assistant director with UFA who arrived in the US in 1924 and, after a stint with a Wagnerian opera company and in a Broadway chorus, left for Hollywood. Vidor made his directorial debut in 1931 with the self-financed short, "The Bridge", which landed him a contract with MGM. In 1932 he co-directed his first feature, "The Mask of Fu Manchu", one of the finest screen adaptations of the Sax Rohmer novels. Vidor was noted for his ability to impart a technical fluency to routine subjects; among the best of his prolific output were "Ladies in Retirement" (1941), "Love Me or Leave Me" (1955) and "The Joker Is Wild" (1957). Vidor was also responsible for the trailblazing psychological study, "Blind Alley" (1939), and the two Rita Hayworth vehi-

cles that cemented her stardom: the arresting musical, "Cover Girl" (1944), and the steamy noir thriller, "Gilda" (1946).

MILESTONES:

Served as infantry lieutenant during WWI

Worked as assistant cutter and assitant director at UFA studios, Berlin, in early 1920s

1924: Moved to USA; sang with English Grand opera company; worked in Broadway chorus and as longshoreman

Moved to Hollywood; worked as assistant to Alexander Korda; worked as assistant director, editor and scriptwriter in late 1920s

1931: Directed first independent short, "The Bridge"

1932: Joined MGM; directed first feature, "The Mask of Fu Manchu" (uncredited; co-directed with Charles Brabin)

1933: Directed first solo feature, "Sensation Hunters"

1939: Joined Columbia Pictures

1949: Quit Columbia after dispute with Harry Cohn; settled breach-of-contract suit out of court; returned to MGM

1956: Formed Aurora Productions

1959: Suffered heart attack in Vienna while filming "Magic Flame" (completed by George Cukor as "Song Without End")

BORN: King Wallis Vidor in Galveston, Texas, 02/08/1894

DEATH: in Paso Robles, California, 11/01/1982

NATIONALITY: American

EDUCATION: Peacock Military Academy, San Antonio, Texas

AWARDS: Venice Film Festival Best Director Award "Wedding Night" 1935

Edinburgh Film Festival Special Prize for Life Achievement 1964

Directors Guild of America D. W. Griffith Award 1957

Los Angeles Film Critics Association Career Achievement Award 1977

Honorary Oscar 1978 for cinematic achievement and innovation

BIOGRAPHY

King Vidor's films range across all genres, but they are unified by a concern with the struggle for selfhood in a pluralistic, mass society. Influenced both by D.W. Griffith's realism and Sergei Eisenstein's montage aesthetic, Vidor has come closer to reconciling these strains than any other American director.

Raised in Texas, Vidor shot local events for national newsreel companies before forming the Hotex Motion Picture Company in Houston in 1914. Moving to Hollywood with his actress wife Florence, he supported himself with a variety of production jobs before settling at Universal as a writer. His first directing work in Hollywood was independently produced. He made a series of ten inspirational shorts in 1918, followed by "The Turn in the Road" (1919), an extremely successful feature with Vidor's Christian Science beliefs as thematic material.

After a series of further successes released through Robertson-Cole and First National between 1919 and 1921, the director founded "Vidor Village," a small studio from which he planned to produce independently. The experiment failed, but in the meantime Florence Vidor had become a star, and Vidor directed several films featuring her before beginning work for the Metro and Goldwyn studios in 1922. The merger which created MGM in 1924 also made Vidor a senior director for the company, and his fifth film for the young studio, "The Big Parade" (1925), was a landmark critical and popular success.

"The Big Parade" was the first serious screen treatment of WWI, and its harrowing story of a disinterested heir (John Gilbert) experiencing passion, fear and loss in wartime struck a responsive chord. The film, reportedly one of the most profitable silent films ever produced, made Gilbert a star, vaulted MGM to front-rank studio status and gave Vidor unheard-of creative control.

Vidor's record as a bankable director accounts for the freedom with which he was able to make the unusual urban parable, "The Crowd" (1928). Though a financial failure, the film garnered further prestige for MGM and reinforced Vidor's now international reputation for stylistic experimentation and uncompromising concern for social issues. Subsequent critical milestones were "Hallelujah" (1929), a pioneering black film; "Street Scene" (1931), an adaptation of Elmer Rice's socially conscious drama; and "Our Daily Bread" (1934), the story of a Depression agricultural cooperative, clearly indebted to Soviet montage filmmaking. Notable box-office successes for Vidor were "The Champ" (1931) and "Stella Dallas" (1937). Vidor was instrumental in founding the Screen Directors'

Guild in 1936, and alongside John Ford, Frank Capra and Ernst Lubitsch, was a central figure in 30s American filmmaking.

After some three weeks' work on "The Wizard of Oz" (1939) and the spectacular and innovative location Technicolor photography of "Northwest Passage" (1940), Vidor became frustrated with MGM's apparent lack of commitment to his increasingly epochal vision of American life. His "An American Romance" (1944) was drastically cut by MGM and led him to sever ties with the studio where, except for prestigious loan-outs, he had been directing for over 20 years.

Vidor's epic "Duel in the Sun" (1947) pioneered the "adult" western genre, but he quit the project before completion and the final result is the product of several directorial hands, as well as producer David O. Selznick. After his episode of the omnibus film "On Our Merry Way" (1948) was cut by producer Benedict Bogeaus, Vidor signed with Warner Bros. for what would eventually be a three-picture deal. The first of these projects was "The Fountainhead" (1949), which skillfully combined novelist Ayn Rand's radical egoism with the director's own, more quizzical, individualism. The story of an architect's battle with professional and social hypocrisy, the film was among Vidor's most fully realized productions of the postwar period. Although equally striking, "Beyond the Forest" (1949) was thematically bizarre: the tale of a small-town doctor's wife (Bette Davis) and her ambitions ended Davis' 20-year career at Warners amid poor box-office returns and much resentment.

On concluding his deal with Warners, Vidor experimented as an independent producer with two films, "Japanese War Bride" (1952) and, in the same year, "Ruby Gentry"—the last picture to fully manifest his bleak point of view and operatic visual style. His last three features were the inconclusive and bloodless "Man Without a Star" (1955) and the spectacles "War and Peace" (1956) and "Solomon and Sheba" (1959).

Vidor spent his last years producing two

short films on metaphysics, lecturing at film schools and retrospectives of his work, and trying to interest producers in various projects, including a film based on his investigation of the 1924 William Desmond Taylor murder case.

Vidor's darkly humanistic vision, accompanied (especially in the 1925–35 period) by a striking and eclectic visual style, made him one of the most influential directors of his time. His oeuvre is as rich, diverse and intelligent as any in the history of cinema.

MILESTONES:

1909–1910: Worked in Galveston's first movie theater, the Globe, as ticket-taker and part-time projectionist

Became amateur newsreel photographer, shooting local events and selling them to newsreel companies

1915: Shot first film (two-reeler), "In Tow" (date approximate)

1915: Drove to Hollywood (financed trip by shooting footage for Ford Company's advertising newsreel)

Submitted original scripts to Universal under pseudonym, Charles K Wallis

1918: Directed shorts about reform work of Judge Willis Brown

1919: Debut as film director with "The Turn in the Road"

1920: Formed Vidor Village studio

1922: Joined MGM after Vidor Village shut down

1925: Directed first hit, "The Big Parade"

1929: Filmed first sound feature, "Hallelujah"

1959: Retired from directing

Became instructor for UCLA graduate cinema class in the 1960s

1974: Directed two short documentaries, "Truth and Illusion"

BIBLIOGRAPHY:

"A Tree Is a Tree" King Vidor, 1953; autobiography; reprinted in 1977

"King Vidor" John Baxter, 1976

BORN: Jean Bonaventure de Vigo in Paris, France, 04/26/1905

DEATH: in Paris, France, 10/26/1934

NATIONALITY: French

EDUCATION: attended several boarding schools including the Boys School of St. Cloud until 1917

attended a boarding school in Nimes (under the name, Jean Sales) and other boarding schools at Millau and Chartes after death of father

BIOGRAPHY

Battling chronic lung disease throughout his life, branded a traitor's son by his fellow countrymen, dead at the untimely age of 29, Jean Vigo left a truncated cinema legacy of four films. Despite his meager output, Vigo has become one of the most influential French filmmakers of the century, even if it was an honor he would never live to see. At the time of their release, the films now considered Vigo's three masterpieces, "A propos de Nice" (1929), "Zero de conduite" (1933) and "L'Atalante" (1934), were largely vilified by the critics, ignored by the public, recut and butchered by producers and exhibitors. Not until the late 1940s, during the postwar art cinema movement, was Vigo's work rediscovered and finally appreciated for its unique combination of lyric realism and daring surrealism and for its and poetic simplicity.

Vigo's life was one of constant turmoil. A sickly child who suffered from respiratory disease, Vigo was constantly shuttled in and out of hospitals and sanitariums. Both his parents were intensely involved in politics, leaving no time for the care of a child, and Jean found himself passed from relative to relative and boarding school to boarding school. During Jean's young adulthood, his father, Eugene Bonaventure de Vigo (a.k.a. Miguel Almereyda), a left-wing political activist, was accused by the French government of collaborating with Germany in a scheme to end WWI, and he was put on trial as a traitor. But before Almereyda was to appear at his trial, he was found strangled in his jail cell. Embittered over the questionable circumstances behind his father's death, Vigo became embroiled in a campaign to clear his father's name, but frequent relapses of his illness somewhat diluted his efforts. In 1926, Vigo began to attend classes at the Sorbonne, sparking his interest in cinema.

In 1928, Vigo traveled to Paris, where, through meetings with Claude Autant-Lara and Germaine Dulac, he became an assistant cameraman to the noted French cinematographer Burel on "Venus." After receiving a 100,000-franc gift from his father-in-law, Vigo purchased a Debrie camera and proceeded to shoot an independent documentary, "A propos de Nice."

As with such innovators as Griffith and Welles, Vigo's genius was in incorporating past trends and reshaping them into a new film style that future filmmakers can adopt and amend. With "A propos de Nice," "Zero de conduite" and "L'Atalante," Vigo consolidated the formalistic expressiveness of the silent French avant-garde, the open naturalism of the American silent cinema of von Stroheim and Chaplin, and the blasting immediacy of Dziga Vertov's Kino Pravda newsreel. Vigo reshaped these strands into a cinema of stylized realism. His films were poetic studies of small details and processes transformed into celebrations of mythic moments.

"A propos de Nice" uses satirical exaggerations and sexual imagery to explode a seemingly gentle travelogue into a subversive expose of a way of life. "Taris Champion de Natation"

(1931), his second film, enlisted a toned-down surrealism which undercut a celebratory profile of a famous swimmer. In its depiction of an authoritarian adult world in a French boarding school, "Zero de conduite" employed an opposition between formalist caricature and a hyper-real depiction of a child's world view to criticize stifling regimentation and conservatism. And in "L'Atalante," Vigo wove a simple, graceful narrative into a celebratory ode to movement and the present tense. In these films, Vigo strove to create a new, immediate style that was later to achieve full expression in the open cinema of Welles and Renoir and retooled into the French New Wave essays of Jean-Luc Godard.

But the bright promise of Vigo in pursuit of a new film style was suddenly crushed when, on October 5, 1934, a few days after the opening of "L'Atalante," Jean Vigo succumbed to rheumatic septicameia. However, by its lyrical grace and sparkling immediacy, Vigo's scant film work has endured and re-shaped cinema, its towering contradictions and poetic sensibility ever fresh and new.

MILESTONES:

After death of father, adopted by grand-mother's husband, photographer Gabriel Aubes who taught him photography

1926: Sent to sanatorium at Font-Romeu for his tuberculosis

1928: Moved to Nice to work at Franco-Film's new production studio

1929: First film assignment as assistant cameraman on film, "Venus"

1930: Film directing debut with "A Propos de Nice"

1933: Third film, "Zero de conduite" removed from circulation by censors because it was considered "anti-France" (except for cine-club screenings, not shown again in France until 1945)

QUOTES:

The annual Jean Vigo Prize is awarded in his memory, generally to a young and promising filmmaker.

Thomas Vinterberg

BORN: in Copenhagen, Denmark, 05/19/1969

NATIONALITY: Danish

EDUCATION: National Film School of Denmark, Copenhagen, Denmark, 1993

AWARDS: Cannes Film Festival Jury Prize "Festen/Celebration" 1998; shared with Claude Miller's "La Classe niege/The Class Trip"

European Film Academy Discovery 98 Award "Festen/The Celebration" 1998; tied with Erick Zonca's "La Vie revee des anges/The Dreamlife of Angels"

Amanda Award Best Nordic Film "Festen/The Celebration" 1998; Norwegian film award

Los Angeles Film Critics Association Award Best Foreign Film "The Celebration" 1998

New York Film Critics Circle Award Best Foreign Language Film "The Celebration" 1998

Guldbagge Award Best Foreign Film "The Celebration" 1998

Independent Spirit Award Best Foreign Film "Festen/The Celebration" 1999

BIOGRAPHY

In danger of becoming as well known for his good looks as for his movies, Danish filmmaker Thomas Vinterberg entered into the spirit of child's play with fellow director Lars von Trier ("Breaking the Waves" 1996), taking a "Vow of Chastity" as part of their "Dogma 95" and finding liberation in the self-imposed limits. Though the tireless self-promoter won both praise and scorn for his half-serious, half tongue-in-cheek embrace of Dogma 95, with some parties sneering he wasn't exactly "reinventing the wheel" by walking in the footprints of Cassavetes, De Sica and Altman, he certainly backed all the talk with a brilliant film adhering to the manifesto's edicts, "Festen/The Celebration" (1998), an expertly paced melodrama employing child abuse as a catalyst to explore unbridled machismo, patriarchal arrogance and the prevalence of Danish racism. His feature debut, "De Storste helte/The Greatest Heroes" (1996), had been a fairly typical example of the "road movie" genre and paled in comparison.

Vinterberg became established with his thesis film "Last Round" (1993), which won the jury and producer's awards at the International Student Film Festival in Munich and first prize in Tel Aviv. He followed with the TV drama "Dregen der Gik Baglaens/The Boy Who Walked Backwards" (1995) and "The Greatest Heroes" before hitting the mother lode of critical acclaim with "The Celebration." Wishing to evoke the dramatic breadth of Strindberg and the cinematic panache of Bergman, Vinterberg unleashed his video cameras (fudging Dogma 95 principles a bit by later blowing the video up to the prescribed 35mm) on an upperclass, dysfunctional Danish family, with friends, spouses and lovers in tow, as they mark the patriarch's 60th birthday. When the oldest son Christian, displaying the melancholy and mordant wit of a latter-day Hamlet, calmly accuses his father of incest before the assembled, it sets the stage for a long night (and even the next morning) of revelation, and the frenetic handheld camera movements perfectly captured the film's nervous evocation of moral chaos. The running gag is how the party never ends, that no matter what appalling act has just been disclosed, the guests never drop their sense of propriety. Their attitude is, "Let's have our coffee."

"The Celebration" is an audacious film, in keeping with its creator's brashness, but time will tell if it, von Trier's "The Idiots" (1998) and Soren Kragh-Jacobsen's "Mifune" (1999) are the only products of Dogma 95's gimmicky genre. Though the style worked for "The Celebration", it must be said that screenwriters Vinterberg and Mogens Rukov supplied outstanding raw material for the experiment, a story so compelling that audiences forgave the film's grainy texture and lack of conventional polish. If the director adheres to the manifesto's rules for subsequent films, one wonders if moviegoers will have continued patience for such a "home movies" flavor. Certainly the onus will be on Vinterberg to provide scintillating tales that take the viewers' minds off what they are missing.

MILESTONES:

Grew up in a journalists' commune in Copenhagen

1993: Thesis film, "Last Round", won the jury and producer's awards at the International Student Film Festival in Munich and first prize in Tel Aviv; co-written with Bo hr. Hansen

1994: Wrote (again with Hansen) and directed the 36-minute "Drengen der gik baglaens/The Boy Who Walked Backwards" for Danish TV; also produced

1995: With Lars von Trier, issued 'Dogme 95/Dogma 95', a manifesto for making films; declaration of principles ("vow of chastity") included shooting on location in 35mm color with hand-held cameras and no unnatural sound or music and adhering to a very Aristotelian allegiance of time; disallowed any "genre" movies or "superficial action"

1996: First feature, "De Storste helte/The Greatest Heroes", starred Danish actors Ulrich Thomsen and Thomas Bo Larsen; third screenwriting collaboration with Hansen; picture did not subscribe to Dogma 95 doctrine

1998: First film made under Dogma 95, "Festen/The Celebration", reunited him with Thomsen and Larsen; co-wrote with Mogens

Rukov; also contributed an uncredited cameo as a taxi driver

1999: Signed to direct first English-language feature "The Third Lie"

QUOTES:

The Vow of Chastity

I swear to submit to the following set of rules drawn up and confirmed by Dogma 95:

1. Shooting must be done on location. Props and sets must not be brought in. (If a particular prop is necessary for the story, a location must be chosen where the prop is to be found.)

2. The sound must never be produced apart from the images or vice versa. (Music must not be used unless it occurs where the scene is being shot.)

3. The camera must be hand-held. And movement or immobility attainable in the hand is permitted. (The film must not take place where the camera is standing; shooting must take place where the film takes place.)

4. The film must be in colour. Special lighting is not acceptable. (If there is too little light for exposure the scene must be cut or a single lamp be attached to the camera.)

5. Optical work and filters are forbidden.

6. The film must not contain superficial action. (Murders, weapons, etc., must not occur.)

7. Temporal and geographic alienation are forbidden. (That is to say that the film takes place here and now.)

8. Genre movies are not acceptable.

9. The film format must be Academy 35 mm.

10. The director must not be credited.

"Europe has a complex about America. Often the American culture is like rolling over Europe; we have McFries on every corner, things like that. So I think it is important not to give in to much and start to serve the American territories with our films. We have to do what we do. And those who want to see it, see it."—Thomas Vinterberg, to John Anderson, in *Los Angeles Times*, October 18, 1998.

"Shooting on video was a compromise I didn't like . . . But we couldn't afford it [35mm]. In the beginning I said we wouldn't do the film on video. Then we were told we could have 35mm—as long as we used only three actors. We needed 50. But you gain something from video, namely the hidden camera. You can do things with that you can't with a 35mm.

" . . . Shooting normally you can shoot the speech and then shoot the reaction shot. But when you need the sound to be recorded at the same time you have to do the reaction shot every time. We filmed a huge amount of material— 64 hours. Sometimes we'd use three cameras at once, all needing sound. There would be booms and wires all over the place. Sometimes we had the actors holding the cameras. In the scene where Christian faints at the reception the sound engineer was swinging the microphone to make a swooshing, dizzy-like sound and Christian was holding the camera."—Vinterberg, quoted in *Sight and Sound*, February 1999

"Many people in Denmark are quite enlightened and support the values of the welfare state, but due to competition over jobs, there are an increasing number of unemployed and working-class people who are becoming quite racist. And because of very nationalistic traditions, and the fact that the country is small and homogenous, these problems are on the rise . . . we have ultranationalistic parties who basically support Nazism. If you look at France, someone like Le Pen, who's a complete Nazi, received 18 percent of the vote. It's all over the place and that worries me.

"But to be completely honest, the reference to the black guy in the film came about because the actor playing the part is a very close friend of mine. He moved to New York and I thought, 'I'll bring him back, I'll have to give him a part in the film.' I think it's quite common in filmmaking for good things to come out of banalitites."—Vinterberg, to Richard Porton in *Cineaste*, Volume XXIV, Numbers 2–3.

BORN: Holger Bernard Mischwitzki in Riga, German-occupied Latvia, 11/25/1942

SOMETIMES CREDITED AS:
Holger Mischwitzki

NATIONALITY: German

EDUCATION: Humanistisches Gymnasium left before completion

Werkkunstschule Offenbach, Germany art school

Hochschule fur Bildende Kunste Berlin, Germany art college

AWARD: Los Angeles Film Critics Association Award Best Independent/Experimental Film "Fear of Emptiness" 1985

BIOGRAPHY

One of the more eccentric figures to emerge from the New German Cinema movement, Rosa von Praunheim (ne Holger Mischwitski) studied painting in Berlin before apprenticing with openly gay filmmakers Gregory J. Markopoulos and Werner Schroeter. He made several short films in the late 1960s—the first was "Von Rosa von Praunheim" in 1967—and moved into TV work with 1970s' "Die Bettwurst/The Bedroll". Von Praunheim first garnered notice with the documentary "Sisters of the Revolution" (1969), which examined the women's liberation movement and included a segment on homosexuals who supported feminist causes. The satirical "It Is Not the Homosexual Who Is Perverted, But the Situation in Which He Lives" (1970) follows the "coming out" process of one young man and engendered some controversy for its depictions of stereotypical gay men caught up in what was perceived as a self-destructive lifestyle.

Von Praunheim has remained a more marginal figure than contemporaries such as Volker Schlondorff and Wim Wenders, preferring to address issues of politics and sexuality, especially gay and lesbian sexuality and AIDS, than to reach a broader mainstream audience. He also has again and again courted controversy with his films. "Army of Lovers or Revolt of the Perverts" (1979) examined segments of the gay rights movement in the USA and pointed up the fragmentation of the leadership into groups with self-aggrandizing agendas. Not all of his work focused exclusively on gay themes, either (i.e., "Red Love" 1982); von Praunheim was also interested in people living on the margins of society and many of his films openly challenge the complacent views of audiences. He has dabbled in thrillers ("Horror Vacui" 1984; "Der Biss/The Bite" 1985) as well as profiled cabaret artists from the 1920s and 30s. Working in tandem with American documentarian Phil Zwickler, von Praunheim crafted a trilogy ("Silence = Death", "Positive" and "Fire Under Your Ass"—the latter remains unreleased in the USA) which examined the effects of the AIDS crisis in NYC. In 1995, he produced, directed and played himself in "Neurosia: 50 Years of Perversity", an autobiographical feature structured after Orson Welles' 1941 classic "Citizen Kane" with a journalist investigating the murder of infamous filmmaker Rosa von Praunheim. More recently, he helmed the documentary "Gay Courage: 100 Years of the Gay Movement" (1998) which featured historical reenactments.

MILESTONES:
Raised in East Berlin and Frankfurt
Studied painting in Berlin
Worked as apprentice to filmmakers Gregory J. Markopoulos and Werner Schroeter

1967: Directed first 16mm (12 minute) short, "Von Rosa von Praunheim"

1969: Helmed the documentary "Sisters of the Revolution" which examined the women's rights movement

1970: Made the feature-length TV movie "Die Bettwurst/The Bedroll"

1970: Directed the satire on gay life, "It Is Not the Homosexual Who Is Perverse, But the Situation in Which He Lives"

1975: Produced, directed, shot and appeared in the documentary "Underground and Emigrants"

1977: Wrote, directed and produced "Berlin Bettwurst", a sequel to "Die Bettwurst"

1982: Investigated the underground cabaret scene of Berlin in "Stadt der Verlorenen Seelen/City of Lost Souls"

1984: Helmed the thriller "Horror Vacui"

1990: Examined the effects of the AIDS crisis in NYC in "Schweigen = Tod/Silence = Death" and "Positive"; both made in collaboration with Phil Zwickler

1992: Wrote, produced and directed the biographical docudrama "Ich Bin Meine Eigene Frau/I Am My Own Woman", based on the life of German transvestite Charlotte von Mahsldorf

1995: Directed, produced and played himself in the autobiographical comedy "Neurosia: 50 Years of Perversity"

1996: Appeared as himself in "I Was a Jewish Sex Worker", a documentary directed by Phillip B. Roth

1998: Directed the documentary "Gay Courage: 100 Years of the Gay Movement"

QUOTES:

"I thought gay people could overthrow the government and have greater sexual freedom. Now, I think even bourgeois gay people have the right to live a bourgeois gay life. If they want to marry, they can, and if they want to go to the military, they can. I think they should be recognized as openly gay and lesbian. . . . I can't force them to be revolutionaries."—Rosa von Praunheim

Josef von Sternberg

BORN: Jonas Sternberg in Vienna, Austria, 05/29/1894

DEATH: in Hollywood, California, 12/22/1969

NATIONALITY: Austrian

EDUCATION: Jamaica High School, Jamaica, New York; attended briefly

AWARD: Venice Film Festival Best Cinematography Award "The Devil Is A Woman" 1935; award shared with Lucien Ballard

BIOGRAPHY

Once considered one of Hollywood's premier directors, Josef von Sternberg is now remembered chiefly for his seven films with Marlene Dietrich. Actually, his main contribution to cinema is probably his handling of lighting and mise-en-scene. Sternberg (the "von" was added, as with his fellow Austrian Erich von Stroheim, to lend glamour to his name) was first and foremost a master cinematographer (the only one, in fact, who was able to use the American Society of Cinematographers credit "A.S.C." after his name on a directorial credit). He only made one color film (the unfortunate "Jet Pilot" 1957), but the rich textures of his cinematic spaces attained a color of their own; if he learned anything from the experiments of early German cinema, it was the establishment, through "expressionist" use of light and dark, of "Stimmung" (atmosphere). Even when the plot line of his film was diffuse, its stunning visuals took on a life of their own. Whether a Sternberg film is set in a small German town or an outpost in Morocco, sunny Spain or a misty Japanese island, the Russian Imperial court or the California coast, it is part of a distinct universe.

Sternberg's first films were made in Hollywood, and his very first, "The Salvation Hunters" (1925), was an immediate success. The great German actor Emil Jannings, whom Sternberg brought to the US to star in "The Last Command" (1928) as a Russian general dispossessed by the Revolution, recommended that he return to Europe to direct the film version of Heinrich Mann's "The Blue Angel" (1930). The film, Germany's first sound production, made an international star not only of Dietrich but of Sternberg himself, and the two were welcomed back to Hollywood with great fanfare, initiating a collaboration that would, in the space of five years, make film history with "Morocco" (1930), "Dishonored" (1931), "Shanghai Express" (1932), "Blonde Venus" (1932), "The Scarlet Empress" (1934) and "The Devil Is a Woman" (1935).

While "The Blue Angel," based on a literary source, employed a certain degree of realism to tell its tale of an authoritarian schoolmaster smitten with a free-spirited cabaret entertainer, the Hollywood films seem to deal with aspects of the Eternal Feminine, as personified by the sometimes glamorous and mysterious, sometimes mischievous and witty, sometimes earthy, always feisty Dietrich, whose very presence gives a decidedly feminist cast to all these films.

Of Sternberg's post-Dietrich films, three are notable: 1937's uncompleted "I, Claudius", which might have been his finest film he had not run into problems with financial backers; "The Shanghai Gesture" (1941), a delightfully dark piece of suspense and exoticism in which Gene Tierney, Ona Munson, and Victor Mature together assume the Dietrich persona; and the director's own favorite project, "The Saga of

Anatahan" (1952), a poetic study of Japanese soldiers isolated on an island at the end of WWII. "Anatahan" can be seen as a virtual encyclopedia of the possibilities inherent in black-and-white cinematography.

COMPANIONS:

wife: Riza Royce. Married in 1926; divorced in 1930

wife: Jeanne Annette MacBride. Secretary; married in 1943; was 21 at time of marriage; worked as Von Sternberg's secretary; had two children together

MILESTONES:

1901: Sent for by father who was living in the USA

1904: Returned to Vienna

1908: Moved back to USA (Long Island)

Worked as apprentice at aunt's millinery store and as stock clerk for lace store

Changed first name to Josef and left home at 17

1914: Film patcher, then chief assistant to the director general, with World Film Company, Fort Lee, NJ

1917: Joined Army Signal Corps; helped make training films

1919: First credit as assistant director, "The Mystery of the Yellow Room" (dir. Emile Chautard)

1923: Moved to Hollywood; first work as assistant director on "By Divine Right"

1924: Added "von" to name at suggestion of actor Elliot Dexter while working as scenarist and assistant on "By Divine Right"

1925: Directorial debut, "The Salvation Hunters"

1926: Joined Paramount as assistant director

1930: Moved to Germany, directed UFA's first sound film, "The Blue Angel" (first of seven films with Marlene Dietrich)

1937: Went to England to work for Alexander Korda on "I Claudius"

1941: Filmed documentary "The Town" for US Office of War Information

1947: Taught class in film directing at USC

Semi-retired during mid 1950s

1953: Last film shot in Jjapan, "The Saga of Anatahan"

1959–1963: Taught course on the aethetics of film at UCLA

QUOTES:

"No theory of the cinema is viable unless it considers Josef von Sternberg one of its major talents"—John Baxter in "Hollywood in the Thirties."

"I am Marlene and Marlene is me"—Josef von Sternberg.

He received the George Eastman House Medal of Honor in 1957.

Made honorary member of the Akademie der Kunste, Berlin in 1960.

BIBLIOGRAPHY:

"Fun in a Chinese Laundry" Josef Von Sternberg, 1965; autobiography

"The Cinema of Josef Von Sternberg" J. Baxter, 1971

"Sternberg" Peter Baxter; collection of reviews and critical essays on Sternberg's films

Erich von Stroheim

BORN: Erich Oswald Stroheim in Vienna, Austria, 09/22/1885

SOMETIMES CREDITED AS:
Erich Oswald Hans Carl Maria Stroheim

DEATH: in Maurepas, France, 05/12/1957

NATIONALITY: Austrian

CITIZENSHIP: United States, 1926

AWARD: National Board of Review Award Best Acting "La grande illusion/Grand Illusion" 1938; one of 22 performers cited; shared award with co-stars Dita Parlo, Jean gabin and Pierre Fresnay

BIOGRAPHY

Erich Stroheim adopted his 'von', the mark of nobility, somewhere between his native Vienna, where he grew up working in his father's straw hat factory, and Hollywood, where he joined D.W. Griffith's ensemble around 1914, playing mainly villains. As America entered WWI and anti-German sentiment grew, Stroheim

cultivated the image of the implacable, autocratic Hun, which inspired the studio tag line, "the man you love to hate."

In fact, his true aspiration was directing. "Blind Husbands" (1919) provided Stroheim with a successful debut—he not only directed, but wrote, designed the sets and starred. The film earned him a reputation as a master of physical detail and psychological sophistication flavored by a European sensibility. "The Devil's Passkey" (1920) and "Foolish Wives" (1922) also amplified his reputation for tales of adultery, as well as spendthrift production. To the Hollywood establishment, Stroheim's most annoying trait was his penchant for lengthy, psychologically intricate movies, and he invariably fell afoul of studio editing and interference. "Foolish Wives" was reduced by a third, and he was fired from "Merry-Go-Round" (1923) by Universal production chief Irving Thalberg. In perhaps the most famous case of a mangled masterpiece, Stroheim filmed Frank Norris's novel "McTeague" in obsessive detail, producing a 9 1/2 hour masterwork, "Greed" (1925). The horrified studio forced the director to cut the film, but that version was still over

4 hours, so the film was taken out of Stroheim's hands and given first to director Rex Ingram and eventually to editor June Mathis, who pruned it to its present 140-minute running time. Search for the missing footage spawned a virtual cottage industry among devoted archivists and Stroheim devotees.

Hired by MGM to direct the operetta "The Merry Widow" (1925), Stroheim perversely adapted it as a black comedy, replete with the sadism of the decadent Hapsburg empire. He returned to the same subject for "The Wedding March" (1928), a film so long it had to be released in two parts—the second part called "The Honeymoon" in Europe. As brilliant as Stroheim's films were, he seemed willfully ignorant of the havoc his painstaking and expensive production methods wreaked in his relations with financial backers. His most profligate escapade was with Joseph P. Kennedy's money, on the Gloria Swanson vehicle "Queen Kelly" (1928). Stroheim's high-handedness also failed to endear him to stars, and Swanson fired him from the picture, which was never completed, although a "reconstructed" version was issued in 1985. Stroheim's directing career virtually ended with the swashbuckling silent era, as sound and budget-conscious production changed the tenor of filmmaking.

In the 1930s, with the Germans once again on the march, Stroheim returned to acting the horrible Hun. As the commandant of the POW camp in Jean Renoir's "Grand Illusion" (1937), his disdainful demeanor, complete with monocle, would stand as an indelible symbol of the tragic decline of the European aristocracy. Although typecast, he did seem the only actor to inhabit that persona, and it was used with particularly poignant effect in "Sunset Boulevard" (1950). By his death in 1957, he had become an icon of another era, one whose image he had helped create by living up to his self-imposed "von."

MILESTONES:
Served briefly in the Austrian cavalry at 17;

managed father's straw hat manufacturing factory

1909: Arrived in America; worked as salesman, clerk, short story writer, railroad worker and travel agent

1912: Wrote first play, "In the Morning"

1914: Initial film work as an extra in "Captain McLean" and

1915: First screen credit in "Farewell to Thee"

1916: Debut as assistant director, "Intolerance"; also acted

1919: First film as director, star, and screenwriter in "Blind Husbands/The Pinnacle")

1919: Signed contract with Universal

1919: Starred as villain in "The Heart of Humanity"

1922: Fired from "Merry-Go-Round" by Irving Thalberg

Hired by Goldwyn Company early 1920s

1923: Fired from "Greed" by Irving Thalberg, the production head of newly-formed Metro-Goldwyn-Mayer who then hired Rex Ingram to recut the film

1929: Fired from "Queen Kelly" by Joseph Kennedy

1932: Sound film co-directing debut with "Walking Down Broadway" (co-screenwriter; re-directed by Alfred Werker, re-edited and re-titled "Hello, Sister;" no directorial credit; original prints no longer exist)

1934: Attempted suicide (Christmas)

1935: Hired as contract writer at MGM

1936: Quit MGM

1941–1943: Made only stage play appearance in "Arsenic and Old Lace"

Moved to and worked as actor in France; briefly returned to USA to appear in "Sunset Boulevard" (1950)

QUOTES:
"The public at large is not as spiritually poor as the producers imagine. It wants to be shown life as real as it actually is for people: harsh, unexpected, hopeless, fatalistic. I intend to tailor my films in the rough fabric of human

conflicts. Because to make films with the regularity of a sausage machine forces you to make them neither better nor worse than a string of sausages."—von Stroheim, in 1925.

Given the Legion of Honor by French government for his services to film art in 1957.

BIBLIOGRAPHY:

"Paprika" Eric von Stroheim, 1935; novel about gypsy life

"Les Feux de la St. Jean" Eric von Stroheim, 1951; first volume of two

"Les Feux de la St. Jean" Eric von Stroheim 1954, second volume

"Poto-Poto" Eric von Stroheimn, 1956; novel; adaptation of "Queen Kelly" script

"Hollywood Scapegoat: The Biography of Erich von Stroheim" Peter Noble, 1951, Fortune Press

"The Man You Love to Hate" Richard Kozarski; critical and historical study of von Stroheim's career

"Stroheim" Arthur Lenning, 2000, University of Kentucky Press

Lars von Trier

BORN: Lars Trier in Copenhagen, Denmark, 04/30/1956

NATIONALITY: Danish

EDUCATION: University of Copenhagen Copenhagen, Denmark

National Film School of Denmark, Copenhagen, Denmark, 1979–82

AWARDS: Cannes Film Festival Technique Award "The Element of Crime" 1984

Cannes Film Festival Grand Prix "Zentropa/Europa" 1991

Cannes Film Festival Technique Award "Zentropa/Europa" 1991

Stockhom Film Festival Dala Horse "Zentropa/Europa" 1991

Danish Film Academy Robert Statue Award Best Danish Film "Zentropa/Europa" 1991; film won a total of seven Danish Film Academy awards including cinematography, production design, sound, music, editing, special effects

Seattle Film Festival Golden Space Needle "The Kingdom" 1995

Cannes Film Festival Grand Prix "Breaking the Waves" 1996

Felix Best Picture "Breaking the Waves" 1996

New York Film Critics Circle Award Best Director "Breaking the Waves" 1996

National Society of Film Critics Award Best Director "Breaking the Waves" 1996

Cesar Best Foreign Film "Breaking the Waves" 1997

Cannes Film Festival Palme d'Or "Dancer in the Dark" 2000

European Film Academy Award European Film "Dancer in the Dark" 2000

Golden Satellite Best Original Song "I've Seen It All" (from "Dancer in the Dark") 2000 shared with Bjork and Sjon Sigurdsson

Goya Best European Film "Dancer in the Dark" 2000

Independent Spirit Award Best Foreign Film "Dancer in the Dark" 2001

BIOGRAPHY

Lars von Trier has been one of the splashiest talents that Danish—indeed European—cinema has produced in years. His reputation as one of a few genuine "enfants terribles" of cinema in the 1980s and 90s does not stem simply from his call for Ingmar Bergman's death (so that other Scandinavian filmmakers could receive more attention) or his calling Roman Polanski a bad name when his film "Europa" (1991;

"Zentropa" in the USA) failed to receive the Palme d'Or at Cannes. Rather, the attention von Trier has justly received stems from his playful experimentation and the darkly haunting atmosphere he evokes in settings which, whether set in the present or past, somehow seem futuristic and other-worldly. He is best known for his trilogy on the theme of Europe, "The Element of Crime" (1984), "Epidemic" (1987) and especially "Zentropa", which together form a potent allegorical critique of contemporary Continental decay. Sometimes uneven, frequently witty, ever challenging, von Trier's work is perhaps typified by the remarks of the "Leonard Maltin's Film & Video Guide" on "Zentropa": "Though it feels like a stunt, this is a rare contemporary movie that makes one feel privy to the reinvention of cinema."

Part of von Trier's inventiveness stems from his refusal to honor conventions consistently, his blithe shifting of moods from the satirically comic to the ironically tragic. He also wreaks clever variation on recurring symbolism in his oeuvre; water imagery, for instance, occurs in the overflowing bathtub and the flooded train of "Zentropa", the submerged police archives in "The Element of Crime" and the rugged emotionalism of the Scottish coastal waters in his strangely epic love story "Breaking the Waves" (1996). Von Trier's originality also rests on his appropriations; his endlessly tricky films are some of the most densely referential in the international swell of postmodernism. His frequently hilarious and very disturbing "The Kingdom" (1994), made as a miniseries for Dutch TV but also released theatrically, is only the most obvious example. A sly pastiche of TV medical dramas, it openly borrows from and even parodies David Lynch's cult series "Twin Peaks."

The latter connection is apt, for von Trier is, like Lynch, categorizable, if at all, by the admittedly vague but nonetheless bandied-about term "stylist." Obsessed with obsession; drawn to mystery, fantasy and comical horror; lushly romantic at times but deeply critical of romantic love and romanticism, he is a filmmaker who seems to revel in technique but who actually dissolves splits between form and content with his pointed, cinematically evoked social observation. Von Trier finds his spiritual comrades in fellow "stylists" ranging from George Melies, James Whale, Alfred Hitchcock, Joseph von Sternberg, Andrei Tarkovsky, Max Ophuls and R.W. Fassbinder. Sometimes criticized for seeming to favor style over meaning, von Trier does not distinguish between the two.

Rather, like the mesmeric narration voiced by Max von Sydow in "Zentropa", von Trier is overt about his control as auteur, about institutions of social constraint (government, law, medicine) and about the reserve spectators exhibit in addressing films. The process of interpreting cinema is pointed out and questioned; the spectator is both victim and conspirator. Hypnosis, used both metaphorically and reflexively, recurs in his films, often commenting on the filmgoing experience itself, perhaps most memorably in the voice-overs of "Zentropa." His films at once hypnotize the spectator and yet constantly call attention to the very process of viewer manipulation in which cinema indulges. As von Trier has noted, "Cinema and hypnotism have a lot in common; mainly 'make believe'. Film is a series of fixed shots which give a false impression of movement. Just like hypnosis, film is based on repetition."

Just as viewer and viewed overlap in von Trier's films, so does the image reflexively fold in upon itself. "Epidemic" features films within the film and "Zentropa", mixing black-and-white with color, piles superimpositions upon back projections, sometimes layering the image seven-fold. In a similar but more thematic vein, von Trier considers other important dichotomies which, in true deconstructionist fashion, he implodes. The law and crime are very close in von Trier's films—in "The Element of Crime" the aging detective who serves as mentor to the protagonist requires that a private eye must merge his identity with that of the criminal he's investigating. A physician within "Epidemic", meanwhile, spreads the disease he's fighting, while in "The Kingdom" another doctor transplants a diseased organ into his own body. A woman in "Breaking the Waves" proves her fidelity by being as promiscuous as possible, while the feckless US hero of "Zentropa", in a collapsing of innocence and duplicity, is manipulated by post-WWII reconstructionists and neo-fascists alike.

As von Trier continues to enjoy international success with the strange, unsettling films he has completed, he has also been working on a lengthy feature whose funding arrangements have inspired him to finish only three minutes worth of the film each year. He plans to finish the film, called "Dimension", in 2024 and doubtless, von Trier will have explored many more of the dimensions of cinema before it is completed.—Written by David Lugowski

MILESTONES:

1977: Made a student film, "Orkide gartneren/ The Orchid Gardener", which helped him gain admission to the Danish Film School

1983: Made the medium-length (60 mins.) film, "Liberation Pictures/Image of a Relief", which he wrote and directed, as a graduate school project; won second prize at an annual European Film School Competition and was promptly picked up by Britain's Channel 4

1984: Feature film debut, "The Element of Crime", which he wrote and directed; was the first film in his "Europe" trilogy; also played the role of "Schmuck of Ages"

1989: Appeared as an actor only in the Danish children's film, "A World of Difference"

1991: Began making the film "Dimension" in three-minute segments to be finished each year; the film is scheduled to be completed in the year 2024

1991: Made third and last film in his "European" trilogy, "Europa/Zentropa"

1994: Made a miniseries for Dutch TV, "The Kingdom", which was then transferred to 35mm film and received an international release theatrically

1995: Films were subject of a retrospective held by Lincoln Center in NYC

1995: With fellow Dane Thomas Vinterberg, issued Dogme 95, a manifesto on cinema requiring helmers to take a "vow of Chastity" and shoot films with no score, using natural light and other techniques

1996: Garnered critical acclaim for "Breaking the Waves"

1998: Helmed the second film made under Dogme 95, "The Idiots"

2000: Directed the musical feature "Dancer in the Dark", starring Bjork; also co-wrote lyrics to songs; shared a Best Original Song Oscar nomination for "I've Seen It All"

Andy Wachowski

BORN: Andrew Wachowski in Chicago, Illinois, 12/29/1967

NATIONALITY: American

EDUCATION: Emerson College, Boston, Massachusetts; dropped out

AWARD: Saturn Award Direction "The Matrix" 2000; shared with brother

BIOGRAPHY

The younger half of the writing-directing-producing team The Wachowski Brothers, Andy Wachowski dropped out of Emerson College in Boston to pursue a career in show business.

Collaborating with his older brother Larry, the duo completed their first script which was optioned by producer Dino De Laurentiis and eventually became the Warner Bros. feature "Assassins" (1995). Another writer polished the script, so the finished product, starring Sylvester Stallone and Antonio Banderas as hit men, veered between generic actioner and character study and ended up a box-office disappointment.

The Wachowskis chose a chancy project for their directorial debut, "Bound" (1996), a romance-thriller featuring Jennifer Tilly and Gina Gershon as criminal lesbians in love. Drawing on influences as varied as Billy Wilder ("Double Indemnity" 1944), Roman Polanski ("Chinatown" 1974) and Sam Raimi ("The Evil Dead" 1983), the brothers set out to create a modern film noir that would invert the genre. With its elaborately stylish camerawork and intriguing story, "Bound" fell into the category of work that one either loved or hated. Receiving generally appreciative reviews, it found a limited, but appreciative audience.

On the other hand, "The Matrix" (1999), the proposed first in a trilogy of futuristic spectaculars that borrowed heavily from such diverse sources as the Bible, "Alice in Wonderland", Hong Kong action flicks and mythology, proved a popular success. Over a period of more than five years, the brothers developed the story for this comic book come to life, penning 14 drafts and overseeing the design of some 500 storyboards. The arduous shoot required the actors (including Keanu Reeves, Laurence Fishburne, Hugo Weaving and Carrie-Anne Moss) to undergo extensive physical conditioning so the film's innovative, special effects-driven set pieces would have a unique visual flair. The meticulous planning paid off as the film opened at Number One and quickly grossed over $100 million, virtually assuring that the other parts of the trilogy would be successes. After nearly a four-year wait, "Matrix Reloaded" (2003), the second installment, hit theaters.

MILESTONES:

Raised in the Midwest

1995: Had first produced screenplay, co-writing "Assassins" with brother Larry

1996: With brother Larry, co-directed, co-wrote, and co-executive produced "Bound"

1999: Co-wrote and co-directed the hit sci-fi actioner "The Matrix", starring Keanu Reevs

2003: With brother Larry, co-wrote and co-directed "The Matrix Reloaded"

Completed the trilogy with "The Matrix: Revelations" (lensed 2001–2002)

QUOTES:

"We wanted to make an independent feature, something that could push the boundaries of a genre film and still remain entertaining."—The Wachowski brothers quoted in the press kit for "Bound."

"We don't like the idea of selling ourselves. We hate the 'film by' credit at the top of a movie. It is so egotistical."—Andy Wachowski quoted in *USA Today*, April 5, 1999.

About writing "The Matrix": Andy Warchowski told *The New York Times* (April 5, 1999): "The script was a synthesis of ideas that sort of came together at a moment when we were interested in a lot of things: making mythology relevant in a modern context, relating quantum physics to Zen Buddhism, investigating your own life. . . . We started out thinking of this as a comic book. We filled notebook after notebook with ideas. Essentially, that's where the script came from."

BIBLIOGRAPHY:

"The Art of 'The Matrix' " Larry & Andy Wachowski, 2001, Newmarket

Larry Wachowski

BORN: Laurence Wachowski in Chicago, Illinois, 06/21/1965

NATIONALITY: American

EDUCATION: Bard College Annandale-on-Hudson, New York dropped out after attending for two years

AWARD: Saturn Award Direction "The Matrix" 2000; shared with brother

BIOGRAPHY

With his younger brother Andy, Larry Wachowski saw their first screenplay produced when "Assassins" (1995) made it to the screen as a vehicle for Sylvester Stallone who played an assassin who is being hunted by another younger hit man (Antonio Banderas). While the final result (with a script polished by yet another writer) was found uneven by critics and was a box-office disappointment, it nevertheless gave the Wachowskis entree in Hollywood.

Born and raised in Chicago, the Wachowskis jokingly claim to have begun their collaboration as toddlers. Both dropped out of college to pursue showbiz and both overcame some major hurdles to complete a far more unusual undertaking, "Bound" (1996), which they co-directed, co-wrote, and co-executive produced. The film, a modern twist on the film noir genre, starred Jennifer Tilly and Gina Gershon as criminal lesbian lovers on the run. The brothers, both married, downplayed their involvement somewhat and turned the focus on the actresses cast. While they claimed it was not difficult for them to create believable gay women protagonists, no doubt the gay community's negative reaction to perceived negative portrayals of lesbian and gay characters (as in 1991's "The Silence of the Lambs" and

1992's "Basic Instinct") was taken into consideration. The press, both before and after its premiere, was generally positive and the film found a limited, albeit appreciative, audience.

On the other hand, "The Matrix" (1999), the proposed first in a trilogy of futuristic spectaculars that borrowed heavily from such diverse sources as the Bible, "Alice in Wonderland", Hong Kong action flicks and mythology, proved a popular success. Over a period of more than five years, the brothers developed the story for this comic book come to life, penning 14 drafts and overseeing the design of some 500 storyboards. The arduous shoot required the actors (including Keanu Reeves, Laurence Fishburne, Hugo Weaving and Carrie-Anne Moss) to undergo extensive physical conditioning so the film's innovative, special-effects-driven set pieces would have a unique visual flair. The meticulous planning paid off as the film opened at Number One and quickly grossed over $100 million, virtually assuring that the other parts of the trilogy would be successful. After a wait of nearly four years, part two, "Matrix Reloaded" (2003) hit movie screens.

MILESTONES:

Raised in the Midwest

1995: Had first screenplay produced, "Assassins"; co-written with brother Andy

1996: With brother, co-directed, co-wrote and co-executive produced "Bound"

1999: Co-wrote and co-directed the hit sci-fi actioner "The Matrix", starring Keanu Reeves

2003: With brother Andy, wrote and directed the second part of the trilogy "The Matrix Reloaded"

Wrapped the trilogy with "The Matrix: Revelations" (lensed 2001–2002)

QUOTES:

"You talk to people and they always ask, 'Why are action movies so dumb?' We hope people are more interested in a more intelligent approach. We hope they are not just intertested in what we call McDonald's movies, the standard you-know-what-you-get [films]."—Larry Warchowski quoted in *USA Today*, April 5, 1999.

"Maybe we'll just retire with a two-film retrospective. We're jsut so tired at this point."— Larry Warchowski quoted in *The New York Times*, April 5, 1999.

BIBLIOGRAPHY:

"The Art of 'The Matrix' " Larry & Andy Wachowski, 2001, Newmarket

Andrzej Wajda

BORN: in Suwalki, Poland, 03/06/1926

NATIONALITY: Polish

EDUCATION: Academy of Fine Arts, Cracow, Poland painting attended for three years; did not graduate

State Film School, Lodz, Poland, 1950–52; began career making short films

AWARDS: Cannes Film Festival Special Jury Prize "Kanal" 1957

Moscow Film Festival Gold Medal "Kanal" 1957 in the category of feature films by young directors

Berlin Film Festival Best Director Award "Ashes and Diamonds" 1962

Milan Film Festival Golden Globe "Landscape After Battle" 1971

Colombo Film Festival First Prize "Landscape After Battle" 1971

Moscow Film Festival Gold Medal "The Birchwood" 1971

San Sebastian Film Festival Silver Conch "The Wedding" 1973

Moscow Film Festival Gold Medal "The Promised Land" 1975

Chicago Film Festival Golden Hugo "The Promised Land" 1975

Cannes Film Festival FIPRESCI Prize "Man of Marble" 1978

Cannes Film Festival Ecumenical Award

(Mixed Catholic and Protestant Jury) "Rough Treatment" 1979

New York Film Critics Circle Special Award 1981; cited along with Krzysztof Zanussi for "the artistry and independent spirit of Polish filmmakers . . . as demonstrated in their films"

Cannes Film Festival Palme d'Or "Man of Iron" 1981

Prix Louis Delluc "Danton" 1982

Cesar Best Director "Danton" 1983

Felix Lifetime Achievement Award 1990; also known as European Film Award

Berlin Film Festival Silver Bear for Lifetime Contribution to the Art of Cinema "Holy Week" 1996

Berlin Film Festival Lifetime Achievement Award 1998

Venice Film Festival Golden Lion for Career Achievement 1998

Honorary Oscar 1999; honored as "one of the most respected filmmakers of our time, a man whose films have given audiences around the world an artist's view of history, democracy and freedom, and who in so doing has himself become a symbol of courage and hope for millions of people in postwar Europe"; presented on March 26, 2000

BIOGRAPHY

By far the best-known film director working in Poland, Andrzej Wajda has achieved the status, both in his life and his work, of a symbol for his beleaguered country. The son of a cavalry officer killed in WWII, Wajda joined the Resistance as a teenager. Later, he studied at the Fine Arts Academy in Krakow for three years before transferring in 1950 to the newly opened State Film School in Lodz, where he learned technique directing several short films.

Wajda's first feature film, "Pokolenie/A Generation" (1954), traced the fate of several young people living under the Nazi Occupation. It was followed in 1957 by "Kanal/They Love Life" a grim tribute to the Warsaw Uprising of 1944, when Red Army units were unable or unwilling to come to the aid of the city. Wajda completed his trilogy on the effects of WWII with his best-known early film, the controversial "Popiol i Diament/Ashes and Diamonds" (1958), which dealt with the undeclared civil war of 1945–46 between elements of the anti-Communist Home Army and the security forces established by the Communist Party–dominated government. Based on a Jerzy Andrzejewski novel, the film incisively depicted the corruption and idealism coloring both sides of the struggle. In keeping with Wajda's tragic sense of Polish history, the idealistic representative of each faction is killed, and both sides remain controlled by the corrupt—whether greedy politicians or arrogant aristocrats.

In addition to adapting literary works to the screen ("The Birch-Wood" 1970, "The Wedding" 1972, "The Young Girls of Wilko" 1979), Wajda has consistently drawn on Polish history for material suited to his tragic sensibility—from the fate of lancers serving under Napoleon in "Popioly/Ashes" (1965) to the harsh industrialization of Lodz in "Ziemia Obiecana/Land of Promise" (1975). It was in the late 1970s, however, that his films became a virtual barometer of social unrest and rebellion. "Czlowiek z Marmuru/Man of Marble" (1977) and "Bez Znieczulenia/Without Anesthesia" (1979) depict the oppression, respectively, of the worker and the intellectual in contemporary Poland. In the later film, a journalist discovers that he has taken the wrong

side in a literary prize discussion and subsequently loses his university lectureship, as well as such special privileges as the opportunity to read foreign news magazines. Unable to cope with the simultaneous collapse of his marriage, he is driven to suicide. "Man of Marble," with a plot which echoes "Citizen Kane", traces a student filmmaker's attempt to reconstruct the story of Birkut, a Stakhanovite bricklayer and former propaganda hero who mysteriously fell from favor and went to an unmarked grave after the 1967 unrest.

That film's sequel "Czlowiek z Zelaza/Man of Iron" (1981), charted the beginnings of the Solidarity movement, using newsreel footage and featuring Solidarity leader Lech Walesa in both its documentary and directed segments. The events of August 1980 are seen through the eyes of Winkiel, an alcoholic reporter whom the secret police try to use in order to defame the movement. Although essentially a tribute to Solidarity's success, the film ends with a Party official laughingly dismissing the accord between union and government as a mere piece of paper. It also earned a 1981 Oscar nomination as Best Foreign-Language Film.

Following the military crackdown of the winter of 1981, Wajda moved to France to make "Danton" (1982), a consideration of the dual nature of revolution. The grim tone of the film is hardly surprising given the fate of Solidarity, and of his own "Unit X" film production unit, which was to be dismantled in 1983. He headed to Germany for "Eine Liebe in Deutschland/A Love in Germany" (1983), dealing with the tragic and forbidden relationship between a German woman and a Polish prisoner-of-war under the Third Reich. In 1989, with the astounding liberalization in Poland, Andrzej Wajda was not only elected as Solidarity candidate to the Sejm (the Polish parliament), but was able to realize a long-cherished project about Jewish-Polish pedagogue Janusz "Korczak" (1989), who died, along with his wards, in a Nazi death camp.

Into the 90s, Wajda has continued to create disturbing films, often returning to the familiar setting of WWII-era Poland. "The Ring With the Crowned Eagle" (1993), a look at Polish history with particular attention on the 1944 Warsaw Ghetto Uprising. "Nastazja/Natasha" (1994) was a fascinating two-character retelling of the final chapter of "The Idiot", cast with Japanese Kabuki actors. The director returned to the Warsaw uprising with "Wielki Tydzien/Holy Week" (1996), which examined the event through the efforts of a Jewish woman seeking asylum with an intellectual. Most recently, Wajda depicted a metaphysical relationship with lesbian overtones in "Panna Nikt/Miss Nobody" (1997).

MILESTONES:

1942: Became Polish Resistance fighter at age 16 (date approximate)

Made first short films while attending film school in Lodz

1953: Served as assistant to director Aleksander Ford on "Five Boys From Barska Street"

1953: Co-wrote and directed diploma film "Three Stories"

1954: Feature directing debut, "Pokolenie/A Generation"

1955: Directed first documentary, "Ide ku sloncu/I Walk to the Sun"

1957: First of Wajda's film to examine the Warsaw uprising, "Kanal/They Love Life"

1958: Earned international attention with "Popiol i diament/Ashes and Diamonds"

1959: Debut as theater director, "A Hatful of Rain"

1962: First credit as a TV director, "Interview with Ballmayer"

1965: Helmed the expensive historical romance "Popioly/Ashes"

Concentrated on stage directing in the 1970s

1975: "Land and Promise" received an Academy Award nomination for Best Foreign-Language Film

1977: Helmed "Czlowiek z marmuru/Man of Marble", employing a cinema verite style

1979: "The Young Girls of Wilko/The Maids of Wilko" received Academy Award nomination for Best Foreign-Language Film

1981: "Czlowiek z Zalaza/Man of Iron" earned Oscar nomination as Best Foreign-Language Film

1982: Garnered further praise for his adaptation of "Danton", starring Gerard Depardieu

1989: Elected Senator in Polish government (Solidarity Party representative)

1993: Focused on the Warsaw Uprising in "The Ring with the Crowned Eagle"

1994: Helmed "Natasha", featuring two Japanese Kabuki actors in a drama based on the final chapter of Dosetevski's "The Idiot"

1996: Revisited familiar themes in "Holy Week", focusing on a Jewish woman who seeks asylum from an intellectual during the Warsaw Ghetto uprising

1997: Helmed "Panna Nikt/Miss Nobody", a feature with lesbian overtones in its central relationship between a teenager and a New Age hippie

1999: Helmed "Pan Tadeusz/The Last Foray in Lithuania"; selected as Poland's official entry for the Best Foreign-Language Academy Award

2002: Directed "Zemsta/The Vengeance", starring Roman Polanski

AFFILIATION: Roman Catholic

QUOTES:

His name is pronounced AHN-Jay VY-da.

In April 2000, Wajda donated his honorary Academy Award to Jagiellonian University in Krakow, Poland.

"The greatest difficulties I have are with myself."—Andrzej Wajda

"I am often asked why I bother myself with the theatre, whose works disappear with time and are so easily forgotten, since I can make films which last foreverm always having a chance to move and entertain future generations. It is precisely this ephemeral and transitory nature that truly and profoundly binds me to the theatre, for it is not only the meed of immorality and the wish to live on that constitute the natural human need—it is also the awareness of nothingness and death that attracts us, and with age even more so."—Wajda in 1990

Raoul Walsh

BORN: in New York, New York, 03/11/1887

DEATH: 12/04/1980

NATIONALITY: American

EDUCATION: Seton Hall University, South Orange, New Jersey

BIOGRAPHY

Raoul Walsh's film career spanned more than half a century, encompassing acting, writing scenarios and directing. He began as an actor in 1909 in westerns made by the Pathe brothers. He signed with D.W. Griffith in 1912, appearing as the young Pancho Villa in Christy Cabanne's "The Life of General Villa" (1912) and as John Wilkes Booth in "Birth of a Nation" (1915). "Villa" also marked Walsh's first directing experience; he shot the Mexican documentary sequence for the film, persuading Villa himself to re-stage the battle of Durango. From there, it was on to one- and two-reelers and then features, most of them under contract to Fox between 1916 and 1928. Many of these films were minor efforts, but several are among his better accomplishments: "Evangeline" (1919); "The Thief of Bagdad," with Douglas Fairbanks (1924); the WWI classic "What Price Glory?" (1926); "Sadie Thompson," with Gloria Swanson (1928); and "Me, Gangster" (1928).

The 1930s were a variable period for Walsh as he spent some time at Paramount making, among other films, genial but rather bland musicals which lacked his distinctive grit and clearly interested him little. This period, though, does include the likably rowdy comedies "Me

and My Gal" (1932) and "Sailor's Luck" (1933), the lusty brawling of "The Bowery" (1933) and "Under Pressure" (1935) and the offbeat semi-Western "Wild Girl" (1932). A recognizable style and recurrent thematic interests were beginning to emerge in Walsh's work.

Walsh's career took a dramatic turn in 1939 when he assumed direction of "The Roaring Twenties" for Warner Bros. It began a fruitful 15-year association with that studio, in whose productive and creative environment Walsh flourished. At Warners, Walsh associated with first-rate talent at all levels. From these collaborations emerged a body of films that demonstrated Walsh's remarkable talent for different genres.

Walsh directed four first-rate examples of film noir and/or romantic melodrama: "They Drive By Night" (1940), "High Sierra" (1941), "The Man I Love" (1946) and "White Heat" (1949). "High Sierra" and "White Heat," among the very best gangster films, demonstrate Walsh's mastery of action; his style is wonderfully straightforward and unpretentious but not without flair and bravura. "They Drive By Night" and "The Man I Love" focus more on relationships than on action. Ida Lupino's role in the latter, an unusually feisty entry in the "women's film" genre, film calls attention to Walsh's continued interest in, and sympathy with, strong women characters.

Most of Walsh's westerns are skillfully made if traditional action-oriented films such as "They Died With Their Boots On" (1941). However, "Pursued" (1947), with its strong Freudian undertones, introduced the psychological western and belies the notion that Walsh's style and technique were always simple and direct. "Colorado Territory" (1949) is an affecting and effective reworking of "High Sierra."

"Objective Burma!" (1945) is one of the outstanding war films of the 1940s and amply showcases Walsh's talents. Critic Jean-Pierre Couroson has observed of this film: "Seen purely in terms of direction . . . Walsh's control over pace and space, narrative and detail, performance and logistics, is total."

After his contract with Warners expired in 1953, Walsh continued working for another 11 years, but his successes were limited. Among his better films from this later period were the Western "The Tall Men" (1955) and the story of a canny, land-buying club "hostess" (a prostitute in the source novel), "The Revolt of Mamie Stover" (1956). Still, Walsh's long and productive career surely mark him for consideration among the best craftsman working in the heyday of the Hollywood studio system.

COMPANION:

wife: Miriam Cooper. Actor; first wife; married 1916, divorced 1927; starred in many of his films

MILESTONES:

1910: Stage acting debut

1912: Film acting debut

1912: Assistant director to D.W. Griffith

1914: Film co-directing debut (with Christy Cabanne), "The Life of General Villa"

1915: Played John Wilkes Booth in "The Birth of a Nation"

1929: Began wearing eye patch after losing an eye during the shooting of Hollywood's first outdoor sound film, "In Old Arizona"

1964: Retired after losing sight in other eye

BIBLIOGRAPHY:

"Each Man in His Time" Raoul Walsh, 1974 Farrar, Straus & Giroux; autobiography

Andy Warhol

BORN: Andrew Warhola in Pittsburgh, Pennsylvania, 08/06/1927

DEATH: in New York, New York, 02/22/1987

NATIONALITY: American

EDUCATION: Schenley High School, Pittsburgh, Pennsylvania

University of Pittsburgh, Pittsburgh, Pennsylvania; enrolled with plans to become a teacher; transferred to Carnegie Institute

Carnegie Institute of Technology, painting and graphics design, BFA, 1949; school later changed name to Carnegie-Mellon University

BIOGRAPHY

Pioneer of the Pop Art movement of the 1960s who transplanted his sometimes witty, sometimes boring explorations of popular culture from the canvas to the screen. Warhol acquired a 16mm camera in 1963 and made his first "underground" film, "Kiss", the same year. It combined the deliberately nonprofessional techniques endorsed by the American avant-garde with Warhol's own camp sensibility and the ironic banality of his "serial" artwork.

Warhol's film work falls into a silent and a sound phase, the first of which reached its apex in "Sleep" (1964), a six-hour study of a slumbering man conveyed via a virtually stationary camera. Glacially indifferent to the question of viewer involvement, "Sleep" is not so much "watched" as it is "experienced."

Warhol was prolific in his idiosyncratic, voyeuristic brand of "cinema verite", churning out product at an assembly-line clip of roughly one film a week during the period 1964–65. He trained his camera on the motley band of freaks, musicians and social register slummers that trooped through his Felliniesque "Factory." In an ironic inversion of the Hollywood studio system, Warhol elevated the more prominent "players" into underground "superstars": the beautiful, tragic Candy Darling, Joe Dallesandro, Holly Woodlawn, Jackie Curtis, et al.

Although all of Warhol's films were governed by his peculiar sensibility, he assembled a nucleus of capable technicians, such as Paul Morrissey and Chuck Wein, who made various—uncredited—contributions, often in the master's absence.

Warhol entered his "sound phase" with "Harlot" (1965) and continued to crank out such influential films as "Vinyl" (1965), based upon Anthony Burgess's "A Clockwork Orange", which launched the tragic career and cruel exploitation of socialite/superstar Edie Sedgwick. In 1966 he produced his most enduring and definitive work, "The Chelsea Girls", a crazed showcase of Factory stalwarts which synthesized the enthusiasms and strategies encompassed by his previous work. The film was projected on two adjacent screens, each of which depicted unrelated situations. Its relative popularity ("The Chelsea Girls" was the first Warhol film to surface in "real" movie houses), inspired a more commercial, or at least less arcane, approach to filmmaking.

While such post–Chelsea Girls" films as "Lonesome Cowboys" (1969) continued to use typically Warholian alienation effects (extreme long takes, "strobe" cuts, etc.), they also relied on previously disdained qualities such as plot and characterization. By the time the Factory closed, after an attempt on Warhol's life in June of 1968, Morrissey had inserted his more formal concerns into the Warhol formula, producing a series of bizarre sex farces that proved more accessible to a popular audience (although they gradually reverted into self-parody). By the mid-1970s, Morrissey was turning out Gothic romps affixed with

Warhol's brand name, although they were only vaguely indebted to the Factory style.

Though he had effectively closed the filmmaking chapter of his career after the release of "Andy Warhol's Bad" (dir. Jed Johnson, 1977), Warhol continued to satisfy his voyeuristic appetites with a Polaroid camera that he toted on his late-night revels until his untimely death in 1987.

MILESTONES:

1949: Moved to New York after graduating from college

Earned reputation as leading illustrator through 1950s

1962: First one-man show in New York

1962–1963: Began attending underground/avant-garde film screenings

Shot first film on trip to Los Angeles

1963: Made first "serial" film, "Kiss"

1964: Joined by scenarist Ronald Tevel and assistant director Chuck Wein

1964: Shot first sound film, "Harlot" (70 mins) in December

1965: Paul Morrissey joined Warhol's entourage

1965: Made "Vinyl," an adaptation of Anthony Burgess's "A Clockwork Orange"; also film debut of Edie Sedgwick

1965: "Produced" debut record album of "The Velvet Underground and Nico"

1966: Made "The Chelsea Girls," whose commercial success precipitated more mainstream projects

1968: Seriously wounded after being shot twice by Valerie Solanis on June 4

1968: While Warhol recuperated, Morrissey wrote and directed "Flesh," the first "Warhol" film which Warhol did not direct

1969: Founded *Interview* magazine

1977: After "Andy Warhol's Bad" (directed by Jed Johnson), ended filmmaking career (though he directed several music videos in the 1980s)

1983: Started own cable TV talk show

BIBLIOGRAPHY:

"The Philosophy of Andy Warhol: From A to B and Back Again" Andy Warhol, 1988

"The Andy Warhol Diaries" Andy Warhol; edited by Pat Hackett, 1989, Warner Books

"Andy Warhol" Wayne Koestenbaum, 2001, Penguin; issued as part of the Penguin Lives series

John Waters

BORN: in Baltimore, Maryland, 04/22/1946

NATIONALITY: American

EDUCATION: attended a Catholic high school for boys

BIOGRAPHY

John Waters once stated that having someone vomit while watching one of his movies was like getting a standing ovation. Although a slow but steady integration into mainstream filmmaking has tempered that kind of thinking, the openly gay Waters remains one of cinema's most audacious practitioners.

Born into an upper-middle-class Catholic family, Waters grew up in Baltimore, which serves as the locale of all his movies. Childhood interests in car accidents and murders marked him as a unique personality. As a teenager, he began making 8mm films, largely influenced by the experimental and exploitation films that he sought out while skipping school. His crude early short films, sporting titles like "Hag in a Black Leather Jacket" (1964) and "Eat Your Makeup" (1966), were screened only in the Baltimore area, but did spark the genesis of Waters' Dreamland Productions stock company. Made up of his friends and neighbors, the Dreamlanders came to include Divine, a 300-pound transvestite, and Edith Massey, a snaggle-toothed barmaid and thrift-shop owner, as well as Mink Stole, Cookie Mueller, Mary Vivian Pearce, Danny Mills, Alan Wendl and David Lochary.

Waters' first 16mm sound feature, "Multiple Maniacs" (1971), established the pattern for most of his work: a complex plot involving a "family"; vicious attacks on middle-class manners and morals, religion and other sacred cows; and an overriding mission to offend even the most jaded moviegoer. "Pink Flamingos" (1972), made for $10,000, was Waters' first film to receive national distribution, becoming a hit on the midnight movie circuit. Divine played "the filthiest person alive"; she finds her title challenged by the Marbles (Stole and Lochary), who kidnap women, have their servant rape them with a syringe and then sell the babies to lesbian couples. The film assaults the viewer with a barrage of repellent images, such as the hefty Massey splayed out in a play pen wearing a bra and girdle and covered with the half-eaten eggs that are her passion. The notorious finale, in which Divine eats dog excrement, remains one of the most sickening sights captured on film. Nonetheless, Waters plays everything on a broadly comic scale. Dialogue is ridiculously melodramatic and performances are overblown. The sets, designed by Waters' regular art director (and later, production designer) Vincent Peranio, are the essence of kitsch. As bad taste is elevated to a new aesthetic, the audience must laugh to keep from gagging. The act of attending and professing to enjoy one of Waters' midnight movies became a safe way to thumb one's nose at the establishment during the "Me Decade."

Divine returned to star in "Female Trouble" (1975), Waters' rumination on fashion, fame and criminality. The film demonstrated that the director had discovered the last exploitable subject in film—the idea of taste itself. In "Desperate Living" (1977), Waters' satire became sharper. Mink Stole starred as Peggy Gravel, a suburban housewife recovering from a breakdown. When Peggy's husband is killed, she and her maid escape to Mortville, a community of criminals presided over by the despotic Queen Carlotta (Massey). The expected disgusting gags are present—sex changes, rabies injections, roach eating, death-by-dog-food. But the anarchistic tone of Waters' earlier films has given way to more pointed commentary on class and gender roles, as Peggy is stripped of her middle-class pretensions.

Waters made his move out of the midnight movie ghetto in 1981 with "Polyester." He toned down the visually gross elements but compensated with a gimmick worthy of one of his heroes, producer/director William Castle. Audience members were given scratch'n'sniff "Odorama" cards, which they were cued to use by numbers flashing on the screen. Scents ranged from roses to dirty sneakers. Divine played Francine Fishpaw, a housewife beset by family problems; her philandering husband owns a porn theater, her daughter is a high school harlot and her son is the dreaded Baltimore Foot Stomper! Francine goes over the edge but is rescued by drive-in owner Tod Tomorrow, played by former teen idol Tab Hunter in a delightfully mannered performance. The film plays like a hyperbolic "woman's picture" from Hollywood's golden age, complete with a ludicrous happy ending. Once again, bourgeois attitudes are Waters' favorite target.

Throughout the 1980s, Waters published numerous cheeky articles in film and music magazines, extolling the virtues of Pia Zadora, *The National Enquirer* and other campy topics. "Hairspray" (1988), a smart and lively quasi-musical about the racial integration of a popular Baltimore teen TV program in the early 60s, established Waters as a bankable and moderately mainstream director. He continued in a similar vein with "Cry-Baby" (1990), a charming

spoof of Elvis and 50s juvenile delinquent flicks. Featuring an auspicious performance from Johnny Depp—then fresh from TV—as the sensitive protagonist, the film did not fare well at the box office. It did once again demonstrate Waters' penchant for casting past icons. Patricia Hearst, David Nelson, and Tracy Lords were among the cast. "Serial Mom" (1994) marked a career milestone for the former renegade auteur. Waters had a significant budget ($13 million), name stars (i.e., Kathleen Turner, Sam Waterston), and reams of positive press. Yet, Waters had difficulty finding financing for subsequent feature films. Having survived several members of his stock company and finding the mainstream increasingly attuned to his distinctive take on American life, Waters' assaults on good taste have grown less angry, savage, and scattershot. Nonetheless, he continues to be one of cinema's most potent satirists.

To that end, the director had made frequent TV appearances, such as on "Politically Incorrect", which have extended his fame. He was one of those featured in the American Movie Classics' documentary "Ballyhoo: The Hollywood Sideshow" (1996). Additionally, Waters has made acting appearances not only in his own films (i.e., the psychiatrist suggesting electroshock therapy for a Caucasian girl in love with an African American in "Hairspray") but also in the film of others (e.g., the 1986 CBS TV-movie "Passion Flower", the 1989 feature "Homer and Eddie"). In 1997, he was again the subject of media attention when "Pink Flamingos" was re-released in an slightly modified (outtakes were added) 25th anniversary edition.

MILESTONES:

Grew up in Lutherville, a suburb of Baltimore, Maryland

Began working as a puppeteer at age 12, performing for 3–4 children's birthday parties per week: handled all aspects of production: writing scripts, designing advertising, printing flyers, designing sets, et al.

1964: Directed first 8mm short, "Hag in a Black Leather Jacket", at age 19

Had three of his 8mm shorts shown simultaneously under the umbrella title, "Roman Candles"; first collaboration with actors Divine and Mink Stole

1970: Feature film debut as director, writer, producer, cinematographer and editor, "Mondo Trasho"

1971: First feature starring Divine, "Multiple Maniacs"

Attended court trials of the Manson gang, Patty Hearst, and serial killer Richard Ramirez

1975: "Pink Flamingos" was closed down in Hicksville, NY; Waters fined $5,000 for obscenity

1975: "Pink Flamingos" was accepted into the permanent collection of the Musum of Modern Art

1981: First studio-backed feature, "Polyester"; employed "Odorama" a gimmick involving the distribution of scratch-and-sniff cards to be used with visual cues in the film

1986: Made cameo appearance as car salesman in Jonathan Demme's "Something Wild"

1986: Had role in TV-movie "Passion Flower" (CBS)

1988: Directed his most profitable feature (to date) "Hairspray"; first film with Ricki Lake; last film with Divine

1991: Honored with a 7-day career retrospective, "Midnight Madness: The Films of John Waters", at the Angelika Theater in NYC

1994: First Hollywood A-list film (major stars; $13 million budget), "Serial Mom"

1996: Participated on-camera in "Ballyhoo! The Hollywood Sideshow" (American Movie Classics)

1997: Provided a character voice on the animated Fox series "The Simpsons"

1997: "Pink Flamingos" was re-released in a 25th anniversary edition

1998: Helmed "Pecker", a semi-autobiographical portrait of a teenaged photographer

AFFILIATION: Roman Catholic

QUOTES:

Waters reported that he was expelled from the New York University Film School for smoking pot according to *USA Today,* (April 12, 1994). He also cheerfully admits to years of LSD use.

"I think he's probably a genius," she [Kathleen Turner, star of 'Serial Mom'] says of Waters. 'Quite frankly, you don't create your own genre and an international audience completely outside a system—and in spite of the Hollywood system—unless you have one hell of a lot of talent.' "—quoted in "John Waters' Weirdness Runs Deep" by Luaine Lee in *Daily News,* April 12, 1994.

"How could I have sold out? . . . My movie stars a 300-pound transvestite and Tab Hunter."—Waters to *New York Post* after being accused of selling out by making the relatively commercial movie, "Polyester" (1981).

"In our neighborhood, you always left the garbageman liquor at Christmas. I always wished that garbagemen were my secret friends. I love when they pull up in Baltimore and go 'Hoo!' That's when you have to run out and give them liquor or money or whatever."—John Waters, talking to Ann Magnuson in "Moveable Blood Feast" in *Paper,* May 1994.

"I don't make films about things I hate," Waters says. "What always makes me laugh are people who have very extreme taste and think they're very normal. That to me is the funniest . . . I respect that. I don't look down on it, I'm IN AWE of it. Like people who have on the most hideous outfit and think they really look good. Who am I to say they don't really?"—Waters quoted in "Diving in New Waters" by Frank DeCaro in *Newsday,* April 11, 1994.

February 7, 1985 was declared "John Waters Day" in Baltimore, Maryland.

BIBLIOGRAPHY:

"Crackpot" John Waters, 1986, Macmillan; essays
"Shock Value" John Waters; essays
"Trash Trio" John Waters

BORN: in England, 1954

NATIONALITY: English

BIOGRAPHY

British director whose output preceding the 1994 feature film sequel to the successful comedy "City Slickers" (1991) "City Slickers II: The Legend of Curly's Gold" was marked by a comedic feature which bombed and an amusing TV series "Mr. Bean" (HBO, 1992–94). Weiland's feature directorial debut, "Leonard Part 6" (1987) was so bad that its star and producer Billy Cosby reportedly recommended audiences stay away. His next effort was a charming trifle, "Bernard and the Genie" (1992), which aired on English TV before materializing on US cable and video shelves. Featuring superior performances from British comics Rowan Atkinson and Lenny Henry, this was the story of a Black genie (Henry) who grants wishes to a recently fired exec. Weiland collaborated with Atkinson again on TV's "Mr. Bean", directing the bulgy eyed comic as an eccentric character who makes rather ordinary situations extraordinary merely by participating in them.

Weiland's commercial fortunes improved when he directed the saddle sore sequel "City Slickers II" (1994), a high-profile assignment which lassoed most of the first film's original cast, including Billy Crystal and Jack Palance. The story of the Slickers search for buried treasure in the Wild West, this continuation did respectably at the box office but lacked the snap of the original.

MILESTONES:

1987: Feature directorial debut, "Leonard, Part 6"

1992–1994: TV directorial debut, "Mr. Bean"

BORN: Peter Lindsay Weir in Sydney, Australia, 08/21/1944

NATIONALITY: Australian

EDUCATION: Scots College, Sydney, Australia
University of Sydney Sydney, Australia art and law dropped out at age 19

AWARDS: Australian Film Institute Award Best Film "Three to Go" 1970 shared award with Brian Hannant and Oliver Howes; Weir directed the segment entitled "Michael"

Australian Film Institute Award Best Film "Homesdale" 1971

Australian Film Institute Raymond Longford Award 1990

Cesar Best Foreign Film "Dead Poets Society" 1991

European Film Academy International Award "The Truman Show" 1998

Florida Film Critics Circle Award Best Director "The Truman Show" 1998

Film Critics Circle of Australia Award Best Foreign Film "The Truman Show" 1998

BAFTA David Lean Award for Best Achievement in Direction "The Truman Show" 1999

Australian Screen Directors Association (ASDA) Lifetime Achievement Award 2001; initial presentation

BIOGRAPHY

Peter Weir briefly attended Sydney University, dropped out to join his father's real estate business, and left that job for a trip to Europe in 1966. Upon his return, he took a job at a TV station and, in his free time, began making short films full of anti-establishment attitudes. In 1969, he signed on with the Commonwealth Film Unit as an assistant cameraman and production designer, which led to opportunities to direct a number of short films and eventually features.

Weir's contribution to the Australian film renaissance of the late 1970s lay in his ability to portray the imminent disruption of the rational world by irrational forces hovering just beyond our mundane lives. His reputation as the most stylish of the new Australian directors was built on his charting of that country's landscape and cultural oddities with a sense of wonder.

Weir's first feature, "The Cars That Ate Paris" (1974), portrayed the terror lurking beneath a sleepy Outback town called Paris which profits from highway disasters. It is a Gothic horror story laced with fetishistic black humor. He created another kind of haunting atmosphere for "Picnic at Hanging Rock" (1975), in which a turn-of-the-century girls' school picnic in the Australian bush turns tragic. Weir contrasted the imported and repressive cultural values of the English-style boarding school with the unsettling but liberating influence of the natural environment of Hanging Rock, where the girls' sexuality is stirred by the phallic and frankly unrefined rock.

The accumulation of details around a motif also shaped "The Last Wave" (1977), in which water is used functionally in the narrative as well as thematically, until all civilization seems at the mercy of an enormous tidal wave prophesied by an ignored aborigine. Weir's early films portrayed a stable society on the verge of collapse both from fear and from events beyond its control, and never more so than in "Gallipoli" (1981). A culturally underdeveloped society, made strong by the values of camaraderie and loyalty, is forced by duty into war in service of an empire devoid of concern for anything but its privileged classes. The film made the isolationism of Australia comprehensible in a context of snobbish, exploitative and incompetent British rule and its international success helped establish the screen career of Mel Gibson.

Australian films of the 70s and early 80s tended to avoid male/female psychology and romance, but in "The Year of Living Dangerously" (1982), Weir dealt with the animal attraction of an endangered species, Caucasian observers in the Third World. An Australian journalist (Mel Gibson) and an embassy employee (Sigourney Weaver) fall in love in the midst of political unrest in 1965 Jakarta. Once again, Weir sharply evokes a palpable sense of place and time in this underrated film which, although mishandled by its American distributor, did land Weir his first Hollywood picture.

In the thriller "Witness" (1985), Weir sensitively recreated the simple but disciplined virtues of the Amish, in pointed contrast to the corrupt world of urban police politics. Harrison Ford gave an acclaimed performance as John Book, a tough and honest cop who functions in both worlds. The film also demonstrated that Weir could adeptly handle Hollywood's requirements for glossy romance and compelling action sequences and he was rewarded with his first Oscar nomination as Best Director. Ford gave an underrated tour-de-force performance as an idealistic inventor who packs up his family and leaves America for an untainted village in Central America in Weir's next film, "The Mosquito Coast" (1986). His own "American" qualities, however, contain the seeds for disaster. The film revealed a darker side than seen in Weir's previous work though this may also be attributed, in some part, to Paul Schrader's adaptation of Paul Theroux's hard-hitting novel. Robin Williams' exuberance enhanced the comic edges of "Dead Poets Society" (1989), a popular depiction of an American private boys' school and its repressive response to ideas about individuality and sensitivity. The film's lectures on the value of poetry and a new way of seeing seem addressed more to Hollywood than an educational elite. For his efforts, Weir earned a second Academy Award nomination as Best Director.

Weir truly went Hollywood with his next outing, the light romantic comedy "Green Card" (1990). A genial and inconsequential outing, it provided the English-language debut for the shambling French hunk Gerard Depardieu well matched by leading lady Andie Mac-Dowell. Weir earned a surprise Best Original Screenplay Oscar nomination. He returned to more substantial issues with "Fearless" (1993), a drama about people's varying reactions to tragedy starring Jeff Bridges, Rosie Perez, and John Turturro. After a five year absence, the director returned to motion pictures with "The Truman Show" (1998), which provided a rare dramatic role for comic actor Jim Carrey as an insurance salesman who, in a Pirandellian twist, discovers his life has been the basis for a television show.

MILESTONES:

Dropped out of college

Traveled on a Greek ship to England

Found an unused closed-circuit TV camera aboard ship and, with several friends, created shows for the other passengers

Met his future wife in England; married

Returned to Australia

1967: Began working in TV as a stagehand at Australia's ATN 7

1967: Short film directing debut, "Count Vim's Last Exercise"

1968: Short film acting debut (also director), "The Life and Flight of the Reverend Buckshotte"

1969–1973: Employed by Commonwealth Film Institute (now Film Australia)

1970: Directed and wrote 30-minute segment "Michael" of ominibus feature "Three to Go"

1971: Directed his first medium-length featurette, "Homesdale" (50 mins)

1974: Directed and co-wrote first feature film, "The Cars That Ate Paris"

1981: Won international recognition with "Gallipoli"; first screen collaboration with Mel Gibson

1982: Reteamed with Gibson on "The Year of Living Dangerously"

1985: US directing debut, "Witness", starring Harrison Ford; earned first Oscar nomination as Best Director

1986: Directed Ford in "The Mosquito Coast"

1989: Scored hit with "Dead Poets Society"; earned second Best Director Oscar nod

1990: Was nominated for a third Oscar as screenwriter of "Green Card"

1993: Helmed the flawed but unsuccessful "Fearless"

1998: Directed Jim Carrey in rare dramatic role in "The Truman Show"; received Best Director Oscar nomination

Helmed "Master and Commander/The Far Side of the World" (lensed 2002), an adaptation of Patrick O'Brien's series of action-adventure novels

QUOTES:

Various sources list Mr. Weir's date of birth as June 21, August 8 and August 21.

Paul Weitz

BORN: Paul John Weitz in New York, New York, 1965

NATIONALITY: American

EDUCATION: Collegiate School, New York, New York

Wesleyan University, Middletown, Connecticut, film, BFA

BIOGRAPHY

Screenwriter and director Paul Weitz first gained notice when he and his younger brother Chris (along with Todd Alcott) contributed to the screenplay for the Dream-Works/PDI computer animated feature "Antz" (1998). For this film, the writers created a movie that would have appeal for adults as well as children. A cleverly written exploration of individuality in the face of society's predetermined roles, "Antz" starred Woody Allen in what was easily his funniest role in the better part of a decade. Allen voiced Z-4195, the drone dissatisfied with his station in life who, for the love of high-class ant Princess Bala (Sharon Stone), undertakes a great adventure, becomes a hero, finds the elusive Insectopia, and foils the plans of coup minded General Mandible (Gene Hackman). With visual gags to entertain children and sophisticated social commentary that spoke to adults, "Antz" proved a crowd-pleaser, its character-driven screenplay setting it apart from Disney's similarly themed Pixar computer animated "A Bug's Life" (also 1998).

Paul and Chris Weitz come from a Hollywood background, their mother is Academy Award nominated actress Susan Kohner, father fashion designer John Weitz, grandfather famed talent agent Paul Kohner, grandmother Mexican actress Lupita Tovar, and uncle producer Pancho Kohner. Keeping the family business alive, the Weitz brothers collaborated on their next project as well, Paul as director and Chris as producer (and reportedly uncredited co-director) of 1999's teen comedy "American Pie", the brothers' take on a tale of four high school seniors who go to great lengths in their attempts to lose their virginity. "American Pie", the modern equivalent of the teen sex comedies prevalent in the early 80s (i.e., "Porky's" 1981; "Fast Times At Ridgemont High" 1982) captured that era's crudely funny look at teen sexuality, as well as incorporated a somewhat sensitive look at friendships and relationships. Featuring an ensemble cast made up primarily of virtual unknowns, "American Pie" was positioned to become a summer sleeper hit, its trailer creating audience buzz.

Before achieving success in film, Weitz received some acclaim as a playwright, with "Mango Tea" produced by New York's Ensemble Studio Theater (EST) and performed off-Broadway featuring Marisa Tomei and Rob Morrow. Other plays of Weitz's produced by EST include "All for One" and "Captive", the latter leading to his first film credit. This lurid story of a couple who finds that taking a hostage serves as romantic inspiration was adapted by writer-director Karl Slovin into "Sex and the Other Man" (1995), starring Kari Wuhrer and Ron Eldard as a dysfunctional couple, and Stanley Tucci as Wuhrer's boss, taken hostage by the couple whose presence cures Eldard's impotence. Weitz also had writing credits in Daisy von Scherler Mayer's "Madeline" (1998), as co-lyricist of the song "The Cuckoo and the Nightingale." Additionally, Weitz and brother Chris teamed up to pen the pilot episode of the 1998 remake series "Fantasy Island" (ABC).—Written by Jane O'Donnell

MILESTONES:

Playwriting debut, "Mango Tea"; produced by New York's Ensemble Studio Theatre (EST) starring Marisa Tomei and Rob Morrow

Had two subsequent plays, "Captive" and "All for One", produced by EST

1994: With brother Chris, sold spec script "Rhode Island Smith and the Theme Park of Doom"

1995: Writer-director Karl Slovin adapted "Captive" as the film "Sex and the Other Man", starring Stanley Tucci, Ron Eldard and Kari Wuhrer

1996: Collaborated with brother on script for film version of 1960s TV sitcom "My Favorite Martian"; eventually replaced on project

1998: Co-wrote the song "The Cuckoo and the Nightingale" for the children's film "Madeline"; had originally written a draft of the script with brother that was subsequently set aside; uncle Poncho Kohner was one of the film's producers

1998: Penned an episode of the remake series "Fantasy Island" (ABC)

1998: With brother Chris and Todd Alcott, received credit for the screenplay of the animated comedy "Antz"

1999: Directed the teen comedy "American Pie", with brother Chris producing (and reportedly co-directing)

2001: With brother, co-directed "Down to Earth", a remake of "Heaven Can Wait", starring Chris Rock; also contributed to the screenplay

2002: Along with brother Chris and Peter Hedges wrote "About a Boy"; received an Oscar nomination for Adapted Screenplay

Orson Welles

BORN: George Orson Welles in Kenosha, Wisconsin, 05/06/1915

DEATH: 10/09/1985

NATIONALITY: American

EDUCATION: Todd School, Woodstock, Illinois, 1931

AWARDS: National Board of Review Award Best American Film "Citizen Kane" 1941; one of ten films cited

National Board of Review Award Best Acting "Citizen Kane" 1941; one of 21 performers cited

New York Film Critics Circle Award Best Picture "Citizen Kane" 1941

Oscar Best Writing (Original Screenplay) "Citizen Kane" 1941; co-written by Herman J. Mankiewicz

Cannes Film Festival Grand Prix "Othello"

1952; shared with Renato Catellani's "Two Cents Worth of Hope"

Cannes Film Festival Best Actor Award "Compulsion" 1959; shared with co-stars Bradford Dillman and Dean Stockwell

Cannes Film Festival 20th Anniversary Prize "Chimes at Midnight" 1966; also cited for his "contribution to world cinema"

Honorary Oscar 1970; for overall work in motion pictures

American Film Institute Life Achievement Award 1975

Grammy Best Spoken Word Recording (Album) "Great American Documents" 1976; shared with Henry Fonda, Helen Hayes and James Earl Jones

Los Angeles Film Critics Association Career Achievement Award 1978

Grammy Best Spoken Word Recording (Album) "Citizen Kane (Original Motion Picture Soundtrack)" 1978

Grammy Best Spoken Word, Documentary or Drama Recording (Album) "Donovan's Brain" 1981

Directors Guild of America D W Griffith Award 1984; for lifetime achievement

Los Angeles Film Critics Association Award Best Documentary "It's All True" 1993; award shared with Myron Meisel, Bill Krohn and Richard Wilson

BIOGRAPHY

Orson Welles' pioneering, influential cinema was imaginative, ambitious and technically daring. His baroque cinematic style created a dense moral universe in which every action had tangled—and usually tragic—human repercussions. Before his dramatic arrival in Hollywood, Welles had carved a considerable reputation in theater and radio. At 18 he was a successful actor at the experimental Gate Theatre in Ireland; at 19, he made his Broadway debut as Tybalt in "Romeo and Juliet." A series of collaborations with director/producer John Houseman led to their participation in the New York Federal Theatre Project. Their first great success was Welles' staging of an all-black 'voodoo' "Macbeth," which demonstrated Welles' penchant for stretching existing forms beyond established limits. Welles and Houseman eventually formed their own repertory company, the Mercury Theatre, enjoying success with their 1937 production of "Julius Caesar," which Welles rewrote and set in contemporary Fascist Italy.

Soon Welles was also directing the Mercury players in weekly, hour-long radio dramas for CBS. Once again he stretched the medium, exploiting radio's intimacy to heighten narrative immediacy, most notoriously with the Halloween 1938 broadcast of H.G. Wells' "War of the Worlds." Concocted news bulletins and eyewitness accounts were so authentic in "reporting" the landing of hostile Martians in New Jersey that the broadcast caused a panic among unsuspecting listeners. Seeking to capitalize on

Welles' notoriety, RKO brought him to Hollywood to produce, direct, write and act in two films for $225,000 plus total creative freedom and a percentage of the profits. It was the most generous offer a Hollywood studio had ever made to an untested filmmaker.

After several projects (among them an adaptation of Joseph Conrad's "Heart of Darkness") came to naught, the 25 year-old Welles made what is generally described as the most stunning debut in the history of film. Initially called "American" and later retitled "Citizen Kane," Welles' film was a bold, brash and inspired tour-de-force that told its story from several different perspectives, recounting the rise and corruption of an American tycoon, Charles Foster Kane (modeled on publishing magnate William Randolph Hearst). With the brashness of someone new to Hollywood, Welles pushed existing filmmaking techniques as far as they would go, creating a new and distinctive film aesthetic.

Among the innovative elements of Welles' style exhibited in "Citizen Kane" were: 1) composition in depth: the use of extreme deep focus cinematography to connect distant figures in space; 2) complex "mise-en-scene," in which the frame overflowed with action and detail; 3) low-angle shots that revealed ceilings and made characters, especially Kane, seem simultaneously dominant and trapped; 4) long takes; 5) a fluid, moving camera that expanded the action beyond the frame and increased the importance of off-screen space; and 6) the creative use of sound as a transition device (Thatcher wishes a young Charles "Merry Christmas . . . " and completes the phrase " . . . and a Happy New Year" to a grown Charles years later) and to create visual metaphors (as in the opera montage where the image of the flickering backstage lamp combined with Susan Kane's faint singing and a whirring noise to symbolize her imminent breakdown and subsequent suicide attempt).

Although well received by the critics, "Citizen

Kane" faced distribution and exhibition problems exacerbated by Hearst's negative campaign, and it fared poorly at the box office. Welles' second film for RKO, an adaptation of Booth Tarkington's "The Magnificent Ambersons" (1942), was a more conventional, less flamboyant film that utilized many of the same techniques Welles had developed for "Kane" to evoke a richly textured recollection of turn-of-the-century America. But with Welles off to South America to shoot a semi-documentary (the never-completed "It's All True") jointly sponsored by RKO and the US government, the studio severely edited the film, deleting 43 minutes. Even in its truncated form, "Ambersons" remains a dark, compelling look at nature of wealth, class and progress in America. Before he left for South America, Welles supervised the filming of "Journey Into Fear" (1942), whose direction is credited to Norman Foster. Welles co-starred and co-wrote the screenplay with Joseph Cotten; the result was an intriguing but muddled thriller. When "Ambersons" proved a commercial failure, it was a blow from which Welles' reputation would never recover. Welles and the Mercury Players were dismissed from RKO. "The Stranger" (1946), produced by independent Sam Spiegel, had Welles directing himself as a Nazi war criminal hiding in a small town, but it was devoid of the characteristic Welles touch. He regained his filmmaking flair with "The Lady From Shanghai" (1948), a stunning film noir in which Welles and his wife Rita Hayworth co-starred. (Already separated before the collaboration began, she filed for divorce once filming was completed.) The hall-of-mirrors finale is a superb example of Welles' gift for the audacious visual image.

Welles' next film proved to be the first of an informal, impressive Shakespeare trilogy, an eccentric, atmospheric version of "Macbeth" (1948) in which the actors were encouraged to speak with thick Scottish burrs. Its center-piece—a sequence that begins with Macbeth's

decision to kill the king, includes the murder and ends with the discovery of the crime by Macduff—was captured in a single ten-minute take. The film, however, was not successful and was dismissed at the Venice Film Festival. Four years later, he answered his critics with a striking version of "Othello" (1952), which won the Grand Prix at Cannes. The final film in the trilogy was the triumphant "Chimes at Midnight/Falstaff" (1966) which Welles, who by this time was of the correct girth to play Falstaff, fashioned from five of Shakespeare's historical plays. As a separate narrative, Falstaff's tale is a bitter one of deteriorating friendship passing from privilege to neglect. It ranks among Welles' greatest achievements.

After the failure of "Macbeth," Welles began a self-imposed, ten-year exile from Hollywood. His follow-up to "Othello," "Mr. Arkadin/Confidential Report" (1955), was an acerbic profile of a powerful man that showed signs of the brilliance that marked "Kane," but was hindered by an episodic narrative and spotty acting. Welles returned to Hollywood to act in and direct "Touch of Evil" (1958), a film noir masterpiece. From its stunning long-take opening of a car bombing to its tragic denouement, it reiterated his overarching vision of the world as an exacting moral network where each human act has endless and unforeseen moral consequences. His adaptation of Kafka's "The Trial" (1962), a nightmarish extension of that vision, depicted a society completely devoid of a moral sense, where empty procedure replaced principle. "The Immortal Story" (1968) was a satisfying, minor work made for French television, an adaptation of an Isak Dinesen story. His final completed film, "F For Fake" (1973), a diverting collage of documentary and staged footage that investigated the line separating reality and illusion, celebrated all tricksters—including its director, who sometimes stated that if he had not become a director, he would have been a magician.

At the time of his death, "The Other Side of

the Wind," a project he had begun filming in the 1970s, remained unfinished. Obviously autobiographical, it was the story of a famous filmmaker (played by Welles' good friend, John Huston) struggling to find financing for his film, just as Welles was forced to do many times. As an unseen fragment, it was a sad and ironic end for a filmmaking maverick who set the standards for the modern narrative film and the man who was, in the words of Martin Scorsese, "responsible for inspiring more people to be film directors than anyone else in history of the cinema."

COMPANION:

wife: Rita Hayworth. Actor, dancer; married in 1943; divorced in 1947; popular film star of the 1940s and 50s in such films as "You Were Never Lovelier" (1942), "Gilda" (1952) and "Miss Sadie Thompson" (1953); worked once with Welles, on "The Lady from Shanghai" (1948)

MILESTONES:

Born with anomalies of the spine which caused Welles pain throughout his life

Moved to Chicago as a child

First stage appearance, a walk-on bit in the Chicago Opera's production of "Samson and Delilah" at age five; then played "Madame Butterfly' "s child "Trouble"

Parents separated when Welles was six; traveled after divorce

1927: Became ward of Chicago doctor, Maurice Bernstein, at age 12 (date approximate)

1931: Began tour of Ireland

1931: First leading stage role at Dublin's Gate Theater in "Jew Suss"

1932: Returned to USA

1934: Broadway acting debut (as Tybalt) in "Romeo and Juliet"

1934: Co-directed and acted in short film, "The Hearts of Age"

1934: Radio acting debut

1936: First major stage success as director,

"Macbeth" (for Federal Theater Project, Harlem); featured an all-black cast which later went to Broadway and toured the country; often referred to as the "voodoo Macbeth" due to the Haitian setting and African-influenced witchcraft theme

1937: Formed Mercury Theater with John Houseman

1937–1938: During one Broadway season, helmed four major successes for the Mercury Theatre, beginning with a modern-dress "Julius Caesar"; generally hailed as one of the great stage talents of the day

1938: Made national headlines with CBS radio broadcast (for "Mercury Theatre of the Air") of H.G. Wells' "The War of the Worlds" (the night of October 30)

1938: First short film as solo director, "Too Much Johnson" (also co-producer; writer); was to be incorporated into play of same name which never made it to Broadway; sole extant print allegedly lost in fire in 1970

Signed by RKO; given carte blanche; originally planned several other films, including an adaptation of "Heart of Darkness," before settling on the less ambitious "Citizen Kane"

1940: Was voice-over narrator of RKO's "Swiss Family Robinson"

1941: Feature film directing, producing, acting and co-writing (with Herman Mankiewicz) debut, "Citizen Kane"

1942: Just before completion of shooting of second film, "The Magnificent Ambersons," was sent by RKO (through a Nelson Rockefeller-run government office) as cultural ambassador to South America to keep positive relations with USA; shot footage for omnibus film "It's All True"; due to wartime flying restrictions unable to directly supervise editing of "Ambersons" from Brazil; film subsequently taken out of his hands and edited by Robert Wise with new footage added; after new ownership at RKO, Welles' contract ended

1943: With romantic leading role as Rochester

in "Jane Eyre" began acting in films directed by others

Rejected by draft board (due to asthma and flat feet); during remaining war years had various radio shows and worked as a journalist, often praising his friend, President Roosevelt

1946: Directed and starred in (for producer Sam Spiegel/Sam S. Eagle) only commercially successful directorial effort, "The Stranger"

Self-imposed exile in Europe; had trouble with back taxes

1953: TV acting debut in Peter Brook's "King Lear"

1954: Hosted BBC series, "The Orson Welles Sketchbook" (date approximate)

1955: Wrote and starred in the stage play "Moby Dick—Rehearsed"; performed in London

Returned to USA for starring role on Broadway in own production of "King Lear"; hired first as actor, then director, of Charlton Heston screen vehicle "Touch of Evil"

Moved back to Europe

Returned to USA in 1970s

Regularly seen in TV commercials for Paul Masson wines in 1980s

1993: Reconstruction of substantial parts of "It's All True" publicly premiered at New York Film Festival

1998: Restored version of "Touch of Evil" using Welles' 17-page memo as guideline premiered

QUOTES:

There was a special issue of the film journal *Persistence of Vision* dedicated to Welles.

BIBLIOGRAPHY:

"The Fabulous Orson Welles" Peter Noble, 1956, Hutchinson

"The Cinema of Orson Welles" Peter Bogdanovich, 1961, Film Library of the Museum of Modern Art

"The Films of Orson Welles" Charles Higham, 1970

"The Panic Broadcast: Portrait of an Event" Howard Koch, 1970, Little, Brown; introductory interview by Arthur C. Clarke

"A Ribbon of Dreams: The Cinema of Orson Welles" Peter Cowie, 1973, A.S. Barnes & Co. Inc.; re-issued by Da Capo Press in 1983

"Focus on Orson Welles" Ronald Gottesman (editor), 1976, Prentice-Hall

"American Visions: The Films of Chaplin, Ford, Capra and Welles, 1936–1941" Charles J. Maland, 1977, Arno Press

"Orson Welles: A Critical View" Andre Bazin; Jonathan Rosenbaum (translator), 1978, Elm Tree Books; foreword by Francois Truffaut and profile by Jean Cocteau

"Orson Welles" Joseph McBride, 1972, Viking; re-issued in 1977 under title "Orson Welles: Actor and Director" by Harvest/HBJ Books

"Orson Welles: The Rise and Fall of an American Genius" Charles Higham, 1985

"The Making of Citizen Kane" Robert L. Carringer, 1985, University of California Press

"Orson Welles: A Biography" Barbara Leaming, 1985, Viking

"Citizen Welles: A Biography of Orson Welles" Frank Brady, 1989, Scribner

"Orson Welles: A Bio-Bibliography" Bret Wood, 1990, Greenwood Press

"The Complete Films of Orson Welles" James Howard, 1991, Carol Publishing Group

"This Is Orson Welles" Orson Welles and Peter Bogdanovich; Jonathan Rosenbaum (editor), 1992, HarperCollins; reissued in 1998 with a new introduction by Bogdanovich and published by Da Capo Press.

"The Magnificent Ambersons: A Reconstruction" Robert L. Carringer, 1993, University of California Press

"Orson Welles: The Road to Xanadu" Simon Callow, 1995, Viking

"Rosebud: The Story of Orson Welles" David Thomson, 1996, Alfred A. Knopf

"Orson Welles, Shakespeare and Popular Culture" Michael A. Anderegg, 1999, Columbia University Press

BORN: William Augustus Wellman in Brookline, Massachusetts, 02/29/1896

SOMETIMES CREDITED AS:
"Wild Bill"

DEATH: in Brentwood, California, 12/09/1975

NATIONALITY: American

EDUCATION: was sports star in high school; impressed and made acquaintance of Douglas Fairbanks, who saw him playing ice hockey

AWARDS: Oscar Best Writing (Original Story) "A Star Is Born" 1937; shared with Robert Carson

National Board of Review Award Best Director "The Ox-Bow Incident" 1943; Tay Garnett and Michael Curtiz also cited

Directors Guild of America D. W. Griffith Award 1973; cited with David Lean

BIOGRAPHY

Versatile director whose prolific output was mostly unexceptional but which included a number of cinematic gems.

After an aimless, misspent youth, including a stint in the foreign legion, Wellman became an ace pilot in WWI. He was discharged as a war hero after his plane was shot down and, in 1918, was stationed as a flight instructor at an air base in Southern California. He was then invited to Hollywood by Douglas Fairbanks, whom he had met and befriended before the war.

Garbed in full military splendor, Wellman greeted Fairbanks and was promptly offered a substantial part in "Knickerbocker Buckaroo" (1919); he found the experience unbearable, and acting an unmanly undertaking. He opted instead for a directing career and worked his way up the ranks; has first job, as a messenger, involved delivering fan notices to his estranged first wife, Helene Chadwick. Wellman made his directorial debut with Fox in 1923 and, over the course of four years, graduated from low-profile westerns to major productions; in 1927 he directed "Wings," the first film to win an Academy Award.

Wellman went on to prove a capable, well-rounded technician, and was responsible for such excellent, diverse films as "Public Enemy" (1931), the definitive Cagney gangster film; the original "A Star Is Born" (1937), for which he earned a best screenplay Oscar; "Nothing Sacred" (1937), a scathingly funny screwball comedy; and "The Ox-Bow Incident" (1943), a didactic drama about lynching. He also directed two fine war films, "The Story of GI Joe" (1945) and "Battleground" (1949). Among his later wives were singer-dancer Margery Chapin and actress Dorothy Coonan, whom he directed in "Wild Boys of the Road" (1933).

COMPANIONS:

wife: Helene Chadwick. Actor; first wife; married 1918; separated after a month; later divorced

wife: Margery Chapin. Singer, dancer; married in 1925; together for a short time

wife: Marjorie Crawford. mMrried in 1931; divorced

wife: Dorothy Coonan. Actor; fourth wife; starred in Wellman's 1933 film "Wild Boys of The Road"; married in March 1934

MILESTONES:

Joined a pro minor-league hockey team

1917–1918: Joined Foreign Legion, then Lafayette Flying Corps; plane shot down during WWI; sustained lasting back injuries; awarded Croix de Guerre and other honors

1918: Returned to Boston as war hero; authored (with a ghost writer) his story, "Go, Get 'Em"

1918: While a flight instructor at Rockwell Field, San Diego, became friendly with Hollywood figures

1919: On invitation from Douglas Fairbanks, made film acting debut in "Knickerbocker Buckaroo"

Unhappy with acting, decided to become a director; worked at Goldwyn as messenger boy (including delivering fan mail to his estranged wife), propman, and then assistant director

1921: Moved to Fox as assistant director

1923: Took over direction of "The Eleventh Hour" from mentor Bernard J Durning

1923: Solo directing debut, "The Man Who Won"

After succession of successful low-rent films, asked for raise and was fired

1925: Joined MGM as assistant director

1925: Resumed full-fledged directing chores at MGM with "The Boob" (released after his Columbia effort, "When Husbands Flirt")

1927: Directed first major success (winner of the first Academy Award for best picture), "Wings"

1936: First film as co-screenwriter (also director), "The Robin Hood of El Dorado"

1938: First film as producer (also director), "Men with Wings"

QUOTES:

Always the aviator, Wellman's body was cremated and strewn over the US by plane.

He was awarded Croix de Guerre in 1918.

Received five US citations.

BIBLIOGRAPHY:

"A Short Time for Insanity" William A. Wellman, 1974; autobiography

"Growing Old Gracefully" William A. Wellman, 1975

"William A. Wellman" Frank T. Thompson, 1983, Scarecrow Press; foreword by Barbara Stanwyck

Wim Wenders

BORN: Wilhelm Ernst Wenders in Dusseldorf, Germany, 08/14/1945

NATIONALITY: German

EDUCATION: completed secondary school in Oberhausen in 1965

University of Freiburg, Freiburg, Germany, philosophy and medicine, 1965; took job in hospital as orderly; transferred out

transferred to university in Dusseldorf; remained for one semester then went to Paris

Hochschule fur Film und Fernsehen, Munich, Germany, 1967–70; school founded in 1967; Wenders made seven films during attendance, two of which were officially produced by the school

AWARDS: Cannes Film Festival FIPRESCI Prize "Kings of the Road" 1976

Cannes Film Festival Palme d'Or "Paris, Texas" 1984

Cannes Film Festival FIPRESCI Prize "Paris, Texas" 1984

BAFTA Award Best Director "Paris, Texas" 1984

Cannes Film Festival Best Director Award "Wings of Desire" 1987

Los Angeles Film Critics Association Award Best Foreign Film "Wings of Desire" 1988

Cannes Film Festival Grand Jury Prize "Far Away, So Close" 1993

Venice Film Festival International Critics Prize "Beyond the Clouds" 1995; shared award with Michelangelo Antonioni; film also tied for prize with "Cyclo"

Deutscher Filmpreis Film Band in Gold for Best Director "The End of the Violence" 1998

Edinburgh International Film Festival Standard Life Audience Award "Buena Vista Social Club" 1999

European Film Award European Documentary of the Year "Buena Vista Social Club" 1999

National Board of Review Best Documentary "Buena Vista Social Club" 1999

Los Angeles Film Critics Association Award Best Documentary "Buena Vista Social Club" 1999

New York Film Critics Circle Award Best Non-Fiction Film "Buena Vista Social Club" 1999

Broadcast Film Critics Association Award Best Documentary "Buena Vista Social Club" 1999

Florida Film Critics Circle Award Best Documentary "Buena Vista Social Club" 1999

Online Film Critics Society Award Best Documentary "Buena Vista Social Club" 1999

National Society of Film Critics Award Best Nonfiction Film "Buena Vista Social Club" 1999

Golden Satellite Best Documentary "Buena Vista Social Club" 1999

Berlin Film Festival Silver Bear Jury Prize "The Million Dollar Hotel" 2000

BIOGRAPHY

One of the best-known directors of the New German Cinema, Wim Wenders grew up glued to the American Forces Network, fascinated not only by the music but by all things American. Raised a Catholic, he briefly entertained ambitions for the priesthood but abandoned them by the age of 18 as rock 'n' roll had become a more powerful influence. (His movies to this day reflect a continued steady love affair with American pop music, and he counts rock artists like U2's Bono, Nick Cave, Lou Reed and Ry Cooder as personal friends and collaborators.) Wenders, whose father was a surgeon, would become increasingly immersed in the counterculture and eventually give up his studies in

medicine and philosophy and move to Paris where he discovered the Cinematheque Francais, often viewing as many as five feature films a day. Before he enrolled in the newly founded Munich Film School in 1967, the seeds of the "art house" style he would use to explore the impact of American culture on post–World War II German life were already germinating.

Wenders made seven films while a student, culminating with his first feature (16mm) "Summer in the City" (1970), dedicated to the Kinks, and began associations with director of photography Robby Muller and editor Peter Przygodda, important players in his development as a filmmaker. Both were present for his first professional feature, "The Goalie's Anxiety at the Penalty Kick" (1972), which attracted considerable critical attention, not all of it favorable. Based on a novel by Peter Handke, a Wenders friend (who had also worked on one of the student films and would write "Wrong Move" 1975 and collaborate with Wenders on "Wings of Desire" 1987), it is the first of his dramas of alienation in which restless, unrooted individuals (in this case, the beaten goalie) wander through haunted, sterile, but bleakly beautiful landscapes. The meandering, almost non-existent story left some people cold, but it was a prototype for the non-narrative structure he would master in his later films.

Wenders' team concept included actors as well, and he cast Rudiger Vogler, who had appeared in "Goalie's Anxiety", as the star of the "road movies", a trilogy on which the team continued to learn and improve. "Alice in the Cities" (1974), his first film shot partially in the USA, savages the America that had obsessed him since his youth while showing his eye and ear for inconsequential scenes that build into a subtle mood. Wenders continued his exploration of "the notion of identity" in "Wrong Move", the alienated journalist whose friendship with a little girl helps him rediscover personal relationships in "Alice" replaced by a blocked writer rambling through Germany accompanied by various social outcasts he has met. The last and best of the trilogy, "Kings of the Road" (1976), containing even less dramatic content than its predecessors, established him as a major figure in the New German Cinema. Focusing on the relationship that develops between two men as they travel in a van along the border between East and West Germany, this lonely and introspective film offers a promise of self-realization at the end that is more positive than in any of his earlier films.

"The American Friend" (1977), based on Patricia Highsmith's novel "Ripley's Game" and strongly echoing Alfred Hitchcock's "Strangers on a Train", won Wenders international attention. Featuring appearances by six filmmakers (including cameos by Samuel Fuller and Nicholas Ray, two of the directors most admired by Wenders), the picture explores the unlikely and accidental friendship between Jonathan (frequent Wenders' player Bruno Ganz), a terminally-ill picture restorer and framemaker, and Ripley (Dennis Hopper), an American underworld figure who manipulates Jonathan into committing a series of murders. This story allows Wenders to focus on German/American cultural tensions and to explore the exigencies of international filmmaking dominated by Hollywood and American interests. He then co-directed Ray's death project, "Lightning Over Water" (1979), helping Ray record the agonizing details of his battle with cancer. As long as Ray dominates, the film is a remarkable study of courage, but when the baton passes to Wenders, it, unfortunately, staggers to its conclusion.

In 1978, Wenders went to the United States under contract to direct "Hammett" for Francis Ford Coppola, but after numerous difficulties with the script and Coppola, less than 30 percent of Wenders' original film made it into the final version released in 1983. The project cost him four years of his creative energies, and he would indirectly document the problems he encountered on it in "The State of Things"

(1983), filmed during a long hiatus in the shooting of the detective picture. As frustrating as his work on "Hammett" had been, "Paris, Texas" (1984), based on a script by Sam Shepard about a reunion between a drifter and his family, returned him to the familiar terrain of the "road movie", an odyssey, if you will, of a man's journey to self-recognition. Winner of the Palme d'Or at Cannes in 1984, it featured the stunning work of Muller and Przygodda and, in Wenders' own words, benefited from Shepard's involvement. "For once I was making a movie that wasn't meandering all over the place. That's what Sam brought to this movie of mine as an American writer; forward movement, which is very American in a way." Wenders' conclusion that alienation and existential angst are about the same on both sides of the Atlantic produced one of the fondest, most ambivalent movies ever made about America by a European.

Wenders returned to Berlin to make "Wings of Desire," a lyrical, mostly black-and-white fantasia (remade as "City of Angels" 1998) starring Ganz as an angel who wanders the city, yearning for a physical, human existence. Many of the best moments of the film have no particular dramatic purpose but simply reveal what it is like to be forever an observer, almost making us understand Lucifer's choice in renouncing heaven for the suffering (the feeling) of Hell. The relative commercial success of the film, which earned Wenders the Best Director award at Cannes in 1987, led to the production of a sequel, "Faraway, So Close" (1993), which failed artistically because of too many plot strands forced arbitrarily on a private, meditative movie. "Until the End of the World" (1991) was a metaphysical detective romp of global dimensions, with William Hurt, Sam Neill, Solveig Dommartin and others pursuing each other around the world in search of a camera that enables blind people to "see." Half post-modernist road movie, half self-indulgent meditation on the nature of the recorded image, the result is a disappointingly banal exploration of some of Wenders' most cherished themes, as awful a film as a good director can make.

In "Lisbon Story", Wenders cast Vogler as a German sound recordist summoned across Europe by a postcard from a disillusioned director friend. When he arrives in Portugal, the director has vanished, leaving behind silent footage shot on an old hand-cranked camera (perhaps inspired by Wenders' participation in that year's "Lumiere and Company"). Unfortunately, his customary non-story, improvised during shooting, amounts to little more than a indigestible investigation into the nature of cinema, and can go only so far on its ambling charm. Much as he had for Ray, Wenders showed his affection for Michelangelo Antonioni by agreeing to direct the framing sequences of "Beyond the Clouds" (also 1995), a film that showed no diminishing in the old master's technical expertise. "The End of Violence" (1997), Wenders' first American film since "Paris, Texas", fell somewhere between art-house and commercial cinema, making the argument that compromising one's style to work in America is ultimately corrupting. Despite the gentleness and thoughtfulness of the approach and a beautifully clear widescreen image (Wenders' first film in Cinemascope) of Los Angeles looking better than it has in recent years, the dialogue readings were quicker, there were fewer extended scenes, and the shots lacked the poetic resonance of his best work, perhaps as a result of the abbreviated shooting schedule dictated by the busy schedules of the participants.

COMPANIONS:

wife: Edda Koechl. Married in 1968; divorced in 1974

wife: Ronee Blakley. Actor; married 1979, divorced 1981; wrote and performed "Lightning Over Water" song for Wenders' film of the same name; also appeared in picture

wife: Donata Schmidt. Married in 1979; divorced in 1981

Solveig Dommartin. Actor, editor; has acted in a number of Wenders' films, including "Wings of Desire" (1987) and "Until the End of the World" (1991)

MILESTONES:

Moved to Oberhausen while still a juvenile; began attending the city's annual short film festival

1966: Began, but did not complete, application to the Ecole des Beaux-Arts, Paris (to Wenders' dislike, program required a preliminary course in life drawing); studied privately with Johnny Friedlander; frequented the Cinematheque Francaise; applied to IDHEC but was not accepted

1966–1967: First short film as director, "Schauplatze/Locations" (16mm, 10 mins); no longer extant

Worked as critic for journal *Filmkritik* and newspaper *Die Suddeutsche Zeitung*

First collaboration with director of photography Robby Muller on the student film "Alabama: 2000 Light Years" (35mm, 22 mins)

1969: First collaboration with writer Peter Handke on the independent short "3 American LPs" (16mm, 15 mins); Wenders and Handke appear in the film driving a car

1970: Feature film directing, producing and writing debut, "Summer in the City"; made as graduation project; first collaboration with editor Peter Przygodda; film is "dedicated to the Kinks"

1970: Along with 11 other filmmakers, formed Filmverlag der Autoren/The Filmmaker's Company to insure the distribution of their films

1971: Professional feature directing and co-writing (with Peter Handke) debut, "The Goalie's Anxiety at the Penalty Kick"; first of nine collaborations (to date) with actor Rudiger Vogler

1974: First of three "road movies" with Vogler, "Alice in the Cities"

1975: Second movie of trilogy, "Wrong Move"

1976: Established his own production company, Road Movies Produktion

1976: Completed trilogy with "Kings of the Road"

1977: Won international attention for "The American Friend", starring Dennis Hopper and Bruno Ganz

1979: Co-directed (with Nicholas Ray) "Lightning Over Water", detailing Ray's fight to finish his life at work while battling cancer

1982: Indirectly documented his difficulties making first US feature "Hammett" in "The State of Things", a self-referential film that contrasts American and European filmmaking styles

1984: Directed "Paris, Texas", an English-language film with screenplay by Sam Shepard; guitarist Ry Cooder supplied the haunting, plaintive score

1985: First collaboration with editor Solveig Dommartin, the documentary "Tokyo-Ga"

1987: Made "Wings of Desire", starring Ganz as an angel who wanders Berlin, yearning for a physical, human existence

1991: Became chair of the newly founded European Film Academy

1991: Expressed disappointment with the 2 1/2 cut of "Until the End of the World" that was released; alternate version (more than twice as long), though still problematic, revealed what the director had been after

1995: Participated in the "Lumiere and Company" project, shooting a scene with the original hand-cranking camera

1995: Collaborated with Michelangelo Antonioni on "Beyond the Clouds", writing and directing the "frames" between the segments helmed by the Italian master; hired as an insurance policy in case Antonioni's health prevented him from finishing movie; last collaboration (to date) with Robby Muller as director of photography

1997: Helmed "The End of Violence", scripted by Nicholas Klein; first feature since "Wings of Desire" to secure US distribution; director Sam Fuller portrayed Gabriel Byrne's father

1998: "City of Angels", loosely based on "Wings of Desire" was released

1999: Helmed the documentary "Buena Vista Social Club", focusing on Cuba musicians tracked down by Ry Cooder; film was nominated for a Best Feature Documentary Academy Award

2000: Directed "The Million Dollar Hotel", starring Mel Gibson (Bono who collaborated with Wenders and Klein on the screenplay was originally slated to act in film); Bono had performed on the soundtrack for "The End of Violence"; Wenders has directed music videos for the band; released theatrically in the USA in 2001

AFFILIATION: Raised Roman Catholic

QUOTES:

"Some of my favorite films are extremely violent. I saw 'Taxi Driver' again and I was amazed at how violent it was. A lot of my favorite films deal with violence, and Sam Fuller's films deal with it very explicitly. But they deal with it in such a way that you know why it occurs. You see it coming and you know what happens afterwards. There's not necessarily a reason for it, but you feel why it happens and sometimes you even understand why it happens. I think violence is a very important part of contemporary life, so why should it be kept out of movies? That's not my argument. My argument is that it should be treated as what it is, so people can understand it instead of savouring it. Violence is strictly a consumer product in movies now, not a story element."—Wim Wenders in *Sight and Sound*, May 1997.

"When Bono first sent me a draft of it, just to get my opinion, not to be involved as director, I thought, great characters. I was taken by the ambience of it, and the story. Mel Gibson's company, Icon, was developing it at the time. Then, a few years later, Bono approached me about directing it. And so I met with him and Nicholas [Klein], and we worked on it for two years. And during that time, the script became 'The Billion Dollar Hotel', because it had become a science fiction story set in the future. I worked on that with them while I was doing 'Beyond the Clouds' and 'Lisbon Story'.

"So Nicholas and I came here last May, to get the film going. And even though it's not a big-budget film, it's complicated because it's a project which calls for a lot of production work. So when it became clear that it would take a little more time to get things going . . . I decided to make another movie ['The End of Violence']."—Wenders quoted in *Moviemaker*, October 1997.

BIBLIOGRAPHY:

"The Act of Seeing" Wim Wenders, 1997; collection of essays

"My Time with Antonioni" Wim Wenders, 2000, Faber and Faber

Lina Wertmuller

BORN: Arcangela Felice Assunta Wertmuller von Elgg Spanol Von Braueich in Rome, Italy, 08/14/1928

SOMETIMES CREDITED AS:
George Brown
Nathan Wich

NATIONALITY: Italian

EDUCATION: attended, and thrown out of, numerous Catholic schools; eventually earned teacher's certificate

entered law school at same time as drama school, eventually dropping the former to concentrate on the latter

Stanislavskyan Academy of Theater, Rome, Italy, 1951

AWARDS: Locarno Film Festival Silver Sail Award "I basilischi/The Lizards" 1963

Cannes Film Festival Best Director Award "The Seduction of Mimi" 1972

Women in Film Crystal Award 1985

BIOGRAPHY

This European director's grotesque/comic treatments of weighty political, social and sexual themes earned her a sizeable cult following in the mid-1970s.

Wertmuller was born to a family of Swiss aristocrats; her father, a lawyer, dominated his family and young Lina constantly fought with him. A product of a Roman Catholic education, Wertmuller brought her domestic battles into the classroom and, as she approached college age, could boast of having been thrown out of fifteen schools. Her father wanted her to attend law school but Wertmuller decided, at the instigation of a friend, to enroll in theater school. After her graduation in 1951 she became an itinerant theatrical jack-of-all-trades, traveling through Europe as a producer of avant-garde plays, puppeteer, stage manager, set designer, publicist and radio/TV scriptwriter. Through an acquaintance with Marcello Mastroianni, Wertmuller was introduced to Federico Fellini, who offered her a production position on his film "8 1/2" (1962).

Through her work on this production Wertmuller developed a desire to direct her own film. Enlisting the services of several technicians from "8 1/2", Wertmuller (with the financial backing of Fellini) made her first film, "The Lizards," in 1963. A second film, "Let's Talk About Men" (1965), performed decently at the box office, but when she had difficulty obtaining funding for a third film, Wertmuller returned to her work in the theater and TV.

Wertmuller re-emerged as a major film director through her friendship with actor Giancarlo Giannini, who had already established a reputation as a popular stage star. Wertmuller directed him in a TV production, "Rita the Mosquito" (1966); Giannini then recommended a play she had written, "Two Plus Two Are No Longer Four," to Franco Zeffirelli, who agreed to produce it with Giannini starring. The critical and financial success of this production was the breakthrough Wertmuller needed.

Giannini and Wertmuller now agreed to collaborate on films. Their first production, "The Seduction of Mimi," a comic examination of sexual role-playing and political maneuvering, garnered Wertmuller the best director award at the 1972 Cannes Film Festival. Their next film, "Love and Anarchy" (1973), won Giannini the best actor award at Cannes and, booked for distribution in New York in 1974, gave American critics a first look at a new directorial sensibility. Its success prompted the release of "The Seduction of Mimi" in the USA.

The release of these films created an almost instantaneous cult around Wertmuller, which was fueled by the release of "All Screwed Up" (1974) and "Let's Talk About Men" and culminated with the release of "Swept Away "(1974) and "Seven Beauties" (1975). These films combined heavy-handed caricature with extended, often violent, political and sexual debate. Wertmuller's satirical thrust was so broad that both feminists and anti-feminists, liberals and conservatives flocked to her films. On the whole, however, Wertmuller's women characters were treated with contempt—from the shrill, ultra-chic Mariangela Melato in "Swept Away" and "Summer Night" (1986) to the Felliniesque, wide-angle exaggerations of "The Seduction of Mimi" and "Seven Beauties." Her male characters were not much more sympathetic, but their broad, macho posturing and chauvinism was

tempered by the Chaplinesque pathos of Giannini's performances—particularly his pathologically comic Pasqualino in "Seven Beauties."

After "Seven Beauties," Wertmuller's reputation took a sharp downward turn. Her first American film, "The End of the World in Our Usual Bed in a Night Full of Rain" (1978), was both a critical and financial flop and her subsequent, sporadic productions have failed to recapture her audience.

COMPANION:

husband: Enrico Job. Sculptor, conceptual artist, production designer, costume designer; married in 1968

MILESTONES:

After drama school co-founded an experimental theater group, then worked with controversial puppet theater company

Acted in, managed and designed sets for stage productions, and wrote a number of scripts for TV before being introduced (by old friend actress Flora Carabella, now married to Marcello Mastroianni) to Federico Fellini

1962: Hired as assistant to Fellini on "8 1/2"

1963: Feature writing and directing debut, "I basilischi/The Lizards"

1966: First collaboration with actor Giancarlo Giannini, the TV film "Rita la zanzara/Rita the Mosquito"; Wertmuller took credit under her own name only for musical sequences, taking credit for overall direction under the name George Brown

1967: Had play "Due piu non fa piu quattro/Two and Two Are no Longer Four" staged by Franco Zeffirelli

1972: Came to international attention as writer and director of "The Seduction of Mimi"

1974: First producing credit, "Seven Beauties", which she also wrote and directed

Formed Liberty Films production company with Giancarlo Giannini; first film under Liberty banner, "The End of the World . . . " (1978)

QUOTES:
Wertmuller, presumably due to male prejudice in the Italian TV industry, took credit as George

Brown for the direction of the 1966 TV film "Rita the Mosquito." (She took credit under her own name only for the musical sequences.)

James Whale

BORN: in Dudley, West Midlands, England, 07/22/1889

DEATH: 05/29/1957

NATIONALITY: English

EDUCATION: Dudley School of Arts and Crafts, Dudley, West Midlands, England

BIOGRAPHY

One of the most distinctive, gifted and unusual filmmaking talents of his era, James Whale was Universal Studios' most prestigious director of the 1930s ("It's a Whale of a picture!" often publicized his work). Yet, after his ten-year career in Hollywood ended, he faded for decades into an undeserved obscurity. Even though his surrealistic "Remember Last Night?" (1935) became a minor cult favorite of the influential *Cahiers du Cinema* critics, Whale was generally overlooked by the flood of French and later British and American "auteur" criticism of the 50s and 60s. Such criticism tended to romantically lionize long-standing veterans who were read as "survivors" within an impersonal system; the ones who obviously fought the system; directors whose styles and themes remained consistent even though they worked internationally; or those who either died young or were artistically silenced by their government or studio heads. Whale, who seemed to abruptly scorn his craft, just did not seem to fit any category. Being gay obviously hindered any possible interest in his oeuvre during the 60s; in recent years, though, it has had precisely the opposite effect.

Whale came from a very poor family but, being bright, sensitive and ambitious, he was determined to find an outlet for his quiet, insistent need for self-expression. Having known poverty, he also desperately wanted success; once he had achieved fame and fortune in Hollywood, he was noted for both saving his earnings diligently and for trading in on US Anglophilia, sometimes making his background seem far more aristocratic. Whale worked for a time as a newspaper cartoonist before serving in WWI, during which he discovered theater while in a German prisoner of war camp. Upon his return to England, Whale embarked on a stage career, trying his hand rather unsuccessfully at acting, doing better at set designing and eventually striking pay dirt with directing. In 1928, he enjoyed a tremendous, if unexpected, success on the London stage with R.C. Sherriff's moving war drama "Journey's End" and repeated its triumph the following year on Broadway.

Whale was the right man in the right place at the right time. Hollywood, converting to sound cinema, raided the stage for talent experienced with dialogue, and Whale rode the wave to Tinseltown. The position of "dialogue director" was created to help established silent film directors, and Whale's best-known credit as such was Howard Hughes' landmark "Hell's Angel's" (1930). He actually directed a number of interior dialogue scenes, and did his best to browbeat a performance out of sexy but insecure neophyte Jean Harlow. A 1930 film of "Journey's End", with its fine dialogue and action confined largely to a foxhole, was perfectly suited to the technical limitations of early sound cinema, and Whale firmly assumed the director's chair with his remarkably assured first effort.

Whale consolidated his position at Universal with the tender, moving and very adult first version of "Waterloo Bridge" (1931). He did himself one better when he requested "Frankenstein", leading already assigned director Robert Florey to be dropped from the project. Even more than its companion piece, Tod Browning's "Dracula" (1931), "Frankenstein" marked the full-fledged emergence of horror as a viable, regular genre in American cinema and, still moving and powerful, stands as a landmark of genre filmmaking. It made Boris Karloff a major star and catapulted Whale to the position of Universal's resident ace director.

The financial and critical success of "Frankenstein" meant that Universal regularly tried to get Whale to direct other horror films. To some extent he resisted (for years in the case of a sequel to "Frankenstein"), yet he also enjoyed the chances to express his penchant for Expressionistic lighting and set design, campy gallows humor, and theatrical portraits of bizarre, indeed monstrous, yet often likable outsiders. "The Invisible Man" (1933) proved to be a special effects bonanza, a compelling study of megalomania and a showcase for the gifts of Whale's character favorites and the marvelous voice of Claude Rains in the title role. Even greater were two films which clinched Whale's position as arguably the greatest director of horror films in the history of the cinema. "The Old Dark House" (1932) was at once the exciting apotheosis of the menacing mansion subgenre, a brilliant exercise in acting and directorial style, and an affectionate yet sharp parody of English family life. More famous and flamboyant still is the film often claimed as Whale's greatest, the sequel he finally agreed to make, "Bride of Frankenstein" (1935), a film full of touching and fantastic moments, remarkable technical virtuosity and a rich control of tones and moods ranging

from religious sentiment to horror to parody. Whale had become one of a handful of directors in the studio system to attain such unusual control over his personal projects, but as long as the box office responded, Carl Laemmle Sr. and Jr. of Universal were content to let Whale play and kept upping his paycheck.

The attention paid to Whale's horror films has, over the years, almost completely obscured his versatility. His only other well-known films are an excellent version of Dumas' swashbuckling classic "The Man in the Iron Mask" (1939) and the greatest version of the landmark stage musical drama "Show Boat" (1936), handsomely shot, lovingly detailed, and featuring memorable performances from Paul Robeson, Helen Morgan, Irene Dunne and others. Yet his other films, both projects he chose and even films he was asked to helm, are remarkably consistent in their fluid, stylized camerawork, and their mix of offbeat humor and British, indeed often Continental, grace. His abiding interest in the stage was reflected in his merging of the arts to create a truly theatrical cinema.

Almost all of Whale's films are literary or stage adaptations that allowed the director to highlight his films as performances, by tracking through the walls of sets or staging scenes as playlets. Examples include his splendidly stylized comic frou-frou "By Candlelight" (1933) and the delicious period jaunt "The Great Garrick" (1937). He obsessed over mirror shots to point out differences between social appearance and reality, as in his compellingly grim portrait of marriage, "The Kiss Before the Mirror" (1933). Strictly in terms of technical virtuosity, Whale had few peers, and he worked regularly with such gifted collaborators as cinematographers Arthur Edeson and John J. Mescall, writers R.C. Sherriff and Benn Levy, editor Ted Kent, and set designer Charles D. Hall. He also assembled a regular stock company of, typically British, character players (Ernest Thesiger, E.E. Clive, Colin Clive, Una

O'Connor) to portray the rich gallery of eccentrics peopling his whimsical yet sharply observed worlds. He was able to turn genre conventions on their head, as with his bizarre, almost incomprehensible mix of screwball comedy and murder mystery "Remember Last Night?" (1935). Whale could, though, also play it straight, so to speak, as with his unsung masterpiece, "One More River" (1934). Another portrait of troubled marriage and the tentativeness of status and relationships, this beautiful adaptation of John Galsworthy's last novel captures its period so well one could swear it was made in England. It also depicts a range of emotions so well that it belies critical dismissal of Whale as a cold, competent technician with a snide wit.

The Laemmles, in a bid to move Universal from the second rank to the big leagues, overextended themselves financially by 1936 and, when cost-cutters moved in, the sympathetic atmosphere Whale had enjoyed quickly evaporated. His war drama, "The Road Back" (1937), was cut to placate Nazi Party protests over its representation of WWI Germany, and the studio quickly assigned its leading talent to B-pictures to get their high-priced employee to scrap his contract. Lesser films like "Wives Under Suspicion" (1938) have their interest, and Whale certainly had moments amid the sometimes ridiculous jungle epic "Green Hell" (1940) but, having saved his money, he simply bade farewell to the industry. Being ill-treated had led him to become increasingly difficult to work with; stories have also circulated that Universal may have hinted at invoking the standard "moral turpitude" clause in studio contracts to force the gay filmmaker out. At any rate, Whale took up painting and continued the life he had begun in 1930 with lover David Lewis, who had worked his way up to producer via RKO, MGM and finally Warners.

Whale worked only for a few days on "They Dare Not Love" (1941) before differences arose, even though his contract led to his receiving screen credit. He did occasional stage work but only worked in film again for "Hello Out There", a never-released, 40-minute segment of an omnibus film produced in 1949. Whale traveled abroad a great deal as his partnership with Lewis (though not their friendship) ended after 20 years and he met Pierre Fogel, who lived with him from the early 50s on. Sadly, a long, slow, painful decline in health set in, and Whale drowned in his swimming pool under suspicious circumstances in 1957. Years later it was revealed that his death had been a suicide, motivated by depression over increasing physical infirmity. Film historian William K. Everson was for years one of Whale's few champions, though a very thoroughly researched biography came from James Curtis in 1982. In 1995, Mark Gatiss' newer bio, which gave more emphasis to Whale's homosexuality and British character, and a fascinating, highly enjoyable novel, "Father of Frankenstein", penned by Christopher Bram with the aging Whale as protagonist, were published. (The latter was adapted as the 1998 feature "Gods and Monsters" with Ian McKellen playing Whale.) Changing attitudes about homosexuality, the rise of gay biographies and academic studies, and the financial viability of such efforts meant that Whale would finally get some of the attention he had deserved for years.—Written by David Lugowski

MILESTONES:

Began acting while a POW in WWI; after war worked in British theater as actor and designer, then director

1918: Moved to London to pursue stage career

1924: Began working with the Oxford Players for three seasons; worked with, among others, John Gielgud, Flora Robson, Alan Napier and Raymond Massey

1928: Directed and did the settings for the plays, "Fortunato and the Lady from Alfaqueque" and "The Dreamers" in England, working with the likes of and up-and-coming

John Gielgud and the established Gwen Ffrangcon-Davies

1928: Breakthrough stage success, "Journey's End", a play by R. C. Sherriff with settings and direction by Whale

1929: Successfully restaged "Journey's End" on Broadway

1929: Moved to Hollywood; first film credit, dialogue director of "The Love Doctor", directed by Melville Brown and starring Richard Dix

1930: Served as dialogue director of "Hell's Angels" and also, uncredited director on some scenes

1930: Made full-fledged directing debut, "Journey's End" (adaptation of his London and Broadway stage success)

1930: Signed contract with Universal Studios (date approximate)

1930: Last stage work for over a decade, "Badger's Green" by R. C. Sherriff, with settings and direction by Whale, and "The Violet" and "One Two Three", two one-act plays by Ferenc Molnar, in which Whale directed Ruth Gordon

1931: First film for Universal, "Waterloo Bridge"

1931: Replaced Robert Florey as director of "Frankenstein"

1935: Made last of four classic horror films, "Bride of Frankenstein"

1936: Whale's expensive filming of "Show Boat" not completed in time to save Universal from receivership; executive producers Carl Laemmle Sr. and Jr. replaced by more cost-conscious executives appointed by a bank

1937: Film sequel to "All Quiet on the Western Front", "The Road Back", taken away from Whale and re-edited to offset official protests from Nazi Germany

1937–1938: Whale loaned out to Warner Bros. and MGM, respectively, for two films, "The Great Garrick" and "Port of Seven Seas"

1939: Made "The Man in the Iron Mask" for the independent Edward Small Productions

1940: Last film for Universal, "Green Hell"

1941: Began but did not finish "They Dare Not Love" for Columbia; replaced by Charles Vidor but his contract stipulated that he receive screen credit

1944: Briefly returned to Broadway work during WWII; directed "Hand in Glove" for the Playhouse Theater, but the play's run was short

Turned down an offer from David O. Selznick to be put under contract as a director at $1,000 a week

1949: One-shot return to film directing: "Hello, Out There", a 40-minute, one-set segment produced at a TV studio to be used in an RKO anthology film; never released

Turned down an offer by producer William Dozier to film an adaptation of H. G. Wells' "The Food of the Gods"

1951: Last work as a director: helmed a production of the play, "Pagan in the Parlour", at the Pasadena Playhouse, and later arranged to take the play briefly to England

BIBLIOGRAPHY:

"James Whale" James Curtis, 1982, Scarecrow Press; biography

"James Whale: A Biography, or The Would-Be Gentleman" Mark Gatiss, 1995, Cassell

"Father of Frankenstein" Christopher Bram, 1995; fictional novel with Whale, in his declining later days, as the protagonist; basis of 1998 feature "Gods and Monsters"

BORN: Samuel Wilder in Sucha, Galicia, Austria (now part of Poland), 06/22/1906

SOMETIMES CREDITED AS:
Billie Wilder

DEATH: in Los Angeles, California, 03/27/2002

NATIONALITY: Austrian

CITIZENSHIP: United States, 1939

EDUCATION: attended realgymnasium (high school) in Vienna, Austria

University of Vienna Vienna, Austria law left after one year to work as a copy boy and then as a reporter for *Die Stunde*

AWARDS: New York Film Critics Circle Award Best Director "The Lost Weekend" 1945

Oscar Best Director "The Lost Weekend" 1945

Oscar Best Writing (Adapted Screenplay) "The Lost Weekend" 1945; award shared with Charles Brackett

Cannes Film Festival Grand Prix "The Lost Weekend" 1946

Writers Guild of America Award Best-Written American Drama "Sunset Boulevard" 1950; award shared with Charles Brackett and D. M. Marshman Jr.

Golden Globe Award Best Director "Sunset Boulevard" 1950

Oscar Best Writing (Story and Screenplay) "Sunset Boulevard" 1950; shared award with Charles Brackett and D. M. Marshman Jr.

Venice Film Festival International Prize "Big Carnival" 1951; one of three films cited

Golden Globe Award Best Screenplay "Sabrina" 1954; award shared with Samuel Taylor and Ernest Lehman

Writers Guild of America Award Best-Written American Comedy "Sabrina" 1954; award shared with Samuel Taylor and Ernest Lehman

Writers Guild of America Laurel Award for Achievement 1956; award shared with Charles Brackett

Writers Guild of America Award Best-Written American Comedy "Love in the Afternoon" 1957; award shared with I.A.L. Diamond

Golden Globe Award Best Motion Picture-Comedy "Some Like it Hot" 1959

Writers Guild of America Award Best-Written American Comedy "Some Like It Hot" 1959; award shared with I.A.L. Diamond

New York Film Critics Circle Award Best Motion Picture "The Apartment" 1960; tied with "Sons and Lovers"

New York Film Critics Circle Award Best Director "The Apartment" 1960; tied with Jack Cardiff for "Sons and Lovers"

New York Film Critics Circle Award Best Writing "The Apartment" 1960; award shared with I.A.L. Diamond

Golden Globe Award Best Motion Picture-Comedy "The Apartment" 1960

Oscar Best Picture "The Apartment" 1960

Oscar Best Director "The Apartment" 1960

Oscar Best Writing (Story and Screenplay) "The Apartment" 1960; award shared with I.A.L. Diamond

British Film Academy Award Best Film "The Apartment" 1960; producer and director

Directors Guild of America Award Outstanding Directorial Achievement in Feature Film "The Apartment" 1960

Writers Guild of America Award Best-Written American Comedy "The Apartment" 1960; award shared with I.A.L. Diamond

Directors Guild of America D. W. Griffith Award 1985; for lifetime achievement

American Film Institute Life Achievement Award 1986

Irving G. Thalberg Memorial Award 1987; presented by the Academy of Motion Picture Arts and Sciences

Kennedy Center Honors Lifetime Achievement Award 1990

Preston Sturges Award for Outstanding Achievements in Both Writing and Directing 1991; given jointly by the Directors Guild of America and the Writers Guild of America West

Felix Lifetime Achievement 1992

PEN Lifetime Achievement Award in Screenwriting 1993; first time award given; awarded December 5, 1993

Los Angeles Film Critics Association Career Achievement Award 1994

Writers Guild Foundation Career Achievement Award for Excellence in the Art of Screenwriting 1995

Producers Guild of America David O. Selznick Award 1996; presented for lifetime achievement

German Film Prize for Lifetime Achievement 1997; cited with Jennifer Jones and German poster designer Klaus Dill

BIOGRAPHY

First and foremost a writer, Billy Wilder, by his own admission, became a director to protect his scripts, having frequently bounced onto a set to express his fury at their misinterpretation in other hands. Sometimes criticized for tempering the harshness of his vision in deference to the box office, he operated with assurance across genre boundaries, compiling an impressive body of work featuring language over character, its wit and astringent bite setting his oeuvre refreshingly apart from mainstream Hollywood fare. With the help of co-writer Raymond Chandler, he produced a masterpiece of film noir, "Double Indemnity" (1944), which he followed with "The Lost Weekend" (1945), a social problem play that despite its unconvincing, upbeat ending delivers a brutally

uncompromising look at an alcoholic. Wilder, who created a variation on the comedy of manners and seduction of his mentor Ernst Lubitsch in films such as "Sabrina" (1954) and "Love in the Afternoon" (1957), mixed black comedy with farce for "Some Like It Hot" (1959), his most purely entertaining movie, and alienated Hollywood with arguably the greatest Tinseltown insider's tale, the cruel and haunting "Sunset Boulevard" (1950).

Wilder's initial foray to film was extremely fortuitous. Co-writing the screenplay for "Menschen am Sonntag/People on Sunday" (1929) brought him into collaboration with future Hollywood players Robert and Curt Siodmak, Edgar G. Ulmer and Fred Zinnemann, all of whom joined him at the huge German studio UFA on the strength of its overwhelming success. At UFA he wrote scores of scripts for silents and talkies, including two notable 1931 films. Gerhard Lamprecht's "Emil und die Detektive" and "Der Mann, der Seinen Morder Sucht", which reteamed him with director Robert Siodmak. Hitler's ascent to power, however, convinced him that Germany was no place for a Jew (his mother, stepfather and grandmother would all perish at Auschwitz). Wasting no time, he sold his possessions and slipped out of Berlin on the night train to Paris, where he shared directing duties with Alexander Esway on "Mauvaise graine/Bad Blood" (1933), a fast-paced movie about young auto thieves. His sale of a story to Columbia Pictures gave him his first American credit ("Adorable" 1933) and financed his trip to California, but his unfamiliarity with English made it tough to eke out a living as a writer, despite a brain burgeoning with script ideas.

Success finally came Wilder's way when Paramount producer Arthur Hornblower matched him with veteran screenwriter Charles Brackett on Ernst Lubitsch's "Bluebeard's Eighth Wife" (1938), inaugurating a storied partnership that would produce 14 screenplays and earn the pair two shared Oscars ("The Lost

Weekend" and "Sunset Boulevard"). Running his innumerable ideas past Brackett who sifted the grain from the chaff, Wilder enjoyed an incredibly volatile relationship with his co-author behind closed doors, but the two joined forces to terrorize Paramount's front office and make life miserable for actors and directors who took liberties with their scripts. Their second screenplay for Lubitsch, "Ninotchka" (1939), provided Greta Garbo with the wonderfully comic role of an icy Russian agent who melts for playboy Melvyn Douglas and earned them their first Academy Award nomination. They also wrote for Howard Hawks ("Ball of Fire", 1941) and Mitchell Leisen ("Midnight" 1939, "Arise, My Love" 1940, "Hold Back the Dawn" 1941), a director Wilder deemed incompetent, before the studio, expecting him to fail, gave him his first directing assignment, "The Major and the Minor" (1942).

To Paramount's surprise, Wilder triumphed with the sparkling, sexy farce about a working girl (Ginger Rogers, 30 at the time) who pretends to be a 12-year-old to save train fare. When Army major Ray Milland finds himself smitten by the supposed pre-teen, he doesn't quite know what to do (after all, he's no pedophile), but the censors did, turning a blind eye toward the potentially risque situations as everything was in good fun. His second picture, the war-time thriller "Five Graves to Cairo" (1943, with Erich von Stroheim as German Field Marshal Rommel), was a box-office success as well, and the two films that followed firmly established his directing star with their scrutiny of human weakness. The lust-driven insurance agent (Fred MacMurray) and calculating married woman (Barbara Stanwyck) of "Double Indemnity" plus the hopeless alcoholic (Ray Milland) of "The Lost Weekend" (which earned him a Best Director Academy Award) are at the front of a long line of Wilder characters whose squalid motives enhance the cynicism of his films. Though he had begun writing comedies and would always

be the master of the wisecrack, the Austrian-born director had looked closely at his adopted country and found a black spot at the center of the American dream.

Wilder, who had returned to Germany (as a civilian with the rank of colonel) to serve in the Psychological Warfare Division and, working under CBS president William Paley, written a 400-page manual to help reconstruct the German film industry, brilliantly captured the bewildering moral climate of the late 40s with the underrated political satire "A Foreign Affair" (1948). Despite a star-reviving turn by Marlene Dietrich as a torch singer with Nazis in her past and an equally good job by straight-arrow Jean Arthur investigating black marketeering in post-war Berlin, this extremely acerbic study of the clash between American and European values was too much too soon with the war and its wounds still fresh in mind, prompting critics to attack its "tastelessness." "Sunset Boulevard", his last project with Brackett, restored his box office clout and gave us Gloria Swanson as the half-mad silent star stuck in a time-warp, spouting the unforgettable "I AM big! It's the pictures that got small!" and "All right, Mr. DeMille, I'm ready for my close-up" as she descends the staircase, a frightening specter of dementia in the film's closing moment.

Sans Brackett, Wilder was responsible for one of the darkest pictures ever to come from a commercial studio, "Ace in the Hole/The Big Carnival" (1951), starring Kirk Douglas as an embittered reporter who stumbles on the story of a man trapped in a cave-in and ruthlessly exploits the "human interest" angle to his own ends by postponing a rescue for six days. Vast crowds arrive to enjoy the potential tragedy, a carnival moves in to exploit the crowds, the man dies, and Wilder offers not one scrap of compassion, not a morsel of hope for the human race in a film that flopped in its day but seems curiously contemporary now. He then embarked on a succession of successful adaptations of plays, beginning with "Stalag 17"

(1953), the exuberant prison-camp comedy that revealed the charisma of its Oscar-winning Best Actor William Holden and set the stage for everything from "The Great Escape" (1965) to "Hogan's Heroes" (CBS, 1965–71). After the romantic satire "Sabrina" and "The Seven Year Itch" (1955), in which the dreamy humor is sometimes overwhelmed by the prodigious presence of Marilyn Monroe, he slipped in the Lindbergh biopic "The Spirit of St. Louis" before returning to the theater as the source of "Witness for the Prosecution" (both 1957).

Wilder began his second great writing partnership with I.A.L. Diamond on the elegant romantic comedy "Love in the Afternoon" (1957), an emphatic tribute to Lubitsch that paired Gary Cooper and Audrey Hepburn. Coop was too long in the tooth for the gamine Hepburn, but the director shot him in the shadows to keep him a mysterious figure (and mitigate the extremeness of their particular May–December match), resulting in a first-class film practically stolen by Maurice Chevalier as Hepburn's private-eye father. Their second project together was the delightful, gender-bending "Some Like It Hot" (1959), presenting Monroe at her luscious best ("Jell-O on springs"), Tony Curtis (when not in drag) doing Cary Grant, and Jack Lemmon at the beginning of his long association with Wilder. There are those who consider it his best film. Certainly, it is a screwball masterpiece right to the end when Lemmon, taking off his wig and declaring himself a man to his intended, Joe E. Brown, prompts the famous last line from the amorous millionaire: "Well, nobody's perfect." As Brown would say, "Zowee!"

Although Wilder and Diamond would co-write all the director's subsequent work, they reached their zenith (award-wise) on "The Apartment" (1960), a quiet, sad, often bitter comedy about the perennial conflict between love and money, earning Wilder three Academy Awards for producing, directing and writing (with Diamond). art director Alexander Trauner, a collaborator on five other Wilder

efforts, contributed handsomely, picking up an Oscar for designing the dehumanizing interior of the vast insurance office with its geometric rows of desks and clicking business machines. Again on display was the moral frailty of the cheating boss (MacMurray) and the spineless, insurance clerk (Lemmon) who lends out his apartment to his superiors for their extra-marital affairs, obtaining a promotion and the coveted key to the executive washroom. However, love wins out in the end for Lemmon, who gets his girl, the pert, pixieish Shirley MacLaine, showing for the first time the depth of her talent as MacMurray's discarded mistress. MacMurray received so much negative mail as the perfect heel that he never again took a role where his character could be questioned.

Wilder's hot streak continued with the machine-gun paced comedy "One, Two, Three" (1961), starring James Cagney as a West Berlin-based Coca-Cola executive, and "Irma La Douce" (1963), the overly-long (but still successful) music-less film based on a French musical about an inept cop (Lemmon) who falls for a prostitute (MacLaine). "Kiss Me, Stupid" (1964), condemned by the Catholic Legion of Decency for allowing adultery to go unpunished, began his commercial slide, and the improbably positive ending of the otherwise savage satire that followed, "The Fortune Cookie" (1966), represented, according to some critics (who were obviously forgetting "The Lost Weekend"), a failure of his nerve. His time had passed. Though blessed with the talents of Lemmon and Walter Matthau ("The Front Page" 1974, "Buddy, Buddy" 1981) and Holden ("Fedora" 1978), he never again had a hit, though his atypical, but extremely personal "The Private Life of Sherlock Holmes" (1970) and sadly underrated "Avanti!" (1972) gain in stature with each passing year.

The string of box-office failures forced Wilder reluctantly into retirement, but he remained a vibrant link to Old Hollywood, always ready to oblige with a trademark quip, especially when accepting the many lifetime achievement awards that came his way. A marvelous director of actors, he coaxed career performances out of Milland, Swanson, Holden, Curtis, Lemmon, Monroe and Rogers, to name only a few, and who can't love a guy that at one time or another infuriated almost every segment of the movie-going population. He brought to the screen an outsider's sharp satirical eye for American absurdity and cruelty, and a master scenarist's skill at rendering those absurdities within a dozen variations. Some were bitter, some sweet, but all were marked by intelligence, clarity and even affection, with just a touch of innocence. Whether you prefer the earlier darker version ("Double Indemnity", "Sunset Boulevard") or the more freewheeling later one ("Some Like It Hot", "The Apartment"), there can be no denying Wilder was a master storyteller with a great ear for a memorable line.—Written by Greg Senf

MILESTONES:

1914: Moved to Vienna at age 8 (date approximate)

Joined staff of *Die Stunde* as journalist

Moved to Berlin aged 20; worked various jobs including crime reporter and (allegedly) arts critic, dancer and gigolo

1929: First film as co-screenwriter (with Curt Siodmak), the pseudo-documentary "Menschen am Sonntag/People on Sunday", co-directed by Robert Siodmak and Edgar G. Ulmer

1929–1933: Worked as a screenwriter for UFA; among his sound pictures was Gerhard Lamprecht's version of "Emil and the Detectives" (1931)

1933: Fled from Nazi Germany to Paris

1933: In France, made co-directing debut with Alexander Esway on "Mauvaise Graine/Bad Blood"; also co-wrote script

1933: First Hollywood credit, "Adorable", (shared a "from story" credit as film was based on 1931 German picture "Ihre Hoheit befiehlt")

1934: Moved to Hollywood via Mexico; shared a room and "a can of soup a day" with actor Peter Lorre

1934: First screen credits after moving to Hollywood; "One Exciting Adventure" (co-story) and "Music in the Air" (as co-writer, billed as 'Billie Wilder'); latter starred Gloria Swanson

1936: Teamed with Charles Brackett; first produced script, Ernst Lubitsch's "Bluebeard's Eighth Wife" (1938)

1939: With Brackett and Walter Reisch, co-wrote Lubitsch's "Ninotchka"; received first of 20 Academy Award nominations

1941: Scripted (with Brackett) Howard Hawks' "Ball of Fire"; Oscar-nominated for Best Original Story; also received Best Screenplay nomination (shared with Brackett) for "Hold Back the Dawn"

1942: Hollywood directing debut (also co-writer with Brackett), "The Major and the Minor", starring Ray Milland and Ginger Rogers

1943: First film directing actor Erich von Stroheim, "Five Graves to Cairo"

1944: Co-author (with Raymond Chandler) and director of "Double Indemnity", starring Barbara Stanwyck and Fred MacMurray; received first Best Director Academy Award nomination; also shared Best Screenplay nomination

1945: Returned to Berlin as colonel in charge of US Army Psychological Warfare Division

1945: Captured first two Oscars for direction and script (written with Brackett) for "The Lost Weekend", starring Milland as an alcoholic in relentless pursuit of the next drink

1948: Savagely sent-up America's military presence in post–World War II Berlin in "Foreign Affair"

1950: Directed last collaboration with Charles Brackett, "Sunset Boulevard", collecting two more Oscar nominations (and a win for Best Screenplay); starred Swanson, William Holden and von Stroheim

1951: First film as producer, "Ace in the Hole/ The Big Carnival"; also directed and co-wrote

1953: Directed first of three successive adaptations of stage plays, "Stalag 17", picking up an Oscar nomination for Best Director; second film with Holden (who picked up a Best Actor statue)

1954: Helmed and co-adapted "Sabrina", earning Academy Award nominations for Best Director and Best Screenplay; third film with Holden

1955: First time directing Marilyn Monroe, "The Seven Year Itch"

1957: Picked up Oscar nomination for directing "Witness for the Prosecution", adapted from the play by Agatha Christie

1957: First collaboration with co-writer and producer I.A.L. Diamond, "Love in the Afternoon"; has been called "Wilder's most emphatic tribute to Lubitsch," a romantic comedy of the greatest elegance and charm

1959: Received Oscar nominations for directing and co-writing (with Diamond) "Some Like It Hot", starring Monroe, Tony Curtis and Jack Lemmon

1960: Won three Academy Awards, Best Picture, Best Director and Best Original Screenplay (shared with Diamond) for "The Apartment", which reunited him with MacMurray and Lemmon; first screen collaboration with Shirley MacLaine

1963: Reteamed with MacLaine and Lemmon for "Irma la Douce", his last box-office hit

1964: "Kiss Me Stupid" condemned by the Legion of Decency

1966: Final Oscar nomination for writing (with Diamond) "The Fortune Cookie", starring Lemon; also directed; Walter Matthau received Best Supporting Actor Oscar

1968: "Promises, Promises", a musical by Neil Simon, Burt Bacharach and Hal David based on "The Apartment", opened on Broadway; produced by David Merrick

1970: Extremely personal Wilder film, "The Private Life of Sherlock Holmes", received only a moderately warm reception at the time of its release

1972: Helmed, produced and co-wrote (with Diamond) the underrated comedy "Avanti!", starring Lemmon and Juliet Mills

1972: "Sugar", an ill-fated musical adaptation of "Some Like It Hot" with a score by Jule Styne, opened on Broadway; produced by Merrick

1974: Reunited with Lemmon and Matthau for ill-fated remake of "The Front Page"

1978: Mined the themes of "Sunset Boulevard" in "Fedora", starring Holden as fading producer Dutch Detweiler; adapted from a short story by Tom Tryon about a Garboesque star

1981: Final film as writer-director, "Buddy Buddy", starring Lemmon and Matthau

1993: Andrew Lloyd Webber's stage musical based on "Sunset Boulevard" returned Wilder to public consciousness

1995: Approached by director Cameron Crowe to play cameo role of a legendary agent (Dickie Fox) and mentor to "Jerry Maguire"; Wilder refused role

QUOTES:

"People will do anything for money. Except some people. They will do almost anything for money."—Billy Wilder.

"All that's left on the cutting-room floor when I'm through are cigarette butts, chewing gum wrappers and tears. A director must be a policeman, a midwife, a psychoanalyst, a sycophant, and a bastard."—Billy Wilder.

In late 1989, Wilder put 94 works of art (many by modern masters) up for auction at Christie's in New York City.

Awarded the Grand National Prize of Austria in October 1985.

On working with Marilyn Monroe in "Some Like It Hot": "You can learn to live with an actress who is temperamental, if she is consistent as well as tough. But Marilyn would throw you for a loop. She would have a week where she was flawless, never missed a mark or forgot a line. Then, the next week, a total mental block would descend on her. She'd look at me and say, 'What's the name of the picture?'

"After redoing the same shot 42 times I took her aside and hugged her and said, to calm her down, 'Don't worry, Marilyn,' and she looked at me with wide-open eyes and said, 'Don't worry about what?'

"But she was absolutely unique. They try to imitate her. It's not the same.

"She had something like Garbo had: When she was on-screen, the voltage increased tenfold . . . Her simplest lines have a third dimension of sensuality.

"She could give a great delivery of a joke. She would stand there with those cement boobs of hers and the innocence in her eyes. The mouth-watering flesh package. She would look around in amazement and ask, 'Why do people look at me?' And, like Garbo, on celluloid it comes out amplified. Damn thing just jumps off the screen at you."—Billy Wilder quoted in *New York Newsday*, May 10, 1991.

At the 1994 Academy Awards ceremony, Fernando Trueba, director of the winning contender for Best Foreign-Language Film, "Belle Epoque", tipped his hat to his guru by saying, "I would like to believe in God so that I could thank Him, but I just believe in Billy Wilder. So thank you, Billy Wilder." Wilder called him the next day and said "It's God!"—and later told the *Los Angeles Times* "I wish he hadn't said that [because] people start crossing themselves when they see me!"—From GQ, October 1994.

About serving with the Psychological Warfare Division in Germany after World War II: "One day a letter came from the director of the Passion Play in Oberammergau. He was requesting permission to perform the play, with Anton Lang as Jesus. I translated the letter and was asked my opinion. Anton Lang was a Nazi, so I said, 'Permission granted, but the nails have to be real.' "—Billy Wilder to *Los Angeles Times*, February 17, 1997.

In March 2000, Wilder was presented with the Federal Republic of Germany's Knight Commander's Cross (badge and star).

BIBLIOGRAPHY:
"Billy Wilder in Hollywood" Maurice Zolotow, 1977, G.P. Putnam's Sons
"Wilder Times" Kevin Lally, 1996, Henry Holt & Co; biography
"On Sunset Boulevard: The Life and Times of Billy Wilder" Ed Sikov, 1998, Hyperion
"Conversations With Wilder" Cameron Crowe, 1999

Michael Winterbottom

BORN: in Blackburn, Lancastershire, England, 03/29/1961

NATIONALITY: British

EDUCATION: Oxford University, Oxford, England English
   studied filmmaking in Bristol and in London after graduating from Oxford

AWARDS: Edinburgh Film Festival Michael Powell Award "Jude" 1996

British Independent Film Award Best British Independent Film "Wonderland" 1999
   Berlin Film Festival Award The Golden Bear "In This World" 2002; for best film that reflected the central theme of the festival

BIOGRAPHY
A talented and intelligent British filmmaker of intense and often introspective relationship dramas, Michael Winterbottom studied film in Bristol and London after completing a degree in English at Oxford. He first worked in the

industry when he got a job in the cutting room at Thames Television, and made the transition to director via two well-received documentaries, "Ingmar Bergman: The Magic Lantern" and "Ingmar Bergman: The Director" (both 1988), profiling the revered Swedish filmmaker. Winterbottom then formed a semi-regular working relationship with screenwriter Frank Cottrell Boyce when they teamed for a couple of youth-oriented TV comedy-dramas, beginning with "The Strangers" (1989), which received a BAFTA nomination as Best Educational Film. His fondness for quirky, personal projects, sometimes whimsical but often austere, featuring small casts enacting emotional and class struggles, continued via the road picture "Under the Sun" (1991) and the acclaimed "Love Lies Bleeding" (BBC2, 1992), also for TV.

Winterbottom did a good job helming installments of TV series, including the two-hour premiere of "Cracker" subtitled "The Mad Woman in the Attic" (Granada, 1993; aired in the US on A&E in 1994), and he also helmed the "Death at the Bar" episode for "The Inspector Alleyn Mysteries" (BBC/PBS, 1995). A breakthrough, though, came with his four-part serial, "Family" (BBC, 1994), an acclaimed study of a dysfunctional Irish working-class family written by Roddy Doyle. Some of Winterbottom's work, including an edited-down version of "Family", had played well at film festivals, but it was not until "Butterfly Kiss" (1995) that he made a film directly for feature release. An odd, often engaging and touching tale which revisits the road film genre in its mix of lesbian love and serial murder, it showed Winterbottom's promising talent for actors as well as his penchant for emotional extremes and flashy shock cuts. His stylish, personal and often socially committed touch also showed in his study of a multiple sclerosis victim, "Go Now" (1995).

A number of qualities which his work had manifested were present in his most ambitious undertaking to date, an adaptation of Thomas Hardy's bleak, difficult but rewarding novel

"Jude the Obscure." Retitled "Jude" (1996), Winterbottom's film suggested his ongoing debts to Bergman and to Francois Truffaut, as well as his admirably restless if not always successful attempts at distancing effects. Very handsomely shot and produced, and featuring a mature star performance by Kate Winslet, the film was generally well received, despite the challenges of its length, austerity and mixed ambitions. Winterbottom also set himself challenges anew with his present-day historical study of potent emotional bonds formed that are explored in "Welcome to Sarajevo" (1997). Debuting in competition at the Cannes Film Festival, the film received praise for its restrained, yet disturbing examination of the effects of war. In 2002, Winterbottom directed the musical drama "24 Hour Party People," a feature that intertwines music, sex, drugs and a lot of partying people.—Written by David Lugowski

MILESTONES:

Grew up in Blackburn

First worked in the film and TV industries with a job in the cutting room at Thames Television

1988: First work as director: made two TV documentaries about Swedish filmmaker Ingmar Bergman, "Ingmar Bergman: The Magic Lantern" (for Channel 4) and "Ingmar Bergman: The Director" (for ITV)

1989–1990: First worked with screenwriter Frank Cottrell Boyce on the made-for-TV young adult dramas, "The Strangers" and "Forget About Me"

1993: Directed opening two-hour TV-movie installment of the British crime drama series, "Cracker"; opening episode entitled "Cracker: The Mad Woman in the Attic"

1994: Breakthrough work, and first TV miniseries work, the four-part BBC/RTE serial drama, "Family"; a two-hour pared-down version of the program also played at a number of film festivals

1994: Along with Andrew Eaton, formed production company, Revolution Films, in March, while "Family" was in post-production

1995: Directed first feature film, "Butterfly Kiss"

1996: Helmed the underrated adaptation of "Jude", starring Christopher Eccleston and Kate Winslet

1997: Directed the based-on-fact "Welcome to Sarajevo", an ironically titled film about a British journalist who develops a bond with a Bosnian child

1999: Won praise for "Wonderland", which premiered at the Cannes Film Festival; released theatrically in the USA in 2000

2000: Helmed "The Claim", an adaptation of "The Mayor of Casterbridge" set in 1860s California

2002: Directed "24 Hour Party People", a drama about the British electronica musical group New Order

2002: Helmed "Going Mad in Hollywood" (lensed 2002), a drama about filmmaker Lindsay Anderson's friendship with writer David Sherwin

Robert Wise

BORN: Robert Earl Wise, Jr. in Winchester, Indiana, 09/10/1914

SOMETIMES CREDITED AS:
Robert E. Wise

NATIONALITY: American

EDUCATION: Franklin College of Indiana, Franklin, Indiana; quit after one year in the 1930s at the height of the Depression

AWARDS: Cannes Film Festival Critics Prize "The Set-Up" 1949

New York Film Critics Award Best Picture "West Side Story" 1961; Wise was the producer

Golden Globe Award Best Motion Picture-Musical "West Side Story" 1961; Wise was the producer

Directors Guild of America Award Outstanding Directorial Achievement in Feature Film "West Side Story" 1961; award shared with Jerome Robbins

Oscar Best Picture "West Side Story" 1961; shared award

Oscar Best Director "West Side Story" 1961; shared with Jerome Robbins

Golden Globe Award Best Motion Picture—Musical/Comedy "The Sound of Music" 1965; Wise was the producer

Directors Guild of America Award Outstanding Directorial Achievement in Feature Film "The Sound of Music" 1965

Oscar Best Picture "The Sound of Music" 1965; shared award

Oscar Best Director "The Sound of Music" 1965

Irving G Thalberg Memorial Award 1966; presented by the Academy of Motion Picture Arts and Sciences

Directors Guild of America Honorary Lifetime Membership 1983; cited with Elia Kazan

Directors Guild of America Robert Aldrich Award 1984; presented for extraordinary service to the DGA; initial presentation of the award

Directors Guild of America D. W. Griffith Award 1988; for lifetime achievement

Eastman Second Century Award 1991; award given by Eastman Kodak to honor "individuals for their continuing contribution to the development of young talent in the entertainment industry"; presented by Robert Mitchum

ASCAP Opus Award 1997; initial presentation of the award

American Society of Cinematographers Board of Governors Award 1997

Broadcast Film Critics Association Life Achievement Award 1997

American Film Institute Life Achievement Award 1998

Society of Motion Picture & Television Art Directors Award Outstanding Contribution to Cinematic Imagery 1999

Directors Guild of America President's Award 2001; second recipient of award which is presented intermittently

Producers Guild of America Milestone Award 2002

BIOGRAPHY

Veteran Hollywood craftsman Robert Wise directed 39 films from 1944 to 1989, establishing a reputation for proficiency in such a wide variety of genres as to cause some critics to say there is no Wise style. At the beginning of his career, he worked with equal facility in horror ("The Curse of the Cat People" 1944), film noir ("Born to Kill" 1947), Westerns ("Blood on the Moon" 1948), sports ("The Set-Up" 1949) and sci-fi ("The Day the Earth Stood Still" 1951), probably making his best films early on, before big budgets raised the stakes and made him a more cautious filmmaker. Still, you can't take those four Oscars away from him for directing and producing "West Side Story" (1961) and "The Sound of Music" (1965), and though critics may not have applauded, audiences approved his liberating the musicals from their stylized sets and taking them to the streets (and Alps).

In the decade that followed the Hoosier's arrival in Hollywood, Wise made a name for himself as an editor at RKO, earning an Oscar nomination for his work on Orson Welles' "Citizen Kane" (1941) and even doing a little uncredited directing for Welles' "The Magnificent Ambersons" (1942). An even greater influence than Welles on the young Wise was the producer Val Lewton who tapped him to take over for Gunther von Fritsch as director of the stylish horror picture "The Curse of the Cat

People". Wise's first three directorial projects (also "Mademoiselle Fifi" 1944 and "Body Snatchers" 1945) were all under Lewton's aegis, and he benefited from his mentor's taste for literate material, psychological drama and the film noir style.

RKO finally gave Wise his first 'A' film budget for the ambitious Western "Blood on the Moon", starring Robert Mitchum, but it was his last film at RKO, the boxing feature "The Set-Up", that established him as a leading Hollywood talent. Praised for its uncompromising realism, the virtuoso editing of the fight sequences and the quasi- expressionistic reaction shots of the animalistic ringside crowd, "The Set-Up" won the Critics' Prize at Cannes but did not earn Wise a new contract with the studio. He departed for a three-year nonexclusive contract with 20th Century Fox, where he helmed the landmark sci-fi classic "The Day the Earth Stood Still", making a serious statement in a genre without any tradition or respectability. Its story of an extraterrestrial emissary of peace (Michael Rennie) was blatantly anti-nuclear in the middle of the Cold War and a significant step in sci-fi's development away from the simple-mindedness of the past (i.e., the Buck Rogers serial).

Wise entered the MGM fold to direct the multifaceted tale of a company power struggle, "Executive Suite" (1954), the first of four collaborations with screenwriter Ernest Lehman that would also include the Academy Award–winning "West Side Story" and "The Sound of Music." He reteamed for the second time with Lehman on "Somebody Up There Likes Me" (1956), adapted from the autobiography of the middleweight boxing champion Rocky Graziano. Wise's biggest hit of the 50s offered an outstanding star turn by Paul Newman (in his second film role) plus noteworthy debuts by Steve McQueen and Robert Loggia and picked up an Oscar for Joseph Ruttenberg's photography. Wise earned his first Oscar nomination as Best Director for "I Want to Live!" (1958), a gritty prison drama about condemned criminal Barbara Graham, which did win Susan Hayward the statuette as Best Actress.

For the balance of his career, Wise continued to pursue a varied course, often returning to genres in which he had previously distinguished himself. In horror, many consider "The Haunting" (1963) the finest supernatural story of the 60s. He revisited sci-fi at the helm of "The Andromeda Strain" (1971) and "Star Trek—The Movie" (1979) and even trod once again in the very large footprints left by "West Side Story" and "The Sound of Music", faltering with "Star!" (1968) and "Rooftops" (1989), his last movie to date. Wise's thirst for diversity extended to his casts and crews. In a town where longtime associations are common, Wise never employed the same cinematographer more than twice, and that occurred on only eight occasions. In recognition of his body of work, the American Society of Cinematographers honored him with their Board of Directors Governors Award in 1997, and the American Film Institute presented him with a Lifetime Achievement Award the following year. The honors may have been a bit premature, however, as Wise returned to the director's chair for the 2000 Showtime remake of the TV-movie "A Storm in Summer."—Written by Greg Senf

MILESTONES:

Grew up in Connorsville, Indiana

1933: After dropping out of college moved to Southern California, where his brother worked as an accountant at RKO Pictures

1933–1934: Hired by RKO as general editing gofer; promoted to apprentice sound editor after nine months; then music editor (i.e., "The Gay Divorcee" 1934 and "Top Hat" 1935)

1937: Moved up to assistant picture editor, working under William Hamilton

1939: First three films as co-editor (with Hamilton); "Fifth Avenue Girl", "The Story of Vernon and Irene Castle" and "The Hunchback of Notre Dame"

1940: First two films as sole editor; "My Favorite Wife" and "Dance, Girl, Dance"

Edited both "Citizen Kane" (1941) and "The Magnificent Ambersons" (1942) for Orson Welles; earned Oscar nomination for his work on "Citizen Kane"

1944: First film as co-director (due to illness and slowness of project's original director, Gunther von Fritsch), "The Curse of the Cat People"

1944: First film as sole director, "Mademoiselle Fifi"

1947: Helmed the supertough cult film noir "Born to Kill"; uncharacteristically mean-spirited for Wise

1949: Made first boxing picture "The Set-Up", starring Robert Ryan

RKO (then in the hands of Howard Hughes) dropped Wise's contract; departed for three-year, nonexclusive contract with 20th Century Fox

1951: Directed the sci-fi classic "The Day the Earth Stood Still"

Teamed with two former RKO editors, director Mark Robson and producer Theron Warth, to form Aspen Productions; company released only two pictures, Wise's "The Captive City" (1952) and Robson's "Return to Paradise" (1953)

1954: Brought into MGM fold to direct "Executive Suite"; following its preview, MGM signed Wise to three-year contract

1956: Provided Paul Newman his big break in "Somebody Up There Likes Me", the boxing tale of Rocky Graziano; Wise's biggest hit of the 1950s

1958: Received second Oscar nomination (this time for Best Director) for "I Want to Live!", starring Susan Hayward

1959: First film as producer, "Odds Against Tomorrow"; also directed

1961: Co-directed "West Side Story" with Jerome Robbins; also was one of the film's producers; won Best Director Oscar and Best Picture Oscar

1963: Completed original commitment to MGM with a return to the horror genre, "The Haunting"

1965: Earned third and fourth Oscars for directing and producing "The Sound of Music", starring Julie Andrews

1968: Experienced box-office failure with "Star!", a biopic of Gertrude Lawrence starring Julie Andrews

1970: Joined with Robson (again), James Bridges and former Paramount vice president Bernard Sonnenfield to form the Filmmaker's Group

1971: Produced and directed film adaptation of Michael Cricton's first novel "The Andromeda Strain"

1979: Boarded the Enterprise to direct "Star Trek—The Motion Picture"

1989: Directed last feature to date, "Rooftops", an urban B musical about a teenaged white male, his forbidden Hispanic girlfriend, drug pushers and a form of "combat dancing" (martial arts without the sound of bones snapping)

1996: Screen acting debut in John Landis' "The Stupids"

1998: Received American Film Institute Life Achievement Award

2000: Returned to directing at the helm of the Showtime remake of the TV-movie "A Storm in Summer"

AFFILIATION: Past president, Academy of Motion Picture Arts and Sciences (1984–1987)

Member, Board of Governors of Academy of Motion Picture Arts and Sciences

Past president, Directors Guild of America (1971–1975)

Member, Board of Trustees, American Film Institute

QUOTES:

The library of the Directors Guild of America was named in honor of Wise in 1998.

Received the first Sidney P. Solow Memorial Award from the Technology Council (1992)

"In 1947, I had just finished editing a film called 'My Favorite Wife', when my boss asked if I knew Orson Welles. The studio had just given him a green light, and he needed an editor. I was aware of his remarkable record on the stage in New York and on radio but had never met him. To meet him, I visited a stage where he was shooting a test. We chatted for just a few minutes and I headed back to the editing department. My boss told me Orson had already called and wanted me to edit 'Citizen Kane'. It was an incredible experience.

"I've been asked many times if Orson looked over my shoulder and directed the editing. He never came into the editing room. I worked with him as I had with any other director. I would take notes on his comments when we ran dailies. There was a lot of give and take. There was a certain timing and rhythm he was after."—Robert Wise, from American Society of Cinematographers press material on the occasion of his receiving their Board of Governors Award

"On 'I Want to Live!' Susan Hayward wanted us to use a cameraman that she liked very much, someone who had made other pictures with her and had a knack for the glamorous look. Well, he had been last on my list for this particular drama, which was a gritty sort of crime story, the Barbara Graham murder trial piece.

"I had liked [Lionel] Curly Lindon's texture on a couple of films that he gave a documentary-like look to. So, I had a set-to with Susan Hayward and then a stand-off. Her agent finally got us to meet. And she said, 'So-and-so is free to do this,' and I said he won't be able to give us the documentary look we want. She finally decided to go along with us and won the Academy Award for best actress. But she sure watched the rushes."—Robert Wise in *Daily Variety,* February 21, 1997

Inducted into the Producers Guild Hall of Fame in 1999

BORN: in Canton, China, 05/01/1946

SOMETIMES CREDITED AS:
Ng Yu-Sum
Wu Yu-Sheng
Wu Yusen

NATIONALITY: Chinese

AWARDS: Hong Kong Film Award Best Director "The Killer" 1989

Hong Kong Film Award Best Editing "A Bullet to the Head" 1990

Hong Kong Film Award Best Editing "Hard Boiled" 1992; shared award

MTV Movie Award Best Action Sequence "Face/Off" 1998

MTV Movie Award Best Action Sequence "Mission: Impossible 2" 2001

BIOGRAPHY

Hailed by action star Jean-Claude Van Damme as "the Martin Scorsese of Asia," Woo was a legendary action director in the burgeoning Hong Kong film industry before emigrating to Hollywood to direct Van Damme in "Hard Target" (1993). Reportedly the first Asian to direct a major Hollywood studio film, Woo made his name with action-packed, emotionally florid movies with titles like "The Killer" (1989), "A Bullet in the Head" (1990), and "Hard-Boiled" (1992). Enthusiastically embraced by "hip" Brit and American critics while dismissed as a chopsocky poseur by skeptics, this bold visual stylist stages kinetic scenes of over-the-top gunplay with fluid camera movements, extremely long takes, and meticulous choreography of movement. The work of celebrated Western helmers Sergio Leone and Sam Peckinpah inspire his action scenes. Classic American gangster films—as well as their French and Japanese variations—

have informed his selection of iconography. Woo was forced to tone down the carnage, reduce the body count and greatly slow down the pace of his action to appease uninitiated audiences for his American debut.

In a 1993 interview with journalist Bob Strauss in *Pulse!*, Woo explained: "I choreograph action like you'd design a dancing sequence in a musical . . . I have a sense of the beauty and the rhythm of the action, the atmosphere and the action's emotional arc. Everything is clear in my mind before I shoot. But like a musical, the rhythm and movement have to be filmed precisely as you thought it out."

Unapologetically sentimental and melodramatic, Woo does not tailor his work for the intelligentsia. After more than a decade of churning out kung fu movies and wacky comedies, he struck pay dirt with "A Better Tomorrow" (1986). Reputedly the highest grossing film in Hong Kong history, the film generated two popular sequels. (Woo directed the first two of the series.) "A Better Tomorrow" is credited with creating the modern HK gangster film. Woo's preference for romantic heroes—even when they are ostensibly criminals—rather than the "realistic" variety favored by Hollywood has affected the trajectory of the genre in Hong Kong.

Though blood-soaked, his films are marked by their old-fashioned morality and chastely gallant attitudes toward women. The demands of friendship and loyalty are his major recurring themes. There is no explicit sexuality in his work, though critics have noted a marked homoerotic tension between his heroes and villains. Unlike Hollywood features, Woo's good guys are just as ruthless as the bad.

In Hong Kong, Woo's leading man of choice was matinee idol Chow Yun-fat. Woo and Chow collaborated on five HK films, prompting British critics to liken their collaboration to that of John

Ford and John Wayne, while the director compares them to Scorsese and De Niro. "Hard-Boiled", their last film before Woo left for Hollywood, opened in NYC in a restored director's cut in the highly competitive summer of 1993. Also scheduled to open in July of that year was "Hard Target", but after a preview audience (stocked with Van Damme fans) hooted at the over-the-top action and balked at Woo's use of hypnotic slow-motion, elegant dissolves and fades, the release was delayed. A standard action editor was brought in to "punch up" (and dumb down) the footage. Though quite tame by HK standards, the film turned out to be a solid commercial success, despite the extensive re-editing.

Two years passed before Woo found a suitable script to make his American directing debut. During that interlude, the Hollywood newcomer endured countless meetings and watched several projects fade away, including an opportunity to collaborate with Scorsese. Despite his stated preference for a smaller project, he was convinced to take on directing chores for the $54 million "Broken Arrow" (1996), a pulse-pounding, non-stop actioner starring Christian Slater and John Travolta as rival pilots battling over two nuclear warheads. In addition to working with genuine American stars, the film allowed Woo to try his hand at a special effects-driven thriller. Though lacking the poetry of his HK work, "Broken Arrow" offered awesome action set pieces and racked up impressive box-office receipts.

Woo's career continued at the breakneck speed of his signature action sequences. He directed the 1997 hit "Face/Off" and signed a lucrative film deal with Tri-Star in 1998. He directed Tom Cruise in the blockbuster "Mission Impossible 2" (2001) and reteamed once again with Nicolas Cage in the WWII drama "Windtalkers (2002).—Written by Kent Greene

MILESTONES:

1951: Moved from Guandong provice in China to Hong Kong with his parents

Lived on the streets with his parents for over a year

1967: At age 19, joined a theater company established by the Chinese Student Weekly, a periodical (date approximate)

Began making Super-8 and 16 millimeter shorts

1969: Hired for the entry level position of production assistant at Cathay Film Studio

1971: Worked his way up to assistant director; went to work for the busy production facility of the Shaw Brothers

Became assistant director to celebrated filmmaker Zhang Che, the master of "martial chivalry" epics

1974: Directed first feature "The Young Dragons"; produced by Golden Harvest, a rival studio to the Shaw Brothers' (date approximate)

Directed a kung fu quickie in Korea entitled "The Hand of Death/Shaolin Men/Countdown in Kung-Fu"; first major exposure for future international action star Jackie Chan

1986: Directed "A Better Tomorrow", the highest-grossing film in Hong Kong history; first collaboration with actor Chow Yun-Fat and producer Tsui Hark

1993: American directorial debut, "Hard Target"

With Terrence Chang, formed WCG Productions

1997: Helmed blockbuster action flick "Face/Off" starring John Travolta and Nicolas Cage

1998: WCG Prods. signed to two-year, first-look production deal at TriStar

2000: Helmed "Mission: Impossible 2", with Tom Cruise reprising his role of Ethan Hunt

2002: Reunited with Nicolas Cage with the WWII drama "Windtalkers" about Navajo code breakers

Executive produced the USA Network pilot "Red Skies"

QUOTES:

"I never count the number of squibs that are being used in my films. It's the rhythm that is important"—Woo quoted in the British genre film magazine *Samhian,* undated.

"This time, Woo's ballistic ballet features two cops—jazz buff Tequila (Chow Yun-Fat) and undercover man Tony (Tony Leung, NOT of "The Lover")—whose electric "pas de deux" bespeaks that intense love between men, albeit the kind best expressed through the unbridled spray of bullets. Their target is gangster boss and number-one-son-of-a-bitch Johnny, who's stashed his smuggled weapons in a hospital's basement morgue. When Tony 'n' Tequila discover it, Johnny threatens to blow the place up. Enter Tequila's love interest, Teresa, who plays

tag-team rescue by frantically escorting droves of limping, confused patients (gunshot victims, perhaps?) from the burning hospital before it . . . Wait! The babies! What about all those squirming babies?"—David D. Kim, review of "Hard-Boiled", *Village Voice,* June 22, 1993.

"He's a tremendous filmmaker. I love the poetry of his images."—Tom Cruise, who was directed by Woo in "Mission: Impossible 2"

BIBLIOGRAPHY:

"John Woo: The Films" Kenneth E. Hall, 1999, McFarland

Edward D Wood, Jr

BORN: in Poughkeepsie, New York, 10/10/1924

SOMETIMES CREDITED AS:
Akdov Telmig
Daniel Davis
Dick Trent
Johnny Carpenter
Ed Wood

DEATH: 12/10/1978

NATIONALITY: American

EDUCATION: Northwestern University Evanston, Illinois studied acting for a time after WWII

BIOGRAPHY

Widely regarded as the creator of some of the worst films in the history of cinema, Wood drifted to Hollywood in 1947 and worked for a time as a stunt double and as an extra, with the already established dream of writing and directing his own films. Wood did manage to write, photograph and direct a short film in 1948, "Streets of Laredo", but was unable to get together the money to add on any soundtrack.

It would not be until 1953 that Wood was able to make his first feature—and one of his most famous—"Glen or Glenda?" As was typical of all of Wood's output, the film was made extremely cheaply, quickly and, one might add, poorly. A longstanding affection for the then broken-down former horror star Bela Lugosi resulted in some largely incoherent ramblings by Lugosi grafted onto a cliched and stilted yet hilarious screenplay about a man with an inordinate fondness for wearing angora sweaters. Full of lousy acting and incredibly inept technical credits, the film is one of a half dozen Wood efforts that literally gives credence to the phrase "it's so bad that it's good." It is of course easy to sense that Wood made his films with a certain tongue in cheek, and yet "Glen or Glenda?", as with his later efforts, has too much that seems to be intended soberly and too much that is poorly done to be entirely justified as a sly wink at audiences for schlock cinema. At the same time "Glen" is also one of Wood's most personal films, a genuinely heartfelt plea for tolerance for those who gain not only sexual pleasure but also comfort and a universally deserved sense of human identity via cross-dressing.

Wood continued to make films on a semi-regular basis until the early 1960s. Many of them were largely one-person efforts, and so it is difficult to lay the blame on—or give the credit to—anyone else but Wood. He formed an instantly recognizable stock company: Lugosi; bald, 300-pound wrestler Tor Johnson; the ghoulish, wasp-waisted Vampira; aging 30s leading man and character actor Lyle Talbot; talentless blonde leading lady Dolores Fuller; eccentric "psychic" The Great Criswell, and others. Many of his films fall squarely into the realm of science-fiction and horror, including "Bride of the Monster" (1956), "Night of the Ghouls" (1959) and, his most (in)famous epic, "Plan 9 from Outer Space" (1958). Replete with paper plate-like flying saucers, a chiropractor with a cape over his face standing in for Lugosi (who died during early production), and a ridiculous plot about raising the dead in order to conquer Earth, "Plan 9" has been called the worst film ever made. While any such judgments are instantly disputable, the film is certainly not the least entertaining film of all time, and its portentous narration, oddly enough, unerringly satirizes so many movie conventions it's almost eerie.

In the 60s Wood's fortunes went even farther downhill, despite a reportedly happy marriage to his second wife. He continued to indulge his penchant for the lurid by writing screenplays and trash novels under several pseudonyms. His achievements included the books "To Make a Homo", "Raped in the Grass", "Night Time Lez" and "Toni: Black Tigress." Late in the decade and into the early 70s he also began making a number of erotic features such as "The Photographer" (1969), in which a nudie photographer is assaulted by a group of fetishistic women. Later softcore credits include "Necromania" and "The Only House" (both 1971, and his last directing credits), and screenplays for the likes of "Dropout Wife" (1972), "Fugitive Girls" (1974), and "Beach Bunnies" (1976). An alcoholic for years, Wood died in poverty several years before his renaissance—which hit a new peak with Tim Burton's affectionate biopic "Ed Wood" (1994)—got underway.—Written by David Lugowski

MILESTONES:

1942: Joined the Marine Corps at age 17

Served as a Marine in WWII; reportedly wore pink panties and a pink bra underneath his battle fatigues during the invasion of Tarawa; had his teeth knocked out from a Japanese gun butt

1947: Moved to Hollywood with a play, "The Casual Company", which quickly folded (date approximate)

1948: Directed first film, the short, "Street of Laredo", which he also wrote and photographed; musical soundtrack was never added and film was never released

1951: Produced first film, the short, "The Sun Was Setting", which he also wrote and directed

1953: Wrote and directed first feature-length film, "Glen or Glenda?" (aka "I Led Two Lives/I Changed My Sex/He or She?"), in which he also played the title role; acting credit has him billed as "Daniel Davis"

1954: First screenplay credit on a film he did not also direct, "The Lawless Rider", for which he also supplied the original story; received screen credit as "Johnny Carpenter"; film was directed by legendary Western film stuntman, stunt coordinator and actor Yakima Canutt

1956–1958: Directed most famous film, "Plan 9 from Outer Space", which he also wrote and edited; production began in 1956 but was not released until two years later; film later feted in many quarters as "the worst film ever made"

1960: Directed last film for a decade, "The Sinister Urge"

1965: First credit as assistant director, "Orgy of the Dead", produced and directed by Stephen C. Apostolof (credited as A. C. Stephen); Wood also wrote screenplay

1969: First screenplay in the genre of erotica, "The Photographer", in which he also played the role of "Mr. Murphy"

1970: Returned to directing with the erotic film, "Take It Out in Trade", which he also wrote and edited

1971: Directed last films, "Necromania" and "The Only House", both erotic films for which he also wrote the screenplays

1976: Last screenplay and last collaboration with Stephen C. Apostolof, "The Beach Bunnies"

1999: Previously unproduced screenplay, "I Woke Up Early the Day I Died" made into film starring Billy Zane

BIBLIOGRAPHY:

"Death of a Transvestite" Edward D. Wood Jr.; novel

"To Make a Homo" Edward D. Wood Jr.; novel

"Raped in the Grass" Edward D. Wood Jr.; novel

"Night Time Lez" Edward D. Wood Jr.; novel

"Watts—The Difference" Edward D. Wood Jr.; novel

"It Takes One to Know One" Edward D. Wood Jr.; novel

"Young, Black and Gay" Edward D. Wood Jr.; novel

"Toni: Black Tigress" Edward D. Wood Jr.; novel

"Hollywood Rat Race" Edward D. Wood Jr.; memoirs

Sam Wood

BORN: Samuel Grosvenor Wood in Philadelphia, Pennsylvania, 07/10/1883

SOMETIMES CREDITED AS:
Chad Applegate

DEATH: in Hollywood, California, 09/22/1949

NATIONALITY: American

BIOGRAPHY
Began his career as an actor, moved behind the camera as assistant to Cecil B. DeMille in 1915 and made his directorial debut in 1920 with "Double Speed." Wood displayed a certain flair for complementing the talents of whatever stars he was handed, turning out a number of Gloria Swanson vehicles at Paramount in the early 1920s ("Bluebeard's Eight Wife" 1923 etc.), and hitting his modest stride at MGM in the 30s. His output includes two Marx Brothers films, the durable soap opera "Madame X" (1937), the unjustly overlooked "Lord Jeff" (1938) and "Ivy" (1947), the poignant dramas "Goodbye Mr. Chips" (1939) and "Kitty Foyle" (1940), and the literary adaptations "Our Town" (1940) and "Kings Row" (1942). A number of Wood's films stand largely on the strength of their casts and production crews, and he did occasionally have the out-and-out stinker (e.g., "For Whom the Bell Tolls" 1943).

A conservative in politics as well as in film practice, Wood testified before HUAC in 1947. Father of actress K.T. (Katherine) Stevens (nee Gloria Wood), who played a supporting role in "Kitty Foyle" and enjoyed short-lived leading lady status in the 1940s.

FAMILY:
daughter: K. T. Stevens. Actor; born on July 19, 1919 appeared in her father's "Kitty Foyle" (1940); married and divorced actor Hugh Marlowe; died of lung cancer on June 13, 1994

MILESTONES:

1908: Film acting debut

1915: Assistant director to Cecil B. DeMille

1920: Directing debut at Paramount, "Double Speed"

1939: Directed some scenes of "Gone With the Wind" when George Cukor was removed from the film and replacement Victor Fleming was taken ill

President of Motion Picture Alliance for the Preservation of American Ideals

1947: Testified as a "friendly witness" before the House Un-American Activities Committee

1949: Directed last films, "Ambush" and "The Stratton Story"

QUOTES:

Legend has it that one way to test Ernest Hemingway's reportedly awesome gift for profanity was to mention director Sam Wood; the author was known to have intensely disliked the bowdlerized 1943 film adaptation of his novel, "For Whom the Bell Tolls" as directed by Wood.

Received Oscar nominations for Best Director for "Goodbye, Mr. Chips" (1939), "Kitty Foyle" (1940), and "Kings Row" (1942).

William Wyler

BORN: in Mulhausen, Germany, 07/01/1902

DEATH: in Beverly Hills, California, 07/27/1981

NATIONALITY: German

CITIZENSHIP: United States 1928

EDUCATION: L'Ecole Superieure de Commerce, Lausanne, Switzerland

Paris Conservatoire, Paris, France, violin; studied occasionally over several months

AWARDS: Oscar Best Director "Mrs. Miniver" 1942

National Board of Review Award Best Documentary "Memphis Belle" 1944; one of five films cited

New York Film Critics Circle Special Award "The Fighting Lady" 1945

National Board of Review Award Best Director "The Best Years of Our Lives" 1946

New York Film Critics Circle Award Best Director "The Best Years of Our Lives" 1946

Oscar Best Director "The Best Years of Our Lives" 1946

National Board of Review Award Best Director "The Desperate Hours" 1955

Cannes Film Festival Palme d'Or "Friendly Persuasion" 1957

Golden Globe Award Best Director "Ben-Hur" 1959

Directors Guild of America Award Outstanding Directorial Achievement in Feature Film "Ben-Hur" 1959

Oscar Best Director "Ben-Hur" 1959

Irving G Thalberg Memorial Award 1965; presented by the Academy of Motion Picture Arts and Sciences

Directors Guild of America D. W. Griffith Award 1966 for lifetime career achievement

American Film Institute Life Achievement Award 1976

BIOGRAPHY

Few film directors have demonstrated the depth, range, longevity, and sensitivity that William Wyler gave to the American screen. Yet like many of the early Hollywood destiny shapers, Wyler possessed neither a background in the arts nor even an all-American upbringing. Born in Alsace-Lorraine of German-Swiss-Jewish parentage, he was schooled in Switzerland

and prepared for a career as a haberdasher in Paris. During a visit to his parents' home in 1920 he met Carl Laemmle, his mother's cousin from America and president of Universal Studios. Laemmle, a former clothing merchant himself, had no problem coaxing young Willie into working for him in America.

Wyler spent the next year in the publicity department of Universal's New York offices. He was then transferred to Hollywood and accepted several menial studio jobs until 1925, when he was offered the chance to cut his directorial teeth on low-budget westerns. By 1928, he had completed two dozen two-reelers, seven feature-length westerns and one comedy. He was also granted his United States citizenship that year.

Over the next decade Wyler built a reputation as a director of popular and respectable film adaptations of classic literary works and contemporary theater. In 1936, he signed with Samuel Goldwyn Productions and established a working relationship with playwright Lillian Hellman. They reworked her controversial Broadway drama, "The Children's Hour," into a sensitive (if sanitized) film titled "These Three" (1936). At this time Wyler also teamed with cameraman Gregg Toland, who would develop the deep-focus technique that would enhance such Wyler films as "The Little Foxes" (1941), another Hellman collaboration. "Dodsworth" (1936), "Dead End" (1937) and "Jezebel" (1938) followed, all critical and commercial successes. Wyler's amazing string of hits continued with "Wuthering Heights" (1939), "The Letter" (1940) and "The Little Foxes." Oscar-nominated for all three films, Wyler won his first Academy Award for "Mrs. Miniver" (1942), an uplifting tale of a British family's fortitude in the face of the hardships of WWII.

Ironically, later that year Wyler was commissioned as a major in the US Army Air Force. While stationed in England he produced documentaries and undertook several dangerous missions to gather air combat footage. Over Italy he suffered injuries that left him partially deaf. Following the war he ended his long association with Goldwyn on an exceptionally high note with "The Best Years Of Our Lives" (1946), a story of three returning American war veterans which won Wyler his second Oscar and proved to be the top box-office draw of the decade. In 1947, he rallied to counteract the stinging accusations of the Congressional HUAC investigations of Hollywood by helping to form, along with John Huston and Phillip Dunne, the Committee for the First Amendment. In 1948, he and fellow directors Frank Capra, George Stevens and Samuel Briskin formed their own production company, Liberty Films, which was later taken over by Paramount.

"The Heiress" (1949) found Wyler demonstrating his knack for bringing rich, visual staging to the literary classics. During the 1950s Wyler's work embraced several genres: urban melodrama ("Detective Story" 1951), romantic comedy ("Roman Holiday" 1953), and western ("The Big Country" 1958). He capped the decade with "Ben-Hur" (1959), the Biblical spectacle that garnered a record 11 Academy Awards including best picture and best director—Wyler's third Oscar.

The next ten years presented a variety of cinematic challenges for Wyler, including his first musical, "Funny Girl" (1968). That Barbra Streisand won an Oscar in this, her debut film, owed something to the Wyler touch, which had guided so many other performers to award-winning performances. His last film, "The Liberation of L.B. Jones" (1970), proved a critical and box-office disappointment and Wyler retired shortly thereafter. In 1976, he became the third recipient of the prestigious Life Achievement Award from the American Film Institute.

COMPANIONS:

wife: Margaret Sullavan. Actor; married in 1934; divorced in 1936

Bette Davis. Actor; began on-again, off-again relationship in the late 1930s; collaborated on three films together: "Jezebel" (1938),

"The Lettter" (1940) and "The Little Foxes" (1941)

MILESTONES:

1920: Invited to US by cousing Carl Laemmle, head of Universal Studios

Began career at Universal Studios, New York as shipping clerk; then worked in foreign publicity

1921: Transferred to Universal City, Hollywood

1922: Immigrated to USA

1923: First film as assistant director, "The Hunchback of Notre Dame"

1925: Film directing debut at age 23, "Crook Busters"

1936: Left Universal; began working for independent producer Samuel Goldwyn; first collaboration with cinematographer Gregg Toland

1942–1945: Served in England with US Air Force during WWII; produced, wrote and co-photographed documentary, "Memphis Belle" (1944) and co-directed (with John Sturges) documentary "Thunderbolt" (1945); discharged as lieutenant colonel

AFFILIATION: Jewish

QUOTES:

While serving with the US Air Force in England during WWII, Wyler made two documentaries about bombing assignments over Germany; "Memphis Belle" (1944) and "Thunderbolt" (1945; co-directed with John Sturges). In 1990, Wyler's daughter Catherine made her feature film producing debut (with David Puttnam)—"Memphis Belle."

He received the Air Medal after serving with US bomber troops in England.

Under his direction, a record 35 actors received Oscar nominations and 13 won the award (14, if you count supporting actor Oscar winner Walter Brennan in "Come and Get It", co-directed by Wyler and Howard Hawks).

BIBLIOGRAPHY:

"A Talent for Trouble: The Life of Hollywood's Most Acclaimed Director, William Wyler" Jan Herman, 1996, G.P. Putnam's Sons

Zhang Yimou

BORN: in Shaanxi Province, China, 1950

SOMETIMES CREDITED AS:
Cheung Aau Mau

NATIONALITY: Chinese

EDUCATION: Beijing Film Academy, Beijing, China, 1978–88

AWARDS: Berlin Film Festival Golden Bear "Red Sorghum" 1988; director

New York Film Critics Circle Award Best Foreign Language Film "Raise the Red Lantern" 1992

Cannes Film Festival Grand Prix du Jury "To Live" 1994; award shared with Nikita Mikhalkov's "Burnt by the Sun"

BAFTA Award Best Foreign Film "To Live" 1994

National Board of Review Award Best Foreign Film "Shanghai Triad" 1995

National Board of Review Freedom of Expression Award 1995; special award for Zhang Yimou's fight against censorship in China

Venice Film Festival Golden Lion "Not One Less" 1999

Berlin Film Festival Silver Bear Grand Jury Prize "Not One Less" 2000

Chinese Golden Cock Film Award Best Director "The Road Home" 2000; tied with Chen Guo-xing ("Sudden Appearance")

Chinese Flower Film Award Best Director "The Road Home" 2000

Sundance Film Festival Audienc Award (World Cinema) "The Road Home" 2001

BIOGRAPHY

A leading filmmaker of China's "Fifth Generation" who began as a cinematographer and has shot films by directors Chen Kaige and Wu Tianming, Zhang Yimou made an auspicious directorial debut with "Red Sorghum" (1987), which won the Golden Bear at the 1988 Berlin Festival. Set in the remote Shandong province in the 1930s and rich with mythical overtones, "Red Sorghum" uses minimal dialogue, haunting music and stunning visuals to tell the story of a meek young bride who develops into the forceful head of her husband's winery after his death.

His second feature, "Ju Dou" (1990) about a young wife, sold to a brutal old man, who has an affair with his son in order to provide her husband with an heir, became embroiled in controversy when it was submitted as Best Foreign Film to the Motion Picture Academy's nominating committee by the Chinese government and then was officially withdrawn because the film had not been theatrically released in China. The Motion Picture Academy then hastily changed its eligibility rules to allow "Ju Dou" to compete for an Oscar.

Zhang continued his streak of critically acclaimed films with "Raise the Red Lantern" (1991), a strikingly filmed drama about the trouble a man's latest addition to his bevy of wives causes. He followed up with a lighter but still powerful film, "The Story of Qiu Ju" (1992), about a tenacious farmer determined to right a wrong done to her husband. As with all Zhang's films, it starred Gong Li, an intelligent, naturalistic actress who aptly embodied the tension between the graceful surface of cultural tradition and the turbulence of youth and

injustice towards women which all his films explore. The importance of gender roles in maintaining hierarchies in Chinese society again fueled Zhang's story of a prostitute's travails, "Shanghai Triad" (1995), while the family of "To Live" (1994) endures the turbulence of the 1940s through the 70s, a key transition period in contemporary Chinese history.—Written by David Lugowski

COMPANION:

Gong Li. Actor; starred in Zhang's "Red Sorghum", "Ju Dou", "Raise the Red Lantern" and "The Story of Qiu Ju"; no longer together

MILESTONES:

1966: Due to the Cultural Revolution, studies suspended and sent to work in the countryside, first on farms in Shanxi province and later as a laborer in a spinning mill

1982: Assigned to work in the Guangxi Film Studio

1982: Debut as feature cinematographer, "One and Eight"

1985: Transferred to the pioneering Xi'an Film Studio

1987: Feature-film directing debut, "Red Sorghum"

1991: Directed the internationally acclaimed "Raise the Red Latern"

1994: Won award at Cannes for "To Live"

1997: Debut as opera director with production of "Turandot" at the Teatro Comunale in Florence, Italy; reportedly the first Chinese director of an Italian opera production

1997: Helmed the comedy "Keep Cool"

1999: Earned critical praise for "Not One Less", a look at contemporary China as seen through the story of a young schoolteacher and an unruly student; screened at Venice; set to be released theatrically in the USA in 2000

2001: "The Road Home", a drama about a woman recalling her courtship with her now deceased husband, screened at Sundance

2002: Directed "Hero", starring Jet Li and

Maggie Cheung; received a nomination for Best Foreign Language Film

QUOTES:

"To Live" was officially banned by the Chinese government, although many in Zhang's hometown saw it through videos. However, when the film was shown at the Cannes Film Festival in 1994, the infuriated regime issued strict new rules concerning foreign investment in Chinese film projects. Zhang, himself, told *The New York Times*, February 27, 1995: "Now I feel more constrained. I feel like I'm being watched all the time."

"Film is a collective effort. The director is empowered to allow everyone to exercise his talents. To my mind, that is a sensible way of working. I believe some directors behave like leaders. The crew follows their orders. I don't like that method—it's not my way. Moreover, I think that therein lies the essential difference between a cineaste and a writer or painter."— Zhang Yimou in press kit for "Shanghai Triad"

Franco Zeffirelli

BORN: in Florence, Italy, 02/12/1923

NATIONALITY: Italian

EDUCATION: Accademia di Belle Arti Florence, Italy

Florence University Florence, Italy architecture, 1941–46

AWARDS: Tony Special Award 1962 for design and direction of Old Vic Theatre's production of "Romeo and Juliet"

National Board of Review Best Director "Romeo and Juliet" 1968

BIOGRAPHY

Franco Zeffirelli's distinctive career reflects his reverence for the classics of music and literature. Nearly all his films are adaptations, lavish productions utilizing lush locations, extravagant sets and sumptuous costumes. In fact, the very qualities which embellish also tend to impair his work. His films are so well researched that the audience is often overwhelmed with detail. A daring filmmaker, Zeffirelli is not afraid to pursue risky projects which challenge the predictable world of commercial filmmaking.

Zeffirelli's roots are in the theater, especially opera. Ironically, his name is taken from a Mozart aria in "Cosi fan tutte." His mother chose the name "Zeffiretti" or "little breezes" from the aria, but his name was misspelled in the birth register as "Zeffirelli."

His formal education was in architecture at the University of Florence. However, after seeing Laurence Olivier's film of "Henry V" (1945), Zeffirelli decided it was the stage which truly ignited him. That same year, he began his career as a theatrical set designer, working as an assistant to a scenic painter in the Teatro della Pergola in Florence. It was here that he met his mentor, Luchino Visconti, who hired him as an assistant director on "La Terra Trema" (1948). Visconti's influence over Zeffirelli was profound, especially in their passionate attention to detail.

Although Zeffirelli would work with Visconti on two other films, "Bellissima" (1951) and "Senso" (1954), he spent much of the 1950s and 1960s immersed in the theater, designing costumes and sets and directing a variety of productions, from Tennessee Williams to Shakespeare, as well as guiding opera diva Maria Callas through some of her greatest performances. In 1967, Zeffirelli caught the attention of the film world with "The Taming of the Shrew." He managed to maintain a delicate equilibrium between his two stars, Richard Burton and Elizabeth Taylor, and in the process created a film which was true to the spirit of the original play, though it was criticized as a bowdlerization.

In November 1966, while editing "The Taming of the Shrew," Zeffirelli heard of widespread destruction caused by flooding in Florence. He and a hastily assembled crew shot a documentary for Italian television depicting the devastation, and Richard Burton did the narration. The film helped raise over $20 million toward the restoration of the city and its valuable works of art.

Zeffirelli's name is still most closely associated with his next film, "Romeo and Juliet" (1968). In a bit of inspired casting, Zeffirelli chose two teenage actors, Olivia Hussey and Leonard Whiting, to play the leads. This version of Shakespeare's tragedy was consonant with the 1960s and included a nude love scene. A box-office smash, "Romeo and Juliet" also earned Academy Awards for cinematography and costume design.

Few Zeffirelli films since "Romeo and Juliet" have realized such widespread popularity. "Brother Sun, Sister Moon" (1973), the life of St. Francis of Assisi, was a box-office failure, although a recent resurgence of interest has elevated the film to a kind of cult status. Zeffirelli's television presentation, "Jesus of Nazareth," first broadcast in 1977, exhibited his masterful ability to direct spectacle and to render a sensitive subject intelligently. These qualities were also evident in "La Traviata" (1983). In this extraordinary film, his decision to deconstruct the images of the famed opera while sustaining the melody serves the opera most eloquently. Applying the same techniques to his next cinematic opera, "Otello" (1986), however, failed to produce the same results.

Though film critics have chastised him for his unabashed sentimentality (especially in his remake of "The Champ," 1979) and extravagant productions, these are also the qualities that have made him popular with film audiences, as well as theater and opera patrons around the world.

MILESTONES:

Worked as radio actor in Florence and Rome

1947: Acted in Luigi Zampa's feature "L'Onorevole Angelina"

Assistant to Luchino Visconti

1949: First professional stage design for Visconti's production of "Troilus and Cressida"

1957: Feature film directing debut, "Camping"

1966: Made documentary on Florence floods, "Florence: Days of Destruction"; narration by Richard Burton

1967: Co-produced, co-wrote and directed English language film adaptation, "The Taming of the Shrew"

1968: Had international hit with his filming of Shakespeare's "Romeo and Juliet"

1977: Directed the TV miniseries, "Jesus of Nazareth"

1979: Helmed the remake of "The Champ"

1983: Recreated his staging of "La Traviata" as a film; also served as production designer

1990: Put Mel Gibson through the paces as Shakespeare's "Hamlet"

1994: Elected to a seat in Italy's senate

1996: Returned to features directing an adaptation of "Charlotte Bronte's 'Jane Eyre' "

1999: Directed the autobiographical feature "Tea With Mussolini"

NATIONALITY: American, 05/14/52

EDUCATION: Northern Illinois University, De Kalb, Illinois; transferred after two years

University of Southern California, Los Angeles, California, film, BFA, 1973

AWARDS: Student Academy Award "A Field of Honor" 1973

Los Angeles Film Critics Association Special Award "Who Framed Roger Rabbit" 1988

Golden Globe Award Best Director "Forrest Gump" 1994

NATO/ShoWest Director of the Year Award "Forrest Gump" 1994; presented by National Association of Theater Owners

Directors Guild of America Award Outstanding Directorial Achievement in Feature Film "Forrest Gump" 1994

Oscar Best Director "Forrest Gump" 1994

American Cinema Editors Golden Eddie Award 2000

BIOGRAPHY

This gifted producer-writer-director is best-known for his zesty if fairly traditional Hollywood entertainments. With a flair for special effects and an impressive track record for eliciting strong performances, Zemeckis is the star graduate of the "Spielberg School of Genre Filmmaking." After directing and co-writing several small projects which Spielberg produced, he demonstrated that he could also helm blockbusters of his own. This billion-dollar director of nostalgic period pieces, fast-paced adventures, and eye-popping fantasies also displays a penchant for the macabre, as displayed in the popular TV series "Tales From the Crypt" (HBO, 1989–96), which he co-executive produced and occasionally directed, and the black comedy feature "Death Becomes Her" (1992).

As a filmmaking student at USC, Zemeckis met kindred soul and future screenwriting partner Bob Gale. While many of their peers genuflected before European art films, the Two Bobs grooved to American genre fare. Zemeckis earned his stripes by netting a Student Academy Award for the 1973 film "Field of Honor", which caught the attention of alums John Milius and Steven Spielberg, who offered the Bobs a development deal for what eventually became "1941" (1979), the poorly received WWII comedy directed by Spielberg. The year before, though, Gale and Zemeckis made their feature debut with "I Wanna Hold Your Hand" (1978), a cheery romp about early Beatlemania, which Zemeckis also directed. But, neither their first film nor their enjoyably adolescent follow-up, "Used Cars" (1980), stimulated much box-office action. They did, however, get the attention of Michael Douglas, who hired Zemeckis to helm the hit romantic adventure "Romancing the Stone" (1984).

With Gale producing and co-writing, Zemeckis directed the immensely popular, clever, and surprisingly poignant "Back to the Future" (1985) and its two time-traveling sequels (1989 and 1990) for Amblin Entertainment. In between the first and second "Future" installments, the duo created "Go to the Head of the Class" (NBC, 1986), a darkly comic hour-long installment of Steven Spielberg's fantasy anthology series "Amazing Stories." This memorable outing featured Christopher Lloyd and Mary Stuart Masterson in a tale co-written by Gale and directed by Zemeckis. He and Gale also provided a surprisingly hard-boiled action script for Walter Hill's riveting "Trespass" (1992).

Without his partner, Zemeckis crafted "Who Framed Roger Rabbit" (1988), a bravura example of integrating live action with animation and a major blockbuster for Disney and Amblin. He has also branched out into producing for network TV ("Johnny Bago", CBS 1993) and features ("The Public Eye" 1992). After the relative commercial disappointment of "Death Becomes Her"—a gruesome comic showcase for Meryl Streep, Goldie Hawn, Bruce Willis, and Oscar-winning FX—Zemeckis took on an unusual project. With the sometimes fanciful and often moving comedy-drama "Forrest Gump" (1994), the skillful toymaker proved that he could successfully tackle a large-scale story that foregrounded human elements. Adapted from the book by Winston Groom, the film has been described as essentially a picaresque novel for the screen as it covers three tumultuous decades in the life of America as seen through the innocent eyes of a child-like Southerner. Tom Hanks delivered a bravura performance in this critical and commercial hit which seamlessly integrated special effects within a realistic storyline. For his efforts Zemeckis was rewarded with the DGA award and the Academy Award for Best Director.

Biding his time after such a monumental success, Zemeckis chose to wait nearly three years before helming his next project, the ponderous adaptation of Carl Sagan's "Contact" (1997). Despite terrific special effects, that film bogged down in its addressing of big themes like spirituality and technology. The piece's pretentious tone alienated most reviewers and audiences didn't exactly embrace the movie either. There was another gap of three years, during which the director participated in the Showtime documentary series "In the 20th Century" by probing America's reaction to its vices in "Robert Zemeckis on Smoking, Drinking and Drugging in the 20th Century: The Pursuit of Happiness" (1999). Back on the big screen, he enjoyed the one-two punch of "What Lies Beneath" and "Cast Away" (both 2000) clearly demonstrated the filmmaker's strengths and weaknesses. "What Lies Beneath" proved to be a somewhat high concept but pedestrian thriller enlivened only by the histrionics of star Michelle Pfeiffer. "Cast Away" was far more intriguing, however. Reteaming with Hanks, the movie maker took risks with the project that eventually paid off in terms of critical kudos and a hefty box office. In presenting this story of a Federal Express employee who survives a plane crash and washes up on a deserted island, Zemeckis proved his capabilities. The expository sequences moved at a brisk pace and the airline crash was presented in harrowing detail. The bulk of the film, set on the island with only Hanks center stage easily might have devolved into maudlin claptrap. Under Zemeckis' watchful eye and through Hanks' bravura acting, though, the audience is drawn into the story. Eschewing a soundtrack or much dialogue, this section played almost like a silent film. The director overstepped in the final third when Hanks' character returns to civilization and the screenplay falters.

MILESTONES:

Born and raised on the south side of Chicago

Began making 8mm films in high school

1971: Met future writing partner Bob Gale at USC

1972: Directed first "professional" short "The Lift", an 8-minute student film

1973: Made award-winning 14-minute student film "A Field of Honor"

Screened "A Field of Honor" for Steven Spielberg and John Milius who helped him and Gale get a development deal for an original screenplay that became "1941"

1978: Feature film directorial debut, "I Wanna Hold Your Hand"; also co-wrote script with Gale

1979: Co-wrote with Gale, "1941", a sprawling comedy directed by Steven Spielberg

1980: Helmed the comedy "Used Cars"

1984: Enjoyed box-office hit as director of the adventure love story "Romancing the Stone"

1985: With Gale co-wrote the blockbuster "Back to the Future"; also directed

1986: TV directing debut, "Go to the Head of the Class", an episode of "Amazing Stories"

1988: Directed the live-action and animated combination "Who Framed Roger Rabbit"

1989–1996: TV producing debut as one of the co-executive producers of "Tales From the Crypt", an HBO horror anthology series

Helmed the sequels "Back to the Future II" (1989) and "Back to the Future III" (1990) back to back

1991: TV acting debut, "Parker Lewis Can't Lose!", a Fox sitcom that featured his then-wife Mary Ellen Trainor

1992: Feature debut as executive producer, "The Public Eye"

1992: Directed with mixed results the black comedy "Death Becomes Her", featuring Meryl Streep and Goldie Hawn

1992: Scripted and executive produced "Trespass", helmed by Walter Hill

1993: Produced first network TV series, "Johnny Bago," a CBS adventure-comedy series

1993: Created and produced "Tales from the Cryptkeeper", an ABC animated series

1994: Directed the box-office hit "Forrest Gump", starring Tom Hanks; film won eight Academy Awards, including one for Best Director

1995: Was one of the executive producers of the feature "Tales From the Crypt Presents Demon Knight"

1997: Helmed the screen adaptation of Carl Sagan's book "Contact"; also produced

1998: Served as a producer on the remake of "The House on Haunted Hill"

1999: Made "Robert Zemeckis on Smoking, Drinking and Drugging in the 20th Century: In Pursuit of Happiness" for Showtime

2000: Reunited with Tom Hanks as producer and director of "Cast Away", filmed over a stretch of time in 1999–2000 with a break for Hanks to lose weight

2000: During break from filming "Cast Away", produced and helmed the thriller "What Lies Beneath", starring Harrison Ford and Michelle Pfeiffer; film released before "Cast Away"

QUOTES:

Some sources list 1952 as the year of Mr. Zemeckis' birth.

Zemeckis was the first recipient of USC's Mary Pickford Alumni Award in 1995.

In October 1998, Zemeckis donated $5 million to the University of Southern California for the creation of a cutting-edge digital arts studio, known as the Robert Zemeckis Center for Digital Arts.

On discussing his and partner Bob Gale's taste in movies while in film school: "We like[d] Clint Eastwood movies, and we didn't get Godard."—Robert Zemeckis in *Premiere*, December 1989.

"Johnny Bago," an hour-long action-comedy with the emphasis on comedy, will follow the fractured tales of an ex-con named Johnny Tenuti [Peter Dobson], who's running for his life in a secondhand RV. Johnny Winnebago—Johnny Bago get it? We're not making this up. The series will debut on CBS in the spring. So what's this show like, Mr. Zemeckis? "Well, if you can imagine a Ralph Kramden for the '90s mixed with 'The Fugitive,' 'Route 66,' and 'On the Road with Charles Kuralt,' that's what 'Johnny Bago' is like," the producer-director said. "We like to call it a random exploration of the burgs and byways of America . . . "—From *Daily News*, January 21, 1993.

With deep emotional underpinnings, it ["Forrest Gump"] is not the sort of frenetic comedy that one would expect from Zemeckis. "One of the first conversations we had about this movie," [actor Tom] Hanks recalls, "was that this movie broke all his rules drilled into him to work on basic storytelling levels. There's no jeopardy. There's no clock running. Bob is a master at explaining the illogical, as in the 'Back to the Future' movies, and having them make sense. But this is the opposite. He had to take this emotional story and put it in the trappings of a special effects epic in a way that was so natural, it served the human elements of the story, instead of how he usually works, where it serves the fantastic elements of the story."— From "Reality Bites Back" by David Kronke, *Los Angeles Times Calendar*, July 3, 1994.

David Zucker

BORN: in Milwaukee, Wisconsin, 10/16/1947

NATIONALITY: American

EDUCATION: University of Wisconsin, Madison, Madison, Wisconsin, film, BA, 1970

BIOGRAPHY

With his younger brother Jerry and high school pal Jim Abrahams, David Zucker is responsible for a series of corny, but often hilarious, spoofs of popular movie genres. The Zucker brothers first collaborated on comic Super-8 films they made as they were growing up in suburban Wisconsin. After completing studies at the University of Wisconsin, he and his brother teamed with Abrahams to form the multimedia troupe Kentucky Fried Theater, which combined live-action with video and film. Relocating to L.A. in 1972, the trio opened a West Coast branch of their show and over a four-year period became a critical and audience success.

The three raised enough money to finance a collection of short parodies that became the raunchy indie "The Kentucky Fried Movie" (1977). The team, often referred to as ZAZ, first enjoyed mainstream success with "Airplane!" (1980), a gag-filled parody of disaster epics that successfully cast such stalwarts as Lloyd Bridges, Peter Graves, Robert Stack and Leslie Nielsen against type. Reteaming with Nielsen, the Zucker brothers and Abrahams oversaw the cult hit "Police Squad" (ABC, 1982), a short-lived sitcom that parodied the cop drama. When the series premiered, few were prepared

for its zany mix of slapstick, sight gags and puns and it last a mere six episodes.

Undaunted by their lack of small screen success, Zucker and company turned their attentions to the big screen again and fashioned the delightful spy spoof "Top Secret!" (1984), featuring Val Kilmer as an Elvis-like surfer battling Nazis and Communists in East Germany with the aid of the French Resistance. They followed with the above average comedy "Ruthless People" (1986) which showcased the abilities of Bette Midler, Danny DeVito, Helen Slater and Bill Pullman. The trio next brought to the screen a feature based on their TV sitcom. "The Naked Gun: From the Files of Police Squad!" (1988), which David Zucker directed solo, proved to be an hilarious romp headlined by the deadpan Nielsen. Its box-office success led to two sequels of varying quality. Atypically, Zucker served as a producer of the romantic drama "A Walk in the Clouds" (1995) before returning to form as co-scenarist and co-producer of the dopey "High School High" (1996), followed by a stint co-scripting and helming the raunchy flop "BASEketball" (1998), with "South Park" creators Trey Parker and Matt Stone attempting to launch a new sport. In 2000 he served as the producer of the short-lived TV series "Absolutely True" and was one of the producers of the surprise hit thriller "Phone Booth" (2002), and 2003 saw the release of his next behind-the-camera effort, the uneven "My Boss' Daughter," which sat on the shelf for two years before the sudden heat behind star Ashton Kutcher's career prompted a release.

FAMILY:

brother: Jerry Zucker. director, producer, screen-writer have often worked together; made a cameo appearance in "The Naked Gun 2 1/2"

MILESTONES:

1969: With brother Jerry Zucker and friend Jim Abrahams, founded the Kentucky Fried The-atre in Madison, Wisconsin

1972: Moved to L.A.

1977: First film as co-writer and actor, "Ken-tucky Fried Movie"

1980: First film as co-director and producer (co-executive), "Airplane!"; also co-writer)

1988: Solo directing debut (also co-executive producer and co-writer), "The Naked Gun: From the Files of Police Sqaud!"

1991: Signed 3 to 5-year deal with Columbia Pictures Entertainment (writing/producing/ directing) after contract expired at Para-mount

1995: Served a producer of the dramatic "A Walk in the Clouds"

1999: Signed with Gil Netter by NBC to develop TV series

QUOTES:

"We write for ourselves, what we think is funny. It's not that we're trying to write stuff like 'Well, the kids will like this.' We actually do take responsibility for liking the stuff we write."—David Zucker in *Daily News*, March 14, 1994

Jerry Zucker

BORN: in Milwaukee, Wisconsin, 03/11/1950

NATIONALITY: American

EDUCATION: University of Wisconsin-Madison, Madison, Wisconsin, education

BIOGRAPHY

Created, with brother David and college friend Jim Abrahams, a series of hilarious spoofs of popular movie genres. After a raunchy debut with "The Kentucky Fried Movie" (1977), the team first enjoyed mainstream success with "Airplane" (1980), and followed it with "Top Secret!" (1984), about an Elvis-like surfer (Val Kilmer) battling Nazi-Communists in East Ger-many with the aid of the French Resistance.

Zucker made his solo debut and scored a huge success with the supernatural thriller-romance, "Ghost" (1990). The movie was one of year's top box office grossing films, and earned Whoopi Goldberg an Oscar.

FAMILY:

brother: David Zucker. Screenwriter, producer, director

MILESTONES:

1969: With brother David and friend Jim Abra-hams, formed the Kentucky Fried Theatre in Madison

1977: First film as co-writer and actor, "Ken-tucky Fried Movie"

1980: First film as co-director and producer (co-executive), "Airplane!" (Also co-writer)

1990: Solo directing debut, "Ghost"

1991: Executive produced the sequel "The Naked Gun 2 1/2: The Smell of Fear"

1995: Directed and produced "First Knight", a retelling of the Camelot myth

1997: Served a producer on the romantic comedy "My Best Friend's Wedding"

2001: Returned to directing with the frenetic comedy "Rat Race"; also produced